STATISTICAL TABLES
AND INDEX

58/B3 **Flixecourt**
69/D4 **Flize, Fran**
66/D4 **Floing, Fra**
66/H4 **Flonheim,**
58/F5 **Florange, I**
60/U3 **Floreffe, B**
68/D3 **Florennes**

OXFORD UNIVERSITY PRESS
WALTON STREET, OXFORD OX2 6DP

Oxford New York Athens
Auckland Bangkok Bombay
Calcutta Cape Town Dar es Salaam
Delhi Florence Hong Kong Istanbul Karachi
Kuala Lumpur Madras Madrid Melbourne
Mexico City Nairobi Paris Singapore
Taipei Tokyo Toronto

and associated companies in
Berlin Ibadan

Oxford is a trade mark of Oxford University Press

This edition is not available in the USA

Rachel Carson quote reprinted by permission of
Frances Collin, Trustee, Copyright © 1958 by Rachel
Carson. Copyright renewed by Roger A. Christie

BRITISH LIBRARY
CATALOGUING IN PUBLICATION DATA

Data available

LIBRARY OF CONGRESS
CATALOGING-IN-PUBLICATION DATA

Data available

ISBN 0-19-869252-8

Map Projections

The original idea of a conic projection is to cap the globe with a cone, and then project onto the cone from the planet's center the lines of latitude and longitude (the parallels and meridians). To produce a working map, the cone is simply cut open and laid flat. The conic projection used here is a modification of this idea. A cone can be made tangent to any standard parallel you choose. One popular version of a conic projection, the Lambert Conformal Conic, uses two standard parallels near the top and bottom of the map to further reduce errors of scale.

Because this projection shows correct areas with relatively little distortion of shapes, it is commonly used to plot maps of the continents. However, because of improved accuracy, the Optimal Conformal projection was used for all of the continent maps in this atlas.

S imply stated, the map-maker's challenge is to project the earth's curved surface onto a flat plane. To achieve this elusive goal, cartographers have developed map projections — equations which govern this conversion of geographic data.

This section explores some of the most widely used projections. It also introduces a new projection, Hammond's Optimal Conformal.

GENERAL PRINCIPLES AND TERMS

The earth rotates around its axis once a day. Its end points are the North and South poles; the line circling the earth midway between the poles is the equator. The arc from the equator to either pole is divided into 90 degrees of latitude. The equator represents 0° latitude. Circles of equal latitude, called parallels, are traditionally shown at every fifth or tenth degree.

The equator is divided into 360 degrees. Lines circling the globe from pole to pole through the degree points on the equator are called meridians, or great circles. All meridians are equal in length, but by international agreement the meridian passing through the Greenwich Observatory near London has been chosen as the prime meridian or 0° longitude. The distance in degrees from the prime meridian to any point east or west is its longitude.

While meridians are all equal in length, parallels become shorter as they approach the poles. Whereas one degree of latitude represents approximately 69 miles (112 km.) anywhere on the globe, a degree of longitude varies from 69 miles (112 km.) at the equator to zero at the poles. Each degree of latitude and longitude is divided into 60 minutes. One minute of latitude equals one nautical mile (1.15 land miles or 1.85 km.).

HOW TO FLATTEN A SPHERE: THE ART OF CONTROLLING DISTORTION

There is only one way to represent a sphere with absolute precision: on a globe. All attempts to project our planet's surface onto a plane unevenly stretch or tear the sphere as it flattens, inevitably distorting shapes, distances, area (sizes appear larger or smaller than actual size), angles or direction.

Since representing a sphere on a flat plane always creates distortion, only the parallels or the meridians (or some other set of lines) can maintain the same length as on a globe of corresponding scale. All other lines must be either too long or too short. Accordingly, the scale on a flat map cannot be true everywhere; there will always be different scales in different parts of a map. On world maps or very large areas, variations in scale may be extreme. Most maps seek to preserve either true area relationships (equal area projections) or true angles and shapes (conformal projections); some attempt to achieve overall balance.

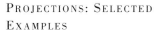

PROJECTIONS: SELECTED EXAMPLES

Mercator (Fig. 1): This projection is especially useful because all compass directions appear as straight lines, making it a valuable navigational tool. Moreover, every small region conforms to its shape on a globe — hence the name conformal. But because its meridians are evenly-spaced vertical lines which never converge (unlike the globe), the horizontal parallels must be drawn farther and farther apart at higher latitudes to maintain a correct relationship. Only the equator is true to scale, and the size of areas in the higher latitudes is dramatically distorted.

Robinson (Fig. 2): To create the thematic maps in Global Relationships and the two-page world map in the Maps of the World section, the Robinson projection was used. It combines elements of both conformal and equal area projections to show the whole earth with relatively true shapes and reasonably equal areas. Conic (Fig. 3): This projection has been used frequently for air navigation charts and to create most of the national and regional maps in this atlas. (See text in margin at left).

HAMMOND'S OPTIMAL CONFORMAL

As its name implies, this new conformal projection presents the optimal view of an area by reducing shifts in scale over an entire region to the minimum degree possible. While conformal maps generally preserve all small shapes, large shapes can become very distorted because of varying scales, causing considerable inaccuracy in distance measurements. The concept underlying the Optimal Conformal is that for any region on the globe, there is an ideal projection for which scale variation can be made as small as possible. Consequently, unlike other projections, the Optimal Conformal does not use one standard formula to construct a map. Each map is a unique projection — the optimal projection for that particular area.

In practice, the cartographer first defines the map subject, then, working on a computer, draws a band around the region to be mapped. Next, a sophisticated software program evaluates the size and shape of the region to determine the most accurate way to project it. The result is the most distortion-free conformal map possible, and the most

OXFORD

HAMMOND

ESSENTIAL
ATLAS

OF THE WORLD

OXFORD UNIVERSITY PRESS

OXFORD   MELBOURNE   TORONTO

1994

Contents

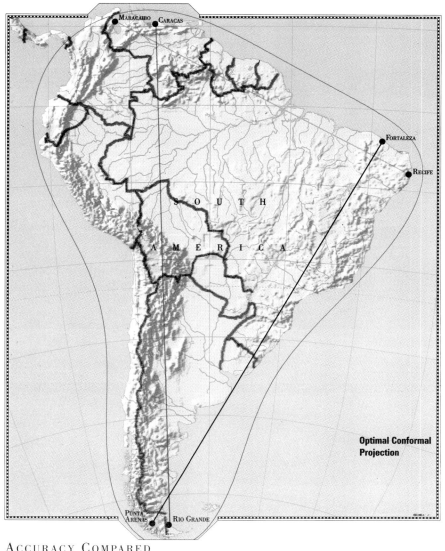

Optimal Conformal Projection

ACCURACY COMPARED

CITIES	SPHERICAL (TRUE) DISTANCE	OPTIMAL CONFORMAL DISTANCE	LAMBERT AZIMUTHAL DISTANCE
CARACAS TO RIO GRANDE	4,443 MI. (7,149 KM.)	4,429 MI. (7,126 KM.)	4,316 MI. (6,944 KM.)
MARACAIBO TO RECIFE	2,834 MI. (4,560 KM.)	2,845 MI. (4,578 KM.)	2,817 MI. (4,533 KM.)
FORTALEZA TO PUNTA ARENAS	3,882 MI. (6,246 KM.)	3,907 MI. (6,266 KM.)	3,843 MI. (6,163 KM.)

Continent maps drawn using the Lambert Azimuthal Equal Area projection (Fig. 4) contain distortions ranging from 2.3 percent for Europe up to 15 percent for Asia. The Optimal Conformal cuts that **distortion in half, improving distance measurements on these continent maps. Less distortion means greater visual fidelity, so the shape of a continent on an Optimal projection** **its True shape. The table above compares measurements on the Optimal projection to those of the Lambert Azimuthal Equal Area projection for selected cities.**

accurate projections that have ever been made. All of the continents maps in this atlas (with the exception of Antarctica) have been drawn using this projection.

PROJECTIONS COMPARED

Because the true shapes of earth's landforms are unfamiliar to most people, distinguishing between various projections can be difficult. The following diagrams reveal the distortions introduced by several commonly used projections. By using a simple face with familiar shapes as the starting point (The Plan), it is easy to see the benefits — and drawbacks — of each. Think of the facial features as continents. Note that distortion appears not only in the features themselves, but in the changing shapes, angles and areas of the background grid, or graticule.

Figure 5: The Plan
The Plan indicates that the continents are either perfect concentric circles

or are true straight lines *on the earth*. They should appear that way on a "perfect" map.

Figure 6: Orthographic Projection
This view shows the continents on the earth as seen from space. The facial features occupy half of the earth, which is all that you can see from this perspective. As you move outward towards the edge, note how the eyes become elliptical, the nose appears larger and less straight, and the mouth is curved into a smile.

Figure 7: Mercator
This cylindrical projection preserves angles exactly, but the mouth is now smiling broadly, and shows extreme distortion at the map's outer edge. This rapid expansion as you move away from the map's center is typified by the extreme enlargement of Greenland found on Mercator world maps (also see Fig. 1).

Figure 8: Peters
The Peters projection is a square equal area projection elongated, or stretched vertically, by a factor of two. While representing areas in their correct proportions, it does not closely resemble the Plan, and angles, local shapes and global relations are significantly distorted.

Figure 9: Hammond's Optimal Conformal
As you can see, this projection minimizes inaccuracies between the angles and shapes of the Plan, yielding a near-perfect map of the given area, up to a complete hemisphere. Like all conformal maps, the Optimal projection preserves every angle exactly, but it is more successful than previous projections at spreading the inevitable curvature across the entire map. Note that the sides of the triangle appear almost straight while correctly containing more than 180°. And though the eyes are slightly too large, it is the only map with eyes which appear concentric. Both mathematically and visually, it offers the best conformal map that can be made of the ideal Plan. All continent maps in this atlas are drawn on this projection.

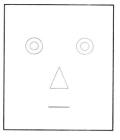

Figure 5
The Plan

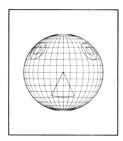

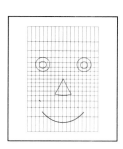

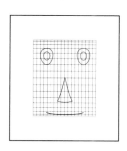

Figure 8
Peters Projection

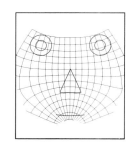

Figure 9
Optimal Conformal Projection

Using This Atlas

How to Locate Information Quickly
Our Maps of the World section is organized by continent. If you're looking for a major region of the world, consult the Contents on page two.

Australia
Page/Location:
Area: 2,966,136 sq
7,682,300 s
Population: 17,?
Capital: Can⁺

World Reference Guide
This concise guide lists the countries of the world alphabetically. If you're looking for the largest scale map of any country, you'll find a page and alpha-numeric reference at a glance, as well as information about each country, including its flag.

Merlimont, Fra⸱.
⸱⸱/F4 **Mersch**, Luxembou
68/A3 **Mers-les-Bains**, France
69/F4 **Mertert**, Luxembourg
69/F4 **Mertesdorf**, Germany
69/G6 **Mertzwiller**, France
68/B5 **Méru**, France
68/B2 **Merville**, France
69/F2 **Merzenich**, Germany
69/F5 **Merzig**, Germany
⸱⸱⸱4 **Messancy**, Belg⸱⸱
⸱⸱⸱⸱⸱**+⸱ttet** Bel⸱⸱

Master Index
When you're looking for a specific place or physical feature, your quickest route is the Master Index. This 45,000-entry alphabetical index lists both the page number and alpha-numeric reference for major places and features in Maps of the World.

This new atlas is created from a unique digital database, and its computer-generated maps represent a new phase in map-making technology.

HOW COMPUTER-GENERATED MAPS ARE MADE

To build a digital database capable of generating this world atlas, the latitude and longitude of every significant town, river, coastline, boundary, transportation network and peak elevation was researched and digitized. Hundreds of millions of data points describing every important geographic feature are organized into thousands of different map feature codes.

There are no maps in this unique system. Rather, it consists entirely of coded points, lines and polygons. To create a map, cartographers simply determine what specific information they wish to show, based upon considerations of scale, size, density and importance of different features.

New technology developed by Hammond describes and re-configures coastlines, borders and other linework to fit a variety of map scales and projections. A computerized type placement program allows thousands of map labels to be placed accurately in minutes.

Each section of this atlas has been designed to be both easy and enjoyable to use. Familiarizing yourself with its organization will help you to benefit fully from its use.

WORLD FLAGS AND REFERENCE GUIDE

This colorful section portrays each nation of the world, its flag, important geographical data, such as size, population and capital, and its location in the Maps of the World section.

GLOBAL RELATIONSHIPS

Three thematic chapters highlight social and cultural factors providing a fresh perspective on the world today.

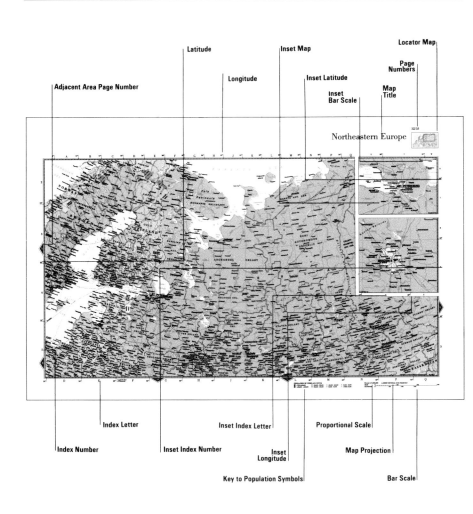

Latitude — Inset Map — Locator Map

Adjacent Area Page Number — Longitude — Inset Latitude — Page Numbers

Inset Bar Scale — Map Title

Northeastern Europe

Index Letter — Inset Index Letter — Proportional Scale

Index Number — Inset Index Number — Inset Longitude — Map Projection

Inset Longitude

Key to Population Symbols — Bar Scale

SYMBOLS USED ON MAPS OF THE WORLD

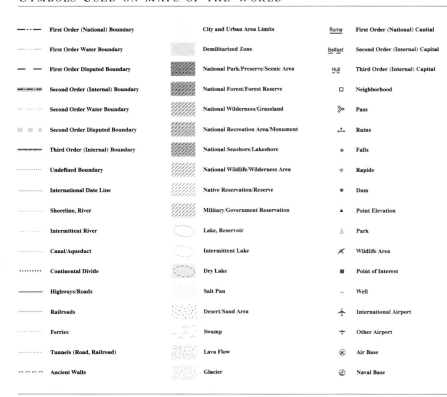

First Order (National) Boundary	City and Urban Area Limits	Rome — First Order (National) Capital
First Order Water Boundary	Demilitarized Zone	Belfast — Second Order (Internal) Capital
First Order Disputed Boundary	National Park/Preserve/Scenic Area	Hull — Third Order (Internal) Capital
Second Order (Internal) Boundary	National Forest/Forest Reserve	▫ Neighborhood
Second Order Water Boundary	National Wilderness/Grassland	⫽ Pass
Second Order Disputed Boundary	National Recreation Area/Monument	⸫ Ruins
Third Order (Internal) Boundary	National Seashore/Lakeshore	● Falls
Undefined Boundary	National Wildlife/Wilderness Area	✳ Rapids
International Date Line	Native Reservation/Reserve	● Dam
Shoreline, River	Military/Government Reservation	▲ Point Elevation
Intermittent River	Lake, Reservoir	⚘ Park
Canal/Aqueduct	Intermittent Lake	✗ Wildlife Area
Continental Divide	Dry Lake	■ Point of Interest
Highways/Roads	Salt Pan	⌣ Well
Railroads	Desert/Sand Area	✈ International Airport
Ferries	Swamp	✛ Other Airport
Tunnels (Road, Railroad)	Lava Flow	⊗ Air Base
Ancient Walls	Glacier	⊘ Naval Base

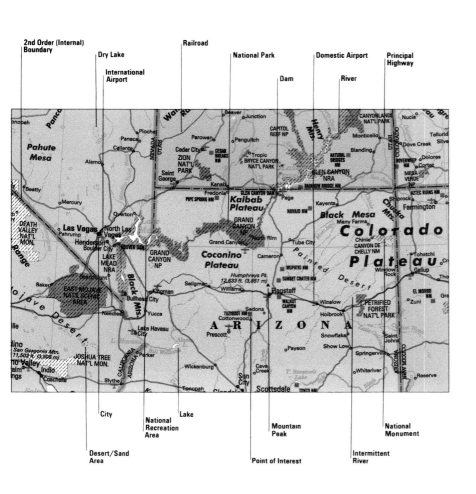

2nd Order (Internal) Boundary · Dry Lake · Railroad · National Park · Domestic Airport · Principal Highway · International Airport · Dam · River · City · National Recreation Area · Lake · Mountain Peak · National Monument · Desert/Sand Area · Point of Interest · Intermittent River

PRINCIPAL MAP ABBREVIATIONS

ABOR. RSV.	ABORIGINAL RESERVE	IND. RES.	INDIAN RESERVATION	NWR	NATIONAL WILDLIFE
ADMIN.	ADMINISTRATION	INT'L	INTERNATIONAL		RESERVE
AFB	AIR FORCE BASE	IR	INDIAN RESERVATION	OBL.	OBLAST
AMM. DEP.	AMMUNITION DEPOT	ISTH.	ISTHMUS	OCC.	OCCUPIED
ARCH.	ARCHIPELAGO	JCT.	JUNCTION	OKR.	OKRUG
ARPT.	AIRPORT	L.	LAKE	PAR.	PARISH
AUT.	AUTONOMOUS	LAG.	LAGOON	PASSG.	PASSAGE
B.	BAY	LAKESH.	LAKESHORE	PEN.	PENINSULA
BFLD.	BATTLEFIELD	MEM.	MEMORIAL	PK.	PEAK
BK.	BROOK	MIL.	MILITARY	PLAT.	PLATEAU
BOR.	BOROUGH	MISS.	MISSILE	PN	PARK NATIONAL
BR.	BRANCH	MON.	MONUMENT	PREF.	PREFECTURE
C.	CAPE	MT.	MOUNT	PROM.	PROMONTORY
CAN.	CANAL	MTN.	MOUNTAIN	PROV.	PROVINCE
CAP.	CAPITAL	MTS.	MOUNTAINS	PRSV.	PRESERVE
C.G.	COAST GUARD	NAT.	NATURAL	PT.	POINT
CHAN.	CHANNEL	NAT'L	NATIONAL	R.	RIVER
CO.	COUNTY	NAV.	NAVAL	RA	RECREATION AREA
CR.	CREEK	NB	NATIONAL	RA.	RANGE
CTR.	CENTER		BATTLEFIELD	REC.	RECREATION(AL)
DEP.	DEPOT	NBP	NATIONAL	REF.	REFUGE
DEPR.	DEPRESSION		BATTLEFIELD PARK	REG.	REGION
DEPT.	DEPARTMENT	NBS	NATIONAL	REP.	REPUBLIC
DES.	DESERT		BATTLEFIELD SITE	RES.	RESERVOIR,
DIST.	DISTRICT	NHP	NATIONAL HISTORICAL		RESERVATION
DMZ	DEMILITARIZED ZONE		PARK	RVWY.	RIVERWAY
DPCY.	DEPENDENCY	NHPP	NATIONAL HISTORICAL	SA.	SIERRA
ENG.	ENGINEERING		PARK AND PRESERVE	SD.	SOUND
EST.	ESTUARY	NHS	NATIONAL HISTORIC	SEASH.	SEASHORE
FD.	FIORD, FJORD		SITE	SO.	SOUTHERN
FED.	FEDERAL	NL	NATIONAL LAKESHORE	SP	STATE PARK
FK.	FORK	NM	NATIONAL MONUMENT	SPR., SPRS.	SPRING, SPRINGS
FLD.	FIELD	NMEMP	NATIONAL MEMORIAL	ST.	STATE
FOR.	FOREST		PARK	STA.	STATION
FT.	FORT	NMILP	NATIONAL MILITARY	STM.	STREAM
G.	GULF		PARK	STR.	STRAIT
GOV.	GOVERNOR	NO.	NORTHERN	TERR.	TERRITORY
GOVT.	GOVERNMENT	NP	NATIONAL PARK	TUN.	TUNNEL
GD.	GRAND	NPP	NATIONAL PARK AND	TWP.	TOWNSHIP
GT.	GREAT		PRESERVE	VAL.	VALLEY
HAR.	HARBOR	NPRSV	NATIONAL PRESERVE	VILL.	VILLAGE
HD.	HEAD	NRA	NATIONAL	VOL.	VOLCANO
HIST.	HISTORIC(AL)		RECREATION AREA	WILD.	WILDLIFE,
HTS.	HEIGHTS	NRSV	NATIONAL RESERVE		WILDERNESS
I., IS.	ISLAND(S)	NS	NATIONAL SEASHORE	WTR.	WATER

THE PHYSICAL WORLD

These relief maps of the continents are derived from a digital cartographic database and drawn on a new Optimal Conformal Projection. They present the relationships of land and sea forms with startling realism.

MAPS OF THE WORLD

These detailed regional maps are arranged by continent, and introduced by a physical map of that continent which utilizes Hammond's new Optimal Conformal projection.

On the regional maps, individual colors for each country highlight political divisions. A country's color remains the same on all regional maps. These maps also provide considerable information by locating numerous political and physical geographic features.

WORLD STATISTICS

World Statistics lists the dimensions of the earth's principal mountains, islands, rivers and lakes, along with other useful geographic information.

MASTER INDEX

This is an A-Z listing of names found on the political maps. It also has its own abbreviation list which, along with other Index keys, appears on page 122.

MAP SCALES

A map's scale is the relationship of any length on the map to an identical length on the earth's surface. A scale of 1:3,000,000 means that one inch on the map represents 3,000,000 inches (47 miles, 76 km.) on the earth's surface. A 1:1,000,000 scale is larger than a 1:3,000,000 scale, just as 1/1 is larger than 1/3.

The most densely populated areas are shown at a scale of 1:1,170,000, while selected metropolitan areas are covered at either 1:587,000 or 1:1,170,000. Other populous areas are presented at 1:3,500,000 and 1:7,000,000. Large regions and continent maps, as well as the United States, Canada, Russia, Pacific and World have smaller scales.

World Flags and Reference Guide

Afghanistan
Page/Location: 61/H2
Area: 250,775 sq. mi.
  649,507 sq. km.
Population: 16,450,000
Capital: Kabul
Largest City: Kabul
Highest Point: Noshaq
Monetary Unit: afghani

Albania
Page/Location: 49/F2
Area: 11,100 sq. mi.
  28,749 sq. km.
Population: 3,335,000
Capital: Tiranë
Largest City: Tiranë
Highest Point: Korab
Monetary Unit: lek

Algeria
Page/Location: 82/F2
Area: 919,591 sq. mi.
  2,381,740 sq. km.
Population: 26,022,000
Capital: Algiers
Largest City: Algiers
Highest Point: Tahat
Monetary Unit: Algerian dinar

Andorra
Page/Location: 37/F1
Area: 188 sq. mi.
  487 sq. km.
Population: 53,000
Capital: Andorra la Vella
Largest City: Andorra la Vella
Highest Point: Coma Pedrosa
Monetary Unit: Fr. franc, Sp. peseta

Angola
Page/Location: 87/C3
Area: 481,351 sq. mi.
  1,246,700 sq. km.
Population: 8,668,000
Capital: Luanda
Largest City: Luanda
Highest Point: Morro de Môco
Monetary Unit: kwanza

Antigua and Barbuda
Page/Location: 101/J4
Area: 171 sq. mi.
  443 sq. km.
Population: 64,000
Capital: St. John's
Largest City: St. John's
Highest Point: Boggy Peak
Monetary Unit: East Caribbean dollar

Argentina
Page/Location: 91/C4
Area: 1,072,070 sq. mi.
  2,776,661 sq. km.
Population: 32,664,000
Capital: Buenos Aires
Largest City: Buenos Aires
Highest Point: Cerro Aconcagua
Monetary Unit: Argentine peso

Armenia
Page/Location: 55/H5
Area: 11,506 sq. mi.
  29,800 sq. km.
Population: 3,283,000
Capital: Yerevan
Largest City: Yerevan
Highest Point: Alagez
Monetary Unit: Armenian ruble

Australia
Page/Location: 74
Area: 2,966,136 sq. mi.
  7,682,300 sq. km.
Population: 17,288,000
Capital: Canberra
Largest City: Sydney
Highest Point: Mt. Kosciusko
Monetary Unit: Australian dollar

Austria
Page/Location: 45/L3
Area: 32,375 sq. mi.
  83,851 sq. km.
Population: 7,666,000
Capital: Vienna
Largest City: Vienna
Highest Point: Grossglockner
Monetary Unit: schilling

Azerbaijan
Page/Location: 55/H4
Area: 33,436 sq. mi.
  86,600 sq. km.
Population: 7,029,000
Capital: Baku
Largest City: Baku
Highest Point: Bazardyuzyu
Monetary Unit: Azerbaijani ruble

Bahamas
Page/Location: 101/F2
Area: 5,382 sq. mi.
  13,939 sq. km.
Population: 252,000
Capital: Nassau
Largest City: Nassau
Highest Point: 207 ft. (63 m)
Monetary Unit: Bahamian dollar

Bahrain
Page/Location: 60/F3
Area: 240 sq. mi.
  622 sq. km.
Population: 537,000
Capital: Manama
Largest City: Manama
Highest Point: Jabal Dukhān
Monetary Unit: Bahraini dinar

Bangladesh
Page/Location: 70/E3
Area: 55,126 sq. mi.
  142,776 sq. km.
Population: 116,601,000
Capital: Dhaka
Largest City: Dhaka
Highest Point: Keokradong
Monetary Unit: taka

Barbados
Page/Location: 101/K5
Area: 166 sq. mi.
  430 sq. km.
Population: 255,000
Capital: Bridgetown
Largest City: Bridgetown
Highest Point: Mt. Hillaby
Monetary Unit: Barbadian dollar

Belarus
Page/Location: 30/F3
Area: 80,154 sq. mi.
  207,600 sq. km.
Population: 10,200,000
Capital: Minsk
Largest City: Minsk
Highest Point: Dzerzhinskaya
Monetary Unit: Belarusian ruble

Belgium
Page/Location: 42/C2
Area: 11,781 sq. mi.
  30,513 sq. km.
Population: 9,922,000
Capital: Brussels
Largest City: Brussels
Highest Point: Botrange
Monetary Unit: Belgian franc

Belize
Page/Location: 100/D4
Area: 8,867 sq. mi.
  22,966 sq. km.
Population: 228,000
Capital: Belmopan
Largest City: Belize City
Highest Point: Victoria Peak
Monetary Unit: Belize dollar

Benin
Page/Location: 85/F4
Area: 43,483 sq. mi.
  112,620 sq. km.
Population: 4,832,000
Capital: Porto-Novo
Largest City: Cotonou
Highest Point: Nassoukou
Monetary Unit: CFA franc

Bhutan
Page/Location: 70/E2
Area: 18,147 sq. mi.
  47,000 sq. km.
Population: 1,598,000
Capital: Thimphu
Largest City: Thimphu
Highest Point: Kula Kangri
Monetary Unit: ngultrum

Bolivia
Page/Location: 92/F7
Area: 424,163 sq. mi.
  1,098,582 sq. km.
Population: 7,157,000
Capital: La Paz; Sucre
Largest City: La Paz
Highest Point: Nevado Ancohuma
Monetary Unit: Bolivian peso

Bosnia and Herzegovina
Page/Location: 50/C3
Area: 19,940 sq. mi.
  51,129 sq. km.
Population: 4,124,256
Capital: Sarajevo
Largest City: Sarajevo
Highest Point: Maglič
Monetary Unit: —

Botswana
Page/Location: 87/D5
Area: 224,764 sq. mi.
  582,139 sq. km.
Population: 1,258,000
Capital: Gaborone
Largest City: Gaborone
Highest Point: Tsodilo Hills
Monetary Unit: pula

Brazil
Page/Location: 90/D3
Area: 3,284,426 sq. mi.
  8,506,663 sq. km.
Population: 155,356,000
Capital: Brasília
Largest City: São Paulo
Highest Point: Pico da Neblina
Monetary Unit: cruzeiro real

Brunei
Page/Location: 72/D2
Area: 2,226 sq. mi.
  5,765 sq. km.
Population: 398,000
Capital: Bandar Seri Begawan
Largest City: Bandar Seri Begawan
Highest Point: Bukit Pagon
Monetary Unit: Brunei dollar

Bulgaria
Page/Location: 51/G4
Area: 42,823 sq. mi.
  110,912 sq. km.
Population: 8,911,000
Capital: Sofia
Largest City: Sofia
Highest Point: Musala
Monetary Unit: lev

Burkina Faso
Page/Location: 85/E3
Area: 105,869 sq. mi.
  274,200 sq. km.
Population: 9,360,000
Capital: Ouagadougou
Largest City: Ouagadougou
Highest Point: 2,405 ft. (733 m)
Monetary Unit: CFA franc

Burma
Page/Location: 71/G3
Area: 261,789 sq. mi.
  678,034 sq. km.
Population: 42,112,000
Capital: Rangoon
Largest City: Rangoon
Highest Point: Hkakabo Razi
Monetary Unit: kyat

Burundi
Page/Location: 87/E1
Area: 10,747 sq. mi.
  27,835 sq. km.
Population: 5,831,000
Capital: Bujumbura
Largest City: Bujumbura
Highest Point: 8,760 ft. (2,670 m)
Monetary Unit: Burundi franc

Cambodia
Page/Location: 69/D3
Area: 69,898 sq. mi.
  181,036 sq. km.
Population: 7,146,000
Capital: Phnom Penh
Largest City: Phnom Penh
Highest Point: Phnum Aoral
Monetary Unit: riel

Cameroon
Page/Location:
Area: 183,568 sq. mi.
475,441 sq. km.
Population: 11,390,000
Capital: Yaoundé
Largest City: Douala
Highest Point: Mt. Cameroon
Monetary Unit: CFA franc

Canada
Page/Location:
Area: 3,851,787 sq. mi.
9,976,139 sq. km.
Population: 26,835,331
Capital: Ottawa
Largest City: Toronto
Highest Point: Mt. Logan
Monetary Unit: Canadian dollar

Cape Verde
Page/Location:
Area: 1,557 sq. mi.
4,033 sq. km.
Population: 387,000
Capital: Praia
Largest City: Praia
Highest Point: 9,282 ft. (2,829 m)
Monetary Unit: Cape Verde escudo

Central African Republic
Page/Location:
Area: 242,000 sq. mi.
626,780 sq. km.
Population: 2,952,000
Capital: Bangui
Largest City: Bangui
Highest Point: Mt. Kayagangiri
Monetary Unit: CFA franc

Chad
Page/Location:
Area: 495,752 sq. mi.
1,283,998 sq. km.
Population: 5,122,000
Capital: N'Djamena
Largest City: N'Djamena
Highest Point: Emi Koussi
Monetary Unit: CFA franc

Chile
Page/Location:
Area: 292,257 sq. mi.
756,946 sq. km.
Population: 13,287,000
Capital: Santiago
Largest City: Santiago
Highest Point: Nevado Ojos del Salado
Monetary Unit: Chilean peso

China
Page/Location:
Area: 3,691,000 sq. mi.
9,559,690 sq. km.
Population: 1,151,487,000
Capital: Beijing
Largest City: Shanghai
Highest Point: Mt. Everest
Monetary Unit: yuan

Colombia
Page/Location:
Area: 439,513 sq. mi.
1,138,339 sq. km.
Population: 33,778,000
Capital: Bogotá
Largest City: Bogotá
Highest Point: Pico Cristóbal Colón
Monetary Unit: Colombian peso

Comoros
Page/Location:
Area: 719 sq. mi.
1,862 sq. km.
Population: 477,000
Capital: Moroni
Largest City: Moroni
Highest Point: Karthala
Monetary Unit: Comorian franc

Congo
Page/Location:
Area: 132,046 sq. mi.
342,000 sq. km.
Population: 2,309,000
Capital: Brazzaville
Largest City: Brazzaville
Highest Point: Lékéti Mts.
Monetary Unit: CFA franc

Costa Rica
Page/Location:
Area: 19,575 sq. mi.
50,700 sq. km.
Population: 3,111,000
Capital: San José
Largest City: San José
Highest Point: Cerro Chirripó Grande
Monetary Unit: Costa Rican colón

Croatia
Page/Location:
Area: 22,050 sq. mi.
56,538 sq. km.
Population: 4,601,469
Capital: Zagreb
Largest City: Zagreb
Highest Point: Veliki Troglav
Monetary Unit: Croatian dinar

Cuba
Page/Location:
Area: 44,206 sq. mi.
114,494 sq. km.
Population: 10,732,000
Capital: Havana
Largest City: Havana
Highest Point: Pico Turquino
Monetary Unit: Cuban peso

Cyprus
Page/Location:
Area: 3,473 sq. mi.
8,995 sq. km.
Population: 709,000
Capital: Nicosia
Largest City: Nicosia
Highest Point: Olympus
Monetary Unit: Cypriot pound

Czech Republic
Page/Location:
Area: 30,449 sq. mi.
78,863 sq. km.
Population: 10,291,927
Capital: Prague
Largest City: Prague
Highest Point: Sněžka
Monetary Unit: Czech koruna

Denmark
Page/Location:
Area: 16,629 sq. mi.
43,069 sq. km.
Population: 5,133,000
Capital: Copenhagen
Largest City: Copenhagen
Highest Point: Yding Skovhøj
Monetary Unit: Danish krone

Djibouti
Page/Location:
Area: 8,880 sq. mi.
23,000 sq. km.
Population: 346,000
Capital: Djibouti
Largest City: Djibouti
Highest Point: Moussa Ali
Monetary Unit: Djibouti franc

Dominica
Page/Location:
Area: 290 sq. mi.
751 sq. km.
Population: 86,000
Capital: Roseau
Largest City: Roseau
Highest Point: Morne Diablotin
Monetary Unit: Dominican dollar

Dominican Republic
Page/Location:
Area: 18,704 sq. mi.
48,443 sq. km.
Population: 7,385,000
Capital: Santo Domingo
Largest City: Santo Domingo
Highest Point: Pico Duarte
Monetary Unit: Dominican peso

Ecuador
Page/Location:
Area: 109,483 sq. mi.
283,591 sq. km.
Population: 10,752,000
Capital: Quito
Largest City: Guayaquil
Highest Point: Chimborazo
Monetary Unit: sucre

Egypt
Page/Location:
Area: 386,659 sq. mi.
1,001,447 sq. km.
Population: 54,452,000
Capital: Cairo
Largest City: Cairo
Highest Point: Mt. Catherine
Monetary Unit: Egyptian pound

El Salvador
Page/Location:
Area: 8,260 sq. mi.
21,393 sq. km.
Population: 5,419,000
Capital: San Salvador
Largest City: San Salvador
Highest Point: Santa Ana
Monetary Unit: Salvadoran colón

Equatorial Guinea
Page/Location:
Area: 10,831 sq. mi.
28,052 sq. km.
Population: 379,000
Capital: Malabo
Largest City: Malabo
Highest Point: Pico de Santa Isabel
Monetary Unit: CFA franc

Eritrea
Page/Location:
Area: 45,410 sq. mi.
117,600 sq. km.
Population: 2,614,700
Capital: Åsmera
Largest City: Åsmera
Highest Point: Soira
Monetary Unit: birr

Estonia
Page/Location:
Area: 17,413 sq. mi.
45,100 sq. km.
Population: 1,573,000
Capital: Tallinn
Largest City: Tallinn
Highest Point: Munamägi
Monetary Unit: kroon

Ethiopia
Page/Location:
Area: 426,366 sq. mi.
1,104,300 sq. km.
Population: 50,576,300
Capital: Addis Ababa
Largest City: Addis Ababa
Highest Point: Ras Dashen Terara
Monetary Unit: birr

Fiji
Page/Location:
Area: 7,055 sq. mi.
18,272 sq. km.
Population: 744,000
Capital: Suva
Largest City: Suva
Highest Point: Tomaniivi
Monetary Unit: Fijian dollar

Finland
Page/Location:
Area: 130,128 sq. mi.
337,032 sq. km.
Population: 4,991,000
Capital: Helsinki
Largest City: Helsinki
Highest Point: Kahperusvaara
Monetary Unit: markka

France
Page/Location:
Area: 210,038 sq. mi.
543,998 sq. km.
Population: 56,596,000
Capital: Paris
Largest City: Paris
Highest Point: Mont Blanc
Monetary Unit: French franc

Gabon
Page/Location:
Area: 103,346 sq. mi.
267,666 sq. km.
Population: 1,080,000
Capital: Libreville
Largest City: Libreville
Highest Point: Mt. Iboundji
Monetary Unit: CFA franc

Gambia
Page/Location:
Area: 4,127 sq. mi.
10,689 sq. km.
Population: 875,000
Capital: Banjul
Largest City: Banjul
Highest Point: 98 ft. (30 m)
Monetary Unit: dalasi

Georgia
Page/Location:
Area: 26,911 sq. mi.
69,700 sq. km.
Population: 5,449,000
Capital: Tbilisi
Largest City: Tbilisi
Highest Point: Kazbek
Monetary Unit: Georgian ruble

Germany
Page/Location:
Area: 137,753 sq. mi.
356,780 sq. km.
Population: 79,548,000
Capital: Berlin
Largest City: Berlin
Highest Point: Zugspitze
Monetary Unit: Deutsche mark

Ghana
Page/Location:
Area: 92,099 sq. mi.
238,536 sq. km.
Population: 15,617,000
Capital: Accra
Largest City: Accra
Highest Point: Afadjoto
Monetary Unit: cedi

Greece
Page/Location:
Area: 50,944 sq. mi.
131,945 sq. km.
Population: 10,043,000
Capital: Athens
Largest City: Athens
Highest Point: Mt. Olympus
Monetary Unit: drachma

Grenada
Page/Location:
Area: 133 sq. mi.
344 sq. km.
Population: 84,000
Capital: St. George's
Largest City: St. George's
Highest Point: Mt. St. Catherine
Monetary Unit: East Caribbean dollar

World Flags and Reference Guide

Guatemala
Page/Location: 100/C4
Area: 42,042 sq. mi.
108,889 sq. km.
Population: 9,266,000
Capital: Guatemala
Largest City: Guatemala
Highest Point: Tajumulco
Monetary Unit: quetzal

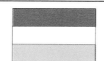

Guinea
Page/Location: 84/C4
Area: 94,925 sq. mi.
245,856 sq. km.
Population: 7,456,000
Capital: Conakry
Largest City: Conakry
Highest Point: Mt. Nimba
Monetary Unit: Guinea franc

Guinea-Bissau
Page/Location: 84/B3
Area: 13,948 sq. mi.
36,125 sq. km.
Population: 943,000
Capital: Bissau
Largest City: Bissau
Highest Point: 689 ft. (210 m)
Monetary Unit: Guinea-Bissau peso

Guyana
Page/Location: 92/G2
Area: 83,000 sq. mi.
214,970 sq. km.
Population: 1,024,000
Capital: Georgetown
Largest City: Georgetown
Highest Point: Mt. Roraima
Monetary Unit: Guyana dollar

Haiti
Page/Location: 101/G4
Area: 10,694 sq. mi.
27,697 sq. km.
Population: 6,287,000
Capital: Port-au-Prince
Largest City: Port-au-Prince
Highest Point: Pic la Selle
Monetary Unit: gourde

Honduras
Page/Location: 100/D4
Area: 43,277 sq. mi.
112,087 sq. km.
Population: 4,949,000
Capital: Tegucigalpa
Largest City: Tegucigalpa
Highest Point: Cerro de las Minas
Monetary Unit: lempira

Hungary
Page/Location: 50/D2
Area: 35,919 sq. mi.
93,030 sq. km.
Population: 10,558,000
Capital: Budapest
Largest City: Budapest
Highest Point: Kékes
Monetary Unit: forint

Iceland
Page/Location: 37/N7
Area: 39,768 sq. mi.
103,000 sq. km.
Population: 260,000
Capital: Reykjavík
Largest City: Reykjavík
Highest Point: Hvannadalshnúkur
Monetary Unit: króna

India
Page/Location: 73/C3
Area: 1,269,339 sq. mi.
3,287,558 sq. km.
Population: 869,515,000
Capital: New Delhi
Largest City: Calcutta
Highest Point: Nanda Devi
Monetary Unit: Indian rupee

Indonesia
Page/Location: 75/E4
Area: 788,430 sq. mi.
2, 042,034 sq. km.
Population: 19,560,000
Capital: Jakarta
Largest City: Jakarta
Highest Point: Puncak Jaya
Monetary Unit: rupiah

Iran
Page/Location: 60/F2
Area: 636,293 sq. mi.
1,648,000 sq. km.
Population: 59,051,000
Capital: Tehran
Largest City: Tehran
Highest Point: Qolleh-ye Damāvand
Monetary Unit: Iranian rial

Iraq
Page/Location: 60/D2
Area: 172,476 sq. mi.
446,713 sq. km.
Population: 19,525,000
Capital: Baghdad
Largest City: Baghdad
Highest Point: Haji Ibrahim
Monetary Unit: Iraqi dinar

Ireland
Page/Location: 36/A4
Area: 27,136 sq. mi.
70,282 sq. km.
Population: 3,489,000
Capital: Dublin
Largest City: Dublin
Highest Point: Carrantuohill
Monetary Unit: Irish pound

Israel
Page/Location: 59/K5
Area: 7,847 sq. mi.
20,324 sq. km.
Population: 4,558,000
Capital: Jerusalem
Largest City: Tel Aviv-Yafo
Highest Point: Har Meron
Monetary Unit: shekel

Italy
Page/Location: 30/E4
Area: 116,303 sq. mi.
301,225 sq. km.
Population: 57,772,000
Capital: Rome
Largest City: Rome
Highest Point: Monte Rosa
Monetary Unit: Italian lira

Ivory Coast
Page/Location: 84/D5
Area: 124,504 sq. mi.
322,465 sq. km.
Population: 12,978,000
Capital: Yamoussoukro
Largest City: Abidjan
Highest Point: Mt. Nimba
Monetary Unit: CFA franc

Jamaica
Page/Location: 101/F4
Area: 4,411 sq. mi.
11,424 sq. km.
Population: 2,489,000
Capital: Kingston
Largest City: Kingston
Highest Point: Blue Mountain Pk.
Monetary Unit: Jamaican dollar

Japan
Page/Location: 63/M4
Area: 145,730 sq. mi.
377,441 sq. km.
Population: 124,017,000
Capital: Tokyo
Largest City: Tokyo
Highest Point: Fujiyama
Monetary Unit: yen

Jordan
Page/Location: 60/C2
Area: 35,000 sq. mi.
90,650 sq. km.
Population: 3,413,000
Capital: Amman
Largest City: Amman
Highest Point: Jabal Ramm
Monetary Unit: Jordanian dinar

Kazakhstan
Page/Location: 56/G5
Area: 1,048,300 sq. mi.
2,715,100 sq. km.
Population: 16,538,000
Capital: Alma-Ata
Largest City: Alma-Ata
Highest Point: Khan-Tengri
Monetary Unit: Kazakhstani ruble

Kenya
Page/Location: 83/M7
Area: 224,960 sq. mi.
582,646 sq. km.
Population: 25,242,000
Capital: Nairobi
Largest City: Nairobi
Highest Point: Mt. Kenya
Monetary Unit: Kenya shilling

Kiribati
Page/Location: 79/H5
Area: 291 sq. mi.
754 sq. km.
Population: 71,000
Capital: Bairiki
Largest City: —
Highest Point: Banaba Island
Monetary Unit: Australian dollar

Korea, North
Page/Location: 63/K3
Area: 46,540 sq. mi.
120,539 sq. km.
Population: 21,815,000
Capital: P'yŏngyang
Largest City: P'yŏngyang
Highest Point: Paektu-san
Monetary Unit: North Korean won

Korea, South
Page/Location: 63/K4
Area: 38,175 sq. mi.
98,873 sq. km.
Population: 43,134,000
Capital: Seoul
Largest City: Seoul
Highest Point: Halla-san
Monetary Unit: South Korean won

Kuwait
Page/Location: 60/E3
Area: 6,532 sq. mi.
16,918 sq. km.
Population: 2,204,000
Capital: Al Kuwait
Largest City: Al Kuwait
Highest Point: 951 ft. (290 m)
Monetary Unit: Kuwaiti dinar

Kyrgyzstan
Page/Location: 68/B3
Area: 76,641 sq. mi.
198,500 sq. km.
Population: 4,291,000
Capital: Bishkek
Largest City: Bishkek
Highest Point: Pik Pobedy
Monetary Unit: Kyrgyz ruble

Laos
Page/Location: 69/C2
Area: 91,428 sq. mi.
236,800 sq. km.
Population: 4,113,000
Capital: Vientiane
Largest City: Vientiane
Highest Point: Phou Bia
Monetary Unit: kip

Latvia
Page/Location: 52/E4
Area: 24,595 sq. mi.
63,700 sq. km.
Population: 1,681,000
Capital: Riga
Largest City: Riga
Highest Point: Gaizina Kalns
Monetary Unit: Latvian ruble, lat

Lebanon
Page/Location: 59/K5
Area: 4,015 sq. mi.
10,399 sq. km.
Population: 3,385,000
Capital: Beirut
Largest City: Beirut
Highest Point: Qurnat as Sawdā'
Monetary Unit: Lebanese pound

Lesotho
Page/Location: 88/E3
Area: 11,720 sq. mi.
30,355 sq. km.
Population: 1,801,000
Capital: Maseru
Largest City: Maseru
Highest Point: Thabana-Ntlenyana
Monetary Unit: loti

Liberia
Page/Location:
Area: 43,000 sq. mi.
111,370 sq. km.
Population: 2,730,000
Capital: Monrovia
Largest City: Monrovia
Highest Point: Mt. Wuteve
Monetary Unit: Liberian dollar

Libya
Page/Location:
Area: 679,358 sq. mi.
1,759,537 sq. km.
Population: 4,353,000
Capital: Tripoli
Largest City: Tripoli
Highest Point: Picco Bette
Monetary Unit: Libyan dinar

Liechtenstein
Page/Location:
Area: 61 sq. mi.
158 sq. km.
Population: 28,000
Capital: Vaduz
Largest City: Vaduz
Highest Point: Grauspitz
Monetary Unit: Swiss franc

Lithuania
Page/Location:
Area: 25,174 sq. mi.
65,200 sq. km.
Population: 3,690,000
Capital: Vilnius
Largest City: Vilnius
Highest Point: Nevaišių
Monetary Unit: talonas

Luxembourg
Page/Location:
Area: 999 sq. mi.
2,587 sq. km.
Population: 388,000
Capital: Luxembourg
Largest City: Luxembourg
Highest Point: Ardennes Plateau
Monetary Unit: Luxembourg franc

Macedonia
Page/Location:
Area: 9,889 sq. mi.
25,713 sq. km.
Population: 1,909,136
Capital: Skopje
Largest City: Skopje
Highest Point: Korab
Monetary Unit: denar

Madagascar
Page/Location:
Area: 226,657 sq. mi.
587,041 sq. km.
Population: 12,185,000
Capital: Antananarivo
Largest City: Antananarivo
Highest Point: Maromokotro
Monetary Unit: Malagasy franc

Malawi
Page/Location:
Area: 45,747 sq. mi.
118, 485 sq. km.
Population: 9,438,000
Capital: Lilongwe
Largest City: Blantyre
Highest Point: Mulanje Mts.
Monetary Unit: Malawi kwacha

Malaysia
Page/Location:
Area: 128,308 sq. mi.
332,318 sq. km.
Population: 17,982,000
Capital: Kuala Lumpur
Largest City: Kuala Lumpur
Highest Point: Gunung Kinabalu
Monetary Unit: ringgit

Maldives
Page/Location:
Area: 115 sq. mi.
298 sq. km.
Population: 226,000
Capital: Male
Largest City: Male
Highest Point: 20 ft. (6 m)
Monetary Unit: rufiyaa

Mali
Page/Location:
Area: 464,873 sq. mi.
1,204,021 sq. km.
Population: 8,339,000
Capital: Bamako
Largest City: Bamako
Highest Point: Hombori Tondo
Monetary Unit: CFA franc

Malta
Page/Location:
Area: 122 sq. mi.
316 sq. km.
Population: 356,000
Capital: Valletta
Largest City: Sliema
Highest Point: 830 ft. (253 m)
Monetary Unit: Maltese lira

Marshall Islands
Page/Location:
Area: 70 sq. mi.
181 sq. km.
Population: 48,000
Capital: Majuro
Largest City: —
Highest Point: 20 ft. (6 m)
Monetary Unit: U.S. dollar

Mauritania
Page/Location:
Area: 419,229 sq. mi.
1,085, 803 sq. km.
Population: 1,996,000
Capital: Nouakchott
Largest City: Nouakchott
Highest Point: Kediet Ijill
Monetary Unit: ouguiya

Mauritius
Page/Location:
Area: 790 sq. mi.
2,046 sq. km.
Population: 1,081,000
Capital: Port Louis
Largest City: Port Louis
Highest Point: 2,713 ft. (827 m)
Monetary Unit: Mauritian rupee

Mexico
Page/Location:
Area: 761,601 sq. mi.
1,972,546 sq. km.
Population: 90,007,000
Capital: Mexico City
Largest City: Mexico City
Highest Point: Citlaltépetl
Monetary Unit: Mexican peso

Micronesia
Page/Location:
Area: 271 sq. mi.
702 sq. km.
Population: 108,000
Capital: Kolonia
Largest City: —
Highest Point: —
Monetary Unit: U.S. dollar

Moldova
Page/Location:
Area: 13,012 sq. mi.
33,700 sq. km.
Population: 4,341,000
Capital: Kishinev
Largest City: Kishinev
Highest Point: 1,408 ft. (429 m)
Monetary Unit: Moldovan ruble

Monaco
Page/Location:
Area: 368 acres
149 hectares
Population: 30,000
Capital: Monaco
Largest City: —
Highest Point: —
Monetary Unit: French franc

Mongolia
Page/Location:
Area: 606,163 sq. mi.
1,569, 962 sq. km.
Population: 2,247,000
Capital: Ulaanbaatar
Largest City: Ulaanbaatar
Highest Point: Tavan Bogd Uul
Monetary Unit: tughrik

Morocco
Page/Location:
Area: 172,414 sq. mi.
446,550 sq. km.
Population: 26,182,000
Capital: Rabat
Largest City: Casablanca
Highest Point: Jebel Toubkal
Monetary Unit: Moroccan dirham

Mozambique
Page/Location:
Area: 303,769 sq. mi.
786,762 sq. km.
Population: 15,113,000
Capital: Maputo
Largest City: Maputo
Highest Point: Monte Binga
Monetary Unit: metical

Namibia
Page/Location:
Area: 317,827 sq. mi.
823,172 sq. km.
Population: 1,521,000
Capital: Windhoek
Largest City: Windhoek
Highest Point: Brandberg
Monetary Unit: rand

Nauru
Page/Location:
Area: 7.7 sq. mi.
20 sq. km.
Population: 9,000
Capital: Yaren (district)
Largest City: —
Highest Point: 230 ft. (70 m)
Monetary Unit: Australian dollar

Nepal
Page/Location:
Area: 54,663 sq. mi.
141,557 sq. km.
Population: 19,612,000
Capital: Kathmandu
Largest City: Kathmandu
Highest Point: Mt. Everest
Monetary Unit: Nepalese rupee

Netherlands
Page/Location:
Area: 15,892 sq. mi.
41,160 sq. km.
Population: 15,022,000
Capital: The Hague; Amsterdam
Largest City: Amsterdam
Highest Point: Vaalserberg
Monetary Unit: Netherlands guilder

New Zealand
Page/Location:
Area: 103,736 sq. mi.
268,676 sq. km.
Population: 3,309,000
Capital: Wellington
Largest City: Auckland
Highest Point: Mt. Cook
Monetary Unit: New Zealand dollar

Nicaragua
Page/Location:
Area: 45,698 sq. mi.
118,358 sq. km.
Population: 3,752,000
Capital: Managua
Largest City: Managua
Highest Point: Pico Mogotón
Monetary Unit: córdoba

Niger
Page/Location:
Area: 489,189 sq. mi.
1,267,000 sq. km.
Population: 8,154,000
Capital: Niamey
Largest City: Niamey
Highest Point: Bagzane
Monetary Unit: CFA franc

Nigeria
Page/Location:
Area: 357,000 sq. mi.
924,630 sq. km.
Population: 122,471,000
Capital: Abuja
Largest City: Lagos
Highest Point: Dimlang
Monetary Unit: naira

Norway
Page/Location:
Area: 125,053 sq. mi.
323,887 sq. km.
Population: 4,273,000
Capital: Oslo
Largest City: Oslo
Highest Point: Glittertjnden
Monetary Unit: Norwegian krone

Oman
Page/Location:
Area: 120,000 sq. mi.
310,800 sq. km.
Population: 1,534,000
Capital: Muscat
Largest City: Muscat
Highest Point: Jabal ash Shām
Monetary Unit: Omani rial

Pakistan
Page/Location:
Area: 310,403 sq. mi.
803,944 sq. km.
Population: 117,490,000
Capital: Islamabad
Largest City: Karachi
Highest Point: K2 (Godwin Austen)
Monetary Unit: Pakistani rupee

Panama
Page/Location:
Area: 29,761 sq. mi.
77,082 sq. km.
Population: 2,476,000
Capital: Panamá
Largest City: Panamá
Highest Point: Barú
Monetary Unit: balboa

Papua New Guinea
Page/Location:
Area: 183,540 sq. mi.
475,369 sq. km.
Population: 3,913,000
Capital: Port Moresby
Largest City: Port Moresby
Highest Point: Mt. Wilhelm
Monetary Unit: kina

Paraguay
Page/Location:
Area: 157,047 sq. mi.
406,752 sq. km.
Population: 4,799,000
Capital: Asunción
Largest City: Asunción
Highest Point: Sierra de Amambay
Monetary Unit: guaraní

World Flags and Reference Guide

Peru
Page/Location: 92/C5
Area: 496,222 sq. mi.
1,285,215 sq. km.
Population: 22,362,000
Capital: Lima
Largest City: Lima
Highest Point: Nevado Huascarán
Monetary Unit: nuevo sol

Philippines
Page/Location: 67/D5
Area: 115,707 sq. mi.
299,681 sq. km.
Population: 65,759,000
Capital: Manila
Largest City: Manila
Highest Point: Mt. Apo
Monetary Unit: Philippine peso

Poland
Page/Location: 39/K2
Area: 120,725 sq. mi.
312,678 sq. km.
Population: 37,800,000
Capital: Warsaw
Largest City: Warsaw
Highest Point: Rysy
Monetary Unit: zloty

Portugal
Page/Location: 46/A3
Area: 35,549 sq. mi.
92,072 sq. km.
Population: 10,388,000
Capital: Lisbon
Largest City: Lisbon
Highest Point: Serra da Estrela
Monetary Unit: Portuguese escudo

Qatar
Page/Location: 60/F3
Area: 4,247 sq. mi.
11,000 sq. km.
Population: 518,000
Capital: Doha
Largest City: Doha
Highest Point: Dukhān Heights
Monetary Unit: Qatari riyal

Romania
Page/Location: 51/F3
Area: 91,699 sq. mi.
237,500 sq. km.
Population: 23,397,000
Capital: Bucharest
Largest City: Bucharest
Highest Point: Moldoveanul
Monetary Unit: leu

Russia
Page/Location: 56/H3
Area: 6,592,812 sq. mi.
17,075,400 sq. km.
Population: 147,386,000
Capital: Moscow
Largest City: Moscow
Highest Point: El'brus
Monetary Unit: Russian ruble

Rwanda
Page/Location: 87/E1
Area: 10,169 sq. mi.
26,337 sq. km.
Population: 7,903,000
Capital: Kigali
Largest City: Kigali
Highest Point: Karisimbi
Monetary Unit: Rwanda franc

Saint Kitts and Nevis
Page/Location: 101/J4
Area: 104 sq. mi.
269 sq. km.
Population: 40,000
Capital: Basseterre
Largest City: Basseterre
Highest Point: Mt. Misery
Monetary Unit: East Caribbean dollar

Saint Lucia
Page/Location: 101/J5
Area: 238 sq. mi.
616 sq. km.
Population: 153,000
Capital: Castries
Largest City: Castries
Highest Point: Mt. Gimie
Monetary Unit: East Caribbean dollar

Saint Vincent and the Grenadines
Page/Location: 101/J5
Area: 150 sq. mi.
388 sq. km.
Population: 114,000
Capital: Kingstown
Largest City: Kingstown
Highest Point: Soufrière
Monetary Unit: East Caribbean dollar

San Marino
Page/Location: 45/K5
Area: 23.4 sq. mi.
60.6 sq. km.
Population: 23,000
Capital: San Marino
Largest City: San Marino
Highest Point: Monte Titano
Monetary Unit: Italian lira

São Tomé and Príncipe
Page/Location: 82/G7
Area: 372 sq. mi.
963 sq. km.
Population: 128,000
Capital: São Tomé
Largest City: São Tomé
Highest Point: Pico de São Tomé
Monetary Unit: dobra

Saudi Arabia
Page/Location: 60/D4
Area: 829,995 sq. mi.
2,149,687 sq. km.
Population: 17,870,000
Capital: Riyadh
Largest City: Riyadh
Highest Point: Jabal Sawdā'
Monetary Unit: Saudi riyal

Senegal
Page/Location: 84/B3
Area: 75,954 sq. mi.
196,720 sq. km.
Population: 7,953,000
Capital: Dakar
Largest City: Dakar
Highest Point: Fouta Djallon
Monetary Unit: CFA franc

Seychelles
Page/Location: 80/H5
Area: 145 sq. mi.
375 sq. km.
Population: 69,000
Capital: Victoria
Largest City: Victoria
Highest Point: Morne Seychellois
Monetary Unit: Seychellois rupee

Sierra Leone
Page/Location: 84/B4
Area: 27,925 sq. mi.
72,325 sq. km.
Population: 4,275,000
Capital: Freetown
Largest City: Freetown
Highest Point: Loma Mansa
Monetary Unit: leone

Singapore
Page/Location: 72/B3
Area: 226 sq. mi.
585 sq. km.
Population: 2,756,000
Capital: Singapore
Largest City: Singapore
Highest Point: Bukit Timah
Monetary Unit: Singapore dollar

Slovakia
Page/Location: 39/K4
Area: 18,924 sq. mi.
49,014 sq. km.
Population: 4,991,168
Capital: Bratislava
Largest City: Bratislava
Highest Point: Gerlachovský Štít
Monetary Unit: Slovak koruna

Slovenia
Page/Location: 50/B3
Area: 7,898 sq. mi.
20,251 sq. km.
Population: 1,891,864
Capital: Ljubljana
Largest City: Ljubljana
Highest Point: Triglav
Monetary Unit: tolar

Solomon Islands
Page/Location: 78/E6
Area: 11,500 sq. mi.
29,785 sq. km.
Population: 347,000
Capital: Honiara
Largest City: Honiara
Highest Point: Mt. Makarakomburu
Monetary Unit: Solomon Islands dollar

Somalia
Page/Location: 83/Q6
Area: 246,200 sq. mi.
637,658 sq. km.
Population: 6,709,000
Capital: Mogadishu
Largest City: Mogadishu
Highest Point: Shimber Berris
Monetary Unit: Somali shilling

South Africa
Page/Location: 88/C3
Area: 455,318 sq. mi.
1,179,274 sq. km.
Population: 40,601,000
Capital: Cape Town; Pretoria
Largest City: Johannesburg
Highest Point: Injasuti
Monetary Unit: rand

Spain
Page/Location: 46/C2
Area: 194,881 sq. mi.
504,742 sq. km.
Population: 39,385,000
Capital: Madrid
Largest City: Madrid
Highest Point: Pico de Teide
Monetary Unit: peseta

Sri Lanka
Page/Location: 70/D6
Area: 25,332 sq. mi.
65,610 sq. km.
Population: 17,424,000
Capital: Colombo
Largest City: Colombo
Highest Point: Pidurutalagala
Monetary Unit: Sri Lanka rupee

Sudan
Page/Location: 83/L5
Area: 967,494 sq. mi.
2,505,809 sq. km.
Population: 27,220,000
Capital: Khartoum
Largest City: Omdurman
Highest Point: Jabal Marrah
Monetary Unit: Sudanese pound

Suriname
Page/Location: 93/G3
Area: 55,144 sq. mi.
142,823 sq. km.
Population: 402,000
Capital: Paramaribo
Largest City: Paramaribo
Highest Point: Juliana Top
Monetary Unit: Suriname guilder

Swaziland
Page/Location: 89/E2
Area: 6,705 sq. mi.
17,366 sq. km.
Population: 859,000
Capital: Mbabane
Largest City: Mbabane
Highest Point: Emlembe
Monetary Unit: lilangeni

Sweden
Page/Location: 37/E3
Area: 173,665 sq. mi.
449,792 sq. km.
Population: 8,564,000
Capital: Stockholm
Largest City: Stockholm
Highest Point: Kebnekaise
Monetary Unit: krona

Switzerland
Page/Location: 45/H3
Area: 15,943 sq. mi.
41,292 sq. km.
Population: 6,784,000
Capital: Bern
Largest City: Zürich
Highest Point: Dufourspitze
Monetary Unit: Swiss franc

Syria
Page/Location: 60/C1
Area: 71,498 sq. mi.
　　　185,180 sq. km.
Population: 12,966,000
Capital: Damascus
Largest City: Damascus
Highest Point: Jabal ash Shaykh
Monetary Unit: Syrian pound

Taiwan
Page/Location: 67/D3
Area: 13,971 sq. mi.
　　　36,185 sq. km.
Population: 16,609,961
Capital: Taipei
Largest City: Taipei
Highest Point: Yü Shan
Monetary Unit: new Taiwan dollar

Tajikistan
Page/Location: 56/H6
Area: 55,251 sq. mi.
　　　143,100 sq. km.
Population: 5,112,000
Capital: Dushanbe
Largest City: Dushanbe
Highest Point: Communism Peak
Monetary Unit: Tajik ruble

Tanzania
Page/Location: 87/F2
Area: 363,708 sq. mi.
　　　942,003 sq. km.
Population: 26,869,000
Capital: Dar es Salaam
Largest City: Dar es Salaam
Highest Point: Kilimanjaro
Monetary Unit: Tanzanian shilling

Thailand
Page/Location: 69/C3
Area: 198,455 sq. mi.
　　　513,998 sq. km.
Population: 56,814,000
Capital: Bangkok
Largest City: Bangkok
Highest Point: Doi Inthanon
Monetary Unit: baht

Togo
Page/Location: 85/F4
Area: 21,622 sq. mi.
　　　56,000 sq. km.
Population: 3,811,000
Capital: Lomé
Largest City: Lomé
Highest Point: Mt. Agou
Monetary Unit: CFA franc

Tonga
Page/Location: 79/H7
Area: 270 sq. mi.
　　　699 sq. km.
Population: 102,000
Capital: Nuku'alofa
Largest City: Nuku'alofa
Highest Point: Kao Island
Monetary Unit: pa'anga

Trinidad and Tobago
Page/Location: 101/J5
Area: 1,980 sq. mi.
　　　5,128 sq. km.
Population: 1,285,000
Capital: Port-of-Spain
Largest City: Port-of-Spain
Highest Point: El Cerro del Aripo
Monetary Unit: Trin. & Tobago dollar

Tunisia
Page/Location: 82/G1
Area: 63,378 sq. mi.
　　　164,149 sq. km.
Population: 8,276,000
Capital: Tunis
Largest City: Tunis
Highest Point: Jabal ash Sha'nabī
Monetary Unit: Tunisian dinar

Turkey
Page/Location: 59/C2
Area: 300,946 sq. mi.
　　　779,450 sq. km.
Population: 58,581,000
Capital: Ankara
Largest City: Istanbul
Highest Point: Mt. Ararat
Monetary Unit: Turkish lira

Turkmenistan
Page/Location: 56/F6
Area: 188,455 sq. mi.
　　　488,100 sq. km.
Population: 3,534,000
Capital: Ashkhabad
Largest City: Ashkhabad
Highest Point: Rize
Monetary Unit: Turkmen ruble

Tuvalu
Page/Location: 78/G5
Area: 9.8 sq. mi.
　　　25.3 sq. km.
Population: 9,000
Capital: Fongafale
Largest City: —
Highest Point: 16 ft. (5 m)
Monetary Unit: Australian dollar

Uganda
Page/Location: 83/M7
Area: 91,076 sq. mi.
　　　235,887 sq. km.
Population: 18,690,000
Capital: Kampala
Largest City: Kampala
Highest Point: Margherita Peak
Monetary Unit: Ugandan shilling

Ukraine
Page/Location: 54/D2
Area: 233,089 sq. mi.
　　　603,700 sq. km.
Population: 51,704,000
Capital: Kiev
Largest City: Kiev
Highest Point: Goverla
Monetary Unit: Ukrainian ruble

United Arab Emirates
Page/Location: 60/F4
Area: 32,278 sq. mi.
　　　83,600 sq. km.
Population: 2,390,000
Capital: Abu Dhabi
Largest City: Dubayy
Highest Point: Hajar Mts.
Monetary Unit: Emirian dirham

United Kingdom
Page/Location: 36
Area: 94,399 sq. mi.
　　　244,493 sq. km.
Population: 57,515,000
Capital: London
Largest City: London
Highest Point: Ben Nevis
Monetary Unit: pound sterling

United States
Page/Location: 104
Area: 3,623,420 sq. mi.
　　　9,384,658 sq. km.
Population: 252,502,000
Capital: Washington
Largest City: New York
Highest Point: Mt. McKinley
Monetary Unit: U.S. dollar

Uruguay
Page/Location: 91/E3
Area: 72,172 sq. mi.
　　　186,925 sq. km.
Population: 3,121,000
Capital: Montevideo
Largest City: Montevideo
Highest Point: Cerro Catedral
Monetary Unit: Uruguayan peso

Uzbekistan
Page/Location: 56/G5
Area: 173,591 sq. mi.
　　　449,600 sq. km.
Population: 19,906,000
Capital: Tashkent
Largest City: Tashkent
Highest Point: Khodzha-Pir'yakh
Monetary Unit: Uzbek ruble

Vanuatu
Page/Location: 78/F6
Area: 5,700 sq. mi.
　　　14,763 sq. km.
Population: 170,000
Capital: Vila
Largest City: Vila
Highest Point: Tabwemasana
Monetary Unit: vatu

Vatican City
Page/Location: 48/C2
Area: 108.7 acres
　　　44 hectares
Population: 1,000
Capital: —
Largest City: —
Highest Point: —
Monetary Unit: Italian lira

Venezuela
Page/Location: 92/E2
Area: 352,143 sq. mi.
　　　912,050 sq. km.
Population: 20,189,000
Capital: Caracas
Largest City: Caracas
Highest Point: Pico Bolívar
Monetary Unit: bolívar

Vietnam
Page/Location: 69/D2
Area: 128,405 sq. mi.
　　　332,569 sq. km.
Population: 67,568,000
Capital: Hanoi
Largest City: Ho Chi Minh City
Highest Point: Fan Si Pan
Monetary Unit: dong

Western Samoa
Page/Location: 79/H6
Area: 1,133 sq. mi.
　　　2,934 sq. km.
Population: 190,000
Capital: Apia
Largest City: Apia
Highest Point: Mt. Silisili
Monetary Unit: tala

Yemen
Page/Location: 60/E5
Area: 188,321 sq. mi.
　　　487,752 sq. km.
Population: 10,063,000
Capital: Sanaa
Largest City: Aden
Highest Point: Nabī Shu'ayb
Monetary Unit: Yemeni rial

Yugoslavia
Page/Location: 50/E3
Area: 38,989 sq. mi.
　　　102,173 sq. km.
Population: 11,371,275
Capital: Belgrade
Largest City: Belgrade
Highest Point: Ðaravica
Monetary Unit: Yugoslav new dinar

Zaire
Page/Location: 80/E5
Area: 905,063 sq. mi.
　　　2,344,113 sq. km.
Population: 37,832,000
Capital: Kinshasa
Largest City: Kinshasa
Highest Point: Margherita Peak
Monetary Unit: zaire

Zambia
Page/Location: 87/E3
Area: 290,586 sq. mi.
　　　752,618 sq. km.
Population: 8,446,000
Capital: Lusaka
Largest City: Lusaka
Highest Point: Sunzu
Monetary Unit: Zambian kwacha

Zimbabwe
Page/Location: 87/E4
Area: 150,803 sq. mi.
　　　390,580 sq. km.
Population: 10,720,000
Capital: Harare
Largest City: Harare
Highest Point: Inyangani
Monetary Unit: Zimbabwe dollar

Environmental Concerns

DESERTIFICATION AND ACID RAIN DAMAGE

- ▨ AREAS OF PRODUCTIVE DRYLANDS DESERTIFIED BY EARLY 1980'S
- ● AREAS OF DAMAGE FROM ACID RAIN AND OTHER AIRBORNE POLLUTANTS

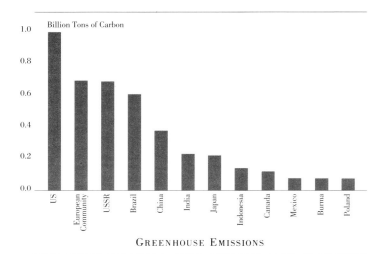

Billion Tons of Carbon

1.0
0.8
0.6
0.4
0.2
0.0

US · European Community · USSR · Brazil · China · India · Japan · Indonesia · Canada · Mexico · Burma · Poland

GREENHOUSE EMISSIONS

CARBON DIOXIDE EQUIVALENTS, 1987 NET EMISSIONS

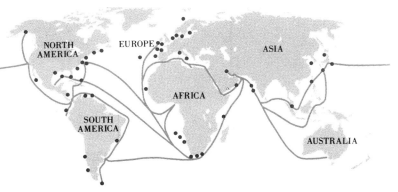

MAIN TANKER ROUTES AND MAJOR OIL SPILLS

—— ROUTES OF VERY LARGE CRUDE OIL CARRIERS · ● MAJOR OIL SPILLS

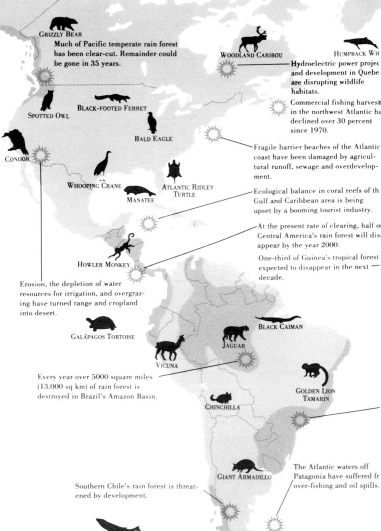

GRIZZLY BEAR

Much of Pacific temperate rain forest has been clear-cut. Remainder could be gone in 35 years.

WOODLAND CARIBOU

HUMPBACK WH

Hydroelectric power projec and development in Quebe are disrupting wildlife habitats.

Commercial fishing harves in the northwest Atlantic ha declined over 30 percent since 1970.

Fragile barrier beaches of the Atlantic coast have been damaged by agricultural runoff, sewage and overdevelopment.

Ecological balance in coral reefs of th Gulf and Caribbean area is being upset by a booming tourist industry.

At the present rate of clearing, half o Central America's rain forest will dis appear by the year 2000.

One-third of Guinea's tropical forest expected to disappear in the next decade.

SPOTTED OWL · BLACK-FOOTED FERRET · BALD EAGLE

CONDOR

WHOOPING CRANE · MANATEE · ATLANTIC RIDLEY TURTLE

HOWLER MONKEY

Erosion, the depletion of water resources for irrigation, and overgrazing have turned range and cropland into desert.

GALÁPAGOS TORTOISE

BLACK CAIMAN

JAGUAR

VICUÑA

Every year over 5000 square miles (13,000 sq km) of rain forest is destroyed in Brazil's Amazon Basin.

CHINCHILLA

GOLDEN LION TAMARIN

GIANT ARMADILLO

The Atlantic waters off Patagonia have suffered fr over-fishing and oil spills.

Southern Chile's rain forest is threatened by development.

BLUE WHALE

Acid Rain

Acid rain of nitric and sulfuric acids has killed all life in thousands of lakes, and over 15 million acres (6 million hectares) of virgin forest in Europe and North America are dead or dying.

Deforestation

Each year, 50 million acres (20 million hectares) of tropical rainforests are being felled by loggers. Trees remove carbon dioxide from the atmosphere and are vital to the prevention of soil erosion.

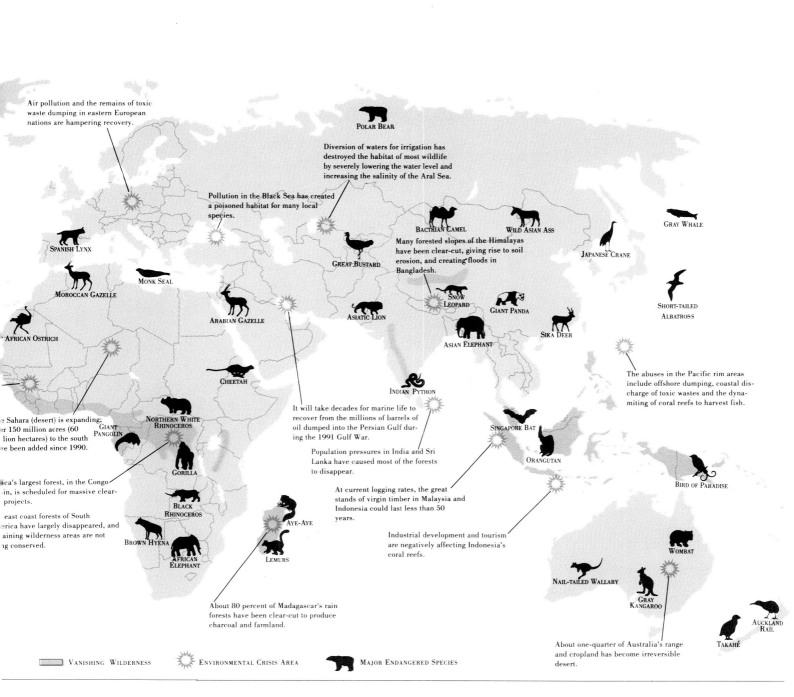

Air pollution and the remains of toxic waste dumping in eastern European nations are hampering recovery.

POLAR BEAR

Diversion of waters for irrigation has destroyed the habitat of most wildlife by severely lowering the water level and increasing the salinity of the Aral Sea.

Pollution in the Black Sea has created a poisoned habitat for many local species.

SPANISH LYNX

MOROCCAN GAZELLE

MONK SEAL

GREAT BUSTARD

BACTRIAN CAMEL

WILD ASIAN ASS

GRAY WHALE

JAPANESE CRANE

Many forested slopes of the Himalayas have been clear-cut, giving rise to soil erosion, and creating floods in Bangladesh.

ARABIAN GAZELLE

ASIATIC LION

SNOW LEOPARD

GIANT PANDA

SHORT-TAILED ALBATROSS

AFRICAN OSTRICH

ASIAN ELEPHANT

SIKA DEER

The abuses in the Pacific rim areas include offshore dumping, coastal discharge of toxic wastes and the dynamiting of coral reefs to harvest fish.

CHEETAH

INDIAN PYTHON

e Sahara (desert) is expanding; er 150 million acres (60 lion hectares) to the south ve been added since 1990.

GIANT PANGOLIN

NORTHERN WHITE RHINOCEROS

It will take decades for marine life to recover from the millions of barrels of oil dumped into the Persian Gulf during the 1991 Gulf War.

SINGAPORE BAT

GORILLA

Population pressures in India and Sri Lanka have caused most of the forests to disappear.

ORANGUTAN

BIRD OF PARADISE

ica's largest forest, in the Congo in, is scheduled for massive clearprojects.

At current logging rates, the great stands of virgin timber in Malaysia and Indonesia could last less than 50 years.

east coast forests of South erica have largely disappeared, and aining wilderness areas are not g conserved.

BLACK RHINOCEROS

AYE-AYE

Industrial development and tourism are negatively affecting Indonesia's coral reefs.

WOMBAT

BROWN HYENA

AFRICAN ELEPHANT

LEMURS

NAIL-TAILED WALLABY

GRAY KANGAROO

About 80 percent of Madagascar's rain forests have been clear-cut to produce charcoal and farmland.

AUCKLAND RAIL

TAKAHÉ

About one-quarter of Australia's range and cropland has become irreversible desert.

VANISHING WILDERNESS   ENVIRONMENTAL CRISIS AREA   MAJOR ENDANGERED SPECIES

Extinction

Biologists estimate that over 50,000 plant and animal species inhabiting the world's rain forests are disappearing each year due to pollution, unchecked hunting and the destruction of natural habitats.

Air Pollution

Billions of tons of industrial emissions and toxic pollutants are released into the air each year, depleting our ozone layer, killing our forests and lakes with acid rain and threatening our health.

Water Pollution

Only 3 percent of the earth's water is fresh. Pollution from cities, farms and factories has made much of it unfit to drink. In the developing world, most sewage flows untreated into lakes and rivers.

Ozone Depletion

The layer of ozone in the stratosphere shields earth from harmful ultraviolet radiation. But man-made gases are destroying this vital barrier, increasing the risk of skin cancer and eye disease.

Population

CURRENT POPULATION COMPARISONS

EACH AREA'S SIZE IS PROPORTIONATE TO ITS POPULATION

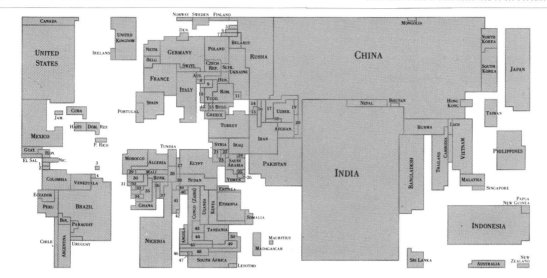

COUNTRIES INDICATED BY NUMBER

1	COSTA RICA	10	BOSNIA AND	20	TAJIKISTAN	30	SENEGAL
2	PANAMA		HERCEGOVINA	21	LEBANON	31	GUINEA-BISSAU
3	TRINIDAD AND	11	MOLDOVA	22	JORDAN	32	GUINEA
	TOBAGO	12	ALBANIA	23	ISRAEL	33	SIERRA LEONE
4	GUYANA	13	MACEDONIA	24	KUWAIT	34	LIBERIA
5	ESTONIA	14	GEORGIA	25	UNITED ARAB	35	IVORY COAST
6	LATVIA	15	ARMENIA		EMIRATES	36	TOGO
7	LITHUANIA	16	AZERBAIJAN	26	OMAN	37	BENIN
8	SLOVENIA	17	KAZAKHSTAN	27	LIBYA	38	CHAD
9	CROATIA	18	TURKMENISTAN	28	NIGER	39	CENTRAL AFRICAN
		19	KYRGYZSTAN	29	MAURITANIA		REPUBLIC

40	CONGO	51	CYPRUS
41	CAMEROON	52	CAPE VERDE
42	GABON	53	GAMBIA
43	RWANDA	54	EQUATORIAL GUINEA
44	BURUNDI	55	BAHRAIN
45	ZAMBIA	56	QATAR
46	NAMIBIA	57	BRUNEI
47	BOTSWANA	58	SOLOMON ISLANDS
48	ZIMBABWE		
49	MOZAMBIQUE		
50	MALAWI		

PROJECTED POPULATION COMPARISONS - 2020

EACH AREA'S SIZE IS PROPORTIONATE TO ITS POPULATION

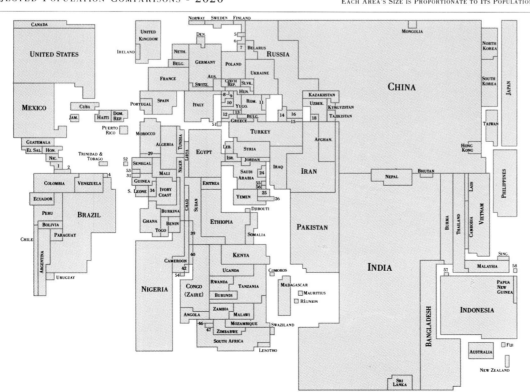

ALASKA

ME

3.5 PERCENT OR MO

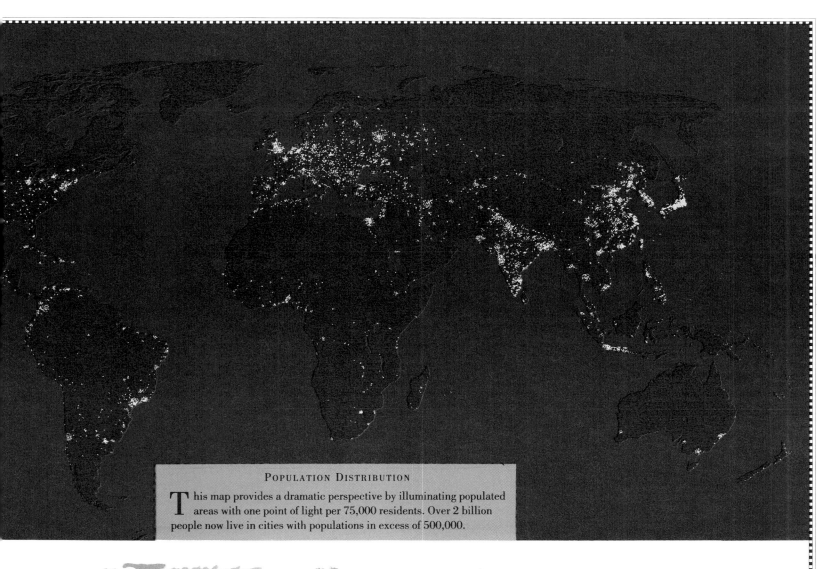

POPULATION DISTRIBUTION

This map provides a dramatic perspective by illuminating populated areas with one point of light per 75,000 residents. Over 2 billion people now live in cities with populations in excess of 500,000.

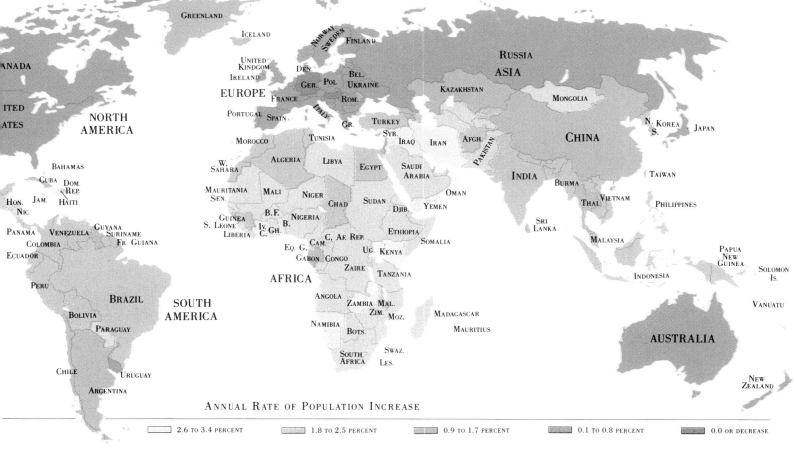

ANNUAL RATE OF POPULATION INCREASE

2.6 TO 3.4 PERCENT   1.8 TO 2.5 PERCENT   0.9 TO 1.7 PERCENT   0.1 TO 0.8 PERCENT   0.0 OR DECREASE

Standards of Living

EUROPE

NORTH AMERICA

ASIA

AFRICA

SOUTH AMERICA

AUSTRALIA

LITERATE PERCENT OF POPULATION

80 AND ABOVE	40-59	0-19
60-79	20-39	

EUROPE

NORTH AMERICA

ASIA

AFRICA

SOUTH AMERICA

AUSTRALIA

YEARS OF LIFE EXPECTANCY (MEN AND WOMEN)

70 AND ABOVE	50-59	0-39
60-69	40-49	

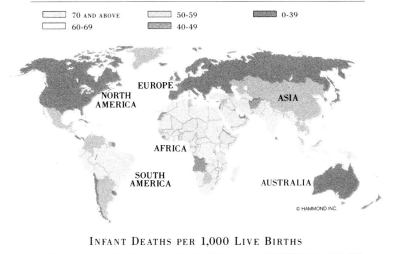

EUROPE

NORTH AMERICA

ASIA

AFRICA

SOUTH AMERICA

AUSTRALIA

© HAMMOND INC.

INFANT DEATHS PER 1,000 LIVE BIRTHS

150 AND MORE	50-99	0-24
100-149	25-49	

GREEN

ALASKA

CANADA

UNITED STATES

UNITED STATES
The economic and political influence of women has risen substantially. In a number of fields, women's salaries are now nearly equal to men's.

MEXICO

BAHAMAS

CUBA

JAM. DOM. REP.

HAITI

BEL. HON.

GUAT. EL SAL. NIC.

C.R.

PANAMA

VENEZUELA GUYANA

COLOMBIA

SURINAME

FR. GUIANA.

ECUADOR

SOUTH AMERICA
Political unrest, rising inflation and slow economic growth continue to thwart efforts to bring unity and prosperity to the nations of South America

LATIN AMERICA
The gulf between rich and poor continues to widen, despite efforts to reform oppressive governments, increase literacy and relieve overburdened cities.

PERU

BRAZIL

BOLIVIA

PARAGUAY

CHILE

URUGUAY

ARGENTINA

COMPARISON OF EUROPEAN, U.S. AND JAPANESE WORKERS

COUNTRY	SCHEDULED WEEKLY HOURS	ANNUAL LEAVE DAYS/HOLIDAYS	ANNUAL HOURS WORKED
GERMANY	39	42	1708
NETHERLANDS	40	43.5	1740
BELGIUM	38	31	1748
AUSTRIA	39.3	38	1751
FRANCE	39	34	1771
ITALY	40	39	1776
UNITED KINGDOM	39	33	1778
LUXEMBOURG	40	37	1792
FINLAND	40	37	1792
SWEDEN	40	37	1792
SPAIN	40	36	1800
DENMARK	40	34	1816
NORWAY	40	30	1848
GREECE	40	28	1864
IRELAND	40	28	1864
UNITED STATES	40	22	1912
SWITZERLAND	41.5	30.5	1913
PORTUGAL	45	36	2025
JAPAN	44	23.5	2116

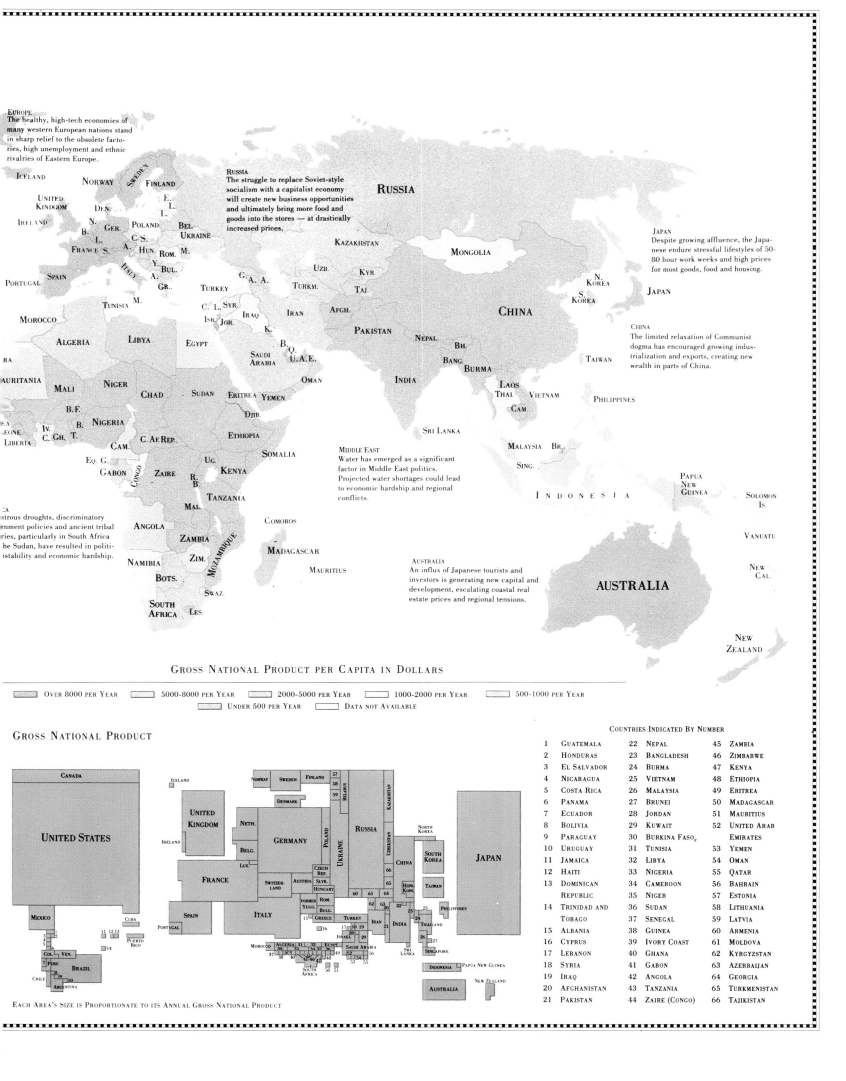

EUROPE
The healthy, high-tech economies of many western European nations stand in sharp relief to the obsolete factories, high unemployment and ethnic rivalries of Eastern Europe.

RUSSIA
The struggle to replace Soviet-style socialism with a capitalist economy will create new business opportunities and ultimately bring more food and goods into the stores — at drastically increased prices.

JAPAN
Despite growing affluence, the Japanese endure stressful lifestyles of 50-80 hour work weeks and high prices for most goods, food and housing.

CHINA
The limited relaxation of Communist dogma has encouraged growing industrialization and exports, creating new wealth in parts of China.

MIDDLE EAST
Water has emerged as a significant factor in Middle East politics. Projected water shortages could lead to economic hardship and regional conflicts.

AUSTRALIA
An influx of Japanese tourists and investors is generating new capital and development, escalating coastal real estate prices and regional tensions.

...trous droughts, discriminatory ...rnment policies and ancient tribal ...ries, particularly in South Africa ...he Sudan, have resulted in politi-...nstability and economic hardship.

GROSS NATIONAL PRODUCT PER CAPITA IN DOLLARS

OVER 8000 PER YEAR   5000-8000 PER YEAR   2000-5000 PER YEAR   1000-2000 PER YEAR   500-1000 PER YEAR
UNDER 500 PER YEAR   DATA NOT AVAILABLE

GROSS NATIONAL PRODUCT

EACH AREA'S SIZE IS PROPORTIONATE TO ITS ANNUAL GROSS NATIONAL PRODUCT

COUNTRIES INDICATED BY NUMBER

1	GUATEMALA	22	NEPAL	45	ZAMBIA
2	HONDURAS	23	BANGLADESH	46	ZIMBABWE
3	EL SALVADOR	24	BURMA	47	KENYA
4	NICARAGUA	25	VIETNAM	48	ETHIOPIA
5	COSTA RICA	26	MALAYSIA	49	ERITREA
6	PANAMA	27	BRUNEI	50	MADAGASCAR
7	ECUADOR	28	JORDAN	51	MAURITIUS
8	BOLIVIA	29	KUWAIT	52	UNITED ARAB
9	PARAGUAY	30	BURKINA FASO		EMIRATES
10	URUGUAY	31	TUNISIA	53	YEMEN
11	JAMAICA	32	LIBYA	54	OMAN
12	HAITI	33	NIGERIA	55	QATAR
13	DOMINICAN	34	CAMEROON	56	BAHRAIN
	REPUBLIC	35	NIGER	57	ESTONIA
14	TRINIDAD AND	36	SUDAN	58	LITHUANIA
	TOBAGO	37	SENEGAL	59	LATVIA
15	ALBANIA	38	GUINEA	60	ARMENIA
16	CYPRUS	39	IVORY COAST	61	MOLDOVA
17	LEBANON	40	GHANA	62	KYRGYZSTAN
18	SYRIA	41	GABON	63	AZERBAIJAN
19	IRAQ	42	ANGOLA	64	GEORGIA
20	AFGHANISTAN	43	TANZANIA	65	TURKMENISTAN
21	PAKISTAN	44	ZAIRE (CONGO)	66	TAJIKISTAN

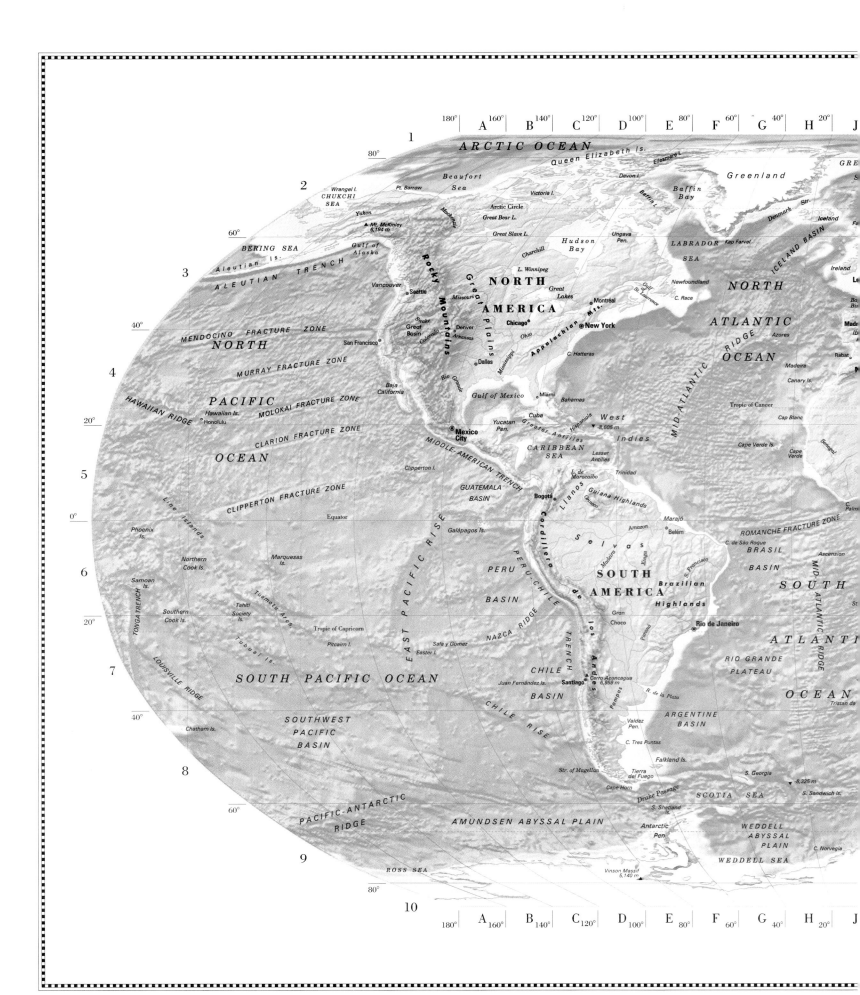

1

ARCTIC OCEAN

80°

Queen Elizabeth Is.

Beaufort
Sea

Ellesmere I.

Greenland GRE

2

Wrangel I.
CHUKCHI
SEA

Pt. Barrow

Devon I.

Baffin
Bay

Str.

Denmark

Iceland

Fa

Victoria I.

Yukon

▲ Mt. McKinley
6,194 m

Arctic Circle

Great Bear L.

Baffin

LABRADOR

Kap Farvel

ICELAND BASIN

60°

BERING SEA

Great Slave L.

Hudson
Bay

Ungava
Pen.

SEA

Ireland

Gulf of
Alaska

Churchill

Le

3

Aleutian Is.

ALEUTIAN   TRENCH

Vancouver

Seattle

Rocky Mountains

L. Winnipeg

Great
Lakes

Montréal

NORTH
AMERICA

C. Race

NORTH

Newfoundland

ATLANTIC

Ba
Bi

Missouri

Chicago

New York

40°

MENDOCINO   FRACTURE   ZONE

Denver

Great
Plains

Ohio

Appalachian Mts.

Madr

NORTH

Snake
Great
Basin

Colorado

Arkansas

OCEAN

Ib

San Francisco

RIDGE

Azores

4

MURRAY FRACTURE ZONE

Dallas

Mississippi

C. Hatteras

Madeira

PACIFIC

Baja
California

Rio Grande

Gulf of Mexico

Miami

Bahamas

MID-ATLANTIC

Canary Is.

20°

HAWAIIAN RIDGE

Hawaiian Is.
Honolulu

MOLOKAI FRACTURE ZONE

Yucatan
Pen.

Cuba

Greater Antilles

West

Hispaniola

▼ -8,605 m

Indies

Tropic of Cancer

Cap Blanc

CLARION FRACTURE ZONE

Mexico
City

CARIBBEAN
SEA

Lesser
Antilles

Cape Verde Is.

Cape
Verde

OCEAN

MIDDLE-AMERICAN TRENCH

Trinidad

Senegal

5

Clipperton I.

GUATEMALA
BASIN

Bogotá

L. de
Maracaibo

Llanos

Orinoco

Guiana Highlands

C
Palm

Line Islands

Equator

Galápagos Is.

Cordillera

Marajó

Amazon

ROMANCHE FRACTURE ZONE

Phoenix
Is.

Belém

C. de São Roque

Ascension

BRASIL

6

Northern
Cook Is.

Marquesas
Is.

PERU
BASIN

PERU-CHILE

Selvas

Madeira

Xingu

S.Francisco

BASIN

S

Samoan
Is.

SOUTH
AMERICA

Brazilian
Highlands

MID-ATLANTIC RIDGE

Southern
Cook Is.

Tahiti
Society
Is.

Tuamotu Arch.

Gran
Choco

Rio de Janeiro

20°

TONGA TRENCH

Tubuai Is.

Tropic of Capricorn

Pitcairn I.

Safa y Gomez

NAZCA RIDGE

Paraná

ATLANTI

Easter I.

Andes

RIO GRANDE
PLATEAU

7

LOUISVILLE RIDGE

EAST PACIFIC RISE

CHILE

Juan Fernández Is.

Santiago

Cerro Aconcagua
6,959 m

R. de la Plata

Pampas

OCEAN

Tristan da

SOUTH PACIFIC OCEAN

BASIN

CHILE   RISE

ARGENTINE
BASIN

40°

Chatham Is.

SOUTHWEST
PACIFIC
BASIN

Valdez
Pen.

C. Tres Puntas

Falkland Is.

8

Str. of Magellan

Tierra
del Fuego

S. Georgia

▼ -8,325 m

S. Sandwich Is.

Cape Horn

Drake Passage

SCOTIA   SEA

S. Shetland
Is.

60°

PACIFIC-ANTARCTIC
RIDGE

AMUNDSEN ABYSSAL PLAIN

Antarctic
Pen.

WEDDELL
ABYSSAL
PLAIN

C. Norvegia

9

ROSS SEA

Vinson Massif
5,140 m

WEDDELL SEA

80°

10

World

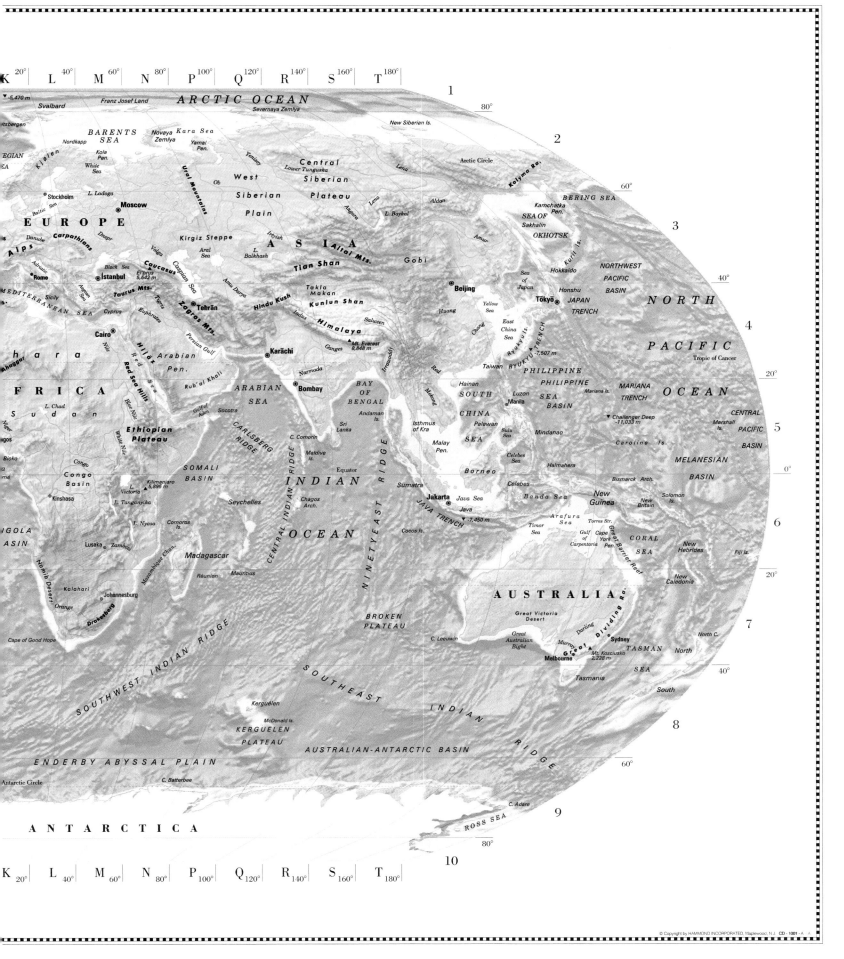

K 20° **L** 40° **M** 60° **N** 80° **P** 100° **Q** 120° **R** 140° **S** 160° **T** 180°

▼-5,470 m
Svalbard Franz Josef Land ARCTIC OCEAN 1
Spitsbergen Severnaya Zemlya 80°
BARENTS Novaya Kara Sea New Siberian Is.
Nordkapp SEA Zemlya Yamal 2
Kola Pen. Pen. Arctic Circle
EGIAN Klałen White Sea Central Kolyma Ra. BERING SEA 60°
SEA Sea West Lower Tunguska Siberian Kamchatka
Stockholm L. Ladoga Siberian Plateau Pen. 3
Baltic Moscow Ob Plain Lena SEA OF Sakhalin
Sea Plain Angara Lena L. Baykal Aldan OKHOTSK Kuril Is.
E U R O P E Kirgiz Steppe Irtysh A S I A Altai Mts. Amur Hokkaido NORTHWEST 40°
Danube Carpathians Aral L.Balkhash Gobi Sea PACIFIC
Alps Dnepr Sea Tian Shan Beijing of Honshu BASIN N O R T H
Black Sea El'brus Caspian Sea Takla Japan Tōkyō JAPAN
Adriatic İstanbul 5,642 m Makan Huang Yellow TRENCH 4
Rome Aegean Caucasus Kunlun Shan Chang Sea East P A C I F I C
MEDITERRANEAN SEA Taurus Mts. Tehrān Hindu Kush Himalaya China Ryukyu Is.
Sicily Zagros Mts. Indus Saluaen Sea RYUKYU TRENCH 20°
Cyprus Tigris ▲Mt. Everest -7,507 m
Cairo Euphrates Persian Gulf Ganges 8,848 m Irrawaddy Taiwan PHILIPPINE MARIANA Tropic of Cancer
h a r a Nile Karāchi Narmada Hainan PHILIPPINE TRENCH O C E A N
Ahaggar Hilaz Arabian Rub'al Khali BAY SOUTH Luzon SEA Mariana Is. CENTRAL 5
F R I C A Red Sea Hills Pen. OF CHINA Manila BASIN ▼Challenger Deep PACIFIC
L. Chad Blue Nile ARABIAN BENGAL Palawan -11,033 m Marshall BASIN
S u d a n Gulf of SEA Andaman SEA Sulu Is.
Niger White Nile Aden Socotra CARLSBERG Is. Isthmus Malay Sea Caroline Is.
gos Bioka RIDGE Sri Lanka of Kra Pen. Mindanao MELANESIAN
Congo C. Comorin Celebes Halmahera BASIN
mé Congo SOMALI Maldive Borneo Sea 0°
a Basin Kilimanjaro BASIN Is. Equator Celebes
Kinshasa L.Victoria 5,895 m Seychelles INDIAN Sumatra Banda Sea New New
L. Tanganyika Chagos Java Sea Guinea Britain Solomon
NGOLA L. Nyasa Comoros Arch. Jakarta Java Bismarck Arch. Is. 6
ASIN Lusaka Zambez Is. OCEAN JAVA TRENCH Timor Arafura New
Madagascar Cocos Is. ▲-7,450 m Sea Gulf Sea CORAL Hebrides
Namib Réunion Torres Str. of Cape SEA
Desert Mauritius Carpentaria York New
Kalahari Pen. Caledonia 20°
Orange Johannesburg NINETYEAST RIDGE A U S T R A L I A Fiji Is.
Drakesberg BROKEN 7
Cape of Good Hope CENTRAL INDIAN RIDGE PLATEAU Great Victoria TASMAN
C. Leeuwin Desert Murray Sydney North C.
Great Darling Great Dividing Ra. North 40°
SOUTHWEST INDIAN RIDGE Australian Melbourne Mt. Kosciusko SEA
Kerguélen Bight 2,228 m
McDonald Is. SOUTHEAST Tasmania South
KERGUELEN INDIAN 8
PLATEAU AUSTRALIAN-ANTARCTIC BASIN RIDGE 60°
ENDERBY ABYSSAL PLAIN
Antarctic Circle C. Batterbee C. Adare 9
A N T A R C T I C A ROSS SEA
80°
10

K 20° **L** 40° **M** 60° **N** 80° **P** 100° **Q** 120° **R** 140° **S** 160° **T** 180°

POPULATION OF CITIES AND TOWNS

SCALE 1:81,700,000   ROBINSON PROJECTION   STANDARD PARALLELS 38°N AND 38°S

◉ OVER 5,000,000   ⊙ 500,000 - 1,999,999
● 2,000,000 - 4,999,999   ○ UNDER 500,000

MILES   0   1000   2000   3000   4000
KILOMETERS 0   1000   2000   3000   4000

Europe

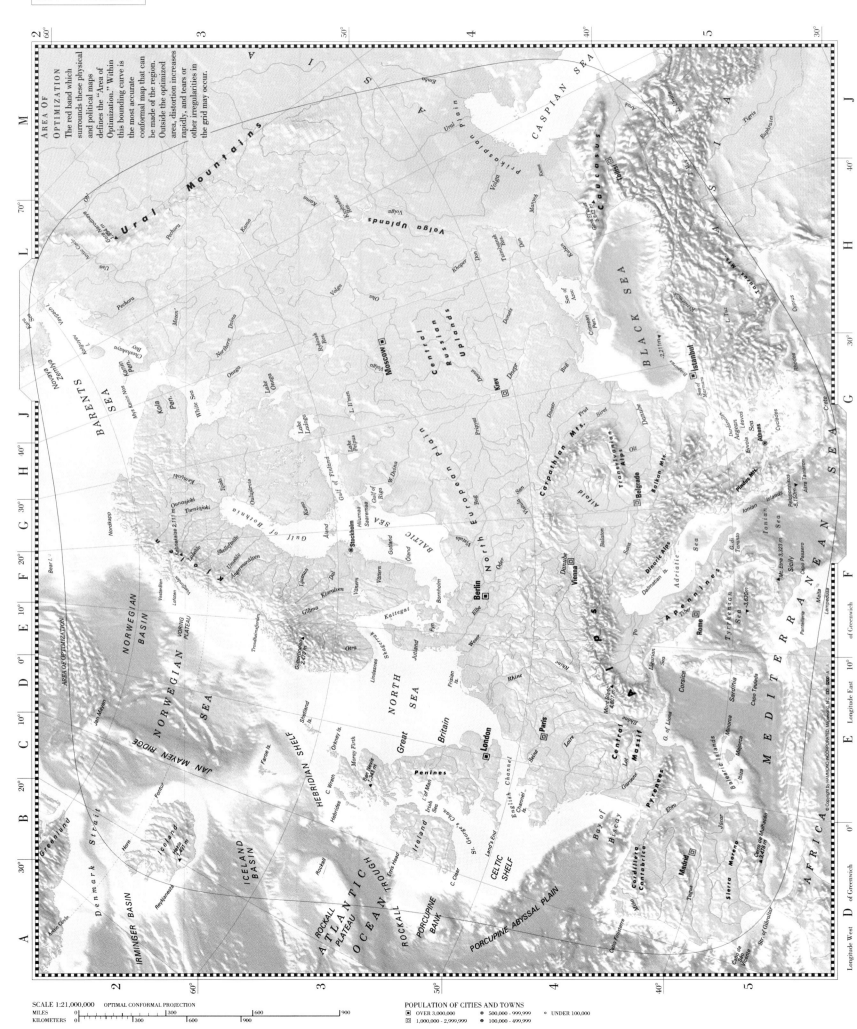

© Copyright by HAMMOND INCORPORATED Maplewood, N.J. DD-6500-A-1.A

AREA OF OPTIMIZATION
The red band which surrounds these physical and political maps defines the "Area of Optimization." Within this bounding curve is the most accurate conformal map that can be made of the optimized area, distortion increases rapidly, and tears or other irregularities in the grid may occur.

SCALE 1:21,000,000   OPTIMAL CONFORMAL PROJECTION

MILES	0		300	600	900
KILOMETERS	0	300	600	900	

POPULATION OF CITIES AND TOWNS

▫ OVER 3,000,000   ● 500,000 - 999,999   ○ UNDER 100,000
▣ 1,000,000 - 2,999,999   ● 100,000 - 499,999

Asia

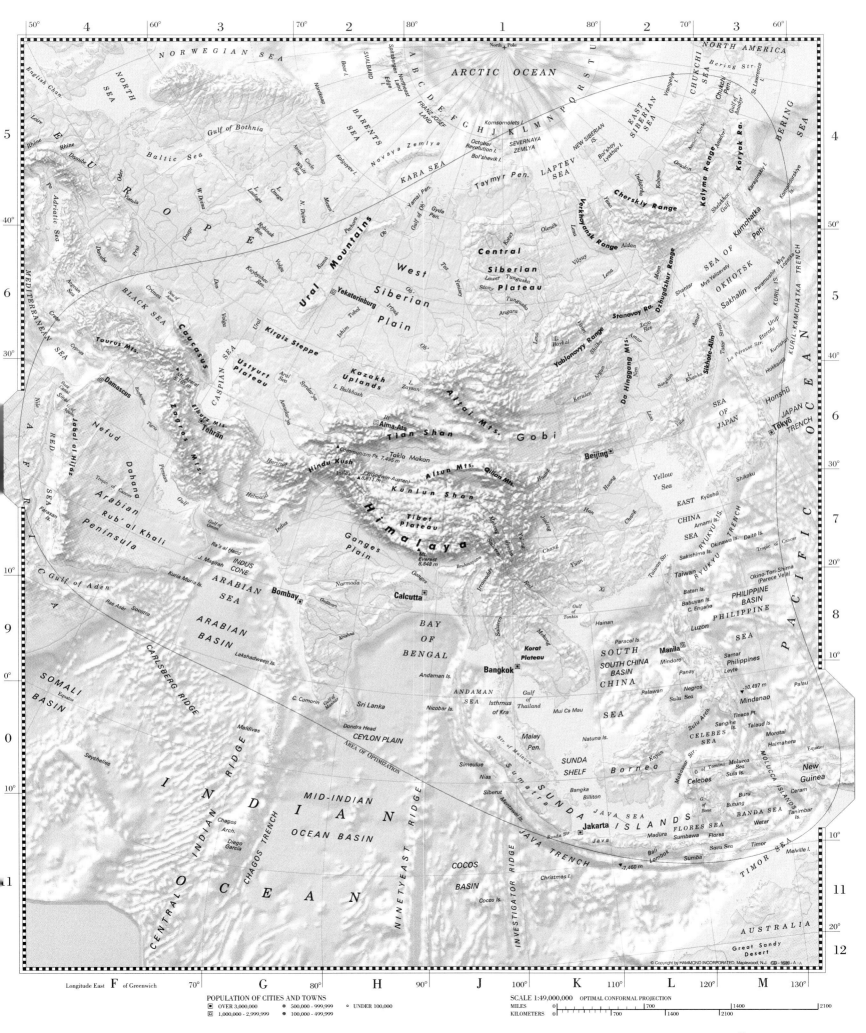

Africa

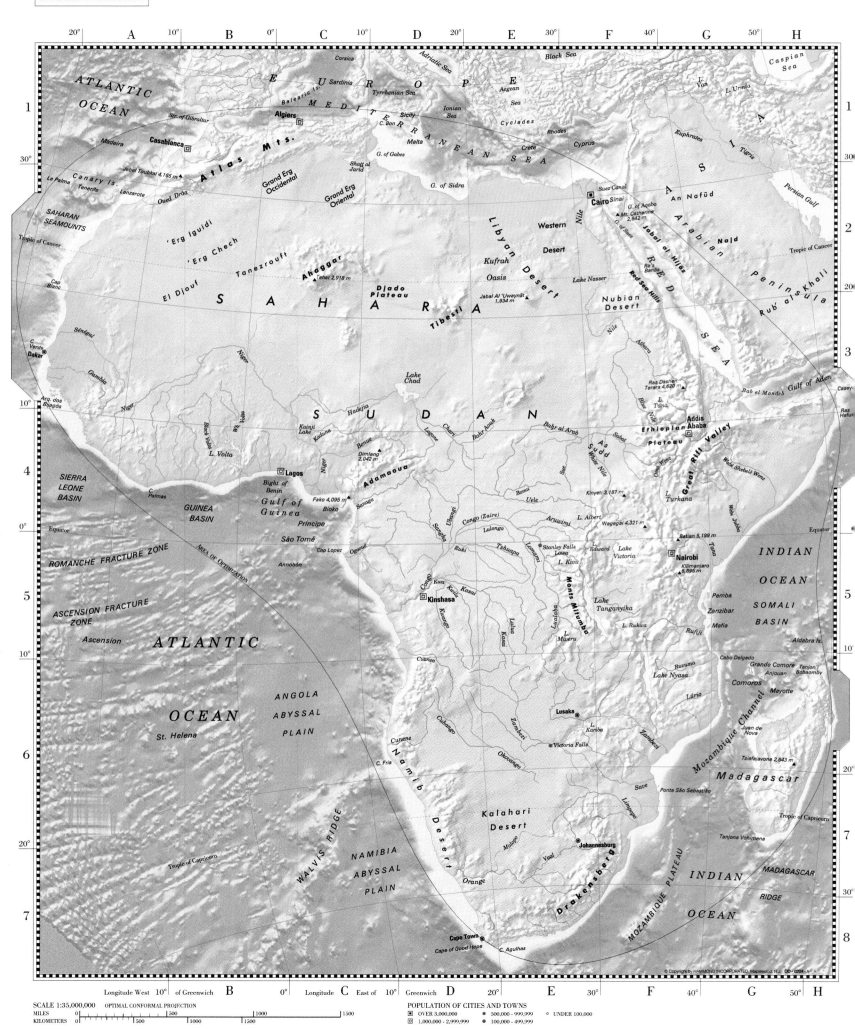

SCALE 1:35,000,000   OPTIMAL CONFORMAL PROJECTION

MILES 0   500   1000   1500

KILOMETERS 0   500   1000   1500

Longitude West 10° of Greenwich   B   0°   Longitude   C   East of   10°   Greenwich   D   20°   E   30°   F   40°   G   50°   H

POPULATION OF CITIES AND TOWNS

▣ OVER 3,000,000   ● 500,000 - 999,999
◉ 1,000,000 - 2,999,999   ● 100,000 - 499,999   ○ UNDER 100,000

South America

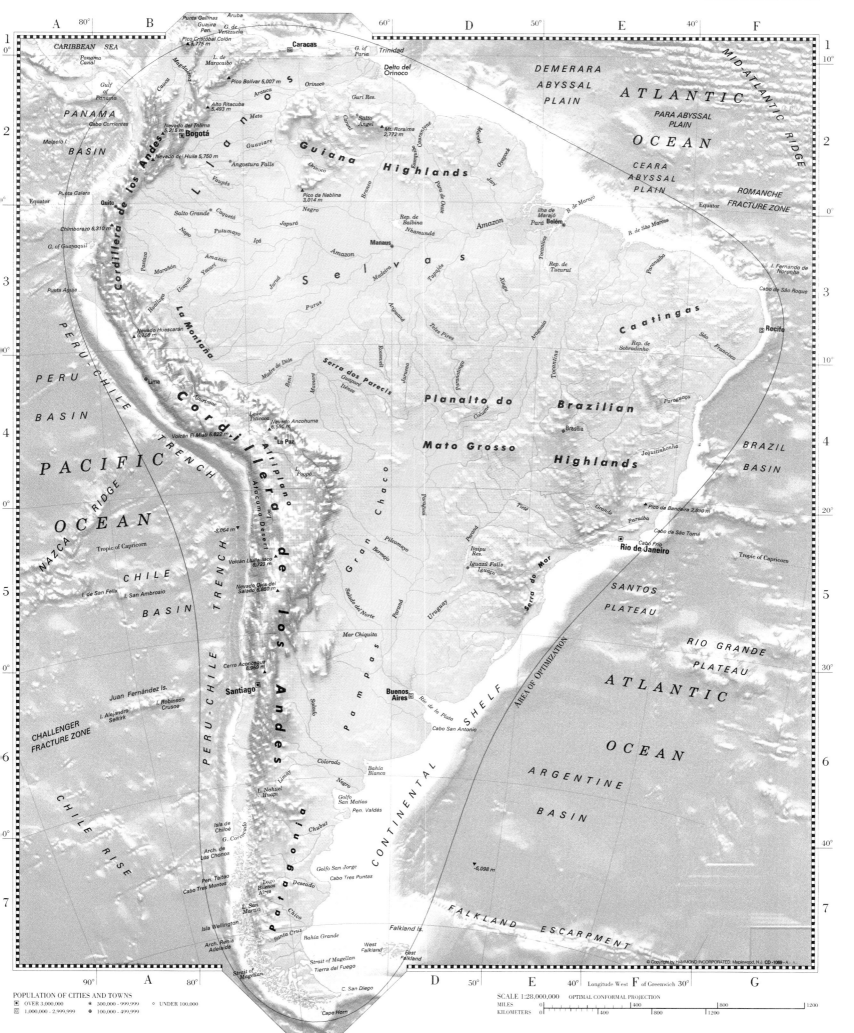

CARIBBEAN SEA

Punta Gallinas
Guajira Pen.
Aruba
Pico Cristóbal Colón ▲ 5,775 m
G. de Venezuela
Caracas
G. of Paria
Trinidad

Panama Canal
L. de Maracaibo
Orinoco
Delta del Orinoco

Gulf of Panama
▲ Pico Bolívar 5,007 m
Guri Res.

PANAMA
BASIN
Cabo Corrientes
Alto Ritacuba 5,493 m
Arauca
Meta

Malpelo I.
Nevado del Tolima 5,215 m
Bogotá
Salto Angel
Mt. Roraima 2,772 m

Punta Galera
Nevado del Huila 5,750 m
Guaviare
Cuand

Equator
Quito
Angostura Falls
Orinoco

Chimborazo 6,310 m
Caquetá
Salto Grande
Pico da Neblina 3,014 m
Branco
Pará
Belém

G. of Guayaquil
Napo
Putumayo
Içá
Negro
Rep. de Balbina
Nhamundá
B. de Marajó
Ilha de Marajó

Punta Aguja
Pastaza
Amazon
Japurá
Amazon
Manaus
Amazon
B. de São Marcos

Marañón
Ucayali
Yavarí
Jurúa
Madeira
Tapajós
Xingu
Tocantins
Rep. de Tucuruí

Nevado Huascarán 6,768 m
Purus
Tapajós
Araguaia
Paranaíba
Cabo de São Roque

Lima
Huallaga
Madre de Dios
Roosevelt
Teles Pires
Araguaia
Caatingas
Recife

Apurímac
Beni
Mamoré
Guaporé
Iténez
Tocantins
São Francisco
Rep. de Sobradinho

Lake Titicaca
Nevado Ancohuma 6,550 m
Serra dos Parecis
Juruena
Paranatinga
Planalto do
Brazilian

La Paz
Volcán El Misti 5,822 m
Guaporé
Mato Grosso
Highlands
Brasília
Jequitinhonha

L. Poopó
8,064 m
Gran Chaco
Pilcomayo
Pilcomayo
Grande
Pico da Bandeira 2,890 m

Volcán Llullaillaco 6,723 m
Bermejo
Paraguay
Itaipú Res.
Paraná
Paraíba
Cabo de São Tomé

Nevado Ojos del Salado 6,880 m
Salado del Norte
Iguazú Falls
Iguazú
Rio de Janeiro
Cabo Frío

Cerro Aconcagua 6,959 m
Paraná
Uruguay
Tietê
Serra do Mar
SANTOS PLATEAU

Juan Fernández Is.
Santiago
Mar Chiquita
Paraná
RIO GRANDE PLATEAU

I. de San Félix
I. San Ambrosio
Salado
Buenos Aires
Río de la Plata

I. Alejandro Selkirk
I. Robinson Crusoe
Cabo San Antonio

Colorado
Bahía Blanca
ARGENTINE BASIN

Negro
Linay
Golfo San Matías
Pen. Valdés

Isla de Chiloé
L. Nahuel Huapi
Chubut

G. Corcovado
Golfo San Jorge
Cabo Tres Puntas
−6,098 m

Arch. de Los Chonos
Deseado

Pen. Taitao
Cabo Tres Montes
Lago Buenos Aires
Chico
Santa Cruz

Isla Wellington
Bahía Grande
Falkland Is.

Arch. Reina Adelaida
West Falkland
East Falkland

Strait of Magellan
Tierra del Fuego
Cape Horn
C. San Diego

Llanos
Guiana Highlands
Selvas
Cordillera de los Andes
La Montaña
Cordillera de los Andes
Altiplano
Atacama Desert
Cordillera de los Andes
Patagonia

DEMERARA ABYSSAL PLAIN
ATLANTIC OCEAN
MID-ATLANTIC RIDGE

PARA ABYSSAL PLAIN
CEARA ABYSSAL PLAIN
ROMANCHE FRACTURE ZONE

Equator
I. Fernando de Noronha

BRAZIL BASIN

PACIFIC OCEAN
NAZCA RIDGE
PERU-CHILE TRENCH
PERU-CHILE TRENCH

PERU-CHILE BASIN
CHILE BASIN

Tropic of Capricorn
Tropic of Capricorn

CHALLENGER FRACTURE ZONE

CHILE RISE

AREA OF OPTIMIZATION
CONTINENTAL SHELF
ATLANTIC OCEAN

FALKLAND ESCARPMENT

POPULATION OF CITIES AND TOWNS
- ▣ OVER 3,000,000
- ⊡ 1,000,000 - 2,999,999
- ● 500,000 - 999,999
- ● 100,000 - 499,999
- ○ UNDER 100,000

SCALE 1:28,000,000   OPTIMAL CONFORMAL PROJECTION
MILES   0   400   800   1200
KILOMETERS   0   400   800   1200

Longitude West of Greenwich

North America

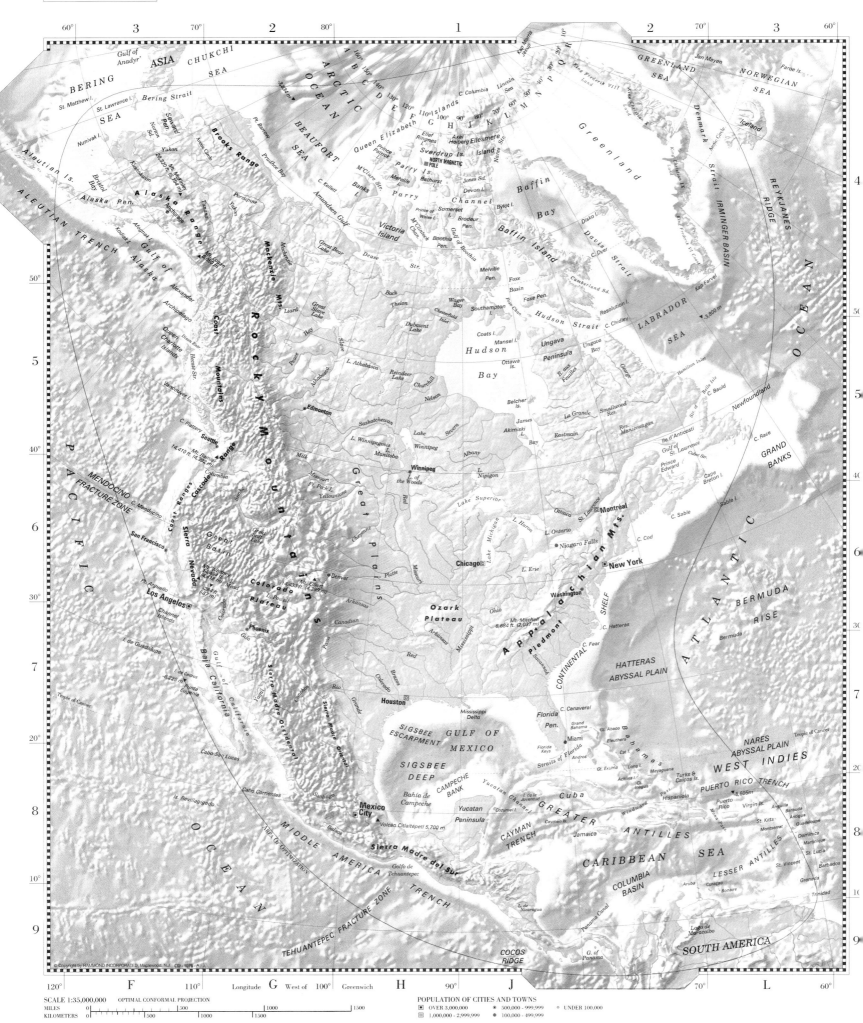

SCALE 1:35,000,000   OPTIMAL CONFORMAL PROJECTION

MILES 0   500   1000   1500
KILOMETERS 0   500   1000   1500

POPULATION OF CITIES AND TOWNS
■ OVER 3,000,000   ● 500,000 - 999,999   ○ UNDER 100,000
◨ 1,000,000 - 2,999,999   ● 100,000 - 499,999

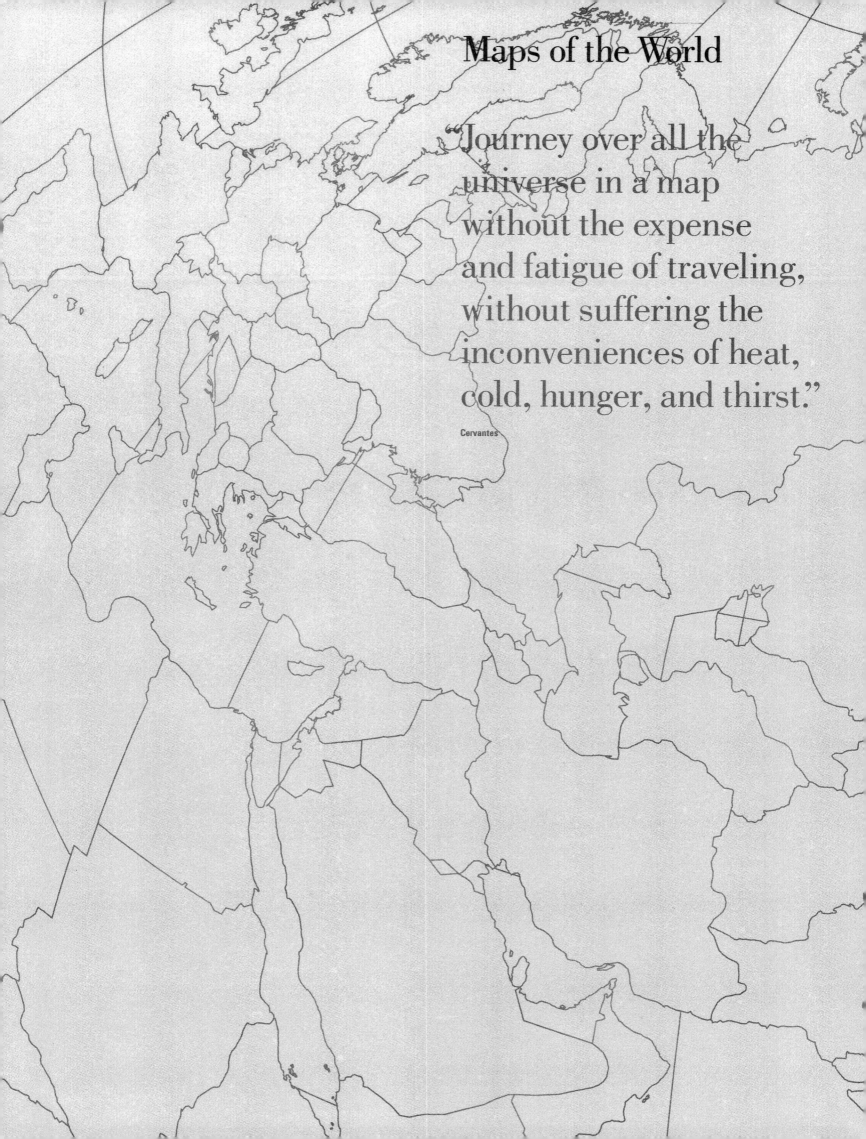

Maps of the World

"Journey over all the
universe in a map
without the expense
and fatigue of traveling,
without suffering the
inconveniences of heat,
cold, hunger, and thirst."

Cervantes

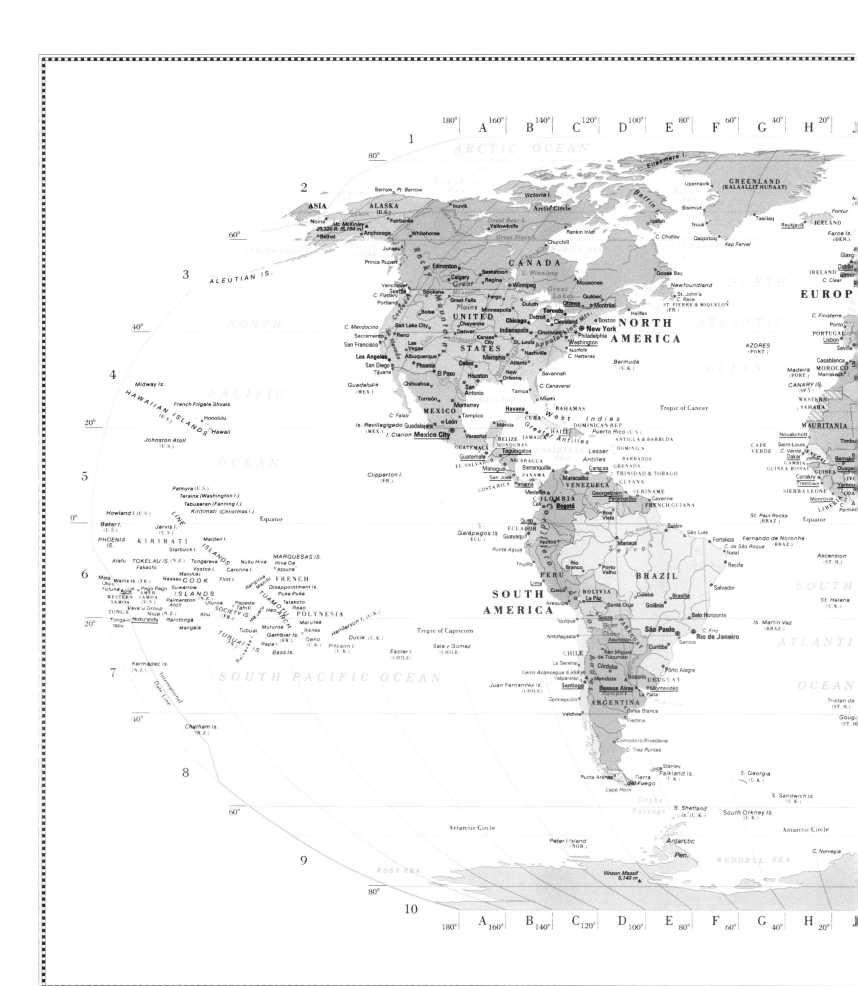

ARCTIC OCEAN

80°

ASIA

ALASKA
(U.S.)

Barrow   Pt. Barrow

Victoria I.

Arctic Circle

Inuvik

GREENLAND
(KALAALLIT NUNAAT)

Upernavik

Ellesmere I.

Baffin I.

Sisimiut

Fontur

Nome   Mt. McKinley
20,320 ft. (6,194 m)

Fairbanks

Yellowknife
Great Bear L.

Rankin Inlet

Iqaluit

Nuuk

Tasiilaq

ICELAND

60°

Bethel

Anchorage

Whitehorse

Great Slave L.

Churchill

C. Chidley

Qaqortoq

Kap Farvel

Reykjavik

Faroe Is.
(DEN.)

ALEUTIAN IS.

Prince Rupert

Vancouver

Seattle

C. Flattery

Portland

Edmonton

Calgary

Saskatoon

Regina

Winnipeg

L. Winnipeg

Moosonee

CANADA

Québec

Goose Bay

Newfoundland

St. John's

C. Race
ST. PIERRE & MIQUELON
(FR.)

NORTH

EUROPE

Glasg

Dublin
IRELAND Birmin

C. Clear

40°

NORTH

Spokane

Great Falls

Boise

Fargo

Duluth

Ottawa

Montréal

Halifax

C. Finisterre

PORTUGAL
Lisbon

ATLANTIC

C. Mendocino

Sacramento

San Francisco

Salt Lake City

Reno

Las
Vegas

Minneapolis

Cheyenne

Denver

UNITED

Kansas
City

Chicago

Indianapolis

St. Louis

Detroit

Cincinnati

Cleveland

Boston

New York

Philadelphia

Washington

NORTH

AMERICA

AZORES
(PORT.)

Seville

Casablanca
MOROCCO
Marrakech

OCEAN

Los Angeles

San Diego

Tijuana

Albuquerque

Phoenix

STATES

Nashville

Memphis

Atlanta

Norfolk

C. Hatteras

Bermuda
(U.K.)

Madeira
(PORT.)

CANARY IS.
(SP.)

WESTERN
SAHARA

Guadalupe
(MEX.)

Chihuahua

El Paso

Dallas

Houston

San
Antonio

New
Orleans

Savannah

C. Canaveral

Tampa

Tropic of Cancer

MAURITANIA

Nouakchott

Is. Revillagigedo Guadalajara
(MEX.)   I. Clarion Mexico City

MEXICO

Torreón

Tampico

Monterrey

Veracruz

León

Mérida

Havana

CUBA

BAHAMAS

West   Indies

DOMINICAN REP.

Puerto Rico (U.S)

CAPE
VERDE

Saint-Louis

C. Verde
Dakar

Timbu

SENEG

40°

Midway Is.

French Frigate Shoals

HAWAIIAN ISLANDS
(U.S.)

Honolulu

Hawaii

Johnston Atoll
(U.S.)

PACIFIC

GUATEMALA

Guatemala

EL SALVADOR

BELIZE
HONDURAS

Tegucigalpa

NICARAGUA

JAMAICA

Greater   Antilles

CARIBBEAN

Lesser

Antilles

HAITI

ANTIGUA & BARBUDA

DOMINICA

BARBADOS

GRENADA

TRINIDAD & TOBAGO

GAMBIA
GUINEA-BISSAU

Conakry
Freetown

SIERRA LEONE

GUINEA

Ouaga

IVO

Yamou

COA

20°

Managua

Barranquilla

San José

PANAMA

SEA

Caracas

Medellín

Cali

COLOMBIA

Bogotá

VENEZUELA

Maracaibo

Georgetown

Paramaribo

GUYANA

SURINAME

FRENCH GUIANA

Cayenne

Monrovia

LIBERIA

Palmas

Clipperton I.
(FR.)

COSTA RICA

Panamá

Boa
Vista

St. Paul Rocks
(BRAZ.)

Equator

0°

Palmyra (U.S.)

Teraina (Washington I.)

Tabuaeran (Fanning I.)

Kiritimati (Christmas I.)

Equator

Quito

ECUADOR

Galápagos Is.
(ECU.)

Guayaquil

Punta Aguja

Belém

São Luís

Fortaleza

Fernando de Noronha
(BRAZ.)

C. de São Roque

Natal

OCEAN

Howland I. (U.S.)

Jarvis I.
(U.S.)

Baker I.
(U.S.)

PHOENIX
IS.

KIRIBATI

Malden I.

Starbuck I.

LINE   ISLANDS

Iquitos

PERU

Trujillo

Manaus

Selva

Amazon

Rio
Branco

Porto
Velho

BRAZIL

Recife

Ascension
(ST. H.)

Equator

SOUTH

Atafu

TOKELAU IS. (N.Z.)

Fakaofo

Nassau

Vostok I.

Caroline I.

MARQUESAS IS.

Nuku Hiva

Hiva Oa

Atuona

Lima

Cusco

BOLIVIA

La Paz

Cuiabá

Brasília

Salvador

St. Helena
(U.K.)

6

Mata   Wallis Is. (FR.)

Utu   Pago Pago

Futuna   AMER.

WESTERN   SAMOA

SAMOA   (U.S.)

TONGA

COOK

Suwarrow

Manihiki

Rangiroa

Manihi

Flint I.

FRENCH

Disappointment Is.

Puka Puka

ISLANDS

Palmerston (N.Z.)

Tatakoto

Papeete   Tahiti

Reao

Uturoa

SOUTH

AMERICA

Arequipa

Sucre

Santa Cruz

Goiânia

Belo Horizonte

Is. Martin Vaz
(BRAZ.)

Tonga-o   Niue (N.Z.)

Vava'u Group

tapu   Nuku'alofa

Rarotonga

Mangaia

SOCIETY IS.
(FR.)

Atiu

TUAMOTCH

Hikueru

Marutea

Gran

Chaco

PARAGUAY

Curitiba

São Paulo

C. Frio

Rio de Janeiro

Santos

20°

TUBUAI

Tubuai

Mururoa

Gambier Is.
(FR.)

Rapa I.

Rikitea

Oeno
(U.K.)

Henderson I. (U.K.)

Ducie (U.K.)

Tropic of Capricorn

Iquique

Antofagasta

Asunción

CHILE

San Miguel
de Tucumán

Pôrto Alegre

ATLANTI

7

Kermadec Is.
(N.Z.)

Bass Is.

Pitcairn I.
(U.K.)

Easter I.
(CHILE)

Sala y Gomez
(CHILE)

Cerro Aconcagua 6,959 m

La Serena

Valparaíso

Mendoza

Córdoba

Rosario

URUGUAY

OCEAN

International   Date Line

SOUTH PACIFIC OCEAN

Juan Fernández Is.
(CHILE)

Concepción

Santiago

Buenos Aires

Montevideo

La Plata

Pampas

Tristan da
(ST. H.)

40°

Chatham Is.
(N.Z.)

ARGENTINA

Valdivia

Bahía Blanca

Viedma

Gougu
(ST. H

8

Comodoro Rivadavia

C. Tres Puntas

Stanley

Falkland Is.
(U.K.)

S. Georgia
(U.K.)

60°

Punta Arenas

Tierra
del Fuego

Cape Horn

S. Sandwich Is.
(U.K.)

Antarctic Circle

Drake
Passage

S. Shetland
Is. (U.K.)

South Orkney Is.
(U.K.)

Antarctic Circle

Peter I Island
(NOR.)

Antarctic

Pen.

WEDDELL SEA

C. Norvegia

9

ROSS SEA

Vinson Massif
5,140 m

80°

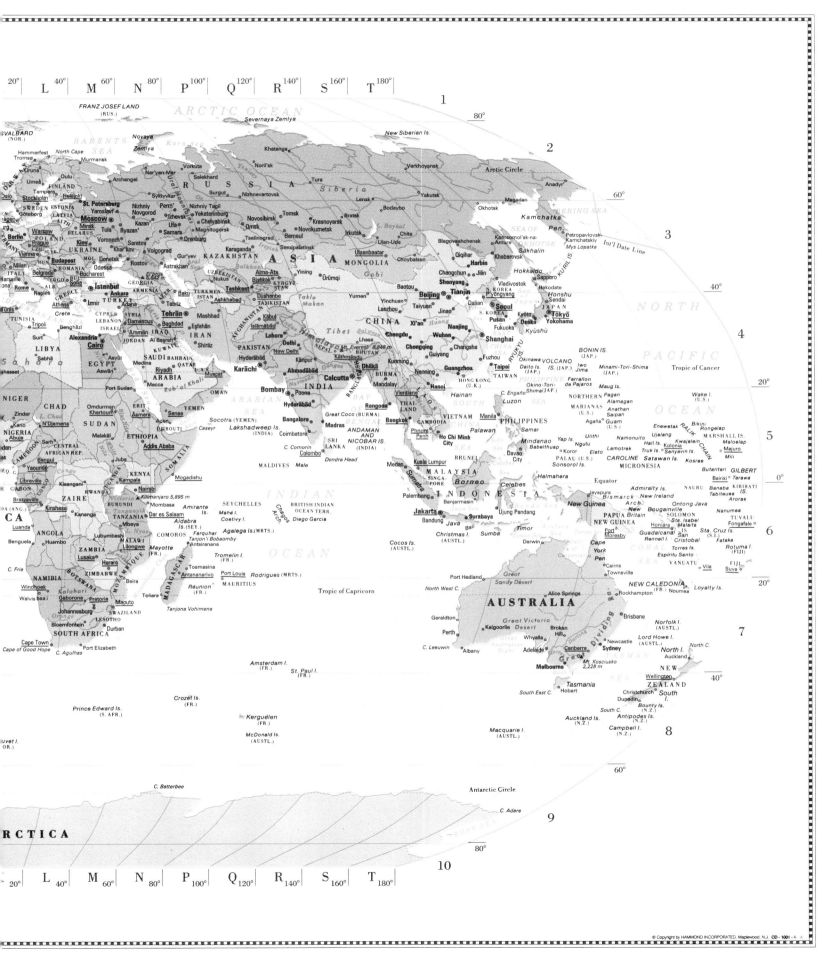

POPULATION OF CITIES AND TOWNS
- ◉ OVER 5,000,000
- ● 2,000,000 - 4,999,999
- ◎ 500,000 - 1,999,999
- ○ UNDER 500,000

SCALE 1:81,700,000   ROBINSON PROJECTION   STANDARD PARALLELS 38°N AND 38°S
MILES 0 1000 2000 3000 4000
KILOMETERS 0 1000 2000 3000 4000

© Copyright by HAMMOND INCORPORATED, Maplewood, N.J. OD - 1001 - A A

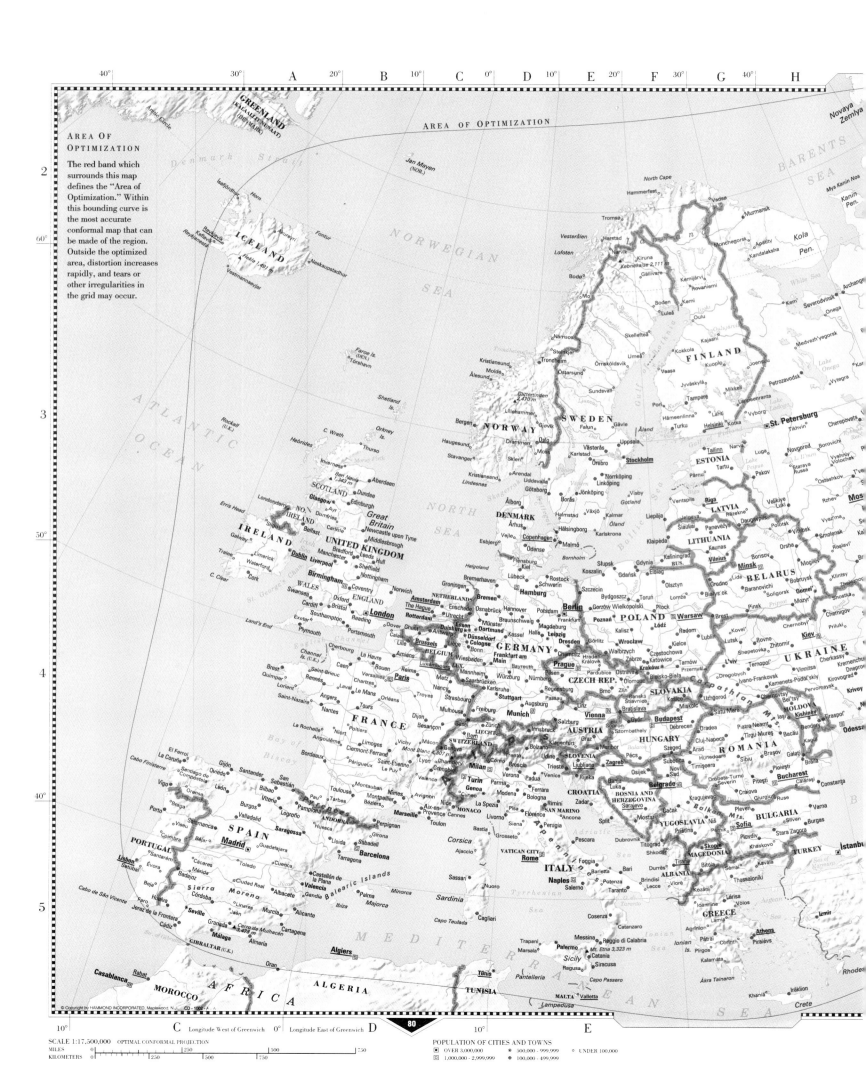

AREA OF OPTIMIZATION

AREA OF
OPTIMIZATION

The red band which
surrounds this map
defines the "Area of
Optimization." Within
this bounding curve is
the most accurate
conformal map that can
be made of the region.
Outside the optimized
area, distortion increases
rapidly, and tears or
other irregularities in
the grid may occur.

GREENLAND
(KALAALLIT NUNAAT)
(DENMARK)

Arctic Circle

Jan Mayen
(NOR.)

NORWEGIAN

SEA

BARENTS

SEA

Novaya
Zemlya

Denmark Strait

ICELAND

Faroe Is.
(DEN.)

ATLANTIC

OCEAN

NORTH

SEA

UNITED KINGDOM

IRELAND

NORWAY

SWEDEN

FINLAND

DENMARK

GERMANY

FRANCE

SPAIN

PORTUGAL

ITALY

POLAND

UKRAINE

BELARUS

ROMANIA

HUNGARY

AUSTRIA

CZECH REP.

SLOVAKIA

BULGARIA

GREECE

TURKEY

MEDITERRANEAN

SEA

AFRICA

ALGERIA

TUNISIA

MOROCCO

SCALE 1:17,500,000 OPTIMAL CONFORMAL PROJECTION
MILES 0 250 500 750
KILOMETERS 0 250 500 750

POPULATION OF CITIES AND TOWNS
◼ OVER 3,000,000   ◉ 500,000 - 999,999   ○ UNDER 100,000
◻ 1,000,000 - 2,999,999   ◉ 100,000 - 499,999

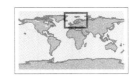

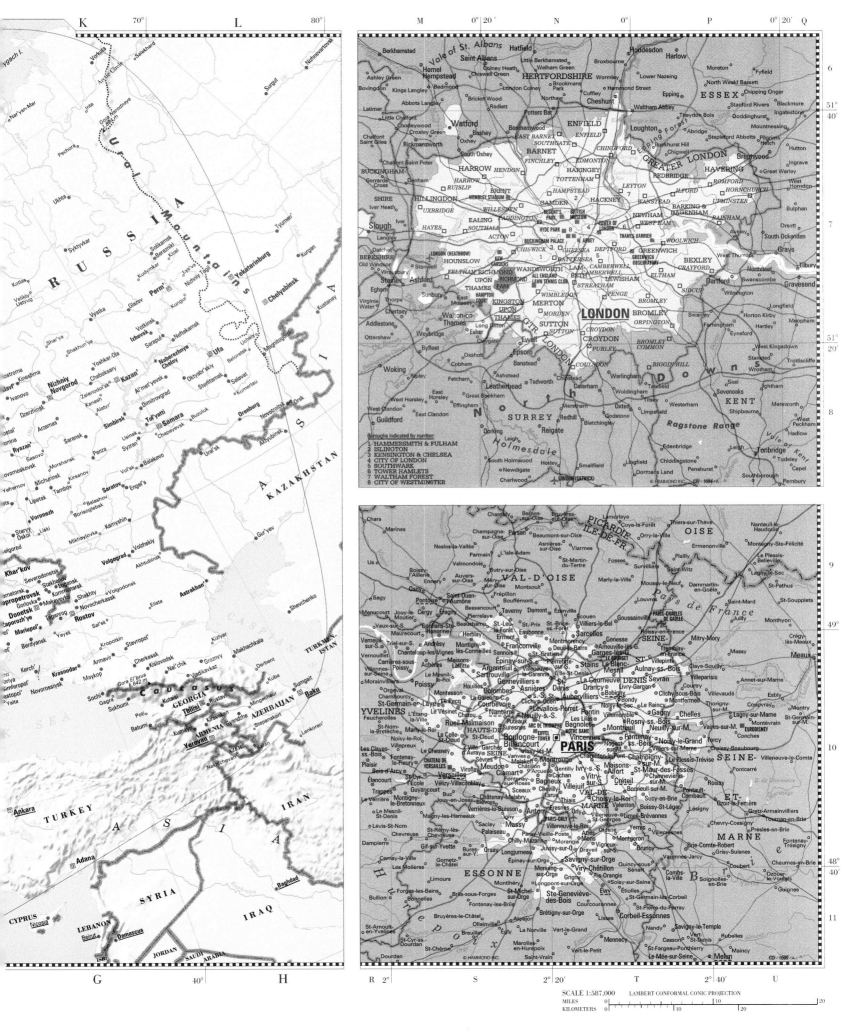

Northeastern Ireland, Northern England and Wales

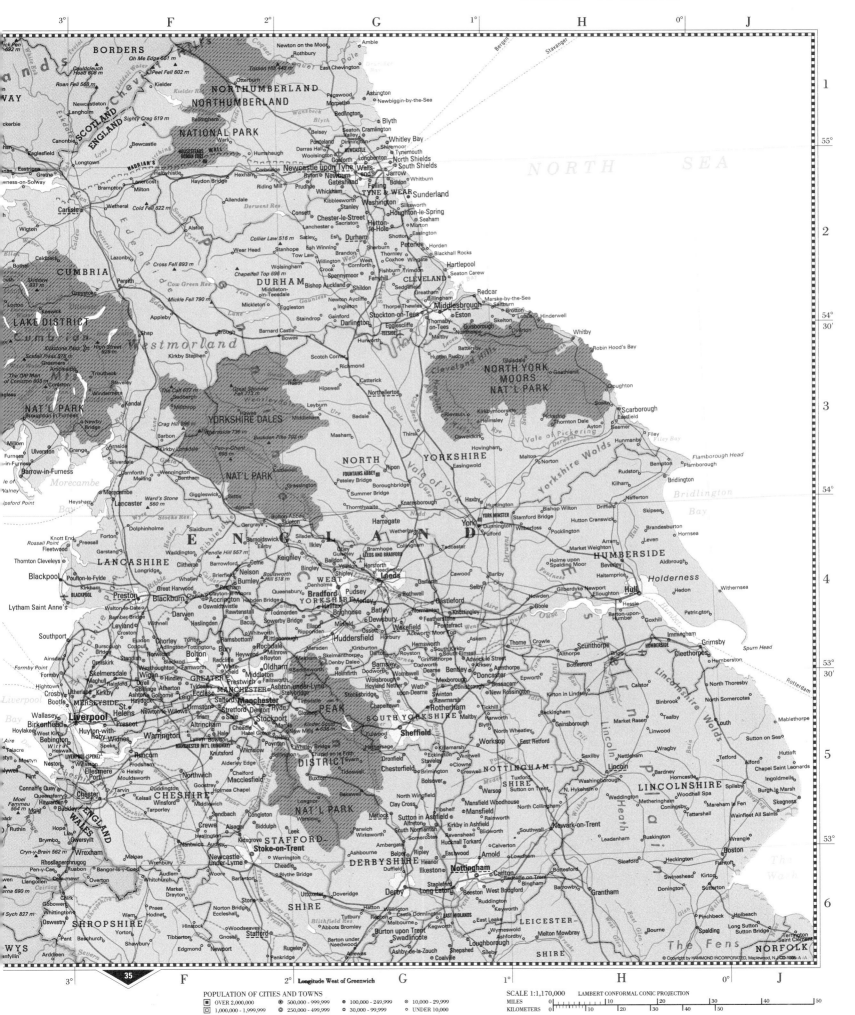

NORTH SEA

BORDERS

NORTHUMBERLAND
NORTHUMBERLAND
NATIONAL PARK

Scotland
England

Newcastle upon Tyne

TYNE & WEAR
Sunderland

CUMBRIA

LAKE DISTRICT

DURHAM

CLEVELAND
Middlesbrough

NORTH YORK
MOORS
NAT'L PARK

YORKSHIRE DALES

NAT'L PARK

NORTH
YORKSHIRE

Vale of Pickering

Scarborough

York
YORK MINSTER

HUMBERSIDE

E N G L A N D

LANCASHIRE

WEST
YORKSHIRE

Bradford
Leeds

Holderness

Hull

Blackpool

Preston

Blackburn

Liverpool

GREATER
MANCHESTER

Manchester

PEAK

DISTRICT

SOUTH YORKSHIRE

Sheffield

MERSEYSIDE

CHESHIRE

ENGLAND
WALES

NAT'L PARK

STAFFORD-
SHIRE
Stoke-on-Trent

DERBYSHIRE

NOTTINGHAM-
SHIRE

LINCOLNSHIRE

Lincoln

Derby

Nottingham

EAST MIDLANDS

LEICESTER-
SHIRE

NORFOLK

The Fens

WYS

SHROPSHIRE

POPULATION OF CITIES AND TOWNS

Symbol	Population	Symbol	Population	Symbol	Population
▣	OVER 2,000,000	⬤	500,000 - 999,999	●	100,000 - 249,999	⊙	10,000 - 29,999
▢	1,000,000 - 1,999,999	●	250,000 - 499,999	●	30,000 - 99,999	○	UNDER 10,000

SCALE 1:1,170,000   LAMBERT CONFORMAL CONIC PROJECTION

MILES 0 ... 10 ... 20 ... 30 ... 40 ... 50

KILOMETERS 0 ... 10 ... 20 ... 30 ... 40 ... 50

Longitude West of Greenwich

© Copyright by HAMMOND INCORPORATED, Maplewood, N.J.

Southern England and Wales

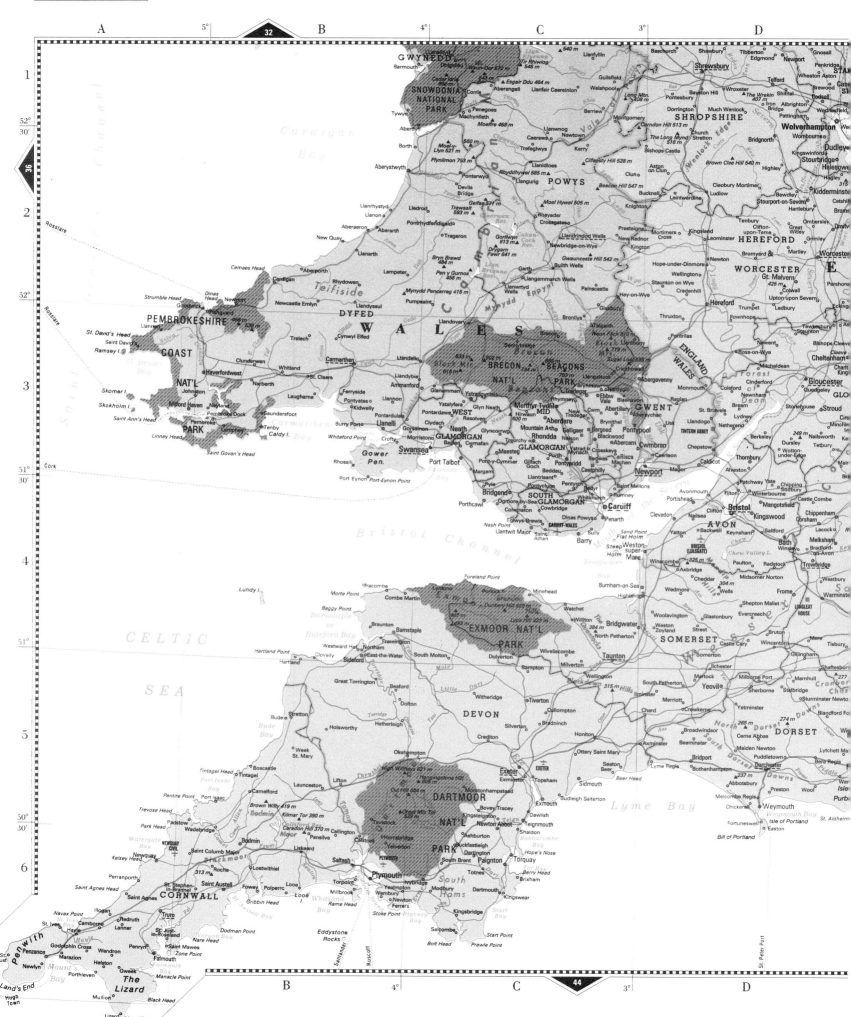

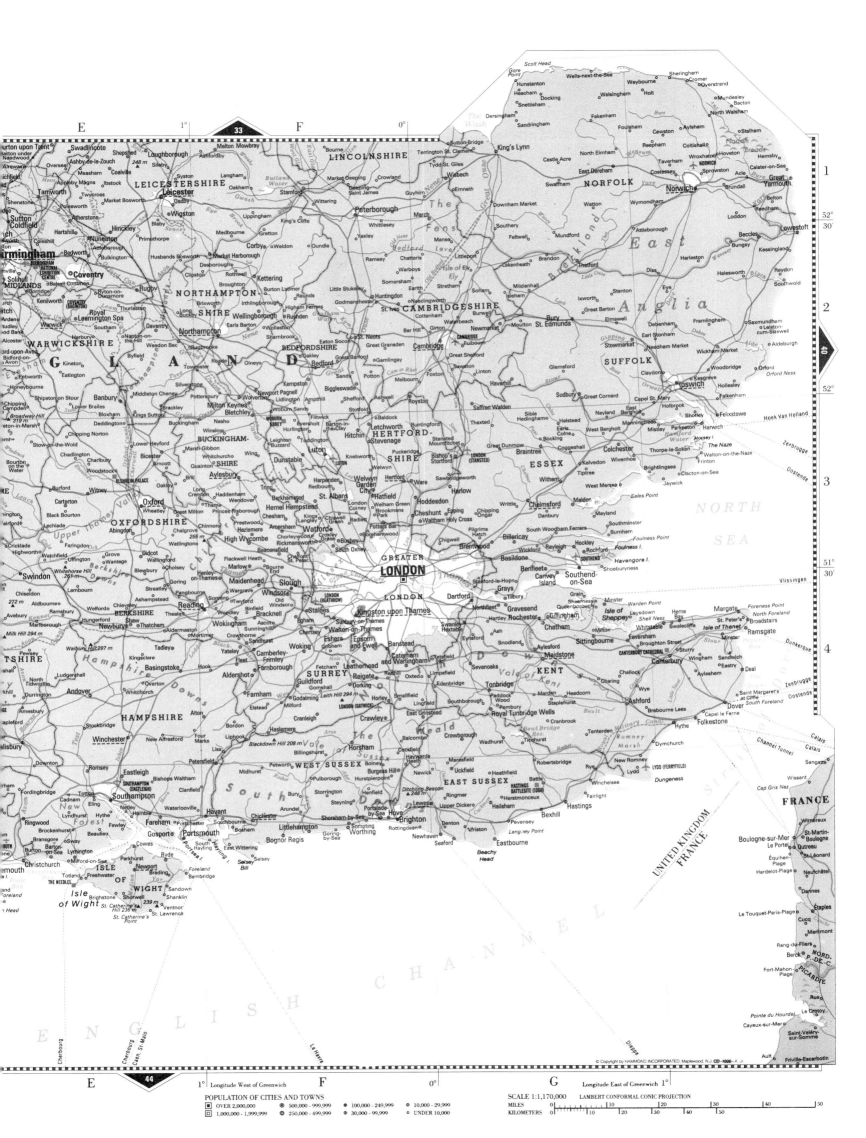

United Kingdom, Ireland

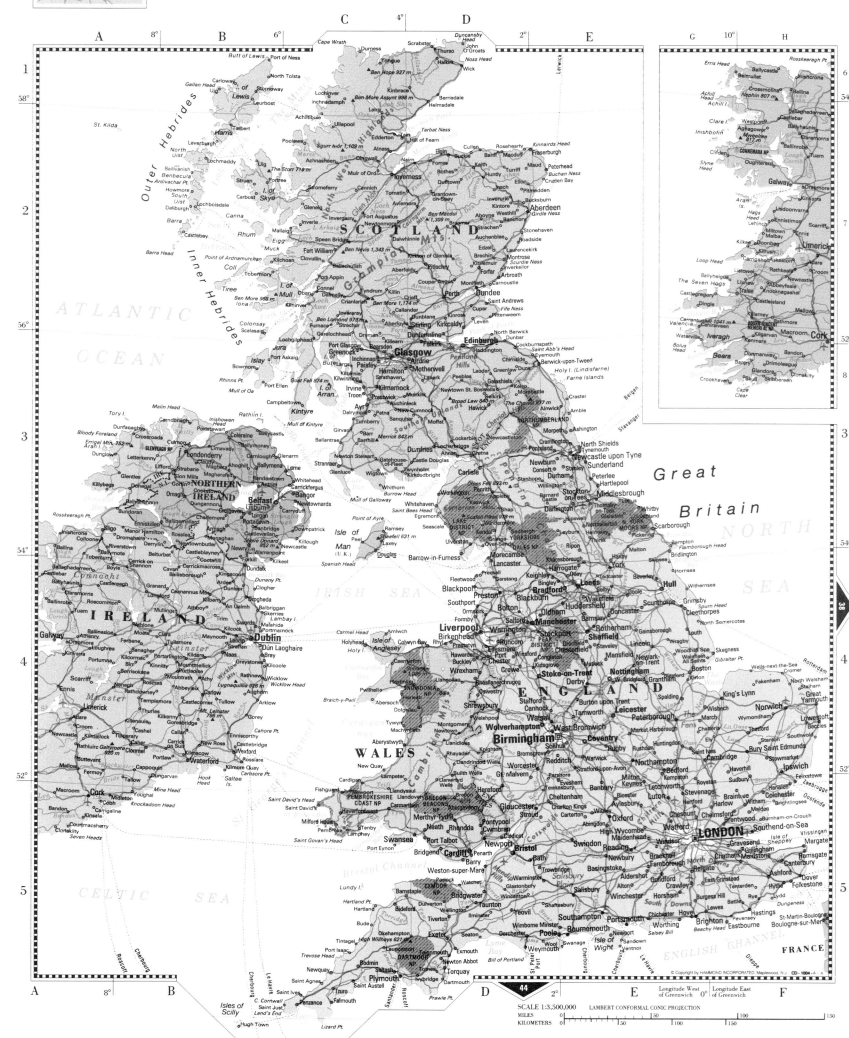

SCALE 1:3,500,000   LAMBERT CONFORMAL CONIC PROJECTION

MILES

KILOMETERS

Longitude West of Greenwich 0° Longitude East of Greenwich

© Copyright by HAMMOND INCORPORATED, Maplewood, N.J.   CD · 1004 · A · A

Scandinavia and Finland, Iceland

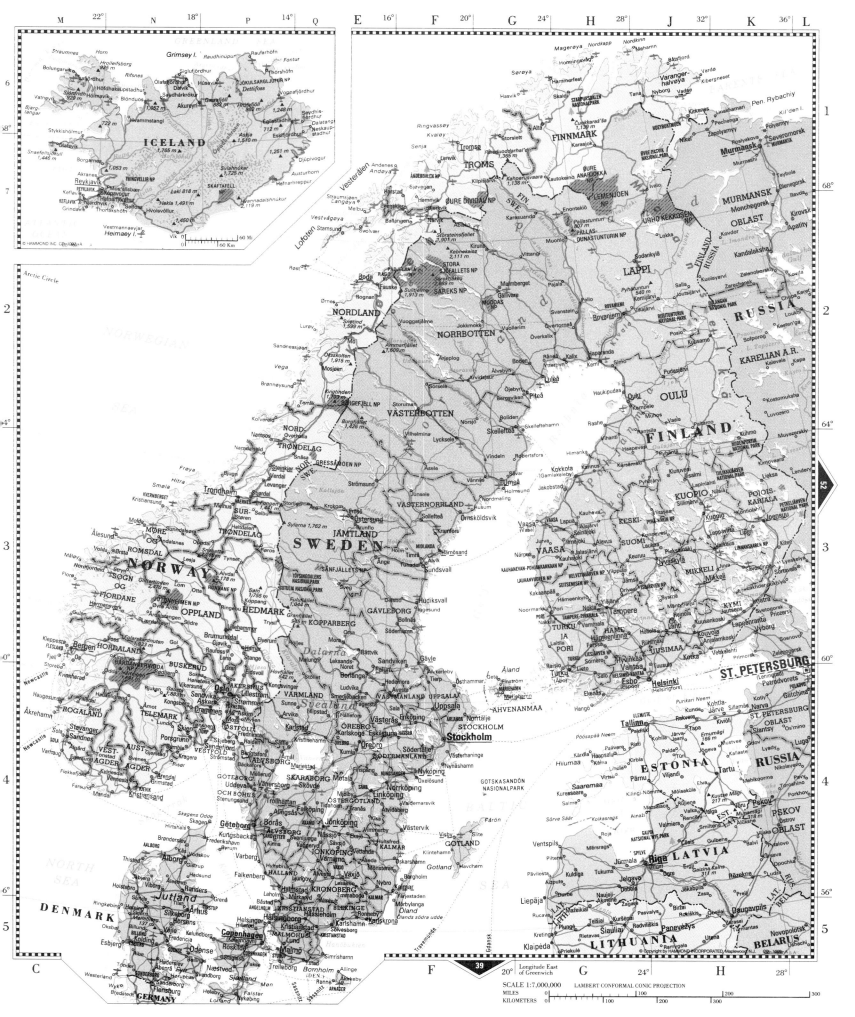

North Central Europe

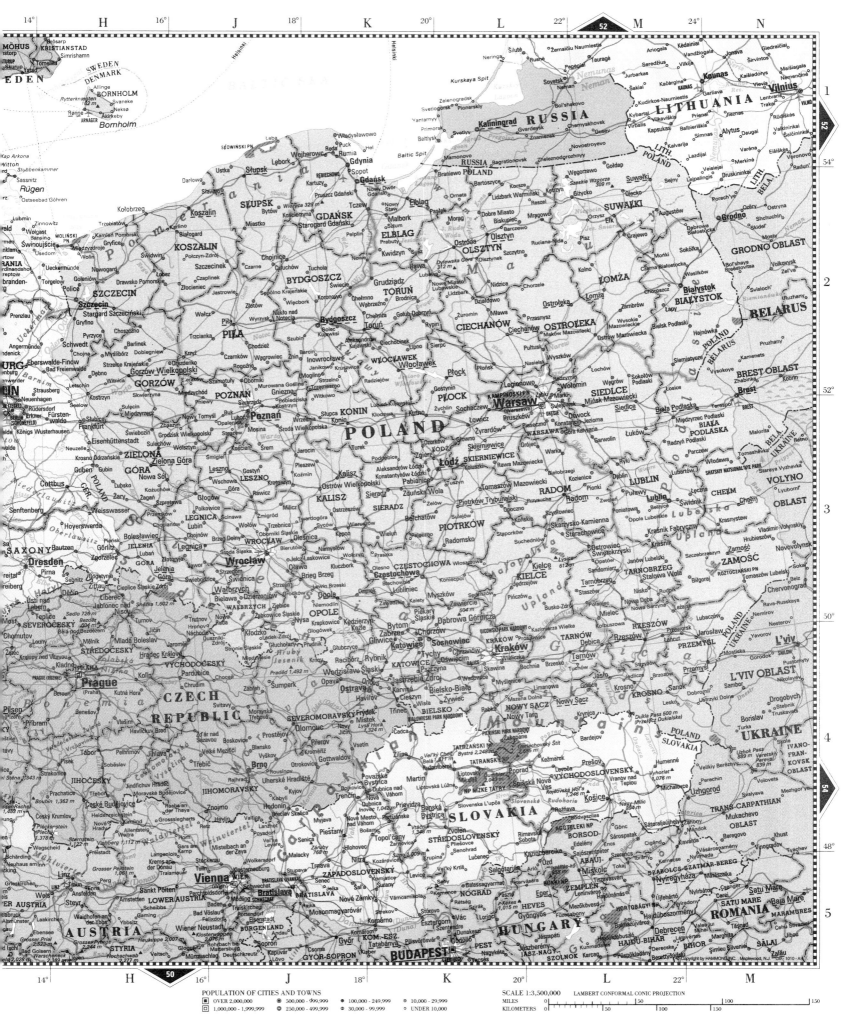

Netherlands, Northwestern Germany

5° Longitude East of Greenwich

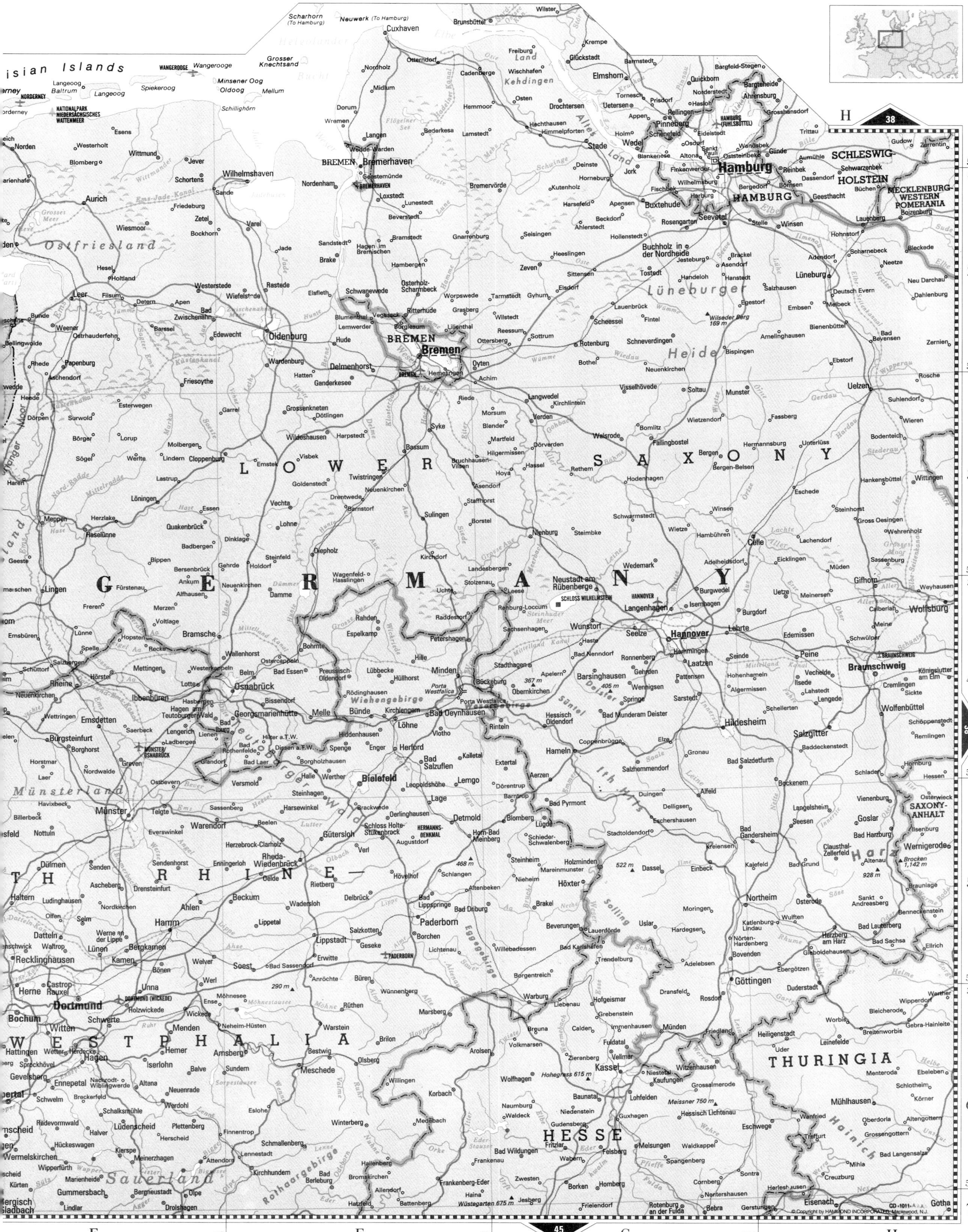

38

SCHLESWIG-HOLSTEIN

MECKLENBURG-WESTERN POMERANIA

H

L O W E R   S A X O N Y

G E R M A N Y

NORTH   R H I N E -   WESTPHALIA

HESSE

THURINGIA

SAXONY-ANHALT

Ostfriesland

Münsterland

Sauerland

Lüneburger Heide

Harz

Hamburg
HAMBURG

BREMEN
Bremen

Bremerhaven
BREMERHAVEN

Oldenburg

Osnabrück

Münster

Bielefeld

Dortmund

HANNOVER
Hannover

Braunschweig

Hildesheim

Salzgitter

Göttingen

Kassel

Paderborn

Wilhelmshaven

Lüneburg

Cuxhaven

POPULATION OF CITIES AND TOWNS

■ OVER 2,000,000
□ 1,000,000 – 1,999,999
● 500,000 – 999,999
◉ 250,000 – 499,999
⊕ 100,000 – 249,999
⊕ 30,000 – 99,999
⊙ 10,000 – 29,999
○ UNDER 10,000

SCALE 1:1,170,000   LAMBERT CONFORMAL CONIC PROJECTION

MILES 0   10   20   30   40   50

KILOMETERS 0   10   20   30   40   50

CD-1011-A-A

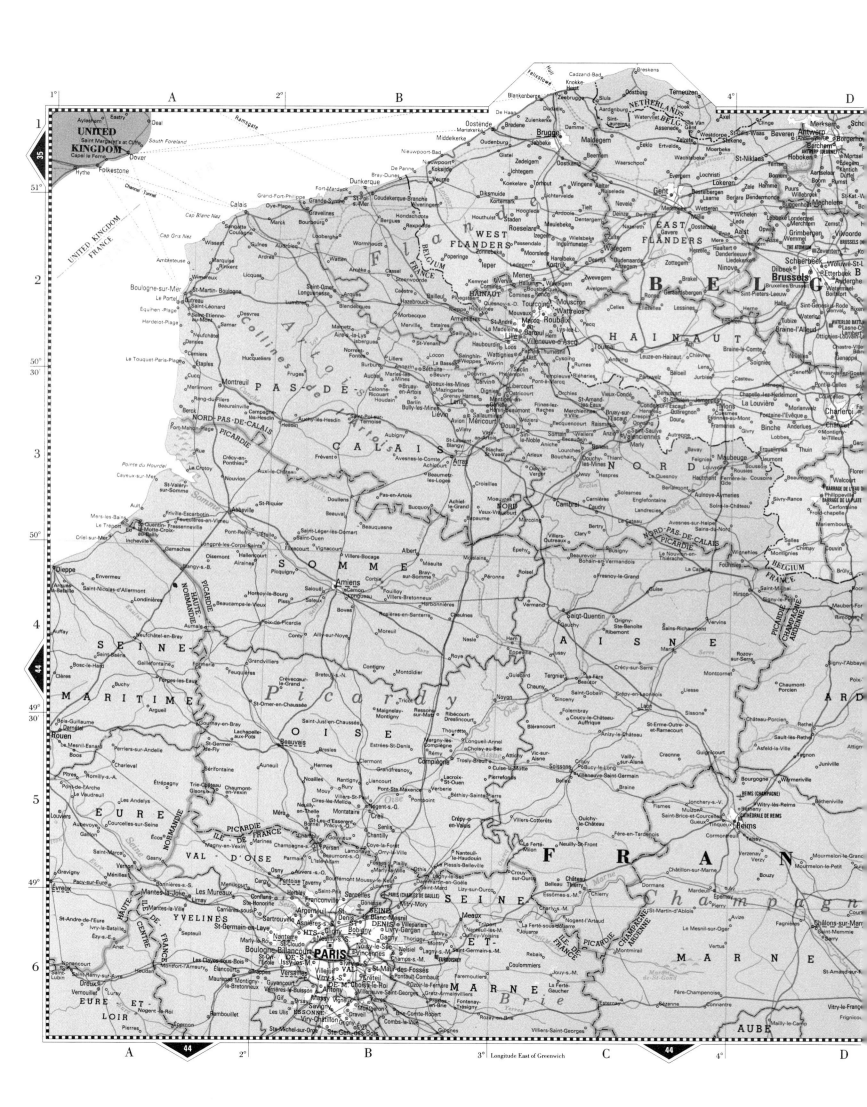

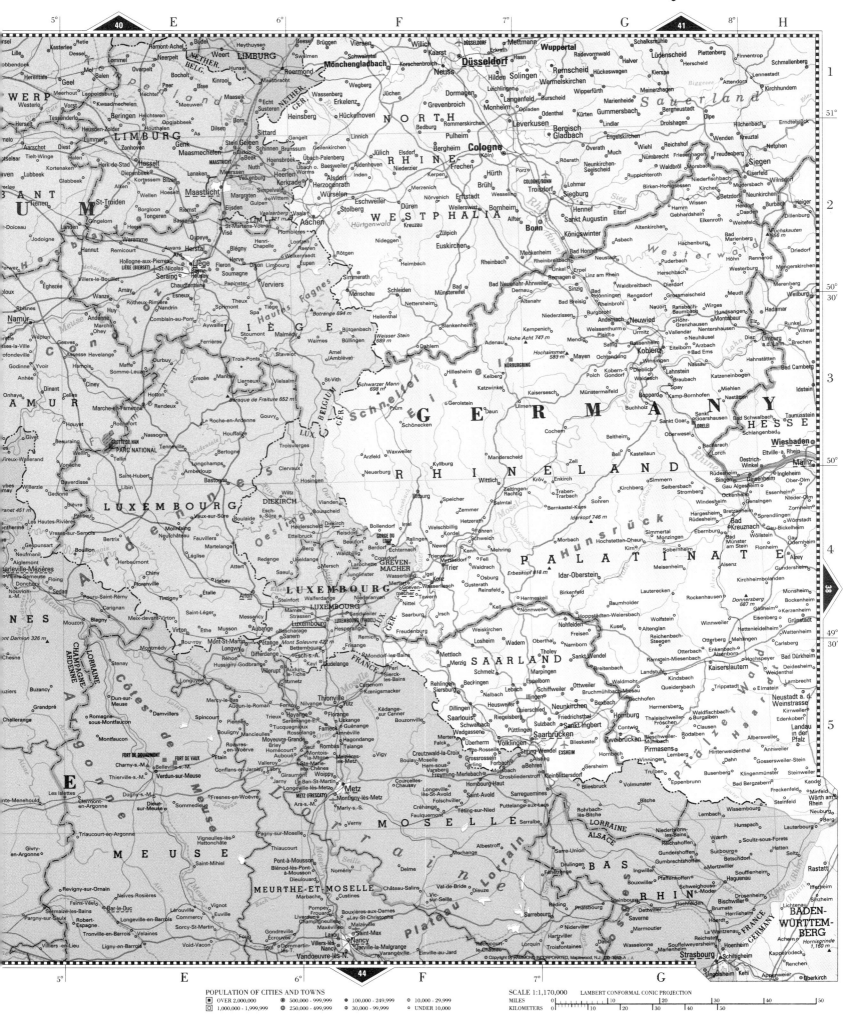

POPULATION OF CITIES AND TOWNS

◼ OVER 2,000,000	● 500,000 - 999,999	● 100,000 - 249,999	○ 10,000 - 29,999
▣ 1,000,000 - 1,999,999	● 250,000 - 499,999	● 30,000 - 99,999	○ UNDER 10,000

SCALE 1:1,170,000 LAMBERT CONFORMAL CONIC PROJECTION

MILES 0 — 10 — 20 — 30 — 40 — 50

KILOMETERS 0 — 10 — 20 — 30 — 40 — 50

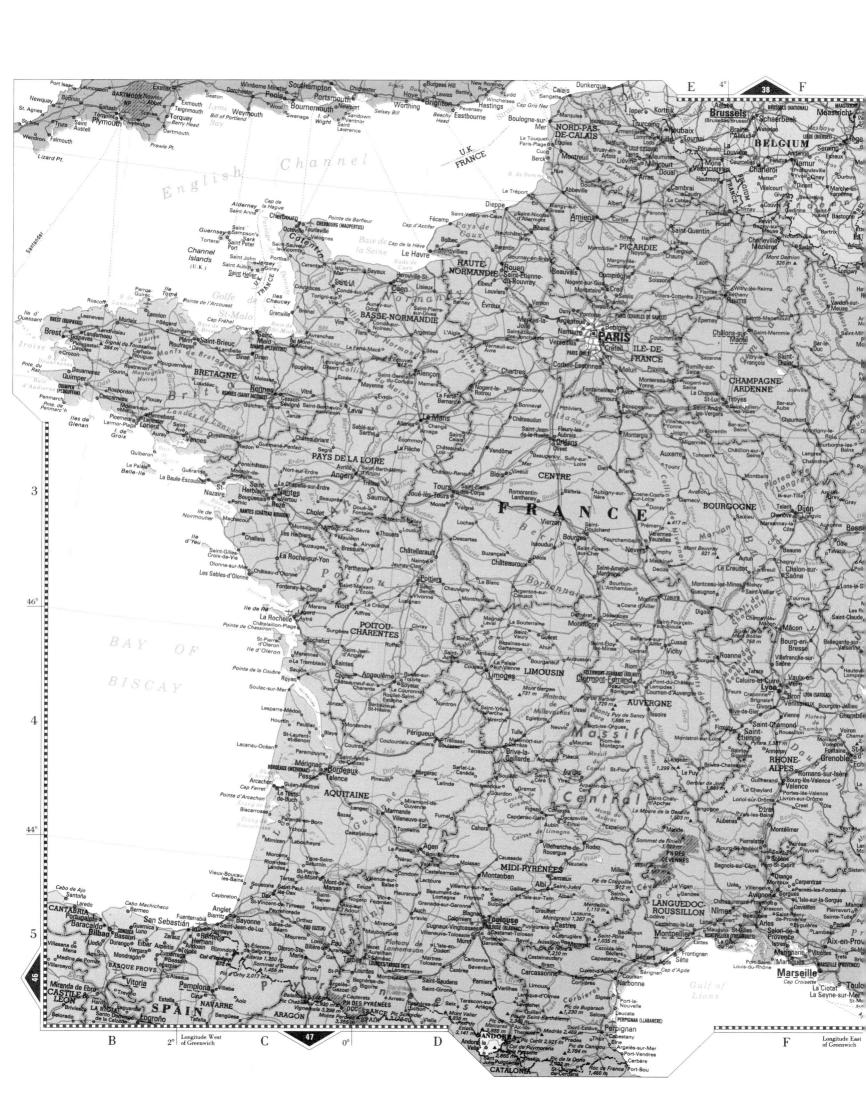

West Central Europe

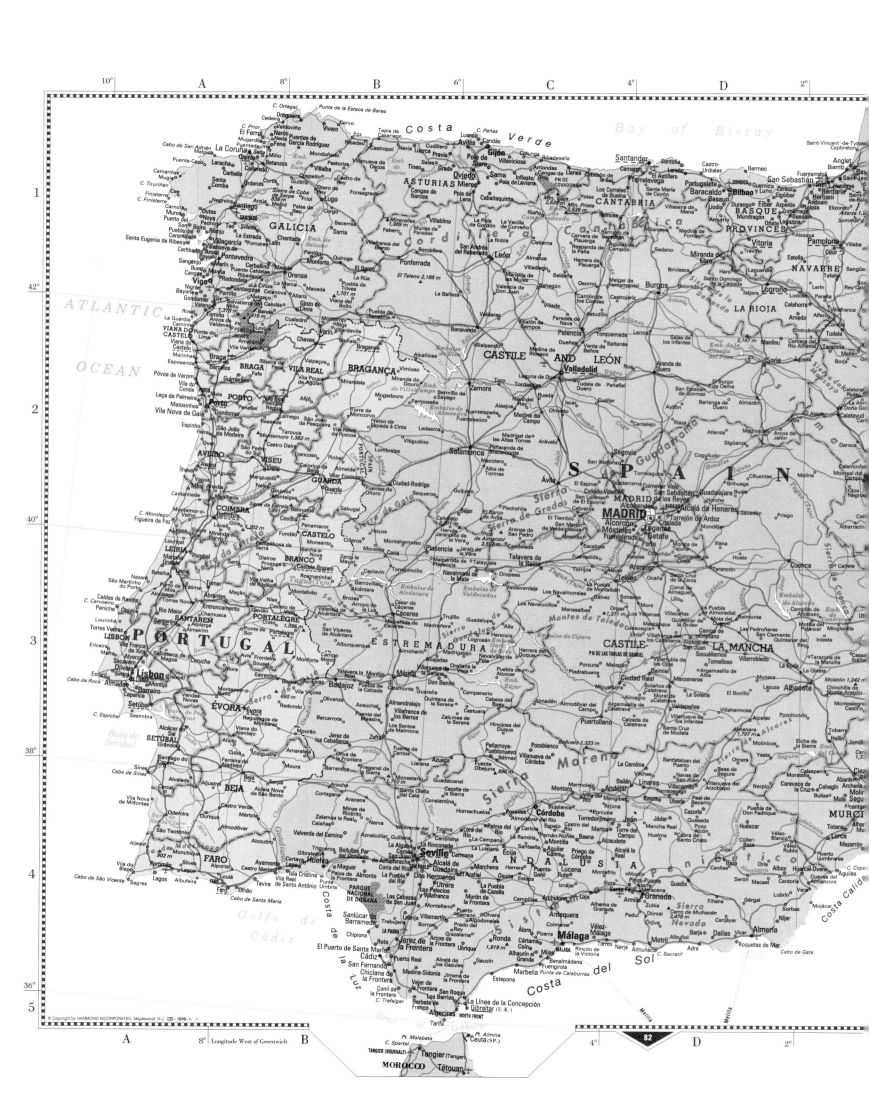

Spain, Portugal

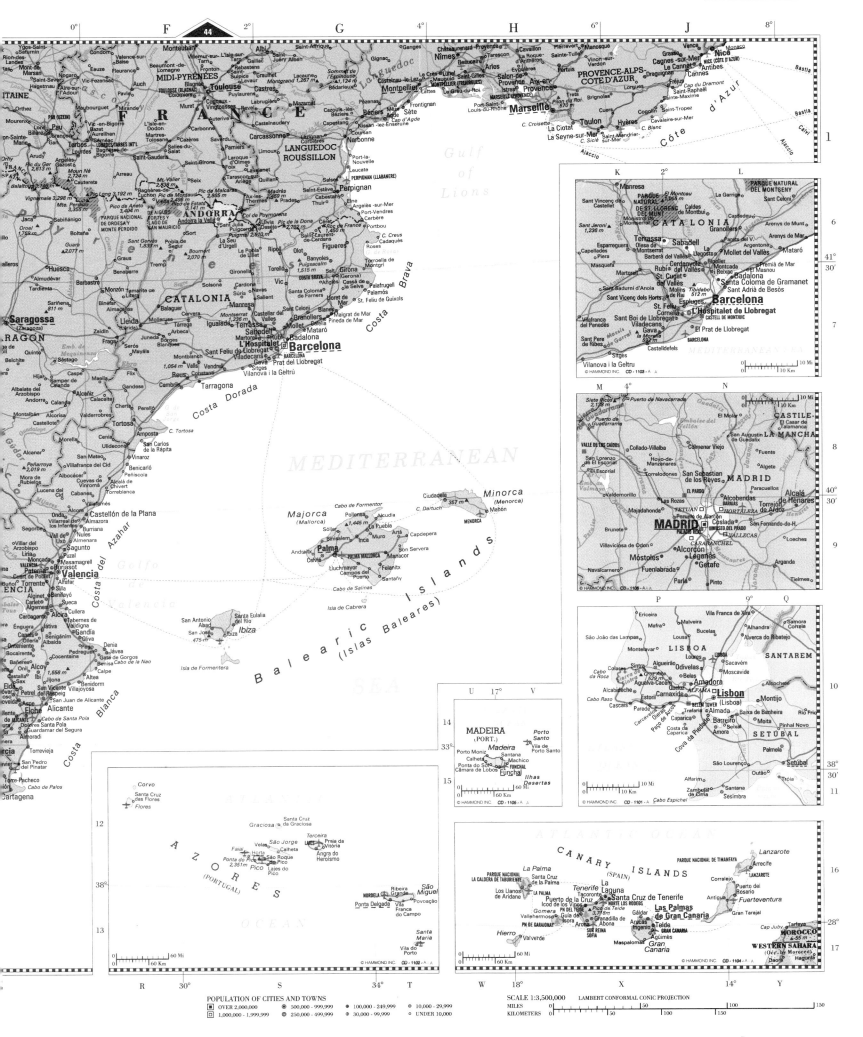

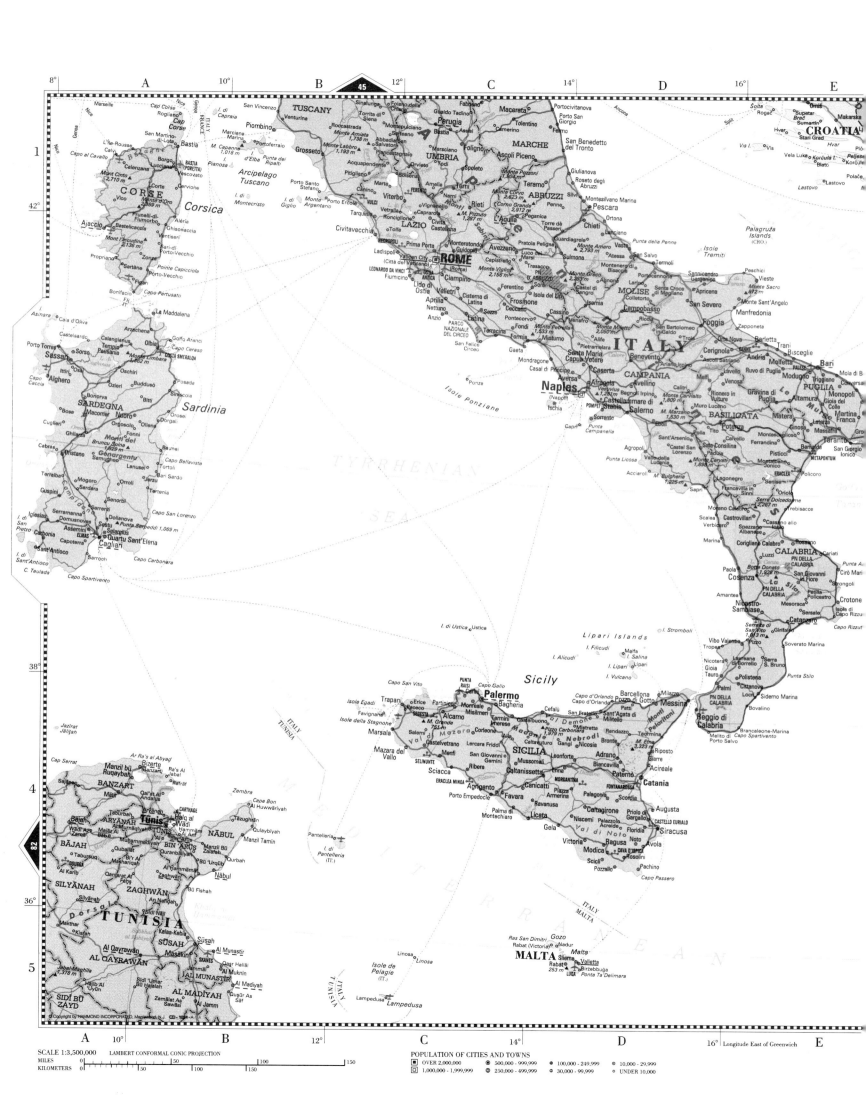

Southern Italy, Albania, Greece

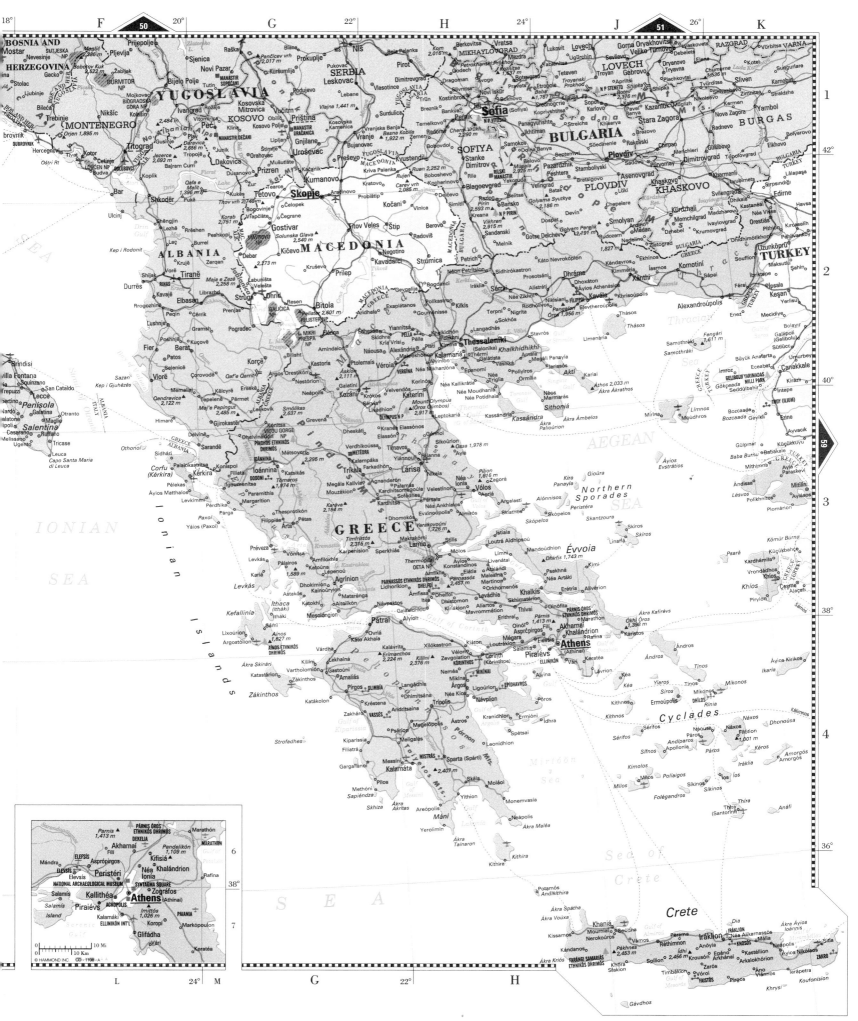

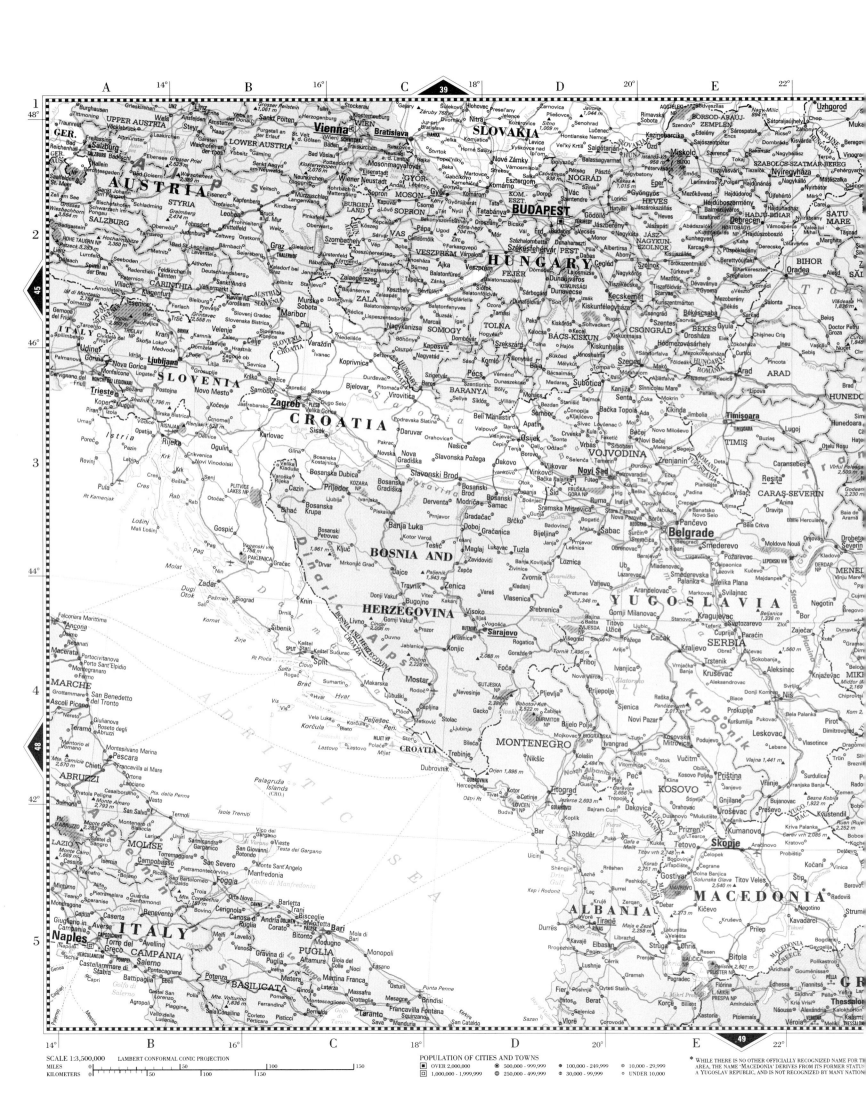

Hungary, Northern Balkan States

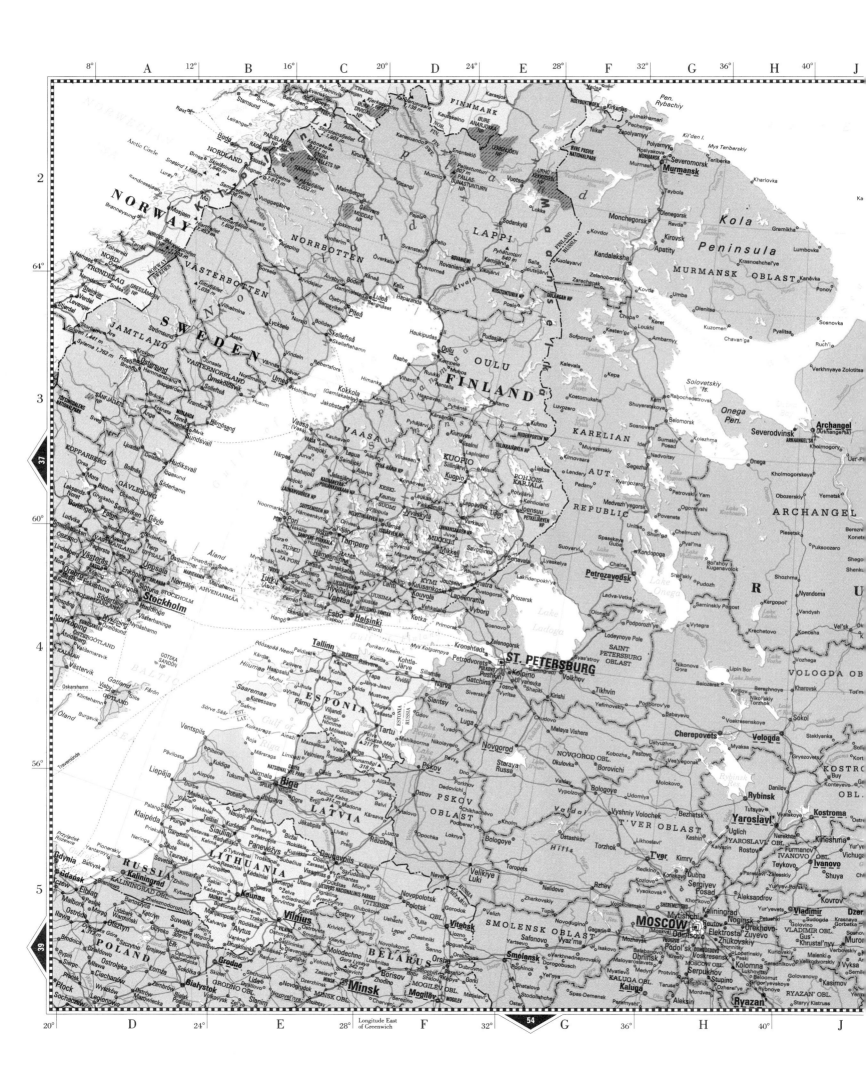

Northeastern Europe

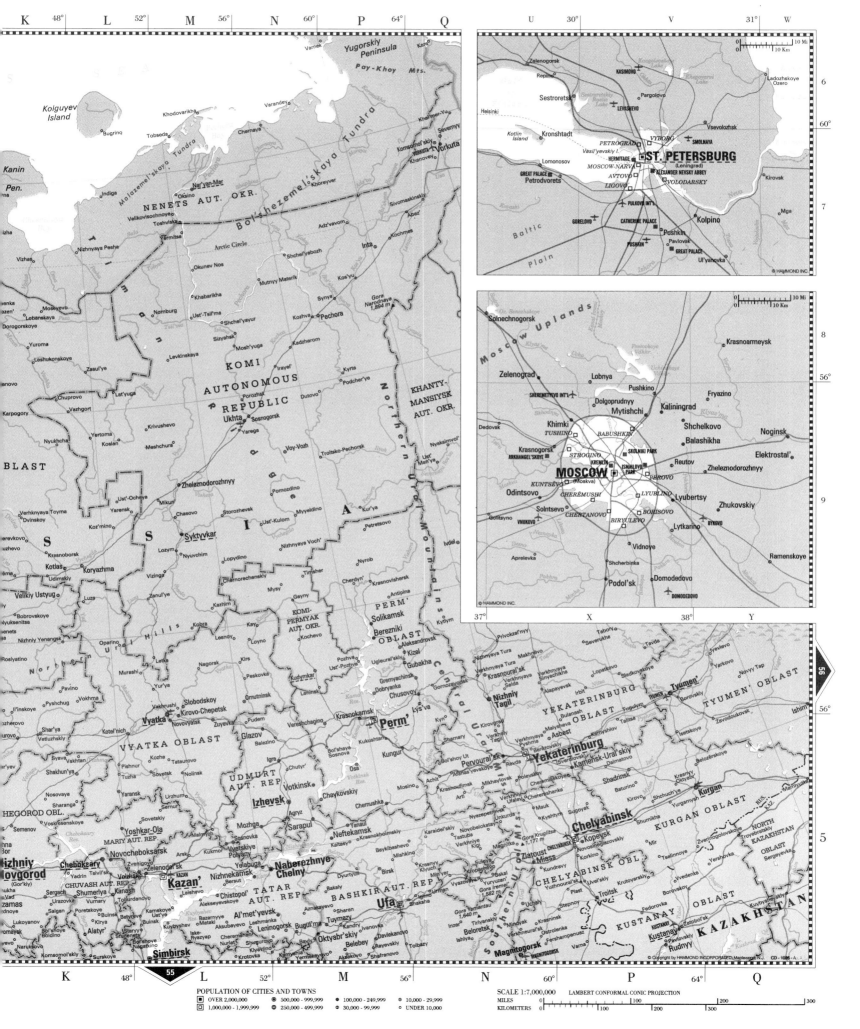

Southeastern Europe

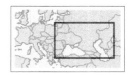

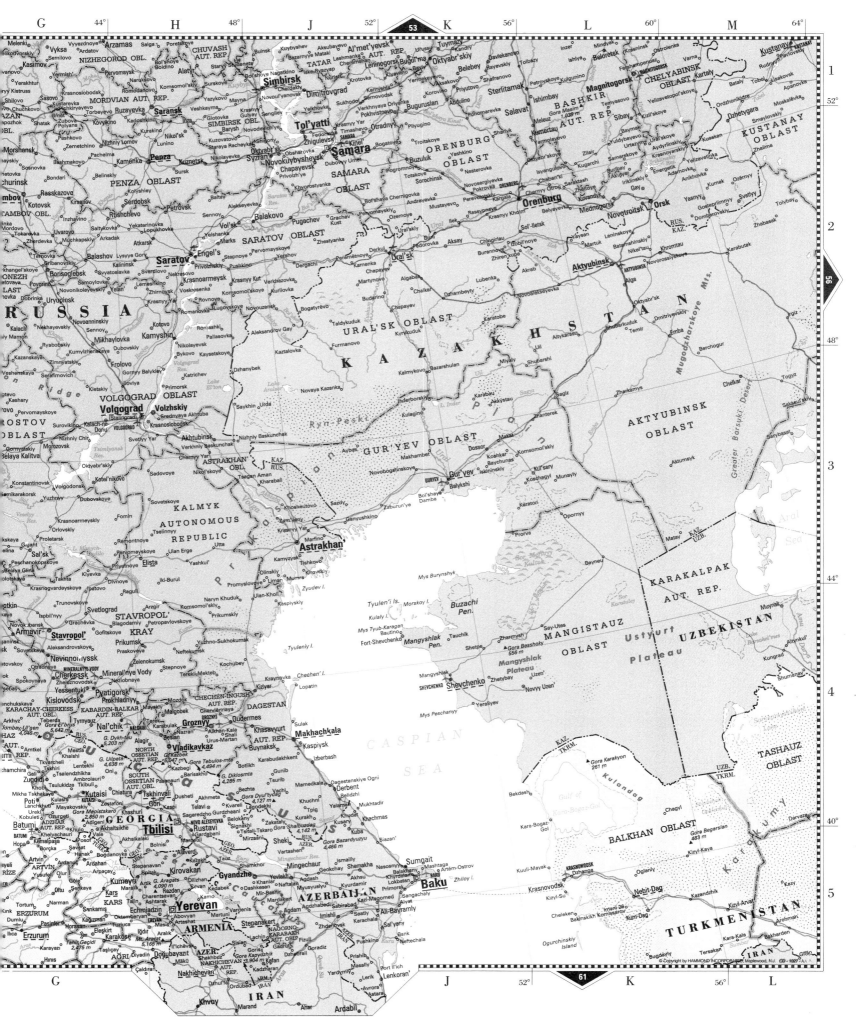

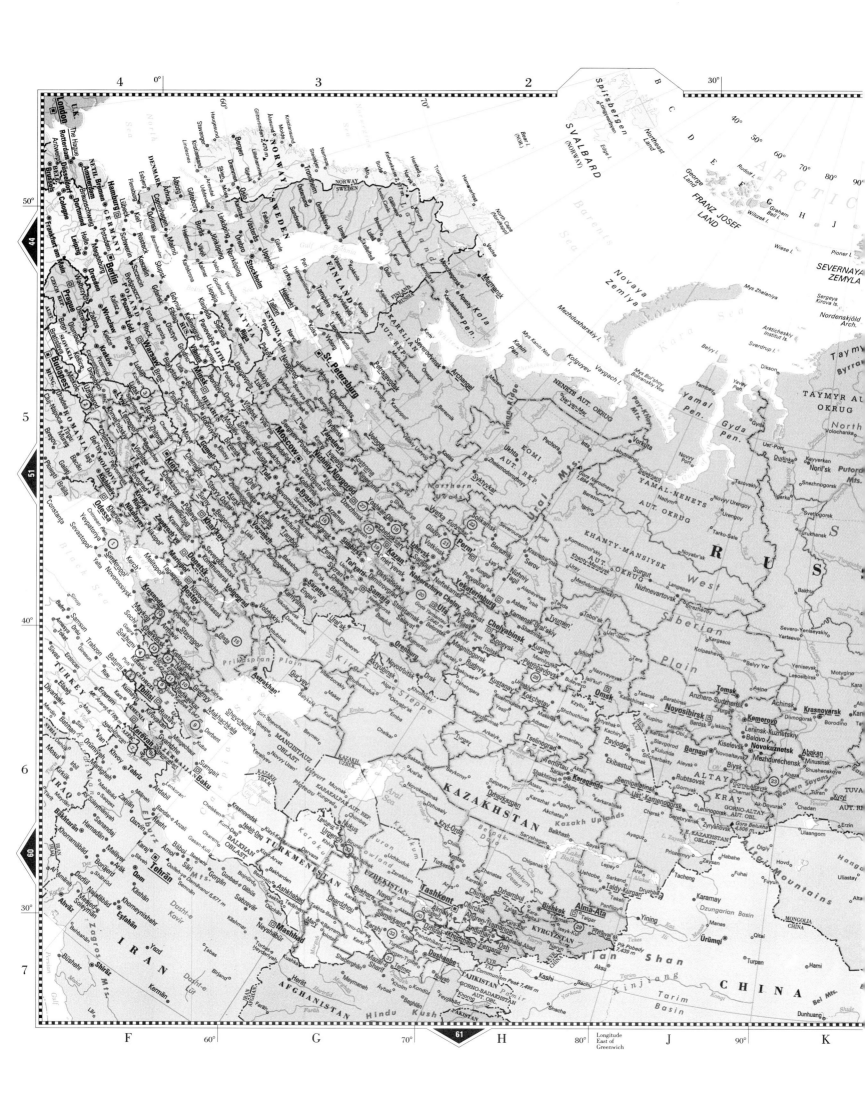

Russia and Neighboring Countries

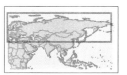

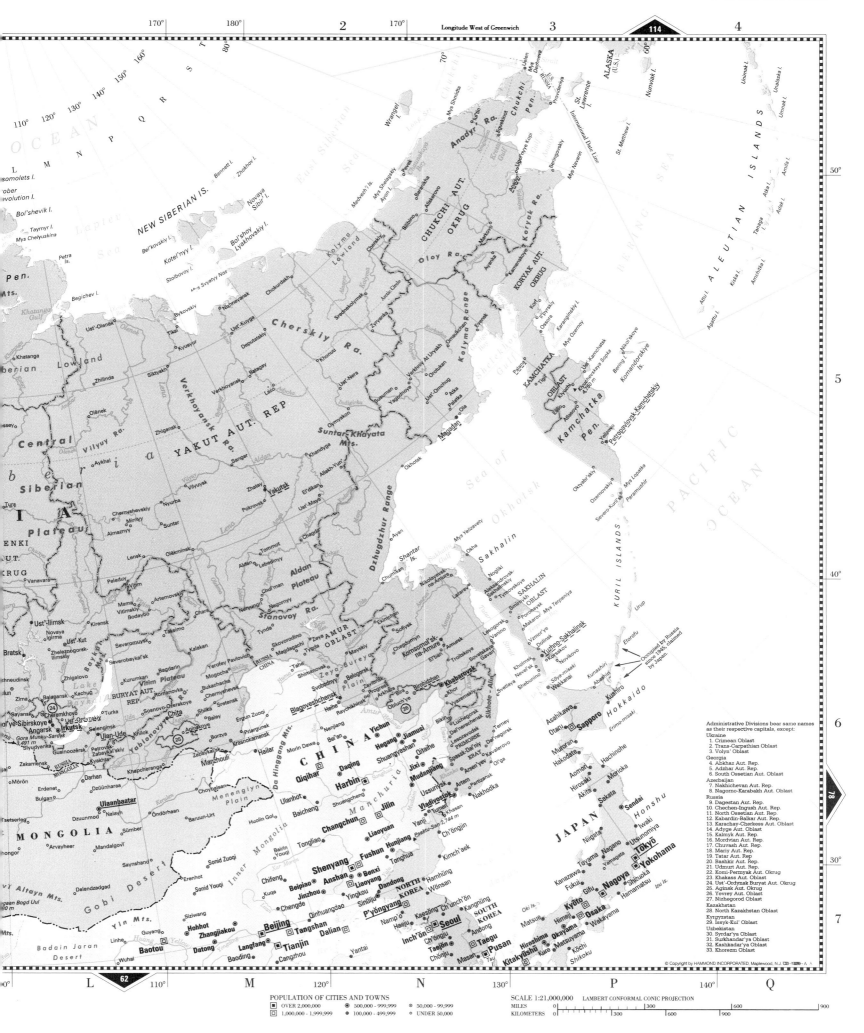

Asia

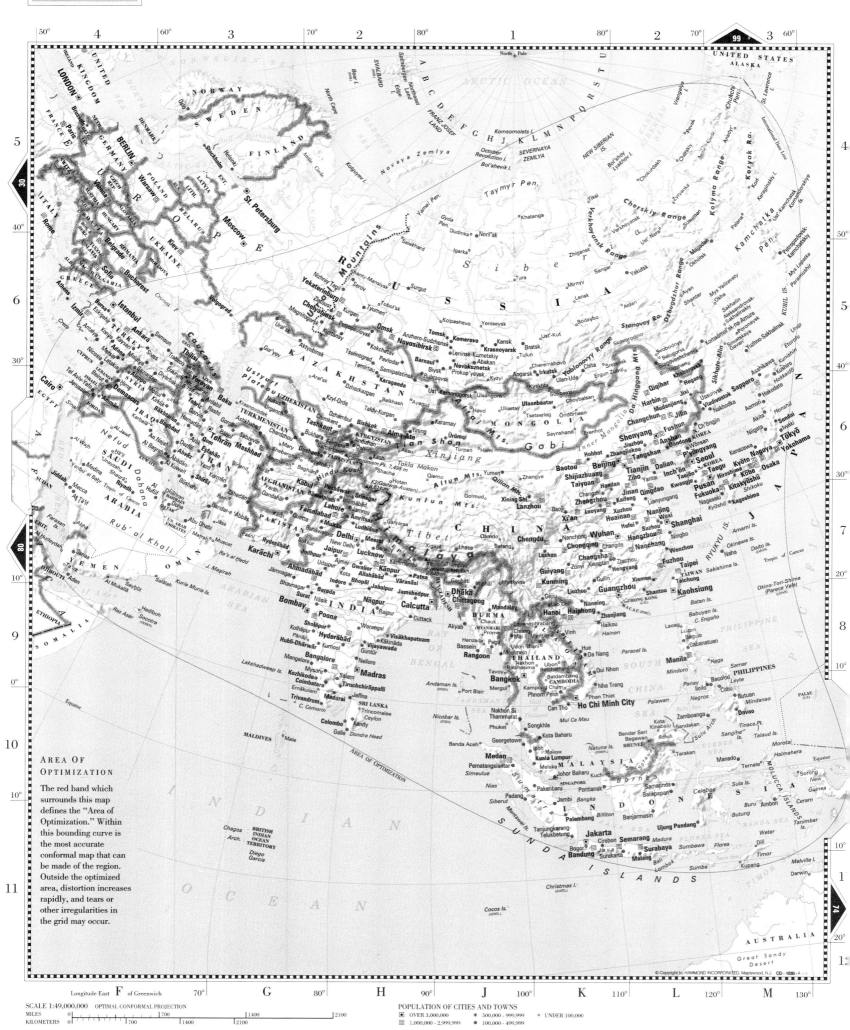

AREA OF OPTIMIZATION

The red band which surrounds this map defines the "Area of Optimization." Within this bounding curve is the most accurate conformal map that can be made of the region. Outside the optimized area, distortion increases rapidly, and tears or other irregularities in the grid may occur.

SCALE 1:49,000,000   OPTIMAL CONFORMAL PROJECTION

MILES	0		700	1400		2100
KILOMETERS	0		700	1400	2100	

Longitude East **F** of Greenwich   70°   **G**   80°   **H**   90°   **J**   100°   **K**   110°   **L**   120°   **M**   130°

POPULATION OF CITIES AND TOWNS

▣ OVER 3,000,000   ● 500,000 - 999,999   ○ UNDER 100,000
▣ 1,000,000 - 2,999,999   ● 100,000 - 499,999

Eastern Mediterranean Region

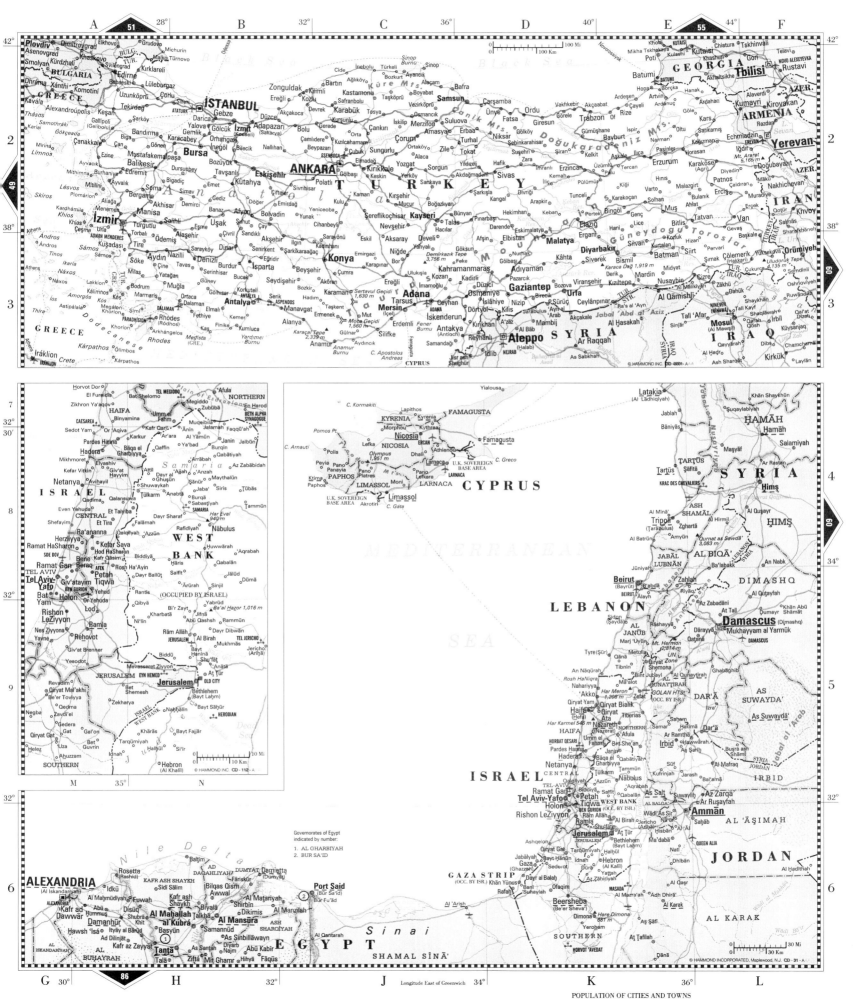

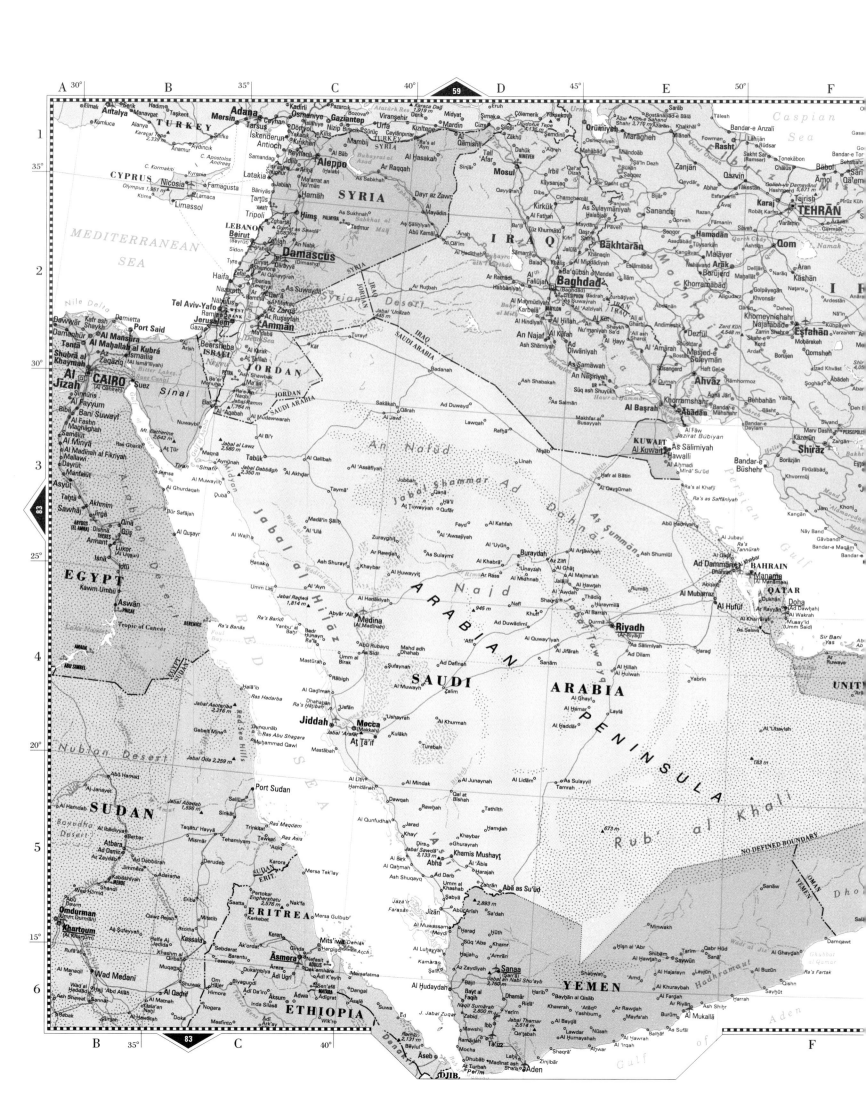

Southwestern Asia

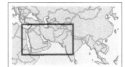

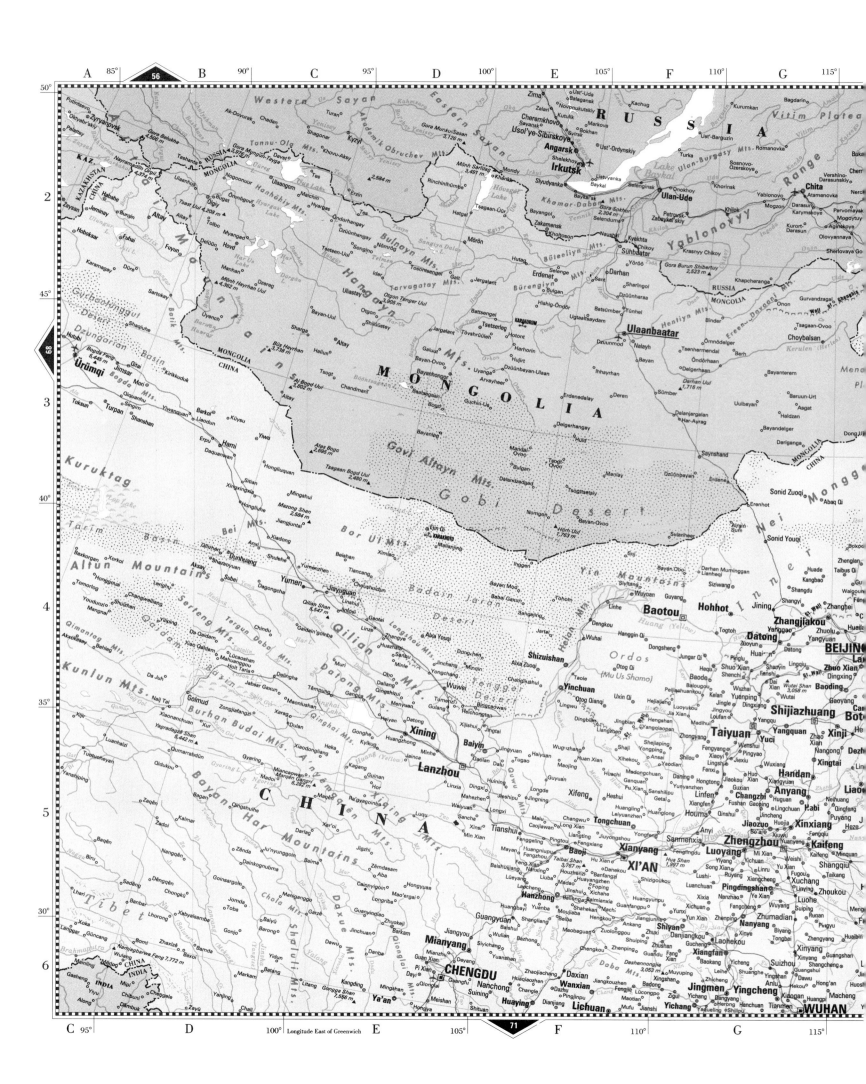

Eastern Asia

38°

SŎRAKSAN NAT'L PARK
Inje
Yangyang
Hongch'ŏn
ODAESAN
NAT'L PARK
Kangnŭng
Paektŏk-san 1,350 m
P'yŏngch'ang
▲ Nogwak-san 1,321 m
Wŏnju
Samch'ŏk
KANGWŎN-DO
CH'UNGCH'ŎNG
Chech'ŏn
Ulchin
KYŎNGSANG-BUKTO

2

Ullŭng I.
(South Korea)

S O U T H

Yŏngju
Ponghwa
Yŏng-yang

Liancourt Rocks
(Disputed between Japan
and South Korea)

S E A   O F   J A P A N

63

Ch'ŏmch'ŏn
Andong
Sangju
Ch'ŏngsong
Yŏngdŏk
Sŏnsan
Uisŏng
Yŏngdŏk
Kumi
Kimch'ŏn

K O R E A

P'ohang

36°

Kimch'ŏn
TAEGU-
JIKHALSI
Taegu
KYŎNGSANG-
BUKTO
KYŎNGSANG-
NAMDO

Pirgong-san
1,192 m
Hwayang

OKI
ISLANDS
Dōgo
Saigō
OKI
DAISEN-OKI
NAT'L PARK
Dōzen

Koma
Kaga

Mikuni
Sakai
Fukui

Kyŏngsan
Kyŏngju
KYŎNGJU NAT'L PARK
SILLA TOMBS
PULGUK-SA

Takefu
Tsuruga

Miryang
Ulsan
Kaji-san 1,240 m
Samnangjin

Ch'angwŏn
Kimhae

Masan
Chinhae
KIMHAE
Ûiryŏng

SAN'IN KAIGIN
NATIONAL PARK

3

UNITED NATIONS MEMORIAL CEM.
PUSAN-JIKHALSI
Koje Island
Ch'ŏngmu
Shinhyŏn

Hirata
Izumo IZUMO
Oda

Sakaiminato
Jizō-zaki
Matsue
YONAGO
Yonago
Daisen-oki
TOTTORI
Iwami
TOTTORI
Toyo-oka
Miyazu

Kurayoshi
Daisen 1,711 m

Wasa
Hyō-no-sen 1,510 m
Tottori

Kyōga-misaki
Wakasa
Bay
Maizuru
Takahama
Imazu
Obama

PUSAN

Wakasa
Fukuchiyama

Tsuruga
Mikuni
Nagao

SOUTH KOREA

Hino-misaki
Taisha

SHIMANE

Tsuyama

Fukuchiyama
Sonobe
KYŌTO
Kameoka

CHUGOKU
KINKI
HYŌGO

Kyōto
Otsu

Koso'ng
HALLYŎ-HAESANG
NAT'L PARK
Chonghyŏn
Kara-saki

Hamada

Götsu

Shōbara
Tōjō

Niimi

Takahashi
OKAYAMA
Sōja

NORAKUEN GARDEN

Kurashiki

Nishiwaki
Ono
Sanda
Shimamoto
HIMEJI CASTLE
Himeji
Yokawa
Awaji
Kōbe

Nagaokakyō
Takatsuki

Hirakata
Yao
Nara

34°

Chejú I.
SOUTH KOREA
JAPAN
Tsu Island
Izuhara

Ko-saki

Masuda

Miyoshi

Kanmuri-yama 1,339 m

HIROSHIMA

Fuchū
Ibara
Kasaoka

Akō
Okayama
Izumi-Sano
OSAKA
Izumi
Sakaide
Shōdo
I.
Sumoto
Kainan
Gojō
YOSHINO-
KUMANO

Hagi

Nagato
Ōtake
Onomichi
Takamatsu
Takehara
Kure
HIROSHIMA
PEACE MEMORIAL PARK

SETO-NAIKAI
NAT'L PARK
Kan'onji
Zentsūji
KAGAWA
TOKUSHIMA

Naruto
Wakayama
Arida

NARA
OSAKA
Hashimoto
Katsuura

Tsu Island
TSUSHIMA
Izuhara

YAMAGUCHI
Yamaguchi

Shimonoseki

Onoda
Hōfu
Tokuyama
Kudamatsu
Iwakuni
Yanai

Kan'on
Imabari
Hōjō

Iyo
Saijō
Niihama
Keda

Shikoku
I.
Komatsushima
Katsura

TOKUSHIMA
Tokushima

Hakken-san 1,915 m
Shirakawa-tōge

WAKAYAMA
Shingū

Iki
IKI

Ube
UBE

CHŪGOKU
KYŪSHŪ

SETO-NAIKAI
NAT'L PARK

MATSUYAMA
Matsuyama

TOKUSHIMA

Tanabe

Kitakyūshū
Nogata
KITAKYŪSHŪ
Yukuhashi

Nakatsu
Usa

ŌITA
ŌITA

Nagahama

EHIME
Ōzu

KŌCHI
Nankoku
Ishizuchi-san 1,982 m
Tsurugi-san
1,955 m

Kumano

Fukuoka
Iizuka
Tagawa
FUKUOKA
Amagi

Yawatahama

Sakawa

Kōchi
KŌCHI
Aki
Kaifu
Muroto

Hirado
Karatsu
Saga
Tosu
Kurume
Yanagawa
Yamaga

Beppu
Hiji
ŌITA
Ōita

Uwajima
Yoshida
Ine

Tosa
Susaki

Muroto-zaki

Imari
SAGA
Kashima
Ōkawa
Yamaga

Usuki

Saiki

Kubokawa

Tosa Bay

SAIKAI
NAT'L PARK
KAMIGOTŌ
Sasebo

Ōmuta
Yamaga

ASO NAT'L PARK
Yufu-san 1,787 m
Taketa

Tsukumi

Nakamura

4

GOTŌ
ISLANDS
Fukue I.
SAIKAI
NAT'L PARK
FUKUE
Fukue I.

NAGASAKI
Ōmura
NAGASAKI
Nagasaki
NAGASAKI PEACE PARK
Isahaya

Unzen-dake
▲1,359 m
Shimabara

KUMAMOTO
Kumamoto
KUMAMOTO

Aso-san 1,592 m

Sumoto
Sukumo
Tosashimizu
Ashizuri-misaki

S h i k o k u

J A P A N

Nomo-zaki
Tachibana
Bay
Hondo

Yatsushiro

SHIKOKU
KYŪSHŪ
Saiki

Amakusa
Sea
Ushibuka

Minamata
UNZEN-AMAKUSA
NATIONAL PARK

Nobeoka
Kumimi-dake 1,739 m
Hyūga

Kyūshū Highs

Hitoyoshi
MIYAZAKI

32°

P A C I F I C

Akune
Izumi
Ōkuchi
Saito
Takanabe
Sadowara

E A S T
C H I N A

Shimo-
koshiki
I.
Kushikino
Sendai
KAGOSHIMA
Miyanojō
Kirishima-yama
▲1,700 m
Kobayashi

MIYAZAKI
Miyazaki

Makurazaki
Nomo-misaki
Kaseda

Kagoshima
KAGOSHIMA
Tarumizu
Kanoya
Kushima
Kokubu
Miyakonojō
Nichinan

K y ū s h ū

S E A

Jūin

Ôsumi Pen.
Koyama
Kanoya

O C E A N

Sata-misaki

Nishino'omote

ŌSUMI   ISLANDS
N28E Naha

Tanega I.

Kamiyaku
Yaku I.
Nakatane

KIRISHIMA-YAKU NAT'L PARK

Central and Southern Japan

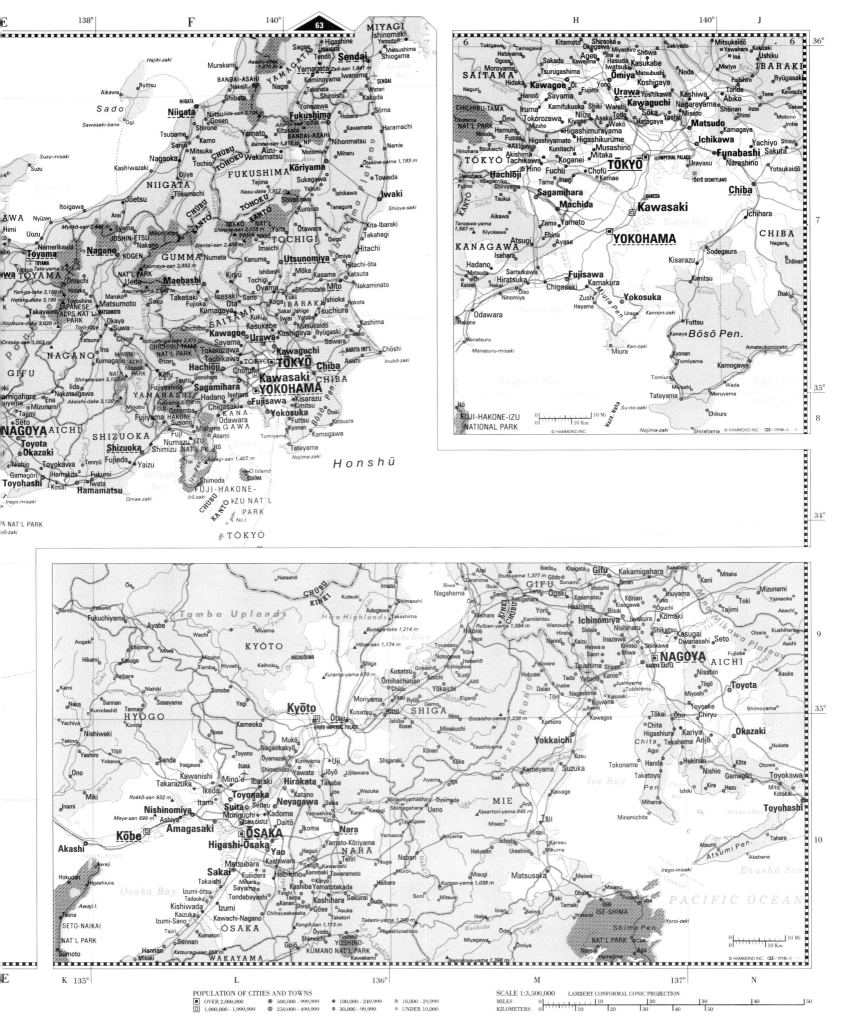

Northeastern China

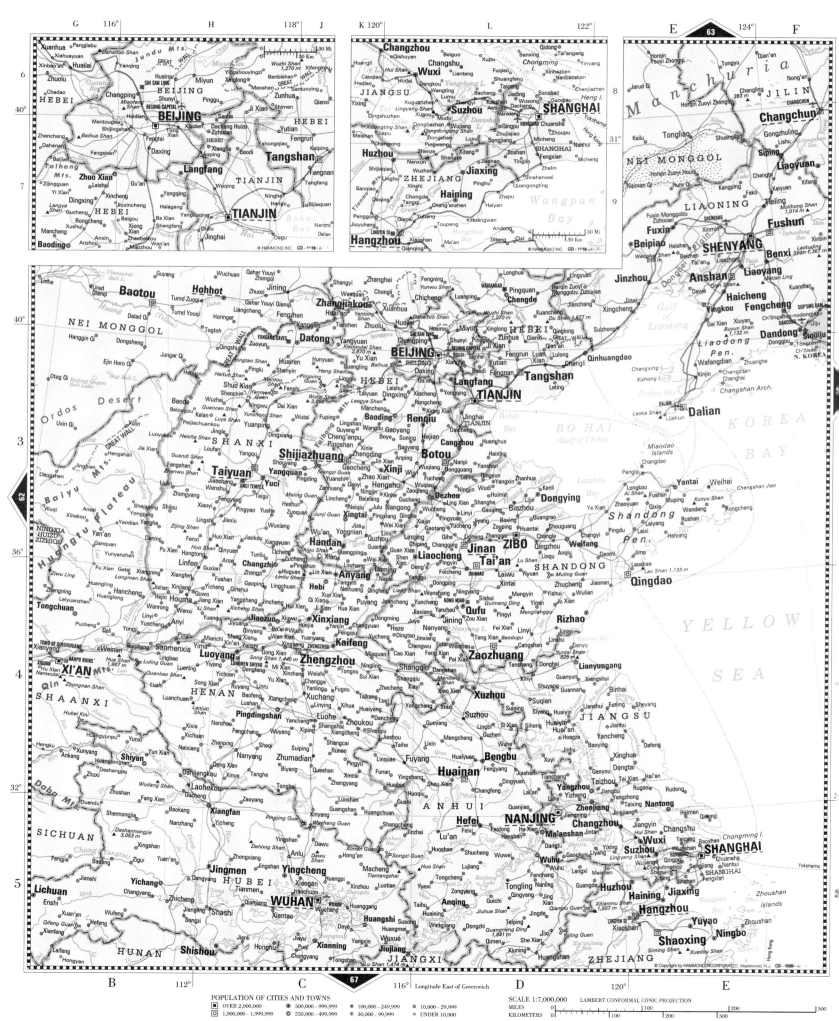

Southeastern China, Taiwan, Philippines

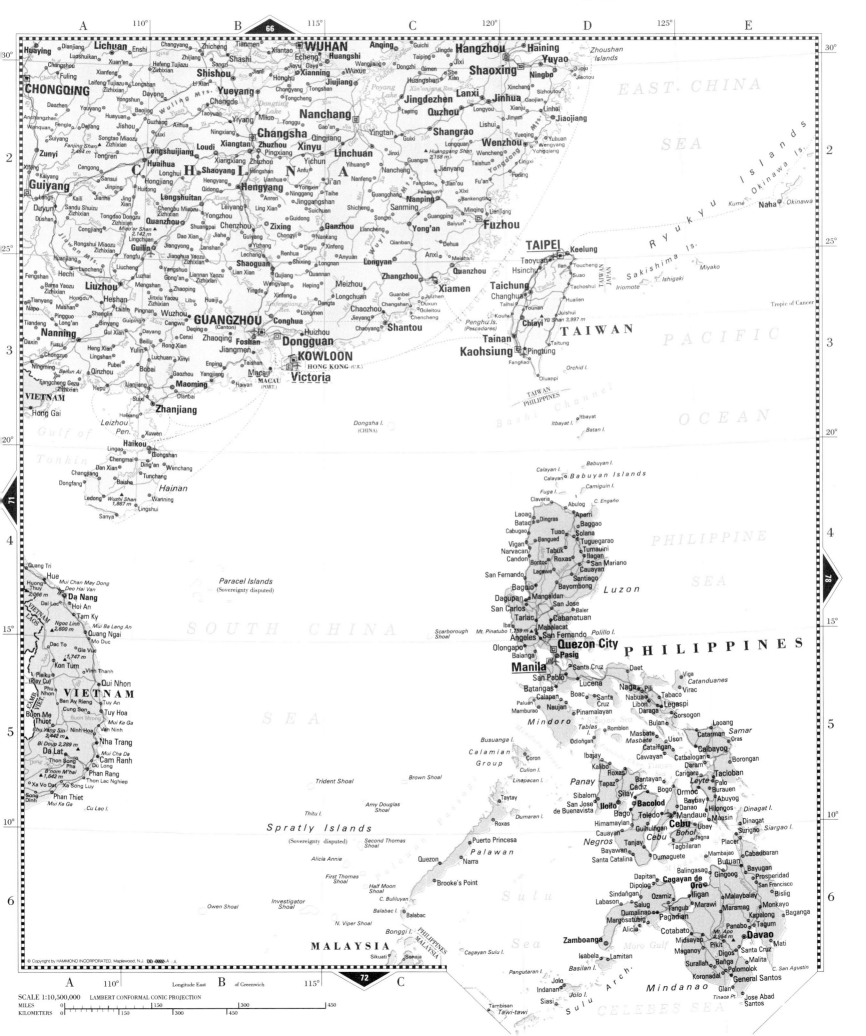

Central Asia

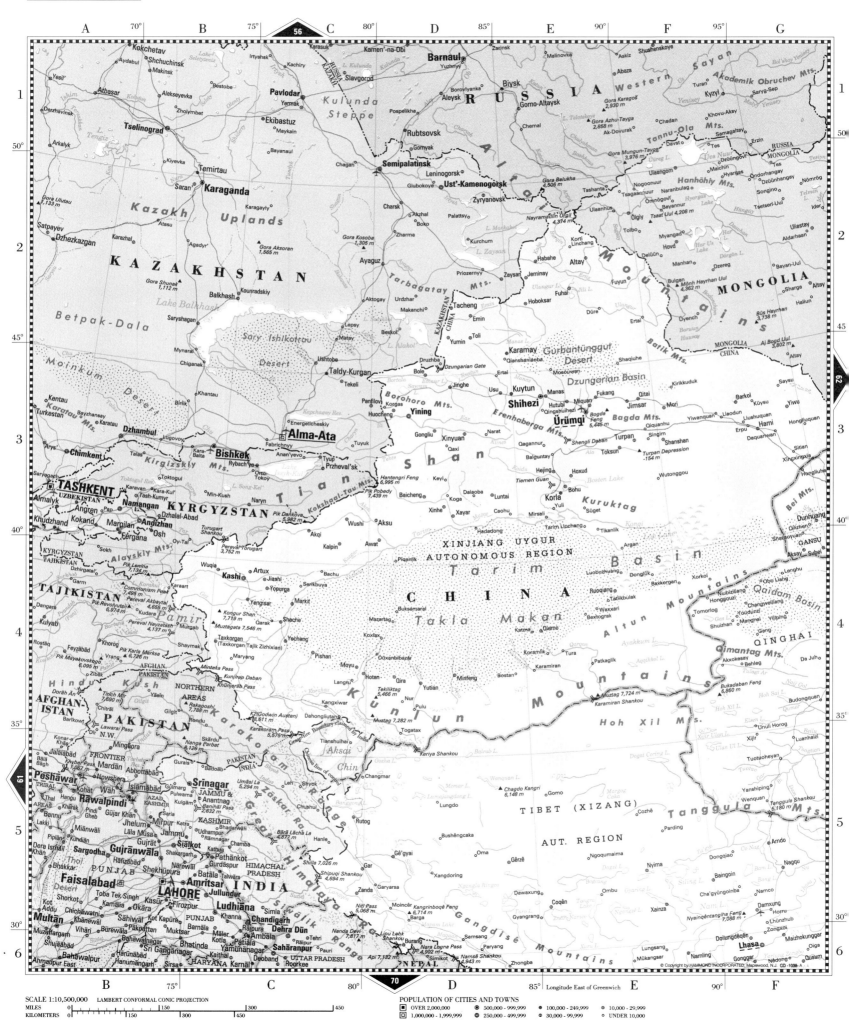

Eastern Burma, Thailand, Indochina

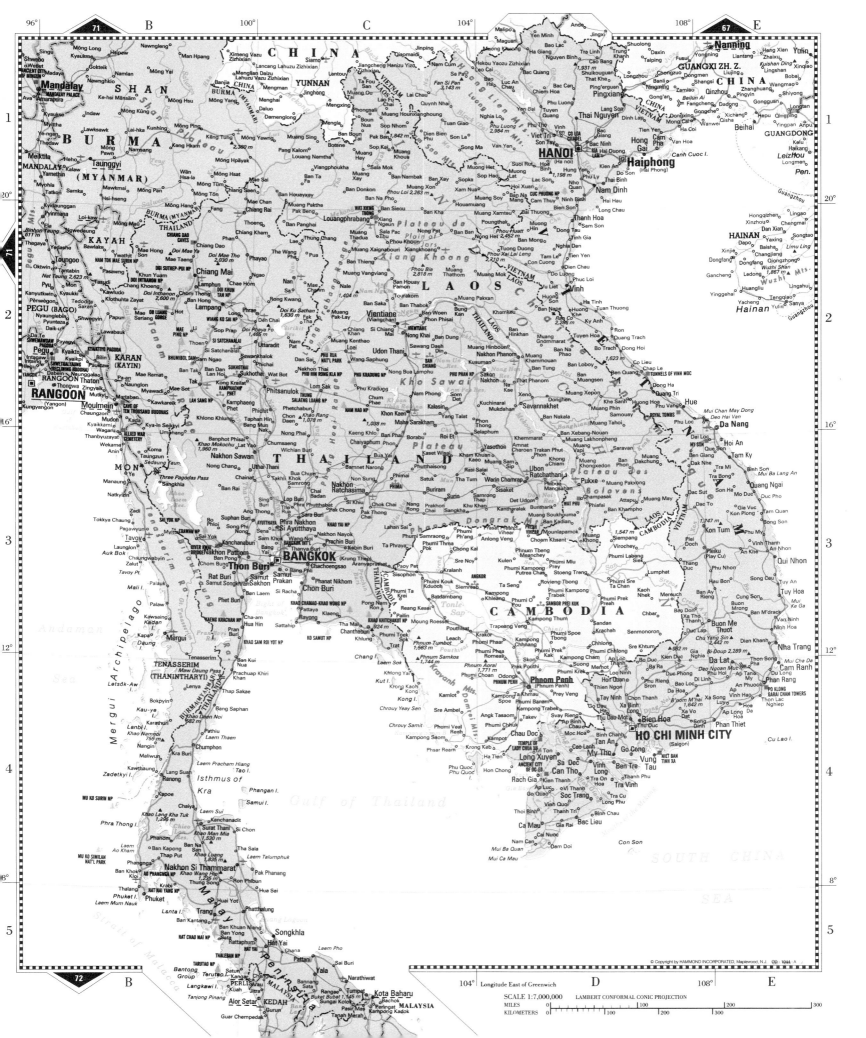

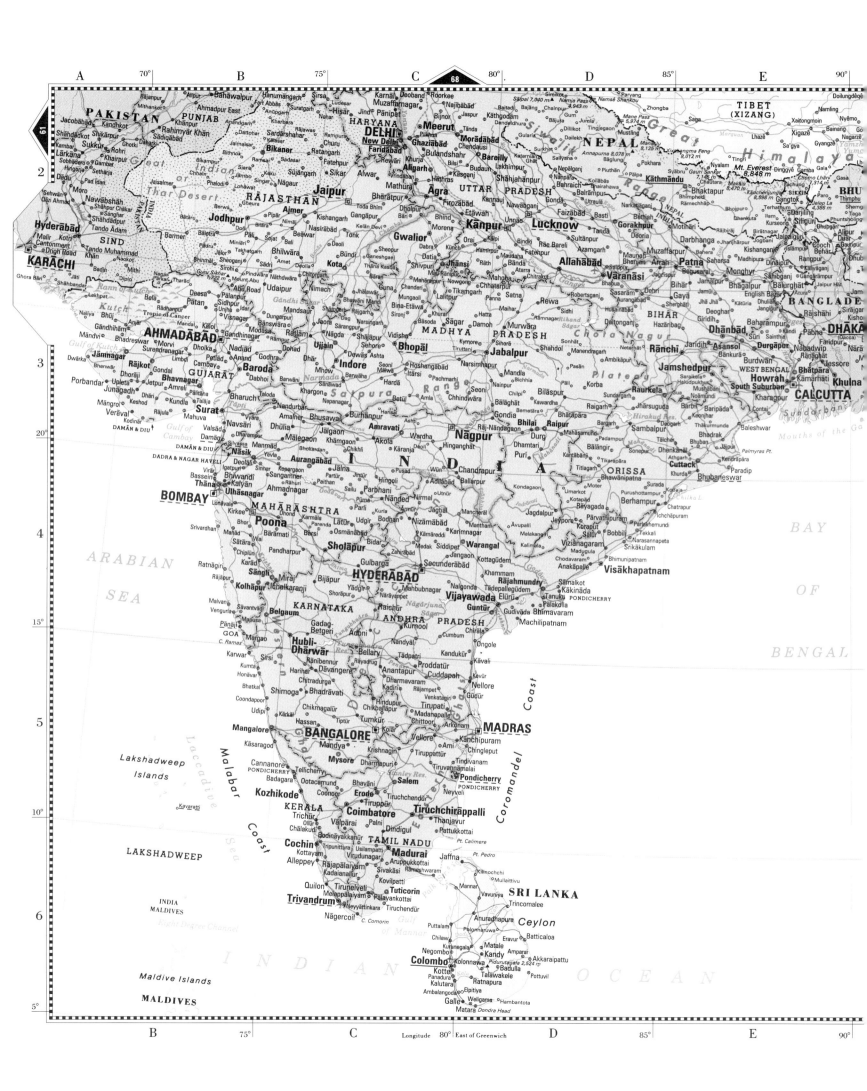

Southern Asia

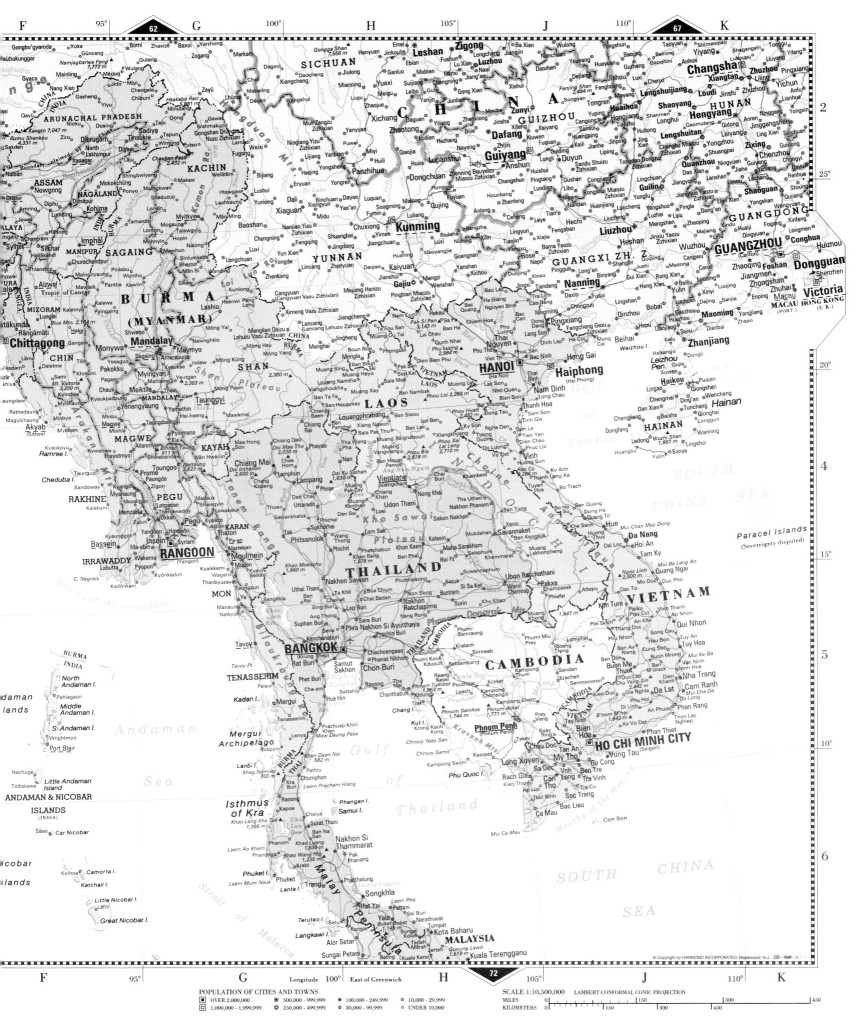

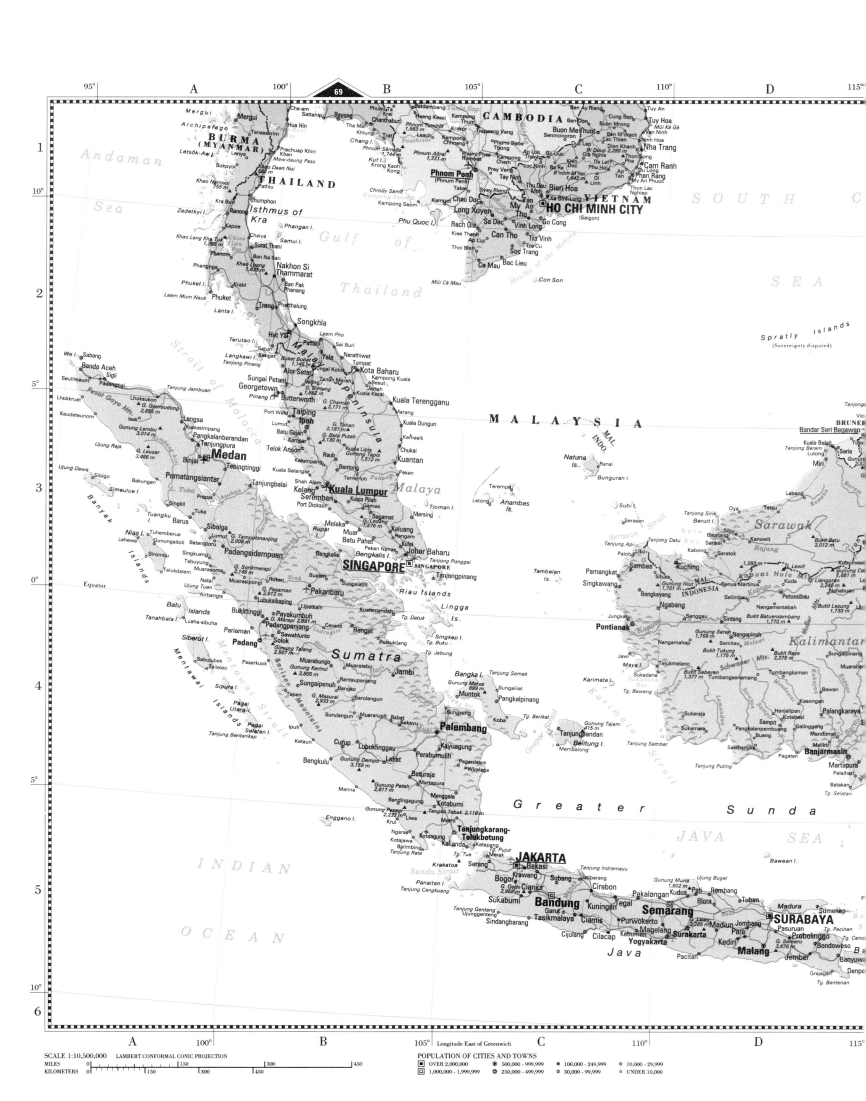

Southeastern Asia

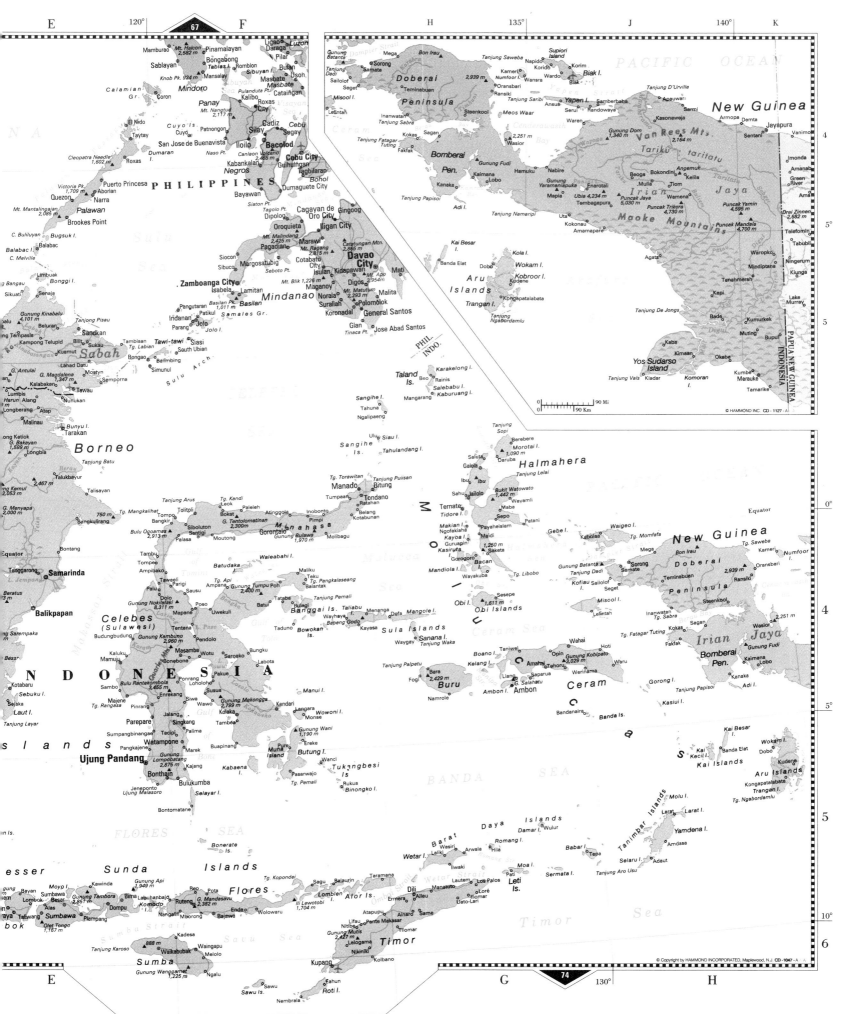

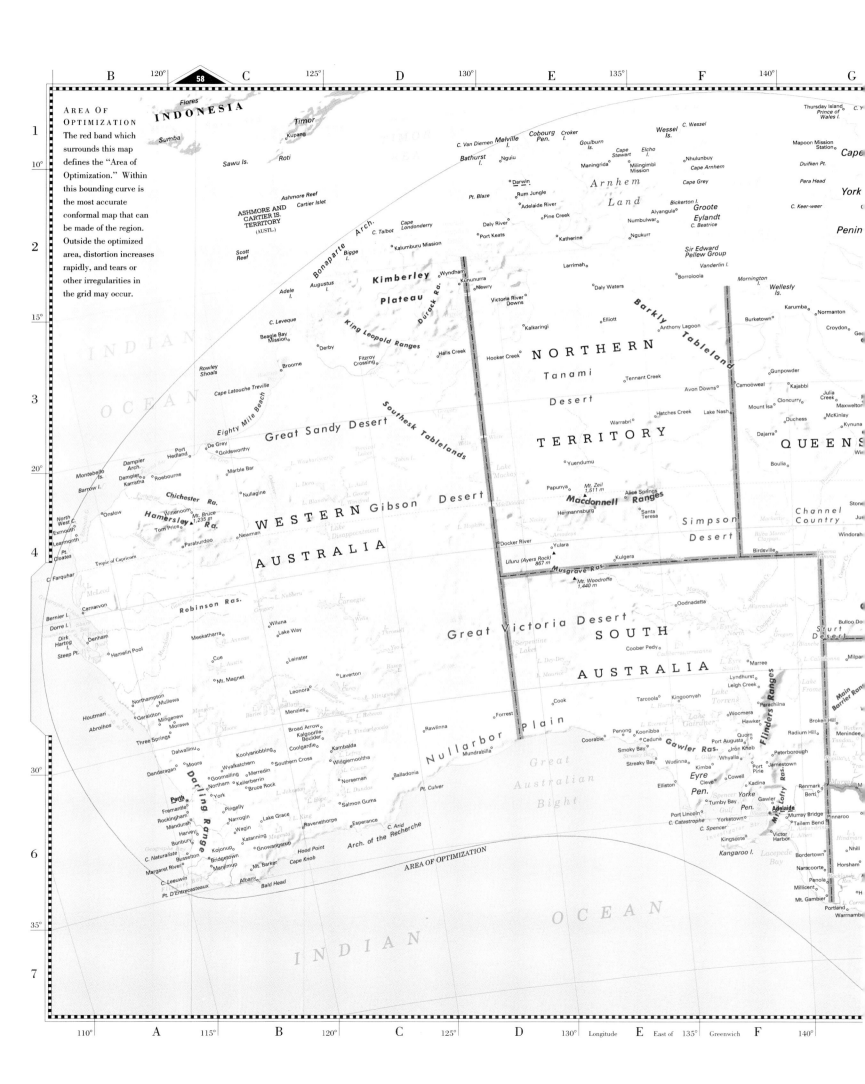

AREA OF OPTIMIZATION The red band which surrounds this map defines the "Area of Optimization." Within this bounding curve is the most accurate conformal map that can be made of the region. Outside the optimized area, distortion increases rapidly, and tears or other irregularities in the grid may occur.

INDONESIA

Flores

Timor

Sumba

Sawu Is.

Kupang

Roti

Ashmore Reef
Cartier Islet

ASHMORE AND CARTIER IS. TERRITORY (AUSTL.)

Scott Reef

Bonaparte Arch.

Adele I.

Augustus I.

Bigge I.

Cape Londonderry

Kalumburu Mission

Kimberley Plateau

Durack Ra.

Wyndham

C. Talbot

C. Van Diemen   Melville I.   Bathurst I.   Nguiu

Darwin

Pt. Blaze

Rum Jungle

Adelaide River

Pine Creek

Daly River

Port Keats

Katherine

Cobourg Pen.   Croker I.   Goulburn Is.   Cape Stewart   Elcho I.   Wessel Is.   C. Wessel

Maningrida   Milingimbi Mission   Nhulunbuy   Cape Arnhem

Cape Grey

Arnhem Land

Numbulwar   Alyangula   **Groote Eylandt**   C. Beatrice

Ngukurr

Mapoon Mission Station   Cape Y
Duifken Pt.
Pera Head
C. Keer-weer
York Penin

NORTHERN

Newry

Victoria River Downs

Kalkaringi

Hooker Creek

Larrimah

Daly Waters

Elliott

Anthony Lagoon

Sir Edward Pellew Group
Vanderlin I.
Borroloola
Mornington I.   Wellesly Is.
Karumba   Normanton
Burketown   Croydon   Gee

Barkly Tableland

King Leopold Ranges

C. Leveque

Beagle Bay Mission

Derby

Fitzroy Crossing

Halls Creek

Southesk Tablelands

TERRITORY

Tanami Desert

Tennant Creek

Warrabri

Avon Downs

Camooweal   Kajabbi   Gunpowder

Mount Isa   Cloncurry   Julia Creek   Maxwelton
Duchess   McKinlay
Dajarra   Kynuna

QUEENS

Rowley Shoals

Broome

Cape Latouche Treville

Eighty Mile Beach

Great Sandy Desert

L. Waukarlycarly

Percival Lakes

Tobin L.

L. White

Mt. Zeil 1,511 m

Papunya

Hermannsburg

Yuendumu

Lake Mackay

Boulia

Hatches Creek   Lake Nash

Alice Springs   Santa Teresa

Macdonnell Ranges

Montebello Is.   Dampier Arch.   *Barrow I.*

Port Hedland   De Grey   Goldsworthy

Marble Bar

Chichester Ra.

Hamersley Ra.   Wittenoom   Mt. Bruce 1,235 m   Tom Price   Ra.

Paraburdoo

Newman

Nullagine

L. Dora

L. Auld

L. Blanche

L. George

L. Winifred

Dampier Karratha

Roebourne

Onslow

North West C.

Exmouth

Learmonth

Pt. Cloates

Tropic of Capricorn

WESTERN Gibson Desert

Lake Disappointment

L. Hopkins

L. Neeley

L. Amadeus

MacDonnell

Docker River   Yulara

Uluru (Ayers Rock) 867 m   Kulgera

Mt. Woodroffe 1,440 m

Simpson Desert

Birdsville

Channel Country

Marketinnie

Windorah

AUSTRALIA

Musgrave Ras.

Oodnadatta

L. Woorandinna

C. Farquhar

L. McLeod

Bernier I.   *Dorre I.*   *Dirk Hartog I.*   Steep Pt.

Carnarvon

Denham

Hamelin Pool

Robinson Ras.

L. Nabberu

Gregory

L. Carnegie

L. Wells

Meekatharra

Wiluna

Lake Way

Cue

Austin

Mt. Magnet

Leinster

Laverton

Leonora

L. Throssell

Yeo L.

Serpentine Lakes

L. Dey-Dey   L. Maurice

Great Victoria Desert

Coober Pedy

Cook

SOUTH

Marree

Lyndhurst

Leigh Creek

Tarcoola   Kingoonya

L. Eyre North

L. Blanche

Sturt Desert

Bulloo Down

Milpar

AUSTRALIA

Northampton   Mullewa

Geraldton   Mingenew

Morawa

Three Springs

Houtman Abrolhos

Dalwallinu

Dandaragan   Moora

Wyalkatchem   Merredin

Koolyanobbing

Southern Cross

Broad Arrow

Kalgoorlie-Boulder

Coolgardie

Kambalda   Widgiemooltha

Norseman

Balladonia

Menzies

Forrest

Rawlinna

Coorabie

Mundrabilla

Nullarbor Plain

Pt. Culver

Great Australian Bight

Penong   Koonibba   Ceduna

Smoky Bay

Streaky Bay

Wudinna

Kimba

Penong

L. Everard

L. Gairdner

L. Torrens

Woomera

Hawker

Parachilna

Broken Hill

Radium Hill

Flinders Ranges

Menindee

Tandou L.

Main Barrier Range

Peterborough

Jamestown

Port Augusta   Quorn

Iron Knob

Whyalla

Cleve   Cowell

Kadina

Port Pirie

Renmark   Berri

L. Frome

Darling Range

Perth

Fremantle

Rockingham

Mandurah

Harvey

Bunbury

C. Naturaliste   Busselton

Margaret River

C. Leeuwin   Pt. D'Entrecasteaux

Northam   Kellerberrin

York

Pingelly

Narrogin

Wagin

Kojonup

Katanning

Bridgetown

Manjimup

Mt. Barker

Albany   Bald Head

Bruce Rock

Lake Grace

Ravensthorpe

L. King

L. Hope

Salmon Gums

Esperance

C. Arid

Hood Point   Cape Knob

Arch. of the Recherche

Gnowangerup

Eyre Pen.

Elliston

Tumby Bay

Port Lincoln

C. Catastrophe   C. Spencer

Kangaroo I.

Kingscote

Wudinna

Yorke Pen.

Spencer Gulf

Gawler

Yorketown

Adelaide

Murray Bridge

Tailem Bend

Victor Harbor

Bordertown

Naracoorte

Penola

Millicent

Mt. Gambier

Portland

Warrnamb

Pinnaroo

Nhill

Horsham

INDIAN OCEAN

AREA OF OPTIMIZATION

OCEAN

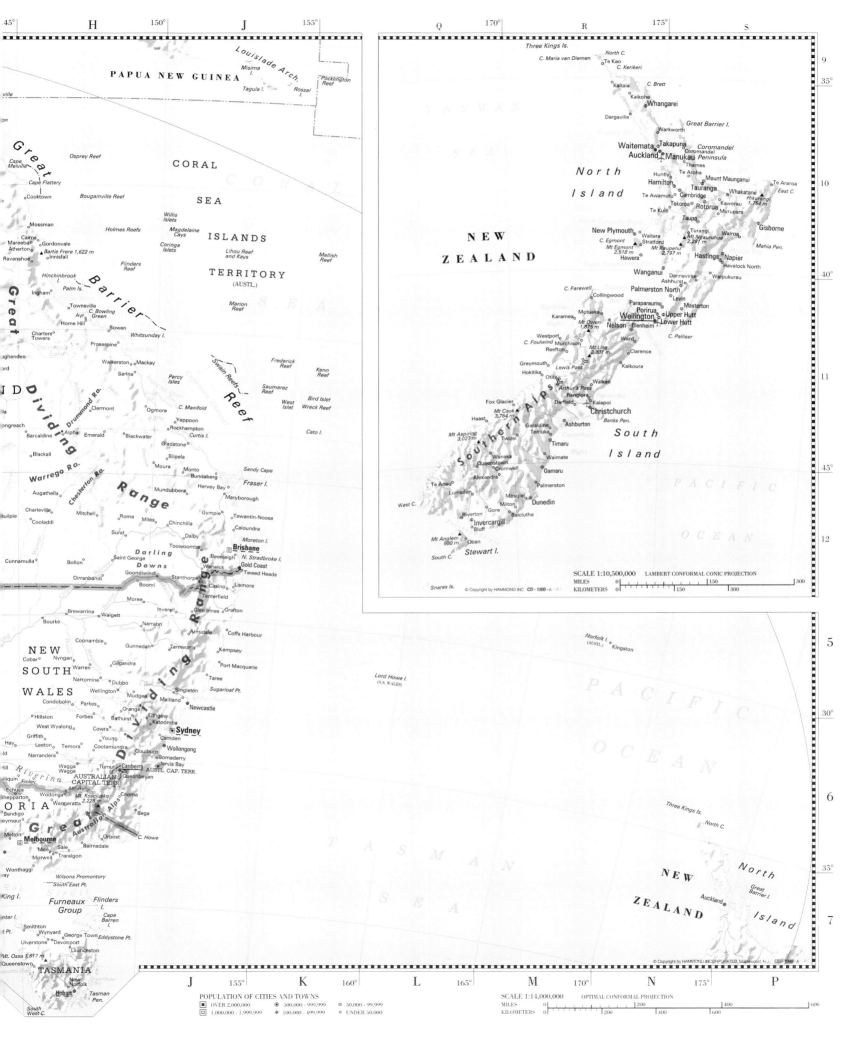

Northeastern Australia

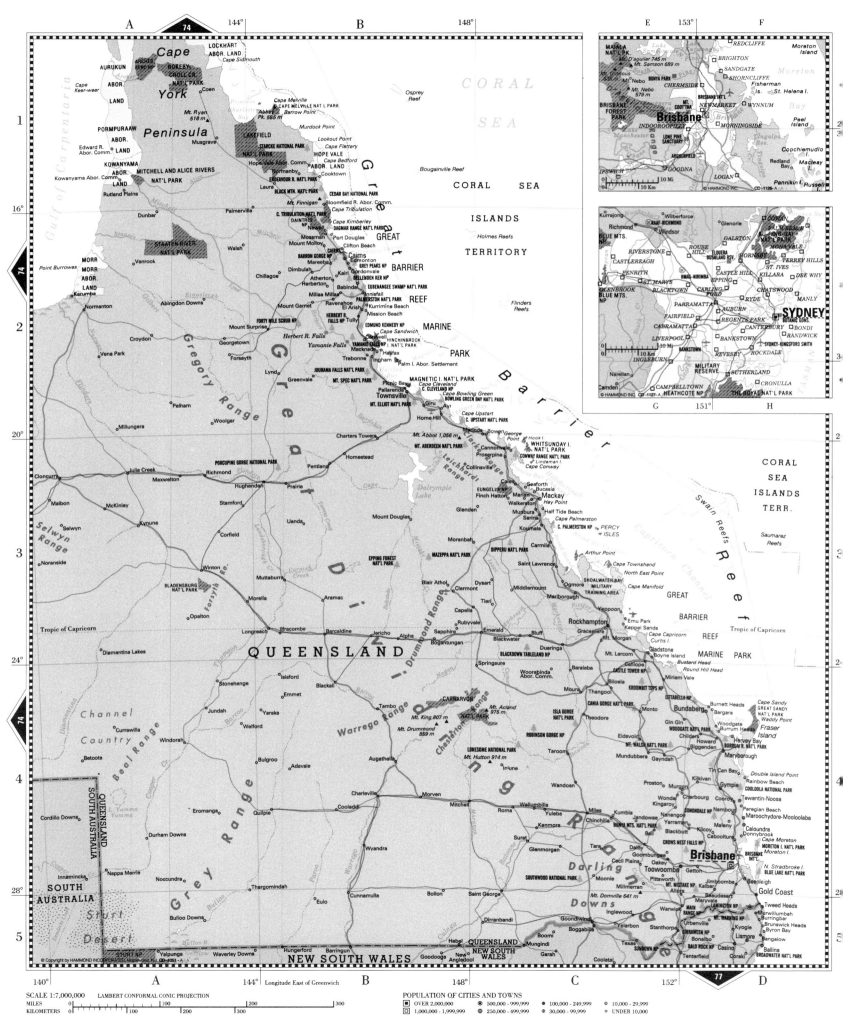

POPULATION OF CITIES AND TOWNS

■ OVER 2,000,000	● 500,000 – 999,999 ● 100,000 – 249,999 ◉ 10,000 – 29,999
▣ 1,000,000 – 1,999,999	● 250,000 – 499,999 ● 30,000 – 99,999 ◦ UNDER 10,000

Southeastern Australia

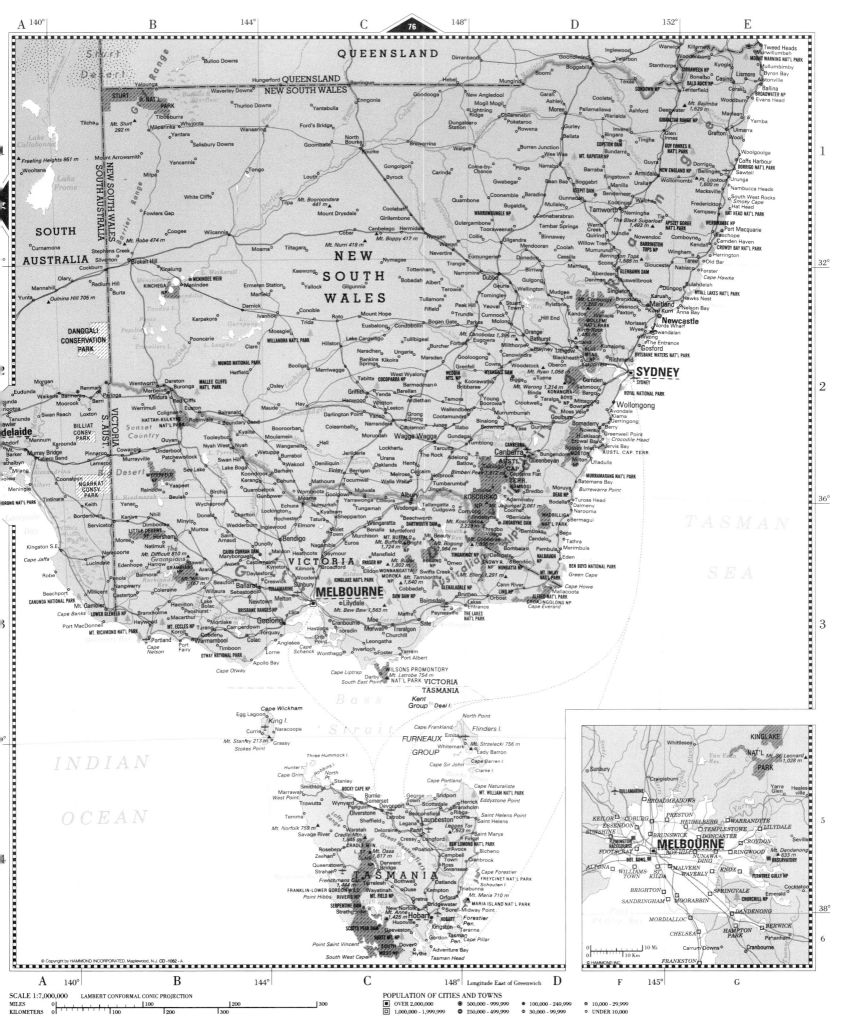

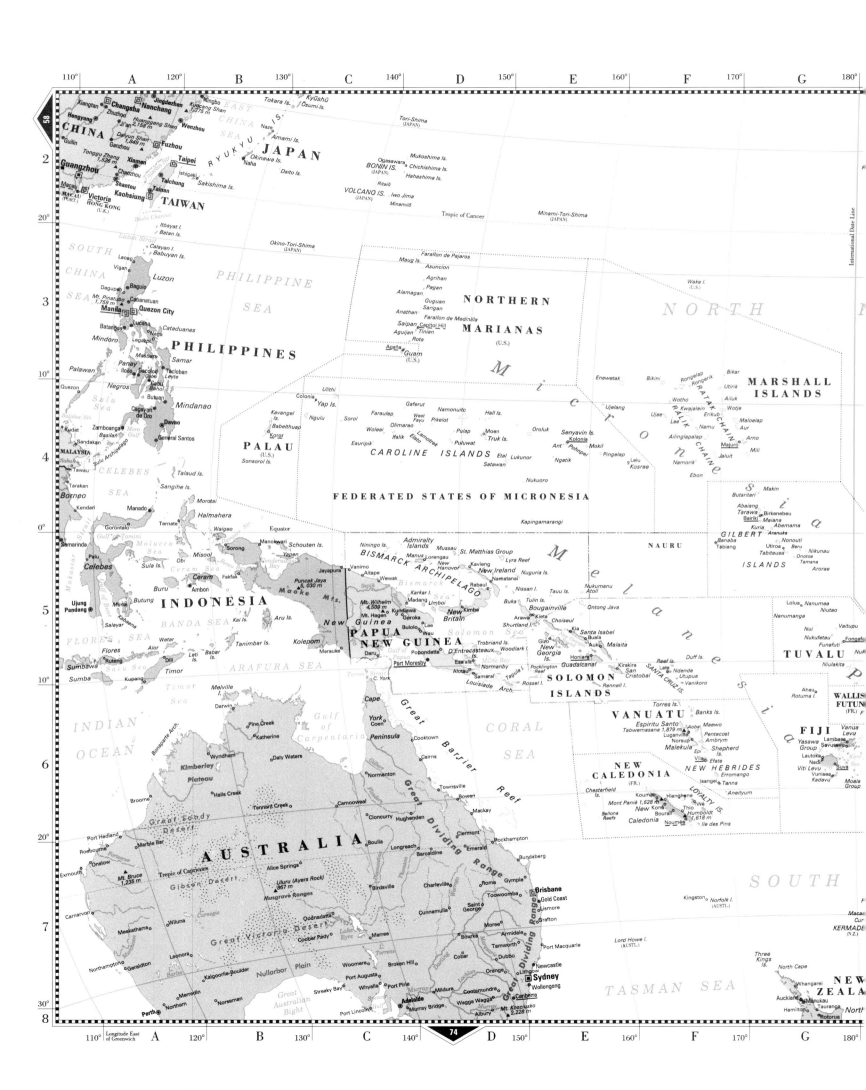

Central Pacific Ocean

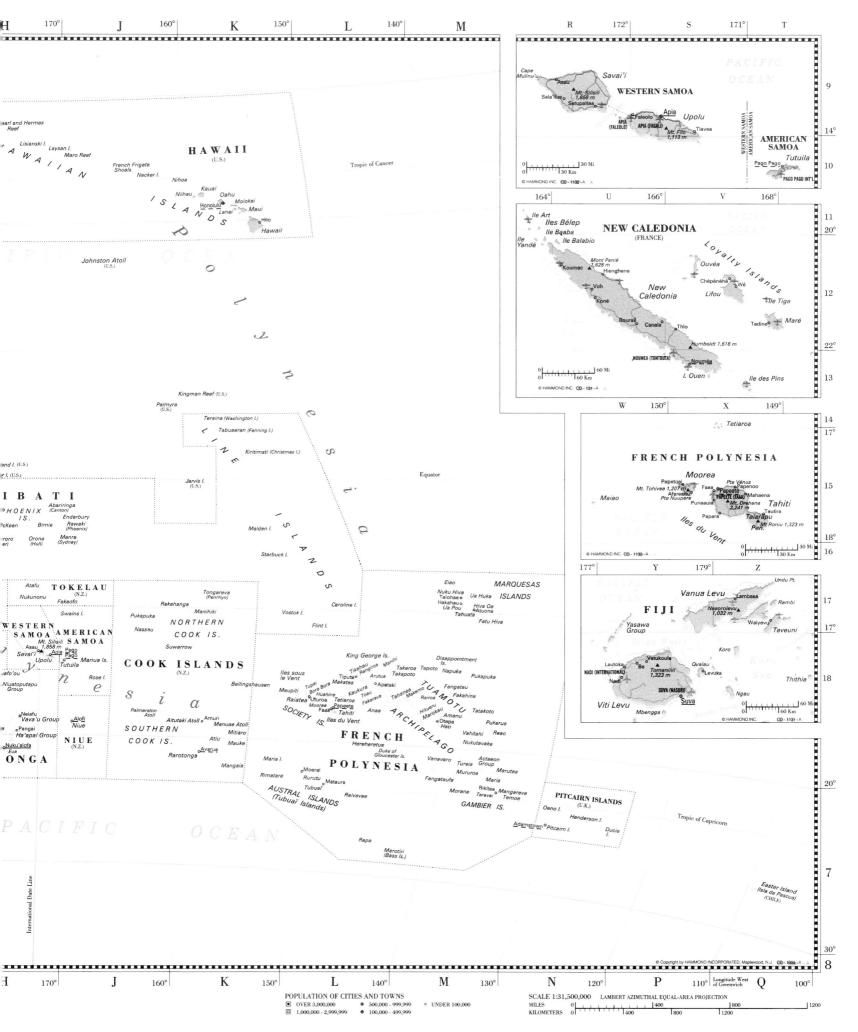

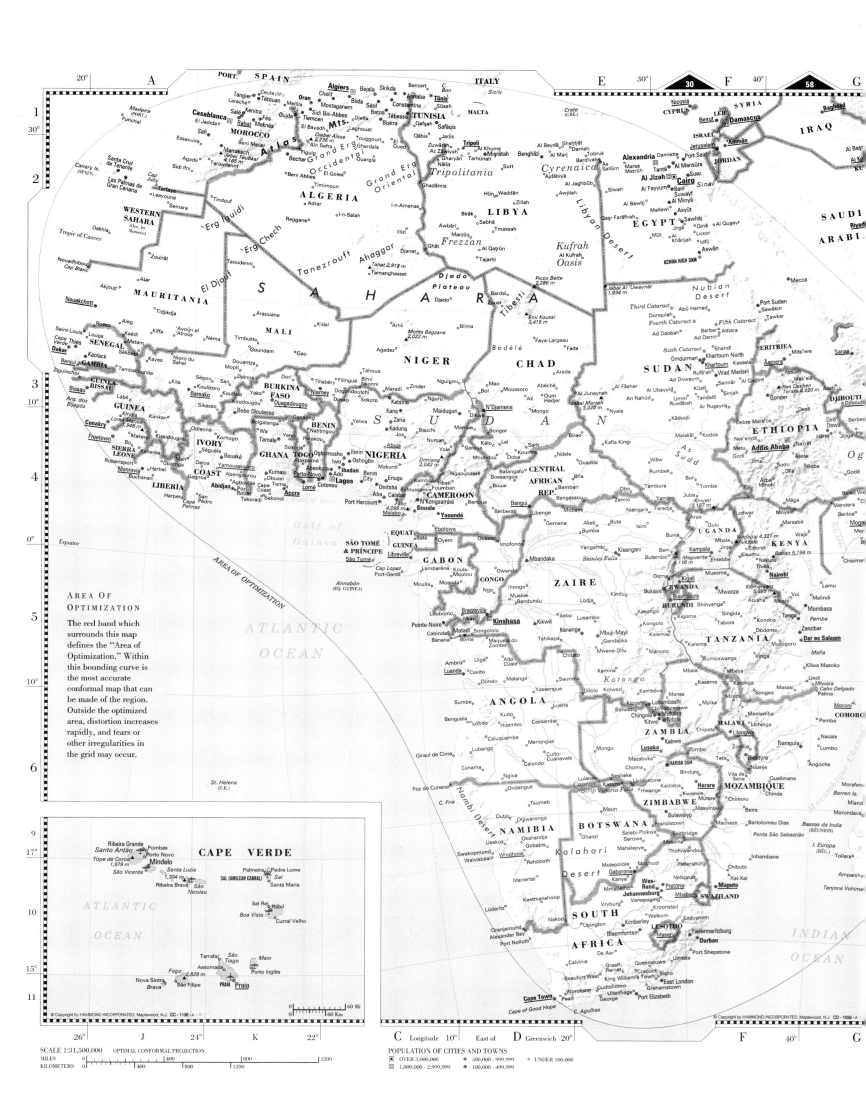

AREA OF OPTIMIZATION

The red band which surrounds this map defines the "Area of Optimization." Within this bounding curve is the most accurate conformal map that can be made of the region. Outside the optimized area, distortion increases rapidly, and tears or other irregularities in the grid may occur.

SCALE 1:31,500,000   OPTIMAL CONFORMAL PROJECTION

MILES

KILOMETERS

POPULATION OF CITIES AND TOWNS

▣ OVER 3,000,000   ⊛ 500,000 - 999,999   ○ UNDER 100,000
▢ 1,000,000 - 2,999,999   ⊙ 100,000 - 499,999

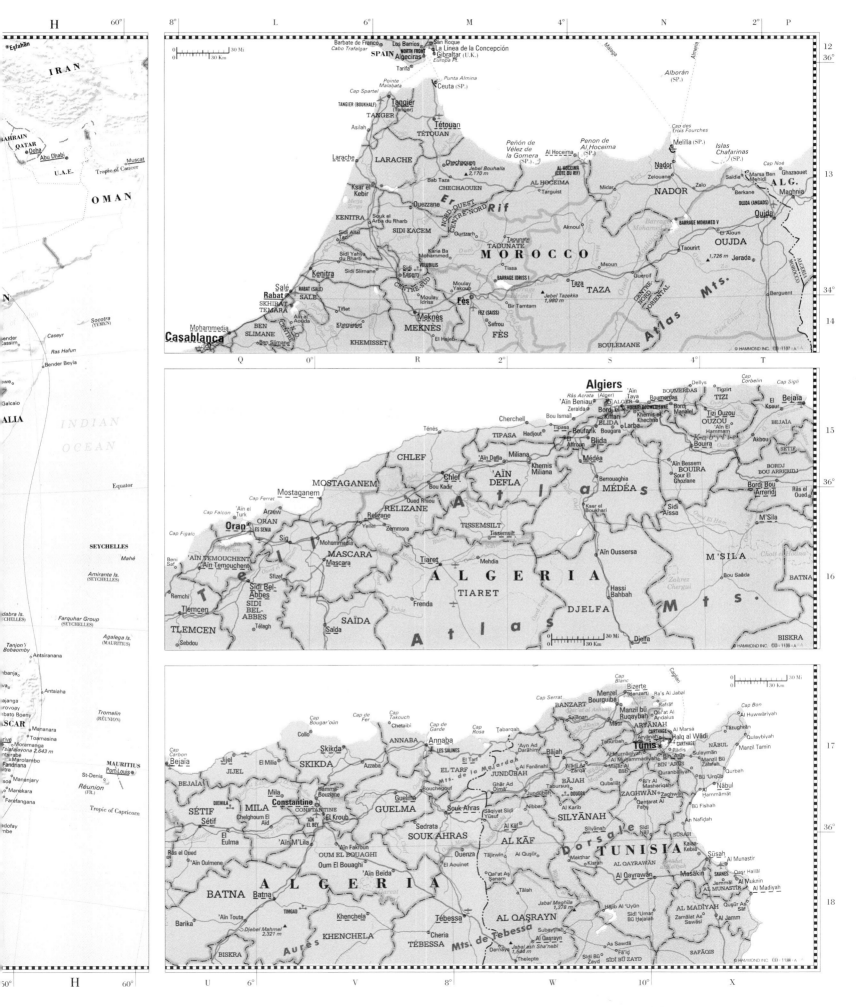

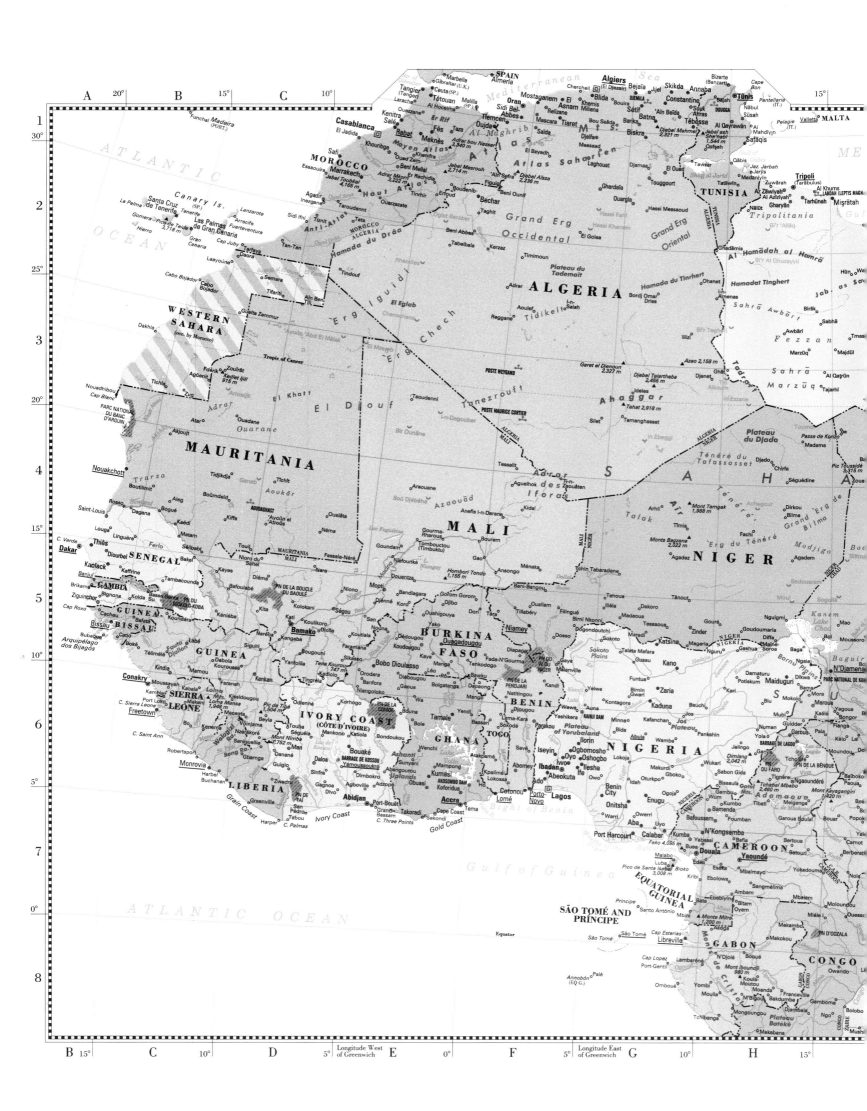

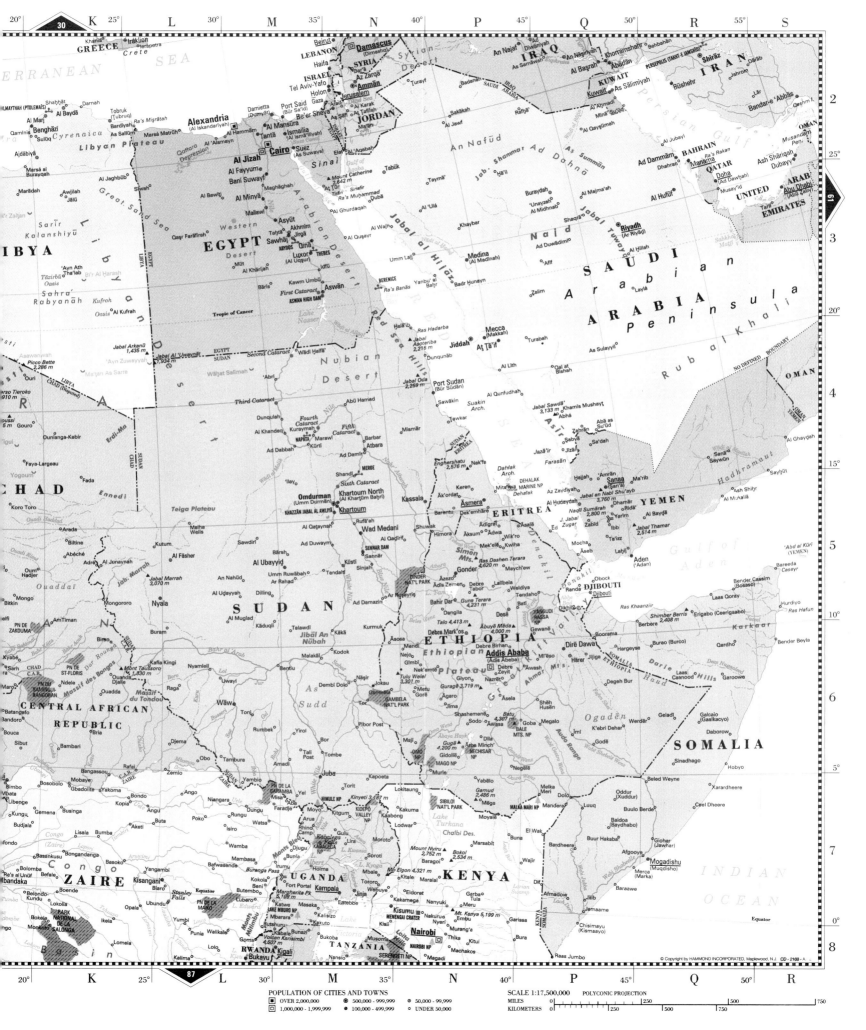

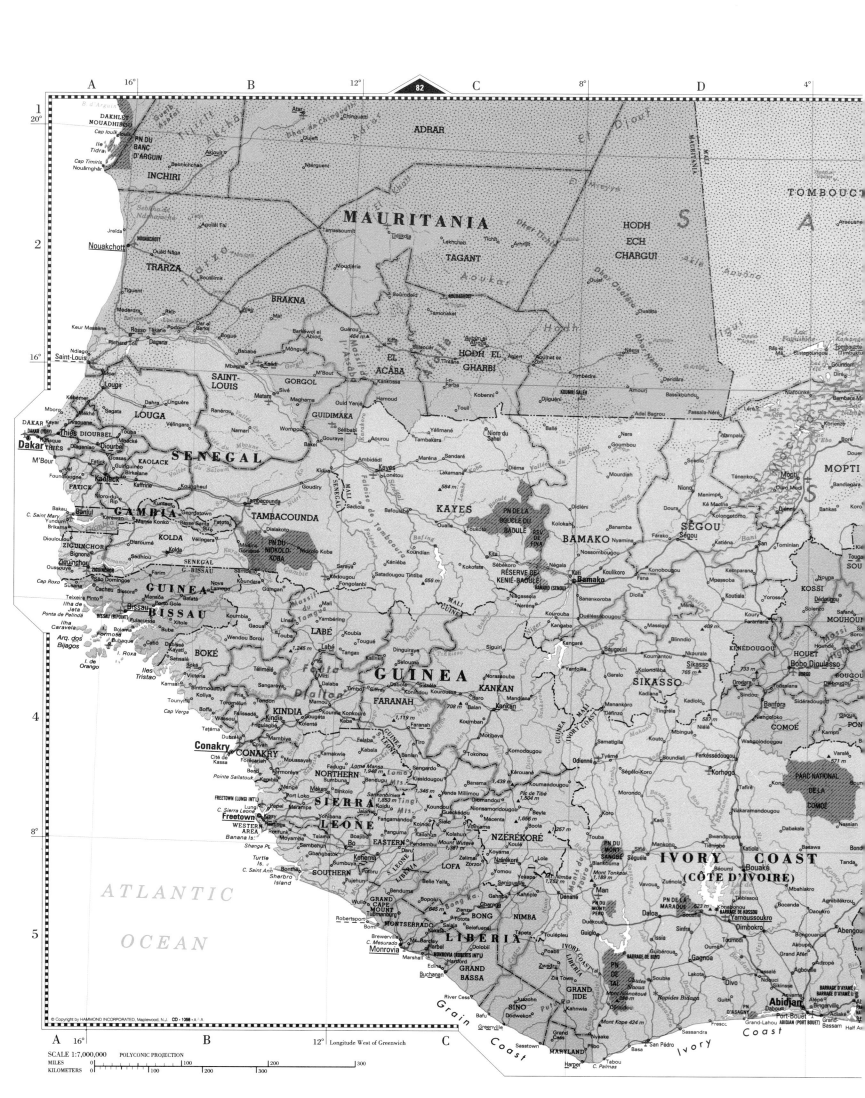

A 16°   B   12°   82   C   8°   D   4°

1
20°

B. d'Arguin
DAKHLET
NOUADHIBOU
Cap Ioulk
Ile Tidra
PN DU BANC D'ARGUIN
Cap Timiris
Nouâmghâr
INCHIRI
Bennichchab

Atar
Chinguetti
Oujen
Akjoujt
N'terguent

ADRAR

TOMBOUCT

MAURITANIA

Tidjikdja
Lekhcheb
Tichît
Arhrijît
HODH ECH CHARGUI

S

TAGANT

A

2

Nouakchott
NOUAKCHOTT
Ouâd-Nâga

TRARZA

Boutilimit
Tiguent
Mederdra
Rkiz
Lac Rkiz
Aleg

BRAKNA

Moudjéria
Baûmdeid
Tamohaket

Aoukâr

Hodh

NOUABIGHOT
Oualâta
Néma

S

Keur Massène
Rosso Tekane
Richard Toll
Dagana
Podor
Dar el Barka
Bogué
Mbout

Boutilimit
Bababé
Kaédi
Mônguel
Guérou
464 m
Kiffa
Billsouâr
Aydun el Aroû
Adjert
Koubat ez Zbil
Koumbi Saleh
Deridâra
Bassikounou
Fassala-Néré

16°
Saint-Louis
Ndiago
SAINT-LOUIS

EL ACÂBA

HODH EL GHARBI

Nara

Mbao
Kébémer
Louga
Dahra
Linguère
Ranérou
Matam
Maghama
Ould Yenjé
Hamoud
Touil
Kobenni
Djiguéni
Timbédra
Amourj
Adel Bagrou

DAKAR
Thiès DIOURBEL
Touba
Mbacké
LOUGA
Vélingara
Namari
Sélibabi
GUIDIMAKA
Yélimané
Nioro du Sahel
Ballé
Goumbou
Nampala
Nara

Dakar THIÈS
M'Bour
Fatick
Gossas
Diourbel
Koungheul
Goudiry
Wompou
Bakel
Gouraye
Aourou
Tambakara
Diéma
Mourdiah
Ké Macina
Mopti

SENEGAL

KAOLACK
Guinguinéo
Birkelane
Kaffrine
Tambacounda
Kidira
Kayes
Lakamané
Lonétou
Niono
Ségou

PATICK
Nioro du Rip
Kuntaur
Georgetown
SAINT-LOUIS

GAMBIA
Banjul
Kerewan

TAMBACOUNDA
Dialakoto
PN DE LA BOUCLE DU BAOULÉ
RSV DE FINA
BAMAKO

SÉGOU

SCALE 1:7,000,000   POLYCONIC PROJECTION

MILES 0 ___ 100 ___ 200 ___ 300
KILOMETERS 0 ___ 100 ___ 200 ___ 300

A 16°   B   12° Longitude West of Greenwich   C

© Copyright by HAMMOND INCORPORATED, Maplewood, N.J.   CD · 1058 · A · A

West Africa

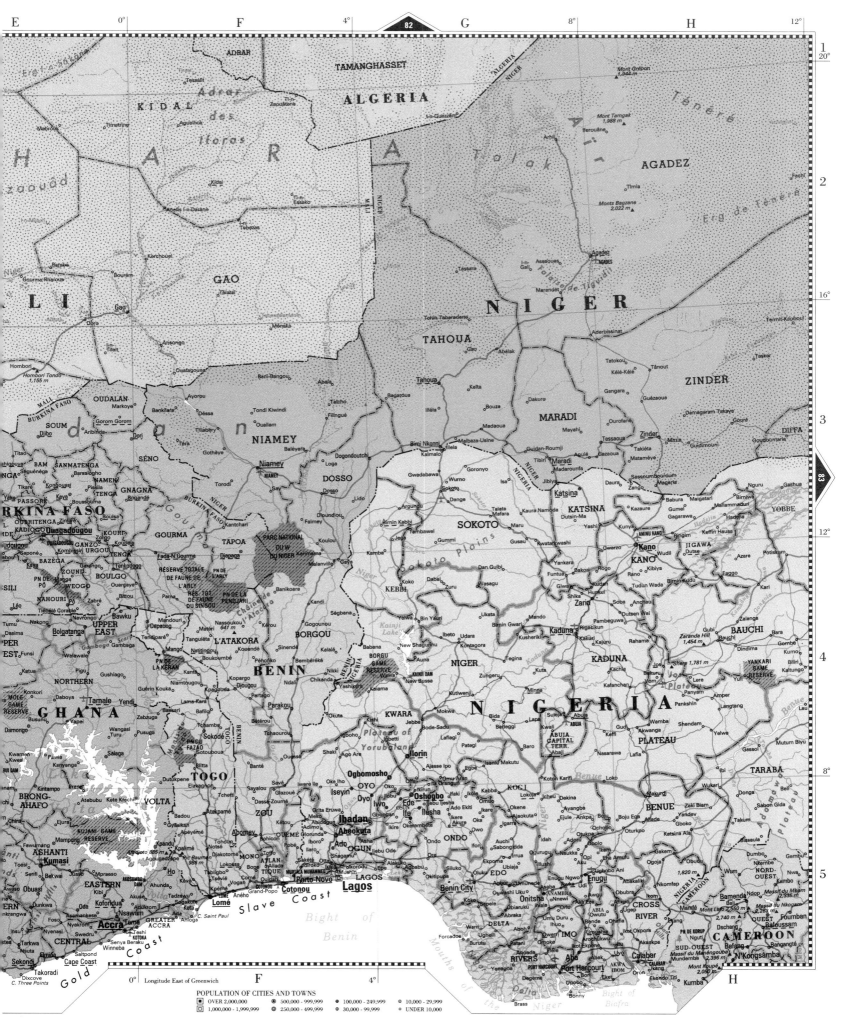

Northeastern Africa

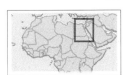

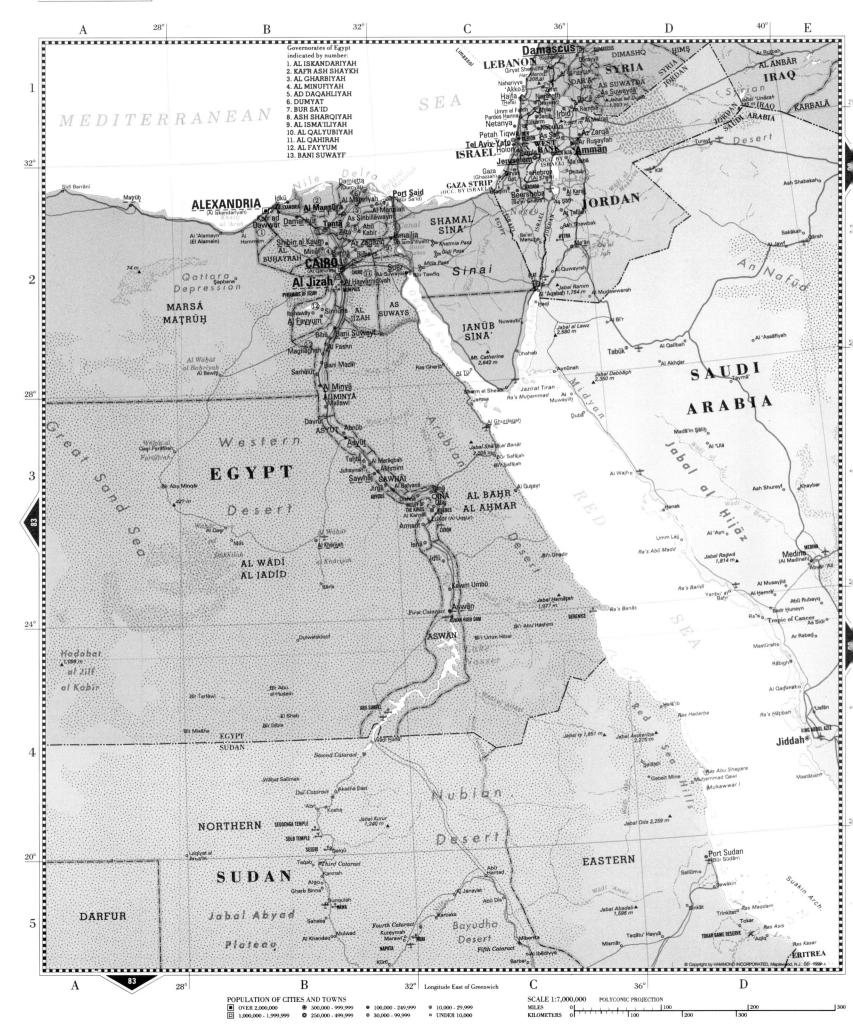

Southern Africa

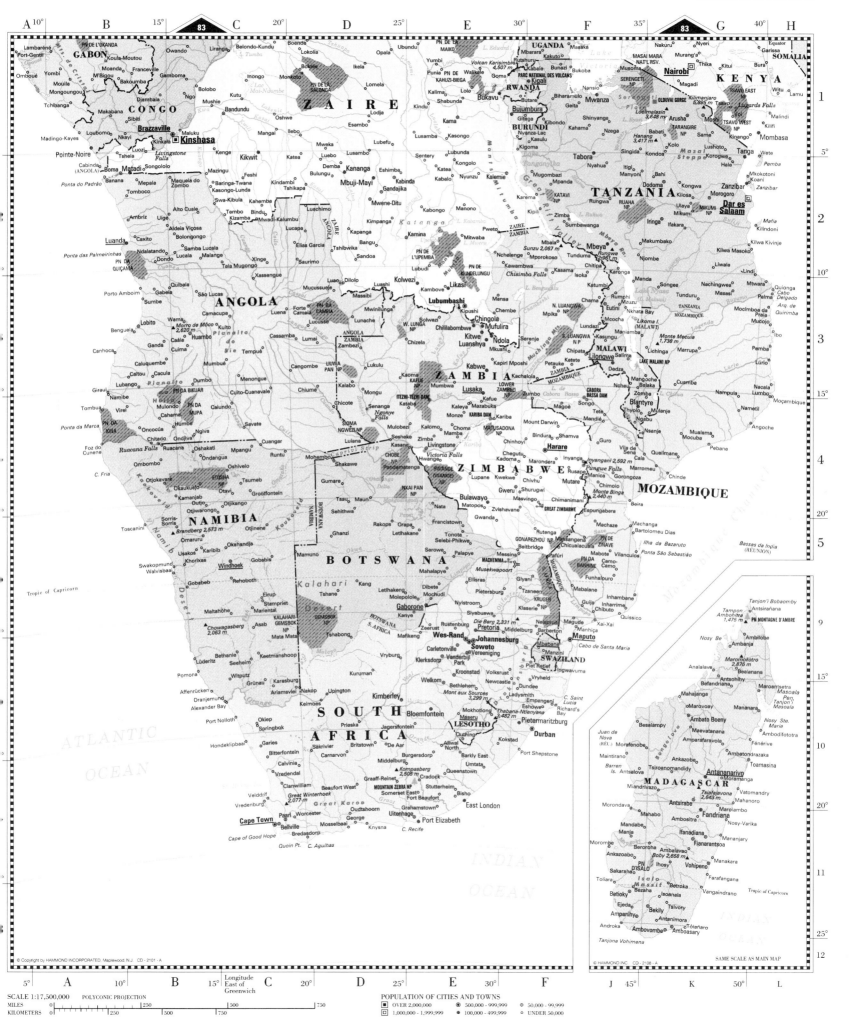

SCALE 1:17,500,000   POLYCONIC PROJECTION

MILES

KILOMETERS

POPULATION OF CITIES AND TOWNS

■ OVER 2,000,000   ● 500,000 - 999,999   ○ 50,000 - 99,999
□ 1,000,000 - 1,999,999   ● 100,000 - 499,999   ○ UNDER 50,000

SAME SCALE AS MAIN MAP

© HAMMOND INC.   CD - 2108 - A

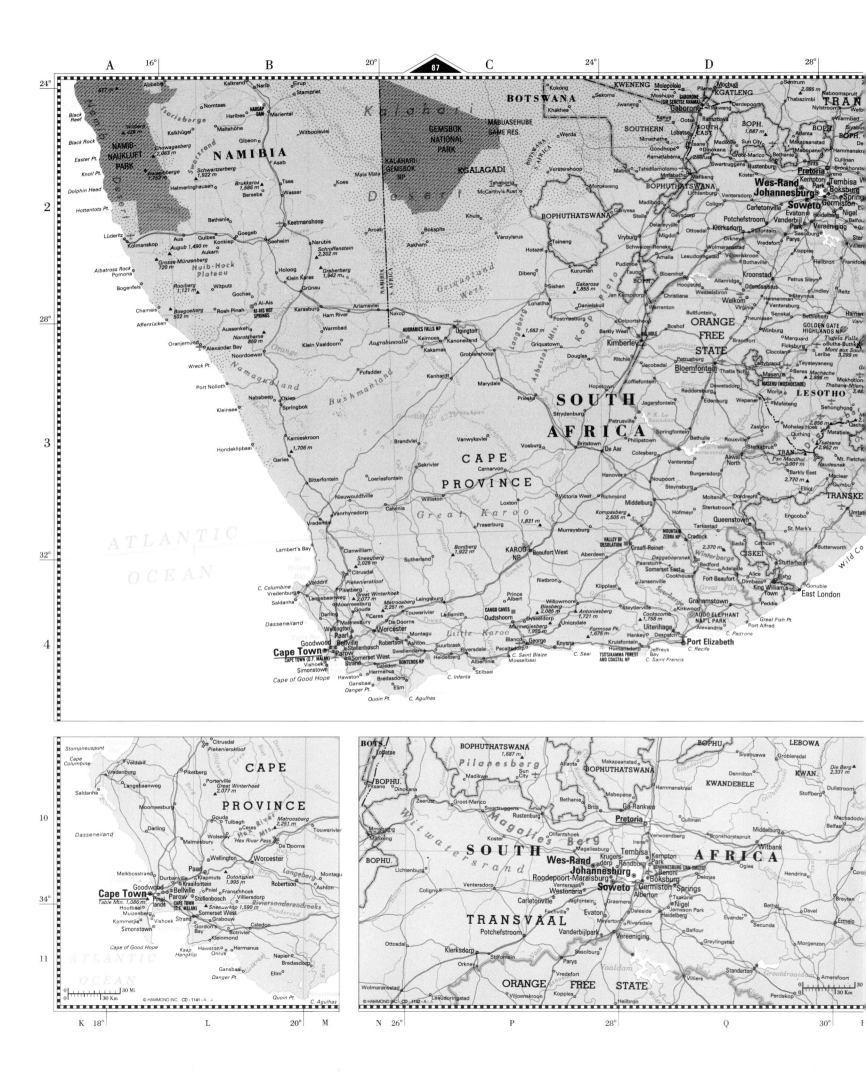

South Africa

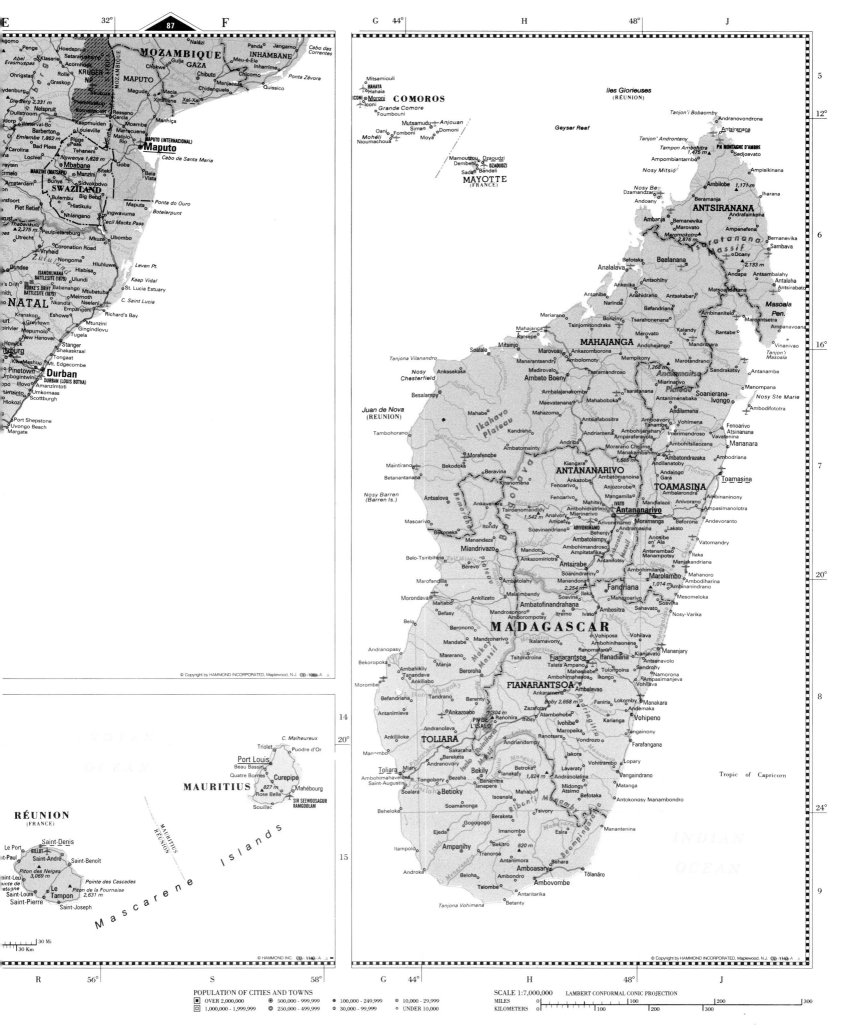

South America

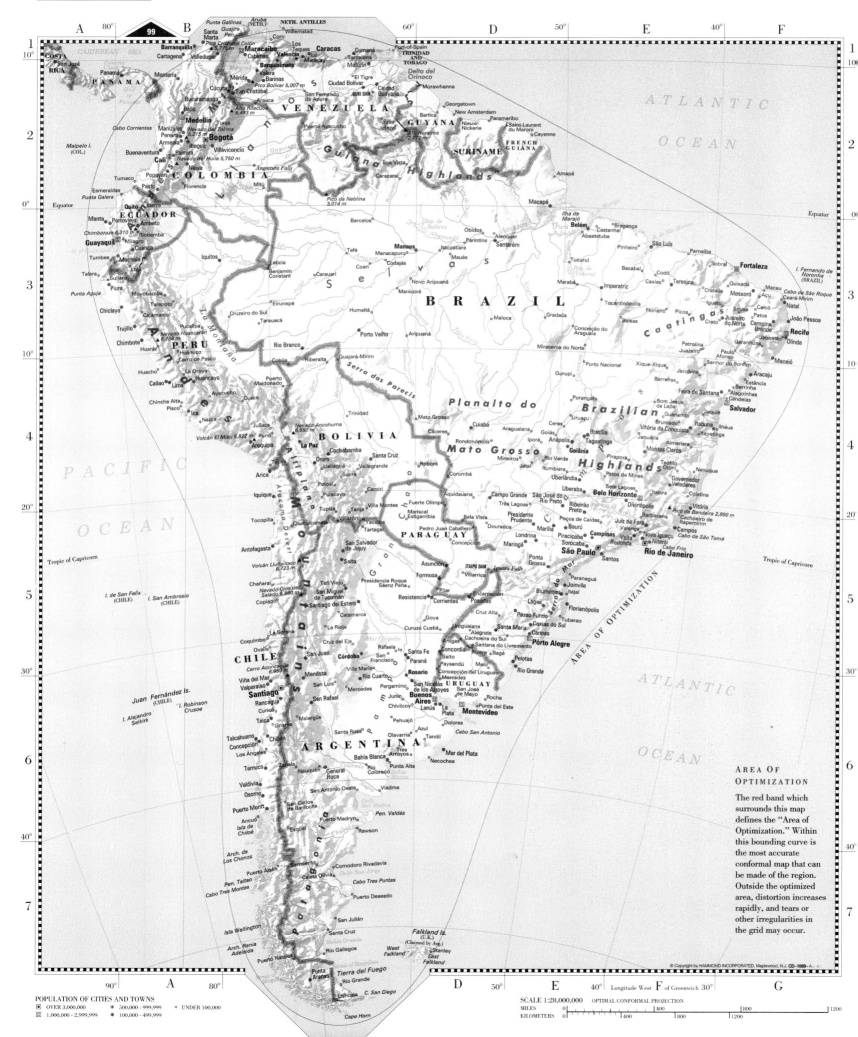

Southern South America

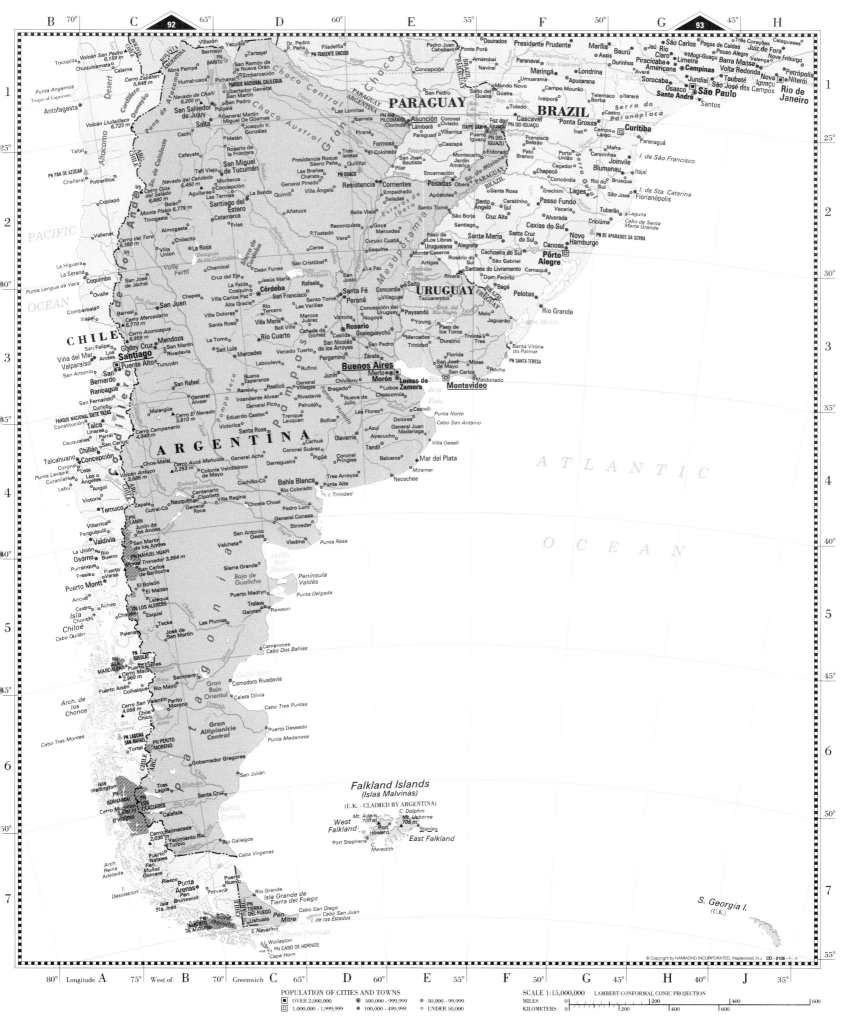

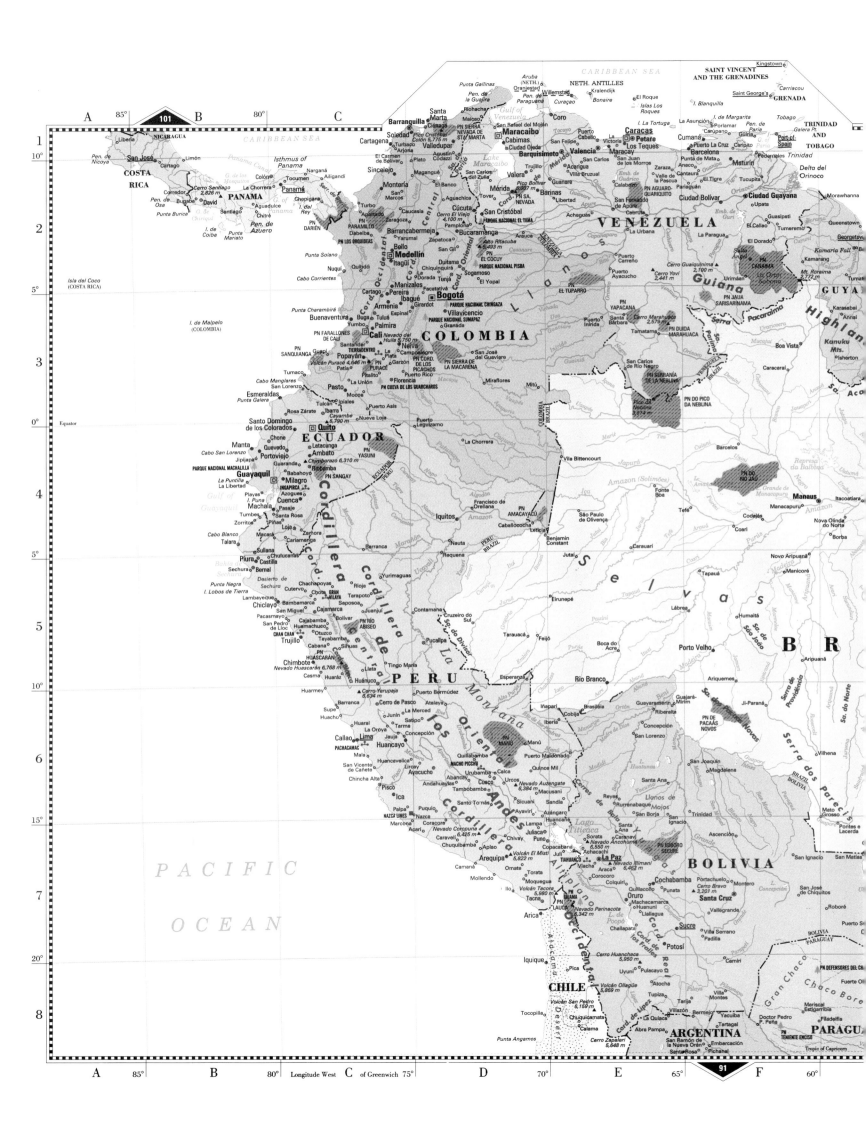

Northern South America

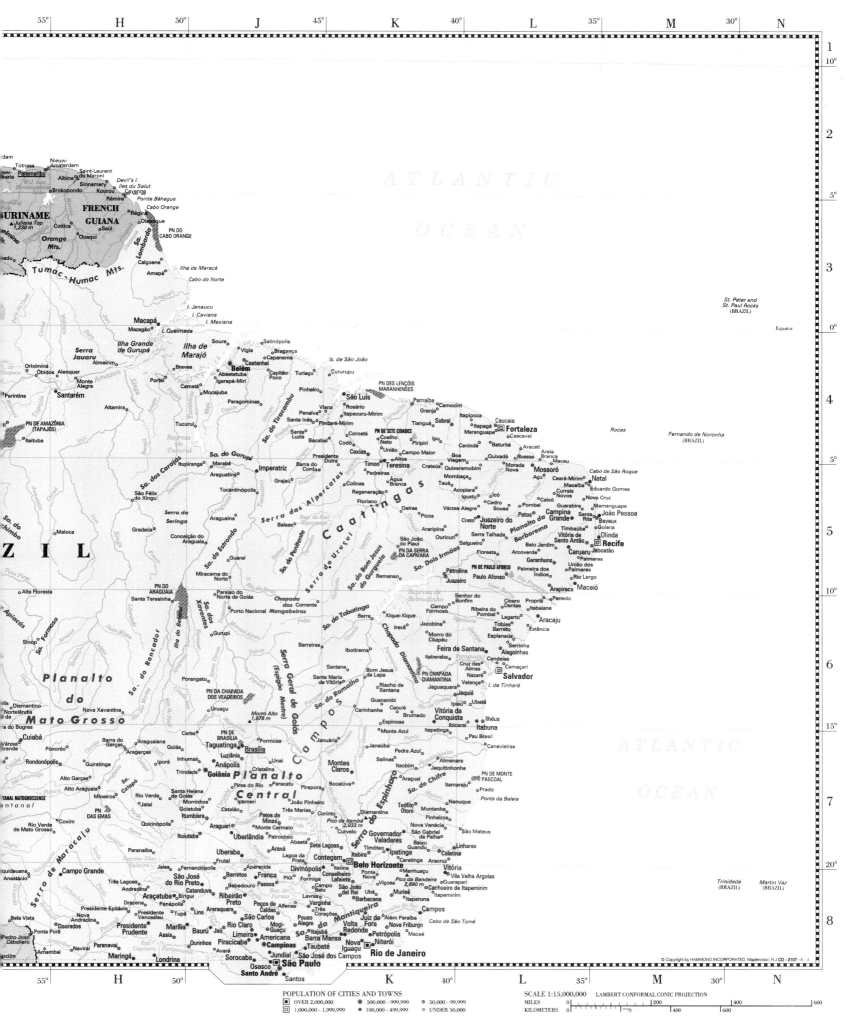

Northeastern Brazil

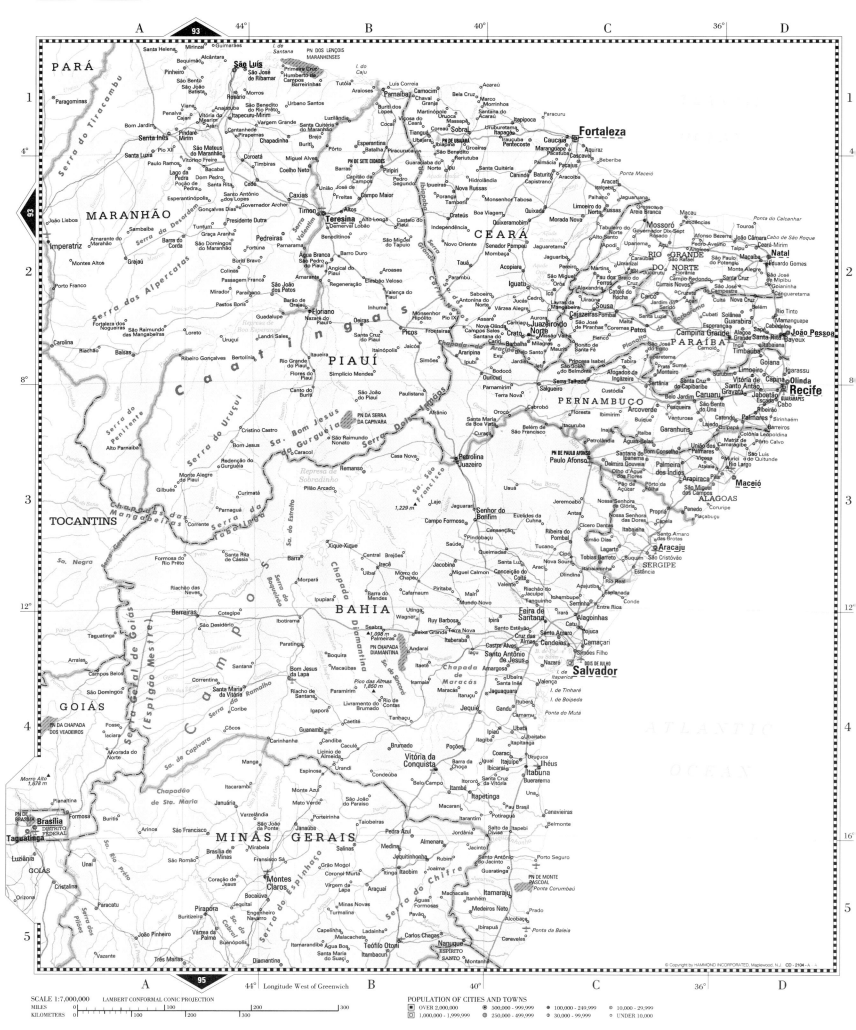

Southeastern Brazil

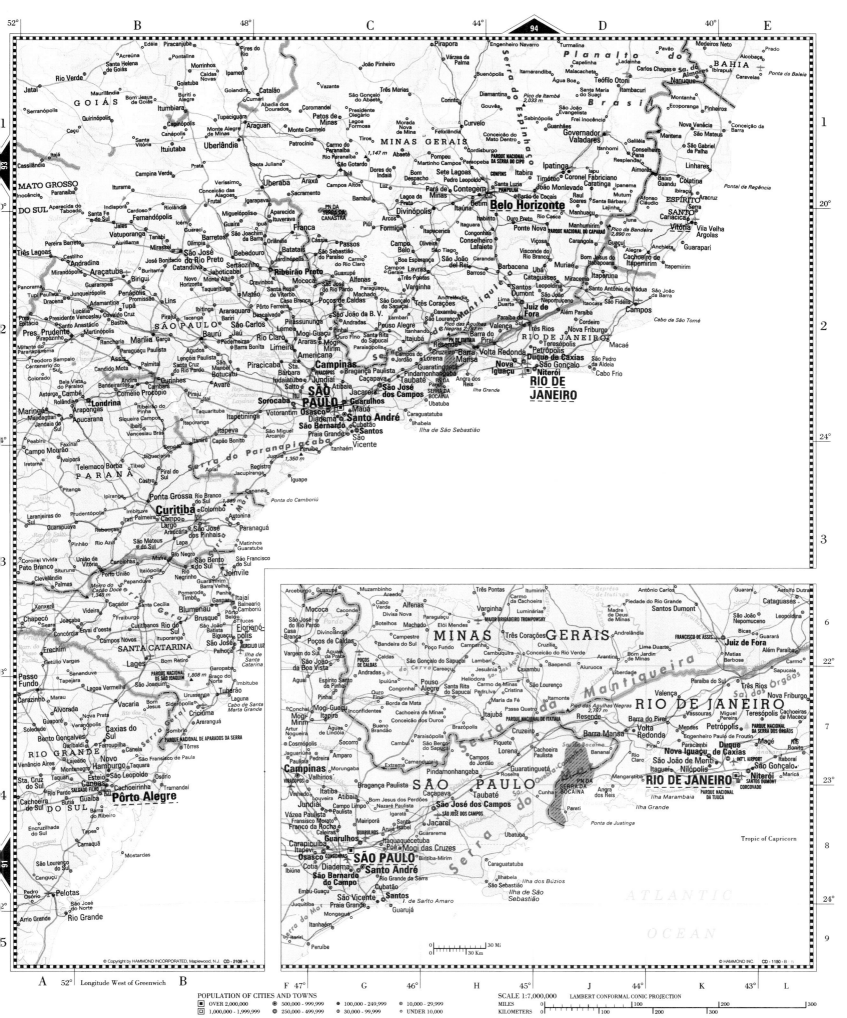

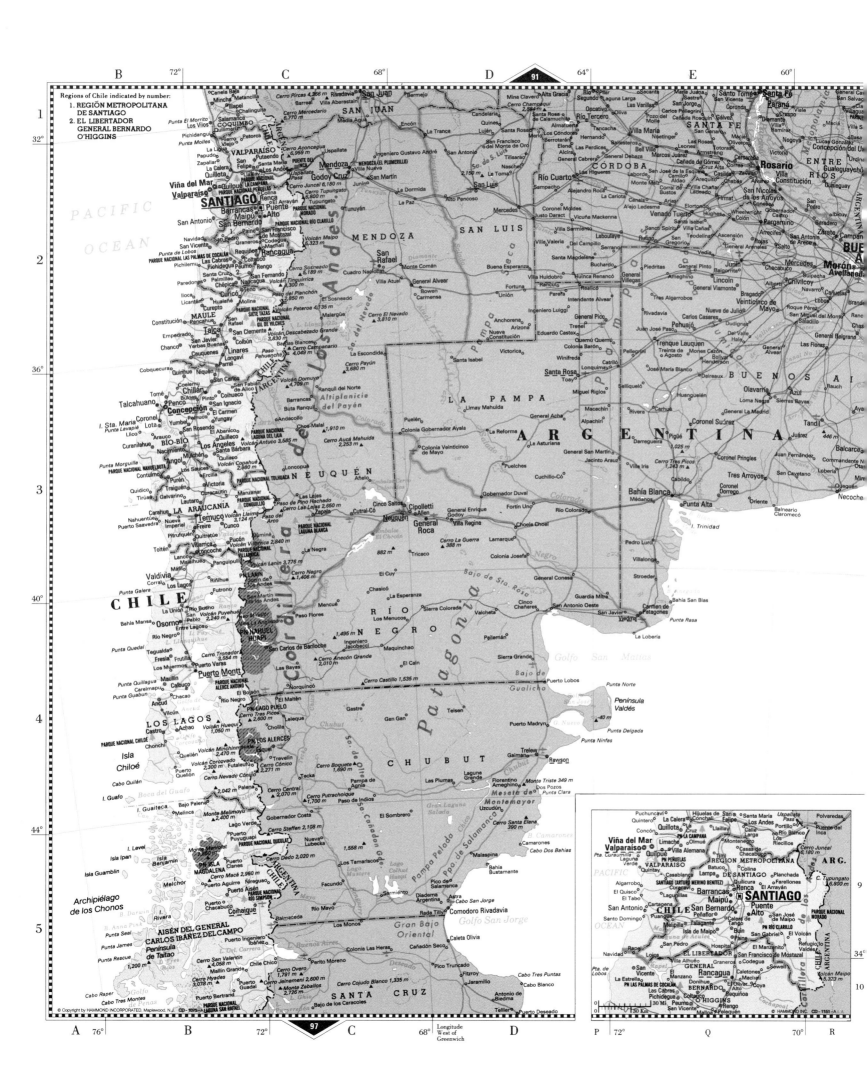

Southern Chile and Argentina

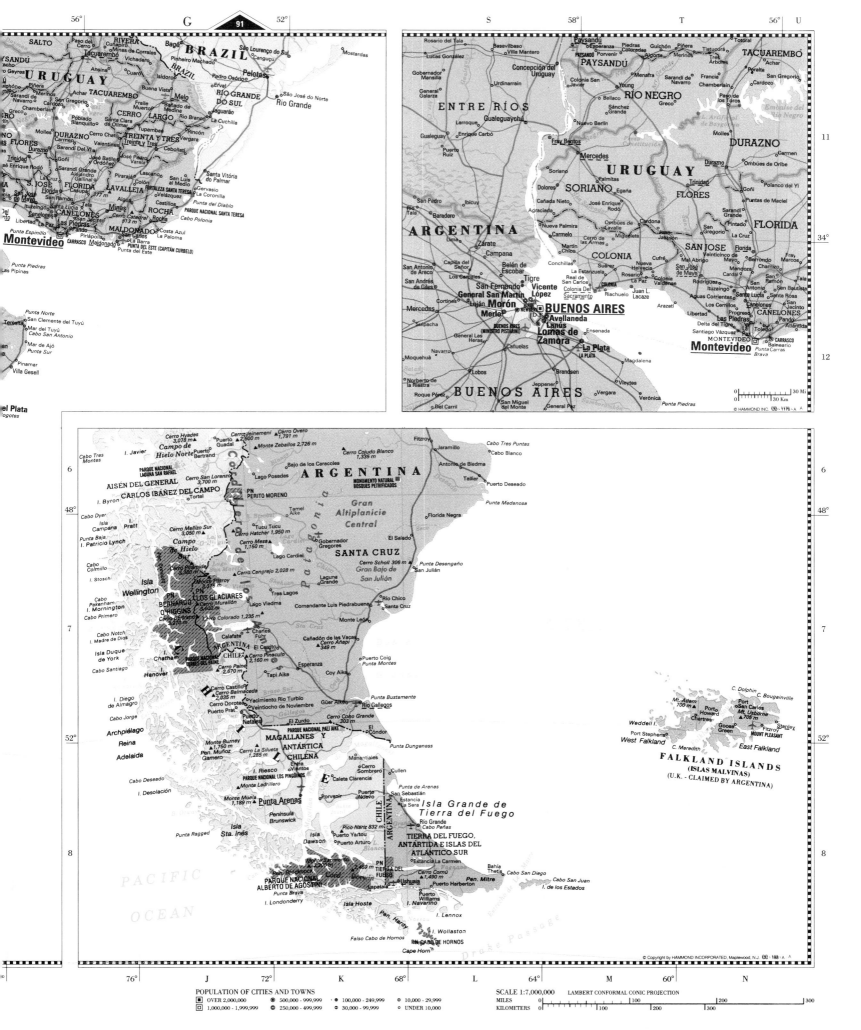

POPULATION OF CITIES AND TOWNS

- ■ OVER 2,000,000
- ▣ 1,000,000 – 1,999,999
- ● 500,000 – 999,999
- ◉ 250,000 – 499,999
- ◦ 100,000 – 249,999
- • 30,000 – 99,999
- · 10,000 – 29,999
- ○ UNDER 10,000

SCALE 1:7,000,000   LAMBERT CONFORMAL CONIC PROJECTION

MILES 0 · · · 100 · · · 200 · · · 300

KILOMETERS 0 · · · 100 · · · 200 · · · 300

Antarctica

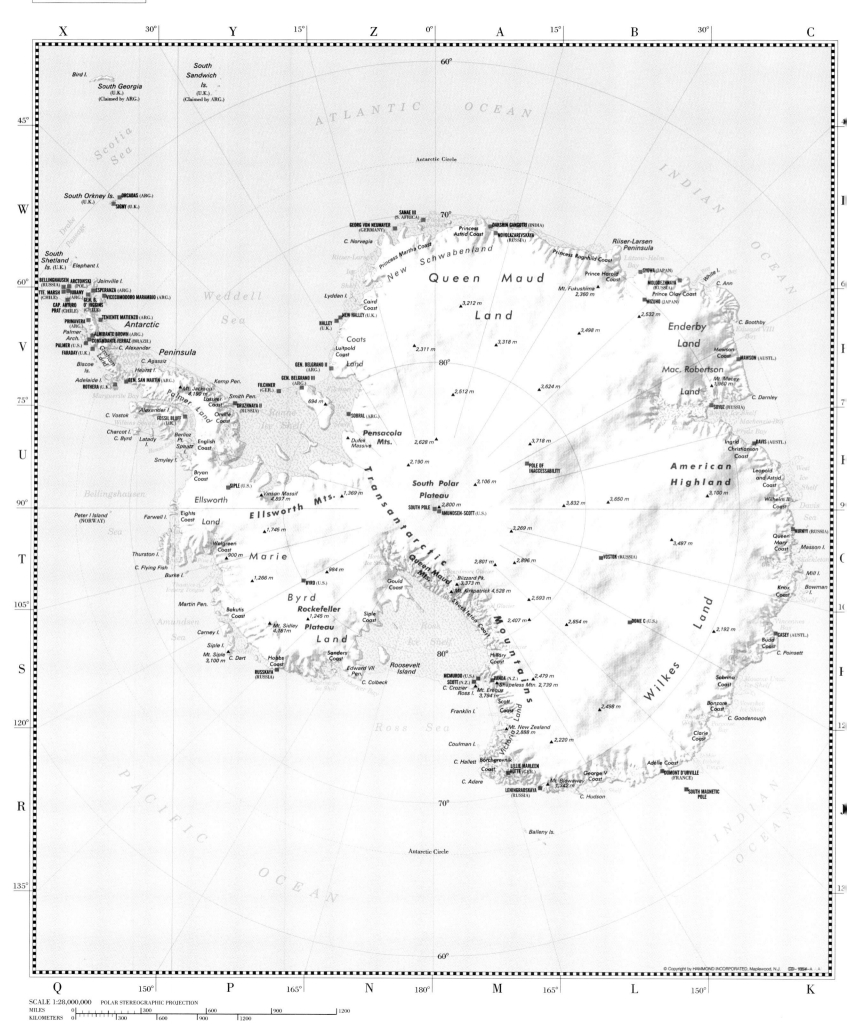

SCALE 1:28,000,000   POLAR STEREOGRAPHIC PROJECTION

MILES
KILOMETERS

North America

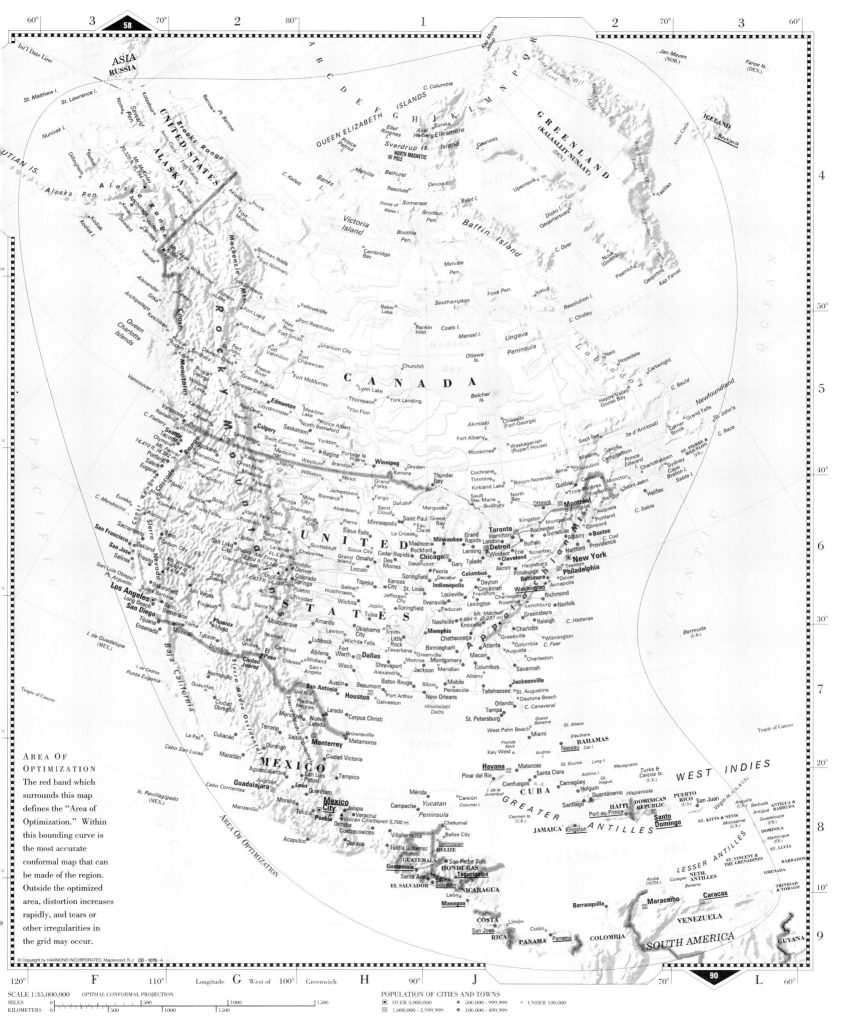

Middle America and Caribbean

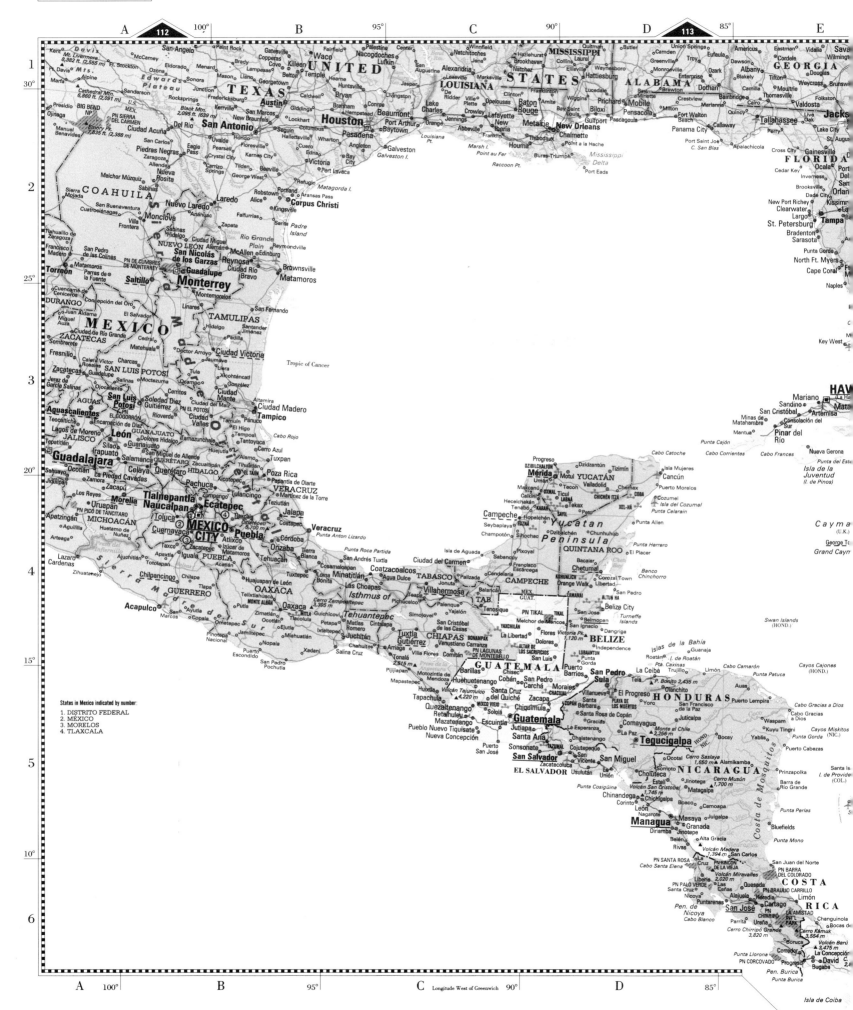

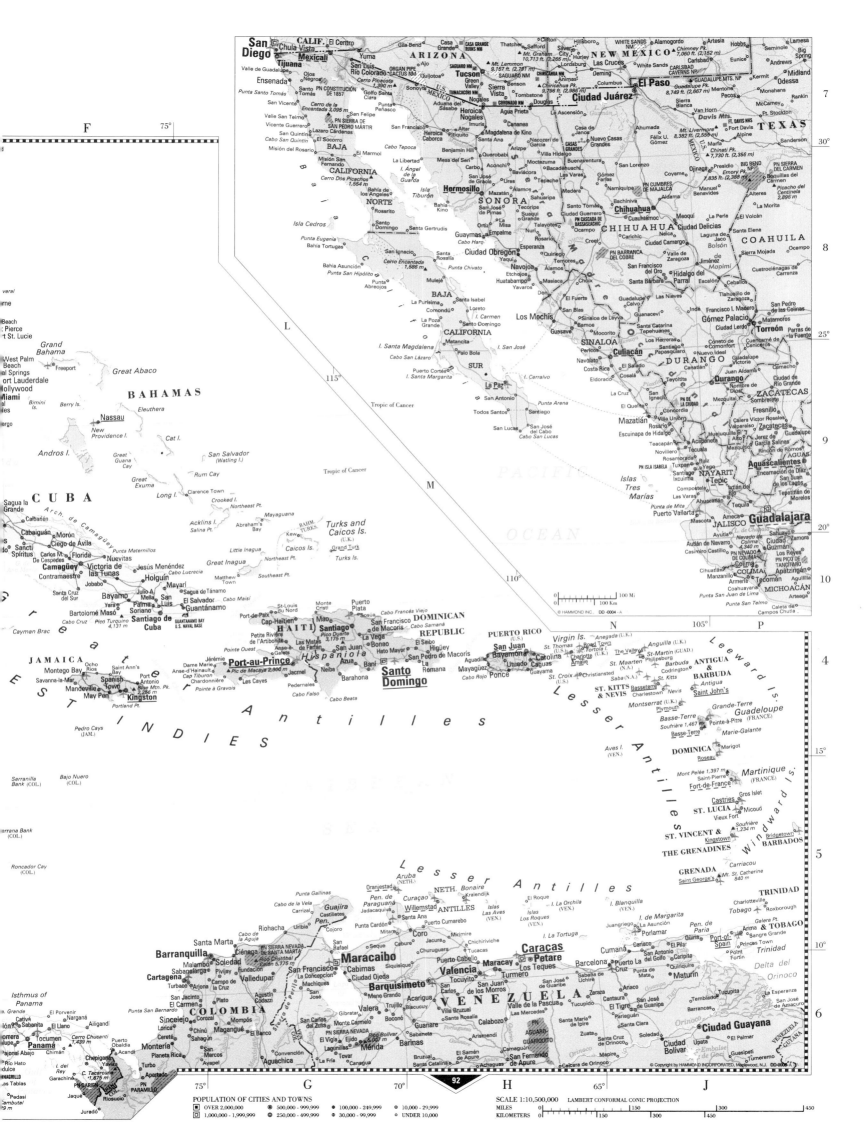

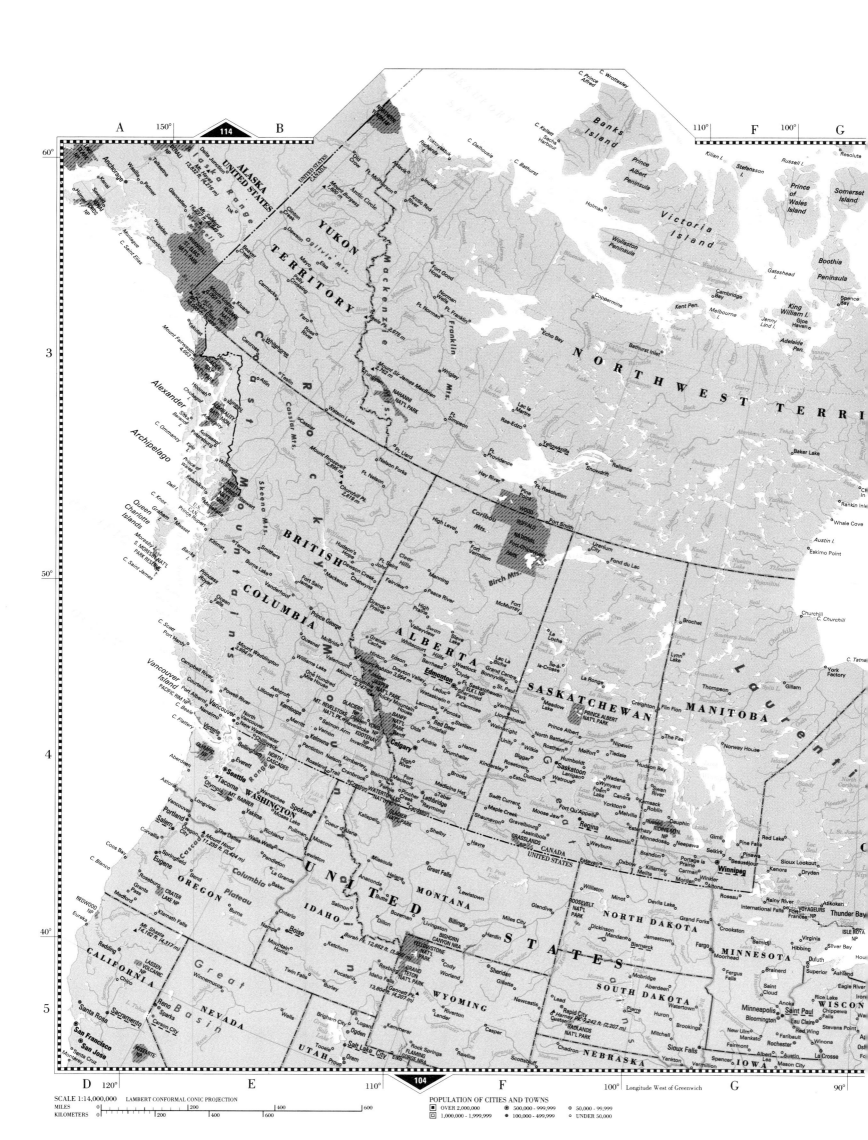

Canada

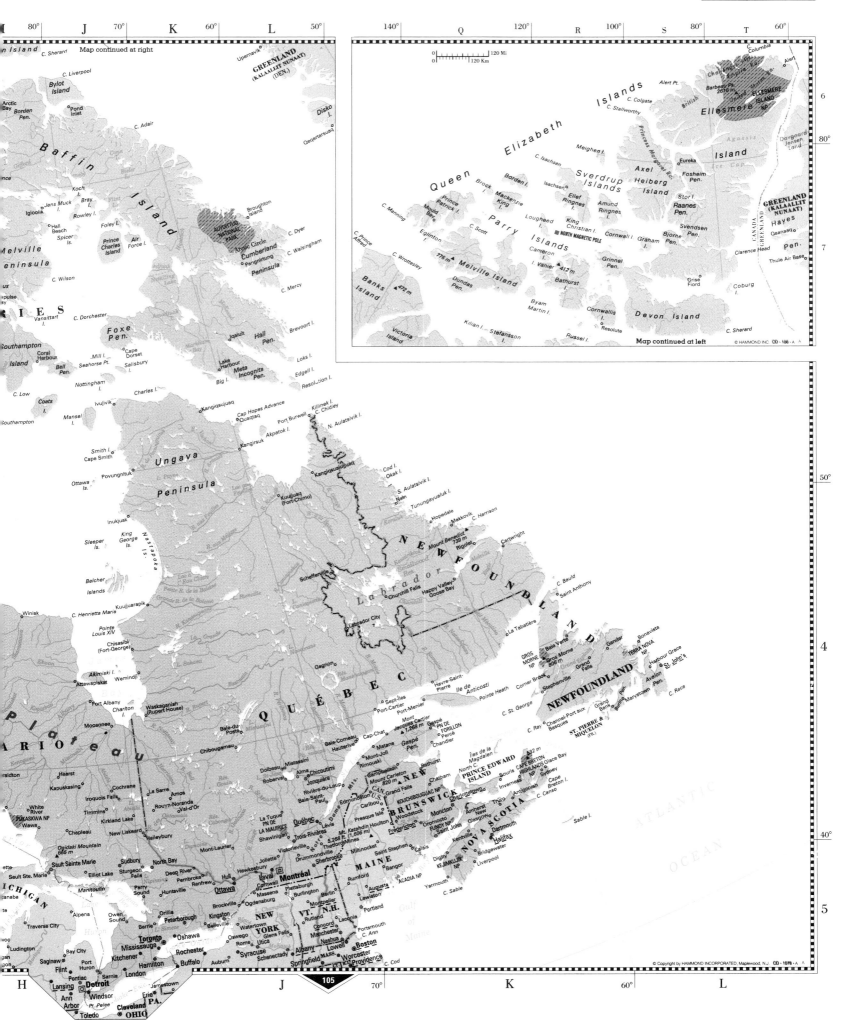

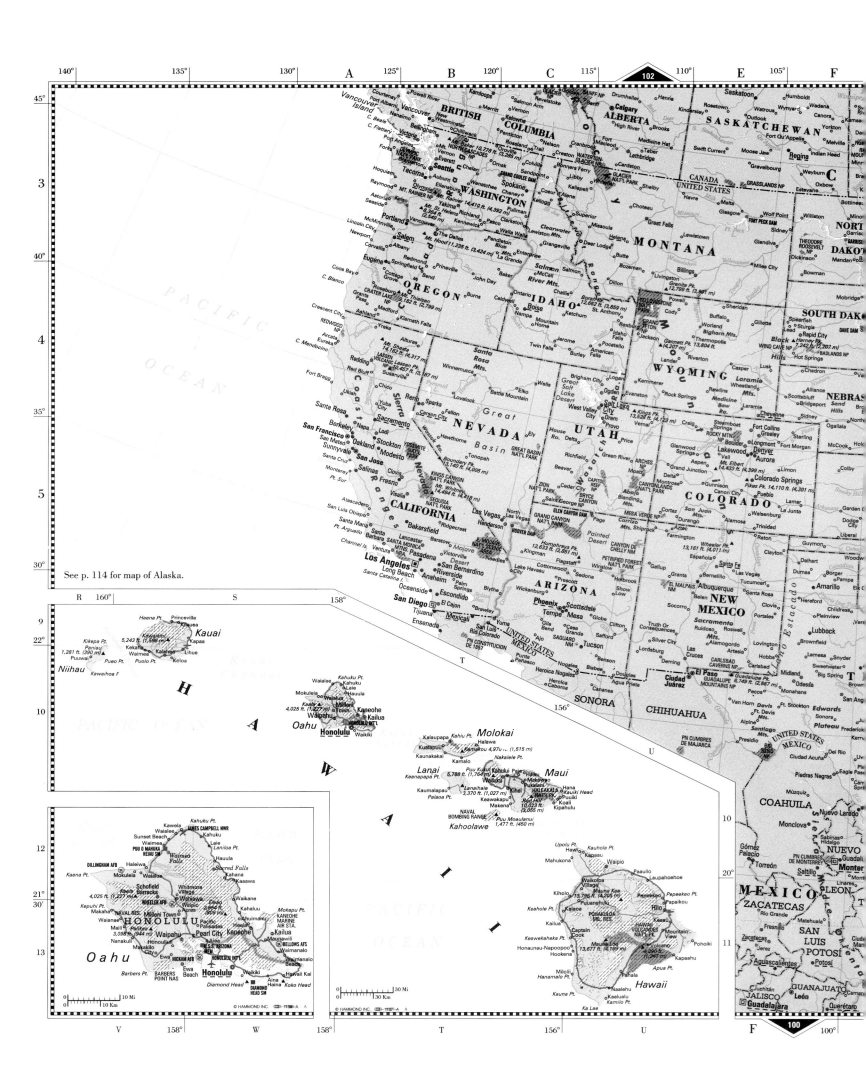

United States

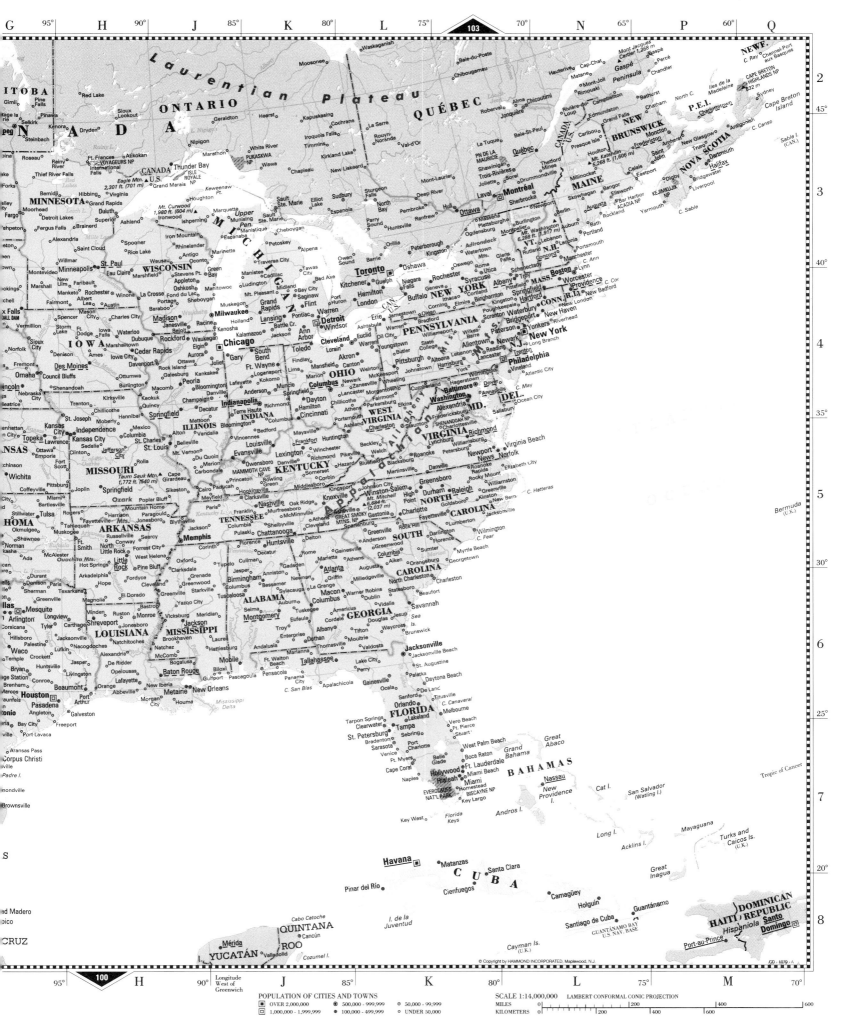

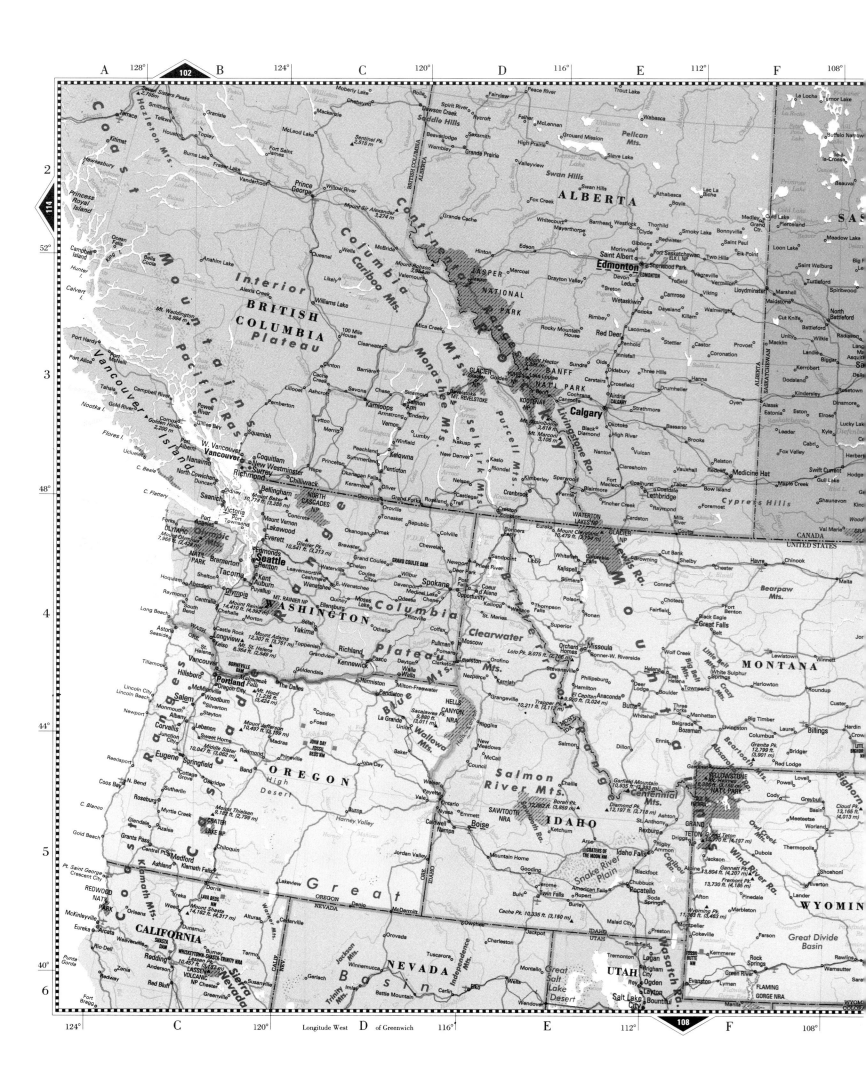

Southwestern Canada, Northwestern United States

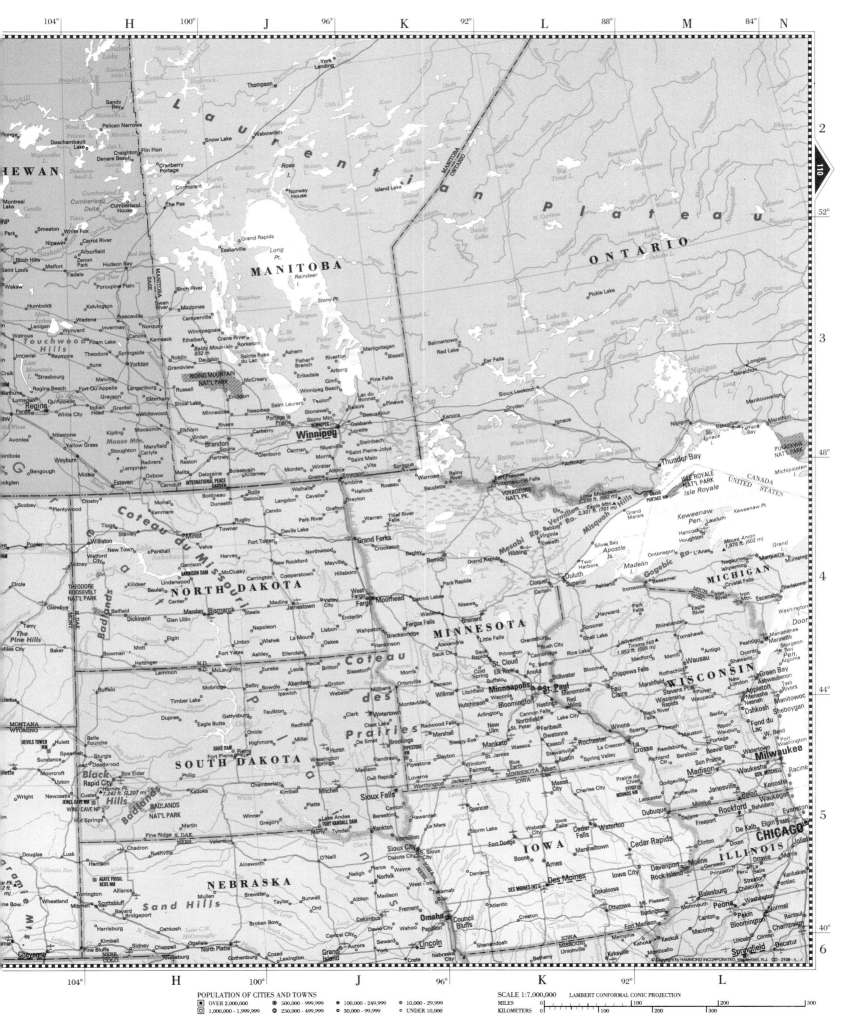

Southwestern United States

POPULATION OF CITIES AND TOWNS

- ◻ OVER 2,000,000
- ◻ 1,000,000 - 1,999,999
- ⬤ 500,000 - 999,999
- ● 250,000 - 499,999
- ● 100,000 - 249,999
- ● 30,000 - 99,999
- • 10,000 - 29,999
- · UNDER 10,000

SCALE 1:7,000,000   LAMBERT CONFORMAL CONIC PROJECTION

MILES 0   100   200   300

KILOMETERS 0   100   200   300

© Copyright by HAMMOND INCORPORATED, Maplewood, N.J.

Southeastern Canada, Northeastern United States

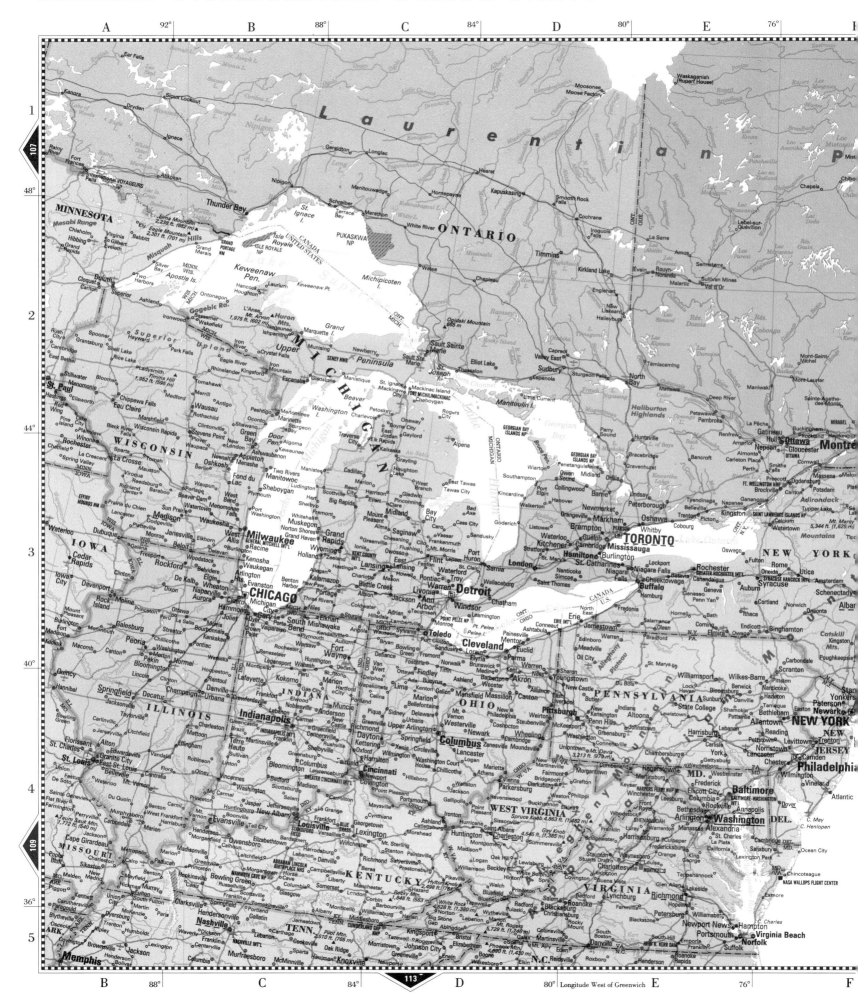

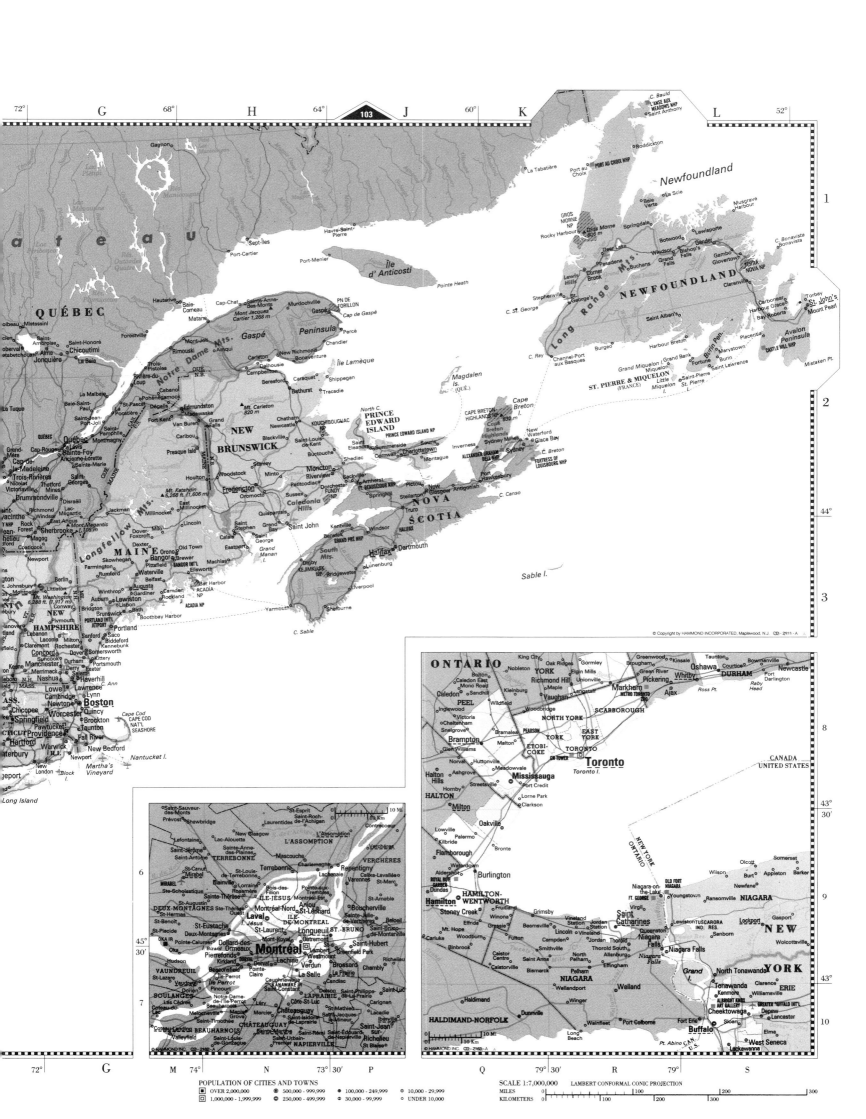

Southeastern United States

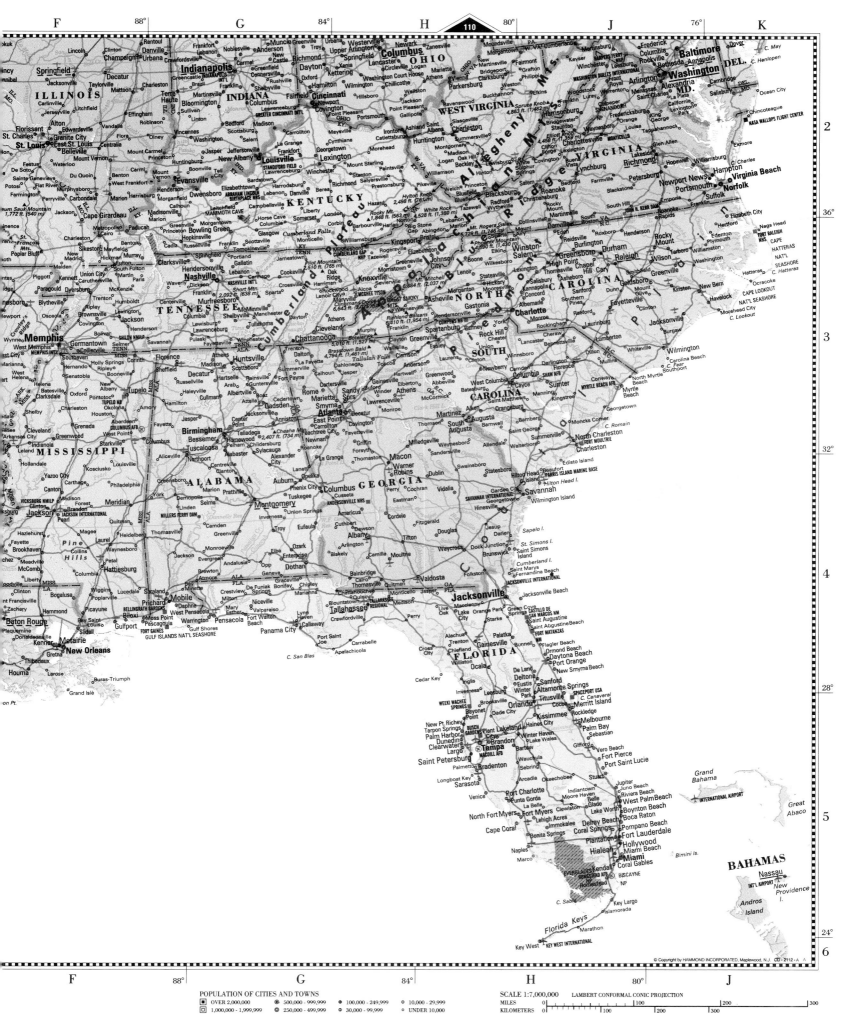

POPULATION OF CITIES AND TOWNS

■ OVER 2,000,000	● 500,000 - 999,999
□ 1,000,000 - 1,999,999	● 250,000 - 499,999

● 100,000 - 249,999   ○ 10,000 - 29,999
● 30,000 - 99,999   ○ UNDER 10,000

SCALE 1:7,000,000   LAMBERT CONFORMAL CONIC PROJECTION

MILES 0 | 100 | 200 | 300
KILOMETERS 0 | 100 | 200 | 300

© Copyright by HAMMOND INCORPORATED, Maplewood, N.J. CD-2112-A-A

Alaska

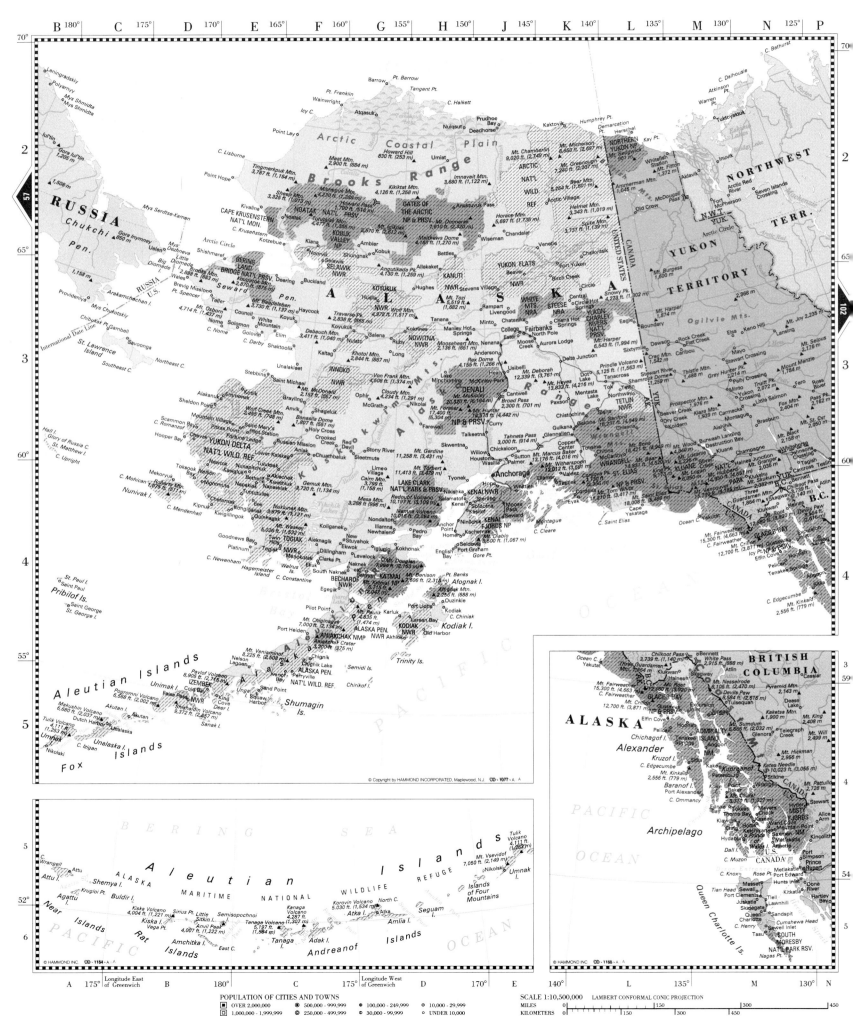

Los Angeles, New York-Philadelphia-Washington

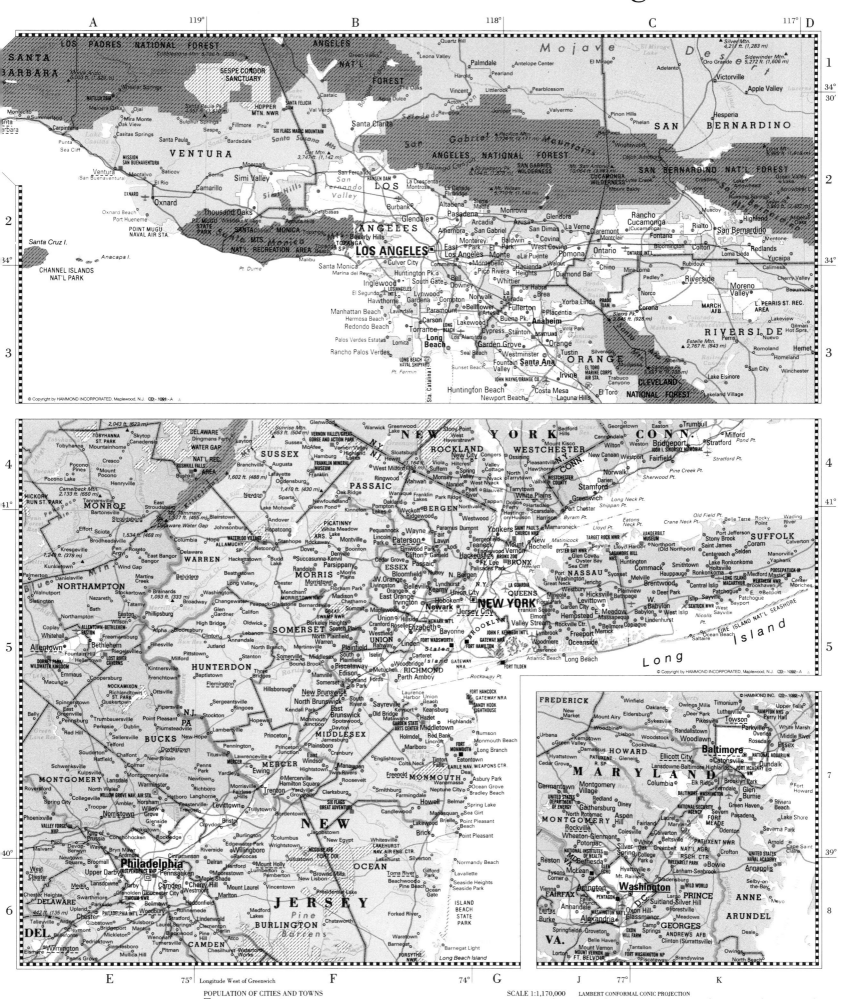

Seattle, San Francisco, Detroit, Chicago

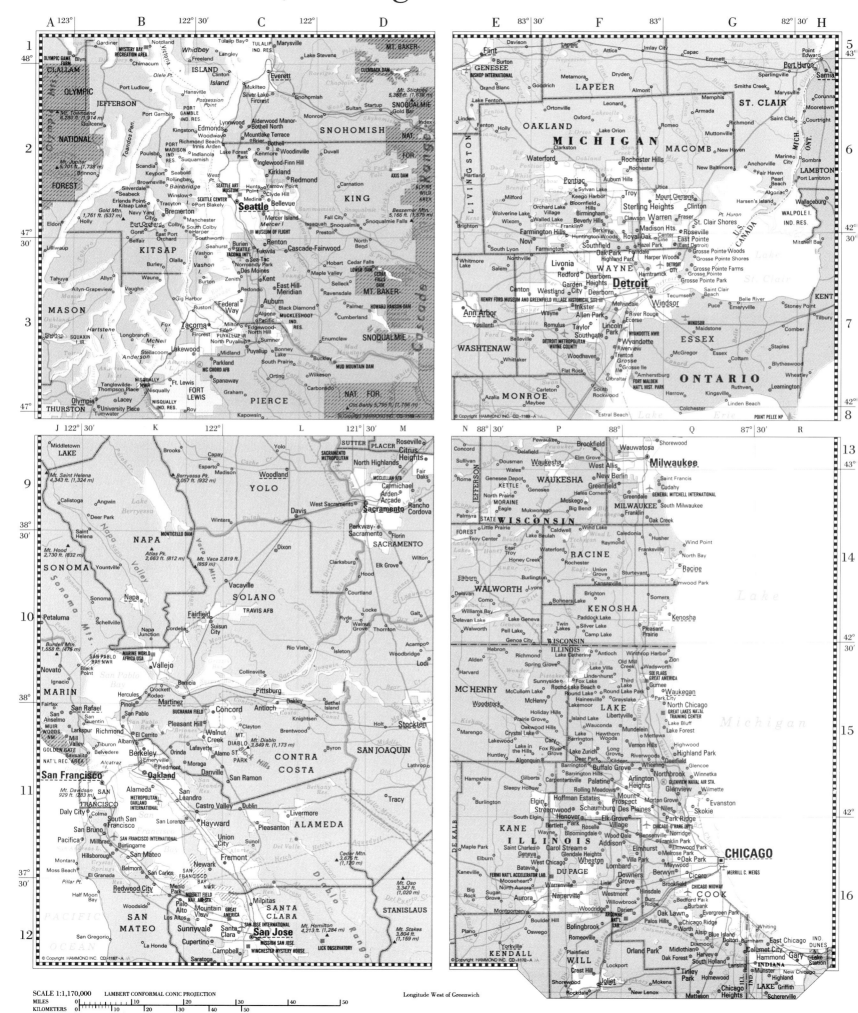

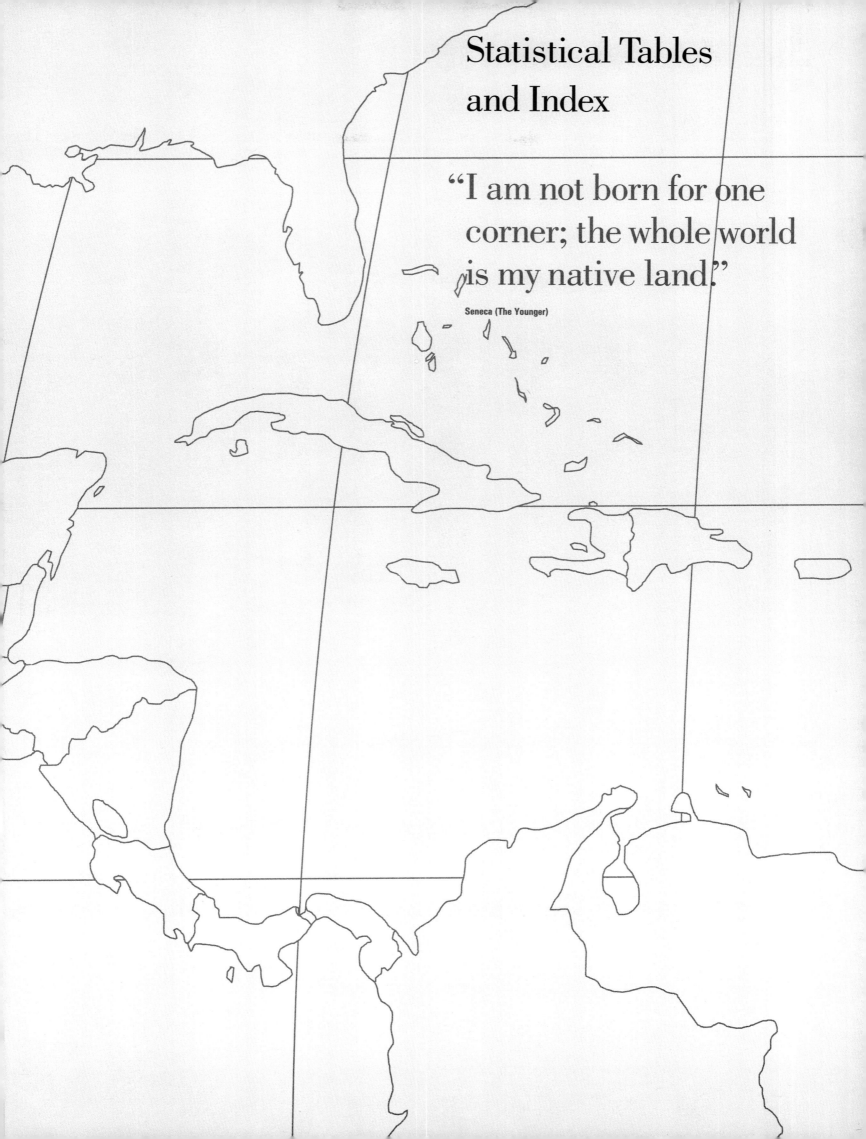

Statistical Tables and Index

"I am not born for one corner; the whole world is my native land."

Seneca (The Younger)

Time Zones of the World

165° W	150° W	135° W	120° W	105° W	90° W	75° W	60° W	45° W	30° W	15° W	0°
1 A.M.	2 A.M.	3 A.M.	4 A.M.	5 A.M.	6 A.M.	7 A.M.	8 A.M.	9 A.M.	10 A.M.	11 A.M.	NOON

GREENLAND

9 A.M.

11 A.M.

Nuuk

ICELAND
Reykjavík

3 A.M.
ALASKA

Anchorage

Whitehorse

CANADA

Edmonton

Winnipeg

NEWFOUNDLAND
8:30 A.M.

Montreal

Halifax

Seattle

Boise

Detroit

Chicago

Denver

UNITED STATES

Washington

New York

San Francisco

Los
Angeles

Phoenix

Atlanta

BERMUDA

Houston

AZORES

IRELAND

UNITED
KINGDOM

London

Paris

FRAN

Mo

ANDORRA

Madrid

PORTUGAL

SPAIN

Algiers

MOROCCO

ALGER

CANARY
Is.

W. SAHARA

Honolulu

HAWAII

MEXICO

Miami

BAHAMAS

Mexico City

CUBA

PUERTO
RICO

DOM.
HAITI REP.

ANT. & BARB.

BELIZE

JAMAICA ST. KITTS & NEVIS

DOMINICA

GUATEMALA

HONDURAS

ST. LUCIA

BARBADOS

EL SALVADOR

NICARAGUA

ST. VINC. & GRENS.

GRENADA

COSTA RICA

PANAMA

TRINIDAD AND TOBAGO

VENEZUELA

GUYANA

Bogotá

COLOMBIA

SUR. FR. GUIANA

ECUADOR

Manaus

KIRIBATI

2:30 A.M.
MARQUESAS
Is.

PERU

BRAZIL

Recife

ASCENSION

Lima

La Paz

BOLIVIA

TAHITI

FRENCH POLYNESIA

3:30A.M.
PITCAIRN I.

EASTER I.

PARAGUAY

Rio de
Janeiro

CHILE

Santiago

URUGUAY

Buenos Aires

ARGENTINA

TRISTAN DA CUNHA

MAURITANIA

CAPE
VERDE

Dakar

SENEGAL

MALI

GAMBIA

BURKINA
FASO

GUINEA-BISSAU

GUINEA

IVORY
COAST

GHANA

SIERRA LEONE

LIBERIA

EQUAT. G.
SÃO TO
PRÍN

TIME ZONES OF THE WORLD

STANDARD TIME ZONES

3 A.M.	4 A.M.	5 A.M.	6 A.M.

AREAS USING HALF HOUR DEVIATIONS

5:30 P.M.

FALKLAND
Is.

SOUTH GEORGIA

© Copyright HAMMOND INCORPORATED, Maplewood, N.J.

1 A.M.	2 A.M.	3 A.M.	4 A.M.	5 A.M.	6 A.M.	7 A.M.	8 A.M.	9 A.M.	10 A.M.	11 A.M.	NOON

ARCTIC OCEAN

FRANZ JOSEF LAND

SVALBARD

WRANGEL I.

RUSSIA

Anadyr

2 P.M.
FINLAND
Helsinki
St. Petersburg

Magadan

SWEDEN

EST.
LAT.
LITH.
RUS.

Stockholm

Moscow

Yekaterinburg

Novosibirsk

ALASKA

2 A.M.

Berlin
POLAND
BELARUS
4 P.M.
Kiev
UKRAINE
4 P.M.
Volgograd

KAZAKHSTAN

Irkutsk
Chita

CZECH
Vienna SLVK.
HUN.

6 P.M.

MONGOLIA

8 P.M.

ROMANIA
BOSN.
YUGO.
BULGARIA
ALB. MAC.

GEO. 4 P.M.
ARM. AZER. Baku
UZBEKISTAN
Tashkent
KYRGYZSTAN
TAJIKISTAN

Beijing

Vladivostok

N. KOREA
Seoul
S. KOREA

JAPAN
Tokyo

MONDAY SUNDAY

GREECE
Istanbul
Athens
TURKEY

TURKMENISTAN

CHINA

MALTA
CYPRUS
LEB.
SYRIA
ISRAEL JOR.

Tehran
IRAN
3:30 P.M.

AFGHANISTAN
4:30 P.M.

5 P.M.
PAKISTAN

5:40 P.M.
NEPAL BHU.

HAWAII

Tripoli
IRAQ
KUWAIT

TAIWAN

LIBYA
Cairo
EGYPT

Riyadh
SAUDI
ARABIA

BAHRAIN
QATAR
U.A.E.

Karachi

Delhi
INDIA
Calcutta
BANG.

BURMA
6:30
P.M.
LAOS

HONG KONG

9 P.M.

NORTHERN
MARIANAS

INTERNATIONAL DATE LINE

CHAD
Khartoum
SUDAN
ERIT.
YEMEN
DJIBOUTI

OMAN

5:30 P.M.
Bombay

THAI-
LAND
Bangkok
CAMB.

MARSHALL
ISLANDS

C. AFR. REP.
ETHIOPIA

SRI
LANKA

5:30
P.M.

VIETNAM

Manila

FED. STATES OF
MICRONESIA

Ndjamena

MALDIVES

MALAYSIA
BRUNEI
SING.

PHILIPPINES

CONGO
ZAIRE
(CONGO)
RWANDA
BURUNDI

KENYA
SOMALIA

SEYCHELLES

NAURU

KIRIBATI

UGANDA

TANZANIA
Dar es
Salaam

BRITISH INDIAN
OCEAN TERR.

6:30 P.M.

Jakarta INDONESIA

PAPUA
NEW GUINEA

SOLOMON
ISLANDS

TUVALU

2 P.M.

ANGOLA
ZAMBIA
MALAWI
COMOROS

COCOS
IS.

TOKELAU

W. SAMOA

NAMIBIA
ZIMB.
MOZAMBIQUE

MADAGASCAR

MAURITIUS

Darwin

VANUATU

FIJI

AMER.
SAMOA

TONGA

BOTSWANA
Johannesburg
SWAZILAND
SOUTH
AFRICA
LESOTHO

9:30
P.M.

AUSTRALIA

11:30 P.M.
NORFOLK I.

1 A.M.

Cape Town

Perth

Adelaide

Sydney

LORD HOWE I.
10:30
P.M.

NEW
ZEALAND
Wellington
12:45 A.M.

PRINCE
EDWARD IS.

CROZET IS.

CHATHAM
IS.

World Statistics

ELEMENTS OF THE SOLAR SYSTEM

	Mean Distance from Sun: in Miles	in Kilometers	Period of Revolution around Sun	Period of Rotation on Axis	Equatorial Diameter in Miles	in Kilometers	Surface Gravity (Earth = 1)	Mass (Earth = 1)	Mean Density (Water = 1)	Number of Satellites
Mercury	35,990,000	57,900,000	87.97 days	59 days	3,032	4,880	0.38	0.055	5.5	0
Venus	67,240,000	108,200,000	224.70 days	243 days†	7,523	12,106	0.90	0.815	5.25	0
Earth	93,000,000	149,700,000	365.26 days	23h 56m	7,926	12,755	1.00	1.00	5.5	1
Mars	141,730,000	228,100,000	687.00 days	24h 37m	4,220	6,790	0.38	0.107	4.0	2
Jupiter	483,880,000	778,700,000	11.86 years	9h 50m	88,750	142,800	2.87	317.9	1.3	16
Saturn	887,130,000	1,427,700,000	29.46 years	10h 39m	74,580	120,020	1.32	95.2	0.7	23
Uranus	1,783,100,000	2,870,500,000	84.01 years	17h 24m†	31,600	50,900	0.93	14.6	1.3	15
Neptune	2,795,500,000	4,498,800,000	164.79 years	17h 50m	30,200	48,600	1.23	17.2	1.8	8
Pluto	3,667,900,000	5,902,800,000	247.70 years	6.39 days(?)	1,500	2,400	0.03(?)	0.01(?)	0.7(?)	1

† Retrograde motion

DIMENSIONS OF THE EARTH

	Area in: Sq. Miles	Sq. Kilometers
Superficial area	196,939,000	510,073,000
Land surface	57,506,000	148,941,000
Water surface	139,433,000	361,132,000

	Distance in: Miles	Kilometers
Equatorial circumference	24,902	40,075
Polar circumference	24,860	40,007
Equatorial diameter	7,926.4	12,756.4
Polar diameter	7,899.8	12,713.6
Equatorial radius	3,963.2	6,378.2
Polar radius	3,949.9	6,356.8

Volume of the Earth	2.6×10^{11} cubic miles	10.84×10^{11} cubic kilometers
Mass or weight	6.6×10^{21} short tons	6.0×10^{21} metric tons
Maximum distance from Sun	94,600,000 miles	152,000,000 kilometers
Minimum distance from Sun	91,300,000 miles	147,000,000 kilometers

OCEANS AND MAJOR SEAS

	Area in: Sq. Miles	Sq. Kms.	Greatest Depth in: Feet	Meters
Pacific Ocean	64,186,000	166,241,700	36,198	11,033
Atlantic Ocean	31,862,000	82,522,600	28,374	8,648
Indian Ocean	28,350,000	73,426,500	25,344	7,725
Arctic Ocean	5,427,000	14,056,000	17,880	5,450
Caribbean Sea	970,000	2,512,300	24,720	7,535
Mediterranean Sea	969,000	2,509,700	16,896	5,150
South China Sea	895,000	2,318,000	15,000	4,600
Bering Sea	875,000	2,266,250	15,800	4,800
Gulf of Mexico	600,000	1,554,000	12,300	3,750
Sea of Okhotsk	590,000	1,528,100	11,070	3,370
East China Sea	482,000	1,248,400	9,500	2,900
Yellow Sea	480,000	1,243,200	350	107
Sea of Japan	389,000	1,007,500	12,280	3,740
Hudson Bay	317,500	822,300	846	258
North Sea	222,000	575,000	2,200	670
Black Sea	185,000	479,150	7,365	2,245
Red Sea	169,000	437,700	7,200	2,195
Baltic Sea	163,000	422,170	1,506	459

THE CONTINENTS

	Area in: Sq. Miles	Sq. Kms.	Percent of World's Land
Asia	17,128,500	44,362,815	29.5
Africa	11,707,000	30,321,130	20.2
North America	9,363,000	24,250,170	16.2
South America	6,875,000	17,806,250	11.8
Antarctica	5,500,000	14,245,000	9.5
Europe	4,057,000	10,507,630	7.0
Australia	2,966,136	7,682,300	5.1

MAJOR SHIP CANALS

	Length in: Miles	Kms.	Minimum Depth in: Feet	Meters
Volga-Baltic, Russia	225	362	–	–
Baltic-White Sea, Russia	140	225	16	5
Suez, Egypt	100.76	162	42	13
Albert, Belgium	80	129	16.5	5
Moscow-Volga, Russia	80	129	18	6
Volga-Don, Russia	62	100	–	–
Göta, Sweden	54	87	10	3
Kiel (Nord-Ostsee), Germany	53.2	86	38	12
Panama Canal, Panama	50.72	82	41.6	13
Houston Ship, U.S.A.	50	81	36	11

LARGEST ISLANDS

	Area in: Sq. Miles	Sq. Kms.
Greenland	840,000	2,175,600
New Guinea	305,000	789,950
Borneo	290,000	751,100
Madagascar	226,400	586,376
Baffin, Canada	195,928	507,454
Sumatra, Indonesia	164,000	424,760
Honshu, Japan	88,000	227,920
Great Britain	84,400	218,896
Victoria, Canada	83,896	217,290
Ellesmere, Canada	75,767	196,236
Celebes, Indonesia	72,986	189,034
South I., New Zealand	58,393	151,238
Java, Indonesia	48,842	126,501
North I., New Zealand	44,187	114,444
Newfoundland, Canada	42,031	108,860
Cuba	40,533	104,981
Luzon, Philippines	40,420	104,688
Iceland	39,768	103,000
Mindanao, Philippines	36,537	94,631
Ireland	31,743	82,214
Sakhalin, Russia	29,500	76,405
Hispaniola, Haiti & Dom. Rep.	29,399	76,143

	Area in: Sq. Miles	Sq. Kms.
Hokkaido, Japan	28,983	75,066
Banks, Canada	27,038	70,028
Ceylon, Sri Lanka	25,332	65,610
Tasmania, Australia	24,600	63,710
Svalbard, Norway	23,957	62,049
Devon, Canada	21,331	55,247
Novaya Zemlya (north isl.), Russia	18,600	48,200
Marajó, Brazil	17,991	46,597
Tierra del Fuego, Chile & Argentina	17,900	46,360
Alexander, Antarctica	16,700	43,250
Axel Heiberg, Canada	16,671	43,178
Melville, Canada	16,274	42,150
Southhampton, Canada	15,913	41,215
New Britain, Papua New Guinea	14,100	36,519
Taiwan, China	13,836	35,835
Kyushu, Japan	13,770	35,664
Hainan, China	13,127	33,999
Prince of Wales, Canada	12,872	33,338
Spitsbergen, Norway	12,355	31,999
Vancouver, Canada	12,079	31,285
Timor, Indonesia	11,527	29,855
Sicily, Italy	9,926	25,708

	Area in: Sq. Miles	Sq. Kms.
Somerset, Canada	9,570	24,786
Sardinia, Italy	9,301	24,090
Shikoku, Japan	6,860	17,767
New Caledonia, France	6,530	16,913
Nordaustlandet, Norway	6,409	16,599
Samar, Philippines	5,050	13,080
Negros, Philippines	4,906	12,707
Palawan, Philippines	4,550	11,785
Panay, Philippines	4,446	11,515
Jamaica	4,232	10,961
Hawaii, United States	4,038	10,458
Viti Levu, Fiji	4,010	10,386
Cape Breton, Canada	3,981	10,311
Mindoro, Philippines	3,759	9,736
Kodiak, Alaska, U.S.A.	3,670	9,505
Cyprus	3,572	9,251
Puerto Rico, U.S.A.	3,435	8,897
Corsica, France	3,352	8,682
New Ireland, Papua New Guinea	3,340	8,651
Crete, Greece	3,218	8,335
Anticosti, Canada	3,066	7,941
Wrangel, Russia	2,819	7,301

PRINCIPAL MOUNTAINS

	Height in : Feet	Meters		Height in : Feet	Meters		Height in : Feet	Meters
erest, Nepal-China	29,028	8,848	Llullaillaco, Chile-Argentina	22,057	6,723	Blanc, France	15,771	4,807
2 (Godwin Austen), Pakistan-China	28,250	8,611	Nevada Ancohuma, Bolivia	21,489	6,550	Klyuchevskaya Sopka, Russia	15,584	4,750
akalu, Nepal-China	27,789	8,470	Chimborazo, Ecuador	20,561	6,267	Fairweather, Br. Col., Canada	15,300	4,663
aulagiri, Nepal	26,810	8,172	McKinley, Alaska	20,320	6,194	Dufourspitze (Mte. Rosa), Italy-Switzerland	15,203	4,634
anga Parbat, Pakistan	26,660	8,126	Logan, Yukon, Canada	19,524	5,951	Ras Dashen, Ethiopia	15,157	4620
nnapurna, Nepal	26,504	8,078	Cotopaxi, Ecuador	19,347	5,897	Matterhorn, Switzerland	14,691	4,478
kaposhi, Pakistan	25,550	7,788	Kilimanjaro, Tanzania	19,340	5,895	Whitney, California, U.S.A.	14,494	4,418
ongur Shan, China	25,325	7,719	El Misti, Peru	19,101	5,822	Elbert, Colorado, U.S.A.	14,433	4,399
rich Mir, Pakistan	25,230	7,690	Pico Cristóbal Colón, Colombia	18,947	5,775	Rainier, Washington, U.S.A.	14,410	4,392
ongqa Shan, China	24,790	7,556	Huila, Colombia	18,865	5,750	Shasta, California, U.S.A.	14,162	4,317
mmunism Peak, Tajikistan	24,590	7,495	Citlaltépetl (Orizaba), Mexico	18,701	5,700	Pikes Peak, Colorado, U.S.A.	14,110	4,301
abedy Peak, Kyrgyzstan	24,406	7,439	Damavand, Iran	18,606	5,671	Finsteraarhorn, Switzerland	14,022	4, 274
omo Lhari, Bhutan-China	23,997	7,314	El'brus, Russia	18,510	5,642	Mauna Kea, Hawaii, U.S.A.	13,796	4,205
uztag, China	23,891	7,282	St. Elias, Alaska, U.S.A.-Yukon, Canada	18,008	5,489	Mauna Loa, Hawaii, U.S.A.	13,677	4,169
erro Aconcagua, Argentina	22,831	6,959	Dykh-tau, Russia	17,070	5,203	Jungfrau, Switzerland	13,642	4,158
os del Salado, Chile-Argentina	22,572	6,880	Batian (Kenya), Kenya	17,058	5,199	Grossglockner, Austria	12,457	3,797
nete, Chile-Argentina	22,546	6,872	Ararat, Turkey	16,946	5,165	Fujiyama, Japan	12,389	3,776
upungato, Chile-Argentina	22,310	6,800	Vinson Massif, Antarctica	16,864	5,140	Cook, New Zealand	12,349	3,764
ssis, Argentina	22,241	6,779	Margherita (Ruwenzori), Africa	16,795	5,119	Etna, Italy	10,902	3,323
ercedario, Argentina	22,211	6,770	Kazbek, Georgia-Russia	16,558	5,047	Kosciusko, Australia	7,310	2,228
uascarán, Peru	22,205	6,768	Puncak Jaya, Indonesia	16,503	5,030	Mitchell, North Carolina, U.S.A.	6,684	2,037

LONGEST RIVERS

	Length in : Miles	Kms.		Length in : Miles	Kms.		Length in : Miles	Kms.
le, Africa	4,145	6,671	Indus, Asia	1,800	2,897	Don, Russia	1,222	1,967
mazon, S. America	3,915	6,300	Danube, Europe	1,775	2,857	Red, U.S.A.	1,222	1,966
ang Jiang (Yangtze), China	3,900	6,276	Salween, Asia	1,770	2,849	Columbia, U.S.A.-Canada	1,214	1,953
ississippi-Missouri-Red Rock, U.S.A.	3,741	6,019	Brahmaputra, Asia	1,700	2,736	Saskatchewan, Canada	1,205	1,939
'-Irtysh-Black Irtysh, Russia-Kazakhstan	3,362	5,411	Euphrates, Asia	1,700	2,736	Peace-Finlay, Canada	1,195	1,923
nisey-Angara, Russia	3,100	4,989	Tocantins, Brazil	1,677	2,699	Tigris, Asia .	1,181	1,901
uang He (Yellow), China	2,877	4,630	Xi (Si), China	1,650	2,601	Darling, Australia	1,160	1,867
mur-Shilka-Onon, Asia	2,744	4,416	Amudar'ya, Asia	1,616	2,601	Angara, Russia	1,135	1,827
ena, Russia	2,734	4,400	Nelson-Saskatchewan, Canada	1,600	2,575	Sungari, Asia	1,130	1,819
ongo (Zaire), Africa	2,718	4,374	Orinoco, S. America	1,600	2,575	Pechora, Russia	1,124	1,809
ackenzie-Peace-Finlay, Canada	2,635	4,241	Zambezi, Africa	1,600	2,575	Snake, U.S.A.	1,038	1,670
ekong, Asia	2,610	4,200	Paraguay, S. America	1,584	2,549	Churchill, Canada	1,000	1,609
issouri-Red Rock, U.S.A.	2,564	4,125	Kolyma, Russia	1,562	2,514	Pilcomayo, S. America	1,000	1,609
ger, Africa	2,548	4,101	Ganges, Asia	1,550	2,494	Uruguay, S. America	994	1.600
araná-La Plata, S. America	2,450	3,943	Ural, Russia-Kazakhstan	1,509	2,428	Platte-N. Platte, U.S.A.	990	1,593
ississippi, U.S.A.	2,348	3,778	Japurá, S. America	1,500	2,414	Ohio, U.S.A.	981	1,578
urray-Darling, Australia	2,310	3,718	Arkansas, U.S.A.	1,450	2,334	Magdalena, Colombia	956	1,538
olga, Russia	2,194	3,531	Colorado, U.S.A.-Mexico	1.450	2,334	Pecos, U.S.A.	926	1,490
adeira, S. America	2,013	3,240	Negro, S. America	1,400	2,253	Oka, Russia	918	1,477
urus, S. America	1,995	3,211	Dnieper, Russia-Belarus-Ukraine	1,368	2,202	Canadian, U.S.A.	906	1,458
ukon, Alaska-Canada	1,979	3,185	Orange, Africa	1,350	2,173	Colorado, Texas, U.S.A.	894	1,439
. Lawrence, Canada-U.S.A.	1,900	3,058	Irrawaddy, Burma	1,325	2,132	Dniester, Ukraine-Moldova	876	1,410
o Grande, Mexico-U.S.A.	1,885	3,034	Brazos, U.S.A.	1,309	2,107	Fraser, Canada	850	1,369
rdar'ya-Naryn, Asia	1,859	2,992	Ohio-Allegheny, U.S.A.	1,306	2,102	Rhine, Europe	820	1,319
io Francisco, Brazil	1,811	2,914	Kama, Russia	1,252	2,031	Northern Dvina, Russia	809	1,302

PRINCIPAL NATURAL LAKES

	Area in: Sq. Miles	Sq. Kms.	Max. Depth in: Feet	Meters		Area in: Sq. Miles	Sq. Kms.	Max. Depth in: Feet	Meters
aspian Sea, Asia	143,243	370,999	3,264	995	Lake Eyre, Australia	3,500-0	9,000-0	–	–
ake Superior, U.S.A.-Canada	31,820	82,414	1,329	405	Lake Titicaca, Peru-Bolivia	3,200	8,288	1, 000	305
ake Victoria, Africa	26,724	69,215	270	82	Lake Nicaragua, Nicaragua	3,100	8,029	230	70
ake Huron, U.S.A.-Canada	23,010	59,596	748	228	Lake Athabasca, Canada	3,064	7,936	400	122
ake Michigan, U.S.A.	22,400	58,016	923	281	Reindeer Lake, Canada	2,568	6,651	–	–
ral Sea, Kazakhstan-Uzbekistan	15,830	41,000	213	65	Lake Turkana (Rudolf), Africa	2,463	6,379	240	73
ake Tanganyika, Africa	12,650	32,764	4,700	1,433	Issyk-Kul', Kyrgyzstan	2,425	6,281	2,303	702
ake Baykal, Russia	12,162	31,500	5,316	1,620	Lake Torrens, Australia	2,230	5,776	–	–
eat Bear Lake, Canada	12,096	31,328	1,356	413	Vänern, Sweden	2,156	5,584	328	100
ake Nyasa (Malawi), Africa	11,555	29,928	2,320	707	Nettilling Lake, Canada	2,140	5,543	–	–
eat Slave Lake, Canada	11,031	28,570	2,015	614	Lake Winnipegosis, Canada	2,075	5,374	38	12
ake Erie, U.S.A.-Canada	9,940	25,745	210	64	Lake Mobutu Sese Seko (Albert), Africa	2,075	5,374	160	49
ake Winnipeg, Canada	9,417	24,390	60	18	Kariba Lake, Zambia-Zimbabwe	2,050	5,310	295	90
ake Ontario, U.S.A.-Canada	7,540	19,529	775	244	Lake Nipigon, Canada	1,872	4,848	540	165
ake Ladoga, Russia	7,104	18,399	738	225	Lake Mweru, Zaire-Zambia	1,800	4,662	60	18
ake Balkhash, Kazakhstan	7,027	18,200	87	27	Lake Manitoba, Canada	1,799	4,659	12	4
ake Maracaibo, Venezuela	5,120	13,261	100	31	Lake Taymyr, Russia	1,737	4,499	85	26
ake Chad, Africa	4,000 –	10,360 –			Lake Khanka, China-Russia	1,700	4,403	33	10
	10,000	25,900	25	8	Lake Kioga, Uganda	1,700	4,403	25	8
ake Onega, Russia	3,710	9,609	377	115	Lake of the Woods, U.S.A.-Canada	1,679	4,349	70	21

Index of the World

This index is a comprehensive listing of the places and geographic features found in the atlas. Names are arranged in strict alphabetical order, without regard to hyphens or spaces. Every name is followed by the country or area to which it belongs. Except for cities, towns, countries and cultural areas, all entries include a reference to feature type, such as province, river, island, peak, and so on. The page number and alpha-numeric code appear in green to the left of each listing. The page number directs you to the largest scale map on which the name can be found. The code refers to the grid squares formed by the horizontal and vertical lines of latitude and longitude on each map. Following the letters from left to right and the numbers from top to bottom helps you to locate quickly the square containing the place or feature. Inset maps have their own alpha-numeric codes. Names that are accompanied by a point symbol are indexed to the symbol's location on the map. Other names are indexed to the initial letter of the name. When a map name contains a subordinate or alternate name, both names are listed in the index. To conserve space and provide room for more entries, many abbreviations are used in this index. The primary abbreviations are listed below.

Index Abbreviations

A
Ab,Can	Alberta
Acad.	Academy
ACT	Australian Capital Territory
A.F.B.	Air Force Base
Afld.	Airfield
Afg.	Afghanistan
Afr.	Africa
Ak,US	Alaska
Al,US	Alabama
Alb.	Albania
Alg.	Algeria
Amm. Dep.	Ammunition Depot
And.	Andorra
Ang.	Angola
Angu.	Anguilla
Ant.	Antarctica
Anti.	Antigua and Barbuda
Ar,US	Arkansas
Arch.	Archipelago
Arg.	Argentina
Arm.	Armenia
Arpt.	Airport
Aru.	Aruba
ASam.	American Samoa
Ash.	Ashmore and Cartier Islands
Aus.	Austria
Austl.	Australia
Aut.	Autonomous
Az,US	Arizona
Azer.	Azerbaijan
Azor.	Azores

B
Bahm.	Bahamas
Bahr.	Bahrain
Bang.	Bangladesh
Bar.	Barbados
BC,Can	British Columbia
Bela.	Belarus
Belg.	Belgium
Belz.	Belize
Ben.	Benin
Berm.	Bermuda
Bfld.	Battlefield
Bhu.	Bhutan
Bol.	Bolivia
Bor.	Borough
Bosn.	Bosnia and Hercegovina
Bots.	Botswana
Braz.	Brazil
Brln.	British Indian Ocean Territory
Bru.	Brunei
Bul.	Bulgaria
Burk.	Burkina
Buru.	Burundi
BVI	British Virgin Islands

C
Ca,US	California
CAfr.	Central African Republic
Camb.	Cambodia
Camr.	Cameroon
Can.	Canada
Can.	Canal
Canl.	Canary Islands
Cap.	Capital
Cap. Dist.	Capital District

Cap. Terr.	Capital Territory
Cay.	Cayman Islands
C.G.	Coast Guard
Chan.	Channel
Chl.	Channel Islands
Co.	County
Co,US	Colorado
Col.	Colombia
Com.	Comoros
Cont.	Continent
CpV.	Cape Verde Islands
CR	Costa Rica
Cr.	Creek
Cro.	Croatia
CSea.	Coral Sea Islands Territory
Ct,US	Connecticut
Ctr.	Center
Ctry.	Country
Cyp.	Cyprus
Czh.	Czech Republic

D
DC,US	District of Columbia
De,US	Delaware
Den.	Denmark
Depr.	Depression
Dept.	Department
Des.	Desert
DF	Distrito Federal
Dist.	District
Djib.	Djibouti
Dom.	Dominica
Dpcy.	Dependency
DRep.	Dominican Republic

E
Ecu.	Ecuador
Emb.	Embankment
Eng.	Engineering
Eng,UK	England
EqG.	Equatorial Guinea
Erit.	Eritrea
ESal.	El Salvador
Est.	Estonia
Eth.	Ethiopia
Eur.	Europe

F
Falk.	Falkland Islands
Far.	Faroe Islands
Fed. Dist.	Federal District
Fin.	Finland
Fl,US	Florida
For.	Forest
Fr.	France
FrAnt.	French Southern and Antarctic Lands
FrG.	French Guiana
FrPol.	French Polynesia

G
Ga,US	Georgia
Galp.	Galapagos Islands
Gam.	Gambia
Gaza	Gaza Strip
GBis.	Guinea-Bissau
Geo.	Georgia
Ger.	Germany

Gha.	Ghana
Gib.	Gibraltar
Glac.	Glacier
Gov.	Governorate
Govt.	Government
Gre.	Greece
Grld.	Greenland
Gren.	Grenada
Grsld.	Grassland
Guad.	Guadeloupe
Guat.	Guatemala
Gui.	Guinea
Guy.	Guyana

H
Har.	Harbor
Hi,US	Hawaii
Hist.	Historic(al)
HK	Hong Kong
Hon.	Honduras
Hts.	Heights
Hun.	Hungary

I
Ia,US	Iowa
Ice.	Iceland
Id,US	Idaho
Il,US	Illinois
IM	Isle of Man
In,US	Indiana
Ind. Res.	Indian Reservation
Indo.	Indonesia
Int'l	International
Ire.	Ireland
Isl., Isls.	Island, Islands
Isr.	Israel
Isth.	Isthmus
It.	Italy
IvC.	Ivory Coast

J
Jam.	Jamaica
Jor.	Jordan

K
Kaz.	Kazakhstan
Kiri.	Kiribati
Ks,US	Kansas
Kuw.	Kuwait
Ky,US	Kentucky
Kyr.	Kyrgyzstan

L
La,US	Louisiana
Lab.	Laboratory
Lag.	Lagoon
Lakesh.	Lakeshore
Lat.	Latvia
Lcht.	Liechtenstein
Ldg.	Landing
Leb.	Lebanon
Les.	Lesotho
Libr.	Liberia
Lith.	Lithuania
Lux.	Luxembourg

M
Ma,US	Massachusetts
Macd.	Macedonia
Madg.	Madagascar
Madr.	Madeira
Malay.	Malaysia
Mald.	Maldives
Malw.	Malawi
Mart.	Martinique
May.	Mayotte
Mb,Can	Manitoba
Md,US	Maryland

Me,US	Maine
Mem.	Memorial
Mex.	Mexico
Mi,US	Michigan
Micr.	Micronesia, Federated States of
Mil.	Military
Mn,US	Minnesota
Mo,US	Missouri
Mol.	Moldova
Mon.	Monument
Mona.	Monaco
Mong.	Mongolia
Monts.	Montserrat
Mor.	Morocco
Moz.	Mozambique
Mrsh.	Marshall Islands
Mrta.	Mauritania
Mrts.	Mauritius
Ms,US	Mississippi
Mt.	Mount
Mt,US	Montana
Mtn., Mts.	Mountain, Mountains
Mun. Arpt.	Municipal Airport

N
NAm.	North America
Namb.	Namibia
NAnt.	Netherlands Antilles
Nat'l	National
Nav.	Naval
NB,Can	New Brunswick
Nbrhd.	Neighborhood
NC,US	North Carolina
NCal.	New Caledonia
ND,US	North Dakota
Ne,US	Nebraska
Neth.	Netherlands
Nf,Can	Newfoundland
Nga.	Nigeria
NH,US	New Hampshire
NI,UK	Northern Ireland
Nic.	Nicaragua
NJ,US	New Jersey
NKor.	North Korea
NM,US	New Mexico
NMar.	Northern Mariana Islands
Nor.	Norway
NS,Can	Nova Scotia
Nv,US	Nevada
NW,Can	Northwest Territories
NY,US	New York
NZ	New Zealand

O
Obl.	Oblast
Oh,US	Ohio
Ok,US	Oklahoma
On,Can	Ontario
Or,US	Oregon

P
Pa,US	Pennsylvania
PacUS	Pacific Islands, U.S.
Pak.	Pakistan
Pan.	Panama
Par.	Paraguay
Par.	Parish

PE,Can	Prince Edward Island
Pen.	Peninsula
Phil.	Philippines
Phys. Reg.	Physical Region
Pitc.	Pitcairn Islands
Plat.	Plateau
PNG	Papua New Guinea
Pol.	Poland
Port.	Portugal
Poss.	Possession
Pkwy.	Parkway
PR	Puerto Rico
Pref.	Prefecture
Prov.	Province
Prsv.	Preserve
Pt.	Point

Q
Qu,Can	Quebec

R
Rec.	Recreation(al)
Ref.	Refuge
Reg.	Region
Rep.	Republic
Res.	Reservoir, Reservation
Reun.	Réunion
RI,US	Rhode Island
Riv.	River
Rom.	Romania
Rsv.	Reserve
Rus.	Russia
Rvwy.	Riverway
Rwa.	Rwanda

S
SAfr.	South Africa
SAm.	South America
SaoT.	São Tomé and Príncipe
SAr.	Saudi Arabia
Sc,UK	Scotland
SC,US	South Carolina
SD,US	South Dakota
Seash.	Seashore
Sen.	Senegal
Sey.	Seychelles
SGeo.	South Georgia and Sandwich Islands
Sing.	Singapore
Sk,Can	Saskatchewan
SKor.	South Korea
SLeo.	Sierra Leone
Slov.	Slovenia
Slvk.	Slovakia
SMar.	San Marino
Sol.	Solomon Islands
Som.	Somalia
Sp.	Spain
Spr., Sprs.	Spring, Springs
SrL.	Sri Lanka
Sta.	Station
StH.	Saint Helena
Str.	Strait
StK.	Saint Kitts and Nevis
StL.	Saint Lucia
StP.	Saint Pierre and Miquelon
StV.	Saint Vincent and the Grenadines
Sur.	Suriname

Sval.	Svalbard
Swaz.	Swaziland
Swe.	Sweden
Swi.	Switzerland

T
Tah.	Tahiti
Tai.	Taiwan
Taj.	Tajikistan
Tanz.	Tanzania
Ter.	Terrace
Terr.	Territory
Thai.	Thailand
Tn,US	Tennessee
Tok.	Tokelau
Trg.	Training
Trin.	Trinidad and Tobago
Trkm.	Turkmenistan
Trks.	Turks and Caicos Islands
Tun.	Tunisia
Tun.	Tunnel
Turk.	Turkey
Tuv.	Tuvalu
Twp.	Township
Tx,US	Texas

U
UAE	United Arab Emirates
Ugan.	Uganda
UK	United Kingdom
Ukr.	Ukraine
Uru.	Uruguay
US	United States
USVI	U.S. Virgin Islands
Ut,US	Utah
Uzb.	Uzbekistan

V
Va,US	Virginia
Val.	Valley
Van.	Vanuatu
VatC.	Vatican City
Ven.	Venezuela
Viet.	Vietnam
Vill.	Village
Vol.	Volcano
Vt,US	Vermont

W
Wa,US	Washington
Wal,UK	Wales
Wall.	Wallis and Futuna
WBnk.	West Bank
Wi,US	Wisconsin
Wild.	Wildlife, Wilderness
WSah.	Western Sahara
WSam.	Western Samoa
WV,US	West Virginia
Wy,US	Wyoming

Y
Yem.	Yemen
Yk,Can	Yukon Territory
Yugo.	Yugoslavia

Z
Zam.	Zambia
Zim.	Zimbabwe

A

42/B2 Aa (riv.), Fr.
40/D5 Aa (riv.), Ger.
41/G5 Aa (riv.), Ger.
43/F2 Aachen, Ger.
40/C5 Aalburg, Neth.
45/J2 Aalen, Ger.
40/B4 Aalsmeer, Neth.
42/D2 Aalst, Belg.
40/D5 Aalten, Neth.
42/C1 Aalter, Belg.
45/H3 Aarau, Swi.
45/H3 Aare (riv.), Swi.
43/D2 Aarschot, Belg.
42/D1 Aartselaar, Belg.
62/E5 Aba, China
85/G5 Aba, Nga.
83/M7 Aba, Zaire
60/D5 Abā as Su'ūd, SAr.
92/G5 Abacaxis (riv.), Braz.
86/C5 Abadab, Jabal (peak), Sudan
60/E2 Ābādān, Iran
60/F2 Ābādeh, Iran
95/C1 Abaeté, Braz.
93/J4 Abaetetuba, Braz.
78/G4 Abaiang (atoll), Kiri.
104/D4 Abajo (mts.), Ut,US
56/K4 Abakan, Rus.
92/D6 Abancay, Peru
62/G3 Abaq Qi, China
46/E3 Abarán, Sp.
79/H5 Abariringa (Canton) (atoll), Kiri.
60/F2 Abar Kūh, Iran
63/N3 Abashiri, Japan
56/H5 Abay, Kaz.
83/N6 Ābaya Hayk' (lake), Eth.
68/F1 Abaza, Rus.
48/B1 Abbadia San Salvatore, It.
42/A3 Abbeville, Fr.
112/E4 Abbeville, La,US
113/H3 Abbeville, SC,US
32/E2 Abbey Head (pt.), Sc,UK
76/B3 Abbot (mt.), Austl.
98/T Abbot Ice Shelf, Ant.
33/G6 Abbots Bromley, Eng,UK
34/D5 Abbotsbury, Eng,UK
31/M6 Abbots Langley, Eng,UK
61/K2 Abbottābād, Pak.
40/B4 Abcoude, Neth.
59/E3 'Abd al 'Azīz, Jabal (mts.), Syria
55/K1 Abdulino, Rus.
83/K5 Abéché, Chad
89/E2 Abel Erasmuspas (pass), SAfr.
78/G4 Abemama (atoll), Kiri.
84/E5 Abengourou, IvC.
38/E1 Åbenrå, Den.
45/J2 Abens (riv.), Ger.
85/F5 Abeokuta, Nga.
32/D5 Aber, Wal,UK
34/B2 Aberaeron, Wal,UK
34/C1 Aberangell, Wal,UK
34/B2 Aberath, Wal,UK
34/C3 Abercarn, Wal,UK
34/C3 Aberdare, Wal,UK
32/D6 Aberdaron, Wal,UK
102/G2 Aberdeen (lake), NW,Can
36/D2 Aberdeen, Sc,UK
113/F3 Aberdeen, Ms,US
107/J4 Aberdeen, SD,US
106/C4 Aberdeen, Wa,US
34/B1 Aberdyfi, Wal,UK
36/D2 Aberfeldy, Sc,UK
36/C2 Aberfoyle, Sc,UK
34/C3 Abergavenny, Wal,UK
32/E5 Abergele, Wal,UK
34/B2 Aberporth, Wal,UK
32/D6 Abersoch, Wal,UK
34/C3 Abersychan, Wal,UK
108/B2 Abert (lake), Or,US
34/C3 Abertillery, Wal,UK
34/B2 Aberystwyth, Wal,UK
60/D5 Abhā, SAr.
60/E1 Abhar, Iran
83/P5 Abhe Bad (lake), Djib., Eth.
84/D5 Abidjan, IvC.
65/J7 Abiko, Japan
109/H3 Abilene, Ks,US
112/D3 Abilene, Tx,US
35/E3 Abingdon, Eng,UK
110/D4 Abingdon, Va,US
111/R10 Abino (pt.), On,Can
109/F3 Abiquiu, NM,US
110/E1 Abitibi (lake), On,Can
110/D1 Abitibi (riv.), On,Can
55/G4 Abkhaz Aut. Rep., Geo.
86/B3 Abnūb, Egypt
84/E5 Aboisso, IvC.
85/F5 Abomey, Ben.
50/E2 Abony, Hun.
73/E2 Aborlan, Phil.
37/G3 Åbo (Turku), Fin.
36/D2 Aboyne, Sc,UK
67/D4 Abra (riv.), Phil.
101/G3 Abraham's Bay, Bahm.
46/A3 Abrantes, Port.
91/C1 Abra Pampa, Arg.
86/B4 'Abrī, Sudan
31/P7 Abridge, Eng,UK
50/F2 Abrud, Rom.
48/C1 Abruzzi (reg.), It.
48/C2 Abruzzo Nat'l Park, It.
106/F4 Absaroka (range), Mt, Wy,US
60/F4 Abū al Abyaḑ (isl.), UAE
61/F4 Abu Dhabi (Abū Ẓaby) (cap.), UAE
86/C5 Abū Dīs, Sudan
86/B4 Abu el-Husein, Bîr (well), Egypt
86/C5 Abū Hamad, Sudan
86/C4 Abu Hashim, Bi'r (well), Egypt
59/H6 Abū Ḩummuş, Egypt
85/G4 Abuja (cap.), Nga.
85/G4 Abuja Cap. Terr., Nga.
59/H6 Abū Kabīr, Egypt
60/D2 Abū Kamāl, Syria
65/G2 Abukuma (hills), Japan
65/G2 Abukuma (riv.), Japan
67/D4 Abulog, Phil.
86/A3 Abu Minqâr, Bîr (well), Egypt
92/E6 Abunã (riv.), Bol.
92/E5 Abunã (riv.), Braz.
70/B3 Abu Road, India
86/D4 Abu Shagara, Ras (cape), Sudan
86/B4 Abu Simbel (ruins), Egypt
83/N5 Ābuyē Mēda (peak), Eth.
67/E5 Abuyog, Phil.
61/F4 Abū Ẓaby (Abu Dhabi) (cap.), UAE
48/A4 Abyaḑ, Ar Ra's al (cape), Tun.
86/B3 Abydos (ruins), Egypt
111/G2 Acadia Nat'l Park, Me,US
94/C3 Acajutiba, Braz.
101/N9 Acaponeta, Mex.
100/B4 Acapulco, Mex.
94/B1 Acaraú, Braz.
94/B1 Acaraú (riv.), Braz.
94/C2 Acari, Braz.
92/G5 Acari (riv.), Braz.
101/H6 Acarigua, Ven.
100/B4 Acatlán, Mex.
85/E5 Accra (cap.), Gha.
33/F4 Accrington, Eng,UK
96/B4 Achao, Chile
85/H2 Achegour (well), Niger
63/K2 Acheng, China
31/S10 Achères, Fr.
42/B3 Achicourt, Fr.
42/B3 Achiel-le-Grand, Fr.
111/N6 Achigan (riv.), Qu,Can
56/K4 Achinsk, Rus.
84/D2 Achmîm (well), Mrta.
36/C2 Achnasheen, Sc,UK
43/G3 Acht, Hohe (peak), Ger.
48/D4 Acireale, It.
101/G3 Acklins (isl.), Bahm.
33/G4 Ackworth Moor Top, Eng,UK
76/C4 Acland (peak), Austl.
35/H1 Acle, Eng,UK
96/C2 Aconcagua, Cerro (peak), Arg.
94/C2 Acopiara, Braz.
45/H4 Acqui Terme, It.
74/F6 Acraman (lake), Austl.
92/E6 Acre (riv.), Braz., Peru
95/B1 Acreúna, Braz.
49/L7 Acropolis, Gre.
79/M7 Actaeon Group (isls.), FrPol.
31/N7 Acton, Eng,UK
115/B2 Acton, Ca,US
94/C2 Açu, Braz.
96/Q9 Aculeo (lake), Chile
110/D3 Ada, Oh,US
109/H4 Ada, Ok,US
50/E3 Ada, Yugo.
103/J1 Adair (cape), NW,Can
46/C2 Adaja (riv.), Sp.
114/C6 Adak (isl.), Ak,US
114/C6 Adak (str.), Ak,US
97/M7 Adam (peak), Falk.
95/B2 Adamantina, Braz.
85/H5 Adamawa (plat.), Camr., Nga.
106/D3 Adams (lake), BC,Can
106/C4 Adams (peak), Wa,US
59/C3 Adana, Turk.
51/K5 Adapazarı, Turk.
98/M Adare (cape), Ant.
44/C5 Adarza (mtn.), Fr.
45/H4 Adda (riv.), It.
83/M4 Ad Dabbah, Sudan
60/D3 Ad Dahnā' (des.), SAr.
83/M5 Ad Damazin, Sudan
83/M4 Ad Damīr, Sudan
60/F3 Ad Dammām, SAr.
59/H6 Ad Daqahlīyah (gov.), Egypt
60/F3 Ad Dawḩah (Doha) (cap.), Qatar
59/H6 Ad Dilinjāt, Egypt
83/N6 Addis Ababa (cap.), Eth.
116/Q16 Addison, Il,US
60/D2 Ad Dīwānīyah, Iraq
31/M7 Addlestone, Eng,UK
88/D4 Addo Elephant Nat'l Park, SAfr.
83/M5 Ad Duwaym, Sudan
98/V Adelaide (isl.), Ant.
77/A2 Adelaide, Austl.
102/G2 Adelaide (pen.), NW,Can
88/D4 Adelaide, SAfr.
115/C1 Adelanto, Ca,US
74/C3 Adèle (isl.), Austl.
41/G5 Adelebsen, Ger.
98/K Adélie (coast), Ant.
83/Q5 Aden (gulf), Afr., Asia
60/D6 Aden, Yem.
41/H2 Adendorf, Ger.
73/H4 Adi (isl.), Indo.
45/J4 Adige (Etsch) (riv.), It.
83/N5 Ādīgrat, Eth.
70/C4 Adilābād, India
85/E2 Adiora (well), Mali
110/F2 Adirondack (mts.), NY,US
83/N6 Ādīs Ābeba (Addis Ababa) (cap.), Eth.
83/N5 Ādīs Zemen, Eth.
60/C6 Ādī Ugri, Erit.
59/D3 Adıyaman, Turk.
51/H2 Adjud, Rom.
100/B3 Adjuntas (res.), Mex.
33/F4 Adlington, Eng,UK
74/D2 Admiralty (gulf), Austl.
103/H1 Admiralty (inlet), NW,Can
78/D5 Admiralty (isls.), PNG
116/B2 Admiralty (inlet), Wa,US
114/M4 Admiralty I. Nat'l Mon., Ak,US
65/L9 Ado (riv.), Japan
85/F5 Ado, Nga.
65/M9 Adogawa, Japan
70/C4 Ādoni, India
44/C5 Adour (riv.), Fr.
46/D4 Adra, Sp.
48/D4 Adrano, It.
82/E2 Adrar, Alg.
84/B1 Adrar (reg.), Mrta.
82/E1 Adrar bou Nasser (peak), Mor.
85/F1 Adrar des Iforas (mts.), Mali
83/K5 Adré, Chad
45/K4 Adria, It.
110/C3 Adrian, Mi,US
35/F5 Adur (riv.), Eng,UK
83/N5 Ādwa, Eth.
33/G4 Adwick le Street, Eng,UK
57/P3 Adycha (riv.), Rus.
55/G4 Adzhar Aut. Rep., Geo.
53/N2 Adz'va (riv.), Rus.
49/J3 Aegean (sea), Gre., Turk.
38/F1 Aerø (isl.), Den.
34/B2 Aeron (riv.), Wal,UK
32/E1 Ae, Water of (riv.), Sc,UK
85/F5 Afadjoto (peak), Gha.
79/X15 Afareaitu, FrPol.
59/M8 Afek Nat'l Park, Isr.
44/B3 Aff (riv.), Fr.
61/H2 Afghanistan
83/Q7 Afgooye, Som.
94/C2 Afogados da Ingàzeira, Braz.
114/H3 Afognak (isl.), Ak,US
114/H4 Afognak (mtn.), Ak,US
84/C2 Afollé (reg.), Mrta.
95/D2 Afonso Cláudio, Braz.
48/D2 Afragola, It.
80/* Africa
59/D2 Afşin, Turk.
40/C2 Afsluitdijk (IJsselmeer) (dam), Neth.
41/F5 Afte (riv.), Ger.
106/F5 Afton, Wy,US
59/K5 'Afula, Isr.
59/B2 Afyon, Turk.
82/H4 Agadem, Niger
85/G2 Agadez, Niger
85/H2 Agadez (dept.), Niger
82/D1 Agadir, Mor.
81/H6 Agalega (isls.), Mrts.
85/F2 Agamor (well), Mali
78/D3 Agaña (cap.), Guam
65/F2 Agano (riv.), Japan
83/N6 Āgaro, Eth.
71/F3 Agartala, India
98/V Agassiz (cape), Ant.
103/T6 Agassiz (ice field), NW,Can
109/G2 Agate Fossil Beds Nat'l Mon., Ne,US
114/A5 Agattu (isl.), Ak,US
114/A5 Agattu (str.), Ak,US
85/G5 Agbor, Nga.
84/D5 Agboville, IvC.
55/H5 Agdam, Azer.
44/E5 Agde, Fr.
44/E5 Agde, Cap d' (cape), Fr.
44/D4 Agen, Fr.
65/H7 Ageo, Japan
38/E1 Agerbæk, Den.
41/E6 Agger (riv.), Ger.
50/E1 Aggteleki Nat'l Park, Hun.
32/B3 Aghagallon, NI,UK
60/E2 Āghā Jārī, Iran
101/N8 Agiabampo, Estero de (bay), Mex.
62/G1 Aginskoye, Rus.
32/B1 Agivey, NI,UK
44/E5 Agly (riv.), Fr.
51/G3 Agnita, Rom.
65/M10 Ago, Japan
45/H4 Agogna (riv.), It.
115/B2 Agoura Hills, Ca,US
44/D5 Agout (riv.), Fr.
70/C2 Āgra, India
48/E2 Agri (riv.), It.
55/H5 Ağri (Ararat) (peak), Turk.
48/C4 Agrigento, It.
78/D3 Agrihan (isl.), NMar.
49/G3 Agrinion, Gre.
96/C3 Agrio (riv.), Arg.
48/D2 Agropoli, It.
53/M4 Agryz, Rus.
101/G6 Aguachica, Col.
101/H4 Aguadilla, PR
100/C4 Agua Dulce, Mex.
101/E6 Aguadulce, Pan.
95/F7 Aguaí, Braz.
47/P10 Agualva-Cacém, Port.
100/D4 Aguan (riv.), Hon.
95/B2 Aguapeí (riv.), Braz.
101/N7 Agua Prieta, Mex.
101/H6 Aguaro-Guariquito Nat'l Park, Ven.
95/A1 Águas (hills), Braz.
94/C3 Águas Belas, Braz.
100/A3 Aguascalientes, Mex.
100/A3 Aguascalientes (state), Mex.
95/G6 Águas da Prata, Braz.
95/G7 Águas de Lindóia, Braz.
94/B5 Águas Formosas, Braz.
95/B1 Aguavermelha (res.), Braz.
95/B2 Agudos, Braz.
46/A2 Águeda, Port.
46/B2 Agueda (riv.), Sp.
82/C3 Agüenit, WSah.
65/M10 Agui, Japan
78/D3 Aguijan (isl.), NMar.
46/C4 Aguilar, Sp.
46/C1 Aguilar de Campóo, Sp.
91/C2 Aguilares, Arg.
46/E4 Aguilas, Sp.
101/P10 Aguililla de Iturbide, Mex.
47/X17 Agüimes, Canl.,Sp.
101/G5 Aguja (cape), Col.
88/M11 Agulhas (cape), SAfr.
95/C2 Agulhas Negras (peak), Braz.
73/E5 Agung (vol.), Indo.
67/E6 Agusan (riv.), Phil.
101/G5 Agustín Codazzi, Col.
82/G3 Ahaggar (plat.), Alg.
40/E4 Ahaus, Ger.
43/F3 Ahbach (riv.), Ger.
59/E2 Ahlat, Turk.
41/E5 Ahlen, Ger.
70/B3 Ahmadābād, India
70/B4 Ahmadnagar, India
61/K3 Ahmadpur East, Pak.
83/P6 Ahmar (mts.), Eth.
32/B2 Ahoghill, NI,UK
43/F3 Ahr (riv.), Ger.
41/H1 Ahrensburg, Ger.
41/F5 Ahse (riv.), Ger.
101/P9 Ahuacatlán, Mex.
104/W13 Ahuimanu, Hi,US
101/N7 Ahumada, Mex.
60/E2 Ahvāz, Iran
37/F4 Ahvenanmaa (prov.), Fin.
88/B2 Ai-Ais Hot Springs, Namb.
66/B2 Aibag Gol (riv.), China
65/E3 Aichi (pref.), Japan
104/W13 Aiea, Hi,US
44/E4 Aigoual (mtn.), Fr.
44/F4 Aigues (riv.), Fr.
47/F1 Aigues Tortes y Lago de San Mauricio Nat'l Park, Sp.
81/Q16 Aiguille, Cap de l' (cape), Alg.
65/F1 Aikawa, Japan
113/H3 Aiken, SC,US
101/F6 Ailigandí, Pan.
78/F4 Ailinglapalap (atoll), Mrsh.
32/C1 Ailsa Craig (isl.), Sc,UK
78/G3 Ailuk (atoll), Mrsh.
66/C5 Aimen Guan (pass), China
95/D1 Aimorés, Braz.
44/F4 Ain (riv.), Fr.
81/V18 'Aïn Beïda, Alg.
81/S15 'Aïn Beniau, Alg.
82/D2 'Aïn Ben Tili, Mrta.
81/S15 'Aïn Bessem, Alg.
81/R15 'Aïn Defla, Alg.
81/Q16 'Aïn el Turk, Alg.
81/V17 'Aïn Fakroun, Alg.
81/V17 'Aïn M'Lila, Alg.
49/G3 Aínos (peak), Gre.
49/G3 Aínos Nat'l Park, Gre.
81/U18 'Aïn Oulmene, Alg.
81/S16 'Aïn Oussersa, Alg.
33/E4 Ainsdale, Eng,UK
82/E1 'Aïn Sefra, Alg.
109/H2 Ainsworth, Ne,US
81/S15 'Aïn Taya, Alg.
81/Q16 'Aïn Temouchent, Alg.
81/U18 'Aïn Touta, Alg.
85/G2 Aïr (plat.), Niger
106/E3 Airdrie, Ab,Can
36/D3 Airdrie, Sc,UK
42/D5 Aire (riv.), Fr.
33/G4 Aire (riv.), Eng,UK
42/B2 Aire, Canal de (can.), Fr.
33/E5 Aire, Point of (pt.), Wal,UK
42/B2 Aire-sur-la-Lys, Fr.
103/J2 Air Force (isl.), NW,Can
33/F3 Airton, Eng,UK
45/J2 Aisch (riv.), Ger.
42/D3 Aiseau-Presles, Belg.
96/B5 Aisén del General Carlos Ibáñez del Campo (reg.), Chile
66/E3 Ai Shan (mtn.), China
114/L3 Aishihik, Yk,Can
43/E3 Aisne (riv.), Belg.
42/C4 Aisne (dept.), Fr.
42/C5 Aisne (riv.), Fr.
82/E1 Aïssa (peak), Alg.
65/M9 Aitō, Japan
79/J6 Aitutaki (atoll), Cookls.
51/F2 Aiud, Rom.
95/J7 Aiuruoca (riv.), Braz.
44/F5 Aix-en-Provence, Fr.
44/F4 Aix-les-Bains, Fr.
49/H4 Aíyina, Gre.
49/H3 Aíyion, Gre.
65/F2 Aizu-Wakamatsu, Japan
71/F3 Aīzwal, India
43/A2 Ajaccio, Fr.
43/A2 Ajaccio (gulf), Fr.
111/R8 Ajax, On,Can
62/D3 Aj Bogd (peak), Mong.
82/K1 Ajdābiyā, Libya
83/C5 Aj Janayet, Sudan
50/C2 Ajka, Hun.
70/B2 Ajmer, India
108/D4 Ajo, Az,US
46/D1 Ajo, Cabo de (cape), Sp.
100/A4 Ajuchitlán, Mex.
65/F1 Aka (riv.), Japan
65/N10 Akabane, Japan
65/F1 Akademik Obruchev (mts.), Rus.
63/F3 Akaishi-dake (mtn.), Japan
86/B4 Akasha East, Sudan
64/D3 Akashi, Japan
65/K10 Akashi (str.), Japan
68/B4 Akbaytal (pass), Taj.
81/T15 Akbou, Alg.
59/D2 Akçaabat, Turk.
59/D3 Akçakale, Turk.
51/K5 Akçakoca, Turk.
84/B2 Akchâr (reg.), Mrta.
59/C2 Akdağmadeni, Turk.
60/G4 Akdar, Al Jabal (mts.), Oman
65/N9 Akechi, Japan
37/D3 Akershus (co.), Nor.
83/K7 Aketi, Zaire
55/G4 Akhaltsikhe, Geo.
45/H3 Akharnaí, Gre.
45/G3 Akhelóos (riv.), Gre.
55/A2 Akhisar, Turk.
86/B3 Akhmīm, Egypt
55/H3 Akhtuba (riv.), Rus.
55/H2 Akhtubinsk, Rus.
54/E2 Akhtyrka, Ukr.
84/C4 Aki, Japan
65/H7 Aki (riv.), Japan
65/H7 Akigawa, Japan
102/H3 Akimiski (isl.), NW,Can
65/H7 Akishima, Japan
63/N4 Akita, Japan
84/B2 Akjoujt, Mrta.
70/D6 Akkaraipattu, SrL.
59/K5 'Akko, Isr.
84/D2 'Aklé 'Aouâna (dune), Mali, Mrta.
64/D3 Akō, Japan
82/H7 Akoga, Gabon
70/C3 Akola, India
83/N4 Āk'ordat, Erit.
85/F5 Akosombo (dam), Gha.
103/K2 Akpatok (isl.), NW,Can
68/C3 Akqi, China
49/J2 Ákrathos, Ákra (cape), Gre.
37/C4 Åkrehamn, Nor.
49/G4 Akrítas, Ákra (cape), Gre.
109/G2 Akron, Co,US
110/D3 Akron, Oh,US
68/C4 Aksai Chin (reg.), China, India
59/C2 Aksaray, Turk.
62/C4 Aksay, China
55/K2 Aksay, Kaz.
59/B2 Akşehir, Turk.
59/B2 Akşehir (lake), Turk.
68/C2 Aksoran (peak), Kaz.
68/D3 Aksu, China
68/C3 Aksu (riv.), China
68/C2 Aksu (riv.), Kaz.
83/N5 Āksum, Eth.
49/J2 Aktí (pen.), Gre.
55/L2 Aktyubinsk, Kaz.
55/L2 Aktyubinsk Obl., Kaz.
64/B4 Akune, Japan
37/N6 Akureyri, Ice.
114/E5 Akutan (isl.), Ak,US
114/E5 Akutan (passg.), Ak,US
85/G5 Akwa Ibom (state), Nga.
71/F3 Akyab (Sittwe), Burma
55/L2 Ak"yar, Rus.
51/K5 Akyazı, Turk.
62/B3 Ala (riv.), China
113/G3 Alabama (state), US
113/G4 Alabama (riv.), Al,US
113/G3 Alabaster, Al,US
59/C2 Alaca, Turk.
59/C2 Alaçam, Turk.
113/H4 Alachua, Fl,US
55/H4 Alagir, Rus.
44/E4 Alagnon (riv.), Fr.
94/D2 Alagoa Grande, Braz.
94/D3 Alagoas (state), Braz.
94/C4 Alagoinhas, Braz.
46/B2 Alagón (riv.), Sp.
37/G3 Alajärvi, Fin.
100/E5 Alajuela, CR
68/D2 Alakol' (lake), Kaz.
86/B2 Al 'Alamayn (El Alamein), Egypt
78/D3 Alamagan (isl.), NMar.
60/E2 Al 'Amārah, Iraq
60/F3 'Alāmarvdasht (riv.), Iran
116/K11 Alameda, Ca,US
100/E5 Alamikamba, Nic.
100/B3 Alamo, Mex.
108/D4 Alamo (lake), Az,US
116/K11 Alamo, Ca,US
108/D3 Alamo, Nv,US
109/F4 Alamogordo, NM,US
101/N8 Álamos, Mex.
109/F3 Alamosa, Co,US
37/G3 Åland (isls.), Fin.
38/F2 Aland (riv.), Ger.
59/C3 Alanya, Turk.
89/J7 Alaotra (lake), Madg.
113/H4 Alapaha (riv.), Ga,US
51/K5 Alaplı, Turk.
46/D3 Alarcón (res.), Sp.
59/B2 Alaşehir, Turk.
59/L6 Al 'Āsimah (gov.), Jor.
114/* Alaska (state), US
114/J4 Alaska (gulf), Ak,US
114/F4 Alaska (pen.), Ak,US
114/H3 Alaska (range), Ak,US
114/B5 Alaska Maritime Nat'l Wild. Ref., Ak,US
114/G4 Alaska Pen. Nat'l Wild. Ref., Ak,US
45/H5 Alassio, It.
53/K5 Alatyr', Rus.
55/H4 Alaverdi, Arm.
37/G3 Alavus, Fin.
32/D5 Alaw (riv.), Wal,UK
32/D5 Alaw, Llyn (lake), Wal,UK
68/B4 Alayskiy (mts.), Kyr.
57/R3 Alazeya (riv.), Rus.
60/E2 Al 'Azīzīyah, Iraq
82/H1 Al 'Azīzīyah, Libya
45/H4 Alba, It.
51/F2 Alba (co.), Rom.
59/D3 Al Bāb, Syria
46/E3 Albacete, Sp.
86/C3 Al Baḩr al Aḩmar (gov.), Egypt
51/F2 Alba Iulia, Rom.
59/K5 Al Balqā' (gov.), Jor.
86/C3 Al Balyanā, Egypt
111/F1 Albanel (lake), Qu,Can
49/F2 Albania
74/B5 Albany, Austl.
103/H3 Albany (riv.), On,Can
116/K11 Albany, Ca,US
113/G4 Albany, Ga,US
110/C4 Albany, Ky,US
110/F3 Albany (cap.), NY,US
106/C4 Albany, Or,US
60/E2 Al Başrah, Iraq
74/G2 Albatross (bay), Austl.
88/A2 Albatross (pt.), Namb.
86/B2 Al Bawīţī, Egypt
83/K1 Al Bayḑā, Libya
113/H3 Albemarle, NC,US
113/J2 Albemarle (sound), NC,US
45/H4 Albenga, It.
46/C2 Alberche (riv.), Sp.
74/E5 Alberga (riv.), Austl.
77/A2 Albert (inlet), Austl.
74/F7 Albert (lake), Austl.
43/E2 Albert (can.), Belg.
42/B4 Albert, Fr.
83/M7 Albert (lake), Ugan., Zaire
102/E3 Alberta (prov.), Can.
96/E2 Alberti, Arg.
50/D2 Albertirsa, Hun.
107/K5 Albert Lea, Mn,US
83/M7 Albert Nile (riv.), Ugan.
97/J8 Alberto de Agostini Nat'l Park, Chile
88/Q13 Alberton, SAfr.
45/G4 Albertville, Fr.
113/G3 Albertville, Al,US
44/E5 Albi, Fr.
45/H4 Albino, It.
110/C3 Albion, Mi,US
109/H2 Albion, Ne,US
59/L4 Al Biqā' (gov.), Leb.
59/K5 Al Biqā' (Bekaa) (val.), Leb.
59/K6 Al Bīrah, WBnk.
40/B5 Alblasserdam, Neth.
37/D4 Ålborg, Den.
46/D4 Albox, Sp.
34/D1 Albrighton, Eng,UK
46/A4 Albufeira, Port.
59/H6 Al Buḩayrah (gov.), Egypt
45/H3 Albula (riv.), Swi.
108/F4 Albuquerque, NM,US
46/B3 Alburquerque, Sp.
77/C3 Albury, Austl.
47/P10 Alcabideche, Port.
46/A3 Alcácer do Sal, Port.
46/C4 Alcalá de Guadaira, Sp.
46/D2 Alcalá de Henares, Sp.
46/D4 Alcalá la Real, Sp.
48/C4 Alcamo, It.
47/E2 Alcanadre (riv.), Sp.
47/E2 Alcanar, Sp.
47/E2 Alcañiz, Sp.
46/B3 Alcantara (res.), Sp.
46/E4 Alcantarilla, Sp.
46/D3 Alcarez (range), Sp.
116/K11 Alcatraz (isl.), Ca,US
46/D3 Alcaudete, Sp.
46/D3 Alcázar de San Juan, Sp.
35/E2 Alcester, Eng,UK
47/E3 Alcira, Sp.
113/H3 Alcoa, Tn,US
46/D2 Alcobendas, Sp.
47/Q10 Alcochete, Port.
47/E2 Alcora, Sp.
46/D2 Alcorcón, Sp.
113/H3 Alcovy (riv.), Ga,US
47/E3 Alcoy, Sp.
81/G5 Aldabra (isls.), Sey.
112/B4 Aldama, Mex.
57/N4 Aldan, Rus.
57/N4 Aldan (plat.), Rus.
57/P3 Aldan (riv.), Rus.
68/G2 Aldarhaan, Mong.
35/E4 Aldbourne, Eng,UK
33/H4 Aldbrough, Eng,UK
35/H2 Alde (riv.), Eng,UK
35/H2 Aldeburgh, Eng,UK
87/B2 Aldeia Viçosa, Ang.
43/F2 Aldenhoven, Ger.
32/B2 Aldergrove, NI,UK
33/F5 Alderley Edge, Eng,UK
35/E4 Aldermaston, Eng,UK
111/Q9 Aldershot, On,Can
35/F4 Aldershot, Eng,UK
116/C2 Alderwood Manor-Bothell North, Wa,US
112/E4 Aldine, Tx,US
35/E1 Aldridge, Eng,UK
84/B2 Aleg, Mrta.
95/D2 Alegre, Braz.
91/E2 Alegrete, Braz.
90/A6 Alejandro Selkirk (isl.), Chile
54/E2 Aleksandriya, Ukr.
52/H4 Aleksandrov, Rus.
53/N4 Aleksandrovsk, Rus.
63/N1 Aleksandrovsk-Sakhalinskiy, Rus.
33/K2 Aleksandrów Kujawski, Pol.
39/K3 Aleksandrów Łódzki, Pol.
68/B1 Alekseyevka, Kaz.
54/F2 Alekseyevka, Rus.
52/H5 Aleksin, Rus.
50/E4 Aleksinac, Yugo.
95/L8 Além Paraíba, Braz.
44/D2 Alençon, Fr.
93/H4 Alenquer, Braz.
104/T10 Alenuihaha (chan.), Hi,US
59/D3 Aleppo (Ḩalab), Syria
96/B4 Alerce Andino Nat'l Park, Chile
103/S6 Alert (pt.), NW,Can
50/F2 Aleşd, Rom.
45/H4 Alessandria, It.
37/C3 Ålesund, Nor.
114/E5 Aleutian (isls.), Ak,US
114/G4 Aleutian (range), Ak,US
98/V Alexander (cape), Ant.
98/V Alexander (isl.), Ant.
114/L4 Alexander (arch.), Ak,US
113/G3 Alexander City, Al,US
75/Q12 Alexandra, NZ
94/C2 Alexandria, Braz.
49/H2 Alexándria, Gre.
51/G4 Alexandria, Rom.
112/E4 Alexandria, La,US
107/K4 Alexandria, Mn,US
115/J8 Alexandria, Va,US
59/G6 Alexandria (Al Iskandarīyah), Egypt
77/A2 Alexandrina (lake), Austl.
49/J2 Alexandroúpolis, Gre.
106/C2 Alexis Creek, BC,Can
68/D1 Aley (riv.), Rus.
68/D1 Aleysk, Rus.
47/E3 Alfafar, Sp.
60/D2 Al Fallūjah, Iraq
47/P10 Alfama, Port.
47/P11 Alfarim, Port.
46/E1 Alfaro, Sp.
83/L5 Al Fāsher, Sudan
86/B2 Al Fashn, Egypt
60/D1 Al Fatḩah, Iraq
60/E3 Al Fāw, Iraq
86/B2 Al Fayyūm, Egypt
43/F3 Alfbach (riv.), Ger.
41/G5 Alfeld, Ger.
95/H6 Alfenas, Braz.
49/G4 Alfiós (riv.), Gre.
33/J5 Alford, Eng,UK
77/D3 Alfred Nat'l Park, Austl.
33/G5 Alfreton, Eng,UK
35/G5 Alfriston, Eng,UK
43/G2 Alfter, Ger.
55/L2 Alga, Kaz.
37/C4 Ålgård, Nor.
46/C4 Algeciras, Sp.
47/E3 Algemesí, Sp.
81/S15 Alger (Algiers) (cap.), Alg.
82/F2 Algeria
41/G4 Algermissen, Ger.
47/N8 Algete, Sp.
86/B2 Al Gharbīyah (gov.), Egypt
48/A2 Alghero, It.
86/C3 Al Ghurdaqah, Egypt
81/S15 Algiers (Alger) (cap.), Alg.
47/E3 Alginet, Sp.
88/D4 Algoa (bay), SAfr.
92/D4 Algodón (riv.), Peru
116/P15 Algonquin, Il,US
47/P10 Algueirão, Port.
60/D2 Al Ḩadīthah, Iraq
59/E3 Al Ḩaḑr, Iraq
61/G4 Al Ḩajar ash Sharqī (mts.), Oman
61/G5 Al Ḩallānīyah (isl.), Oman
46/D4 Alhama de Granada, Sp.
46/E4 Alhama de Murcia, Sp.
115/B2 Alhambra, Ca,US
86/B2 Al Ḩammām, Egypt
47/Q10 Alhandra, Port.
59/E3 Al Ḩasakah, Syria
46/C4 Alhaurín el Grande, Sp.
86/B2 Al Ḩawāmidīyah, Egypt
60/E2 Al Ḩayy, Iraq
60/D2 Al Ḩillah, Iraq
60/D2 Al Hindīyah, Iraq
81/N13 Al Hoceima, Mor.
81/N13 Al Hoceima (isl.), Sp.
60/E3 Al Hufūf, SAr.
59/A2 Aliağa, Turk.
49/G2 Aliákmon (riv.), Gre.
49/G2 Aliákmonos (lake), Gre.
60/E2 'Alī al Gharbī, Iraq
60/E2 'Alī ash Sharqī, Iraq
112/C3 Alibates Flint Quarries Nat'l Mon., Tx,US
55/J5 Ali-Bayramly, Azer.
86/C5 Al Ibēdiyya, Sudan
51/J5 Alibeyköy, Turk.
47/E3 Alicante, Sp.
76/A1 Alice (riv.), Austl.
48/E3 Alice (pt.), It.
112/D5 Alice, Tx,US
74/E4 Alice Springs, Austl.
113/F3 Aliceville, Al,US
67/D6 Alicia, Phil.
67/C6 Alicia Annie (shoal)
48/D3 Alicudi (isl.), It.
70/C2 Alīgarh, India
60/E2 Alīgudarz, Iran
82/J8 Alima (riv.), Congo
37/E4 Alingsås, Swe.
70/B2 Alīpur, Pak.
70/E2 Alīpur Duār, India
59/G6 Al Iskandarīyah (gov.), Egypt
59/G6 Al Iskandarīyah (Alexandria), Egypt
86/C2 Al Ismā'īlīyah (gov.), Egypt
86/C2 Al Ismā'īlīyah (Ismalia), Egypt
88/D3 Aliwal North, SAfr.
83/K2 Al Jaghbūb, Libya
81/X18 Al Jamm, Tun.
59/K5 Al Janūb (gov.), Leb.
86/B2 Al Jīzah, Egypt
86/B2 Al Jīzah (gov.), Egypt
83/K5 Al Junaynah, Sudan
46/A4 Aljustrel, Port.
81/W17 Al Kāf, Tun.
81/W17 Al Kāf (gov.), Tun.
59/K6 Al Karak, Jor.
59/L6 Al Karak (gov.), Jor.
86/C3 Al Karnak, Egypt
43/E2 Alken, Belg.
61/G4 Al Khābūrah, Oman
59/K6 Al Khalīl (Hebron), WBnk.
60/D2 Al Khāliş, Iraq
86/B5 Al Khandaq, Sudan
86/B3 Al Khārijah, Egypt
83/M4 Al Kharţūm Baḩrī (Khartoum North), Sudan
60/F3 Al Khobar, SAr.
82/H1 Al Khums, Libya
40/B3 Alkmaar, Neth.
82/H3 Alkoum (well), Alg.
60/D2 Al Kūfah, Iraq
83/K3 Al Kufrah, Libya
60/E2 Al Kūt, Iraq
50/E3 Al Kuwait (Kuwait) (cap.), Kuw.
59/K4 Al Lādhiqīyah (Latakia), Syria
70/D2 Allahābād, India
107/G3 Allan, Sk,Can
107/G3 Allan (hills), Sk,Can
111/R9 Allanburg, On,Can
71/G4 Allanmyo, Burma
107/L3 Allan Water (riv.), On,Can
82/H1 'Allāq (well), Libya
86/C4 'Allāqī, Wādī al (dry riv.), Egypt
110/C3 Allegan, Mi,US
105/K4 Allegheny (mts.), US
110/E3 Allegheny (plat.), Pa,US
110/E3 Allegheny (riv.), Pa,US
96/D3 Allen, Arg.
34/B5 Allen (riv.), Eng,UK
32/B5 Allen, Bog of (swamp), Ire.
33/F2 Allendale, Eng,UK
113/H3 Allendale, SC,US
100/A2 Allende, Mex.
116/F7 Allen Park, Mi,US
115/E5 Allentown, Pa,US
70/C6 Alleppey, India
41/G3 Aller (riv.), Ger.
41/H4 Allerkanal (can.), Ger.
45/J3 Allgäu (mts.), Aus., Ger.
109/G2 Alliance, Ne,US
110/D3 Alliance, Oh,US
44/E3 Allier (riv.), Fr.
44/D3 Allones, Fr.
111/G1 Alma, Qu,Can
110/C3 Alma, Mi,US
109/H2 Alma, Ne,US
68/C3 Alma-Ata (cap.), Kaz.
46/A3 Almada, Port.
46/C3 Almadén, Sp.
60/B3 Al Madīnah al Fikrīyah, Egypt
81/X18 Al Madīyah, Tun.
81/X18 Al Madīyah (gov.), Tun.
59/L5 Al Mafraq, Jor.
96/D2 Almafuerte, Arg.
82/E1 Al Maghrib (reg.), Alg., Mor.
46/D3 Almagro, Sp.
59/H6 Al Maḩallah al Kubrá, Egypt
59/H6 Al Maḩmūdīyah, Egypt
60/D2 Al Maḩmūdīyah, Iraq
59/E3 Al Mālikīyah, Syria
68/A3 Almalyk, Uzb.
60/F3 Al Manāmah (Manama) (cap.), Bahr.
108/B2 Almanor (lake), Ca,US
47/E3 Almansa, Sp.
59/H6 Al Manşūra, Egypt

124
Al Man – Arlin

59/H6 **Al Manzilah**, Egypt
46/D4 **Almanzora** (riv.), Sp.
46/C2 **Almanzor, Pico de** (peak), Sp.
86/B3 **Al Marāghah**, Egypt
82/K1 **Al Marj**, Libya
94/B4 **Almas** (peak), Braz.
93/J6 **Almas** (riv.), Braz.
59/J6 **Al Maṭarīyah**, Egypt
59/E3 **Al Mawṣil** (Mosul), Iraq
60/D1 **Al Mayādin**, Syria
47/E3 **Almazora**, Sp.
41/F5 **Alme** (riv.), Ger.
46/A3 **Almeirim**, Port.
40/D4 **Almelo**, Neth.
94/B5 **Almenara**, Braz.
46/D3 **Almenara** (mtn.), Sp.
46/B2 **Almendra** (res.), Sp.
46/B3 **Almendralejo**, Sp.
40/C4 **Almere**, Neth.
46/D4 **Almería**, Sp.
47/D4 **Almería** (gulf), Sp.
53/M5 **Al'met'yevsk**, Rus.
37/E4 **Älmhult**, Swe.
46/C5 **Almina** (pt.), Sp.
86/B2 **Al Minūfīyah** (gov.), Egypt
86/B2 **Al Minyā**, Egypt
86/B3 **Al Minyā** (gov.), Egypt
60/D2 **Al Miqdādiyah**, Iraq
97/J7 **Almirante Montt** (gulf), Chile
49/H3 **Almirós**, Gre.
49/J5 **Almiroú** (gulf), Gre.
46/C3 **Almodóvar del Campo**, Sp.
46/C4 **Almodóvar del Río**, Sp.
36/D2 **Almond** (riv.), Sc,UK
31/U11 **Almont** (riv.), Fr.
110/E2 **Almonte**, On,Can
46/B4 **Almonte**, Sp.
47/E3 **Almoradí**, Sp.
95/D1 **Almores** (range), Braz.
60/E3 **Al Mubarraz**, SAr.
83/L5 **Al Muglad**, Sudan
81/X18 **Al Muknīn**, Tun.
81/X18 **Al Munastīr**, Tun.
81/X18 **Al Munastīr** (gov.), Tun.
46/D4 **Almuñécar**, Sp.
36/C2 **Alness**, Sc,UK
79/J6 **Alofi** (cap.), Niue
78/H6 **Alofi** (isl.), Wall.
71/G2 **Along**, India
49/H3 **Alónnisos** (isl.), Gre.
73/F5 **Alor** (isls.), Indo.
46/C4 **Álora**, Sp.
72/B2 **Alor Setar**, Malay.
78/E6 **Alotau**, PNG
40/D5 **Alpen**, Ger.
110/D2 **Alpena**, Mi,US
94/A2 **Alpercatas** (mts.), Braz.
94/A2 **Alpercatas** (riv.), Braz.
40/B4 **Alphen aan de Rijn**, Neth.
46/A3 **Alpiarça**, Port.
112/C4 **Alpine**, Tx,US
106/F5 **Alpine**, Wy,US
46/B4 **Alportel**, Port.
45/G4 **Alps** (mts.), Eur.
65/F3 **Alps-Minami Nat'l Park**, Japan
61/G4 **Al Qābil**, Oman
83/N5 **Al Qaḍīrif**, Sudan
86/B2 **Al Qāhirah** (Cairo) (cap.), Egypt
59/E3 **Al Qāmishlī**, Syria
86/B3 **Al Qaṣr**, Egypt
81/W18 **Al Qaṣrayn**, Tun.
81/W18 **Al Qaṣrayn** (gov.), Tun.
83/M5 **Al Qaṭaynah**, Sudan
82/H3 **Al Qaṭrūn**, Libya
81/X18 **Al Qayrawān**, Tun.
81/W18 **Al Qayrawān** (gov.), Tun.
59/K5 **Al Qunayṭirah** (prov.), Syria
86/C3 **Al Quṣayr**, Egypt
59/L4 **Al Quṣayr**, Syria
59/L5 **Al Quṭayfah**, Syria
35/E1 **Alrewas**, Eng,UK
38/F1 **Als** (isl.), Den.
45/G2 **Alsace** (reg.), Fr.
38/D5 **Alsace, Ballon d'** (mtn.), Fr.
33/F5 **Alsager**, Eng,UK
106/F3 **Alsask**, Sk,Can
46/D1 **Alsasua**, Sp.
43/F2 **Alsdorf**, Ger.
38/E3 **Alsfeld**, Ger.
116/Q16 **Alsip**, Il,US
41/H1 **Alster** (riv.), Ger.
33/F2 **Alston**, Eng,UK
33/F4 **Alt** (riv.), Eng,UK
37/G1 **Alta**, Nor.
115/B2 **Altadena**, Ca,US
93/G6 **Alta Floresta**, Braz.
96/D1 **Alta Gracia**, Arg.
100/D5 **Alta Gracia**, Nic.
68/D1 **Altai** (mts.), Asia
113/H4 **Altamaha** (riv.), Ga,US
93/H4 **Altamira**, Braz.
100/B3 **Altamira**, Mex.
113/H4 **Altamonte Springs**, Fl,US
48/E2 **Altamura**, It.
100/C4 **Altar de los Sacrificios** (ruins), Guat.
62/B2 **Altay**, China
56/J4 **Altay** (kray), Rus.
45/H3 **Altdorf**, Swi.
45/J2 **Altdorf bei Nürnberg**, Ger.
47/E3 **Altea**, Sp.
41/E6 **Altena**, Ger.
41/F5 **Altenau** (riv.), Ger.
41/F5 **Altenbeken**, Ger.
38/G3 **Altenburg**, Ger.
39/G2 **Altentreptow**, Ger.
101/P8 **Alteres**, Mex.
40/D5 **Alter Rhein** (riv.), Ger.
41/G1 **Altes Land** (reg.), Ger.
33/H4 **Althorpe**, Eng,UK
92/E7 **Altiplano** (plat.), Bol., Peru
38/F2 **Altmark** (reg.), Ger.
45/J2 **Altmühl** (riv.), Ger.
45/K3 **Altmünster**, Aus.
94/A4 **Alto** (peak), Braz.
93/H7 **Alto Araguaia**, Braz.
87/C2 **Alto Cuale**, Ang.
35/F4 **Alton**, Eng,UK
110/B4 **Alton**, Il,US
77/F5 **Altona**, Austl.
107/J3 **Altona**, Mb,Can
110/E3 **Altoona**, Pa,US
94/A3 **Alto Parnaíba**, Braz.
92/D6 **Alto Purús** (riv.), Peru
94/B2 **Altos**, Braz.
94/C2 **Alto Santo**, Braz.
33/F5 **Altrincham**, Eng,UK
62/C4 **Altun** (mts.), China
100/D4 **Altun Ha** (ruins), Belz.
108/B2 **Alturas**, Ca,US
109/H4 **Altus**, Ok,US
109/H4 **Altus** (res.), Ok,US
109/H4 **Altus A.F.B.**, Ok,US
83/M5 **Al Ubayyiḍ**, Sudan
83/L5 **Al Uḍayyah**, Sudan
32/E5 **Alun** (riv.), Wal,UK
86/C3 **Al Uqṣur** (Luxor), Egypt
54/E3 **Alushta**, Ukr.
83/L3 **Al 'Uwaynāt** (peak), Sudan
109/H3 **Alva**, Ok,US
35/E2 **Alvechurch**, Eng,UK
46/A3 **Alverca**, Port.
47/P10 **Alverca do Ribatejo**, Port.
37/E4 **Alvesta**, Swe.
34/D4 **Alveston**, Eng,UK
112/E4 **Alvin**, Tx,US
37/F3 **Älvkarleby**, Swe.
37/E4 **Älvsborg** (co.), Swe.
37/G2 **Älvsbyn**, Swe.
86/B3 **Al Wādī al Jadīd** (gov.), Egypt
70/C2 **Alwar**, India
62/E4 **Alxa Youqi**, China
62/F4 **Alxa Zuoqi**, China
39/N1 **Alytus**, Lith.
45/K2 **Alz** (riv.), Ger.
45/H4 **Alzano Lombardo**, It.
43/F4 **Alzette** (riv.), Lux.
86/C2 **Al 'Aqabah**, Jor.
92/D4 **Amacayacú Nat'l Park**, Col.
60/B4 **Amada** (ruins), Egypt
74/E4 **Amadeus** (lake), Austl.
83/M6 **Amadi**, Sudan
103/J2 **Amadjuak** (lake), NW,Can
46/A3 **Amadora**, Port.
65/L10 **Amagasaki**, Japan
64/B4 **Amagi**, Japan
65/F3 **Amagi-san** (mtn.), Japan
73/G4 **Amahai**, Indo.
64/A4 **Amakusa** (sea), Japan
37/E4 **Åmål**, Swe.
62/G1 **Amalat** (riv.), Rus.
49/G4 **Amaliás**, Gre.
70/C3 **Amalner**, India
91/E1 **Amambaí**, Braz.
93/H8 **Amambaí** (riv.), Braz.
78/B2 **Amami** (isls.), Japan
48/E3 **Amantea**, It.
79/L6 **Amanu** (atoll), FrPol.
94/B2 **Amarante**, Braz.
46/A2 **Amarante**, Port.
69/B1 **Amarapura**, Burma
94/C4 **Amargosa**, Braz.
108/C3 **Amargosa** (dry riv.), Ca, Nv,US
112/C3 **Amarillo**, Tx,US
48/D1 **Amaro** (peak), It.
59/C2 **Amasya**, Turk.
65/J7 **Amatsukominato**, Japan
42/E2 **Amay**, Belg.
93/H4 **Amazon** (riv.), SAm.
93/G4 **Amazônia** (Tapajós) Nat'l Park, Braz.
70/C4 **Ambajogai**, India
61/L2 **Ambāla**, India
70/D6 **Ambalangoda**, SrL.
89/H8 **Ambalavao**, Madg.
89/J6 **Ambanja**, Madg.
89/H6 **Ambaro** (bay), Madg.
92/C4 **Ambato**, Ecu.
89/H7 **Ambato Boeny**, Madg.
89/H8 **Ambatofinandrahana**, Madg.
89/H7 **Ambatolampy**, Madg.
89/H7 **Ambatondrazaka**, Madg.
49/H4 **Ámbelos, Ákra** (cape), Gre.
45/J2 **Amberg**, Ger.
33/G5 **Ambergate**, Eng,UK
70/D3 **Ambikāpur**, India
89/J6 **Ambilobe**, Madg.
89/J7 **Ambinanínony**, Madg.
33/G1 **Amble**, Eng,UK
115/E5 **Ambler**, Pa,US
33/F3 **Ambleside**, Eng,UK
42/A2 **Ambleteuse**, Fr.
43/F3 **Amblève** (riv.), Belg.
89/H9 **Amboasary**, Madg.
89/J6 **Ambohitra, Tampon** (peak), Madg.
73/G4 **Ambon**, Indo.
73/G4 **Ambon** (isl.), Indo.
89/H8 **Ambositra**, Madg.
89/H9 **Ambovombe**, Madg.
87/B2 **Ambriz**, Ang.
78/F6 **Ambrym** (isl.), Van.
114/B6 **Amchitka** (isl.), Ak,US
114/B6 **Amchitka** (passg.), Ak,US
101/P9 **Ameca**, Mex.
43/F3 **Amel**, Belg.
40/C2 **Ameland** (isl.), Neth.
40/B5 **Amer** (chan.), Neth.
98/F **American** (highland), Ant.
116/M9 **American** (riv.), Ca,US
116/B3 **American** (lake), Wa,US
95/C2 **Americana**, Braz.
106/E5 **American Falls**, Id,US
108/D2 **American Falls** (res.), Id,US
108/E2 **American Fork**, Ut,US
79/J6 **American Samoa** (terr.), US
113/G3 **Americus**, Ga,US
45/L3 **Ameringkogel** (peak), Aus.
40/C4 **Amersfoort**, Neth.
35/F3 **Amersham**, Eng,UK
98/E **Amery Ice Shelf**, Ant.
107/K5 **Ames**, Ia,US
35/E4 **Amesbury**, Eng,UK
49/H3 **Ámfissa**, Gre.
57/N3 **Amga** (riv.), Rus.
57/T3 **Amguema** (riv.), Rus.
63/M1 **Amgun'** (riv.), Rus.
111/H2 **Amherst**, NS,Can
116/F7 **Amherstburg**, On,Can
48/B1 **Amiata** (peak), It.
42/B4 **Amiens**, Fr.
57/U4 **Amila** (isl.), Ak,US
81/H5 **Amirante** (isls.), Sey.
107/H2 **Amisk** (lake), Sk,Can
112/C4 **Amistad** (res.), Mex., US
109/G5 **Amistad Nat'l Rec. Area**, Tx,US
109/K5 **Amite** (riv.), La,US
70/C3 **Amla**, India
114/D6 **Amlia** (isl.), Ak,US
32/D5 **Amlwch**, Wal,UK
59/K6 **'Ammān** (cap.), Jor.
34/C3 **Amman** (riv.), Wal,UK
34/C3 **Ammanford**, Wal,UK
37/E2 **Ammarfjället** (peak), Swe.
114/K2 **Ammerman** (mtn.), Yk,Can
45/J2 **Ammersee** (lake), Ger.
106/F5 **Ammon**, Id,US
69/D3 **Amnat Charoen**, Thai.
43/F5 **Amnéville**, Fr.
61/H2 **Āmol**, Iran
47/P10 **Amora**, Port.
49/J4 **Amorgós** (isl.), Gre.
113/F3 **Amory**, Ms,US
110/E1 **Amos**, Qu,Can
89/J8 **Ampangalana** (can.), Madg.
89/H9 **Ampanihy**, Madg.
70/D6 **Amparai**, SrL.
95/G7 **Amparo**, Braz.
89/J6 **Ampasindava** (bay), Madg.
47/F2 **Amposta**, Sp.
35/F2 **Ampthill**, Eng,UK
111/H1 **Amqui**, Qu,Can
70/C3 **Amravati**, India
70/B3 **Amreli**, India
60/C2 **'Amrīt** (ruins), Syria
61/K2 **Amritsar**, India
38/E1 **Amrun** (isl.), Ger.
40/B4 **Amstel** (riv.), Neth.
40/B4 **Amstelveen**, Neth.
29/N7 **Amsterdam** (isl.), FrAnt.
40/B4 **Amsterdam** (cap.), Neth.
110/F3 **Amsterdam**, NY,US
40/C5 **Amsterdam-Rijnkanaal** (can.), Neth.
45/L2 **Amstetten**, Aus.
83/K5 **Am Timan**, Chad
58/F5 **Amudar'ya** (riv.), Asia
114/D5 **Amukta** (passg.), Ak,US
103/S7 **Amund Rignes** (isl.), NW,Can
98/D **Amundsen** (bay), Ant.
98/S **Amundsen** (sea), Ant.
102/D1 **Amundsen** (gulf), NW,Can
98/A **Amundsen-Scott**, Ant.
63/M1 **Amur** (riv.), China, Rus.
79/K6 **Amuri**, CookIs.
57/N4 **Amur Obl.**, Rus.
46/D1 **Amurrio**, Sp.
63/M1 **Amursk**, Rus.
86/C5 **'Amur, Wādī** (dry riv.), Sudan
67/C5 **Amy Douglas** (shoal)
59/K4 **Amyūn**, Leb.
79/L6 **Anaa** (atoll), FrPol.
57/L3 **Anabar** (riv.), Rus.
115/A2 **Anacapa** (isl.), Ca,US
101/J6 **Anaco**, Ven.
106/E4 **Anaconda**, Mt,US
109/H4 **Anadarko**, Ok,US
57/T3 **Anadyr'**, Rus.
57/U3 **Anadyr'** (gulf), Rus.
57/T3 **Anadyr'** (range), Rus.
58/S3 **Anadyr'** (riv.), Rus.
49/J4 **Anáfi** (isl.), Gre.
60/D2 **'Ānah**, Iraq
115/C3 **Anaheim**, Ca,US
106/B2 **Anahim Lake**, BC,Can
100/A2 **Anáhuac**, Mex.
112/E4 **Anahuac**, Tx,US
70/D4 **Anakāpalle**, India
89/H6 **Analalava**, Madg.
89/J7 **Analamaitso** (plat.), Madg.
101/F3 **Ana María** (gulf), Cuba
72/C3 **Anambas** (isls.), Indo.
85/G5 **Anambra** (state), Nga.
59/C3 **Anamur**, Turk.
59/C3 **Anamur** (pt.), Turk.
64/D4 **Anan**, Japan
70/B3 **Anand**, India
70/C5 **Anantapur**, India
61/L2 **Anantnag**, India
68/C3 **Anan'yevo**, Kyr.
54/F3 **Anapa**, Rus.
97/K7 **Añapi** (peak), Arg.
93/J7 **Anápolis**, Braz.
93/H4 **Anapu** (riv.), Braz.
93/G8 **Anastácio**, Braz.
78/D3 **Anathan** (isl.), NMar.
59/B2 **Anatolia** (reg.), Turk.
91/D2 **Añatuya**, Arg.
92/F3 **Anauá** (riv.), Braz.
111/Q9 **Ancaster**, On,Can
67/A2 **Anchangzhen**, China
116/G6 **Anchor** (bay), Mi,US
114/J3 **Anchorage**, Ak,US
111/G2 **Ancienne-Lorette**, Qu,Can
92/E7 **Ancohuma** (peak), Bol.
45/K5 **Ancona**, It.
96/B4 **Ancud**, Chile
96/B4 **Ancud** (gulf), Chile
63/K2 **Anda**, China
92/D6 **Andahuaylas**, Peru
89/J7 **Andaingo Gara**, Madg.
37/C3 **Åndalsnes**, Nor.
46/C4 **Andalusia** (aut. comm.), Sp.
113/G4 **Andalusia**, Al,US
71/F5 **Andaman** (sea), Asia
71/F5 **Andaman** (isls.), India
71/F5 **Andaman & Nicobar Is.** (terr.), India
89/J6 **Andapa**, Madg.
42/A4 **Andelle** (riv.), Fr.
37/F1 **Andenes**, Nor.
43/E3 **Andenne**, Belg.
37/F1 **Ånderdalen Nat'l Park**, Nor.
42/D3 **Anderlues**, Belg.
43/G3 **Andernach**, Ger.
114/N2 **Anderson** (riv.), NW,Can
108/B2 **Anderson**, Ca,US
110/C3 **Anderson**, In,US
113/H3 **Anderson**, SC,US
112/E4 **Anderson**, Tx,US
116/B3 **Anderson** (isl.), Wa,US
90/C4 **Andes** (mts.), SAm.
37/F1 **Andfjorden** (fjord), Nor.
70/C4 **Andhra Pradesh** (state), India
49/H5 **Andikíthira** (isl.), Gre.
89/J7 **Andilamena**, Madg.
60/E2 **Andīmeshk**, Iran
49/J4 **Andíparos** (isl.), Gre.
95/B2 **Andira**, Braz.
68/B3 **Andizhan**, Uzb.
46/D1 **Andoain**, Sp.
64/A2 **Andong**, SKor.
64/A2 **Andong** (lake), SKor.
47/F1 **Andorra**
47/E2 **Andorra**, Sp.
47/F1 **Andorra la Vella** (cap.), And.
35/E4 **Andover**, Eng,UK
115/F5 **Andover**, NJ,US
37/E1 **Andøya** (isl.), Nor.
95/G7 **Andradas**, Braz.
95/B2 **Andradina**, Braz.
47/G3 **Andraitx**, Sp.
89/H7 **Andranomavo** (riv.), Madg.
114/C6 **Andreanof** (isls.), Ak,US
95/J6 **Andrelândia**, Braz.
31/S10 **Andrésy**, Fr.
112/C3 **Andrews**, Tx,US
48/E2 **Andria**, It.
89/H8 **Andringitra** (mts.), Madg.
89/J6 **Androntany** (cape), Madg.
101/F3 **Andros** (isl.), Bahm.
49/J4 **Ándros** (isl.), Gre.
110/G2 **Androscoggin** (riv.), Me, NH,US
46/C3 **Andújar**, Sp.
96/C4 **Anecón Grande** (peak), Arg.
96/E4 **Anegada** (bay), Arg.
101/J4 **Anegada** (isl.), BVi.
101/J4 **Anegada** (passage), NAm.
85/F5 **Aného**, Togo
78/G7 **Aneityum** (isl.), Van.
47/F1 **Aneto, Pico de** (peak), Sp.
67/B2 **Anfu**, China
91/B1 **Angamos** (pt.), Chile
62/E1 **Angara** (riv.), Rus.
62/E1 **Angarsk**, Rus.
37/E3 **Ånge**, Swe.
41/E5 **Angel** (riv.), Ger.
101/M8 **Ángel de la Guarda** (isl.), Mex.
67/D4 **Angeles**, Phil.
115/B2 **Angeles Nat'l Forest**, Ca,US
112/E4 **Angelina** (riv.), Tx,US
38/E1 **Angeln** (reg.), Ger.
92/F2 **Angel, Salto** (falls), Ven.
116/F6 **Angelus** (lake), Mi,US
73/J4 **Angemuk** (mtn.), Indo.
37/E2 **Ångermanälven** (riv.), Swe.
39/H2 **Angermünde**, Ger.
44/C3 **Angers**, Fr.
94/C2 **Angicos**, Braz.
69/C3 **Angkor** (ruins), Camb.
69/D4 **Angk Tasaom**, Camb.
75/Q12 **Anglem** (peak), NZ
32/D5 **Anglesey** (isl.), Wal,UK
44/C5 **Anglet**, Fr.
112/E4 **Angleton**, Tx,US
43/D3 **Anglin** (riv.), Fr.
69/C2 **Ang Nam Ngum** (lake), Laos
83/L7 **Ango**, Zaire
96/B3 **Angol**, Chile
87/C3 **Angola**
110/C3 **Angola**, In,US
100/C4 **Angostura** (res.), Mex.
44/D4 **Angoulême**, Fr.
47/S12 **Angra do Heroísmo**, Azor.,Port.
95/J8 **Angra dos Reis**, Braz.
68/B3 **Angren**, Uzb.
69/C3 **Ang Thong**, Thai.
83/K7 **Angu**, Zaire
101/J4 **Anguilla** (isl.), UK
114/G2 **Angutikada** (peak), Ak,US
93/H8 **Anhanduí** (riv.), Braz.
43/D3 **Anhée**, Belg.
71/K2 **Anhua**, China
66/D4 **Anhui** (prov.), China
114/G4 **Aniakchak** (crater), Ak,US
114/G4 **Aniakchak Nat'l Mon. & Prsv.**, Ak,US
42/C3 **Aniche**, Fr.
108/F3 **Animas** (riv.), Co, NM,US
50/E3 **Anina**, Rom.
63/N2 **Aniva** (bay), Rus.
37/H3 **Anjalamkoski**, Fin.
70/B3 **Anjār**, India
65/N10 **Anjō**, Japan
111/N6 **Anjou**, Qu,Can
44/C3 **Anjou** (hist. reg.), Fr.
89/H6 **Anjouan** (isl.), Com.
59/C2 **Ankara** (cap.), Turk.
89/H7 **Ankaratra, Massif** (plat.), Madg.
112/C2 **Ankaree** (riv.), Co,US
89/H8 **Ankazoabo**, Madg.
69/E3 **An Khe**, Viet.
39/G2 **Anklam**, Ger.
69/D3 **Anlong Veng**, Camb.
40/D2 **Anloo**, Neth.
66/C5 **Anlu**, China
98/D **Ann** (cape), Ant.
111/G3 **Ann** (cape), Ma,US
110/E4 **Anna** (lake), Va,US
81/V17 **Annaba**, Alg.
45/K1 **Annaberg-Buchholz**, Ger.
59/L4 **An Nabk**, Syria
32/B3 **Annaclone**, NI,UK
60/C3 **An Nafūd** (des.), SAr.
83/L5 **An Nahūd**, Sudan
60/D2 **An Najaf**, Iraq
36/B3 **Annalee** (riv.), Ire.
32/C3 **Annalong**, NI,UK
69/D2 **Annamitique, Chaîne** (mts.), Laos, Viet.
33/E2 **Annan**, Sc,UK
36/D3 **Annan** (riv.), Sc,UK
115/J8 **Annandale**, Va,US
40/B3 **Anna Pavlowna**, Neth.
96/B5 **Anna Pink** (bay), Chile
115/K8 **Annapolis** (cap.), Md,US
70/D2 **Annapurna** (mtn.), Nepal
60/C3 **An Naqb, Ra's**, Jor.
116/E7 **Ann Arbor**, Mi,US
60/E2 **An Nāṣirīyah**, Iraq
77/C4 **Anne** (peak), Austl.
74/B5 **Annean** (lake), Austl.
45/G4 **Annecy**, Fr.
31/U10 **Annet-sur-Marne**, Fr.
69/E3 **An Nhon**, Viet.
113/G3 **Anniston**, Al,US
82/F8 **Annobón** (isl.), EqG.
44/F4 **Annonay**, Fr.
44/E2 **An Nu'manīyah**, Iraq
65/M10 **Anō**, Japan
47/K7 **Anoia** (riv.), Sp.
107/K4 **Anoka**, Mn,US
89/J7 **Anosibe an' Ala**, Madg.
85/G2 **Ânou-Zeggarene** (wadi), Niger
69/E4 **An Phuoc**, Viet.
66/D5 **Anqing**, China
41/F5 **Anröchte**, Ger.
43/E2 **Ans**, Belg.
45/J2 **Ansbach**, Ger.
101/G4 **Anse-d'Hainault**, Haiti
45/L2 **Ansfelden**, Aus.
71/J2 **Anshun**, China
74/D2 **Anson** (bay), Austl.
112/D3 **Anson**, Tx,US
63/K4 **Ansŏng**, SKor.
78/E4 **Ant** (atoll), Micr.
35/H1 **Ant** (riv.), Eng,UK
59/D3 **Antakya** (Antioch), Turk.
89/J6 **Antalaha**, Madg.
59/B3 **Antalya**, Turk.
59/B3 **Antalya** (gulf), Turk.
89/H7 **Antananarivo** (cap.), Madg.
89/H7 **Antananarivo** (prov.), Madg.
98/W **Antarctic** (pen.), Ant.
98/* **Antarctica**
95/B4 **Antas** (riv.), Braz.
42/D5 **Ante** (riv.), Fr.
46/C4 **Antequera**, Sp.
109/H3 **Anthony**, Ks,US
108/F4 **Anthony**, NM,US
82/D2 **Anti-Atlas** (mts.), Mor.
45/G5 **Antibes**, Fr.
111/J1 **Anticosti** (isl.), Qu,Can
44/D2 **Antifer, Cap d'** (cape), Fr.
110/B2 **Antigo**, Wi,US
111/J2 **Antigonish**, NS,Can
101/J4 **Antigua** (isl.), Ant. & Barb.
101/J4 **Antigua and Barbuda**
59/K5 **Anti-Lebanon** (mts.), Leb.
116/L10 **Antioch**, Ca,US
116/P15 **Antioch**, Il,US
59/D3 **Antioch** (Antakya), Turk.
29/T8 **Antipodes** (isls.), NZ
109/J4 **Antlers**, Ok,US
91/B1 **Antofagasta**, Chile
42/C2 **Antoing**, Belg.
89/J6 **Antongil** (bay), Madg.
88/C4 **Antoniesberg** (peak), SAfr.
95/B3 **Antonina**, Braz.
109/F3 **Antonito**, Co,US
100/B4 **Anton Lizardo** (pt.), Mex.
31/S10 **Antony**, Fr.
32/B2 **Antrim**, NI,UK
32/B2 **Antrim** (dist.), NI,UK
32/B1 **Antrim** (mts.), NI,UK
89/H7 **Antsalova**, Madg.
89/H7 **Antsirabe**, Madg.
89/J6 **Antsiranana**, Madg.
89/J6 **Antsiranana** (prov.), Madg.
89/H6 **Antsohihy**, Madg.
96/C3 **Antuco** (vol.), Chile
43/E1 **Antwerp** (prov.), Belg.
42/D1 **Antwerp** (Antwerpen), Belg.
70/D6 **Anuradhapura**, SrL.
114/B6 **Anvil** (vol.), Ak,US
67/C2 **Anxi**, China
66/C3 **Anyang**, China
62/D4 **A'nyêmaqên** (mts.), China
66/B4 **Anyi**, China
63/M2 **Anyuy** (riv.), Rus.
42/C2 **Anzegem**, Belg.
56/J4 **Anzhero-Sudzhensk**, Rus.
42/C3 **Anzin**, Fr.
48/C2 **Anzio**, It.
65/L9 **Aogaki**, Japan
69/B4 **Ao Kham** (pt.), Thai.
63/N3 **Aomori**, Japan
49/G2 **Aóos** (riv.), Gre.
69/B4 **Ao Phangnga Nat'l Park**, Thai.
69/D3 **Aoral** (peak), Camb.
45/G4 **Aosta**, It.
84/C2 **Aoudaghost** (ruins), Mrta.
83/K5 **Aouk** (riv.), CAfr., Chad
84/C2 **Aoukar** (reg.), Mrta.
82/F2 **Aoulef**, Alg.
65/M10 **Aoyama**, Japan
82/J3 **Aozou**, Chad
112/B4 **Apache** (mts.), Tx,US
113/G4 **Apalachicola**, Fl,US
95/B4 **Aparados da Serra Nat'l Park**, Braz.
95/C2 **Aparecida**, Braz.
95/B2 **Aparecida do Taboado**, Braz.
67/D4 **Aparri**, Phil.
101/F6 **Apartadó**, Col.
79/L6 **Apataki**, FrPol.
50/D3 **Apatin**, Yugo.
52/G2 **Apatity**, Rus.
101/P10 **Apatzingán**, Mex.
100/B4 **Apaxtla**, Mex.
69/D4 **Ap Binh Chau**, Viet.
40/C4 **Apeldoorn**, Neth.
40/C4 **Apeldoornsch** (can.), Neth.
41/E2 **Apen**, Ger.
30/E4 **Apennines** (mts.), It.
72/C3 **Api** (cape), Indo.
73/E5 **Api** (peak), Indo.
68/D5 **Api** (mtn.), Nepal
79/H6 **Apia** (cap.), WSam.
93/G6 **Apiacás** (mts.), Braz.
95/B3 **Apiaí**, Braz.
69/D4 **Ap Loc Thanh**, Viet.
69/E4 **Ap Long Hoa**, Viet.
69/D4 **Ap Luc**, Viet.
67/E6 **Apo** (mt.), Phil.
94/C2 **Apodi**, Braz.
94/C2 **Apodi** (riv.), Braz.
79/R9 **Apolima** (str.), WSam.
95/B1 **Aporé** (riv.), Braz.
110/B2 **Apostle** (isls.), Wi,US
91/E2 **Apóstoles**, Arg.
59/C3 **Apostolos Andreas** (cape), Cyp.
105/K4 **Appalachian** (mts.), US
40/D2 **Appingedam**, Neth.
33/F2 **Appleby**, Eng,UK
35/E1 **Appleby Magna**, Eng,UK
111/S9 **Appleton**, NY,US
110/B2 **Appleton**, Wi,US
115/C1 **Apple Valley**, Ca,US
48/D2 **Apricena**, It.
48/C2 **Aprilia**, It.
54/F3 **Apsheronsk**, Rus.
77/E1 **Apsley Gorge Nat'l Park**, Austl.
69/E4 **Ap Tan My**, Viet.
104/U11 **Apua** (pt.), Hi,US
45/J4 **Apuane** (mts.), It.
95/B2 **Apucarana**, Braz.
101/H6 **Apure** (riv.), Ven.
92/D6 **Apurímac** (riv.), Peru
69/E4 **Ap Vinh Hao**, Viet.
86/C2 **Aqaba** (gulf), Asia
60/B3 **Aqaba** (gulf), Egypt, SAr.
86/D5 **'Aqīq**, Sudan
68/E4 **Aqqikkol** (lake), China
60/D1 **'Aqrah**, Iraq
93/G8 **Aquidauana**, Braz.
93/G8 **Aquidauana** (riv.), Braz.
94/C1 **Aquiraz**, Braz.
44/C4 **Aquitaine** (reg.), Fr.
62/D4 **Ar** (riv.), China
65/F2 **Ara** (riv.), Japan
83/L5 **'Arab** (riv.), Sudan
113/G3 **Arab**, Al,US
86/C2 **'Arabah, Wādī** (dry riv.), Egypt
60/D3 **Arabian** (pen.), Asia
61/H5 **Arabian** (sea), Asia
86/C3 **Arabian** (des.), Egypt
59/L5 **'Arab, Jabal al** (mts.), Syria
86/B2 **'Arab, Kalīj al** (gulf), Egypt
54/E4 **Araç** (riv.), Turk.
94/C3 **Aracaju**, Braz.
94/C2 **Aracati**, Braz.
95/B2 **Araçatuba**, Braz.
46/B4 **Aracena**, Sp.
94/C3 **Araci**, Braz.
95/D1 **Aracruz**, Braz.
94/B5 **Araçuaí**, Braz.
94/B5 **Araçuaí** (riv.), Braz.
50/E2 **Arad**, Rom.
50/E2 **Arad** (co.), Rom.
83/K4 **Arada**, Chad
60/F1 **Ārādān**, Iran
60/D4 **'Arafāt, Jabal** (mtn.), SAr.
78/C5 **Arafura** (sea), Austl., Indo.
93/H7 **Aragarças**, Braz.
55/H4 **Aragats, Gora** (peak), Arm.
47/E2 **Aragon** (aut. comm.), Sp.
46/E1 **Aragón** (riv.), Sp.
93/J5 **Araguaia** (riv.), Braz.
93/H5 **Araguaia Nat'l Park**, Braz.
93/J5 **Araguaína**, Braz.
95/B1 **Araguari**, Braz.
93/H3 **Araguari** (riv.), Braz.
93/J7 **Araguari** (riv.), Braz.
95/C1 **Araguari** (Valhas) (riv.), Braz.
93/J5 **Araguatins**, Braz.
65/F2 **Arai**, Japan
94/B1 **Araioses**, Braz.
60/E2 **Arāk**, Iran
114/D3 **Arakamchechan** (isl.), Rus.
71/F3 **Arakan** (mts.), Burma
49/G3 **Árakhthos** (riv.), Gre.
31/H5 **Araks** (riv.), Eur., Asia
56/G5 **Aral** (sea), Uzb., Kaz.
56/G5 **Aral'sk**, Kaz.
55/H2 **Aralsor** (lake), Kaz.
60/F2 **Ārān**, Iran
36/H7 **Aran** (isl.), Ire.
36/A4 **Aran** (isls.), Ire.
46/D2 **Aranda de Duero**, Sp.
50/E3 **Arandelovac**, Yugo.
46/D2 **Aranjuez**, Sp.
32/E6 **Aran Mawddwy** (mtn.), Wal,UK
112/D5 **Aransas Pass**, Tx,US
78/G4 **Aranuka** (atoll), Kiri.
94/C3 **Arapiraca**, Braz.
59/D2 **Arapkir**, Turk.
95/B2 **Arapongas**, Braz.
95/B4 **Araranguá**, Braz.
95/B2 **Araraquara**, Braz.
95/C2 **Araras**, Braz.
77/B3 **Ararat**, Austl.
94/A1 **Arari**, Braz.
94/B2 **Araripe** (hills), Braz.
94/B2 **Araripina**, Braz.
55/H5 **Aras** (riv.), Asia
84/C2 **Aratane** (well), Mrta.
94/B2 **Aratas** (res.), Braz.
92/F4 **Arauá** (riv.), Braz.
92/D2 **Arauca**, Col.
95/B3 **Araucária**, Braz.
78/E5 **Arawa**, PNG
95/C1 **Araxá**, Braz.
83/N6 **Ārba Minch'**, Eth.
107/H2 **Arborfield**, Sk,Can
107/J3 **Arborg**, Mb,Can
36/D2 **Arbroath**, Sc,UK
44/F5 **Arc** (riv.), Fr.
45/G4 **Arc** (riv.), Fr.
44/C4 **Arcachon**, Fr.
44/C4 **Arcachon** (lag.), Fr.
44/C4 **Arcachon, Pointe d'** (pt.), Fr.
115/B2 **Arcadia**, Ca,US
113/H5 **Arcadia**, Fl,US
108/A2 **Arcata**, Ca,US
31/S10 **Arc de Triomphe**, Fr.
52/J2 **Archangel** (Arkhangel'sk), Rus.
52/H3 **Archangel Obl.**, Rus.
46/E3 **Archena**, Sp.
76/A1 **Archer** (riv.), Austl.
76/A1 **Archer Bend Nat'l Park**, Austl.
112/D3 **Archer City**, Tx,US
108/E3 **Arches Nat'l Park**, Ut,US
46/C4 **Archidona**, Sp.
96/C3 **Arco** (pass), Arg.
45/J4 **Arco**, It.
106/E5 **Arco**, Id,US
95/C2 **Arcos**, Braz.
46/C4 **Arcos de la Frontera**, Sp.
94/C3 **Arcoverde**, Braz.
28/A1 **Arctic** (ocean)
114/F2 **Arctic** (coast. pl.), Ak,US
114/J2 **Arctic Nat'l Wild. Ref.**, Ak,US
114/M2 **Arctic Red River**, NW,Can
51/G5 **Arda** (riv.), Bul.
59/E2 **Ardahan**, Turk.
60/F2 **Ardakān**, Iran
37/C3 **Årdalstangen**, Nor.
59/E2 **Ardanuç**, Turk.
33/E6 **Arddleen**, Wal,UK
44/F4 **Ardèche** (riv.), Fr.
116/M9 **Arden-Arcade**, Ca,US
43/E4 **Ardennes** (for.), Eur.
42/D4 **Ardennes** (dept.), Fr.
43/D4 **Ardennes, Canal des** (can.), Fr.
59/E2 **Ardeşen**, Turk.
32/C3 **Ardglass**, NI,UK
46/B3 **Ardila** (riv.), Sp.
109/H4 **Ardmore**, Ok,US
115/E5 **Ardmore**, Pa,US
42/C2 **Ardooie**, Belg.
32/C3 **Ards** (dist.), NI,UK
32/C3 **Ards** (pen.), NI,UK
37/E3 **Åre**, Swe.
95/G6 **Areado**, Braz.
94/C2 **Areia Branca**, Braz.
101/N9 **Arena** (pt.), Mex.
108/B3 **Arena** (pt.), Ca,US
93/G6 **Arenápolis**, Braz.
46/C2 **Arenas de San Pedro**, Sp.
97/K8 **Arenas, Punta de** (pt.), Arg.
37/D4 **Arendal**, Nor.
40/C6 **Arendonk**, Belg.
32/E6 **Arenig Fawr** (mtn.), Wal,UK
47/L6 **Arenys de Mar**, Sp.
47/L6 **Arenys de Munt**, Sp.
92/D7 **Arequipa**, Peru
46/C2 **Arévalo**, Sp.
45/J5 **Arezzo**, It.
44/C5 **Arga** (riv.), Sp.
46/D3 **Argamasilla de Alba**, Sp.
46/C3 **Argamasilla de Calatrava**, Sp.
47/N9 **Arganda**, Sp.
45/G5 **Argens** (riv.), Fr.
44/C2 **Argentan**, Fr.
45/G4 **Argentera** (peak), It.
31/S10 **Argenteuil**, Fr.
91/C4 **Argentina**
97/J7 **Argentino** (lake), Arg.
47/L6 **Argentona**, Sp.
51/G3 **Argeş** (co.), Rom.
51/G3 **Argeş** (riv.), Rom.
61/J2 **Arghandab** (riv.), Afg.
83/M4 **Argo**, Sudan
49/H4 **Argolis** (gulf), Gre.
43/E5 **Argonne** (for.), Fr.
49/H4 **Árgos**, Gre.
49/G3 **Argostólion**, Gre.
42/A4 **Argueil**, Fr.
108/B4 **Arguello** (pt.), Ca,US
84/A1 **Arguin** (bay), Mrta.
63/H1 **Argun** (riv.), China, Rus.
68/E2 **Argut** (riv.), Rus.
74/D3 **Argyle** (lake), Austl.
82/C3 **Arhreijît** (well), Mrta.
37/D4 **Århus**, Den.
48/D2 **Ariano Irpino**, It.
46/C1 **Arianza** (riv.), Sp.
92/D7 **Arica**, Chile
74/C6 **Arid** (cape), Austl.
64/D3 **Arida**, Japan
115/A1 **Arido** (mt.), Ca,US
44/D5 **Ariège** (riv.), Fr.
51/K5 **Arifiye**, Turk.
59/K6 **Arīḥā** (Jericho), WBnk.
109/G3 **Arikaree** (riv.), Co,US
101/J5 **Arima**, Trin.
93/G6 **Arinos** (riv.), Braz.
92/F5 **Aripuanã** (riv.), Braz.
92/F5 **Ariquemes**, Braz.
86/C2 **'Arīsh, Wādī al** (dry riv.), Egypt
89/H7 **Arivonimamo**, Madg.
47/E2 **Arize** (riv.), Fr.
108/D4 **Arizona** (state), US
101/F5 **Arjona**, Col.
46/C4 **Arjona**, Sp.
112/E3 **Arkadelphia**, Ar,US
36/C2 **Arkaig, Loch** (lake), Sc,UK
68/A1 **Arkalyk**, Kaz.
109/K4 **Arkansas** (riv.), US
112/E3 **Arkansas** (state), US
113/F3 **Arkansas City**, Ar,US
109/H3 **Arkansas City**, Ks,US
83/K3 **Arkanū** (peak), Libya
52/J2 **Arkhangel'sk** (Archangel), Rus.
32/B6 **Arklow**, Ire.
39/G1 **Arkona, Kap** (cape), Ger.
70/C5 **Arkonam**, India
33/G4 **Arksey**, Eng,UK
56/H2 **Arkticheskiy Institut** (isls.), Rus.
46/C1 **Arlanza** (riv.), Sp.
46/C1 **Arlazón** (riv.), Sp.
44/F5 **Arles**, Fr.
42/C3 **Arleux**, Fr.
113/G4 **Arlington**, Ga,US
107/K4 **Arlington**, Mn,US
112/D3 **Arlington**, Tx,US
115/J8 **Arlington**, Va,US

125
Arlin – Baldy

116/Q15 **Arlington Heights,** Il,US
43/E4 **Arlon,** Belg.
85/F4 **Arly Nat'l Park,** Burk.
116/G6 **Armada,** Mi,US
32/B3 **Armagh,** NI,UK
32/B3 **Armagh** (dist.), NI,UK
44/F3 **Armançon** (riv.), Fr.
95/B2 **Armando Laydner** (res.), Braz.
86/C3 **Armant,** Egypt
55/G3 **Armavir,** Rus.
45/G5 **Arme, Cap d'** (cape), Fr.
55/H4 **Armenia**
92/C3 **Armenia,** Col.
42/B2 **Armentières,** Fr.
101/P10 **Armería,** Mex.
77/D1 **Armidale,** Austl.
46/D4 **Armilla,** Sp.
32/B1 **Armoy,** NI,UK
96/E2 **Armstrong,** Arg.
106/D3 **Armstrong,** BC,Can
33/G4 **Armthorpe,** Eng,UK
70/C4 **Armūr,** India
103/J3 **Arnaud** (riv.), Qu,Can
59/J4 **Arnauti** (cape), Cyp.
35/E3 **Arncott,** Eng,UK
46/D1 **Arnedo,** Sp.
42/B2 **Arnèke,** Fr.
109/H3 **Arnett,** Ok,US
74/F2 **Arnhem** (bay), Austl.
74/F2 **Arnhem** (cape), Austl.
40/C5 **Arnhem,** Neth.
74/E2 **Arnhem Land** (reg.), Austl.
70/C5 **Arni,** India
45/J5 **Arno** (riv.), It.
78/G4 **Arno** (atoll), Mrsh.
33/G5 **Arnold,** Eng,UK
45/K3 **Arnoldstein,** Aus.
44/E3 **Arnon** (riv.), Fr.
31/T10 **Arnouville-lès-Gonesse,** Fr.
110/E2 **Arnprior,** On,Can
41/F6 **Arnsberg,** Ger.
33/F3 **Arnside,** Eng,UK
38/F3 **Arnstadt,** Ger.
41/G6 **Arolsen,** Ger.
44/E3 **Aron** (riv.), Fr.
47/X16 **Arona,** Canl.
42/B4 **Aronde** (riv.), Fr.
78/G5 **Arorae** (atoll), Kiri.
73/H5 **Aro Usu** (cape), Indo.
31/S11 **Arpajon,** Fr.
42/B2 **Arques,** Fr.
70/D2 **Arrah,** India
83/M5 **Ar Rahad,** Sudan
93/H6 **Arraias** (riv.), Braz.
33/H4 **Arram,** Eng,UK
60/D2 **Ar Ramādī,** Iraq
59/L5 **Ar Ramthā,** Jor.
36/C3 **Arran** (isl.), Sc,UK
59/D3 **Ar Raqqah,** Syria
42/B3 **Arras,** Fr.
59/L4 **Ar Rastan,** Syria
47/F1 **Arrats** (riv.), Fr.
47/Y16 **Arrecife,** Canl.
96/E2 **Arrecifes,** Arg.
44/B2 **Arrée** (mts.), Fr.
100/C4 **Arriaga,** Mex.
95/A5 **Arrio Grande,** Braz.
60/E4 **Ar Riyāḑ** (Riyadh) (cap.), SAr.
44/F3 **Arroux** (riv.), Fr.
46/B3 **Arroyo de la Luz,** Sp.
108/B4 **Arroyo Grande,** Ca,US
59/L5 **Ar Ruşayfah,** Jor.
83/M5 **Ar Ruşayriş,** Sudan
60/F4 **Ar Ruways,** SAr.
63/L3 **Arsen'yev,** Rus.
79/T11 **Art** (isl.), NCal.
49/G3 **Árta,** Gre.
49/G3 **Arta** (gulf), Gre.
46/A1 **Arteijo,** Sp.
63/L3 **Artem,** Rus.
100/E3 **Artemisa,** Cuba
115/B3 **Artesia,** Ca,US
109/F4 **Artesia,** NM,US
76/C3 **Arthur** (pt.), Austl.
75/R11 **Arthur's** (pass), NZ
91/E3 **Artigas,** Uru.
42/A2 **Artois** (reg.), Fr.
42/B2 **Artois, Collines de l'** (hills), Fr.
95/F7 **Artur Nogueira,** Braz.
68/C4 **Artux,** China
59/E2 **Artvin,** Turk.
73/H5 **Aru** (isls.), Indo.
83/M7 **Arua,** Ugan.
101/H5 **Aruba** (isl.), Neth.
95/G8 **Arujá,** Braz.
35/F5 **Arun** (riv.), Eng,UK
71/F2 **Arunachal Pradesh** (state), India
35/F5 **Arundel,** Eng,UK
70/C6 **Aruppukkottai,** India
73/F3 **Arus** (cape), Indo.
87/G1 **Arusha,** Tanz.
79/L6 **Arutua** (atoll), FrPol.
83/L7 **Aruwimi** (riv.), Zaire
62/E2 **Arvayheer,** Mong.
37/F2 **Arvidsjaur,** Swe.
37/E4 **Arvika,** Swe.
108/C4 **Arvin,** Ca,US
110/B2 **Arvon** (peak), Mi,US
81/X17 **Aryānah** (gov.), Tun.
68/A3 **Arys',** Kaz.
44/B3 **Arz** (riv.), Fr.
53/J5 **Arzamas,** Rus.
41/G4 **Arzen,** Ger.
81/Q16 **Arzew,** Alg.
43/F3 **Arzfeld,** Ger.
46/A1 **Arzúa,** Sp.
43/E1 **As,** Belg.
45/K1 **Aš,** Czh.
37/D4 **Ås,** Nor.
60/E2 **Asadābād,** Iran
84/D5 **Asagny Nat'l Park,** IvC.
72/A3 **Asahan** (riv.), Indo.
64/C3 **Asahi** (riv.), Japan
65/G2 **Asahi-Bandai Nat'l Park,** Japan
63/N3 **Asahi-dake** (mtn.), Japan
83/N3 **Asahikawa,** Japan
65/H7 **Asaka,** Japan
65/M9 **Asake** (riv.), Japan
83/P5 **Āsalē,** Erit.
65/F2 **Asama-yama** (mtn.), Japan
70/E3 **Asansol,** India
82/J3 **Asawanwah** (well), Libya
53/P4 **Asbest,** Rus.
88/C3 **Asbestos** (mts.), SAfr.
115/F5 **Asbury Park,** NJ,US
100/D4 **Ascención** (bay), Mex.
28/J6 **Ascension** (isl.), StH.
41/E5 **Ascheberg,** Ger.
38/F3 **Aschersleben,** Ger.
48/A1 **Asco** (riv.), Fr.
48/C1 **Ascoli Piceno,** It.
48/D2 **Ascoli Satriano,** It.
35/F4 **Ascot,** Eng,UK
83/P5 **Āseb,** Erit.
83/N6 **Āsela,** Eth.
51/G4 **Asenovgrad,** Bul.
62/G2 **Asgat,** Mong.
35/G4 **Ash,** Eng,UK
35/E4 **Ashampstead,** Eng,UK
85/E5 **Ashanti** (reg.), Gha.
85/E5 **Ashanti** (uplands), Gha.
33/G5 **Ashbourne,** Eng,UK
74/B4 **Ashburton** (riv.), Austl.
75/R11 **Ashburton,** NZ
34/C5 **Ashburton,** Eng,UK
35/E1 **Ashby** (can.), Eng,UK
33/G6 **Ashby-de-la-Zouch,** Eng,UK
34/D3 **Ashchurch,** Eng,UK
106/C3 **Ashcroft,** BC,Can
113/J3 **Asheboro,** NC,US
107/J3 **Ashern,** Mb,Can
113/H3 **Asheville,** NC,US
107/M2 **Asheweig** (riv.), On,Can
31/M7 **Ashford,** Eng,UK
35/F1 **Ashfordby,** Eng,UK
111/Q8 **Ashgrove,** On,Can
75/S11 **Ashhurst,** NZ
33/G1 **Ashington,** Eng,UK
65/L10 **Ashiya,** Japan
64/C4 **Ashizuri-misaki** (cape), Japan
81/W17 **Ashkal** (lake), Tun.
61/G1 **Ashkhabad** (cap.), Trkm.
109/H3 **Ashland,** Ks,US
110/D4 **Ashland,** Ky,US
110/D3 **Ashland,** Oh,US
106/C5 **Ashland,** Or,US
110/B2 **Ashland,** Wi,US
107/J4 **Ashley,** ND,US
31/M6 **Ashley Green,** Eng,UK
74/C2 **Ashmore** (reef), Austl.
74/C2 **Ashmore and Cartier Is.** (terr.), Austl.
59/L4 **Ash Shamāl** (gov.), Leb.
60/D2 **Ash Shāmīyah,** Iraq
61/G3 **Ash Shāriqah,** UAE
59/E3 **Ash Sharqāt,** Iraq
59/H6 **Ash Sharqīyah** (gov.), Egypt
70/C3 **Ashta,** India
110/D3 **Ashtabula,** Oh,US
31/N8 **Ashtead,** Eng,UK
106/F4 **Ashton,** Id,US
33/F5 **Ashton-in-Makerfield,** Eng,UK
33/F5 **Ashton-under-Lyne,** Eng,UK
110/B2 **Ashwaubenon,** Wi,US
35/F2 **Ashwell,** Eng,UK
58/* **Asia**
81/L13 **Asilah,** Mor.
48/A2 **Asinara** (gulf), It.
48/A2 **Asinara** (isl.), It.
56/J4 **Asino,** Rus.
60/D5 **'Asīr** (mts.), SAr., Yemen
86/D5 **Asis, Ras** (cape), Sudan
59/E2 **Aşkale,** Turk.
33/E3 **Askam in Furness,** Eng,UK
37/D4 **Asker,** Nor.
33/G4 **Askern,** Eng,UK
37/D4 **Askim,** Nor.
49/G2 **Áskion** (peak), Gre.
37/P6 **Askja** (crater), Ice.
83/N4 **Āsmera** (cap.), Erit.
31/T9 **Asnières-sur-Oise,** Fr.
31/S10 **Asnières-sur-Seine,** Fr.
64/B4 **Aso Nat'l Park,** Japan
83/M5 **Āsosa,** Eth.
64/B4 **Aso-san** (mtn.), Japan
86/D4 **Asoteriba, Jabal** (peak), Sudan
33/E2 **Aspatria,** Eng,UK
47/E3 **Aspe,** Sp.
108/F3 **Aspen,** Co,US
115/J7 **Aspen Hill,** Md,US
112/C3 **Aspermont,** Tx,US
47/F1 **Aspin, Col d'** (pass), Fr.
75/Q11 **Aspiring** (peak), NZ
49/H3 **Asprópirgos,** Gre.
106/G2 **Asquith,** Sk,Can
84/C2 **'Assâba, Massif de l'** (reg.), Mrta.
59/D3 **As Sabkhah,** Syria
59/K6 **Aş Şāfī,** Jor.
60/E3 **As Sālimīyah,** Kuw.
60/E4 **As Sālimīyah,** SAr.
83/L1 **As Sallūm,** Egypt
59/K5 **As Salţ,** Jor.
71/F2 **Assam** (state), India
60/E2 **As Samāwah,** Iraq
59/H6 **As Santah,** Egypt
59/K5 **Aş Şarīḩ,** Jor.
42/D2 **Asse,** Belg.
48/A3 **Assemini,** It.
40/D2 **Assen,** Neth.
42/C1 **Assenede,** Belg.
82/J1 **As Sidr,** Libya
59/H6 **As Sinbillāwayn,** Egypt
107/G3 **Assiniboia,** Sk,Can
106/E3 **Assiniboine** (peak), BC,Can
107/J3 **Assiniboine** (riv.), Mb,Can
110/F1 **Assinika** (lake), Qu,Can
95/B2 **Assis,** Braz.
47/G1 **Assou** (riv.), Fr.
83/M6 **As Sudd** (reg.), Sudan
60/E1 **As Sulaymānīyah,** Iraq
60/E3 **Aş Şummān** (mts.), SAr.
59/L5 **As Suwaydā',** Syria
59/L5 **As Suwaydā'** (dist.), Syria
60/D2 **Aş Şuwayrah,** Iraq
86/C2 **As Suways** (gov.), Egypt
86/C2 **As Suways** (Suez), Egypt
40/C6 **Asten,** Neth.
45/H4 **Asti,** It.
95/L6 **Astolfo Dutra,** Braz.
35/E2 **Aston,** Eng,UK
34/D2 **Aston on Clun,** Eng,UK
95/B2 **Astorga,** Braz.
106/C4 **Astoria,** Or,US
55/J3 **Astrakhan',** Rus.
55/H3 **Astrakhan Obl.,** Rus.
46/B1 **Asturias** (aut. comm.), Sp.
35/E2 **Astwood Bank,** Eng,UK
65/L10 **Asuka,** Japan
65/N9 **Asuke,** Japan
78/D3 **Asuncion** (isl.), NMar.
91/E2 **Asunción** (cap.), Par.
100/B4 **Asunción Ixtaltepec,** Mex.
83/M7 **Aswa** (riv.), Ugan.
86/C3 **Aswān,** Egypt
86/C4 **Aswān** (gov.), Egypt
86/C4 **Aswan High** (dam), Egypt
86/B3 **Asyūt,** Egypt
86/B3 **Asyūt** (gov.), Egypt
86/C2 **Asyūţī, Wādī al** (dry riv.), Egypt
91/C2 **Atacama** (des.), Chile
91/C1 **Atacama, Puna de** (plat.), Arg.
85/F4 **Atacora** (range), Ben.
79/H5 **Atafu** (atoll), Tok.
85/F5 **Atakpamé,** Togo
94/C3 **Atalaia,** Braz.
65/F3 **Atami,** Japan
84/B1 **Atar,** Mrta.
46/D4 **Atarfe,** Sp.
70/D2 **Atarra,** India
62/D3 **Atas Bogd** (peak), Mong.
108/B4 **Atascadero,** Ca,US
59/D3 **Atatürk** (res.), Turk.
83/M4 **Atbara,** Sudan
83/M4 **Atbara** (Atbarah) (riv.), Eth., Sudan
68/A1 **Atbasar,** Kaz.
109/K5 **Atchafalaya** (bay), La,US
113/F4 **Atchafalaya** (riv.), La,US
109/J3 **Atchison,** Ks,US
85/E5 **Atebubu,** Gha.
37/G1 **Ateelva** (riv.), Nor.
101/P9 **Atengo** (riv.), Mex.
48/C1 **Aterno** (riv.), It.
42/C2 **Ath,** Belg.
106/E2 **Athabasca,** Ab,Can
102/E3 **Athabasca** (riv.), Ab,Can
102/F3 **Athabasca** (lake), Ab, Sk,Can
107/H2 **Athapapuskow** (lake), Mb,Can
82/K1 **Āthār Ţulmaythah** (Ptolemaīs) (ruins), Libya
113/G3 **Athens,** Al,US
113/H3 **Athens,** Ga,US
110/D4 **Athens,** Oh,US
113/G3 **Athens,** Tn,US
112/E3 **Athens,** Tx,US
49/H4 **Athens** (Athínai) (cap.), Gre.
49/L7 **Athens** (Athínai) (inset) (cap.), Gre.
35/E1 **Atherstone,** Eng,UK
33/F4 **Atherton,** Eng,UK
31/T10 **Athis-Mons,** Fr.
38/B4 **Athlone,** Ire.
49/J2 **Áthos** (peak), Gre.
82/J5 **Ati,** Chad
95/G8 **Atibaia,** Braz.
95/G7 **Atibaia** (riv.), Braz.
110/B1 **Atikokan,** On,Can
79/K7 **Atiu** (isl.), Cookls.
115/F4 **Atka** (isl.), Ak,US
55/H2 **Atkarsk,** Rus.
114/M2 **Atkinson** (pt.), NW,Can
113/G3 **Atlanta** (cap.), Ga,US
112/E3 **Atlanta,** Tx,US
28/G3 **Atlantic** (ocean)
107/K5 **Atlantic,** Ia,US
115/G5 **Atlantic Beach,** NY,US
85/F5 **Atlantique** (prov.), Ben.
82/E2 **Atlas** (mts.), Afr.
116/K10 **Atlas** (peak), Ca,US
82/E1 **Atlas Saharien** (mts.), Alg., Mor.
114/M4 **Atlin** (lake), BC,Can
100/B4 **Atlixco,** Mex.
113/G4 **Atmore,** Al,US
82/B3 **Atoui** (dry riv.), Mrta.
61/G1 **Atrak** (riv.), Iran
92/C2 **Atrato** (riv.), Col.
65/H7 **Atsugi,** Japan
65/N10 **Atsumi,** Japan
65/N10 **Atsumi** (pen.), Japan
59/K6 **Aţ Ţafīlah,** Jor.
60/D4 **Aţ Ţā'if,** SAr.
59/L5 **At Tall,** Syria
113/G3 **Attalla,** Al,US
103/H3 **Attawapiskat** (riv.), On,Can
41/E6 **Attendorn,** Ger.
45/K3 **Attersee** (lake), Aus.
42/C5 **Attichy,** Fr.
35/E2 **Attleborough,** Eng,UK
35/H2 **Attleborough,** Eng,UK
114/A5 **Attu** (isl.), Ak,US
86/C2 **Aţ Ţūr,** Egypt
59/K6 **Aţ Ţūr,** WBnk.
60/D6 **At Turbah,** Yem.
96/D2 **Atuel** (riv.), Arg.
37/F4 **Åtvidaberg,** Swe.
108/B3 **Atwater,** Ca,US
109/G3 **Atwood,** Ks,US
100/E4 **Auas,** Hon.
43/E4 **Aubange,** Belg.
42/D6 **Aube** (dept.), Fr.
44/F2 **Aube** (riv.), Fr.
44/F4 **Aubenas,** Fr.
31/T10 **Aubervilliers,** Fr.
42/C6 **Aubetin** (riv.), Fr.
42/A5 **Aubette** (riv.), Fr.
44/E4 **Aubin,** Fr.
44/E4 **Aubrac** (mts.), Fr.
113/G3 **Auburn,** Al,US
108/B3 **Auburn,** Ca,US
110/C3 **Auburn,** In,US
111/G2 **Auburn,** Me,US
109/J2 **Auburn,** Ne,US
110/E3 **Auburn,** NY,US
116/C3 **Auburn,** Wa,US
116/F6 **Auburn Hills,** Mi,US
96/C3 **Aucá Mahuida** (peak), Arg.
44/D5 **Auch,** Fr.
42/B3 **Auchel,** Fr.
36/D2 **Auchenblae,** Sc,UK
32/E2 **Auchencairn,** Sc,UK
36/C3 **Auchinleck,** Sc,UK
75/R10 **Auckland,** NZ
29/S8 **Auckland** (isls.), NZ
44/E5 **Aude** (riv.), Fr.
42/D2 **Auderghem,** Belg.
44/A3 **Audierne** (bay), Fr.
33/F6 **Audlem,** Eng,UK
33/F5 **Audley,** Eng,UK
83/P6 **Audo** (range), Eth.
43/E5 **Audun-le-Tiche,** Fr.
45/K1 **Aue,** Ger.
41/E2 **Aue** (riv.), Ger.
41/F3 **Aue** (riv.), Ger.
45/K1 **Auerbach,** Ger.
45/J2 **Auerbach in der Oberpfalz,** Ger.
32/A3 **Augher,** NI,UK
32/B3 **Aughnacloy,** NI,UK
88/C3 **Augrabies Falls Nat'l Park,** SAfr.
88/C3 **Augrabiesvalle** (falls), SAfr.
45/J2 **Augsburg,** Ger.
88/A2 **Augub** (peak), Namb.
48/D4 **Augusta,** It.
48/D4 **Augusta** (gulf), It.
113/H3 **Augusta,** Ga,US
111/G2 **Augusta** (cap.), Me,US
41/F5 **Augustdorf,** Ger.
39/M2 **Augustów,** Pol.
74/C3 **Augustus** (isl.), Austl.
69/B3 **Auk Bok** (isl.), Burma
74/C4 **Auld** (lake), Austl.
47/M9 **Aulencia** (riv.), Sp.
31/T10 **Aulnay-sous-Bois,** Fr.
44/B2 **Aulne** (riv.), Fr.
42/C3 **Aulnoye-Aymeries,** Fr.
42/B5 **Aunette** (riv.), Fr.
88/B2 **Auob** (dry riv.), Namb.
88/C2 **Auobrivier** (dry riv.), SAfr.
78/G4 **Aur** (atoll), Mrsh.
70/C4 **Aurangābād,** India
70/D3 **Aurangābād,** India
44/B3 **Auray,** Fr.
45/D5 **Aureilhan,** Fr.
41/E2 **Aurich,** Ger.
95/B2 **Auriflama,** Braz.
44/E4 **Aurillac,** Fr.
94/C2 **Aurora,** Braz.
109/F3 **Aurora,** Co,US
116/P16 **Aurora,** Il,US
109/J3 **Aurora,** Mo,US
109/H2 **Aurora,** Ne,US
76/A1 **Aurukun Abor. Land,** Austl.
110/C2 **Au Sable** (riv.), Mi,US
39/K3 **Auschwitz** (Oświęcim), Pol.
44/E5 **Aussillon,** Fr.
37/C4 **Aust-Agder** (co.), Nor.
74/B5 **Austin** (lake), Austl.
102/G2 **Austin** (isl.), NW,Can
107/K5 **Austin,** Mn,US
108/C3 **Austin,** Nv,US
112/D4 **Austin** (cap.), Tx,US
74/* **Australia**
77/C3 **Australian Alps** (mts.), Austl.
77/D3 **Australian Cap. Terr.,** Austl.
45/L3 **Austria**
37/P7 **Austurhorn** (pt.), Ice.
42/B3 **Authie** (riv.), Fr.
101/P10 **Autlán de Navarro,** Mex.
42/B5 **Automne** (riv.), Fr.
44/F3 **Autun,** Fr.
44/E4 **Auvergne** (reg.), Fr.
31/S9 **Auvers-sur-Oise,** Fr.
44/D4 **Auvézère** (riv.), Fr.
44/E3 **Auxerre,** Fr.
44/F3 **Auxonne,** Fr.
113/D2 **Aux Sables** (riv.), On,Can
103/K2 **Auyuittuq Nat'l Park,** NW,Can
92/D6 **Auzangate** (peak), Peru
44/E3 **Avallon,** Fr.
111/K2 **Avalon** (pen.), Nf,Can
95/B2 **Avaré,** Braz.
35/E4 **Avebury,** Eng,UK
43/A2 **Aveiro,** Port.
46/A2 **Aveiro** (dist.), Port.
31/P7 **Aveley,** Eng,UK
42/C2 **Avelgem,** Belg.
96/F2 **Avellaneda,** Arg.
48/D2 **Avellino,** It.
42/A4 **Avelon** (riv.), Fr.
108/B3 **Avenal,** Ca,US
42/A6 **Aver** (riv.), Fr.
48/D2 **Aversa,** It.
101/J4 **Aves** (isl.), Ven.
37/F3 **Avesta,** Swe.
44/D4 **Aveyron** (riv.), Fr.
43/C1 **Avezzano,** It.
36/D2 **Aviemore,** Sc,UK
44/F5 **Avignon,** Fr.
45/C2 **Ávila de los Caballeros,** Sp.
43/C1 **Avilés,** Sp.
42/B3 **Avion,** Fr.
46/B3 **Avis,** Port.
32/B6 **Avoca,** Ire.
32/B6 **Avoca** (riv.), Ire.
48/D4 **Avola,** It.
44/E2 **Avon,** Fr.
34/D4 **Avon** (co.), Eng,UK
34/C6 **Avon** (riv.), Eng,UK
34/D4 **Avon** (riv.), Eng,UK
35/E2 **Avon** (riv.), Eng,UK
35/E5 **Avon** (riv.), Eng,UK
32/B6 **Avonbeg** (riv.), Ire.
107/G3 **Avonlea,** Sk,Can
32/B6 **Avonmore** (riv.), Ire.
34/D4 **Avonmouth,** Eng,UK
44/C2 **Avranches,** Fr.
42/B4 **Avre** (riv.), Fr.
44/C3 **Avrillé,** Fr.
65/L10 **Awaji,** Japan
64/D3 **Awaji** (isl.), Japan
59/L5 **A'waj, Nahr al** (riv.), Syria
43/E2 **Awans,** Belg.
83/N6 **Āwasa,** Eth.
83/P5 **Āwash Wenz** (riv.), Eth.
88/A2 **Awasibberge** (peak), Namb.
82/H2 **Awbārī,** Libya
36/C2 **Awe, Loch** (lake), Sc,UK
83/K2 **Awjilah,** Libya
37/P6 **Axarfjördhur** (bay), Ice.
34/D4 **Axbridge,** Eng,UK
34/D4 **Axe** (riv.), Eng,UK
34/D5 **Axe** (riv.), Eng,UK
40/A6 **Axel,** Neth.
103/S7 **Axel Heiberg** (isl.), NW,Can
85/E5 **Axim,** Gha.
49/H2 **Axios** (riv.), Gre.
34/D5 **Axminster,** Eng,UK
53/N5 **Ay** (riv.), Rus.
64/D3 **Ayabe,** Japan
96/F3 **Ayacucho,** Arg.
92/D6 **Ayacucho,** Peru
68/D2 **Ayaguz,** Kaz.
68/D2 **Ayaguz** (riv.), Kaz.
68/E4 **Ayakkum** (lake), China
65/M10 **Ayama,** Japan
84/E5 **Ayamé, Barrage d'** (dam), IvC.
46/B4 **Ayamonte,** Sp.
59/C2 **Ayancık,** Turk.
101/F6 **Ayapel,** Col.
65/H7 **Ayase,** Japan
92/D6 **Ayaviri,** Peru
61/J1 **Aybak,** Afg.
59/N8 **'Aybāl, Jabal** (Har Eval) (mtn.), WBnk.
59/A3 **Aydın,** Turk.
59/C3 **Aydıncık,** Turk.
74/E5 **Ayers Rock** (Uluru) (peak), Austl.
49/J3 **Áyios Evstrátios** (isl.), Gre.
49/J5 **Áyios Ioánnis, Ákra** (cape), Gre.
49/J5 **Áyios Nikólaos,** Gre.
35/F3 **Aylesbury,** Eng,UK
35/G4 **Aylesford,** Eng,UK
35/H2 **Aylesham,** Eng,UK
102/F2 **Aylmer** (lake), NW,Can
35/H1 **Aylsham,** Eng,UK
59/D3 **'Ayn al 'Arab,** Syria
83/K2 **'Ayn Ath Tha'lab,** Libya
60/D1 **'Ayn, Ra's al,** Syria
83/K3 **'Ayn Zuwayyah** (well), Libya
57/S3 **Ayon** (isl.), Rus.
47/E3 **Ayora,** Sp.
82/D3 **'Ayoûn 'Abd el Mâlek** (well), Mrta.
76/B2 **Ayr,** Austl.
36/C3 **Ayr,** Sc,UK
36/C3 **Ayr** (riv.), Sc,UK
32/D3 **Ayre, Point of** (pt.), Eng,UK
33/H3 **Ayton,** Eng,UK
51/H4 **Aytos,** Bul.
44/C3 **Aytré,** Fr.
100/B4 **Ayutla,** Mex.
69/C3 **Ayutthaya** (ruins), Thai.
59/A2 **Ayvacık,** Turk.
59/A2 **Ayvalık,** Turk.
43/E3 **Aywaille,** Belg.
47/F3 **Azahar** (coast), Sp.
65/M9 **Azaj,** Japan
106/C5 **Azalea,** Or,US
70/D2 **Azamgarh,** India
92/D6 **Azángaro,** Peru
82/G2 **Azao** (peak), Alg.
85/E2 **Azaouâd** (reg.), Mali
85/G2 **Azaouak, Vallée de l'** (wadi), Mali, Niger
59/D3 **A'zāz,** Syria
55/H4 **Azerbaijan**
83/N5 **Āzezo,** Eth.
68/E1 **Azhu-Tayga, Gora** (peak), Rus.
92/C4 **Azogues,** Ecu.
47/R12 **Azores** (aut. reg.), Port.
47/R12 **Azores** (isls.), Port.
54/F3 **Azov,** Rus.
54/E3 **Azov** (sea), Rus., Ukr.
46/D1 **Azpeitia,** Sp.
108/F3 **Aztec,** NM,US
108/E3 **Aztec Ruins Nat'l Mon.,** NM,US
101/G4 **Azua,** DRep.
46/C3 **Azuaga,** Sp.
65/M9 **Azuchi,** Japan
101/F6 **Azuero** (pen.), Pan.
96/F3 **Azul,** Arg.
65/G2 **Azuma-san** (mtn.), Japan
65/F2 **Azumaya-san** (mtn.), Japan
45/G5 **Azur, Côte d'** (coast), Fr.
115/C2 **Azuza,** Ca,US
81/V17 **Azzaba,** Alg.
59/L5 **Az Zabadānī,** Syria
86/B2 **Az Zaqāzīq,** Egypt
45/K4 **Azzano Decimo,** It.
59/L5 **Az Zarqā',** Jor.
82/H1 **Az Zāwiyah,** Libya

B

79/Y18 **Ba,** Fiji
69/E3 **Ba** (riv.), Viet.
79/U11 **Baaba** (isl.), NCal.
59/N9 **Ba'al Hazor** (Tall 'Āşūr) (mtn.), WBnk.
45/H3 **Baar,** Swi.
80/G4 **Baarawe,** Som.
40/C4 **Baarn,** Neth.
62/D2 **Baatsagaan,** Mong.
61/J2 **Baba** (mts.), Afg.
51/F4 **Baba** (peak), Bul.
54/D4 **Baba Burnu** (pt.), Turk.
51/J3 **Babadag,** Rom.
51/H5 **Babaeski,** Turk.
92/C4 **Babahoyo,** Ecu.
73/G5 **Babar** (isl.), Indo.
87/G1 **Babati,** Tanz.
34/C5 **Babbacombe** (bay), Eng,UK
107/L4 **Babbitt,** Mn,US
108/C3 **Babbitt,** Nv,US
81/G3 **Bab el Mandeb** (str.), Afr., Asia
78/C4 **Babelthuap** (isl.), Palau
54/A2 **Babia Gora** (peak), Pol.
71/H3 **Babian** (riv.), China
106/B2 **Babine** (lake), BC,Can
102/D3 **Babine** (riv.), BC,Can
60/F1 **Bābol,** Iran
67/D4 **Babuyan** (isls.), Phil.
60/D2 **Babylon** (ruins), Iraq
115/G5 **Babylon,** NY,US
94/A2 **Bacabal,** Braz.
93/H4 **Bacajá** (riv.), Braz.
73/G4 **Bacan** (isl.), Indo.
51/H2 **Bacău,** Rom.
51/H2 **Bacău** (co.), Rom.
69/D1 **Bac Can,** Viet.
69/D1 **Bac Giang,** Viet.
102/G2 **Back** (riv.), NW,Can
110/E2 **Back** (lake), On,Can
115/K7 **Back** (riv.), Md,US
50/D3 **Bačka** (reg.), Yugo.
50/D3 **Bačka Palanka,** Yugo.
50/D3 **Bačka Topola,** Yugo.
45/H2 **Backnang,** Ger.
34/D4 **Backwell,** Eng,UK
69/D4 **Bac Lieu,** Viet.
69/D1 **Bac Ninh,** Viet.
67/D5 **Bacolod,** Phil.
69/D1 **Bac Quang,** Viet.
50/D2 **Bácsalmás,** Hun.
50/D2 **Bács-Kiskun** (co.), Hun.
35/H1 **Bacton,** Eng,UK
33/F4 **Bacup,** Eng,UK
107/H4 **Bad** (riv.), SD,US
70/C5 **Badagara,** India
62/E3 **Badain Jaran** (des.), China
46/B3 **Badajoz,** Sp.
47/L7 **Badalona,** Sp.
110/D3 **Bad Axe,** Mi,US
41/F6 **Bad Berleburg,** Ger.
43/G2 **Bad Breisig,** Ger.
38/F1 **Bad Doberan,** Ger.
41/G5 **Bad Driburg,** Ger.
45/M2 **Baden,** Aus.
45/H2 **Baden-Baden,** Ger.
45/H2 **Baden-Württemberg** (state), Ger.
41/F4 **Bad Essen,** Ger.
39/H2 **Bad Freienwalde,** Ger.
41/H5 **Bad Gandersheim,** Ger.
45/K3 **Bad Goisern,** Aus.
41/H5 **Bad Harzburg,** Ger.
38/E3 **Bad Hersfeld,** Ger.
45/H1 **Bad Homburg vor der Höhe,** Ger.
43/G2 **Bad Honnef,** Ger.
61/J4 **Badīn,** Pak.
45/K3 **Bad Ischl,** Aus.
45/G2 **Bad Kreuznach,** Ger.
45/G3 **Bad Krozingen,** Ger.
107/H4 **Badlands** (uplands), ND,US
107/H5 **Badlands** (hills), SD,US
107/H5 **Badlands Nat'l Park,** SD,US
41/H6 **Bad Langensalza,** Ger.
41/H5 **Bad Lauterberg,** Ger.
41/F3 **Bad Lippspringe,** Ger.
45/H2 **Bad Mergentheim,** Ger.
41/G4 **Bad Munder am Deister,** Ger.
43/F2 **Bad Münstereifel,** Ger.
45/H1 **Bad Nauheim,** Ger.
41/G4 **Bad Nenndorf,** Ger.
43/G2 **Bad Neuenahr-Ahrweiler,** Ger.
45/J1 **Bad Neustadt an der Saale,** Ger.
41/F4 **Bad Oeynhausen,** Ger.
38/F2 **Bad Oldesloe,** Ger.
41/G5 **Bad Pyrmont,** Ger.
61/J3 **Bādrāh,** Pak.
38/G5 **Bad Reichenhall,** Ger.
41/H5 **Bad Sachsa,** Ger.
41/H4 **Bad Salzdetfurth,** Ger.
41/F4 **Bad Salzuflen,** Ger.
38/F3 **Bad Salzungen,** Ger.
41/F5 **Bad Sassendorf,** Ger.
38/F2 **Bad Schwartau,** Ger.
38/F2 **Bad Segeberg,** Ger.
41/G6 **Bad Sooden-Allendorf,** Ger.
45/J3 **Bad Tölz,** Ger.
70/D6 **Badulla,** SrL.
45/M3 **Bad Vöslau,** Aus.
41/G6 **Bad Wildungen,** Ger.
41/E2 **Bad Zwischenahn,** Ger.
46/C4 **Baena,** Sp.
95/J6 **Baependi,** Braz.
43/F2 **Baesweiler,** Ger.
46/D4 **Baeza,** Sp.
85/H5 **Bafang,** Camr.
103/H1 **Baffin** (isl.), NW,Can
103/K1 **Baffin** (bay), Can.,Grld.
112/D5 **Baffin** (bay), Tx,US
82/H7 **Bafia,** Camr.
84/D4 **Bafing** (riv.), Gui., IvC.
84/C3 **Bafing** (riv.), Gui., Mali
85/H5 **Bafoussam,** Camr.
59/C2 **Bafra,** Turk.
84/B2 **Bafrechié** (well), Mrta.
83/L7 **Bafwasende,** Zaire
66/B3 **Bag** (salt lake), China
82/H5 **Baga,** Nga.
67/E6 **Baganga,** Phil.
85/G3 **Bagaroua,** Niger
68/E3 **Bagda** (mts.), China
97/G1 **Bagé,** Braz.
67/D4 **Baggao,** Phil.
34/B4 **Baggy** (pt.), Eng,UK
60/D2 **Baghdad** (Baghdād) (cap.), Iraq
48/C3 **Bagheria,** It.
61/J1 **Baghlān,** Afg.
34/C3 **Baglan,** Wal,UK
107/K4 **Bagley,** Mn,US
44/D5 **Bagnères-de-Bigorre,** Fr.
31/S10 **Bagneux,** Fr.
31/T10 **Bagnolet,** Fr.
44/F4 **Bagnols-sur-Cèze,** Fr.
67/D5 **Bago,** Phil.
84/D3 **Bagoe** (riv.), IvC., Mali
69/B2 **Bago** (Pegu) (div.), Burma
67/D4 **Baguio,** Phil.
82/J5 **Baguirmi** (reg.), Chad
85/H2 **Bagzane** (peak), Niger
101/F2 **Bahamas**
70/E3 **Baharampur,** India
68/B6 **Bahāwalnagar,** Pak.
61/K3 **Bahāwalpur,** Pak.
87/G2 **Bahi,** Tanz.
94/B4 **Bahia** (state), Braz.
100/D4 **Bahía** (isls.), Hon.
101/M8 **Bahia Asunción,** Mex.
96/E3 **Bahía Blanca,** Arg.
101/M8 **Bahía de los Angeles,** Mex.
70/D3 **Bahía Honda,** Cuba
101/M8 **Bahía Kino,** Mex.
101/M8 **Bahía Tortugas,** Mex.
83/N5 **Bahir Dar,** Eth.
61/G4 **Bahlah,** Oman
70/D2 **Bahraich,** India
60/F3 **Bahrain**
60/F3 **Bahrain** (gulf), Bahr., SAr.
80/E3 **Baḩr al Arab** (riv.), Sudan
60/D2 **Baḩr al Milḩ** (lake), Iraq
80/D4 **Bahr Aouk** (riv.), CAfr., Chad
86/B2 **Baḩrīyah, Al Wāḩāt al** (oasis), Egypt
66/C2 **Bai** (riv.), China
66/C4 **Bai** (riv.), China
51/F2 **Baia Mare,** Rom.
51/F2 **Baia Sprie,** Rom.
82/J6 **Baïbokoum,** Chad
63/J2 **Baicheng,** China
68/D3 **Baicheng,** China
51/G3 **Băicoi,** Rom.
83/P7 **Baidoa,** Som.
66/D5 **Baidong** (lake), China
111/G1 **Baie-Comeau,** Qu,Can
103/J3 **Baie-du-Poste,** Qu,Can
111/G2 **Baie-Saint-Paul,** Qu,Can
111/K1 **Baie Verte,** Nf,Can
66/G7 **Baigou** (riv.), China
66/C3 **Baihua Shan** (mtn.), China
60/D2 **Ba'ījī,** Iraq
57/L4 **Baikal** (Baykal) (lake), Rus.
33/G4 **Baildon,** Eng,UK
46/D3 **Bailén,** Sp.
51/F3 **Băileşti,** Rom.
42/B2 **Bailleul,** Fr.
62/E5 **Bailong** (riv.), China
66/C4 **Bailu** (riv.), China
33/H5 **Bain** (riv.), Eng,UK
113/G4 **Bainbridge,** Ga,US
116/B2 **Bainbridge** (isl.), Wa,US
68/D4 **Bairab** (lake), China
114/F3 **Baird** (inlet), Ak,US
112/D3 **Baird,** Tx,US
78/G4 **Bairiki** (cap.), Kiri.
77/C3 **Bairnsdale,** Austl.
59/L6 **Bā'ir, Wādī** (riv.), Jor.
44/D5 **Baïse** (riv.), Fr.
70/D2 **Baitadi,** Nepal
69/D2 **Bai Thuong,** Viet.
47/P10 **Baixa de Banheira,** Port.
94/B4 **Baixa Grande,** Braz.
95/D1 **Baixo Guandu,** Braz.
62/E4 **Baiyin,** China
66/B3 **Baiyu** (mts.), China
67/C2 **Baiyun,** China
97/J7 **Baja** (pt.), Chile
50/D2 **Baja,** Hun.
101/L8 **Baja California** (pen.), Mex.
101/L7 **Baja California Norte** (state), Mex.
101/M8 **Baja California Sur** (state), Mex.
81/W17 **Bājah,** Tun.
81/W17 **Bājah** (gov.), Tun.
73/F5 **Bajawa,** Indo.
50/D4 **Bajina Bašta,** Yugo.
77/E1 **Bajmba** (peak), Austl.
50/D3 **Bajmok,** Yugo.
101/F4 **Bajo Nuevo** (isl.), Col.
68/C2 **Bakanas** (riv.), Kaz.
73/E3 **Bakayan** (peak), Indo.
84/B3 **Bakel,** Sen.
102/G2 **Baker** (lake), NW,Can
97/J6 **Baker** (riv.), Chile
79/H4 **Baker** (isl.), PacUS
108/C4 **Baker,** Ca,US
107/G4 **Baker,** Mt,US
108/D3 **Baker,** Nv,US
106/D4 **Baker,** Or,US
106/C3 **Baker** (peak), Wa,US
108/C4 **Bakersfield,** Ca,US
33/G5 **Bakewell,** Eng,UK
54/E3 **Bakhchisaray,** Ukr.
54/E2 **Bakhmach,** Ukr.
60/E2 **Bākhtarān,** Iran
60/F3 **Bakhtegān** (lake), Iran
37/P6 **Bakkaflói** (bay), Ice.
87/B1 **Bakoumba,** Gabon
84/C4 **Bakoye** (riv.), Gui., Mali
55/J4 **Baku** (cap.), Azer.
98/S **Bakutis** (coast), Ant.
92/E6 **Bala** (mts.), Bol.
32/E6 **Bala,** Wal,UK
73/E2 **Balabac** (str.), Malay., Phil.
67/C6 **Balabac,** Phil.
67/C6 **Balabac** (isl.), Phil.
59/L5 **Ba'labakk,** Leb.
79/U12 **Balabio** (isl.), NCal.
60/D2 **Balad,** Iraq
70/D3 **Bālāghāt,** India
48/A1 **Balagne** (range), Fr.
47/F2 **Balaguer,** Sp.
44/C5 **Balaïtous** (mtn.), Fr.
87/F3 **Balaka,** Malw.
53/J4 **Balakhna,** Rus.
55/H1 **Balakovo,** Rus.
61/H1 **Bālā Morghab,** Afg.
51/G2 **Bălan,** Rom.
100/C4 **Balancán,** Mex.
67/D5 **Balanga,** Phil.
69/E3 **Ba Lang An** (cape), Viet.
70/D3 **Bālāngir,** India
53/X9 **Balashikha,** Rus.
55/G2 **Balashov,** Rus.
50/D1 **Balassagyarmat,** Hun.
50/C2 **Balaton** (lake), Hun.
50/C2 **Balatonfüred,** Hun.
92/F4 **Balbina** (res.), Braz.
96/F3 **Balcarce,** Arg.
32/E2 **Balcary** (pt.), Sc,UK
51/J4 **Balchik,** Bul.
75/Q12 **Balclutha,** NZ
35/F4 **Balcombe,** Eng,UK
112/D4 **Balcones Escarpment** (plat.), Tx,US
74/B7 **Bald** (pt.), Austl.
113/H2 **Bald** (peak), Va,US
35/F3 **Baldock,** Eng,UK
77/E1 **Bald Rock Nat'l Park,** Austl.
115/C2 **Baldwin Park,** Ca,US
107/H3 **Baldy** (peak), Mb,Can

41/F4 Belm, Ger.
115/F5 Belmar, NJ,US
116/K11 Belmont, Ca,US
94/C4 Belmonte, Braz.
100/D4 Belmopan (cap.), Belz.
42/C2 Beloeil, Belg.
111/P6 Beloeil, Qu,Can
63/K1 Belogorsk, Rus.
50/F4 Belogradchik, Bul.
95/D1 Belo Horizonte, Braz.
109/H3 Beloit, Ks,US
110/B3 Beloit, Wi,US
94/C3 Belo Jardim, Braz.
52/G2 Belomorsk, Rus.
87/C1 Belondo-Kundu, Zaire
54/F3 Belorechensk, Rus.
53/N5 Beloretsk, Rus.
50/E4 Beloševac, Yugo.
51/H4 Beloslav, Bul.
56/J4 Belovo, Rus.
52/H3 Beloye (lake), Rus.
33/G5 Belper, Eng,UK
33/G1 Belsay, Eng,UK
106/F4 Belt, Mt,US
40/D3 Belterwijde (lake), Neth.
35/H1 Belton, Eng,UK
112/D4 Belton, Tx,US
115/K7 Beltsville, Md,US
51/H2 Bel'tsy, Mol.
115/E5 Beltzville (lake), Pa,US
68/E2 Belukha, Gora (peak), Rus.
110/B3 Belvidere, Il,US
76/B3 Belyando (riv.), Austl.
56/G2 Belyy (isl.), Rus.
38/G2 Belzig, Ger.
39/M3 Bełżyce, Pol.
89/H7 Bemaraha (plat.), Madg.
89/H7 Bemarivo (riv.), Madg.
46/B1 Bembibre, Sp.
35/E5 Bembridge, Eng,UK
107/K4 Bemidji, Mn,US
40/C5 Bemmel, Neth.
33/H3 Bempton, Eng,UK
77/C3 Benalla, Austl.
46/C4 Benalmádena, Sp.
46/C2 Benavente, Sp.
112/D5 Benavides, Tx,US
32/B1 Benbane Head (pt.), NI,UK
77/D3 Ben Boyd Nat'l Park, Austl.
32/B3 Benburb, NI,UK
106/C4 Bend, Or,US
85/G5 Bendel (state), Nga.
114/F2 Bendeleben (mtn.), Ak,US
51/J2 Bendery, Mol.
77/C3 Bendigo, Austl.
59/M8 Bene Beraq, Isr.
103/L3 Benedict (mtn.), Nf,Can
32/D1 Beneraid (hill), Sc,UK
45/L2 Benešov, Czh.
48/D2 Benevento, It.
35/G3 Benfleet, Eng,UK
70/E4 Bengal (bay), Asia
66/D4 Bengbu, China
83/K1 Benghāzī, Libya
69/D3 Ben Giang, Viet.
72/B3 Bengkalis, Indo.
72/B3 Bengkalis (isl.), Indo.
72/C3 Bengkayang, Indo.
72/B4 Bengkulu, Indo.
107/G3 Bengough, Sk,Can
37/E4 Bengtsfors, Swe.
87/B3 Benguela, Ang.
87/F3 Bengweulu (lake), Zam.
92/E6 Beni (riv.), Bol.
83/L7 Beni, Zaire
82/E1 Beni Abbes, Alg.
47/F2 Benicarló, Sp.
116/K10 Benicia, Ca,US
47/E3 Benidorm, Sp.
47/E3 Benifayó, Sp.
82/D1 Beni Mellal, Mor.
85/F4 Benin
85/F5 Benin (bight), Ben., Nga.
85/G5 Benin City, Nga.
82/E1 Beni Ounif, Alg.
47/F3 Benisa, Sp.
96/B5 Benjamin (isl.), Chile
112/D3 Benjamin, Tx,US
92/D4 Benjamin Constant, Braz.
101/M7 Benjamín Hill, Mex.
109/G2 Benkelman, Ne,US
32/D5 Benllech, Wal,UK
36/C2 Ben Lomond (mtn.), Sc,UK
77/C4 Ben Lomond Nat'l Park, Austl.
36/D2 Ben Macdui (mtn.), Sc,UK
36/C2 Ben More (mtn.), Sc,UK
32/C1 Bennane Head (pt.), Sc,UK
57/R2 Bennett (isl.), Rus.
113/J3 Bennettsville, SC,US
36/C2 Ben Nevis (mtn.), Sc,UK
111/F3 Bennington, Vt,US
88/Q13 Benoni, SAfr.
89/J6 Be, Nosy (isl.), Madg.
82/H6 Bénoué Nat'l Park, Camr.
69/D2 Ben Quang, Viet.
116/Q16 Bensenville, Il,US
45/H2 Bensheim, Ger.
108/E5 Benson, Az,US
107/K4 Benson, Mn,US
33/F3 Bentham, Eng,UK
41/E4 Bentheim, Ger.
83/L6 Bentiu, Sudan
33/G4 Bentley, Eng,UK
95/B4 Bento Gonçalves, Braz.
112/E3 Benton, Ar,US
110/B4 Benton, Il,US
110/B4 Benton, Ky,US
72/B3 Bentong, Malay.
110/C3 Benton Harbor, Mi,US
112/E2 Bentonville, Ar,US
69/D4 Ben Tre, Viet.
85/G4 Benue (riv.), Nga.
85/G5 Benue (state), Nga.
50/D3 Beočin, Yugo.
50/E3 Beograd (Belgrade) (cap.), Yugo.
64/B4 Beppu, Japan
64/B4 Beppu (bay), Japan
82/E1 Beraber (well), Alg.
32/A2 Beragh, NI,UK
49/F2 Berat, Alb.
73/E4 Beratus (peak), Indo.
73/H4 Berau (bay), Indo.
73/E3 Berau (riv.), Indo.
83/G5 Berbera, Som.
82/J7 Berberati, CAfr.
92/G2 Berbice (riv.), Guy.
42/D1 Berchem, Belg.
45/K3 Berchtesgaden, Ger.
45/K3 Berchtesgaden Nat'l Park, Ger.
42/A3 Berck, Fr.
54/D2 Berdichev, Ukr.
56/J4 Berdsk, Rus.
54/F3 Berdyansk, Ukr.
110/C4 Berea, Ky,US
54/B2 Beregovo, Ukr.
85/E5 Berekum, Gha.
86/C4 Berenice (ruins), Egypt
34/D5 Bere Regis, Eng,UK
111/H2 Beresford, NB,Can
107/J5 Beresford, SD,US
50/E2 Berettyo (riv.), Hun.
50/E2 Berettyóújfalu, Hun.
54/D1 Berezina (riv.), Bela.
53/N4 Berezniki, Rus.
88/B4 Berg (riv.), SAfr.
59/A2 Bergama, Turk.
45/H4 Bergamo, It.
40/B3 Bergen, Neth.
37/C3 Bergen, Nor.
41/G3 Bergen-Belsen, Ger.
115/F5 Bergenfield, NJ,US
40/B6 Bergen op Zoom, Neth.
44/D4 Bergerac, Fr.
40/C6 Bergeyk, Neth.
43/F2 Bergheim, Ger.
41/E6 Bergisch Gladbach, Ger.
41/E5 Bergkamen, Ger.
41/E6 Bergneustadt, Ger.
40/C2 Bergum, Neth.
40/D2 Bergumermeer (lake), Neth.
70/D4 Berhampur, India
72/C4 Berikat (cape), Indo.
57/S4 Bering (isl.), Rus.
114/E3 Bering (str.), Rus., Ak,US
43/E1 Beringen, Belg.
114/E2 Bering Land Bridge Nat'l Prsv., Ak,US
72/B4 Beritarikap (cape), Indo.
46/D4 Berja, Sp.
40/D4 Berkel (riv.), Ger.
40/B5 Berkel, Neth.
34/D3 Berkeley, Eng,UK
116/K11 Berkeley, Ca,US
115/F5 Berkeley Heights, NJ,US
31/M6 Berkhamsted, Eng,UK
116/F6 Berkley, Mi,US
98/W Berkner (isl.), Ant.
51/F4 Berkovitsa, Bul.
35/E4 Berkshire (co.), Eng,UK
35/E4 Berkshire Downs (uplands), Eng,UK
42/C5 Berlare, Belg.
40/C5 Berlicum, Neth.
39/G2 Berlin (cap.), Ger.
111/G2 Berlin, NH,US
98/V Berlioz (pt.), Ant.
50/E5 Bermejo (riv.), Arg.
91/D1 Bermejo, Bol.
46/D1 Bermeo, Sp.
99/L6 Bermuda (isl.), UK
45/G3 Bern (cap.), Swi.
92/B5 Bernal, Peru
48/E2 Bernalda, It.
108/F4 Bernalillo, NM,US
102/D1 Bernard (riv.), NW,Can
97/J7 Bernardo O'Higgins Nat'l Park, Chile
115/G5 Bernardsville, NJ,US
44/D2 Bernay, Fr.
38/F3 Bernburg, Ger.
41/F2 Berne (riv.), Ger.
45/G3 Bernese Alps (range), Swi.
31/S9 Bernes-sur-Oise, Fr.
74/A4 Bernier (isl.), Austl.
102/G1 Bernier (bay), NW,Can
45/J3 Bernina, Passo del (pass), Swi.
42/C3 Bernissart, Belg.
43/G4 Bernkastel-Kues, Ger.
89/H8 Beroroha, Madg.
45/L2 Beroun, Czh.
45/K2 Berounka (riv.), Czh.
50/C5 Berovo, Macd.
44/F5 Berre (lag.), Fr.
34/C1 Berriew, Wal,UK
81/S15 Berrouaghia, Alg.
101/F2 Berry (isls.), Bahm.
44/D3 Berry (hist. reg.), Fr.
116/K9 Berryessa (lake), Ca,US
116/K9 Berryessa (peak), Ca,US
34/C6 Berry Head (pt.), Eng,UK
112/E2 Berryville, Ar,US
82/H7 Bertoua, Camr.
97/J7 Bertrand (peak), Arg.
43/E4 Bertrix, Belg.
78/G5 Beru (atoll), Kiri.
72/D3 Beruit (isl.), Malay.
77/G5 Berwick, Austl.
111/H2 Berwick, NB,Can
36/D3 Berwick-upon-Tweed, Eng,UK
32/E6 Berwyn (mts.), Wal,UK
116/Q16 Berwyn, Il,US
115/E5 Berwyn-Devon, Pa,US
44/E4 Bès (riv.), Fr.
89/H7 Besalampy, Madg.
44/G3 Besançon, Fr.
73/E4 Besar (peak), Indo.
44/F3 Besbre (riv.), Fr.
56/F6 Beshahr, Iran
50/E3 Beška, Yugo.
39/K4 Beskids (mts.), Pol.
55/H4 Beslan, Rus.
50/F4 Besna Kobila (peak), Yugo.
107/G2 Besnard (lake), Sk,Can
33/G4 Bessacarr, Eng,UK
31/S9 Bessancourt, Fr.
51/J2 Bessarabia (reg.), Mol.
36/B3 Bessbrook, NI,UK
113/G3 Bessemer, Al,US
110/B2 Bessemer, Mi,US
116/D2 Bessemer (mtn.), Wa,US
55/K3 Besshoky, Gora (peak), Kaz.
42/D6 Best, Neth.
41/F6 Bestwig, Ger.
48/A1 Betanzos, Sp.
81/M14 Beth (riv.), Mor.
59/N7 Beth Alpha Synagogue Nat'l Park, Isr.
109/J2 Bethany, Mo,US
32/D5 Bethesda, Wal,UK
115/J8 Bethesda, Md,US
88/E3 Bethlehem, SAfr.
115/F5 Bethlehem, Pa,US
59/K6 Bethlehem (Bayt Laḩm), WBnk.
115/G5 Bethpage, NY,US
107/G3 Bethune, Sk,Can
42/B2 Béthune, Fr.
42/A4 Béthune (riv.), Fr.
95/C1 Betim, Braz.
89/H8 Betioky, Madg.
68/A2 Betpak-Dala (des.), Kaz.
43/G6 Betschdorf, Fr.
59/K5 Bet She'an, Isr.
59/M9 Bet Shemesh, Isr.
111/G1 Betsiamites (riv.), Qu,Can
89/H7 Betsiboka (riv.), Madg.
63/J3 Bette (peak), Libya
43/F4 Bettembourg, Lux.
70/D2 Bettiah, India
70/C4 Betūl, India
40/C5 Betuwe (reg.), Neth.
32/E5 Betws-y-Coed, Wal,UK
43/G6 Betzdorf, Ger.
107/H4 Beulah, ND,US
40/D3 Beulakerwijde (lake), Neth.
35/G4 Beult (riv.), Eng,UK
43/D2 Beuningen, Neth.
44/D3 Beuvron (riv.), Fr.
31/U10 Beuvronne (riv.), Fr.
42/B2 Beuvry, Fr.
42/D3 Bevensen, Ger.
41/E4 Bever (riv.), Ger.
42/D2 Beveren, Belg.
33/H4 Beverley, Eng,UK
115/B2 Beverly Hills, Ca,US
116/F6 Beverly Hills, Mi,US
41/G5 Beverungen, Ger.
40/B4 Beverwijk, Neth.
33/F1 Bewcastle, Eng,UK
34/D2 Bewdley, Eng,UK
35/G4 Bewl Bridge (res.), Eng,UK
43/G5 Bexbach, Ger.
35/G5 Bexhill, Eng,UK
31/P7 Bexley (bor.), Eng,UK
51/J5 Beykoz, Turk.
42/A6 Beyne-Heusay, Belg.
51/K5 Beypazarı, Turk.
58/B2 Beyşehir, Turk.
59/B3 Beyşehir (lake), Turk.
50/D3 Bezdan, Yugo.
45/L1 Bezděz (peak), Czh.
52/H4 Bezhetsk, Rus.
44/E5 Béziers, Fr.
70/E3 Bhabua, India
70/E3 Bhadrak, India
70/C5 Bhadrāvati, India
70/E4 Bhadreswar, India
70/E3 Bhāgalpur, India
61/K2 Bhakkar, Pak.
70/E2 Bhaktapur, Nepal
71/G3 Bhamo, Burma
70/C2 Bharatpur, India
70/C3 Bharuch, India
70/E3 Bhātāpāra, India
61/K2 Bhatinda, India
70/E4 Bhatkal, India
70/E3 Bhātpāra, India
70/C5 Bhavāni, India
70/C3 Bhavnagar, India
70/C3 Bhawāni Mandi, India
70/D4 Bhawānipatna, India
70/D3 Bhilai, India
70/B2 Bhīlwāra, India
70/C4 Bhīma (riv.), India
70/D4 Bhīmavaram, India
70/D4 Bhimunipatnam, India
70/C2 Bhind, India
70/B3 Bhīnmāl, India
70/B4 Bhiwandi, India
70/E2 Bhojpur, Nepal
70/C3 Bhopāl, India
70/B4 Bhor, India
70/E3 Bhuban, India
70/E3 Bhubaneswar, India
70/A3 Bhūj, India
69/B2 Bhumibol (dam), Thai.
70/C3 Bhusawal, India
70/E2 Bhutan
68/F5 Bi (riv.), China
92/E4 Biá (riv.), Braz.
84/E5 Bia (riv.), Gui., IvC.
42/B3 Biache-Saint-Vaast, Fr.
82/G7 Biafra (bight), Afr.
73/J4 Biak (isl.), Indo.
39/M2 Biała Podlaska, Pol.
39/M3 Biała Podlaska (prov.), Pol.
39/L3 Białobrzegi, Pol.
39/J2 Białogard, Pol.
39/K4 Białowieski Nat'l Park, Pol.
39/M2 Białystok, Pol.
39/M2 Białystok (prov.), Pol.
45/J3 Bianca (peak), It.
48/D4 Biancavilla, It.
83/L7 Biaro, Zaire
44/C5 Biarritz, Fr.
86/B2 Bibā, Egypt
95/K6 Bicas, Braz.
51/H2 Bicaz, Rom.
35/E4 Bicester, Eng,UK
74/F2 Bickerton (isl.), Austl.
50/D2 Bicske, Hun.
84/D5 Bidaga (rapids), IvC.
70/C4 Bīdar, India
111/G3 Biddeford, Me,US
35/F4 Biddulph, Eng,UK
34/B4 Bideford, Eng,UK
34/B4 Bideford (Barnstaple) (bay), Eng,UK
35/E2 Bidford on Avon, Eng,UK
69/E3 Bi Doup (peak), Viet.
47/E1 Bidouze (riv.), Fr.
87/B4 Bíe (plat.), Ang.
39/M2 Biebrza (riv.), Pol.
45/G3 Biel, Swi.
39/J3 Bielawa, Pol.
41/F4 Bielefeld, Ger.
103/J1 Bieler (lake), NW,Can
39/K4 Bielsko (prov.), Pol.
39/K4 Bielsko-Biała, Pol.
39/M2 Bielsk Podlaski, Pol.
69/D4 Bien Hoa, Viet.
69/D4 Bien Son, Viet.
103/J3 Bienville (lake), Qu,Can
40/B5 Biesbosch (reg.), Neth.
40/D5 Biesme (riv.), Fr.
45/G4 Bietschhorn (peak), Swi.
31/S10 Bièvre (riv.), Fr.
31/S10 Bièvres, Fr.
48/D2 Biferno (riv.), It.
77/B2 Big (des.), Austl.
103/J2 Big (isl.), NW,Can
102/D1 Big (riv.), NW,Can
51/H5 Biga, Turk.
51/H5 Bigadiç, Turk.
106/F4 Big Belt (mts.), Mt,US
112/C4 Big Bend Nat'l Park, Tx,US
109/K4 Big Black (riv.), Ms,US
108/H2 Big Blue (riv.), Ks, Ne,US
34/C6 Bigbury (bay), Eng,UK
114/D2 Big Diomede (isl.), Rus.
107/K4 Big Fork (riv.), Mn,US
106/G2 Biggar, Sk,Can
43/G1 Biggasee (lake), Ger.
74/D2 Bigge (isl.), Austl.
41/E6 Bigge (riv.), Ger.
41/E6 Biggesee (res.), Ger.
31/P8 Biggin Hill, Eng,UK
35/F2 Biggleswade, Eng,UK
88/D3 Big Hole, SAfr.
106/E4 Big Hole (riv.), Mt,US
106/F4 Bighorn (lake), Mt, Wy,US
106/G4 Bighorn (mts.), Mt, Wy,US
106/G4 Bighorn (riv.), Mt, Wy,US
108/E1 Bighorn (basin), Wy,US
102/F4 Bighorn Canyon Nat'l Rec. Area, Mt,US
112/C4 Big Lake, Tx,US
108/D2 Big Lost (riv.), Id,US
116/P14 Big Muskego (lake), Wi,US
84/A3 Bignona, Sen.
110/C3 Big Rapids, Mi,US
106/G2 Big River, Sk,Can
116/N16 Big Rock (cr.), Il,US
113/H4 Big Saltilla (cr.), Ga,US
109/G3 Big Sandy (cr.), Co,US
113/F2 Big Sandy (riv.), Tn,US
108/E2 Big Sandy (riv.), Wy,US
107/J5 Big Sioux (riv.), Ia, SD,US
112/C3 Big Spring, Tx,US
107/J4 Big Stone (lake), Mn, SD,US
110/D4 Big Stone Gap, Va,US
106/F4 Big Timber, Mt,US
102/H3 Big Trout (lake), On,Can
115/B2 Big Tujunga (canyon), Ca,US
95/B3 Biguaçu, Braz.
108/D2 Big Wood (riv.), Id,US
50/B3 Bihać, Yugo.
70/E3 Bihār, India
70/E3 Bihār (state), India
50/F2 Bihor (co.), Rom.
42/A4 Bihorel, Fr.
84/A4 Bijagós (isls.), GBis.
70/C4 Bijāpur, India
60/E1 Bījār, Iran
50/D3 Bijeljina, Bosn.
50/D4 Bijelo Polje, Yugo.
70/C2 Bijnor, India
70/B2 Bīkaner, India
78/G3 Bikar (atoll), Mrsh.
63/L2 Bikin, Rus.
63/M2 Bikin (riv.), Rus.
78/F3 Bikini (atoll), Mrsh.
87/C4 Bikuar Nat'l Park, Moz.
69/B3 Bilauktaung (range), Burma, Thai.
74/G5 Bilba Morea Claypan (lake), Austl.
46/D1 Bilbao, Sp.
86/B2 Bilbays, Egypt
50/D4 Bileća, Bosn.
59/B2 Bilecik, Turk.
51/K5 Bilecik (prov.), Turk.
39/M3 Biłgoraj, Pol.
57/S3 Bilibino, Rus.
69/B2 Bilin (riv.), Burma
77/C2 Billabong (cr.), Austl.
41/H1 Bille (riv.), Ger.
41/E5 Billerbeck, Ger.
44/C5 Billère, Fr.
35/G3 Billericay, Eng,UK
77/B2 Billiat Consv. Park, Austl.
33/F5 Billinge, Eng,UK
33/G2 Billingham, Eng,UK
106/F4 Billings, Mt,US
35/F4 Billingshurst, Eng,UK
58/K10 Billiton (isl.), Indo.
108/D4 Bill Williams (riv.), Az,US
76/C4 Biloela, Austl.
113/F4 Biloxi, Ms,US
70/C2 Bilsi, India
43/E2 Bilzen, Belg.
73/E5 Bima, Indo.
77/D2 Bimberi (peak), Austl.
101/F2 Bimini (isls.), Bahm.
70/C3 Bina-Etāwa, India
81/X17 Bin 'Arūs (gov.), Tun.
111/Q9 Binbrook, On,Can
33/H5 Binbrook, Eng,UK
42/D3 Binche, Belg.
62/G2 Binder, Mong.
70/D2 Bindki, India
87/C2 Bindu, Zaire
87/F4 Bindura, Zim.
47/F2 Binéfar, Sp.
35/F4 Binfield, Eng,UK
87/F4 Binga (mtn.), Moz.
45/G2 Bingen, Ger.
84/E5 Bingerville, IvC.
33/H6 Bingham, Eng,UK
110/F3 Binghamton, NY,US
53/G4 Bingley, Eng,UK
59/E2 Bingöl, Turk.
66/D4 Binhai, China
69/D4 Binh Chanh, Viet.
69/D4 Binh Chau, Viet.
71/G4 Binhon (peak), Burma
69/E3 Binh Son, Viet.
72/A3 Binjai, Indo.
73/E3 Binongko (isl.), Indo.
72/B2 Bintang (peak), Malay.
71/J3 Binyang, China
66/D3 Binzhou, China
96/B3 Bío-Bío (reg.), Chile
96/B3 Bío-Bío (riv.), Chile
50/B4 Biograd, Cro.
50/D4 Biogradska Nat'l Park, Yugo.
82/G7 Bioko (isl.), EqG.
70/C3 Bīr, India
82/H2 Birāk, Libya
82/H2 Bi'r al Ghuzayyil (well), Libya
83/K2 Bi'r al Ḩarash (well), Libya
70/E2 Birātnagar, Nepal
102/E3 Birch (mts.), Ab,Can
107/G2 Birch Hills, Sk,Can
107/H2 Birch River, Mb,Can
98/X Bird (isl.), Ant.
75/K4 Bird Islet (isl.), Austl.
77/D2 Birds Rock (peak), Austl.
59/D3 Birecik, Turk.
95/B2 Birigui, Braz.
95/G8 Biritiba-Mirim, Braz.
61/G2 Bīrjand, Iran
78/G4 Birkenebeu, Kiri.
33/E5 Birkenhead, Eng,UK
45/J3 Birkkarspitze (peak), Aus.
51/H2 Bîrlad, Rom.
51/H2 Bîrlad (riv.), Rom.
68/B3 Birlik, Kaz.
35/E2 Birmingham, Eng,UK
113/G3 Birmingham, Al,US
116/F6 Birmingham, Mi,US
45/K3 Birnhorn (peak), Aus.
79/H5 Birnie (isl.), Kiri.
85/G3 Birni Nkonni, Niger
63/L2 Birobidzhan, Rus.
84/D3 Bîr Ounâne (well), Mali
45/G3 Birse (riv.), Swi.
53/M5 Birsk, Rus.
52/E4 Biržai, Lith.
51/F4 Bis (lake), Rom.
65/M9 Bisai, Japan
108/E5 Bisbee, Az,US
44/C4 Biscarrosse, Fr.
44/C4 Biscarrosse (lag.), Fr.
44/B4 Biscay (bay), Eur.
113/H5 Biscayne Nat'l Park, Fl,US
48/E2 Bisceglie, It.
45/G2 Bischheim, Fr.
45/K3 Bischofshofen, Aus.
43/G6 Bischwiller, Fr.
98/V Biscoe (isls.), Ant.
101/H6 Biscucuy, Ven.
60/D4 Bīshah (dry riv.), SAr.
68/B3 Bishkek (cap.), Kyr.
108/C3 Bishop, Ca,US
33/G2 Bishop Auckland, Eng,UK
34/D2 Bishops Castle, Eng,UK
34/D3 Bishops Cleeve, Eng,UK
111/L1 Bishop's Falls, Nf,Can
35/G3 Bishop's Stortford, Eng,UK
35/E5 Bishops Waltham, Eng,UK
33/H4 Bishop Wilton, Eng,UK
82/G1 Biskra, Alg.
39/L2 Biskupiec, Pol.
67/E6 Bislig, Phil.
111/Q9 Bismarck, On,Can
78/D5 Bismarck (arch.), PNG
78/D5 Bismarck (sea), PNG
107/H4 Bismarck (cap.), ND,US
59/E3 Bismil, Turk.
84/B4 Bissau (cap.), GBis.
41/F4 Bissendorf, Ger.
107/K3 Bissett, Mb,Can
51/G2 Bistrița, Rom.
51/G2 Bistrița-Năsăud (co.), Rom.
92/E2 Bita (riv.), Col.
82/H7 Bitam, Gabon
43/F4 Bitburg, Ger.
43/G5 Bitche, Fr.
82/J5 Bitkin, Chad
59/E2 Bitlis, Turk.
50/E5 Bitola, Macd.
50/C5 Bitonto, It.
51/G3 Bitrița (riv.), Rom.
86/C2 Bitter (lakes), Egypt
106/E4 Bitterroot (range), Id, Mt,US
73/G3 Bitung, Indo.
82/H5 Biu, Nga.
65/M9 Biwa, Japan
64/E3 Biwa (lake), Japan
109/J4 Bixby, Ok,US
59/H6 Biyalā, Egypt
56/J4 Biysk, Rus.
111/N7 Bizard (isl.), Qu,Can
81/W17 Bizerte (Banzart), Tun.
37/M6 Bjargtangar (pt.), Ice.
38/G1 Bjärred, Swe.
50/C3 Bjelovar, Cro.
103/S7 Bjorne (pen.), NW,Can
35/E1 Blaby, Eng,UK
39/K3 Blachownia, Pol.
54/D4 Black (sea), Asia, Eur.
110/B1 Black (bay), On,Can
107/L2 Black (riv.), On,Can
114/M3 Black (mtn.), Yk,Can
69/C1 Black (riv.), China
54/D4 Black (sea), Eur.
45/H2 Black (for.), Ger.
88/A2 Black (pt.), Namb.
34/A6 Black (pt.), Eng,UK
34/C3 Black (mtn.), Wal,UK
34/C3 Black (mts.), Wal,UK
109/K3 Black (riv.), Ar, Mo,US
108/D4 Black (mts.), Az,US
108/E4 Black (riv.), Az,US
116/L11 Black (hills), Ca,US
116/G5 Black (riv.), Mi,US
108/F4 Black (range), NM,US
110/F3 Black (riv.), NY,US
107/H5 Black (hills), SD, Wy,US
107/L4 Black (riv.), Wi,US
35/E3 Black Bourton, Eng,UK
33/F4 Blackburn, Eng,UK
32/D1 Blackcraig (hill), Sc,UK
69/C1 Black (Da) (riv.), Viet.
106/E3 Black Diamond, Ab,Can
35/F4 Blackdown (hill), Eng,UK
34/C5 Blackdown (hills), Eng,UK
76/C3 Blackdown Tableland Nat'l Park, Austl.
106/F4 Black Eagle, Mt,US
106/E5 Blackfoot, Id,US
106/E5 Blackfoot (res.), Id,US
33/G2 Blackhall Rocks, Eng,UK
32/C2 Black Head (pt.), NI,UK
108/E3 Black Mesa (upland), Az,US
34/B6 Blackmoor (upland), Eng,UK
31/P6 Blackmore, Eng,UK
76/B1 Black Mountain Nat'l Park, Austl.
33/E4 Blackpool, Eng,UK
88/A2 Black Reef (pt.), Namb.
110/B2 Black River Falls, Wi,US
108/C2 Black Rock (des.), Nv,US
33/F4 Blackrod, Eng,UK
110/D4 Blacksburg, Va,US
113/H3 Blackshear (lake), Ga,US
110/E4 Blackstone, Va,US
77/D1 Black Sugarloaf (peak), Austl.
76/G8 Blacktown, Austl.
111/H2 Blackville, NB,Can
84/E4 Black Volta (riv.), Afr.
113/G3 Black Warrior (riv.), Al,US
76/C3 Blackwater, Austl.
32/B4 Blackwater (riv.), Ire.
36/A4 Blackwater (riv.), Ire.
35/G3 Blackwater (riv.), Eng,UK
32/B3 Blackwater (riv.), NI,UK
109/J3 Blackwater (riv.), Mo,US
109/H3 Blackwell, Ok,US
34/C3 Blackwood, Wal,UK
115/K6 Bladensburg, Md,US
76/A3 Bladensburg Nat'l Park, Austl.
32/D2 Bladnoch (riv.), Sc,UK
32/E6 Blaenau-Ffestiniog, Wal,UK
34/C3 Blaenavon, Wal,UK
44/D5 Blagnac, Fr.
51/F4 Blagoevgrad, Bul.
63/K1 Blagoveshchensk, Rus.
106/G2 Blaine Lake, Sk,Can
111/N6 Blainville, Qu,Can
109/H2 Blair, Ne,US
106/E3 Blairmore, Ab,Can
115/F5 Blairstown, NJ,US
44/F2 Blaise (riv.), Fr.
51/F2 Blaj, Rom.
113/G4 Blakely, Ga,US
82/B3 Blanc (cape), Mrta.
96/E3 Blanca (bay), Arg.
92/C5 Blanca (range), Peru
46/E3 Blanca, Sp.
47/E4 Blanca (coast), Sp.
109/F4 Blanca (peak), NM,US
74/C4 Blanche (lake), Austl.
74/C5 Blanche (lake), Austl.
45/G4 Blanc, Mont (mtn.), Fr., It.
42/A2 Blanc Nez (cape), Fr.
97/K6 Blanco (riv.), Arg.
97/K8 Blanco (lake), Chile
96/C1 Blanco (riv.), Chile
100/D6 Blanco (cape), CR
92/B4 Blanco (cape), Peru
106/B5 Blanco (cape), Or,US
109/H5 Blanco (riv.), Tx,US
34/D5 Blandford Forum, Eng,UK
108/E3 Blanding, Ut,US
47/G2 Blanes, Sp.
47/G1 Blanes, Serre de (mtn.), Fr.
39/G4 Blanice (riv.), Czh.
42/C1 Blankenberge, Belg.
43/F3 Blankenheim, Ger.
101/J5 Blanquilla (isl.), Ven.
39/J4 Blansko, Czh.
87/G4 Blantyre, Malw.
44/F3 Blanzy, Fr.
40/C4 Blaricum, Neth.
38/E1 Blåvands Huk (pt.), Den.
44/B2 Blavet (riv.), Fr.
74/D2 Blaze (pt.), Austl.
41/H2 Bleckede, Ger.
42/E2 Blégny, Belg.
42/C2 Bléharies, Belg.
50/B2 Bleiburg, Aus.
41/H6 Bleicherode, Ger.
40/B4 Bleiswijk, Neth.
37/E4 Blekinge (co.), Swe.
75/R11 Blenheim, NZ
35/E3 Blenheim Palace, Eng,UK
45/G4 Bléone (riv.), Fr.
42/C4 Blérancourt, Fr.
88/C4 Blesberg (peak), SAfr.
31/N8 Bletchingley, Eng,UK
35/F3 Bletchley, Eng,UK
35/E2 Blewbury, Eng,UK
81/S15 Blida, Alg.
33/G5 Blidworth, Eng,UK
43/G5 Blies (riv.), Fr., Ger.
43/G5 Bliesbruck, Fr.
43/G5 Blieskastel, Ger.
79/Y18 Bligh Water (sound), Fiji
73/F2 Blik (mt.), Phil.
33/G6 Blithfield (res.), Eng,UK
98/L Blizzard (peak), Ant.
40/B4 Bloemendaal, Neth.
88/D3 Bloemfontein, SAfr.
88/D3 Bloemhofdam (res.), SAfr.
44/D3 Blois, Fr.
40/C3 Blokker, Neth.
107/J3 Bloodvein (riv.), Mb, On,Can
36/A3 Bloody Foreland (pt.), Ire.
110/B2 Bloomer, Wi,US
115/F5 Bloomfield, NJ,US
108/F3 Bloomfield, NM,US
116/F6 Bloomfield Hills, Mi,US
116/P16 Bloomingdale, Il,US
115/C2 Bloomington, Ca,US
110/B3 Bloomington, Il,US
110/C4 Bloomington, In,US
107/K4 Bloomington, Mn,US
72/D5 Blora, Indo.
113/G4 Blountstown, Fl,US
98/L Blowaway (peak), Ant.
35/E3 Bloxham, Eng,UK
34/E1 Bloxwich, Eng,UK
45/K1 Blšanka (riv.), Czh.
45/H3 Bludenz, Aus.
71/F3 Blue (mtn.), India
112/D3 Blue (riv.), Ok,US
106/D4 Blue (mts.), Or, Wa,US
107/K5 Blue Earth, Mn,US
110/D4 Bluefield, Va,US
110/D4 Bluefield, WV,US
100/E5 Bluefields, Nic.
116/Q16 Blue Island, Il,US
108/C2 Bluejoint (lake), Or,US
76/D4 Blue Lake Nat'l Park, Austl.
108/F3 Blue Mesa (res.), Co,US
101/F4 Blue Mountain (pk.), Jam.
77/D2 Blue Mountains Nat'l Park, Austl.
74/F2 Blue Mud (bay), Austl.
83/M5 Blue Nile (riv.), Eth., Sudan
102/E2 Bluenose (lake), NW,Can
113/G3 Blue Ridge, Ga,US
113/H2 Blue Ridge (mts.), NC, Va,US
75/Q12 Bluff, NZ
110/C3 Bluffton, In,US
95/B3 Blumenau, Braz.
33/G1 Blyth, Eng,UK
33/G5 Blyth, Eng,UK
35/H2 Blyth (riv.), Eng,UK
33/F6 Blythe (riv.), Eng,UK
108/D4 Blythe, Ca,US
33/F6 Blythe Bridge, Eng,UK
113/F3 Blytheville, Ar,US
69/D4 B'nom M'hai (peak), Viet.
84/C5 Bo, SLeo.
67/D5 Boac, Phil.
100/D5 Boaco, Nic.
95/C2 Boa Esperança, Braz.
94/A2 Boa Esperança (res.), Braz.
73/G4 Boano (isl.), Indo.
103/H2 Boas (riv.), NW,Can
94/C2 Boa Viagem, Braz.
92/F3 Boa Vista, Braz.
80/K10 Boa Vista (isl.), CpV.
113/G3 Boaz, Al,US
71/J3 Bobai, China
81/G6 Bobaomby (cape), Madg.
70/D4 Bobbili, India
42/B6 Bobigny, Fr.
45/H2 Böblingen, Ger.
84/D4 Bobo Dioulasso, Burk.
50/D4 Bobotov Kuk (peak), Yugo.
50/F4 Bobovdol, Bul.
39/H3 Bóbr (riv.), Pol.
54/G2 Bobrov, Rus.
54/D1 Bobruysk, Bela.
89/H8 Boby (peak), Madg.
92/E5 Boca do Acre, Braz.
95/J7 Bocaina (mts.), Braz.
94/E5 Bocaiúva, Braz.
113/H5 Boca Raton, Fl,US
100/D5 Bocay, Nic.
39/L4 Bochnia, Pol.
43/E1 Bocholt, Belg.
40/D5 Bocholt, Ger.
41/E6 Bochum, Ger.
41/H4 Bockenem, Ger.
35/G3 Bocking, Eng,UK
101/G6 Boconó, Ven.
43/D3 Bocq (riv.), Belg.
82/J7 Boda, CAfr.
57/M4 Bodaybo, Rus.
78/F3 Bode (riv.), Ger.
108/B3 Bodega (bay), Ca,US
40/C4 Bodegraven, Neth.
82/J4 Bodélé (depr.), Chad
37/G2 Boden, Swe.
45/H3 Bodensee (Constance) (lake), Ger., Swi.
70/C4 Bodhan, India
70/C5 Bodināyakkanūr, India
34/B6 Bodmin, Eng,UK
34/B5 Bodmin Moor (upland), Eng,UK
37/E2 Bodø, Nor.
62/C2 Bodonchiyn (riv.), Mong.
50/E1 Bodrog (riv.), Hun.
59/A3 Bodrum, Turk.
69/D4 Bo Duc, Viet.
88/A2 Boegoeberg (peak), Namb.
40/C5 Boekel, Neth.
87/D1 Boende, Zaire
109/K4 Boeuf (riv.), Ar, La,US
113/F4 Bogalusa, La,US
77/C1 Bogan (riv.), Austl.
85/E3 Bogandé, Burk.
50/D3 Bogatić, Yugo.
39/H3 Bogatynia, Pol.
59/C2 Boğazlıyan, Turk.
63/E5 Bogcang (riv.), China
62/E2 Bogd, Mong.
62/B3 Bogda (mts.), China
68/E3 Bogda Feng (peak), China
35/F5 Bognor Regis, Eng,UK
43/D4 Bogny-sur-Meuse, Fr.
67/D5 Bogo, Phil.
77/C3 Bogong (peak), Austl.
77/C3 Bogong Nat'l Park, Austl.

Bogor - Bucur

72/C5 **Bogor,** Indo.
92/D3 **Bogotá** (cap.), Col.
50/E5 **Bogovinje,** Macd.
70/E3 **Bogra,** Bang.
32/E1 **Bogrie** (hill), Sc,UK
84/B2 **Bogué,** Mrta.
66/D3 **Bohai** (bay), China
66/E3 **Bohai** (str.), China
66/D3 **Bo Hai** (Chihli) (gulf), China
42/C4 **Bohain-en-Vermandois,** Fr.
45/K1 **Bohemia** (reg.), Czh.
41/G3 **Böhme** (riv.), Ger.
41/F4 **Bohmte,** Ger.
67/D6 **Bohol** (isl.), Phil.
71/J4 **Bo Ho Su,** Viet.
48/D2 **Boiano,** It.
94/C4 **Boipeda** (isl.), Braz.
46/A1 **Boiro,** Sp.
95/B1 **Bois** (riv.), Braz.
31/S10 **Bois-d'Arcy,** Fr.
106/D5 **Boise** (cap.), Id,US
106/E5 **Boise** (riv.), Id,US
109/G3 **Boise City,** Ok,US
42/A5 **Bois-Guillaume,** Fr.
107/H3 **Boissevain,** Mb,Can
31/S9 **Boissy-l'Aillerie,** Fr.
31/T10 **Boissy-Saint-Léger,** Fr.
41/H2 **Boizenburg,** Ger.
82/C2 **Bojador** (cape), WSah.
39/J4 **Bojkovice,** Czh.
61/G1 **Bojnūrd,** Iran
84/B4 **Boké** (comm.), Gui.
87/D1 **Bokele,** Zaire
37/C4 **Boknafjorden** (fjord), Nor.
83/N7 **Bokol** (peak), Kenya
82/J5 **Bokoro,** Chad
88/E2 **Boksburg,** SAfr.
84/B4 **Bolama,** GBis.
61/J3 **Bolān** (pass), Pak.
46/D3 **Bolaños de Calatrava,** Sp.
44/D2 **Bolbec,** Fr.
51/H3 **Boldeşti-Scăeni,** Rom.
33/G2 **Boldon,** Eng,UK
85/E4 **Bole,** Gha.
39/H3 **Bolesławiec,** Pol.
85/E4 **Bolgatanga,** Gha.
116/P16 **Bolingbrook,** Il,US
96/E3 **Bolívar,** Arg.
109/J3 **Bolivar,** Mo,US
110/B5 **Bolivar,** Tn,US
101/G6 **Bolívar** (pk.), Ven.
92/F7 **Bolivia**
43/F4 **Bollendorf,** Ger.
44/F4 **Bollène,** Fr.
45/G3 **Bolligen,** Swi.
33/F5 **Bollin** (riv.), Eng,UK
33/F5 **Bollington,** Eng,UK
37/F3 **Bollnäs,** Swe.
46/B4 **Bollullos Par del Condado,** Sp.
35/F5 **Bolney,** Eng,UK
87/C1 **Bolobo,** Zaire
45/J4 **Bologna,** It.
52/G4 **Bologoye,** Rus.
83/J7 **Bolomba,** Zaire
63/M2 **Bolon'** (lake), Rus.
87/C2 **Bolongongo,** Ang.
69/D3 **Bolovens** (plat.), Laos
48/B1 **Bolsena** (lake), It.
55/K2 **Bol'shaya Khobda** (riv.), Kaz.
55/K1 **Bol'shaya Kinel'** (riv.), Rus.
53/P2 **Bol'shaya Rogovaya** (riv.), Rus.
53/N2 **Bol'shaya Synya** (riv.), Rus.
63/L2 **Bol'shaya Ussurka** (riv.), Rus.
57/L2 **Bol'shevik** (isl.), Rus.
53/M2 **Bol'shezemel'skaya** (tundra), Rus.
56/F2 **Bol'shoy Bolvanskiy Nos** (pt.), Rus.
55/H2 **Bol'shoy Irgiz** (riv.), Rus.
57/Q2 **Bol'shoy Lyakhovskiy** (isl.), Rus.
55/J2 **Bol'shoy Uzen'** (riv.), Kaz., Rus.
62/D1 **Bol'shoy Yenisey** (riv.), Rus.
33/G5 **Bolsover,** Eng,UK
40/C2 **Bolsward,** Neth.
34/C6 **Bolt Head** (pt.), Wal,UK
111/Q8 **Bolton,** On,Can
33/F4 **Bolton,** Eng,UK
33/G4 **Bolton Abbey,** Eng,UK
51/K5 **Bolu,** Turk.
51/K5 **Bolu** (prov.), Turk.
59/B2 **Bolvadin,** Turk.
87/B2 **Boma,** Zaire
77/D2 **Bomaderry,** Austl.
70/B4 **Bombay,** India
73/H4 **Bomberai** (pen.), Indo.
94/C3 **Bom Conselho,** Braz.
95/C1 **Bom Despacho,** Braz.
71/G2 **Bomi,** China
94/A1 **Bom Jardim,** Braz.
95/J6 **Bom Jardin de Minas,** Braz.
94/A3 **Bom Jesus,** Braz.
95/B4 **Bom Jesus,** Braz.
94/B3 **Bom Jesus da Gurguéia** (mts.), Braz.
94/B4 **Bom Jesus da Lapa,** Braz.
95/B1 **Bom Jesus de Goiás,** Braz.
95/D2 **Bom Jesus do Itabapoana,** Braz.
95/G8 **Bom Jesus dos Perdões,** Braz.
41/G3 **Bomlitz,** Ger.
95/B3 **Bom Retiro,** Braz.
83/L6 **Bomu** (riv.), Zaire
81/X17 **Bon** (cape), Tun.
114/K3 **Bona** (mtn.), Ak,US
101/H5 **Bonaire** (isl.), NAnt.
100/C4 **Bonampak** (ruins), Mex.
101/G4 **Bonao,** DRep.
74/C2 **Bonaparte** (arch.), Austl.
114/F3 **Bonasila** (mtn.), Ak,US
111/H1 **Bonaventure,** Qu,Can
111/H1 **Bonaventure** (riv.), Qu,Can
111/L1 **Bonavista** (bay), Nf,Can
111/L1 **Bonavista** (cape), Nf,Can
45/J4 **Bondeno,** It.
76/H8 **Bondi,** Austl.
83/K7 **Bondo,** Zaire
84/E4 **Bondoukou,** IvC.
72/D5 **Bondowoso,** Indo.
73/F4 **Bone** (gulf), Indo.
41/E5 **Bönen,** Ger.
73/F5 **Bonerate** (isls.), Indo.
68/F5 **Bong** (lake), China
84/C5 **Bong** (co.), Libr.
84/C5 **Bong** (range), Libr.
73/F1 **Bongabong,** Phil.
83/K7 **Bongandanga,** Zaire
73/E2 **Bongao,** Phil.
73/E2 **Bonggi** (isl.), Malay.
73/F4 **Bongka** (riv.), Indo.
89/H7 **Bongolava** (uplands), Madg.
82/J5 **Bongor,** Chad
83/K6 **Bongos** (mts.), CAfr.
69/E3 **Bong Son,** Viet.
112/D3 **Bonham,** Tx,US
42/D1 **Bonheiden,** Belg.
48/A2 **Bonifacio** (str.), Fr., It.
113/G4 **Bonifay,** Fl,US
78/D2 **Bonin** (isls.), Japan
113/H5 **Bonita Springs,** Fl,US
100/D4 **Bonito** (pk.), Hon.
43/G2 **Bonn,** Ger.
31/S11 **Bonnelles,** Fr.
106/D3 **Bonners Ferry,** Id,US
106/E4 **Bonner-West Riverside,** Mt,US
107/K3 **Bonnet** (lake), Mb,Can
31/T10 **Bonneuil-sur-Marne,** Fr.
45/G3 **Bonneville,** Fr.
106/C4 **Bonneville** (dam), Or, Wa,US
116/C3 **Bonney Lake,** Wa,US
106/F2 **Bonnyville,** Ab,Can
88/C4 **Bontberg** (peak), SAfr.
88/C4 **Bontebok Nat'l Park,** SAfr.
73/E5 **Bonthain,** Indo.
84/B5 **Bonthe,** SLeo.
67/D4 **Bontoc,** Phil.
50/D2 **Bonyhád,** Hun.
98/J **Bonzare** (coast), Ant.
42/D1 **Boom,** Belg.
107/K5 **Boone,** Ia,US
113/H2 **Boone,** NC,US
113/F3 **Booneville,** Ms,US
115/F5 **Boonton,** NJ,US
62/D2 **Bööntsagaan** (lake), Mong.
110/C4 **Boonville,** In,US
77/C1 **Booroondara** (peak), Austl.
42/A5 **Boos,** Fr.
111/G3 **Boothbay Harbor,** Me,US
98/D **Boothby** (cape), Ant.
102/G1 **Boothia** (gulf), NW,Can
102/G1 **Boothia** (pen.), NW,Can
33/E5 **Bootle,** Eng,UK
82/H8 **Booué,** Gabon
88/D2 **Bophuthatswana** (ind. homeland), SAfr.
43/G3 **Boppard,** Ger.
77/C1 **Boppy** (peak), Austl.
94/B3 **Boqueirão** (mts.), Braz.
96/C4 **Boquete** (peak), Arg.
83/N7 **Bor** (dry riv.), Kenya
53/K4 **Bor,** Rus.
83/M6 **Bor,** Sudan
59/C3 **Bor,** Turk.
50/F3 **Bor,** Yugo.
79/K6 **Bora Bora** (isl.), FrPol.
106/E4 **Borah** (peak), Id,US
37/E4 **Borås,** Swe.
60/F3 **Borāzjān,** Iran
92/G4 **Borba,** Braz.
44/D3 **Borbonnais** (hist. reg.), Fr.
94/C2 **Borborema** (plat.), Braz.
50/E3 **Borča,** Yugo.
41/F5 **Borchen,** Ger.
98/M **Borchgrevink** (coast), Ant.
59/E2 **Borçka,** Turk.
40/D4 **Borculo,** Neth.
95/G7 **Borda da Mata,** Braz.
44/C4 **Bordeaux,** Fr.
103/R7 **Borden** (isl.), NW,Can
103/H2 **Borden** (pen.), NW,Can
115/F5 **Bordentown,** NJ,US
33/F1 **Borders** (reg.), Sc,UK
81/T15 **Bordj Bou Arreridj,** Alg.
47/G4 **Bordj el Bahri** (cape), Alg.
81/S15 **Bordj el Kiffan,** Alg.
81/S15 **Bordj Manaïel,** Alg.
82/G2 **Bordj Omar Driss,** Alg.
35/F4 **Bordon,** Eng,UK
31/N7 **Borehamwood,** Eng,UK
37/E2 **Børgefjell Nat'l Park,** Nor.
41/G5 **Borgentreich,** Ger.
40/D3 **Borger,** Neth.
112/C3 **Borger,** Tx,US
42/D1 **Borgerhout,** Belg.
37/F4 **Borgholm,** Swe.
41/F4 **Borgholzhausen,** Ger.
41/E4 **Borghorst,** Ger.
45/G4 **Borgo San Dalmazzo,** It.
85/F4 **Borgou** (prov.), Ben.
85/F4 **Borgu Game Rsv.,** Nga.
54/B2 **Borislav,** Ukr.
55/G2 **Borisoglebsk,** Rus.
52/F5 **Borisov,** Bela.
89/H6 **Boriziny,** Madg.
40/D5 **Borken,** Ger.
40/D1 **Borkum** (isl.), Ger.
37/E3 **Borlänge,** Swe.
45/H4 **Bormida** (riv.), It.
40/C6 **Born,** Neth.
38/G3 **Borna,** Ger.
40/C2 **Borndiep** (chan.), Neth.
40/D4 **Borne,** Neth.
42/D1 **Bornem,** Belg.
72/E3 **Borneo** (isl.), Asia
43/F2 **Bornheim,** Ger.
39/H1 **Bornholm** (co.), Den.
39/H1 **Bornholm** (isl.), Den.
39/H1 **Bornholmsgat** (chan.), Swe.
85/H3 **Borno** (state), Nga.
46/C4 **Bornos,** Sp.
82/H5 **Bornu** (plains), Nga.
83/L6 **Boro** (riv.), Sudan
68/D3 **Borohoro** (mts.), China, Kaz.
67/E5 **Borongan,** Phil.
33/G3 **Boroughbridge,** Eng,UK
52/G4 **Borovichi,** Rus.
50/D3 **Borovo,** Cro.
54/B3 **Borşa,** Rom.
63/H1 **Borshchovochnyy** (mts.), Rus.
50/E1 **Borsod-Abaúj-Zemplén** (co.), Hun.
40/A6 **Borssele,** Neth.
68/D3 **Bortala** (riv.), China
34/B2 **Borth,** Wal,UK
60/F2 **Borūjen,** Iran
60/E2 **Borūjerd,** Iran
62/D3 **Bor Ul** (mts.), China
62/H1 **Borzya,** Rus.
48/A2 **Bosa,** It.
50/C3 **Bosanska Dubica,** Bosn.
50/C3 **Bosanska Gradiška,** Bosn.
50/C3 **Bosanska Kostajnica,** Bosn.
50/C3 **Bosanska Krupa,** Bosn.
50/D3 **Bosanski Brod,** Bosn.
50/C3 **Bosanski Petrovac,** Bosn.
50/D3 **Bosanski Šamac,** Bosn.
83/Q5 **Bosaso** (Bender Cassim), Som.
34/B5 **Boscastle,** Eng,UK
71/J3 **Bose,** China
35/F5 **Bosham,** Eng,UK
40/B4 **Boskoop,** Neth.
39/J4 **Boskovice,** Czh.
50/D3 **Bosna** (riv.), Bosn.
50/C3 **Bosnia and Hercegovina**
65/G3 **Bōsō** (pen.), Japan
83/J7 **Bosobolo,** Zaire
51/J5 **Bosporus** (str.), Turk.
108/F4 **Bosque Farms,** NM,US
97/K6 **Bosques Petrificados Natural Mon.,** Arg.
82/J6 **Bossangoa,** CAfr.
112/E3 **Bossier City,** La,US
68/E3 **Bosten** (lake), China
33/H6 **Boston,** Eng,UK
112/E3 **Boston** (mts.), Ar,US
111/G3 **Boston** (cap.), Ma,US
112/E3 **Boston,** Tx,US
50/D3 **Bosut** (riv.), Cro.
70/B3 **Botād,** India
76/H8 **Botany** (bay), Austl.
113/H3 **Boteler** (peak), NC,US
89/F2 **Botelerpunt** (pt.), SAfr.
95/G6 **Botelhos,** Braz.
49/J1 **Botev** (peak), Bul.
51/F4 **Botevgrad,** Bul.
89/E2 **Bothaspas** (pass), SAfr.
33/E2 **Bothel,** Eng,UK
116/C2 **Bothell,** Wa,US
34/D5 **Bothenhampton,** Eng,UK
37/G2 **Bothnia** (gulf), Fin., Swe.
54/C3 **Botoşani,** Rom.
51/H2 **Botoşani** (co.), Rom.
66/D3 **Botou,** China
69/D2 **Bo Trach,** Viet.
43/F3 **Botrange** (mtn.), Belg.
87/D5 **Botswana**
48/E3 **Botte Donato** (peak), It.
33/H4 **Bottesford,** Eng,UK
33/H6 **Bottesford,** Eng,UK
107/H3 **Bottineau,** ND,US
40/D5 **Bottrop,** Ger.
95/B2 **Botucatu,** Braz.
111/L1 **Botwood,** Nf,Can
84/D4 **Bou** (riv.), IvC.
84/D5 **Bouaflé,** IvC.
84/D5 **Bouaké,** IvC.
82/J6 **Bouar,** CAfr.
45/K2 **Boubín** (peak), Czh.
83/J6 **Bouca,** CAfr.
111/P6 **Boucherville,** Qu,Can
84/C3 **Boucle du Baoulé Nat'l Park,** Mali
82/E1 **Boudenib,** Mor.
85/E2 **Boû Djébéha** (well), Mali
81/S15 **Boufarik,** Alg.
31/S9 **Bouffémont,** Fr.
76/B1 **Bougainville** (reef), Austl.
97/N7 **Bougainville** (cape), Falk.
78/E5 **Bougainville** (isl.), PNG
81/S15 **Bougara,** Alg.
81/V17 **Bougar'oûn** (cape), Alg.
84/D4 **Bougouni,** Mali
84/E4 **Bougouriba** (prov.), Burk.
44/C3 **Bouguenais,** Fr.
81/M13 **Bouhalla** (peak), Mor.
81/V17 **Bou Hamdane** (riv.), Alg.
81/S15 **Bouira,** Alg.
81/S15 **Bou Ismaïl,** Alg.
81/R15 **Bou Kadir,** Alg.
78/B8 **Boulder,** Austl.
109/F2 **Boulder,** Co,US
106/E4 **Boulder,** Mt,US
108/D4 **Boulder City,** Nv,US
116/P16 **Boulder Hill,** Il,US
85/E4 **Boulgo** (prov.), Burk.
85/E3 **Boulkiemde** (prov.), Burk.
44/C3 **Boulogne** (riv.), Fr.
31/S10 **Boulogne-Billancourt,** Fr.
42/A2 **Boulogne-sur-Mer,** Fr.
33/F4 **Boulsworth** (hill), Eng,UK
81/S15 **Boumerdas,** Alg.
47/F1 **Boumort** (mtn.), Sp.
114/K3 **Boundary,** Yk,Can
108/C3 **Boundary** (peak), Nv,US
115/F5 **Bound Brook,** NJ,US
84/D4 **Boundiali,** IvC.
108/E2 **Bountiful,** Ut,US
29/T8 **Bounty** (isls.), NZ
115/B2 **Bouquet** (canyon), Ca,US
110/C3 **Bourbonnais,** Il,US
42/B2 **Bourbourg,** Fr.
81/L14 **Bou Regreg** (riv.), Mor.
85/F2 **Bouressa** (wadi), Mali
44/F3 **Bourg-en-Bresse,** Fr.
44/E3 **Bourges,** Fr.
44/F4 **Bourg-lès-Valence,** Fr.
44/B3 **Bourgneuf** (bay), Fr.
42/D5 **Bourgogne,** Fr.
44/E3 **Bourgogne** (reg.), Fr.
44/F4 **Bourgoin-Jallieu,** Fr.
35/F1 **Bourne,** Eng,UK
31/M8 **Bourne** (riv.), Eng,UK
35/F3 **Bourne End,** Eng,UK
35/E5 **Bournemouth,** Eng,UK
35/E2 **Bournville,** Eng,UK
36/A4 **Bourn-Vincent Mem. Nat'l Park,** Ire.
41/E3 **Bourtanger Moor** (reg.), Ger.
35/E3 **Bourton on the Water,** Eng,UK
81/T15 **Bou Sellam** (riv.), Alg.
84/B2 **Boutilimit,** Mrta.
29/K8 **Bouvet** (isl.), Nor.
42/C5 **Bouzy,** Fr.
41/G5 **Bovenden,** Ger.
40/D3 **Bovenwijde** (lake), Neth.
34/C5 **Bovey Tracey,** Eng,UK
31/M6 **Bovingdon,** Eng,UK
45/J4 **Bovolone,** It.
106/E3 **Bow** (riv.), Ab,Can
107/J4 **Bowdle,** SD,US
33/F5 **Bowdon,** Eng,UK
76/C3 **Bowen,** Austl.
40/C5 **Bowen Merwede** (can.), Neth.
33/G3 **Bowes,** Eng,UK
108/E4 **Bowie,** Az,US
115/K8 **Bowie,** Md,US
106/F3 **Bow Island,** Ab,Can
76/B2 **Bowling Green** (cape), Austl.
110/C4 **Bowling Green,** Ky,US
109/K3 **Bowling Green,** Mo,US
110/D3 **Bowling Green,** Oh,US
76/B2 **Bowling Green Bay Nat'l Park,** Austl.
98/G **Bowman** (isl.), Ant.
103/J2 **Bowman** (bay), NW,Can
107/H4 **Bowman,** ND,US
111/S8 **Bowmanville,** Nf,Can
33/E2 **Bowness-on-Solway,** Eng,UK
73/F4 **Bowokan** (isls.), Indo.
77/D2 **Bowral,** Austl.
106/C2 **Bowron** (riv.), BC,Can
107/H4 **Box Elder,** SD,US
77/C3 **Box Hill,** Austl.
77/G5 **Box Hill,** Austl.
40/C5 **Boxmeer,** Neth.
40/C5 **Boxtel,** Neth.
59/C2 **Boyabat,** Turk.
77/D2 **Boyd-Konangra Nat'l Park,** Austl.
107/K5 **Boyer** (riv.), Ia,US
106/E2 **Boyle,** Ab,Can
32/B4 **Boyne** (riv.), Ire.
110/C2 **Boyne City,** Mi,US
113/H5 **Boynton Beach,** Fl,US
106/F5 **Boysen** (res.), Wy,US
49/J3 **Bozcaada** (isl.), Turk.
106/F4 **Bozeman,** Mt,US
59/C3 **Bozkir,** Turk.
82/J6 **Bozoum,** CAfr.
59/B2 **Bozüyük,** Turk.
45/G4 **Bra,** It.
42/D2 **Brabant** (prov.), Belg.
35/G4 **Brabourne Lees,** Eng,UK
50/C4 **Brač** (isl.), Cro.
48/B1 **Bracciano** (lake), It.
110/E2 **Bracebridge,** On,Can
52/B3 **Bräcke,** Swe.
112/C4 **Brackettville,** Tx,US
35/E2 **Brackley,** Eng,UK
35/F4 **Bracknell,** Eng,UK
95/B4 **Braço do Norte,** Braz.
50/F2 **Brad,** Rom.
48/D2 **Bradano** (riv.), It.
32/D3 **Bradda Head** (pt.), IM,UK
113/H5 **Bradenton,** Fl,US
33/G4 **Bradford,** Eng,UK
110/E3 **Bradford,** Pa,US
34/D4 **Bradford on Avon,** Eng,UK
35/E5 **Brading,** Eng,UK
115/F5 **Bradley Beach,** NJ,US
34/C5 **Bradninch,** Eng,UK
112/D4 **Brady,** Tx,US
114/L3 **Braeburn,** Yk,Can
36/D2 **Braemar,** Sc,UK
46/A2 **Braga,** Port.
46/A2 **Braga** (dist.), Port.
96/E2 **Bragado,** Arg.
93/J4 **Bragança,** Braz.
46/B2 **Bragança,** Port.
46/B2 **Bragança** (dist.), Port.
95/G7 **Bragança Paulista,** Braz.
58/J7 **Brahmaputra** (riv.), Asia
32/D6 **Braich-y-Pwll** (pt.), Wal,UK
32/B2 **Braid** (riv.), NI,UK
51/H3 **Brăila,** Rom.
51/H3 **Brăila** (co.), Rom.
42/D2 **Braine-l'Alleud,** Belg.
42/D2 **Braine-le-Comte,** Belg.
107/K4 **Brainerd,** Mn,US
35/G3 **Braintree,** Eng,UK
88/C3 **Brak** (riv.), SAfr.
41/F2 **Brake,** Ger.
42/C2 **Brakel,** Belg.
41/G5 **Brakel,** Ger.
84/B2 **Brakna** (reg.), Mrta.
111/Q8 **Bramalea,** On,Can
33/G4 **Bramhope,** Eng,UK
111/Q8 **Brampton,** On,Can
33/F2 **Brampton,** Eng,UK
41/E4 **Bramsche,** Ger.
92/F4 **Branco** (riv.), Braz.
87/B5 **Brandberg** (peak), Namb.
38/G2 **Brandenburg,** Ger.
38/G2 **Brandenburg** (state), Ger.
33/H4 **Brandesburton,** Eng,UK
107/J3 **Brandon,** Mb,Can
35/G2 **Brandon,** Eng,UK
113/H5 **Brandon,** Fl,US
113/F3 **Brandon,** Ms,US
96/F2 **Brandsen,** Arg.
39/K1 **Braniewo,** Pol.
35/E5 **Bransgore,** Eng,UK
111/J2 **Bras d'Or** (lake), NS,Can
94/A4 **Brasília** (cap.), Braz.
94/A5 **Brasília de Minas,** Braz.
94/A4 **Brasília Nat'l Park,** Braz.
95/D1 **Brasil, Planalto do** (plat.), Braz.
51/G3 **Braşov,** Rom.
51/G3 **Braşov** (co.), Rom.
40/B6 **Brasschaat,** Belg.
113/H3 **Brasstown Bald** (peak), Ga,US
39/J4 **Bratislava** (cap.), Slvk.
39/J4 **Bratislava** (reg.), Slvk.
57/L4 **Bratsk,** Rus.
111/F3 **Brattleboro,** Vt,US
100/E5 **Braulio Carrillo,** CR
45/K2 **Braunau am Inn,** Aus.
41/H5 **Braunlage,** Ger.
41/H4 **Braunschweig** (Brunswick), Ger.
34/B4 **Braunton,** Eng,UK
80/J11 **Brava** (isl.), CpV.
47/G2 **Brava** (coast), Sp.
97/T12 **Brava** (pt.), Uru.
92/F7 **Bravo** (peak), Bol.
108/D4 **Brawley,** Ca,US
103/J2 **Bray** (isl.), NW,Can
32/B5 **Bray,** Ire.
44/D3 **Braye** (riv.), Fr.
32/B5 **Bray Head** (pt.), Ire.
42/B4 **Bray-sur-Somme,** Fr.
90/D3 **Brazil**
110/C4 **Brazil,** In,US
90/E4 **Brazilian** (plat.), Braz.
95/H7 **Brazópolis,** Braz.
112/D4 **Brazos** (riv.), Tx,US
97/K7 **Brazo Sur** (riv.), Arg.
87/C1 **Brazzaville** (cap.), Congo
50/D3 **Brčko,** Bosn.
38/J2 **Brda** (riv.), Pol.
45/K2 **Brdy** (mts.), Czh.
115/C3 **Brea,** Ca,US
34/D3 **Bream,** Eng,UK
51/G3 **Breaza,** Rom.
36/D2 **Brechin,** Sc,UK
40/B6 **Brecht,** Belg.
107/J4 **Breckenridge,** Mn,US
41/E6 **Breckerfeld,** Ger.
35/G2 **Breckland** (reg.), Eng,UK
97/K8 **Brecknock** (pen.), Chile
39/J4 **Břeclav,** Czh.
34/C3 **Brecon,** Wal,UK
34/C3 **Brecon Beacons** (mts.), Wal,UK
34/C3 **Brecon Beacons Nat'l Park,** Wal,UK
40/B5 **Breda,** Neth.
42/B1 **Bredene,** Belg.
43/E1 **Bree,** Belg.
88/L10 **Breë** (riv.), SAfr.
50/F5 **Bregalinca** (riv.), Macd.
45/H3 **Bregenz,** Aus.
37/M6 **Breidhafjördhur** (bay), Ice.
94/B1 **Brejo,** Braz.
94/C2 **Brejo Santo,** Braz.
41/F2 **Bremen,** Ger.
41/F2 **Bremen** (state), Ger.
76/E7 **Bremer** (riv.), Austl.
41/F1 **Bremerhaven,** Ger.
116/B2 **Bremerton,** Wa,US
41/G2 **Bremervörde,** Ger.
34/C4 **Brendon** (hills), Eng,UK
112/D4 **Brenham,** Tx,US
32/E5 **Brenig, Llyn** (lake), Wal,UK
44/F3 **Brenne** (riv.), Fr.
45/J3 **Brenner** (Brennerpass) (pass), Aus.
31/N7 **Brent** (bor.), Eng,UK
31/N7 **Brent** (res.), Eng,UK
31/N7 **Brent** (riv.), Eng,UK
45/J4 **Brenta** (riv.), It.
31/P7 **Brentwood,** Eng,UK
116/L11 **Brentwood,** Ca,US
115/G5 **Brentwood,** NY,US
45/J4 **Brescia,** It.
42/A4 **Bresle** (riv.), Fr.
45/J3 **Bressanone,** It.
44/C3 **Bressuire,** Fr.
39/M2 **Brest,** Bela.
44/A2 **Brest,** Fr.
39/M2 **Brest Obl.,** Bela.
44/B2 **Bretagne** (mts.), Fr.
44/B2 **Bretagne** (reg.), Fr.
89/R15 **Bretagne** (pt.), Reun.
31/S11 **Brétigny-sur-Orge,** Fr.
106/E2 **Breton,** Ab,Can
111/K2 **Breton** (cape), NS,Can
75/R10 **Brett** (cape), NZ
31/S11 **Breuillet,** Fr.
40/B4 **Breukelen,** Neth.
93/H4 **Breves,** Braz.
103/K2 **Brevoort** (isl.), NW,Can
111/G2 **Brewer,** Me,US
34/D1 **Brewood,** Eng,UK
109/H2 **Brewster,** Ne,US
106/D3 **Brewster,** Wa,US
113/G4 **Brewton,** Al,US
50/B3 **Brežice,** Slov.
51/G3 **Brezoi,** Rom.
83/K6 **Bria,** CAfr.
45/G4 **Briançon,** Fr.
34/C2 **Brianne, Lyn** (res.), Wal,UK
115/F5 **Brick,** NJ,US
31/M6 **Bricket Wood,** Eng,UK
36/A4 **Bride** (riv.), Ire.
32/D3 **Bride,** IM,UK
112/E4 **Bridge City,** Tx,US
34/C4 **Bridgend,** Wal,UK
108/C3 **Bridgeport,** Ca,US
111/F3 **Bridgeport,** Ct,US
109/G2 **Bridgeport,** Ne,US
110/D4 **Bridgeport,** WV,US
106/F4 **Bridger,** Mt,US
101/K5 **Bridgetown** (cap.), Bar.
77/C4 **Bridgewater,** Austl.
111/H2 **Bridgewater,** NS,Can
110/E4 **Bridgewater,** Va,US
34/D1 **Bridgnorth,** Eng,UK
111/G2 **Bridgton,** Me,US
34/D4 **Bridgwater,** Eng,UK
34/C4 **Bridgwater** (bay), Eng,UK
33/H3 **Bridlington,** Eng,UK
33/H3 **Bridlington** (bay), Eng,UK
34/D5 **Bridport,** Eng,UK
31/U10 **Brie** (reg.), Fr.
31/T10 **Brie-Comte-Robert,** Fr.
39/J3 **Brieg Brzeg,** Pol.
40/B5 **Brielle,** Neth.
115/F5 **Brielle,** NJ,US
33/F4 **Brierfield,** Eng,UK
45/G3 **Brig,** Swi.
33/H4 **Brigg,** Eng,UK
45/H3 **Brig-Glis,** Swi.
108/D2 **Brigham City,** Ut,US
33/G4 **Brighouse,** Eng,UK
35/E5 **Brighstone,** Eng,UK
35/H3 **Brightlingsea,** Eng,UK
76/F6 **Brighton,** Austl.
77/F5 **Brighton,** Austl.
35/F5 **Brighton,** Eng,UK
109/F3 **Brighton,** Co,US
44/F4 **Brignais,** Fr.
44/G5 **Brignoles,** Fr.
31/S11 **Briis-sous-Forges,** Fr.
84/A3 **Brikama,** Gam.
35/E3 **Brill,** Eng,UK
93/H8 **Brillante** (riv.), Braz.
41/F6 **Brilon,** Ger.
33/G5 **Brimington,** Eng,UK
49/E2 **Brindisi,** It.
34/E3 **Brinkworth,** Eng,UK
46/A1 **Brion,** Sp.
116/K11 **Briones** (res.), Ca,US
76/D4 **Brisbane ,** Austl.
76/F6 **Brisbane** (riv.), Austl.
76/E6 **Brisbane For. Park,** Austl.
76/E6 **Brisbane** (inset), Austl.
77/C3 **Brisbane Ranges Nat'l Park,** Austl.
77/D2 **Brisbane Waters Nat'l Park,** Austl.
34/B4 **Bristol** (chan.), UK
34/D4 **Bristol,** Eng,UK
114/F4 **Bristol** (bay), Ak,US
115/F5 **Bristol,** Pa,US
113/H2 **Bristol,** Tn,US
109/H4 **Bristow,** Ok,US
114/K2 **British** (mts.), Yk,Can, Ak,US
102/D3 **British Columbia** (prov.), Can.
103/S6 **British Empire** (range), NW,Can
58/G10 **British Indian Ocean Terr.**
88/P12 **Brits,** SAfr.
44/B2 **Brittany** (reg.), Fr.
107/J4 **Britton,** SD,US
44/D4 **Brive-la-Gaillarde,** Fr.
34/C6 **Brixham,** Eng,UK
35/F2 **Brixworth,** Eng,UK
39/J4 **Brno,** Czh.
76/C3 **Broad** (sound), Austl.
114/J3 **Broad** (pass), Ak,US
113/H3 **Broad** (riv.), NC, SC,US
110/E1 **Broadback** (riv.), Qu,Can
36/D3 **Broad Law** (mtn.), Sc,UK
77/F5 **Broadmeadows,** Austl.
76/C3 **Broad Sound** (chan.), Austl.
35/H4 **Broadstairs,** Eng,UK
35/E5 **Broadstone,** Eng,UK
107/G4 **Broadus,** Mt,US
77/E1 **Broadwater Nat'l Park,** Austl.
35/E2 **Broadway,** Eng,UK
35/E2 **Broadway** (hill), Eng,UK
34/D5 **Broadwindsor,** Eng,UK
103/R7 **Brock** (isl.), NW,Can
41/H5 **Brocken** (peak), Ger.
35/E5 **Brockenhurst,** Eng,UK
111/G3 **Brockton,** Ma,US
110/F2 **Brockville,** On,Can
102/G1 **Brodeur** (pen.), NW,Can
115/E4 **Brodhead** (cr.), Pa,US
39/K2 **Brodnica,** Pol.
40/B3 **Broek Op Langedijk,** Neth.
77/D2 **Broken** (bay), Austl.
109/J3 **Broken Arrow,** Ok,US
109/H2 **Broken Bow,** Ne,US
109/J4 **Broken Bow,** Ok,US
109/J4 **Broken Bow** (lake), Ok,US
77/B1 **Broken Hill,** Austl.
112/B3 **Brokeoff** (mts.), NM,US
31/P7 **Bromley,** Eng,UK
31/P7 **Bromley** (bor.), Eng,UK
31/P7 **Bromley Common,** Eng,UK
34/D2 **Bromsgrove,** Eng,UK
34/D2 **Bromyard,** Eng,UK
44/F4 **Bron,** Fr.
37/D4 **Brønderslev,** Den.
85/E5 **Brong-Ahafo** (reg.), Gha.
45/H4 **Broni,** It.
34/C3 **Bronllys,** Wal,UK
37/E2 **Brønnøysund,** Nor.
111/Q9 **Bronte,** On,Can
48/D4 **Bronte,** It.
115/G5 **Bronx** (co.), NY,US
67/C6 **Brooke's Point,** Phil.
116/Q16 **Brookfield,** Il,US
109/J3 **Brookfield,** Mo,US
116/P13 **Brookfield,** Wi,US
113/F4 **Brookhaven,** Ms,US
115/H5 **Brookhaven,** NY,US
107/J4 **Brookings,** SD,US
115/G5 **Brooklyn** (Kings) (co.), NY,US
115/K7 **Brooklyn Park,** Md,US
31/N6 **Brookmans Park,** Eng,UK
106/F3 **Brooks,** Ab,Can
114/E2 **Brooks** (mtn.), Ak,US
114/F2 **Brooks** (range), Ak,US
113/H4 **Brooksville,** Fl,US
115/E6 **Broomall,** Pa,US
111/P7 **Brossard,** Qu,Can
33/H2 **Brotton,** Eng,UK
33/F2 **Brough,** Eng,UK
111/R8 **Brougham,** On,Can
32/B2 **Broughshane,** NI,UK
35/F2 **Broughton,** Eng,UK
33/E3 **Broughton in Furness,** Eng,UK
35/G4 **Broughton Street,** Eng,UK
40/A5 **Brouwersdam** (dam), Neth.
67/C5 **Brown** (shoal)
34/D2 **Brown Clee** (hill), Eng,UK
112/C3 **Brownfield,** Tx,US
35/E1 **Brownhills,** Eng,UK
106/E3 **Browning,** Mt,US
35/E5 **Brownsea** (isl.), Eng,UK
115/F6 **Browns Mills,** NJ,US
113/F3 **Brownsville,** Tn,US
112/D5 **Brownsville,** Tx,US
34/B5 **Brown Willy** (hill), Eng,UK
112/D4 **Brownwood,** Tx,US
31/N6 **Broxbourne,** Eng,UK
42/B3 **Bruay-en-Artois,** Fr.
42/C3 **Bruay-sur-l'Escaut,** Fr.
74/B4 **Bruce** (peak), Austl.
110/D2 **Bruce** (pen.), On,Can
45/G2 **Bruche** (riv.), Fr.
43/G5 **Bruchmühlbach-Miesau,** Ger.
45/H2 **Bruchsal,** Ger.
41/G5 **Brucht** (riv.), Ger.
45/K3 **Bruck an der Grossglockner-strasse,** Aus.
50/C1 **Bruck an der Leitha,** Aus.
45/L3 **Bruck an der Mur,** Aus.
38/F5 **Bruckmühl,** Ger.
34/D4 **Brue** (riv.), Eng,UK
42/C1 **Bruges** (Brugge), Belg.
40/D6 **Brüggen,** Ger.
43/F2 **Brühl,** Ger.
88/B2 **Brukkaros** (peak), Namb.
94/B4 **Brumado,** Braz.
43/G6 **Brumath,** Fr.
40/D4 **Brummen,** Neth.
37/D3 **Brumunddal,** Nor.
48/A2 **Bruncu Spina** (peak), It.
35/H1 **Brundall,** Eng,UK
42/D4 **Brune** (riv.), Fr.
108/D2 **Bruneau** (riv.), Id, Nv,US
72/D2 **Brunei**
43/J3 **Brunico,** It.
31/T10 **Brunoy,** Fr.
41/G1 **Brunsbüttel,** Ger.
43/E2 **Brunssum,** Neth.
77/F5 **Brunswick,** Austl.
97/J8 **Brunswick** (pen.), Chile
113/H4 **Brunswick,** Ga,US
111/G3 **Brunswick,** Me,US
110/D3 **Brunswick,** Oh,US
41/H4 **Brunswick** (Braunschweig), Ger.
95/B3 **Brusque,** Braz.
42/D2 **Brussels** (Bruxelles) (cap.), Belg.
34/D4 **Bruton,** Eng,UK
31/S11 **Bruyères-le-Châtel,** Fr.
31/S9 **Bruyères-sur-Oise,** Fr.
44/C2 **Bruz,** Fr.
98/U **Bryan** (coast), Ant.
110/C3 **Bryan,** Oh,US
112/D4 **Bryan,** Tx,US
54/E1 **Bryansk,** Rus.
54/E1 **Bryansk Obl.,** Rus.
108/D3 **Bryce Canyon Nat'l Park,** Ut,US
33/E5 **Brymbo,** Wal,UK
34/C2 **Bryn Brawd** (mtn.), Wal,UK
34/C3 **Brynithel,** Wal,UK
34/C3 **Brynmawr,** Wal,UK
39/J3 **Brzeg Dolny,** Pol.
39/L4 **Brzesko,** Pol.
39/M4 **Brzozów,** Pol.
69/C3 **Bua Yai,** Thai.
84/B4 **Buba,** GBis.
84/B4 **Bubaque,** GBis.
60/E3 **Būbiyan** (isl.), Kuw.
31/S10 **Buc,** Fr.
59/B3 **Bucak,** Turk.
92/D2 **Bucaramanga,** Col.
47/P10 **Bucelas,** Port.
103/J1 **Buchan** (gulf), NW,Can
84/C5 **Buchanan,** Libr.
109/H5 **Buchanan** (lake), Tx,US
111/K1 **Buchans,** Nf,Can
51/H3 **Bucharest** (Bucureşti) (cap.), Rom.
41/G2 **Buchholz in der Nordheide,** Ger.
108/B4 **Buchon** (pt.), Ca,US
33/F3 **Buckden Pike** (mtn.), Eng,UK
41/G4 **Bückeburg,** Ger.
34/C6 **Buckfastleigh,** Eng,UK
110/D4 **Buckhannon,** WV,US
31/P7 **Buckhurst Hill,** Eng,UK
36/D2 **Buckie,** Sc,UK
110/F2 **Buckingham,** Qu,Can
35/F3 **Buckingham,** Eng,UK
31/N7 **Buckingham Palace,** Eng,UK
35/F3 **Buckinghamshire** (co.), Eng,UK
33/E5 **Buckley,** Wal,UK
34/D2 **Bucknell,** Eng,UK
36/D2 **Bucksburn,** Sc,UK
111/H2 **Buctouche,** NB,Can
51/H3 **București** (Bucharest) (cap.), Rom.

129

Bucyr – Caraj

110/D3 **Bucyrus,** Oh,US
50/D2 **Budaörs,** Hun.
50/D2 **Budapest** (cap.), Hun.
70/C2 **Budaun,** India
98/H **Budd** (coast), Ant.
116/B3 **Budd** (inlet), Wa,US
115/F5 **Budd Lake,** NJ,US
34/B5 **Bude,** Eng,UK
34/B5 **Bude** (bay), Eng,UK
40/C6 **Budel,** Neth.
38/E1 **Büdelsdorf,** Ger.
45/H1 **Büdingen,** Ger.
83/J7 **Budjala,** Zaire
34/C5 **Budleigh Salterton,** Eng,UK
50/D4 **Budva,** Yugo.
51/J2 **Budzhak** (reg.), Mol., Ukr.
82/G7 **Buea,** Camr.
115/C3 **Buena Park,** Ca,US
92/C3 **Buenaventura,** Col.
109/F3 **Buena Vista,** Co,US
110/E4 **Buena Vista,** Va,US
96/B4 **Bueno** (riv.), Chile
96/F2 **Buenos Aires** (cap.), Arg.
96/C5 **Buenos Aires** (lake), Arg.
96/E3 **Buenos Aires** (prov.), Arg.
97/S12 **Buenos Aires** (inset) (cap.), Arg.
94/C4 **Buerarema,** Braz.
46/A1 **Bueu,** Sp.
77/C3 **Buffalo** (peak), Austl.
106/E2 **Buffalo** (lake), Ab,Can
89/E2 **Buffalo** (riv.), SAfr.
112/E2 **Buffalo** (riv.), Ar,US
107/K4 **Buffalo,** Mn,US
109/J3 **Buffalo,** Mo,US
111/S10 **Buffalo,** NY,US
109/H3 **Buffalo,** Ok,US
107/H4 **Buffalo,** SD,US
113/G3 **Buffalo** (riv.), Tn,US
106/G4 **Buffalo,** Wy,US
116/Q15 **Buffalo Grove,** Il,US
106/F2 **Buffalo Narrows,** Sk,Can
77/B1 **Buffalo Riv. Overflow** (swamp), Austl.
88/B3 **Buffelsrivier** (dry riv.), SAfr.
113/G3 **Buford,** Ga,US
51/G3 **Buftea,** Rom.
54/B1 **Bug** (riv.), Eur.
51/K2 **Bug** (estuary), Ukr.
92/C3 **Buga,** Col.
100/E6 **Bugaba,** Pan.
44/E5 **Bugarach, Pic de** (peak), Fr.
35/E2 **Bugbrooke,** Eng,UK
72/D5 **Bugel** (pt.), Indo.
42/D1 **Buggenhout,** Belg.
50/C3 **Bugojno,** Bosn.
73/E2 **Bugsuk** (isl.), Phil.
53/M5 **Bugul'ma,** Rus.
55/K1 **Buguruslan,** Rus.
62/D4 **Buh** (riv.), China
59/D3 **Buhayrat al Asad** (lake), Turk.
60/D2 **Buḩayrat ath Tharthār** (lake), Iraq
106/E5 **Buhl,** Id,US
51/H2 **Buhuşi,** Rom.
85/E4 **Bui** (dam), Gha.
85/E4 **Bui Gorge** (res.), Gha.
34/C2 **Builth Wells,** Wal,UK
96/D9 **Buin,** Chile
46/C4 **Bujalance,** Sp.
50/E4 **Bujanovac,** Yugo.
51/H3 **Bujor,** Rom.
87/E1 **Bujumbura** (cap.), Buru.
39/J2 **Buk,** Pol.
78/E5 **Buka** (isl.), PNG
62/H1 **Bukachacha,** Rus.
68/F4 **Bukadaban Feng** (peak), China
60/E1 **Būkān,** Iran
87/E1 **Bukavu,** Zaire
69/C5 **Buket Bubat** (peak), Malay.
56/G6 **Bukhara,** Uzb.
62/A2 **Bukhtarma** (riv.), Kaz.
72/B4 **Bukittinggi,** Indo.
50/E1 **Bükki Nat'l Park,** Hun.
87/F1 **Bukoba,** Tanz.
72/B4 **Buku** (cape), Indo.
67/D5 **Bulan,** Phil.
70/C2 **Bulandshahr,** India
59/E2 **Bulanık,** Turk.
73/F3 **Bulawa** (peak), Indo.
87/E5 **Bulawayo,** Zim.
114/B5 **Buldir** (isl.), Ak,US
62/C2 **Bulgan** (riv.), Mong.
51/G4 **Bulgaria**
48/D2 **Bulgheria** (peak), It.
67/C6 **Buliluyan** (cape), Phil.
76/F7 **Bulimba** (cr.), Austl.
35/E2 **Bulkington,** Eng,UK
106/B2 **Bulkley** (riv.), BC,Can
32/B1 **Bull** (pt.), NI,UK
46/E3 **Bullas,** Sp.
77/C3 **Buller** (peak), Austl.
108/D4 **Bullhead City,** Az,US
43/F3 **Büllingen,** Belg.
31/R11 **Bullion,** Fr.
76/A5 **Bulloo** (riv.), Austl.
109/J3 **Bull Shoals** (lake), Ar, Mo,US
42/B3 **Bully-les-Mines,** Fr.
62/D2 **Bulnayn** (mts.), Mong.
96/B3 **Bulnes,** Chile
78/D5 **Bulolo,** PNG
31/G7 **Bulphan,** Eng,UK
73/F5 **Bulukumba,** Indo.
87/D2 **Bulungu,** Zaire
83/K7 **Bumba,** Zaire
83/N7 **Buna,** Kenya
65/L9 **Bunaga-take** (peak), Japan
87/F1 **Bunazi,** Tanz.
74/B6 **Bunbury,** Austl.
76/D4 **Bundaberg,** Austl.
41/F4 **Bünde,** Ger.
70/C2 **Būndi,** India
35/H2 **Bungay,** Eng,UK
72/C3 **Bunguran** (isl.), Indo.
83/M7 **Bunia,** Zaire
113/H4 **Bunnell,** Fl,US
40/C4 **Bunnik,** Neth.
47/E3 **Buñol,** Sp.
40/C4 **Bunschoten,** Neth.
35/F3 **Buntingford,** Eng,UK
76/C4 **Bunya Mountains Nat'l Park,** Austl.
59/C2 **Bünyan,** Turk.
76/E6 **Bunya Park,** Austl.
73/E3 **Bunyu** (isl.), Indo.
69/E3 **Buon Me Thuot,** Viet.
69/E3 **Buon Mrong,** Viet.
94/C3 **Buquim,** Braz.
83/N8 **Bura,** Kenya
83/L5 **Buram,** Sudan
83/M7 **Buranga** (pass), Ugan.
83/Q6 **Burao** (Burco), Som.
113/F4 **Buras-Triumph,** La,US
67/D5 **Burauen,** Phil.
60/D3 **Buraydah,** SAr.
43/H2 **Burbach,** Ger.
115/B2 **Burbank,** Ca,US
116/Q16 **Burbank,** Il,US
83/Q6 **Burco** (Burao), Som.
76/B3 **Burdekin** (riv.), Austl.
116/J10 **Burdell** (mtn.), Ca,US
59/B3 **Burdur,** Turk.
70/E3 **Burdwān,** India
35/H1 **Bure** (riv.), Eng,UK
41/F5 **Büren,** Ger.
40/C5 **Buren,** Neth.
62/E2 **Bürengiyn** (mts.), Mong.
31/S10 **Bures-sur-Yvette,** Fr.
61/K2 **Būrewāla,** Pak.
63/L1 **Bureya** (mts.), Rus.
63/L1 **Bureya** (riv.), Rus.
35/E3 **Burford,** Eng,UK
51/H4 **Burgas,** Bul.
51/H4 **Burgas** (bay), Bul.
51/H4 **Burgas** (reg.), Bul.
41/H4 **Burgdorf,** Ger.
45/M3 **Burgenland** (prov.), Aus.
111/K2 **Burgeo,** Nf,Can
88/D3 **Burgersdorp,** SAfr.
114/L2 **Burgess** (mtn.), Yk,Can
35/F5 **Burgess Hill,** Eng,UK
37/E2 **Burgfjället** (peak), Swe.
33/J5 **Burgh le Marsh,** Eng,UK
45/K2 **Burglengenfeld,** Ger.
46/D1 **Burgos,** Sp.
41/E4 **Burgsteinfurt,** Ger.
44/F3 **Burgundy** (hist. reg.), Fr.
41/G3 **Burgwedel,** Ger.
62/D4 **Burhan Budai** (mts.), China
59/A2 **Burhaniye,** Turk.
70/C3 **Burhānpur,** India
100/E6 **Burica** (pen.), CR, Pan.
100/E6 **Burica** (pt.), Pan.
36/C5 **Burien,** Wa,US
111/L2 **Burin,** Nf,Can
111/K2 **Burin** (pen.), Nf,Can
69/C3 **Buriram,** Thai.
95/B2 **Buritama,** Braz.
94/B1 **Buriti,** Braz.
95/B1 **Buriti Alegre,** Braz.
94/B2 **Buriti Bravo,** Braz.
94/A4 **Buritis,** Braz.
95/C1 **Buritizeiro,** Braz.
47/E3 **Burjasot,** Sp.
112/D3 **Burkburnett,** Tx,US
98/S **Burke** (isl.), Ant.
115/J8 **Burke,** Va,US
106/B2 **Burke Channel** (inlet), BC,Can
85/E3 **Burkina Faso**
106/E5 **Burley,** Id,US
116/K11 **Burlingame,** Ca,US
111/Q9 **Burlington,** On,Can
109/G3 **Burlington,** Co,US
107/L5 **Burlington,** Ia,US
109/J3 **Burlington,** Ks,US
113/J2 **Burlington,** NC,US
115/F5 **Burlington,** NJ,US
111/F2 **Burlington,** Vt,US
116/P14 **Burlington,** Wi,US
71/G2 **Burma** (Myanmar)
51/K3 **Burnas** (lake), Ukr.
112/D4 **Burnet,** Tx,US
97/J8 **Burney** (peak), Chile
108/B2 **Burney,** Ca,US
35/G3 **Burnham on Crouch,** Eng,UK
34/D4 **Burnham on Sea,** Eng,UK
77/C4 **Burnie-Somerset,** Austl.
33/F4 **Burnley,** Eng,UK
105/D5 **Burns,** Or,US
102/E2 **Burnside** (riv.), NW,Can
106/B2 **Burns Lake,** BC,Can
107/J2 **Burntwood** (riv.), Mb,Can
35/E1 **Burntwood,** Eng,UK
77/B2 **Buronga,** Austl.
62/E2 **Burqin** (riv.), China
75/H6 **Burragorang** (lake), Austl.
49/G4 **Burrel,** Alb.
77/D2 **Burrendong** (res.), Austl.
77/D2 **Burrewarra** (pt.), Austl.
47/E3 **Burriana,** Sp.
77/D2 **Burrinjuck** (res.), Austl.
76/A2 **Burrowes** (pt.), Austl.
32/D2 **Burrow Head** (pt.), Sc,UK
116/Q16 **Burr Ridge,** Il,US
76/D4 **Burrum River Nat'l Park,** Austl.
34/B3 **Burry** (inlet), Wal,UK
34/B3 **Burry Port,** Wal,UK
51/J5 **Bursa,** Turk.
51/J5 **Bursa** (prov.), Turk.
86/C3 **Būr Safājah,** Egypt
59/J6 **Būr Sa'īd** (gov.), Egypt
59/J6 **Būr Sa'īd** (Port Said), Egypt
41/E6 **Burscheid,** Ger.
33/F4 **Burscough Bridge,** Eng,UK
86/D5 **Būr Sūdān** (Port Sudan), Sudan
111/S9 **Burt,** NY,US
86/C2 **Būr Tawfīq,** Egypt
35/E5 **Burton,** Eng,UK
116/E6 **Burton,** Mi,US
35/F2 **Burton Latimer,** Eng,UK
35/E1 **Burton upon Trent,** Eng,UK
73/G4 **Buru** (isl.), Indo.
59/H6 **Burullus, Buḩayrat al** (lag.), Egypt
87/E1 **Burundi**
62/F2 **Burun Shibertuy** (peak), Rus.
94/A2 **Buruticupu** (riv.), Braz.
114/L3 **Burwash Landing,** Yk,Can
35/G2 **Burwell,** Eng,UK
109/H2 **Burwell,** Ne,US
35/F5 **Bury,** Eng,UK
57/M4 **Buryat Aut. Rep.,** Rus.
55/J3 **Burynshyk** (pt.), Kaz.
35/G2 **Bury Saint Edmunds,** Eng,UK
45/H4 **Busalla,** It.
32/B1 **Bush** (riv.), NI,UK
62/C2 **Büs Hayrhan** (peak), Mong.
31/M7 **Bushey,** Eng,UK
115/E4 **Bushkill** (falls), Pa,US
88/B3 **Bushmanland** (reg.), SAfr.
32/B1 **Bushmills,** NI,UK
83/K7 **Businga,** Zaire
37/D3 **Buskerud** (co.), Nor.
39/L3 **Busko-Zdrój,** Pol.
74/B6 **Busselton,** Austl.
83/L6 **Busseri** (riv.), Sudan
40/C4 **Bussum,** Neth.
97/K7 **Bustamente** (pt.), Arg.
76/C4 **Bustard** (pt.), Austl.
51/G3 **Buşteni,** Rom.
45/H4 **Busto Arsizio,** It.
67/C5 **Busuanga** (isl.), Phil.
83/K7 **Buta,** Zaire
87/E1 **Butare,** Rwa.
78/G4 **Butaritari** (atoll), Kiri.
106/B3 **Bute** (inlet), BC,Can
36/C3 **Bute** (isl.), Sc,UK
62/E2 **Büteeliyn** (mts.), Mong.
87/E1 **Butembo,** Zaire
95/B4 **Butiá,** Braz.
110/E3 **Butler,** Pa,US
73/F5 **Buton** (isl.), Indo.
31/S9 **Butry-sur-Oise,** Fr.
106/E4 **Butte,** Mt,US
72/B2 **Butterworth,** Malay.
67/D6 **Butung** (isl.), Indo.
55/G2 **Buturlinovka,** Rus.
45/H1 **Butzbach,** Ger.
38/F2 **Bützow,** Ger.
83/Q7 **Buulo Berde,** Som.
83/P7 **Buur Hakaba,** Som.
41/G2 **Buxtehude,** Ger.
33/G5 **Buxton,** Eng,UK
52/J4 **Buy,** Rus.
55/H4 **Buynaksk,** Rus.
84/D5 **Buyo, Barrage de** (dam), IvC.
63/H2 **Buyr** (lake), Mong.
51/J5 **Büyükçekmece,** Turk.
59/B3 **Büyük Menderes** (riv.), Turk.
66/E2 **Buyun Shan** (peak), China
55/J3 **Buzachi** (pen.), Kaz.
51/H3 **Buzău,** Rom.
51/H3 **Buzău** (co.), Rom.
51/H3 **Buzău** (riv.), Rom.
50/E3 **Buziaş,** Rom.
95/H8 **Búzios** (isl.), Braz.
55/K1 **Buzuluk,** Rus.
51/F4 **Byala Slatina,** Bul.
103/R7 **Byam Martin** (chan.), NW,Can
103/R7 **Byam Martin** (isl.), NW,Can
39/J2 **Bydgoszcz,** Pol.
39/J2 **Bydgoszcz** (prov.), Pol.
35/E2 **Byfield,** Eng,UK
31/M8 **Byfleet,** Eng,UK
54/D1 **Bykhov,** Bela.
32/E5 **Bylchau,** Wal,UK
103/J1 **Bylot** (isl.), NW,Can
115/G5 **Byram** (pt.), NY,US
98/U **Byrd** (cape), Ant.
98/L **Byrd** (glac.), Ant.
97/J6 **Byron** (isl.), Chile
56/K2 **Byrranga** (mts.), Rus.
39/K4 **Bystrá** (peak), Slvk.
57/N3 **Bytantay** (riv.), Rus.
39/K3 **Bytom,** Pol.
39/J1 **Bytów,** Pol.

C

69/D2 **Ca** (riv.), Viet.
87/C3 **Caála,** Ang.
94/B2 **Caatingas** (reg.), Braz.
67/E6 **Cabadbaran,** Phil.
101/F3 **Cabaiguán,** Cuba
108/F4 **Caballo** (res.), NM,US
46/C1 **Cabañaquinta,** Sp.
67/D4 **Cabanatuan,** Phil.
34/C2 **Caban Coch** (res.), Wal,UK
111/G2 **Cabano,** Qu,Can
94/D2 **Cabedelo,** Braz.
44/E5 **Cabestany,** Fr.
46/C3 **Cabeza del Buey,** Sp.
46/C1 **Cabezón de la Sal,** Sp.
101/G5 **Cabimas,** Ven.
87/B2 **Cabinda,** Ang.
94/D3 **Cabo,** Braz.
82/C2 **Cabo Bojador,** WSah.
95/D2 **Cabo Frio,** Braz.
110/E2 **Cabonga** (res.), Qu,Can
76/D4 **Caboolture,** Austl.
93/H3 **Cabo Orange Nat'l Park,** Braz.
87/F4 **Cabora Bassa** (lake), Moz.
111/J2 **Cabot** (str.), Nf, NS,Can
95/G6 **Cabo Verde,** Braz.
46/C4 **Cabra,** Sp.
94/A5 **Cabral** (mts.), Braz.
76/G8 **Cabramatta,** Austl.
48/A3 **Cabras,** It.
47/G3 **Cabrera** (isl.), Sp.
106/F3 **Cabri,** Sk,Can
46/E3 **Cabriel** (riv.), Sp.
94/C3 **Cabrobó,** Braz.
67/D4 **Cabugao,** Phil.
101/H5 **Cabure,** Ven.
95/B3 **Caçador,** Braz.
50/E4 **Čačak,** Yugo.
95/H8 **Caçapava,** Braz.
48/A2 **Caccia** (cape), It.
92/G7 **Cáceres,** Braz.
46/B3 **Cáceres,** Sp.
31/S10 **Cachan,** Fr.
96/Q10 **Cachapoal** (riv.), Chile
108/B3 **Cache** (cr.), Ca,US
106/E5 **Cache** (peak), Id,US
106/C3 **Cache Creek,** BC,Can
84/A3 **Cacheu,** GBis.
93/G5 **Cachimbo** (mts.), Braz.
95/A4 **Cachoeira do Sul,** Braz.
95/J7 **Cachoeira Paulista,** Braz.
95/L7 **Cachoeiras de Macacu,** Braz.
95/B4 **Cachoeirinha,** Braz.
95/D2 **Cachoeiro de Itapemirim,** Braz.
95/G6 **Caconde,** Braz.
95/B1 **Caçu,** Braz.
87/B3 **Cacula,** Ang.
94/B4 **Caculé,** Braz.
47/G1 **Cadaques,** Sp.
39/K4 **Čadca,** Slvk.
112/E3 **Caddo** (mts.), Ar,US
34/C1 **Cader Idris** (mtn.), Wal,UK
74/E5 **Cadibarrawirracanna** (lake), Austl.
110/C2 **Cadillac,** Mi,US
67/D5 **Cadiz,** Phil.
46/B4 **Cádiz,** Sp.
46/B4 **Cádiz** (gulf), Sp.
110/C4 **Cadiz,** Ky,US
35/E5 **Cadnam,** Eng,UK
44/C2 **Caen,** Fr.
34/D3 **Caerleon,** Wal,UK
32/D5 **Caernarfon,** Wal,UK
32/D5 **Caernarfon** (bay), Wal,UK
34/C3 **Caerphilly,** Wal,UK
34/C1 **Caersws,** Wal,UK
59/M7 **Caesarea Nat'l Park,** Isr.
42/B2 **Caëstre,** Fr.
94/B4 **Caetité,** Braz.
91/C2 **Cafayate,** Arg.
67/D6 **Cagayan de Oro,** Phil.
67/C6 **Cagayan Sulu** (isl.), Phil.
48/A3 **Cagliari,** It.
48/A3 **Cagliari** (gulf), It.
45/G5 **Cagnes-sur-Mer,** Fr.
92/D3 **Caguán** (riv.), Col.
101/H4 **Caguas,** PR
87/B4 **Cahama,** Ang.
36/B4 **Cahore** (pt.), Ire.
44/D4 **Cahors,** Fr.
95/B4 **Cai** (riv.), Braz.
93/H7 **Caiapó** (mts.), Braz.
93/H7 **Caiapó** (riv.), Braz.
101/F3 **Caibarién,** Cuba
94/C2 **Caicó,** Braz.
101/G3 **Caicos** (isls.), Trks.
95/G8 **Caieiras,** Braz.
42/A4 **Cailly** (riv.), Fr.
69/D4 **Cai Nuoc,** Viet.
98/Y **Caird** (coast), Ant.
114/G3 **Cairn** (mtn.), Ak,US
77/B3 **Cairn Curran** (dam), Austl.
36/D2 **Cairngorm** (mts.), Sc,UK
32/C2 **Cairn Pat** (hill), Sc,UK
32/C2 **Cairnryan,** Sc,UK
76/B2 **Cairns,** Austl.
32/D1 **Cairnsmore of Carsphairn** (mtn.), Sc,UK
113/G4 **Cairo,** Ga,US
110/B4 **Cairo,** Il,US
86/B2 **Cairo** (Al Qāhirah) (cap.), Egypt
35/H1 **Caister on Sea,** Eng,UK
33/H5 **Caistor,** Eng,UK
111/Q9 **Caistor Centre,** On,Can
111/Q9 **Caistorville,** On,Can
87/B3 **Caitou,** Ang.
87/C4 **Caiundo,** Ang.
66/C5 **Caizi** (lake), China
92/C5 **Cajabamba,** Peru
92/C5 **Cajamarca,** Peru
94/C2 **Cajazeiras,** Braz.
100/E3 **Cajón** (pt.), Cuba
94/B1 **Caju** (isl.), Braz.
85/H5 **Calabar,** Nga.
101/H6 **Calabozo,** Ven.
48/E3 **Calabria** (reg.), It.
48/E3 **Calabria Nat'l Park,** It.
46/C4 **Calaburras, Punta de** (pt.), Sp.
50/F4 **Calafat,** Rom.
46/E1 **Calahorra,** Sp.
42/A2 **Calais,** Fr.
111/H2 **Calais,** Me,US
42/A2 **Calais, Canal de** (can.), Fr.
91/C2 **Calalaste** (mts.), Arg.
91/C1 **Calama,** Chile
67/C5 **Calamian Group** (isls.), Phil.
50/F3 **Călan,** Rom.
67/D5 **Calapan,** Phil.
51/H3 **Călăraşi,** Rom.
51/H3 **Călăraşi** (co.), Rom.
46/E3 **Calasparra,** Sp.
46/E2 **Calatayud,** Sp.
116/L12 **Calaveras** (res.), Ca,US
67/D4 **Calayan,** Phil.
67/D4 **Calayan** (isl.), Phil.
67/D5 **Calbayog,** Phil.
96/B4 **Calbuco,** Chile
92/D6 **Calca,** Peru
94/D2 **Calcanhar, Ponta do** (pt.), Braz.
112/E4 **Calcasieu** (riv.), La,US
110/F2 **Calcium,** NY,US
70/E3 **Calcutta,** India
46/A3 **Caldas da Rainha,** Port.
95/B1 **Caldas Novas,** Braz.
33/E2 **Caldbeck,** Eng,UK
41/G6 **Calden,** Ger.
33/G4 **Calder** (riv.), Eng,UK
114/M4 **Calder** (mtn.), Ak,US
47/L6 **Caldes de Montbui,** Sp.
33/F2 **Caldew** (riv.), Eng,UK
34/D3 **Caldicot,** Wal,UK
106/D5 **Caldwell,** Id,US
112/D4 **Caldwell,** Tx,US
34/B3 **Caldy** (isl.), Wal,UK
88/D3 **Caledon** (riv.), Les., SAfr.
111/Q8 **Caledon East,** On,Can
111/H2 **Caledonia** (hills), NB,Can
47/G2 **Calella,** Sp.
96/Q9 **Calera de Tango,** Chile
101/P9 **Calera Víctor Rosales,** Mex.
101/P10 **Caleta de Campos Chutla,** Mex.
96/D5 **Caleta Olivia,** Arg.
108/D4 **Calexico,** Ca,US
33/F3 **Calf, The** (mtn.), Eng,UK
106/E3 **Calgary,** Ab,Can
47/S12 **Calheta,** Azor.,Port.
47/U15 **Calheta,** Madr.,Port.
113/G3 **Calhoun,** Ga,US
110/C4 **Calhoun,** Ky,US
92/C3 **Cali,** Col.
46/E4 **Calida, Costa** (coast), Sp.
108/D3 **Caliente,** Nv,US
101/M8 **California** (gulf), Mex.
108/B3 **California** (state), US
110/E4 **California,** Md,US
109/J3 **California,** Mo,US
91/D1 **Calilegua Nat'l Park,** Arg.
51/G3 **Călimăneşti,** Rom.
70/C5 **Calimere** (pt.), India
115/C2 **Calimesa,** Ca,US
100/C3 **Calkiní,** Mex.
77/A1 **Callabonna** (lake), Austl.
36/C2 **Callander,** Sc,UK
92/C6 **Callao,** Peru
113/G4 **Callaway,** Fl,US
96/Q9 **Calle Larga,** Chile
34/B6 **Callington,** Eng,UK
47/E3 **Callosa de Ensarriá,** Sp.
47/E3 **Callosa de Segura,** Sp.
34/D4 **Calne,** Eng,UK
42/B3 **Calonne-Ricouart,** Fr.
48/D2 **Calore** (riv.), It.
76/D4 **Caloundra,** Austl.
47/F3 **Calpe,** Sp.
34/B6 **Calstock,** Eng,UK
48/D4 **Caltagirone,** It.
48/D4 **Caltanissetta,** It.
44/F4 **Caluire-et-Cuire,** Fr.
116/Q16 **Calumet** (riv.), Il,US
116/Q16 **Calumet City,** Il,US
87/B3 **Caluquembe,** Ang.
106/A3 **Calvert** (isl.), BC,Can
33/G5 **Calverton,** Eng,UK
115/K7 **Calverton,** Md,US
115/H5 **Calverton,** NY,US
47/G3 **Calviá,** Sp.
88/B3 **Calvinia,** SAfr.
46/C2 **Calvitero** (mtn.), Sp.
35/G2 **Cam** (riv.), Eng,UK
94/C4 **Camaçari,** Braz.
87/C3 **Camacupa,** Ang.
101/F3 **Camagüey,** Cuba
101/F3 **Camagüey** (arch.), Cuba
45/J5 **Camaiore,** It.
94/C4 **Camamu,** Braz.
94/C4 **Camamu** (bay), Braz.
92/D7 **Camaná,** Peru
95/B4 **Camaquã,** Braz.
95/A4 **Camaquã** (riv.), Braz.
47/V15 **Câmara de Lobos,** Madr.,Port.
45/G5 **Camarat** (cape), Fr.
46/D1 **Camargo,** Sp.
115/A2 **Camarillo,** Ca,US
46/A1 **Camariñas,** Sp.
100/D4 **Camarón** (cape), Hon.
96/D5 **Camarones** (bay), Arg.
46/B4 **Camas,** Sp.
69/D4 **Ca Mau,** Viet.
69/D4 **Ca Mau** (cape), Viet.
46/A1 **Cambados,** Sp.
95/B2 **Cambará,** Braz.
70/B3 **Cambay,** India
70/B3 **Cambay** (gulf), India
95/B2 **Cambé,** Braz.
35/F4 **Camberley Frimley,** Eng,UK
31/N7 **Camberwell,** Eng,UK
69/D3 **Cambodia**
95/C3 **Camboriú, Ponta do** (pt.), Braz.
34/A6 **Camborne,** Eng,UK
42/C3 **Cambrai,** Fr.
34/C2 **Cambrian** (mts.), Wal,UK
110/D3 **Cambridge,** On,Can
75/S10 **Cambridge,** NZ
35/G2 **Cambridge,** Eng,UK
111/G3 **Cambridge,** Ma,US
110/E4 **Cambridge,** Md,US
107/K4 **Cambridge,** Mn,US
110/D3 **Cambridge,** Oh,US
35/G2 **Cambridgeshire** (co.), Eng,UK
47/F2 **Cambrils,** Sp.
95/G7 **Cambuí,** Braz.
95/H6 **Cambuquira,** Braz.
101/E6 **Cambutal** (mt.), Pan.
77/D2 **Camden,** Austl.
31/N7 **Camden** (bor.), Eng,UK
113/G4 **Camden,** Al,US
112/E3 **Camden,** Ar,US
111/G2 **Camden,** Me,US
115/E6 **Camden,** NJ,US
113/H3 **Camden,** SC,US
109/J3 **Camdenton,** Mo,US
87/D3 **Cameia Nat'l Park,** Ang.
34/B6 **Camel** (riv.), Eng,UK
115/E4 **Camelback** (mtn.), Pa,US
34/B5 **Camelford,** Eng,UK
103/R7 **Cameron** (isl.), NW,Can
108/E4 **Cameron,** Az,US
112/E4 **Cameron,** La,US
109/J3 **Cameron,** Mo,US
112/D4 **Cameron,** Tx,US
82/H7 **Cameroon**
93/J4 **Cametá,** Braz.
42/A2 **Camiers,** Fr.
67/D4 **Camiguin** (isl.), Phil.
113/G4 **Camilla,** Ga,US
92/F8 **Camiri,** Bol.
87/F5 **Camo-Camo,** Moz.
94/B1 **Camocim,** Braz.
71/F6 **Camorta** (isl.), India
42/A3 **Campagne,** Fr.
96/F2 **Campana,** Arg.
97/J7 **Campana** (isl.), Chile
96/C2 **Campanario** (peak), Arg.
48/D2 **Campanella** (cape), It.
95/H6 **Campanha,** Braz.
48/D2 **Campania** (reg.), It.
29/T8 **Campbell** (isl.), NZ
116/L12 **Campbell,** Ca,US
106/A2 **Campbell Island,** BC,Can
106/B3 **Campbell River,** BC,Can
110/C4 **Campbellsville,** Ky,US
111/H2 **Campbellton,** NB,Can
76/G9 **Campbelltown,** Austl.
111/Q9 **Campbellville,** On,Can
111/R9 **Campden,** On,Can
100/C4 **Campeche,** Mex.
100/C4 **Campeche** (bay), Mex.
100/C4 **Campeche** (state), Mex.
107/H3 **Camperville,** Mb,Can
95/G6 **Campestre,** Braz.
69/D1 **Cam Pha,** Viet.
48/A3 **Campidano** (range), It.
46/C4 **Campillos,** Sp.
94/D2 **Campina Grande,** Braz.
95/F7 **Campinas,** Braz.
95/B1 **Campina Verde,** Braz.
92/C3 **Campoalegre,** Col.
48/D2 **Campobasso,** It.
95/C2 **Campo Belo,** Braz.
46/D3 **Campo de Criptana,** Sp.
101/G5 **Campo de la Cruz,** Col.
94/B3 **Campo Formoso,** Braz.
93/H8 **Campo Grande,** Braz.
91/G2 **Campo Largo,** Braz.
95/G8 **Campo Limpo Paulista,** Braz.
94/B2 **Campo Maior,** Braz.
46/B3 **Campo Maior,** Port.
45/H4 **Campomorone,** It.
95/A3 **Campo Mourão,** Braz.
94/C2 **Campo Redondo,** Braz.
46/C1 **Camporredondo** (res.), Sp.
95/D2 **Campos,** Braz.
94/A4 **Campos** (reg.), Braz.
95/C1 **Campos Altos,** Braz.
94/A4 **Campos Belos,** Braz.
47/G3 **Campos del Puerto,** Sp.
95/H7 **Campos do Jordão,** Braz.
95/C2 **Campos Gerais,** Braz.
95/B3 **Campos Novos,** Braz.
94/B2 **Campos Sales,** Braz.
115/K8 **Camp Springs,** Md,US
112/E4 **Campti,** La,US
69/E4 **Cam Ranh,** Viet.
106/E2 **Camrose,** Ab,Can
69/D1 **Cam Thuy,** Viet.
102/* **Canada**
96/E2 **Cañada de Gómez,** Arg.
109/H4 **Canadian** (riv.), US
112/C3 **Canadian,** Tx,US
96/C5 **Cañadon Grande** (mts.), Arg.
101/G6 **Canagua,** Ven.
92/F2 **Canaima Nat'l Park,** Ven.
51/H5 **Çanakkale,** Turk.
51/H5 **Çanakkale** (prov.), Turk.
79/U12 **Canala,** NCal.
96/E2 **Canals,** Arg.
47/E3 **Canals,** Sp.
110/E3 **Canandaigua,** NY,US
101/M7 **Cananea,** Mex.
95/C3 **Cananéia,** Braz.
47/X16 **Canary Islands** (aut. comm.), Sp.
100/D5 **Cañas,** CR
101/P9 **Canatlán,** Mex.
113/H4 **Canaveral** (cape), Fl,US
94/C4 **Canavieiras,** Braz.
77/D2 **Canberra** (cap.), Austl.
42/A3 **Canche** (riv.), Fr.
100/D3 **Cancún,** Mex.
46/C1 **Candás,** Sp.
111/N7 **Candiac,** Qu,Can
95/B2 **Candido Mota,** Braz.
72/D5 **Canding** (cape), Indo.
107/G2 **Candle** (lake), Sk,Can
107/J3 **Cando,** ND,US
67/D4 **Candon,** Phil.
95/B4 **Canela,** Braz.
45/H4 **Canelli,** It.
97/F2 **Canelones,** Uru.
97/F2 **Canelones** (dept.), Uru.
46/A1 **Cangas,** Sp.
46/B1 **Cangas de Narcea,** Sp.
46/C1 **Cangas de Onís,** Sp.
72/C5 **Cangkuang** (cape), Indo.
88/C4 **Cango Caves,** SAfr.
87/D3 **Cangombe,** Ang.
97/J7 **Cangrejo** (peak), Arg.
94/D2 **Canguaretama,** Braz.
95/A4 **Canguçu,** Braz.
66/D3 **Cangzhou,** China
69/D1 **Canh Cuoc** (isl.), Viet.
87/B3 **Canhoca,** Ang.
76/C4 **Cania Gorge Nat'l Park,** Austl.
103/K3 **Caniapiscau** (lake), Qu,Can
103/K3 **Caniapiscau** (riv.), Qu,Can
48/C4 **Canicatti,** It.
44/E5 **Canigou, Pic de** (peak), Fr.
59/D2 **Canik** (mts.), Turk.
46/D4 **Caniles,** Sp.
94/C2 **Canindé,** Braz.
94/B2 **Canindé** (riv.), Braz.
59/C2 **Çankırı,** Turk.
73/F1 **Canlaon** (vol.), Phil.
106/E3 **Canmore,** Ab,Can
70/C5 **Cannanore,** India
48/E2 **Canne** (ruins), It.
43/F5 **Canner** (riv.), Fr.
45/G5 **Cannes,** Fr.
36/C2 **Cannich,** Sc,UK
34/D1 **Cannock,** Eng,UK
107/H4 **Cannonball** (riv.), ND,US
107/K4 **Cannon Falls,** Mn,US
95/B4 **Canoas,** Braz.
95/B3 **Canoas** (riv.), Braz.
77/D2 **Canobolas** (peak), Austl.
106/F2 **Canoe** (lake), Sk,Can
95/B3 **Canoinhas,** Braz.
33/F1 **Canonbie,** Sc,UK
109/F3 **Canon City,** Co,US
107/H3 **Canora,** Sk,Can
111/J2 **Canso** (cape), Can.
46/C1 **Cantabria** (aut. comm.), Sp.
44/E4 **Cantal** (plat.), Fr.
46/A2 **Cantanhede,** Port.
101/J6 **Cantaura,** Ven.
76/H8 **Canterbury,** Austl.
75/R11 **Canterbury** (bight), NZ
35/H4 **Canterbury,** Eng,UK
69/D4 **Can Tho,** Viet.
46/C4 **Cantillana,** Sp.
94/B3 **Canto do Buriti,** Braz.
110/B3 **Canton,** Il,US
116/E7 **Canton,** Mi,US
113/F3 **Canton,** Ms,US
110/F2 **Canton,** NY,US
110/D3 **Canton,** Oh,US
109/H3 **Canton,** Ok,US
107/J5 **Canton,** SD,US
112/E3 **Canton,** Tx,US
79/H5 **Canton** (Abariringa) (atoll), Kiri.
67/B3 **Canton** (Guangzhou), China
45/H4 **Cantù,** It.
96/F2 **Cañuelas,** Arg.
77/B3 **Canunda Nat'l Park,** Austl.
35/G3 **Canvey Island,** Eng,UK
106/G2 **Canwood,** Sk,Can
112/C3 **Canyon,** Tx,US
108/E3 **Canyon de Chelly Nat'l Mon.,** Az,US
108/E3 **Canyonlands Nat'l Park,** Ut,US
69/D1 **Cao Bang,** Viet.
67/A2 **Caodu** (riv.), China
69/D4 **Cao Lanh,** Viet.
92/E2 **Capanaparo** (riv.), Ven.
93/J4 **Capanema,** Braz.
48/B1 **Capanne** (peak), It.
45/J5 **Capannori,** It.
95/B3 **Capão Bonito,** Braz.
95/D2 **Caparaó Nat'l Park,** Braz.
46/A3 **Caparica,** Port.
111/H1 **Cap-Chat,** Qu,Can
111/F2 **Cap-de-la-Madeleine,** Qu,Can
76/B3 **Cape** (riv.), Austl.
88/C3 **Cape** (prov.), SAfr.
77/D4 **Cape Barren** (isl.), Austl.
111/J2 **Cape Breton** (highlands), NS,Can
111/J2 **Cape Breton** (isl.), NS,Can
111/J2 **Cape Breton Highlands Nat'l Park,** NS,Can
76/B2 **Cape Cleveland Nat'l Park,** Austl.
85/E5 **Cape Coast,** Gha.
111/G3 **Cape Cod Nat'l Seashore,** Ma,US
113/H5 **Cape Coral,** Fl,US
113/J3 **Cape Fear** (riv.), NC,US
109/K3 **Cape Girardeau,** Mo,US
113/K3 **Cape Hatteras Nat'l Seashore,** NC,US
114/E2 **Cape Krusenstern Nat'l Mon.,** Ak,US
31/Q8 **Capel,** Eng,UK
94/C3 **Capela,** Braz.
32/E5 **Capel-Curig,** Wal,UK
95/D1 **Capelinha,** Braz.
47/K6 **Capellades,** Sp.
35/H4 **Capel le Ferne,** Eng,UK
113/J3 **Cape Lookout Nat'l Seashore,** NC,US
35/H2 **Capel Saint Mary,** Eng,UK
76/B1 **Cape Melville Nat'l Park,** Austl.
76/C3 **Cape Palmerston Nat'l Park,** Austl.
115/K7 **Cape Saint Claire,** Md,US
88/B4 **Cape Town** (cap.), SAfr.
76/B2 **Cape Tribulation Nat'l Park,** Austl.
76/B2 **Cape Upstart Nat'l Park,** Austl.
80/K9 **Cape Verde**
76/A1 **Cape York** (pen.), Austl.
101/G4 **Cap-Haïtien,** Haiti
48/A2 **Capicciola** (pt.), Fr.
93/J4 **Capim** (riv.), Braz.
94/D2 **Capina,** Braz.
95/B1 **Capinópolis,** Braz.
95/B2 **Capirara** (res.), Braz.
112/B3 **Capitan** (mts.), NM,US
93/J4 **Capitão Poco,** Braz.
108/E3 **Capitol Reef Nat'l Park,** Ut,US
94/A4 **Capivara** (mts.), Braz.
93/H8 **Capivara** (res.), Braz.
95/J6 **Capivari** (riv.), Braz.
50/C4 **Čapljina,** Bosn.
48/D3 **Capo d'Orlando,** It.
48/A3 **Capoterra,** It.
48/A1 **Capraia** (isl.), It.
110/D2 **Capreol,** On,Can
48/D2 **Capri,** It.
76/C3 **Capricorn** (cape), Austl.
76/C3 **Capricorn** (chan.), Austl.
87/D4 **Caprivi Strip** (reg.), Namb.
112/C3 **Cap Rock Escarpment** (cliffs), Tx,US
112/C3 **Caprock, The** (cliffs), NM,US
111/G2 **Cap-Rouge,** Qu,Can
45/G5 **Cap Roux, Pointe du** (pt.), Fr.
109/G3 **Capulin Volcano Nat'l Mon.,** NM,US
92/D4 **Caquetá** (riv.), Col.
47/N9 **Carabanchel** (nrbhd.), Sp.
51/G3 **Caracal,** Rom.
101/H5 **Caracas** (cap.), Ven.
34/B5 **Caradon** (hill), Eng,UK
95/H8 **Caraguatatuba,** Braz.
95/H8 **Caraguatatuba** (bay), Braz.
96/B3 **Carahue,** Chile
93/H5 **Carajás** (mts.), Braz.

Caran – Chen

95/D2 **Carandaí**, Braz.
95/D2 **Carangola**, Braz.
50/F3 **Caransebeş**, Rom.
48/D2 **Carapelle** (riv.), It.
95/G8 **Carapicuíba**, Braz.
111/H2 **Caraquet**, NB,Can
50/E3 **Caraş-Severin** (co.), Rom.
100/E4 **Caratasca** (lag.), Hon.
95/D1 **Caratinga**, Braz.
92/E4 **Carauarí**, Braz.
94/C2 **Caraúbas**, Braz.
46/E3 **Caravaca de la Cruz**, Sp.
84/A4 **Caravela** (isl.), GBis.
91/F2 **Carazinho**, Braz.
46/A1 **Carballino**, Sp.
46/A1 **Carballo**, Sp.
107/J3 **Carberry**, Mb,Can
81/U17 **Carbon** (cape), Alg.
116/C3 **Carbon** (riv.), Wa,US
48/A3 **Carbonara** (cape), It.
48/D4 **Carbonara, Pizzo** (peak), It.
110/B4 **Carbondale**, Il,US
110/F3 **Carbondale**, Pa,US
48/A3 **Carbonia**, It.
47/E3 **Carcagente**, Sp.
96/E2 **Carcaraña**, Arg.
44/E5 **Carcassonne**, Fr.
47/P10 **Carcavelos**, Port.
46/E3 **Carche** (mtn.), Sp.
102/C2 **Carcross**, Yt,Can
47/L6 **Cardedeu**, Sp.
97/K7 **Cardiel** (lake), Arg.
34/C4 **Cardiff** (cap.), Wal,UK
34/B2 **Cardigan**, Wal,UK
47/F2 **Cardona**, Sp.
95/B2 **Cardoso**, Braz.
106/E3 **Cardston**, Ab,Can
50/F2 **Carei**, Rom.
44/C2 **Carentan**, Fr.
50/F4 **Carev vrh** (peak), Macd.
74/C5 **Carey** (lake), Austl.
44/B2 **Carhaix-Plouguer**, Fr.
96/E3 **Carhué**, Arg.
95/D2 **Cariacica**, Braz.
101/J5 **Cariaco**, Ven.
92/C4 **Cariamanga**, Ecu.
48/E3 **Cariati**, It.
101/G5 **Caribbean** (sea)
106/C2 **Cariboo** (mts.), BC,Can
102/E3 **Caribou** (mts.), Ab,Can
110/B1 **Caribou** (lake), On,Can
114/L3 **Caribou**, Yk,Can
106/F5 **Caribou** (range), Id,US
111/G2 **Caribou**, Me,US
67/D5 **Carigara**, Phil.
94/B4 **Carinhanha**, Braz.
94/A4 **Carinhanha** (riv.), Braz.
48/C3 **Carini**, It.
45/K3 **Carinthia** (prov.), Aus.
101/J5 **Caripito**, Ven.
94/B2 **Cariri Novos** (mts.), Braz.
109/G3 **Carizzo** (cr.), NM, Tx,US
47/E3 **Carlet**, Sp.
111/H2 **Carleton** (peak), NB,Can
111/H2 **Carleton** (riv.), NS,Can
111/H1 **Carleton**, Qu,Can
88/D2 **Carletonville**, SAfr.
108/C2 **Carlin**, Nv,US
76/H8 **Carlingford**, Austl.
32/B3 **Carlingford** (mtn.), Ire.
32/B3 **Carlingford Lough** (inlet), Ire.
110/B4 **Carlinville**, Il,US
111/Q9 **Carlisle**, On,Can
33/F2 **Carlisle**, Eng,UK
44/D5 **Carlit** (peak), Fr.
96/E2 **Carlos Casares**, Arg.
95/D1 **Carlos Chagas**, Braz.
101/F3 **Carlos M. De Cespedes**, Cuba
32/B6 **Carlow**, Ire.
32/B6 **Carlow** (co.), Ire.
109/F4 **Carlsbad**, NM,US
109/F4 **Carlsbad Caverns Nat'l Park**, NM,US
33/G6 **Carlton**, Eng,UK
107/K4 **Carlton**, Mn,US
111/Q9 **Carluke**, On,Can
107/H3 **Carlyle**, Sk,Can
109/K3 **Carlyle** (lake), Il,US
102/C2 **Carmacks**, Yk,Can
45/G4 **Carmagnola**, It.
107/J3 **Carman**, Mb,Can
34/B3 **Carmarthen**, Wal,UK
34/B3 **Carmarthen** (bay), Wal,UK
44/E4 **Carmaux**, Fr.
110/C4 **Carmel**, In,US
32/D5 **Carmel Head** (pt.), Wal,UK
59/K5 **Carmel, Mount** (Har Karmel) (mtn.), Isr.
96/F2 **Carmelo**, Uru.
101/M8 **Carmen** (isl.), Mex.
101/N7 **Carmen** (riv.), Mex.
110/B4 **Carmi**, Il,US
116/M9 **Carmichael**, Ca,US
95/L6 **Carmo**, Braz.
95/C1 **Carmo do Paranaíba**, Braz.
95/C2 **Carmo do Rio Claro**, Braz.
46/C4 **Carmona**, Sp.
32/B1 **Carnanmore** (mtn.), NI,UK
74/A4 **Carnarvon**, Austl.
88/C3 **Carnarvonleegte** (dry riv.), SAfr.
76/B4 **Carnarvon Nat'l Park**, Austl.
47/P10 **Carnaxide**, Port.
32/C2 **Carncastle**, NI,UK
107/H3 **Carnduff**, Sk,Can
32/D5 **Carnedd Dafydd** (mtn.), Wal,UK
32/E5 **Carnedd Llewelyn** (mtn.), Wal,UK
74/C5 **Carnegie** (lake), Austl.
98/S **Carney** (isl.), Ant.
33/F3 **Carnforth**, Eng,UK
42/C3 **Carnières**, Fr.
32/B2 **Carnlough**, NI,UK
94/C2 **Carnoió**, Braz.
82/J7 **Carnot**, CAfr.
46/A1 **Carnota**, Sp.
36/D2 **Carnoustie**, Sc,UK
36/B4 **Carnsore** (pt.), Ire.
102/D2 **Carnwath** (riv.), NW,Can
110/D3 **Caro**, Mi,US
94/A2 **Carolina**, Braz.
101/H4 **Carolina**, PR
79/K5 **Caroline** (isl.), Kiri.
78/D4 **Caroline** (isls.), Micr.
116/P16 **Carol Stream**, Il,US
54/B2 **Carpathian** (mts.), Eur.
45/J4 **Carpenedolo**, It.
74/F2 **Carpentaria** (gulf), Austl.
116/P15 **Carpentersville**, Il,US
44/F4 **Carpentras**, Fr.
45/J4 **Carpi**, It.
115/A2 **Carpinteria**, Ca,US
116/B3 **Carr** (inlet), Wa,US
113/G4 **Carrabelle**, Fl,US
45/J4 **Carrara**, It.
32/D6 **Carreg Ddu** (pt.), Wal,UK
101/J5 **Carriacou** (isl.), Gren.
32/C2 **Carrickfergus**, NI,UK
32/C2 **Carrickfergus** (dist.), NI,UK
32/A2 **Carrickmore**, NI,UK
31/S10 **Carrières-sous-Poissy**, Fr.
32/B3 **Carrigatuke** (mtn.), NI,UK
107/J4 **Carrington**, ND,US
46/C1 **Carrión** (riv.), Sp.
101/G5 **Carrizal**, Col.
104/E4 **Carrizo** (mts.), Az,US
112/C2 **Carrizo** (cr.), NM,US
112/D4 **Carrizo Springs**, Tx,US
109/F4 **Carrizozo**, NM,US
113/G3 **Carrollton**, Ga,US
110/C4 **Carrollton**, Ky,US
109/J3 **Carrollton**, Mo,US
107/H2 **Carrot** (riv.), Sk,Can
107/H2 **Carrot River**, Sk,Can
32/C2 **Carrowdore**, NI,UK
32/C2 **Carryduff**, NI,UK
59/D2 **Çarşamba**, Turk.
115/B3 **Carson**, Ca,US
108/C3 **Carson** (riv.), Nv,US
108/C3 **Carson** (sink), Nv,US
108/C3 **Carson City** (cap.), Nv,US
32/D1 **Carsphairn**, Sc,UK
106/E3 **Carstairs**, Ab,Can
96/Q9 **Cartagena**, Chile
101/F5 **Cartagena**, Col.
47/E4 **Cartagena**, Sp.
92/C3 **Cartago**, Col.
100/E6 **Cartago**, CR
46/C4 **Cártama**, Sp.
46/A3 **Cartaxo**, Port.
46/B4 **Cartaya**, Sp.
75/A1 **Carter** (peak), Austl.
115/F5 **Carteret**, NJ,US
113/G3 **Cartersville**, Ga,US
35/E3 **Carterton**, Eng,UK
48/B4 **Carthage** (ruins), Tun.
109/J3 **Carthage**, Mo,US
113/F3 **Carthage**, Ms,US
113/G2 **Carthage**, Tn,US
112/E3 **Carthage**, Tx,US
74/C2 **Cartier Islet** (isl.), Austl.
103/L3 **Cartwright**, Nf,Can
94/D3 **Caruaru**, Braz.
92/F1 **Carúpano**, Ven.
109/K3 **Caruthersville**, Mo,US
42/B2 **Carvin**, Fr.
46/A3 **Carvoeiro** (cape), Port.
116/P15 **Cary**, Il,US
113/J3 **Cary**, NC,US
81/L14 **Casablanca**, Mor.
95/F6 **Casa Branca**, Braz.
101/N7 **Casa de Janos**, Mex.
108/E4 **Casa Grande**, Az,US
108/E4 **Casa Grande Nat'l Mon.**, Az,US
48/D2 **Casal di Principe**, It.
45/J4 **Casalecchio di Reno**, It.
45/H4 **Casale Monferrato**, It.
84/A3 **Casamance** (riv.), Sen.
94/B3 **Casa Nova**, Braz.
49/F3 **Casarano**, It.
101/N7 **Casas Grandes** (ruins), Mex.
101/N8 **Cascada de Bassaseachic Nat'l Park**, Mex.
106/C5 **Cascade** (range), Can., US
106/D4 **Cascade** (res.), Id,US
116/C3 **Cascade-Fairwood**, Wa,US
89/R15 **Cascades** (pt.), Reun.
47/P10 **Cascais**, Port.
111/H1 **Cascapédia** (riv.), Qu,Can
94/C2 **Cascavel**, Braz.
45/J5 **Cascina-Navacchio**, It.
116/B3 **Case** (inlet), Wa,US
48/D2 **Caserta**, It.
98/H **Casey**, Ant.
98/D **Casey** (bay), Ant.
81/H3 **Caseyr** (cape), Som.
106/C4 **Cashmere**, Wa,US
96/E2 **Casilda**, Arg.
101/P10 **Casimiro Castillo**, Mex.
77/E1 **Casino**, Austl.
115/A2 **Casitas** (lake), Ca,US
92/C5 **Casma**, Peru
47/E2 **Caspe**, Sp.
107/G5 **Casper**, Wy,US
56/F6 **Caspian** (sea), Eur., Asia
47/G2 **Cassà de la Selva**, Sp.
87/D3 **Cassai** (riv.), Ang.
87/D3 **Cassamba**, Ang.
48/E3 **Cassano allo Ionio**, It.
110/D3 **Cass City**, Mi,US
95/C2 **Cássia**, Braz.
102/C3 **Cassiar** (mts.), BC,Can
95/B1 **Cassilândia**, Braz.
48/C2 **Cassino**, It.
109/J3 **Cassville**, Mo,US
115/B2 **Castaic**, Ca,US
115/B1 **Castaic** (lake), Ca,US
47/E3 **Castalla**, Sp.
93/J4 **Castanhal**, Braz.
48/D4 **Castelbuono**, It.
45/K5 **Castelfidardo**, It.
48/C3 **Castellammare** (gulf), It.
48/D2 **Castellammare di Stabia**, It.
45/G4 **Castellamonte**, It.
47/G2 **Castellar del Vallès**, Sp.
47/K7 **Castelldefels**, Sp.
47/L7 **Castell de Montjuic**, Sp.
48/D4 **Castello Eurialo** (ruins), It.
47/E3 **Castellón de la Plana**, Sp.
59/N9 **Castel Nat'l Park**, Isr.
44/D5 **Castelnaudary**, Fr.
44/E5 **Castelnau-le-Lez**, Fr.
46/B3 **Castelo Branco**, Port.
46/B2 **Castelo Branco** (dist.), Port.
94/B2 **Castelo do Piauí**, Braz.
44/D4 **Castelsarrasin**, Fr.
48/C4 **Castelvetrano**, It.
95/B2 **Castilho**, Braz.
92/B5 **Castilla**, Peru
46/C2 **Castille and León** (aut. comm.), Sp.
46/D3 **Castille-La Mancha** (aut. comm.), Sp.
101/G5 **Castilletes**, Col.
96/C4 **Castillo** (peak), Arg.
113/H4 **Castillo de San Marcos Nat'l Mon.**, Fl,US
97/G2 **Castillos**, Uru.
35/G1 **Castle Acre**, Eng,UK
36/A4 **Castlebar**, Ire.
34/D4 **Castle Cary**, Eng,UK
32/B3 **Castlecaulfield**, NI,UK
34/D4 **Castle Combe**, Eng,UK
108/E3 **Castle Dale**, Ut,US
32/B2 **Castledawson**, NI,UK
33/G6 **Castle Donnington**, Eng,UK
32/E2 **Castle Douglas**, Sc,UK
33/G4 **Castleford**, Eng,UK
106/D3 **Castlegar**, BC,Can
76/H8 **Castle Hill**, Austl.
32/D2 **Castle Kennedy**, Sc,UK
77/C3 **Castlemaine**, Austl.
76/G8 **Castlereagh**, Austl.
32/B1 **Castlerock**, NI,UK
109/F3 **Castle Rock**, Co,US
107/L5 **Castle Rock** (lake), Wi,US
76/C4 **Castle Tower Nat'l Park**, Austl.
32/D3 **Castletown**, IM,UK
32/C3 **Castlewellan**, NI,UK
106/F2 **Castor**, Ab,Can
82/D6 **Castos** (riv.), Libr.
44/E5 **Castres**, Fr.
40/B3 **Castricum**, Neth.
101/J5 **Castries** (cap.), StL.
95/B3 **Castro**, Braz.
96/B4 **Castro**, Chile
94/C4 **Castro Alves**, Braz.
46/C4 **Castro del Río**, Sp.
46/B1 **Castro de Rey**, Sp.
41/E5 **Castrop-Rauxel**, Ger.
46/D1 **Castro-Urdiales**, Sp.
116/K11 **Castro Valley**, Ca,US
48/E3 **Castrovillari**, It.
46/C3 **Castuera**, Sp.
101/F3 **Cat** (isl.), Bahm.
107/K3 **Cat** (lake), On,Can
78/B3 **Cataduanes** (isl.), Phil.
95/L6 **Cataguases**, Braz.
67/D5 **Catainğan**, Phil.
73/F1 **Catainğan**, Phil.
51/K5 **Çatalağzı**, Turk.
95/C1 **Catalão**, Braz.
51/J5 **Çatalca**, Turk.
108/E4 **Catalina**, Az,US
47/F2 **Catalonia** (aut. comm.), Sp.
91/C2 **Catamarca**, Arg.
67/D5 **Catanduanes** (isl.), Phil.
95/B2 **Catanduva**, Braz.
48/D4 **Catania**, It.
48/D4 **Catania** (gulf), It.
48/E3 **Catanzaro**, It.
73/F1 **Catarman**, Indo.
67/D5 **Catarman**, Phil.
47/E3 **Catarroja**, Sp.
74/E7 **Catastrophe** (cape), Austl.
101/G6 **Catatumbo** (riv.), Col., Ven.
73/F2 **Catatungan** (mtn.), Phil.
113/H3 **Catawba** (riv.), NC, SC,US
67/D5 **Catbalogan**, Phil.
97/G2 **Catedral** (peak), Uru.
94/D3 **Catende**, Braz.
31/N8 **Caterham**, Eng,UK
86/C2 **Catherine, Mount** (Jabal Katrīnah) (mtn.), Egypt
101/F6 **Cativá**, Pan.
110/D4 **Catlettsburg**, Ky,US
75/K4 **Cato** (isl.), Austl.
100/D3 **Catoche** (cape), Mex.
94/C2 **Catolé do Rocha**, Braz.
45/K5 **Catria** (peak), It.
92/F3 **Catrimani** (riv.), Braz.
34/D2 **Catshill**, Eng,UK
110/F3 **Catskill** (mts.), NY,US
43/F5 **Cattenom**, Fr.
33/G3 **Catterick**, Eng,UK
94/C4 **Catu**, Braz.
67/D4 **Cauayan**, Phil.
67/D6 **Cauayan**, Phil.
92/C2 **Cauca** (riv.), Col.
94/C1 **Caucaia**, Braz.
92/C2 **Caucasia**, Col.
54/G4 **Caucasus** (mts.), Eur.
47/E3 **Caudete**, Sp.
42/C3 **Caudry**, Fr.
33/F1 **Cauldcleuch** (mtn.), Sc,UK
96/B2 **Cauquenes**, Chile
44/D4 **Caussade**, Fr.
48/D4 **Cava d'Ispica** (ruins), It.
46/B2 **Cávado** (riv.), Port.
44/F5 **Cavaillon**, Fr.
107/J3 **Cavalier**, ND,US
82/D6 **Cavalla** (riv.), IvC., Libr.
84/D5 **Cavalla** (Cavally) (riv.), IvC., Libr.
48/A1 **Cavallo, Capo al** (cape), Fr.
32/A4 **Cavan** (co.), Ire.
108/E4 **Cave Creek**, Az,US
93/J3 **Caviana**, Braz.
51/F2 **Cavnic**, Rom.
67/D5 **Cawayan**, Phil.
77/B2 **Cawndilla** (lake), Austl.
33/G4 **Cawood**, Eng,UK
35/H1 **Cawston**, Eng,UK
95/J6 **Caxambu**, Braz.
94/B2 **Caxias**, Braz.
95/B4 **Caxias do Sul**, Braz.
100/D4 **Caxinas** (pt.), Hon.
87/B2 **Caxito**, Ang.
59/B2 **Çay**, Turk.
92/C3 **Cayambe** (vol.), Ecu.
113/H3 **Cayce**, SC,US
51/L5 **Çaycuma**, Turk.
59/E2 **Çayeli**, Turk.
93/H3 **Cayenne** (cap.), FrG.
101/F4 **Cayman Brac** (isl.), Cay.
100/E4 **Cayman Islands**, UK
100/E4 **Cayos Cajones** (isls.), Hon.
100/E5 **Cayos Miskitos** (isls.), Nic.
50/B3 **Cazin**, Bosn.
46/D4 **Cazorla**, Sp.
46/C1 **Cea** (riv.), Sp.
94/C3 **Ceará** (state), Braz.
94/D2 **Ceará-Mirim**, Braz.
97/G2 **Cebollatí** (riv.), Uru.
67/D5 **Cebu**, Phil.
67/D6 **Cebu** (isl.), Phil.
48/C2 **Ceccano**, It.
89/E2 **Cecil Macks** (pass), Swaz.
45/J5 **Cecina**, It.
48/E3 **Cecita** (lake), It.
107/H2 **Cedar** (lake), Mb,Can
110/E2 **Cedar** (lake), On,Can
116/L11 **Cedar** (mtn.), Ca,US
107/L5 **Cedar** (riv.), Ia,US
115/F6 **Cedar** (cr.), NJ,US
116/C3 **Cedar** (riv.), Wa,US
76/B1 **Cedar Bay Nat'l Park**, Austl.
109/G3 **Cedar Bluff** (res.), Ks,US
108/D3 **Cedar Breaks Nat'l Mon.**, Ut,US
108/D3 **Cedar City**, Ut,US
112/D3 **Cedar Creek** (res.), Tx,US
107/K5 **Cedar Falls**, Ia,US
115/F5 **Cedar Grove**, NJ,US
113/H4 **Cedar Key**, Fl,US
107/L5 **Cedar Rapids**, Ia,US
113/G3 **Cedartown**, Ga,US
108/B2 **Cedarville**, Ca,US
46/A1 **Cedeira**, Sp.
94/C2 **Cedro**, Braz.
101/L8 **Cedros** (isl.), Mex.
46/A1 **Cee**, Sp.
83/Q7 **Ceel Dheere**, Som.
83/Q5 **Ceerigaabo** (Erigabo), Som.
48/D3 **Cefalù**, It.
32/D5 **Cefni** (riv.), Wal,UK
33/E6 **Cefn-mawr**, Wal,UK
46/C2 **Cega** (riv.), Sp.
50/D2 **Cegléd**, Hun.
46/E3 **Cehegín**, Sp.
51/F2 **Cehu Silvaniei**, Rom.
33/E6 **Ceiriog** (riv.), Wal,UK
54/F4 **Çekerek** (riv.), Turk.
46/B1 **Čelanova**, Sp.
100/D3 **Celarain** (pt.), Mex.
100/A3 **Celaya**, Mex.
32/B5 **Celbridge**, Ire.
73/F3 **Celebes** (sea), Asia
73/E4 **Celebes** (Sulawesi) (isl.), Indo.
110/C3 **Celina**, Oh,US
50/B2 **Celje**, Slov.
50/C2 **Celldömölk**, Hun.
44/E2 **Celle** (riv.), Fr.
41/H3 **Celle**, Ger.
34/A4 **Celtic** (sea), Eur.
34/B2 **Cemaes Head** (pt.), Wal,UK
72/D3 **Cemaru** (peak), Indo.
46/E3 **Cenajo** (res.), Sp.
73/H4 **Cenderawasih** (bay), Indo.
91/C4 **Centenario**, Arg.
95/B2 **Centenario do Sul**, Braz.
108/D4 **Centennial** (wash), Az,US
106/E4 **Centennial** (mts.), Id,US
107/H4 **Center**, ND,US
112/E4 **Center**, Tx,US
115/G5 **Centereach**, NY,US
116/F7 **Center Line**, Mi,US
115/H5 **Center Moriches**, NY,US
113/G3 **Center Point**, Al,US
113/G3 **Centerville**, Tn,US
112/E4 **Centerville**, Tx,US
45/J4 **Cento**, It.
96/C4 **Central** (peak), Arg.
94/B3 **Central**, Braz.
85/E5 **Central** (reg.), Gha.
59/K5 **Central** (dist.), Isr.
83/J6 **Central African Republic**
106/G3 **Central Butte**, Sk,Can
109/H2 **Central City**, Ne,US
92/C5 **Central, Cordillera** (range), SAm.
110/B4 **Centralia**, Il,US
106/C4 **Centralia**, Wa,US
115/G5 **Central Islip**, NY,US
61/H3 **Central Makrān** (range), Pak.
44/E4 **Central, Massif** (plat.), Fr.
93/J7 **Central, Planalto** (plat.), Braz.
106/C5 **Central Point**, Or,US
57/L3 **Central Siberian** (plat.), Rus.
53/N4 **Central Ural** (mts.), Rus.
44/D3 **Centre** (reg.), Fr.
81/L14 **Centre** (reg.), Mor.
81/M13 **Centre Nord** (reg.), Mor.
81/M14 **Centre Sud** (reg.), Mor.
113/G3 **Centreville**, Al,US
44/D4 **Céou** (riv.), Fr.
50/D3 **Čepin**, Cro.
73/G4 **Ceram** (isl.), Indo.
73/G4 **Ceram** (sea), Indo.
48/A2 **Ceraso** (cape), It.
47/L7 **Cerdanyola del Vallès**, Sp.
44/D4 **Cère** (riv.), Fr.
45/J4 **Cerea**, It.
91/D2 **Ceres**, Arg.
93/J7 **Ceres**, Braz.
88/B4 **Ceres**, SAfr.
101/F6 **Cereté**, Col.
31/S9 **Cergy**, Fr.
48/D2 **Cerignola**, It.
51/J5 **Çerkezköy**, Turk.
51/J3 **Cernavodă**, Rom.
31/R10 **Cernay-la-Ville**, Fr.
34/D5 **Cerne Abbas**, Eng,UK
101/N9 **Cerralvo** (isl.), Mex.
32/E5 **Cerrig-y-Druidion**, Wal,UK
49/F2 **Cërrik**, Alb.
100/A3 **Cerritos**, Mex.
100/B3 **Cerro Azul**, Mex.
96/C3 **Cerro Colorados** (res.), Arg.
101/L7 **Cerro de la Encantada** (peak), Mex.
101/M8 **Cerro Dos Picachos** (peak), Mex.
101/M8 **Cerro Encantada** (peak), Mex.
97/G2 **Cerro Largo** (dept.), Uru.
101/M7 **Cerro Pinacote** (peak), Mex.
48/D2 **Cervaro** (riv.), It.
48/D2 **Cervati** (peak), It.
47/F2 **Cervera**, Sp.
45/K4 **Cervia**, It.
48/D2 **Cervialto** (peak), It.
45/K4 **Cervignano del Friuli**, It.
95/H7 **Cervo** (hills), Braz.
46/B1 **Cervo**, Sp.
92/D2 **César** (riv.), Col.
45/K4 **Cesena**, It.
45/K4 **Cesenatico**, It.
52/E4 **Cēsis**, Lat.
45/L2 **České Budějovice**, Czh.
39/H4 **Českomoravská Vysočina** (upland), Czh.
45/L2 **Český Krumlov**, Czh.
50/C3 **Česma** (riv.), Cro.
49/K3 **Çeşme**, Turk.
59/A2 **Çeşme**, Turk.
31/T11 **Cesson**, Fr.
44/C2 **Cesson-Sévigné**, Fr.
84/C5 **Cestos** (riv.), Libr.
50/C4 **Cetina** (riv), Cro.
50/D4 **Cetinje**, Yugo.
46/D2 **Ceurda del Pozo** (res.), Sp.
46/C5 **Ceuta**, Sp.
44/E5 **Cévennes** (mts.), Fr.
44/E4 **Cévennes Nat'l Park**, Fr.
59/C3 **Ceyhan**, Turk.
59/E3 **Ceylânpınar**, Turk.
70/D6 **Ceylon** (isl.), SrL.
44/F4 **Cèze** (riv.), Fr.
44/C5 **Chabarrou** (peak), Fr.
92/E2 **Chacabuco**, Arg.
92/C5 **Chachapoyas**, Peru
69/C3 **Chachoengsao**, Thai.
108/F3 **Chaco** (dry riv.), NM,US
112/B3 **Chaco** (mesa), NM,US
91/D2 **Chaco Austral** (plain), Arg.
92/G8 **Chaco Boreal** (plain), Par.
91/D1 **Chaco Central** (plain), Arg.
91/E2 **Chaco Nat'l Park**, Arg.
100/D4 **Chacujal** (ruins), Guat.
83/J4 **Chad**
82/H5 **Chad** (lake), Afr.
69/E4 **Cha Da** (cape), Viet.
35/E3 **Chadlington**, Eng,UK
109/G2 **Chadron**, Ne,US
51/J2 **Chadyr-Lunga**, Mol.
81/N13 **Chafarinas** (isls.), Sp.
68/D5 **Chagdo Kangri** (peak), China
58/G10 **Chagos** (arch.), Brln.
61/H3 **Chāh Behār** (Bandar Beheshtī), Iran
100/C4 **Chahuites**, Mex.
69/C3 **Chainat**, Thai.
69/C3 **Chaiyaphum**, Thai.
70/C5 **Chālakudi**, India
100/D5 **Chalatenango**, ESal.
83/N7 **Chalbi** (des.), Kenya
63/H2 **Chalchyn** (riv.), Mong.
111/H2 **Chaleur** (bay), NB, Qu,Can
31/M7 **Chalfont Saint Giles**, Eng,UK
31/M7 **Chalfont Saint Peter**, Eng,UK
35/E3 **Chalgrove**, Eng,UK
31/U10 **Chalifert** (can.), Fr.
112/C4 **Chalk** (mts.), Tx,US
44/C3 **Challans**, Fr.
103/T6 **Challenger** (mtn.), NW,Can
43/D5 **Challerange**, Fr.
106/E4 **Challis**, Id,US
35/G4 **Challock**, Eng,UK
42/D6 **Châlons-sur-Marne**, Fr.
44/F3 **Chalon-sur-Saône**, Fr.
60/F1 **Chālūs**, Iran
45/K2 **Cham**, Ger.
108/F3 **Chama** (riv.), Co, NM,US
72/B2 **Chamah** (peak), Malay.
61/J2 **Chaman**, Pak.
61/L2 **Chamba**, India
70/C2 **Chambal** (riv.), India
44/F4 **Chambaran** (plat.), Fr.
111/G2 **Chamberlain** (lake), Me,US
107/J5 **Chamberlain**, SD,US
114/K2 **Chamberlin** (mtn.), Ak,US
110/E4 **Chambersburg**, Pa,US
44/F4 **Chambéry**, Fr.
87/F3 **Chambeshi** (riv.), Zam.
111/P7 **Chambly**, Qu,Can
31/S9 **Chambly**, Fr.
31/S10 **Chambourcy**, Fr.
59/F3 **Chamchamāl**, Iraq
44/F4 **Chamechaude** (mtn.), Fr.
91/C3 **Chamical**, Arg.
45/G4 **Chamonix-Mont-Blanc**, Fr.
114/L3 **Champagne**, Yk,Can
42/C6 **Champagne** (reg.), Fr.
44/F2 **Champagne-Ardennes** (reg.), Fr.
31/S9 **Champagne-sur-Oise**, Fr.
110/B3 **Champaign**, Il,US
96/D1 **Champaqui** (peak), Arg.
43/F6 **Champigneulles**, Fr.
31/T10 **Champigny-sur-Marne**, Fr.
110/F2 **Champlain** (lake), Can., US
100/C4 **Champotón**, Mex.
42/B6 **Champs-sur-Marne**, Fr.
91/B2 **Chañaral**, Chile
46/B4 **Chança** (riv.), Port.
92/C5 **Chan Chan** (ruins), Peru
96/B2 **Chanco**, Chile
114/J2 **Chandalar** (riv.), Ak,US
70/C2 **Chandausi**, India
70/C3 **Chanderi**, India
61/L2 **Chandigarh**, India
111/H1 **Chandler**, Qu,Can
114/H2 **Chandler** (riv.), Ak,US
112/D3 **Chandler**, Ok,US
70/C4 **Chandrapur**, India
66/C5 **Chang** (lake), China
66/B8 **Chang** (riv.), China
69/C3 **Chang** (isl.), Thai.
63/K3 **Changbai** (peak), China
63/K3 **Changbai** (mts.), China, NKor.
66/F2 **Changchun**, China
66/D5 **Changdang** (lake), China
67/B2 **Changde**, China
64/A2 **Changgi-ap** (cape), SKor.
67/D3 **Changhua**, Tai.
63/K5 **Changhŭng**, SKor.
66/D3 **Changli**, China
66/D2 **Changping**, China
63/J4 **Changsan-got** (cape), NKor.
67/B2 **Changsha**, China
66/E5 **Changshu**, China
71/J2 **Changshun**, China
63/K4 **Changsŏng**, SKor.
100/E6 **Changuinola**, Pan.
64/A3 **Ch'angwŏn**, SKor.
66/E3 **Changxing** (isl.), China
66/D5 **Chang** (Yangtze) (riv.), China
66/C3 **Changzhi**, China
66/D5 **Changzhou**, China
69/E2 **Chan May Dong** (cape), Viet.
35/H4 **Channel** (tunnel), UK, Fr.
108/C4 **Channel** (isls.), Ca,US
76/A4 **Channel Country** (plain), Austl.
44/B2 **Channel Islands**, UK
108/B4 **Channel Islands Nat'l Park**, Ca,US
111/K2 **Channel-Port aux Basques**, Nf,Can
46/B1 **Chantada**, Sp.
31/S10 **Chanteloup-les-Vignes**, Fr.
69/C3 **Chanthaburi**, Thai.
42/B5 **Chantilly**, Fr.
102/G2 **Chantrey** (inlet), NW,Can
109/J3 **Chanute**, Ks,US
66/D5 **Chao** (lake), China
63/H4 **Chaobai** (riv.), China
69/C3 **Chao Phraya** (riv.), Thai.
63/J2 **Chaor** (riv.), China
67/C3 **Chaoyang**, China
67/C3 **Chaozhou**, China
94/B4 **Chapada Diamantina Nat'l Park**, Braz.
94/A4 **Chapada dos Veadeiros Nat'l Park**, Braz.
94/B1 **Chapadinha**, Braz.
110/F1 **Chapais**, Qu,Can
101/P9 **Chapala** (lake), Mex.
55/J1 **Chapayevsk**, Rus.
95/A3 **Chapecó**, Braz.
33/G5 **Chapel en le Frith**, Eng,UK
33/F2 **Chapelfell Top** (mtn.), Eng,UK
113/J3 **Chapel Hill**, NC,US
42/D3 **Chapelle-Lez-Herlaimont**, Belg.
33/J5 **Chapel Saint Leonards**, Eng,UK
33/G5 **Chapeltown**, Eng,UK
116/D2 **Chaplain** (lake), Wa,US
69/D2 **Chap Le**, Viet.
110/D2 **Chapleau**, On,Can
106/G3 **Chaplin**, Sk,Can
109/G2 **Chappell**, Ne,US
57/M4 **Chara** (riv.), Rus.
92/C3 **Charambirá** (pt.), Col.
49/L6 **Charandra** (riv.), Gre.
91/D2 **Charata**, Arg.
100/A3 **Charcas**, Mex.
98/U **Charcot** (isl.), Ant.
34/D5 **Chard**, Eng,UK
56/G6 **Chardzhou**, Trkm.
81/N14 **Charef, Oued** (riv.), Mor.
44/C4 **Charente** (riv.), Fr.
31/T10 **Charenton-le-Pont**, Fr.
82/J5 **Chari** (riv.), Chad
61/J1 **Chārīkār**, Afg.
35/G4 **Charing**, Eng,UK
109/J2 **Chariton** (riv.), Ia, Mo,US
35/E3 **Charlbury**, Eng,UK
32/B3 **Charlemont**, NI,UK
42/D3 **Charleroi**, Belg.
42/D2 **Charleroi à Bruxelles, Canal de** (can.), Belg.
103/J2 **Charles** (isl.), NW,Can
110/F4 **Charles** (cape), Va,US
107/K5 **Charles City**, Ia,US
110/B4 **Charleston**, Il,US
109/K3 **Charleston**, Mo,US
113/F3 **Charleston**, Ms,US
108/D2 **Charleston**, Nv,US
113/J3 **Charleston**, SC,US
110/D4 **Charleston** (cap.), WV,US
43/D4 **Charleville-Mézières**, Fr.
110/C2 **Charlevoix**, Mi,US
106/B2 **Charlotte** (lake), BC,Can
110/C3 **Charlotte**, Mi,US
113/H3 **Charlotte**, NC,US
101/J4 **Charlotte Amalie** (cap.), USVI
110/E4 **Charlottesville**, Va,US
111/J2 **Charlottetown** (cap.), PE,Can
101/J5 **Charlotteville**, Trin.
103/H3 **Charlton** (isl.), NW,Can
34/D3 **Charlton Kings**, Eng,UK
31/N8 **Charlwood**, Eng,UK
44/F3 **Charolais** (mts.), Fr.
31/R9 **Chars**, Fr.
68/D2 **Charsk**, Kaz.
76/B3 **Charters Towers**, Austl.
44/D2 **Chartres**, Fr.
68/C3 **Charyn** (riv.), Kaz.
68/D1 **Charysh** (riv.), Rus.
96/F2 **Chascomús**, Arg.
106/D3 **Chase**, BC,Can
44/F4 **Chassezac** (riv.), Fr.
44/C3 **Chassiron, Pointe de** (pt.), Fr.
44/C3 **Châteaubriant**, Fr.
44/C3 **Château-d'Olonne**, Fr.
44/D2 **Châteaudun**, Fr.
111/N7 **Châteauguay**, Qu,Can
44/F5 **Châteaurenard-Provence**, Fr.
44/D3 **Château-Renault**, Fr.
44/D3 **Châteauroux**, Fr.
42/C5 **Château-Thierry**, Fr.
42/D3 **Châtelet**, Belg.
44/D3 **Châtellerault**, Fr.
31/S10 **Châtenay-Malabry**, Fr.
109/J2 **Chatfield**, Mn,US
111/H2 **Chatham**, NB,Can
110/D3 **Chatham**, On,Can
97/J7 **Chatham** (isl.), Chile
35/G4 **Chatham**, Eng,UK
115/F5 **Chatham**, NJ,US
31/S10 **Châtillon**, Fr.
44/F3 **Châtillon-sur-Seine**, Fr.
31/S10 **Chatou**, Fr.
70/D4 **Chatrapur**, India
76/H8 **Chatswood**, Austl.
115/B2 **Chatsworth** (res.), Ca,US
113/G3 **Chatsworth**, Ga,US
113/G4 **Chattahoochee**, Fl,US
113/G4 **Chattahoochee** (riv.), Fl, Ga,US
113/G3 **Chattanooga**, Tn,US
35/G2 **Chatteris**, Eng,UK
44/C2 **Chaucey** (isls.), Fr.
43/E2 **Chaudfontaine**, Belg.
111/G2 **Chaudière** (riv.), Qu,Can
69/D4 **Chau Doc**, Viet.
71/F3 **Chauk**, Burma
71/G2 **Chaukan** (pass), India
42/B4 **Chaulnes**, Fr.
31/U10 **Chaumes-en-Brie**, Fr.
44/F2 **Chaumont**, Fr.
42/A5 **Chaumont-en-Vexin**, Fr.
42/D4 **Chaumont-Porcien**, Fr.
57/T3 **Chaunskaya** (bay), Rus.
42/C4 **Chauny**, Fr.
110/E3 **Chautauqua** (lake), NY,US
44/D3 **Chauvigny**, Fr.
94/B1 **Chaval**, Braz.
46/B2 **Chaves**, Port.
69/D1 **Chay** (riv.), Viet.
92/E7 **Chayana** (riv.), Bol.
53/M4 **Chaykovskiy**, Rus.
33/G6 **Cheadle**, Eng,UK
113/G3 **Cheaha** (peak), Al,US
45/K1 **Cheb**, Czh.
53/K4 **Cheboksary**, Rus.
53/K4 **Cheboksary** (res.), Rus.
110/C2 **Cheboygan**, Mi,US
81/M13 **Chechaouene**, Mor.
55/H4 **Chechen'** (isl.), Rus.
55/H4 **Chechen-Ingush Aut. Rep.**, Rus.
82/D3 **Chech, 'Erg** (des.), Afr.
64/A2 **Chech'ŏn**, SKor.
109/J4 **Checotah**, Ok,US
111/J2 **Chedabucto** (bay), NS,Can
34/D4 **Cheddar**, Eng,UK
71/F4 **Cheduba** (isl.), Burma
111/S10 **Cheektowaga**, NY,US
110/D1 **Cheepash** (riv.), On,Can
110/D1 **Cheepay** (riv.), On,Can
63/L1 **Chegdomyn**, Rus.
87/F4 **Chegutu**, Zim.
106/C4 **Chehalis**, Wa,US
45/G5 **Cheiron, Cime du** (peak), Fr.
63/K5 **Cheju**, SKor.
63/K5 **Cheju** (isl.), SKor.
63/K5 **Cheju** (str.), SKor.
106/C4 **Chelan**, Wa,US
106/C4 **Chelan** (lake), Wa,US
33/F5 **Chelford**, Eng,UK
81/V17 **Chelghoum El Aïd**, Alg.
55/L3 **Chelkar**, Kaz.
31/T10 **Chelles**, Fr.
39/M3 **Chełm**, Pol.
39/M3 **Chełm** (prov.), Pol.
35/G3 **Chelmer** (riv.), Eng,UK
39/K2 **Chełmno**, Pol.
35/G3 **Chelmsford**, Eng,UK
39/K2 **Chełmża**, Pol.
77/G6 **Chelsea**, Austl.
31/N7 **Chelsea**, Eng,UK
31/N7 **Chelsea & Kensington** (bor.), Eng,UK
111/Q8 **Cheltenham**, On,Can
34/D3 **Cheltenham**, Eng,UK
53/P5 **Chelyabinsk**, Rus.
53/P5 **Chelyabinsk Obl.**, Rus.
57/L2 **Chelyuskina** (cape), Rus.
87/E3 **Chembe**, Zam.
38/G3 **Chemnitz**, Ger.
67/A2 **Chen** (riv.), China

61/K2 **Chenāb** (riv.), India, Pak.
82/E2 **Chenachane** (well), Alg.
106/D4 **Cheney,** Wa,US
66/C3 **Cheng'anpu,** China
66/D2 **Chengde,** China
66/E3 **Chengshan Jiao** (cape), China
31/T10 **Chennevières-sur-Marne,** Fr.
44/F3 **Chenòve,** Fr.
67/B2 **Chenzhou,** China
51/G5 **Chepelare,** Bul.
79/V12 **Chépénéhé,** NCal.
96/C2 **Chépica,** Chile
101/F6 **Chepigana,** Pan.
34/D3 **Chepstow,** Wal,UK
53/M4 **Cheptsa** (riv.), Rus.
44/D3 **Cher** (riv.), Fr.
113/J3 **Cheraw,** SC,US
44/C2 **Cherbourg,** Fr.
81/S15 **Cherchell,** Alg.
62/E1 **Cheremkhovo,** Rus.
52/H4 **Cherepovets,** Rus.
81/V17 **Cherf** (riv.), Alg.
81/S16 **Chergui** (lake), Alg.
81/V18 **Cheria,** Alg.
54/E2 **Cherkassy,** Ukr.
54/D2 **Cherkassy Obl.,** Ukr.
55/G3 **Cherkessk,** Rus.
76/E6 **Chermside,** Austl.
53/M2 **Chernaya** (riv.), Rus.
54/D2 **Chernigov,** Ukr.
54/D2 **Chernigov Obl.,** Ukr.
51/H4 **Cherni Lom** (riv.), Bul.
51/F4 **Cherni Vrŭkh** (peak), Bul.
54/C2 **Chernovtsy,** Ukr.
54/C2 **Chernovtsy Obl.,** Ukr.
53/N4 **Chernushka,** Rus.
62/H1 **Chernyshevsk,** Rus.
109/H3 **Cherokee,** Ok,US
112/E2 **Cherokees** (lake), Ok,US
71/F2 **Cherrapunjee,** India
108/D3 **Cherry Creek,** Nv,US
115/E6 **Cherry Hill,** NJ,US
115/D3 **Cherry Valley,** Ca,US
57/Q3 **Cherskiy** (range), Rus.
31/M7 **Chertsey,** Eng,UK
51/G4 **Cherven Bryag,** Bul.
54/C2 **Chervonograd,** Ukr.
35/E3 **Cherwell** (riv.), Eng,UK
110/C3 **Chesaning,** Mi,US
110/E4 **Chesapeake** (bay), Md, Va,US
35/F3 **Chesham,** Eng,UK
33/F5 **Cheshire** (co.), Eng,UK
33/F5 **Cheshire** (plain), Eng,UK
53/K2 **Cheshskaya** (bay), Rus.
31/N6 **Cheshunt,** Eng,UK
33/F5 **Chester,** Eng,UK
108/B2 **Chester,** Ca,US
106/F3 **Chester,** Mt,US
115/F5 **Chester,** NJ,US
115/E6 **Chester,** Pa,US
113/H3 **Chester,** SC,US
102/G2 **Chesterfield** (inlet), NW,Can
78/E7 **Chesterfield** (isls.), NCal.
33/G5 **Chesterfield,** Eng,UK
89/H7 **Chesterfield, Nosy** (isl.), Madg.
33/G2 **Chester-le-Street,** Eng,UK
76/B3 **Chesterton** (range), Austl.
111/G2 **Chesuncook** (lake), Me,US
100/D4 **Chetumal** (bay), Belz., Mex.
100/D4 **Chetumal,** Mex.
106/C2 **Chetwynd,** BC,Can
31/T10 **Chevilly-Larue,** Fr.
31/S10 **Chevreuse,** Fr.
31/T10 **Chevry-Cossigny,** Fr.
34/D4 **Chew** (riv.), Eng,UK
106/D3 **Chewelah,** Wa,US
34/D4 **Chew Valley** (lake), Eng,UK
109/H4 **Cheyenne,** Ok,US
107/H4 **Cheyenne** (riv.), SD, Wy,US
107/G5 **Cheyenne** (cap.), Wy,US
109/G3 **Cheyenne Wells,** Co,US
70/C3 **Chhatarpur,** India
70/C3 **Chhindwāra,** India
69/D3 **Chhlong,** Camb.
66/D4 **Chi** (riv.), China
69/C2 **Chi** (riv.), Thai.
69/B2 **Chiang Dao** (caves), Thai.
69/B2 **Chiang Mai,** Thai.
69/B2 **Chiang Rai,** Thai.
48/C1 **Chiani** (riv.), It.
100/C4 **Chiapas** (state), Mex.
55/G4 **Chiatura,** Geo.
45/H4 **Chiavari,** It.
45/H3 **Chiavenna,** It.
67/D3 **Chiayi,** Tai.
65/G3 **Chiba,** Japan
65/G3 **Chiba** (pref.), Japan
110/F1 **Chibougamau,** Qu,Can
110/F1 **Chibougamau** (lake), Qu,Can
110/F1 **Chibougamau** (riv.), Qu,Can
114/D3 **Chibukak** (pt.), Ak,US
89/F2 **Chibuto,** Moz.
116/Q16 **Chicago,** Il,US
116/Q16 **Chicago Heights,** Il,US
116/Q16 **Chicago Ridge,** Il,US
114/L4 **Chichagof** (isl.), Ak,US
61/K2 **Chīchāwatni,** Pak.
66/C2 **Chicheng,** China
100/D3 **Chichén Itzá** (ruins), Mex.
74/B4 **Chichester** (range), Austl.
35/F5 **Chichester,** Eng,UK
65/F3 **Chichibu,** Japan
65/F3 **Chichibu-Tama Nat'l Park,** Japan
100/D5 **Chichigalpa,** Nic.
78/D2 **Chichishima** (isls.), Japan
113/G3 **Chickamauga** (lake), Tn,US
109/H4 **Chickasha,** Ok,US
34/D5 **Chickerell,** Eng,UK
46/B4 **Chiclana de la Frontera,** Sp.
92/C5 **Chiclayo,** Peru
96/C4 **Chico** (riv.), Arg.
96/D5 **Chico** (riv.), Arg.
108/B3 **Chico,** Ca,US
111/F3 **Chicopee,** Ma,US
87/D4 **Chicote,** Ang.
111/G1 **Chicoutimi,** Qu,Can
31/P8 **Chiddingstone,** Eng,UK
103/K2 **Chidley** (cape), Nf,Can
113/H4 **Chiefland,** Fl,US
69/D1 **Chiem Hoa,** Viet.
45/K3 **Chiemsee** (lake), Ger.
48/C1 **Chienti** (riv.), It.
69/B4 **Chieo Lan** (res.), Thai.
43/E5 **Chiers** (riv.), Fr.
45/J3 **Chiese** (riv.), It.
48/D1 **Chieti,** It.
35/E4 **Chieveley,** Eng,UK
63/H3 **Chifeng,** China
94/B5 **Chifre** (mts.), Braz.
65/F3 **Chigasaki,** Japan
114/G4 **Chiginagak** (mtn.), Ak,US
111/H2 **Chignecto** (bay), NB,Can
31/P7 **Chigwell,** Eng,UK
65/L10 **Chihayaakasaka,** Japan
66/D3 **Chihli** (Bo Hai) (gulf), China
101/N8 **Chihuahua,** Mex.
101/N8 **Chihuahua** (state), Mex.
109/H3 **Chikaskia** (riv.), Ks,US
70/C5 **Chikballāpur,** India
70/C3 **Chikhli,** India
70/C5 **Chikmagalūr,** India
62/G1 **Chikoy** (riv.), Rus.
64/B4 **Chikugo** (riv.), Japan
65/F2 **Chikuma** (riv.), Japan
65/H8 **Chikura,** Japan
70/D4 **Chilakalūrupet,** India
100/B4 **Chilapa,** Mex.
70/C6 **Chilaw,** SrL.
106/C3 **Chilcotin** (riv.), BC,Can
113/G3 **Childersburg,** Al,US
112/C3 **Childress,** Tx,US
90/B6 **Chile**
100/D5 **Chile** (mt.), Hon.
91/C2 **Chilecito,** Arg.
87/E3 **Chililabombwe,** Zam.
70/E4 **Chilka** (lake), India
106/C3 **Chilko** (lake), BC,Can
114/L4 **Chilkoot** (pass), BC,Can, Ak,US
96/B3 **Chillán,** Chile
110/B3 **Chillicothe,** Il,US
109/J3 **Chillicothe,** Mo,US
110/D4 **Chillicothe,** Oh,US
106/C3 **Chilliwack,** BC,Can
31/S10 **Chilly-Mazarin,** Fr.
96/B4 **Chiloé** (isl.), Chile
96/B4 **Chiloé Nat'l Park,** Chile
106/C5 **Chiloquin,** Or,US
100/B4 **Chilpancingo,** Mex.
35/F3 **Chiltern** (hills), Eng,UK
87/G4 **Chilwa** (lake), Malw.
101/F6 **Chimán,** Pan.
42/D3 **Chimay,** Belg.
56/F5 **Chimbay,** Uzb.
92/C4 **Chimborazo** (vol.), Ecu.
92/C5 **Chimbote,** Peru
68/A3 **Chimkent,** Kaz.
101/N7 **Chimney** (peak), NM.,US
71/F3 **Chin** (state), Burma
63/K5 **Chin** (isl.), SKor.
58/J6 **China**
100/D5 **Chinandega,** Nic.
112/B4 **Chinati** (mts.), Tx,US
101/P8 **Chinati** (peak), Tx.,US
92/C6 **Chincha Alta,** Peru
102/E3 **Chinchaga** (riv.), Ab,Can
110/F4 **Chincoteague,** Va,US
71/F3 **Chindwin** (riv.), Burma
92/D3 **Chingaza Nat'l Park,** Col.
31/P7 **Chingford,** Eng,UK
70/C5 **Chingleput,** India
87/E3 **Chingola,** Zam.
84/B1 **Chinguetti, Dhar de** (hills), Mrta.
64/A3 **Chinhae,** SKor.
87/F4 **Chinhoyi,** Zim.
114/H4 **Chiniak** (cape), Ak,US
61/K2 **Chiniot,** Pak.
69/D3 **Chinit** (riv.), Camb.
83/K6 **Chinko** (riv.), CAfr.
108/E3 **Chinle** (dry riv.), Az, Ut,US
35/F3 **Chinnor,** Eng,UK
65/F3 **Chino,** Japan
115/C2 **Chino,** Ca,US
106/F3 **Chinook,** Mt,US
101/F6 **Chinú,** Col.
87/F3 **Chipata,** Zam.
66/D3 **Chiping,** China
46/B4 **Chipiona,** Sp.
113/G4 **Chipley,** Fl,US
70/B4 **Chiplūn,** India
113/G4 **Chipola** (riv.), Fl,US
34/D4 **Chippenham,** Eng,UK
107/K4 **Chippewa** (riv.), Mn,US
110/B2 **Chippewa** (riv.), Wi,US
110/B2 **Chippewa Falls,** Wi,US
35/E2 **Chipping Campden,** Eng,UK
35/E3 **Chipping Norton,** Eng,UK
31/P6 **Chipping Ongar,** Eng,UK
34/D3 **Chipping Sodbury,** Eng,UK
31/N8 **Chipstead,** Eng,UK
111/H2 **Chiputneticook** (lakes), NB,Can, Me,US
100/D5 **Chiquimula,** Guat.
92/D2 **Chiquinquirá,** Col.
90/C6 **Chiquita, Mar** (lake), Arg.
90/A3 **Chira** (riv.), Peru
70/D4 **Chīrāla,** India
68/A3 **Chirchik,** Uzb.
82/H3 **Chirfa,** Niger
101/N7 **Chiricahua** (peak), Az.,US
108/E4 **Chiricahua Nat'l Mon.,** Az,US
114/G4 **Chirikof** (isl.), Ak,US
100/E6 **Chiriquí** (gulf), Pan.
33/E6 **Chirk,** Eng,UK
36/D3 **Chirnside,** Sc,UK
51/G4 **Chirpan,** Bul.
100/E6 **Chirripó Grande** (mt.), CR
100/E6 **Chirripó Nat'l Park,** CR
65/N10 **Chiryu,** Japan
103/J3 **Chisasibi** (Fort-George), Qu,Can
100/C4 **Chisec,** Guat.
35/E3 **Chiseldon,** Eng,UK
110/A2 **Chisholm,** Mn,US
61/K3 **Chishtiān Mandi,** Pak.
83/P8 **Chisimayu,** Som.
50/E2 **Chişineu Criş,** Rom.
53/L5 **Chistopol',** Rus.
31/M6 **Chiswell Green,** Eng,UK
31/N7 **Chiswick,** Eng,UK
65/M10 **Chita,** Japan
65/M10 **Chita** (bay), Japan
65/M10 **Chita** (pen.), Japan
62/G1 **Chita,** Rus.
87/B4 **Chitado,** Ang.
87/F2 **Chitipa,** Malw.
70/B3 **Chitorgarh,** India
63/N3 **Chitose,** Japan
70/C5 **Chitradurga,** India
70/D2 **Chitrakut,** India
101/E6 **Chitré,** Pan.
71/F3 **Chittagong,** Bang.
70/C5 **Chittoor,** India
87/D4 **Chiume,** Ang.
45/G4 **Chivasso,** It.
101/M8 **Chivato** (pt.), Mex.
96/E2 **Chivilcoy,** Arg.
81/R15 **Chlef,** Alg.
81/R15 **Chlef** (riv.), Alg.
69/D3 **Choam Khsant,** Camb.
96/C1 **Choapa** (riv.), Chile
87/D4 **Chobe Nat'l Park,** Bots.
39/K4 **Choč** (peak), Slvk.
39/J4 **Choceň,** Czh.
39/H3 **Chocianów,** Pol.
108/D4 **Chocolate** (mts.), Ca,US
45/K1 **Chodov,** Czh.
39/J2 **Chodzież,** Pol.
65/F3 **Chōfu,** Japan
65/H7 **Chofū,** Japan
78/E5 **Choiseul** (isl.), Sol.
31/T10 **Choisy-le-Roi,** Fr.
39/H2 **Chojna,** Pol.
39/J2 **Chojnice,** Pol.
39/H3 **Chojnów,** Pol.
63/N4 **Chokai-san** (mtn.), Japan
112/D4 **Choke Canyon** (res.), Tx,US
62/D5 **Chola** (mts.), China
44/C3 **Cholet,** Fr.
35/E3 **Cholsey,** Eng,UK
100/D5 **Choluteca** (riv.)
100/D5 **Choluteca,** Hon.
87/E4 **Choma,** Zam.
64/A2 **Chŏmch'on,** SKor.
70/E2 **Chomo Lhāri** (mtn.), Bhu.
45/K1 **Chomutov,** Czh.
65/J7 **Chōnan,** Japan
63/K4 **Ch'ŏnan,** SKor.
69/C3 **Chon Buri,** Thai.
96/B4 **Chonchi,** Chile
92/B4 **Chone,** Ecu.
63/K3 **Ch'ŏngjin,** NKor.
63/K4 **Ch'ŏngju,** SKor.
69/C3 **Chong Kal,** Camb.
66/L8 **Chongming** (isl.), China
67/A2 **Chongqing,** China
64/A2 **Ch'ŏngsong,** SKor.
63/K4 **Chŏnju,** SKor.
96/A5 **Chonos** (arch.), Chile
69/D4 **Chon Thanh,** Viet.
33/F4 **Chorley,** Eng,UK
31/M7 **Chorleywood,** Eng,UK
54/C2 **Chortkov,** Ukr.
39/K3 **Chorzów,** Pol.
65/G3 **Chōshi,** Japan
39/H2 **Choszczno,** Pol.
92/C5 **Chota,** Peru
106/E4 **Choteau,** Mt,US
88/A2 **Chowagasberg** (peak), Namb.
113/J2 **Chowan** (riv.), NC,US
62/G2 **Choybalsan,** Mong.
75/R11 **Christchurch,** NZ
35/E5 **Christchurch,** Eng,UK
35/E5 **Christchurch** (bay), Eng,UK
114/L4 **Christian** (sound), Ak,US
88/D2 **Christiana,** SAfr.
110/D4 **Christiansburg,** Va,US
106/F2 **Christine** (riv.), Ab,Can
58/K11 **Christmas** (isl.), Austl.
79/K4 **Christmas** (Kiritimati) (atoll), Kiri.
39/H4 **Chrudim,** Czh.
39/K3 **Chrzanów,** Pol.
68/B3 **Chu** (riv.), Kaz.
69/D2 **Chu** (riv.), Viet.
66/E4 **Chuanchang** (riv.), China
106/E5 **Chubbuck,** Id,US
65/F2 **Chūbu** (prov.), Japan
96/C4 **Chubut** (prov.), Arg.
96/D4 **Chubut** (riv.), Arg.
101/F6 **Chucanti** (mt.), Pan.
64/C3 **Chūgoku** (mts.), Japan
64/C3 **Chūgoku** (prov.), Japan
72/B3 **Chukai,** Malay.
63/M1 **Chukchagirskoye** (lake), Rus.
57/U3 **Chukchi** (pen.), Rus.
57/S3 **Chukchi Aut. Okr.,** Rus.
114/D3 **Chukotskiy, Mys** (pt.), Rus.
108/C4 **Chula Vista,** Ca,US
92/B5 **Chulucanas,** Peru
56/J4 **Chulym** (riv.), Rus.
68/E1 **Chulyshman** (riv.), Rus.
51/G4 **Chumerna** (peak), Bul.
69/B4 **Chumphon,** Thai.
56/K4 **Chuna** (riv.), Rus.
63/K4 **Ch'unch'ŏn,** SKor.
63/K4 **Ch'ungju,** SKor.
64/A3 **Ch'ungmu,** SKor.
57/L3 **Chunya** (riv.), Rus.
91/C1 **Chuquicamata,** Chile
45/H3 **Chur,** Swi.
71/F3 **Churachandpur,** India
33/F4 **Church,** Eng,UK
102/D3 **Churchill** (peak), BC,Can
102/G3 **Churchill,** Mb,Can
102/G3 **Churchill** (cape), Mb,Can
102/G3 **Churchill** (riv.), Mb, Sk,Can
103/K3 **Churchill** (riv.), Nf,Can
106/F1 **Churchill** (lake), Sk,Can
102/G3 **Churchill** (riv.), Mb, Sk,Can
77/G5 **Churchill Nat'l Park,** Austl.
34/D1 **Church Stretton,** Eng,UK
33/G6 **Churnet** (riv.), Eng,UK
70/B2 **Churu,** India
101/H5 **Churuguara,** Ven.
108/E3 **Chuska** (mts.), Az, NM,US
53/N4 **Chusovaya** (riv.), Rus.
53/N4 **Chusovoy,** Rus.
53/K5 **Chuvash Aut. Rep.,** Rus.
64/A2 **Chuwang-san Nat'l Park,** SKor.
71/H2 **Chuxiong,** China
62/B1 **Chuya** (riv.), Rus.
69/E3 **Chu Yang Sin** (peak), Viet.
65/M9 **Chūzu,** Japan
72/C5 **Ciamis,** Indo.
48/C2 **Ciampino,** It.
72/C5 **Cianjur,** Indo.
116/Q16 **Cicero,** Il,US
94/C3 **Cícero Dantas,** Braz.
48/C2 **Cicero Nat'l Park,** It.
59/C2 **Cide,** Turk.
39/L2 **Ciechanów,** Pol.
39/K2 **Ciechanów** (prov.), Pol.
39/K2 **Ciechocinek,** Pol.
101/F3 **Ciego de Avilla,** Cuba
101/G5 **Ciénaga,** Col.
101/E3 **Cienfuegos,** Cuba
39/H3 **Cieplice Śląskie Zdrój,** Pol.
39/K4 **Cieszyn,** Pol.
46/E3 **Cieza,** Sp.
59/B2 **Çifteler,** Turk.
46/D3 **Cigüela** (riv.), Sp.
59/C2 **Cihanbeyli,** Turk.
101/P10 **Cihuatlán,** Mex.
46/C3 **Cijara** (res.), Sp.
72/C5 **Cijulang,** Indo.
72/C5 **Cilacap,** Indo.
34/C2 **Cilfaesty** (hill), Wal,UK
109/G3 **Cimarron,** Ks,US
109/H3 **Cimarron** (riv.), Ks, Ok,US
112/B2 **Cimarron** (range), NM,US
50/F2 **Cîmpeni,** Rom.
51/F2 **Cîmpia Turzii,** Rom.
51/G3 **Cîmpina,** Rom.
51/G3 **Cîmpulung,** Rom.
51/G2 **Cîmpulung Moldovenesc,** Rom.
47/F1 **Cinca** (riv.), Sp.
50/C4 **Cincar** (peak), Bosn.
110/C4 **Cincinnati,** Oh,US
96/C3 **Cinco Saltos,** Arg.
34/D3 **Cinderford,** Eng,UK
51/F3 **Cîndrelu** (peak), Rom.
59/B3 **Çine,** Turk.
43/E3 **Ciney,** Belg.
115/F6 **Cinnaminson,** NJ,US
100/C4 **Cintalapa,** Mex.
48/A1 **Cinto** (mtn.), Fr.
50/C4 **Čiovo** (isl.), Cro.
96/D3 **Cipolletti,** Arg.
107/G4 **Circle,** Mt,US
110/D4 **Circleville,** Oh,US
72/C5 **Cirebon,** Indo.
34/E3 **Cirencester,** Eng,UK
48/E3 **Cirò Marina,** It.
44/C4 **Ciron** (riv.), Fr.
88/D4 **Ciskei** (ind. homeland), SAfr.
51/G3 **Cisnădie,** Rom.
96/B5 **Cisnes** (riv.), Chile
44/D3 **Cisse** (riv.), Fr.
48/C2 **Cisterna di Latina,** It.
100/B4 **Citlaltépetl** (mt.), Mex.
116/M9 **Citrus Heights,** Ca,US
45/K5 **Città di Castello,** It.
48/E3 **Cittanova,** It.
100/A2 **Ciudad Acuna,** Mex.
101/J6 **Ciudad Bolívar,** Ven.
101/N8 **Ciudad Camargo,** Mex.
100/C4 **Ciudad del Carmen,** Mex.
101/N8 **Ciudad Delicias,** Mex.
101/P9 **Ciudad de Río Grande,** Mex.
47/G3 **Ciudadela,** Sp.
101/J6 **Ciudad Guayana,** Ven.
101/N8 **Ciudad Guerrero,** Mex.
101/P10 **Ciudad Guzmán,** Mex.
101/N7 **Ciudad Juárez,** Mex.
101/P8 **Ciudad Lerdo,** Mex.
100/B3 **Ciudad Madero,** Mex.
100/B3 **Ciudad Mante,** Mex.
100/B2 **Ciudad Miguel Alemán,** Mex.
101/N8 **Ciudad Obregón,** Mex.
101/G5 **Ciudad Ojeda,** Ven.
46/D3 **Ciudad Real,** Sp.
100/B2 **Ciudad Río Bravo,** Mex.
46/B2 **Ciudad-Rodrigo,** Sp.
100/B3 **Ciudad Valles,** Mex.
100/B3 **Ciudad Victoria,** Mex.
54/F4 **Civa Burnu** (pt.), Turk.
45/K3 **Cividale del Friuli,** It.
48/C1 **Civita Castellana,** It.
48/B1 **Civitavecchia,** It.
59/B2 **Çivril,** Turk.
66/C3 **Ci Xian,** China
59/E3 **Cizre,** Turk.
46/E1 **Cizur,** Sp.
35/H3 **Clacton on Sea,** Eng,UK
34/C2 **Claerwen** (res.), Wal,UK
44/D3 **Clain** (riv.), Fr.
102/E3 **Claire** (lake), Ab,Can
108/B2 **Clair Engle** (lake), Ca,US
44/D3 **Claise** (riv.), Fr.
31/S10 **Clamart,** Fr.
35/F5 **Clanfield,** Eng,UK
113/G3 **Clanton,** Al,US
111/Q9 **Clappison's Corners,** On,Can
96/D4 **Clara** (pt.), Arg.
36/A4 **Clare** (riv.), Ire.
110/C3 **Clare,** Mi,US
115/C2 **Claremont,** Ca,US
111/F3 **Claremont,** NH,US
109/J3 **Claremore,** Ok,US
77/E1 **Clarence** (riv.), Austl.
74/E2 **Clarence** (str.), Austl.
103/T7 **Clarence** (pt.), NW,Can
75/R11 **Clarence,** NZ
111/S9 **Clarence,** NY,US
101/G3 **Clarence Town,** Bahm.
112/C3 **Clarendon,** Tx,US
106/E3 **Claresholm,** BC,Can
98/J **Clarie** (coast), Ant.
107/J4 **Clark,** SD,US
77/D4 **Clarke** (isl.), Austl.
76/B3 **Clarke** (range), Austl.
106/E3 **Clark Fork** (riv.), Id, Mt,US
113/H3 **Clark Hill** (lake), Ga, SC,US
110/D4 **Clarksburg,** WV,US
113/F3 **Clarksdale,** Ms,US
111/Q8 **Clarkson,** On,Can
116/F6 **Clarkston,** Mi,US
106/D4 **Clarkston,** Wa,US
112/E3 **Clarksville,** Ar,US
113/G2 **Clarksville,** Tn,US
112/E3 **Clarksville,** Tx,US
95/B1 **Claro** (riv.), Braz.
42/C3 **Clary,** Fr.
32/D1 **Clatteringshaws Loch** (lake), Sc,UK
32/A2 **Claudy,** NI,UK
41/H5 **Clausthal-Zellerfeld,** Ger.
67/D4 **Claveria,** Phil.
116/F6 **Clawson,** Mi,US
109/H3 **Clay Center,** Ks,US
33/G5 **Clay Cross,** Eng,UK
35/H2 **Claydon,** Eng,UK
31/U10 **Claye-Souilly,** Fr.
31/M7 **Claygate,** Eng,UK
32/D3 **Clay Head** (pt.), IM,UK
115/E6 **Claymont,** De,US
116/L11 **Clayton,** Ca,US
113/H3 **Clayton,** Ga,US
109/G3 **Clayton,** NM,US
109/J4 **Clayton,** Ok,US
33/F4 **Clayton-le-Moors,** Eng,UK
97/S11 **Clé** (stream), Arg.
102/E3 **Clear** (hills), Ab,Can
36/H8 **Clear** (cape), Ire.
108/B3 **Clear** (lake), Ca,US
114/J4 **Cleare** (cape), Ak,US
107/J4 **Clear Lake,** SD,US
106/C3 **Clearwater,** BC,Can
113/H5 **Clearwater,** Fl,US
106/D4 **Clearwater** (mts.), Id,US
107/K4 **Clearwater** (riv.), Mn,US
32/E2 **Cleator Moor,** Eng,UK
112/D3 **Cleburne,** Tx,US
33/H4 **Cleethorpes,** Eng,UK
34/D3 **Cleeve** (hill), Eng,UK
113/H3 **Clemson,** SC,US
34/D2 **Cleobury Mortimer,** Eng,UK
73/E1 **Cleopatra Needle** (mtn.), Phil.
42/A4 **Clères,** Fr.
43/E3 **Clerf** (riv.), Belg., Lux.
42/B5 **Clermont,** Fr.
34/D4 **Clevedon,** Eng,UK
76/B2 **Cleveland** (cape), Austl.
33/G2 **Cleveland** (co.), Eng,UK
33/G3 **Cleveland** (hills), Eng,UK
113/F3 **Cleveland,** Ms,US
106/E3 **Cleveland** (peak), Mt,US
110/D3 **Cleveland,** Oh,US
113/G3 **Cleveland,** Tn,US
112/E4 **Cleveland,** Tx,US
95/A3 **Clevelândia,** Braz.
36/A4 **Clew** (bay), Ire.
113/H5 **Clewiston,** Fl,US
42/B6 **Clichy,** Fr.
31/T10 **Clichy-sous-Bois,** Fr.
34/D4 **Clifton,** Eng,UK
108/E4 **Clifton,** Az,US
115/F5 **Clifton,** NJ,US
112/D4 **Clifton,** Tx,US
113/J2 **Clifton Forge,** Va,US
34/D2 **Clifton upon Teme,** Eng,UK
42/C5 **Clignon** (riv.), Fr.
113/H3 **Clingmans** (mtn.), Tn,US
106/C3 **Clinton,** BC,Can
107/L5 **Clinton,** Ia,US
110/B3 **Clinton,** Il,US
113/F4 **Clinton,** La,US
116/G6 **Clinton,** Mi,US
116/F6 **Clinton** (riv.), Mi,US
109/J3 **Clinton,** Mo,US
113/F3 **Clinton,** Ms,US
113/J3 **Clinton,** NC,US
115/F5 **Clinton,** NJ,US
115/F4 **Clinton** (res.), NJ,US
109/H4 **Clinton,** Ok,US
113/H3 **Clinton,** SC,US
102/F2 **Clinton-Colden** (lake), NW,Can
102/B2 **Clinton Creek,** Yk,Can
115/K8 **Clinton** (Surrattsville), Md,US
110/D3 **Clio,** Mi,US
28/D5 **Clipperton** (isl.), Fr.
35/F2 **Clipston,** Eng,UK
33/F4 **Clitheroe,** Eng,UK
74/A4 **Cloates** (pt.), Austl.
32/B4 **Clogherhead,** Ire.
32/B4 **Clogher Head** (pt.), Ire.
32/C3 **Cloghy,** NI,UK
36/B4 **Clonmel,** Ire.
41/F3 **Cloppenburg,** Ger.
107/K4 **Cloquet,** Mn,US
91/E2 **Clorinda,** Arg.
32/E1 **Closeburn,** Sc,UK
106/G4 **Cloud** (peak), Wy,US
112/B3 **Cloudcroft,** NM,US
114/G3 **Cloudy** (mtn.), Ak,US
32/B2 **Cloughmills,** NI,UK
33/H3 **Cloughton,** Eng,UK
34/B4 **Clovelly,** Eng,UK
108/B3 **Cloverdale,** Ca,US
108/C3 **Clovis,** Ca,US
109/G4 **Clovis,** NM,US
36/C2 **Clovullin,** Sc,UK
33/G5 **Clowne,** Eng,UK
51/F2 **Cluj** (co.), Rom.
51/F2 **Cluj-Napoca,** Rom.
34/C2 **Clun,** Eng,UK
34/B3 **Clunderwen,** Wal,UK
45/G3 **Cluses,** Fr.
45/H4 **Clusone,** It.
32/E5 **Clwyd** (co.), Wal,UK
33/E5 **Clwyd** (riv.), Wal,UK
33/E5 **Clwydian** (range), Wal,UK
34/C3 **Clydach,** Wal,UK
111/H2 **Clyde** (riv.), NS,Can
106/E2 **Clyde,** NW,Can
36/C3 **Clyde** (riv.), Sc,UK
36/C3 **Clyde, Firth of** (inlet), Sc,UK
34/C2 **Clywedog** (riv.), Wal,UK
111/R8 **CN Tower,** On,Can
46/B2 **Côa** (riv.), Port.
108/C4 **Coachella,** Ca,US
32/B2 **Coagh,** NI,UK
100/A2 **Coahuila** (state), Mex.
106/E3 **Coaldale,** Ab,Can
109/H4 **Coalgate,** Ok,US
106/E3 **Coalhurst,** Ab,Can
32/B2 **Coalisland,** NI,UK
35/E1 **Coalville,** Eng,UK
108/E2 **Coalville,** Ut,US
94/C4 **Coaraci,** Braz.
92/F4 **Coari,** Braz.
92/F5 **Coari** (riv.), Braz.
102/C2 **Coast** (mts.), BC, Yk,Can
104/B4 **Coast** (ranges), Ca,US
113/H4 **Coastal** (plain), US
100/B4 **Coatepec,** Mex.
111/G2 **Coaticook,** Qu,Can
103/H2 **Coats** (isl.), NW,Can
98/Y **Coats Land** (reg.), Ant.
100/C4 **Coatzacoalcos,** Mex.
100/D3 **Coba** (ruins), Mex.
46/B1 **Coba de Serpe, Sierra de** (mtn.), Sp.
100/C4 **Cobán,** Guat.
77/D3 **Cobberas** (peak), Austl.
115/B1 **Cobblestone** (mtn.), Ca,US
107/K2 **Cobham** (riv.), Mb, On,Can
31/M8 **Cobham,** Eng,UK
74/E2 **Cobourg** (pen.), Austl.
110/E3 **Cobourg,** On,Can
96/B3 **Cobquecura,** Chile
77/F5 **Coburg,** Austl.
103/T7 **Coburg** (isl.), NW,Can
45/J1 **Coburg,** Ger.
47/E3 **Cocentaina,** Sp.
92/E7 **Cochabamba,** Bol.
70/C6 **Cochin,** India
113/H3 **Cochran,** Ga,US
106/E3 **Cochrane,** Ab,Can
110/D1 **Cochrane,** On,Can
97/J8 **Cockburn** (chan.), Chile
36/D3 **Cockburnspath,** Sc,UK
33/E2 **Cockermouth,** Eng,UK
88/D4 **Cockscomb** (peak), SAfr.
92/A2 **Coco** (isl.), CR
100/E5 **Coco** (riv.), Hon.
113/H4 **Cocoa,** Fl,US
108/D4 **Coconino** (plat.), Az,US
77/C2 **Cocoparra Nat'l Park,** Austl.
58/J11 **Cocos** (Keeling) (isls.), Austl.
103/K3 **Cod** (isl.), Nf,Can
33/G3 **Cod Beck** (riv.), Eng,UK
96/C2 **Codegua,** Chile
51/G3 **Codlea,** Rom.
94/B2 **Codó,** Braz.
45/H4 **Codogno,** It.
101/J4 **Codrington,** Anti.
45/K4 **Codroipo,** It.
34/D1 **Codsall,** Eng,UK
106/F4 **Cody,** Wy,US
94/B2 **Coelho Neto,** Braz.
41/E5 **Coesfeld,** Ger.
29/M6 **Coetivy** (isl.), Sey.
106/D4 **Coeur d'Alene,** Id,US
106/D4 **Coeur d'Alene** (lake), Id,US
40/D3 **Coevorden,** Neth.
109/J3 **Coffeyville,** Ks,US
77/E1 **Coffs Harbour,** Austl.
35/G3 **Coggeshall,** Eng,UK
48/A2 **Coghinas** (lake), It.
44/C4 **Cognac,** Fr.
100/E6 **Coiba** (isl.), Pan.
97/K7 **Coig** (riv.), Arg.
96/B5 **Coihaique,** Chile
96/C3 **Coihueco,** Chile
70/C5 **Coimbatore,** India
46/A2 **Coimbra,** Port.
46/A2 **Coimbra** (dist.), Port.
46/C4 **Coín,** Sp.
47/P10 **Coina** (riv.), Port.
44/F4 **Coise** (riv.), Fr.
92/E2 **Cojedes** (riv.), Ven.
101/G5 **Cojoro,** Ven.
96/C5 **Cojudo Blanco** (peak), Arg.
100/D5 **Cojutepeque,** ESal.
106/F5 **Cokeville,** Wy,US
77/B3 **Colac,** Austl.
109/H2 **Colamus** (riv.), Ne,US
47/P10 **Colares,** Port.
95/D1 **Colatina,** Braz.
98/P **Colbeck** (cape), Ant.
96/C2 **Colbún,** Chile
109/G3 **Colby,** Ks,US
35/G3 **Colchester,** Eng,UK
106/F2 **Cold** (lake), Ab, Sk,Can
33/F2 **Cold Fell** (mtn.), Eng,UK
106/F2 **Cold Lake,** Ab,Can
107/K4 **Cold Spring,** Mn,US
112/E4 **Coldspring,** Tx,US
109/H3 **Coldwater,** Ks,US
110/C3 **Coldwater,** Mi,US
35/E3 **Cole** (riv.), Eng,UK
34/D3 **Coleford,** Eng,UK
112/D4 **Coleman,** Tx,US
59/E3 **Çölemerik,** Turk.
32/B1 **Coleraine,** NI,UK
32/B1 **Coleraine** (dist.), NI,UK
88/D3 **Colesberg,** SAfr.
35/E2 **Coleshill,** Eng,UK
115/J7 **Colesville,** Md,US
106/D4 **Colfax,** Wa,US
103/S6 **Colgate** (cape), NW,Can
96/C5 **Colhué Huapí** (lake), Arg.
69/D2 **Co Lieu,** Viet.
101/P10 **Colima,** Mex.
101/P10 **Colima** (state), Mex.
96/C2 **Colina,** Chile
94/A2 **Colinas,** Braz.
46/D2 **Collado-Villalba,** Sp.
114/J3 **College,** Ak,US
115/K8 **College Park,** Md,US
112/D4 **College Station,** Tx,US
45/G4 **Collegno,** It.
77/D1 **Collie,** Austl.
74/C3 **Collier** (bay), Austl.
33/G2 **Collier Law** (hill), Eng,UK
113/F3 **Collierville,** Tn,US
34/B6 **Colliford** (res.), Eng,UK
33/G4 **Collingham,** Eng,UK
110/D2 **Collingwood,** On,Can
75/R11 **Collingwood,** NZ
113/F4 **Collins,** Ms,US
109/J3 **Collinsville,** Ok,US
110/E4 **Collinsville,** Va,US
81/V17 **Collo,** Alg.
45/G2 **Colmar,** Fr.
46/D2 **Colmenar Viejo,** Sp.
97/J7 **Colmillo** (cape), Chile
32/D1 **Colmonell,** Sc,UK
35/E3 **Coln** (riv.), Eng,UK
33/F4 **Colne,** Eng,UK
35/G3 **Colne** (riv.), Eng,UK
31/N6 **Colney Heath,** Eng,UK
43/F2 **Cologne** (Köln), Ger.
31/S10 **Colombes,** Fr.
92/D3 **Colombia**
95/B3 **Colombo,** Braz.
70/C6 **Colombo** (cap.), SrL.
44/D5 **Colomiers,** Fr.
96/E2 **Colón,** Arg.
96/F2 **Colón,** Arg.
101/F6 **Colón,** Pan.
78/C4 **Colonia,** Micro.
97/F2 **Colonia** (dept.), Uru.
97/F2 **Colonia Del Sacramento,** Uru.
94/D3 **Colônia Leopoldina,** Braz.
97/K7 **Colorado** (peak), Arg.
96/D3 **Colorado** (riv.), Arg.
95/B2 **Colorado,** Braz.
108/D4 **Colorado** (riv.), Mex., US
108/E3 **Colorado** (plat.), US
108/F3 **Colorado** (state), US
112/D4 **Colorado** (riv.), Tx,US
109/F3 **Colorado City,** Co,US
112/C3 **Colorado City,** Tx,US
108/E3 **Colorado Nat'l Mon.,** Co,US
91/C2 **Colorados, Desagües de los** (marsh), Arg.
109/F3 **Colorado Springs,** Co,US
92/E7 **Colquiri,** Bol.
106/G4 **Colstrip,** Mt,US
32/D1 **Colt** (hill), Sc,UK
96/C2 **Coltauco,** Chile
35/H1 **Coltishall,** Eng,UK
115/C2 **Colton,** Ca,US
115/F5 **Colts Neck,** NJ,US
90/D4 **Coluene** (riv.), Braz.
102/E3 **Columbia** (mtn.), Ab,Can
106/C2 **Columbia** (mts.), BC,Can
103/T6 **Columbia** (cape), NW,Can
106/C4 **Columbia** (riv.), Can., US
106/D4 **Columbia** (plat.), US
110/C4 **Columbia,** Ky,US
112/E3 **Columbia,** La,US
115/K7 **Columbia,** Md,US
109/J3 **Columbia,** Mo,US
113/F4 **Columbia,** Ms,US
113/H3 **Columbia** (cap.), SC,US
113/G3 **Columbia,** Tn,US
106/E3 **Columbia Falls,** Mt,US
88/B4 **Columbine** (cape), SAfr.
113/G3 **Columbus,** Ga,US
110/C4 **Columbus,** In,US
113/F3 **Columbus,** Ms,US
106/F4 **Columbus,** Mt,US
109/H2 **Columbus,** Ne,US
115/F5 **Columbus,** NJ,US
108/F5 **Columbus,** NM,US
110/D4 **Columbus** (cap.), Oh,US
112/D4 **Columbus,** Tx,US
108/B3 **Colusa,** Ca,US
102/D2 **Colville** (lake), NW,Can
114/H2 **Colville** (riv.), Ak,US
106/D3 **Colville,** Wa,US
116/B3 **Colvos** (passg.), Wa,US
34/D2 **Colwall,** Eng,UK
34/C4 **Colwinston,** Wal,UK
32/E5 **Colwyn Bay,** Wal,UK
45/K4 **Comacchio,** It.
45/K4 **Comacchio, Valli di** (lag.), It.
112/D4 **Comanche,** Tx,US
96/F3 **Comandante Nicanor Otamendi,** Arg.
51/H2 **Comăneşti,** Rom.
51/G3 **Comarnic,** Rom.
100/D5 **Comayagua,** Hon.
91/B3 **Combarbalá,** Chile
34/B4 **Combe Martin,** Eng,UK
32/C2 **Comber,** NI,UK
31/T11 **Combs-la-Ville,** Fr.
76/C4 **Comet** (riv.), Austl.
71/F3 **Comilla,** Bang.
42/B2 **Comines,** Belg.
42/C2 **Comines,** Fr.
115/G5 **Commack,** NY,US
44/E3 **Commentry,** Fr.
115/B2 **Commerce,** Ca,US
43/E6 **Commercy,** Fr.

132

Comm – Dalqū

103/H2 Committee (bay), NW,Can
68/B4 Communism (Kommunizma) (peak), Taj.
45/H4 Como, It.
45/H3 Como (lake), It.
116/P14 Como (lake), Wi,US
96/D5 Comodoro Rivadavia, Arg.
84/D4 Comoé (prov.), Burk.
84/E4 Comoé Nat'l Park, IvC.
70/C6 Comorin (cape), India
89/G5 Comoros
106/B3 Comox, BC,Can
42/B5 Compiègne, Fr.
101/P9 Compostela, Mex.
115/B3 Compton, Ca,US
112/C4 Comstock, Tx,US
84/B4 Conakry (cap.), Gui.
84/B4 Conakry (comm.), Gui.
44/B3 Concarneau, Fr.
95/E1 Conceição da Barra, Braz.
95/B1 Conceição das Alagoas, Braz.
93/J5 Conceição do Araguaia, Braz.
94/C3 Conceição do Coité, Braz.
95/D1 Conceição do Mato Dentro, Braz.
95/H6 Conceição do Rio Verde, Braz.
92/F7 Concepción (lake), Bol.
96/B3 Concepción, Chile
91/E1 Concepción, Par.
92/C6 Concepción, Peru
100/A3 Concepción del Oro, Mex.
96/F2 Concepción del Uruguay, Arg.
108/B4 Conception (pt.), Ca,US
95/F7 Conchal, Braz.
109/F4 Conchas (lake), NM,US
31/U10 Conches, Fr.
109/G5 Concho (riv.), Tx,US
101/N8 Conchos (riv.), Mex.
116/K11 Concord, Ca,US
113/H3 Concord, NC,US
111/G3 Concord (cap.), NH,US
91/E3 Concordia, Arg.
95/A3 Concórdia, Braz.
109/H3 Concordia, Ks,US
106/C3 Concrete, Wa,US
69/D2 Con Cuong, Viet.
101/F3 Condado, Cuba
75/J5 Condamine (riv.), Austl.
42/C3 Condé-sur-L'Escaut, Fr.
44/C2 Condé-sur-Noireau, Fr.
76/C4 Condomine (riv.), Austl.
106/C4 Condon, Or,US
43/D3 Condroz (plat.), Belg.
113/G4 Conecuh (riv.), Al,US
45/K4 Conegliano, It.
112/B2 Conejos, Co,US
31/S10 Conflans-Sainte-Honorine, Fr.
115/G4 Congers, NY,US
67/B3 Conghua, China
33/F5 Congleton, Eng,UK
80/D5 Congo
83/K7 Congo (basin), Afr.
87/C1 Congo (riv.), Afr.
95/D2 Congonhas, Braz.
96/C3 Conguillio Nat'l Park, Chile
96/C4 Cónico, Cerro (Nevado) (peak), Arg., Chile
46/B4 Conil de la Frontera, Sp.
33/H5 Coningsby, Eng,UK
33/G5 Conisbrough, Eng,UK
33/E3 Coniston, Eng,UK
33/E3 Coniston Water (lake), Eng,UK
32/C2 Conlig, NI,UK
103/J1 Conn (lake), NW,Can
36/A4 Connacht (prov.), Ire.
33/E5 Connah's Quay, Wal,UK
110/D3 Conneaut, Oh,US
111/G2 Connecticut (riv.), US
111/F3 Connecticut (state), US
36/C2 Connel, Sc,UK
110/E3 Connellsville, Pa,US
36/H7 Connemara Nat'l Park, Ire.
110/C4 Connersville, In,US
36/A3 Conn, Lough (lake), Ire.
97/K7 Cono Grande (peak), Arg.
76/D4 Conondale Nat'l Park, Austl.
44/E4 Conques, Fr.
106/F3 Conrad, Mt,US
100/B1 Conroe, Tx.,US
112/E4 Conroe, Tx,US
95/D2 Conselheiro Lafaiete, Braz.
95/D1 Conselheiro Pena, Braz.
33/G2 Consett, Eng,UK
115/E5 Conshohocken, Pa,US
100/E3 Consolación del Sur, Cuba
69/D4 Con Son (isl.), Viet.
45/H3 Constance (Bodensee) (lake), Ger., Swi.
51/J3 Constanța, Rom.
51/J3 Constanța (co.), Rom.
47/F2 Constantí, Sp.
46/C4 Constantina, Sp.
81/V17 Constantine, Alg.
81/V17 Constantine (gov.), Alg.
114/G4 Constantine (cape), Ak,US
96/B2 Constitución, Chile
97/T11 Constitución (res.), Uru.
101/L7 Constitución de 1857 Nat'l Park, Mex.
46/D3 Consuegra, Sp.
70/E3 Contai, India
45/K4 Contarina, It.
94/B4 Contas (riv.), Braz.
95/C1 Contegem, Braz.
42/B4 Contigny, Fr.
106/C2 Continental (ranges), Ab, BC,Can
116/L11 Contra Costa (can.), Ca,US
101/F3 Contramaestre, Cuba
46/E3 Contreras (res.), Sp.
114/J3 Controller (bay), Ak,US
96/B3 Contulmo, Chile
102/E2 Contwoyto (lake), NW,Can
42/B4 Conty, Fr.
101/G6 Convención, Col.
48/E2 Conversano, It.
76/C3 Conway (cape), Austl.
112/E3 Conway, Ar,US
111/G3 Conway, NH,US
113/J3 Conway, SC,US
76/C3 Conway Range Nat'l Park, Austl.
32/E5 Conway, Vale of (val.), Wal,UK
32/E5 Conwy, Wal,UK
32/D5 Conwy (bay), Wal,UK
32/E5 Conwy (riv.), Wal,UK
70/E2 Cooch Behār, India
76/F7 Coochiemudlo (isl.), Austl.
97/K8 Cook (bay), Chile
75/R11 Cook (str.), NZ
114/H3 Cook (inlet), Ak,US
113/G2 Cookeville, Tn,US
98/L Cook Ice Shelf, Ant.
79/J6 Cook Islands (terr.), NZ
75/R11 Cook, Mount (peak), NZ
32/B2 Cookstown, NI,UK
32/B2 Cookstown (dist.), NI,UK
77/B3 Coola Coola (swamp), Austl.
32/B4 Cooley (pt.), Ire.
76/D4 Cooloola Nat'l Park, Austl.
77/D3 Cooma, Austl.
70/B5 Coondapoor, India
70/C5 Coonoor, India
74/F5 Cooper (cr.), Austl.
112/E3 Cooper, Tx,US
107/J4 Cooperstown, ND,US
77/A3 Coorong Nat'l Park, Austl.
113/G3 Coosa (riv.), Al,US
106/B5 Coos Bay, Or,US
77/D2 Cootamundra, Austl.
115/G5 Copague, NY,US
96/C3 Copahué (vol.), Chile
100/D5 Copán (ruins), Hon.
46/E4 Cope (cape), Sp.
32/C2 Copeland (isl.), NI,UK
38/G1 Copenhagen (København) (cap.), Den.
49/F2 Copertino, It.
77/D1 Copeton (dam), Austl.
91/B2 Copiapó, Chile
45/J4 Copparo, It.
41/G4 Coppenbrügge, Ger.
112/D4 Copperas Cove, Tx,US
102/E2 Coppermine (riv.), NW,Can
33/F4 Coppull, Eng,UK
51/G2 Copșa Mică, Rom.
33/F1 Coquet (riv.), Eng,UK
33/G1 Coquet Dale (val.), Eng,UK
91/B2 Coquimbo, Chile
96/C1 Coquimbo (reg.), Chile
51/G4 Corabia, Rom.
94/A5 Coração de Jesus, Braz.
76/C1 Coral (sea)
113/H5 Coral Gables, Fl,US
75/J2 Coral Sea Is. (terr.), Austl.
113/H5 Coral Springs, Fl,US
115/H5 Coram, NY,US
44/E2 Corbeil-Essonnes, Fr.
81/T15 Corbelin (cape), Alg.
42/B4 Corbie, Fr.
44/E5 Corbieres (mts.), Fr.
110/C4 Corbin, Ky,US
33/F2 Corbridge, Eng,UK
35/F2 Corby, Eng,UK
95/K7 Corcovado (mon.), Braz.
96/B4 Corcovado (gulf), Chile
96/B4 Corcovado (vol.), Chile
100/E6 Corcovado Nat'l Park, CR
95/D2 Cordeiro, Braz.
113/H4 Cordele, Ga,US
109/H4 Cordell (New Cordell), Ok,US
45/K4 Cordenons, It.
92/D3 Cordillera de los Picachos Nat'l Park, Col.
91/D3 Córdoba, Arg.
91/D3 Córdoba (mts.), Arg.
96/E2 Córdoba (prov.), Arg.
100/B4 Córdoba, Mex.
46/C4 Córdoba, Sp.
114/J3 Cordova (peak), Ak,US
46/E1 Corella, Sp.
94/C2 Coremas, Braz.
92/G3 Corentyne (riv.), Guy.
49/F3 Corfu (Kérkira) (isl.), Gre.
46/B3 Coria, Sp.
46/B4 Coria del Río, Sp.
77/D2 Coricudgy (peak), Austl.
48/E3 Corigliano Calabro, It.
75/J3 Coringa Islets (isls.), Austl.
49/H4 Corinth (ruins), Gre.
113/F3 Corinth, Ms,US
49/H4 Corinth (Kórinthos), Gre.
95/C1 Corinto, Braz.
100/D5 Corinto, Nic.
46/A1 Coristanco, Sp.
48/C4 Corleone, It.
51/H5 Çorlu, Turk.
42/D5 Cormontreuil, Fr.
107/H2 Cormorant, Mb,Can
107/H2 Cormorant (lake), Mb,Can
34/C1 Corndon (hill), Wal,UK
95/B2 Cornélio Procópio, Braz.
103/K2 Cornelius Grinnel (bay), NW,Can
47/L7 Cornella, Sp.
77/C3 Corner (inlet), Austl.
111/K1 Corner Brook, Nf,Can
110/E3 Corning, NY,US
76/B3 Cornish (cr.), Austl.
45/J4 Corno alle Scale (peak), It.
97/L8 Cornú (peak), Arg.
103/S7 Cornwall (isl.), NW,Can
110/F2 Cornwall, On,Can
111/J2 Cornwall, PE,Can
34/B6 Cornwall (co.), Eng,UK
103/S7 Cornwallis (isl.), NW,Can
101/H5 Coro, Ven.
80/J9 Coroa (mtn.), CpV.
94/A2 Coroatá, Braz.
92/E7 Corocoro, Bol.
95/C1 Coromandel, Braz.
70/D5 Coromandel (coast), India
75/S10 Coromandel, NZ
75/S10 Coromandel (pen.), NZ
67/D5 Coron, Phil.
115/C3 Corona, Ca,US
109/F4 Corona, NM,US
100/E6 Coronado (bay), CR
106/F2 Coronation, Ab,Can
102/E2 Coronation (gulf), NW,Can
96/E1 Coronda, Arg.
96/B3 Coronel, Chile
96/E3 Coronel Dorrego, Arg.
95/D1 Coronel Fabriciano, Braz.
96/D2 Coronel Moldes, Arg.
91/E2 Coronel Oviedo, Par.
96/E3 Coronel Pringles, Arg.
96/E3 Coronel Suárez, Arg.
95/A3 Coronel Vivida, Braz.
92/D7 Coropuna (peak), Peru
101/F6 Corozal, Col.
100/D4 Corozal Town, Belz.
112/D5 Corpus Christi, Tx,US
46/D3 Corral de Almaguer, Sp.
96/E2 Corral de Bustos, Arg.
47/Y16 Corralejo, Canl.
77/B3 Corrangamite (lake), Austl.
100/E6 Corredor, CR
94/A3 Corrente, Braz.
94/A4 Corrente (riv.), Braz.
95/B1 Corrente (riv.), Braz.
36/A4 Corrib, Lough (lake), Ire.
91/E2 Corrientes, Arg.
100/E3 Corrientes (cape), Cuba
92/C4 Corrientes (riv.), Ecu., Peru
34/C1 Corris, Wal,UK
48/A1 Corse (cape), Fr.
48/A1 Corse (reg.), Fr.
32/D1 Corserine (mtn.), Sc,UK
32/C1 Corsewall (pt.), Sc,UK
34/D4 Corsham, Eng,UK
48/A1 Corsica (Corse) (isl.), Fr.
112/D3 Corsicana, Tx,US
48/A1 Corte, Fr.
108/E3 Cortez, Co,US
45/K3 Cortina d'Ampezzo, It.
110/E3 Cortland, NY,US
84/B4 Corubal (riv.), GBis.
46/A3 Coruche, Port.
59/E2 Çoruh (riv.), Turk.
92/G7 Corumbá, Braz.
95/B1 Corumbá (riv.), Braz.
94/C5 Corumbaú (pt.), Braz.
94/C3 Coruripe, Braz.
106/C4 Corvallis, Or,US
34/D2 Corve (riv.), Eng,UK
47/R12 Corvo (isl.), Azor.
48/C1 Corvo (peak), It.
33/E6 Corwen, Wal,UK
48/E3 Cosenza, It.
110/D3 Coshocton, Oh,US
100/D5 Cosigüina (pt.), Nic.
46/D2 Coslada, Sp.
95/F7 Cosmópolis, Braz.
44/E3 Cosne-Cours-sur-Loire, Fr.
46/B1 Cospeito, Sp.
91/D3 Cosquín, Arg.
44/D3 Cosson (riv.), Fr.
115/C3 Costa Mesa, Ca,US
100/E5 Costa Rica
101/N9 Costa Rica, Mex.
35/H1 Costessey, Eng,UK
51/G3 Costești, Rom.
116/M10 Cosumnes (riv.), Ca,US
67/D6 Cotabato, Phil.
84/D5 Côte d'Ivoire (Ivory Coast)
44/F3 Côte d'Or (uplands), Fr.
94/A4 Cotegipe, Braz.
44/C2 Cotentin (pen.), Fr.
111/N7 Côte-Saint-Luc, Qu,Can
34/B3 Cothi (riv.), Wal,UK
95/G8 Cotia, Braz.
85/F5 Cotonou, Ben.
34/D4 Cotswolds (hills), Eng,UK
106/C5 Cottage Grove, Or,US
39/H3 Cottbus, Ger.
35/G2 Cottenham, Eng,UK
108/D4 Cottonwood, Az,US
112/D2 Cottonwood (riv.), Ks,US
109/F5 Cottonwood (dry riv.), Tx,US
112/D4 Cotulla, Tx,US
31/U10 Coubert, Fr.
44/C4 Coubre, Pointe de la (pt.), Fr.
42/C5 Coucy-le-Château-Auffrique, Fr.
42/B1 Coudekerque-Branche, Fr.
44/E5 Couguille, Pic de (peak), Fr.
44/D2 Coulaines, Fr.
106/D4 Coulee City, Wa,US
98/M Coulman (isl.), Ant.
42/C6 Coulommiers, Fr.
110/E2 Coulonge (riv.), Qu,Can
44/D4 Coulounieix-Chamiers, Fr.
31/N8 Coulsdon, Eng,UK
106/D4 Council, Id,US
107/K5 Council Bluffs, Ia,US
109/H3 Council Grove, Ks,US
36/D2 Coupar Angus, Sc,UK
31/U10 Coupvray, Fr.
31/S10 Courbevoie, Fr.
42/D3 Courcelles, Belg.
43/F5 Courcelles-Chaussy, Fr.
31/T11 Courcouronnes, Fr.
44/E4 Cournon-d'Auvergne, Fr.
102/D4 Courtenay, BC,Can
111/S8 Courtice, On,Can
42/C2 Courtrai (Kortrijk), Belg.
31/T10 Courtry, Fr.
44/C2 Coutances, Fr.
106/F3 Coutts, Ab,Can
42/D3 Couvin, Belg.
47/P10 Cova da Piedade, Port.
46/C1 Covadonga Nat'l Park, Sp.
51/H3 Covasna, Rom.
50/G3 Covasna (co.), Rom.
35/E2 Coventry, Eng,UK
35/E1 Coventry (can.), Eng,UK
46/B2 Covilhã, Port.
115/C2 Covina, Ca,US
113/H3 Covington, Ga,US
110/C4 Covington, Ky,US
113/F3 Covington, Tn,US
110/E4 Covington, Va,US
76/H8 Cowan, Austl.
74/C6 Cowan (lake), Austl.
34/C4 Cowbridge, Wal,UK
35/E5 Cowes, Eng,UK
33/F2 Cow Green (res.), Eng,UK
106/C4 Cowlitz (riv.), Wa,US
113/H3 Cowpens Nat'l Bfld., SC,US
77/D2 Cowra, Austl.
33/G2 Coxhoe, Eng,UK
93/H7 Coxim, Braz.
31/T9 Coye-la-Forêt, Fr.
109/H2 Cozad, Ne,US
100/D3 Cozumel, Mex.
100/D3 Cozumel (isl.), Mex.
77/C4 Cradle (peak), Austl.
77/C4 Cradle Mountain-Lake Saint Clair Nat'l Park, Austl.
88/D4 Cradock, SAfr.
114/K3 Crag (mtn.), Yk,Can
33/F3 Crag (hill), Eng,UK
108/F2 Craig, Co,US
32/C2 Craigavad, NI,UK
32/B3 Craigavon, NI,UK
32/B3 Craigavon (dist.), NI,UK
77/F5 Craigieburn, Austl.
107/G3 Craik, Sk,Can
45/J2 Crailsheim, Ger.
51/F3 Craiova, Rom.
33/G1 Cramlington, Eng,UK
32/A1 Crana (riv.), Ire.
107/H2 Cranberry Portage, Mb,Can
34/D5 Cranborne Chase (for.), Eng,UK
77/C3 Cranbourne, Austl.
106/E3 Cranbrook, BC,Can
35/G4 Cranbrook, Eng,UK
115/F5 Cranbury, NJ,US
112/C4 Crane, Tx,US
107/J3 Crane River, Mb,Can
115/F5 Cranford, NJ,US
35/F4 Cranleigh, Eng,UK
42/C5 Craonne, Fr.
51/F2 Crasna (riv.), Rom.
106/C5 Crater (lake), Or,US
106/C5 Crater Lake Nat'l Park, Or,US
106/E5 Craters of the Moon Nat'l Mon., Id,US
94/B2 Crateús, Braz.
48/E3 Crati (riv.), It.
94/C2 Crato, Braz.
95/C2 Cravinhos, Braz.
110/C3 Crawfordsville, In,US
113/G4 Crawfordville, Fl,US
35/F4 Crawley, Eng,UK
31/P7 Cray (riv.), Eng,UK
31/P7 Crayford, Eng,UK
106/F4 Crazy (mts.), Mt,US
42/A3 Crécy-en-Ponthieu, Fr.
34/D2 Credenhill, Eng,UK
111/Q8 Credit (riv.), On,Can
34/C5 Crediton, Eng,UK
102/F3 Cree (lake), Sk,Can
102/F3 Cree (riv.), Sk,Can
32/D2 Cree (riv.), Sc,UK
32/D2 Creetown, Sc,UK
31/U10 Crégy-lès-Meaux, Fr.
107/H2 Creighton, Sk,Can
42/B5 Creil, Fr.
45/H4 Crema, It.
41/H4 Cremlingen, Ger.
45/J4 Cremona, It.
42/B5 Crépy-en-Valois, Fr.
50/B3 Cres (isl.), Cro.
108/A2 Crescent City, Ca,US
96/E2 Crespo, Arg.
44/F4 Crest, Fr.
116/P16 Crest Hill, Il,US
115/C2 Crestline, Ca,US
106/D3 Creston, BC,Can
107/K5 Creston, Ia,US
113/G4 Crestview, Fl,US
33/G5 Creswell, Eng,UK
49/J5 Crete (isl.), Gre.
49/J5 Crete (sea), Gre.
109/H2 Crete, Ne,US
31/T10 Créteil, Fr.
47/G1 Creus (cape), Sp.
44/D3 Creuse (riv.), Fr.
43/F5 Creutzwald-la-Croix, Fr.
45/J4 Crevalcore, It.
47/E3 Crevillente, Sp.
33/F5 Crewe, Eng,UK
34/D5 Crewkerne, Eng,UK
36/C2 Crianlarich, Sc,UK
32/D6 Criccieth, Wal,UK
95/B4 Criciúma, Braz.
34/C3 Crickhowell, Wal,UK
35/E3 Cricklade, Eng,UK
36/D2 Crieff, Sc,UK
42/A3 Criel-sur-Mer, Fr.
32/E2 Criffell (hill), Eng,UK
54/E3 Crimean (pen.), Ukr.
54/E3 Crimean Obl., Ukr.
82/H7 Cristal (mts.), Gabon
94/A5 Cristalina, Braz.
101/G5 Cristóbal (pk.), Col.
50/F2 Criștul Alb (riv.), Rom.
51/G2 Cristuru Secuiesc, Rom.
50/E2 Crișul Negru (riv.), Rom.
93/H6 Crixás-Açu (riv.), Braz.
49/G2 Crna Reka (riv.), Macd.
77/D3 Croajingolong Nat'l Park, Austl.
50/B3 Croatia
111/F2 Croche (riv.), Qu,Can
72/E3 Crocker (range), Malay.
32/E1 Crocketford, Sc,UK
112/E4 Crockett, Tx,US
77/D2 Crocodile (pt.), Austl.
115/K7 Crofton, Md,US
34/B3 Crofty, Wal,UK
32/B6 Croghan (mtn.), Ire.
44/F5 Croisette (cape), Fr.
31/T10 Croissy-Beaubourg, Fr.
107/L3 Croix (lake), Can., US
74/E2 Croker (isl.), Austl.
35/H1 Cromer, Eng,UK
75/Q12 Cromwell, NZ
69/E3 Crong A Na (riv.), Viet.
76/H9 Cronulla, Austl.
33/G2 Crook, Eng,UK
101/G3 Crooked (isl.), Bahm.
107/J4 Crookston, Mn,US
33/E5 Crosby, Eng,UK
107/H3 Crosby, ND,US
112/C3 Crosbyton, Tx,US
31/T10 Crosne, Fr.
65/H5 Cross (riv.), Camr., Nga.
107/J2 Cross (lake), Mb,Can
113/H4 Cross City, Fl,US
112/F3 Crossett, Ar,US
33/F2 Cross Fell (mtn.), Eng,UK
106/E3 Crossfield, Ab,Can
32/C3 Crossgar, NI,UK
34/C2 Crossgates, Wal,UK
32/D1 Crosshill, Sc,UK
34/C3 Crosskeys, Wal,UK
32/B3 Crossmaglen, NI,UK
32/E2 Crossmichael, Sc,UK
85/H5 Cross River (state), Nga.
113/G3 Crossville, Tn,US
33/F4 Croston, Eng,UK
48/E3 Crotone, It.
35/G3 Crouch (riv.), Eng,UK
42/C5 Crouy-sur-Ourq, Fr.
106/G4 Crow Agency, Mt,US
35/G4 Crowborough, Eng,UK
77/E1 Crowdy Bay Nat'l Park, Austl.
110/E2 Crowe (riv.), On,Can
106/F5 Crowheart, Wy,US
35/F1 Crowland, Eng,UK
33/H4 Crowle, Eng,UK
112/E4 Crowley, La,US
113/F3 Crowley's (ridge), Ar,US
107/K4 Crow, North Fork (riv.), Mn,US
110/C3 Crown Point, In,US
108/E4 Crownpoint, NM,US
103/H1 Crown Prince Frederik (isl.), NW,Can
76/D4 Crows Nest Falls Nat'l Park, Austl.
35/F4 Crowthorne, Eng,UK
31/M7 Croxley Green, Eng,UK
77/G5 Croydon, Austl.
31/N7 Croydon (bor.), Eng,UK
29/M8 Crozet (isls.), FrAnt.
98/M Crozier (cape), Ant.
44/A2 Crozon, Fr.
36/E2 Cruden Bay, Sc,UK
32/B2 Crumlin, NI,UK
33/E2 Crummock Water (lake), Eng,UK
43/E5 Crusnes (riv.), Fr.
101/F4 Cruz (cape), Cuba
96/E2 Cruz Alta, Arg.
91/F2 Cruz Alta, Braz.
47/P10 Cruz Alta (mtn.), Port.
94/C4 Cruz das Almas, Braz.
91/D3 Cruz del Eje, Arg.
95/J7 Cruzeiro, Braz.
92/D5 Cruzeiro do Sul, Braz.
95/J6 Cruzília, Braz.
50/D3 Crvenka, Yugo.
33/E5 Cryn-y-Brain (mtn.), Wal,UK
108/C3 Crystal Bay, Nv,US
112/D4 Crystal City, Tx,US
110/B2 Crystal Falls, Mi,US
116/P15 Crystal Lake, Il,US
50/E2 Csongrád, Hun.
50/E2 Csongrád (co.), Hun.
50/C2 Csorna, Hun.
50/E2 Csorvás, Hun.
50/D2 Csóványos (peak), Hun.
60/D2 Ctesiphon (ruins), Iraq
87/D4 Cuando (riv.), Ang.
87/C4 Cuangar, Ang.
87/C2 Cuango (riv.), Ang.
87/B2 Cuanza (riv.), Ang.
47/E3 Cuart de Poblet, Sp.
96/D2 Cuarto (riv.), Arg.
100/A2 Cuatrociénagas, Mex.
101/F3 Cuba
109/K3 Cuba, Mo,US
87/C4 Cubango (riv.), Ang.
95/G8 Cubatão, Braz.
59/C2 Çubuk, Turk.
115/C2 Cucamonga (Rancho Cucamonga), Ca,US
92/E2 Cuchivero (riv.), Ven.
35/F4 Cuckfield, Eng,UK
35/G5 Cuckmere (riv.), Eng,UK
69/D1 Cuc Phuong Nat'l Park, Viet.
92/D2 Cúcuta, Col.
116/Q14 Cudahy, Wi,US
70/C5 Cuddalore, India
70/C5 Cuddapah, India
33/F5 Cuddington, Eng,UK
46/B1 Cudillero, Sp.
33/G4 Cudworth, Eng,UK
46/C2 Cuéllar, Sp.
92/C4 Cuenca, Ecu.
46/D2 Cuenca, Sp.
46/E2 Cuenca (range), Sp.
100/B4 Cuernavaca, Mex.
112/D4 Cuero, Tx,US
44/G5 Cuers, Fr.
92/C3 Cueva de los Guarcharos Nat'l Park, Col.
46/E4 Cuevas del Almanzora, Sp.
31/N6 Cuffley, Eng,UK
51/F3 Cugir, Rom.
44/D5 Cugnaux-Vingtcasses, Fr.
93/G7 Cuiabá, Braz.
93/G7 Cuiabá (riv.), Braz.
40/C5 Cuijk, Neth.
87/C2 Cuilo (riv.), Ang.
87/C3 Cuima, Ang.
94/C2 Cuité, Braz.
87/C4 Cuito (riv.), Ang.
87/C4 Cuito-Cuanavale, Ang.
92/F4 Cuiuni (riv.), Braz.
59/E3 Çukurca, Turk.
69/E4 Cu Lao (isl.), Viet.
32/A1 Culdaff (riv.), Ire.
40/C5 Culemborg, Neth.
93/H6 Culene (riv.), Braz.
77/C1 Culgoa (riv.), Austl.
101/N9 Culiacán, Mex.
67/D5 Culion (isl.), Phil.
46/D4 Cúllar Baza, Sp.
36/D2 Cullen, Sc,UK
47/E3 Cullera, Sp.
46/A1 Culleredo, Sp.
113/G3 Cullman, Al,US
34/C5 Cullompton, Eng,UK
32/B2 Cullybackey, NI,UK
32/A1 Culmore, NI,UK
76/B5 Culoga (riv.), Austl.
110/E4 Culpeper, Va,US
74/C6 Culver (pt.), Austl.
115/B2 Culver City, Ca,US
101/J5 Cumaná, Ven.
103/K2 Cumberland (pen.), NW,Can
103/K2 Cumberland (sound), NW,Can
107/H2 Cumberland (lake), Sk,Can
113/G3 Cumberland (plat.), US
113/H4 Cumberland (isl.), Ga,US
113/G2 Cumberland (falls), Ky,US
110/C4 Cumberland (lake), Ky,US
113/G2 Cumberland (riv.), Ky, Tn,US
110/E4 Cumberland, Md,US
110/D4 Cumberland Gap Nat'l Hist. Park, Tn,US
107/H2 Cumberland House, Sk,Can
101/N8 Cumbres de Majalca Nat'l Park, Mex.
100/A2 Cumbres de Monterrey Nat'l Park, Mex.
33/F2 Cumbria (co.), Eng,UK
33/E3 Cumbrian (mts.), Eng,UK
70/C4 Cumbum, India
59/C3 Çumra, Turk.
114/M5 Cumshewa (pt.), BC,Can
96/B3 Cunco, Chile
87/B4 Cunene (riv.), Ang.
45/G4 Cuneo, It.
69/E3 Cung Son, Viet.
95/J8 Cunha, Braz.
37/H1 Čuokkaraš'ša (peak), Nor.
45/G4 Cuorgnè, It.
36/D2 Cupar, Sc,UK
116/K12 Cupertino, Ca,US
50/E4 Ćuprija, Yugo.
101/H5 Curaçao (isl.), NAnt.
96/C3 Curacautín, Chile
96/B3 Curanilahue, Chile
92/C4 Curaray (riv.), Ecu., Peru
96/Q9 Curaumilla (pt.), Chile
50/F2 Curcubăta (peak), Rom.
44/E3 Cure (riv.), Fr.
89/S15 Curepipe, Mrts.
96/B2 Curepto, Chile
96/C2 Curicó, Chile
95/B3 Curitiba, Braz.
95/B3 Curitibanos, Braz.
32/B5 Curragh, The, Ire.
94/C2 Currais Novos, Braz.
109/K3 Current (riv.), Ar, Mo,US
108/D2 Currie, Nv,US
51/G3 Curtea de Argeș, Rom.
50/E2 Curtici, Rom.
76/C3 Curtis (isl.), Austl.
78/H8 Curtis (isl.), NZ
93/G4 Curuá (riv.), Braz.
93/H5 Curuá (riv.), Braz.
92/D5 Curuçú (riv.), Braz.
72/B4 Curup, Indo.
93/K4 Cururupu, Braz.
91/E2 Curuzú Cuatiá, Arg.
95/C1 Curvelo, Braz.
105/J2 Curwood (mtn.), Mi,US
92/D6 Cusco, Peru
32/B1 Cushendall, NI,UK
32/B3 Cusher (riv.), NI,UK
109/H4 Cushing, Ok,US
44/E3 Cusset, Fr.
113/G3 Cusseta, Ga,US
106/G4 Custer, Mt,US
107/H5 Custer, SD,US
94/C3 Custódia, Braz.
34/C5 Cut (hill), Eng,UK
106/E3 Cut Bank, Mt,US
92/C5 Cutervo, Peru
113/G4 Cuthbert, Ga,US
106/F2 Cut Knife, Sk,Can
96/C3 Cutral-Có, Arg.
70/E3 Cuttack, India
41/F1 Cuxhaven, Ger.
108/C4 Cuyama (riv.), Ca,US
73/F1 Cuyo, Phil.
73/F1 Cuyo (isls.), Phil.
92/F2 Cuyuni (riv.), Guy., Ven.
34/C3 Cwm, Wal,UK
34/C3 Cwmafan, Wal,UK
34/C3 Cwmbran, Wal,UK
107/H5 C.W. McConaughy (lake), Ne,US
49/J4 Cyclades (isls.), Gre.
110/C4 Cynthiana, Ky,US
34/B3 Cynwyl Elfed, Wal,UK
106/F3 Cypress (hills), Ab, Sk,Can
115/B3 Cypress, Ca,US
59/J4 Cyprus
83/K1 Cyrenaica (reg.), Libya
34/B3 Cywyn (riv.), Wal,UK
39/J2 Czaplinek, Pol.
39/M2 Czarna Biał ostocka, Pol.
39/J2 Czarnków, Pol.
39/H4 Czech Republic
39/K3 Częstochowa, Pol.
39/K3 Częstochowa (prov.), Pol.
39/J2 Czł uchów, Pol.

D

67/D2 Da (riv.), China
66/B4 Daba (mts.), China
50/D2 Dabas, Hun.
60/C3 Dabbāgh, Jabal (mtn.), SAr.
92/C2 Dabeiba, Col.
70/B3 Dabhoi, India
69/D1 Da (Black) (riv.), Viet.
116/B2 Dabob (bay), Wa,US
83/Q6 Daborow, Som.
84/D5 Dabou, IvC.
70/C2 Dabra, India
39/M2 Dąbrowa Biał ostocka, Pol.
39/K3 Dąbrowa Górnicza, Pol.
45/J2 Dachau, Ger.
69/D3 Dac Sut, Viet.
69/D3 Dac To, Viet.
113/H4 Dade City, Fl,US
73/H4 Dadi (cape), Indo.
70/B4 Dadra & Nagar Haveli (terr.), India
61/J3 Dādu, Pak.
70/D6 Daduru (riv.), SrL.
69/B4 Daen Noi (peak), Thai.
67/D5 Daet, Phil.
71/J2 Dafang, China
84/B2 Dagana, Sen.
55/H3 Dagestan Aut. Rep., Rus.
88/D4 Daggaboersnek (pass), SAfr.
76/B2 Dagmar Range Nat'l Park, Austl.
71/H2 Daguan, China
76/E6 D'Aguilar (mtn.), Austl.
76/E6 D'Aguilar (range), Austl.
63/K2 Daguokui (peak), China
67/D4 Dagupan, Phil.
68/E5 Dagzê (lake), China
66/C2 Dahaituo Shan (mtn.), China
58/D7 Dahana (des.), SAr.
70/B4 Dāhānu, India
70/A2 Daharki, Pak.
66/B2 Dahei (riv.), China
63/K2 Daheiding (peak), China
63/J2 Da Hinggang (mts.), China
83/N4 Dahlak (arch.), Erit.
113/H3 Dahlonega, Ga,US
39/G3 Dahme (riv.), Ger.
69/D4 Da Hoa, Viet.
66/C5 Dahong (mtn.), China
59/E3 Dahūk, Iraq
66/C2 Dai (lake), China
65/M9 Daian, Japan
65/G2 Daigo, Japan
70/D2 Dailekh, Nepal
32/D1 Dailly, Sc,UK
69/E3 Dai Loc, Viet.
46/D3 Daimiel, Sp.
112/E3 Daingerfield, Tx,US
76/B2 Daintree Nat'l Park, Austl.
65/E3 Daiō-zaki (pt.), Japan
96/E3 Daireaux, Arg.
64/C3 Dai-sen (mtn.), Japan
64/C3 Daisen-Oki Nat'l Park, Japan
65/L10 Daitō, Japan
78/C2 Daito (isls.), Japan
84/A3 Dakar (cap.), Sen.
84/A3 Dakar (reg.), Sen.
86/B3 Dākhilah, Wāḥāt ad (oasis), Egypt
82/B3 Dakhla, WSah.
84/A1 Dakhlet Nouadhibou (reg.), Mrta.
69/D3 Dak Nhe, Viet.
85/G3 Dakoro, Niger
109/H2 Dakota City, Ne,US
50/E4 Dakovica, Yugo.
50/D3 Dakovo, Yugo.
98/A Dakshin Gangotri, Ant.
30/E2 Dal (riv.), Swe.
62/H3 Dalai (salt lake), China
59/B3 Dalaman, Turk.
62/F2 Dalanjargalan, Mong.
37/E3 Dalarna (reg.), Swe.
69/E4 Da Lat, Viet.
37/Q6 Dalatangi (pt.), Ice.
32/E2 Dalbeattie, Sc,UK
76/C4 Dalby, Austl.
86/B4 Dal Cataract (falls), Sudan
40/D4 Dalfsen, Neth.
112/C2 Dalhart, Tx,US
111/H1 Dalhousie, NB,Can
114/N1 Dalhousie (cape), NW,Can
71/H2 Dali, China
66/B3 Dali (riv.), China
46/D4 Dalías, Sp.
63/H3 Daling (riv.), China
50/D3 Dalj, Cro.
114/M4 Dall (isl.), Ak,US
114/F3 Dall (lake), Ak,US
112/D3 Dallas, Tx,US
106/C4 Dalles, The, Or,US
85/F3 Dallol Bosso (wadi), Mali, Niger
36/C2 Dalmally, Sc,UK
50/C4 Dalmatia (reg.), Cro.
32/D1 Dalmellington, Sc,UK
63/M3 Dal'negorsk, Rus.
63/L2 Dal'nerechensk, Rus.
84/D5 Daloa, IvC.
86/B4 Dalqū, Sudan

133

Dalry – Dorki

76/B3 Dalrymple (lake), Austl.
36/C3 Dalrymple, Sc,UK
113/G3 Dalton, Ga,US
70/D3 Daltonganj, India
33/E3 Dalton-in-Furness, Eng,UK
36/C2 Dalwhinnie, Sc,UK
74/E2 Daly (riv.), Austl.
102/H2 Daly (bay), NW,Can
116/K11 Daly City, Ca,US
68/F5 Dam (riv.), China
70/B3 Damān, India
70/B3 Damān & Diu (terr.), India
59/H6 Damanhūr, Egypt
73/G5 Damar (isl.), Indo.
115/J7 Damascus, Md,US
59/L5 Damascus (Dimashq) (cap.), Syria
82/H5 Damaturu, Nga.
60/F1 Damavānd (mtn.), Iran
69/D4 Dam Doi, Viet.
35/E5 Damerham, Eng,UK
61/F1 Dāmghān, Iran
59/H6 Damietta (Dumyāţ), Egypt
66/C3 Daming, China
43/D4 Damion (mtn.), Fr.
31/U9 Dammartin-en-Goële, Fr.
42/C1 Damme, Belg.
41/F3 Damme, Ger.
70/C3 Damoh, India
85/E4 Damongo, Gha.
74/B4 Dampier (arch.), Austl.
73/H4 Dampier (str.), Indo.
69/C4 Damrei (mts.), Camb.
40/D2 Damsterdiep (riv.), Neth.
43/E5 Damvillers, Fr.
66/B4 Dan (riv.), China
113/H2 Dan (riv.), NC,US
83/P5 Danakil (reg.), Djib.
84/C5 Danané, IvC.
69/E2 Da Nang, Viet.
67/D5 Danao, Phil.
35/G3 Danbury, Eng,UK
77/G5 Dandenong, Austl.
77/G5 Dandenong (cr.), Austl.
77/G5 Dandenong (mtn.), Austl.
33/F5 Dane (riv.), Eng,UK
62/D4 Dang (riv.), China
88/B4 Danger (pt.), SAfr.
77/B2 Danggali Consv. Park, Austl.
83/N5 Dangila, Eth.
100/D4 Dangriga, Belz.
52/J4 Danilov, Rus.
66/B4 Danjiangkou, China
66/B4 Danjiangkou (res.), China
54/F1 Dankov, Rus.
68/C3 Dankova, Pik (peak), Kyr.
113/G3 Dannelly (res.), Al,US
38/F2 Dannenberg, Ger.
75/S11 Dannevirke, NZ
30/F4 Danube (riv.), Eur.
51/J3 Danube (delta), Rom.
51/H3 Danube, Borcea Branch (riv.), Rom.
51/J3 Danube, Mouths of the, Rom.
51/J3 Danube, Sfîntu Gheorghe Branch (riv.), Rom.
51/J3 Danube, Sulina Branch (riv.), Rom.
116/L11 Danville, Ca,US
110/C3 Danville, Il,US
110/C4 Danville, Ky,US
110/E4 Danville, Va,US
85/F4 Dapaong, Togo
113/G4 Daphne, Al,US
67/D6 Dapitan, Phil.
63/K2 Daqing, China
66/H7 Daqing (riv.), China
61/H2 Daqq-e Patargān (lake), Afg., Iran
59/L5 Dar'ā, Syria
61/F3 Dārāb, Iran
51/H1 Darabani, Rom.
67/D5 Daraga, Phil.
67/D5 Daram, Phil.
50/E4 Đaravica (peak), Yugo.
59/L5 Dārayyā, Syria
70/E2 Darbhanga, India
114/F3 Darby (cape), Ak,US
115/E6 Darby, Pa,US
50/D3 Darda, Cro.
109/J4 Dardanelle (lake), Ar,US
51/H5 Dardanelles (str.), Turk.
77/G5 Darebin (cr.), Austl.
59/D2 Darende, Turk.
31/P8 Darent (riv.), Eng,UK
87/G2 Dar es Salaam (cap.), Tanz.
75/R11 Darfield, NZ
45/J4 Darfo, It.
75/R10 Dargaville, NZ
32/B5 Dargle (riv.), Ire.
62/F2 Darhan (peak), Mong.
83/Q6 Darie (hills), Som.
115/G4 Darien, Ct,US
113/H4 Darien, Ga,US
116/Q16 Darien, Il,US
101/F6 Darien Nat'l Park, Pan.
62/G2 Dariganga, Mong.
70/E2 Darjiling, India
74/B6 Darling (range), Austl.
77/B2 Darling (riv.), Austl.
76/C4 Darling Downs (upland), Austl.
33/G2 Darlington, Eng,UK
113/J3 Darlington, SC,US
39/J1 Darłowo, Pol.
45/H2 Darmstadt, Ger.
83/K1 Darnah, Libya
81/W18 Darnāya, Tun.
42/A5 Darnétal, Fr.
98/E Darnley (cape), Ant.
102/D2 Darnley (bay), NW,Can
33/G1 Darras Hall, Eng,UK
61/G1 Darreh Gaz, Iran
83/K6 Dar Rounga (reg.), CAfr.
98/R Dart (cape), Ant.
34/C6 Dart (riv.), Eng,UK
31/P7 Dartford, Eng,UK
34/C6 Dartington, Eng,UK
34/B5 Dartmoor (upland), Eng,UK
34/C5 Dartmoor Nat'l Park, Eng,UK
77/C3 Dartmouth (res.), Austl.
111/J2 Dartmouth, NS,Can
34/C6 Dartmouth, Eng,UK
33/G4 Darton, Eng,UK
47/G3 Dartuch (cape), Sp.
78/D5 Daru, PNG
50/C3 Daruvar, Cro.
73/E3 Darvel (bay), Malay.
33/F4 Darwen, Eng,UK
74/E2 Darwin, Austl.
96/B5 Darwin (bay), Chile
97/K8 Darwin (mts.), Chile
61/H2 Daryācheh-ye Sīstān (lake), Iran
63/H3 Dashengtang (peak), China
66/B5 Dashennongjia (peak), China
83/N5 Dashen, Ras (peak), Eth.
61/F2 Dasht-e Kavīr (des.), Iran
61/G2 Dasht-e Lūt (des.), Iran
61/H2 Dasht-e Mārgow (des.), Afg.
61/H3 Dasht Kaur (riv.), Pak.
41/G5 Dassel, Ger.
88/B4 Dasseneiland (isl.), SAfr.
31/M7 Datchet, Eng,UK
69/D4 Dat Do, Viet.
70/C2 Datia, India
108/F4 Datil, NM,US
66/C2 Datong, China
62/D4 Datong (mts.), China
62/D4 Datong (riv.), China
41/E5 Datteln, Ger.
72/C3 Datu (cape), Malay.
72/B3 Datuk (cape), Indo.
37/H4 Daugava (riv.), Lat.
52/E4 Daugava (riv.), Lat.
52/E5 Daugavpils, Lat.
47/F3 Daun, Ger.
69/B3 Daung (isl.), Burma
107/H3 Dauphin, Mb,Can
107/J3 Dauphin (lake), Mb,Can
70/C5 Dāvangere, India
67/E6 Davao, Phil.
107/L5 Davenport, Ia,US
106/D4 Davenport, Wa,US
35/E2 Daventry, Eng,UK
103/T6 Davgaard-Jensen (reg.), Grld.
100/E6 David, Pan.
109/H2 David City, Ne,US
107/G3 Davidson, Sk,Can
116/K11 Davidson (mtn.), Ca,US
98/F Davis (sea), Ant.
98/F Davis (sta.), Ant.
99/M3 Davis (str.), Can., Grld.
116/L9 Davis, Ca,US
110/E4 Davis (peak), Pa,US
112/B4 Davis (mts.), Tx,US
53/M5 Davlekanovo, Rus.
84/D5 Davo (riv.), IvC.
45/H3 Davos, Swi.
62/C1 Davst, Mong.
83/N7 Dawa Wenz (riv.), Afr.
66/D4 Dawen (riv.), China
34/C5 Dawlish, Eng,UK
76/C4 Dawson (riv.), Austl.
114/L3 Dawson, Yk,Can
97/K8 Dawson (isl.), Chile
113/G4 Dawson, Ga,US
106/C2 Dawson Creek, BC,Can
66/C5 Dawu Shan (mtn.), China
60/G4 Dawwah, Oman
44/C5 Dax, Fr.
66/D3 Daxing, China
71/G3 Daying (riv.), China
97/F1 Dayman (riv.), Uru.
67/B2 Dayong, China
59/K6 Dayr al Balaḩ, Gaza
60/D1 Dayr az Zawr, Syria
86/B3 Dayrūt, Egypt
106/E2 Daysland, Ab,Can
110/C4 Dayton, Oh,US
113/G3 Dayton, Tn,US
106/D4 Dayton, Wa,US
113/H4 Daytona Beach, Fl,US
88/D3 De Aar, SAfr.
59/K6 Dead (sea), Isr., Jor.
107/H4 Deadwood, SD,US
77/C3 Deal (isl.), Austl.
35/H4 Deal, Eng,UK
115/G5 Deal, NJ,US
106/B2 Dean (riv.), BC,Can
34/D3 Dean, Forest of (for.), Eng,UK
91/D3 Deán Funes, Arg.
116/F7 Dearborn, Mi,US
116/F7 Dearborn Heights, Mi,US
33/G4 Dearne, Eng,UK
33/G4 Dearne (riv.), Eng,UK
114/N4 Dease (riv.), BC,Can
102/F2 Dease (str.), NW,Can
108/C3 Death Valley Nat'l Mon., Ca, Nv,US
50/E5 Debar, Macd.
114/G3 Debauch (mtn.), Ak,US
35/H2 Deben (riv.), Eng,UK
35/H2 Debenham, Eng,UK
39/L3 Dębica, Pol.
40/C4 De Bilt, Neth.
39/L3 Dęblin, Pol.
39/H2 Dębno, Pol.
114/J3 Deborah (mtn.), Ak,US
83/N6 Debre Birhan, Eth.
50/E2 Debrecen, Hun.
83/N5 Debre Mark'os, Eth.
83/N5 Debre Tabor, Eth.
83/N6 Debre Zeyit, Eth.
113/G3 Decatur, Al,US
113/G3 Decatur, Ga,US
110/B4 Decatur, Il,US
110/C3 Decatur, In,US
112/D3 Decatur, Tx,US
44/E4 Decazeville, Fr.
70/C5 Deccan (plat.), India
39/H3 Děčín, Czh.
44/E3 Decize, Fr.
35/E3 Deddington, Eng,UK
40/D3 Dedemsvaart, Neth.
96/C5 Dedo (peak), Arg.
84/E3 Dédougou, Burk.
87/F3 Dedza, Malw.
32/B4 Dee (riv.), Ire.
32/D1 Dee (riv.), Sc,UK
36/D2 Dee (riv.), Sc,UK
33/E5 Dee (riv.), Wal,UK
32/A4 Deel (riv.), Ire.
35/F1 Deeping Saint James, Eng,UK
112/E2 Deep River, On,Can
114/F5 Deer (isl.), Ak,US
116/Q15 Deerfield, Il,US
111/K1 Deer Lake, Nf,Can
42/C2 Deerlijk, Belg.
106/E4 Deer Lodge, Mt,US
115/G5 Deer Park, NY,US
106/D4 Deer Park, Wa,US
70/B3 Deesa, India
76/H8 Dee Why, Austl.
83/Q6 Deex Nugaaleed (dry river), Som.
92/F8 Defensores del Chaco Nat'l Park, Par.
110/C3 Defiance, Oh,US
113/G4 De Funiak Springs, Fl,US
32/E5 Deganwy, Wal,UK
83/P6 Degeh Bur, Eth.
111/G2 Dégelis, Qu,Can
45/K2 Deggendorf, Ger.
74/B4 De Grey (riv.), Austl.
42/C1 De Haan, Belg.
83/P4 Dehalak (isl.), Erit.
83/P4 Dehalak Marine Nat'l Park, Erit.
61/L2 Dehra Dūn, India
70/D3 Dehri, India
42/C2 Deinze, Belg.
41/G4 Deister (mts.), Ger.
51/F2 Dej, Rom.
110/B3 De Kalb, Il,US
83/N4 Dek'emhāre, Eth.
113/H4 De Land, Fl,US
108/C4 Delano, Ca,US
61/H2 Delārām, Afg.
106/G2 Delarode (lake), Sk,Can
116/N14 Delavan, Wi,US
110/F3 Delaware (riv.), US
110/F4 Delaware (state), US
110/D3 Delaware, Oh,US
115/F4 Delaware Water Gap Nat'l Rec. Area, NJ, Pa,US
41/F5 Delbrück, Ger.
96/D2 Del Campillo, Arg.
50/F5 Delčevo, Macd.
40/D4 Delden, Neth.
40/D2 De Leijen (lake), Neth.
45/G3 Delémont, Swi.
40/B5 Delft, Neth.
40/D2 Delfzijl, Neth.
96/E4 Delgada (pt.), Arg.
87/H3 Delgado (cape), Moz.
62/D2 Delger (riv.), Mong.
62/F2 Delgerhaan, Mong.
62/E2 Delgerhangay, Mong.
70/C2 Delhi, India
54/E5 Delice (riv.), Turk.
40/B5 De Lier, Neth.
48/D5 Delimara, Ponta Ta' (pt.), Malta
106/G3 Delisle, Sk,Can
41/G5 Delligsen, Ger.
107/J5 Dell Rapids, SD,US
88/Q13 Delmas, SAfr.
43/F6 Delme, Fr.
41/F3 Delme (riv.), Ger.
41/F2 Delmenhorst, Ger.
94/C3 Delmiro Gouveia, Braz.
109/F3 Del Norte, Co,US
49/J4 Delos (ruins), Gre.
49/H3 Delphi (ruins), Gre.
110/C3 Delphos, Oh,US
115/F5 Delran, NJ,US
113/H5 Delray Beach, Fl,US
112/C4 Del Rio, Tx,US
108/E3 Delta, Co,US
108/D3 Delta, Ut,US
97/T12 Delta del Tigre, Uru.
116/M11 Delta-Mendota (can.), Ca,US
113/H4 Deltona, Fl,US
62/C2 Delüün, Mong.
116/L11 Del Valle (lake), Ca,US
53/M5 Dēma (riv.), Rus.
46/D1 Demanda (range), Sp.
114/K2 Demarcation (pt.), Ak,US
87/D2 Demba, Zaire
83/M6 Dembī Dolo, Eth.
40/B7 Demer (riv.), Belg.
108/F4 Deming, NM,US
92/F3 Demini (riv.), Braz.
38/G2 Demmin, Ger.
113/G3 Demopolis, Al,US
72/B4 Dempo (peak), Indo.
42/C3 Denain, Fr.
83/P5 Denakil (reg.), Erit., Eth.
114/H3 Denali Nat'l Park & Prsv., Ak,US
107/H2 Denare Beach, Sk,Can
33/E5 Denbigh, Wal,UK
40/B2 Den Burg, Neth.
33/G4 Denby Dale, Eng,UK
42/D2 Dender (riv.), Belg.
42/D2 Denderleeuw, Belg.
42/D1 Dendermonde, Belg.
40/D4 Denekamp, Neth.
74/A5 Denham (sound), Austl.
40/D4 Den Ham, Neth.
31/M7 Denham, Eng,UK
40/B3 Den Helder, Neth.
33/G4 Denholme, Eng,UK
47/G3 Denia, Sp.
77/C2 Deniliquin, Austl.
108/C2 Denio, Nv,US
114/H4 Denison (mtn.), Ak,US
107/K5 Denison, Ia,US
112/D3 Denison, Tx,US
59/B3 Denizli, Turk.
98/G Denman (glac.), Ant.
37/C5 Denmark
99/D3 Denmark (str.), NAm
72/E5 Denpasar, Indo.
42/C2 Dentergem, Belg.
35/G5 Denton, Eng,UK
112/D3 Denton, Tx,US
74/A6 D'Entrecasteaux (pt.), Austl.
78/D5 D'Entrecasteaux (isls.), PNG
109/F3 Denver (cap.), Co,US
115/F5 Denville, NJ,US
70/C2 Deoband, India
70/D3 Deogarh, India
70/E3 Deoghar, India
70/B4 Deolāli, India
70/C2 Deoli, India
44/D3 Déols, Fr.
70/D2 Deoria, India
42/B1 De Panne, Belg.
40/C6 De Peel (reg.), Neth.
111/S10 Depew, NY,US
42/C2 De Pinte, Belg.
31/N7 Deptford, Eng,UK
83/P7 Dera (dry riv.), Som.
61/K2 Dera Ghāzi Khān, Pak.
61/K2 Dera Ismā'īl Khān, Pak.
55/J4 Derbent, Rus.
33/G6 Derby, Eng,UK
109/H3 Derby, Ks,US
33/G6 Derbyshire (co.), Eng,UK
51/F3 Đerdap Nat'l Park, Yugo.
50/E2 Derecske, Hun.
62/F2 Deren, Mong.
36/A4 Derg, Lough (lake), Ire.
112/E4 De Ridder, La,US
59/E3 Derik, Turk.
44/B2 Déroute (passg.), Fr., Chl,UK
32/A4 Derravaragh, Lough (lake), Ire.
32/B6 Derry (riv.), Ire.
111/G3 Derry, NH,US
32/C3 Derryboy, NI,UK
36/B3 Derrylin, NI,UK
35/G1 Dersingham, Eng,UK
50/C3 Derventa, Bosn.
32/B1 Dervock, NI,UK
77/C4 Derwent (riv.), Austl.
33/F2 Derwent (res.), Eng,UK
33/E2 Derwent (riv.), Eng,UK
33/G5 Derwent (riv.), Eng,UK
33/H4 Derwent (riv.), Eng,UK
32/E2 Derwent Water (lake), Eng,UK
96/D2 Desaguadero (riv.), Arg.
92/E7 Desaguadero (riv.), Bol.
35/F2 Desborough, Eng,UK
96/C2 Descabezado Grande (vol.), Chile
95/C2 Descalvado, Braz.
107/H2 Deschambault Lake, Sk,Can
108/B2 Deschutes (riv.), Or,US
83/N5 Desē, Eth.
91/C6 Deseado (riv.), Arg.
97/J8 Deseado (cape), Chile
97/L7 Desengaño (pt.), Arg.
47/V15 Desertas (isl.), Madr.,Port.
66/B4 Deshengpu, China
107/J4 De Smet, SD,US
107/K5 Des Moines (cap.), Ia,US
107/K5 Des Moines (riv.), Ia, Mo,US
116/C3 Des Moines, Wa,US
54/D2 Desna (riv.), Rus., Ukr.
97/J8 Desolación (isl.), Chile
88/D4 Desolation, Valley of (val.), SAfr.
94/A2 Desordem (mts.), Braz.
109/K3 De Soto, Mo,US
88/D4 Despatch, SAfr.
116/Q15 Des Plaines, Il,US
116/P16 Des Plaines (riv.), Il,US
38/G3 Dessau, Ger.
43/E1 Dessel, Belg.
42/C1 Destelbergen, Belg.
114/L3 Destruction Bay, Yk,Can
50/E3 Deta, Rom.
41/F5 Detmold, Ger.
116/F7 Detroit, Mi,US
116/F7 Detroit (riv.), On,Can, Mi,US
107/K4 Detroit Lakes, Mn,US
37/P6 Dettifoss (falls), Ice.
77/D2 Deua Nat'l Park, Austl.
31/S10 Deuil-la-Barre, Fr.
42/B2 Deûle (riv.), Fr.
40/B6 Deurne, Belg.
40/C6 Deurne, Neth.
45/L3 Deutschlandsberg, Aus.
111/N6 Deux-Montagnes, Qu,Can
111/M7 Deux-Montagnes (lake), Qu,Can
50/F3 Deva, Rom.
50/E2 Dévaványa, Hun.
59/C2 Develi, Turk.
40/D4 Deventer, Neth.
36/D2 Deveron (riv.), Sc,UK
49/H2 Devil's (isl.), FrG.
109/G5 Devils (riv.), Tx,US
107/J3 Devils Lake, ND,US
114/M4 Devils Paw (mtn.), BC,Can, Ak,US
108/C3 Devils Postpile Nat'l Mon., Ca,US
107/G4 Devils Tower Nat'l Mon., Wy,US
51/G5 Devin, Bul.
112/D4 Devine, Tx,US
35/E4 Devizes, Eng,UK
51/H4 Devnya, Bul.
49/G2 Devoll (riv.), Alb.
106/E2 Devon, Ab,Can
103/S7 Devon (isl.), NW,Can
34/C5 Devon (co.), Eng,UK
77/C4 Devonport, Austl.
51/K5 Devrek, Turk.
54/D4 Devrek (riv.), Turk.
54/E4 Devrez (riv.), Turk.
72/A3 Dewa (pt.), Indo.
70/C3 Dewās, India
112/E2 Dewey, Ok,US
109/H2 De Witt, Ne,US
33/G4 Dewsbury, Eng,UK
111/G2 Dexter, Me,US
74/D5 Dey-Dey (lake), Austl.
60/E2 Dez (riv.), Iran
60/E2 Dezfūl, Iran
114/E2 Dezhneva, Mys (pt.), Rus.
66/D3 Dezhou, China
86/C2 Dhahab, Egypt
70/F3 Dhākā (Dacca) (cap.), Bang.
70/D3 Dhamtari, India
70/E3 Dhānbād, India
70/E2 Dhankuta, Nepal
70/C3 Dhār, India
70/B3 Dharampur, India
70/B3 Dhāri, India
70/C5 Dharmapuri, India
70/C5 Dharmavaram, India
70/D2 Dhaulāgiri (peak), Nepal
49/H3 Dhelfoí (Delphi) (ruins), Gre.
70/E3 Dhenkānāl, India
49/K2 Dhidhimótikhon, Gre.
49/H3 Dhírfis (peak), Gre.
60/F5 Dhofar (reg.), Oman
70/B3 Dholka, India
70/C2 Dholpur, India
70/B4 Dhond, India
49/J4 Dhonoúsa (isl.), Gre.
70/B3 Dhorāji, India
49/J2 Dhráma, Gre.
43/F4 Dhronbach (riv.), Ger.
70/E2 Dhubri, India
70/B3 Dhūlia, India
70/E3 Dhuliān, India
70/E2 Dhupgāri, India
49/J5 Dia (isl.), Gre.
45/G4 Diable, Cime du (peak), Fr.
114/H4 Diablo (mtn.), Ak,US
116/L11 Diablo (mt.), Ca,US
108/B3 Diablo (range), Ca,US
112/B4 Diablo (plat.), Tx,US
97/G2 Diablo, Punta del (pt.), Uru.
95/G8 Diadema, Braz.
95/E2 Diamante, Arg.
96/D2 Diamante (riv.), Arg.
74/G4 Diamantina (riv.), Austl.
95/D1 Diamantina, Braz.
94/B3 Diamantina (mts.), Braz.
93/G6 Diamantino, Braz.
77/G5 Diamond (cr.), Austl.
106/E4 Diamond (peak), Id,US
115/C3 Diamond Bar, Ca,US
104/W13 Diamond Head (crater), Hi,US
66/L8 Dianshan (lake), China
85/F3 Diapaga, Burk.
98/J Dibble Iceberg Tongue, Ant.
87/E5 Dibete, Bots.
86/B4 Dibis, Bîr (well), Egypt
112/E4 Diboll, Tx,US
71/F2 Dibrugarh, India
59/F3 Dibs, Iraq
112/C3 Dickens, Tx,US
107/H4 Dickinson, ND,US
113/G2 Dickson, Tn,US
59/E3 Dicle (riv.), Turk.
40/D5 Didam, Neth.
35/E3 Didcot, Eng,UK
106/E3 Didsbury, Ab,Can
61/K3 Didwāna, India
89/E2 Die Berg (peak), SAfr.
84/E4 Diébougou, Burk.
102/F3 Diefenbaker (lake), Sk,Can
97/J7 Diego de Almagro (isl.), Chile
58/G10 Diego Garcia (isl.), BrIn.
43/E4 Diekirch (dist.), Lux.
41/F5 Diemel (riv.), Ger.
40/B4 Diemen, Neth.
69/C1 Dien Bien Phu, Viet.
69/D2 Dien Chau, Viet.
69/E3 Dien Khanh, Viet.
43/E2 Diepenbeek, Belg.
40/D4 Diepenveen, Neth.
41/F3 Diepholz, Ger.
42/A4 Dieppe, Fr.
43/E2 Diest, Belg.
83/P7 Dif, Kenya
85/H3 Diffa (dept.), Niger
43/E4 Differdange, Lux.
77/B3 Difficult (peak), Austl.
71/G2 Digboi, India
111/H2 Digby, NS,Can
45/G4 Digne, Fr.
44/E3 Digoin, Fr.
67/E6 Digos, Phil.
70/C3 Digras, India
42/D2 Dijle (Dyle) (riv.), Belg.
44/F3 Dijon, Fr.
83/P5 Dikhil, Djib.
59/H6 Dikirnis, Egypt
55/H4 Diklosmta, Gora (peak), Geo.
42/B1 Diksmuide, Belg.
82/H5 Dikwa, Nga.
83/N6 Dīla, Eth.
42/D2 Dilbeek, Belg.
73/G5 Dili, Indo.
41/H2 Dillenburg, Ger.
83/L5 Dilling, Sudan
43/F5 Dillingen, Ger.
113/J3 Dillon, SC,US
87/D3 Dilolo, Zaire
43/E1 Dilsen, Belg.
71/F2 Dimāpur, India
59/L5 Dimashq (Damascus) (cap.), Syria
84/D5 Dimbokro, IvC.
51/G3 Dîmbovița (co.), Rom.
57/P2 Dimitriya Lapteva (str.), Rus.
51/G4 Dimitrovgrad, Bul.
55/J1 Dimitrovgrad, Rus.
50/F4 Dimitrovgrad, Yugo.
82/H6 Dimlang (peak), Nga.
59/K5 Dimona, Isr.
59/K6 Dimona, Hare (mtn.), Isr.
67/E6 Dinagat, Phil.
67/E5 Dinagat (isl.), Phil.
70/E2 Dinājpur, Bang.
44/B2 Dinan, Fr.
43/D3 Dinant, Belg.
59/B2 Dinar, Turk.
44/B2 Dinard, Fr.
49/E1 Dinaric Alps (range), Bosn., Cro.
34/B2 Dinas (pt.), Wal,UK
34/C4 Dinas Powys, Wal,UK
83/N5 Dinder Nat'l Park, Eth.
70/C5 Dindigul, India
45/K2 Dingolfing, Ger.
67/D4 Dingras, Phil.
32/C2 Dingwall, Sc,UK
66/C3 Dingxing, China
66/C3 Dingyuan, China
69/D1 Dinh Lap, Viet.
41/E5 Dinkel (riv.), Ger.
41/F3 Dinklage, Ger.
33/G1 Dinnington, Eng,UK
103/E2 Dinosaur, Co,US
108/E2 Dinosaur Nat'l Mon., Co, Ut,US
40/D5 Dinslaken, Ger.
106/G3 Dinsmore, Sk,Can
40/B5 Dintel Mark (riv.), Neth.
108/C3 Dinuba, Ca,US
40/D5 Dinxperlo, Neth.
84/C4 Dion (riv.), Gui.
84/A3 Diourbel, Sen.
84/A3 Diourbel (reg.), Sen.
71/F2 Diphu, India
61/J4 Diplo, Pak.
67/D6 Dipolog, Phil.
76/C3 Dipperu Nat'l Park, Austl.
84/E2 Diré, Mali
75/G2 Direction (cape), Austl.
83/P6 Dirē Dawa, Eth.
100/D5 Diriamba, Nic.
74/A5 Dirk Hartog (isl.), Austl.
82/H4 Dirkou, Niger
40/B5 Dirksland, Neth.
108/E3 Dirty Devil (riv.), Ut,US
74/C4 Disappointment (lake), Austl.
79/L6 Disappointment (isls.), FrPol.
77/B3 Discovery (bay), Austl.
86/C3 Dishnā, Egypt
103/L2 Disko (isl.), Grld.
33/F5 Disley, Eng,UK
115/C3 Disneyland, Ca,US
43/E2 Dison, Belg.
70/F2 Dispur, India
111/G2 Disraëli, Qu,Can
35/H2 Diss, Eng,UK
41/F4 Dissen am Teutoburger Wald, Ger.
32/E2 Distington, Eng,UK
115/J8 District of Columbia (cap.), US
97/S12 Distrito Federal (fed. dist.), Arg.
94/A4 Distrito Féderal (fed. dist.), Braz.
100/B4 Distrito Federal (state), Mex.
59/H6 Disūq, Egypt
35/F6 Ditchling Beacon (hill), Eng,UK
48/D4 Dittaino (riv.), It.
61/K4 Diu (isl.), India
70/B3 Diu, Damān and (terr.), India
50/D4 Diva (riv.), Yugo.
44/D3 Dive (riv.), Fr.
95/C2 Divinópolis, Braz.
32/B2 Divis (mtn.), NI,UK
92/D5 Divisor (mts.), Braz.
84/D5 Divo, IvC.
59/D2 Divriği, Turk.
114/M4 Dixon (chan.), Ak,US
116/L10 Dixon, Ca,US
110/B3 Dixon, Il,US
102/C3 Dixon Entrance (chan.), BC,Can
59/E2 Diyadin, Turk.
59/E3 Diyarbakır, Turk.
59/H6 Diyarb Najm, Egypt
82/H3 Djado, Niger
82/H3 Djado (plat.), Niger
82/G1 Djamaa, Alg.
87/B1 Djambala, Congo
82/G3 Djanet, Alg.
81/S16 Djelfa, Alg.
81/U17 Djemila (ruins), Alg.
84/D3 Djénné, Mali
85/E3 Djibo, Burk.
83/P5 Djibouti
83/P5 Djibouti (cap.), Djib.
32/B5 Djouce (mtn.), Ire.
85/F4 Djougou, Ben.
83/M7 Djugu, Zaire
30/G3 Dnepr (riv.), Eur.
54/E2 Dneprodzerzhinsk, Ukr.
54/E2 Dnepropetrovsk, Ukr.
54/E2 Dnepropetrovsk Obl., Ukr.
54/D3 Dnestr (riv.), Eur.
62/E5 Do (riv.), China
85/E3 Do (lake), Mali
82/J6 Doba, Chad
115/G4 Dobbs Ferry, NY,US
52/D4 Dobele, Lat.
38/G3 Döbeln, Ger.
73/H4 Doberai (pen.), Indo.
50/D3 Doboj, Bosn.
39/L2 Dobre Miasto, Pol.
51/H4 Dobruja (reg.), Bul., Rom.
54/D1 Dobrush, Bela.
53/N4 Dobryanka, Rus.
95/D1 Doce (riv.), Braz.
35/G1 Docking, Eng,UK
113/H4 Dock Junction, Ga,US
91/D1 Doctor Pedro P. Peña, Par.
50/F2 Doctor Petru Groza, Rom.
110/F1 Doda (lake), Qu,Can
32/B5 Dodder (riv.), Ire.
31/P7 Doddinghurst, Eng,UK
59/A3 Dodecanese (isls.), Turk.
109/G3 Dodge City, Ks,US
110/B3 Dodgeville, Wi,US
34/B6 Dodman (pt.), Wal,UK
87/G2 Dodoma, Tanz.
49/G3 Dodoni (ruins), Gre.
106/F3 Dodsland, Sk,Can
33/G4 Dodworth, Eng,UK
40/D4 Doesburg, Neth.
40/D5 Doetinchem, Neth.
68/E5 Dogai Coring (lake), China
59/D2 Doğankent (riv.), Turk.
64/C2 Dōgo (isl.), Japan
85/G3 Dogondoutchi, Niger
59/F2 Doğubayazıt, Turk.
59/E2 Doğukaradeniz (mts.), Turk.
60/F3 Doha (Ad Dawḩah) (cap.), Qatar
70/B3 Dohad, India
69/B2 Doi Inthanon Nat'l Park, Thai.
69/B2 Doi Khun Tan Nat'l Park, Thai.
46/B1 Doiras (res.)
94/B3 Dois Irmãos (mts.), Braz.
69/B2 Doi Suthep-Pui Nat'l Park, Thai.
40/D2 Dokkum, Neth.
40/C2 Dokkumer Ee (riv.), Neth.
111/F1 Dolbeau, Qu,Can
44/F3 Dôle, Fr.
34/C1 Dolgellau, Wal,UK
48/A3 Dolianova, It.
63/N2 Dolinsk, Rus.
51/F3 Dolj (co.), Rom.
111/N7 Dollard-des-Ormeaux, Qu,Can
41/E2 Dollard (Dollart) (bay), Ger., Neth.
38/D5 Doller (riv.), Fr.
50/C5 Dolmen (ruins), It.
45/J3 Dolomite Alps (Alpi Dolomitiche) (range), It.
97/F3 Dolores, Arg.
100/D4 Dolores, Guat.
47/E3 Dolores, Sp.
96/F2 Dolores, Uru.
108/E3 Dolores, Co,US
108/E3 Dolores (riv.), Co, Ut,US
100/A3 Dolores Hidalgo, Mex.
97/N7 Dolphin (cape), Falk.
88/A2 Dolphin (pt.), Namb.
102/E1 Dolphin and Union (str.), NW,Can
33/F4 Dolphinholme, Eng,UK
34/B5 Dolton, Eng,UK
116/Q16 Dolton, Il,US
69/D2 Do Luong, Viet.
73/J4 Dom (peak), Indo.
45/H3 Domat-Ems, Swi.
45/K2 Domažlice, Czh.
45/G2 Dombasle-sur-Meurthe, Fr.
55/G4 Dombay-Ul'gen, Gora (peak), Geo.
50/D2 Dombóvár, Hun.
44/E3 Domérat, Fr.
91/C1 Domeyko (mts.), Chile
101/J4 Dominica
101/H4 Dominican Republic
40/C6 Dommel (riv.), Belg., Neth.
69/D3 Dom Noi (res.), Thai.
53/X9 Domodedovo, Rus.
45/H3 Domodossola, It.
31/S9 Domont, Fr.
91/F3 Dom Pedrito, Braz.
94/A2 Dom Pedro, Braz.
73/E5 Dompu, Indo.
50/D2 Dömsöd, Hun.
48/A3 Domusnovas, It.
96/C3 Domuyo (vol.), Arg.
76/C5 Domvilk (peak), Austl.
50/B2 Domžale, Slov.
44/C3 Don (riv.), Fr.
101/N8 Don, Mex.
50/D2 Don (ridge), Rus.
55/G3 Don (riv.), Rus.
33/G3 Don (riv.), Eng,UK
36/D2 Don (riv.), Sc,UK
32/D2 Donaghadee, NI,UK
32/B2 Donaghmore, NI,UK
113/F4 Donaldsonville, La,US
46/B4 Doñana Nat'l Park, Sp.
44/E5 Dona, Pic de la (peak), Fr.
39/H4 Donau (Danube) (riv.), Aus., Ger.
46/C3 Don Benito, Sp.
77/G5 Doncaster, Austl.
33/G4 Doncaster, Eng,UK
87/B2 Dondo, Ang.
70/D6 Dondra Head (pt.), SrL.
36/A3 Donegal (bay), Ire.
32/A1 Donegal (co.), Ire.
54/F3 Donetsk, Ukr.
54/F3 Donetsk Obl., Ukr.
67/B3 Dong (riv.), China
71/J5 Dong (riv.), Viet.
85/H5 Donga (riv.), Camr., Nga.
71/H2 Dongchuan, China
71/J3 Dong Dang, Viet.
66/E5 Dongdongting Shan (mtn.), China
40/B5 Dongen, Neth.
67/B3 Dongguan, China
69/D2 Dong Ha, Viet.
69/D2 Donghen, Laos
69/D2 Dong Hoi, Viet.
66/E2 Dongliao (riv.), China
69/D4 Dong Noi (riv.), Viet.
66/D3 Dongping (lake), China
67/C3 Dongsha (isl.), China
66/E4 Dongtai, China
66/L9 Dongtaio (riv.), China
69/D2 Dong Tau, Viet.
67/B2 Dongting (lake), China
66/D3 Dongying, China
96/Q10 Donihue, Chile
33/H6 Donington, Eng,UK
102/C2 Donjek (riv.), Yk,Can
50/C3 Donji Vakuf, Bosn.
32/D1 Doon (riv.), Sc,UK
114/H2 Doonerak (mtn.), Ak,US
32/D1 Doon, Loch (lake), Sc,UK
110/C2 Door (pen.), Wi,US
40/C4 Doorn, Neth.
88/B3 Doorn (riv.), SAfr.
74/C4 Dora (lake), Austl.
47/F2 Dorada (coast), Sp.
61/K1 Do Rāh (pass), Afg.
68/B4 Dorāh Ān (pass), Pak.
45/G4 Dora Riparia (riv.), It.
111/H2 Dorchester, NB,Can
103/J2 Dorchester (cape), NW,Can
34/D5 Dorchester, Eng,UK
44/D4 Dordogne (riv.), Fr.
40/B5 Dordrecht, Neth.
106/G2 Dore (lake), Sk,Can
44/E4 Dore (mts.), Fr.
44/E4 Dore (riv.), Fr.
95/C1 Dores do Indaiá, Braz.
48/A2 Dorgali, It.
62/C2 Dörgön (lake), Mong.
85/E3 Dori, Burk.
111/M7 Dorion, Qu,Can
31/N8 Dorking, Eng,UK

135

Elwy – Foča

32/E5 Elwy (riv.), Wal,UK
35/G2 Ely, Eng,UK
107/L4 Ely, Mn,US
108/D3 Ely, Nv,US
35/G2 Ely, Isle of (reg.), Eng,UK
110/D3 Elyria, Oh,US
43/G3 Elzbach (riv.), Ger.
41/G4 Elze, Ger.
61/F1 Emāmshahr, Iran
93/H7 Emas Nat'l Park, Braz.
55/L2 Emba, Kaz.
55/K3 Emba (riv.), Kaz.
91/D1 Embarcación, Arg.
113/E2 Embarras (riv.), Il,US
92/D5 Embira (riv.), Braz.
95/C1 Emborcaçao (res.), Braz.
95/G8 Embu-Guaçu, Braz.
41/E2 Emden, Ger.
71/H2 Emei, China
77/G5 Emerald, Austl.
107/J3 Emerson, Mb,Can
116/K11 Emeryville, Ca,US
59/B2 Emet, Turk.
45/J4 Emilia-Romagna (reg.), It.
68/D2 Emin (riv.), China
109/K3 Eminence, Mo,US
51/H4 Emine, Nos (cape), Bul.
59/B2 Emirdağ, Turk.
59/C3 Emirgazi, Turk.
89/E2 Emlembe (peak), Swaz.
40/D3 Emlichheim, Ger.
37/E4 Emmaboda, Swe.
115/E5 Emmaus, Pa,US
40/C3 Emmeloord, Neth.
40/D3 Emmen, Neth.
45/G2 Emmendingen, Ger.
41/G5 Emmer (riv.), Ger.
41/E5 Emmerbach (riv.), Ger.
40/D5 Emmerich, Ger.
106/D5 Emmett, Id,US
35/G1 Emneth, Eng,UK
112/E3 Emory, Tx,US
101/P8 Emory (peak), Tx.,US
101/M8 Empalme, Mex.
89/E3 Empangeni, SAfr.
91/E2 Empedrado, Arg.
96/B2 Empedrado, Chile
109/H3 Emporia, Ks,US
110/E4 Emporia, Va,US
41/E4 Emsbüren, Ger.
41/E4 Emsdetten, Ger.
40/D2 Ems (Eems) (riv.), Ger., Neth.
41/E2 Ems-Jade (can.), Ger.
41/E3 Emsland (reg.), Ger.
41/E3 Emstek, Ger.
37/H4 Emumägi (hill), Est.
53/J1 Emur (riv.), China
65/E3 Ena, Japan
106/G5 Encampment, Wy,US
101/L7 Encantada (mt.), Mex.
101/M8 Encantado (mt.), Mex.
91/E2 Encarnación, Par.
101/P9 Encarnación de Díaz, Mex.
84/E5 Enchi, Gha.
106/C4 Encinitas, Ca,US
77/A2 Encounter (bay), Austl.
95/A4 Encruzilhada do Sul, Braz.
73/F5 Ende, Indo.
76/B1 Endeavour River Nat'l Park, Austl.
79/H5 Enderbury (atoll), Kiri.
106/D3 Enderby, BC,Can
98/D Enderby Land (reg.), Ant.
107/J4 Enderlin, ND,US
110/E3 Endicott, NY,US
92/D6 Ene (riv.), Peru
78/F3 Enewetak (atoll), Mrsh.
31/N7 Enfield, Eng,UK
31/N7 Enfield (bor.), Eng,UK
67/D4 Engaño (cape), Phil.
55/H2 Engel's, Rus.
43/G2 Engelskirchen, Ger.
40/D2 Engelsmanplaat (isl.), Neth.
95/K7 Engenheiro Paulo de Froutin, Braz.
41/F4 Enger, Ger.
72/E5 Enggano (isl.), Indo.
83/N4 Enghershatu (peak), Erit.
40/D2 Enghien, Belg.
36/D4 England, UK
110/E2 Englehart, On,Can
115/F5 Englewood, NJ,US
115/G5 Englewood, NJ,US
98/V English (coast), Ant.
107/K3 English (riv.), On,Can
44/B2 English (chan.), Eur.
70/E3 English Bāzār, India
115/F5 Englishtown, NJ,US
109/H3 Enid, Ok,US
40/C3 Enkhuizen, Neth.
37/F4 Enköping, Swe.
48/D4 Enna, It.
83/K4 Ennedi (plat.), Chad
41/E6 Ennepe (riv.), Ger.
41/E6 Ennepetal, Ger.
35/E4 Ennery, Fr.
41/F5 Enningerloh, Ger.
106/F4 Ennis, Mt,US
112/D3 Ennis, Tx,US
45/L3 Enns (riv.), Aus.
76/E6 Enoggera (res.), Austl.
113/H3 Enoree (riv.), SC,US
40/D4 Enschede, Neth.
41/E6 Ense, Ger.
101/L7 Ensenada, Mex.
66/B5 Enshi, China
83/M7 Entebbe, Ugan.
45/K2 Entenbühl (peak), Ger.
113/G4 Enterprise, Al,US
96/F2 Entre Ríos (prov.), Arg.
94/C3 Entre Rios, Braz.
46/A3 Entroncamento, Port.
85/G5 Enugu, Nga.
116/D3 Enumclaw, Wa,US
65/N10 Enushū (sea), Japan
42/A4 Envermeu, Fr.
45/H2 Enz (riv.), Ger.
65/F3 Enzan, Japan
43/F4 Enzbach (riv.), Ger.
40/C4 Epe, Neth.
42/C5 Épernay, Fr.
78/F6 Epi (isl.), Van.
49/H4 Epidaurus (ruins), Gre.
45/G2 Épinal, Fr.
31/S10 Épinay-sur-Orge, Fr.
31/S10 Épinay-sur-Seine, Fr.
49/G3 Epirus (reg.), Gre.
43/F5 Eppelborn, Ger.
76/H8 Epping, Austl.
31/P6 Epping, Eng,UK
76/B3 Epping Forest Nat'l Park, Austl.
31/N8 Epsom, Eng,UK
33/H4 Epworth, Eng,UK
82/G7 Equatorial Guinea
71/H2 Er (lake), China
48/E2 Eraclea (ruins), It.
48/C4 Eraclea Minoa (ruins), It.
31/S9 Éragny, Fr.
70/D6 Eravur, SrL.
69/B3 Erawan Nat'l Park, Thai.
45/H4 Erba, It.
59/D2 Erbaa, Turk.
38/D4 Erbeskopf (peak), Ger.
96/B3 Ercilla, Chile
59/C2 Erciş, Turk.
42/C3 Erclin (riv.), Fr.
50/D2 Érd, Hun.
63/K3 Erdao (riv.), China
51/H5 Erdek, Turk.
51/H5 Erdek (gulf), Turk.
59/C3 Erdemli, Turk.
62/G3 Erdene, Mong.
62/E2 Erdenedalay, Mong.
83/K4 Erdi-Ma (plat.), Chad
45/J2 Erding, Ger.
44/C3 Erdre (riv.), Fr.
98/M Erebus (vol.), Ant.
95/A3 Erechim, Braz.
62/G2 Ereen Davaanī (mts.), Mong.
51/K5 Ereğli, Turk.
59/C3 Ereğli, Turk.
68/D3 Erenhaberga (mts.), China
62/G3 Erenhot, China
51/K5 Erenler, Turk.
93/G4 Erepecu (lake), Braz.
42/C3 Eresma (riv.), Sp.
82/E1 Erfoud, Mor.
43/F1 Erft (riv.), Ger.
43/F2 Erftstadt, Ger.
38/F3 Erfurt, Ger.
59/D2 Ergani, Turk.
82/H3 'Erg Chech (des.), Afr.
82/H3 'Erg du Ténéré (des.), Niger
51/H5 Ergene Nehri (riv.), Turk.
82/D2 'Erg Iguidi (des.), Afr.
83/J5 Erguig (riv.), Chad
63/H1 Ergun (riv.), China, Rus.
106/D3 Erickson, BC,Can
107/J3 Erickson, Mb,Can
110/D3 Erie (lake), Can., US
111/S9 Erie (can.), NY,US
110/D3 Erie, Pa,US
83/Q5 Erigabo, Som.
107/J3 Eriksdale, Mb,Can
78/F4 Erikub (atoll), Mrsh.
49/G4 Erímanthos (peak), Gre.
63/N3 Erimo-misaki (cape), Japan
83/N4 Eritrea
40/D6 Erkelenz, Ger.
43/G2 Erkner, Ger.
40/D6 Erkrath, Ger.
45/J2 Erlangen, Ger.
66/F2 Erlongshan (res.), China
34/C6 Erme (riv.), Eng,UK
40/C4 Ermelo, Neth.
89/E2 Ermelo, SAfr.
59/C3 Ermenek, Turk.
31/T9 Ermenonville, Fr.
31/S10 Ermont, Fr.
49/J4 Ermoúpolis, Gre.
40/C4 Erndtebrück, Ger.
44/C2 Ernée (riv.), Fr.
70/C5 Erode, India
42/D3 Erquelinnes, Belg.
82/E1 Er Rachidīa, Mor.
81/M13 Er Rif (mts.), Mor.
34/B2 Errigal (mtn.), Ire.
78/F6 Erromango (isl.), Van.
41/H4 Erse (riv.), Ger.
62/B2 Ertix (riv.), China
95/B3 Erval d'Oeste, Braz.
110/D4 Erwin, Tn,US
41/F5 Erwitte, Ger.
49/F2 Erzen (riv.), Alb.
45/K1 Erzgebirge (Krušné Hory) (mts.), Czh., Ger.
59/D2 Erzincan, Turk.
59/D2 Erzurum, Turk.
78/D5 Esa'ala, PNG
83/L7 Esambo, Zaire
63/N3 Esashi, Japan
37/D5 Esbjerg, Den.
31/U10 Esbly, Fr.
37/H3 Esbo (Espoo), Fin.
94/D3 Escada, Braz.
108/E3 Escalante (riv.), Ut,US
113/G4 Escambia (riv.), Fl,US
110/C2 Escanaba, Mi,US
42/C3 Escaudain, Fr.
42/C3 Escaut (riv.), Belg., Fr.
43/E6 Esch (riv.), Fr.
42/B5 Esches (riv.), Fr.
43/E5 Esch-sur-Alzette, Lux.
41/H6 Eschwege, Ger.
43/F2 Eschweiler, Ger.
108/C4 Escondido, Ca,US
101/N9 Escuinapa de Hidalgo, Mex.
100/C5 Escuintla, Guat.
59/N7 Esdraelon, Plain of (plain), Isr.
82/H7 Eséka, Camr.
41/E1 Esens, Ger.
47/F1 Esera (riv.), Sp.
60/F2 Eşfahān, Iran
34/C1 Esgair Ddu (mtn.), Wal,UK
33/G2 Esh, Eng,UK
31/M7 Esher, Eng,UK
87/D2 Eshimba, Zaire
33/G2 Esh Winning, Eng,UK
33/E2 Esk (riv.), Eng,UK
33/H3 Esk (riv.), Eng,UK
33/E1 Eskdale (val.), Sc,UK
59/C2 Eskil, Turk.
37/F4 Eskilstuna, Swe.
59/D2 Eskimalatya, Turk.
114/M2 Eskimo (lakes), NW,Can
59/B2 Eskişehir, Turk.
48/C1 Esla (riv.), Sp.
60/E2 Eslāmābād, Iran
41/F6 Eslohe, Ger.
59/B2 Eşme, Turk.
98/E3 Esmeraldas, Ecu.
43/E2 Esneux, Belg.
110/D2 Espanola, On,Can
109/F4 Española, NM,US
47/K6 Esparreguera, Sp.
47/F4 Espelkamp, Ger.
94/D2 Esperança, Braz.
74/C6 Esperance, Austl.
94/B1 Esperantina, Braz.
94/A2 Esperantinópolis, Braz.
106/B3 Esperanza (inlet), BC,Can
46/A3 Espichel (cape), Port.
92/D3 Espinal, Col.
94/B5 Espinhaço (mts.), Braz.
46/A2 Espinho, Port.
97/F2 Espinillo (pt.), Uru.
94/B4 Espinosa, Braz.
95/D1 Espírito Santo (state), Braz.
95/G7 Espírito Santo do Pinhal, Braz.
78/F6 Espíritu Santo (isl.), Van.
94/C3 Esplanada, Braz.
47/L7 Esplugues, Sp.
37/H3 Espoo (Esbo), Fin.
96/C4 Esquel, Arg.
91/E3 Esquina, Arg.
82/D1 Essaouira, Mor.
41/G5 Esse (riv.), Ger.
40/B6 Essen, Belg.
41/E6 Essen, Ger.
77/F5 Essendon, Austl.
92/G2 Essequibo (riv.), Guy.
116/G7 Essex, On,Can
31/P6 Essex (co.), Eng,UK
115/K7 Essex, Md,US
45/H2 Esslingen, Ger.
31/S11 Essonne (dept.), Fr.
31/T11 Essonne (riv.), Fr.
97/E2 Estados (isl.), Arg.
60/F3 Eşţahbān, Iran
94/C3 Estância, Braz.
97/E8 Estancia La Carmen, Arg.
97/E8 Estancia La Sera, Arg.
47/F1 Estats, Pico de (peak), Sp.
89/E3 Estcourt, SAfr.
100/E3 Este (pt.), Cuba
41/G2 Este (riv.), Ger.
45/J4 Este, It.
50/B4 Esteio, Braz.
100/D5 Estelí, Nic.
46/D1 Estella, Sp.
115/C3 Estelle (mtn.), Ca,US
46/C4 Estepa, Sp.
46/C4 Estepona, Sp.
45/M3 Esterhazy, Sk,Can
87/G7 Esterias (cape), Gabon
45/G5 Estéron (riv.), Fr.
107/H3 Estevan, Sk,Can
40/C4 Estinnes-Au-Mont, Belg.
33/G2 Eston, Eng,UK
52/E4 Estonia
46/A3 Estoril, Port.
46/B2 Estrela, Serra da (mtn.), Port.
46/A3 Estrela, Serra da (range), Port.
94/B3 Estrelto (mts.), Braz.
46/B3 Estremadura (aut. comm.), Sp.
46/B3 Estremoz, Port.
93/J5 Estrondo (mts.), Braz.
50/D2 Esztergom, Hun.
78/E4 Étal (atoll), Micr.
42/A2 Étaples, Fr.
62/C2 Etāwah, India
107/H3 Ethelbert, Mb,Can
83/N6 Ethiopia
83/N6 Ethiopian (plat.), Eth.
65/M9 Eti (riv.), Japan
31/T11 Étiolles, Fr.
48/D4 Etna, Monte (Mount Etna) (vol.), It.
111/Q8 Etobicoke, On,Can
114/E3 Etolin (str.), Ak,US
63/P3 Etorofu (isl.), Rus.
87/C4 Etosha Nat'l Park, Namb.
87/C4 Etosha Pan (salt pan), Namb.
51/G4 Etropole, Bul.
65/F2 Etsu-Joshin Kogen Nat'l Park, Japan
59/M8 Et Taiyiba, Isr.
43/F4 Ettelbruck, Lux.
40/B5 Etten-Leur, Neth.
42/D2 Etterbeek, Belg.
59/M8 Et Tīra, Isr.
45/H2 Ettlingen, Ger.
33/E1 Ettrick Pen (mtn.), Sc,UK
42/A3 Eu, Fr.
79/H7 Eua (isl.), Tonga
76/B2 Eubenangee Swamp Nat'l Park, Austl.
110/D3 Euclid, Oh,US
94/C3 Euclides da Cunha, Braz.
75/H7 Eucumbene (lake), Austl.
113/F3 Eudora, Ar,US
113/G4 Eufaula, Al,US
109/J4 Eufaula, Ok,US
109/H4 Eufaula (lake), Ok,US
106/C4 Eugene, Or,US
101/L8 Eugenia (pt.), Mex.
83/B1 Eume (lake), Sp.
76/C3 Eungella Nat'l Park, Austl.
112/E4 Eunice, La,US
109/G4 Eunice, NM,US
43/F2 Eupen, Belg.
58/D6 Euphrates (riv.), Asia
44/D2 Eure (riv.), Fr.
103/S6 Eureka, NW,Can
103/S7 Eureka (sound), NW,Can
108/A2 Eureka, Ca,US
106/E3 Eureka, Mt,US
108/D3 Eureka, Nv,US
107/J4 Eureka, SD,US
42/B6 Eurodisney, Fr.
81/M12 Europa (pt.), Gib.
87/G5 Europa (isl.), Reun.
30/* Europe
40/B5 Europoort, Neth.
43/F2 Euskirchen, Ger.
113/H4 Eustis, Fl,US
38/F1 Eutin, Ger.
87/F3 Eutini, Malw.
106/B2 Eutsuk (lake), BC,Can
33/F4 Euxton, Eng,UK
110/E1 Évain, Qu,Can
103/H2 Evans (str.), NW,Can
110/E1 Evans (lake), Qu,Can
109/F2 Evans, Co,US
109/F3 Evans (mtn.), Co,US
116/Q15 Evanston, Il,US
106/F5 Evanston, Wy,US
110/C4 Evansville, In,US
109/F2 Evansville, Wy,US
110/C3 Evart, Mi,US
88/D2 Evaton, SAfr.
60/F3 Evaz, Iran
107/K4 Eveleth, Mn,US
57/L3 Evenki Aut. Okr., Rus.
35/E3 Evenlode (riv.), Eng,UK
77/D3 Everard (cape), Austl.
74/F6 Everard (lake), Austl.
34/D4 Evercreech, Eng,UK
31/P6 Everett, Wa,US
42/C1 Evergem, Belg.
113/H5 Everglades Nat'l Park, Fl,US
113/G4 Evergreen, Al,US
116/D6 Evergreen Park, Il,US
35/F3 Eversholt, Eng,UK
41/E5 Everswinkel, Ger.
35/E2 Evesham, Eng,UK
49/G3 Évinos (riv.), Gre.
46/B3 Évora, Port.
46/A3 Évora (dist.), Port.
42/A5 Évreux, Fr.
44/C2 Évron, Fr.
49/H4 Evrótas (riv.), Gre.
31/T11 Évry, Fr.
49/H3 Évvoia (gulf), Gre.
49/H3 Évvoia (isl.), Gre.
104/V13 Ewa, Hi,US
104/V13 Ewa Beach, Hi,US
31/N7 Ewell, Eng,UK
115/F5 Ewing, NJ,US
109/J3 Excelsior Springs, Mo,US
34/C5 Exe (riv.), Eng,UK
34/C5 Exeter, Eng,UK
111/G3 Exeter, NH,US
34/C5 Exminster, Eng,UK
34/C4 Exmoor Nat'l Park, Eng,UK
110/F4 Exmore, Va,US
74/A4 Exmouth (gulf), Austl.
97/J7 Exmouth (pen.), Chile
34/C5 Exmouth, Eng,UK
103/L3 Exploits (riv.), Nf,Can
95/G7 Extrema, Braz.
94/C2 Exu, Braz.
101/F3 Exuma (sound), Bahm.
33/G5 Eyam, Eng,UK
87/F1 Eyasi (lake), Tanz.
35/H2 Eye, Eng,UK
35/F1 Eye (brook), Eng,UK
36/D3 Eyemouth, Sc,UK
59/N9 Eyn Hemed Nat'l Park, Isr.
31/P7 Eynsford, Eng,UK
74/F6 Eyre (pen.), Austl.
74/F5 Eyre North (lake), Austl.
74/F5 Eyre South (lake), Austl.
31/T9 Ézanville, Fr.
49/K3 Ezine, Turk.
82/H3 Ezzane (well), Alg.

F

79/L6 Faaa, FrPol.
112/B4 Fabens, Tx,US
48/B1 Fabero, Sp.
38/F1 Fåborg, Den.
45/K5 Fabriano, It.
92/D3 Facatativá, Col.
42/C2 Faches-Thumesnil, Fr.
83/K4 Fada, Chad
85/F3 Fada-N'Gourma, Burk.
45/J4 Faenza, It.
83/J6 Fafa (riv.), CAfr.
46/A2 Fafe, Port.
83/P6 Fafen Shet' (riv.), Eth.
51/G3 Făgăraş, Rom.
37/E4 Fagersta, Swe.
97/L8 Fagnano (lake), Arg.
84/D2 Faguibine (lake), Mali
47/S12 Faial (isl.), Azor.,Port.
33/F4 Failsworth, Eng,UK
114/J3 Fairbanks, Ak,US
116/J11 Fairfax, Ca,US
115/J8 Fairfax, Va,US
76/G8 Fairfield, Austl.
116/K10 Fairfield, Ca,US
115/G4 Fairfield, Ct,US
106/F4 Fairfield, Mt,US
110/C4 Fairfield, Oh,US
112/D4 Fairfield, Tx,US
35/E3 Fairford, Eng,UK
111/F3 Fair Haven, Vt,US
32/B1 Fair Head (pt.), NI,UK
115/K7 Fairland, Md,US
115/F5 Fair Lawn, NJ,US
115/F5 Fairless Hills, Pa,US
35/G5 Fairlight, Eng,UK
107/K5 Fairmont, Mn,US
110/D4 Fairmont, WV,US
116/M9 Fair Oaks, Ca,US
112/B2 Fairplay, Co,US
106/D1 Fairview, Ab,Can
109/H3 Fairview, Ok,US
114/L4 Fairweather (cape), Ak,US
114/L4 Fairweather (mtn.), BC,Can, Ak,US
116/C3 Fairwood-Cascade, Wa,US
61/K2 Faisalabad, Pak.
49/J5 Faistós (ruins), Gre.
70/D2 Faizābād, India
79/M6 Fakahina (isl.), FrPol.
79/H5 Fakaofo (atoll), Tok.
79/L6 Fakarava (atoll), FrPol.
35/G1 Fakenham, Eng,UK
82/G7 Fako (peak), Camr.
38/G1 Fakse Bugt (bay), Den.
34/B6 Fal (riv.), Eng,UK
81/Q16 Falcon (cape), Alg.
112/D5 Falcon (res.), Mex., US
45/K5 Falconara Marittima, It.
84/C3 Falémé (riv.), Mali, Sen.
79/S9 Faleolo, WSam.
112/D5 Falfurrias, Tx,US
106/D2 Falher, Ab,Can
37/E4 Falkenberg, Swe.
35/H2 Falkenham, Eng,UK
97/M8 Falkland Islands (Islas Malvinas) (dpcy.), UK
37/E4 Falköping, Swe.
41/G3 Fallingbostel, Ger.
108/C3 Fallon, Nv,US
111/G3 Fall River, Ma,US
115/J8 Falls Church, Va,US
109/J2 Falls City, Ne,US
34/A6 Falmouth, Eng,UK
34/A6 Falmouth (bay), Eng,UK
101/G4 Falso (cape), DRep.
97/K8 Falso Cabo de Hornos (cape), Chile
38/G1 Falster (isl.), Den.
51/H2 Fălticeni, Rom.
37/E3 Falun, Swe.
59/J4 Famagusta, Cyp.
43/F5 Fameck, Fr.
43/E3 Famenne (reg.), Belg.
66/D5 Fanchang, China
81/G7 Fandriana, Madg.
32/B4 Fane (riv.), Ire.
79/L6 Fangatau (isl.), FrPol.
79/L7 Fangataufa (isl.), FrPol.
67/C2 Fangcun, China
67/C2 Fangdao, China
67/D3 Fangliao, Tai.
67/A2 Fanjing (peak), China
79/K4 Fanning (Tabuaeran) (atoll), Kiri.
38/E1 Fanø (isl.), Den.
45/K5 Fano, It.
69/C1 Fan Si Pan (peak), Viet.
59/H6 Fāqūs, Egypt
83/L7 Faradje, Zaire
81/G7 Faradofay, Madg.
81/G7 Farafangana, Madg.
86/A3 Farāfirah, Wāḩāt al (oasis), Egypt
61/H2 Farāh, Afg.
61/H2 Farāh (riv.), Afg.
108/B3 Farallon (isls.), Ca,US
78/D3 Farallon de Medinilla (isl.), NMar.
78/D2 Farallon de Pajaros (isl.), NMar.
92/C3 Farallones de Cali Nat'l Park, Col.
84/C4 Faranah (comm.), Gui.
89/H8 Faraony (riv.), Madg.
78/D4 Faraulep (atoll), Micr.
42/D3 Farciennes, Belg.
35/E5 Fareham, Eng,UK
75/R11 Farewell (cape), NZ
107/J4 Fargo, ND,US
107/K4 Faribault, Mn,US
70/C2 Farīdābād, India
70/E3 Farīdpur, Bang.
35/E3 Faringdon, Eng,UK
59/H6 Fāriskūr, Egypt
111/G2 Farmington, Me,US
116/F7 Farmington, Mi,US
109/K3 Farmington, Mo,US
108/E3 Farmington, NM,US
116/F7 Farmington Hills, Mi,US
110/E4 Farmville, Va,US
35/F4 Farnborough, Eng,UK
35/F4 Farnham, Eng,UK
31/P7 Farningham, Eng,UK
33/F4 Farnworth, Eng,UK
102/C2 Faro, Yk,Can
46/B4 Faro, Port.
46/A4 Faro (dist.), Port.
30/D2 Faroe (isls.), Den.
37/F4 Fårön (isl.), Swe.
82/H6 Faro Nat'l Park, Camr.
74/A4 Farquhar (cape), Austl.
81/H5 Farquhar (isls.), Sey.
95/B4 Farroupilha, Braz.
70/C2 Farrukhābād, India
49/H3 Fársala, Gre.
106/F5 Farson, Wy,US
37/C4 Farsund, Nor.
60/F5 Fartak, Ra's (pt.), Yem.
99/N4 Farvel (cape), Grld.
98/T Farwell (isl.), Ant.
60/F3 Fasā, Iran
48/E2 Fasano, It.
41/H3 Fassberg, Ger.
54/D2 Fastov, Ukr.
73/H4 Fatagar Tuting (cape), Indo.
79/J6 Fataka (isl.), Sol.
70/B2 Fatehpur, India
70/D2 Fatehpur, India
84/A3 Fatick (reg.), Sen.
46/A3 Fátima, Port.
60/C4 Fāţimah (dry riv.), SAfr.
59/D2 Fatsa, Turk.
79/M6 Fatu Hiva (isl.), FrPol.
84/C4 Faucilles (mts.), Fr.
32/A2 Faughan (riv.), NI,UK
107/J4 Faulkton, SD,US
37/E2 Fauske, Nor.
48/C4 Favara, It.
35/G4 Faversham, Eng,UK
35/E5 Fawley, Eng,UK
102/H3 Fawn (riv.), On,Can
37/M7 Faxaflói (bay), Ice.
95/B2 Faxinal, Braz.
83/J4 Faya-Largeau, Chad
113/G3 Fayette, Al,US
109/J3 Fayette, Mo,US
113/F4 Fayette, Ms,US
112/E2 Fayetteville, Ar,US
113/G3 Fayetteville, Ga,US
113/J3 Fayetteville, NC,US
113/G3 Fayetteville, Tn,US
85/F4 Fazao (mts.), Gha., Togo
85/F4 Fazao Nat'l Park, Togo
36/A4 Feale (riv.), Ire.
113/J3 Fear (cape), NC,US
108/B3 Feather (riv.), Ca,US
33/G4 Featherstone, Eng,UK
42/A2 Fécamp, Fr.
116/C3 Federal Way, Wa,US
32/A2 Feeny, NI,UK
50/F2 Fehérgyarmat, Hun.
38/F1 Fehmarn (isl.), Ger.
38/F1 Fehmarn Belt (str.), Ger., Den.
66/D4 Fei (riv.), China
95/D2 Feia (lake), Braz.
42/C3 Feignies, Fr.
66/D4 Fei Huang (riv.), China
94/C3 Feira de Santana, Braz.
45/L3 Feistritz (riv.), Aus.
50/D2 Fejér (co.), Hun.
47/P3 Felanitx, Sp.
37/H2 Feldberg (peak), Ger.
45/K3 Feldkirch, Aus.
45/L3 Feldkirchen in Kärnten, Aus.
35/H3 Felixstowe, Eng,UK
101/N7 Félix U. Gómez, Mex.
33/G2 Felling, Eng,UK
41/G6 Felsberg, Ger.
31/M7 Feltham, Eng,UK
35/G2 Feltwell, Eng,UK
66/C4 Fen (riv.), China
45/A1 Fene, Sp.
59/C3 Fener (pt.), Turk.
43/G6 Fénétrange, Fr.
49/J3 Fengári (peak), Gre.
63/J3 Fengcheng, China
66/D5 Fengle (riv.), China
66/B5 Fengnan, China
66/D3 Fengrun, China
63/J1 Fengshui (peak), China
66/C2 Fengzhen, China
114/C5 Fenimore (passg.), Ak,US
35/G2 Fens, The (reg.), Eng,UK
116/E6 Fenton, Mi,US
54/E3 Feodosiya, Ukr.
81/V17 Fer, Cap de (cape), Alg.
61/G2 Ferdows, Iran
48/C2 Ferentino, It.
48/C1 Ferento (ruins), It.
68/B3 Fergana, Uzb.
107/J4 Fergus Falls, Mn,US
102/F2 Ferguson (lake), NW,Can
84/D4 Ferkéssédougou, IvC.
45/L3 Ferlach, Aus.
82/C4 Ferlo (reg.), Sen.
84/B3 Ferlo, Vallée du (wadi), Sen.
32/A3 Fermanagh (dist.), NI,UK
115/B3 Fermin (pt.), Ca,US
48/C1 Fermo, It.
113/H4 Fernandina Beach, Fl,US
93/M4 Fernando de Noronha (isl.), Braz.
95/B2 Fernandópolis, Braz.
46/C4 Fernán-Núñez, Sp.
115/K7 Ferndale, Md,US
116/F7 Ferndale, Mi,US
35/E5 Ferndown, Eng,UK
106/E3 Fernie, BC,Can
77/G5 Ferntree Gully Nat'l Park, Austl.
48/E2 Ferrandina, It.
45/J4 Ferrara, It.
46/A3 Ferreira do Alentejo, Port.
44/C4 Ferret (cape), Fr.
112/F4 Ferriday, La,US
113/F4 Ferriday, La,US
33/G2 Ferryhill, Eng,UK
34/B3 Ferryside, Wal,UK
45/M3 Fertő (Neusiedler See) (lake), Aus., Hun.
40/C2 Ferwerd, Neth.
81/M13 Fès, Mor.
87/C2 Feshi, Zaire
113/F2 Festus, Mo,US
31/M8 Fetcham, Eng,UK
51/H3 Feteşti, Rom.
31/R10 Feucherolles, Fr.
45/J2 Feucht, Ger.
103/J3 Feuilles (lake), Qu,Can
103/J3 Feuilles (riv.), Qu,Can
44/F4 Feurs, Fr.
61/K1 Feyzābād, Afg.
82/H2 Fezzan (reg.), Libya
32/E6 Ffestiniog, Wal,UK
81/G7 Fianarantsoa, Madg.
89/H8 Fianarantsoa (prov.), Madg.
82/J6 Fianga, Chad
88/D3 Ficksburg, SAfr.
45/J4 Fidenza, It.
84/C4 Fié (riv.), Gui., Mali
51/G3 Fieni, Rom.
49/F2 Fier, Alb.
49/G1 Fierzë (lake), Alb.
36/D2 Fife Ness (pt.), Sc,UK
81/Q16 Figalo (cape), Alg.
44/E4 Figeac, Fr.
46/A2 Figueira da Foz, Port.
47/G1 Figueres, Sp.
82/E1 Figuig, Mor.
89/G8 Fiherenana (riv.), Madg.
78/G6 Fiji
98/X Filchner Ice Shelf, Ant.
33/H3 Filey, Eng,UK
33/H3 Filey (bay), Eng,UK
51/F3 Filiaşi, Rom.
48/D3 Filicudi (isl.), It.
85/F3 Filingué, Niger
49/J2 Filippoi (ruins), Gre.
37/E4 Filipstad, Swe.
115/B2 Fillmore, Ca,US
108/D3 Fillmore, Ut,US
79/S9 Filo (peak), WSam.
34/D3 Filton, Eng,UK
98/Z Fimbul Ice Shelf, Ant.
82/J8 Fimi (riv.), Zaire
45/H4 Finale Ligure, It.
84/C3 Fina Rsv., Mali
31/N7 Finchley, Eng,UK
36/D2 Findhorn (riv.), Sc,UK
110/D3 Findlay, Oh,US
77/D4 Fingal, Austl.
103/K2 Finger (lake), On,Can
110/E3 Finger (lakes), NY,US
44/E4 Finiels, Sommet de (peak), Fr.
59/B3 Finike, Turk.
46/A1 Finisterre (cape), Sp.
74/F5 Finke (riv.), Austl.
45/K3 Finkenstein, Aus.
37/H2 Finland
52/E4 Finland (gulf), Eur.
102/D3 Finlay (riv.), BC,Can
112/B4 Finlay (mts.), Tx,US
41/E6 Finnentrop, Ger.
116/C2 Finn Hill-Inglewood, Wa,US
76/B1 Finnigan (peak), Austl.
37/G1 Finnmark (co.), Nor.
37/E4 Finspång, Swe.
32/A3 Fintona, NI,UK
48/B1 Fiora (riv.), It.
45/J4 Fiorenzuola d'Arda, It.
116/C2 Fircrest-Silver Lake, Wa,US
45/J5 Firenze (Florence), It.
96/E2 Firmat, Arg.
44/F4 Firminy, Fr.
70/C2 Firozābād, India
61/K2 Firozpur, India
60/F3 Fīrūzābād, Iran
88/B3 Fischbacher (mts.), Aus.
88/B2 Fish (riv.), Namb.
88/C3 Fish (riv.), SAfr.
33/G2 Fishburn, Eng,UK
98/E Fisher (glac.), Ant.
107/J3 Fisher (bay), Mb,Can
103/H2 Fisher (str.), NW,Can
107/J3 Fisher Branch, Mb,Can
76/F6 Fisherman (isl.), Austl.
34/B3 Fishguard, Wal,UK
54/F4 Fisht, Gora (peak), Rus.
33/J6 Fishtoft, Eng,UK
79/S8 Fito (peak), WSam.
114/L2 Fitton (mtn.), Yk,Can
113/H4 Fitzgerald, Ga,US
106/B3 Fitz Hugo (sound), BC,Can
97/J7 Fitzroy (peak), Arg.
76/C3 Fitzroy (riv.), Austl.
103/R7 Fitzwilliam (str.), NW,Can
48/C2 Fiumicino, It.
32/A3 Fivemiletown, NI,UK
37/C3 Fjell, Nor.
35/F3 Flackwell Heath, Eng,UK
109/G3 Flagler, Co,US
113/H4 Flagler Beach, Fl,US
108/E4 Flagstaff, Az,US
110/B2 Flambeau (riv.), Wi,US
111/Q9 Flamborough, On,Can
33/H3 Flamborough, Eng,UK
33/H3 Flamborough Head (pt.), Eng,UK
38/G2 Fläming (hills), Ger.
106/F5 Flaming Gorge Nat'l Rec. Area, Ut, Wy,US
107/K2 Flanagan (riv.), On,Can
42/B2 Flanders (reg.), Belg., Fr.
107/J4 Flandreau, SD,US
114/L3 Flat Creek, Yk,Can
106/E4 Flathead (lake), Mt,US
106/E4 Flathead (riv.), Mt,US
34/C4 Flat Holm (isl.), Eng,UK
109/K3 Flat River, Mo,US
116/F7 Flat Rock, Mi,US
76/B1 Flattery (cape), Austl.
106/B3 Flattery (cape), Wa,US
35/F4 Fleet, Eng,UK
33/E4 Fleetwood, Eng,UK
37/C4 Flekkefjord, Nor.
115/F5 Flemington, NJ,US
38/E1 Flensburg, Ger.
43/E2 Fleron, Belg.
44/C2 Flers, Fr.
42/D3 Fleurus, Belg.
44/D3 Fleury-les-Aubrais, Fr.
40/C4 Flevoland (prov.), Neth.
42/B2 Flimby, Eng,UK
74/A6 Flinders (bay), Austl.
77/D3 Flinders (isl.), Austl.
74/F6 Flinders (ranges), Austl.
75/C2 Flinders (reefs), Austl.
76/A2 Flinders (riv.), Austl.
107/L3 Flindt (riv.), On,Can
107/H2 Flin Flon, Mb,Can
102/J3 Flint (lake), NW,Can
79/K6 Flint (isl.), Kiri.
33/E5 Flint, Wal,UK
113/G4 Flint (riv.), Ga,US
109/H3 Flint (hills), Ks,US
116/F5 Flint, Mi,US
35/F3 Flitwick, Eng,UK
41/F1 Flögelner See (lake), Ger.
39/G3 Flöha (riv.), Ger.
110/B4 Flora, Il,US
115/G5 Floral Park, NY,US
43/F5 Florange, Fr.
42/D3 Floreffe, Belg.
113/G3 Florence, Al,US
108/E4 Florence, Az,US
109/F3 Florence, Co,US
113/J3 Florence, SC,US
45/J5 Florence (Firenze), It.
92/C3 Florencia, Col.
42/D3 Florennes, Belg.
96/E3 Flores (riv.), Arg.
106/B3 Flores (isl.), BC,Can
100/D4 Flores, Guat.
73/F5 Flores (isl.), Indo.
73/E5 Flores (sea), Indo.
47/R12 Flores (isl.), Azor.,Port.
97/F2 Flores (dept.), Uru.
94/C3 Floresta, Braz.
112/D4 Floresville, Tx,US
115/F5 Florham Park, NJ,US
94/B2 Floriano, Braz.
95/B3 Florianópolis, Braz.
101/F3 Florida, Cuba
101/E3 Florida (str.), NAm.
97/F2 Florida, Uru.
97/F2 Florida (dept.), Uru.
113/H4 Florida (state), US
113/H5 Florida (bay), Fl,US
113/H5 Florida Keys (isls.), Fl,US
48/C4 Floridia, It.
116/M10 Florin, Ca,US
49/G2 Flórina, Gre.
113/K3 Florissant, Mo,US
37/C3 Florø, Nor.
112/C3 Floydada, Tx,US
40/C3 Fluessen (lake), Neth.
48/A3 Flumendosa (riv.), It.
110/D3 Flushing, Mi,US
40/A6 Flushing (Vlissingen), Neth.
78/D5 Fly (riv.), PNG
98/T Flying Fish (cape), Ant.
37/P6 Fnjóská (riv.), Ice.
107/H3 Foam Lake, Sk,Can
50/D4 Foča, Bosn.

136
Focşa – Geret

51/H3 Focşani, Rom.
48/D2 Foggia, It.
80/J10 Fogo (isl.), CpV.
45/L3 Fohnsdorf, Aus.
38/E1 Föhr (isl.), Ger.
44/D5 Foix, Fr.
37/C3 Folarskardnuten (peak), Nor.
37/D2 Folda (fjord), Nor.
49/J4 Folégandros (isl.), Gre.
103/J2 Foley (isl.), NW,Can
48/C1 Foligno, It.
35/H4 Folkestone, Eng,UK
113/H4 Folkston, Ga,US
48/B1 Follonica (gulf), It.
102/F3 Fond du Lac (riv.), Sk,Can
110/B3 Fond du Lac, Wi,US
48/C2 Fondi, It.
37/D3 Fongen (peak), Nor.
46/B1 Fonsagrada, Sp.
100/D5 Fonseca (gulf), NAm.
44/F4 Fontaine, Fr.
44/E2 Fontainebleau, Fr.
42/D3 Fontaine-L'Evêque, Belg.
115/C2 Fontana, Ca,US
44/C3 Fontenay-le-Comte, Fr.
31/S10 Fontenay-le-Fleury, Fr.
31/S11 Fontenay-les-Briis, Fr.
31/T10 Fontenay-sous-Bois, Fr.
31/U10 Fontenay-Trésigny, Fr.
106/F5 Fontenelle (res.), Wy,US
45/G4 Font Sancte, Pic de la (peak), Fr.
37/P6 Fontur (pt.), Ice.
77/F5 Footscray, Austl.
114/H3 Foraker (mtn.), Ak,US
43/F5 Forbach, Fr.
77/D2 Forbes, Austl.
46/A1 Forcarey, Sp.
45/J2 Forchheim, Ger.
116/E7 Ford (lake), Mi,US
35/E5 Fordingbridge, Eng,UK
112/E3 Fordyce, Ar,US
34/C4 Foreland (pt.), Eng,UK
35/E5 Foreland, The (pt.), Eng,UK
106/F3 Foremost, Ab,Can
35/H4 Foreness (pt.), Eng,UK
113/F3 Forest, Ms,US
77/D4 Forestier (cape), Austl.
111/G1 Forestville, Qu,Can
115/K8 Forestville, Md,US
44/E4 Forez (mts.), Fr.
36/D2 Forfar, Sc,UK
31/S11 Forges-les-Bains, Fr.
111/H1 Forillon Nat'l Park, Qu,Can
32/B3 Forkill, NI,UK
45/K4 Forlì, It.
33/E4 Formby, Eng,UK
33/E4 Formby (pt.), Eng,UK
47/F3 Formentera (isl.), Sp.
47/G3 Formentor, Cabo de (cape), Sp.
48/C2 Formia, It.
95/C2 Formiga, Braz.
91/E2 Formosa, Arg.
94/A4 Formosa, Braz.
93/G6 Formosa (mts.), Braz.
84/A4 Formosa (isl.), GBis.
88/C4 Formosa (peak), SAfr.
94/A4 Formoso (riv.), Braz.
45/J5 Fornacelle, It.
36/D2 Forres, Sc,UK
113/F3 Forrest City, Ar,US
37/G3 Forssa, Fin.
76/A3 Forsyth (range), Austl.
113/H3 Forsyth, Ga,US
106/G4 Forsyth, Mt,US
61/K3 Fort Abbās, Pak.
94/C1 Fortaleza, Braz.
97/G2 Fortaleza Santa Teresa, Uru.
88/D4 Fort Beaufort, SAfr.
106/F4 Fort Benton, Mt,US
108/B3 Fort Bragg, Ca,US
109/H4 Fort Cobb (res.), Ok,US
109/F2 Fort Collins, Co,US
112/C4 Fort Davis, Tx,US
43/E5 Fort de Douaumont, Fr.
101/J5 Fort-de-France (cap.), Mart.
43/E5 Fort de Vaux, Fr.
107/K5 Fort Dodge, Ia,US
87/D3 Forte Cameia, Ang.
111/S10 Fort Erie, On,Can
74/B4 Fortescue (riv.), Austl.
110/A1 Fort Frances, On,Can
113/F4 Fort Gaines, Al,US
111/R9 Fort George, On,Can
103/J3 Fort-George (Chisasibi), Qu,Can
109/J4 Fort Gibson, Ok,US
112/E2 Fort Gibson (lake), Ok,US
82/C3 Fort-Gouraud, Mrta.
36/C2 Forth (riv.), Sc,UK
36/D2 Forth, Firth of (inlet), Sc,UK
111/G2 Fort Kent, Me,US
113/H5 Fort Lauderdale, Fl,US
115/F5 Fort Lee, NJ,US
109/F2 Fort Lupton, Co,US
106/E3 Fort Macleod, Ab,Can
107/L5 Fort Madison, Ia,US
113/H4 Fort Matanzas Nat'l Mon., Fl,US
102/E3 Fort McMurray, Ab,Can
110/C2 Fort Michilimackinac, Mi,US
109/G2 Fort Morgan, Co,US
113/J3 Fort Moultrie, SC,US
113/H5 Fort Myers, Fl,US
102/D3 Fort Nelson (riv.), BC,Can
33/F4 Forton, Eng,UK
48/D2 Fortore (riv.), It.
113/G3 Fort Payne, Al,US
106/G4 Fort Peck (lake), Mt,US
113/H5 Fort Pierce, Fl,US
107/H4 Fort Pierre, SD,US
83/M7 Fort Portal, Ugan.
107/H3 Fort Qu'Appelle, Sk,Can
107/J5 Fort Randall (dam), SD,US
106/B2 Fort Saint James, BC,Can
102/D3 Fort Saint John, BC,Can
106/E2 Fort Saskatchewan, Ab,Can
109/J3 Fort Scott, Ks,US
55/J3 Fort-Shevchenko, Kaz.
112/E3 Fort Smith, Ar,US
112/C4 Fort Stockton, Tx,US
109/F4 Fort Sumner, NM,US
107/J4 Fort Totten, ND,US
94/A2 Fortuna, Braz.
111/L2 Fortune, Nf,Can
111/L2 Fortune (bay), Nf,Can
34/D5 Fortuneswell, Eng,UK
109/F4 Fort Union Nat'l Mon., NM,US
113/G4 Fort Walton Beach, Fl,US
115/J8 Fort Washington Park, Md,US
110/C3 Fort Wayne, In,US
36/C2 Fort William, Sc,UK
112/D3 Fort Worth, Tx,US
107/H4 Fort Yates, ND,US
76/B2 Forty Mile Scrub Nat'l Park, Austl.
67/B3 Foshan, China
103/S7 Fosheim (pen.), NW,Can
33/G3 Foss (riv.), Eng,UK
45/G4 Fossano, It.
31/T9 Fosses, Fr.
43/D3 Fosses-la-Ville, Belg.
106/C4 Fossil, Or,US
106/F5 Fossil Butte Nat'l Mon., Wy,US
110/D3 Fostoria, Oh,US
44/C2 Fougères, Fr.
83/N3 Foul (bay), Egypt, Sudan
35/G3 Foulness (isl.), Eng,UK
35/G3 Foulness (pt.), Eng,UK
33/H4 Foulness (riv.), Eng,UK
35/H1 Foulsham, Eng,UK
85/H5 Foumban, Camr.
109/F3 Fountain, Co,US
115/C3 Fountain Valley, Ca,US
112/E3 Fourche La Fave (riv.), Ar,US
35/E4 Four Marks, Eng,UK
42/D4 Fourmies, Fr.
114/D5 Four Mountains (isls.), Ak,US
89/R15 Fournaise, Piton de la (peak), Reun.
84/B4 Fouta Djallon (reg.), Gha.
75/Q12 Foveaux (str.), NZ
34/B6 Fowey, Eng,UK
34/B6 Fowey (riv.), Eng,UK
77/B1 Fowlers Gap, Austl.
60/E1 Fowman, Iran
114/M3 Fox (mtn.), Yk,Can
114/E5 Fox (isls.), Ak,US
110/B3 Fox (riv.), Il, Wi,US
106/D2 Fox Creek, Ab,Can
103/H2 Foxe (chan.), NW,Can
103/J2 Foxe (pen.), NW,Can
103/J2 Foxe Basin (sound), NW,Can
75/R11 Fox Glacier, NZ
116/P15 Fox Lake, Il,US
35/G2 Foxton, Eng,UK
106/F3 Fox Valley, Sk,Can
32/A2 Foyle (riv.), NI,UK
32/A1 Foyle, Lough (inlet), Ire., NI,UK
46/B1 Foz, Sp.
87/B4 Foz do Cunene, Ang.
91/F2 Foz do Iguaçu, Braz.
47/F2 Fraga, Sp.
95/B3 Fraiburgo, Braz.
92/E7 Frailes (range), Bol.
42/C3 Frameries, Belg.
35/H2 Framlingham, Eng,UK
95/C2 Franca, Braz.
49/E2 Francavilla Fontana, It.
44/D3 France
31/T9 France, Pays de (plain), Fr.
44/E5 France, Roc de (mtn.), Fr.
102/C2 Frances (lake), Yk,Can
100/E3 Frances (cape), Cuba
101/H4 Francés Viejo (cape), DRep.
87/B1 Franceville, Gabon
45/G3 Franche-Comté (reg.), Fr.
107/J5 Francis Case (lake), SD,US
100/C4 Francisco Escárcega, Mex.
101/P8 Francisco I. Madero, Mex.
87/E5 Francistown, Bots.
95/G8 Franco da Rocha, Braz.
106/B2 Francois (lake), BC,Can
31/S10 Franconville, Fr.
40/C2 Franeker, Neth.
41/F6 Frankenberg-Eder, Ger.
110/D3 Frankenmuth, Mi,US
110/C3 Frankfort, In,US
110/C4 Frankfort (cap.), Ky,US
39/H2 Frankfurt, Ger.
45/H1 Frankfurt am Main, Ger.
45/J2 Frankische Alb (mts.), Ger.
45/H1 Fränkische Saale (riv.), Ger.
45/J2 Fränkische Schweiz (reg.), Ger.
77/C3 Frankland (cape), Austl.
98/M Franklin (isl.), Ant.
114/N1 Franklin (bay), NW,Can
102/D2 Franklin (mts.), NW,Can
114/G1 Franklin (pt.), Ak,US
110/C4 Franklin, In,US
110/C4 Franklin, Ky,US
113/H3 Franklin, NC,US
113/G3 Franklin, Tn,US
112/D4 Franklin, Tx,US
110/E4 Franklin, Va,US
116/P14 Franklin, Wi,US
110/E4 Franklin, WV,US
106/D3 Franklin D. Roosevelt (lake), Wa,US
115/F4 Franklin Lakes, NJ,US
77/C4 Franklin-Lower Gordon Wild Rivers Nat'l Park, Austl.
116/Q16 Franklin Park, Il,US
115/G5 Franklin Square, NY,US
91/F2 Fransisco Beltrão, Braz.
95/G8 Fransisco Morato, Braz.
94/B5 Fransisco Sá, Braz.
56/F2 Franz Josef Land (arch.), Rus.
76/D4 Fraser (isl.), Austl.
106/B2 Fraser (lake), BC,Can
106/C3 Fraser (riv.), BC,Can
116/G6 Fraser, Mi,US
36/D2 Fraserburgh, Sc,UK
106/B2 Fraser Lake, BC,Can
77/C3 Fraser Nat'l Park, Austl.
45/H3 Frauenfeld, Swi.
96/F2 Fray Bentos, Uru.
108/C4 Frazier Park, Ca,US
43/F2 Frechen, Ger.
74/A5 Frecinet (estuary), Austl.
88/E3 Fred (mtn.), SAfr.
38/E1 Fredericia, Den.
75/J4 Frederick (reef), Austl.
110/E4 Frederick, Md,US
109/H4 Frederick, Ok,US
112/D4 Fredericksburg, Tx,US
110/E4 Fredericksburg, Va,US
111/H2 Fredericton (cap.), NB,Can
37/D4 Frederikshavn, Den.
108/D3 Fredonia, Az,US
109/J3 Fredonia, Ks,US
110/E3 Fredonia, NY,US
37/D4 Fredrikstad, Nor.
109/H3 Freedom, Ok,US
115/F5 Freehold, NJ,US
77/A1 Freeling Heights (peak), Austl.
101/F2 Freeport, Bahm.
110/B3 Freeport, Il,US
115/G5 Freeport, NY,US
112/E4 Freeport, Tx,US
112/D5 Freer, Tx,US
84/B4 Freetown (cap.), SLeo.
44/B2 Fréhel (cape), Fr.
38/G3 Freib (riv.), Ger.
39/G3 Freiberg, Ger.
38/G3 Freiberger Mulde (riv.), Ger.
95/D1 Frei Inocêncio, Braz.
96/B3 Freire, Chile
43/G4 Freisen, Ger.
45/J2 Freising, Ger.
45/L2 Freistadt, Aus.
39/G3 Freital, Ger.
45/G5 Fréjus, Fr.
34/B4 Fremington, Eng,UK
116/L11 Fremont, Ca,US
110/C3 Fremont, Mi,US
109/H2 Fremont, Ne,US
110/D3 Fremont, Oh,US
108/E3 Fremont (riv.), Ut,US
106/F5 Fremont (peak), Wy,US
110/D2 French (riv.), On,Can
79/J2 French Frigate (shoals), Hi,US
93/H3 French Guiana (dpcy.), Fr.
106/G3 Frenchman (riv.), Can., US
109/G2 Frenchman (cr.), Ne,US
111/R8 Frenchman's (bay), On,Can
77/C4 Frenchmans Cap (peak), Austl.
79/M6 French Polynesia (terr.), Fr.
81/R16 Frenda, Alg.
31/S9 Frépillon, Fr.
93/H5 Fresco (riv.), Braz.
35/E5 Freshwater, Eng,UK
96/B4 Fresia, Chile
31/S10 Fresnes, Fr.
101/P9 Fresnillo de González Echeverría, Mex.
108/C3 Fresno, Ca,US
77/D4 Freycinet Nat'l Park, Austl.
43/F5 Freyming-Merlebach, Fr.
45/K2 Freyung, Ger.
87/B4 Fria (cape), Namb.
91/C2 Frias, Arg.
45/G3 Fribourg, Swi.
45/H1 Friedberg, Ger.
41/E2 Friedeburg, Ger.
45/H1 Friedrichsdorf, Ger.
45/H3 Friedrichshafen, Ger.
43/G5 Friedrichsthal, Ger.
41/G7 Frielendorf, Ger.
45/G2 Friesenheim, Ger.
40/C2 Friesland (prov.), Neth.
41/E2 Friesoythe, Ger.
35/F4 Frimley, Eng,UK
35/H3 Frinton, Eng,UK
28/G7 Frio (cape), Braz.
109/H5 Frio (riv.), Tx,US
41/G6 Fritzlar, Ger.
45/K3 Friuli-Venezia Giula (reg.), It.
32/E2 Frizington, Eng,UK
103/K2 Frobisher (bay), NW,Can
106/F1 Frobisher (lake), Sk,Can
33/F5 Frodsham, Eng,UK
37/D3 Frohavet (bay), Nor.
42/D3 Froidchapelle, Belg.
55/G2 Frolovo, Rus.
77/B1 Frome (lake), Austl.
74/F5 Frome (riv.), Austl.
34/D4 Frome, Eng,UK
34/D2 Frome (riv.), Eng,UK
34/D5 Frome (riv.), Eng,UK
109/F2 Front (range), Co,US
44/E5 Frontignan, Fr.
110/E4 Front Royal, Va,US
48/C2 Frosinone, It.
37/E3 Frösö, Swe.
98/J Frost (glac.), Ant.
43/F6 Frouard, Fr.
37/D3 Frøya (isl.), Nor.
103/H2 Frozen (str.), NW,Can
111/Q9 Fruitland, On,Can
50/D3 Fruška Gora Nat'l Park, Yugo.
95/B2 Frutal, Braz.
96/B4 Frutillar, Chile
39/K4 Frýdek-Místek, Czh.
66/C5 Fu (riv.), China
66/D3 Fucheng, China
38/E3 Fuchskaute (peak), Ger.
43/H2 Fuchskauten (peak), Ger.
64/C3 Fuchū, Japan
66/D5 Fuchun (riv.), China
73/H4 Fudi (mtn.), Indo.
67/D2 Fuding, China
47/Y16 Fuenaventura (isl.), Canl.
46/C4 Fuengirola, Sp.
46/D2 Fuenlabrada, Sp.
47/N8 Fuente, Sp.
47/E4 Fuente-Álamo, Sp.
46/B3 Fuente del Maestre, Sp.
46/C3 Fuente Obejuna, Sp.
46/E1 Fuenterrabiá, Sp.
46/C4 Fuentes de Andalucía, Sp.
101/N8 Fuerte (riv.), Mex.
67/D4 Fuga (isl.), Phil.
78/F3 Fuhne (riv.), Ger.
41/H4 Fuhse (riv.), Ger.
65/F3 Fuji, Japan
65/F3 Fuji (riv.), Japan
65/F3 Fujieda, Japan
65/F3 Fuji-Hakone-Izu Nat'l Park, Japan
65/L10 Fujiidera, Japan
65/H7 Fujimi, Japan
65/H7 Fujino, Japan
65/F3 Fujinomiya, Japan
65/F3 Fujioka, Japan
65/F3 Fujisawa, Japan
65/J7 Fujishiro, Japan
65/M9 Fujiwara, Japan
65/F3 Fujiyama (mtn.), Japan
65/F3 Fujiyoshida, Japan
64/D3 Fukuchiyama, Japan
64/A4 Fukue, Japan
64/A4 Fukue (isl.), Japan
64/E2 Fukui, Japan
64/E3 Fukui (pref.), Japan
64/B4 Fukuoka, Japan
64/B4 Fukuoka (pref.), Japan
65/E3 Fukuroi, Japan
98/C Fukushima (peak), Ant.
65/G2 Fukushima, Japan
65/F2 Fukushima (pref.), Japan
64/C3 Fukuyama, Japan
61/J2 Fūlādī (mtn.), Afg.
35/G2 Fulbourn, Eng,UK
45/H1 Fulda, Ger.
33/G4 Fulford, Eng,UK
67/A2 Fuling, China
115/C3 Fullerton, Ca,US
115/E5 Fullerton (Whitehall), Pa,US
111/Q9 Fulton, On,Can
110/B4 Fulton, Ky,US
109/K3 Fulton, Mo,US
110/E3 Fulton, NY,US
37/E3 Fulufjället (peak), Swe.
33/F4 Fulwood, Eng,UK
44/D4 Fumel, Fr.
65/H7 Funabashi, Japan
78/G5 Funafuti (atoll), Tuv.
101/G5 Fundación, Col.
111/H2 Fundy (bay), NB, NS,Can
111/H2 Fundy Nat'l Park, NB,Can
87/F5 Funhalouro, Moz.
52/J4 Furmanov, Rus.
36/C2 Furnace, Sc,UK
95/H6 Furnas (res.), Braz.
77/C4 Furneaux Group (isls.), Austl.
41/E3 Fürstenau, Ger.
50/C2 Fürstenfeld, Aus.
45/J2 Fürstenfeldbruck, Ger.
39/H2 Fürstenwalde, Ger.
45/K2 Furth im Wald, Ger.
63/N4 Furukawa, Japan
103/H2 Fury and Hecla (str.), NW,Can
66/B4 Fushan, China
66/E3 Fushan, China
63/J3 Fushun, China
65/M9 Fuso, Japan
65/H7 Fussa, Japan
45/J3 Füssen, Ger.
65/M10 Futami, Japan
50/D3 Futog, Yugo.
96/B4 Futrono, Chile
65/F3 Futtsu, Japan
78/H6 Futuna (isl.), Wall.
59/H6 Fuwah, Egypt
71/H3 Fuxian (lake), China
63/J3 Fuxin, China
66/C4 Fuyang, China
67/B2 Fuyi (riv.), China
63/J2 Fuyu, China
39/L5 Füzesabony, Hun.
67/C2 Fuzhou, China
31/P6 Fyfield, Eng,UK
38/F1 Fyn (co.), Den.
37/D5 Fyn (isl.), Den.

G

83/Q6 Gaalkacyo (Galcaio), Som.
40/D5 Gaanderen, Neth.
40/C2 Gaast, Neth.
44/C5 Gabas (riv.), Fr.
108/C3 Gabbs, Nv,US
87/B3 Gabela, Ang.
82/H1 Gabes (gulf), Tun.
82/H7 Gabon
88/D2 Gaborone (cap.), Bots.
51/G4 Gabrovo, Bul.
50/D4 Gacko, Bosn.
70/C4 Gadag-Betgeri, India
113/G3 Gadsden, Al,US
51/G3 Găeşti, Rom.
48/C2 Gaeta, It.
48/C2 Gaeta (gulf), It.
113/H3 Gaffney, SC,US
52/G5 Gagarin, Rus.
84/D5 Gagnoa, IvC.
111/G1 Gagnon, Qu,Can
31/T10 Gagny, Fr.
54/G4 Gagra, Geo.
50/A2 Gail (riv.), Aus.
44/D5 Gaillac, Fr.
45/K3 Gailtaler Alps (mts.), Aus.
96/D4 Gaiman, Arg.
113/H4 Gainesville, Fl,US
113/H3 Gainesville, Ga,US
109/J3 Gainesville, Mo,US
112/D3 Gainesville, Tx,US
33/G2 Gainford, Eng,UK
33/H5 Gainsborough, Eng,UK
74/F6 Gairdner (lake), Austl.
115/J7 Gaithersburg, Md,US
52/E4 Gaizina Kalns (peak), Lat.
88/C2 Gakarosa (peak), SAfr.
46/D2 Galapagar, Sp.
36/D3 Galashiels, Sc,UK
51/J3 Galaţi, Rom.
51/H3 Galaţi (co.), Rom.
49/F2 Galatina, It.
49/F2 Galatone, It.
110/D4 Galax, Va,US
49/H3 Galaxídhiou, Gre.
73/G3 Galela, Indo.
110/B3 Galena, Il,US
96/B3 Galera (pt.), Chile
92/B3 Galera (pt.), Ecu.
101/J5 Galera (pt.), Trin.
110/B3 Galesburg, Il,US
36/A4 Galey (riv.), Ire.
32/B2 Galgorm, NI,UK
52/J4 Galich, Rus.
39/L3 Galicia (reg.), Pol., Ukr.
46/A1 Galicia (aut. comm.), Sp.
50/E5 Galičica Nat'l Park, Macd.
59/K5 Galilee, Sea of (Tiberias) (lake), Isr.
110/D3 Galion, Oh,US
113/G2 Gallatin, Tn,US
70/D6 Galle, SrL.
97/K7 Gallegos (riv.), Arg.
101/G5 Gallinas (pt.), Col.
112/B3 Gallinas (mts.), NM,US
49/E2 Gallipoli, It.
51/H5 Gallipoli (pen.), Turk.
51/H5 Gallipoli (Gelibolu), Turk.
110/D4 Gallipolis, Oh,US
37/G2 Gällivare, Swe.
48/C3 Gallo (cape), It.
32/D2 Galloway, Mull of (pt.), Sc,UK
108/E4 Gallup, NM,US
31/R10 Gally (riv.), Fr.
62/D2 Galt, Mong.
116/M10 Galt, Ca,US
36/A4 Galtymore (mtn.), Ire.
62/E2 Galuut, Mong.
96/B3 Galvarino, Chile
112/E4 Galveston, Tx,US
112/E4 Galveston (bay), Tx,US
112/E4 Galveston (isl.), Tx,US
96/E2 Gálvez, Arg.
36/A4 Galway, Ire.
36/A4 Galway (bay), Ire.
69/D1 Gam (riv.), Viet.
88/C2 Gamagara (dry riv.), SAfr.
65/E3 Gamagōri, Japan
70/E2 Gamba, China
85/E4 Gambaga Scarp (escarp.), Gha., Togo
70/A2 Gambat, Pak.
83/M6 Gambēla, Eth.
83/M6 Gambela Nat'l Park, Eth.
84/B3 Gambia
84/A3 Gambia (Gambie) (riv.), Afr.
79/M7 Gambier (isls.), FrPol.
111/L1 Gambo, Nf,Can
87/C1 Gamboma, Congo
88/C4 Gamka (riv.), SAfr.
88/B3 Gamkab (dry riv.), Namb.
35/F2 Gamlingay, Eng,UK
52/D2 Gammelstad, Swe.
65/M9 Gamo, Japan
39/G5 Gamsfeld (peak), Aus.
83/N7 Gamud (peak), Eth.
67/C2 Gan (riv.), China
110/E2 Gananoque, On,Can
87/D2 Gandajika, Zaire
111/L1 Gander, Nf,Can
111/L1 Gander (lake), Nf,Can
41/F2 Ganderkesee, Ger.
70/B3 Gāndhīhām, India
70/B3 Gandhinagar, India
70/B3 Gāndhi Sāgar (res.), India
47/E3 Gandía, Sp.
94/C4 Gandu, Braz.
84/C2 Ganeb (well), Mrta.
70/C2 Gangāpur, India
70/E2 Gangārāmpur, India
68/D5 Gangdisê (mts.), China
43/F2 Gangelt, Ger.
70/E3 Ganges (riv.), India
48/D4 Gangi, It.
70/E2 Gangtok, India
59/N8 Gan Hashlosha Nat'l Park, Isr.
106/F5 Gannett (peak), Wy,US
68/F4 Gansu (prov.), China
82/H6 Ganye, Nga.
67/B2 Ganzhou, China
85/E3 Ganzourgou (prov.), Burk.
85/E2 Gao, Mali
85/E2 Gao (reg.), Mali
66/C3 Gaocheng, China
67/D2 Gaojian, China
84/E4 Gaoua, Burk.
66/C3 Gaoyang, China
66/D4 Gaoyou (lake), China
45/G4 Gap, Fr.
62/D5 Gar (riv.), China
70/E3 Garai (riv.), Bang.
83/L7 Garamba Nat'l Park, Zaire
94/C3 Garanhuns, Braz.
83/N7 Garba Tula, Kenya
38/E2 Garbsen, Ger.
95/B2 Garça, Braz.
94/B3 Garças (riv.), Braz.
31/S10 Garches, Fr.
46/C3 Garcia de Sota (res.), Sp.
44/F5 Gard (riv.), Fr.
45/J4 Garda (lake), It.
81/V17 Garde, Cap de (cape), Alg.
38/F2 Gardelegen, Ger.
115/B3 Gardena, Ca,US
113/H3 Garden City, Ga,US
109/G3 Garden City, Ks,US
116/F7 Garden City, Mi,US
115/G5 Garden City, NY,US
106/A2 Gardener Canal (inlet), BC,Can
115/C3 Garden Grove, Ca,US
61/J2 Gardēz, Afg.
111/G2 Gardiner, Me,US
106/F4 Gardiner, Mt,US
79/H5 Gardner (Nikumaroro) (atoll), Kiri.
36/C2 Garelochhead, Sc,UK
82/G2 Garet el Djenoun (peak), Alg.
106/E4 Garfield (peak), Mt,US
115/F5 Garfield, NJ,US
33/G4 Garforth, Eng,UK
44/D4 Gargan (mtn.), Fr.
31/T10 Garges-lès-Gonesse, Fr.
33/F4 Gargrave, Eng,UK
70/C3 Garhākotā, India
95/B4 Garibaldi, Braz.
83/N8 Garissa, Kenya
112/D3 Garland, Tx,US
32/D2 Garlieston, Sc,UK
45/J3 Garmisch-Partenkirchen, Ger.
109/J3 Garnett, Ks,US
77/B2 Garnpung (lake), Austl.
44/D4 Garonne (riv.), Fr.
85/E2 Garou (lake), Mali
82/H6 Garoua, Camr.
82/H6 Garoua Boulaï, Camr.
47/K7 Garraf (range), Sp.
32/D6 Garreg, Wal,UK
41/F3 Garrel, Ger.
107/H4 Garrison, ND,US
107/H4 Garrison (dam), ND,US
32/C1 Garron (pt.), NI,UK
103/H2 Garry (bay), NW,Can
102/F2 Garry (lake), NW,Can
33/F4 Garstang, Eng,UK
45/L2 Garsten, Aus.
41/H6 Garte (riv.), Ger.
44/D3 Gartempe (riv.), Fr.
34/C2 Garth, Wal,UK
72/C5 Garut, Indo.
32/B2 Garvagh, NI,UK
39/L3 Garwolin, Pol.
116/R16 Gary, In,US
92/C3 Garzón, Col.
58/F4 Gas (lake), China
37/P6 Gæsafjöll (peak), Ice.
110/C3 Gas City, In,US
109/J3 Gasconade (riv.), Mo,US
44/C5 Gascony (reg.), Fr.
74/B5 Gascoyne (riv.), Austl.
95/B3 Gaspar, Braz.
72/C4 Gaspar (riv.), Indo.
111/H1 Gaspé, Qu,Can
111/H1 Gaspé (pen.), Qu,Can
111/H1 Gaspé, Cap de (cape), Qu,Can
111/S9 Gasport, NY,US
113/J2 Gaston (lake), NC, Va,US
113/H3 Gastonia, NC,US
59/J4 Gata (cape), Cyp.
46/B2 Gata (range), Sp.
46/D4 Gata, Cabo de (cape), Sp.
52/F4 Gatchina, Rus.
32/D2 Gatehouse-of-Fleet, Sc,UK
102/F1 Gateshead (isl.), NW,Can
33/G2 Gateshead, Eng,UK
114/H2 Gates of the Arctic Nat'l Pk. & Prsv., Ak,US
112/D4 Gatesville, Tx,US
115/G5 Gateway Nat'l Rec. Area, NJ, NY,US
44/C3 Gâtine (hills), Fr.
110/F2 Gatineau, Qu,Can
110/F2 Gatineau (riv.), Qu,Can
43/H4 Gau-Bickelheim, Ger.
71/F2 Gauhāti, India
33/G2 Gaunless (riv.), Eng,UK
70/E2 Gauripur, India
70/E2 Gauri Sankar (mtn.), Nepal
37/D4 Gausta (peak), Nor.
52/E4 Gauya Nat'l Park, Lat.
47/G2 Gavà, Sp.
49/J5 Gávdhos (isl.), Gre.
41/E1 Gave de Pau (riv.), Fr.
42/C2 Gavere, Belg.
37/F3 Gävle, Swe.
37/E3 Gävleborg (co.), Swe.
77/A2 Gawler, Austl.
74/F6 Gawler (ranges), Austl.
62/D3 Gaxun (lake), China
55/L2 Gay, Rus.
110/D4 Gay (peak), WV,US
63/K3 Gaya (riv.), China
70/E3 Gayā, India
85/F4 Gaya, Niger
110/C2 Gaylord, Mi,US
54/D2 Gaysin, Ukr.
59/K6 Gaza (Ghazzah), Gaza
59/J6 Gaza Strip
59/D3 Gaziantep, Turk.
63/H1 Gazimur (riv.), Rus.
45/G2 Gazon de Faing (peak), Fr.
83/K7 Gbadolite, Zaire
84/C5 Gbarnga, Libr.
39/K1 Gdańsk, Pol.
39/K1 Gdańsk (prov.), Pol.
39/K1 Gdańsk (gulf), Pol., Rus.
39/K1 Gdynia, Pol.
66/D5 Ge (lake), China
45/J1 Gebaberg (peak), Ger.
73/G3 Gebe (isl.), Indo.
86/D4 Gebeit Mine, Sudan
51/J5 Gebze, Turk.
72/C5 Gede (peak), Indo.
59/M9 Gedera, Isr.
59/B2 Gediz, Turk.
59/A2 Gediz (riv.), Turk.
43/E1 Geel, Belg.
77/C3 Geelong, Austl.
74/A5 Geelvink (chan.), Austl.
41/E3 Geeste, Ger.
41/F2 Geeste (riv.), Ger.
41/H2 Geesthacht, Ger.
68/D5 Gê'gyai, China
41/G4 Gehrden, Ger.
34/C2 Geifas (mtn.), Wal,UK
102/F3 Geikie (riv.), Sk,Can
43/F2 Geilenkirchen, Ger.
65/M10 Geinō, Japan
45/H2 Geislingen an der Steige, Ger.
71/H3 Gejiu, China
83/L6 Gel (riv.), Sudan
48/D4 Gela, It.
48/D4 Gela (gulf), It.
83/Q6 Geladī, Eth.
40/C4 Gelderland (prov.), Neth.
40/C5 Geldermalsen, Neth.
40/D5 Geldern, Ger.
40/C6 Geldrop, Neth.
43/E2 Geleen, Neth.
54/F3 Gelendzhik, Rus.
51/H5 Gelibolu (Gallipoli), Turk.
34/C3 Gelligaer, Wal,UK
40/E5 Gelsenkirchen, Ger.
43/D2 Gembloux, Belg.
83/J7 Gemena, Zaire
40/C5 Gemert, Neth.
51/J5 Gemlik, Turk.
51/J5 Gemlik (gulf), Turk.
45/K3 Gemona del Friuli, It.
88/C2 Gemsbok-Kalahari Nat'l Park, SAfr.
88/C2 Gemsbok Nat'l Park, Bots.
114/G3 Gemuk (mtn.), Ak,US
63/J1 Gen (riv.), China
83/N6 Genalē Wenz (riv.), Eth.
42/D2 Genappe, Belg.
48/A3 Genargentu (mts.), It.
59/E2 Genç, Turk.
40/D5 Gendringen, Neth.
40/C5 Gendt, Neth.
40/D3 Genemuiden, Neth.
96/D3 General Acha, Arg.
96/D2 General Alvear, Arg.
96/F2 General Belgrano, Arg.
96/E2 General Cabrera, Arg.
96/B5 General Carrera (lake), Chile
97/F3 General Juan Madariaga, Arg.
97/S12 General Las Heras, Arg.
91/C1 General Martín Miguel de Güemes, Arg.
96/E2 General Pico, Arg.
91/D2 General Pinedo, Arg.
67/E6 General Santos, Phil.
51/J4 General-Toshevo, Bul.
96/E2 General Viamonte, Arg.
96/E2 General Villegas, Arg.
110/E3 Genesee (riv.), NY,US
107/L5 Geneseo, Il,US
110/E3 Geneseo, NY,US
113/G4 Geneva, Al,US
116/P16 Geneva, Il,US
109/H2 Geneva, Ne,US
110/E3 Geneva, NY,US
116/P14 Geneva (lake), Wi,US
45/G3 Geneva (Genève), Swi.
45/G3 Geneva (Léman) (lake), Fr., Swi.
45/H2 Gengenbach, Ger.
54/E3 Genichesk, Ukr.
46/C4 Genil (riv.), Sp.
43/E2 Genk, Belg.
40/C5 Gennep, Neth.
31/S10 Gennevilliers, Fr.
45/H4 Genoa (Genova), It.
45/H4 Genova (gulf), It.
42/C1 Gent-Brugge (can.), Belg.
72/C5 Genteng (cape), Indo.
42/C1 Gent (Ghent), Belg.
74/A6 Geographe (bay), Austl.
74/A4 Geographe (chan.), Austl.
74/C4 George (lake), Austl.
77/D2 George (lake), Austl.
76/C3 George (pt.), Austl.
103/K3 George (riv.), Qu,Can
88/C4 George, SAfr.
113/H4 George (lake), Fl,US
56/E1 George Land (isl.), Rus.
76/G9 Georges (riv.), Austl.
111/Q8 Georgetown, On,Can
100/E4 George Town (cap.), Cay.
92/G2 Georgetown (cap.), Guy.
113/H4 Georgetown, Ga,US
110/C4 Georgetown, Ky,US
113/J3 Georgetown, SC,US
112/D4 Georgetown, Tx,US
98/L George V (coast), Ant.
98/V George VI (sound), Ant.
112/D4 George West, Tx,US
55/G4 Georgia
106/B3 Georgia (str.), Can., US
113/G3 Georgia (state), US
110/D2 Georgian Bay Islands Nat'l Park, On,Can
74/F4 Georgina (riv.), Austl.
51/H4 Georgi Traykov, Bul.
41/F4 Georgsmarienhütte, Ger.
38/G3 Gera, Ger.
42/C2 Geraardsbergen, Belg.
94/A3 Geral (mts.), Braz.
94/A4 Geral de Goiás (Espigão Mestre) (range), Braz.
75/R11 Geraldine, NZ
74/A5 Geraldton, Austl.
110/C1 Geraldton, On,Can
44/F4 Gerbier de Jonc (mtn.), Fr.
41/H3 Gerdau (riv.), Ger.
114/H3 Gerdine (mtn.), Ak,US
51/L5 Gerede, Turk.
61/H2 Gereshk, Afg.
45/J3 Geretsried, Ger.

108/C2 **Gerlach,** Nv,US
39/L4 **Gerlachovský Štít** (peak), Slvk.
115/J7 **Germantown,** Md,US
113/F3 **Germantown,** Tn,US
38/E3 **Germany**
45/J2 **Germering,** Ger.
88/E2 **Germiston,** SAfr.
43/F3 **Gerolstein,** Ger.
47/G2 **Gerona** (Girona), Sp.
47/E1 **Ger, Pic du** (peak), Fr.
42/D3 **Gerpinnes,** Belg.
31/M7 **Gerrards Cross,** Eng,UK
44/D5 **Gers** (riv.), Fr.
43/G5 **Gersheim,** Ger.
40/E5 **Gescher,** Ger.
41/F5 **Geseke,** Ger.
83/P6 **Gestro Wenz** (riv.), Eth.
46/D2 **Getafe,** Sp.
43/E2 **Gete** (riv.), Belg.
107/J4 **Gettysburg,** SD,US
95/A3 **Getúlio Vargas,** Braz.
98/S **Getz Ice Shelf,** Ant.
43/E2 **Geul** (riv.), Belg., Neth.
72/A3 **Geureudong** (peak), Indo.
59/E2 **Gevaş,** Turk.
41/E6 **Gevelsberg,** Ger.
50/F5 **Gevgelija,** Macd.
83/P5 **Gewanē,** Eth.
89/H6 **Geyser** (reef), Madg.
51/K5 **Geyve,** Turk.
68/B4 **Gez** (riv.), China
82/G1 **Ghadāmis,** Libya
86/C3 **Ghadir, Bi'r** (well), Egypt
85/E4 **Ghana**
87/D5 **Ghanzi,** Bots.
86/B5 **Gharb Binna,** Sudan
82/F1 **Ghardaïa,** Alg.
82/H1 **Gharyān,** Libya
82/H3 **Ghāt,** Libya
82/J5 **Ghazal** (riv.), Chad
81/P13 **Ghazaouet,** Alg.
70/C2 **Ghaziābād,** India
61/J2 **Ghaznī,** Afg.
59/K6 **Ghazzah** (Gaza), Gaza
62/G2 **Ghengis Khan Wall** (ruins), Mong.
42/C1 **Ghent** (Gent), Belg.
51/H2 **Gheorghe Gheorghiu-Dej,** Rom.
51/G2 **Gheorgheni,** Rom.
51/F2 **Gherla,** Rom.
96/C5 **Ghio** (lake), Arg.
70/A2 **Ghotki,** Pak.
51/H2 **Ghūrīān,** Afg.
69/D4 **Gia Nghia,** Viet.
88/E3 **Giant's Castle** (peak), SAfr.
48/D4 **Giarre,** It.
69/E3 **Gia Vuc,** Viet.
106/E2 **Gibbons,** Ab,Can
46/B4 **Gibraleón,** Sp.
46/B4 **Gibraltar** (str.), Afr., Eur.
111/R8 **Gibraltar** (pt.), On,Can
46/C4 **Gibraltar** (dpcy.), UK
116/F7 **Gibraltar,** Mi,US
77/E1 **Gibraltar Range Nat'l Park,** Austl.
74/D4 **Gibson** (des.), Austl.
112/D4 **Giddings,** Tx,US
86/C2 **Gidi** (pass), Egypt
83/N6 **Gidollē,** Eth.
44/E3 **Gien,** Fr.
45/J2 **Giengen an der Brenz,** Ger.
44/F4 **Gier** (riv.), Fr.
45/H1 **Giessen,** Ger.
40/B5 **Giessendam,** Neth.
42/B6 **Gif,** Fr.
103/H1 **Gifford** (riv.), NW,Can
113/H5 **Gifford,** Fl,US
41/H4 **Gifhorn,** Ger.
31/S10 **Gif-sur-Yvette,** Fr.
65/E3 **Gifu,** Japan
65/E3 **Gifu** (pref.), Japan
33/F3 **Giggleswick,** Eng,UK
48/B1 **Giglio** (isl.), It.
46/C1 **Gijón,** Sp.
108/D4 **Gila** (riv.), Az, NM,US
108/D4 **Gila Bend,** Az,US
108/E4 **Gila Cliff Dwellings Nat'l Mon.,** NM,US
33/H4 **Gilberdyke Newport,** Eng,UK
76/A2 **Gilbert** (riv.), Austl.
78/G5 **Gilbert** (isls.), Kiri.
110/A2 **Gilbert,** Mn,US
96/C2 **Gil de Vilches Nat'l Park,** Chile
34/C3 **Gilfach Goch,** Wal,UK
32/B3 **Gilford,** NI,UK
115/F6 **Gilford Park,** NJ,US
61/K1 **Gilgit** (riv.), Pak.
74/F6 **Gilles** (lake), Austl.
107/G4 **Gillette,** Wy,US
106/B3 **Gillies Bay,** BC,Can
34/D4 **Gillingham,** Eng,UK
35/G4 **Gillingham,** Eng,UK
112/E3 **Gilmer,** Tx,US
61/K1 **Gilqit** (riv.), Pak.
63/K1 **Gilyuy** (riv.), Rus.
40/B5 **Gilze,** Neth.
83/N6 **Gīmbī,** Eth.
107/J3 **Gimli,** Mb,Can
47/F1 **Gimone** (riv.), Fr.
65/M9 **Ginan,** Japan
43/E2 **Gingelom,** Belg.
67/E6 **Gingoog,** Phil.
48/E2 **Ginosa,** It.
46/B1 **Ginzo de Limia,** Sp.
83/Q7 **Giohar,** Som.
48/D3 **Gioia** (gulf), It.
48/E2 **Gioia del Colle,** It.
48/D3 **Gioia Tauro,** It.
49/J3 **Gioüra** (isl.), Gre.
35/G2 **Gipping** (riv.), Eng,UK
92/D3 **Girardot,** Col.
87/B4 **Giraul,** Ang.
80/D6 **Giraul de Cima,** Ang.
59/D2 **Giresun,** Turk.
70/E3 **Gīrīdīh,** India
48/E3 **Girifalco,** It.
31/N7 **Girling** (res.), Eng,UK
47/G2 **Girona** (Gerona), Sp.
44/C4 **Gironde** (riv.), Fr.
77/D1 **Girraween Nat'l Park,** Austl.
35/G2 **Girton,** Eng,UK
32/D1 **Girvan,** Sc,UK
32/D1 **Girvan, Water of** (riv.), Sc,UK
75/S10 **Gisborne,** NZ
42/A5 **Gisors,** Fr.
42/B1 **Gistel,** Belg.
87/E1 **Gitega,** Buru.
52/B2 **Gittsfjället** (peak), Swe.
45/H3 **Giubiasco,** Swi.
48/C1 **Giulianova,** It.
51/G4 **Giurgiu,** Rom.
51/G3 **Giurgiu** (co.), Rom.
59/M8 **Giv'atayim,** Isr.
43/D3 **Givet,** Fr.
44/F4 **Givors,** Fr.
43/D6 **Givry-en-Argonne,** Fr.
87/F5 **Giyani,** SAfr.
83/N6 **Giyon,** Eth.
86/B2 **Giza, Pyramids of** (Jīzah) (ruins), Egypt
57/R3 **Gizhiga** (bay), Rus.
39/L1 **Giżycko,** Pol.
49/G2 **Gjirokastër,** Alb.
37/D3 **Gjøvik,** Nor.
49/F2 **Gjuhëzës, Kep i** (cape), Alb.
111/K2 **Glace Bay,** NS,Can
106/D3 **Glacier,** BC,Can
106/C3 **Glacier** (peak), Wa,US
114/L4 **Glacier Bay Nat'l Park & Prsv.,** Ak,US
106/D3 **Glacier Nat'l Park,** Can., US
40/D5 **Gladbeck,** Ger.
76/C3 **Gladstone,** Austl.
110/C3 **Gladwin,** Mi,US
33/H3 **Glaisdale,** Eng,UK
30/E2 **Glåma** (riv.), Nor.
43/G4 **Glan** (riv.), Ger.
67/E6 **Glan,** Phil.
34/C3 **Glanamman,** Wal,UK
42/D4 **Gland** (riv.), Fr.
45/H3 **Glarus Alps** (range), Swi.
34/C2 **Glasbury,** Wal,UK
36/C3 **Glasgow,** Sc,UK
110/C4 **Glasgow,** Ky,US
106/G3 **Glasgow,** Mt,US
32/D6 **Glaslyn** (riv.), Wal,UK
32/D3 **Glass** (riv.), IM,UK
112/D2 **Glass** (mts.), Ok,US
112/C4 **Glass** (mts.), Tx,US
115/K8 **Glassmanor-Oxon Hill,** Md,US
34/D4 **Glastonbury,** Eng,UK
53/M4 **Glazov,** Rus.
35/G2 **Glemsford,** Eng,UK
33/H6 **Glen** (riv.), Eng,UK
77/C3 **Glenaladale Nat'l Park,** Austl.
110/E4 **Glen Allen,** Va,US
32/C2 **Glenarm,** NI,UK
32/C2 **Glenarm** (riv.), NI,UK
32/B2 **Glenavy,** NI,UK
77/D2 **Glenbawn** (dam), Austl.
107/J3 **Glenboro,** Mb,Can
76/G8 **Glenbrook,** Austl.
115/K7 **Glen Burnie,** Md,US
108/E3 **Glen Canyon Nat'l Rec. Area,** Az, Ut,US
32/E1 **Glencaple,** Sc,UK
89/E3 **Glencoe,** SAfr.
116/Q15 **Glencoe,** Il,US
115/G5 **Glen Cove,** NY,US
108/D4 **Glendale,** Az,US
115/B2 **Glendale,** Ca,US
106/C5 **Glendale,** Or,US
116/P16 **Glendale Heights,** Il,US
107/G4 **Glendive,** Mt,US
109/F2 **Glendo** (res.), Wy,US
115/C2 **Glendora,** Ca,US
32/B1 **Glendun** (riv.), NI,UK
77/B3 **Glenelg** (riv.), Austl.
32/A2 **Glenelly** (riv.), NI,UK
32/D2 **Glenluce,** Sc,UK
36/C2 **Glen Mòr** (val.), Sc,UK
115/E6 **Glenolden,** Pa,US
114/M4 **Glenora,** BC,Can
76/H8 **Glenorie,** Austl.
109/H4 **Glenpool,** Ok,US
112/D3 **Glen Rose,** Tx,US
110/F3 **Glens Falls,** NY,US
32/B2 **Glenshane** (pass), NI,UK
115/E5 **Glenside,** Pa,US
32/D1 **Glentrool,** Sc,UK
107/H4 **Glen Ullin,** ND,US
116/Q15 **Glenview,** Il,US
111/Q8 **Glen Williams,** On,Can
108/F3 **Glenwood Springs,** Co,US
49/L7 **Glifáhda,** Gre.
41/H1 **Glinde,** Ger.
37/D3 **Glittertinden** (peak), Nor.
39/K3 **Gliwice,** Pol.
108/E4 **Globe,** Az,US
39/H5 **Gloggnitz,** Aus.
39/J3 **Głogów,** Pol.
39/J3 **Głogówek,** Pol.
89/H5 **Glorieuses, Iles** (isls.), Reun.
76/E6 **Glorious** (mtn.), Austl.
114/D3 **Glory of Russia** (cape), Ak,US
33/G5 **Glossop,** Eng,UK
110/F2 **Gloucester,** On,Can
34/D3 **Gloucester,** Eng,UK
115/E6 **Gloucester City,** NJ,US
34/D3 **Gloucestershire** (co.), Eng,UK
34/D3 **Gloucester, Vale of** (val.), Eng,UK
111/L1 **Glovertown,** Nf,Can
39/K3 **Głowno,** Pol.
39/J3 **Głubczyce,** Pol.
39/J3 **Głuchołazy,** Pol.
38/E1 **Glücksburg,** Ger.
41/G1 **Glückstadt,** Ger.
54/E2 **Glukhov,** Ukr.
32/B4 **Glyde** (riv.), Ire.
34/C3 **Glyncorrwg,** Wal,UK
32/C2 **Glynn,** NI,UK
34/C3 **Glyn Neath,** Wal,UK
39/H4 **Gmünd,** Aus.
85/E3 **Gnagna** (prov.), Burk.
41/G2 **Gnarrenburg,** Ger.
39/J2 **Gniezno,** Pol.
50/E4 **Gnjilane,** Yugo.
34/D1 **Gnosall,** Eng,UK
64/C3 **Gō** (riv.), Japan
70/B4 **Goa** (state), India
70/F2 **Goālpāra,** India
36/C3 **Goat Fell** (mtn.), Sc,UK
33/H3 **Goathland,** Eng,UK
83/N6 **Goba,** Eth.
87/C5 **Gobabeb,** Namb.
62/E3 **Gobi** (des.), China, Mong.
64/D4 **Gobō,** Japan
33/E6 **Gobowen,** Eng,UK
40/D5 **Goch,** Ger.
69/D4 **Go Cong,** Viet.
35/F4 **Godalming,** Eng,UK
69/D4 **Go Dau Ha,** Viet.
70/D4 **Godāvari** (riv.), India
83/P6 **Godē,** Eth.
50/F3 **Godeanu** (peak), Rom.
110/D3 **Goderich,** On,Can
70/B3 **Godhra,** India
35/F2 **Godmanchester,** Eng,UK
73/F4 **Godo** (mtn.), Indo.
65/M9 **Gōdo,** Japan
50/D2 **Gödöllő,** Hun.
34/A6 **Godolphin Cross,** Eng,UK
96/C2 **Godoy Cruz,** Arg.
107/K2 **Gods** (lake), Mb,Can
107/K2 **Gods** (riv.), Mb,Can
103/H2 **Gods Mercy** (bay), NW,Can
31/N8 **Godstone,** Eng,UK
99/M3 **Godthåb** (Nuuk), Grld.
68/C4 **Godwin Austen** (K2) (peak), China, Pak.
110/E1 **Goéland** (lake), Qu,Can
40/A5 **Goerce,** Neth.
40/A6 **Goes,** Neth.
110/B2 **Gogebic** (range), Mi,US
70/D2 **Gogra** (riv.), India
41/G3 **Gohbach** (riv.), Ger.
94/D2 **Goiana,** Braz.
93/J7 **Goiânia,** Braz.
94/D2 **Goianinha,** Braz.
93/H7 **Goiás,** Braz.
95/B1 **Goiás** (state), Braz.
95/B1 **Goiatuba,** Braz.
40/C5 **Goirle,** Neth.
64/D3 **Gojō,** Japan
54/E4 **Gok** (riv.), Turk.
64/B4 **Gokase** (riv.), Japan
65/M9 **Gokashō,** Japan
51/G5 **Gökçeada** (isl.), Turk.
59/D2 **Göksun,** Turk.
59/K5 **Golan Heights** (reg.), Syria
59/C2 **Gölbaşı,** Turk.
59/D3 **Gölbaşı,** Turk.
33/F5 **Golborne,** Eng,UK
116/B2 **Gold** (mtn.), Wa,US
39/M1 **Gołdap,** Pol.
106/B5 **Gold Beach,** Or,US
76/D4 **Gold Coast,** Austl.
85/E5 **Gold Coast** (reg.), Gha.
106/D3 **Golden,** BC,Can
109/F3 **Golden,** Co,US
106/C4 **Goldendale,** Wa,US
38/F3 **Goldene Aue** (reg.), Ger.
116/J11 **Golden Gate** (chan.), Ca,US
88/E3 **Golden Gate Highlands Nat'l Park,** SAfr.
106/B3 **Golden Hinde** (peak), BC,Can
41/F3 **Goldenstedt,** Ger.
108/C3 **Goldfield,** Nv,US
106/B3 **Gold River,** BC,Can
113/J3 **Goldsboro,** NC,US
112/D4 **Goldthwaite,** Tx,US
59/E2 **Göle,** Turk.
39/H2 **Goleniów,** Pol.
59/B3 **Gölhisar,** Turk.
112/D4 **Goliad,** Tx,US
59/D2 **Gölköy,** Turk.
62/C4 **Golmud,** China
60/F2 **Golpāyegān,** Iran
51/K5 **Gölpazarı,** Turk.
39/K2 **Golub-Dobrzyń,** Pol.
51/H4 **Golyama Kamchiya** (riv.), Bul.
51/G5 **Golyama Syutkya** (peak), Bul.
51/G5 **Golyam Perelik** (peak), Bul.
87/E1 **Goma,** Zaire
54/D1 **Gomel',** Bela.
54/C2 **Gomel' Obl.,** Bela.
47/X16 **Gomera** (isl.), Canl.
31/S10 **Gometz-le-Châtel,** Fr.
101/P8 **Gómez Palacio,** Mex.
38/F2 **Gommern,** Ger.
35/F4 **Gomshall,** Eng,UK
61/G2 **Gonābād,** Iran
87/F5 **Gonarezhou Nat'l Park,** Zim.
101/G4 **Gonâve** (gulf), Haiti
61/G1 **Gonbad-e Qābūs,** Iran
94/A2 **Gonçalves Dias,** Braz.
70/D2 **Gondā,** India
70/B3 **Gondal,** India
83/N5 **Gonder,** Eth.
70/D3 **Gondia,** India
46/A2 **Gondomar,** Port.
46/A1 **Gondomar,** Sp.
51/H5 **Gönen,** Turk.
31/T10 **Gonesse,** Fr.
71/F2 **Gongbo'gyamda,** China
71/H2 **Gongga** (peak), China
62/E4 **Gonghe,** China
85/H4 **Gongola** (riv.), Nga.
85/H4 **Gongola** (state), Nga.
77/C1 **Gongolgon,** Austl.
66/F2 **Gongzhuling,** China
112/D4 **Gonzales,** Tx,US
100/B3 **González,** Mex.
98/J **Goodenough** (cape), Ant.
88/B4 **Good Hope, Cape of** (cape), SAfr.
106/E5 **Gooding,** Id,US
109/G3 **Goodland,** Ks,US
76/E7 **Goodna,** Austl.
34/B3 **Goodwick,** Wal,UK
88/B4 **Goodwood,** SAfr.
40/C4 **Gooimeer** (lake), Neth.
33/H4 **Goole,** Eng,UK
40/D4 **Goor,** Neth.
107/H2 **Goose** (lake), Mb,Can
104/B3 **Goose** (lake), Ca, Or,US
103/K3 **Goose Bay-Happy Valley,** Nf,Can
33/F5 **Goostrey,** Eng,UK
45/H2 **Göppingen,** Ger.
69/D4 **Go Quao,** Viet.
39/J3 **Góra,** Pol.
39/L3 **Góra Kalwaria,** Pol.
70/D2 **Gorakhpur,** India
50/D4 **Goražde,** Bosn.
100/E5 **Gorda** (pt.), Nic.
108/A2 **Gorda** (pt.), Ca,US
77/C4 **Gordon** (lake), Austl.
82/J6 **Goré,** Chad
83/N6 **Gorē,** Eth.
75/Q12 **Gore,** NZ
35/G1 **Gore** (pt.), Eng,UK
114/H4 **Gore** (pt.), Ak,US
59/D2 **Görele,** Turk.
44/B2 **Gorey,** Chl,UK
61/F1 **Gorgān,** Iran
43/F4 **Gorge du Loup,** Lux.
84/B3 **Gorgol** (reg.), Mrta.
84/B2 **Gorgol** (riv.), Mrta.
55/H4 **Gori,** Geo.
40/B5 **Gorinchem,** Neth.
35/E3 **Goring,** Eng,UK
35/F5 **Goring by Sea,** Eng,UK
45/K4 **Gorizia,** It.
51/F3 **Gorj** (co.), Rom.
54/D1 **Gorki,** Bela.
52/J4 **Gor'kiy** (res.), Rus.
53/K4 **Gor'kiy** (Nizhniy Novgorod), Rus.
39/L4 **Gorlice,** Pol.
39/H3 **Görlitz,** Ger.
34/C2 **Gorllwyn** (mtn.), Wal,UK
54/F2 **Gorlovka,** Ukr.
32/B4 **Gormanston,** Ire.
111/R8 **Gormley,** On,Can
51/G4 **Gorna Oryakhovitsa,** Bul.
50/E3 **Gornji Milanovac,** Yugo.
50/C4 **Gornji Vakuf,** Bosn.
56/J4 **Gorno-Altay Aut. Obl.,** Rus.
68/E1 **Gorno-Altaysk,** Rus.
56/H6 **Gorno-Badakhstan Aut. Obl.,** Taj.
53/J4 **Gorodets,** Rus.
78/D5 **Goroka,** PNG
73/H4 **Gorong** (isl.), Indo.
73/F3 **Gorontalo,** Indo.
34/B3 **Gorseinon,** Wal,UK
40/D4 **Gorssel,** Neth.
32/A2 **Gortin,** NI,UK
54/C2 **Goryn'** (riv.), Bela., Ukr.
39/H2 **Gorzów** (prov.), Pol.
39/H2 **Gorzów Wielkopolski,** Pol.
64/D3 **Gōse,** Japan
65/F2 **Gosen,** Japan
33/G2 **Gosforth,** Eng,UK
63/N3 **Goshogawara,** Japan
41/H5 **Goslar,** Ger.
50/B3 **Gospić,** Cro.
35/E5 **Gosport,** Eng,UK
50/E5 **Gostivar,** Macd.
39/J3 **Gostyń,** Pol.
39/K2 **Gostynin,** Pol.
37/D4 **Göteborg,** Swe.
37/D4 **Göteborg och Bohus** (co.), Swe.
82/H6 **Gotel** (mts.), Camr., Nga.
65/F3 **Gotemba,** Japan
41/H7 **Gotha,** Ger.
109/G2 **Gothenburg,** Ne,US
37/F4 **Gotland** (isl.), Swe.
64/A4 **Gotō** (isls.), Japan
51/F5 **Gotse Delchev,** Bul.
37/F4 **Gotska Sandön Nat'l Park,** Swe.
64/C3 **Gōtsu,** Japan
41/G5 **Göttingen,** Ger.
40/B4 **Gouda,** Neth.
28/J8 **Gough** (isl.), StH.
110/F1 **Gouin** (res.), Qu,Can
110/C2 **Goulais** (riv.), On,Can
77/D2 **Goulburn,** Austl.
74/E2 **Goulburn** (isls.), Austl.
77/D2 **Goulburn** (riv.), Austl.
98/P **Gould** (coast), Ant.
112/F3 **Gould,** Ar,US
84/E2 **Goundam,** Mali
85/H3 **Gouré,** Niger
88/C4 **Gourits** (riv.), SAfr.
85/F3 **Gourma** (prov.), Burk.
85/F3 **Gourma** (reg.), Burk.
85/E2 **Gourma-Rharous,** Mali
42/A5 **Gournay-en-Bray,** Fr.
83/J4 **Gouro,** Chad
31/T9 **Goussainville,** Fr.
59/D2 **Goušu** (riv.), Turk.
95/D1 **Gouvêa,** Braz.
42/B5 **Gouvieux,** Fr.
54/C2 **Goverla** (peak), Ukr.
95/D1 **Governador Valadares,** Braz.
62/D3 **Govĭ Altayn** (mts.), Mong.
61/H3 **Gowd-e-Zereh** (lake), Afg.
34/B3 **Gower** (pen.), Wal,UK
33/H4 **Goxhill,** Eng,UK
91/E2 **Goya,** Arg.
33/F5 **Goyt** (riv.), Eng,UK
65/M9 **Gozaisho-yama** (peak), Japan
68/D4 **Gozha** (lake), China
48/D4 **Gozo** (isl.), Malta
88/D4 **Graaff-Reinet,** SAfr.
40/D4 **Graafschap** (reg.), Neth.
38/B2 **Graberberg** (peak), Namb.
38/F2 **Grabow,** Ger.
50/B3 **Gračac,** Cro.
50/D3 **Gračanica,** Bosn.
113/G4 **Graceville,** Fl,US
100/E5 **Gracias a Dios** (cape), Nic.
47/S12 **Graciosa** (isl.), Azor.,Port.
50/D3 **Gradačac,** Bosn.
93/H5 **Gradaús,** Braz.
46/B1 **Grado,** Sp.
35/F2 **Grafham Water** (lake), Eng,UK
77/E1 **Grafton,** Austl.
76/B2 **Grafton** (passg.), Austl.
107/J3 **Grafton,** ND,US
110/D4 **Grafton,** WV,US
102/C3 **Graham** (isl.), BC,Can
103/S7 **Graham** (isl.), NW,Can
101/N7 **Graham** (peak), Az.,US
112/D3 **Graham,** Tx,US
116/C3 **Graham,** Wa,US
56/G1 **Graham Bell** (isl.), Rus.
98/V **Graham Land** (reg.), Ant.
38/D4 **Grahamstown,** SAfr.
35/G4 **Grain,** Eng,UK
84/C5 **Grain Coast** (reg.), Libr.
94/A2 **Grajaú,** Braz.
93/J4 **Grajaú** (riv.), Braz.
39/M2 **Grajewo,** Pol.
44/D4 **Gramat** (plat.), Fr.
36/C2 **Grampian** (mts.), Sc,UK
77/B3 **Grampians Nat'l Park,** Austl.
40/D3 **Gramsbergen,** Neth.
37/D3 **Gran,** Nor.
32/D3 **Granada,** Col.
100/D5 **Granada,** Nic.
46/D4 **Granada,** Sp.
97/K7 **Gran Altiplanicie Central** (plat.), Arg.
97/K7 **Gran Bajo de San Julián** (val.), Arg.
96/C5 **Gran Bajo Oriental** (val.), Arg.
112/D3 **Granbury,** Tx,US
109/F2 **Granby,** Co,US
47/X17 **Gran Canaria** (isl.), Canl.
90/C5 **Gran Chaco** (plain), SAm.
111/H2 **Grand** (lake), NB,Can
111/K1 **Grand** (lake), Nf,Can
103/J3 **Grand** (riv.), Qu,Can
66/D4 **Grand** (can.), China
32/B5 **Grand** (can.), Ire.
108/D3 **Grand** (canyon), Az,US
109/J3 **Grand** (riv.), Ia, Mo,US
109/J5 **Grand** (lake), La,US
110/C2 **Grand** (isl.), Mi,US
112/E2 **Grand** (riv.), Mo,US
111/S9 **Grand** (isl.), NY,US
107/H4 **Grand** (riv.), SD,US
101/F2 **Grand Bahama** (isl.), Bahm.
111/L2 **Grand Bank,** Nf,Can
84/C5 **Grand Bassa** (co.), Libr.
84/E5 **Grand-Bassam,** IvC.
111/H2 **Grand Bay,** NB,Can
116/E6 **Grand Blanc,** Mi,US
108/D3 **Grand Canyon Nat'l Park,** Az,US
84/C5 **Grand Cape Mount** (co.), Libr.
100/E4 **Grand Cayman** (isl.), Cay.
106/F2 **Grand Centre,** Ab,Can
106/D4 **Grand Coulee** (dam), Wa,US
97/K7 **Grande** (bay), Arg.
97/K8 **Grande** (riv.), Arg.
92/F7 **Grande** (riv.), Bol.
95/K8 **Grande** (isl.), Braz.
95/J7 **Grande** (riv.), Braz.
101/F6 **Grande** (pt.), Pan.
97/T11 **Grande** (stream), Uru.
106/D2 **Grande Cache,** Ab,Can
89/G5 **Grande Comore** (isl.), Com.
48/C1 **Grande, Corno** (peak), It.
93/H4 **Grande de Gurupá,** Braz.
48/C4 **Grande, Monte** (peak), It.
106/D2 **Grande Prairie,** Ab,Can
82/H4 **Grand 'Erg de Bilma** (des.), Niger
82/E1 **Grand Erg Occidental** (des.), Alg.
82/G1 **Grand Erg Oriental** (des.), Alg.
112/C4 **Grande, Rio** (riv.), Mex., US
42/B1 **Grande-Synthe,** Fr.
101/J4 **Grande-Terre** (isl.), Guad.
111/H2 **Grand Falls,** NB,Can
111/L1 **Grand Falls,** Nf,Can
106/D3 **Grand Forks,** BC,Can
107/J4 **Grand Forks,** ND,US
42/B2 **Grand-Fort-Philippe,** Fr.
110/C3 **Grand Haven,** Mi,US
109/H2 **Grand Island,** Ne,US
113/F4 **Grand Isle,** La,US
84/D5 **Grand Jide** (co.), Libr.
108/E3 **Grand Junction,** Co,US
109/J3 **Grand Lake O'The Cherokees** (lake), Ok,US
111/H2 **Grand Manan** (isl.), NB,Can
107/L4 **Grand Marais,** Mn,US
42/C6 **Grand Marin** (riv.), Fr.
111/F2 **Grand-Mère,** Qu,Can
111/K2 **Grand Miquelon** (isl.), StP.
45/G3 **Grand Mont Ruan** (mtn.), Fr.
46/A3 **Grândola,** Port.
107/L4 **Grand Portage Nat'l Mon.,** Mn,US
43/D5 **Grandpré,** Fr.
107/J2 **Grand Rapids,** Mb,Can
110/C3 **Grand Rapids,** Mi,US
107/K4 **Grand Rapids,** Mn,US
44/F5 **Grand Rhône** (riv.), Fr.
106/F5 **Grand Teton Nat'l Park,** Wy,US
101/G3 **Grand Turk,** Trks.
31/M6 **Grand Union** (can.), Eng,UK
107/H3 **Grandview,** Mb,Can
106/D4 **Grandview,** Wa,US
96/C2 **Graneros,** Chile
37/E3 **Granfjället** (peak), Swe.
33/F3 **Grange,** Eng,UK
114/L3 **Granger** (mtn.), Yk,Can
106/D4 **Grangeville,** Id,US
106/B2 **Granisle,** BC,Can
106/F4 **Granite** (peak), Mt,US
110/B4 **Granite City,** Il,US
94/B1 **Granja,** Braz.
96/D5 **Gran Laguna Salada** (lake), Arg.
47/G2 **Granollers,** Sp.
45/G4 **Gran Paradiso Nat'l Park,** It.
45/J3 **Gran Pilastro** (peak), It.
47/Y16 **Gran Tarajal,** Canl.,Sp.
33/H6 **Grantham,** Eng,UK
36/D2 **Grantown-on-Spey,** Sc,UK
108/F4 **Grants,** NM,US
110/A2 **Grantsburg,** Wi,US
106/C5 **Grants Pass,** Or,US
92/C5 **Gran Vilaya** (ruins), Peru
107/H1 **Granville** (lake), Mb,Can
44/C2 **Granville,** Fr.
116/B3 **Grapeview-Allyn,** Wa,US
41/F2 **Grasberg,** Ger.
33/E3 **Grasmere,** Eng,UK
45/G5 **Grasse,** Fr.
111/Q9 **Grassie,** On,Can
33/G3 **Grassington,** Eng,UK
106/G3 **Grasslands Nat'l Park,** Sk,Can
50/B2 **Gratkorn,** Aus.
44/E5 **Graulhet,** Fr.
94/D3 **Gravatá,** Braz.
40/C5 **Grave,** Neth.
106/G3 **Gravelbourg,** Sk,Can
42/B2 **Gravelines,** Fr.
110/E2 **Gravenhurst,** On,Can
31/Q7 **Gravesend,** Eng,UK
42/A5 **Gravigny,** Fr.
48/E2 **Gravina di Puglia,** It.
101/G4 **Gravois** (pt.), Haiti
44/F3 **Gray,** Fr.
110/C2 **Grayling,** Mi,US
31/P7 **Grays,** Eng,UK
106/F5 **Grays** (lake), Id,US
106/B4 **Grays** (har.), Wa,US
116/P15 **Grayslake,** Il,US
107/H3 **Grayson,** Sk,Can
45/L3 **Graz,** Aus.
77/C4 **Great** (lake), Austl.
107/G3 **Great** (plains), Can., US
28/E3 **Great** (lakes), NAm.
108/C2 **Great** (basin), US
101/F2 **Great Abaco** (isl.), Bahm.
39/L5 **Great Alföld** (plain), Hun.
74/D6 **Great Australian** (bight), Austl.
101/F3 **Great Bahama** (bank), Bahm.
35/F2 **Great Barford,** Eng,UK
75/S10 **Great Barrier** (isl.), NZ
76/B2 **Great Barrier Reef Marine Park,** Austl.
35/G2 **Great Barton,** Eng,UK
108/D3 **Great Basin Nat'l Park,** Nv,US
102/D2 **Great Bear** (lake), NW,Can
109/H3 **Great Bend,** Ks,US
31/M8 **Great Bookham,** Eng,UK
88/C3 **Great Brak** (riv.), SAfr.
36/E3 **Great Britain** (isl.), UK
29/P5 **Great Coco** (isl.), Burma
35/G2 **Great Cornard,** Eng,UK
106/F5 **Great Divide** (basin), Wyo,US
75/H7 **Great Dividing** (range), Austl.
33/H4 **Great Driffield,** Eng,UK
35/G3 **Great Dunmow,** Eng,UK
85/F5 **Greater Accra** (reg.), Gha.
101/G4 **Greater Antilles** (arch.), NAm.
55/L3 **Greater Barsuki** (des.), Kaz.
31/P7 **Greater London** (co.), Eng,UK
33/F5 **Greater Manchester** (co.), Eng,UK
72/C4 **Greater Sunda** (isls.), Indo.
101/F3 **Great Exuma** (isl.), Bahm.
106/F4 **Great Falls,** Mt,US
88/D4 **Great Fish** (pt.), SAfr.
88/D4 **Great Fish** (riv.), SAfr.
35/F2 **Great Gransden,** Eng,UK
101/F3 **Great Guana Cay** (isl.), Bahm.
33/G2 **Greatham,** Eng,UK
33/F4 **Great Harwood,** Eng,UK
70/D2 **Great Himalaya** (range), Asia
101/G3 **Great Inagua** (isl.), Bahm.
70/A2 **Great Indian** (des.), India, Pak.
88/C3 **Great Karoo** (reg.), SAfr.
88/D4 **Great Kei** (riv.), SAfr.
34/D2 **Great Malvern,** Eng,UK
35/E3 **Great Milton,** Eng,UK
34/B5 **Great Mis Tor** (hill), Eng,UK
115/G5 **Great Neck,** NY,US
71/F6 **Great Nicobar** (isl.), India
35/G1 **Great Ouse** (riv.), Eng,UK
77/C4 **Great Oyster** (bay), Austl.
113/J3 **Great Pee Dee** (riv.), SC,US
87/F2 **Great Rift** (val.), Afr.
87/F2 **Great Ruaha** (riv.), Tanz.
108/D2 **Great Salt** (lake), Ut,US
108/D2 **Great Salt Lake** (des.), Ut,US
109/F3 **Great Sand Dunes Nat'l Mon.,** Co,US
86/A3 **Great Sand Sea** (des.), Egypt, Libya
74/C4 **Great Sandy** (des.), Austl.
108/B2 **Great Sandy** (des.), Or,US
76/D4 **Great Sandy Nat'l Park,** Austl.
84/B4 **Great Scarcies** (riv.), Gui., SLeo.
35/G2 **Great Shelford,** Eng,UK
33/F3 **Great Shunner Fell** (mtn.), Eng,UK
102/E2 **Great Slave** (lake), NW,Can
113/H3 **Great Smoky Mts. Nat'l Park,** NC, Tn,US
115/G5 **Great South** (bay), NY,US
35/G4 **Great Stour** (riv.), Eng,UK
69/B3 **Great Tenasserim** (riv.), Burma
34/B5 **Great Torrington,** Eng,UK
74/D5 **Great Victoria** (des.), Austl.
66/B3 **Great Wall** (ruins), China
31/P7 **Great Warley,** Eng,UK
77/C4 **Great Western Tiers** (mts.), Austl.
88/B4 **Great Winterhoek** (peak), SAfr.
34/D2 **Great Witley,** Eng,UK
35/H1 **Great Yarmouth,** Eng,UK
59/F3 **Great Zab** (riv.), Iraq, Turk.
87/F5 **Great Zimbabwe** (ruins), Zim.
85/H2 **Grébon** (peak), Niger
59/K4 **Greco** (cape), Cyp.
48/D2 **Greco** (peak), It.
46/C2 **Gredos** (range), Sp.
30/F5 **Greece**
109/F2 **Greeley,** Co,US
103/S6 **Greely** (fjord), NW,Can
77/D3 **Green** (cape), Austl.
110/C4 **Green** (riv.), Ky,US
107/M4 **Green** (bay), Mi, Wi,US
108/E3 **Green** (riv.), Ut, Wy,US
111/G3 **Green** (mts.), Vt,US
110/B2 **Green Bay,** Wi,US
115/K7 **Greenbelt,** Md,US
110/C4 **Greencastle,** In,US
113/H4 **Green Cove Springs,** Fl,US
116/Q14 **Greendale,** Wi,US
113/H2 **Greeneville,** Tn,US
110/C4 **Greenfield,** In,US
111/F3 **Greenfield,** Ma,US
116/P14 **Greenfield,** Wi,US
111/P7 **Greenfield Park,** Qu,Can
115/K7 **Green Haven,** Md,US
32/C2 **Greenisland,** NI,UK
99/R2 **Greenland** (sea)
99/N2 **Greenland** (Kalaallit Nunaat) (dpcy.), Den.
36/D3 **Greenlaw,** Sc,UK
36/C3 **Greenock,** Sc,UK
114/K2 **Greenough** (mtn.), Ak,US
111/R8 **Green River,** On,Can
108/E3 **Green River,** Ut,US
106/F5 **Green River,** Wy,US
113/G3 **Greensboro,** Al,US
113/J2 **Greensboro,** NC,US
110/C4 **Greensburg,** In,US
110/E3 **Greensburg,** Pa,US
111/Q9 **Greensville,** On,Can
108/E5 **Green Valley,** Az,US
115/J7 **Green Valley,** Md,US
84/C5 **Greenville,** Libr.
113/G4 **Greenville,** Al,US
108/B2 **Greenville,** Ca,US
110/C4 **Greenville,** Ky,US
110/C3 **Greenville,** Mi,US
113/F3 **Greenville,** Ms,US
113/J3 **Greenville,** NC,US
110/C3 **Greenville,** Oh,US
113/H3 **Greenville,** SC,US
112/D3 **Greenville,** Tx,US
116/D3 **Greenwater** (riv.), Wa,US
31/P7 **Greenwich** (bor.), Eng,UK
115/G4 **Greenwich,** Ct,US
111/R8 **Greenwood,** On,Can
113/F3 **Greenwood,** Ms,US
115/F4 **Greenwood** (lake), NJ, NY,US
113/H3 **Greenwood,** SC,US
113/H3 **Greenwood** (lake), SC,US
109/J4 **Greers Ferry** (lake), Ar,US
32/B6 **Greese** (riv.), Ire.
40/D6 **Grefrath,** Ger.
92/D5 **Gregório** (riv.), Braz.
74/C5 **Gregory** (lake), Austl.
74/D4 **Gregory** (lake), Austl.
74/F5 **Gregory** (lake), Austl.
76/A2 **Gregory** (range), Austl.
107/J5 **Gregory,** SD,US
39/G1 **Greifswald,** Ger.
39/G1 **Greifwalder Bodden** (bay), Ger.
50/B2 **Greimberg** (peak), Aus.
38/G3 **Greiz,** Ger.
53/N4 **Gremyachinsk,** Rus.
37/D4 **Grenå,** Den.
101/J5 **Grenada**
113/F3 **Grenada,** Ms,US
45/G3 **Grenchen,** Swi.
107/H3 **Grenfell,** Sk,Can
44/F4 **Grenoble,** Fr.
74/G2 **Grenville** (cape), Austl.
37/E2 **Gressåmoen Nat'l Park,** Nor.
33/E2 **Greta** (riv.), Eng,UK
33/F3 **Greta** (riv.), Eng,UK
107/J3 **Gretna,** Mb,Can
33/E2 **Gretna,** Sc,UK
113/F4 **Gretna,** La,US
35/F1 **Gretton,** Eng,UK
31/U10 **Gretz-Armainvilliers,** Fr.
40/B5 **Grevelingendam** (dam), Neth.
41/E4 **Greven,** Ger.
49/G2 **Grevená,** Gre.
40/D6 **Grevenbroich,** Ger.
43/F4 **Grevenmacher** (dist.), Lux.
38/F2 **Grevesmühlen,** Ger.
40/A5 **Grevlingen** (chan.), Neth.
74/F2 **Grey** (cape), Austl.
76/A5 **Grey** (range), Austl.
111/K2 **Grey** (riv.), Nf,Can
32/C2 **Grey** (pt.), NI,UK
32/C2 **Grey Abbey,** NI,UK
106/F4 **Greybull,** Wy,US
114/L3 **Grey Hunter** (peak), Yk,Can
75/R11 **Greymouth,** NZ
76/B2 **Grey Peaks Nat'l Park,** Austl.

138

Greys – Hayra

33/F2 Greystoke, Eng,UK
32/B5 Greystones, Ire.
89/E3 Greytown, SAfr.
43/D2 Grez-Doiceau, Belg.
34/B6 Gribbin (pt.), Eng,UK
40/C2 Griend (isl.), Neth.
113/G3 Griffin, Ga,US
77/C2 Griffith, Austl.
116/R16 Griffith, In,US
42/B6 Grigny, Fr.
77/C4 Grim (cape), Austl.
42/D2 Grimbergen, Belg.
34/D2 Grimley, Eng,UK
38/G1 Grimmen, Ger.
111/Q9 Grimsby, On,Can
33/H4 Grimsby, Eng,UK
37/N6 Grimsey (isl.), Ice.
37/D4 Grimstad, Nor.
103/S7 Grinnel (pen.), NW,Can
50/B2 Grintavec (peak), Slov.
88/E3 Griqualand East (reg.), SAfr.
88/C2 Griqualand West (reg.), SAfr.
42/A2 Gris Nez (cape), Fr.
31/U10 Grisy-Suisnes, Fr.
116/K10 Grizzly (bay), Ca,US
50/C3 Grmeč (mtn.), Bosn.
43/D1 Grobbendonk, Belg.
39/J3 Grodków, Pol.
39/M2 Grodno, Bela.
52/E5 Grodno Obl., Bela.
39/J2 Grodzisk Wielkopolski, Pol.
40/D4 Groenlo, Neth.
112/D4 Groesbeck, Tx,US
40/C5 Groesbeek, Neth.
44/B3 Groix (isl.), Fr.
39/L3 Grójec, Pol.
38/F1 Grömitz, Ger.
40/E4 Gronau, Ger.
40/D2 Groningen, Neth.
40/D2 Groningen (prov.), Neth.
45/J3 Gronlait (peak), It.
88/C4 Groot (riv.), SAfr.
74/F2 Groote Eylandt (isl.), Austl.
40/D2 Grootegast, Neth.
87/C4 Grootfontein, Namb.
88/D2 Groot-Marico (riv.), SAfr.
88/C3 Grootvloer (salt pan), SAfr.
101/J5 Gros Islet, StL.
111/K1 Gros Morne (peak), Nf,Can
111/K1 Gros Morne Nat'l Park, Nf,Can
44/F3 Grosne (riv.), Fr.
41/G6 Grossalmerode, Ger.
41/E3 Grosse Aa (riv.), Ger.
116/F7 Grosse Ile, Mi,US
88/A2 Grosse Münzenberg (peak), Namb.
43/G2 Grosse Nister (riv.), Ger.
41/F3 Grossenkneten, Ger.
116/G7 Grosse Pointe, Mi,US
116/G7 Grosse Pointe Farms, Mi,US
116/G7 Grosse Pointe Park, Mi,US
116/G7 Grosse Pointe Shores, Mi,US
116/G7 Grosse Pointe Woods, Mi,US
45/K2 Grosser Arber (peak), Ger.
41/G3 Grosser Aue (riv.), Ger.
38/F3 Grosser Beer-Berg (peak), Ger.
45/L3 Grosser Bösenstein (peak), Aus.
41/F1 Grosser Knechtsand (isl.), Ger.
39/H4 Grosser Peilstein (peak), Aus.
45/L3 Grosser Priel (peak), Aus.
39/H5 Grosser Pyhrgas (peak), Aus.
45/K2 Grosser Rachel (peak), Ger.
41/E2 Grosses Meer (lake), Ger.
50/A2 Grosses Wiesbachhorn (peak), Aus.
48/B1 Grosseto, It.
45/H2 Grossgerau, Ger.
45/K3 Grossglockner (peak), Aus.
41/H1 Grosshansdorf, Ger.
45/H5 Grosso (cape), Fr.
43/F5 Grossrosseln, Ger.
43/E2 Grote Gete (riv.), Belg.
43/D1 Grote Nete (riv.), Belg.
107/J4 Groton, SD,US
48/E2 Grottaglie, It.
43/E3 Grotte de Han, Belg.
47/E1 Grottes de Bétharram, Fr.
81/L14 Grou (riv.), Mor.
106/D2 Grouard Mission, Ab,Can
110/D1 Groundhog (riv.), On,Can
40/C2 Grouw, Neth.
35/E3 Grove, Eng,UK
109/J3 Grove, Ok,US
108/B4 Grover City, Ca,US
112/E4 Groves, Tx,US
115/J8 Groveton, Va,US
55/H4 Groznyy, Rus.
51/H4 Grudovo, Bul.
39/K2 Grudziądz, Pol.
33/E2 Grune (pt.), Eng,UK
54/F1 Gryazi, Rus.
39/H2 Gryfice, Pol.
39/H2 Gryfino, Pol.
96/B4 Guabun (pt.), Chile
101/F3 Guacanayabo (gulf), Cuba
95/D2 Guaçuí, Braz.
101/P9 Guadalajara, Mex.
46/D2 Guadalajara, Sp.
78/E6 Guadalcanal (isl.), Sol.
46/E4 Guadalentín (riv.), Sp.
46/D3 Guadalimlar (riv.), Sp.
47/N8 Guadalix (riv.), Sp.
47/E2 Guadalope (riv.), Sp.
46/D4 Guadalquivir (riv.), Sp.
94/B2 Guadalupe, Braz.
101/F6 Guadalupe, Pan.
46/C3 Guadalupe (range), Sp.
112/B4 Guadalupe (peak), Tx,US
112/D4 Guadalupe (riv.), Tx,US
112/B4 Guadalupe Mts. Nat'l Park, Tx,US
47/M8 Guadarrama (pass), Sp.
46/C2 Guadarrama (range), Sp.
46/C3 Guadarrama (riv.), Sp.
101/J4 Guadeloupe (dpcy.), Fr.
101/J4 Guadeloupe (passage), NAm.
46/B4 Guadiana (riv.), Sp., Port.
46/D4 Guadiana Menor (riv.), Sp.
46/D4 Guadix, Sp.
96/B4 Guafo (chan.), Chile
96/B4 Guafo (isl.), Chile
95/B4 Guaíba, Braz.
95/B4 Guaiba (riv.), Braz.
92/F2 Guaiquinima (peak), Ven.
95/B2 Guaíra, Braz.
96/B4 Guaiteca (isl.), Chile
92/E6 Guajará-Mirim, Braz.
101/G5 Guajira (pen.), Col., Ven.
108/B3 Gualala, Ca,US
48/C1 Gualdo Tadino, It.
96/F2 Gualeguay, Arg.
96/F2 Gualeguay (riv.), Arg.
96/F2 Gualeguaychú, Arg.
96/D4 Gualicho (val.), Arg.
78/D3 Guam (isl.), PacUS
96/B5 Guamblin (isl.), Chile
95/K7 Guanabara (bay), Braz.
100/A3 Guanajuato, Mex.
100/A3 Guanajuato (state), Mex.
94/B4 Guanambi, Braz.
101/H6 Guanare, Ven.
101/H6 Guanare (riv.), Ven.
66/C3 Guancen Shan (mtn.), China
66/B3 Guandi Shan (mtn.), China
71/K3 Guangdong (prov.), China
66/D5 Guangming Ding (peak), China
71/J3 Guangxi Zhuangzu Zizhiqu (aut. reg.), China
67/C2 Guangze, China
67/B3 Guangzhou (Canton), China
95/D1 Guanhães, Braz.
101/J6 Guanipa (riv.), Ven.
101/F3 Guantánamo, Cuba
66/G6 Guanting (res.), China
66/D4 Guanyun, China
95/B4 Guaporé, Braz.
92/F6 Guaporé (riv.), Braz.
94/A4 Guara (riv.), Braz.
47/E1 Guara (peak), Sp.
94/D2 Guarabira, Braz.
93/J5 Guaraí, Braz.
95/B3 Guaramirim, Braz.
92/C4 Guaranda, Ecu.
95/D2 Guarapari, Braz.
95/B3 Guarapuava, Braz.
95/B2 Guararapes, Braz.
95/G8 Guararema, Braz.
94/C5 Guaratinga, Braz.
95/H7 Guaratinguetá, Braz.
95/B3 Guaratuba, Braz.
46/B2 Guarda, Port.
46/B2 Guarda (dist.), Port.
46/B3 Guareña, Sp.
92/E2 Guárico (res.), Ven.
101/H6 Guárico (riv.), Ven.
95/G9 Guarujá, Braz.
95/G8 Guarulhos, Braz.
101/N8 Guasave, Mex.
100/C4 Guatemala
100/C5 Guatemala (cap.), Guat.
95/G6 Guaxupé, Braz.
101/H4 Guayama, PR
92/C4 Guayaquil, Ecu.
92/B4 Guayaquil (gulf), Ecu.
92/E6 Guayaramerín, Bol.
101/M8 Guaymas, Mex.
53/N4 Gubakha, Rus.
39/H3 Guben, Ger.
39/H3 Gubin, Pol.
54/F2 Gubkin, Rus.
62/E2 Guchin-Us, Mong.
47/E2 Gúdar (range), Sp.
41/G6 Gudensberg, Ger.
55/H4 Gudermes, Rus.
70/D4 Gudivāda, India
70/C5 Gūdūr, India
46/D1 Guecho, Sp.
84/B1 Guelb Azefal (mts.), Mrta.
81/V17 Guelma, Alg.
110/D3 Guelph, On,Can
82/C2 Guelta Zemmur, WSah.
43/F5 Guénange, Fr.
44/B3 Guérande, Fr.
44/D3 Guéret, Fr.
46/D1 Guernica y Luno, Sp.
44/B2 Guernsey (isl.), ChI,UK
100/B4 Guerrero (state), Mex.
44/F3 Gueugnon, Fr.
85/H3 Guézaoua, Niger
83/N6 Gugē (peak), Eth.
78/D3 Guguan (isl.), NMar.
67/B3 Gui (riv.), China
47/X16 Guía de Isora, Sp.
92/F2 Guiana Highlands (mts.), SAm.
100/B4 Guichicovi, Mex.
82/H6 Guidder, Camr.
84/B3 Guidimaka (reg.), Mrta.
48/C2 Guidonia, It.
84/D5 Guiglo, IvC.
31/U11 Guignes, Fr.
42/C5 Guignicourt, Fr.
67/D5 Guihulngan, Phil.
31/M8 Guildford, Eng,UK
44/F4 Guilherand, Fr.
71/K2 Guilin, China
103/J3 Guillaume-Delisle (lake), Qu,Can
46/B4 Guillena, Sp.
34/C1 Guilsfield, Wal,UK
46/A2 Guimarães, Port.
66/D4 Guimeng Ding (mtn.), China
84/C4 Guinea
82/F7 Guinea (gulf), Afr.
84/B3 Guinea-Bissau
44/B2 Guingamp, Fr.
44/A2 Guipavas, Fr.
93/H7 Guiratinga, Braz.
101/J5 Güiria, Ven.
33/G2 Guisborough, Eng,UK
42/C4 Guise, Fr.
33/G4 Guiseley, Eng,UK
46/B1 Guitiriz, Sp.
67/B2 Guiyang, China
71/J2 Guiyang, China
71/J2 Guizhou (prov.), China
44/C4 Gujan-Mestras, Fr.
70/B3 Gujarāt (state), India
61/K2 Gūjar Khān, Pak.
61/K2 Gujrānwāla, Pak.
61/K2 Gujrāt, Pak.
54/F2 Gukovo, Rus.
62/E4 Gulang, China
70/C4 Gulbarga, India
43/G3 Guldenbach (riv.), Ger.
67/C3 Guleitou, China
113/F4 Gulfport, Ms,US
113/G4 Gulf Shores, Al,US
56/G5 Gulistan, Uzb.
63/J2 Guliya (peak), China
32/B2 Gulladuff, NI,UK
106/F3 Gull Lake, Sk,Can
59/C3 Gülnar, Turk.
43/E2 Gulpen, Neth.
83/M7 Gulu, Ugan.
51/G4 Gŭlŭbovo, Bul.
87/D4 Gumare, Bots.
65/F2 Gumma (pref.), Japan
41/E6 Gummersbach, Ger.
54/E4 Gümüşhacıköy, Turk.
59/D2 Gümüşhane, Turk.
83/N5 Guna (peak), Eth.
70/C3 Guna, India
59/E2 Güneydogu Toroslar (mts.), Turk.
107/J2 Gunisao (lake), Mb,Can
107/J2 Gunisao (riv.), Mb,Can
77/D1 Gunnedah, Austl.
108/F3 Gunnison, Co,US
108/F3 Gunnison (riv.), Co,US
108/E3 Gunnison, Ut,US
68/B4 Gunt (riv.), Taj.
113/G3 Guntersville, Al,US
113/G3 Guntersville (lake), Al,US
70/D4 Guntūr, India
45/J2 Günz (riv.), Ger.
45/J2 Gunzenhausen, Ger.
66/C4 Guo (riv.), China
83/N6 Guragē (peak), Eth.
51/G2 Gura Humorului, Rom.
91/F2 Gural (mts.), Braz.
62/B2 Gurbantünggut (des.), China
61/L2 Gurdāspur, India
94/B3 Gurguéia (riv.), Braz.
101/J6 Guri, Embalse de (res.), Ven.
45/L3 Gurk (riv.), Aus.
45/K3 Gurkthaler (mts.), Aus.
116/Q15 Gurnee, Il,US
51/J5 Gürsu, Turk.
93/J6 Gurupi, Braz.
93/J4 Gurupi (mts.), Braz.
94/A1 Gurupi (riv.), Braz.
70/B3 Guru Sikhar (mtn.), India
62/G2 Gurvandzagal, Mong.
55/J3 Gur'yev, Kaz.
55/J3 Gur'yev Obl., Kaz.
52/J5 Gus'-Khrustal'nyy, Rus.
48/A3 Guspini, It.
38/G2 Güstrow, Ger.
41/F5 Gütersloh, Ger.
109/H4 Guthrie, Ok,US
109/G4 Guthrie, Tx,US
37/E3 Gutulia Nat'l Park, Nor.
92/G3 Guyana
31/S10 Guyancourt, Fr.
113/H2 Guyandotte (riv.), WV,US
66/B2 Guyang, China
44/C4 Guyenne (reg.), Fr.
77/E1 Guy Fawkes Riv. Nat'l Park, Austl.
35/G1 Guyhirn, Eng,UK
109/G3 Guymon, Ok,US
62/F4 Guyuan, China
62/H3 Guyuan, China
101/N7 Guzmán (lake), Mex.
61/H3 Gwādar, Pak.
70/C2 Gwalior, India
87/E5 Gwanda, Zim.
35/F1 Gwash (riv.), Eng,UK
34/C2 Gwaunceste (mtn.), Wal,UK
39/J2 Gwda (riv.), Pol.
34/A6 Gweek, Eng,UK
34/D3 Gwent (co.), Wal,UK
33/E5 Gwersyllt, Wal,UK
87/E4 Gweru, Zim.
77/D1 Gwydir (riv.), Austl.
32/D5 Gwynedd (co.), Wal,UK
55/H4 Gyandzhe, Azer.
63/D5 Gyaring (lake), China
85/F5 Gyasikan, Gha.
56/H2 Gyda (pen.), Rus.
76/D4 Gympie, Austl.
71/G4 Gyobingauk, Burma
50/E2 Gyoma, Hun.
50/D2 Gyöngyös, Hun.
50/C2 Győr, Hun.
50/C2 Győr-Sopron (co.), Hun.
50/E2 Gyula, Hun.

H

42/D2 Haacht, Belg.
40/D4 Haaksbergen, Neth.
42/D2 Haaltert, Belg.
40/E6 Haan, Ger.
79/H6 Ha'apai Group (isls.), Tonga
37/H2 Haapavesi, Fin.
52/D4 Haapsalu, Est.
45/J2 Haar, Ger.
45/G2 Haardt (mts.), Ger.
40/B4 Haarlem, Neth.
75/Q11 Haast, NZ
61/J3 Hab (riv.), Pak.
43/E4 Habay, Belg.
60/D2 Habbānīyah, Iraq
71/F3 Habiganj, Bang.
65/L10 Habikino, Japan
63/N3 Haboro, Japan
41/F3 Hache (riv.), Ger.
63/N5 Hachijō (isl.), Japan
65/F3 Hachiōji, Japan
115/C3 Hacienda Heights, Ca,US
59/C2 Hacılar, Turk.
115/F5 Hackensack, NJ,US
115/F5 Hackettstown, NJ,US
31/N7 Hackney (bor.), Eng,UK
69/D1 Ha Coi, Viet.
45/H1 Hadamar, Ger.
65/F3 Hadano, Japan
86/D4 Hadarba, Ras (cape), Sudan
83/J4 Haddad (wadi), Chad
35/F3 Haddenham, Eng,UK
36/D3 Haddington, Sc,UK
115/E6 Haddonfield, NJ,US
115/E6 Haddon (Westmont), NJ,US
61/G4 Ḩadd, Ra's al (pt.), Oman
85/H3 Hadejia (riv.), Nga.
41/F1 Hadelner (can.), Ger.
59/K5 Hadera, Isr.
38/E1 Haderslev, Den.
59/C3 Hadım, Turk.
81/S15 Hadjout, Alg.
50/E2 Hadjú-Bihar (co.), Hun.
102/F1 Hadley (bay), NW,Can
31/Q8 Hadlow, Eng,UK
33/F1 Hadrian's Wall (ruins), Eng,UK
37/E1 Hadselfjorden (fjord), Nor.
63/K4 Haeju, NKor.
104/S9 Haena (pt.), Hi,US
59/D2 Hafik, Turk.
61/K2 Hāfizābād, Pak.
37/N7 Hafnarfjördhur, Ice.
60/E3 Ḩafr al Bāţin, SAr.
60/E2 Haft Gel, Iran
81/H3 Hafun, Ras (pt.), Som.
114/F4 Hagemeister (isl.), Ak,US
41/E6 Hagen, Ger.
41/E4 Hagen am Teutoburger Wald, Ger.
38/F2 Hagenow, Ger.
109/F4 Hagerman, NM,US
110/E4 Hagerstown, Md,US
64/B3 Hagi, Japan
69/D1 Ha Giang, Viet.
34/D2 Hagley, Eng,UK
43/F5 Hagondange, Fr.
36/A4 Hags Head (pt.), Ire.
107/G2 Hague, Sk,Can
44/C2 Hague, Cap de la (cape), Fr.
43/G6 Haguenau, Fr.
40/B4 Hague, The ('s-Gravenhage) (cap.), Neth.
78/D2 Hahashima (isl.), Jap.
41/H6 Hahle (riv.), Ger.
43/G3 Hahnenbach (riv.), Ger.
66/D3 Hai (riv.), China
65/L10 Haibara, Japan
63/J3 Haicheng, China
69/D1 Hai Duong, Viet.
59/K5 Haifa (dist.), Isr.
59/K5 Haifa (Hefa), Isr.
43/H2 Haiger, Ger.
69/D1 Hai Hau, Viet.
67/B3 Haikou, China
63/H2 Hailar, China
63/J2 Hailar (riv.), China
110/E2 Haileybury, On,Can
35/G5 Hailsham, Eng,UK
71/J4 Hainan (prov.), China
67/B3 Hainan (str.), China
42/B2 Hainaut (prov.), Belg.
45/H1 Hainburg, Ger.
113/H4 Haines City, Fl,US
114/L3 Haines Junction, Yk,Can
41/H6 Hainich (mts.), Ger.
66/L9 Haining, China
69/D1 Haiphong (Hai Phong), Viet.
101/G4 Haiti
69/E2 Hai Van (pass), Viet.
71/K3 Haixia (str.), China
66/D4 Haizhou (bay), China
39/L5 Hajdú-Bihar (co.), Hun.
50/E2 Hajdúböszormény, Hun.
50/E2 Hajdúdorog, Hun.
50/E2 Hajdúhadház, Hun.
50/E2 Hajdúnánás, Hun.
50/E2 Hajdúszoboszló, Hun.
65/F1 Hajiki-zaki (pt.), Japan
39/M2 Hajnówka, Pol.
71/F2 Hājo, India
79/L5 Hakahau, Fr.Pol.
64/D3 Hakken-san (mtn.), Japan
63/N3 Hakodate, Japan
65/H7 Hakone, Japan
65/H8 Hakone-Fuji-Izu Nat'l Park, Japan
65/E2 Hakui, Japan
65/M10 Hakusan, Japan
65/E2 Haku-san (mtn.), Japan
65/E2 Hakusan Nat'l Park, Japan
61/J3 Hāla, Pak.
59/D3 Ḩalab (Aleppo), Syria
60/E1 Ḩalabjah, Iraq
86/D4 Ḩalā'ib, Sudan
37/D4 Halden, Nor.
38/F2 Haldensleben, Ger.
111/Q10 Haldimand, On,Can
62/G2 Haldzan, Mong.
87/G2 Hale, Tanz.
33/F5 Hale, Eng,UK
104/T10 Haleakala Nat'l Park, Hi,US
43/E2 Halen, Belg.
116/P14 Hales Corners, Wi,US
34/D2 Halesowen, Eng,UK
35/H2 Halesworth, Eng,UK
113/G3 Haleyville, Al,US
84/E5 Half Assini, Gha.
67/C6 Half Moon (shoal)
116/K12 Half Moon Bay, Ca,US
59/K6 Ḩalḩūl, WBnk.
110/E2 Haliburton (hills), On,Can
76/B2 Halifax (bay), Austl.
111/J2 Halifax (cap.), NS,Can
33/G4 Halifax, Eng,UK
61/G3 Halīl (riv.), Iran
114/H1 Halkett (cape), Ak,US
103/K2 Hall (pen.), NW,Can
78/E4 Hall (isls.), Micr.
114/D3 Hall (isl.), Ak,US
37/E4 Halland (co.), Swe.
63/K5 Halla-san (mtn.), SKor.
42/D2 Halle, Belg.
41/F4 Halle, Ger.
37/E4 Hällefors, Swe.
45/K3 Hallein, Aus.
42/A4 Hallencourt, Fr.
38/F3 Halle-Neustadt, Ger.
98/M Hallett (cape), Ant.
112/D4 Hallettsville, Tx,US
107/J3 Hallock, Mn,US
38/B4 Hallu (riv.), Fr.
42/B3 Hallue (riv.), Fr.
42/C2 Halluin, Fr.
64/A3 Hallyŏ Haesang Nat'l Park, SKor.
73/G3 Halmahera (isl.), Indo.
73/G4 Halmahera (sea), Indo.
37/E4 Halmstad, Swe.
81/X17 Ḩalq al Wādī, Tun.
37/E4 Hälsingborg, Swe.
35/G3 Halstead, Eng,UK
40/B5 Halsteren, Neth.
62/C4 Haltang (riv.), China
33/H4 Haltemprice, Eng,UK
41/E5 Haltern, Ger.
111/Q8 Halton Hills, On,Can
33/F2 Haltwhistle, Eng,UK
41/E6 Halver, Ger.
41/E3 Halverder Aa (riv.), Ger.
42/C4 Ham, Fr.
64/C3 Hamada, Japan
60/E2 Hamadān, Iran
59/L4 Ḩamāh, Syria
65/M10 Hamajima, Japan
65/E3 Hamakita, Japan
65/E3 Hamamatsu, Japan
37/D3 Hamar, Nor.
86/C3 Ḩamāţah, Jabal (mtn.), Egypt
70/D6 Hambantota, SrL.
35/E5 Hamble, Eng,UK
33/G3 Hambleton (hills), Eng,UK
41/G3 Hambühren, Ger.
41/G1 Hamburg, Ger.
41/H1 Hamburg (state), Ger.
112/F3 Hamburg, Ar,US
110/E3 Hamburg, NY,US
37/G3 Häme (prov.), Fin.
37/G3 Hämeenkyrö, Fin.
37/H3 Hämeenlinna, Fin.
74/A5 Hamelin Pool (bay), Austl.
41/G4 Hameln, Ger.
74/B4 Hamersley (range), Austl.
35/H3 Hamford Water (inlet), Eng,UK
63/K3 Hamgyŏng (mts.), NKor.
63/K4 Hamhŭng, NKor.
62/C3 Hami, China
103/L3 Hamilton (inlet), Nf,Can
111/Q9 Hamilton, On,Can
75/S10 Hamilton, NZ
36/C3 Hamilton, Sc,UK
113/G3 Hamilton, Al,US
116/L12 Hamilton (mt.), Ca,US
106/E4 Hamilton, Mt,US
110/C4 Hamilton, Oh,US
112/D4 Hamilton, Tx,US
70/D2 Hamīrpur, India
81/V17 Hamma-Bouziane, Alg.
81/X17 Hammāmāt (gulf), Tun.
81/Q16 Hamman, Oued el (riv.), Alg.
42/D1 Hamme, Belg.
41/F2 Hamme (riv.), Ger.
37/G1 Hammerfest, Nor.
31/N7 Hammersmith & Fulham (bor.), Eng,UK
40/D5 Hamminkeln, Ger.
116/R16 Hammond, In,US
113/F4 Hammond, La,US
43/E1 Hamont-Achel, Belg.
35/E4 Hampshire (co.), Eng,UK
35/E4 Hampshire Downs (hills), Eng,UK
31/N7 Hampstead, Eng,UK
110/E4 Hampton, Va,US
31/M7 Hampton Court, Eng,UK
77/G6 Hampton Park, Austl.
82/H1 Ḩamrā (upland), Libya
116/F7 Hamtramck, Mi,US
65/H7 Hamura, Japan
66/C5 Han (riv.), China
67/C3 Han (riv.), China
63/K4 Han (riv.), SKor.
63/N4 Hanamaki, Japan
104/U11 Hanamalo (pt.), Hi,US
63/M5 Hanamatsu, Japan
87/G1 Hanang (peak), Tanz.
110/B2 Hancock, Mi,US
65/M10 Handa, Japan
66/C3 Handan, China
35/E1 Handsworth, Eng,UK
108/C3 Hanford, Ca,US
62/D2 Hangayn (mts.), Mong.
34/C5 Hangingstone (hill), Eng,UK
88/L11 Hangklip (cape), SAfr.
68/B5 Hangu, Pak.
66/L9 Hangzhou, China
62/C2 Hanhöhiy (mts.), Mong.
59/E2 Hani, Turk.
107/J4 Hankinson, ND,US
107/G3 Hanley, Sk,Can
106/F3 Hanna, Ab,Can
106/G5 Hanna, Wy,US
65/L10 Hannan, Japan
109/K3 Hannibal, Mo,US
65/H7 Hannō, Japan
41/G4 Hannover, Ger.
43/E2 Hannut, Belg.
37/E5 Hanöbukten (bay), Swe.
69/D1 Hanoi (Ha Noi) (cap.), Viet.
110/D2 Hanover, On,Can
97/J7 Hanover (isl.), Chile
111/F3 Hanover, NH,US
116/P16 Hanover Park, Il,US
70/C2 Hānsi, India
68/D3 Hantengri Feng (peak), China
103/J2 Hantzsch (riv.), NW,Can
70/B2 Hanumāngarh, India
62/E2 Hanuy (riv.), Mong.
62/F5 Hanzhong, China
79/L6 Hao (atoll), FrPol.
37/H2 Haparanda, Swe.
103/K3 Happy Valley-Goose Bay, Nf,Can
62/D4 Har (lake), China
62/C2 Har (lake), Mong.
62/F2 Haraa (riv.), Mong.
65/G2 Haramachi, Japan
61/K2 Harappa (ruins), Pak.
87/F4 Harare (cap.), Zim.
62/F2 Har-Ayrag, Mong.
84/C5 Harbel, Libr.
63/K2 Harbin, China
111/L2 Harbour Breton, Nf,Can
35/E2 Harbury, Eng,UK
70/C3 Hardā, India
37/C3 Hardangervidda Nat'l Park, Nor.
88/B2 Hardap (dam), Namb.
41/H3 Hardau (riv.), Ger.
41/G5 Hardegsen, Ger.
40/D3 Hardenberg, Neth.
40/C4 Harderwijk, Neth.
106/G4 Hardin, Mt,US
61/L3 Hardwār, India
97/K8 Hardy (pen.), Chile
111/L1 Hare (bay), Nf,Can
42/C2 Harelbeke, Belg.
41/E3 Haren, Ger.
40/D2 Haren, Neth.
83/P6 Hārer, Eth.
59/N8 Har Eval (Jabal 'Aybāl) (mtn.), WBnk.
83/P6 Hargeysa, Som.
51/G2 Harghita (co.), Rom.
51/G2 Harghita (peak), Rom.
72/B4 Hari (riv.), Indo.
70/C5 Harihar, India
64/D3 Harima (sound), Japan
40/B5 Haringvliet (chan.), Neth.
61/H2 Harīrūd (riv.), Afg.
110/D4 Harlan, Ky,US
32/D6 Harlech, Wal,UK
35/H2 Harleston, Eng,UK
40/C2 Harlingen, Neth.
112/D5 Harlingen, Tx,US
35/F3 Harlington, Eng,UK
31/P6 Harlow, Eng,UK
106/F4 Harlowton, Mt,US
40/B4 Harmelen, Neth.
42/B3 Harnes, Fr.
106/D5 Harney (lake), Or,US
106/D5 Harney (val.), Or,US
107/H5 Harney (peak), SD,US
37/F3 Härnösand, Swe.
101/M8 Haro (cape), Mex.
46/D1 Haro, Sp.
35/F3 Harpenden, Eng,UK
114/L3 Harper (mtn.), Yk,Can
84/D5 Harper, Libr.
114/K3 Harper (mtn.), Ak,US
112/D2 Harper, Ks,US
116/G7 Harper Woods, Mi,US
110/E1 Harricana (riv.), Qu,Can
113/G3 Harriman, Tn,US
74/F6 Harris (lake), Austl.
110/B4 Harrisburg, Il,US
109/G2 Harrisburg, Ne,US
38/E1 Harrislee, Ger.
88/E3 Harrismith, SAfr.
106/C3 Harrison (lake), BC,Can
103/L3 Harrison (cape), Nf,Can
114/H1 Harrison (bay), Ak,US
112/E2 Harrison, Ar,US
109/G2 Harrison, Ne,US
115/G5 Harrison, NY,US
110/E4 Harrisonburg, Va,US
110/C4 Harrodsburg, Ky,US
33/G4 Harrogate, Eng,UK
31/M7 Harrow (bor.), Eng,UK
109/J3 Harry S Truman (res.), Mo,US
41/G2 Harsefeld, Ger.
41/F5 Harsewinkel, Ger.
37/F1 Harstad, Nor.
102/C2 Hart (riv.), Yk,Can
108/C2 Hart (lake), Or,US
88/C3 Hartbeesrivier (dry riv.), SAfr.
37/C3 Hårteigen (peak), Nor.
40/B5 Hartelkanaal (can.), Neth.
110/C3 Hartford City, In,US
109/H2 Hartington, Ne,US
34/B5 Hartland, Eng,UK
34/B4 Hartland (pt.), Eng,UK
34/D2 Hartlebury, Eng,UK
33/G2 Hartlepool, Eng,UK
31/P7 Hartley, Eng,UK
107/H3 Hartney, Mb,Can
88/D3 Harts (riv.), SAfr.
115/G4 Hartsdale, NY,US
113/G3 Hartselle, Al,US
35/E1 Hartshill, Eng,UK
116/B3 Hartstene (isl.), Wa,US
113/H3 Hartwell, Ga,US
113/H3 Hartwell (lake), Ga, SC,US
77/C4 Hartz Mtn. Nat'l Park, Austl.
43/G6 Hartzviller, Fr.
61/K3 Hārūnābād, Pak.
73/E3 Harun, Bukit (peak), Indo.
68/F2 Har Us (lake), Mong.
62/D2 Har-Us (riv.), Mong.
61/H2 Hārūt (riv.), Afg.
116/Q16 Harvey, Il,US
107/J4 Harvey, ND,US
35/H3 Harwich, Eng,UK
33/G5 Harworth, Eng,UK
70/C2 Haryana (state), India
41/H5 Harz (mts.), Ger.
41/E3 Hase (riv.), Ger.
41/E3 Haselünne, Ger.
65/M9 Hashima, Japan
64/D3 Hashimoto, Japan
82/D2 Hasi el Farsía (well), WSah.
61/K3 Hāsilpur, Pak.
112/D3 Haskell, Tx,US
35/F4 Haslemere, Eng,UK
33/F4 Haslingden, Eng,UK
33/F5 Haslington, Eng,UK
70/C5 Hassan, India
103/S7 Hassel (sound), NW,Can
43/E2 Hasselt, Belg.
40/D3 Hasselt, Neth.
45/J1 Hassfurt, Ger.
81/S16 Hassi Bahbah, Alg.
82/G1 Hassi Messaoud, Alg.
37/E4 Hässleholm, Swe.
75/S10 Hastings, NZ
35/G5 Hastings, Eng,UK
110/C3 Hastings, Mi,US
107/K4 Hastings, Mn,US
109/H2 Hastings, Ne,US
115/G4 Hastings-on-Hudson, NY,US
65/H7 Hasuda, Japan
81/W18 Ḩaţab (riv.), Tun.
65/M9 Hatashō, Japan
115/E5 Hatboro, Pa,US
108/F4 Hatch, NM,US
69/B5 Hat Chao Mai Nat'l Park, Thai.
97/J7 Hatcher (peak), Arg.
50/F3 Haţeg, Rom.
31/N6 Hatfield, Eng,UK
77/E1 Hat Head Nat'l Park, Austl.
33/G5 Hathersage, Eng,UK
70/C2 Hāthras, India
60/C4 Ḩāţibah, Ra's (pt.), SAr.
69/D4 Ha Tien, Viet.
69/D2 Ha Tinh, Viet.
69/B5 Hat Nai Yang Nat'l Park, Thai.
65/H7 Hatogaya, Japan
101/H4 Hato Mayor, DRep.
65/H7 Hatoyama, Japan
70/C3 Hatta, India
77/B2 Hattah-Kulkyne Nat'l Park, Austl.
40/D4 Hattem, Neth.
41/F2 Hatten, Ger.
113/K3 Hatteras (cape), NC,US
113/F4 Hattiesburg, Ms,US
41/E6 Hattingen, Ger.
33/G6 Hatton, Eng,UK
50/D2 Hatvan, Hun.
69/C5 Hat Yai, Thai.
69/E3 Hau Bon, Viet.
42/B2 Haubourdin, Fr.
83/Q6 Haud (reg.), Eth., Som.
37/C4 Haugesund, Nor.
69/D4 Hau Giang (riv.), Viet.
37/H2 Haukipudas, Fin.
115/G5 Hauppauge, NY,US
75/S10 Hauraki (gulf), NZ
47/E1 Hauskoa (mtn.), Fr.
82/D1 Haut Atlas (mts.), Mor.
44/D2 Haute-Normandie (reg.), Fr.
111/G1 Hauterive, Qu,Can
43/E3 Hautes Fagnes (uplands), Belg.
42/C3 Hautmont, Fr.
31/S10 Hauts-de-Seine (dept.), Fr.
100/E3 Havana (La Habana) (cap.), Cuba
79/V13 Havannah (chan.), NCal.
35/F5 Havant, Eng,UK
108/D4 Havasu (lake), Az, Ca,US
39/G2 Havel (riv.), Ger.
38/G2 Havelland (reg.), Ger.
113/J3 Havelock, NC,US
75/S10 Havelock North, NZ
35/G3 Havengore (isl.), Eng,UK
34/B3 Haverfordwest, Wal,UK
35/G2 Haverhill, Eng,UK
111/G3 Haverhill, Ma,US
31/P7 Havering (bor.), Eng,UK
39/K4 Havířov, Czh.
41/E5 Havixbeck, Ger.
39/H4 Havlíčkuv Brod, Czh.
106/F3 Havre, Mt,US
111/J1 Havre-Saint-Pierre, Qu,Can
51/H5 Havsa, Turk.
104/S10 Hawaii (state), US
104/U11 Hawaii (isl.), Hi,US
79/H2 Hawaiian (isls.), Hi,US
104/U11 Hawaii Volcanoes Nat'l Park, Hi,US
60/E3 Ḩawallī, Kuw.
33/E5 Hawarden, Wal,UK
107/J5 Hawarden, Ia,US
75/R10 Hawera, NZ
33/F3 Hawes, Eng,UK
33/F2 Haweswater (res.), Eng,UK
36/D3 Hawick, Sc,UK
77/E2 Hawke (cape), Austl.
75/S10 Hawke (bay), NZ
76/G8 Hawkesbury (riv.), Austl.
106/A2 Hawkesbury (isl.), BC,Can
110/F2 Hawkesbury, On,Can
60/E2 Hawr al Ḩammār (lake), Iraq
59/H6 Ḩawsh 'Īsá, Egypt
115/B3 Hawthorne, Ca,US
108/C3 Hawthorne, Nv,US
33/G3 Haxby, Eng,UK
76/C3 Hay (pt.), Austl.
102/E3 Hay (riv.), Ab, NW,Can
65/H7 Hayama, Japan
43/F5 Hayange, Fr.
33/F5 Haydock, Eng,UK
33/F2 Haydon Bridge, Eng,UK
102/G3 Hayes (riv.), Mb,Can
102/G2 Hayes (riv.), NW,Can
103/T7 Hayes (pen.), Grld.
31/M7 Hayes, Eng,UK
114/J3 Hayes (mtn.), Ak,US
34/A6 Hayle, Eng,UK
34/A6 Hayle (riv.), Eng,UK
35/F5 Hayling (isl.), Eng,UK
112/E3 Haynesville, La,US
34/C2 Hay on Wye, Wal,UK
51/H5 Hayrabolu, Turk.

139

Hays – Hunte

109/H3 Hays, Ks,US
109/H3 Haysville, Ks,US
116/K11 Hayward, Ca,US
110/B2 Hayward, Wi,US
35/F5 Haywards Heath, Eng,UK
61/G3 Hazār (mtn.), Iran
110/D4 Hazard, Ky,US
70/E3 Hazāribag, India
42/B2 Hazebrouck, Fr.
33/F5 Hazel Grove, Eng,UK
116/F7 Hazel Park, Mi,US
103/R7 Hazen (str.), NW,Can
114/E3 Hazen (bay), Ak,US
40/B4 Hazerswoude-Dorp, Neth.
113/F4 Hazlehurst, Ms,US
35/F3 Hazlemere, Eng,UK
115/F5 Hazlet, NJ,US
106/B2 Hazleton (mts.), BC,Can
110/F3 Hazleton, Pa,US
65/N10 Hazu, Japan
35/G1 Heacham, Eng,UK
35/G4 Headcorn, Eng,UK
33/G4 Headingley, Eng,UK
108/B3 Healdsburg, Ca,US
77/G5 Healesville, Austl.
33/G6 Heanor, Eng,UK
29/P8 Heard (isl.), Austl.
112/D4 Hearne, Tx,US
98/V Hearst (isl.), Ant.
110/D1 Hearst, On,Can
107/H4 Heart (riv.), ND,US
111/J1 Heath (pt.), Qu,Can
76/G9 Heathcote Nat'l Park, Austl.
35/G5 Heathfield, Eng,UK
112/D5 Hebbronville, Tx,US
33/F4 Hebden Bridge, Eng,UK
66/G6 Hebei (prov.), China
112/E3 Heber Springs, Ar,US
66/C4 Hebi, China
30/C3 Hebrides (isls.), Sc,UK
36/A2 Hebrides, Outer (isls.), Sc,UK
109/H2 Hebron, Ne,US
59/K6 Hebron (Al Khalīl), WBnk.
114/M5 Hecate (str.), BC,Can
71/J3 Hechi, China
43/E1 Hechtel, Belg.
33/H6 Heckington, Eng,UK
107/J4 Hecla, SD,US
103/R7 Hecla and Griper (bay), NW,Can
106/D3 Hector (peak), Ab,Can
37/E3 Hedemora, Swe.
37/D3 Hedmark (co.), Nor.
33/H4 Hedon, Eng,UK
41/E4 Heek, Ger.
40/B3 Heemskerk, Neth.
40/B3 Heemstede, Neth.
40/D4 Heerde, Neth.
40/C3 Heerenveen, Neth.
40/B3 Heerhugowaard, Neth.
43/E2 Heerlen, Neth.
43/E2 Heers, Belg.
40/C5 Heesch, Neth.
40/C6 Heeze, Neth.
59/K5 Ḥefa (Haifa), Isr.
66/D5 Hefei, China
63/L2 Hegang, China
45/H3 Hegau (reg.), Ger.
65/L10 Heguri, Japan
62/D4 Hei (riv.), China
66/B3 Heicha Shan (mtn.), China
38/E1 Heide, Ger.
77/G5 Heidelberg, Austl.
45/H2 Heidelberg, Ger.
89/E2 Heidelberg, SAfr.
113/F4 Heidelberg, Ms,US
40/D5 Heiden, Ger.
63/K1 Heihe, China
38/F1 Heikendorf, Ger.
88/D2 Heilbron, SAfr.
45/H2 Heilbronn, Ger.
38/F1 Heiligenhafen, Ger.
40/D6 Heiligenhaus, Ger.
41/H6 Heiligenstadt, Ger.
63/L2 Heilong (Amur) (riv.), China
40/B3 Heiloo, Neth.
37/N7 Heimaey (isl.), Ice.
40/D4 Heino, Neth.
37/H3 Heinola, Fin.
40/D6 Heinsberg, Ger.
66/C3 Heituo Shan (mtn.), China
65/M9 Heiwa, Japan
66/D3 Hejian, China
59/D2 Hekimhan, Turk.
65/M10 Hekinan, Japan
37/N7 Hekla (vol.), Ice.
62/F4 Helan (mts.), China
40/D6 Helden, Neth.
113/F3 Helena, Ar,US
106/E4 Helena (cap.), Mt,US
38/D1 Helgoland (isl.), Ger.
38/D1 Helgoländer Bucht (bay), Ger.
60/F3 Ḥelleh (riv.), Iran
40/D4 Hellendoorn, Neth.
43/F3 Hellenthal, Ger.
40/B5 Hellevoetsluis, Neth.
46/E3 Hellín, Sp.
106/D4 Hells Canyon Nat'l Rec. Area, Id, Or,US
61/H2 Helmand (riv.), Afg.
38/F3 Helme (riv.), Ger.
114/K2 Helmet (mtn.), Ak,US
40/C6 Helmond, Neth.
33/G3 Helmsley, Eng,UK
38/F2 Helmstedt, Ger.
108/E3 Helper, Ut,US
33/F5 Helsby, Eng,UK
37/E4 Helsingør, Den.
37/H3 Helsinki (Helsingfors) (cap.), Fin.
34/A6 Helston, Eng,UK
37/G3 Helvetinjärven Nat'l Park, Fin.
42/C2 Hem, Fr.
42/B2 Hem (riv.), Fr.
31/M6 Hemel Hempstead, Eng,UK
41/E6 Hemer, Ger.
115/D3 Hemet, Ca,US
41/G4 Hemmingen, Ger.
41/G1 Hemmoor, Ger.
112/E4 Hemphill, Tx,US
115/G5 Hempstead, NY,US
35/H1 Hemsby, Eng,UK
33/G4 Hemsworth, Eng,UK
66/B4 Henan (prov.), China
46/D2 Henares (riv.), Sp.
44/C5 Hendaye, Fr.
51/K5 Hendek, Turk.
96/E2 Henderson, Arg.
79/N7 Henderson (isl.), Pitc.
110/C4 Henderson, Ky,US
113/J2 Henderson, NC,US
108/D3 Henderson, Nv,US
113/F3 Henderson, Tn,US
112/E3 Henderson, Tx,US
113/H3 Hendersonville, NC,US
113/G2 Hendersonville, Tn,US
31/N7 Hendon, Eng,UK
40/B5 Hendrik-Ido-Ambacht, Neth.
89/D3 Hendrik Verwoerdam (res.), SAfr.
35/F5 Henfield, Eng,UK
66/L8 Heng (isl.), China
71/G2 Hengduan (mts.), China
40/D4 Hengelo, Neth.
66/C3 Heng Shan (mtn.), China
66/C3 Hengshui, China
67/B2 Hengyang, China
42/B3 Hénin-Beaumont, Fr.
35/E2 Henley-in-Arden, Eng,UK
35/F3 Henley-on-Thames, Eng,UK
44/B3 Hennebont, Fr.
43/G2 Hennef, Ger.
43/E2 Henri-Chapelle, Belg.
112/D3 Henrietta, Tx,US
103/H3 Henrietta Maria (cape), On,Can
114/M5 Henry (cape), BC,Can
108/E3 Henry (mts.), Ut,US
109/J4 Henryetta, Ok,US
42/C3 Hensies, Belg.
62/F2 Hentiyn (mts.), Mong.
71/G4 Henzada, Burma
37/N6 Heradhsvötn (riv.), Ice.
61/H2 Herāt, Afg.
47/G1 Hérault (riv.), Fr.
76/B2 Herbert (riv.), Austl.
106/G3 Herbert, Sk,Can
76/B2 Herbert Riv. Falls Nat'l Park, Austl.
31/S10 Herblay, Fr.
50/D4 Hercegnovi, Yugo.
116/K10 Hercules, Ca,US
41/E6 Herdecke, Ger.
43/G2 Herdorf, Ger.
100/E6 Heredia, CR
34/D2 Hereford, Eng,UK
112/C3 Hereford, Tx,US
34/D2 Hereford & Worcester (co.), Eng,UK
79/L6 Hereheretue (isl.), FrPol.
51/J5 Hereke, Turk.
46/C3 Herencia, Sp.
43/D1 Herentals, Belg.
41/F4 Herford, Ger.
109/H3 Herington, Ks,US
45/H3 Herisau, Swi.
43/E2 Herk (riv.), Belg.
43/E2 Herk-de-Stad, Belg.
62/G2 Herlen (riv.), Mong.
113/F2 Hermann, Mo,US
41/H3 Hermannsburg, Ger.
42/B5 Hermes, Fr.
106/D4 Hermiston, Or,US
59/K5 Hermon (mtn.), Leb., Syria
115/B3 Hermosa Beach, Ca,US
101/M8 Hermosillo, Mex.
96/E2 Hernando, Arg.
113/F3 Hernando, Ms,US
46/E1 Hernani, Sp.
42/D2 Herne, Belg.
41/E5 Herne, Ger.
35/H4 Herne Bay, Eng,UK
37/D4 Herning, Den.
59/N9 Herodian (ruins), WBnk.
59/N9 Herodion Nat'l Park, WBnk.
101/M7 Heroica Caborca, Mex.
101/M7 Heroica Nogales, Mex.
100/D4 Herrero (pt.), Mex.
44/D5 Hers (riv.), Fr.
41/E6 Herscheid, Ger.
114/L2 Herschel, Yk,Can
43/D1 Herselt, Belg.
43/E2 Herstal, Belg.
35/G5 Herstmonceux, Eng,UK
41/E5 Herten, Ger.
35/F3 Hertford, Eng,UK
31/N6 Hertfordshire (co.), Eng,UK
43/E2 Herve, Belg.
76/D4 Hervey Bay, Austl.
41/H5 Herzberg am Harz, Ger.
41/F5 Herzebrock-Clarholz, Ger.
42/C2 Herzele, Belg.
59/M8 Herzliyya, Isr.
45/J2 Herzogenaurach, Ger.
50/B1 Herzogenburg, Aus.
43/F2 Herzogenrath, Ger.
43/D3 Hesbaye (plat.), Belg.
71/J3 Heshan, China
43/F4 Hesperange, Lux.
115/C2 Hesperia, Ca,US
114/M3 Hess (riv.), Yk,Can
41/G6 Hesse (state), Ger.
41/F5 Hessel (riv.), Ger.
41/G6 Hessisch Lichtenau, Ger.
41/G4 Hessisch Oldendorf, Ger.
33/H4 Hessle, Eng,UK
33/E5 Heswall, Eng,UK
107/H4 Hettinger, ND,US
33/G2 Hetton-le-Hole, Eng,UK
41/E5 Heubach (riv.), Ger.
39/H5 Heukuppe (peak), Aus.
43/E1 Heusden-Zolder, Belg.
43/F5 Heusweiler, Ger.
44/D2 Hève, Cap de la (cape), Fr.
50/E2 Heves, Hun.
39/L5 Heves (co.), Hun.
115/G5 Hewlett (pt.), NY,US
33/F2 Hexham, Eng,UK
63/H3 Hexigten Qi, China
88/L10 Hex River (mts.), SAfr.
88/L10 Hex River (pass), SAfr.
33/F3 Heysham, Eng,UK
40/C6 Heythuysen, Neth.
33/F4 Heywood, Eng,UK
66/C4 Heze, China
113/H5 Hialeah, Fl,US
109/J3 Hiawatha, Ks,US
107/K4 Hibbing, Mn,US
77/C4 Hibbs (pt.), Austl.
114/M4 Hickman (mtn.), BC,Can
110/B4 Hickman, Ky,US
113/H3 Hickory, NC,US
115/G5 Hicksville, NY,US
65/E3 Hida (riv.), Japan
65/H7 Hidaka, Japan
64/D4 Hidaka (riv.), Japan
100/B3 Hidalgo (state), Mex.
101/N8 Hidalgo del Parral, Mex.
41/F4 Hiddenhausen, Ger.
47/W17 Hierro (isl.), Canl.
41/E2 Hieve (lake), Ger.
65/H7 Higashikurume, Japan
65/H7 Higashimurayama, Japan
65/G1 Higashine, Japan
65/L10 Higashi-Ōsaka, Japan
65/K10 Higashiura, Japan
65/H7 Higashiyamato, Japan
106/C5 High (des.), Or,US
35/F2 Higham Ferrers, Eng,UK
34/D4 Highbridge, Eng,UK
115/F5 High Bridge, NJ,US
112/E4 High Island, Tx,US
115/C2 Highland, Ca,US
116/R16 Highland, In,US
116/Q15 Highland Park, Il,US
116/F7 Highland Park, Mi,US
115/F6 Highland Park, NJ,US
34/D2 Highley, Eng,UK
107/J4 Highmore, SD,US
113/H3 High Point, NC,US
106/D2 High Prairie, Ab,Can
107/H2 High Rock (lake), Mb,Can
33/F3 High Street (mtn.), Eng,UK
33/E4 Hightown, Eng,UK
115/F5 Hightstown, NJ,US
34/B5 High Willhays (hill), Eng,UK
35/E3 Highworth, Eng,UK
35/F3 High Wycombe, Eng,UK
101/H4 Higüey, DRep.
59/H6 Hihyā, Egypt
37/J3 Hiidenportin Nat'l Park, Fin.
52/D4 Hiiumaa (isl.), Est.
60/C3 Hijāz, Jabal al (mts.), SAr.
64/B4 Hiji, Japan
96/Q9 Hijuelas de Conchalí, Chile
65/L9 Hikami, Japan
64/E3 Hikone, Japan
79/L6 Hikueru (atoll), FrPol.
75/S10 Hikurangi (peak), NZ
43/H2 Hilchenbach, Ger.
45/J1 Hildburghausen, Ger.
40/D6 Hilden, Ger.
41/G4 Hildesheim, Ger.
98/L Hillary (coast), Ant.
109/H3 Hill City, Ks,US
115/F4 Hillcrest, NY,US
41/F4 Hille, Ger.
40/B4 Hillegom, Neth.
37/E5 Hillerød, Den.
32/B2 Hillhall, NI,UK
31/M7 Hillingdon (bor.), Eng,UK
36/D2 Hill of Fearn, Sc,UK
107/J4 Hillsboro, ND,US
108/F4 Hillsboro, NM,US
110/D4 Hillsboro, Oh,US
106/C4 Hillsboro, Or,US
112/D3 Hillsboro, Tx,US
76/C3 Hillsborough (chan.), Austl.
32/B3 Hillsborough, NI,UK
116/K11 Hillsborough, Ca,US
115/F5 Hillsborough, NJ,US
110/C3 Hillsdale, Mi,US
115/F5 Hillside, NJ,US
32/B3 Hilltown, NI,UK
104/U11 Hilo, Hi,US
67/D5 Hilongos, Phil.
33/E3 Hilpsford (pt.), Eng,UK
113/H3 Hilton Head Island, SC,US
40/C6 Hilvarenbeek, Neth.
40/C4 Hilversum, Neth.
68/C5 Himachal Pradesh (state), India
70/D2 Himalaya, Great (range), Asia
67/D5 Himamaylan, Phil.
64/D3 Himeji, Japan
65/E2 Himi, Japan
83/N5 Himora, Eth.
59/L4 Ḥimş, Syria
114/J3 Hinchinbrook (chan.), Ak,US
76/B2 Hinchinbrook I. Nat'l Park, Austl.
35/E1 Hinckley, Eng,UK
33/H2 Hinderwell, Eng,UK
33/F4 Hindley, Eng,UK
77/B2 Hindmarsh (lake), Austl.
61/J1 Hindu Kush (mts.), Afg., Pak.
70/C5 Hindupur, India
113/H4 Hinesville, Ga,US
70/C3 Hinganghāt, India
61/J3 Hingol (riv.), Pak.
70/C4 Hingoli, India
61/J3 Hingorja, Pak.
59/E2 Hınıs, Turk.
65/H7 Hino, Japan
65/M9 Hino (riv.), Japan
65/H7 Hinode, Japan
46/C3 Hinojosa del Duque, Sp.
64/C3 Hino-misaki (cape), Japan
116/Q16 Hinsdale, Il,US
33/F6 Hinstock, Eng,UK
41/E2 Hinte, Ger.
106/D2 Hinton, Ab,Can
110/D4 Hinton, WV,US
40/B3 Hippolytushoef, Neth.
33/G3 Hipswell, Eng,UK
65/L9 Hira (mts.), Japan
64/A4 Hirado, Japan
64/D3 Hirakata, Japan
70/D3 Hirakud (res.), India
64/C3 Hirata, Japan
65/H7 Hiratsuka, Japan
51/H2 Hîrlău, Rom.
63/N3 Hirosaki, Japan
64/C3 Hiroshima, Japan
64/C3 Hiroshima (pref.), Japan
45/J2 Hirschau, Ger.
42/D4 Hirson, Fr.
51/H3 Hîrşova, Rom.
37/D4 Hirtshals, Den.
34/C3 Hirwaun, Wal,UK
64/E3 Hisai, Japan
70/C2 Hisār, India
62/E2 Hishig-Öndör, Mong.
101/G4 Hispaniola (isl.), DRep., Haiti
65/G2 Hitachi, Japan
65/G2 Hitachi-ōta, Japan
35/F3 Hitchin, Eng,UK
64/B4 Hitoyoshi, Japan
37/C3 Hitra (isl.), Nor.
79/M5 Hiva Oa (isl.), FrPol.
52/B2 Hjartfjellet (peak), Nor.
69/B1 Hka (riv.), Burma
71/G2 Hkakabo (peak), Burma
39/J4 Hlohovec, Slvk.
76/G8 Hmas-Nirimba, Austl.
71/G4 Hmawbi, Burma
85/F5 Ho, Gha.
69/D1 Hoa Binh, Viet.
69/E4 Hoa Da, Viet.
69/C1 Hoang Lien (mts.), Viet.
103/K2 Hoare (bay), NW,Can
65/K2 Hobara, Japan
77/C4 Hobart, Austl.
109/H4 Hobart, Ok,US
98/Q Hobbs (coast), Ant.
109/G4 Hobbs, NM,US
42/D1 Hoboken, Belg.
115/F5 Hoboken, NJ,US
83/Q6 Hobyo, Som.
45/K3 Hochalmspitze (peak), Aus.
69/D4 Ho Chi Minh City (Saigon), Viet.
45/K3 Hochkönig (peak), Aus.
45/L3 Hochschwab (peak), Aus.
43/G3 Hochsimmer (peak), Ger.
35/G3 Hockley, Eng,UK
33/F4 Hodder (riv.), Eng,UK
31/N6 Hoddesdon, Eng,UK
106/G3 Hodgeville, Sk,Can
84/C2 Hodh (reg.), Mrta.
84/D2 Hodh ech Chargui (reg.), Mrta.
84/C2 Hodh el Gharbi (reg.), Mrta.
50/E2 Hódmezővásárhely, Hun.
81/T16 Hodna, Chott el (salt lake), Alg.
33/F6 Hodnet, Eng,UK
39/J4 Hodonín, Czh.
43/E2 Hoegnel (riv.), Belg.
40/B5 Hoekse Waard (polder), Neth.
43/G6 Hoenheim, Fr.
43/E2 Hoensbroek, Neth.
43/E2 Hoeselt, Belg.
40/C4 Hoevelaken, Neth.
40/B5 Hoeven, Neth.
45/J1 Hof, Ger.
118/P15 Hoffman Estates, Il,US
41/G6 Hofgeismar, Ger.
66/B3 Hofong Qagan (salt lake), China
37/P6 Hofsá (riv.), Ice.
37/N7 Hofsjökull (glac.), Ice.
64/B3 Hōfu, Japan
40/C4 Hoge Veluwe Nat'l Park, Neth.
41/G6 Hohegrass (peak), Ger.
45/H3 Hohenems, Aus.
41/H4 Hohenhameln, Ger.
45/H2 Hohenloher Ebene (plain), Ger.
45/K3 Hoher Dachstein (peak), Aus.
45/K3 Hohe Tauern (mts.), Aus.
45/K3 Hohe Tauern Nat'l Park, Aus.
66/B2 Hohhot, China
45/G2 Hohneck (mtn.), Fr.
43/G3 Höhr-Grenzhausen, Ger.
68/F4 Hoh Sai (lake), China
68/F4 Hoh Xil (lake), China
68/E4 Hoh Xil (mts.), China
69/E3 Hoi An, Viet.
112/D2 Hoisington, Ks,US
69/D1 Hoi Xuan, Viet.
64/C4 Hōjō, Japan
75/R11 Hokitika, NZ
63/N3 Hokkaidō (isl.), Japan
65/G2 Hokota, Japan
65/K10 Hokudan, Japan
65/M9 Hokusei, Japan
33/J6 Holbeach, Eng,UK
35/H3 Holbrook, Eng,UK
108/E4 Holbrook, Az,US
109/H4 Holdenville, Ok,US
33/H4 Holderness (pen.), Eng,UK
109/H2 Holdrege, Ne,US
101/F3 Holguín, Cuba
114/G3 Holitna (riv.), Ak,US
110/C3 Holland, Mi,US
113/F3 Hollandale, Ms,US
40/B4 Hollandse IJssel (riv.), Neth.
35/H2 Hollesley, Eng,UK
109/H3 Hollis, Ok,US
108/B3 Hollister, Ca,US
43/E2 Hollogne-aux-Pierres, Belg.
37/H3 Hollola, Fin.
113/F3 Holly Springs, Ms,US
113/H5 Hollywood, Fl,US
37/F3 Holm, Swe.
102/E1 Holman, NW,Can
115/F5 Holmdel, NJ,US
76/C2 Holmes (reefs), Austl.
106/F4 Holmes (peak), Wy,US
33/F5 Holmes Chapel, Eng,UK
31/N8 Holmesdale (val.), Eng,UK
33/H4 Holme upon Spalding Moor, Eng,UK
33/G4 Holmfirth, Eng,UK
98/C Holm-Lützow (bay), Ant.
37/F3 Holmsjön (lake), Swe.
59/K5 Ḥolon, Isr.
37/D4 Holstebro, Den.
113/H2 Holston (riv.), Tn,US
34/B5 Holsworthy, Eng,UK
35/H1 Holt, Eng,UK
40/D4 Holten, Neth.
109/J3 Holton, Ks,US
115/G5 Holtsville, NY,US
32/D5 Holy (isl.), Wal,UK
32/D5 Holyhead, Wal,UK
32/D5 Holyhead (mtn.), Wal,UK
36/E3 Holy (Lindisfarne) (isl.), Eng,UK
109/G2 Holyoke, Co,US
111/F3 Holyoke, Ma,US
33/E5 Holywell, Wal,UK
32/C2 Holywood, NI,UK
38/F5 Holzkirchen, Ger.
41/G5 Holzminden, Ger.
41/E6 Holzwickede, Ger.
88/B3 Hom (dry riv.), Namb.
40/D6 Homberg, Ger.
41/G6 Homberg, Ger.
85/E3 Hombori Tondo (peak), Mali
43/F5 Hombourg-Haut, Fr.
43/G6 Homburg, Ger.
103/K2 Home (bay), NW,Can
43/E5 Homécourt, Fr.
112/E3 Homer, La,US
113/H5 Homestead, Fl,US
113/G3 Homewood, Al,US
116/Q16 Homewood, Il,US
113/F4 Homochitto (riv.), Ms,US
70/B5 Honāvar, India
69/D4 Hon Chong, Viet.
34/C3 Honddu (riv.), Wal,UK
64/B4 Hondo, Japan
109/F4 Hondo (dry riv.), NM,US
112/D4 Hondo, Tx,US
40/D3 Hondsrug (reg.), Neth.
100/D4 Honduras
100/D4 Honduras (gulf), NAm.
108/B2 Honey (lake), Ca,US
35/E2 Honeybourne, Eng,UK
66/C5 Hong (lake), China
66/C4 Hong (riv.), China
71/J2 Hongdu (riv.), China
69/D1 Hon Gai, Viet.
66/C5 Honghu, China
71/J2 Hongjiang, China
67/B3 Hong Kong (dpcy.), UK
66/B3 Hongliu (riv.), China
69/C1 Hong (Red) (riv.), Viet.
71/J3 Hongshui (riv.), China
66/C3 Hongtao Shan (mtn.), China
111/H1 Honguedo (passg.), Qu,Can
66/D4 Hongze (lake), China
78/E5 Honiara (cap.), Sol.
34/C5 Honiton, Eng,UK
104/T10 Honolulu (cap.), Hi,US
69/D4 Hon Quan, Viet.
63/M5 Honshu (isl.), Japan
74/B6 Hood (pt.), Austl.
116/J10 Hood (mt.), Ca,US
106/C4 Hood (mt.), Or,US
106/C4 Hood Canal (inlet), Wa,US
40/B4 Hoofddorp, Neth.
40/C6 Hoogeloon, Neth.
40/B6 Hoogerheide, Neth.
40/D3 Hoogeveen, Neth.
40/D3 Hoogeveense Vaart (can.), Neth.
40/D2 Hoogezand, Neth.
70/E3 Hooghly-Chinsura, India
42/C2 Hooglede, Belg.
40/B6 Hoogstraten, Belg.
76/C3 Hook (isl.), Austl.
35/F4 Hook, Eng,UK
36/B4 Hook Head (pt.), Ire.
110/C3 Hoopeston, Il,US
40/C3 Hoorn, Neth.
40/C3 Hoornse Hop (bay), Neth.
108/D3 Hoover (dam), Az,US
59/E2 Hopa, Turk.
115/F5 Hopatcong, NJ,US
115/F5 Hopatcong (lake), NJ,US
74/C6 Hope (lake), Austl.
106/C3 Hope, BC,Can
33/E5 Hope, Wal,UK
112/E3 Hope, Ar,US
103/K2 Hopes Advance (cape), Qu,Can
34/C6 Hope's Nose (pt.), Eng,UK
34/D2 Hope under Dinmore, Eng,UK
115/F5 Hopewell, NJ,US
110/E4 Hopewell, Va,US
74/D4 Hopkins (lake), Austl.
77/B3 Hopkins (riv.), Austl.
110/C4 Hopkinsville, Ky,US
41/F6 Hoppecke (riv.), Ger.
41/E4 Hopsten, Ger.
106/C4 Hoquiam, Wa,US
114/J2 Horace (mtn.), Ak,US
65/L9 Hōrai-san (peak), Japan
59/E2 Horasan, Turk.
59/K5 Ḥorbat Qesari (ruins), Isr.
33/G4 Horbury, Eng,UK
37/C3 Hordaland (co.), Nor.
33/G2 Horden, Eng,UK
51/G3 Horezu, Rom.
62/F3 Hörh (peak), Mong.
29/S6 Horiara (cap.), Sol.
31/N8 Horley, Eng,UK
45/J2 Horn, Aus.
37/M6 Horn (pt.), Ice.
39/L4 Hornád (riv.), Slvk.
37/E2 Hornavan (lake), Swe.
41/F5 Horn-Bad Meinberg, Ger.
111/Q8 Hornby, On,Can
33/H5 Horncastle, Eng,UK
31/P7 Hornchurch, Eng,UK
110/E3 Hornell, NY,US
110/C1 Hornepayne, On,Can
97/L8 Horn (Hornos) (cape), Chile
97/L8 Hornos Nat'l Park, Cabo de, Chile
42/A4 Hornoy-le-Bourg, Fr.
76/H8 Hornsby, Austl.
33/H4 Hornsea, Eng,UK
38/E1 Hornum Odde (cape), Ger.
63/N3 Horoshiri-dake (mtn.), Japan
34/B6 Horrabridge, Eng,UK
109/F2 Horse (cr.), Ne, Wy,US
110/C4 Horse Cave, Ky,US
106/C2 Horsefly (lake), BC,Can
37/D5 Horsens, Den.
35/H3 Horsey (isl.), Eng,UK
33/G4 Horsforth, Eng,UK
77/B3 Horsham, Austl.
35/F4 Horsham, Eng,UK
115/F5 Horsham, Pa,US
40/D6 Horst, Neth.
41/E4 Hörstel, Ger.
41/E4 Horstmar, Ger.
47/S12 Horta, Azor.,Port.
47/N9 Horteleza, Sp.
50/E2 Hortobágyi Nat'l Park, Hun.
114/N2 Horton (riv.), NW,Can
31/P7 Horton Kirby, Eng,UK
59/K6 Ḥorvot 'Avedat (ruins), Isr.
59/K6 Ḥorvot Meẓada (Masada) (ruins), Isr.
33/F4 Horwich, Eng,UK
110/D2 Horwood (lake), On,Can
70/C3 Hoshangābād, India
70/C4 Hospet, India
97/K8 Hoste (isl.), Chile
65/E2 Hotaka, Japan
65/E2 Hotaka-dake (mtn.), Japan
68/D4 Hotan (riv.), China
107/H5 Hot Springs, SD,US
112/E3 Hot Springs Nat'l Park, Ar,US
102/E2 Hottah (lake), NW,Can
88/A2 Hottentot (bay), Namb.
88/A2 Hottentots (pt.), Namb.
42/B3 Houdain, Fr.
84/D4 Houet (prov.), Burk.
110/B2 Houghton, Mi,US
110/C2 Houghton Lake, Mi,US
33/G2 Houghton-le-Spring, Eng,UK
31/S10 Houilles, Fr.
111/H2 Houlton, Me,US
65/B4 Houma, China
113/F4 Houma, La,US
31/M7 Hounslow (bor.), Eng,UK
42/B2 Houplines, Fr.
42/A3 Hourdel, Pointe du (pt.), Fr.
108/D3 House (range), Ut,US
106/B2 Houston, BC,Can
109/K3 Houston, Mo,US
113/F3 Houston, Ms,US
112/E4 Houston, Tx,US
40/C4 Houten, Neth.
42/B2 Houthulst, Belg.
74/A5 Houtman Abrolhos (isls.), Austl.
40/C3 Houtribdijk (dam), Neth.
35/F5 Hove, Eng,UK
41/F5 Hövelhof, Ger.
108/E3 Hovenweep Nat'l Mon., Co,US
35/H1 Hoveton, Eng,UK
37/E3 Hovfjället (peak), Swe.
33/H3 Hovingham, Eng,UK
62/E1 Hövsgöl (lake), Mong.
114/H2 Howard (hill), Ak,US
114/G2 Howard (pass), Ak,US
33/H4 Howden, Eng,UK
77/D3 Howe (cape), Austl.
110/D3 Howell, Mi,US
115/F5 Howell, NJ,US
89/E3 Howick, SAfr.
79/H4 Howland (isl.), PacUS
70/E3 Howrah, India
38/E3 Höxter, Ger.
39/H3 Hoyerswerda, Ger.
33/E5 Hoylake, Eng,UK
33/G5 Hoyland Nether, Eng,UK
47/N8 Hoyo-de-Manzanares, Sp.
43/E3 Hoyoux (riv.), Belg.
62/E2 Hoyt Tamir (riv.), Mong.
65/M9 Hozumi, Japan
39/H3 Hradec Králové, Czh.
50/D4 Hrasnica, Bosn.
50/B2 Hrastnik, Slov.
37/M6 Hrolleifsborg (peak), Ice.
39/K4 Hron (riv.), Slvk.
39/J3 Hronov, Czh.
39/M3 Hrubieszów, Pol.
39/J3 Hrubý Jeseník (mts.), Czh.
37/P6 Hrútafjöll (peak), Ice.
62/G5 Hua (peak), China
92/C6 Huacho, Peru
69/B3 Hua Hin, Thai.
79/K6 Huahine (isl.), FrPol.
66/C4 Huai (riv.), China
66/D4 Huai'an, China
62/H5 Huaibei, China
67/A2 Huaihua, China
66/C2 Huailai, China
66/D4 Huainan, China
66/C3 Huairen, China
66/D4 Huaiyin, China
100/B4 Huajuapan de León, Mex.
96/C2 Hualañé, Chile
67/D3 Hualien, Tai.
92/C5 Huallaga (riv.), Peru
92/C5 Huamachuco, Peru
87/C3 Huambo, Ang.
66/C5 Huan (riv.), China
92/C6 Huancavelica, Peru
92/C6 Huancayo, Peru
92/E8 Huanchaca (peak), Bol.
69/C2 Huang (riv.), Laos, Thai.
66/C4 Huangchuan, China
67/C2 Huanggang (peak), China
66/C2 Huangqi (lake), China
66/D5 Huangshan, China
66/C5 Huangshi, China
66/C5 Huangtang (lake), China
66/B4 Huangtu (plat.), China
63/H4 Huang (Yellow) (riv.), China
92/C5 Huánuco, Peru
92/E7 Huanuni, Bol.
92/C6 Huaral, Peru
92/C5 Huaráz, Peru
92/C6 Huarmey, Peru
92/C5 Huascarán (peak), Peru
92/C5 Huascarán Nat'l Park, Peru
66/B4 Hua Shan (peak), China
101/N8 Huatabampo, Mex.
92/E6 Huatunas (lake), Bol.
67/A1 Huaying, China
114/L3 Hubbard (mtn.), Ak,US, Yk,Can
109/H4 Hubbard Creek (res.), Tx,US
66/C5 Hubei (prov.), China
66/B4 Hubei Kou (pass), China
70/C4 Hubli-Dhārwār, India
40/D6 Hückelhoven, Ger.
41/E6 Hückeswagen, Ger.
33/G5 Hucknall Torkard, Eng,UK
42/A2 Hucqueliers, Fr.
33/G4 Huddersfield, Eng,UK
52/C4 Huddinge, Swe.
41/F2 Hude, Ger.
37/F3 Hudiksvall, Swe.
98/L Hudson (cape), Ant.
103/H2 Hudson (bay), Can.
103/J2 Hudson (str.), NW, Qu,Can
111/M7 Hudson, Qu,Can
110/F3 Hudson (riv.), NJ, NY,US
110/F3 Hudson, NY,US
107/H2 Hudson Bay, Sk,Can
102/D3 Hudson's Hope, BC,Can
69/D2 Hue, Viet.
50/F2 Huedin, Rom.
100/C4 Huehuetenango, Guat.
100/B3 Huejutla, Mex.
46/B4 Huelva, Sp.
46/B3 Huelva (riv.), Sp.
96/B4 Huequi (vol.), Chile
46/E4 Huercal-Overa, Sp.
109/F3 Huerfano (riv.), Co,US
47/E1 Huesca, Sp.
46/D4 Huéscar, Sp.
96/F3 Huesos (riv.), Arg.
100/A4 Huetamo de Nuñez, Mex.
70/E3 Hugli (riv.), India
109/G3 Hugo, Co,US
109/J4 Hugo, Ok,US
109/G3 Hugoton, Ks,US
62/H2 Hui (riv.), China
88/B2 Huib-Hock (plat.), Namb.
87/B4 Huíla (plat.), Ang.
96/D2 Huinca Renancó, Arg.
66/E5 Hui Shan (mtn.), China
44/D2 Huisne (riv.), Fr.
40/C5 Huissen, Neth.
52/D3 Huittinen, Fin.
100/C4 Huixtla, Mex.
40/C4 Huizen, Neth.
67/B3 Huizhou, China
63/J5 Hŭksan (arch.), SKor.
62/K2 Hulan (riv.), China
62/F2 Huld, Mong.
107/G4 Hulett, Wy,US
110/F2 Hull, Qu,Can
33/H4 Hull, Eng,UK
33/H4 Hull (riv.), Eng,UK
41/F4 Hüllhorst, Ger.
79/H5 Hull (Orona) (atoll), Kiri.
40/B6 Hulst, Neth.
66/B3 Hulu (riv.), China
62/H2 Hulun (lake), China
63/K1 Huma (riv.), China
92/F5 Humaitá, Braz.
101/N8 Humaya (riv.), Mex.
87/B4 Humbe, Ang.
111/K2 Humber (riv.), Nf,Can
111/R8 Humber (bay), On,Can
111/Q8 Humber (riv.), On,Can
33/H4 Humber (riv.), Eng,UK
33/H4 Humberside (co.), Eng,UK
33/H4 Humberston, Eng,UK
112/E4 Humble, Tx,US
107/G2 Humboldt, Sk,Can
78/F7 Humboldt (peak), NCal.
108/C2 Humboldt (range), Nv,US
108/D2 Humboldt (riv.), Nv,US
113/F3 Humboldt, Tn,US
77/C2 Hume (lake), Austl.
39/L4 Humenné, Slvk.
114/K2 Humphrey (pt.), Ak,US
108/E4 Humphreys (peak), Az,US
33/F1 Humshaugh, Eng,UK
63/J3 Hun (riv.), China
63/K3 Hun (riv.), China
37/N6 Húnaflói (bay), Ice.
71/K2 Hunan (prov.), China
63/L3 Hunchun, China
50/F3 Hunedoara, Rom.
50/F3 Hunedoara (co.), Rom.
38/E3 Hünfeld, Ger.
50/D2 Hungary
45/H1 Hungen, Ger.
35/E4 Hungerford, Eng,UK
62/C2 Hüngüy (riv.), Mong.
69/D1 Hung Yen, Viet.
66/B3 Hunjiang, China
33/H3 Hunmanby, Eng,UK
43/G1 Hunspatch, Fr.
43/G4 Hunsrück (mts.), Ger.
35/G1 Hunstanton, Eng,UK
41/F2 Hunte (riv.), Ger.
77/C4 Hunter (isl.), Austl.
77/D2 Hunter (riv.), Austl.

140

Hunte – Jan

106/A3 Hunter (isl.), BC,Can
114/H3 Hunter (mtn.), Ak,US
110/C4 Huntingburg, In,US
35/F2 Huntingdon, Eng,UK
33/G4 Huntington, Eng,UK
110/C3 Huntington, In,US
115/G5 Huntington, NY,US
110/D4 Huntington, WV,US
115/C3 Huntington Beach, Ca,US
115/B3 Huntington Park, Ca,US
116/F7 Huntington Woods, Mi,US
75/S10 Huntly, NZ
36/D2 Huntly, Sc,UK
114/M4 Hunts Inlet, BC,Can
110/E2 Huntsville, On,Can
113/G3 Huntsville, Al,US
112/E4 Huntsville, Tx,US
40/D5 Hünxe, Ger.
63/H2 Huolin Gol, China
69/D2 Huong Hoa, Viet.
69/D2 Huong Khe, Viet.
69/D2 Huong Son, Viet.
71/J4 Huong Thuy, Viet.
66/B3 Huo Shan (mtn.), China
83/R5 Hurdiyo, Som.
31/S11 Hurepoix (reg.), Fr.
108/E4 Hurley, NM,US
110/D2 Huron (lake), Can., US
116/F7 Huron (riv.), Mi,US
107/J4 Huron, SD,US
110/D4 Hurricane, WV,US
35/F5 Hurstpierpoint, Eng,UK
42/D4 Hurtaut (riv.), Fr.
43/F2 Hürth, Ger.
33/G3 Hurworth, Eng,UK
70/D3 Husainābād, India
35/E2 Husbands Bosworth, Eng,UK
51/J2 Huşi, Rom.
38/E1 Husum, Ger.
109/H3 Hutchinson, Ks,US
107/K4 Hutchinson, Mn,US
33/J5 Huttoft, Eng,UK
76/C4 Hutton (peak), Austl.
31/Q7 Hutton, Eng,UK
33/H4 Hutton Cranswick, Eng,UK
33/G3 Hutton Rudby, Eng,UK
111/Q8 Huttonville, On,Can
66/C3 Hutuo (riv.), China
43/E2 Huy, Belg.
33/F5 Huyton-with-Roby, Eng,UK
66/E5 Huzhou, China
37/P7 Hvannadalshnúkur (peak), Ice.
50/C4 Hvar (isl.), Cro.
37/N7 Hvítá (riv.), Ice.
87/E4 Hwange, Zim.
87/E4 Hwange (Wankie) Nat'l Park, Zim.
96/B5 Hyades (peak), Chile
62/C2 Hyargas, Mong.
62/C2 Hyargas (lake), Mong.
115/K8 Hyattsville, Md,US
33/F5 Hyde, Eng,UK
31/N7 Hyde Park, Eng,UK
70/C4 Hyderābād, India
61/J3 Hyderābād, Pak.
45/G5 Hyères, Fr.
45/G5 Hyères (isls.), Fr.
102/D2 Hyland (riv.), Yk,Can
64/D3 Hyōgo (pref.), Japan
64/D3 Hyō-no-sen (mtn.), Japan
108/E2 Hyrum, Ut,US
35/E5 Hythe, Eng,UK
35/H4 Hythe, Eng,UK
64/B4 Hyūga, Japan
37/H3 Hyvinkää, Fin.

I

94/B4 Iaçu, Braz.
50/A2 Iâf di Montasio (peak), It.
51/H3 Ialomiţa (riv.), Rom.
95/D1 Iapu, Braz.
51/H2 Iaşi, Rom.
51/H2 Iaşi (co.), Rom.
67/C4 Iba, Phil.
85/F5 Ibadan, Nga.
92/C3 Ibagué, Col.
95/B2 Ibaiti, Braz.
67/D5 Ibajay, Phil.
108/D2 Ibapah, Ut,US
50/E4 Ibar (riv.), Yugo.
64/C3 Ibara, Japan
65/L10 Ibaraki, Japan
65/F2 Ibaraki (pref.), Japan
92/C3 Ibarra, Ecu.
91/E2 Ibarreta, Arg.
83/L6 Ibba (riv.), Sudan
41/E4 Ibbenbüren, Ger.
85/F2 Ibdekhene (wadi), Mali
91/E2 Ibera, Esteros de (marshes), Arg.
46/D2 Ibérico, Sistema (range), Sp.
111/P7 Iberville, Qu,Can
64/E3 Ibi (riv.), Japan
47/E3 Ibi, Sp.
95/C1 Ibiá, Braz.
94/B2 Ibiapaba (mts.), Braz.
94/C4 Ibicaraí, Braz.
95/C4 Ibimirim, Braz.
95/B2 Ibitinga, Braz.
95/F8 Ibiúna, Braz.
47/F3 Ibiza, Sp.
47/F3 Ibiza (isl.), Sp.
64/D3 Ibo (riv.), Japan
94/B4 Ibotirama, Braz.
82/H8 Iboundji (peak), Gabon
39/L4 Ibrány, Hun.
86/B2 Ibshawāy, Egypt
35/E1 Ibstock, Eng,UK
73/G3 Ibu (mtn.), Indo.
65/M9 Ibuki, Japan
65/M9 Ibuki-yama (peak), Japan
92/C6 Ica, Peru
37/N7 Iceland
70/B4 Ichalkaranji, India
70/D4 Ichchāpuram, India
65/J7 Ichihara, Japan
65/L9 Ichijima, Japan
65/H7 Ichikawa, Japan
64/E3 Ichinomiya, Japan
63/N4 Ichinoseki, Japan
65/M10 Ichishi, Japan
42/C1 Ichtegem, Belg.
94/C2 Icó, Braz.
114/K4 Icy (bay), Ak,US
114/F1 Icy (cape), Ak,US
114/L4 Icy (str.), Ak,US
109/J4 Idabel, Ok,US
106/E5 Idaho (state), US
106/E5 Idaho Falls, Id,US
70/B3 Idar, India
43/G4 Idarkopf (peak), Ger.
43/G4 Idar-Oberstein, Ger.
65/L10 Ide, Japan
62/D2 Ider (riv.), Mong.
86/C3 Idfū, Egypt
49/J5 Ídhi (peak), Gre.
59/H6 Idkū, Egypt
33/H5 Idle (riv.), Eng,UK
59/D3 Idlib, Syria
50/B3 Idrija, Slov.
81/M13 Idriss I (res.), Mor.
42/B2 Ieper, Belg.
49/J5 Ierápetra, Gre.
87/G2 Ifakara, Tanz.
78/D4 Ifalik (isl.), Micr.
89/H8 Ifanadiana, Madg.
85/G5 Ife, Nga.
65/M10 Iga, Japan
65/M10 Iga (riv.), Japan
95/C2 Igarapava, Braz.
93/J4 Igarapé-Miri, Braz.
94/D2 Igarassu, Braz.
56/J3 Igarka, Rus.
70/B4 Igatpuri, India
59/F2 Iğdır, Turk.
31/P8 Ightham, Eng,UK
114/H2 Igikpak (mtn.), Ak,US
48/A3 Iglesias, It.
110/B1 Ignace, On,Can
51/J5 İğneada (cape), Turk.
31/S10 Igny, Fr.
53/M4 Igra, Rus.
95/B3 Iguaçu (riv.), Braz.
91/F2 Iguaçu Nat'l Park, Braz.
94/B4 Iguaí, Braz.
100/B4 Iguala, Mex.
47/F2 Igualada, Sp.
91/E2 Iguapa (riv.), Braz.
95/C3 Iguape, Braz.
95/C3 Iguape (riv.), Braz.
94/C2 Iguatu, Braz.
91/F2 Iguazu Nat'l Park, Arg.
82/D2 Iguidi, 'Erg (des.), Afr.
89/H8 Ihosy, Madg.
89/G8 Ihotry (lake), Madg.
56/C3 Ii (riv.), Fin.
65/E3 Iida, Japan
65/F2 Iide-san (mtn.), Japan
52/E2 Iijoki (riv.), Fin.
65/M10 Iinan, Japan
37/H3 Iisalmi, Fin.
65/M10 Iitaka, Japan
52/E3 Iitti, Fin.
65/F2 Iiyama, Japan
64/B4 Iizuka, Japan
82/C3 Ijill (peak), Mrta.
40/C4 IJmeer (bay), Neth.
40/B4 IJmuiden, Neth.
84/B2 Ijnaoun (well), Mrta.
37/H2 Ijoki (riv.), Fin.
40/C4 IJssel (riv.), Neth.
40/C3 IJsselmeer (lake), Neth.
40/C3 IJsselmuiden, Neth.
40/C4 IJsselstein, Neth.
91/F2 Ijuí, Braz.
64/B5 Ijūin, Japan
42/B2 Ijzer (riv.), Belg.
53/M5 Ik (riv.), Rus.
89/H7 Ikahavo (plat.), Madg.
49/J4 Ikaría (isl.), Gre.
87/D1 Ikela, Zaire
65/M10 Ikenokoya-yama (peak), Japan
51/F4 Ikhtiman, Bul.
64/A4 Iki (chan.), Japan
64/A4 Iki (isl.), Japan
65/L10 Ikoma, Japan
89/H7 Ikopa (riv.), Madg.
67/D4 Ilagan, Phil.
60/E2 Īlām, Iran
70/E2 Ilam, Nepal
67/D3 Ilan, Tai.
39/K2 Iława, Pol.
83/M4 'Ilay, Sudan
34/D4 Ilchester, Eng,UK
106/G2 Ile-à-la-Crosse, Sk,Can
107/G2 Ile-a-la-Crosse (lake), Sk,Can
87/D1 Ilebo, Zaire
44/E2 Ile-de-France (reg.), Fr.
55/K2 Ilek (riv.), Kaz., Rus.
111/N7 Ile-Perrot, Qu,Can
84/E5 Iles Ehotilés Nat'l Park, IvC.
85/G5 Ilesha, Nga.
31/P7 Ilford, Eng,UK
76/B3 Ilfracombe, Austl.
34/B4 Ilfracombe, Eng,UK
54/E4 Ilgaz, Turk.
59/B2 Ilgın, Turk.
95/H8 Ilhabela, Braz.
95/J8 Ilha Grande (bay), Braz.
95/B1 Ilha Solteira (res.), Braz.
46/A2 Ílhavo, Port.
94/C4 Ilhéus, Braz.
68/C3 Ili (riv.), China, Kaz.
114/G4 Iliamna (lake), Ak,US
114/H3 Iliamna (vol.), Ak,US
67/D6 Iligan, Phil.
59/E3 Ilısu (res.), Turk.
51/H6 Ilium (Troy) (ruins), Turk.
33/G6 Ilkeston, Eng,UK
33/G4 Ilkley, Eng,UK
45/H3 Ill (riv.), Aus.
45/G2 Ill (riv.), Fr.
96/C1 Illapel, Chile
85/G3 Illéla, Niger
45/J3 Iller (riv.), Ger.
46/D2 Illescas, Sp.
92/E7 Illimani (peak), Bol.
43/G5 Illingen, Ger.
110/B4 Illinois (state), US
110/B3 Illinois (riv.), Il,US
34/A6 Illogan, Eng,UK
46/D4 Illora, Sp.
45/G3 Illzach, Fr.
45/J2 Ilm (riv.), Ger.
37/G3 Ilmajoki, Fin.
41/G5 Ilme (riv.), Ger.
52/F4 Il'men' (lake), Rus.
38/F3 Ilmenau, Ger.
41/H2 Ilmenau (riv.), Ger.
34/D5 Ilminster, Eng,UK
92/D7 Ilo, Peru
67/D5 Iloilo, Phil.
85/G4 Ilorin, Nga.
55/H2 Ilovlya (riv.), Rus.
41/H4 Ilse (riv.), Ger.
41/H4 Ilsede, Ger.
41/H5 Ilsenburg, Ger.
51/H5 Ilyas (pt.), Turk.
53/N3 Ilych (riv.), Rus.
45/K2 Ilz (riv.), Ger.
64/C3 Imabari, Japan
65/F2 Imaichi, Japan
89/H8 Imaloto (riv.), Madg.
59/C3 İmamoğlu, Turk.
52/F2 Imandra (lake), Rus.
64/A4 Imari, Japan
37/J3 Imatra, Fin.
64/E3 Imazu, Japan
65/J7 Imba, Japan
95/B4 Imbituba, Braz.
83/P6 Īmī, Eth.
55/J5 Imishli, Azer.
49/L7 Imittós (mtn.), Gre.
108/C2 Imlay, Nv,US
41/G6 Immenhausen, Ger.
45/J3 Immenstadt im Allgäu, Ger.
33/H4 Immingham, Eng,UK
113/H5 Immokalee, Fl,US
114/J2 Imnavait (mtn.), Ak,US
85/G5 Imo (state), Nga.
45/J4 Imola, It.
94/A2 Imperatriz, Braz.
45/H5 Imperia, It.
107/G3 Imperial, Sk,Can
109/G2 Imperial, Ne,US
82/J7 Impfondo, Congo
71/F3 Imphāl, India
51/J5 İmrali (isl.), Turk.
59/D2 İmranlı, Turk.
45/J3 Imst, Aus.
65/E3 Ina, Japan
65/L10 Ina (riv.), Japan
39/H2 Ina (riv.), Pol.
65/M9 Inabe, Japan
65/L10 Inagawa, Japan
65/H7 Inagi, Japan
82/G2 I-n-Amenas, Alg.
65/K10 Inami, Japan
81/M13 Inaouene (riv.), Mor.
37/H1 Inari (lake), Fin.
51/G2 Inău (peak), Rom.
65/G2 Inawashiro (lake), Japan
65/M9 Inazawa, Japan
47/G3 Inca, Sp.
85/F2 I-n-Chaouâg (wadi), Mali
36/C3 Inchinnan, Sc,UK
84/B2 Inchiri (reg.), Mrta.
63/K4 Inch'ŏn, SKor.
82/E3 I-n-Dagouber (well), Mali
95/C1 Indaiá (riv.), Braz.
95/C2 Indaiatuba, Braz.
67/D6 Indanan, Phil.
43/F2 Inde (riv.), Ger.
43/F2 Inden, Ger.
100/D4 Independence, Belz.
108/C3 Independence, Ca,US
109/J3 Independence, Ks,US
109/J3 Independence, Mo,US
108/C2 Independence (mts.), Nv,US
115/E6 Independence Nat'l Hist. Park, Pa,US
94/B2 Independência, Braz.
55/J2 Inder (lake), Kaz.
58/G7 India
29/N6 Indian (ocean)
110/C3 Indiana (state), US
110/E3 Indiana, Pa,US
116/R16 Indiana Dunes Nat'l Lakesh., In,US
110/C4 Indianapolis (cap.), In,US
107/H3 Indian Head, Sk,Can
113/F3 Indianola, Ms,US
113/H5 Indiantown, Fl,US
95/B1 Indiaporã, Braz.
57/Q3 Indigirka (riv.), Rus.
50/E3 Inđija, Yugo.
108/C4 Indio, Ca,US
69/C1 Indochina (reg.), Asia
73/E4 Indonesia
76/E6 Indooroopilly, Austl.
70/C3 Indore, India
72/B4 Indragiri (riv.), Indo.
72/C5 Indramayu (cape), Indo.
70/D4 Indrāvati (riv.), India
44/D3 Indre (riv.), Fr.
44/D3 Indrois (riv.), Fr.
58/F7 Indus (riv.), Asia
61/J4 Indus, Mouths of the, Pak.
59/C2 İnebolu, Turk.
85/E1 I-n-Echaï (well), Mali
59/B2 İnegöl, Turk.
50/E2 Ineu, Rom.
82/D1 Inezgane, Mor.
88/C4 Infanta (cape), SAfr.
100/A4 Infiernillo (res.), Mex.
46/C1 Infiesto, Sp.
94/D2 Ingá, Braz.
92/C4 Ingapirca, Ecu.
31/Q7 Ingatestone, Eng,UK
42/C2 Ingelmunster, Belg.
76/G8 Ingleburn, Austl.
33/G2 Ingleton, Eng,UK
111/Q8 Inglewood, On,Can
115/B3 Inglewood, Ca,US
116/C2 Inglewood-Finn Hill, Wa,US
113/H4 Inglis, Fl,US
62/G1 Ingoda (riv.), Rus.
33/J5 Ingoldmells, Eng,UK
45/J2 Ingolstadt, Ger.
31/Q7 Ingrave, Eng,UK
98/E Ingrid Christianson (coast), Ant.
85/G2 I-n-Guezzâm, Alg.
54/E3 Ingulets (riv.), Ukr.
55/G4 Inguri (riv.), Geo.
94/C3 Inhambupe, Braz.
93/J7 Inhumas, Braz.
32/A1 Inishowen (pen.), Ire.
32/B1 Inishowen Head (pt.), Ire.
116/F7 Inkster, Mi,US
64/C3 Inland (sea), Japan
71/G3 Inle (lake), Burma
85/E2 I-n-Milach (well), Mali
45/K2 Inn (riv.), Eur.
62/G3 Inner Mongolia (reg.), China
41/H4 Innerste (riv.), Ger.
45/K3 Innichen (San Candido), It.
76/B2 Innisfail, Austl.
106/E2 Innisfail, Ab,Can
114/G3 Innoko (riv.), Ak,US
45/J3 Innsbruck, Aus.
34/B5 Inny (riv.), Eng,UK
64/C4 Ino, Japan
87/C1 Inongo, Zaire
39/K4 Inovec (peak), Slvk.
39/K2 Inowrocław, Pol.
85/E1 I-n-Sâkâne, Erg (des.), Mali
82/F2 I-n-Salah, Alg.
36/D2 Insch, Sc,UK
71/G4 Insein, Burma
106/A2 Inside (passg.), BC,Can
53/P2 Inta, Rus.
85/F2 I-n-Tassik (well), Mali
106/B2 Interior (plat.), BC,Can
107/K3 International Falls, Mn,US
69/B2 Inthanon (peak), Thai.
51/H3 Întorsura Buzăului, Rom.
65/G3 Inubō-zaki (pt.), Japan
103/J3 Inukjuak, Qu,Can
97/K8 Inútil (bay), Chile
65/E3 Inuyama, Japan
36/C2 Inveraray, Sc,UK
75/Q12 Invercargill, NZ
77/D1 Inverell, Austl.
36/C2 Invergarry, Sc,UK
36/D2 Inverkeilor, Sc,UK
107/H3 Invermay, Sk,Can
111/J2 Inverness, NS,Can
36/C2 Inverness, Sc,UK
113/G3 Inverness, Al,US
113/H4 Inverness, Fl,US
36/D2 Inverurie, Sc,UK
67/B6 Investigator (shoal)
74/F7 Investigator (str.), Austl.
87/F4 Inyangani (peak), Zim.
114/D2 Inymney, Gora (mtn.), Rus.
108/C3 Inyo (mts.), Ca,US
55/H1 Inza, Rus.
65/J7 Inzai, Japan
49/G3 Ioánnina, Gre.
109/J3 Iola, Ks,US
61/H1 Iolotan', Trkm.
87/B4 Iona Nat'l Park, Ang.
110/C3 Ionia, Mi,US
49/F3 Ionian (sea), Eur.
49/F3 Ionian (isls.), Gre.
49/J4 Íos (isl.), Gre.
84/A2 Iouîk (cape), Mrta.
107/K5 Iowa (state), US
107/L5 Iowa (riv.), Ia,US
107/L5 Iowa City, Ia,US
107/K5 Iowa Falls, Ia,US
95/B1 Ipameri, Braz.
96/B5 Ipan (isl.), Chile
95/C1 Ipanema, Braz.
95/D1 Ipatinga, Braz.
39/K4 Ipel' (Ipoly) (riv.), Hun., Slvk.
92/C3 Ipiales, Col.
94/C4 Ipiaú, Braz.
94/C4 Ipirá, Braz.
72/B3 Ipoh, Malay.
39/K4 Ipoly (Ipel') (riv.), Hun., Slvk.
93/H7 Iporá, Braz.
49/K2 Ipsala, Turk.
76/E7 Ipswich, Austl.
35/H2 Ipswich, Eng,UK
107/J4 Ipswich, SD,US
94/B2 Ipu, Braz.
95/B2 Ipuã, Braz.
94/B2 Ipueiras, Braz.
92/D8 Iquique, Chile
92/D4 Iquitos, Peru
65/M10 Irago (chan.), Japan
65/E3 Irago-misaki (cape), Japan
49/J4 Iráklia (isl.), Gre.
49/J5 Iráklion, Gre.
60/F2 Iran
72/D3 Iran (mts.), Indo., Malay.
61/H3 Īrānshahr, Iran
100/A3 Irapuato, Mex.
60/D2 Iraq
95/B3 Irati, Braz.
73/H4 Irau (mtn.), Indo.
59/K5 Irbid, Jor.
59/L5 Irbid (gov.), Jor.
59/F3 Irbīl, Iraq
94/B3 Irecê, Braz.
36/A4 Ireland
36/B3 Ireland, Northern, UK
32/B5 Ireland's Eye (isl.), Ire.
53/N5 Iremel', Gora (peak), Rus.
34/C2 Irfon (riv.), Wal,UK
85/G2 Irhazer Oua-n-Agadez (wadi), Niger
63/K4 Iri, SKor.
73/H4 Irian Jaya (reg.), Indo.
84/D2 Irîgui (reg.), Mali, Mrta.
55/L2 Iriklinskiy (res.), Rus.
87/G2 Iringa, Tanz.
67/D3 Iriomote (isl.), Japan
93/H4 Iriri (riv.), Braz.
32/C4 Irish (sea), Ire., UK
62/E1 Irkut (riv.), Rus.
62/E1 Irkutsk, Rus.
33/F5 Irlam, Eng,UK
34/D1 Iron Bridge, Eng,UK
50/F3 Iron Gate (gorge), Eur.
110/B2 Iron Mountain, Mi,US
110/B2 Iron River, Mi,US
110/D4 Ironton, Oh,US
110/B2 Ironwood, Mi,US
110/D1 Iroquois Falls, On,Can
65/F3 Irō-zaki (pt.), Japan
54/E1 Irput' (riv.), Bela., Rus.
71/G4 Irrawaddy (riv.), Burma
43/F4 Irrel, Ger.
43/F3 Irsen (riv.), Ger.
33/E3 Irt (riv.), Eng,UK
33/F1 Irthing (riv.), Eng,UK
35/F2 Irthlingborough, Eng,UK
56/G4 Irtysh (riv.), Kaz., Rus.
65/H7 Iruma, Japan
83/L7 Irumu, Zaire
46/E1 Irún, Sp.
36/C3 Irvine, Sc,UK
115/C3 Irvine, Ca,US
112/D3 Irving, Tx,US
115/F5 Irvington, NJ,US
76/C3 Isaac (riv.), Austl.
67/D6 Isabela, Phil.
103/K2 Isabella (bay), NW,Can
103/R7 Isachsen (cape), NW,Can
37/M6 Ísafjardhardjúp (fjord), Ice.
64/B4 Isahaya, Japan
89/H8 Isalo Nat'l Park, Madg.
89/H8 Isalo Ruiniform, Massif (plat.), Madg.
38/G4 Isar (riv.), Aus., Ger.
45/J3 Isarco (Eisack) (riv.), It.
48/C2 Ischia, It.
41/H3 Ise (riv.), Ger.
65/E3 Ise, Japan
65/M10 Ise (bay), Japan
35/F2 Ise (riv.), Eng,UK
65/F3 Isehara, Japan
115/F5 Iselin, NJ,US
45/K2 Isen (riv.), Ger.
45/J4 Iseo (lake), It.
44/F4 Isère (riv.), Fr.
41/E6 Iserlohn, Ger.
48/D2 Isernia, It.
65/F2 Isesaki, Japan
65/E3 Ise-Shima Nat'l Park, Japan
53/Q4 Iset' (riv.), Rus.
85/F5 Iseyin, Nga.
65/L10 Ishi (riv.), Japan
65/F2 Ishibashi, Japan
65/M9 Ishibe, Japan
78/B2 Ishigaki, Japan
67/D3 Ishigaki (isl.), Japan
65/F2 Ishige, Japan
65/G2 Ishikawa, Japan
65/E2 Ishikawa (pref.), Japan
65/N10 Ishiki, Japan
56/H4 Ishim (riv.), Kaz., Rus.
53/R4 Ishim, Rus.
55/L1 Ishimbay, Rus.
65/G1 Ishinomaki, Japan
65/G2 Ishioka, Japan
64/C4 Ishizuchi-san (mtn.), Japan
110/C2 Ishpeming, Mi,US
92/E7 Isiboro Securé Nat'l Park, Bol.
97/G1 Isidoro, Uru.
56/H4 Isil'kul', Rus.
83/L7 Isiro, Zaire
86/C4 Is, Jabal (peak), Sudan
59/D3 İskenderun, Turk.
59/C2 İskilip, Turk.
49/H1 Iskŭr (res.), Bul.
49/H1 Iskŭr (riv.), Bul.
36/D2 Isla (riv.), Sc,UK
46/B4 Isla Cristina, Sp.
96/Q9 Isla de Maipo, Chile
75/C4 Isla Gorge Nat'l Park, Austl.
101/N9 Isla Isabela Nat'l Park, Mex.
61/K2 Islāmābād (cap.), Pak.
96/B5 Isla Magdalena Nat'l Park, Chile
70/E2 Islāmpur, India
100/D3 Isla Mujeres, Mex.
107/K2 Island Lake, Mb,Can
111/K1 Islands (bay), Nf,Can
44/D4 Isle (riv.), Fr.
35/G2 Isleham, Eng,UK
32/D3 Isle of Man, UK
32/D2 Isle of Whithorn, Sc,UK
110/B2 Isle Royale Nat'l Park, Mi,US
31/N7 Islington (bor.), Eng,UK
115/G5 Islip, NY,US
53/X9 Ismailovo Park, Rus.
86/C2 Ismalia (Al Ismā'īlīyah), Egypt
86/C3 Isnā, Egypt
45/J3 Isny, Ger.
65/M10 Isobe, Japan
37/H3 Isojärven Nat'l Park, Fin.
87/F3 Isoka, Zam.
48/C3 Isola del Liri, It.
48/E3 Isola di Capo Rizzuto, It.
59/B3 Isparta, Turk.
44/C5 Ispéguy, Col d' (pass), Fr.
51/H4 Isperikh, Bul.
59/E2 İspir, Turk.
59/J5 Israel
116/C2 Issaquah, Wa,US
40/D5 Issel (riv.), Ger.
40/D5 Isselburg, Ger.
84/D5 Issia, IvC.
44/E4 Issoire, Fr.
44/E3 Issoudun, Fr.
40/D5 Issum, Ger.
68/C3 Issyk-Kul' (lake), Kyr.
42/B6 Issy-les-Moulineaux, Fr.
50/E1 Istállós-kő (peak), Hun.
51/J5 İstanbul, Turk.
51/J5 İstanbul (prov.), Turk.
51/H5 Istranca (mts.), Turk.
44/F5 Istres, Fr.
50/A3 Istria (pen.), Cro.
73/F2 Isulan, Phil.
94/C3 Itabaiana, Braz.
94/D2 Itabaiana, Braz.
94/C3 Itabaianinha, Braz.
95/D2 Itabapoana (riv.), Braz.
94/B4 Itaberaba, Braz.
95/D1 Itabira, Braz.
95/D2 Itabirito, Braz.
95/L7 Itaboraí, Braz.
94/C4 Itabuna, Braz.
93/H5 Itacaiunas (riv.), Braz.
94/A4 Itacarambi, Braz.
92/G4 Itacoatiara, Braz.
92/D5 Itacuaí (riv.), Braz.
95/K7 Itaguaí, Braz.
92/C2 Itagüí, Col.
95/B2 Itaí, Braz.
95/B3 Itaiópolis, Braz.
91/F1 Itaipu (res.), Braz., Par.
93/G4 Itaituba, Braz.
95/B3 Itajaí, Braz.
95/B3 Itajai (riv.), Braz.
95/H7 Itajubá, Braz.
94/C4 Itajuípe, Braz.
65/G3 Itako, Japan
30/E4 Italy
94/C5 Itamaraju, Braz.
95/D1 Itamarandiba, Braz.
95/D1 Itambacuri, Braz.
94/B4 Itambé, Braz.
95/D1 Itambé (peak), Braz.
65/L10 Itami, Japan
71/F2 Itanagar, India
95/G9 Itanhaém, Braz.
95/C2 Itanhandu, Braz.
94/B5 Itanhém, Braz.
95/D1 Itanhém (riv.), Braz.
95/D1 Itanhomi, Braz.
94/B5 Itaobim, Braz.
95/D2 Itaocara, Braz.
94/C1 Itapagé, Braz.
94/C4 Itaparica (isl.), Braz.
95/C2 Itapecerica, Braz.
94/A1 Itapecuru-Mirim, Braz.
95/D2 Itapemirim, Braz.
95/D2 Itaperuna, Braz.
94/B4 Itapetinga, Braz.
95/B2 Itapetininga, Braz.
95/B2 Itapeva, Braz.
95/G8 Itapevi, Braz.
94/C3 Itapicuru (riv.), Braz.
94/A1 Itapicuru (riv.), Braz.
94/C1 Itapipoca, Braz.
95/G7 Itapira, Braz.
94/C4 Itapitanga, Braz.
95/B2 Itaporanga, Braz.
95/G8 Itaquaquecetuba, Braz.
94/B4 Itarantim, Braz.
95/B3 Itararé, Braz.
70/C3 Itārsi, India
94/B4 Itaruçu, Braz.
95/C2 Itatiaia Nat'l Park, Braz.
95/G8 Itatiba, Braz.
95/C2 Itatinga (res.), Braz.
94/B3 Itaueira (riv.), Braz.
95/C2 Itaúna, Braz.
63/N3 Itayanagi, Japan
67/D3 Itbayat (isl.), Phil.
35/E4 Itchen (riv.), Eng,UK
83/K7 Itembiri (riv.), Zaire
92/F6 Iténez (riv.), Bol.
87/E4 Itezhi-Tezhi (dam), Zam.
110/E3 Ithaca, NY,US
49/G3 Ithaca (Itháki) (isl.), Gre.
41/G5 Ith Hils (ridge), Ger.
34/C2 Ithon (riv.), Wal,UK
87/F2 Itigi, Tanz.
65/F3 Itō, Japan
65/E2 Itoigawa, Japan
44/D2 Iton (riv.), Fr.
94/B4 Itororó, Braz.
65/H7 Itsukaichi, Japan
41/F6 Itter (riv.), Ger.
48/A2 Ittiri, It.
95/C2 Itu, Braz.
94/C4 Ituberá, Braz.
92/D5 Ituí (riv.), Braz.
95/B1 Ituiutaba, Braz.
95/B1 Itumbiara, Braz.
95/B1 Itumbiara (res.), Braz.
107/H3 Ituna, Sk,Can
95/B3 Ituporanga, Braz.
95/B1 Iturama, Braz.
95/J6 Itutinga (res.), Braz.
95/C2 Ituverava, Braz.
92/E5 Ituxi (riv.), Braz.
59/H6 Ityāy al Bārūd, Egypt
38/E2 Itzehoe, Ger.
114/C2 Iul'tin, Gora (mtn.), Rus.
95/D2 Iuna, Braz.
95/B3 Ivaí (riv.), Braz.
95/B3 Ivaiporã, Braz.
37/H1 Ivalojoki (riv.), Fin.
45/M2 Ivančice, Czh.
50/D4 Ivangrad, Yugo.
110/D1 Ivanhoe (riv.), On,Can
50/E4 Ivanjica, Yugo.
54/C2 Ivano-Frankovsk, Ukr.
54/C2 Ivano-Frankovsk Obl., Ukr.
52/J4 Ivanovo, Rus.
53/J4 Ivanovo Obl., Rus.
49/J2 Ivaylovgrad (res.), Bul.
53/P3 Ivdel, Rus.
31/M7 Iver, Eng,UK
31/M7 Iver Heath, Eng,UK
82/H7 Ivindo (riv.), Gabon
89/H8 Ivohibe, Madg.
89/J7 Ivondro (riv.), Madg.
84/D5 Ivory Coast (Côte d'Ivoire)
45/G4 Ivrea, It.
42/B6 Ivry-sur-Seine, Fr.
34/C6 Ivybridge, Eng,UK
65/F2 Iwai, Japan
65/G2 Iwaki, Japan
64/C3 Iwakuni, Japan
65/M9 Iwakura, Japan
64/D3 Iwami, Japan
63/N3 Iwamizawa, Japan
65/G1 Iwanuma, Japan
65/E3 Iwata, Japan
63/N4 Iwate-san (mtn.), Japan
65/H7 Iwatsuki, Japan
85/G5 Iwo, Nga.
78/D2 Iwo Jima (isl.), Japan
38/C3 Ixelles, Belg.
100/B4 Ixtaltepec, Mex.
101/P9 Ixtlán del Río, Mex.
35/G2 Ixworth, Eng,UK
62/D1 Iya (riv.), Rus.
64/C4 Iyo, Japan
64/C4 Iyo (sea), Japan
100/D4 Izabal (lake), Guat.
55/H4 Izberbash, Rus.
42/C2 Izegem, Belg.
114/F4 Izembek Nat'l Wild. Ref., Ak,US
53/M4 Izhevsk, Rus.
53/M2 Izhma (riv.), Rus.
114/E5 Izigan (cape), Ak,US
61/G4 Izkī, Oman
51/J3 Izmail, Ukr.
59/A2 İzmir, Turk.
51/J5 İzmit, Turk.
51/J5 İzmit (gulf), Turk.
46/C4 Iznájar, Sp.
51/J5 İznik, Turk.
51/H5 İznik (lake), Turk.
59/L5 Izra', Syria
50/D2 Izsák, Hun.
63/M5 Izu (isls.), Japan
65/F3 Izu (pen.), Japan
100/B4 Izúcar de Matamoros, Mex.
65/H8 Izu-Fuji-Hakone Nat'l Park, Japan
64/A3 Izuhara, Japan
64/D3 Izumi, Japan
65/L10 Izumi-ōtsu, Japan
64/D3 Izumi-Sano, Japan
64/C3 Izumo, Japan
54/F2 Izyum, Ukr.

J

86/B5 Jabal Abyad (plat.), Sudan
59/K4 Jabal Lubnān (gov.), Leb.
46/D3 Jabalón (riv.), Sp.
70/C3 Jabalpur, India
59/K6 Jabālyah, Gaza
42/C1 Jabbeke, Belg.
86/C4 Jabjabah, Wādī (dry riv.), Egypt, Sudan
59/K4 Jablah, Syria
49/G2 Jablanica (mts.), Alb.
39/H3 Jablonec nad Nisou, Czh.
94/D3 Jaboatão, Braz.
95/B2 Jaboticabal, Braz.
50/E3 Jabuka, Yugo.
72/B4 Jabung (cape), Indo.
47/E1 Jaca, Sp.
94/B3 Jacaré (riv.), Braz.
95/C2 Jacareí, Braz.
83/Q5 Jaceel (riv.), Som.
111/G2 Jackman, Me,US
108/D2 Jackpot, Nv,US
112/D3 Jacksboro, Tx,US
113/G4 Jackson, Al,US
108/B3 Jackson, Ca,US
110/C3 Jackson, Mi,US
107/K5 Jackson, Mn,US
109/K3 Jackson, Mo,US
113/F3 Jackson (cap.), Ms,US
106/D5 Jackson (mts.), Nv,US
110/D4 Jackson, Oh,US
113/F3 Jackson, Tn,US
106/F5 Jackson, Wy,US
106/F4 Jackson (lake), Wy,US
113/G3 Jacksonville, Al,US
112/E3 Jacksonville, Ar,US
113/H4 Jacksonville, Fl,US
110/B4 Jacksonville, Il,US
113/J3 Jacksonville, NC,US
112/E4 Jacksonville, Tx,US
113/H4 Jacksonville Beach, Fl,US
101/G4 Jacmel, Haiti
61/J3 Jacobābād, Pak.
94/B3 Jacobina, Braz.
111/H1 Jacques-Cartier (mtn.), Qu,Can
111/G2 Jacques-Cartier (riv.), Qu,Can
91/F2 Jacuí (riv.), Braz.
94/C3 Jacuipe (riv.), Braz.
95/C3 Jacupiranga, Braz.
61/H3 Jaddi (pt.), Pak.
38/E2 Jade (bay), Ger.
41/F2 Jade (riv.), Ger.
41/F2 Jadebusen (bay), Ger.
46/D4 Jaén, Sp.
77/A3 Jaffa (cape), Austl.
70/D6 Jaffna, SrL.
70/D4 Jagdalpur, India
70/D2 Jagdīspur, India
67/D6 Jagna, Phil.
68/C5 Jagraon, India
45/J2 Jagst (riv.), Ger.
70/C4 Jagtiāl, India
94/C4 Jaguaquara, Braz.
97/G2 Jaguarão, Braz.
97/G2 Jaguarão (riv.), Braz.
95/G7 Jaguari (riv.), Braz.
95/B3 Jaguariaíva, Braz.
94/C2 Jaguaribe, Braz.
94/C2 Jaguaribe (riv.), Braz.
95/G7 Jaguariúna, Braz.
94/C2 Jaguaruana, Braz.
77/D3 Jagungal (peak), Austl.
60/F3 Jahrom, Iran
73/G3 Jailolo, Indo.
70/C2 Jaipur, India
70/B2 Jaisalmer, India
50/C3 Jajce, Bosn.
70/E3 Jājpur, India
72/C5 Jakarta (cap.), Indo.
37/G3 Jakobstad, Fin.
109/G4 Jal, NM,US
61/K2 Jalālābād, Afg.
37/G3 Jalasjärvi, Fin.
95/B2 Jales, Braz.
70/C3 Jālgaon, India
82/H6 Jalingo, Nga.
101/P9 Jalisco (state), Mex.
48/A4 Jāliţah, Jazīrat (isl.), Tun.
70/C4 Jālna, India
46/E2 Jalon (riv.), Sp.
70/B2 Jālor, India
70/E2 Jalpaiguri, India
83/K2 Jālū, Libya
78/F4 Jaluit (atoll), Mrsh.
60/E2 Jalūlā', Iraq
83/P7 Jamaame, Som.
85/H4 Jamaare (riv.), Nga.
101/F4 Jamaica
101/F4 Jamaica (chan.), NAm.
70/E3 Jamālpur, Bang.
70/E2 Jamālpur, India
93/G5 Jamanxim (riv.), Braz.
92/F5 Jamari (riv.), Braz.
72/B4 Jambi, Indo.
72/A2 Jambuair (cape), Indo.
105/K1 James (lake), On,Can
103/H3 James (bay), On, Qu,Can
96/B5 James (pt.), Chile
107/J4 James (riv.), ND, SD,US
110/E4 James (riv.), Va,US
115/F5 Jamesburg, NJ,US
102/G1 James Ross (str.), NW,Can
107/J4 Jamestown, ND,US
110/E3 Jamestown, NY,US
113/G2 Jamestown, Tn,US
100/B4 Jamiltepec, Mex.
68/B5 Jammu, India
68/C5 Jammu and Kashmīr (state), India
70/B3 Jāmnagar, India
61/K3 Jāmpur, Pak.
37/H3 Jämsä, Fin.
70/E3 Jamshedpur, India
37/E3 Jämtland (co.), Swe.
70/E3 Jamūi, India
107/H2 Jan (lake), Sk,Can

141
Janak – Kāshā

52/E3 Janakkala, Fin.
94/B4 Janaúba, Braz.
93/J3 Janaucu (isl.), Braz.
95/B2 Jandaia do Sul, Braz.
46/C4 Jándula (riv.), Sp.
110/B3 Janesville, Wi,US
70/C4 Jangaon, India
70/E3 Jangipur, India
39/K2 Janikowo, Pol.
59/K5 Janīn, WBnk.
50/D3 Janja, Bosn.
30/D1 Jan Mayen (isl.), Nor.
50/D2 Jánoshalma, Hun.
39/M3 Janów Lubelski, Pol.
94/A4 Januária, Braz.
86/C2 Janūb Sīnā' (gov.), Egypt
70/C3 Jaora, India
63/M4 Japan
63/L4 Japan (sea), Asia
65/E3 Japanese Alps (range), Japan
65/E2 Japanese Alps Nat'l Park, Japan
92/E4 Japurá (riv.), Braz.
59/D3 Jarābulus, Syria
46/C2 Jaraíz de la Vera, Sp.
59/K5 Jarash, Jor.
82/H1 Jarbah (isl.), Tun.
94/C2 Jardim do Seridó, Braz.
91/E2 Jardín América, Arg.
95/C2 Jardinópolis, Braz.
93/H3 Jari (riv.), Braz.
70/E3 Jaridih, India
82/H1 Jarjīs, Tun.
43/E5 Jarny, Fr.
39/J3 Jarocin, Pol.
39/H3 Jaroměř, Czh.
39/M3 Jarosław, Pol.
33/G2 Jarrow, Eng,UK
69/C2 Jars (plain), Laos
43/F6 Jarville-la-Malgrange, Fr.
79/J5 Jarvis (isl.), PacUS
39/L4 Jasło, Pol.
106/D2 Jasper, Ab,Can
113/G3 Jasper, Al,US
113/H4 Jasper, Fl,US
113/G3 Jasper, Ga,US
110/C4 Jasper, In,US
112/E4 Jasper, Tx,US
106/D2 Jasper Nat'l Park, Ab, BC,Can
70/C2 Jaspur, India
39/J2 Jastrowie, Pol.
39/K4 Jastrzębie Zdroj, Pol.
50/E2 Jászapáti, Hun.
50/D2 Jászárokszállás, Hun.
50/D2 Jászberény, Hun.
50/E2 Jászladány, Hun.
50/E2 Jász-Nagykun-Szolnok (co.), Hun.
95/B1 Jataí, Braz.
92/G4 Jatapu (riv.), Braz.
47/E3 Játiva, Sp.
95/B2 Jaú, Braz.
92/F4 Jaú (riv.), Braz.
92/F3 Jauaperi (riv.), Braz.
93/H4 Jauaru (mts.), Braz.
92/F3 Jaua Sarisarinama Nat'l Park, Ven.
92/C6 Jauja, Peru
45/G3 Jaunpass (pass), Swi.
72/C5 Java (isl.), Indo.
72/D5 Java (sea), Indo.
92/D5 Javari (riv.), Braz.
47/F3 Jávea, Sp.
97/J6 Javier (isl.), Chile
50/D1 Javorie (peak), Slvk.
83/Q7 Jawhar (Giohar), Som.
39/J3 Jawor, Pol.
73/J4 Jaya (peak), Indo.
73/K4 Jayapura, Indo.
112/C3 Jayton, Tx,US
35/H3 Jaywick, Eng,UK
60/D5 Jazā'ir Farasān (isls.), SAr.
39/L3 Jędrzejów, Pol.
38/F2 Jeetze (riv.), Ger.
106/C4 Jefferson (peak), Or,US
112/E3 Jefferson, Tx,US
109/J3 Jefferson City (cap.), Mo,US
110/C4 Jeffersonville, In,US
106/G5 Jeffrey City, Wy,US
96/B5 Jeinemeni (peak), Chile
52/E4 Jēkabpils, Lat.
39/J3 Jelcz-Laskowice, Pol.
39/H3 Jelenia Góra, Pol.
39/H3 Jelenia Góra (prov.), Pol.
70/E2 Jelep (pass), China
52/D4 Jelgava, Lat.
42/C3 Jemappes, Belg.
72/D5 Jember, Indo.
108/F4 Jemez Pueblo, NM,US
73/E4 Jempang (riv.), Indo.
86/C3 Jemsa, Egypt
38/F3 Jena, Ger.
112/E4 Jena, La,US
73/E5 Jeneponto, Indo.
112/E4 Jennings, La,US
102/F2 Jenny Lind (isl.), NW,Can
103/H2 Jens Muck (isl.), NW,Can
94/B4 Jequié, Braz.
94/B5 Jequitinhonha, Braz.
94/C5 Jequitinhonha (riv.), Braz.
81/N13 Jerada, Mor.
101/G4 Jérémie, Haiti
101/P9 Jerez de García Salinas, Mex.
46/B4 Jerez de la Frontera, Sp.
46/B3 Jerez de los Caballeros, Sp.
115/G5 Jericho, NY,US
59/K6 Jericho (Arīḩā), WBnk.
106/E5 Jerome, Id,US
115/F5 Jersey City, NJ,US
110/B4 Jerseyville, Il,US
59/M9 Jerusalem (dist.), Isr.
59/N9 Jerusalem Walls Nat'l Park, Isr.
59/K6 Jerusalem (Yerushalayim) (cap.), Isr.
106/C3 Jervis (inlet), BC,Can
50/B2 Jesenice, Slov.
45/K5 Jesi, It.
70/E3 Jessore, Bang.
113/H4 Jesup, Ga,US
111/N6 Jésus (isl.), Qu,Can
91/D3 Jesús María, Arg.
101/F3 Jesús Menéndez, Cuba
84/A4 Jeta (isl.), GBis.
109/H3 Jetmore, Ks,US
70/B3 Jetpur, India
42/D3 Jeumont, Fr.
41/E1 Jever, Ger.
107/G5 Jewel Cave Nat'l Mon., SD,US
70/D4 Jeypore, India
49/F1 Jezerce (peak), Alb.
39/K2 Jeziorák (lake), Pol.
70/E3 Jhā Jhā, India
70/C3 Jhālawār, India
61/K2 Jhang Sadar, Pak.
70/C2 Jhānsi, India
70/D3 Jhārsuguda, India
61/K2 Jhelum (riv.), India, Pak.
61/K2 Jhelum, Pak.
70/E3 Jiāganj, India
62/F5 Jialing (riv.), China
66/C4 Jialu (riv.), China
63/L2 Jiamusi, China
67/B2 Ji'an, China
67/B3 Jian (riv.), China
69/E1 Jiang (riv.), China
67/B3 Jiangmen, China
66/D4 Jiangsu (prov.), China
66/D5 Jiangxi (prov.), China
66/E5 Jiangyin, China
67/C2 Jianyang, China
67/D2 Jiaojiang, China
63/J3 Jiaolai (riv.), China
66/C4 Jiaozuo, China
68/C4 Jiashi, China
66/E5 Jiaxing, China
62/D4 Jiayuguan, China
51/F2 Jibou, Rom.
61/G4 Jibsh, Ra's (pt.), Oman
39/H3 Jičín, Czh.
39/H4 Jihlava, Czh.
45/L2 Jihočeský (reg.), Czh.
39/J4 Jihomoravský (reg.), Czh.
81/U17 Jijel, Alg.
81/U17 Jijel (gov.), Alg.
51/H2 Jijia (riv.), Rom.
83/P6 Jijiga, Eth.
47/E3 Jijona, Sp.
86/A4 Jilf al Kabīr, Ḩadabat al (upland), Egypt
95/B2 Jilhá (res.), Braz.
39/J4 Jilhava (riv.), Czh.
68/E2 Jili (lake), China
63/K3 Jilin, China
63/J1 Jiliu (riv.), China
47/E2 Jiloca (riv.), Sp.
83/N6 Jīma, Eth.
50/E3 Jimbolia, Rom.
46/C4 Jimena de la Frontera, Sp.
62/B3 Jimsar, China
67/C2 Jin (riv.), China
71/K2 Jin (riv.), China
66/D3 Jinan, China
70/C2 Jīnd, India
39/H4 Jindřichuv Hradec, Czh.
66/B4 Jing (riv.), China
67/C2 Jingdezhen, China
67/B2 Jinggangshan, China
66/D3 Jinghai, China
66/C5 Jingmen, China
67/C2 Jinhua, China
66/C2 Jining, China
66/D4 Jining, China
83/M7 Jinja, Ugan.
100/D5 Jinotega, Nic.
100/D5 Jinotepe, Nic.
66/B4 Jinqian (riv.), China
66/E5 Jinshan, China
71/K2 Jinshi, China
67/D5 Jintotolo (chan.), Phil.
70/C4 Jintūr, India
66/E2 Jinxi, China
67/C2 Jinxi, China
66/E2 Jinzhou, China
92/F6 Ji-Paraná, Braz.
92/F5 Jiparaná (riv.), Braz.
92/B4 Jipijapa, Ecu.
86/B3 Jirgā, Egypt
67/A2 Jishou, China
59/D3 Jisr ash Shughūr, Syria
51/F4 Jiu (riv.), Rom.
67/C2 Jiujiang, China
67/A2 Jiuwan (mts.), China
66/D5 Jixi, China
66/C4 Ji Xian, China
66/D2 Ji Xian, China
86/B2 Jīzah, Pyramids of (Giza) (ruins), Egypt
66/C3 Jize, China
45/L1 Jizera (riv.), Czh.
64/C3 Jizō-zaki (pt.), Japan
60/F5 Jiz', Wādī al (dry riv.), Yem.
95/B3 Joaçaba, Braz.
94/B5 Joaíma, Braz.
94/D2 João Câmara, Braz.
94/A2 João Lisboa, Braz.
95/D1 João Monlevade, Braz.
94/D2 João Pessoa, Braz.
95/C1 João Pinheiro, Braz.
91/D2 Joaquín V. González, Arg.
101/F3 Jobabo, Cuba
46/D4 Jódar, Sp.
70/B2 Jodhpur, India
43/D2 Jodoigne, Belg.
37/J3 Joensuu, Fin.
65/F2 Jōetsu, Japan
43/F5 Joeuf, Fr.
88/E2 Johannesburg, SAfr.
108/C4 Johannesburg, Ca,US
106/D4 John Day, Or,US
106/C4 John Day (riv.), Or,US
106/C4 John Day Fossil Beds Nat'l Mon., Or,US
112/C2 John Martin (res.), Co,US
113/H2 Johnson City, Tn,US
112/D4 Johnson City, Tx,US
109/G3 Johnson (Johnson City), Ks,US
114/M3 Johnsons Crossing, Yk,Can
74/C6 Johnston (lake), Austl.
79/J3 Johnston (atoll), PacUS
34/B3 Johnston, Wal,UK
110/E3 Johnstown, Pa,US
72/B3 Johor Baharu, Malay.
44/E3 Joigny, Fr.
95/B3 Joinvile, Braz.
98/W Joinville (isl.), Ant.
83/M6 Jokau, Sudan
37/F2 Jokkmokk, Swe.
37/P6 Jökulsargljufur Nat'l Park, Ice.
116/P16 Joliet, Il,US
110/F2 Joliette, Qu,Can
112/D4 Jollyville, Tx,US
67/D6 Jolo, Phil.
67/D6 Jolo (isl.), Phil.
72/D5 Jombang, Indo.
45/H3 Jona, Swi.
39/N1 Jonava, Lith.
103/S7 Jones (sound), NW,Can
113/F3 Jonesboro, Ar,US
112/E3 Jonesboro, La,US
32/B3 Jonesborough, NI,UK
37/E4 Jönköping, Swe.
37/E4 Jönköping (co.), Swe.
111/G1 Jonquière, Qu,Can
109/J3 Joplin, Mo,US
60/C2 Jordan
111/R9 Jordan, On,Can
59/K6 Jordan (riv.), Jor., WBnk.
106/G4 Jordan, Mt,US
108/E2 Jordan (riv.), Ut,US
111/R9 Jordan Station, On,Can
106/D5 Jordan Valley, Or,US
97/J7 Jorge (cape), Chile
71/F2 Jorhāt, India
41/G1 Jork, Ger.
112/B3 Jornada del Muerto (val.), NM,US
85/H4 Jos (plat.), Nga.
67/E6 Jose Abad Santos, Phil.
95/B2 José Bonifacio, Braz.
94/B2 José de Freitas, Braz.
74/D2 Joseph Bonaparte (gulf), Austl.
65/F2 Joshin-Etsu Kogen Nat'l Park, Japan
108/D4 Joshua Tree Nat'l Mon., Ca,US
37/C3 Jotunheimen Nat'l Park, Nor.
44/C2 Jouanne (riv.), Fr.
42/C6 Jouarre, Fr.
44/D3 Joué-lès-Tours, Fr.
76/B2 Jourama Falls Nat'l Park, Austl.
112/D4 Jourdanton, Tx,US
40/C3 Joure, Neth.
37/J3 Joutseno, Fin.
31/S10 Jouy-en-Josas, Fr.
31/S9 Jouy-le-Moutier, Fr.
60/G1 Joveyn (riv.), Iran
71/F2 Jowai, India
114/M3 Joy (mtn.), Yk,Can
65/L10 Jōyō, Japan
84/A2 Jreïda, Mrta.
66/B5 Ju (riv.), China
101/P9 Juan Aldama, Mex.
106/B3 Juan de Fuca (str.), Can., US
89/G7 Juan de Nova (isl.), Reun.
90/A6 Juan Fernández (isls.), Chile
101/J5 Juangriego, Ven.
92/C5 Juanjuí, Peru
97/T12 Juan L. Lacaze, Uru.
96/F3 Juárez, Arg.
95/J8 Juatinga (pt.), Braz.
94/B3 Juazeiro, Braz.
94/C2 Juazeiro do Norte, Braz.
83/M7 Juba, Sudan
83/P7 Jubba (riv.), Eth., Som.
47/Y17 Juby (cape), Mor.
46/D3 Júcar (riv.), Sp.
40/D6 Jüchen, Ger.
94/B5 Jucurucu (riv.), Braz.
59/N9 Judaea (reg.), WBnk.
45/L3 Judenburg, Aus.
106/F4 Judith (riv.), Mt,US
86/B3 Juhaynah, Egypt
100/D5 Juigalpa, Nic.
31/U9 Juilly, Fr.
44/E2 Juine (riv.), Fr.
67/D3 Juishui, Tai.
40/D1 Juist (isl.), Ger.
95/K6 Juiz de Fora, Braz.
109/G2 Julesburg, Co,US
92/D7 Juliaca, Peru
45/K3 Julian Alps (mts.), It., Slov.
43/F2 Jülich, Ger.
101/F3 Julio A. Mella, Cuba
61/L2 Jullundur, India
66/C3 Juma (riv.), China
46/E3 Jumilla, Sp.
81/W17 Jūmīn (riv.), Tun.
70/D2 Jumla, Nepal
41/E2 Jümme (riv.), Ger.
70/B3 Junāgadh, India
96/C2 Juncal (peak), Arg., Chile
112/D4 Junction, Tx,US
108/D3 Junction, Ut,US
109/H3 Junction City, Ks,US
106/C4 Junction City, Or,US
95/G8 Jundiaí, Braz.
66/H6 Jundu (mts.), China
81/W17 Jundūbah, Tun.
81/W17 Jundūbah (gov.), Tun.
114/M4 Juneau (cap.), Ak,US
45/G3 Jungfrau (peak), Swi.
92/C6 Junín, Peru
42/D5 Juniville, Fr.
66/C3 Junji Guan (pass), China
113/H5 Juno Beach, Fl,US
95/B2 Junqueirópolis, Braz.
95/E1 Juparaná (lake), Braz.
111/J1 Jupiter (riv.), Qu,Can
113/H5 Jupiter, Fl,US
116/A2 Jupiter (mtn.), Wa,US
95/C3 Juquiá, Braz.
95/F8 Juquitiba, Braz.
83/L6 Jur (riv.), Sudan
44/F3 Jura (mts.), Fr.
44/C5 Jurançon, Fr.
42/C2 Jurbise, Belg.
32/D3 Jurby Head (pt.), IM,UK
52/D4 Jūrmala, Lat.
92/E4 Juruá (riv.), Braz.
92/G6 Juruena (riv.), Braz.
93/G4 Juruti, Braz.
65/M9 Jushiyama, Japan
96/D2 Justo Daract, Arg.
92/E4 Jutaí (riv.), Braz.
100/D5 Jutiapa, Guat.
100/D5 Juticalpa, Hon.
37/D4 Jutland (pen.), Den.
37/H3 Juva, Fin.
100/E3 Juventud (Pinos) (isl.), Cuba
31/T10 Juvisy-sur-Orge, Fr.
66/D4 Juye, China
66/C5 Juzhang (riv.), China
50/E4 Južna Morava (riv.), Yugo.
37/H3 Jyväskylä, Fin.

K

68/C4 K2 (Godwin Austen) (mtn.), China, Pak.
82/F5 Ka (riv.), Nga.
88/C3 Kaap (plat.), SAfr.
52/D3 Kaarina, Fin.
40/D6 Kaarst, Ger.
50/E2 Kaba, Hun.
73/F5 Kabaena (isl.), Indo.
100/D3 Kabah (ruins), Mex.
83/L8 Kabale, Ugan.
83/M7 Kabalega Nat'l Park, Ugan.
87/E2 Kabalo, Zaire
87/E2 Kabamba (lake), Zaire
73/F2 Kabankalan, Phil.
55/G4 Kabardin-Balkar Aut. Rep., Rus.
110/C1 Kabinakagani (lake), On,Can
87/D2 Kabinda, Zaire
81/V17 Kabir (riv.), Alg.
48/A5 Kabīyah (lag.), Tun.
87/D3 Kabompo (riv.), Zam.
87/E2 Kabongo, Zaire
61/J2 Kabul (riv.), Afg.
61/J2 Kābul (Kābol) (cap.), Afg.
73/G3 Kaburuang (isl.), Indo.
87/E3 Kabwe, Zam.
50/E4 Kačanik, Yugo.
114/H4 Kachemak (bay), Ak,US
71/G2 Kachin (state), Burma
70/C6 Kadaianallur, India
69/B3 Kadan (isl.), Burma
45/K1 Kadăn, Czh.
78/G6 Kadavu (isl.), Fiji
82/J7 Kadéï (riv.), CAfr., Congo
51/H5 Kadıköy, Turk.
59/C2 Kadınhanı, Turk.
85/E3 Kadiogo (prov.), Burk.
70/C5 Kadiri, India
59/D3 Kadirli, Turk.
107/H5 Kadoka, SD,US
65/L10 Kadoma, Japan
87/E4 Kadoma, Zim.
85/G4 Kaduna, Nga.
85/G4 Kaduna (riv.), Nga.
85/G4 Kaduna (state), Nga.
83/L5 Kāduqli, Sudan
84/B2 Kaédi, Mrta.
82/H5 Kaélé, Camr.
69/C2 Kaeng Khlo, Thai.
69/B3 Kaeng Krachan Nat'l Park, Thai.
63/K4 Kaesŏng, NKor.
55/H5 Kafan, Arm.
61/J2 Kafar Jar Ghar (mts.), Afg.
88/D4 Kaffraria (reg.), SAfr.
84/B3 Kaffrine, Sen.
83/K6 Kafia Kingi, Sudan
49/J3 Kafirévs, Ákra (cape), Gre.
59/H6 Kafr ad Dawwār, Egypt
59/H6 Kafr ash Shaykh, Egypt
59/H6 Kafr ash Shaykh (gov.), Egypt
59/H6 Kafr az Zayyāt, Egypt
59/N8 Kafr Qari', Isr.
59/M8 Kafr Qāsim, Isr.
87/E4 Kafue, Zam.
87/E4 Kafue (riv.), Zam.
87/E4 Kafue Nat'l Park, Zam.
64/E2 Kaga, Japan
82/J6 Kaga Bandoro, CAfr.
56/G6 Kagan, Uzb.
64/D3 Kagawa (pref.), Japan
51/J5 Kağıthane, Turk.
59/E2 Kağızman, Turk.
64/B5 Kagoshima, Japan
64/B5 Kagoshima (bay), Japan
64/B5 Kagoshima (pref.), Japan
51/J3 Kagul, Mol.
104/W12 Kahana, Hi,US
72/D4 Kahayan (riv.), Indo.
87/C2 Kahemba, Zaire
62/D1 Kahmsara (riv.), Rus.
109/K2 Kahoka, Mo,US
104/T10 Kahoolawe (isl.), Hi,US
37/G1 Kahperusvaara (peak), Fin.
59/D3 Kahramanmaraş, Turk.
61/K3 Kahror Pakka, Pak.
59/D3 Kâhta, Turk.
104/T10 Kahuku (pt.), Hi,US
104/T10 Kahului, Hi,US
87/E1 Kahuzi-Biega Nat'l Park, Zaire
73/H5 Kai (isls.), Indo.
75/R11 Kaiapoi, NZ
108/D3 Kaibab (plat.), Az,US
65/L9 Kaibara, Japan
73/H5 Kai Besar (isl.), Indo.
68/E3 Kaidu (riv.), China
62/G5 Kaifeng, China
64/D4 Kaifu, Japan
73/H5 Kai Kecil (isl.), Indo.
75/R10 Kaikohe, NZ
75/R11 Kaikoura, NZ
71/J2 Kaili, China
104/U11 Kailua, Hi,US
88/B2 Kainab (dry riv.), Namb.
50/B2 Kainach (riv.), Aus.
64/D3 Kainan, Japan
85/G4 Kainji (lake), Nga.
75/R10 Kaipara (har.), NZ
65/H7 Kaisei, Japan
43/G5 Kaiserslautern, Ger.
75/R10 Kaitaia, NZ
68/C6 Kaithal, India
104/T10 Kaiwi (chan.), Hi,US
66/F2 Kaiyuan, China
71/H3 Kaiyuan, China
65/M9 Kaizu, Japan
65/L10 Kaizuka, Japan
30/F2 Kajaani, Fin.
64/A3 Kaji-san (mtn.), SKor.
83/M5 Kākā, Sudan
37/G3 Kakaanpää, Fin.
83/M7 Kakamega, Kenya
65/E3 Kakamigahara, Japan
50/D3 Kakanj, Bosn.
114/M4 Kaketsa (mtn.), BC,Can
54/E3 Kakhovka, Ukr.
54/E3 Kakhovka (res.), Ukr.
70/D4 Kākināda, India
65/L9 Kako (riv.), Japan
84/B4 Kakrima (riv.), Gui.
65/G2 Kakuda, Japan
83/M7 Kakuma, Kenya
83/M8 Kakuto, Ugan.
81/X18 Kalaa-Kebia, Tun.
99/N2 Kalaallit Nunaat (Greenland) (dpcy.), Den.
87/D3 Kalabo, Zam.
55/G2 Kalach, Rus.
56/H4 Kalachinsk, Rus.
55/G2 Kalach-na-Donu, Rus.
71/F3 Kaladan (riv.), Burma
104/U11 Ka Lae (cape), Hi,US
87/D5 Kalahari (des.), Afr.
88/C2 Kalahari-Gemsbok Nat'l Park, SAfr.
49/L7 Kalamáki, Gre.
82/H5 Kalamaloué Nat'l Park, Camr.
49/H2 Kalamariá, Gre.
49/H4 Kalamáta, Gre.
110/C3 Kalamazoo, Mi,US
69/C2 Kalasin, Thai.
61/J3 Kalāt, Pak.
81/X18 Kalbīyah (lake), Tun.
37/N7 Kaldakvísl (riv.), Ice.
41/H5 Kalefeld, Ger.
87/E2 Kalemie, Zaire
39/K3 Kalety, Pol.
74/C6 Kalgoorlie-Boulder, Austl.
51/J4 Kaliakra, Nos (pt.), Bul.
72/C5 Kalianda, Indo.
67/D5 Kalibo, Phil.
87/E1 Kalima, Zaire
72/D4 Kalimantan (reg.), Indo.
59/A3 Kálimnos, Gre.
39/L1 Kaliningrad, Rus.
52/H5 Kaliningrad, Rus.
39/K1 Kaliningrad (lag.), Rus.
52/D5 Kaliningrad Obl., Rus.
55/H2 Kalininsk, Rus.
54/D1 Kalinkovichi, Bela.
83/M8 Kalisizo, Ugan.
106/E3 Kalispell, Mt,US
39/K3 Kalisz, Pol.
39/J3 Kalisz (prov.), Pol.
37/G2 Kalix, Swe.
37/G2 Kalixälv (riv.), Swe.
70/E2 Kāliyāganj, India
110/C2 Kalkaska, Mi,US
49/L7 Kallithea, Gre.
37/E3 Kallsjön (lake), Swe.
37/F4 Kalmar, Swe.
37/E4 Kalmar (co.), Swe.
40/B6 Kalmthout, Belg.
55/H3 Kalmyk Aut. Rep., Rus.
50/D2 Kalocsa, Hun.
104/T10 Kalohi (chan.), Hi,US
70/B3 Kālol, India
87/E4 Kalomo, Zam.
70/C2 Kālpi, India
38/E2 Kaltenkirchen, Ger.
45/F4 Kaltern (Caldaro), It.
70/D6 Kalu (riv.), SrL.
52/H5 Kaluga, Rus.
52/G5 Kaluga Obl., Rus.
38/F1 Kalundborg, Den.
54/C2 Kalush, Ukr.
70/C6 Kalutara, SrL.
70/B4 Kalyān, India
53/M4 Kama (res.), Rus.
53/M3 Kama (riv.), Rus.
87/E1 Kama, Zaire
65/J7 Kamagaya, Japan
63/N4 Kamaishi, Japan
104/T10 Kamakou (peak), Hi,US
65/H7 Kamakura, Japan
68/B5 Kamālia, Pak.
59/C2 Kaman, Turk.
84/E2 Kamango (lake), Mali
70/C4 Kāmāreddi, India
70/E3 Kāmārhāti, India
70/A2 Kambar, Pak.
87/E3 Kambove, Zaire
73/F4 Kambuno (peak), Indo.
57/R4 Kamchatka (pen.), Rus.
57/R4 Kamchatka Obl., Rus.
51/H4 Kamchiya (riv.), Bul.
41/E5 Kamen, Ger.
54/C2 Kamenets-Podol'skiy, Ukr.
50/A3 Kamenjak, Rt (cape), Cro.
55/H1 Kamenka, Rus.
68/D1 Kamen'-na-Obi, Rus.
54/G2 Kamensk-Shakhtinskiy, Rus.
53/P4 Kamensk-Ural'skiy, Rus.
64/D3 Kameoka, Japan
65/M10 Kameyama, Japan
106/D4 Kamiah, Id,US
39/H2 Kamień Pomorski, Pol.
65/H7 Kamifukuoka, Japan
63/N3 Kamiisco, Japan
65/M9 Kamiishizu, Japan
104/U11 Kamilo (pt.), Hi,US
87/E2 Kamina, Zaire
65/G1 Kaminoyama, Japan
114/H4 Kamishak (bay), Ak,US
64/B5 Kamiyaku, Japan
106/C3 Kamloops, BC,Can
69/C4 Kamlot, Camb.
65/L10 Kammaki, Japan
50/B2 Kamnik, Slov.
65/J7 Kamo (riv.), Japan
65/G3 Kamogawa, Japan
64/D3 Kamojima, Japan
45/L2 Kamp (riv.), Aus.
83/M7 Kampala (cap.), Ugan.
72/B3 Kampar (riv.), Indo.
72/B3 Kampar, Malay.
40/C3 Kampen, Neth.
69/B2 Kamphaeng Phet, Thai.
39/L2 Kampinoski Nat'l Park, Pol.
40/D6 Kamp-Lintfort, Ger.
69/D4 Kampong Cham, Camb.
69/D3 Kampong Chhnang, Camb.
69/D3 Kampong Khleang, Camb.
69/C4 Kampong Saom, Camb.
69/C4 Kampong Saom (bay), Camb.
69/D4 Kampong Spoe, Camb.
69/D3 Kampong Thum, Camb.
69/D4 Kampong Trabek, Camb.
69/D4 Kampot, Camb.
73/H4 Kamrau (bay), Indo.
107/H3 Kamsack, Sk,Can
107/H1 Kamuchawie (lake), Sk,Can
100/E6 Kámuk (mt.), CR
55/H2 Kamyshin, Rus.
103/J3 Kanaaupscow (riv.), Qu,Can
108/D3 Kanab (riv.), Az, Ut,US
108/D3 Kanab, Ut,US
114/C6 Kanaga (isl.), Ak,US
114/C6 Kanaga (vol.), Ak,US
65/F3 Kanagawa (pref.), Japan
103/K3 Kanairiktok (riv.), Nf,Can
65/L10 Kanan, Japan
87/D2 Kananga, Zaire
53/K5 Kanash, Rus.
110/D4 Kanawha (riv.), WV,US
65/E2 Kanazawa, Japan
69/B3 Kanchanaburi, Thai.
70/C5 Kānchīpuram, India
52/G2 Kandalaksha, Rus.
52/G2 Kandalaksha (gulf), Rus.
79/Y18 Kandavu (passg.), Fiji
61/J3 Kandhkot, Pak.
70/E3 Kāndi, India
73/F3 Kandi (cape), Indo.
51/K5 Kandıra, Turk.
70/C4 Kandukūr, India
70/D6 Kandy, SrL.
103/T7 Kane Basin (sound), NW,Can
82/H5 Kanem (reg.), Chad
104/W13 Kaneohe, Hi,US
104/W13 Kaneohe (bay), Hi,US
87/D5 Kang, Bots.
59/D2 Kangal, Turk.
72/B2 Kangar, Malay.
74/F7 Kangaroo (isl.), Austl.
60/E2 Kangāvar, Iran
73/E5 Kangean (isls.), Indo.
103/K3 Kangiqsualujjuaq, Qu,Can
103/J2 Kangiqsujuaq, Qu,Can
103/J2 Kangirsuk, Qu,Can
64/A2 Kangnŭng, SKor.
68/D5 Kangrinboqê Feng (peak), China
71/F2 Kangto (peak), China
70/C3 Kanhān (riv.), India
65/N9 Kani, Japan
65/M9 Kanie, Japan
53/K2 Kanin (pen.), Rus.
30/H2 Kanin Nos (pt.), Rus.
50/E2 Kanjiža, Yugo.
110/C3 Kankakee, Il,US
110/C3 Kankakee (riv.), Il, In,Us
84/C4 Kankan, Gui.
84/C4 Kankan (comm.), Gui.
70/D3 Kānker, India
64/C3 Kanmuri-yama (mtn.), Japan
113/H3 Kannapolis, NC,US
70/C2 Kannauj, India
65/H7 Kannon-zaki (pt.), Japan
85/H4 Kano, Nga.
85/H3 Kano (state), Nga.
64/C3 Kan'onji, Japan
64/B5 Kanoya, Japan
70/D2 Kānpur, India
109/H3 Kansas (state), US
109/H3 Kansas (riv.), Ks,US
109/J3 Kansas City, Ks, Mo,US
56/K4 Kansk, Rus.
70/D3 Kantābānji, India
65/F2 Kantō (prov.), Japan
92/G3 Kanuku (mts.), Guy.
65/F2 Kanuma, Japan
114/H2 Kanuti Nat'l Wild. Ref., Ak,US
88/D2 Kanye, Bots.
69/D3 Kaoh Nhek, Camb.
67/D3 Kaohsiung, Tai.
87/B4 Kaokoveld (reg.), Namb.
84/A3 Kaolack, Sen.
84/B3 Kaolack (reg.), Sen.
87/D3 Kaoma, Zam.
104/S9 Kapaa, Hi,US
67/E6 Kapalong, Phil.
87/D2 Kapanga, Zaire
50/E4 Kapaonik (upland), Yugo.
68/C3 Kapchagay, Kaz.
68/C3 Kapchagay (res.), Kaz.
40/B6 Kapellen, Belg.
45/L3 Kapfenberg, Aus.
51/H5 Kapidaği (pen.), Turk.
78/E4 Kapingamarangi (isl.), Micr.
87/E3 Kapiri Mposhi, Zam.
103/H3 Kapiskau (riv.), On,Can
83/M7 Kapoeta, Sudan
50/C2 Kapos (riv.), Hun.
50/C2 Kaposvár, Hun.
39/M1 Kapsukas, Lith.
72/C4 Kapuas (riv.), Indo.
72/D3 Kapuas Hulu (mts.), Indo., Malay.
110/D1 Kapuskasing, On,Can
110/D1 Kapuskasing (riv.), On,Can
50/C2 Kapuvár, Hun.
55/H5 Kapydzhik, Gora (peak), Azer.
53/Q1 Kara (riv.), Rus.
56/G2 Kara (sea), Rus.
55/K4 Kara-Bogaz-Gol (gulf), Trkm.
73/H4 Karabra (riv.), Indo.
59/C2 Karabük, Turk.
59/D3 Karaca (peak), Turk.
59/B2 Karacabey, Turk.
55/G4 Karachay-Cherkass Aut. Obl., Rus.
54/E1 Karachev, Rus.
61/J4 Karāchi, Pak.
70/B4 Karād, India
68/B2 Karaganda, Kaz.
58/R4 Karaginskiy (isl.), Rus.
68/E1 Karagoš (peak), Rus.
70/C5 Kāraikkudi, India
60/F1 Karaj, Iran
55/L3 Karakalpak Aut. Rep., Uzb.
68/C4 Karakax (riv.), China
59/D2 Karakaya (res.), Turk.
73/G3 Karakelong (isl.), Indo.
62/E3 Karakhoto (ruins), China
59/E2 Karakoçan, Turk.
68/C4 Karakoram (range), Asia
68/C4 Karakoram (pass), China, India
84/C3 Karakoro (riv.), Mali, Mrta.
62/E2 Karakorum (ruins), Mong.
59/E2 Karaköse, Turk.
68/B4 Karakul' (lake), Taj.
55/L5 Karakumy (des.), Trkm.
55/K4 Karakyon, Gora (peak), Trkm.
61/H1 Karakyr (peak), Trkm.
73/E4 Karam (riv.), Indo.
59/C3 Karaman, Turk.
68/D2 Karamay, China
75/R11 Karamea, NZ
75/R11 Karamea (bight), NZ
68/D4 Karamiran (riv.), China
68/E4 Karamiran Shankou (pass), China
51/J5 Karamürsel, Turk.
71/G4 Karan (state), Burma
73/E5 Karangasem, Indo.
57/S4 Karanginskiy (bay), Rus.
57/S4 Karanginskiy (isl.), Rus.
70/C3 Kāranja, India
69/B2 Karan (Kayin) (state), Burma
59/C3 Karapınar, Turk.
64/A3 Kara-saki (pt.), Japan
65/M10 Karasu, Japan
51/K5 Karasu, Turk.
68/C1 Karasuk, Rus.
68/C2 Karatal (riv.), Kaz.
68/B3 Karatau, Kaz.
68/A3 Karatau (mts.), Kaz.
64/A4 Karatsu, Japan
49/G3 Karáva (peak), Gre.
68/B2 Karazhal, Kaz.
86/C5 Karbaka, Sudan
60/D2 Karbalā', Iraq
50/E2 Karcag, Hun.
49/G3 Kardhítsa, Gre.
56/D3 Karelian Aut. Rep., Rus.
87/F2 Karema, Tanz.
62/H1 Karenga (riv.), Rus.
87/E4 Kariba (lake), Zam., Zim.
87/E4 Kariba, Zim.
72/C4 Karimata (isl.), Indo.
72/C4 Karimata (str.), Indo.
70/C4 Karīmnagar, India
87/E1 Karisimbi (vol.), Rwa.
65/M10 Kariya, Japan
83/Q6 Karkaar (mts.), Som.
70/B5 Kārkāl, India
78/D5 Karkar (isl.), PNG
54/E3 Karkinitsk (gulf), Ukr.
68/B4 Karla Marksa, Pik (peak), Taj.
50/B3 Karlovac, Slov.
51/G4 Karlovo, Bul.
45/K1 Karlovy Vary (Karlsbad), Czh.
37/E4 Karlshamn, Swe.
37/E4 Karlskoga, Swe.
37/E4 Karlskrona, Swe.
45/H2 Karlsruhe, Ger.
37/E4 Karlstad, Swe.
86/B5 Karmah, Sudan
70/C4 Karmāla, India
59/K5 Karmel, Har (Mount Carmel) (mtn.), Isr.
70/C2 Karnāl, India
70/C4 Karnataka (state), India
112/D4 Karnes City, Tx,US
51/H4 Karnobat, Bul.
50/A2 Kärnten (prov.), Aus.
87/F2 Karonga, Malw.
88/C4 Karoo Nat'l Park, SAfr.
61/K2 Karor, Pak.
73/E5 Karoso (cape), Indo.
59/A3 Kárpathos (isl.), Gre.
74/B4 Karratha, Austl.
88/M11 Kars (riv.), SAfr.
59/E2 Kars, Turk.
56/G6 Karshi, Uzb.
55/M1 Kartaly, Rus.
51/L3 Kartinitsk (gulf), Ukr.
39/K1 Kartuzy, Pol.
60/E2 Kārūn (riv.), Iran
39/K4 Karviná, Czh.
70/B5 Karwar, India
107/L2 Kasabonika (lake), On,Can
70/E3 Kāsai (riv.), India
64/D3 Kasai, Japan
87/C1 Kasai (riv.), Zaire
65/G2 Kasama, Japan
87/F3 Kasama, Zam.
65/M9 Kasamatsu, Japan
87/E4 Kasane, Bots.
64/C3 Kasaoka, Japan
70/C5 Kāsaragod, India
86/D5 Kasar, Ras (cape), Sudan
65/M10 Kasartori-yama (peak), Japan
102/F2 Kasba (lake), NW,Can
64/B5 Kaseda, Japan
70/C2 Kāsganj, India
61/H1 Kashaf (riv.), Iran
60/F2 Kāshān, Iran

142

Kashi – Kohun

68/C4 Kashi, China
65/L10 Kashiba, Japan
64/D3 Kashihara, Japan
64/B4 Kashima, Japan
65/G3 Kashima, Japan
52/H4 Kashin, Rus.
65/H7 Kashiwa, Japan
65/L10 Kashiwara, Japan
65/F2 Kashiwazaki, Japan
61/G1 Kāshmar, Iran
70/A2 Kashmor, Pak.
52/J5 Kasimov, Rus.
73/G4 Kasiruta (isl.), Indo.
73/H4 Kasiui (isl.), Indo.
110/B4 Kaskaskia (riv.), Il,US
106/D3 Kaslo, BC,Can
87/E1 Kasongo, Zaire
87/C2 Kasongo-Lunda, Zaire
55/H4 Kaspiysk, Rus.
83/N4 Kassala, Sudan
49/H3 Kassándra (pen.), Gre.
41/G6 Kassel, Ger.
107/K4 Kasson, Mn,US
59/C2 Kastamonu, Turk.
43/D1 Kasterlee, Belg.
49/G2 Kastoría, Gre.
49/G3 Kastrakíou (lake), Gre.
65/E3 Kasugai, Japan
65/F3 Kasukabe, Japan
87/F1 Kasulu, Tanz.
65/G2 Kasumiga (lake), Japan
87/F3 Kasungu, Malw.
61/K2 Kasūr, Pak.
87/E4 Kataba, Zam.
111/G2 Katahdin (mtn.), Me,US
87/E2 Katanga (reg.), Zaire
65/L10 Katano, Japan
87/F2 Katavi Nat'l Park, Tanz.
71/F6 Katchall (isl.), India
87/D2 Katea, Zaire
87/E2 Katea, Zaire
49/H2 Kateríni, Gre.
114/M4 Kates Needle (mtn.), Ak,US
87/F3 Katete, Zam.
71/G3 Katha, Burma
70/C2 Kāthgodām, India
61/K4 Kathiawar (pen.), India
70/E2 Kāthmāndu (cap.), Nepal
61/L2 Kathua, India
84/C3 Kati, Mali
84/D4 Katiola, IvC.
41/H5 Katlenburg-Lindau, Ger.
114/H4 Katmai (vol.), Ak,US
114/G4 Katmai Nat'l Park & Prsv., Ak,US
39/K3 Katowice, Pol.
39/K3 Katowice (prov.), Pol.
83/M2 Kātrīnā, Jabal (Mt. Catherine) (peak), Egypt
36/C2 Katrine, Loch (lake), Sc,UK
85/G3 Katsina, Nga.
85/G3 Katsina (state), Nga.
85/H5 Katsina Ala (riv.), Camr., Nga.
65/L9 Katsura (riv.), Japan
64/D3 Katsuragi, Japan
65/L10 Katsuragi-san (peak), Japan
65/G2 Katsuta, Japan
65/G3 Katsuura, Japan
110/E1 Kattawagami (riv.), On,Can
87/F3 Katumbi, Malw.
68/E1 Katun' (riv.), Rus.
68/E1 Katun'chuya (riv.), Rus.
40/B4 Katwijk aan Zee, Neth.
45/H2 Katzenbuckel (peak), Ger.
104/S10 Kauai (chan.), Hi,US
104/S9 Kauai (isl.), Hi,US
45/J3 Kaufbeuren, Ger.
112/D3 Kaufman, Tx,US
41/G6 Kaufungen, Ger.
37/G3 Kauhajoki, Fin.
37/G3 Kauhanevan-Pohjankankaan Nat'l Park, Fin.
37/G3 Kauhava, Fin.
104/U10 Kauhola (pt.), Hi,US
104/U10 Kauiki Head (pt.), Hi,US
87/C5 Kaukaveld (mts.), Namb.
79/L6 Kaukura (atoll), FrPol.
104/R9 Kaulakahi (chan.), Hi,US
39/M1 Kaunas, Lith.
39/N1 Kaunas (res.), Lith.
69/B4 Kau-ye (isl.), Burma
50/F5 Kavadarci, Macd.
49/F2 Kavajë, Alb.
49/J2 Kavála, Gre.
63/M3 Kavalerovo, Rus.
62/C5 Kāvali, India
78/C4 Kavangel (isls.), Palau
70/B5 Kavaratti, India
51/J4 Kavarna, Bul.
78/E5 Kavieng, PNG
112/D2 Kaw (lake), Ok,US
86/B5 Kawa (ruins), Sudan
65/L10 Kawachi-Nagano, Japan
65/M10 Kawage, Japan
65/F3 Kawagoe, Japan
65/M9 Kawagoe, Japan
65/F3 Kawaguchi, Japan
104/R10 Kawaihoa (pt.), Hi,US
104/S9 Kawaikini (peak), Hi,US
65/H7 Kawajima, Japan
65/G2 Kawamata, Japan
87/E2 Kawambwa, Zam.
65/L10 Kawanishi, Japan
70/D3 Kawardha, India
110/E2 Kawartha (lakes), On,Can
65/F3 Kawasaki, Japan
65/M9 Kawashima, Japan
104/V12 Kawela Bay (Kawela), Hi,US
75/S10 Kawerau, NZ
86/C3 Kawm Umbū, Egypt
68/D3 Kax (riv.), China
68/C3 Kaxgar (riv.), China
114/L2 Kay (pt.), Yk,Can
85/E4 Kaya, Burk.
82/J6 Kayagangiri (peak), CAfr.
69/B2 Kayah (state), Burma
73/E3 Kayan (riv.), Indo.
84/B3 Kayanga (riv.), Sen.
106/G5 Kaycee, Wy,US
108/E3 Kayenta, Az,US
84/C3 Kayes, Mali
84/C3 Kayes (reg.), Mali
69/B2 Kayin (Karan) (state), Burma
43/F5 Kayl, Lux.
73/G3 Kayoa (isl.), Indo.
59/C2 Kayseri, Turk.
72/B4 Kayuagung, Indo.
68/B2 Kazakh (uplands), Kaz.
56/G5 Kazakhstan
102/F2 Kazan (riv.), NW,Can
53/L5 Kazan', Rus.
51/G4 Kazanlŭk, Bul.
54/D2 Kazatin, Ukr.
55/H4 Kazbek (peak), Geo.
60/F3 Kāzerūn, Iran
39/L3 Kazimierza Wielka, Pol.
50/E1 Kazincbarcika, Hun.
63/N3 Kazuno, Japan
49/J4 Kéa (isl.), Gre.
32/B3 Keady, NI,UK
115/F5 Keansburg, NJ,US
109/H2 Kearney, Ne,US
32/C3 Kearny (pt.), NI,UK
115/F5 Kearny, NJ,US
104/U11 Keawekaheka (pt.), Hi,US
59/D2 Keban (res.), Turk.
37/F2 Kebnekaise (peak), Swe.
83/P6 K'ebri Dehar, Eth.
72/C5 Kebumen, Indo.
50/D2 Kecel, Hun.
50/D2 Kecskemét, Hun.
39/M1 Kėdainiai, Lith.
43/F5 Kédange-sur Canner, Fr.
72/D5 Kediri, Indo.
84/B3 Kédougou, Sen.
39/K3 Kędzierzyn-Koźle, Pol.
116/F6 Keego Harbor, Mi,US
102/D2 Keele (riv.), NW,Can
102/C2 Keele (peak), Yk,Can
67/D2 Keelung, Tai.
111/F3 Keene, NH,US
76/A1 Keer-weer (cape), Austl.
88/B2 Keetmanshoop, Namb.
49/G3 Kefallinía (isl.), Gre.
59/M8 Kefar Sava, Isr.
37/M7 Keflavík, Ice.
71/J5 Ke Ga (cape), Viet.
70/D6 Kegalla, SrL.
33/G6 Kegworth, Eng,UK
43/G6 Kehl, Ger.
33/G4 Keighley, Eng,UK
65/L9 Keihoku, Japan
77/F5 Keilor, Austl.
83/J6 Kéita (riv.), Chad
36/D2 Keith, Sc,UK
111/H2 Kejimkujik Nat'l Park, NS,Can
50/D2 Kékes (peak), Hun.
73/G4 Kelang (isl.), Indo.
72/B3 Kelang, Malay.
85/H3 Kélé-Kélé, Niger
45/J2 Kelheim, Ger.
59/D2 Kelkit, Turk.
59/D2 Kelkit (riv.), Turk.
102/D2 Keller (lake), NW,Can
115/C2 Keller (peak), Ca,US
102/D1 Kellett (cape), NW,Can
106/D4 Kellogg, Id,US
32/B2 Kells, NI,UK
112/D4 Kelly A.F.B., Tx,US
82/J6 Kélo, Chad
106/D3 Kelowna, BC,Can
33/F5 Kelsall, Eng,UK
34/A6 Kelsey Head (pt.), UK
36/D3 Kelso, Sc,UK
106/C4 Kelso, Wa,US
72/B3 Keluang, Malay.
33/G6 Kelvedon, Eng,UK
107/H2 Kelvington, Sk,Can
52/G2 Kem', Rus.
52/G2 Kem' (riv.), Rus.
34/D3 Kemble, Eng,UK
72/D3 Kemena (riv.), Malay.
56/J4 Kemerovo, Rus.
37/H2 Kemi, Fin.
37/H2 Kemijärvi, Fin.
37/H2 Kemijoki (riv.), Fin.
42/B2 Kemmel, Belg.
106/F5 Kemmerer, Wy,US
98/W Kemp (pen.), Ant.
109/H4 Kemp (lake), Tx,US
37/H2 Kempele, Fin.
40/D6 Kempen, Ger.
40/C6 Kempenland (reg.), Belg.
40/B6 Kempisch (can.), Belg.
77/E1 Kempsey, Austl.
35/F2 Kempston, Eng,UK
110/F2 Kempt (lake), Qu,Can
45/J3 Kempten, Ger.
88/E2 Kempton Park, SAfr.
73/E3 Kemul (peak), Indo.
114/H3 Kenai, Ak,US
114/J3 Kenai Fjords Nat'l Park, Ak,US
81/V18 Kenchela (gov.), Alg.
33/F3 Kendal, Eng,UK
113/H5 Kendall, Fl,US
110/C3 Kendallville, In,US
73/F4 Kendari, Indo.
40/D5 Kendel (riv.), Neth., Ger.
70/E3 Kendrāpāra, India
84/D4 Kénédougou (prov.), Burk.
84/C5 Kenema, SLeo.
71/J4 Keng Deng, Laos
87/C1 Kenge, Zaire
69/B1 Kēng Tung, Burma
84/C3 Kenié-Baoulé Rsv., Mali
35/E2 Kenilworth, Eng,UK
81/L13 Kenitra, Mor.
32/D1 Ken, Loch (lake), Sc,UK
107/H3 Kenmare, ND,US
111/S10 Kenmore, NY,US
116/C2 Kenmore, Wa,US
75/K4 Kenn (reef), Austl.
111/G2 Kennebec (riv.), Me,US
111/G3 Kennebunk, Me,US
103/T6 Kennedy (chan.), NW,Can
114/H4 Kennedy (str.), Ak,US
40/B4 Kennemerduinen Nat'l Park, Neth.
113/F4 Kenner, La,US
34/D4 Kennet (can.), Eng,UK
35/E4 Kennet (riv.), Eng,UK
110/B4 Kennett, Mo,US
106/D4 Kennewick, Wa,US
110/C1 Kenogami (riv.), On,Can
114/L3 Keno Hill, Yk,Can
110/A1 Kenora, On,Can
116/Q14 Kenosha, Wi,US
31/N7 Kensington & Chelsea (bor.), Eng,UK
102/F2 Kent (pen.), NW,Can
31/P8 Kent (co.), Eng,UK
33/F3 Kent (riv.), Eng,UK
110/D3 Kent, Oh,US
116/C3 Kent, Wa,US
68/A3 Kentau, Kaz.
77/C3 Kent Group (isls.), Austl.
110/D3 Kenton, Oh,US
110/C4 Kentucky (state), US
110/C4 Kentucky (riv.), Ky,US
113/F2 Kentucky (lake), Ky, Tn,US
35/G4 Kent, Vale of (val.), Eng,UK
111/H2 Kentville, NS,Can
32/D1 Ken, Water of (riv.), Sc,UK
80/F4 Kenya
83/M8 Kenya (mtn.), Kenya
65/H7 Ken-zaki (pt.), Japan
107/L5 Keokuk, Ia,US
70/E3 Keonjhar, India
39/J3 Kępno, Pol.
70/C5 Kerala (state), India
85/F4 Kéran Nat'l Park, Togo
49/H4 Keratéa, Gre.
54/F3 Kerch' (str.), Rus., Ukr.
54/F3 Kerch', Ukr.
106/D3 Keremeos, BC,Can
83/N4 Keren, Erit.
52/G2 Keret' (lake), Rus.
29/N8 Kerguélen (isl.), FrAnt.
75/R9 Kerikeri (cape), NZ
72/B4 Kerinci (peak), Indo.
68/D4 Keriya (riv.), China
68/D4 Keriya Shankou (pass), China
40/C5 Kerkdriel, Neth.
40/D6 Kerken, Ger.
56/G6 Kerki, Trkm.
49/H2 Kerkínis (lake), Gre.
49/F3 Kérkira (Corfu), Gre.
43/F2 Kerkrade, Neth.
40/C5 Kerkwijk, Neth.
78/G7 Kermadec (isls.), NZ
61/G2 Kermān, Iran
112/C4 Kermit, Tx,US
108/C4 Kern (riv.), Ca,US
49/J4 Kéros (isl.), Gre.
113/J2 Kerr (res.), NC, Va,US
109/J4 Kerr (lake), Ok,US
106/F3 Kerrobert, Sk,Can
112/D4 Kerrville, Tx,US
34/C2 Kerry, Wal,UK
81/N13 Kert (riv.), Mor.
62/G2 Kerulen (riv.), China, Mong.
110/D1 Kesagami (riv.), On,Can
51/H5 Keşan, Turk.
63/N4 Kesen'numa, Japan
35/H2 Kesgrave, Eng,UK
70/B3 Keshod, India
59/C2 Keskin, Turk.
37/H3 Keski-Suomi (prov.), Fin.
35/H2 Kessingland, Eng,UK
40/C5 Kesteren, Neth.
33/E2 Keswick, Eng,UK
50/C2 Keszthely, Hun.
56/J4 Ket' (riv.), Rus.
85/F5 Keta, Gha.
56/K2 Keta (riv.), Rus.
114/M4 Ketchikan, Ak,US
106/E5 Ketchum, Id,US
85/E5 Kete Krachi, Gha.
40/C3 Ketelmeer (lake), Neth.
39/L1 Kętrzyn, Pol.
35/F2 Kettering, Eng,UK
110/C4 Kettering, Oh,US
106/D3 Kettle (riv.), Can., US
33/F3 Kettlewell, Eng,UK
40/B4 Keukenhof, Neth.
37/H3 Keuruu, Fin.
40/D5 Kevelaer, Ger.
101/G3 Kew, Trks.
110/B2 Keweenaw (bay), Mi,US
110/B2 Keweenaw (pen.), Mi,US
31/N7 Kew Gardens, Eng,UK
113/H5 Key Largo, Fl,US
34/D4 Keynsham, Eng,UK
115/F5 Keyport, NJ,US
110/E4 Keyser, WV,US
112/D2 Keystone (lake), Ok,US
113/H5 Key West, Fl,US
33/G6 Keyworth, Eng,UK
39/L4 Kežmarok, Slvk.
83/Q5 Khaanziir (cape), Som.
63/M2 Khabarovsk, Rus.
55/J4 Khachmas, Azer.
60/E3 Khafjī, Ra's al, SAr.
70/D2 Khairābād, India
61/J3 Khairpur, Pak.
49/H3 Khalándrion, Gre.
49/H2 Khalkhidhikhi (pen.), Gre.
49/H3 Khalkís, Gre.
62/E1 Khamar-Daban (mts.), Rus.
70/D3 Khamaria, India
61/J4 Khambaliya, India
70/C3 Khāmgaon, India
60/D5 Khamīs Mushayţ, SAr.
70/D4 Khammam, India
61/J1 Khānābād, Afg.
60/E2 Khānaqīn, Iraq
70/C3 Khandwa, India
82/F1 Khanem (well), Alg.
61/K2 Khānewāl, Pak.
49/J5 Khaniá, Gre.
63/L3 Khanka (lake), Rus.
62/E1 Khankh, Mong.
68/C5 Khanna, India
61/K3 Khānpur, Pak.
56/G3 Khanty-Mansiysk, Rus.
56/G3 Khanty-Mansiysk Aut. Okr., Rus.
59/K6 Khān Yūnus, Gaza
69/C3 Khao Chamao-Khao Wong Nat'l Park, Thai.
69/C3 Khao Khitchakut Nat'l Park, Thai.
69/B3 Khao Laem (res.), Thai.
69/B3 Khao Sam Roi Yot Nat'l Park, Thai.
69/C3 Khao Yai Nat'l Park, Thai.
70/E3 Kharagpur, India
68/B5 Kharak, Pak.
61/J3 Kharān, Pak.
70/C3 Khargon, India
86/B3 Khārijah, Al Wāḩāt al (oasis), Egypt
86/C3 Kharīt, Wādī al (dry riv.), Egypt
54/F2 Khar'kov, Ukr.
54/F2 Khar'kov Obl., Ukr.
51/G5 Kharmanli, Bul.
52/J4 Kharovsk, Rus.
81/M13 Kharrour (riv.), Mor.
83/M4 Khartoum (Kharţūm) (cap.), Sudan
83/M4 Khartoum North, Sudan
55/H4 Khasavyurt, Rus.
61/H2 Khāsh (riv.), Afg.
61/H3 Khāsh, Iran
55/G4 Khashuri, Geo.
51/G5 Khaskovo, Bul.
51/G5 Khaskovo (reg.), Bul.
57/L2 Khatanga (gulf), Rus.
57/L2 Khatanga (riv.), Rus.
86/C2 Khatmia (pass), Egypt
61/G3 Khaymah, Ra's al, UAE
83/M4 Khazzān Jabal Al Awliyā (dam), Sudan
81/S15 Khemis el Khechna, Alg.
81/S15 Khemis Miliana, Alg.
81/V18 Khenchela, Alg.
82/D1 Khenifra, Mor.
60/F2 Khersān (riv.), Iran
54/E3 Kherson, Ukr.
54/E3 Kherson Obl., Ukr.
62/G1 Khilok, Rus.
62/F1 Khilok (riv.), Rus.
49/K3 Khíos, Gre.
49/J3 Khíos (isl.), Gre.
51/G4 Khisarya, Bul.
56/G5 Khiva, Uzb.
54/C2 Khmel'nitskiy, Ukr.
61/J2 Khojak (pass), Pak.
69/C3 Khok Samrong, Thai.
61/J1 Kholm, Afg.
63/N2 Kholmsk, Rus.
60/F2 Khomeynīshahr, Iran
69/C2 Khon Kaen, Thai.
55/G2 Khopër (riv.), Rus.
63/M2 Khor (riv.), Rus.
68/B4 Khorog, Taj.
60/E2 Khorramābād, Iran
60/E2 Khorramshahr, Iran
69/C2 Kho Sawai (plat.), Thai.
114/G3 Khotol (mtn.), Ak,US
82/D1 Khouribga, Mor.
71/F3 Khowai, India
61/J2 Khowst, Afg.
49/J2 Khrisoúpolis, Gre.
55/L2 Khromtau, Kaz.
49/J5 Khrysi (isl.), Gre.
69/C2 Khuan Ubon Ratana (res.), Thai.
68/A3 Khudzhand, Taj.
70/E3 Khulna, Bang.
61/L1 Khūnjerāb (pass), Pak.
70/C3 Khurai, India
70/E3 Khurda, India
70/C2 Khurja, India
54/B2 Khust, Ukr.
61/J3 Khuzdār, Pak.
63/L3 Khvalynka, Rus.
60/F2 Khvonsār, Iran
59/F2 Khvoy, Iran
68/B5 Khyber (pass), Afg., Pak.
77/D2 Kiama, Austl.
112/E3 Kiamichi (mts.), Ok,US
33/G2 Kibblesworth, Eng,UK
37/J1 Kibergneset (pt.), Nor.
87/F1 Kibondo, Tanz.
50/E5 Kičevo, Macd.
73/F2 Kidapawan, Phil.
34/D2 Kidderminster, Eng,UK
83/M7 Kidepo Valley Nat'l Park, Ugan.
33/F5 Kidsgrove, Eng,UK
34/B3 Kidwelly, Wal,UK
38/F1 Kiel (bay), Den., Ger.
38/F1 Kiel, Ger.
39/L3 Kielce, Pol.
39/L3 Kielce (prov.), Pol.
33/F1 Kielder, Eng,UK
33/F1 Kielder (res.), Eng,UK
69/D1 Kien An, Viet.
69/D4 Kien Duc, Viet.
69/D4 Kien Thanh, Viet.
41/E6 Kierspe, Ger.
54/D2 Kiev (Kiyev) (cap.), Ukr.
54/D2 Kiev Obl., Ukr.
84/C2 Kiffa, Mrta.
49/L6 Kifisiá, Gre.
60/D2 Kifrī, Iraq
87/F1 Kigali (cap.), Rwa.
87/F1 Kigoma, Tanz.
104/T10 Kihei, Hi,US
64/D4 Kii (chan.), Japan
64/D4 Kii (mts.), Japan
68/D3 Kiines (riv.), China
104/R9 Kikepa (pt.), Hi,US
114/H2 Kikiktat (mtn.), Ak,US
50/E3 Kikinda, Yugo.
87/C2 Kikwit, Zaire
36/C3 Kilbirnie, Sc,UK
111/Q9 Kilbride, On,Can
32/B5 Kildare (co.), Ire.
52/G1 Kil'den (isl.), Rus.
112/E3 Kilgore, Tx,US
33/H3 Kilham, Eng,UK
103/R7 Kilian (isl.), NW,Can
51/K5 Kilimli, Turk.
87/G2 Kilindoni, Tanz.
59/D3 Kilis, Turk.
54/D3 Kiliya, Ukr.
32/B3 Kilkeel, NI,UK
36/B4 Kilkenny, Ire.
32/A6 Kilkenny (co.), Ire.
49/H2 Kilkís, Gre.
106/F2 Killam, Ab,Can
33/G5 Killamarsh, Eng,UK
76/H8 Killara, Austl.
107/J3 Killarney, Mb,Can
36/A4 Killarney, Ire.
107/H4 Killdeer, ND,US
32/D1 Killearn, Sc,UK
112/D4 Killeen, Tx,US
36/C2 Killin, Sc,UK
32/C3 Killinchy, NI,UK
103/K2 Killinek (isl.), NW,Can
49/H4 Killíni (peak), Gre.
32/C3 Killough, NI,UK
32/A2 Killyclogher, NI,UK
32/C3 Killyleagh, NI,UK
32/B5 Kilmacanoge, Ire.
36/C3 Kilmarnock, Sc,UK
34/B5 Kilmar Tor (hill), Eng,UK
32/B6 Kilmichael (pt.), Ire.
32/B1 Kilraghts, NI,UK
32/B2 Kilrea, NI,UK
87/G2 Kilwa Masoko, Tanz.
32/C2 Kilwaughter, NI,UK
36/C3 Kilwinning, Sc,UK
107/H5 Kimball, Ne,US
107/J5 Kimball, SD,US
78/E5 Kimbe, PNG
76/B2 Kimberley (cape), Austl.
74/D3 Kimberley (plat.), Austl.
106/E3 Kimberley, BC,Can
88/D3 Kimberley, SAfr.
63/K3 Kimch'aek, NKor.
64/A2 Kimch'ŏn, SKor.
64/A3 Kimhae, SKor.
65/F3 Kimitsu, Japan
63/K4 Kimje, SKor.
49/J4 Kímolos (isl.), Gre.
54/F1 Kimovsk, Rus.
87/D2 Kimpanga, Zaire
52/H4 Kimry, Rus.
73/E2 Kinabalu, Gunung (peak), Malay.
73/E2 Kinabatangan (riv.), Malay.
106/D2 Kinbasket (lake), BC,Can
106/G3 Kincaid, Sk,Can
110/D2 Kincardine, On,Can
77/B2 Kinchega Nat'l Park, Austl.
87/D2 Kindambi, Zaire
45/L3 Kindberg, Aus.
33/G5 Kinder Scout (mtn.), Eng,UK
84/B4 Kindia, Gui.
84/B4 Kindia (comm.), Gui.
87/E1 Kindu, Zaire
55/J1 Kinel', Rus.
52/J4 Kineshma, Rus.
35/E2 Kineton, Eng,UK
77/C3 King (isl.), Austl.
74/B6 King (lake), Austl.
76/B4 King (peak), Austl.
74/C3 King (sound), Austl.
106/B2 King (isl.), BC,Can
114/N4 King (mtn.), BC,Can
114/K3 King (peak), Yk,Can
76/C4 Kingaroy, Austl.
103/R7 King Christian (isl.), NW,Can
99/P3 King Christian IX Land (reg.), Grld.
99/Q2 King Christian X Land (reg.), Grld.
111/Q8 King City, On,Can
108/B3 King City, Ca,US
109/H4 Kingfisher, Ok,US
99/N3 King Frederik VI Coast (reg.), Grld.
99/Q2 King Frederik VIII Land (reg.), Grld.
79/L6 King George (isl.), FrPol.
110/E4 King George, Va,US
77/C3 Kinglake Nat'l Park, Austl.
74/D3 King Leopold (ranges), Austl.
79/J4 Kingman (reef), PacUS
108/D4 Kingman, Az,US
109/H3 Kingman, Ks,US
115/E5 King of Prussia, Pa,US
108/C3 Kings (riv.), Ca,US
108/E2 Kings (peak), Ut,US
34/C6 Kingsbridge, Eng,UK
108/C3 Kings Canyon Nat'l Park, Ca,US
35/E4 Kingsclere, Eng,UK
35/F1 King's Cliffe, Eng,UK
34/D2 Kingsland, Eng,UK
31/M6 Kings Langley, Eng,UK
35/G1 King's Lynn, Eng,UK
113/H2 Kingsport, Tn,US
35/E2 Kings Sutton, Eng,UK
34/C5 Kingsteignton, Eng,UK
77/C4 Kingston, Austl.
110/E2 Kingston, On,Can
101/F4 Kingston (cap.), Jam.
78/F7 Kingston, Norfl.
110/F3 Kingston, NY,US
77/A3 Kingston South East, Austl.
31/N7 Kingston upon Thames (bor.), Eng,UK
101/J5 Kingstown (cap.), StV.
113/J3 Kingstree, SC,US
86/C3 Kings, Valley of the, Egypt
112/D5 Kingsville, Tx,US
34/D2 Kingswinford, Eng,UK
34/D4 Kingswood, Eng,UK
34/C2 Kington, Eng,UK
102/G2 King William (isl.), NW,Can
88/D4 King William's Town, SAfr.
114/L4 Kinkaid (mtn.), Ak,US
87/B1 Kinkala, Congo
64/D3 Kinki (prov.), Japan
84/B4 Kinkon, Chutes de (falls), Gui.
32/E5 Kinmel, Wal,UK
37/E4 Kinna, Swe.
36/E2 Kinnairds Head (pt.), Sc,UK
64/D3 Kino (riv.), Japan
43/E1 Kinrooi, Belg.
36/D2 Kinross, Sc,UK
111/R8 Kinsale, On,Can
87/C1 Kinshasa (cap.), Zaire
109/H3 Kinsley, Ks,US
113/J3 Kinston, NC,US
85/E4 Kintampo, Gha.
36/D2 Kintore, Sc,UK
32/C1 Kintyre, Mull of (pt.), Sc,UK
65/F2 Kinu (riv.), Japan
83/M7 Kinyeti (peak), Sudan
49/G4 Kiparissía (gulf), Gre.
110/E2 Kipawa (lake), Qu,Can
87/F2 Kipili, Tanz.
107/H3 Kipling, Sk,Can
32/B5 Kippure (mtn.), Ire.
87/E3 Kipushi, Zaire
65/N10 Kira, Japan
49/H3 Kira Panayía (isl.), Gre.
41/F6 Kirchhundem, Ger.
41/F4 Kirchlengern, Ger.
41/G3 Kirchlinteln, Ger.
32/C3 Kircubbin, NI,UK
32/D2 Kircudbright (bay), Sc,UK
57/L4 Kirensk, Rus.
68/B3 Kirgizskiy (mts.), Kyr.
56/F5 Kirgiz Steppe (grsld.), Kaz., Rus.
78/H5 Kiribati
59/D3 Kırıkhan, Turk.
59/C2 Kırıkkale, Turk.
62/C3 Kirikkuduk, China
52/G4 Kirishi, Rus.
64/B5 Kirishima-Yaku Nat'l Park, Japan
64/B5 Kirishima-yama (mtn.), Japan
79/K4 Kiritimati (Christmas) (atoll), Kiri.
33/G4 Kirkburton, Eng,UK
33/F5 Kirkby, Eng,UK
33/G5 Kirkby in Ashfield, Eng,UK
33/F3 Kirkby Lonsdale, Eng,UK
33/H3 Kirkbymoorside, Eng,UK
33/F3 Kirkby Stephen, Eng,UK
36/D2 Kirkcaldy, Sc,UK
32/C2 Kirkcolm, Sc,UK
32/D2 Kirkcowan, Sc,UK
32/D2 Kirkcudbright, Sc,UK
70/B4 Kirkee, India
37/J1 Kirkenes, Nor.
33/F4 Kirkham, Eng,UK
32/D2 Kirkinner, Sc,UK
111/N7 Kirkland, Qu,Can
116/C2 Kirkland, Wa,US
110/D1 Kirkland Lake, On,Can
51/H5 Kırklareli, Turk.
51/H5 Kırklareli (prov.), Turk.
32/D3 Kirkmichael, IM,UK
51/L2 Kirkovgrad Obl., Ukr.
98/M Kirkpatrick (mtn.), Ant.
109/J2 Kirksville, Mo,US
36/D2 Kirkton of Glenisla, Sc,UK
59/F3 Kirkūk, Iraq
43/G4 Kirn, Ger.
54/E1 Kirov, Rus.
55/H4 Kirovakan, Arm.
53/L4 Kirovo-Chepetsk, Rus.
54/E2 Kirovograd, Ukr.
54/D2 Kirovograd Obl., Ukr.
36/D2 Kirriemuir, Sc,UK
55/G1 Kirsanov, Rus.
59/C2 Kırşehir, Turk.
33/H6 Kirton, Eng,UK
33/H5 Kirton in Lindsey, Eng,UK
37/G2 Kiruna, Swe.
65/F2 Kiryū, Japan
83/L7 Kisangani, Zaire
65/F3 Kisarazu, Japan
39/K5 Kisbér, Hun.
56/J4 Kiselevsk, Rus.
70/E2 Kishanganj, India
70/B2 Kishangarh, India
51/J2 Kishinëv (cap.), Mol.
64/D3 Kishiwada, Japan
70/F3 Kishorganj, Bang.
61/L2 Kishtwar, India
116/N15 Kishwaukee (riv.), Il,US
83/M8 Kisii, Kenya
114/B6 Kiska (isl.), Ak,US
114/B5 Kiska (vol.), Ak,US
106/C2 Kiskatinaw (riv.), BC,Can
107/J2 Kiskitto (lake), Mb,Can
50/D2 Kiskőrös, Hun.
50/D2 Kiskunfélegyháza, Hun.
50/D2 Kiskunhalas, Hun.
50/D2 Kiskunmajsa, Hun.
50/D2 Kiskunsági Nat'l Park, Hun.
55/G4 Kislovodsk, Rus.
83/P8 Kismaayo (Chisimayu), Som.
65/E3 Kiso (riv.), Japan
65/M9 Kisogawa, Japan
113/H4 Kissimmee, Fl,US
113/H4 Kissimmee (lake), Fl,US
107/H2 Kississing (lake), Mb,Can
50/E2 Kisújszállás, Hun.
83/M8 Kisumu, Kenya
50/F1 Kisvárda, Hun.
65/G2 Kita (inlet), Japan
84/C3 Kita, Mali
65/M9 Kitagata, Japan
65/G2 Kita-Ibaraki, Japan
65/F2 Kitakata, Japan
64/B4 Kitakyūshū, Japan
83/N7 Kitale, Kenya
63/N3 Kitami, Japan
63/N2 Kitami (mts.), Japan
65/H6 Kitamoto, Japan
110/D3 Kitchener, On,Can
37/J3 Kitee, Fin.
49/H4 Kithira (isl.), Gre.
49/J4 Kithnos (isl.), Gre.
106/A2 Kitimat, BC,Can
106/A2 Kitimat Arm (inlet), BC,Can
116/B2 Kitsap Lake-Erlands Point, Wa,US
115/E4 Kittatinny (mts.), NJ, Pa,US
111/G3 Kittery, Me,US
87/E3 Kitwe, Zam.
45/K3 Kitzbühel, Aus.
45/J2 Kitzingen, Ger.
37/H2 Kiuruvesi, Fin.
37/H2 Kivalo (mts.), Fin.
52/E4 Kiviõli, Est.
87/E1 Kivu (lake), Rwa., Zaire
54/D2 Kiyev (res.), Ukr.
54/D2 Kiyev (Kiev) (cap.), Ukr.
65/H7 Kiyose, Japan
65/M9 Kiyosu, Japan
87/C2 Kizamba, Zaire
53/M4 Kizel, Rus.
68/B4 Kizil (riv.), China
59/C2 Kızılcahamam, Turk.
59/C2 Kizilirmak (riv.), Turk.
59/E3 Kızıltepe, Turk.
55/H4 Kizlyar, Rus.
65/L10 Kizu, Japan
64/E3 Kizu (riv.), Japan
55/L5 Kizyl-Arvat, Trkm.
52/C1 Kjerkestinden (peak), Nor.
37/E2 Kjølen (Kölen) (mts.), Nor., Swe.
50/D3 Kladanj, Bosn.
45/L1 Kladno, Czh.
50/F3 Kladovo, Yugo.
45/L3 Klagenfurt, Aus.
52/D5 Klaipėda, Lith.
106/C5 Klamath (mts.), Ca, Or,US
106/C5 Klamath (riv.), Ca, Or,US
106/C5 Klamath Falls, Or,US
56/B3 Klar (riv.), Swe.
37/E3 Klarälven (riv.), Swe.
40/E3 Klazienaveen, Neth.
43/G5 Kleinblittersdorf, Ger.
111/Q8 Kleinburg, On,Can
39/G3 Kleine Elster (riv.), Ger.
43/E2 Kleine Gete (riv.), Belg.
40/B6 Kleine Nete (riv.), Belg.
88/Q12 Kleinolifants (riv.), SAfr.
37/C3 Kleppestø, Nor.
88/D2 Klerksdorp, SAfr.
40/D5 Kleve, Ger.
54/E1 Klintsy, Rus.
88/E2 Klip (riv.), SAfr.
50/C3 Ključ, Bosn.
39/K2 Kłodawa, Pol.
39/J3 Kłodzko, Pol.
41/F3 Klosterbach (riv.), Ger.
45/M2 Klosterneuburg, Aus.
45/L3 Klosterwappen (peak), Aus.
36/F2 Klötze, Ger.
114/L3 Kluane, Yk,Can
114/K3 Kluane Nat'l Park, Yk,Can
39/K3 Kluczbork, Pol.
114/L3 Klukshu, Yk,Can
40/B5 Klundert, Neth.
41/E3 Klüstenkanal (can.), Ger.
52/J4 Klyaz'ma (riv.), Rus.
57/S4 Klyuchevskaya (peak), Rus.
33/G3 Knaresborough, Eng,UK
35/F3 Knebworth, Eng,UK
107/K2 Knee (lake), Mb,Can
51/G4 Knezha, Bul.
106/B3 Knight (inlet), BC,Can
34/C2 Knighton, Wal,UK
50/C3 Knin, Cro.
45/L3 Knittelfeld, Aus.
50/F4 Knjaževac, Yugo.
74/B6 Knob (cape), Austl.
73/F1 Knob (peak), Phil.
32/B2 Knockcloghrim, NI,UK
32/B1 Knocklayd (mtn.), NI,UK
42/C1 Knokke-Heist, Belg.
88/A2 Knoll (pt.), Namb.
49/J5 Knosós (Knossos) (ruins), Gre.
33/F4 Knott End, Eng,UK
33/G4 Knottingley, Eng,UK
98/G Knox (coast), Ant.
77/G5 Knox, Austl.
114/M4 Knox (cape), BC,Can
113/H3 Knoxville, Tn,US
33/F5 Knutsford, Eng,UK
88/C4 Knysna, SAfr.
63/M2 Ko (peak), Rus.
64/B5 Kobayashi, Japan
64/D3 Kōbe, Japan
38/G1 København (Copenhagen) (cap.), Den.
73/G4 Kobipato (peak), Indo.
43/G3 Koblenz, Ger.
39/N2 Kobrin, Bela.
114/G2 Kobuk (riv.), Ak,US
114/G2 Kobuk Valley Nat'l Park, Ak,US
65/F3 Kobushi-ga-take (mtn.), Japan
51/J5 Kocaeli (prov.), Turk.
50/F5 Kočani, Macd.
50/B3 Kočevje, Slov.
102/J2 Koch (isl.), NW,Can
45/H2 Kocher (riv.), Ger.
64/C4 Kōchi, Japan
64/C4 Kōchi (pref.), Japan
114/H4 Kodiak, Ak,US
114/H4 Kodiak (isl.), Ak,US
114/H4 Kodiak Nat'l Wild. Ref., Ak,US
70/B3 Kodinār, India
83/M6 Kodok, Sudan
51/H2 Kodry (hills), Mol.
42/B1 Koekelare, Belg.
70/D3 Koel (riv.), India
43/F5 Koenigsmacker, Fr.
108/D4 Kofa (mts.), Az,US
73/G4 Kofiau (isl.), Indo.
85/E5 Koforidua, Gha.
65/F3 Kōfu, Japan
65/F2 Koga, Japan
65/H7 Koganei, Japan
38/G1 Køge, Den.
38/G1 Køge Bugt (bay), Den.
84/B4 Kogon (riv.), Gui.
61/K2 Kohāt, Pak.
71/F2 Kohīma, India
52/E4 Kohtla-Järve, Est.
63/K5 Kohŭng, SKor.
100/D4 Kohunlich (ruins), Mex.

143

Koich – Lake

88/A2 **Koichab** (dry riv.), Namb.
114/K3 **Koidern**, Yk,Can
64/A3 **Kōje** (isl.), SKor.
39/L4 **Kojšovská Hol'a** (peak), Slvk.
69/B1 **Kok** (riv.), Burma
65/M10 **Kōka**, Japan
65/J7 **Kokai** (riv.), Japan
68/B3 **Kokand**, Uzb.
68/A1 **Kokchetav**, Kaz.
37/G3 **Kokkola**, Fin.
84/C3 **Kokofata**, Mali
104/W13 **Koko Head** (crater), Hi,US
83/L7 **Kokola**, Zaire
110/C3 **Kokomo**, In,US
70/F2 **Kokrajhar**, India
68/C3 **Kokshaal-Tau** (mts.), Kyr.
42/B1 **Koksijde**, Belg.
103/K3 **Koksoak** (riv.), Qu,Can
88/E3 **Kokstad**, SAfr.
64/B5 **Kokubu**, Japan
52/H1 **Kola** (pen.), Rus.
52/G1 **Kola** (riv.), Rus.
73/F4 **Kolaka**, Indo.
70/C5 **Kolār**, India
50/D4 **Kolašin**, Yugo.
38/G5 **Kolbermoor**, Ger.
39/L3 **Kolbuszowa**, Pol.
84/B3 **Kolda**, Sen.
84/B3 **Kolda** (reg.), Sen.
38/E1 **Kolding**, Den.
37/E2 **Kölen (Kjølen)** (mts.), Nor., Swe.
78/C5 **Kolepom** (isl.), Indo.
52/F4 **Kolgompya** (cape), Rus.
53/K1 **Kolguyev** (isl.), Rus.
70/B4 **Kolhāpur**, India
84/B3 **Koliba** (riv.), Gui.
39/H3 **Kolín**, Czh.
52/D4 **Kolkasrags** (pt.), Lat.
40/D2 **Kollum**, Neth.
40/D7 **Köln (Cologne)**, Ger.
39/L2 **Kolno**, Pol.
54/A1 **Koło**, Pol.
87/G1 **Kolo**, Tanz.
39/H1 **Kołobrzeg**, Pol.
84/C3 **Kolokani**, Mali
54/F1 **Kolomna**, Rus.
54/C2 **Kolomyya**, Ukr.
70/C6 **Kolonnawa**, SrL.
84/D3 **Kolossa** (riv.), Mali
56/J4 **Kolpashevo**, Rus.
52/F4 **Kolpino**, Rus.
50/E3 **Kolubara** (riv.), Yugo
39/K3 **Koluszki**, Pol.
68/A1 **Koluton** (riv.), Kaz.
53/N2 **Kolva** (riv.), Rus.
87/E3 **Kolwezi**, Zaire
57/R2 **Kolyma** (lowland), Rus.
57/R3 **Kolyma** (range), Rus.
57/R3 **Kolyma** (riv.), Rus.
50/F4 **Kom** (peak), Bul.
65/H7 **Koma** (riv.), Japan
50/E2 **Komádi**, Hun.
85/H4 **Komadugu Gana** (riv.), Nga.
85/H3 **Komadugu Yobé** (riv.), Nga.
65/H7 **Komae**, Japan
65/E3 **Komagane**, Japan
65/M9 **Komaki**, Japan
57/S4 **Komandorskiye** (isls.), Rus.
39/K5 **Komárno**, Slvk.
50/D2 **Komárom**, Hun.
50/D2 **Komárom-Esztergom** (co.), Hun.
64/E2 **Komatsu**, Japan
64/D4 **Komatsushima**, Japan
53/L2 **Komi Aut. Rep.**, Rus.
53/M3 **Komi-Permyak Aut. Okr.**, Rus.
50/D2 **Komló**, Hun.
54/F2 **Kommunarsk**, Ukr.
68/B4 **Kommunizma** (Communism) (peak), Taj.
73/E5 **Komodo Isl. Nat'l Park**, Indo.
84/E5 **Komoé** (riv.), IvC.
64/E3 **Komono**, Japan
49/J2 **Komotini**, Gre.
88/D3 **Kompasberg** (peak), SAfr.
51/J2 **Komrat**, Mol.
57/L1 **Komsomolets** (isl.), Rus.
53/P2 **Komsomol'skiy**, Rus.
63/M1 **Komsomol'sk-na-Amure**, Rus.
49/K3 **Kömür** (pt.), Turk.
68/A2 **Kon** (riv.), Kaz.
52/H4 **Konakovo**, Rus.
65/M10 **Kōnan**, Japan
65/M9 **Kōnan**, Japan
77/D2 **Konangra-Boyd Nat'l Park**, Austl.
73/F4 **Konaweha** (riv.), Indo.
62/G1 **Konda** (riv.), Rus.
52/G3 **Kondopoga**, Rus.
61/J1 **Kondūz**, Afg.
69/C4 **Kong** (isl.), Camb.
69/D3 **Kong** (riv.), Laos
63/K4 **Kongju**, SKor.
87/E2 **Kongolo**, Zaire
65/L10 **Kongō-zan** (peak), Japan
37/D4 **Kongsberg**, Nor.
37/E3 **Kongsvinger**, Nor.
68/C4 **Kongur Shan** (peak), China
87/G2 **Kongwa**, Tanz.
39/K3 **Koniecpol**, Pol.
41/H4 **Königslutter am Elm**, Ger.
43/G2 **Königswinter**, Ger.
39/G2 **Königs Wusterhausen**, Ger.
39/K2 **Konin**, Pol.
39/K2 **Konin** (prov.), Pol.
45/G3 **Köniz**, Swi.
50/C4 **Konjic**, Bosn.
88/B2 **Konkiep** (dry riv.), Namb.
84/B4 **Konkouré** (riv.), Gui.
54/E2 **Konotop**, Ukr.
68/E3 **Konqi** (riv.), China
39/L3 **Końskie**, Pol.
39/L2 **Konstancin-Jeziorna**, Pol.
54/F2 **Konstantinovka**, Ukr.
39/K3 **Konstantynów Łódzki**, Pol.
45/H3 **Konstanz**, Ger.
42/D1 **Kontich**, Belg.
37/J3 **Kontiolahti**, Fin.
69/E3 **Kon Tum**, Viet.
59/C3 **Konya**, Turk.
43/F4 **Konz**, Ger.
106/E3 **Koocanusa** (lake), Can., US
106/D3 **Kootenai** (riv.), Id, Mt,US
106/D3 **Kootenay** (lake), BC,Can
106/D3 **Kootenay Nat'l Park**, BC,Can
70/B4 **Kopargaon**, India
37/N7 **Kópavogur**, Ice.
84/D5 **Kope** (peak), IvC.
39/G2 **Köpenick**, Ger.
53/P5 **Kopeysk**, Rus.
54/G4 **Kop Gecidi** (pass), Turk.
83/K7 **Kopia**, Zaire
52/C4 **Köping**, Swe.
73/F5 **Kopondei** (cape), Indo.
37/E3 **Kopparberg** (co.), Swe.
63/M2 **Koppi** (riv.), Rus.
50/C2 **Koprivnica**, Cro.
60/F2 **Kor** (riv.), Iran
65/M9 **Kōra**, Japan
49/G2 **Korab** (peak), Alb.
45/L4 **Korana** (riv.), Bosn., Cro.
70/D4 **Koraput**, India
70/D3 **Korba**, India
41/F6 **Korbach**, Ger.
49/G2 **Korçë**, Alb.
50/C4 **Korčula** (isl.), Cro.
50/C4 **Korčulanski** (chan.), Cro.
60/F1 **Kord Kūy**, Iran
63/J4 **Korea** (bay), China, NKor.
64/A4 **Korea** (str.), Japan, SKor.
63/K3 **Korea, North**
63/K4 **Korea, South**
54/F3 **Korenovsk**, Rus.
84/D4 **Korhogo**, IvC.
49/H4 **Kórinthos (Corinth)**, Gre.
50/C2 **Kőris-hegy** (peak), Hun.
65/G2 **Kōriyama**, Japan
82/J3 **Korizo, Passe de** (pass), Chad
57/R3 **Korkodon** (riv.), Rus.
59/B3 **Korkuteli**, Turk.
68/E3 **Korla**, China
59/J4 **Kormakiti** (cape), Cyp.
50/B4 **Kornat** (isl.), Cro.
79/Z18 **Koro** (isl.), Fiji
78/G6 **Koro** (sea), Fiji
51/K5 **Köroğlu** (peak), Turk.
87/G2 **Korogwe**, Tanz.
67/E6 **Koronadal**, Phil.
49/H2 **Korónia** (lake), Gre.
39/J2 **Koronowo**, Pol.
49/L7 **Koropí**, Gre.
78/C4 **Koror** (cap.), Palau
50/E2 **Körös** (riv.), Hun.
54/D2 **Korosten'**, Ukr.
54/D2 **Korostyshev**, Ukr.
53/P1 **Korotaikha** (riv.), Rus.
82/J4 **Koro Toro**, Chad
114/D5 **Korovin** (vol.), Ak,US
63/N2 **Korsakov**, Rus.
40/D6 **Korschenbroich**, Ger.
38/F1 **Korsør**, Den.
42/C1 **Kortemark**, Belg.
43/E2 **Kortenaken**, Belg.
42/D2 **Kortenberg**, Belg.
43/E2 **Kortessem**, Belg.
42/C2 **Kortrijk**, Belg.
85/H5 **Korup Nat'l Park**, Camr.
58/R3 **Koryak** (range), Rus.
57/S3 **Koryak Aut. Okr.**, Rus.
53/K3 **Koryazhma**, Rus.
65/L10 **Kōryō**, Japan
59/A3 **Kós** (isl.), Gre.
65/E3 **Kosai**, Japan
64/A3 **Ko-saki** (pt.), Japan
69/C3 **Ko Samut Nat'l Park**, Thai.
39/J2 **Kościan**, Pol.
39/J1 **Kościerzyna**, Pol.
77/D3 **Kosciusko** (mt.), Austl.
113/F3 **Kosciusko**, Ms,US
77/D3 **Kosciusko Nat'l Park**, Austl.
65/M10 **Kosei**, Japan
86/B4 **Kosha**, Sudan
65/F3 **Koshigaya**, Japan
61/H2 **Koshk**, Afg.
70/E2 **Kosi** (riv.), India
39/L4 **Košice**, Slvk.
68/C2 **Kosoba, Gora** (peak), Kaz.
50/E4 **Kosovo** (aut. reg.), Yugo.
50/E4 **Kosovo Polje**, Yugo.
50/E4 **Kosovska Mitrovica**, Yugo.
78/F4 **Kosrae** (isl.), Micr.
84/D3 **Kossi** (prov.), Burk.
84/D5 **Kossou** (lake), IvC.
51/F4 **Kostinbrod**, Bul.
54/C2 **Kostopol'**, Ukr.
52/J4 **Kostroma**, Rus.
52/J4 **Kostroma** (riv.), Rus.
52/J4 **Kostroma Obl.**, Rus.
39/H2 **Kostrzyn**, Pol.
39/J2 **Kostrzyn**, Pol.
53/N4 **Kos'va** (riv.), Rus.
53/N2 **Kos'yu** (riv.), Rus.
39/J1 **Koszalin**, Pol.
39/H2 **Koszalin** (prov.), Pol.
70/C2 **Kota**, India
65/N10 **Kōta**, Japan
72/B5 **Kotaagung**, Indo.
72/B2 **Kota Baharu**, Malay.
73/E4 **Kotabaru**, Indo.
72/C4 **Kotabumi**, Indo.
61/K2 **Kot Addu**, Pak.
51/H4 **Kotel**, Bul.
53/L4 **Kotel'nich**, Rus.
55/G3 **Kotel'nikovo**, Rus.
57/P2 **Kotel'nyy** (isl.), Rus.
38/F3 **Köthen**, Ger.
37/H3 **Kotka**, Fin.
52/E3 **Kotka**, Fin.
61/K2 **Kot Kapūra**, India
53/K3 **Kotlas**, Rus.
65/M9 **Kotō**, Japan
50/D4 **Kotor**, Yugo.
55/H2 **Kotovo**, Rus.
55/G1 **Kotovsk**, Rus.
61/J3 **Kotri**, Pak.
70/D4 **Kottagūdem**, India
70/C6 **Kottayam**, India
70/C6 **Kotte**, SrL.
83/K6 **Kotto** (riv.), CAfr.
57/L3 **Kotuy** (riv.), Rus.
114/E2 **Kotzebue** (sound), Ak,US
111/H2 **Kouchibouguac Nat'l Park**, NB,Can
85/E3 **Koudougou**, Burk.
49/J5 **Koufonísion** (isl.), Gre.
114/E2 **Kougarok** (mtn.), Ak,US
67/D3 **Kouhu**, Tai.
103/J2 **Koukdjuak** (riv.), NW,Can
87/B1 **Koula-Moutou**, Gabon
84/D3 **Koulikoro**, Mali
84/B3 **Koulountou** (riv.), Gui., Sen.
84/D3 **Koumbi Saleh** (ruins), Mrta.
82/J6 **Koumra**, Chad
68/C2 **Kounradskiy**, Kaz.
112/E4 **Kountze**, Tx,US
85/H5 **Koupé** (peak), Camr.
85/E3 **Koupela**, Burk.
85/E3 **Kouritenga** (prov.), Burk.
93/H2 **Kourou**, FrG.
82/J4 **Koussi** (peak), Chad
84/D3 **Koutiala**, Mali
37/H3 **Kouvola**, Fin.
50/E3 **Kovačica**, Yugo.
52/F2 **Kovdozero** (lake), Rus.
54/C2 **Kovel'**, Ukr.
70/C6 **Kovilpatti**, India
52/J4 **Kovrov**, Rus.
70/C5 **Kovūr**, India
55/G1 **Kovylkino**, Rus.
61/J1 **Kowkcheh** (riv.), Afg.
61/H2 **Kowl-e Namaksār** (lake), Afg., Iran
67/B3 **Kowloon**, HK
64/B5 **Kōyama**, Japan
51/G4 **Koynare**, Bul.
114/H2 **Koyukuk** (riv.), Ak,US
65/N10 **Kozakai**, Japan
59/C3 **Kozan**, Turk.
49/G2 **Kozáni**, Gre.
50/C3 **Kozara Nat'l Park**, Bosn.
70/C5 **Kozhikode**, India
52/H3 **Kozhozero** (lake), Rus.
53/M2 **Kozhva** (riv.), Rus.
39/L3 **Kozienice**, Pol.
51/F4 **Kozloduy**, Bul.
59/E2 **Kozluk**, Turk.
39/J3 **Koźmin**, Pol.
51/F4 **Koznitsa** (peak), Bul.
39/H3 **Kożuchów**, Pol.
85/F5 **Kpalimé**, Togo
85/F5 **Kpandu**, Gha.
69/B4 **Kra** (isth.), Burma, Thai.
88/D3 **Kraai** (riv.), SAfr.
88/L10 **Kraaifontein**, SAfr.
69/B4 **Krabi**, Thai.
69/D3 **Kracheh**, Camb.
37/D4 **Kragerø**, Nor.
50/E3 **Kragujevac**, Yugo.
45/H2 **Kraichgau** (reg.), Ger.
72/C5 **Krakatoa** (vol.), Indo.
69/C3 **Krakor**, Camb.
39/K3 **Kraków**, Pol.
39/K3 **Kraków** (prov.), Pol.
69/C3 **Kralanh**, Camb.
101/H5 **Kralendijk**, NAnt.
50/E4 **Kraljevo**, Yugo.
45/L1 **Kralupy nad Vltavou**, Czh.
54/F2 **Kramatorsk**, Ukr.
37/F3 **Kramfors**, Swe.
40/B5 **Krammer** (chan.), Neth.
40/D5 **Kranenburg**, Ger.
50/B2 **Kranj**, Slov.
39/J3 **Krapkowice**, Pol.
39/M3 **Kraśnik**, Pol.
39/M3 **Kraśnik Fabryczny**, Pol.
55/H2 **Krasnoarmeysk**, Rus.
54/F3 **Krasnodar**, Rus.
54/F3 **Krasnodar** (kray), Rus.
54/F1 **Krasnogorsk**, Rus.
54/E2 **Krasnograd**, Ukr.
63/H1 **Krasnokamensk**, Rus.
53/M4 **Krasnokamsk**, Rus.
55/H2 **Krasnoslobodsk**, Rus.
56/G4 **Krasnotur'insk**, Rus.
53/P4 **Krasnoural'sk**, Rus.
55/K5 **Krasnovodsk**, Trkm.
56/K4 **Krasnoyarsk**, Rus.
39/M3 **Krasnystaw**, Pol.
55/H2 **Krasnyy Kut**, Rus.
54/F2 **Krasnyy Luch**, Ukr.
54/G3 **Krasnyy Sulin**, Rus.
69/C4 **Kravanh** (mts.), Camb.
72/C5 **Krawang**, Indo.
40/D6 **Krefeld**, Ger.
41/G5 **Kreiensen**, Ger.
49/G3 **Kremastón** (lake), Gre.
54/E2 **Kremenchug**, Ukr.
54/E2 **Kremenchug** (res.), Ukr.
108/F2 **Kremmling**, Co,US
45/L2 **Krems an der Donau**, Aus.
57/T3 **Kresta** (gulf), Rus.
37/G5 **Kretinga**, Lith.
43/F2 **Kreuzau**, Ger.
43/G2 **Kreuztal**, Ger.
82/G7 **Kribi**, Camr.
54/D1 **Krichev**, Bela.
63/N2 **Kril'on, Mys** (cape), Rus.
40/B5 **Krimpen aan de IJssel**, Neth.
70/D4 **Krishna** (riv.), India
70/C5 **Krishnagiri**, India
37/C4 **Kristiansand**, Nor.
37/E4 **Kristianstad**, Swe.
39/H1 **Kristianstad** (co.), Swe.
37/C3 **Kristiansund**, Nor.
37/E4 **Kristinehamn**, Swe.
50/F4 **Kriva Palanka**, Macd.
54/E3 **Krivoy Rog**, Ukr.
50/B3 **Krk**, Cro.
50/C3 **Krka** (riv.), Cro.
39/J3 **Krnov**, Czh.
89/E2 **Krokodil** (riv.), SAfr.
88/D2 **Krokodilrivier** (riv.), SAfr.
54/E2 **Krolevets**, Ukr.
39/J4 **Kroměříž**, Czh.
45/J1 **Kronach**, Ger.
69/C4 **Krong Kaoh Kong**, Camb.
69/D4 **Krong Keb**, Camb.
37/E4 **Kronoberg** (co.), Swe.
52/F4 **Kronshtadt**, Rus.
76/C4 **Kroombit Tops Nat'l Park**, Austl.
88/D2 **Kroonstad**, SAfr.
55/G3 **Kropotkin**, Rus.
39/L4 **Krosno**, Pol.
39/L4 **Krosno** (prov.), Pol.
39/H2 **Krosno Odrzańskie**, Pol.
39/J3 **Krotoszyn**, Pol.
50/B3 **Krško**, Slov.
41/G1 **Kruckau** (riv.), Ger.
87/F5 **Kruger Nat'l Park**, SAfr.
88/P13 **Krugersdorp**, SAfr.
53/N5 **Kruglitsa, Gora** (peak), Rus.
114/A5 **Krugloi** (pt.), Ak,US
40/B6 **Kruibeke**, Belg.
50/D5 **Krujë**, Alb.
51/G5 **Krumovgrad**, Bul.
69/C3 **Krung Thep (Bangkok)** (cap.), Thai.
39/K4 **Krupina**, Slvk.
114/F2 **Krusenstern** (cape), Ak,US
50/E4 **Kruševac**, Yugo.
45/K1 **Krušné Hory** (Erzgebirge) (mts.), Czh., Ger.
39/K2 **Kruszwica**, Pol.
114/L4 **Kruzof** (isl.), Ak,US
54/F3 **Krymsk**, Rus.
39/L4 **Krynica**, Pol.
39/M3 **Krzna** (riv.), Pol.
39/J2 **Krzyż**, Pol.
81/M13 **Ksar el Kebir**, Mor.
66/D4 **Kuai** (riv.), China
72/D3 **Kuala Belait**, Bru.
72/B3 **Kuala Dungun**, Malay.
72/B3 **Kuala Lipis**, Malay.
72/B3 **Kuala Lumpur** (cap.), Malay.
72/B3 **Kuala Pilah**, Malay.
72/B2 **Kuala Terengganu**, Malay.
72/B3 **Kuantan**, Malay.
55/J4 **Kuba**, Azer.
54/F3 **Kuban'** (riv.), Rus.
52/H4 **Kubenskoye** (lake), Rus.
64/C4 **Kubokawa**, Japan
51/H4 **Kubrat**, Bul.
72/D3 **Kuching**, Malay.
49/F2 **Kuçovë**, Alb.
64/B4 **Kudamatsu**, Japan
72/D5 **Kudus**, Indo.
53/M4 **Kudymkar**, Rus.
83/K3 **Kufrah** (oasis), Libya
59/K5 **Kufrinjah**, Jor.
45/K3 **Kufstein**, Aus.
37/J2 **Kuhmo**, Fin.
40/D3 **Kuinder of Tjonger** (riv.), Neth.
69/E1 **Kuishan** (mtn.), China
87/C3 **Kuito**, Ang.
114/M4 **Kuiu** (isl.), Ak,US
85/E5 **Kujani Game Rsv.**, Gha.
39/K2 **Kujawy** (reg.), Pol.
63/N3 **Kuji**, Japan
64/B4 **Kujū-san** (mtn.), Japan
49/G1 **Kukës**, Alb.
65/F2 **Kuki**, Japan
65/J7 **Kukizaki**, Japan
61/G3 **Kūl** (riv.), Iran
50/D3 **Kula**, Yugo.
72/B3 **Kulai**, Malay.
55/J3 **Kulaly** (isl.), Kaz.
55/K4 **Kulandag** (mts.), Trkm.
55/G4 **Kulashi**, Geo.
52/D4 **Kuldīga**, Lat.
52/J5 **Kulebaki**, Rus.
69/D3 **Kulen**, Camb.
77/B2 **Kulkyne-Hattah Nat'l Park**, Austl.
61/L2 **Kullu**, India
45/J1 **Kulmbach**, Ger.
53/J2 **Kuloy** (riv.), Rus.
55/K3 **Kul'sary**, Kaz.
59/C2 **Kulu**, Turk.
56/H4 **Kulunda**, Rus.
68/C1 **Kulunda** (lake), Rus.
68/D1 **Kulunda** (riv.), Rus.
68/C1 **Kulunda Steppe** (grsld.), Kaz., Rus.
61/J1 **Kulyab**, Taj.
55/H3 **Kuma** (riv.), Rus.
65/F2 **Kumagaya**, Japan
64/B4 **Kumamoto**, Japan
64/B4 **Kumamoto** (pref.), Japan
64/E4 **Kumano**, Japan
64/D4 **Kumano** (riv.), Japan
50/E4 **Kumanovo**, Macd.
85/E5 **Kumasi**, Gha.
65/L10 **Kumatori**, Japan
55/G4 **Kumayri**, Arm.
85/H5 **Kumba**, Camr.
85/H5 **Kumbo**, Camr.
55/K5 **Kum-Dag**, Trkm.
67/E2 **Kume** (isl.), Japan
55/K1 **Kumertau**, Rus.
64/A2 **Kumi**, SKor.
65/L10 **Kumiyama**, Japan
37/E4 **Kumla**, Swe.
59/B3 **Kumluca**, Turk.
30/F2 **Kumo** (riv.), Fin.
71/G2 **Kumon** (range), Burma
70/B5 **Kumta**, India
104/U11 **Kumukahi** (cape), Hi,US
63/P3 **Kunashiri** (isl.), Rus.
70/C2 **Kūnch**, India
87/E3 **Kundelungu Nat'l Park**, Zaire
61/K2 **Kundiān**, Pak.
70/B3 **Kundla**, India
37/E4 **Kungsbacka**, Swe.
83/J7 **Kungu**, Zaire
53/N4 **Kungur**, Rus.
50/E2 **Kunhegyes**, Hun.
64/B4 **Kunimi-dake** (mtn.), Japan
72/C5 **Kuningan**, Indo.
65/H7 **Kunitachi**, Japan
68/C4 **Kunjirap Daban** (pass), China
68/C4 **Kunlun** (mts.), China
50/E2 **Kunmadaras**, Hun.
71/H2 **Kunming**, China
63/K4 **Kunsan**, SKor.
66/E5 **Kunshan**, China
50/E2 **Kunszentmárton**, Hun.
66/E3 **Kunyu Shan** (mtn.), China
37/H3 **Kuopio**, Fin.
37/H3 **Kuopio** (prov.), Fin.
50/B3 **Kupa** (riv.), Cro., Slov.
73/F6 **Kupang**, Indo.
56/H4 **Kupino**, Rus.
114/M4 **Kupreanof** (isl.), Ak,US
54/F2 **Kupyansk**, Ukr.
63/L1 **Kur** (riv.), Rus.
55/J5 **Kura** (riv.), Azer., Geo.
65/L9 **Kurama-yama** (peak), Japan
64/C3 **Kurashiki**, Japan
86/B5 **Kuraymah**, Sudan
64/C3 **Kurayoshi**, Japan
60/D1 **Kurdistan** (reg.), Asia
51/G5 **Kŭrdzhali**, Bul.
49/J2 **Kŭrdzhali** (res.), Bul.
64/C3 **Kure**, Japan
59/C2 **Küre** (mts.), Turk.
78/H2 **Kure** (isl.), Hi,US
52/D4 **Kuressaare**, Est.
56/K3 **Kureyka** (riv.), Rus.
53/Q5 **Kurgan**, Rus.
53/Q5 **Kurgan Obl.**, Rus.
61/J1 **Kurgan-Tyube**, Taj.
78/G4 **Kuria** (isl.), Kiri.
60/G5 **Kuria Muria** (isls.), Oman
57/Q5 **Kuril** (isls.), Rus.
76/H8 **Ku-Ring-Gai Nat'l Park**, Austl.
83/M5 **Kurmuk**, Sudan
70/C4 **Kurnool**, India
65/K9 **Kurodashō**, Japan
65/G2 **Kuroiso**, Japan
65/M10 **Kuroso-yama** (peak), Japan
61/K2 **Kurram** (riv.), Pak.
52/D5 **Kuršėnai**, Lith.
70/E2 **Kurseong**, India
54/F2 **Kursk**, Rus.
39/L1 **Kurskaya** (spit), Lith., Rus.
39/L1 **Kurskiy** (lag.), Rus.
54/E2 **Kursk Obl.**, Rus.
50/E4 **Kuršumlija**, Yugo.
59/E3 **Kurtalan**, Turk.
41/E6 **Kürten**, Ger.
86/B5 **Kurtī**, Sudan
83/L6 **Kuru** (riv.), Sudan
55/G4 **Kuruçay** (riv.), Turk.
68/E3 **Kuruktag** (mts.), China
64/B4 **Kurume**, Japan
70/D6 **Kurunegala**, SrL.
86/B4 **Kurur, Jabal** (peak), Sudan
76/E6 **Kurwongbah** (lake), Austl.
59/A3 **Kuşadası**, Turk.
83/M7 **Kusania** (lake), Ugan.
69/C2 **Ku Sathan** (peak), Thai.
65/L9 **Kusatsu**, Japan
65/M9 **Kusatsu**, Japan
65/M10 **Kushida** (riv.), Japan
64/B5 **Kushikino**, Japan
64/B5 **Kushima**, Japan
64/D4 **Kushimoto**, Japan
63/N3 **Kushiro**, Japan
53/Q5 **Kushmurun** (lake), Kaz.
62/F4 **Kushui** (riv.), China
55/J2 **Kushum** (riv.), Kaz.
114/F4 **Kuskokwim** (bay), Ak,US
114/G3 **Kuskokwim** (mts.), Ak,US
114/F3 **Kuskokwim** (riv.), Ak,US
55/M1 **Kustanay**, Kaz.
55/M2 **Kustanay Obl.**, Kaz.
83/M5 **Kūstī**, Sudan
65/M10 **Kusu**, Japan
69/C4 **Kut** (isl.), Thai.
59/B2 **Kütahya**, Turk.
55/G4 **Kutaisi**, Geo.
70/A3 **Kutch** (gulf), India
70/A3 **Kutch** (reg.), India
61/J4 **Kutch, Rann of** (swamp), India, Pak.
39/H4 **Kutná Hora**, Czh.
39/K2 **Kutno**, Pol.
87/C1 **Kutu**, Zaire
83/K5 **Kutum**, Sudan
102/E1 **Kuujjua** (riv.), NW,Can
103/K3 **Kuujjuaq** (Fort-Chimo), Qu,Can
103/J3 **Kuujjuarapik**, Qu,Can
37/J2 **Kuusamo**, Fin.
37/H3 **Kuusankoski**, Fin.
37/H4 **Kuutse Mägi** (mt.), Est.
55/L2 **Kuvandyk**, Rus.
60/E3 **Kuwait**
60/E3 **Kuwait** (Al Kuwait) (cap.), Kuw.
70/D2 **Kuwānā** (riv.), India
64/E3 **Kuwana**, Japan
53/L5 **Kuybyshev** (res.), Rus.
66/B3 **Kuye** (riv.), China
59/F3 **Küysanjaq**, Iraq
52/F2 **Kuyto** (lake), Rus.
68/E3 **Kuytun**, China
68/D2 **Kuytun** (riv.), China
100/E5 **Kuyu Tingni**, Nic.
114/E2 **Kuzitrin** (riv.), Ak,US
55/H1 **Kuznetsk**, Rus.
37/F1 **Kvaløy** (isl.), Nor.
50/B3 **Kvarner** (chan.), Cro.
50/B3 **Kvarnerić** (chan.), Cro.
37/E2 **Kvigtinden** (peak), Nor.
37/C4 **Kvinnherad**, Nor.
87/C1 **Kwa** (riv.), Zaire
69/B3 **Kwai, River** (bridge), Thai.
78/F4 **Kwajelein** (atoll), Mrsh.
88/Q12 **Kwandebele** (homeland), SAfr.
63/K4 **Kwangju**, SKor.
87/C1 **Kwango** (riv.), Zaire
85/G4 **Kwara** (state), Nga.
110/D1 **Kwataboahegan** (riv.), On,Can
87/E4 **Kwekwe**, Zim.
39/K2 **Kwidzyn**, Pol.
83/N5 **Kwīha**, Eth.
80/D5 **Kwilu** (riv.), Zaire
82/J6 **Kyabé**, Chad
69/B2 **Kyaikkami**, Burma
69/B2 **Kyaikto**, Burma
62/F1 **Kyakhta**, Rus.
71/G4 **Kyangin**, Burma
69/D2 **Ky Anh**, Viet.
69/B1 **Kyaukme**, Burma
71/F4 **Kyaukpyu**, Burma
69/B1 **Kyaukse**, Burma
39/J4 **Kyjov**, Czh.
106/F3 **Kyle**, Sk,Can
43/F3 **Kyll** (riv.), Ger.
43/F3 **Kyllburg**, Ger.
35/F2 **Kym** (riv.), Eng,UK
37/H3 **Kymi** (prov.), Fin.
70/C3 **Kymore**, India
83/M7 **Kyoga** (lake), Ugan.
64/D3 **Kyōga-misaki** (cape), Japan
65/F3 **Kyonan**, Japan
64/A3 **Kyŏngju**, SKor.
64/A3 **Kyŏngju Nat'l Park**, SKor.
64/A2 **Kyŏngsang-bukto** (prov.), SKor.
64/A3 **Kyŏngsang-namdo** (prov.), SKor.
64/D3 **Kyōto**, Japan
64/D3 **Kyōto** (pref.), Japan
59/J4 **Kyrenia** (dist.), Cyp.
68/B3 **Kyrgyzstan**
38/G2 **Kyritz**, Ger.
71/H4 **Ky Son**, Viet.
64/B5 **Kyūshū** (isl.), Japan
64/B4 **Kyūshū** (mts.), Japan
64/B4 **Kyūshū** (prov.), Japan
50/F4 **Kyustendil**, Bul.
68/F1 **Kyzyl**, Rus.
56/G5 **Kyzylkum** (des.), Kaz.,Uzb.
56/G5 **Kzyl-Orda**, Kaz.

L

38/G2 **Laage**, Ger.
45/K3 **Laakirchen**, Aus.
46/B4 **La Algaba**, Sp.
100/E6 **La Amistad Int'l Park**
96/B3 **La Araucanía** (reg.), Chile
42/C1 **Laarne**, Belg.
101/N7 **La Ascensión**, Mex.
101/J5 **La Asunción**, Ven.
41/G4 **Laatzen**, Ger.
82/C2 **Laayoune**, WSah.
111/G1 **La Baie**, Qu,Can
46/A1 **La Baña**, Sp.
91/D2 **La Banda**, Arg.
46/C1 **La Bañeza**, Sp.
67/D6 **Labason**, Phil.
42/B2 **La Bassée**, Fr.
44/B3 **La Baule-Escoublac**, Fr.
48/B1 **Labbro** (peak), It.
82/H1 **Labdah** (Leptis Magna) (ruins), Libya
84/B4 **Labé**, Gui.
84/B4 **Labé** (comm.), Gui.
39/H3 **Labe** (Elbe) (riv.), Czh.
113/H5 **La Belle**, Fl,US
50/B3 **Labin**, Cro.
55/G3 **Labinsk**, Rus.
47/G2 **La Bisbal**, Sp.
100/D3 **Labná** (ruins), Mex.
39/L4 **Laborec** (riv.), Slvk.
96/E2 **Laboulaye**, Arg.
103/K3 **Labrador** (reg.), Nf,Can
99/M4 **Labrador** (sea), Can., Grld.
103/K3 **Labrador City**, Nf,Can
92/F5 **Lábrea**, Braz.
73/E2 **Labuk** (bay), Malay.
73/E2 **Labuk** (riv.), Malay.
71/F4 **Labutta**, Burma
49/F2 **Laç**, Alb.
96/C2 **La Calera**, Chile
111/N6 **Lac-Alouette**, Qu,Can
96/C2 **La Campana Nat'l Park**, Chile
115/B2 **La Cañada-Flintridge**, Ca,US
96/E2 **La Carlota**, Arg.
46/C4 **La Carlota**, Sp.
46/D3 **La Carolina**, Sp.
70/B5 **Laccadive** (sea), India
107/J3 **Lac du Bonnet**, Mb,Can
100/D4 **La Ceiba**, Hon.
31/S10 **La Celle-Saint-Cloud**, Fr.
77/A3 **Lacepede** (bay), Austl.
116/B3 **Lacey**, Wa,US
52/H3 **Lacha** (lake), Rus.
42/A5 **Lachapelle-aux-Pots**, Fr.
44/F2 **La Chapelle-Saint-Luc**, Fr.
44/C3 **La Chapelle-sur-Erdre**, Fr.
111/N6 **Lachenaie**, Qu,Can
111/N7 **Lachine**, Qu,Can
77/C2 **Lachlan** (riv.), Austl.
101/F6 **La Chorrera**, Pan.
41/H3 **Lachte** (riv.), Ger.
109/F4 **La Cienega**, NM,US
46/A1 **La Ciñiza**, Sp.
45/F5 **La Ciotat**, Fr.
101/N9 **La Ciudad Nat'l Park**, Mex.
111/S10 **Lackawanna**, NY,US
106/F2 **Lac La Biche**, Ab,Can
111/G2 **Lac-Mégantic**, Qu,Can
34/D4 **Lacock**, Eng,UK
106/E2 **Lacombe**, Ab,Can
100/E6 **La Concepción**, Pan.
101/G5 **La Concepcíon**, Ven.
111/G3 **Laconia**, NH,US
46/A1 **La Coruña**, Sp.
31/T10 **La Courneuve**, Fr.
44/D4 **La Couronne**, Fr.
107/L5 **La Crescent**, Mn,US
115/B2 **La Crescenta-Montrose**, Ca,US
110/B3 **La Crosse**, Wi,US
96/Q9 **La Cruz**, Chile
100/D5 **La Cruz**, CR
101/N9 **La Cruz**, Mex.
69/D1 **Lac Son**, Viet.
72/C1 **Lac Thien**, Viet.
61/L2 **Ladakh** (mts.), Pak., India
77/B3 **Laddon** (riv.), Austl.
39/J3 **Lądek-Zdrój**, Pol.
48/C2 **Ladispoli**, It.
52/F3 **Ladoga** (lake), Rus.
92/D2 **La Dorada**, Col.
97/J8 **Ladrillero** (mtn.), Chile
88/D3 **Ladybrand**, SAfr.
89/E3 **Ladysmith**, SAfr.
110/B2 **Ladysmith**, Wi,US
78/F4 **Lae** (atoll), Mrsh.
78/D5 **Lae**, PNG
100/D5 **La Esperanza**, Hon.
101/J6 **La Esperanza**, Ven.
46/B1 **La Estaca de Bares, Punta de** (cape), Sp.
46/A1 **La Estrada**, Sp.
96/C3 **La Falda**, Arg.
116/K11 **Lafayette**, Ca,US
113/G3 **La Fayette**, Ga,US
110/C3 **Lafayette**, In,US
112/E4 **Lafayette**, La,US
44/D2 **La Ferté-Bernard**, Fr.
44/C2 **La Ferté-Macé**, Fr.
42/C6 **La Ferté-sous-Jouarre**, Fr.
110/E1 **Laflamme** (riv.), Qu,Can
44/C3 **La Flèche**, Fr.
45/L3 **Lafnitz** (riv.), Aus.
111/M6 **Lafontaine**, Qu,Can
45/G4 **La Font Sancte, Pic de** (peak), Fr.
101/G6 **La Fría**, Ven.
71/F6 **Lāfūl**, India
32/B3 **Lagan** (riv.), NI,UK
31/S10 **La Garenne-Colombes**, Fr.
112/B2 **La Garita** (mts.), Co,US
47/L6 **La Garriga**, Sp.
94/C3 **Lagarto**, Braz.
67/D4 **Lagawe**, Phil.
82/H6 **Lagdo** (riv.), Camr.
41/F5 **Lage**, Ger.
95/B3 **Lages**, Braz.
40/C4 **Lage Vaart** (can.), Neth.
82/F1 **Laghouat**, Alg.
31/U9 **Lagny-le-Sec**, Fr.
31/U10 **Lagny-sur-Marne**, Fr.
95/C2 **Lagoa da Prata**, Braz.
95/C1 **Lagoa Formosa**, Braz.
95/B4 **Lagoa Vermelha**, Braz.
94/A2 **Lago da Pedra**, Braz.
96/C4 **Lago Puelo Nat'l Park**, Arg.
85/F5 **Lagos**, Nga.
85/F5 **Lagos** (state), Nga.
46/A4 **Lagos**, Port.
100/A3 **Lagos de Moreno**, Mex.
99/K4 **La Grande** (riv.), Can.
106/D4 **La Grande**, Or,US
45/G4 **La Grande Ruine** (mtn.), Fr.
113/G3 **La Grange**, Ga,US
110/C4 **La Grange**, Ky,US
112/D4 **La Grange**, Tx,US
92/F2 **La Gran Sabana** (plain), Ven.
46/A2 **La Guardia**, Sp.
96/D3 **La Guerra** (peak), Arg.
95/B4 **Laguna**, Braz.
116/M10 **Laguna** (cr.), Ca,US
96/C3 **Laguna Blanca Nat'l Park**, Arg.
46/C2 **Laguna de Duero**, Sp.
96/C3 **Laguna del Laja Nat'l Park**, Chile
115/C3 **Laguna Hills**, Ca,US
97/J6 **Laguna San Rafael Nat'l Park**, Chile
100/C4 **Lagunas de Montebello Nat'l Park**, Mex.
101/G6 **Lagunillas**, Ven.
115/C3 **La Habra**, Ca,US
72/B4 **Lahat**, Indo.
111/H2 **La Have** (riv.), NS,Can
91/B2 **La Higuera**, Chile
60/F1 **Lāhījān**, Iran
38/E3 **Lahn** (riv.), Ger.
43/G3 **Lahnstein**, Ger.
37/E4 **Laholm**, Swe.
61/K2 **Lahore**, Pak.
45/G2 **Lahr**, Ger.
37/H3 **Lahti**, Fin.
82/J6 **Laï**, Chad
69/C1 **Lai Chau**, Viet.
67/A2 **Laifeng Tujiazu Zizhixian**, China
44/D2 **L'Aigle**, Fr.
37/G3 **Laihia**, Fin.
37/G2 **Lainioälven** (riv.), Swe.
37/G3 **Laitila**, Fin.
45/J3 **Laives** (Leifers), It.
66/D3 **Laiwu**, China
66/D3 **Laizhou** (bay), China
96/C3 **Laja** (lake), Chile
95/B4 **Lajeado**, Braz.
94/C3 **Lajedo**, Braz.
47/S12 **Lajes do Pico**, Azor.,Port.
95/D2 **Lajinha**, Braz.
50/D2 **Lajosmizse**, Hun.
109/G3 **La Junta**, Co,US
107/J5 **Lake Andes**, SD,US
115/C2 **Lake Arrowhead**, Ca,US
112/E4 **Lake Charles**, La,US
108/F3 **Lake City**, Co,US
113/H4 **Lake City**, Fl,US
107/K4 **Lake City**, Mn,US
114/H3 **Lake Clark Nat'l Park & Prsv.**, Ak,US
33/E2 **Lake District Nat'l Park**, Eng,UK
115/C3 **Lake Elsinore**, Ca,US
76/B1 **Lakefield Nat'l Park**, Austl.
116/Q15 **Lake Forest**, Il,US
112/E3 **Lake Fork** (res.), Tx,US
108/D4 **Lake Havasu City**, Az,US
115/F5 **Lakehurst**, NJ,US
112/E3 **Lake Jackson**, Tx,US
113/H4 **Lakeland**, Fl,US
106/D3 **Lake Louise**, Ab,Can
87/F3 **Lake Malawi Nat'l Park**, Malw.
83/M8 **Lake Mburo Nat'l Park**, Ugan.
108/D4 **Lake Mead Nat'l Rec. Area**, Az, Nv,US
49/G2 **Lake Mikri Prespa Nat'l Park**, Gre.
115/F4 **Lake Mohawk**, NJ,US
35/G2 **Lakenheath**, Eng,UK
109/J3 **Lake of the Ozarks** (lake), Mo,US

Lake – Lille

37/D3 **Lillehammer**, Nor.
42/B2 **Lillers**, Fr.
37/D4 **Lillestrøm**, Nor.
106/C3 **Lillooet**, BC,Can
106/C3 **Lillooet** (riv.), BC,Can
87/F3 **Lilongwe** (cap.), Malw.
77/G5 **Lilydale**, Austl.
50/D4 **Lim** (riv.), Yugo.
92/C6 **Lima** (cap.), Peru
46/A2 **Lima** (riv.), Port.
107/L4 **Lima** (peak), Mn,US
110/C3 **Lima**, Oh,US
96/Q9 **Limache**, Chile
95/K6 **Lima Duarte**, Braz.
39/L4 **Limanowa**, Pol.
59/J4 **Limassol**, Cyp.
32/B1 **Limavady**, NI,UK
32/A2 **Limavady** (dist.), NI,UK
96/C4 **Limay** (riv.), Arg.
42/A6 **Limay**, Fr.
48/A2 **Limbara** (peak), It.
70/B3 **Limbdi**, India
43/E2 **Limburg** (prov.), Belg.
43/E1 **Limburg** (prov.), Neth.
45/H1 **Limburg an der Lahn**, Ger.
111/Q8 **Limehouse**, On,Can
31/T10 **Limeil-Brévannes**, Fr.
95/C2 **Limeira**, Braz.
36/A4 **Limerick**, Ire.
46/B2 **Limia** (riv.), Sp.
74/F2 **Limmen** (bight), Austl.
49/J3 **Límnos** (isl.), Gre.
94/D2 **Limoeiro**, Braz.
94/C2 **Limoeiro do Norte**, Braz.
44/D4 **Limoges**, Fr.
44/D4 **Limogne** (plat.), Fr.
100/E5 **Limón**, CR
109/G3 **Limon**, Co,US
31/S11 **Limours**, Fr.
44/D4 **Limousin** (mts.), Fr.
44/D4 **Limousin** (reg.), Fr.
44/E5 **Limoux**, Fr.
87/F5 **Limpopo** (riv.), Afr.
31/P8 **Limpsfield**, Eng,UK
69/E2 **Limu** (mtn.), China
67/C5 **Linapacan** (isl.), Phil.
96/C2 **Linares**, Chile
100/B3 **Linares**, Mex.
46/D3 **Linares**, Sp.
67/C2 **Linchuan**, China
96/E2 **Lincoln**, Arg.
111/R9 **Lincoln**, On,Can
99/L1 **Lincoln** (sea), Can., Grld.
33/H5 **Lincoln**, Eng,UK
110/B3 **Lincoln**, Il,US
111/G2 **Lincoln**, Me,US
109/H2 **Lincoln** (cap.), Ne,US
106/B4 **Lincoln Beach**, Or,US
106/B4 **Lincoln City**, Or,US
33/H5 **Lincoln Heath** (woodl.), Eng,UK
116/F7 **Lincoln Park**, Mi,US
115/F5 **Lincoln Park**, NJ,US
33/H5 **Lincolnshire** (co.), Eng,UK
33/H5 **Lincolnshire Wolds** (hills), Eng,UK
113/H3 **Lincolnton**, NC,US
115/F5 **Lincroft**, NJ,US
48/A2 **L'Incudine, Mont** (mtn.), Fr.
40/D3 **Linde** (riv.), Neth.
76/C3 **Lindeman** (isl.), Austl.
92/G2 **Linden**, Guy.
113/G3 **Linden**, Al,US
115/F5 **Linden**, NJ,US
45/H3 **Lindenberg im Allgäu**, Ger.
116/P15 **Lindenhurst**, Il,US
115/G5 **Lindenhurst**, NY,US
115/F6 **Lindenwold**, NJ,US
52/B4 **Lindesberg**, Swe.
87/G3 **Lindi**, Tanz.
36/E3 **Lindisfarne** (Holy) (isl.), Eng,UK
41/E6 **Lindlar**, Ger.
77/D3 **Lind Nat'l Park**, Austl.
110/E2 **Lindsay**, On,Can
108/C3 **Lindsay**, Ca,US
112/D2 **Lindsborg**, Ks,US
79/K4 **Line** (isls.), Kiri.
66/B3 **Linfen**, China
66/C4 **Lingchuan**, China
67/B2 **Lingchuan**, China
40/C5 **Linge** (riv.), Neth.
41/E3 **Lingen**, Ger.
31/N8 **Lingfield**, Eng,UK
72/B3 **Lingga** (isls.), Indo.
43/G6 **Lingolsheim**, Fr.
84/B3 **Linguère**, Sen.
66/D3 **Ling Xian**, China
67/B2 **Ling Xian**, China
66/E5 **Lingyang Shan** (mtn.), China
66/L8 **Lingyen Shan** (mtn.), China
66/E5 **Lingyin Si**, China
67/D2 **Linhai**, China
95/D1 **Linhares**, Braz.
37/E4 **Linköping**, Swe.
66/C3 **Linliu Shan** (mtn.), China
37/J3 **Linnansaaren Nat'l Park**, Fin.
34/A3 **Linney Head** (pt.), Wal,UK
36/C2 **Linnhe, Loch** (inlet), Sc,UK
43/F2 **Linnich**, Ger.
48/C5 **Linosa** (isl.), It.
66/C3 **Linqing**, China
95/B2 **Lins**, Braz.
89/H9 **Linta** (riv.), Madg.
35/G2 **Linton**, Eng,UK
110/C4 **Linton**, In,US
107/H4 **Linton**, ND,US
33/H5 **Linwood**, Eng,UK
66/B4 **Linyi**, China
66/D3 **Linyi**, China
66/D4 **Linyi**, China
45/L2 **Linz**, Aus.
44/E5 **Lions** (gulf), Fr.
48/D3 **Lipari** (isls.), It.
37/J3 **Liperi**, Fin.
54/F1 **Lipetsk**, Rus.
54/F1 **Lipetsk Obl.**, Rus.
92/E8 **Lípez** (range), Bol.
92/E8 **Lípez** (riv.), Bol.
35/F4 **Liphook**, Eng,UK
50/E4 **Lipljan**, Yugo.
39/K2 **Lipno**, Pol.
50/E2 **Lipova**, Rom.
40/E5 **Lippe** (riv.), Ger.
41/F5 **Lippetal**, Ger.
41/F5 **Lippstadt**, Ger.
39/K4 **Liptovský Mikuláš**, Slvk.
77/C3 **Liptrap** (cape), Austl.
68/D5 **Lipu La** (pass), India
68/D5 **Lipu Lehk Shankou** (pass), China
83/M7 **Lira**, Ugan.
87/C1 **Liranga**, Congo
48/C2 **Liri** (riv.), It.
47/E3 **Liria**, Sp.
83/K7 **Lisala**, Zaire
46/A3 **Lisboa** (dist.), Port.
111/G2 **Lisbon**, Me,US
107/J4 **Lisbon**, ND,US
46/A3 **Lisbon** (Lisboa) (cap.), Port.
47/P10 **Lisbon** (Lisboa) (inset) (cap.), Port.
32/B2 **Lisburn**, NI,UK
32/B3 **Lisburn** (dist.), NI,UK
114/E2 **Lisburne** (cape), Ak,US
66/B4 **Li Shan** (mtn.), China
71/H2 **Lishe** (riv.), China
67/C2 **Lishui**, China
79/H2 **Lisianski** (isl.), Hi,US
54/F2 **Lisichansk**, Ukr.
44/D2 **Lisieux**, Fr.
34/B6 **Liskeard**, Eng,UK
116/P16 **Lisle**, Il,US
42/B5 **L'Isle-Adam**, Fr.
44/F5 **L'Isle-sur-!a-Sorgue**, Fr.
77/E1 **Lismore**, Austl.
32/B3 **Lisnacree**, NI,UK
35/F4 **Liss**, Eng,UK
40/B4 **Lisse**, Neth.
31/T11 **Lisses**, Fr.
41/E6 **Lister** (riv.), Ger.
110/D3 **Listowel**, On,Can
71/H2 **Litang** (riv.), China
59/K5 **Līţanī** (riv.), Leb.
110/B4 **Litchfield**, Il,US
107/K4 **Litchfield**, Mn,US
40/C5 **Lith**, Neth.
33/F5 **Litherland**, Eng,UK
77/D2 **Lithgow**, Austl.
52/D5 **Lithuania**
52/E5 **Litovskiy Nat'l Park**, Lith.
76/D4 **Littabella Nat'l Park**, Austl.
113/H4 **Little** (riv.), Ga,US
109/J4 **Little** (riv.), La,US
113/J3 **Little** (riv.), NC,US
109/J4 **Little** (riv.), Ok,US
112/D4 **Little** (riv.), Tx,US
110/D1 **Little Abitibi** (riv.), On,Can
39/J5 **Little Alföld** (plain), Hun.
71/F5 **Little Andaman** (isl.), India
106/F4 **Little Belt** (mts.), Mt,US
31/N6 **Little Berkhamstead**, Eng,UK
106/G4 **Little Bighorn Nat'l Mon.**, Mt,US
109/H2 **Little Blue** (riv.), Ks, Ne,US
33/F4 **Littleborough**, Eng,UK
101/E4 **Little Cayman** (isl.), Cay.
31/M7 **Little Chalfont**, Eng,UK
108/E4 **Little Colorado** (riv.), Az,US
110/D2 **Little Current**, On,Can
110/C1 **Little Current** (riv.), On,Can
34/C5 **Little Dart** (riv.), Eng,UK
77/B3 **Little Desert Nat'l Park**, Austl.
114/E2 **Little Diomede** (isl.), Ak,US
107/K4 **Little Falls**, Mn,US
112/C3 **Littlefield**, Tx,US
107/K4 **Little Fork** (riv.), Mn,US
35/F5 **Littlehampton**, Eng,UK
101/G3 **Little Inagua** (isl.), Bahm.
88/C4 **Little Karoo** (reg.), SAfr.
111/K2 **Little Miquelon** (isl.), StP.
109/J4 **Little Missouri** (riv.), Ar,US
107/H4 **Little Missouri** (riv.), ND, SD,US
71/F6 **Little Nicobar** (isl.), India
35/G2 **Little Ouse** (riv.), Eng,UK
35/G2 **Littleport**, Eng,UK
109/J4 **Little Red** (riv.), Ar,US
112/E3 **Little Rock** (cap.), Ar,US
114/L3 **Little Salmon**, Yk,Can
84/B4 **Little Scarcies** (riv.), Gui., SLeo.
107/K5 **Little Sioux** (riv.), Ia,US
114/B5 **Little Sitkin** (isl.), Ak,US
106/D2 **Little Smoky** (riv.), Ab,Can
108/E2 **Little Snake** (riv.), Co, Wy,US
35/G4 **Little Stour** (riv.), Eng,UK
35/F2 **Little Stukeley**, Eng,UK
111/G2 **Littleton**, NH,US
110/B4 **Little Wabash** (riv.), Il,US
109/G2 **Little White** (riv.), SD,US
106/E5 **Little Wood** (riv.), Id,US
59/F3 **Little Zab** (riv.), Iraq
63/J3 **Liu** (riv.), China
63/K3 **Liu** (riv.), China
67/A3 **Liu** (riv.), China
87/D3 **Liuwa Pan Nat'l Park**, Zam.
71/J3 **Liuzhou**, China
113/H4 **Live Oak**, Fl,US
43/F6 **Liverdun**, Fr.
116/L11 **Livermore**, Ca,US
112/B4 **Livermore** (peak), Tx,US
76/G8 **Liverpool**, Austl.
111/H2 **Liverpool**, NS,Can
114/M2 **Liverpool** (bay), NW,Can
103/J1 **Liverpool** (cape), NW,Can
33/F5 **Liverpool**, Eng,UK
33/E5 **Liverpool** (bay), Eng,UK
33/H2 **Liverton**, Eng,UK
106/F4 **Livingston**, Mt,US
115/F5 **Livingston**, NJ,US
112/E4 **Livingston**, Tx,US
109/J5 **Livingston** (lake), Tx,US
106/E3 **Livingstone** (range), Ab,Can
87/E4 **Livingstone**, Zam.
87/B1 **Livingstone, Chutes de** (Livingstone) (falls), Congo
50/C4 **Livno**, Bosn.
54/F1 **Livny**, Rus.
37/H2 **Livojoki** (riv.), Fin.
116/F7 **Livonia**, Mi,US
45/J5 **Livorno**, It.
94/B4 **Livramento do Brumado**, Braz.
44/F4 **Livron-sur-Drôme**, Fr.
42/B6 **Livry-Gargan**, Fr.
87/G2 **Liwale**, Tanz.
34/A7 **Lizard**, Eng,UK
34/A7 **Lizard** (pt.), Eng,UK
34/A6 **Lizard, The** (pen.), Eng,UK
50/B2 **Ljubljana** (cap.), Slov.
50/C4 **Ljubuški**, Cro.
37/F3 **Ljungan** (riv.), Swe.
37/E4 **Ljungby**, Swe.
52/C3 **Ljusdal**, Swe.
37/E3 **Ljusnan** (riv.), Swe.
96/C2 **Llaillay**, Chile
96/C3 **Llaima** (vol.), Chile
92/E7 **Llallagua**, Bol.
34/B2 **Llanarth**, Wal,UK
32/D5 **Llanberis**, Wal,UK
32/D5 **Llanberis, Pass of** (pass), Wal,UK
96/C2 **Llancañelo** (lake), Arg.
34/C3 **Llandeilo**, Wal,UK
34/D3 **Llandogo**, Wal,UK
34/C3 **Llandovery**, Wal,UK
32/E6 **Llandrillo**, Wal,UK
34/C2 **Llandrindod Wells**, Wal,UK
32/E5 **Llandudno**, Wal,UK
34/C3 **Llandybie**, Wal,UK
34/B2 **Llandyssul**, Wal,UK
34/B3 **Llanelli**, Wal,UK
34/C1 **Llanelltyd**, Wal,UK
32/D6 **Llanenddwyn**, Wal,UK
32/D5 **Llanerchymedd**, Wal,UK
46/C1 **Llanes**, Sp.
34/C1 **Llanfair Caereinion**, Wal,UK
32/E5 **Llanfairfechan**, Wal,UK
32/D5 **Llanfair-Pwllgwyngyll**, Wal,UK
34/C1 **Llanfyllin**, Wal,UK
34/C2 **Llangammarch Wells**, Wal,UK
34/C3 **Llangattock**, Wal,UK
33/E6 **Llangollen**, Wal,UK
34/C2 **Llangurig**, Wal,UK
34/C2 **Llanidloes**, Wal,UK
32/D5 **Llanllyfni**, Wal,UK
34/B3 **Llannon**, Wal,UK
112/D4 **Llano**, Tx,US
109/H5 **Llano** (riv.), Tx,US
108/G4 **Llano Estacado** (plain), NM, Tx,US
34/B2 **Llanon**, Wal,UK
92/D3 **Llanos** (plain), Col., Ven.
96/B4 **Llanquihue** (lake), Chile
33/E5 **Llanrhaeadr**, Wal,UK
34/B2 **Llanrhystyd**, Wal,UK
34/A3 **Llanrian**, Wal,UK
32/E5 **Llanrwst**, Wal,UK
34/C3 **Llanthony**, Wal,UK
34/C3 **Llantrisant**, Wal,UK
34/C4 **Llantwit Major**, Wal,UK
32/E6 **Llanuwchllyn**, Wal,UK
34/C1 **Llanwnog**, Wal,UK
34/C2 **Llanwrtyd Wells**, Wal,UK
33/E5 **Llay**, Wal,UK
34/C2 **Lledrod**, Wal,UK
47/F2 **Lleida** (Lérida), Sp.
100/B3 **Llera**, Mex.
32/D6 **Lleyn** (pen.), Wal,UK
47/F1 **Llobregat** (riv.), Sp.
46/D1 **Llodio**, Sp.
47/G2 **Lloret de Mar**, Sp.
100/E6 **Llorona** (pt.), CR
115/G5 **Lloyd** (pt.), NY,US
106/F2 **Lloydminster**, Ab, Sk,Can
111/K1 **Lloyds** (riv.), Nf,Can
47/G3 **Lluchmayor**, Sp.
91/C1 **Llullaillaco** (vol.), Chile
34/C3 **Llynfi** (riv.), Wal,UK
69/D1 **Lo** (riv.), Viet.
91/C1 **Loa** (riv.), Chile
108/E3 **Loa**, Ut,US
45/H4 **Loano**, It.
47/N8 **Loaoya** (can.), Sp.
88/D2 **Lobatse**, Bots.
96/F3 **Lobería**, Arg.
87/B3 **Lobito**, Ang.
84/D5 **Lobo** (riv.), IvC.
96/F2 **Lobos**, Arg.
92/B5 **Lobos de Tierra** (isl.), Peru
96/B2 **Lobos, Punta de** (pt.), Chile
45/H3 **Locarno**, Swi.
32/D2 **Lochans**, Sc,UK
32/E1 **Locharbriggs**, Sc,UK
40/D4 **Lochem**, Neth.
36/C2 **Lochgilphead**, Sc,UK
32/E1 **Lochmaben**, Sc,UK
42/C1 **Lochristi**, Belg.
36/C2 **Lochy, Loch** (lake), Sc,UK
33/E1 **Lockerbie**, Sc,UK
112/D4 **Lockhart**, Tx,US
110/E3 **Lock Haven**, Pa,US
77/C3 **Lockington**, Austl.
116/P16 **Lockport**, Il,US
111/S9 **Lockport**, NY,US
69/D4 **Loc Ninh**, Viet.
48/E3 **Locri**, It.
109/J3 **Locust** (cr.), Ia, Mo,US
59/M9 **Lod**, Isr.
75/G7 **Loddon** (riv.), Austl.
35/H1 **Loddon**, Eng,UK
35/E4 **Loddon** (riv.), Eng,UK
44/E5 **Lodève**, Fr.
52/G3 **Lodeynoye Pole**, Rus.
106/F3 **Lodge** (cr.), Mt,US
109/G2 **Lodgepole** (cr.), Ne, Wy,US
45/H4 **Lodi**, It.
116/M10 **Lodi**, Ca,US
115/F5 **Lodi**, NJ,US
87/D1 **Lodja**, Zaire
83/N7 **Lodwar**, Kenya
39/K3 **Ł ódź**, Pol.
39/K3 **Ł ódź** (prov.), Pol.
47/N9 **Loeches**, Sp.
69/C2 **Loei**, Thai.
40/C4 **Loenen**, Neth.
84/C5 **Lofa** (co.), Libr.
84/C5 **Lofa** (riv.), Libr.
37/D2 **Lofoten** (isls.), Nor.
33/H2 **Loftus**, Eng,UK
77/C4 **Lofty** (range), Austl.
76/F7 **Logan**, Austl.
114/K3 **Logan** (mtn.), Yk,Can
109/G4 **Logan**, NM,US
110/D4 **Logan**, Oh,US
108/E2 **Logan**, Ut,US
110/D4 **Logan**, WV,US
32/D2 **Logan, Mull of** (pt.), Sc,UK
110/C3 **Logansport**, In,US
82/J6 **Logone** (riv.), Camr., Chad
46/D1 **Logroño**, Sp.
41/G6 **Lohfelden**, Ger.
52/E3 **Lohja**, Fin.
43/G2 **Lohmar**, Ger.
38/E2 **Lohne**, Ger.
41/F3 **Löhne**, Ger.
45/H2 **Lohr**, Ger.
71/G3 **Loi Lun** (range), Burma, China
44/E2 **Loing** (riv.), Fr.
44/C3 **Loir** (riv.), Fr.
44/C3 **Loire** (riv.), Fr.
43/E5 **Loisin** (riv.), Fr.
83/N8 **Loita** (hills), Kenya
92/C4 **Loja**, Ecu.
46/C4 **Loja**, Sp.
42/D1 **Lokeren**, Belg.
87/D1 **Lokolia**, Zaire
83/K8 **Lokolo** (riv.), Zaire
83/J8 **Lokoro** (riv.), Zaire
103/K2 **Loks** (isl.), NW,Can
83/L6 **Lol** (riv.), Sudan
38/F1 **Lolland** (isl.), Den.
106/E4 **Lolo** (peak), Mt,US
87/E1 **Lolo**, Zaire
78/G5 **Lolua**, Tuv.
51/F4 **Lom**, Bul.
84/C4 **Loma** (mts.), Gui., SLeo.
100/B4 **Loma Bonita**, Mex.
115/C2 **Loma Linda**, Ca,US
84/C4 **Loma Mansa** (peak), SLeo.
83/K8 **Lomami** (riv.), Zaire
97/S12 **Lomas de Zamora**, Arg.
116/P16 **Lombard**, Il,US
93/H3 **Lombarda** (mts.), Braz.
45/J4 **Lombardy** (reg.), It.
73/F5 **Lomblen** (isl.), Indo.
73/E5 **Lombok** (isl.), Indo.
85/F5 **Lomé** (cap.), Togo
87/D1 **Lomela**, Zaire
83/K8 **Lomela** (riv.), Zaire
115/B3 **Lomita**, Ca,US
44/E1 **Lomme**, Fr.
43/E1 **Lommel**, Belg.
36/C2 **Lomond, Loch** (lake), Sc,UK
73/E5 **Lompobatang** (peak), Indo.
108/B4 **Lompoc**, Ca,US
69/C2 **Lom Sak**, Thai.
39/M2 **Ł omża**, Pol.
39/M2 **Ł omża** (prov.), Pol.
70/B4 **Lonāvale**, India
96/B3 **Loncoche**, Chile
42/D2 **Londerzeel**, Belg.
42/A4 **Londinières**, Fr.
110/D3 **London**, On,Can
35/F3 **London** (cap.), Eng,UK
110/C4 **London**, Ky,US
31/N6 **London Colney**, Eng,UK
74/D2 **Londonderry** (cape), Austl.
97/J8 **Londonderry** (isl.), Chile
32/A2 **Londonderry**, NI,UK
32/A2 **Londonderry** (dist.), NI,UK
31/N7 **London** (inset) (cap.), Eng,UK
95/B2 **Londrina**, Braz.
109/H4 **Lone Grove**, Ok,US
76/E7 **Lone Pine Sanct.**, Austl.
76/C4 **Lonesome Nat'l Park**, Austl.
101/F3 **Long** (isl.), Bahm.
107/J2 **Long** (pt.), Mb,Can
110/C1 **Long** (lake), On,Can
67/A3 **Long** (riv.), China
57/T2 **Long** (str.), Rus.
34/C1 **Long** (mtn.), Wal,UK
111/F3 **Long** (isl.), NY,US
94/B1 **Longá** (riv.), Braz.
96/C2 **Longaví**, Chile
111/R10 **Long Beach**, On,Can
115/B3 **Long Beach**, Ca,US
115/F6 **Long Beach** (isl.), NJ,US
115/G5 **Long Beach**, NY,US
33/G1 **Longbenton**, Eng,UK
113/H5 **Longboat Key**, Fl,US
115/G5 **Long Branch**, NJ,US
35/E2 **Long Buckby**, Eng,UK
69/D1 **Long Chau**, Viet.
67/C3 **Longchuan**, China
71/G3 **Longchuan**, China
35/F3 **Long Crendon**, Eng,UK
31/N7 **Long Ditton**, Eng,UK
33/G6 **Long Eaton**, Eng,UK
43/E5 **Longeau** (riv.), Fr.
111/G2 **Longfellow** (mts.), Me,US
31/P7 **Longfield**, Eng,UK
36/B4 **Longford**, Ire.
67/B2 **Longhui**, China
115/G5 **Long Island** (sound), Ct,NY,US
31/S10 **Longjumeau**, Fr.
110/C1 **Longlac**, On,Can
34/D4 **Longleat House**, Eng,UK
66/B4 **Longmen Shan** (mtn.), China
66/C4 **Longmen Shiyao** (caves), China
109/F2 **Longmont**, Co,US
34/D1 **Long Mynd, The** (hill), Eng,UK
33/G5 **Longnor**, Eng,UK
69/D4 **Long Phu**, Viet.
31/S11 **Longpont-sur-Orge**, Fr.
111/K2 **Long Range** (mts.), Nf,Can
33/F4 **Longridge**, Eng,UK
62/E4 **Longshou** (mts.), China
33/J6 **Long Sutton**, Eng,UK
33/F2 **Longtown**, Eng,UK
42/B2 **Longuenesse**, Fr.
111/N6 **Longueuil**, Qu,Can
43/E5 **Longuyon**, Fr.
44/F3 **Longvic**, Fr.
112/E3 **Longview**, Tx,US
106/C4 **Longview**, Wa,US
43/E4 **Longwy**, Fr.
69/D4 **Long Xuyen**, Viet.
67/C2 **Longyan**, China
41/E3 **Löningen**, Ger.
44/C5 **Lons**, Fr.
44/F3 **Lons-le-Saunier**, Fr.
34/B6 **Looe**, Eng,UK
34/B6 **Looe** (isl.), Eng,UK
76/B1 **Lookout** (pt.), Austl.
113/J3 **Lookout** (cape), NC,US
87/G1 **Loolmalasin** (peak), Tanz.
106/F2 **Loon Lake**, Sk,Can
40/C5 **Loon op Zand**, Neth.
36/G7 **Loop Head** (pt.), Ire.
42/C2 **Loos**, Fr.
68/F3 **Lop** (lake), China
57/R4 **Lopatka, Mys** (cape), Rus.
69/C3 **Lop Buri**, Thai.
82/G8 **Lopez** (cape), Gabon
40/B5 **Lopik**, Neth.
83/K7 **Lopori** (riv.), Zaire
37/G1 **Lopphavet** (bay), Nor.
61/J3 **Lora** (riv.), Pak.
46/C4 **Lora del Río**, Sp.
61/J3 **Lora, Hāmūn-i-** (lake), Pak.
110/D3 **Lorain**, Oh,US
61/J2 **Loralai**, Pak.
47/E4 **Lorca**, Sp.
75/K6 **Lord Howe** (isl.), Austl.
108/E4 **Lordsburg**, NM,US
43/G3 **Lorelei** (cliff), Ger.
95/H7 **Lorena**, Braz.
73/J5 **Lorentz** (riv.), Indo.
40/C2 **Lorentzsluizen** (dam), Neth.
107/J3 **Lorette**, Mb,Can
83/N7 **Lorian** (swamp), Kenya
101/F6 **Lorica**, Col.
44/B3 **Lorient**, Fr.
81/N13 **L'Oriental** (reg.), Mor.
102/G2 **Lorillard** (riv.), NW,Can
50/D2 **Lorinci**, Hun.
111/Q8 **Lorne Park**, On,Can
45/G3 **Lörrach**, Ger.
43/F6 **Lorrain** (plat.), Fr.
111/N6 **Lorraine**, Qu,Can
45/G2 **Lorraine** (reg.), Fr.
33/E2 **Lorton**, Eng,UK
115/J8 **Lorton**, Va,US
115/B3 **Los Alamitos** , Ca,US
108/B4 **Los Alamos**, Ca,US
109/F4 **Los Alamos**, NM,US
96/C4 **Los Alerces Nat'l Park**, Arg.
116/K12 **Los Altos**, Ca,US
96/C2 **Los Andes**, Chile
96/B3 **Los Ángeles**, Chile
115/B2 **Los Angeles**, Ca,US
115/B2 **Los Angeles** (riv.), Ca,US
108/B3 **Los Banos**, Ca,US
46/C4 **Los Barrios**, Sp.
90/B7 **Los Chonos** (arch.), Chile
46/C1 **Los Corrales de Buelna**, Sp.
97/J7 **Los Glaciares Nat'l Park**, Arg.
43/F4 **Losheim**, Ger.
101/N8 **Los Herreras**, Mex.
39/M2 **Ł osice**, Pol.
50/B3 **Lošinj** (isl.), Cro.
96/B3 **Los Lagos**, Chile
96/B4 **Los Lagos** (reg.), Chile
108/F4 **Los Lunas**, NM,US
101/N8 **Los Mochis**, Mex.
96/B4 **Los Muermos**, Chile
92/C2 **Los Orquideas Nat'l Park**, Col.
46/C4 **Los Palacios y Villafranca**, Sp.
97/J8 **Los Pingüinos Nat'l Park**, Chile
100/A4 **Los Reyes**, Mex.
101/H5 **Los Roques** (isls.), Ven.
46/B3 **Los Santos de Maimona**, Sp.
96/B3 **Los Sauces**, Chile
40/E4 **Losser**, Neth.
101/H5 **Los Teques**, Ven.
108/D1 **Lost River** (range), Id,US
34/B6 **Lostwithiel**, Eng,UK
96/C1 **Los Vilos**, Chile
46/D3 **Los Yébenes**, Sp.
44/D4 **Lot** (riv.), Fr.
96/B3 **Lota**, Chile
61/G1 **Lotfābād**, Trkm.
41/E4 **Lotte**, Ger.
66/B5 **Lou** (riv.), China
69/C2 **Louangphrabang**, Laos
87/B1 **Loubomo**, Congo
44/B2 **Loudéac**, Fr.
67/B2 **Loudi**, China
44/D3 **Loudun**, Fr.
44/F3 **Loue** (riv.), Fr.
84/A3 **Louga**, Sen.
84/B3 **Louga** (reg.), Sen.
33/G6 **Loughborough**, Eng,UK
32/B3 **Loughbrickland**, NI,UK
103/R7 **Lougheed** (isl.), NW,Can
32/B3 **Loughgall**, NI,UK
31/P7 **Loughton**, Eng,UK
110/E4 **Louisa**, Va,US
78/E6 **Louisiade** (arch.), PNG
112/E4 **Louisiana** (state), US
110/C4 **Louisville**, Ky,US
113/F3 **Louisville**, Ms,US
103/J3 **Louis XIV** (pt.), Qu,Can
81/M13 **Loukkos** (riv.), Mor.
46/A4 **Loulé**, Port.
45/K1 **Louny**, Czh.
109/H2 **Loup** (riv.), Ne,US
32/B2 **Loup, The**, NI,UK
31/U10 **L'Ourcq** (can.), Fr.
44/C5 **Lourdes**, Fr.
47/P10 **Loures**, Port.
46/A3 **Louriçal**, Port.
46/A3 **Lourinhã**, Port.
46/A2 **Lousã**, Port.
47/P10 **Lousa**, Port.
32/B4 **Louth** (co.), Ire.
33/H5 **Louth**, Eng,UK
49/H4 **Loutrákion**, Gre.
43/D2 **Louvain** (Leuven), Belg.
95/G8 **Louveira**, Braz.
42/A5 **Louviers**, Fr.
31/T9 **Louvres**, Fr.
42/C3 **Louvroil**, Fr.
42/B2 **Lovaart** (can.), Belg.
52/F4 **Lovat'** (riv.), Bela., Rus.
50/D4 **Lovćen Nat'l Park**, Yugo.
51/G4 **Lovech**, Bul.
51/G4 **Lovech** (reg.), Bul.
109/F2 **Loveland**, Co,US
106/F4 **Lovell**, Wy,US
108/C2 **Lovelock**, Nv,US
45/J4 **Lovere**, It.
109/F4 **Loving**, NM,US
109/G4 **Lovington**, NM,US
52/G2 **Lovozero** (lake), Rus.
103/H2 **Low** (cape), NW,Can
83/L8 **Lowa** (riv.), Zaire
33/H6 **Lowdham**, Eng,UK
111/G3 **Lowell**, Ma,US
88/B2 **Löwen** (dry riv.), Namb.
106/D3 **Lower Arrow** (lake), BC,Can
45/L2 **Lower Austria** (prov.), Aus.
35/E2 **Lower Brailes**, Eng,UK
77/B3 **Lower Glenelg Nat'l Park**, Austl.
77/C4 **Lower Gordon-Franklin Wild Rivers Nat'l Park**, Austl.
35/E3 **Lower Heyford**, Eng,UK
75/R11 **Lower Hutt**, NZ
31/P6 **Lower Nazeing**, Eng,UK
107/K4 **Lower Red** (lake), Mn,US
38/E2 **Lower Saxony** (state), Ger.
56/K3 **Lower Tunguska** (riv.), Rus.
87/E4 **Lower Zambezi Nat'l Park**, Zam.
35/H2 **Lowestoft**, Eng,UK
87/E1 **Lowi** (riv.), Zaire
39/K2 **Ł owicz**, Pol.
32/E1 **Lowther** (hills), Sc,UK
111/Q9 **Lowville**, On,Can
41/F2 **Loxstedt**, Ger.
79/V12 **Loyalty** (isls.), NCal.
50/D3 **Loznica**, Yugo.
54/F2 **Lozovaya**, Ukr.
50/E3 **Lozovik**, Yugo.
66/C5 **Lu** (riv.), China
87/D2 **Luachimo**, Ang.
87/E1 **Lualaba** (riv.), Zaire
66/J6 **Luam** (riv.), China
104/T10 **Lua Makika** (crater), Hi,US
66/D5 **Lu'an**, China
66/D2 **Luan** (riv.), China
46/C1 **Luanco**, Sp.
87/B2 **Luanda** (cap.), Ang.
69/C5 **Luang** (lag.), Thai.
69/B4 **Luang** (peak), Thai.
69/C2 **Luang Prabang** (range), Laos
87/F3 **Luangwa** (riv.), Moz., Zam.
87/E3 **Luanshya**, Zam.
66/D3 **Luan Xian**, China
87/D3 **Luao**, Ang.
46/B1 **Luarca**, Sp.
87/D3 **Luashi**, Zaire
82/G7 **Luba**, EqG.
100/D4 **Lubaantun** (ruins), Belz.
39/M3 **Lubaczów**, Pol.
39/H3 **Lubań**, Pol.
87/B3 **Lubango**, Ang.
39/M3 **Lubartów**, Pol.
39/K2 **Lubawa**, Pol.
41/F4 **Lübbecke**, Ger.
43/D2 **Lubbeek**, Belg.
112/C3 **Lubbock**, Tx,US
38/F2 **Lübeck**, Ger.
87/D1 **Lubefu**, Zaire
39/M3 **Lubelska** (upland), Pol.
83/L8 **Lubero**, Zaire
39/J3 **Lubin**, Pol.
39/M3 **Lublin**, Pol.
39/M3 **Lublin** (prov.), Pol.
39/K3 **Lubliniec**, Pol.
54/E2 **Lubny**, Ukr.
39/J2 **Luboń**, Pol.
39/H3 **Lubsko**, Pol.
87/E2 **Lubudi**, Zaire
72/B4 **Lubuklinggau**, Indo.
72/B3 **Lubuksikaping**, Indo.
87/E3 **Lubumbashi**, Zaire
87/E2 **Lubunda**, Zaire
87/C2 **Lucala**, Ang.
32/B5 **Lucan**, Ire.
69/D1 **Luc An Chau**, Viet.
114/K3 **Lucania** (mtn.), Yk,Can
87/D2 **Lucapa**, Ang.
45/J5 **Lucca**, It.
32/D2 **Luce** (bay), Sc,UK
113/F4 **Lucedale**, Ms,US
95/B2 **Lucélia**, Braz.
67/D5 **Lucena**, Phil.
46/C4 **Lucena**, Sp.
39/K4 **Lučenec**, Slvk.
45/H3 **Lucerne** (Luzern), Swi.
45/H3 **Lucerne** (Vierwaldstättersee) (lake), Swi.
38/F2 **Lüchow**, Ger.
39/G2 **Luckenwalde**, Ger.
70/D2 **Lucknow**, India
106/G3 **Lucky Lake**, Sk,Can
101/F3 **Lucrecia** (cape), Cuba
87/D3 **Lucusse**, Ang.
51/H4 **Luda Kamchiya** (riv.), Bul.
41/E6 **Lüdenscheid**, Ger.
88/A2 **Lüderitz**, Namb.
35/E4 **Ludgershall**, Eng,UK
61/L2 **Ludhiāna**, India
41/E5 **Ludinghausen**, Ger.
110/C3 **Ludington**, Mi,US
34/D2 **Ludlow**, Eng,UK
51/H4 **Ludogorie** (reg.), Bul.
51/G2 **Luduş**, Rom.
37/E3 **Ludvika**, Swe.
45/H2 **Ludwigsburg**, Ger.
39/G2 **Ludwigsfelde**, Ger.
38/F2 **Ludwigslust**, Ger.
87/D2 **Luebo**, Zaire
112/E4 **Lufkin**, Tx,US
52/F4 **Luga**, Rus.
45/H3 **Lugano**, Swi.
54/F2 **Lugansk**, Ukr.
54/F2 **Lugansk Obl.**, Ukr.
41/G5 **Lügde**, Ger.
87/G3 **Lugenda** (riv.), Moz.
34/D2 **Lugg** (riv.), Eng,UK
32/B6 **Lugnaquillia** (mtn.), Ire.
46/B1 **Lugo**, Sp.
50/E3 **Lugoj**, Rom.
41/H2 **Lühe** (riv.), Ger.
87/D4 **Luiana**, Ang.
45/H4 **Luino**, It.
98/X **Luitpold** (coast), Ant.
50/D3 **Lukavac**, Bosn.
87/C1 **Lukenie** (riv.), Zaire
51/G4 **Lukovit**, Bul.
39/M3 **Ł uków**, Pol.
78/E4 **Lukunor** (atoll), Micr.
37/G2 **Luleå**, Swe.
37/G2 **Luleälv** (riv.), Swe.
51/H5 **Lüleburgaz**, Turk.
66/B4 **Luling Guan** (pass), China
80/E4 **Lulonga** (riv.), Zaire
78/G5 **Lulua**, Tuv.
87/D2 **Lulua** (riv.), Zaire
87/D3 **Lumai**, Ang.
68/D5 **Lumajamgdong** (lake), China
113/J3 **Lumberton**, NC,US
112/E4 **Lumberton**, Tx,US
87/H4 **Lumbo**, Moz.
106/D3 **Lumby**, BC,Can
71/F2 **Lumding**, India
43/E2 **Lummen**, Belg.
69/D3 **Lumphat**, Camb.
107/G3 **Lumsden**, Sk,Can
75/Q12 **Lumsden**, NZ
87/D3 **Lunache**, Ang.
39/G1 **Lund**, Swe.
108/D3 **Lund**, Nv,US
87/F5 **Lundi** (riv.), Zim.
34/B4 **Lundy** (isl.), Eng,UK
41/F2 **Lune** (riv.), Ger.
33/F3 **Lune** (riv.), Eng,UK
41/H2 **Lüneburg**, Ger.
41/G2 **Lüneburger Heide** (reg.), Ger.
44/F5 **Lunel**, Fr.
41/E5 **Lünen**, Ger.
111/H2 **Lunenburg**, NS,Can
87/E3 **Lunga** (riv.), Zam.
71/F3 **Lunglei**, India
87/D3 **Lungue-Bungo** (riv.), Ang.
70/B3 **Luni** (riv.), India
66/B3 **Luo** (riv.), China
66/B4 **Luo** (riv.), China
66/C4 **Luohe**, China
66/D4 **Luoma** (lake), China
69/C1 **Luong** (mts.), Viet.
66/C4 **Luoyang**, China
87/B1 **Luozi**, Zaire
87/E4 **Lupane**, Zim.
71/H2 **Lupanshui**, China
51/F3 **Lupeni**, Rom.
71/H2 **Luquan**, China
61/J2 **Lūrah** (riv.), Afg.
110/E4 **Luray**, Va,US
32/B3 **Lurgan**, NI,UK
87/H3 **Lúrio**, Moz.
87/G3 **Lúrio** (riv.), Moz.
87/E4 **Lusaka** (cap.), Zam.
87/E1 **Lusamba**, Zaire
87/D1 **Lusambo**, Zaire
66/D3 **Lu Shan** (mtn.), China
66/C5 **Lu Shan** (peak), China
49/F2 **Lushnje**, Alb.
107/G5 **Lusk**, Wy,US
83/J7 **Lutanga** (riv.), Zaire
115/K7 **Lutherville**, Md,US
40/D1 **Lütjehorn** (isl.), Ger.
35/F3 **Luton**, Eng,UK
54/C2 **Lutsk**, Ukr.
41/F5 **Lutter** (riv.), Ger.
98/C **Lützow-Holm** (bay), Ant.
83/P7 **Luuq**, Som.
107/J5 **Luverne**, Mn,US
43/E4 **Luxembourg**
43/E4 **Luxembourg** (prov.), Belg.
43/F4 **Luxembourg** (cap.), Lux.
43/F4 **Luxembourg** (dist.), Lux.
71/J2 **Lu Xian**, China
86/C3 **Luxor** (Al Uqşur), Egypt
44/C5 **Luy** (riv.), Fr.
66/B3 **Luya Shan** (mtn.), China
95/C1 **Luz**, Braz.
53/L3 **Luza** (riv.), Rus.
45/H3 **Luzern** (Lucerne), Swi.
71/J2 **Luzhou**, China
94/A5 **Luziânia**, Braz.
94/B1 **Luzilândia**, Braz.
67/D4 **Luzon** (isl.), Phil.
54/C2 **L'viv**, Ukr.
54/B2 **L'viv Obl.**, Ukr.
69/C1 **Lwi** (riv.), Burma
53/P3 **Lyapin** (riv.), Rus.
51/G4 **Lyaskovets**, Bul.
37/F2 **Lycksele**, Swe.
35/G5 **Lydd**, Eng,UK
98/Y **Lyddan** (isl.), Ant.
89/E2 **Lydenburg**, SAfr.
34/D3 **Lydney**, Eng,UK
106/F5 **Lyman**, Wy,US
34/C5 **Lyme** (bay), Eng,UK
34/D5 **Lyme Regis**, Eng,UK
35/E5 **Lymington**, Eng,UK
33/F5 **Lymm**, Eng,UK

Łyna – Marin

39/L1 Łyna (riv.), Pol.
32/D5 Lynas (pt.), Wal,UK
115/G5 Lynbrook, NY,US
110/E4 Lynchburg, Va,US
113/H3 Lynches (riv.), SC,US
76/A2 Lynd (riv.), Austl.
35/E5 Lyndhurst, Eng,UK
115/F5 Lyndhurst, NJ,US
33/F1 Lyne (riv.), Eng,UK
37/G1 Lyngen (fjord), Nor.
111/G3 Lynn, Ma,US
113/G4 Lynn Haven, Fl,US
116/C2 Lynnwood, Wa,US
34/C4 Lynton, Eng,UK
115/B3 Lynwood, Ca,US
102/F2 Lynx (lake), NW,Can
44/F4 Lyon, Fr.
109/H3 Lyons, Ks,US
34/C4 Lype (hill), Eng,UK
78/E5 Lyra (reef), PNG
42/B2 Lys (riv.), Fr.
39/K4 Lysá (peak), Czh.
52/E5 Lysaya, Gora (hill), Bela.
39/L3 Łysica (peak), Pol.
42/C2 Lys-lez-Lannoy, Fr.
53/N4 Lys'va, Rus.
34/D5 Lytchett Matravers, Eng,UK
33/E4 Lytham Saint Anne's, Eng,UK
53/X9 Lytkarino, Rus.
106/C3 Lytton, BC,Can
57/F4 Lyubertsy, Rus.
51/H5 Lyubimets, Bul.
54/E2 Lyubotin, Ukr.
54/E1 Lyudinovo, Rus.
34/C3 Lywd (riv.), Wal,UK

M

69/C1 Ma (riv.), Laos, Viet.
59/K5 Ma'alot, Isr.
52/F2 Maanselkä (mts.), Fin.
66/D5 Ma'anshan, China
40/C6 Maarheeze, Neth.
40/C4 Maarssen, Neth.
38/D3 Maas (riv.), Eur.
40/C6 Maasbracht, Neth.
40/D6 Maasbree, Neth.
43/E1 Maaseik, Belg.
67/D5 Maasin, Phil.
43/E2 Maasmechelen, Belg.
40/B5 Maassluis, Neth.
43/E2 Maastricht, Neth.
59/N7 Ma'ayan Harod Nat'l Park, Isr.
67/D4 Mabalacat, Phil.
87/F5 Mabalane, Moz.
33/J5 Mablethorpe, Eng,UK
87/F5 Mabote, Moz.
96/B5 Macá (peak), Chile
95/D2 Macaé, Braz.
94/D2 Macaíba, Braz.
93/H3 Macapá, Braz.
92/C4 Macará, Ecu.
94/B4 Macarani, Braz.
94/C2 Macau, Braz.
67/B3 Macau (cap.), Macau
67/B3 Macau (dpcy.), Port.
78/H7 Macauley (isl.), NZ
92/D3 Macaya (riv.), Col.
101/G4 Macaya (pk.), Haiti
113/H4 Macclenny, Fl,US
33/F5 Macclesfield, Eng,UK
33/F5 Macclesfield (can.), Eng,UK
88/D3 Macdhui (peak), SAfr.
74/D4 MacDonald (lake), Austl.
74/E4 Macdonnell (ranges), Austl.
36/D2 Macduff, Sc,UK
49/G2 Macedonia
49/G2 Macedonia (reg.), Gre., Macd.
94/D3 Maceió, Braz.
94/C2 Maceió (pt.), Braz.
48/C1 Macerata, It.
98/E Macey (peak), Ant.
88/D3 Machache (peak), Les.
95/H6 Machado, Braz.
83/N8 Machakos, Kenya
92/C4 Machala, Ecu.
92/B4 Machalilla Nat'l Park, Ecu.
87/F5 Machanga, Moz.
32/D2 Machars, The (pen.), Sc,UK
74/G5 Machattie (lake), Austl.
87/F5 Machaze, Moz.
87/E5 Machemma (ruins), SAfr.
34/C3 Machen, Wal,UK
66/C5 Macheng, China
111/H2 Machias, Me,US
46/D1 Machichaco (cape), Sp.
47/V15 Machico, Madr.,Port.
65/H7 Machida, Japan
70/D4 Machilipatnam, India
101/G5 Machiques, Ven.
92/D6 Machu Picchu (ruins), Peru
92/F6 Machupo (riv.), Bol.
34/C1 Machynlleth, Wal,UK
51/J3 Măcin, Rom.
84/D3 Macina (reg.), Mali
77/D1 Macintyre (riv.), Austl.
108/E3 Mack, Co,US
76/C3 Mackay, Austl.
74/D4 Mackay (lake), Austl.
98/E MacKenzie (bay), Ant.
76/C3 Mackenzie (riv.), Austl.
106/C2 Mackenzie, BC,Can
114/N2 Mackenzie (riv.), NW,Can
103/C2 Mackenzie (bay), NW, Yk,Can
102/C2 Mackenzie (mts.), NW, Yk,Can
103/R7 Mackenzie King (isl.), NW,Can
110/C2 Mackinac Island, Mi,US
113/F1 Mackinaw (riv.), Il,US
110/C2 Mackinaw City, Mi,US
106/F2 Macklin, Sk,Can
76/F7 Macleay (isl.), Austl.
114/L3 Macmillan (riv.), Yk,Can
48/A2 Macomer, It.
44/F3 Mâcon, Fr.
109/K4 Macon (bayou), Ar, La,US
113/H3 Macon, Ga,US
109/J3 Macon, Mo,US
32/B1 Macosquin, NI,UK
77/C4 Macquarie (har.), Austl.
29/S8 Macquarie (isl.), Austl.
77/C1 Macquarie (riv.), Austl.
98/D Mac-Robertson Land (reg.), Ant.
92/F5 Macuim (riv.), Braz.
74/F5 Macumba (riv.), Austl.
106/C5 Mad (riv.), Ca,US
59/K6 Ma'dabā, Jor.
89/H8 Madagascar
82/H3 Madama, Niger
51/G5 Madan, Bul.
70/C5 Madanapalle, India
78/D5 Madang, PNG
82/H1 Madanīyīn, Tun.
85/G3 Madaoua, Niger
70/F3 Mādārīpur, Bang.
110/E2 Madawaska (riv.), On,Can
111/G2 Madawaska, Me,US
92/F5 Madeira (riv.), Braz.
47/V15 Madeira (isl.), Madr., Port.
47/U14 Madeira (aut. reg.), Port.
107/L4 Madelin (isl.), Wi,US
101/N8 Madera, Mex.
100/D5 Madera (vol.), Nic.
70/E2 Madhipura, India
70/C3 Madhya Pradesh (state), India
92/E6 Madidi (riv.), Bol.
109/H4 Madill, Ok,US
87/B1 Madingo-Kayes, Congo
113/G3 Madison, Al,US
113/H4 Madison, Fl,US
110/C4 Madison, In,US
113/F3 Madison, Ms,US
106/F4 Madison (riv.), Mt,US
109/H2 Madison, Ne,US
115/F5 Madison, NJ,US
107/J4 Madison, SD,US
110/B3 Madison (cap.), Wi,US
110/D4 Madison, WV,US
116/F6 Madison Heights, Mi,US
110/C4 Madisonville, Ky,US
112/E4 Madisonville, Tx,US
72/D5 Madiun, Indo.
62/D5 Madoi, China
45/G2 Madon (riv.), Fr.
48/C4 Madonie Nebrodi (mts.), It.
61/G5 Madrakah, Ra's al (pt.), Oman
70/D5 Madras, India
106/C4 Madras, Or,US
100/B2 Madre (lag.), Mex.
112/D5 Madre (lag.), Tx,US
90/C4 Madre de Dios (riv.), Bol., Peru
97/J7 Madre de Dios (isl.), Chile
44/E5 Madrès (mtn.), Fr.
46/C2 Madrid (aut. comm.), Sp.
46/D2 Madrid (cap.), Sp.
46/D3 Madridejos, Sp.
47/N9 Madrid (inset) (cap.), Sp.
70/D4 Madugula, India
70/C6 Madurai, India
65/F2 Maebashi, Japan
69/C2 Mae Charim, Thai.
69/B2 Mae Ping Nat'l Park, Thai.
34/C3 Maesteg, Wal,UK
69/B2 Mae Tho (peak), Thai.
78/F6 Maewo (isl.), Van.
69/B2 Mae Ya (mtn.), Thai.
87/H2 Mafia (isl.), Tanz.
88/D2 Mafikeng, SAfr.
84/C4 Mafou (riv.), Gui.
95/B3 Mafra, Braz.
46/A3 Mafra, Port.
57/R4 Magadan, Rus.
83/N8 Magadi, Kenya
88/P12 Magalies Berg (range), SAfr.
97/K8 Magallanes (Magellan) (str.), Arg., Chile
97/K8 Magallanes y Antártica Chilena (reg.), Chile
101/G6 Magangué, Col.
67/D6 Maganoy, Phil.
85/H3 Magaria, Niger
67/D4 Magat (riv.), Phil.
109/J4 Magazine (peak), Ar,US
63/K1 Magdagachi, Rus.
111/J2 Magdalen (isls.), Qu,Can
97/T12 Magdalena, Arg.
92/D3 Magdalena (riv.), Col.
101/M7 Magdalena de Kino, Mex.
73/E3 Magdalena, Gunung (peak), Malay.
38/F2 Magdeburg, Ger.
38/F2 Magdeburger Börde (plain), Ger.
75/J3 Magdelaine (cays), Austl.
95/K7 Magé, Braz.
113/F4 Magee, Ms,US
32/C2 Magee, Island (pen.), NI,UK
72/C5 Magelang, Indo.
97/K8 Magellan (Magallanes) (str.), Arg., Chile
74/B6 Magenta (lake), Austl.
37/H1 Magerøya (isl.), Nor.
45/H4 Maggiore (lake), It., Swi.
86/B2 Maghāghah, Egypt
32/B2 Maghera, NI,UK
32/B2 Magherafelt, NI,UK
32/B2 Magherafelt (dist.), NI,UK
81/W18 Maghīla (peak), Tun.
81/P13 Maghnia, Alg.
33/F4 Maghull, Eng,UK
32/B1 Magilligan, NI,UK
32/B1 Magilligan (pt.), NI,UK
50/D3 Maglaj, Bosn.
50/D4 Maglić (peak), Yugo.
49/F2 Maglie, It.
110/D2 Magnetawan (riv.), On,Can
76/B2 Magnetic (passg.), Austl.
76/B2 Magnetic I. Nat'l Park, Austl.
53/N5 Magnitogorsk, Rus.
112/E3 Magnolia, Ar,US
31/S10 Magny-les-Hameaux, Fr.
111/F2 Magog, Qu,Can
83/N6 Mago Nat'l Park, Eth.
34/D3 Magor, Wal,UK
111/H1 Magpie (riv.), Qu,Can
83/L7 Maguerite (peak), Zaire
71/F3 Magwe, Burma
71/F4 Magwe (div.), Burma
60/E1 Mahābād, Iran
70/B4 Mahād, India
79/X15 Mahaena, FrPol.
92/G2 Mahaica, Guy.
89/H6 Mahajamba (bay), Madg.
89/H7 Mahajamba (riv.), Madg.
89/H6 Mahajanga (prov.), Madg.
89/H7 Mahajilo (riv.), Madg.
73/E3 Mahakam (riv.), Indo.
87/E5 Mahalapye, Bots.
60/F2 Mahallāt, Iran
61/G2 Māhān, Iran
70/D3 Mahānadī (riv.), India
84/D4 Mahandiabani (riv.), IvC.
70/C2 Mahārajpur, India
70/B3 Mahārāshtra (state), India
70/D3 Mahāsamund, India
69/C2 Maha Sarakham, Thai.
89/H7 Mahavavy (riv.), Madg.
70/C4 Mahbubnagar, India
61/L2 Mahe, India
81/H5 Mahé (isl.), Sey.
89/S15 Mahébourg, Mrts.
75/S10 Mahia (pen.), NZ
71/G3 Mahlaing, Burma
81/V18 Mahmel (peak), Alg.
70/C2 Mahoba, India
47/H3 Mahón, Sp.
70/B3 Mahuva, India
115/F4 Mahwah, NJ,US
76/E6 Maiala Nat'l Park, Austl.
78/G4 Maiana (atoll), Kiri.
79/W15 Maiao (isl.), FrPol.
92/D1 Maicao, Col.
93/H3 Maicuru (riv.), Braz.
35/F3 Maidenhead, Eng,UK
34/D5 Maiden Newton, Eng,UK
32/D1 Maidens, Sc,UK
116/G7 Maidstone, On,Can
106/F2 Maidstone, Sk,Can
35/G4 Maidstone, Eng,UK
82/H5 Maiduguri, Nga.
42/B4 Maignelay-Montigny, Fr.
36/A4 Maigue (riv.), Ire.
70/D3 Maihar, India
64/E3 Maihara, Japan
83/L8 Maiko Nat'l Park, Zaire
104/V13 Maili, Hi,US
61/K3 Mailsi, Pak.
45/H2 Main (riv.), Ger.
32/B2 Main (riv.), NI,UK
74/G6 Main Barrier (range), Austl.
31/U11 Maincy, Fr.
87/C1 Mai-Ndombe (lake), Zaire
111/G3 Maine (gulf), Can., US
44/C2 Maine (hills), Fr.
36/A4 Maine (riv.), Ire.
111/G2 Maine (state), US
76/C5 Main Range Nat'l Park, Austl.
45/H2 Mainz, Ger.
80/K10 Maio (isl.), CpV.
96/C2 Maipo (vol.), Arg., Chile
96/Q9 Maipo (riv.), Chile
96/F3 Maipú, Arg.
96/C2 Maipú, Chile
45/G4 Maira (riv.), It.
94/B3 Mairi, Braz.
95/G8 Mairiporã, Braz.
101/G3 Maisí (cape), Cuba
31/T10 Maisons-Alfort, Fr.
31/S10 Maisons-Laffitte, Fr.
110/D3 Maitland (riv.), On,Can
43/F5 Maizières-lès-Metz, Fr.
64/D3 Maizuru, Japan
47/N9 Majadahonda, Sp.
49/G2 Maja e Zezë (peak), Alb.
81/W17 Majardah (mts.), Alg., Tun.
81/W17 Majardah (riv.), Tun.
50/E3 Majdanpek, Yugo.
82/J2 Majdūl, Libya
73/E4 Majene, Indo.
83/N6 Majī, Eth.
66/D3 Majia (riv.), China
47/G3 Majorca (Mallorca) (isl.), Sp.
78/G4 Majuro (atoll), Mrsh.
87/B1 Makabana, Congo
104/V13 Makaha, Hi,US
104/V13 Makakilo City, Hi,US
63/N2 Makarov, Rus.
50/C4 Makarska, Cro.
72/E4 Makassar (str.), Indo.
79/L6 Makatea (isl.), FrPol.
89/H8 Makay (massif), Madg.
79/L6 Makemo (atoll), FrPol.
84/B4 Makeni, SLeo.
54/F2 Makeyevka, Ukr.
87/D5 Makgadikgadi (salt pans), Bots.
55/H4 Makhachkala, Rus.
73/G3 Makian (isl.), Indo.
78/G4 Makin (atoll), Kiri.
68/B1 Makinsk, Kaz.
60/C4 Makkah (Mecca), SAr.
50/E2 Makó, Hun.
82/H7 Makokou, Gabon
39/L2 Maków Mazowiecki, Pol.
61/H3 Makran (reg.), Iran, Pak.
61/K3 Makrāna, India
59/F2 Mākū, Iran
87/F2 Makumbako, Tanz.
64/B5 Makurazaki, Japan
114/E5 Makushin (vol.), Ak,US
92/C6 Mala, Peru
70/B5 Malabar (coast), India
82/G7 Malabo (cap.), EqG.
95/D1 Malacacheta, Braz.
69/B5 Malacca (str.), Malay., Thai.
39/J4 Malacky, Slvk.
106/E5 Malad City, Id,US
46/C4 Málaga, Sp.
46/D3 Malagón, Sp.
32/B5 Malahide, Ire.
78/F5 Malaita (isl.), Sol.
83/M6 Malakāl, Sudan
70/D4 Malakangiri, India
101/G5 Malambo, Col.
72/D5 Malang, Indo.
87/C2 Malange, Ang.
96/C2 Malargüe, Arg.
110/E1 Malartic, Qu,Can
73/E5 Malasoro (pt.), Indo.
59/D2 Malatya, Turk.
87/F3 Malawi
69/B5 Malay (pen.), Malay.
52/G4 Malaya Vishera, Rus.
67/E6 Malaybalay, Phil.
60/E2 Malāyer, Iran
72/C2 Malaysia
53/L2 Malazemel'skaya (tundra), Rus.
59/E2 Malazgirt, Turk.
111/G2 Malbaie (riv.), Qu,Can
85/G3 Malbaza-Usine, Niger
39/K1 Malbork, Pol.
44/D5 Malcaras, Pic de (peak), Fr.
38/G2 Malchin, Ger.
62/C2 Malchin, Mong.
42/C1 Maldegem, Belg.
79/K5 Malden (isl.), Kiri.
110/B4 Malden, Mo,US
58/G9 Maldives
35/G3 Maldon, Eng,UK
97/G2 Maldonado, Uru.
97/G2 Maldonado (dept.), Uru.
58/G9 Male (cap.), Mald.
49/H4 Maléa, Ákra (cape), Gre.
70/B3 Mālegaon, India
78/F6 Malekula (isl.), Van.
44/D4 Malemort-sur-Corrèze, Fr.
38/F1 Malente, Ger.
61/L2 Māler Kotla, India
55/H4 Malgobek, Rus.
47/G2 Malgrat de Mar, Sp.
83/L4 Malha Wells, Sudan
106/D5 Malheur (lake), Or,US
106/D5 Malheur (riv.), Or,US
89/S14 Malheureux (cape), Mrts.
84/E2 Mali
69/B3 Mali (isl.), Burma
62/F4 Malian (riv.), China
115/B2 Malibu, Ca,US
83/L4 Malik (wadi), Sudan
54/D2 Malin, Ukr.
73/E3 Malinau, Indo.
87/H1 Malindi, Kenya
42/D1 Malines (Mechelen), Belg.
66/C3 Maling Guan (pass), China
89/H8 Malio (riv.), Madg.
69/D1 Malipo, China
61/J4 Malīr Cantonment, Pak.
67/E6 Malita, Phil.
83/P7 Malka Mari Nat'l Park, Kenya
51/H5 Malkara, Turk.
85/H3 Mallammaduri, Nga.
81/W17 Mallāq, Wādī (riv.), Tun.
86/B3 Mallawī, Egypt
77/B2 Mallee Cliffs Nat'l Park, Austl.
96/Q10 Malleco, Chile
47/G3 Mallorca (Majorca) (isl.), Sp.
36/A4 Mallow, Ire.
37/G2 Malmberget, Swe.
43/F3 Malmédy, Belg.
88/B4 Malmesbury, SAfr.
34/D3 Malmesbury, Eng,UK
38/G1 Malmö, Swe.
39/G1 Malmöhus (co.), Swe.
53/L4 Malmyzh, Rus.
93/H5 Maloca, Braz.
78/G4 Maloelap (atoll), Mrsh.
110/F2 Malone, NY,US
39/L3 Małopolska (upland), Pol.
37/C3 Måløy, Nor.
33/F5 Malpas, Eng,UK
92/B3 Malpelo (isl.), Col.
46/A1 Malpica, Sp.
48/D5 Malta
48/D5 Malta (isl.), Malta
106/G3 Malta, Mt,US
33/G2 Maltby, Eng,UK
33/G5 Maltby, Eng,UK
111/Q8 Malton, On,Can
33/H3 Malton, Eng,UK
87/C1 Maluku, Zaire
37/E3 Malung, Swe.
70/B4 Malvan, India
47/P10 Malveira, Port.
77/G5 Malvern, Austl.
112/E3 Malvern, Ar,US
34/D2 Malvern (Great Malvern), Eng,UK
97/M8 Malvinas, Islas (Falkland Islands) (dpcy.), UK
55/J2 Malyy Uzen' (riv.), Kaz.
62/D1 Malyy Yenisey (riv.), Rus.
43/F6 Malzéville, Fr.
94/D2 Mamanguape, Braz.
115/G5 Mamaroneck, NY,US
87/E4 Mamba, Zam.
67/D6 Mambajao, Phil.
83/L7 Mambasa, Zaire
73/J4 Mamberamo (riv.), Indo.
82/J6 Mambéré (riv.), CAfr.
59/D3 Mambij, Syria
67/D5 Mamburao, Phil.
43/F4 Mamer, Lux.
44/D2 Mamers, Fr.
42/B2 Mametz, Fr.
85/H5 Mamfé, Camr.
110/C4 Mammoth Cave Nat'l Park, Ky,US
113/F2 Mammoth Spring, Ar,US
92/E6 Mamoré (riv.), Bol.
85/E5 Mampong, Gha.
39/L1 Mamry (lake), Pol.
73/E4 Mamuju, Indo.
87/D5 Mamuno, Bots.
93/G4 Mamuri (riv.), Braz.
66/C5 Man (riv.), China
84/D5 Man, IvC.
92/F4 Manacapuru, Braz.
34/A6 Manacle (pt.), UK
47/G3 Manacor, Sp.
73/F3 Manado, Indo.
100/D5 Managua (cap.), Nic.
100/D5 Managua (lake), Nic.
89/J8 Manakara, Madg.
115/F5 Manalapan, NJ,US
60/F3 Manama (Al Manāmah) (cap.), Bahr.
89/H7 Manambaho (riv.), Madg.
89/H7 Manambolo (riv.), Madg.
89/J7 Mananara, Madg.
89/H8 Mananara (riv.), Madg.
89/J8 Mananjary, Madg.
89/H8 Mananjary (riv.), Madg.
68/D2 Manas (lake), China
68/E3 Manas (riv.), China
70/D2 Manāslu (mtn.), Nepal
115/F5 Manasquan, NJ,US
115/F5 Manasquan (riv.), NJ,US
109/F3 Manassa, Co,US
110/E4 Manassas, Va,US
49/G1 Manastir Dečani, Yugo.
49/G1 Manastir Gračanica, Yugo.
49/G1 Manastir Sopoćani, Yugo.
65/H7 Manatsuru, Japan
92/F4 Manaus, Braz.
59/B3 Manavgat, Turk.
107/H2 Manawan (lake), Sk,Can
65/H7 Manazuru-misaki (cape), Japan
32/D3 Man, Calf of (isl.), IM,UK
46/D4 Mancha Real, Sp.
70/C4 Mancherāl, India
76/E6 Manchester (lake), Austl.
33/F5 Manchester, Eng,UK
110/D4 Manchester, Ky,US
111/G3 Manchester, NH,US
113/G3 Manchester, Tn,US
63/J3 Manchuria (reg.), China
60/F3 Mand (riv.), Iran
87/F3 Manda, Tanz.
95/B2 Mandaguari, Braz.
37/C4 Mandal, Nor.
73/K4 Mandala (peak), Indo.
69/B1 Mandalay, Burma
69/A1 Mandalay (div.), Burma
57/L5 Mandalgovĭ, Mong.
60/E2 Mandalī, Iraq
107/H4 Mandan, ND,US
83/J6 Manda Nat'l Park, Chad
66/D4 Mandang Shan (mtn.), China
73/F5 Mandasavu (peak), Indo.
67/D5 Mandaue, Phil.
81/G3 Mandeb, BAb el (str.), Afr., Asia
45/H4 Mandello del Lario, It.
43/F3 Manderscheid, Ger.
101/F4 Mandeville, Jam.
61/L2 Mandi, India
87/F4 Mandié, Moz.
73/G4 Mandiola (isl.), Indo.
70/D3 Mandla, India
38/E1 Mandø (isl.), Den.
49/L6 Mándra, Gre.
89/H9 Mandrare (riv.), Madg.
89/J6 Mandritsara, Madg.
70/C3 Mandsaur, India
74/B6 Mandurah, Austl.
49/E2 Manduria, It.
70/A3 Māndvi, India
70/C3 Māndya, India
70/D2 Mane (pass), Nepal
35/G2 Manea, Eng,UK
70/D3 Manendragarh, India
85/H5 Manéngouba, Massif du (peak), Camr.
45/J4 Manerbio, It.
60/B3 Manfalūt, Egypt
48/D2 Manfredonia, It.
48/E2 Manfredonia (gulf), It.
66/B4 Mang (riv.), China
94/B4 Manga, Braz.
94/A3 Mangabeiras (hills), Braz.
87/C1 Mangai, Zaire
79/K7 Mangaia (isl.), Cookls.
71/F2 Mangaldai, India
67/D4 Mangaldan, Phil.
51/J4 Mangalia, Rom.
70/B5 Mangalore, India
79/M7 Mangareva (isl.), FrPol.
55/K4 Mangistau Obl., Kaz.
73/E3 Mangkalihat (cape), Indo.
61/K2 Mangla, Pak.
92/C3 Manglares (pt.), Col.
85/F4 Mango, Togo
87/G3 Mangoche, Malw.
89/H8 Mangoky (riv.), Madg.
73/G4 Mangole (isl.), Indo.
89/J7 Mangoro (riv.), Madg.
34/D4 Mangotsfield, Eng,UK
70/B3 Mangrol, India
97/G2 Mangueira (lake), Braz.
109/H4 Mangum, Ok,US
55/J3 Mangyshlak (pen.), Kaz.
55/K4 Mangyshlak (plat.), Kaz.
109/H3 Manhattan, Ks,US
106/F4 Manhattan, Mt,US
115/B3 Manhattan Beach, Ca,US
95/D2 Manhuaçu, Braz.
95/D2 Manhumirim, Braz.
49/H4 Máni (pen.), Gre.
89/H7 Mania (riv.), Madg.
87/F4 Manica, Moz.
92/F5 Manicoré, Braz.
92/F5 Manicoré (riv.), Braz.
107/J3 Manicouagan, Mb,Can
111/G1 Manicouagan (res.), Qu,Can
111/G1 Manicouagan (riv.), Qu,Can
111/H1 Manicouagan, Petit Lac (lake), Qu,Can
76/C3 Manifold (cape), Austl.
79/L6 Manihi (isl.), FrPol.
79/J6 Manihiki (atoll), Cookls.
67/D5 Manila (cap.), Phil.
108/E2 Manila, Ut,US
89/J7 Maningory (riv.), Madg.
73/G4 Manipa (str.), Indo.
71/F3 Manipur (state), India
59/A2 Manisa, Turk.
32/D3 Man, Isle of (isl.), UK
110/C2 Manistee, Mi,US
110/C2 Manistee (riv.), Mi,US
102/G3 Manitoba (prov.), Can.
107/J3 Manitoba (lake), Mb,Can
111/H1 Manitou (riv.), Qu,Can
110/D2 Manitoulin (isl.), On,Can
112/B2 Manitou Springs, Co,US
110/C1 Manitouwadge, On,Can
110/C2 Manitowoc, Wi,US
110/F2 Maniwaki, Qu,Can
92/C2 Manizales, Col.
70/C4 Manjlegaon, India
61/L5 Mānjra (riv.), India
107/K4 Mankato, Mn,US
84/D4 Mankono, IvC.
62/F3 Manlay, Mong.
46/D2 Manlleu, Sp.
76/H8 Manly, Austl.
70/B3 Manmād, India
69/B4 Man Mia (peak), Thai.
70/C6 Mannar (gulf), India, SrL.
70/C6 Mannar, SrL.
70/C5 Mannārgudi, India
88/C4 Mannetjiesberg (peak), SAfr.
45/H2 Mannheim, Ger.
103/Q7 Manning (cape), NW,Can
113/H3 Manning, SC,US
35/H3 Manningtree, Eng,UK
84/C5 Mano (riv.), Libr., SLeo.
87/E2 Manono, Zaire
115/H5 Manorville, NY,US
44/F5 Manosque, Fr.
111/G1 Manouane (lake), Qu,Can
111/G1 Manouane (riv.), Qu,Can
79/H5 Manra (Sydney) (atoll), Kiri.
47/F2 Manresa, Sp.
87/E3 Mansa, Zam.
84/B3 Mansa Konko, Gam.
73/F1 Mansalay, Phil.
103/H2 Mansel (isl.), NW,Can
33/G5 Mansfield, Eng,UK
112/E3 Mansfield, La,US
110/D3 Mansfield, Oh,US
33/G5 Mansfield Woodhouse, Eng,UK
92/B4 Manta, Ecu.
73/E2 Mantalingaian (mt.), Phil.
92/C6 Mantaro (riv.), Peru
108/B3 Manteca, Ca,US
95/D1 Mantena, Braz.
42/A6 Mantes-la-Jolie, Fr.
42/A6 Mantes-la-Ville, Fr.
70/C4 Manthani, India
108/E3 Manti, Ut,US
115/G5 Manticock (pt.), NY,US
95/C2 Mantiquiera (range), Braz.
66/C3 Mantou Shan (mtn.), China
45/J4 Mantova, It.
100/E3 Mantua, Cuba
53/K4 Manturovo, Rus.
37/H3 Mäntyharju, Fin.
92/E6 Manú (riv.), Peru
79/J6 Manua (isls.), ASam.
79/K6 Manuae (atoll), Cookls.
104/W13 Manuawili, Hi,US
93/J6 Manuel Alves (riv.), Braz.
72/C5 Manuk (riv.), Indo.
75/R10 Manukau, NZ
92/D6 Manú Nat'l Park, Peru
92/E6 Manuripe (riv.), Bol.
78/D5 Manus (isl.), PNG
115/F5 Manville, NJ,US
112/E4 Many, La,US
55/G3 Manych (riv.), Rus.
55/G3 Manych-Gudilo (lake), Rus.
108/E3 Many Farms, Az,US
87/F2 Manyoni, Tanz.
46/D3 Manzanares, Sp.
47/N8 Manzanares (riv.), Sp.
101/P10 Manzanillo, Mex.
112/B3 Manzano (mts.), NM,US
63/H2 Manzhouli, China
86/C2 Manzilah, Buḩayat al (lake), Egypt
81/W17 Manzil bū Ruqaybah, Tun.
81/X17 Manzil Tamīn, Tun.
89/E2 Manzini, Swaz.
101/G4 Mao, DRep.
73/J4 Maoke (mts.), Indo.
67/B3 Maoming, China
68/D5 Mapam (lake), China
100/C4 Mapastepec, Mex.
101/P8 Mapimí, Bolsón de (val.), Mex.
111/Q8 Maple, On,Can
107/K5 Maple (riv.), Ia,US
107/J4 Maple (riv.), ND,US
106/F3 Maple Creek, Sk,Can
115/F6 Maple Shade, NJ,US
115/F5 Maplewood, NJ,US
74/G2 Mapoon Mission Sta., Austl.
92/G4 Mapuera (riv.), Braz.
70/B4 Mapusa, India
89/F2 Maputo (cap.), Moz.
86/D5 Maqdam, Ras (cape), Sudan
61/J2 Maqor, Afg.
68/D5 Maquan (riv.), China
87/C2 Maquela do Zombo, Ang.
109/K2 Maquoketa (riv.), Ia,US
95/B3 Mar (range), Braz.
93/J5 Marabá, Braz.
93/J3 Maracá (isl.), Braz.
101/G5 Maracaibo, Ven.
101/G6 Maracaibo (lake), Ven.
93/H7 Maracaju (mts.), Braz.
94/B4 Maracás, Braz.
94/B4 Maracás (hills), Braz.
101/H5 Maracay, Ven.
46/D4 Maracena, Sp.
85/G3 Maradi, Niger
85/G3 Maradi (dept.), Niger
60/E1 Marāgheh, Iran
92/E3 Marahuaca (peak), Ven.
109/J3 Marais des Cygnes (riv.), Ks, Mo,US
93/J4 Marajó, Braz.
93/J4 Marajó (bay), Braz.
90/D3 Marajó (isl.), Braz.
67/E6 Maramag, Phil.
95/K8 Marambaia (isl.), Braz.
113/F2 Maramec (riv.), Mo,US
51/F2 Maramureş (co.), Rom.
108/E4 Marana, Az,US
94/C1 Maranguape, Braz.
94/A4 Maranhão (riv.), Braz.
94/A2 Maranhão (state), Braz.
76/C4 Maranoa (riv.), Austl.
92/C4 Marañón (riv.), Peru
84/D5 Maraoue Nat'l Park, IvC.
72/B4 Marapi (peak), Indo.
72/C4 Maras (peak), Indo.
51/H3 Mărăşeşti, Rom.
110/C1 Marathon, On,Can
113/H5 Marathon, Fl,US
112/C4 Marathon, Tx,US
95/A4 Marau, Braz.
67/D6 Marawi, Phil.
86/B5 Marawī, Sudan
34/A6 Marazion, Eng,UK
46/C4 Marbella, Sp.
106/F5 Marbleton, Wy,US
38/E3 Marburg, Ger.
50/C2 Marcali, Hun.
87/B4 Marca, Ponta da (pt.), Ang.
35/G1 March, Eng,UK
44/D3 Marche (mts.), Fr.
45/K5 Marche (reg.), It.
43/E3 Marche-en-Famenne, Belg.
46/C4 Marchena, Sp.
91/D3 Mar Chiquita (lake), Arg.
42/A2 Marck, Fr.
113/H5 Marco, Fl,US
92/C7 Marcona, Peru
106/E3 Marconi (peak), BC,Can
96/E2 Marcos Juárez, Arg.
42/C2 Marcq-en-Baroeul, Fr.
114/J3 Marcus Baker (mtn.), Ak,US
110/F2 Marcy (peak), NY,US
61/K2 Mardān, Pak.
97/F3 Mar del Plata, Arg.
35/G4 Marden, Eng,UK
59/E3 Mardin, Turk.
79/W12 Maré (isl.), NCal.
76/B2 Mareeba, Austl.
36/C2 Maree, Loch (lake), Sc,UK
33/H5 Mareham le Fen, Eng,UK
35/G5 Maresfield, Eng,UK
112/B4 Marfa, Tx,US
34/C3 Margam, Wal,UK
54/E3 Marganets, Ukr.
70/B4 Margao, India
101/J5 Margarita (isl.), Ven.
35/H4 Margate, Eng,UK
44/E4 Margeride (mts.), Fr.
83/L7 Margherita (peak), Ugan.
50/F2 Marghita, Rom.
68/B3 Margilan, Uzb.
68/E5 Margog Caka (lake), China
67/D6 Margosatubig, Phil.
43/E2 Margraten, Neth.
98/V Marguerite (bay), Ant.
77/D4 Maria (peak), Austl.
79/K7 Maria (isl.), FrPol.
77/D4 Maria Island Nat'l Park, Austl.
113/F3 Marianna, Ar,US
113/G4 Marianna, Fl,US
100/E3 Mariano, Cuba
45/K2 Mariánské Lázně (Marienbad), Czh.
106/F3 Marias (riv.), Mt,US
50/B2 Maribor, Slov.
95/L7 Maricá, Braz.
92/E4 Marié (riv.), Braz.
98/S Marie Byrd Land (reg.), Ant.
101/J4 Marie-Galante (isl.), Guad.
37/F3 Mariehamn, Fin.
45/K2 Marienbad (Mariánské Lázně), Czh.
41/E6 Marienheide, Ger.
37/E4 Mariestad, Swe.
113/G3 Marietta, Ga,US
110/D4 Marietta, Oh,US
44/F5 Marignane, Fr.
95/B2 Marília, Braz.
46/A1 Marín, Sp.
115/B3 Marina del Rey, Ca,US

147

Marin – Middl

31/R9 Marines, Fr.
110/C2 Marinette, Wi,US
95/B2 Maringá, Braz.
46/A3 Marinha Grande, Port.
75/J3 Marion (reef), Austl.
113/G3 Marion, Al,US
110/B4 Marion, Il,US
110/C3 Marion, In,US
110/B4 Marion, Ky,US
110/C2 Marion, Mi,US
110/D3 Marion, Oh,US
113/H3 Marion (lake), SC,US
110/D4 Marion, Va,US
108/C3 Mariposa, Ca,US
51/H5 Maritsa (riv.), Bul., Turk.
54/F3 Mariupol', Ukr.
53/K4 Mariy Aut. Rep., Rus.
59/K5 Marj 'Uyūn, Leb.
40/B6 Mark (riv.), Belg.
62/B2 Markakol (lake), Kaz.
83/P7 Marka (Merca), Som.
37/E4 Markaryd, Swe.
40/C4 Marken (isl.), Neth.
40/C4 Markerwaard (polder), Neth.
35/E1 Market Bosworth, Eng,UK
35/F1 Market Deeping, Eng,UK
33/F6 Market Drayton, Eng,UK
35/F2 Market Harborough, Eng,UK
32/B3 Markethill, NI,UK
33/H5 Market Rasen, Eng,UK
33/H4 Market Weighton, Eng,UK
103/J2 Markham (bay), NW,Can
111/R8 Markham, On,Can
39/L2 Marki, Pol.
108/C3 Markleeville, Ca,US
49/L7 Markópoulon, Gre.
55/H2 Marks, Rus.
112/E4 Marksville, La,US
45/K2 Marktredwitz, Ger.
109/J3 Mark Twain (lake), Mo,US
41/E5 Marl, Ger.
115/F5 Marlboro, NJ,US
35/E4 Marlborough, Eng,UK
42/B3 Marles-les-Mines, Fr.
35/F3 Marlow, Eng,UK
115/F6 Marlton, NJ,US
42/C3 Marly, Fr.
31/T9 Marly-la-Ville, Fr.
31/S10 Marly-le-Roi, Fr.
43/F5 Marly-sur-Seille, Fr.
44/D4 Marmande, Fr.
51/H5 Marmara (isl.), Turk.
51/J5 Marmara (sea), Turk.
59/B3 Marmaris, Turk.
92/F5 Marmelos (riv.), Braz.
74/C5 Marmion (lake), Austl.
110/A1 Marmion (lake), On,Can
45/J3 Marmolada (peak), It.
46/C3 Marmolejo, Sp.
42/C6 Marne (dept.), Fr.
44/E2 Marne (riv.), Fr.
43/D6 Marne au Rhin, Canal de la (can.), Fr.
34/D5 Marnhull, Eng,UK
82/J6 Maro, Chad
79/H2 Maro (reef), Hi,US
89/J6 Maroantsetra, Madg.
79/L6 Marokau (atoll), FrPol.
81/G7 Marolambo, Madg.
31/S11 Marolles-en-Hurepoix, Fr.
89/J6 Maromokotro (peak), Madg.
87/F4 Marondera, Zim.
93/H3 Maroni (riv.), FrG., Sur.
76/D4 Maroochydore-Mooloolaba, Austl.
82/H5 Maroua, Camr.
89/H7 Marovoay, Madg.
43/G5 Marpingen, Ger.
33/F5 Marple, Eng,UK
62/D5 Marqên Gangri (peak), China
78/D8 Marquarie (riv.), Austl.
79/M5 Marquesas (isls.), FrPol.
110/C2 Marquette, Mi,US
83/K5 Marrah (mts.), Sudan
82/D1 Marrakech, Mor.
83/N7 Marsabit, Kenya
48/C4 Marsala, It.
83/L1 Marsá Maṭrūḥ, Egypt
31/U10 Marsange (riv.), Fr.
41/F6 Marsberg, Ger.
48/C1 Marsciano, It.
33/G4 Marsden, Eng,UK
40/B3 Marsdiep (chan.), Neth.
44/F5 Marseille, Fr.
112/E4 Marsh (isl.), La,US
106/F2 Marshall, Sk,Can
107/K4 Marshall, Mn,US
109/J3 Marshall, Mo,US
112/E3 Marshall, Tx,US
78/G3 Marshall Islands
107/K5 Marshalltown, Ia,US
109/J3 Marshfield, Mo,US
110/B2 Marshfield, Wi,US
35/E3 Marsh Gibbon, Eng,UK
33/G2 Marske-by-the-Sea, Eng,UK
69/B2 Martaban (gulf), Burma
106/G2 Martensville, Sk,Can
111/G3 Martha's Vineyard (isl.), Ma,US
45/G3 Martigny, Swi.
44/F5 Martigues, Fr.
98/S Martin (pen.), Ant.
39/K4 Martin, Slvk.
113/G3 Martin (lake), Al,US
107/H5 Martin, SD,US
113/F2 Martin, Tn,US
48/E2 Martina Franca, It.
116/K10 Martinez, Ca,US
113/H3 Martinez, Ga,US
100/B3 Martínez de la Torre, Mex.
101/J4 Martinique (passage), Dom., Mart.
101/J5 Martinique (isl.), Fr.
95/B2 Martinópolis, Braz.
110/E4 Martinsburg, WV,US
110/C4 Martinsville, In,US
110/E4 Martinsville, Va,US
28/H7 Martin Vaz (isls.), Braz.
34/D2 Martley, Eng,UK
34/D5 Martock, Eng,UK
47/F2 Martorell, Sp.
46/D4 Martos, Sp.
110/F1 Martre (riv.), Qu,Can
107/J5 Marty, SD,US
64/C3 Marugame, Japan
65/F2 Maruko, Japan
40/D2 Marum, Neth.
64/E2 Maruoka, Japan
79/M7 Marutea (atoll), FrPol.
65/H7 Maruyama, Japan
60/F3 Marv Dasht, Iran
76/D4 Mary (riv.), Austl.
61/H1 Mary, Trkm.
76/D4 Maryborough, Austl.
77/B3 Maryborough, Austl.
113/G4 Mary Esther, Fl,US
107/H3 Maryfield, Sk,Can
84/C5 Maryland (co.), Libr.
110/E4 Maryland (state), US
115/K7 Maryland City, Md,US
32/E2 Maryport, Eng,UK
111/L2 Marystown, Nf,Can
109/H3 Marysville, Ks,US
116/H6 Marysville, Mi,US
116/C1 Marysville, Wa,US
109/J2 Maryville, Mo,US
113/H3 Maryville, Tn,US
48/D2 Marzano (peak), It.
82/H2 Marzūq, Libya
82/H3 Marzūq, Ṣḥrā (des.), Libya
59/K6 Masada (Ḥorvot Meẓada) (ruins), Isr.
87/G1 Masai Steppe (grsld.), Tanz.
83/M8 Masaka, Ugan.
81/X18 Masākin, Tun.
47/E3 Masamagrell, Sp.
73/F4 Masamba, Indo.
64/A3 Masan, SKor.
87/G3 Masasi, Tanz.
100/D5 Masaya, Nic.
67/D5 Masbate, Phil.
67/D5 Masbate (isl.), Phil.
81/R16 Mascara, Alg.
89/S15 Mascarene (isls.), Mrts., Reun.
101/P9 Mascota, Mex.
111/N6 Mascouche, Qu,Can
88/D3 Maseru (cap.), Les.
58/E6 Mashad, Iran
33/G3 Masham, Eng,UK
61/G1 Mashhad, Iran
61/H3 Māshkel, Hāmūn-i- (lake), Pak.
61/H3 Māshkīd (riv.), Iran
55/L1 Masim (peak), Rus.
61/G5 Masira (gulf), Oman
61/G4 Maṣīrah (isl.), Oman
60/E2 Masjed-e Soleymān, Iran
36/A4 Mask, Lough (lake), Ire.
89/J6 Masoala (cape), Madg.
89/J6 Masoala (pen.), Madg.
110/C3 Mason, Mi,US
112/D4 Mason, Tx,US
116/A3 Mason (lake), Wa,US
107/K5 Mason City, Ia,US
47/X17 Maspalomas, Canl.,Sp.
47/K6 Masquefa, Sp.
45/J4 Massa, It.
111/F3 Massachusetts (state), US
111/G3 Massachusetts (bay), Ma,US
48/E2 Massafra, It.
94/B1 Massapê, Braz.
115/G5 Massapequa, NY,US
110/F2 Massena, NY,US
103/S7 Massey (sound), NW,Can
87/D3 Massibi, Ang.
44/E4 Massif Central (plat.), Fr.
110/D3 Massillon, Oh,US
98/G Masson (isl.), Ant.
31/S10 Massy, Fr.
75/S11 Masterton, NZ
40/B5 Mastgat (chan.), Neth.
115/H5 Mastic, NY,US
61/J3 Mastung, Pak.
64/B3 Masuda, Japan
72/B4 Masurai (peak), Indo.
87/F5 Masvingo, Zim.
59/L4 Maṣyāf, Syria
43/F2 Mat (riv.), Alb.
87/B2 Matadi, Zaire
112/C3 Matador, Tx,US
100/D5 Matagalpa, Nic.
110/E1 Matagami (lake), Qu,Can
112/D4 Matagorda (bay), Tx,US
112/D4 Matagorda (isl.), Tx,US
70/D6 Matale, SrL.
84/B3 Matam, Sen.
100/A2 Matamoros, Mex.
100/B2 Matamoros, Mex.
83/K3 Ma'ṭan as Sarra (well), Libya
111/H1 Matane, Qu,Can
111/H1 Matane (riv.), Qu,Can
100/E3 Matanzas, Cuba
95/B2 Matão, Braz.
111/H1 Matapedia (riv.), Qu,Can
96/C2 Mataquito (riv.), Chile
60/C6 Matara (ruins), Egypt
70/D6 Matara, SrL.
73/E5 Mataram, Indo.
47/G2 Mataró, Sp.
79/L7 Mataura, FrPol.
78/H6 Mata Utu (cap.), Wall.
115/F5 Matawan, NJ,US
100/A3 Matehuala, Mex.
48/E2 Matera, It.
101/F3 Maternillos (pt.), Cuba
50/F2 Mátészalka, Hun.
115/C3 Mathews (lake), Ca,US
112/D4 Mathis, Tx,US
70/C2 Mathurā, India
67/E5 Mati, Phil.
95/K6 Matias Barbosa, Braz.
100/B4 Matías Romero, Mex.
81/W17 Mātir, Tun.
33/G5 Matlock, Eng,UK
92/G7 Mato Grosso, Braz.
93/G6 Mato Grosso (plat.), Braz.
95/A1 Mato Grosso do Sul (state), Braz.
87/E5 Matopos, Zim.
46/A2 Matosinhos, Port.
94/B4 Mato Verde, Braz.
61/G4 Maṭraḥ, Oman
94/D3 Matriz de Camaragibe, Braz.
88/B4 Matroosberg (peak), SAfr.
86/A2 Maṭrūḥ, Egypt
86/B2 Maṭrūḥ (gov.), Egypt
89/H8 Matsiatra (riv.), Madg.
65/L10 Matsubara, Japan
65/H7 Matsubushi, Japan
65/H7 Matsuda, Japan
65/H7 Matsudo, Japan
64/C3 Matsue, Japan
63/N3 Matsumae, Japan
65/E2 Matsumoto, Japan
64/E3 Matsusaka, Japan
65/G1 Matsushima, Japan
64/E2 Matsutō, Japan
64/C4 Matsuyama, Japan
110/D1 Mattagami (riv.), On,Can
110/E2 Mattawa, On,Can
45/G4 Matterhorn (pk.), It., Swi.
116/Q16 Matteson, Il,US
114/H2 Matthews (mtn.), Ak,US
101/G3 Matthew Town, Bahm.
64/E2 Mattō, Japan
32/B4 Mattock (riv.), Ire.
110/B4 Mattoon, Il,US
101/J6 Maturín, Ven.
87/E4 Matusadona Nat'l Park, Zim.
73/F2 Matutum (mt.), Phil.
92/G3 Maú (riv.), Braz., Guy.
95/C2 Mauá, Braz.
42/C3 Maubeuge, Fr.
71/G4 Ma-ubin, Burma
36/D2 Maud, Sc,UK
70/D2 Maudaha, India
92/G4 Maués, Braz.
92/G4 Maués Açu (riv.), Braz.
78/D3 Maug (isls.), NMar.
32/D3 Maughold, IM,UK
32/D3 Maughold Head (pt.), IM,UK
44/F5 Mauguio, Fr.
104/T10 Maui (isl.), Hi,US
79/K7 Mauke (isl.), CookIs.
42/A6 Mauldre (riv.), Fr.
96/B2 Maule (reg.), Chile
96/C1 Maule (riv.), Chile
44/C3 Mauléon, Fr.
96/B4 Maullín, Chile
110/C3 Maumee (riv.), In, Oh,US
87/D4 Maun, Bots.
104/U11 Mauna Kea (vol.), Hi,US
104/U11 Mauna Loa (vol.), Hi,US
79/K6 Maupiti (isl.), FrPol.
70/C2 Mau Rānīpur, India
31/S10 Maurecourt, Fr.
42/A6 Maurepas, Fr.
74/E5 Maurice (lake), Austl.
111/F2 Mauricie Nat'l Park, Qu,Can
84/B2 Mauritania
94/C2 Mauriti, Braz.
81/H6 Mauritius
110/B3 Mauston, Wi,US
50/E5 Mavrovo Nat'l Park, Macd.
69/B4 Maw Daung (pass), Thai.
98/D Mawson (coast), Ant.
98/E Mawson (sta.), Ant.
100/D3 Maxcanú, Mex.
43/F6 Maxéville, Fr.
110/F4 May (cape), NJ,US
72/C4 Maya (isl.), Indo.
57/P4 Maya (riv.), Rus.
101/G3 Mayaguana (isl.), Bahm.
101/H4 Mayagüez, PR
61/K1 Mayakovskogo (peak), Taj.
101/F3 Mayarí, Cuba
65/L10 Maya-san (peak), Japan
32/D1 Maybole, Sc,UK
83/N5 Maych'ew, Eth.
43/G3 Mayen, Ger.
44/C2 Mayenne, Fr.
44/C3 Mayenne (riv.), Fr.
106/E2 Mayerthorpe, Ab,Can
110/B4 Mayfield, Ky,US
54/G3 Maykop, Rus.
35/G3 Mayland, Eng,UK
71/G3 Maymyo, Burma
96/C5 Mayo (riv.), Arg.
114/L3 Mayo, Yk,Can
101/N8 Mayo (riv.), Mex.
46/D1 Mayor (cape), Sp.
89/H6 Mayotte (terr.), Fr.
101/F4 May Pen, Jam.
110/D4 Maysville, Ky,US
107/J4 Mayville, ND,US
116/Q16 Maywood, Il,US
87/E4 Mazabuka, Zam.
44/E5 Mazamet, Fr.
48/C4 Mazara (val.), It.
48/C4 Mazara del Vallo, It.
61/J1 Mazār-e Sharīf, Afg.
46/A1 Mazaricos, Sp.
46/E4 Mazarrón, Sp.
92/G2 Mazaruni (riv.), Guy.
100/C5 Mazatenango, Guat.
101/N9 Mazatlán, Mex.
52/D4 Mažeikiai, Lith.
76/B3 Mazeppa Nat'l Park, Austl.
32/B3 Mazetown, NI,UK
42/B3 Mazingarbe, Fr.
87/C2 Mazingu, Zaire
62/D3 Mazong (peak), China
39/L2 Mazury (reg.), Pol.
86/C2 Ma'ān, Jor.
89/E2 Mbabane (cap.), Swaz.
82/H6 Mbabo (peak), Camr.
82/J7 Mbaïki, CAfr.
83/H6 Mbakaou (lake), Camr.
87/F2 Mbala, Zam.
82/H7 Mbalam, Camr.
83/M7 Mbale, Ugan.
82/H7 Mbalmayo, Camr.
85/H6 Mbam (riv.), Camr.
85/H5 Mbam, Massif du (peak), Camr.
83/J7 Mbandaka, Zaire
83/M8 Mbarara, Ugan.
83/J7 Mbata, CAfr.
79/Y18 Mbengga (isl.), Fiji
87/F2 Mbeya, Tanz.
87/F2 Mbeya (range), Tanz.
87/B1 M'Bigou, Gabon
82/G7 Mbini, EqG.
82/H7 Mbini (riv.), EqG.
83/L6 Mbomou (riv.), CAfr.
84/B3 Mboune, Vallée du (wadi), Sen.
84/A3 M'Bour, Sen.
87/D2 Mbuji-Mayi, Zaire
109/J4 McAlester, Ok,US
112/D5 McAllen, Tx,US
106/C2 McBride, BC,Can
106/D4 McCall, Id,US
112/C4 McCamey, Tx,US
116/C3 McChord A.F.B., Wa,US
116/M9 McClellan A.F.B., Ca,US
107/H4 McClusky, ND,US
113/F4 McComb, Ms,US
109/G2 McConaughy (lake), Ne,US
109/G2 McCook, Ne,US
113/H3 McCormick, SC,US
107/J3 McCreary, Mb,Can
108/C2 McDermitt, Nv,US
29/N8 McDonald (isls.), Austl.
114/F3 McDonald (mtn.), Ak,US
114/L2 McDougall (pass), NW, Yk,Can
112/F3 McGehee, Ar,US
113/F3 McGehee, Ar,US
106/C2 McGregor (riv.), BC,Can
116/G7 McGregor, On,Can
116/P15 McHenry, Il,US
79/H5 McKean (atoll), Kiri.
103/K2 McKeand (riv.), NW,Can
110/E3 McKeesport, Pa,US
113/F2 McKenzie, Tn,US
114/H3 McKinley (mtn.), Ak,US
114/J3 McKinley Park, Ak,US
106/B5 McKinleyville, Ca,US
112/D3 McKinney, Tx,US
107/H4 McLaughlin, SD,US
115/J8 McLean, Va,US
106/D2 McLennan, Ab,Can
74/A4 McLeod (lake), Austl.
106/D2 McLeod (riv.), Ab,Can
102/E2 McLeod (bay), NW,Can
106/C2 McLeod Lake, BC,Can
102/F1 M'Clintock (chan.), NW,Can
103/Q7 M'Clure (str.), NW,Can
106/C4 McMinnville, Or,US
113/G3 McMinnville, Tn,US
98/M McMurdo, Ant.
116/B3 McNeil (isl.), Wa,US
87/F3 Mcocha, Malw.
109/H3 McPherson, Ks,US
62/E5 Mê (riv.), China
108/D3 Mead (lake), Az, Nv,US
114/G2 Meade (riv.), Ak,US
106/F2 Meadow Lake, Sk,Can
111/Q8 Meadowvale, On,Can
108/D3 Meadow Valley (riv.), Nv,US
113/F4 Meadville, Ms,US
110/D3 Meadville, Pa,US
94/A1 Mearim (riv.), Braz.
35/E1 Measham, Eng,UK
114/F2 Meat (mtn.), Ak,US
32/B4 Meath (co.), Ire.
107/G2 Meath Park, Sk,Can
31/U10 Meaux, Fr.
60/C4 Mecca (Makkah), SAr.
42/D1 Mechelen (Malines), Belg.
38/F1 Mecklenburger Bucht (bay), Ger.
38/F2 Mecklenburg-Western Pomerania (state), Ger.
87/G3 Mecuia (peak), Moz.
70/C4 Medak, India
72/A3 Medan, Indo.
97/L7 Medanosa (pt.), Arg.
35/F1 Medbourne, Eng,UK
81/S15 Médéa, Alg.
41/F6 Medebach, Ger.
94/B5 Medeiros Neto, Braz.
92/C2 Medellín, Col.
40/C3 Medemblik, Neth.
33/G5 Meden (riv.), Eng,UK
115/H5 Medford, NY,US
106/C5 Medford, Or,US
110/B2 Medford, Wi,US
51/J3 Medgidia, Rom.
51/G2 Mediaş, Rom.
106/D4 Medical Lake, Wa,US
106/F2 Medicine Bow (range), Co, Wy,US
107/G5 Medicine Bow, Wy,US
106/F3 Medicine Hat, Ab,Can
94/B5 Medina, Braz.
35/E5 Medina (riv.), Eng,UK
107/J4 Medina, ND,US
110/D3 Medina, Oh,US
109/H5 Medina, Tx,US
60/C4 Medina (Al Madīnah), SAr.
46/C2 Medina del Campo, Sp.
46/C4 Medina-Sidonia, Sp.
29/K4 Mediterranean (sea)
106/F2 Medley, Ab,Can
55/L2 Mednogorsk, Rus.
55/H2 Medveditsa, Gora (riv.), Rus.
57/S2 Medvezh'i (isls.), Rus.
52/G3 Medvezh'yegorsk, Rus.
31/P8 Medway (riv.), Eng,UK
108/F2 Meeker, Co,US
41/G3 Meerbach (riv.), Ger.
40/D6 Meerbusch, Ger.
43/E1 Meerhout, Belg.
43/E2 Meerssen, Neth.
70/C2 Meerut, India
35/E1 Meese (riv.), Eng,UK
106/F4 Meeteetse, Wy,US
83/N7 Mēga, Eth.
83/P6 Mēgalo, Eth.
111/G2 Megantic (peak), Qu,Can
49/H3 Mégara, Gre.
71/F2 Meghalaya (state), India
59/N7 Megiddo (ruins), Isr.
110/E1 Mégiscane (lake), Qu,Can
110/E1 Mégiscane (riv.), Qu,Can
59/B3 Megista (isl.), Gre.
43/E2 Mehaigne (riv.), Belg.
81/R16 Mehdia, Alg.
41/G1 Mehe (riv.), Ger.
70/C3 Mehkar, India
61/F3 Mehrān (riv.), Iran
60/F2 Mehriz, Iran
70/B3 Mehsāna, India
67/C2 Mei (riv.), China
67/C3 Mei (riv.), China
95/B1 Meia Ponte (riv.), Braz.
82/H6 Meiganga, Camr.
103/R8 Meighen (isl.), NW,Can
63/K3 Meihekou, China
69/A1 Meiktila, Burma
41/H4 Meine, Ger.
41/E6 Meinerzhagen, Ger.
45/J1 Meiningen, Ger.
66/C5 Meishan (res.), China
39/G3 Meissen, Ger.
41/G6 Meissner (peak), Ger.
65/M10 Meiwa, Japan
67/C3 Meizhou, China
82/H7 Mekambo, Gabon
83/N5 Mek'elē, Eth.
81/M14 Meknès, Mor.
58/K8 Mekong (riv.), Asia
73/F4 Mekongga (peak), Indo.
69/D4 Mekong, Mouths of the, Viet.
72/B3 Melaka, Malay.
78/E5 Melanesia (reg.)
70/C6 Melappālaiyam, India
72/D4 Melawi (riv.), Indo.
35/G2 Melbourn, Eng,UK
77/C3 Melbourne, Austl.
102/F2 Melbourne (isl.), NW,Can
33/G6 Melbourne, Eng,UK
113/H4 Melbourne, Fl,US
77/F5 Melbourne (inset), Austl.
96/B5 Melchor (isl.), Chile
100/D4 Melchor de Mencos, Mex.
100/A2 Melchor Múzquiz, Mex.
34/D5 Melcombe Regis, Eng,UK
38/E1 Meldorf, Ger.
50/E3 Melenci, Yugo.
52/J5 Melenki, Rus.
55/K1 Meleuz, Rus.
103/J3 Mélèzes (riv.), Qu,Can
82/J5 Melfi, Chad
48/D2 Melfi, It.
107/G2 Melfort, Sk,Can
37/D3 Melhus, Nor.
81/N13 Melilla, Sp.
96/B5 Melimoyu (peak), Chile
96/Q9 Melipilla, Chile
43/F3 Melissano, It.
107/H3 Melita, Mb,Can
48/D4 Melito di Porto Salvo, It.
54/E3 Melitopol', Ukr.
45/L2 Melk, Aus.
83/P7 Melka Meri, Eth.
34/D4 Melksham, Eng,UK
42/C2 Melle, Belg.
41/F4 Melle, Ger.
81/W17 Mellègue (riv.), Alg.
37/E4 Mellerud, Swe.
46/B1 Mellid, Sp.
33/F3 Melling, Eng,UK
75/K3 Mellish (reef), Austl.
97/J7 Mellizo Sur (peak), Chile
45/J1 Mellrichstadt, Ger.
41/F1 Mellum (isl.), Ger.
45/L1 Mělník, Czh.
97/G2 Melo, Uru.
116/Q16 Melrose Park, Il,US
41/G6 Melsungen, Ger.
33/G4 Meltham, Eng,UK
77/C3 Melton, Austl.
33/H6 Melton Mowbray, Eng,UK
31/T11 Melun, Fr.
74/F2 Melville (bay), Austl.
76/B1 Melville (cape), Austl.
74/E2 Melville (isl.), Austl.
103/L3 Melville (lake), Nf,Can
103/R7 Melville (isl.), NW,Can
103/H2 Melville (pen.), NW,Can
107/H3 Melville, Sk,Can
73/E2 Melville (cape), Phil.
115/G5 Melville, NY,US
116/F7 Melvindale, Mi,US
50/D2 Mélykút, Hun.
68/D5 Mêmar (lake), China
40/D1 Memmert (isl.), Ger.
45/J3 Memmingen, Ger.
69/D4 Memot, Camb.
86/B2 Memphis (ruins), Egypt
116/G6 Memphis, Mi,US
109/J2 Memphis, Mo,US
113/F3 Memphis, Tn,US
112/C3 Memphis, Tx,US
112/E3 Mena, Ar,US
32/D5 Menai (str.), Wal,UK
32/D5 Menai Bridge, Wal,UK
40/C2 Menaldum, Neth.
89/H9 Menarandra (riv.), Madg.
112/D4 Menard, Tx,US
110/B2 Menasha, Wi,US
89/H7 Menavava (riv.), Madg.
72/D4 Mendawai (riv.), Indo.
44/E4 Mende, Fr.
41/E6 Menden, Ger.
114/E4 Mendenhall (cape), Ak,US
59/B3 Menderes, Büyük (riv.), Turk.
95/K7 Mendes, Braz.
83/N6 Mendī, Eth.
43/G3 Mendig, Ger.
34/D4 Mendip (hills), Eng,UK
108/B3 Mendocino, Ca,US
104/B3 Mendocino (cape), Ca,US
96/C2 Mendoza, Arg.
96/C2 Mendoza (prov.), Arg.
89/H9 Mendrare (riv.), Madg.
50/F3 Menedinţi (co.), Rom.
101/G6 Mene Grande, Ven.
59/A2 Menemen, Turk.
42/C2 Menen, Belg.
83/N8 Menengai Crater, Kenya
62/H2 Menengiyn (plain), Mong.
48/C4 Menfi, It.
72/C4 Menggala, Indo.
46/D4 Mengibar, Sp.
66/D4 Menglianggu (mtn.), China
77/B2 Menindee (lake), Austl.
96/B5 Menlolat (peak), Chile
116/K12 Menlo Park, Ca,US
31/T11 Mennecy, Fr.
110/C2 Menominee, Mi,US
110/B3 Menomonee Falls, Wi,US
110/B2 Menomonie, Wi,US
47/H3 Menorca (Minorca) (isl.), Sp.
72/A4 Mentawai (isls.), Indo.
72/A4 Mentawai (str.), Indo.
115/C2 Mentone, Ca,US
112/C4 Mentone, Tx,US
110/D3 Mentor, Oh,US
31/R9 Menucourt, Fr.
73/E3 Menyapa (peak), Indo.
81/W17 Menzel Bourguiba, Tun.
114/M3 Menzie (mtn.), Yk,Can
35/E5 Meon (riv.), Eng,UK
31/Q7 Meopham, Eng,UK
101/N8 Meoqui, Mex.
73/H4 Meos Waar (isl.), Indo.
87/B2 Mepala, Ang.
55/G4 Mepistskaro (peak), Geo.
40/D3 Meppel, Neth.
41/E3 Meppen, Ger.
47/E2 Mequinenzo (res.), Sp.
109/K3 Meramec (riv.), Mo,US
45/J3 Merano, It.
72/D4 Meratus (mts.), Indo.
78/D5 Merauke, Indo.
83/P7 Merca, Som.
45/G4 Mercantour Nat'l Park, Fr.
108/B3 Merced, Ca,US
108/C3 Merced (riv.), Ca,US
96/C1 Mercedario (peak), Arg.
96/D2 Mercedes, Arg.
96/F2 Mercedes, Arg.
97/F2 Mercedes, Uru.
116/C2 Mercer Island, Wa,US
115/F5 Mercerville-Hamilton Square, NJ,US
42/D2 Merchtem, Belg.
111/N7 Mercier, Qu,Can
106/D2 Mercoal, Ab,Can
108/D3 Mercury, Nv,US
103/K2 Mercy (cape), Yk,Can
44/E5 Merdellou (mtn.), Fr.
34/D4 Mere, Eng,UK
97/M8 Meredith (cape), Falk.
112/C3 Meredith (lake), Tx,US
54/F2 Merefa, Ukr.
42/C2 Merelbeke, Belg.
69/D3 Mereuch, Camb.
31/Q8 Mereworth, Eng,UK
63/J2 Mergel (riv.), China
69/B3 Mergui, Burma
69/B4 Mergui (arch.), Burma
42/B3 Méricourt, Fr.
100/D3 Mérida, Mex.
46/B3 Mérida, Sp.
101/G6 Mérida, Ven.
92/D2 Mérida, Ven.
113/F3 Meridian, Ms,US
112/D4 Meridian, Tx,US
116/C2 Meridian-East Hill, Wa,US
44/C4 Mérignac, Fr.
42/D1 Merksem, Belg.
40/B6 Merksplas, Belg.
83/M4 Meroe (ruins), Sudan
59/K5 Meron, Har (mtn.), Isr.
77/F5 Merri (cr.), Austl.
115/G5 Merrick, NY,US
110/B2 Merrill, Wi,US
111/G3 Merrimack, NH,US
34/D5 Merriott, Eng,UK
106/C3 Merritt, BC,Can
113/H4 Merritt Island, Fl,US
33/F5 Mersey (riv.), Eng,UK
33/F5 Merseyside (co.), Eng,UK
59/C3 Mersin, Turk.
72/B3 Mersing, Malay.
31/N8 Merstham, Eng,UK
43/F5 Merten, Fr.
34/C3 Merthyr Tydfil, Wal,UK
31/N7 Merton (bor.), Eng,UK
98/K Mertz (glac.), Ant.
112/C4 Mertzon, Tx,US
42/B5 Méru, Fr.
83/N7 Meru, Kenya
42/B2 Merville, Fr.
40/C5 Merwedekanaal (can.), Neth.
31/S9 Méry-sur-Oise, Fr.
43/F2 Merzenich, Ger.
59/C2 Merzifon, Turk.
43/F5 Merzig, Ger.
97/K7 Mesa (peak), Arg.
114/G3 Mesa (mtn.), Ak,US
108/E4 Mesa, Az,US
107/K4 Mesabi (range), Mn,US
101/M8 Mesa del Seri, Mex.
49/E2 Mesagne, It.
49/J5 Mesarás (gulf), Gre.
108/E3 Mesa Verde Nat'l Park, Co,US
112/C3 Mescalero (ridge), NM,US
41/F6 Meschede, Ger.
45/H4 Mesco, Punta di (pt.), It.
110/F1 Mesgouez (lake), Qu,Can
49/G3 Mesolóngion, Gre.
96/F2 Mesopotamia (reg.), Arg.
60/D2 Mesopotamia (reg.), Iraq
48/E3 Mesoraca, It.
112/D3 Mesquite, Tx,US
82/E1 Mesrouh (peak), Mor.
82/F1 Messaad, Alg.
97/J7 Messier (chan.), Chile
48/D3 Messina, It.
48/D4 Messina (str.), It.
87/F5 Messina, SAfr.
49/H4 Messíni, Gre.
49/H4 Messini (gulf), Gre.
31/U10 Messy, Fr.
51/F5 Mesta (riv.), Bul.
45/K4 Mestre, It.
84/C5 Mesurado (cape), Libr.
111/G1 Métabetchouan, Qu,Can
111/G1 Métabetchouane (riv.), Qu,Can
103/K2 Meta Incognita (pen.), NW,Can
113/F4 Metairie, La,US
91/D2 Metán, Arg.
48/E2 Metapontum (ruins), It.
49/G3 Metéora, Gre.
33/H5 Metheringham, Eng,UK
49/G4 Methóni, Gre.
50/C4 Metković, Cro.
110/B4 Metropolis, Il,US
43/D3 Mettet, Belg.
41/E4 Mettingen, Ger.
43/F5 Mettlach, Ger.
40/D6 Mettmann, Ger.
83/N6 Metu, Eth.
115/F5 Metuchen, NJ,US
43/F5 Metz, Fr.
31/S10 Meudon, Fr.
42/C2 Meulebeke, Belg.
43/E6 Meurthe-et-Moselle (dept.), Fr.
43/E3 Meuse (riv.), Belg., Fr.
42/E6 Meuse (dept.), Fr.
43/E5 Meuse, Cotes de (uplands), Fr.
59/N9 Mevasseret Ẕiyyon, Isr.
33/G5 Mexborough, Eng,UK
112/D4 Mexia, Tx,US
93/J3 Mexiana, Braz.
101/L7 Mexicali, Mex.
100/A3 Mexico
100/B4 México (state), Mex.
109/J5 Mexico (gulf), NAm
109/K3 Mexico, Mo,US
100/B4 Mexico City (cap.), Mex.
60/F2 Meybod, Iran
88/Q13 Meyerton, SAfr.
61/H1 Meymaneh, Afg.
59/K6 Meẓada, Ḥorvot (Masada) (ruins), Isr.
51/F4 Mezdra, Bul.
52/J2 Mezen' (bay), Rus.
53/K2 Mezen' (riv.), Rus.
56/J4 Mezhdurechensk, Rus.
56/E2 Mezhdusharskiy (isl.), Rus.
50/E2 Mezoberény, Hun.
50/E2 Mezokovácsháza, Hun.
50/E2 Mezőkövesd, Hun.
50/E2 Mezőtúr, Hun.
70/C3 Mhow, India
66/D3 Mi (riv.), China
100/B4 Miahuatlán, Mex.
46/C3 Miajadas, Sp.
108/E4 Miami, Az,US
113/H5 Miami, Fl,US
109/J3 Miami, Ok,US
113/H5 Miami Beach, Fl,US
66/B4 Mianchi, China
60/E1 Mīāndoāb, Iran
60/E1 Mīāneh, Iran
115/G4 Mianus (riv.), Ct,US
61/K2 Miānwāli, Pak.
62/E5 Mianyang, China
67/B2 Miao'er (peak), China
66/E3 Miaodao (isls.), China
66/H6 Miaofeng Shan (mtn.), China
53/P5 Miass, Rus.
53/Q5 Miass (riv.), Rus.
39/J2 Miastko, Pol.
86/C5 Miberika, Sudan
106/D2 Mica Creek, BC,Can
39/L4 Michalovce, Slvk.
114/K2 Michelson (mtn.), Ak,US
110/C3 Michigan (lake), Can., US
110/C2 Michigan (state), US
110/C3 Michigan City, In,US
110/C2 Michipicoten (isl.), On,Can
100/A4 Michoacán (state), Mex.
55/G1 Michurinsk, Rus.
33/F2 Mickle Fell (mtn.), Eng,UK
33/F2 Mickleton, Eng,UK
100/E5 Mico (riv.), Nic.
101/J5 Micoud, StL.
78/E3 Micronesia (reg.)
78/D4 Micronesia, Fed. States of
85/G2 Midal (well), Niger
107/H3 Midale, Sk,Can
40/A6 Middelburg, Neth.
88/D3 Middelburg, SAfr.
89/E2 Middelburg, SAfr.
38/E1 Middelfart, Den.
40/B5 Middelharnis, Neth.
42/B1 Middelkerke, Belg.
108/C2 Middle Alkali (lake), Ca,US
71/F5 Middle Andaman (isl.), India
111/F2 Middlebury, Vt,US
112/C4 Middle Concho (riv.), Tx,US
33/G3 Middleham, Eng,UK

Middl – Morri

107/K4 Morris, Mn,US
99/P1 Morris Jesup (cape), Grld.
115/F5 Morris Plains, NJ,US
34/C3 Morriston, Wal,UK
115/F5 Morristown, NJ,US
113/H2 Morristown, Tn,US
115/F5 Morrisville, Pa,US
108/B4 Morro Bay, Ca,US
87/C3 Morro de Môco (peak), Ang.
95/B3 Morro do Capão Doce (hill), Braz.
94/B3 Morro do Chapéu, Braz.
31/T11 Morsang-sur-Orge, Fr.
43/G2 Morsbach, Ger.
55/G1 Morshansk, Rus.
55/J3 Morskoy (isl.), Kaz.
34/B4 Morte (pt.), UK
93/H6 Mortes (riv.), Braz.
35/E4 Mortimer, Eng,UK
34/D2 Mortimers Cross, Eng,UK
110/B3 Morton, Il,US
116/Q15 Morton Grove, Il,US
77/D2 Morton Nat'l Park, Austl.
42/D1 Mortsel, Belg.
44/E3 Morvan (plat.), Fr.
70/B3 Morvi, India
77/C3 Morwell, Austl.
45/A1 Mos, Sp.
45/H2 Mosbach, Ger.
47/P10 Moscavide, Port.
52/G5 Moscow (upland), Rus.
106/D4 Moscow, Id,US
52/H5 Moscow (Moskva) (cap.), Rus.
53/X9 Moscow (Moskva) (inset) (cap.), Rus.
52/H5 Moscow Obl., Rus.
98/H Moscow Univ. Ice Shelf, Ant.
43/F4 Mosel (riv.), Ger.
42/F5 Moselle (dept.), Fr.
43/F5 Moselle (riv.), Fr.
106/D4 Moses Lake, Wa,US
75/R12 Mosgiel, NZ
88/C2 Moshaweng (dry riv.), SAfr.
87/G1 Moshi, Tanz.
39/J2 Mosina, Pol.
37/E2 Mosjøen, Nor.
52/G5 Moskva (riv.), Rus.
53/X9 Moskva (Moscow) (inset) (cap.), Rus.
50/C2 Mosonmagyaróvár, Hun.
109/G4 Mosquero, NM,US
100/E6 Mosquitos (gulf), Pan.
100/E5 Mosquitos, Costa de (coast), Nic.
37/D4 Moss, Nor.
84/E4 Mossi Highlands (upland), Burk.
45/H2 Mössingen, Ger.
33/F4 Mossley, Eng,UK
32/C2 Mossley, NI,UK
94/C2 Mossoró, Braz.
113/F4 Moss Point, Ms,US
32/B1 Moss-side, NI,UK
45/K1 Most, Czh.
81/R16 Mostaganem, Alg.
50/C4 Mostar, Bosn.
46/D2 Móstoles, Sp.
33/E5 Mostyn, Wal,UK
59/E3 Mosul (Al Mawçil), Iraq
100/D4 Motagua (riv.), Guat.
37/E4 Motala, Swe.
66/E2 Motian Ling (mtn.), China
70/D2 Motīhāri, India
65/G2 Motomiya, Japan
37/K1 Motovskiy (gulf), Rus.
46/D4 Motril, Sp.
107/H4 Mott, ND,US
75/R11 Motueka, NZ
100/D3 Motul, Mex.
56/K4 Motygino, Rus.
84/B2 Mougris (well), Mrta.
84/E3 Mouhoun (prov.), Burk.
87/B1 Mouila, Gabon
82/H4 Moul (well), Niger
77/C2 Moulamein (riv.), Austl.
33/F5 Mouldsworth, Eng,UK
44/E3 Moulins, Fr.
69/B2 Moulmein, Burma
81/N13 Moulouya (riv.), Mor.
35/G2 Moulton, Eng,UK
113/H4 Moultrie, Ga,US
113/H3 Moultrie (lake), SC,US
109/J3 Mound City, Ks,US
82/J6 Moundou, Chad
110/D4 Moundsville, WV,US
69/C3 Moung Roessei, Camb.
69/D3 Mounlapamok, Laos
76/B3 Mount Aberdeen Nat'l Park, Austl.
70/B3 Mount Abu, India
102/D2 Mountain (riv.), NW,Can
34/C3 Mountain Ash, Wal,UK
113/G3 Mountain Brook, Al,US
109/J3 Mountain Grove, Mo,US
112/E2 Mountain Home, Ar,US
106/E5 Mountain Home, Id,US
112/E3 Mountain View, Ar,US
116/K12 Mountain View, Ca,US
88/D4 Mountain Zebra Nat'l Park, SAfr.
113/H2 Mount Airy, NC,US
74/B6 Mount Barker, Austl.
77/A2 Mount Barker, Austl.
76/C5 Mount Barney Nat'l Park, Austl.
77/C3 Mount Buffalo Nat'l Park, Austl.
110/C4 Mount Carmel, Il,US
83/M2 Mount Catherine (peak), Egypt
116/G6 Mount Clemens, Mi,US
76/E6 Mount Coot'tha, Austl.
87/F4 Mount Darwin, Zim.
77/B3 Mount Eccles Nat'l Park, Austl.
76/B2 Mount Elliot Nat'l Park, Austl.
77/B3 Mount Emu (cr.), Austl.
77/C4 Mount Field Nat'l Park, Austl.
77/B3 Mount Gambier, Austl.
78/D5 Mount Hagen, PNG
115/F6 Mount Holly, NJ,US
111/Q9 Mount Hope, On,Can
77/D3 Mount Imlay Nat'l Park, Austl.
74/F4 Mount Isa, Austl.
77/D1 Mount Kaputar Nat'l Park, Austl.
115/G4 Mount Kisco, NY,US
116/C2 Mountlake Terrace, Wa,US
115/F6 Mount Laurel, NJ,US
74/F6 Mount Lofty (ranges), Austl.
75/S10 Mount Maunganui, NZ
76/D4 Mount Mistake Nat'l Park, Austl.
110/D3 Mount Morris, Mi,US
76/E6 Mount Nebo, Austl.
31/Q7 Mountnessing, Eng,UK
113/J3 Mount Olive, NC,US
49/H3 Mount Parnes Nat'l Park, Gre.
111/L2 Mount Pearl, Nf,Can
107/L5 Mount Pleasant, Ia,US
110/C3 Mount Pleasant, Mi,US
112/E3 Mount Pleasant, Tx,US
108/E3 Mount Pleasant, Ut,US
116/Q15 Mount Prospect, Il,US
115/K8 Mount Rainier, Md,US
106/C4 Mount Rainier Nat'l Park, Wa,US
106/D3 Mount Revelstoke Nat'l Park, BC,Can
77/B3 Mount Richmond Nat'l Park, Austl.
109/G2 Mount Rushmore Nat'l Mem., SD,US
34/A6 Mount's (bay), Eng,UK
76/B2 Mount Spec Nat'l Park, Austl.
110/D4 Mount Sterling, Ky,US
110/B4 Mount Vernon, Il,US
110/C4 Mount Vernon, In,US
115/G5 Mount Vernon, NY,US
110/D3 Mount Vernon, Oh,US
115/J8 Mount Vernon, Va,US
106/C3 Mount Vernon, Wa,US
76/C4 Mount Walsh Nat'l Park, Austl.
77/E1 Mount Warning Nat'l Park, Austl.
77/D4 Mount William Nat'l Park, Austl.
46/B3 Moura, Port.
44/C5 Mourenx, Fr.
32/B3 Mourne (dist.), NI,UK
32/B3 Mourne (mts.), NI,UK
42/C2 Mouscron, Belg.
82/J5 Moussoro, Chad
31/T9 Moussy-le-Neuf, Fr.
42/C2 Mouvaux, Fr.
94/C3 Moxotó (riv.), Braz.
32/B3 Moy, NI,UK
83/N7 Moyalē, Eth.
82/D1 Moyen Atlas (mts.), Mor.
43/F5 Moyeuvre-Grande, Fr.
32/B2 Moygashel, NI,UK
32/B1 Moyle (dist.), NI,UK
72/E5 Moyo (isl.), Indo.
68/C4 Moyu, China
87/G4 Mozambique
87/G5 Mozambique (chan.), Afr.
52/H5 Mozhaysk, Rus.
53/M4 Mozhga, Rus.
54/D1 Mozyr', Bela.
87/F2 Mpanda, Tanz.
87/C4 Mpangu, Namb.
87/F3 Mpika, Zam.
87/F2 Mporokoso, Zam.
85/E5 Mpraeso, Gha.
39/L2 Mrągowo, Pol.
50/C3 Mrkonjić Grad, Bosn.
81/T16 M'Sila, Alg.
81/T16 M'Sila (riv.), Alg.
81/N13 Msoun (riv.), Mor.
52/G4 Msta (riv.), Rus.
39/L4 Mszana Dolna, Pol.
54/F1 Mtsensk, Rus.
87/H3 Mtwara, Tanz.
87/G4 Mualama, Moz.
69/D2 Muang Gnommarat, Laos
69/C2 Muang Kenthao, Laos
41/G6 Muang Khong, Laos
69/D3 Muang Khongxedon, Laos
69/D3 Muang Lakhonpheng, Laos
69/D1 Muang Soy, Laos
69/C2 Muang Thathom, Laos
69/D2 Muang Xamteu, Laos
69/D2 Muang Xepon, Laos
72/B3 Muar, Malay.
72/B4 Muarabungo, Indo.
61/J4 Muāri (pt.), Pak.
82/H5 Mubi, Nga.
92/F3 Mucajaí (riv.), Braz.
43/G2 Much, Ger.
87/F3 Muchinga (mts.), Zam.
34/D1 Much Wenlock, Eng,UK
32/B2 Muckamore Abbey, NI,UK
87/H3 Mucojo, Moz.
59/C2 Mucur, Turk.
95/D1 Mucuri (riv.), Braz.
87/D3 Mucussueje, Ang.
63/K3 Mudanjiang, China
51/J5 Mudanya, Turk.
63/K2 Muddan (riv.), China
37/F2 Muddus Nat'l Park, Swe.
108/E3 Muddy (riv.), Ut,US
109/H4 Muddy Boggy (cr.), Ok,US
43/G2 Mudersbach, Ger.
77/D2 Mudgee, Austl.
106/G1 Mudjatik (riv.), Sk,Can
116/D3 Mud Mountain (lake), Wa,US
69/B2 Mudon, Burma
97/J8 Muela (peak), Chile
59/N8 Mufjir, Nahr (dry riv.), WBnk.
87/E3 Mufulira, Zam.
46/A1 Mugardos, Sp.
45/K4 Muggia, It.
46/A1 Mugia, Sp.
59/B3 Muğla, Turk.
55/L2 Mugodzharskoye (mts.), Kaz.
87/G2 Mugombazi, Tanz.
86/D4 Muḥammad Qawl, Sudan
86/C3 Muḥammad, Ra's (pt.), Egypt
87/E3 Muhila (mts.), Zaire
45/K2 Mühlviertel (reg.), Aus.
37/H2 Muhos, Fin.
60/C2 Mūḥ, Sabkhat al (lake), Syria
52/D4 Muhu (isl.), Est.
40/C4 Muiden, Neth.
36/C3 Muirkirk, Sc,UK
36/C2 Muir of Ord, Sc,UK
116/J11 Muir Woods Nat'l Mon., Ca,US
63/K4 Muju, SKor.
54/B2 Mukachevo, Ukr.
86/D4 Mukawwar (isl.), Sudan
107/M2 Muketei (riv.), On,Can
59/L5 Mukhayyam al Yarmūk, Syria
116/C2 Mukilteo, Wa,US
65/L10 Mukō, Japan
78/D2 Mukoshima (isls.), Japan
69/B4 Mu Ko Similan Nat'l Park, Thai.
69/B4 Mu Ko Surin Nat'l Park, Thai.
61/K2 Muktsar, India
87/G4 Mulanje, Malw.
114/G4 Mulchatna (riv.), Ak,US
96/B3 Mulchén, Chile
38/G3 Mulde (riv.), Ger.
98/D Mule (pt.), Ant.
46/D4 Mulhacén, Cerro de (mtn.), Sp.
38/F3 Mülhausen, Ger.
40/D6 Mülheim an der Ruhr, Ger.
45/G3 Mulhouse, Fr.
66/D3 Muling (pass), China
63/L2 Muling (riv.), China
79/R9 Mulinu'u (cape), WSam.
61/L2 Mulkila (mtn.), India
32/B5 Mullaghcleevaun (mtn.), Ire.
32/B2 Mullaghmore (mtn.), NI,UK
109/G2 Mullen, Ne,US
72/D4 Muller (mts.), Indo.
45/G3 Müllheim, Ger.
36/B4 Mullingar, Ire.
113/J3 Mullins, SC,US
34/A6 Mullion, Eng,UK
87/C4 Mulondo, Ang.
61/K2 Multān, Pak.
106/C3 Multnomah (falls), Or,US
72/D3 Mulu, Gunung (peak), Malay.
86/B5 Mulwad, Sudan
87/C3 Mumbué, Ang.
87/E3 Mumbwa, Zam.
69/B5 Mum Nauk (pt.), Thai.
69/C3 Mun (riv.), Thai.
73/F4 Muna (isl.), Indo.
37/H4 Munamägi (hill), Est.
45/J2 München (Munich), Ger.
110/C3 Muncie, In,US
116/P15 Mundelein, Il,US
85/H5 Mundemba, Camr.
38/E3 Munden, Ger.
41/G6 Münden, Ger.
35/H1 Mundesley, Eng,UK
35/G2 Mundford, Eng,UK
70/C3 Mungaolī, India
77/B2 Mungo Nat'l Park, Austl.
68/F1 Mungun-Tayga, Gora (peak), Rus.
45/J2 Munich (München), Ger.
110/C2 Munising, Mi,US
57/L4 Munku-Sardyk (peak), Rus.
62/D1 Munku-Sasan (peak), Rus.
97/J8 Muñoz Gamero (pen.), Chile
41/E5 Münster, Ger.
41/H3 Munster, Ger.
36/A4 Munster (prov.), Ire.
116/Q16 Munster, In,US
41/E4 Münsterland (reg.), Ger.
51/F2 Muntele Mare (peak), Rom.
72/C4 Muntok, Indo.
69/D1 Muong Khuong, Viet.
37/G1 Muonioälv (riv.), Swe.
37/G1 Muoniojoki (riv.), Fin.
87/C4 Mupa Nat'l Park, Moz.
83/Q7 Muqdisho (Mogadishu) (cap.), Som.
45/L3 Mur (riv.), Aus.
50/C2 Mura (riv.), Slvk.
59/E2 Muradiye, Turk.
65/F1 Murakami, Japan
97/J7 Murallón (peak), Chile
83/N8 Murang'a, Kenya
59/E2 Murat (riv.), Turk.
54/D5 Murat Dağı (peak), Turk.
74/B5 Murchison (riv.), Austl.
75/R11 Murchison, NZ
47/E4 Murcia, Sp.
46/E4 Murcia (aut. comm.), Sp.
111/H1 Murdochville, Qu,Can
76/B1 Murdock (pt.), Austl.
51/G2 Mureş (co.), Rom.
51/G2 Mureş (riv.), Rom.
44/D5 Muret, Fr.
112/E3 Murfreesboro, Ar,US
113/G3 Murfreesboro, Tn,US
61/H1 Murgab (riv.), Trkm.
72/D5 Muria (peak), Indo.
95/D2 Muriaé, Braz.
61/G3 Mūrīān, Hāmūn-e Jaz (lake), Iran
94/D3 Murici, Braz.
38/G2 Müritz See (lake), Ger.
83/N6 Murle, Eth.
52/G1 Murmansk, Rus.
52/G2 Murmansk Obl., Rus.
65/M10 Muro, Japan
47/G3 Muro, Sp.
52/J5 Murom, Rus.
63/N3 Muroran, Japan
46/A1 Muros, Sp.
64/D4 Muroto, Japan
64/D4 Muroto-zaki (pt.), Japan
39/J2 Murowana Goślina, Pol.
113/G3 Murphy, NC,US
110/B4 Murphysboro, Il,US
77/D2 Murramarang Nat'l Park, Austl.
77/A2 Murray (riv.), Austl.
78/D5 Murray (lake), PNG
110/B4 Murray, Ky,US
113/H3 Murray (lake), SC,US
77/A2 Murray Bridge, Austl.
77/C2 Murrumbidgee (riv.), Austl.
50/C2 Murska Sobota, Slov.
33/G2 Murton, Eng,UK
75/S10 Murupara, NZ
79/M7 Mururoa (isl.), FrPol.
70/D3 Murwāra, India
77/E1 Murwillumbah, Austl.
45/H5 Mürz (riv.), Aus.
45/L3 Mürzzuschlag, Aus.
59/E2 Muş, Turk.
51/F4 Musala (peak), Bul.
61/G3 Musandam (pen.), Oman
65/H7 Musashino, Japan
61/G4 Muscat (Musqaṭ) (cap.), Oman
115/E5 Musconetcong (riv.), NJ,US
115/E5 Muscoy, Ca,US
87/E5 Musekwapoort (pass), SAfr.
74/E5 Musgrave (ranges), Austl.
111/L1 Musgrave Harbour, Nf,Can
70/E3 Mushābani, India
59/N9 Mushāsh, Wādī (dry riv.), WBnk.
87/C1 Mushie, Zaire
72/B4 Musi (riv.), Indo.
116/P14 Muskego, Wi,US
110/C3 Muskegon, Mi,US
110/C3 Muskegon (riv.), Mi,US
110/D4 Muskingum (riv.), Oh,US
109/J4 Muskogee, Ok,US
110/E2 Muskoka (lake), On,Can
87/F1 Musoma, Tanz.
61/G4 Musqaṭ (Muscat) (cap.), Oman
111/J1 Musquaro (riv.), Qu,Can
78/D5 Mussau (isl.), PNG
106/F4 Musselshell (riv.), Mt,US
48/C4 Mussomeli, It.
53/B2 Mustafakemalpaşa, Turk.
73/D2 Mustāng, Nepal
103/H4 Mustang, Ok,US
45/K2 Müstek (peak), Czh.
96/C5 Musters (lake), Arg.
63/K3 Musu-dan (pt.), NKor.
100/D5 Musún (mt.), Nic.
77/D2 Muswellbrook, Austl.
86/B3 Mūt, Egypt
53/C3 Mut, Turk.
94/C4 Mutá, Ponta do (pt.), Braz.
87/F4 Mutare, Zim.
73/F5 Mutis (peak), Indo.
89/H6 Mutsamudu, Com.
63/N3 Mutsu, Japan
95/D1 Mutum, Braz.
55/L4 Muynak, Uzb.
61/K2 Muzaffargarh, Pak.
70/C2 Muzaffarnagar, India
70/E2 Muzaffarpur, India
95/G6 Muzambinho, Braz.
68/D3 Muzat (riv.), China
68/D4 Muztag (peak), China
68/E4 Muztag (peak), China
68/C4 Muztagata (peak), China
87/C2 Mwadi-Kalumbu, Zaire
87/F1 Mwanza, Tanz.
36/H7 Mweelrea (mtn.), Ire.
87/D1 Mweka, Zaire
87/D2 Mwene-Ditu, Zaire
87/E2 Mweru (lake), Zaire, Zam.
77/E2 Myall Lakes Nat'l Park, Austl.
71/G4 Myanaung, Burma
62/C2 Myangad, Mong.
71/G2 Myanmar (Burma)
71/F4 Myaungmya, Burma
71/G3 Myingyan, Burma
71/G2 Myitkyina, Burma
39/J4 Myjava, Slvk.
34/C2 Mynydd Eppynt (mts.), Wal,UK
34/B2 Mynydd Pencarreg (mtn.), Wal,UK
71/F3 Myohaung, Burma
65/F2 Myōkō-san (mtn.), Japan
113/J3 Myrtle Beach, SC,US
106/C5 Myrtle Creek, Or,US
37/D4 Mysen, Nor.
39/K4 Myślenice, Pol.
39/H2 Myślibórz, Pol.
69/E3 My Son (ruins), Viet.
70/C5 Mysore, India
39/K3 Myszków, Pol.
69/D4 My Tho, Viet.
52/H5 Mytishchi, Rus.
45/K2 Mže (riv.), Czh.
87/F3 Mzuzu, Malw.

N

69/C1 Na (riv.), Viet.
45/J2 Naab (riv.), Ger.
40/B5 Naaldwijk, Neth.
40/C4 Naarden, Neth.
32/B5 Naas, Ire.
86/B3 Nababeep, SAfr.
70/E3 Nabadwīp, India
65/H7 Nabari, Japan
65/M10 Nabari (riv.), Japan
41/E5 Nabberu (lake), Austl.
53/M5 Naberezhnye Chelny, Rus.
60/D5 Nabī Shu'ayb, Jabal an (mtn.), Yem.
111/J1 Nabisipi (riv.), Qu,Can
67/D5 Nabua, Phil.
81/K17 Nābul, Tun.
81/K17 Nābul (gov.), Tun.
59/K5 Nābulus, WBnk.
64/D4 Nachi-Katsuura, Japan
39/J3 Náchod, Czh.
41/E6 Nachrodt-Wiblingwerde, Ger.
96/B3 Nacimiento, Chile
112/E4 Nacogdoches, Tx,US
35/G4 Nadder (riv.), Eng,UK
78/G6 Nadi, Fiji
70/B3 Nadiād, India
50/E3 Nădlac, Rom.
81/N13 Nador, Mor.
33/H3 Nafferton, Eng,UK
61/J3 Nag, Pak.
67/D5 Naga, Phil.
64/C4 Nagahama, Japan
64/C4 Nagahama, Japan
65/G1 Nagai, Japan
71/F2 Nāgāland (state), India
65/F2 Nagano, Japan
65/E3 Nagano (pref.), Japan
65/F2 Nagaoka, Japan
64/D3 Nagaokakyō, Japan
65/J7 Nagara, Japan
65/E3 Nagara (riv.), Japan
65/H7 Nagareyama, Japan
77/D1 Nagar Haveli, Dadrak (terr.), India
70/C4 Nāgārjuna Sāgar (res.), India
100/D5 Nagarote, Nic.
114/M5 Nagas (pt.), BC,Can
64/A4 Nagasaki, Japan
64/A4 Nagasaki (pref.), Japan
65/M9 Nagashima, Japan
64/B3 Nagato, Japan
70/B2 Nāgaur, India
70/C3 Nāgda, India
70/C6 Nāgercoil, India
68/F2 Nagoonnuur, Mong.
55/H5 Nagorno-Karabakh Aut. Obl., Azer.
65/E3 Nagoya, Japan
70/C3 Nāgpur, India
62/C5 Nagqu (riv.), China
50/C2 Nagyatád, Hun.
50/E2 Nagyhalász, Hun.
50/E2 Nagykálló, Hun.
50/E2 Nagykanizsa, Hun.
50/D2 Nagykáta, Hun.
50/D2 Nagykőrös, Hun.
50/E1 Nagy-Milic (peak), Hun.
67/E2 Naha, Japan
102/D2 Nahanni Nat'l Park, NW,Can
59/K5 Nahariyya, Isr.
78/D2 Nahashima (isls.), Japan
60/E2 Nahāvand, Iran
43/G4 Nahe (riv.), Ger.
85/E4 Nahouri (prov.), Burk.
96/B3 Nahuelbuta Nat'l Park, Chile
96/C4 Nahuel Huapí Nat'l Park, Arg.
101/N8 Naica, Mex.
62/C4 Naij Gol (riv.), China
64/C3 Naikai-Seto Nat'l Park, Japan
34/D4 Nailsea, Eng,UK
34/D3 Nailsworth, Eng,UK
70/D3 Nainpur, India
36/D2 Nairn, Sc,UK
36/D2 Nairn (riv.), Sc,UK
83/N8 Nairobi (cap.), Kenya
83/N8 Nairobi Nat'l Park, Kenya
60/F2 Najafābād, Iran
60/D3 Najd (des.), SAfr.
46/D1 Nájera, Sp.
70/C2 Najībābād, India
65/K9 Naka, Japan
64/D4 Naka (riv.), Japan
65/G2 Naka (riv.), Japan
65/H7 Nakai, Japan
65/F1 Nakajō, Japan
104/T10 Nakalele (pt.), Hi,US
65/G2 Nakaminato, Japan
64/C4 Nakamura, Japan
65/F2 Nakano, Japan
64/C3 Nakano (lake), Japan
64/B5 Nakatane, Japan
65/E3 Nakatsugawa, Japan
83/N4 Nak'fa, Erit.
55/H5 Nakhichevan', Azer.
55/H5 Nakhichevan Aut. Rep., Azer.
63/L3 Nakhodka, Rus.
69/C3 Nakhon Nayok, Thai.
69/C3 Nakhon Pathom, Thai.
69/D2 Nakhon Phanom, Thai.
69/C3 Nakhon Ratchasima, Thai.
69/C3 Nakhon Sawan, Thai.
69/B4 Nakhon Si Thammarat, Thai.
37/G3 Nakkila, Fin.
39/J2 Nakľo nad Notecią, Pol.
38/F1 Nakskov, Den.
64/A3 Naktong (riv.), SKor.
83/N8 Nakuru, Kenya
106/D3 Nakusp, BC,Can
61/J3 Nāl (riv.), Pak.
62/F2 Nalayh, Mong.
43/F5 Nalbach, Ger.
71/F2 Nalbāri, India
77/D3 Nalbaugh Nat'l Park, Austl.
55/G4 Nal'chik, Rus.
69/C2 Nale, Laos
70/C4 Nalgonda, India
51/K5 Nallıhan, Turk.
46/B1 Nalón (riv.), Sp.
82/H1 Nālūt, Libya
60/F2 Namak (lake), Iran
61/G2 Namakzār-e Shadād (salt dep.), Iran
68/B3 Namangan, Uzb.
88/B3 Namaqualand (reg.), SAfr.
73/J4 Namaripi (cape), Indo.
43/G4 Namborn, Ger.
76/D4 Nambour, Austl.
69/D4 Nam Can, Viet.
69/C1 Nam Cum, Viet.
69/D1 Nam Dinh, Viet.
110/B2 Namekagon (riv.), Wi,US
85/E3 Namemtenga (prov.), Burk.
65/E2 Namerikawa, Japan
87/B5 Namib (des.), Namb.
87/C5 Namibia
88/A2 Namib-Naukluft Park, Namb.
65/G2 Namie, Japan
70/D2 Namja (pass), Nepal
71/G2 Namjagbarwa (peak), China
69/C2 Nam Nao Nat'l Park, Thai.
69/B4 Namnoi (peak), Burma
77/D1 Namoi (riv.), Austl.
78/E4 Namonuito (atoll), Micr.
78/E4 Namorik (atoll), Mrsh.
106/D5 Nampa, Id,US
63/K4 Namp'o, NKor.
87/G4 Nampula, Moz.
68/D6 Namsê Shankou (pass), China
37/D2 Namsos, Nor.
69/B2 Nam Tok Mae Surin Nat'l Park, Thai.
78/F4 Namu (atoll), Mrsh.
69/C2 Nam Un (res.), Thai.
43/D3 Namur, Belg.
43/D3 Namur (prov.), Belg.
39/J3 Namysłów, Pol.
66/B4 Nan (riv.), China
69/C2 Nan, Thai.
69/C2 Nan (riv.), Thai.
106/C3 Nanaimo, BC,Can
104/V13 Nanakuli, Hi,US
65/E2 Nanao, Japan
92/D4 Nanay (riv.), Peru
96/C2 Nancagua, Chile
67/C2 Nanchang, China
67/C2 Nancheng, China
43/F6 Nancy, Fr.
70/C4 Nānded, India
71/G3 Nanding (riv.), China
67/A4 Nandu (riv.), China
70/B3 Nandurbār, India
31/T11 Nandy, Fr.
70/C4 Nandyāl, India
61/K1 Nanga Parbat (mtn.), Pak.
72/D4 Nangapinoh, Indo.
66/C3 Nangong, China
73/F1 Nangtud (mt.), Phil.
66/D4 Nanjing, China
64/C4 Nankoku, Japan
71/J3 Nanliu (riv.), China
63/K3 Nanlou (peak), China
71/J3 Nanning, China
65/M9 Nannō, Japan
32/B4 Nanny (riv.), Ire.
70/D2 Nānpāra, India
67/C2 Nanping, China
65/M10 Nansei, Japan
103/S6 Nansen (sound), NW,Can
87/F1 Nansio, Tanz.
65/F2 Nantai-san (mtn.), Japan
31/S10 Nanterre, Fr.
44/C3 Nantes, Fr.
31/U9 Nanteuil-le-Haudouin, Fr.
110/D3 Nanticoke, On,Can
106/E3 Nanton, Ab,Can
66/E4 Nantong, China
111/G3 Nantucket (isl.), MA,US
33/F5 Nantwich, Eng,UK
34/C3 Nantyglo, Wal,UK
115/F4 Nanuet, NY,US
79/Z18 Nanuku (chan.), Fiji
78/G5 Nanumanga (atoll), Tuv.
78/G5 Nanumea (isl.), Tuv.
95/D1 Nanuque, Braz.
66/C4 Nanwon (res.), China
66/B4 Nanwutai (mtn.), China
66/D4 Nanyang, China
66/D4 Nanyang (lake), China
83/N7 Nanyuki, Kenya
103/J3 Naococane (lake), Qu,Can
70/A3 Naokot, Pak.
63/L2 Naoli (riv.), China
84/D5 Naoua (falls), IvC.
116/K10 Napa, Ca,US
116/K10 Napa (riv.), Ca,US
110/E2 Napanee, On,Can
86/B5 Napata (ruins), Sudan
116/P16 Naperville, Il,US
75/S10 Napier, NZ
88/L11 Napier, SAfr.
113/H5 Naples, Fl,US
48/D2 Naples (Napoli), It.
48/D2 Napoli (gulf), It.
76/A4 Nappa Merrie, Austl.
35/E2 Napton on the Hill, Eng,UK
79/L6 Napuka (isl.), FrPol.
64/D3 Nara, Japan
64/D3 Nara (pref.), Japan
84/D3 Nara, Mali
61/J4 Nāra (riv.), Pak.
68/D5 Nara Logna (pass), Nepal
70/D4 Narasannapeta, India
65/J7 Narashino, Japan
69/C5 Narathiwat, Thai.
70/F3 Nārāyanganj, Bang.
70/C4 Nārāyanpet, India
34/B3 Narberth, Wal,UK
44/E5 Narbonne, Fr.
46/B1 Narcea (riv.), Sp.
49/F2 Nardò, It.
34/B6 Nare (pt.), UK
103/T7 Nares (str.), NW,Can
39/L2 Narew (riv.), Pol.
101/F6 Narganá, Pan.
89/H6 Narinda (bay), Madg.
97/K8 Nariz (peak), Chile
70/D2 Narkatiāganj, India
70/C3 Narmada (riv.), India
59/E2 Narman, Turk.
48/C1 Narni, It.
31/K2 Narodnaya (peak), Rus.
46/A1 Narón, Sp.
61/K2 Nārowāl, Pak.
37/G3 Närpes, Fin.
67/C6 Narra, Phil.
77/D1 Narrabri, Austl.
70/C3 Narsimhapur, India
70/D3 Narsinghgarh, India
64/D3 Naruto, Japan
52/F4 Narva, Est.
52/E4 Narva (riv.), Est., Rus.
67/D4 Narvacan, Phil.
37/F1 Narvik, Nor.
53/M2 Nar'yan-Mar, Rus.
68/C3 Naryn, Kyr.
68/B3 Naryn (riv.), Kyr.
51/G2 Năsăud, Rom.
35/F3 Nash, Eng,UK
34/C4 Nash (pt.), Wal,UK
111/G3 Nashua, NH,US
112/E3 Nashville, Ar,US
113/G2 Nashville (cap.), Tn,US
50/D3 Našice, Cro.
39/L2 Nasielsk, Pol.
70/B4 Nāsik, India
83/M6 Nāşir, Sudan
70/B2 Nasīrābād, India
61/J3 Nasīrābād, Pak.
73/F1 Naso (pt.), Phil.
79/Z17 Nasorolevu (peak), Fiji
114/N4 Nass (riv.), BC,Can
101/F2 Nassau (cap.), Bahm.
97/L8 Nassau (bay), Chile
79/J6 Nassau (isl.), CookIs.
86/C4 Nasser (res.), Egypt
37/E4 Nässjö, Swe.
103/J3 Nastapoka (isls.), NW,Can
38/F1 Næstved, Den.
65/F2 Nasu-dake (mtn.), Japan
69/B2 Nat (peak), Burma
87/E5 Nata, Bots.
110/C1 Natagani (riv.), On,Can
94/D2 Natal, Braz.
89/E3 Natal (prov.), SAfr.
111/J1 Natashquan (riv.), Qu,Can
113/F4 Natchez, Ms,US
112/E4 Natchitoches, La,US
45/G3 Naters, Swi.
79/Z17 Natewa (bay), Fiji
70/B3 Nāthdwāra, India
106/B2 Nation (riv.), BC,Can
108/C4 National City, Ca,US
71/G4 Nattaung (peak), Burma
72/C3 Natuna (isls.), Indo.
108/E3 Natural Bridges Nat'l Mon., Ut,US
74/A6 Naturaliste (cape), Austl.
77/D4 Naturaliste (cape), Austl.
74/A5 Naturaliste (chan.), Austl.
100/B4 Naucalpan, Mex.
88/E3 Naudesnek (pass), SAfr.
67/D5 Naujan, Phil.
52/D4 Naujoji-Akmenė, Lith.
88/A2 Naukluft-Namib Game Rsv., Namb.
78/F5 Nauru
47/N8 Navacarrada (pass), Sp.
108/E3 Navajo Nat'l Mon., Az,US
47/M9 Navalcarnero, Sp.
46/C3 Navalmoral de la Mata, Sp.
32/B4 Navan, Ire.
57/T3 Navarin (cape), Rus.
97/L8 Navarino (isl.), Chile
46/D1 Navarre (aut. comm.), Sp.
96/F2 Navarro, Arg.
34/A6 Navax (pt.), UK
46/B1 Navia, Sp.
46/B1 Navia (riv.), Sp.
96/C2 Navidad, Chile
93/H8 Naviraí, Braz.
51/J3 Năvodari, Rom.
56/G5 Navoi, Uzb.
101/N8 Navojoa, Mex.
101/N9 Navolato, Mex.
49/G3 Návpaktos, Gre.
49/H4 Návplion, Gre.
70/B3 Navsāri, India
103/H1 Navy Board (inlet), NW,Can
70/E3 Nawābganj, Bang.
70/D2 Nawābganj, India
61/J3 Nawābshāh, Pak.
61/G5 Nawş, Ra's (pt.), Oman
49/J4 Náxos (isl.), Gre.
101/P9 Nayarit (state), Mex.
35/G3 Nayland, Eng,UK
62/B2 Nayramadlīn (peak), Mong.
68/B4 Nayzatash, Pereval (pass), Taj.
46/A3 Nazaré, Port.
42/C2 Nazareth, Belg.
59/K5 Nazareth (Naẕerat), Isr.
101/P8 Nazas (riv.), Mex.
92/D6 Nazca, Peru
92/C6 Nazca Lines (ruins), Peru
78/B2 Naze, Japan
35/H3 Naze, The (pt.), Eng,UK
59/B3 Nazilli, Turk.
83/N6 Nazrēt, Eth.
56/H4 Nazyvayevsk, Rus.
87/E2 Nchelenge, Zam.
87/G3 Ncheu, Malw.
87/B2 Ndalatando, Ang.
83/K6 Ndele, CAfr.
78/F6 Ndende (isl.), Sol.
82/J5 N'Djamena (cap.), Chad
82/H8 N'Djolé, Gabon
87/E3 Ndola, Zam.
85/H5 Ndop, Camr.
84/B2 Ndrhamcha, Sebkha de (dry lake), Mrta.
44/C4 Né (riv.), Fr.
49/J5 Néa Alikarnassós, Gre.

Neagh – North

32/B2 Neagh, Lough (lake), NI,UK
49/H3 Néa Ionía, Gre.
74/E4 Neale (lake), Austl.
51/H2 Neamţ (co.), Rom.
114/A6 Near (isls.), Ak,US
34/C3 Neath, Wal,UK
34/C3 Neath (riv.), Wal,UK
32/D3 Neb (riv.), IM,UK
55/K5 Nebit-Dag, Trkm.
76/E6 Nebo (mtn.), Austl.
109/G2 Nebraska (state), US
109/J2 Nebraska City, Ne,US
48/C4 Nebrodi, Madonie (mts.), It.
106/B2 Nechako (riv.), BC,Can
112/E4 Neches (riv.), Tx,US
83/N6 Nechisar Nat'l Park, Eth.
45/H2 Neckar (riv.), Ger.
79/J2 Necker (isl.), Hi,US
96/F3 Necochea, Arg.
48/C1 Necropoli (ruins), It.
46/A1 Neda, Sp.
40/C6 Nederweert, Neth.
40/D4 Neede, Neth.
35/H2 Needham Market, Eng,UK
35/F2 Needingworth, Eng,UK
108/D4 Needles, Ca,US
35/E5 Needles, The (seastacks), UK
110/B2 Neenah, Wi,US
107/J3 Neepawa, Mb,Can
43/E1 Neerpelt, Belg.
41/H2 Neetze (riv.), Ger.
43/F2 Neffelbach (riv.), Ger.
53/M4 Neftekamsk, Rus.
58/C7 Nefud (des.), SAr.
32/D6 Nefyn, Wal,UK
110/C2 Negaunee, Mi,US
83/N6 Negēlē, Eth.
86/D2 Negev (phys. reg.), Isr.
51/G3 Negoiu (peak), Rom.
70/C6 Negombo, SrL.
50/F3 Negotin, Yugo.
50/F5 Negotino, Macd.
94/A3 Negra (mts.), Braz.
92/B5 Negra (pt.), Peru
71/F4 Negrais (cape), Burma
46/A1 Negreira, Sp.
51/H2 Negreşti, Rom.
96/C3 Negro (peak), Arg.
96/D3 Negro (riv.), Arg.
92/F7 Negro (riv.), Bol.
93/G7 Negro (riv.), Braz.
92/F4 Negro (riv.), Braz., Ven.
97/F2 Negro (riv.), Uru., Braz.
67/D6 Negros (isl.), Phil.
101/G4 Neiba, DRep.
89/R15 Neiges, Piton des (peak), Reun.
66/C4 Neihuang, China
66/B2 Nei Monggol (aut. reg.), China
62/G3 Nei Monggol (plat.), China
92/C3 Neiva, Col.
102/G3 Nejanilini (lake), Mb,Can
83/N6 Nejo, Eth.
83/N6 Nek'emtē, Eth.
52/G4 Nelidovo, Rus.
109/H2 Neligh, Ne,US
70/C5 Nellore, India
77/B3 Nelson (cape), Austl.
106/D3 Nelson, BC,Can
102/G3 Nelson (riv.), Mb,Can
97/J7 Nelson (str.), Chile
75/R11 Nelson, NZ
33/F4 Nelson, Eng,UK
34/C3 Nelson, Wal,UK
114/F3 Nelson (isl.), Ak,US
77/E2 Nelson Bay, Austl.
89/E2 Nelspruit, SAfr.
84/D2 Néma, Mrta.
84/D2 Néma, Dhar (hills), Mrta.
45/H4 Nembro, It.
51/H2 Nemira (peak), Rom.
63/J2 Nemor (riv.), China
44/E2 Nemours, Fr.
63/P3 Nemuro, Japan
63/J2 Nen (riv.), China
35/G1 Nene (riv.), Eng,UK
53/M2 Nenets Aut. Okr., Rus.
109/J3 Neosho (riv.), Ks, Mo,US
109/J3 Neosho, Mo,US
58/H7 Nepal
70/D2 Nepālganj, Nepal
70/C3 Nepanagar, India
76/G8 Nepean (riv.), Austl.
110/F2 Nepean, Can.
108/E3 Nephi, Ut,US
36/A3 Nephin (mtn.), Ire.
111/H2 Nepisiguit (riv.), NB,Can
62/H1 Nercha (riv.), Rus.
52/J4 Nerekhta, Rus.
50/D4 Neretva (riv.), Bosn., Cro.
52/E5 Neris (riv.), Lith.
46/D4 Nerja, Sp.
46/B4 Nerva, Sp.
54/C4 Nesebŭr, Bul.
31/S9 Nesles-la-Vallée, Fr.
109/H3 Ness City, Ks,US
41/H6 Nesse (riv.), Ger.
114/M4 Nesselrode (mtn.), Ak,US
36/C2 Ness, Loch (lake), Sc,UK
33/E5 Neston, Eng,UK
49/J2 Néstos (riv.), Gre.
59/M9 Nes Ẕiyyona, Isr.
59/K5 Netanya, Isr.
115/F5 Netcong, NJ,US
41/G5 Nethe (riv.), Ger.
34/D3 Netherend, Eng,UK
40/B5 Netherlands
101/H5 Netherlands Antilles (isls.), Neth.
35/E5 Netley, Eng,UK
48/E3 Neto (riv.), It.
43/H2 Netphen, Ger.
40/D6 Nette (riv.), Ger.
41/H5 Nette (riv.), Ger.
43/G3 Nettebach (riv.), Ger.
43/F3 Nettersheim, Ger.
40/D6 Nettetal, Ger.
103/J2 Nettilling (lake), NW,Can
33/H5 Nettleham, Eng,UK
48/C2 Nettuno, It.
39/G2 Neubrandenburg, Ger.
45/G3 Neuchâtel, Swi.
45/G3 Neuchâtel (lake), Swi.
39/G2 Neuenhagen, Ger.
40/D4 Neuenhaus, Ger.
41/E4 Neuenkirchen, Ger.
41/F3 Neuenkirchen, Ger.
41/E6 Neuenrade, Ger.
43/E4 Neufchâteau, Belg.
44/F2 Neufchâteau, Fr.
42/B5 Neuilly-en-Thelle, Fr.
42/C5 Neuilly-Saint-Front, Fr.
31/T10 Neuilly-sur-Marne, Fr.
31/S10 Neuilly-sur-Seine, Fr.
45/J2 Neumarkt in der Oberpfalz, Ger.
38/E1 Neumünster, Ger.
50/C2 Neunkirchen, Aus.
43/G5 Neunkirchen, Ger.
43/H2 Neunkirchen, Ger.
43/G2 Neunkirchen-Seelscheid, Ger.
96/C3 Neuquén, Arg.
96/C3 Neuquén (prov.), Arg.
96/C3 Neuquén (riv.), Arg.
38/G2 Neuruppin, Ger.
113/J3 Neuse (riv.), NC,US
40/D6 Neuss, Ger.
41/G4 Neustadt am Rübenberge, Ger.
45/J2 Neustadt an der Donau, Ger.
45/H2 Neustadt an der Weinstrasse, Ger.
45/J1 Neustadt bei Coburg, Ger.
38/F1 Neustadt in Holstein, Ger.
38/G2 Neustrelitz, Ger.
45/J2 Neu-Ulm, Ger.
44/G2 Neuves-Maisons, Fr.
41/F1 Neuwerk (isl.), Ger.
43/G3 Neuwied, Ger.
55/V7 Neva (riv.), Rus.
46/D4 Nevada (mts.), Sp.
108/C3 Nevada (state), US
109/J3 Nevada, Mo,US
96/C4 Nevado Cónico (peak), Chile
91/C1 Nevado de Chañi (peak), Arg.
101/P10 Nevado de Colima Nat'l Park, Mex.
91/C2 Nevado del Candado (peak), Arg.
92/C3 Nevado del Huila (peak), Col.
96/C2 Nevado, Sierra del (mts.), Arg.
52/F4 Nevel', Rus.
42/C1 Nevele, Belg.
52/H2 Nevel'sk, Rus.
44/E3 Nevers, Fr.
50/D4 Nevesinje, Bosn.
55/G3 Nevinnomyssk, Rus.
101/J4 Nevis (isl.), StK.
59/C2 Nevşehir, Turk.
92/G3 New (riv.), Guy.
35/E5 New (for.), Eng,UK
110/D4 New (riv.), WV,US
32/E2 New Abbey, Sc,UK
110/C4 New Albany, In,US
113/F3 New Albany, Ms,US
35/E4 New Alresford, Eng,UK
93/G2 New Amsterdam, Guy.
33/H5 New Ancholme (riv.), Eng,UK
116/K11 Newark, Ca,US
115/F5 Newark, NJ,US
110/D3 Newark, Oh,US
33/H5 Newark-on-Trent, Eng,UK
116/G6 New Baltimore, Mi,US
111/G3 New Bedford, Ma,US
116/P14 New Berlin, Wi,US
113/J3 New Bern, NC,US
110/C2 Newberry, Mi,US
113/H3 Newberry, SC,US
33/G1 Newbiggin-by-the-Sea, Eng,UK
112/D4 New Braunfels, Tx,US
34/C2 Newbridge on Wye, Wal,UK
78/D5 New Britain (isl.), PNG
111/F3 New Britain, Ct,US
111/H2 New Brunswick (prov.), Can.
115/F5 New Brunswick, NJ,US
32/A2 New Buildings, NI,UK
33/G2 Newburn, Eng,UK
35/E4 Newbury, Eng,UK
33/F3 Newby Bridge, Eng,UK
78/F6 New Caledonia (terr.), Fr.
79/U12 New Caledonia (isl.), NCal.
115/G4 New Canaan, Ct,US
77/D2 Newcastle, Austl.
111/H2 Newcastle, NB,Can
111/S8 Newcastle, On,Can
89/E2 Newcastle, SAfr.
32/C3 Newcastle, NI,UK
110/C4 New Castle, In,US
110/D3 New Castle, Pa,US
107/G5 Newcastle, Wy,US
34/B2 Newcastle Emlyn, Wal,UK
33/F1 Newcastleton, Sc,UK
33/F5 Newcastle-under-Lyme, Eng,UK
33/G2 Newcastle upon Tyne, Eng,UK
115/G4 New City, NY,US
36/C3 New Cumnock, Sc,UK
70/C2 New Delhi (cap.), India
106/D3 New Denver, BC,Can
31/N8 Newdigate, Eng,UK
115/F5 New Egypt, NJ,US
77/E1 New England Nat'l Park, Austl.
114/F4 Newenham (cape), Ak,US
34/D3 Newent, Eng,UK
111/S9 Newfane, NY,US
103/K3 Newfoundland (prov.), Can.
111/L1 Newfoundland (isl.), Nf,Can
32/D1 New Galloway, Sc,UK
78/E5 New Georgia (isls.), Sol.
78/E5 New Georgia (sound), Sol.
111/J2 New Glasgow, NS,Can
111/N6 New Glasgow, Qu,Can
78/C5 New Guinea (isl.), Indo., PNG
31/P7 Newham (bor.), Eng,UK
111/G3 New Hampshire (state), US
78/D5 New Hanover (isl.), PNG
35/F5 Newhaven, Eng,UK
110/F3 New Haven, Ct,US
116/G6 New Haven, Mi,US
78/F6 New Hebrides (isls.), Van.
115/F5 New Hope, Pa,US
112/F4 New Iberia, La,US
35/G5 Newick, Eng,UK
78/E5 New Ireland (isl.), PNG
110/F3 New Jersey (state), US
110/E3 New Kensington, Pa,US
112/D2 Newkirk, Ok,US
116/Q16 New Lenox, Il,US
110/E2 New Liskeard, On,Can
111/F3 New London, Ct,US
110/B2 New London, Wi,US
34/A6 Newlyn, Eng,UK
109/K3 New Madrid, Mo,US
76/F6 Newmarket, Austl.
110/E2 Newmarket, On,Can
35/G2 Newmarket, Eng,UK
110/D4 New Martinsville, WV,US
106/D4 New Meadows, Id,US
108/F4 New Mexico (state), US
33/F5 New Mills, Eng,UK
113/G3 Newnan, Ga,US
34/D3 Newnham, Eng,UK
77/C4 New Norfolk, Austl.
113/F4 New Orleans, La,US
110/D3 New Philadelphia, Oh,US
75/R10 New Plymouth, NZ
33/F6 Newport, Eng,UK
35/E5 Newport, Eng,UK
34/B2 Newport, Wal,UK
34/D3 Newport, Wal,UK
113/F3 Newport, Ar,US
110/C4 Newport, Ky,US
106/B4 Newport, Or,US
111/G3 Newport, RI,US
110/D5 Newport, Tn,US
111/F2 Newport, Vt,US
106/D3 Newport, Wa,US
115/C3 Newport Beach, Ca,US
110/E4 Newport News, Va,US
35/F2 Newport Pagnell, Eng,UK
113/H4 New Port Richey, Fl,US
101/F3 New Providence (isl.), Bahm.
34/A6 Newquay, Eng,UK
34/B2 New Quay, Wal,UK
34/C2 New Radnor, Wal,UK
111/H1 New Richmond, Qu,Can
115/G5 New Rochelle, NY,US
107/J4 New Rockford, ND,US
35/G5 New Romney, Eng,UK
33/G5 New Rossington, Eng,UK
32/B3 Newry, NI,UK
32/B3 Newry (can.), NI,UK
98/Z New Schwabenland (reg.), Ant.
57/P2 New Siberian (isls.), Rus.
113/H4 New Smyrna Beach, Fl,US
77/C2 New South Wales (state), Austl.
34/D2 Newton, Eng,UK
33/E1 Newton, Sc,UK
109/H3 Newton, Ks,US
111/G3 Newton, Ma,US
115/F4 Newton, NJ,US
112/E4 Newton, Tx,US
34/C5 Newton Abbot, Eng,UK
33/G2 Newton Aycliffe, Eng,UK
34/B6 Newton Ferrers, Eng,UK
33/F5 Newton-le-Willows, Eng,UK
36/C2 Newtonmore, Sc,UK
33/G1 Newton on the Moor, Eng,UK
32/D2 Newton Stewart, Sc,UK
77/B3 Newtown, Austl.
34/C1 Newtown, Wal,UK
107/H4 New Town, ND,US
115/F5 Newtown, Pa,US
32/C2 Newtownabbey, NI,UK
32/C2 Newtownards, NI,UK
36/B3 Newtownbutler, NI,UK
32/B3 Newtownhamilton, NI,UK
36/D3 Newtown Saint Boswells, Sc,UK
32/A2 Newtownstewart, NI,UK
34/C3 New Tredegar, Wal,UK
107/K4 New Ulm, Mn,US
111/J2 New Waterford, NS,Can
106/C3 New Westminster, BC,Can
110/F3 New York (state), US
115/G5 New York, NY,US
75/Q10 New Zealand
98/L New Zealand (peak), Ant.
65/L10 Neyagawa, Japan
34/B3 Neyland, Wal,UK
61/F3 Neyrīz, Iran
61/G1 Neyshābūr, Iran
53/P4 Neyva (riv.), Rus.
70/C5 Neyveli, India
70/C6 Neyyāttinkara, India
54/D2 Nezhin, Ukr.
106/D4 Nezperce, Id,US
72/C3 Ngabang, Indo.
73/H5 Ngabordamlu (cape), Indo.
87/F4 Ngabu, Malw.
82/H5 Ngala, Nga.
68/D5 Ngangla Ringco (lake), China
68/E5 Ngangzê (lake), China
82/H6 Ngaoundéré, Camr.
77/B2 Ngarkat Consv. Park, Austl.
78/E4 Ngatik (isl.), Micr.
79/Z18 Ngau (isl.), Fiji
75/S10 Ngauruhoe (vol.), NZ
69/D2 Nghia Dan, Viet.
69/D1 Nghia Lo, Viet.
87/C4 Ngiva, Ang.
87/C1 Ngo, Congo
69/E4 Ngoan Muc (pass), Viet.
71/J4 Ngoc Linh (peak), Viet.
87/D4 Ngonye (falls), Zam.
63/D5 Ngoring (lake), China
82/H8 Ngounié (riv.), Gabon
82/H5 Nguigmi, Niger
78/C4 Ngulu (atoll), Micr.
72/C2 Ngum (riv.), Laos
69/D1 Nguyen Binh, Viet.
89/E2 Ngwenya (peak), Swaz.
92/G4 Nhamundá (riv.), Braz.
69/E3 Nha Trang, Viet.
84/E3 Niafounké, Mali
111/R9 Niagara (riv.), Can., US
111/R9 Niagara Falls, On,Can
111/R9 Niagara Falls, NY,US
85/F3 Niamey (cap.), Niger
85/F3 Niamey (dept.), Niger
84/C4 Niandan (riv.), Gui.
83/L7 Niangara, Zaire
84/E3 Niangay (lake), Mali
66/C3 Niangzi Guan (pass), China
72/A3 Nias (isl.), Indo.
100/D5 Nicaragua
100/E5 Nicaragua (lake), Nic.
48/E3 Nicastro-Sambiase, It.
45/G5 Nice, Fr.
113/G4 Niceville, Fl,US
64/B5 Nichinan, Japan
74/B4 Nickol (bay), Austl.
71/F6 Nicobar (isls.), India
111/F2 Nicolet, Qu,Can
59/J4 Nicosia (cap.), Cyp.
48/D4 Nicosia, It.
100/D5 Nicoya, CR
100/D6 Nicoya (gulf), CR
100/D6 Nicoya (pen.), CR
33/G4 Nidd (riv.), Eng,UK
45/H1 Nidda, Ger.
43/F2 Nideggen, Ger.
43/G6 Niderviller, Fr.
39/L2 Nidzica, Pol.
38/E1 Niebüll, Ger.
45/G2 Nied (riv.), Fr.
43/F5 Nied (riv.), Ger.
45/K3 Niedere Tauern (mts.), Aus.
39/G3 Niederlausitz (reg.), Ger.
43/H4 Nieder-Olm, Ger.
41/E1 Niedersächsisches Wattenmeer Nat'l Park, Ger.
50/B1 Niederüsterreich (prov.), Aus.
43/F2 Niederzier, Ger.
39/L2 Niegocin (lake), Pol.
41/G5 Nieheim, Ger.
39/J3 Niemodlin, Pol.
41/G3 Nienburg, Ger.
84/D5 Niénokoué (peak), IvC.
42/B2 Nieppe, Fr.
84/B3 Niéri Ko (riv.), Sen.
40/D5 Niers (riv.), Ger.
69/D4 Niet Ban Tinh Xa, Viet.
40/D5 Nieuw-Bergen, Neth.
40/C4 Nieuwegein, Neth.
40/B5 Nieuwerkerk aan de IJssel, Neth.
40/B4 Nieuwkoop, Neth.
40/D3 Nieuwleusen, Neth.
40/C4 Nieuw-Loosdrecht, Neth.
93/G2 Nieuw-Nickerie, Sur.
42/B1 Nieuwpoort, Belg.
40/D3 Nieuw-Schoonebeek, Neth.
59/C3 Niğde, Turk.
88/E2 Nigel, SAfr.
85/G2 Niger
85/G5 Niger (riv.), Afr.
85/G4 Niger (state), Nga.
85/G4 Nigeria
85/G5 Niger, Mouths of the (delta), Nga.
110/D1 Nighthawk (lake), On,Can
46/A1 Nigrán, Sp.
49/H2 Nigríta, Gre.
79/J2 Nihoa (isl.), Hi,US
65/G2 Nihonmatsu, Japan
65/F3 Nii (isl.), Japan
65/F2 Niigata, Japan
65/F2 Niigata (pref.), Japan
64/C4 Niihama, Japan
104/R10 Niihau (isl.), Hi,US
64/C3 Niimi, Japan
65/F2 Niitsu, Japan
65/H7 Niiza, Japan
46/D4 Níjar, Sp.
40/C4 Nijkerk, Neth.
42/D1 Nijlen, Belg.
40/C5 Nijmegen, Neth.
52/F1 Nikel', Rus.
65/F2 Nikkō, Japan
65/F2 Nikkō Nat'l Park, Japan
54/E3 Nikolayev, Ukr.
54/D3 Nikolayev Obl., Ukr.
57/Q4 Nikolayevsk-na-Amure, Rus.
55/H1 Nikol'sk, Rus.
54/E3 Nikopol', Ukr.
59/D2 Niksar, Turk.
50/D4 Nikšić, Yugo.
79/H5 Nikumaroro (Gardner) (atoll), Kiri.
78/G5 Nikunau (isl.), Kiri.
83/M2 Nile (riv.), Afr.
59/H6 Nile (delta), Egypt
116/Q15 Niles, Il,US
110/C3 Niles, Mi,US
110/D3 Niles, Oh,US
95/K7 Nilópolis, Braz.
37/J3 Nilsiä, Fin.
70/B3 Nīmach, India
63/L1 Niman (riv.), Rus.
84/C5 Nimba (peak), IvC.
84/C5 Nimba (co.), Libr.
44/F5 Nîmes, Fr.
98/L Nimrod (glac.), Ant.
43/F4 Nimsbach (riv.), Ger.
83/M7 Nimule Nat'l Park, Sudan
60/D1 Nineveh (ruins), Iraq
96/D4 Ninfas (pt.), Arg.
67/D2 Ningbo, China
66/C4 Ningling, China
66/B3 Ningxia Huizu Zizhiqu (aut. reg.), China
69/D1 Ninh Binh, Viet.
69/E3 Ninh Hoa, Viet.
78/D5 Niningo (isls.), PNG
98/K Ninnis (glac.), Ant.
65/H7 Ninomiya, Japan
42/D2 Ninove, Belg.
109/G2 Niobrara (riv.), Ne,US
84/B3 Niokolo-Koba Nat'l Park, Sen.
84/D3 Niono, Mali
84/B3 Nioro-du-Rip, Sen.
84/B3 Nioro du Sahel, Mali
44/C3 Niort, Fr.
107/H2 Nipawin, Sk,Can
110/B1 Nipigon, On,Can
110/B1 Nipigon (lake), On,Can
110/E2 Nipissing (lake), On,Can
96/C3 Niquén, Chile
65/F3 Nirasaki, Japan
76/H8 Nirimba-Hmas, Austl.
70/C4 Nirmal, India
50/E4 Niš, Yugo.
46/B3 Nisa, Port.
49/H1 Nišava (riv.), Yugo.
48/D4 Niscemi, It.
65/M9 Nishiharu, Japan
64/C3 Nishiki (riv.), Japan
65/L10 Nishinomiya, Japan
64/B5 Nishino'omote, Japan
65/E3 Nishio, Japan
64/D3 Nishiwaki, Japan
39/M3 Nisko, Pol.
116/B3 Nisqually Reach (str.), Wa,US
78/E5 Nissan (isl.), PNG
65/N9 Nisshin, Japan
107/K4 Nisswa, Mn,US
95/K7 Niterói, Braz.
32/E1 Nith (riv.), Sc,UK
32/E1 Nithsdale (val.), Sc,UK
68/C5 Niti (pass), India
39/K4 Nitra, Slvk.
39/K4 Nitra (riv.), Slvk.
53/P4 Nitsa (riv.), Rus.
79/H6 Niuafo'ou (isl.), Tonga
79/H6 Niuatoputapu Group (isls.), Tonga
79/J7 Niue (terr.), NZ
78/G6 Niulakita (isl.), Tuv.
71/H2 Niulan (riv.), China
72/C3 Niut (peak), Indo.
78/G5 Niutau (isl.), Tuv.
42/D2 Nivelles, Belg.
44/E3 Nivernais (hills), Fr.
107/J3 Niverville, Mb,Can
108/C3 Nixon, Nv,US
68/D4 Niya (riv.), China
64/C4 Niyodo (riv.), Japan
70/C4 Nizāmābād, India
53/K4 Nizhegorod Obl., Rus.
53/M4 Nizhnekama (res.), Rus.
53/L5 Nizhnekamsk, Rus.
57/K4 Nizhneudinsk, Rus.
56/H3 Nizhnevartovsk, Rus.
55/G1 Nizhniy Lomov, Rus.
53/K4 Nizhniy Novgorod (Gor'kiy), Rus.
53/N4 Nizhniy Tagil, Rus.
59/D3 Nizip, Turk.
39/K4 Nízke Tatry Nat'l Park, Slvk.
87/F2 Njombe, Tanz.
85/H5 Nkambe, Camr.
87/B1 Nkayi, Congo
87/F3 Nkhata Bay, Malw.
85/H5 Nkogam, Massif du (peak), Camr.
85/H5 N'Kongsamba, Camr.
71/G2 Nmai (riv.), Burma
42/B5 Noailles, Fr.
70/F3 Noākhāli, Bang.
70/E3 Noāmundi, India
114/F2 Noatak (riv.), Ak,US
114/F2 Noatak Nat'l Prsv., Ak,US
64/B4 Nobeoka, Japan
109/H4 Noble, Ok,US
110/C3 Noblesville, In,US
111/Q8 Nobleton, On,Can
63/N3 Noboribetsu, Japan
50/C5 Noci, It.
65/H7 Noda, Japan
81/P13 Noé (cape), Alg.
42/B3 Noeux-les-Mines, Fr.
108/E5 Nogales, Az,US
64/B4 Nogata, Japan
44/D2 Nogent-le-Rotrou, Fr.
31/T10 Nogent-sur-Marne, Fr.
42/B5 Nogent-sur-Oise, Fr.
52/H5 Noginsk, Rus.
76/B4 Nogoa (riv.), Austl.
62/C2 Nogoonuur, Mong.
96/F2 Nogoyá, Arg.
39/K5 Nógrád (co.), Hun.
47/F1 Noguera Pallarosa (riv.), Sp.
64/A2 Nogwak-san (mtn.), SKor.
70/B2 Nohar, India
43/G4 Nohfelden, Ger.
110/E2 Noire (riv.), Qu,Can
44/B2 Noires (mts.), Fr.
44/B3 Noirmoutier (isl.), Fr.
42/B6 Noisiel, Fr.
31/T10 Noisy-le-Grand, Fr.
31/S10 Noisy-le-Roi, Fr.
42/B6 Noisy-le-Sec, Fr.
65/F3 Nojima-zaki (pt.), Japan
37/G3 Nokia, Fin.
73/F4 Nokilalaki (peak), Indo.
61/H3 Nok Kundi, Pak.
82/J7 Nola, CAfr.
77/D2 Nomadgi Nat'l Park, Austl.
114/F3 Nome (cape), Ak,US
64/B5 Nomo-misaki (cape), Japan
64/A4 Nomo-zaki (pt.), Japan
62/D2 Nömrög, Mong.
102/F2 Nonacho (lake), NW,Can
45/G4 None, It.
42/B5 Nonette (riv.), Fr.
66/F1 Nong'an, China
69/D2 Nong Han (res.), Thai.
69/C2 Nong Het, Laos
69/C2 Nong Khai, Thai.
69/C2 Nong Pet, Laos
43/F4 Nonnweiler, Ger.
78/G5 Nonouti (atoll), Kiri.
66/E5 Nonri (isl.), China
63/K4 Nonsan, SKor.
40/A5 Noordbeveland (isl.), Neth.
40/B3 Noorderhaaks (isl.), Neth.
40/B3 Noordhollandsch (can.), Neth.
40/C3 Noordostpolder (polder), Neth.
40/B4 Noordwijk aan Zee, Neth.
40/B4 Noordwijkerhout, Neth.
40/B4 Noordzeekanaal (can.), Neth.
76/D4 Noosa-Tewantin, Austl.
106/B3 Nootka (isl.), BC,Can
106/B3 Nootka (sound), BC,Can
100/B4 Nopala, Mex.
63/L1 Nora (riv.), Rus.
52/B4 Nora, Swe.
73/F2 Norala, Phil.
115/C3 Norco, Ca,US
111/M6 Nord (riv.), Qu,Can
42/C3 Nord (dept.), Fr.
42/B3 Nord, Canal du (can.), Fr.
41/E1 Norden, Ger.
41/F2 Nordenham, Ger.
56/K2 Nordenskjöld (arch.), Rus.
41/E1 Norderney, Ger.
41/E1 Norderney (isl.), Ger.
41/G1 Norderstedt, Ger.
38/F3 Nordhausen, Ger.
41/F1 Nordholz, Ger.
41/E4 Nordhorn, Ger.
37/H1 Nordkapp (North) (cape), Nor.
37/H1 Nordkinn (pt.), Nor.
41/E5 Nordkirchen, Ger.
37/E2 Nordland (co.), Nor.
37/F3 Nordmaling, Swe.
38/E1 Nord-Ostsee (can.), Ger.
85/H5 Nord-Ouest (prov.), Camr.
81/M13 Nord Ouest (reg.), Mor.
44/D1 Nord-Pas-de-Calais (reg.), Fr.
41/E3 Nord-Radde (riv.), Ger.
41/E3 Nord-Sud (can.), Ger.
37/E2 Nord-Trøndelag (co.), Nor.
41/E4 Nordwalde, Ger.
36/B4 Nore (riv.), Ire.
44/E5 Nore, Pic de (peak), Fr.
75/M5 Norfolk (isl.), Austl.
77/C4 Norfolk (peak), Austl.
35/G1 Norfolk (co.), Eng,UK
109/H2 Norfolk, Ne,US
110/E4 Norfolk, Va,US
35/H1 Norfolk Broads (swamp), Eng,UK
109/J3 Norfork (lake), Ar, Mo,US
40/D2 Norg, Neth.
65/E2 Norikura-dake (mtn.), Japan
56/J3 Noril'sk, Rus.
110/B3 Normal, Il,US
76/A2 Norman (riv.), Austl.
109/H4 Norman, Ok,US
78/E6 Normanby (isl.), PNG
116/C3 Normandy Park, Wa,US
33/G4 Normanton, Eng,UK
88/B3 Norotshama (peak), Namb.
107/H3 Norquay, Sk,Can
37/F2 Norrbotten (co.), Swe.
46/B1 Norrea (riv.), Sp.
42/B2 Norrent-Fontes, Fr.
116/Q16 Norridge, Il,US
113/H2 Norris (lake), Tn,US
115/E5 Norristown, Pa,US
37/F4 Norrköping, Swe.
37/F2 Norrland (reg.), Swe.
37/F4 Norrtälje, Swe.
96/E4 Norte (pt.), Arg.
97/F3 Norte (pt.), Arg.
92/G6 Norte (mts.), Braz.
93/J3 Norte, Cabo do (cape), Braz.
97/J6 Norte, Campo de Hielo (glacier), Chile
93/G6 Nortelândia, Braz.
41/G5 Nörten-Hardenberg, Ger.
77/C3 North (pt.), Austl.
77/C4 North (pt.), Austl.
110/D2 North (chan.), On,Can
111/J2 North (cape), PE,Can
30/D3 North (sea), Eur.
75/R9 North (cape), NZ
75/R10 North (isl.), NZ
32/C1 North (chan.), UK
114/D5 North (cape), Ak,US
114/F3 North (peak), Ak,US
50/D4 North Albanian Alps (mts.), Alb., Yugo.
33/G3 Northallerton, Eng,UK
74/B6 Northam, Austl.
34/B4 Northam, Eng,UK
99/* North America
35/F2 Northampton, Eng,UK
35/E2 Northampton (uplands), Eng,UK
110/F3 Northampton, Ma,US
115/F5 Northampton, Pa,US
35/F2 Northamptonshire (co.), Eng,UK
71/F5 North Andaman (isl.), India
103/K3 North Aulatsivik (isl.), Nf,Can
31/N6 Northaw, Eng,UK
36/C2 North Ballachulish, Sc,UK
32/D3 North Barrule (mtn.), IM,UK
106/F2 North Battleford, Sk,Can
110/E2 North Bay, On,Can
106/B5 North Bend, Or,US
115/F5 North Bergen, NJ,US
36/D2 North Berwick, Sc,UK
40/C5 North Brabant (prov.), Neth.
116/Q15 Northbrook, Il,US
115/F5 North Brunswick, NJ,US
109/H3 North Canadian (riv.), Ok,US
107/L2 North Caribou (lake), On,Can
113/H3 North Carolina (state), US
106/C3 North Cascades Nat'l Park, Wa,US
113/J3 North Charleston, SC,US
116/Q15 North Chicago, Il,US
33/H5 North Collingham, Eng,UK
106/C3 North Cowichan, BC,Can
107/H4 North Dakota (state), US
34/D5 North Dorset Downs (uplands), Eng,UK
32/C2 North Down (dist.), NI,UK
35/F4 North Downs (hills), Eng,UK
76/C3 North East (pt.), Austl.
101/G3 Northeast (pt.), Bahm.
114/E3 Northeast (cape), Ak,US
56/C2 Northeast Land (isl.), Sval.
41/G5 Northeim, Ger.
35/G1 North Elmham, Eng,UK
74/E3 Northern (terr.), Austl.
85/E4 Northern (reg.), Gha.
59/K5 Northern (dist.), Isr.
84/B4 Northern (prov.), SLeo.
86/B4 Northern (reg.), Sudan
68/B4 Northern Areas (terr.), Pak.
79/J6 Northern Cook (isls.), CookIs.
30/H2 Northern Dvina (riv.), Rus.
36/B3 Northern Ireland, UK
110/B1 Northern Light (lake), On,Can, Mn,US
78/D3 Northern Marianas, US
56/G3 Northern Sos'va (riv.), Rus.
49/J3 Northern Sporades (isls.), Gre.
53/N3 Northern Ural (mts.), Rus.
53/K4 Northern Uval (hills), Rus.
56/E4 Northern Wals (upland), Rus.
114/K2 Northern Yukon Nat'l Park, Yk,Can
107/K4 Northfield, Mn,US
31/P7 Northfleet, Eng,UK
35/H4 North Foreland (pt.), Eng,UK
113/H5 North Fort Myers, Fl,US
110/D1 North French (riv.), On,Can
38/E1 North Frisian (isls.), Den., Ger.
111/F2 North Hero, Vt,US
116/M9 North Highlands, Ca,US
116/C3 North Hill-Edgewood, Wa,US
40/B3 North Holland (prov.), Neth.
33/H5 North Hykeham, Eng,UK
53/Q5 North Kazakhstan Obl., Rus.
63/K3 North Korea
71/F2 North Lakhimpur, India
108/D3 North Las Vegas, Nv,US
112/E3 North Little Rock, Ar,US
87/F3 North Luangwa Nat'l Park, Zam.
103/R7 North Magnetic Pole, NAm
107/J2 North Moose (lake), Mb,Can
113/J3 North Myrtle Beach, SC,US
37/H1 North (Nordkapp) (cape), Nor.
55/G4 North Ossetian Aut. Rep., Rus.
111/R9 North Pelham, On,Can
34/C4 North Petherton, Eng,UK
76/E6 North Pine (riv.), Austl.
115/F5 North Plainfield, NJ,US
109/G2 North Platte (riv.), US
109/G2 North Platte, Ne,US
113/G3 Northport, Al,US
115/G5 Northport (Old Northport), NY,US
115/J7 North Potomac, Md,US
38/E3 North Rhine-Westphalia (state), Ger.
108/D3 North Rim, Az,US
106/F2 North Saskatchewan (riv.), Ab, Sk,Can
33/G2 North Shields, Eng,UK
56/K2 North Siberian (plain), Rus.
33/J5 North Somercotes, Eng,UK

151
North – Orsay

76/D4 **North Stradbroke** (isl.), Austl.
75/R10 **North Taranaki** (bight), NZ
115/G4 **North Tarrytown,** NY,US
33/H5 **North Thoresby,** Eng,UK
35/E4 **North Tidworth,** Eng,UK
111/S9 **North Tonawanda,** NY,US
33/F1 **North Tyne** (riv.), Eng,UK
111/J2 **Northumberland** (str.), Can.
33/F1 **Northumberland** (co.), Eng,UK
33/F1 **Northumberland Nat'l Park,** Eng,UK
108/B2 **North Umpqua** (riv.), Or,US
102/D4 **North Vancouver,** BC,Can
116/F7 **Northville,** Mi,US
35/H1 **North Walsham,** Eng,UK
31/P6 **North Weald Bassett,** Eng,UK
74/A4 **North West** (cape), Austl.
68/B4 **Northwest Frontier** (prov.), Pak.
111/L1 **North West Gander** (riv.), Nf,Can
36/C2 **North West Highlands** (mts.), Sc,UK
102/E2 **Northwest Territories** (terr.), Can.
33/H5 **North Wheatley,** Eng,UK
33/F5 **Northwich,** Eng,UK
33/G5 **North Wingfield,** Eng,UK
107/J4 **Northwood,** ND,US
111/R8 **North York,** On,Can
33/H3 **North York Moors Nat'l Park,** Eng,UK
33/G3 **North Yorkshire** (co.), Eng,UK
114/F3 **Norton** (bay), Ak,US
114/E3 **Norton** (sound), Ak,US
109/H3 **Norton,** Ks,US
110/D4 **Norton,** Va,US
33/F6 **Norton Bridge,** Eng,UK
110/C3 **Norton Shores,** Mi,US
38/E1 **Nortorf,** Ger.
111/Q8 **Norval,** On,Can
98/Z **Norvegia** (cape), Ant.
43/F2 **Nörvenich,** Ger.
115/B3 **Norwalk,** Ca,US
115/G4 **Norwalk,** Ct,US
110/D3 **Norwalk,** Oh,US
37/B3 **Norway**
107/J2 **Norway House,** Mb,Can
103/S7 **Norwegian** (bay), NW,Can
30/C2 **Norwegian** (sea), Eur.
35/H1 **Norwich,** Eng,UK
110/F3 **Norwich,** NY,US
65/L10 **Nose,** Japan
61/K1 **Noshaq** (mtn.), Pak.
63/N3 **Noshiro,** Japan
51/H4 **Nos Maslen Nos** (pt.), Bul.
72/E2 **Nosong** (cape), Malay.
88/C2 **Nosop** (dry riv.), Bots.
54/D2 **Nosovka,** Ukr.
61/G3 **Noşratābād,** Iran
94/C3 **Nossa Senhora da Glória,** Braz.
94/C3 **Nossa Senhora das Dores,** Braz.
97/J7 **Notch** (cape), Chile
39/J2 **Notec** (riv.), Pol.
48/D4 **Noto,** It.
48/D4 **Noto** (gulf), It.
65/E2 **Noto** (pen.), Japan
48/D4 **Noto Antica** (ruins), It.
65/M9 **Notogawa,** Japan
111/L1 **Notre Dame** (bay), Nf,Can
111/G1 **Notre Dame** (mts.), Qu,Can
111/N7 **Notre-Dame-de-l'Ile-Perrot,** Qu,Can
110/E1 **Nottaway** (riv.), Qu,Can
103/H2 **Nottingham** (isl.), NW,Can
33/G6 **Nottingham,** Eng,UK
33/H5 **Nottinghamshire** (co.), Eng,UK
41/E5 **Nottuln,** Ger.
82/B3 **Nouadhibou,** Mrta.
84/B2 **Nouakchott** (cap.), Mrta.
79/V13 **Nouméa** (cap.), NCal.
88/D3 **Noupoort,** SAfr.
42/A3 **Nouvion,** Fr.
43/D4 **Nouzonville,** Fr.
93/H8 **Nova Andradina,** Braz.
51/F3 **Novaci,** Rom.
94/D2 **Nova Cruz,** Braz.
39/K4 **Nová Dubnica,** Slvk.
95/L7 **Nova Friburgo,** Braz.
50/C3 **Nova Gradiška,** Cro.
95/K7 **Nova Iguaçu,** Braz.
94/C2 **Nova Olinda,** Braz.
92/G4 **Nova Olinda do Norte,** Braz.
50/E3 **Nova Pazova,** Yugo.
95/B4 **Nova Prata,** Braz.
45/H4 **Novara,** It.
94/B2 **Nova Russas,** Braz.
111/J2 **Nova Scotia** (prov.), Can.
94/C3 **Nova Soure,** Braz.
116/J10 **Novato,** Ca,US
50/D4 **Nova Varoš,** Yugo.
95/D1 **Nova Venécia,** Braz.
93/H6 **Nova Xavantina,** Braz.
54/E3 **Novaya Kakhovka,** Ukr.
57/R2 **Novaya Sibir'** (isl.), Rus.
56/E2 **Novaya Zemlya** (isl.), Rus.
51/H4 **Nova Zagora,** Bul.
47/E3 **Novelda,** Sp.
39/J4 **Nové Mesto nad Váhom,** Slvk.
39/K5 **Nové Zámky,** Slvk.
52/F4 **Novgorod,** Rus.
52/G4 **Novgorod Obl.,** Rus.
116/F7 **Novi,** Mi,US
50/E3 **Novi Bečej,** Yugo.
51/F4 **Novi Iskŭr,** Bul.
45/H4 **Novi Ligure,** It.
51/H4 **Novi Pazar,** Bul.
50/E4 **Novi Pazar,** Yugo.
50/D3 **Novi Sad,** Yugo.
95/K6 **Novo** (riv.), Braz.
55/G2 **Novoanninskiy,** Rus.
92/F5 **Novo Aripuanã,** Braz.
53/K4 **Novocheboksarsk,** Rus.
54/G3 **Novocherkassk,** Rus.
54/C2 **Novograd-Volynskiy,** Ukr.
52/E5 **Novogrudok,** Bela.
95/B4 **Novo Hamburgo,** Braz.
95/B2 **Novo Horizonte,** Braz.
56/G5 **Novokazalinsk,** Kaz.
55/J1 **Novokuybyshevsk,** Rus.
56/J4 **Novokuznetsk,** Rus.
98/A **Novolazarevskaya,** Ant.
50/B3 **Novo Mesto,** Slov.
50/E3 **Novo Miloševo,** Yugo.
54/F1 **Novomoskovsk,** Rus.
54/E3 **Novomoskovsk,** Ukr.
94/B2 **Novo Oriente,** Braz.
52/E5 **Novopolotsk,** Bela.
54/F3 **Novorossiysk,** Rus.
54/F3 **Novoshakhtinsk,** Rus.
56/J4 **Novosibirsk,** Rus.
55/L2 **Novotroitsk,** Rus.
54/D2 **Novoukrainka,** Ukr.
54/C2 **Novovolynsk,** Ukr.
53/L4 **Novovyatsk,** Rus.
54/D1 **Novozybkov,** Rus.
50/C3 **Novska,** Cro.
39/K4 **Nový Jičín,** Czh.
55/K4 **Novyy Uzen',** Kaz.
39/L3 **Nowa Dęba,** Pol.
39/J3 **Nowa Ruda,** Pol.
39/M3 **Nowa Sarzyna,** Pol.
39/H3 **Nowa Sól,** Pol.
109/J3 **Nowata,** Ok,US
39/K2 **Nowe,** Pol.
39/K2 **Nowe Miasto Lubawskie,** Pol.
70/C2 **Nowgong,** India
71/F2 **Nowgong,** India
114/H3 **Nowitna** (riv.), Ak,US
114/H3 **Nowitna Nat'l Wild. Ref.,** Ak,US
39/H2 **Nowogard,** Pol.
108/F1 **Nowood** (riv.), Wy,US
61/K2 **Nowshera,** Pak.
39/K1 **Nowy Dwór Gdański,** Pol.
39/L4 **Nowy Sącz,** Pol.
39/L4 **Nowy Sącz** (prov.), Pol.
39/L4 **Nowy Targ,** Pol.
39/J2 **Nowy Tomyśl,** Pol.
46/A1 **Noya,** Sp.
42/B5 **Noye** (riv.), Fr.
42/C4 **Noyon,** Fr.
87/G4 **Nsanje,** Malw.
85/E5 **Nsawam,** Gha.
62/D5 **Nu** (riv.), China
83/M5 **Nūbah** (mts.), Sudan
86/C4 **Nubian** (des.), Sudan
108/E3 **Nucla,** Co,US
112/D4 **Nueces** (riv.), Tx,US
102/G2 **Nueltin** (lake), NW,Can
40/C6 **Nuenen,** Neth.
66/E2 **Nü'er** (riv.), China
100/C5 **Nueva Concepción,** Guat.
100/E3 **Nueva Gerona,** Cuba
97/F2 **Nueva Helvecia,** Uru.
96/B3 **Nueva Imperial,** Chile
92/C3 **Nueva Loja,** Ecu.
97/S11 **Nueva Palmira,** Uru.
100/A2 **Nueva Rosita,** Mex.
101/F3 **Nuevitas,** Cuba
96/D4 **Nuevo** (gulf), Arg.
101/N7 **Nuevo Casas Grandes,** Mex.
101/N9 **Nuevo Ideal,** Mex.
100/B2 **Nuevo Laredo,** Mex.
100/A2 **Nuevo León** (state), Mex.
97/S11 **Nuevo Palmira,** Uru.
78/E5 **Nuguria** (isls.), PNG
79/J2 **Nuhau** (isl.), Hi,US
41/F6 **Nuhne** (riv.), Ger.
78/G5 **Nui** (atoll), Tuv.
65/N10 **Nukata,** Japan
114/F4 **Nuklunek** (mtn.), Ak,US
79/H7 **Nuku'alofa** (cap.), Tonga
78/G5 **Nukufetau** (atoll), Tuv.
79/L5 **Nuku Hiva** (isl.), FrPol.
78/H5 **Nukulaelae** (isl.), Tuv.
78/F5 **Nukumanu** (atoll), PNG
79/H5 **Nukunonu** (atoll), Tok.
78/E4 **Nukuoro** (isl.), Micr.
56/F5 **Nukus,** Uzb.
79/M6 **Nukutavake** (isl.), FrPol.
47/E3 **Nules,** Sp.
74/D6 **Nullarbor** (plain), Austl.
82/H6 **Numan,** Nga.
40/B5 **Numansdorp,** Neth.
65/F2 **Numata,** Japan
65/F3 **Numazu,** Japan
43/G2 **Nümbrecht,** Ger.
73/H4 **Numfoor** (isl.), Indo.
77/G5 **Nunawading,** Austl.
35/E1 **Nuneaton,** Eng,UK
77/D3 **Nungatta Nat'l Park,** Austl.
114/E4 **Nunivak** (isl.), Ak,US
40/C4 **Nunspeet,** Neth.
33/G2 **Nunthorpe,** Eng,UK
63/J1 **Nuomin** (riv.), China
84/C5 **Nuon** (riv.), IvC., Libr.
48/A2 **Nuoro,** It.
68/B2 **Nura** (riv.), Kaz.
43/F3 **Nürburgring,** Ger.
59/D3 **Nurhak,** Turk.
86/B5 **Nuri** (ruins), Sudan
45/J2 **Nürnberg,** Ger.
77/C1 **Nurri** (peak), Austl.
45/H2 **Nürtingen,** Ger.
59/L4 **Nuşarīyah, Jabal an** (mts.), Syria
59/E3 **Nusaybin,** Turk.
114/G4 **Nushagak** (riv.), Ak,US
61/J3 **Nushki,** Pak.
43/E2 **Nuth,** Neth.
115/F5 **Nutley,** NJ,US
99/M3 **Nuuk** (Godthåb), Grld.
79/K15 **Nuupere** (pt.), FrPol.
86/C2 **Nuwaybi',** Egypt
88/L10 **Nuy** (riv.), SAfr.
87/E4 **Nxai Pan Nat'l Park,** Bots.
115/G4 **Nyack,** NY,US
87/F2 **Nyahua,** Tanz.
68/F5 **Nyainqêntanglha Feng** (peak), China
83/K5 **Nyala,** Sudan
83/L6 **Nyamlell,** Sudan
52/J3 **Nyandoma,** Rus.
87/E1 **Nyanza-Lac,** Buru.
87/F3 **Nyasa (Malawi)** (lake), Afr.
38/F1 **Nyborg,** Den.
37/E4 **Nybro,** Swe.
39/L5 **Nyíradony,** Hun.
50/F2 **Nyírbátor,** Hun.
50/E2 **Nyíregyháza,** Hun.
83/N7 **Nyiru** (peak), Kenya
38/F1 **Nykøbing,** Den.
37/F4 **Nyköping,** Swe.
88/E2 **Nylstroom,** SAfr.
37/F4 **Nynäshamn,** Swe.
45/G3 **Nyon,** Swi.
45/K2 **Nýřany,** Czh.
39/J3 **Nysa,** Pol.
106/D5 **Nyssa,** Or,US
63/M4 **Nyūdo-zaki** (pt.), Japan
52/F2 **Nyuk** (lake), Rus.
87/E2 **Nyunzu,** Zaire
65/E2 **Nyūzen,** Japan
84/C5 **Nzérékoré,** Gui.
84/C4 **Nzérékoré** (comm.), Gui.
84/D5 **Nzi** (riv.), IvC.

O

35/E1 **Oadby,** Eng,UK
107/H4 **Oahe** (lake), ND, SD,US
104/V13 **Oahu** (isl.), Hi,US
107/J3 **Oakbank,** Mb,Can
116/Q14 **Oak Creek,** Wi,US
107/J4 **Oakes,** ND,US
116/Q16 **Oak Forest,** Il,US
35/F1 **Oakham,** Eng,UK
110/D4 **Oak Hill,** WV,US
108/C3 **Oakhurst,** Ca,US
116/K11 **Oakland,** Ca,US
115/F4 **Oakland,** NJ,US
116/A3 **Oakland** (bay), Wa,US
116/Q16 **Oak Lawn,** Il,US
35/E3 **Oakley,** Eng,UK
35/F2 **Oakley,** Eng,UK
116/L11 **Oakley,** Ca,US
109/G3 **Oakley,** Ks,US
74/C4 **Oakover** (riv.), Austl.
116/Q16 **Oak Park,** Il,US
116/F7 **Oak Park,** Mi,US
106/C5 **Oakridge,** Or,US
110/C4 **Oak Ridge,** Tn,US
111/R8 **Oak Ridges,** On,Can
34/D3 **Oaksey,** Eng,UK
115/A2 **Oak View,** Ca,US
111/Q9 **Oakville,** On,Can
75/R12 **Oamaru,** NZ
100/B4 **Oaxaca,** Mex.
100/B4 **Oaxaca** (state), Mex.
56/H3 **Ob'** (gulf), Rus.
56/G3 **Ob'** (riv.), Rus.
78/F6 **Oba** (isl.), Van.
110/D2 **Obabika** (lake), On,Can
64/D3 **Obama,** Japan
85/H5 **Oban** (hills), Camr., Nga.
75/Q12 **Oban,** NZ
110/D1 **Obasatika** (riv.), On,Can
65/M10 **Obata,** Japan
91/E6 **Oberá,** Arg.
40/D6 **Oberhausen,** Ger.
39/H3 **Oberlausitz** (reg.), Ger.
109/G3 **Oberlin,** Ks,US
45/H2 **Oberndorf am Neckar,** Ger.
41/G4 **Obernkirchen,** Ger.
43/G4 **Oberthal,** Ger.
45/L3 **Oberwölz,** Aus.
73/G4 **Obi** (isls.), Indo.
73/G4 **Obi** (str.), Indo.
93/G4 **Óbidos,** Braz.
63/N3 **Obihiro,** Japan
50/E4 **Obilić,** Yugo.
65/J7 **Obitsu** (riv.), Japan
69/B2 **Ob Luang Gorge,** Thai.
63/L2 **Obluch'ye,** Rus.
52/H5 **Obninsk,** Rus.
83/P5 **Obock,** Djib.
39/J2 **Oborniki,** Pol.
39/J3 **Oborniki Śląskie,** Pol.
39/J2 **Obra** (riv.), Pol.
50/E3 **Obrenovac,** Yugo.
65/M10 **Ōbu,** Japan
85/E5 **Obuasi,** Gha.
113/H4 **Ocala,** Fl,US
44/C5 **Occabe, Sommet d'** (peak), Fr.
92/E7 **Occidental, Cordillera** (range), SAm.
114/L4 **Ocean** (cape), Ak,US
115/G5 **Ocean Beach,** NY,US
110/F4 **Ocean City,** Md,US
106/B2 **Ocean Falls,** BC,Can
115/F5 **Ocean Grove,** NJ,US
78/* **Oceania**
108/C4 **Oceanside,** Ca,US
115/G5 **Oceanside,** NY,US
69/D4 **Oc-Eo** (ruins), Viet.
55/G4 **Ochamchira,** Geo.
63/P3 **Ochiishi-misaki** (cape), Japan
101/F4 **Ocho Rios,** Jam.
41/E4 **Ochtrup,** Ger.
41/F2 **Ochtum** (riv.), Ger.
35/E3 **Ock** (riv.), Eng,UK
52/C3 **Ockelbo,** Swe.
113/H4 **Ocmulgee** (riv.), Ga,US
51/F2 **Ocna Mureş,** Rom.
113/H3 **Oconee** (lake), Ga,US
113/H3 **Oconee** (riv.), Ga,US
100/D5 **Ocotal,** Nic.
100/A3 **Ocotlán,** Mex.
100/B4 **Ocotlán,** Mex.
44/C2 **Octeville,** Fr.
57/L1 **October Revolution** (isl.), Rus.
85/E5 **Oda,** Gha.
64/C3 **Oda,** Japan
65/M10 **Ōdai,** Japan
64/E3 **Ōdaigahara-san** (mtn.), Japan
86/D4 **Oda, Jabal** (peak), Sudan
63/N3 **Ōdate,** Japan
65/F3 **Odawara,** Japan
37/C3 **Odda,** Nor.
83/P7 **Oddur,** Som.
41/F6 **Odeborn** (riv.), Ger.
46/A4 **Odemira,** Port.
59/A2 **Ödemiş,** Turk.
88/D2 **Odendaalsrus,** SAfr.
38/F1 **Odense,** Den.
41/E6 **Odenthal,** Ger.
115/K7 **Odenton,** Md,US
39/H2 **Oderhaff** (lag.), Ger., Pol.
39/H2 **Oder (Odra)** (riv.), Ger., Pol.
45/K4 **Oderzo,** It.
54/D3 **Odessa,** Ukr.
112/C4 **Odessa,** Tx,US
106/D4 **Odessa,** Wa,US
51/J2 **Odessa Obl.,** Ukr.
44/B2 **Odet** (riv.), Fr.
84/D4 **Odienné,** IvC.
52/H5 **Odintsovo,** Rus.
67/D5 **Odiongan,** Phil.
47/P10 **Odivelas,** Port.
51/H3 **Odobeşti,** Rom.
44/C2 **Odon** (riv.), Fr.
69/D4 **Odongk,** Camb.
40/D3 **Odoorn,** Neth.
51/G2 **Odorheiu Secuiesc,** Rom.
39/H2 **Odra (Oder)** (riv.), Ger., Pol.
50/D3 **Odžaci,** Yugo.
82/J7 **Odzala Nat'l Park,** Congo
65/L9 **Ōe,** Japan
40/B4 **Oegstgeest,** Neth.
94/B2 **Oeiras,** Braz.
41/F5 **Oelde,** Ger.
45/K1 **Oelsnitz,** Ger.
79/M7 **Oeno** (atoll), Pitc.,UK
41/E5 **Oer-Erkenschwick,** Ger.
43/E4 **Oesling** (mts.), Lux.
40/B6 **Oesterdam** (dam), Neth.
45/H2 **Oestrich-Winkel,** Ger.
49/H3 **Oeta Nat'l Park,** Gre.
59/E2 **Of,** Turk.
48/D2 **Ofanto** (riv.), It.
59/K6 **Ofaqim,** Isr.
32/A5 **Offaly** (co.), Ire.
45/H1 **Offenbach,** Ger.
45/G2 **Offenburg,** Ger.
45/G3 **Oftringen,** Swi.
63/M4 **Oga,** Japan
83/P6 **Ogadēn** (reg.), Eth.
64/E3 **Ōgaki,** Japan
109/G2 **Ogallala,** Ne,US
78/D2 **Ogasawara,** Japan
85/G4 **Ogbomosho,** Nga.
108/E2 **Ogden,** Ut,US
110/F2 **Ogdensburg,** NY,US
113/H3 **Ogeechee** (riv.), Ga,US
110/D2 **Ogidaki** (mtn.), On,Can
114/L3 **Ogilvie** (mts.), Yk,Can
102/C2 **Ogilvie** (riv.), Yk,Can
45/J4 **Oglio** (riv.), It.
34/C4 **Ogmore by Sea,** Wal,UK
44/F3 **Ognon** (riv.), Fr.
73/F3 **Ogoamas** (peak), Indo.
107/M3 **Ogoki** (lake), On,Can
107/L3 **Ogoki** (res.), On,Can
107/M3 **Ogoki** (riv.), On,Can
82/G8 **Ogooué** (riv.), Gabon
65/H7 **Ogose,** Japan
51/F4 **Ogosta** (riv.), Bul.
52/E4 **Ogre,** Lat.
65/M9 **Oguchi,** Japan
50/B3 **Ogulin,** Cro.
85/F5 **Ogun** (riv.), Nga.
85/F5 **Ogun** (state), Nga.
55/K5 **Ogurchinskiy** (isl.), Trkm.
82/G2 **Ohanet,** Alg.
76/G8 **O'Hares** (cr.), Austl.
41/E2 **Ohe** (riv.), Ger.
97/J7 **O'Higgins** (lake), Chile
110/B4 **Ohio** (riv.), US
110/D3 **Ohio** (state), US
33/F1 **Oh Me Edge** (hill), Eng,UK
113/H3 **Ohoopee** (riv.), Ga,US
45/K1 **Ohře** (riv.), Czh.
38/F2 **Ohre** (riv.), Ger.
50/E5 **Ohrid** (lake), Alb., Macd.
50/E5 **Ohrid,** Macd.
71/G2 **Oi** (riv.), China
65/H7 **Ōi,** Japan
65/F3 **Ōi** (riv.), Japan
93/H3 **Oiapoque** (riv.), Braz.
47/P10 **Oieras,** Port.
42/B3 **Oignies,** Fr.
110/E3 **Oil City,** Pa,US
40/C5 **Oirschot,** Neth.
42/B5 **Oise** (dept.), Fr.
42/B5 **Oise** (riv.), Fr.
42/C5 **Oise à l'Aisne, Canal de** (can.), Fr.
42/A4 **Oisemont,** Fr.
65/H7 **Ōiso,** Japan
40/C5 **Oisterwijk,** Neth.
42/C3 **Oisy-le-Verger,** Fr.
64/B4 **Ōita,** Japan
64/B4 **Ōita** (pref.), Japan
64/B4 **Ōita** (riv.), Japan
115/A2 **Ojai,** Ca,US
39/K3 **Ojcowski Nat'l Park,** Pol.
65/L10 **Ōji,** Japan
101/P8 **Ojinaga,** Mex.
65/F2 **Ojiya,** Japan
100/A3 **Ojocaliente,** Mex.
91/C2 **Ojos del Salado** (peak), Arg., Chile
101/L7 **Ojos Negros,** Mex.
53/J4 **Oka** (riv.), Rus.
103/K3 **Okak** (isl.), Nf,Can
106/C3 **Okanagan** (lake), BC,Can
106/D3 **Okanagan Falls,** BC,Can
87/B1 **Okanda Nat'l Park,** Gabon
106/D3 **Okanogan,** Wa,US
106/D3 **Okanogan** (riv.), Wa,US
61/K2 **Okāra,** Pak.
87/C4 **Okaukuejo,** Namb.
87/D4 **Okavango Delta** (reg.), Bots.
64/B4 **Ōkawa,** Japan
65/F2 **Okaya,** Japan
64/C3 **Okayama,** Japan
64/C3 **Okayama** (pref.), Japan
65/E3 **Okazaki,** Japan
113/H5 **Okeechobee,** Fl,US
113/H5 **Okeechobee** (lake), Fl,US
65/H7 **Okegawa,** Japan
34/C5 **Okehampton,** Eng,UK
34/B5 **Okement** (riv.), Eng,UK
41/H4 **Oker** (riv.), Ger.
57/Q4 **Okha,** Rus.
49/J3 **Ókhi** (peak), Gre.
57/Q4 **Okhotsk** (sea), Japan, Rus.
64/C2 **Oki** (isls.), Japan
64/C2 **Oki-Daisen Nat'l Park,** Japan
67/E2 **Okinawa** (isls.), Japan
78/C2 **Okino-Tori-Shima (Parece Vela)** (isl.), Japan
71/G4 **Okkan,** Burma
109/H4 **Oklahoma** (state), US
109/H4 **Oklahoma City** (cap.), Ok,US
113/H4 **Oklawaha** (riv.), Fl,US
109/J4 **Okmulgee,** Ok,US
107/K5 **Okoboji** (lakes), Ia,US
113/F3 **Okolona,** Ms,US
106/E3 **Okotoks,** Ab,Can
80/E6 **Okovango** (riv.), Afr.
86/C4 **Oko, Wādī** (dry riv.), Sudan
37/E2 **Oksskolten** (peak), Nor.
55/J1 **Oktyabr'sk,** Rus.
53/M5 **Oktyabr'skiy,** Rus.
52/G4 **Okulovka,** Rus.
63/M3 **Okushiri** (isl.), Japan
65/H7 **Okutama,** Japan
87/D5 **Okwa** (riv.), Bots.
108/C3 **Olancha,** Ca,US
100/D4 **Olanchito,** Hon.
37/F4 **Öland** (isl.), Swe.
37/F4 **Ölands södra udde** (pt.), Swe.
45/G4 **Olan, Pic d'** (peak), Fr.
48/D2 **Olanto** (riv.), It.
108/F3 **Olathe,** Co,US
109/J3 **Olathe,** Ks,US
96/E3 **Olavarría,** Arg.
39/J3 **Oława,** Pol.
41/F5 **Olbach** (riv.), Ger.
48/A2 **Olbia,** It.
45/J2 **Olching,** Ger.
111/S9 **Olcott,** NY,US
116/D3 **Old Baldy** (mtn.), Wa,US
115/F5 **Old Bridge,** NJ,US
114/L2 **Old Crow,** Yk,Can
40/C4 **Oldebroek,** Neth.
41/F2 **Oldenburg,** Ger.
40/D4 **Oldenzaal,** Neth.
33/F4 **Oldham,** Eng,UK
106/E3 **Oldman** (riv.), Ab,Can
32/E3 **Old Man of Coolston, The** (mtn.), Eng,UK
35/F2 **Old Nene** (riv.), Eng,UK
115/G5 **Old Northport** (Northport), NY,US
41/F1 **Oldoog** (isl.), Ger.
111/G2 **Old Town,** Me,US
31/M7 **Old Windsor,** Eng,UK
107/G3 **Old Wives** (lake), Sk,Can
110/E3 **Olean,** NY,US
39/M1 **Olecko,** Pol.
46/A1 **Oleiros,** Sp.
57/N4 **Olekma** (riv.), Rus.
116/B2 **Olele** (pt.), Wa,US
52/G1 **Olenegorsk,** Rus.
57/N2 **Olenek** (bay), Rus.
57/N2 **Olenëk** (riv.), Rus.
68/B1 **Olenty** (riv.), Kaz.
44/C4 **Oléron** (isl.), Fr.
47/K6 **Olesa de Montserrat,** Sp.
39/J3 **Oleśnica,** Pol.
39/K3 **Olesno,** Pol.
41/E5 **Olfen,** Ger.
62/B2 **Ölgiy,** Mong.
46/B4 **Olhão,** Port.
94/C3 **Olho d'Água dos Flores,** Braz.
45/L4 **Olib** (isl.), Cro.
48/A2 **Oliena,** It.
88/B2 **Olifants** (dry riv.), Namb.
88/B3 **Olifants** (riv.), SAfr.
88/E2 **Olifantsrivier** (riv.), SAfr.
78/D4 **Olimarao** (atoll), Micr.
49/H2 **Olimbos (Mount Olympus)** (peak), Gre.
95/B2 **Olímpia,** Braz.
94/D3 **Olinda,** Braz.
94/C3 **Olindina,** Braz.
96/E2 **Oliva,** Arg.
47/E3 **Oliva,** Sp.
46/B3 **Oliva de la Frontera,** Sp.
46/A3 **Olivais,** Port.
95/C2 **Oliveira,** Braz.
46/B3 **Olivenza,** Sp.
106/D3 **Oliver,** BC,Can
44/D3 **Olivet,** Fr.
92/E8 **Ollagüe** (vol.), Bol.
31/S11 **Ollainville,** Fr.
47/E3 **Ollería,** Sp.
70/C5 **Ollūr,** India
96/Q9 **Olmué,** Chile
35/F2 **Olney,** Eng,UK
110/B4 **Olney,** Il,US
115/J7 **Olney,** Md,US
111/J1 **Olomane** (riv.), Qu,Can
39/J4 **Olomouc,** Czh.
67/D5 **Olongapo,** Phil.
44/C3 **Olonne-sur-Mer,** Fr.
44/C5 **Oloron-Sainte-Marie,** Fr.
47/G1 **Olot,** Sp.
57/S3 **Oloy** (range), Rus.
41/E6 **Olpe,** Ger.
41/F6 **Olsberg,** Ger.
40/D4 **Olst,** Neth.
39/L2 **Olsztyn,** Pol.
39/L2 **Olsztyn** (prov.), Pol.
39/L2 **Olsztynek,** Pol.
51/G3 **Olt** (co.), Rom.
51/G4 **Olt** (riv.), Rom.
96/C4 **Olte** (mts.), Arg.
45/G3 **Olten,** Swi.
51/H3 **Olteniţa,** Rom.
51/G3 **Olteţ** (riv.), Rom.
59/E2 **Oltu,** Turk.
59/E2 **Oltu** (riv.), Turk.
67/D3 **Oluanpi,** Tai.
46/C4 **Olvera,** Sp.
116/B3 **Olympia** (cap.), Wa,US
49/G4 **Olympia (Olimbía)** (ruins), Gre.
106/B4 **Olympic** (mts.), Wa,US
106/B4 **Olympic Nat'l Park,** Wa,US
59/J4 **Olympus** (mtn.), Cyp.
106/C4 **Olympus** (peak), Wa,US
49/H2 **Olympus, Mount** (Ólimbos) (peak), Gre.
49/H2 **Olympus Nat'l Park,** Gre.
57/S3 **Olyutorskiy** (bay), Rus.
53/K2 **Oma** (riv.), Rus.
65/E2 **Ōmachi,** Japan
65/F3 **Omae-zaki** (pt.), Japan
32/A2 **Omagh,** NI,UK
32/A2 **Omagh** (dist.), NI,UK
109/J2 **Omaha,** Ne,US
106/D3 **Omak,** Wa,US
61/G4 **Oman**
61/G4 **Oman** (gulf), Asia
87/C4 **Omatako** (riv.), Namb.
73/F5 **Ombai** (str.), Indo.
34/D2 **Ombersley,** Eng,UK
87/B4 **Ombombo,** Namb.
87/A1 **Omboué,** Gabon
48/B1 **Ombrone** (riv.), It.
83/M4 **Omdurman** (Umm Durmān), Sudan
65/H7 **Ōme,** Japan
45/H4 **Omegna,** It.
100/B4 **Ometepec,** Mex.
65/M9 **Ōmihachiman,** Japan
48/E1 **Omiš,** Cro.
65/G2 **Ōmiya,** Japan
114/M4 **Ommaney** (cape), Ak,US
40/D3 **Ommen,** Neth.
62/F2 **Ömnödelger,** Mong.
62/C2 **Ömnögovĭ,** Mong.
48/A2 **Omodeo** (lake), It.
58/Q3 **Omolon** (riv.), Rus.
83/N6 **Omo Nat'l Park,** Eth.
83/N6 **Omo Wenz** (riv.), Eth.
56/H4 **Omsk,** Rus.
51/G3 **Omul** (peak), Rom.
51/H4 **Omurtag,** Bul.
64/B4 **Ōmuta,** Japan
53/M4 **Omutninsk,** Rus.
65/G1 **Onagawa,** Japan
109/J5 **Onalaska,** Tx,US
46/D1 **Oñate,** Sp.
110/C2 **Onaway,** Mi,US
96/E1 **Oncativo,** Arg.
32/D3 **Onchan,** IM,UK
87/B4 **Oncocúa,** Ang.
47/E3 **Onda,** Sp.
87/C4 **Ondangua,** Namb.
39/L4 **Ondava** (riv.), Slvk.
87/C4 **Ondjiva,** Ang.
85/G5 **Ondo** (state), Nga.
62/G2 **Öndörhaan,** Mong.
62/C2 **Öndorhangay,** Mong.
52/H3 **Onega,** Rus.
52/H2 **Onega** (bay), Rus.
52/G3 **Onega** (lake), Rus.
52/H2 **Onega** (pen.), Rus.
52/H3 **Onega** (riv.), Rus.
106/C3 **One Hundred Mile House,** BC,Can
110/F3 **Oneida,** NY,US
109/H2 **O'Neill,** Ne,US
110/F3 **Oneonta,** NY,US
62/E2 **Ongiyn** (riv.), Mong.
70/D4 **Ongole,** India
107/H4 **Onida,** SD,US
47/E3 **Onil,** Sp.
89/G8 **Onilahy** (riv.), Madg.
85/G5 **Onitsha,** Nga.
89/H7 **Onive** (riv.), Madg.
42/C3 **Onnaing,** Fr.
34/D2 **Onny** (riv.), Eng,UK
64/D3 **Ono,** Japan
64/E3 **Ōno,** Japan
64/B4 **Onoda,** Japan
64/C3 **Onomichi,** Japan
62/G1 **Onon** (riv.), Mong., Rus.
78/G5 **Onotoa** (atoll), Kiri.
65/E3 **Ontake-san** (mtn.), Japan
102/H3 **Ontario** (prov.), Can.
110/E3 **Ontario** (lake), Can., US
115/C2 **Ontario,** Ca,US
106/D4 **Ontario,** Or,US
47/E3 **Onteniente,** Sp.
110/B2 **Ontonagon,** Mi,US
78/F5 **Ontong Java** (isl.), Sol.
112/E2 **Oologan** (lake), Ok,US
40/A6 **Oostburg,** Neth.
40/C4 **Oostelijk Flevoland** (polder), Neth.
42/B1 **Oostende,** Belg.
40/B5 **Oosterhout,** Neth.
40/A5 **Oosterschelde** (chan.), Neth.
42/C2 **Oosterzele,** Belg.
42/C1 **Oostkamp,** Belg.
40/C4 **Oostvaarderplassen** (lake), Neth.
40/B4 **Oostzaan,** Neth.
70/C5 **Ootacamund,** India
107/B2 **Ootsa** (lake), BC,Can
87/D1 **Opala,** Zaire
39/J2 **Opalenica,** Pol.
50/B3 **Opatija,** Cro.
39/L3 **Opatów,** Pol.
39/J4 **Opava,** Czh.
113/G3 **Opelika,** Al,US
112/E4 **Opelousas,** La,US
110/E2 **Opeongo** (lake), On,Can
43/E1 **Opglabbeek,** Belg.
40/C5 **Oploo,** Neth.
40/B3 **Opmeer,** Neth.
39/L3 **Opoczno,** Pol.
39/J3 **Opole,** Pol.
39/J3 **Opole** (prov.), Pol.
39/L3 **Opole Lubelskie,** Pol.
113/G4 **Opp,** Al,US
37/D3 **Oppdal,** Nor.
37/D3 **Oppland** (co.), Nor.
106/D4 **Opportunity,** Wa,US
42/D2 **Opwijk,** Belg.
50/E2 **Oradea,** Rom.
50/E4 **Orahovac,** Yugo.
70/C2 **Orai,** India
81/Q16 **Oran,** Alg.
88/B3 **Orange** (riv.), Afr.
77/D2 **Orange,** Austl.
44/F4 **Orange,** Fr.
93/H3 **Orange** (mts.), Sur.
115/C3 **Orange,** Ca,US
115/F5 **Orange,** NJ,US
112/E4 **Orange,** Tx,US
110/E4 **Orange,** Va,US
113/H3 **Orangeburg,** SC,US
88/D3 **Orange Free State** (prov.), SAfr.
113/H4 **Orange Park,** Fl,US
110/D3 **Orangeville,** On,Can
100/D4 **Orange Walk,** Belz.
84/A4 **Orango** (isl.), GBis.
39/G2 **Oranienburg,** Ger.
40/D3 **Oranjekanaal** (can.), Neth.
101/G5 **Oranjestad** (cap.), Aru.
81/Q16 **Oran, Sebkha d'** (lake), Alg.
87/E5 **Orapa,** Bots.
59/M8 **Or 'Aqiva,** Isr.
67/E5 **Oras,** Phil.
51/F3 **Orăştie,** Rom.
50/E3 **Oraviţa,** Rom.
44/E5 **Orb** (riv.), Fr.
46/C1 **Órbigo** (riv.), Sp.
112/B2 **Orchard City,** Co,US
106/E4 **Orchard Homes,** Mt,US
116/F6 **Orchard Lake Village,** Mi,US
67/D3 **Orchid** (isl.), Tai.
45/G4 **Orco** (riv.), It.
44/F3 **Or, Côte d'** (uplands), Fr.
109/H2 **Ord,** Ne,US
46/A1 **Órdenes,** Sp.
47/F1 **Ordesa y Monte Perdido Nat'l Park,** Sp.
66/B3 **Ordos** (des.), China
59/D2 **Ordu,** Turk.
109/G3 **Ordway,** Co,US
37/E4 **Örebro,** Swe.
37/E4 **Örebro** (co.), Swe.
106/C4 **Oregon** (state), US
108/B2 **Oregon Caves Nat'l Mon.,** Or,US
106/C4 **Oregon City,** Or,US
54/F1 **Orël,** Rus.
54/E2 **Orel'** (riv.), Ukr.
54/E1 **Orel Obl.,** Rus.
108/E2 **Orem,** Ut,US
55/K2 **Orenburg,** Rus.
55/K1 **Orenburg Obl.,** Rus.
46/B1 **Orense,** Sp.
49/K2 **Orestiás,** Gre.
35/H2 **Orford,** Eng,UK
35/H2 **Orford Ness** (pt.), UK
108/D4 **Organ Pipe Cactus Nat'l Mon.,** Az,US
95/L7 **Órgãos** (mts.), Braz.
31/S11 **Orge** (riv.), Fr.
31/R10 **Orgeval,** Fr.
51/J2 **Orgeyev,** Mol.
54/D5 **Orhaneli,** Turk.
51/J5 **Orhangazi,** Turk.
62/F2 **Orhon** (riv.), Mong.
44/C5 **Orhy, Pic d'** (peak), Fr.
91/C6 **Oriental** (val.), Arg.
92/D6 **Oriental, Cordillera** (range), SAm.
47/E3 **Orihuela,** Sp.
110/E2 **Orillia,** On,Can
116/K11 **Orinda,** Ca,US
92/F2 **Orinoco** (riv.), Col., Ven.
101/J6 **Orinoco** (delta), Ven.
116/F6 **Orion** (lake), Mi,US
70/D3 **Orissa** (state), India
48/A3 **Oristano,** It.
48/A3 **Oristano** (gulf), It.
37/H3 **Orivesi,** Fin.
93/G4 **Oriximiná,** Braz.
100/B4 **Orizaba,** Mex.
50/D4 **Orjen** (peak), Yugo.
41/F6 **Orke** (riv.), Ger.
30/C3 **Orkney** (isls.), Sc,UK
112/C4 **Orla,** Tx,US
95/C2 **Orlândia,** Braz.
113/H4 **Orlando,** Fl,US
48/D3 **Orlando, Capo d'** (cape), It.
116/Q16 **Orland Park,** Il,US
44/D2 **Orléanais** (hist. reg.), Fr.
44/D3 **Orléans,** Fr.
108/B2 **Orleans,** Ca,US
39/K4 **Orlová,** Czh.
31/T10 **Orly,** Fr.
67/D5 **Ormoc,** Phil.
113/H4 **Ormond Beach,** Fl,US
33/F4 **Ormskirk,** Eng,UK
44/F2 **Ornain** (riv.), Fr.
43/F5 **Orne** (riv.), Fr.
37/E2 **Ørnes,** Nor.
39/L1 **Orneta,** Pol.
37/F3 **Örnsköldsvik,** Swe.
101/N8 **Oro** (riv.), Mex.
45/J3 **Orobie, Alpi** (range), It.
84/D4 **Orodara,** Burk.
47/E1 **Oroel** (peak), Sp.
106/D4 **Orofino,** Id,US
79/L6 **Orohena** (peak), FrPol.
78/E4 **Oroluk** (atoll), Micr.
111/H2 **Oromocto,** NB,Can
48/A1 **Oro, Monte d'** (mtn.), Fr.
79/H5 **Orona** (Hull) (atoll), Kiri.
111/G2 **Orono,** Me,US
59/L4 **Orontes** (riv.), Asia
63/J1 **Oroqen Zizhiqi,** China
73/F2 **Oroquieta,** Phil.
94/C2 **Orós,** Braz.
94/C2 **Orós** (res.), Braz.
48/A2 **Orosei** (gulf), It.
50/E2 **Orosháza,** Hun.
50/D2 **Oroszlány,** Hun.
108/C2 **Orovada,** Nv,US
108/E4 **Oro Valley,** Az,US
108/B3 **Oroville,** Ca,US
106/D3 **Oroville,** Wa,US
31/P7 **Orpington,** Eng,UK
33/F4 **Orrell,** Eng,UK
31/T9 **Orry-la-Ville,** Fr.
37/E3 **Orsa,** Swe.
31/S10 **Orsay,** Fr.

152

Orset – Pearl

31/Q7 **Orsett**, Eng,UK
52/F5 **Orsha**, Bela.
55/L2 **Orsk**, Rus.
50/F3 **Orşova**, Rom.
37/C3 **Ørsta**, Nor.
45/H4 **Orta** (lake), It.
59/C2 **Orta**, Turk.
59/B3 **Ortaca**, Turk.
48/D2 **Orta Nova**, It.
46/B1 **Ortegal** (cape), Sp.
44/C5 **Orthez**, Fr.
46/B1 **Ortigueira**, Sp.
45/J3 **Ortles** (mts.), It., Swi.
92/E6 **Ortón** (riv.), Bol.
63/H2 **Orton** (riv.), China
48/D1 **Ortona**, It.
116/F6 **Ortonville**, Mi,US
107/J4 **Ortonville**, Mn,US
41/H3 **Ortze** (riv.), Ger.
59/F3 **Orūmīyeh**, Iran
92/E7 **Oruro**, Bol.
48/C1 **Orvieto**, It.
98/V **Orville** (coast), Ant.
35/H2 **Orwell** (riv.), Eng,UK
62/H2 **Orxon** (riv.), China
51/F4 **Oryakhovo**, Bul.
59/M8 **Or Yehuda**, Isr.
53/M4 **Osa**, Rus.
109/J3 **Osage** (riv.), Mo,US
109/J3 **Osage Beach**, Mo,US
64/D3 **Ōsaka**, Japan
65/L10 **Osaka** (bay), Japan
64/D3 **Ōsaka** (pref.), Japan
64/L10 **Ōsaka** (inset), Japan
63/K4 **Osan**, SKor.
95/G8 **Osasco**, Braz.
114/C3 **Osborn** (mtn.), Ak,US
109/H3 **Osborne**, Ks,US
113/F3 **Osceola**, Ar,US
38/F2 **Oschersleben**, Ger.
112/B3 **Oscura** (mts.), NM,US
68/B3 **Osh**, Kyr.
87/C4 **Oshakati**, Namb.
111/S8 **Oshawa**, On,Can
63/M3 **Oshima** (pen.), Japan
87/C4 **Oshivelo**, Namb.
107/H5 **Oshkosh**, Ne,US
110/B2 **Oshkosh**, Wi,US
59/F3 **Oshnovīyeh**, Iran
85/G5 **Oshogbo**, Nga.
87/C1 **Oshwe**, Zaire
50/D3 **Osijek**, Cro.
45/K5 **Osimo**, It.
54/D1 **Osipovichi**, Bela.
107/K5 **Oskaloosa**, Ia,US
37/F4 **Oskarshamn**, Swe.
54/F2 **Oskol** (riv.), Rus., Ukr.
37/D4 **Oslo** (cap.), Nor.
70/C4 **Osmānābād**, India
59/C2 **Osmancık**, Turk.
51/K5 **Osmaneli**, Turk.
59/D3 **Osmaniye**, Turk.
41/F4 **Osnabrück**, Ger.
31/S9 **Osny**, Fr.
95/B4 **Osório**, Braz.
96/B4 **Osorno**, Chile
106/D3 **Osoyoos**, BC,Can
76/B1 **Osprey** (reef), Austl.
40/C5 **Oss**, Neth.
77/C4 **Ossa** (peak), Austl.
49/H3 **Ossa** (mtn.), Gre.
46/B3 **Ossa** (range), Port.
85/G5 **Osse** (riv.), Nga.
33/G4 **Ossett**, Eng,UK
115/G4 **Ossining**, NY,US
52/G4 **Ostashkov**, Rus.
41/E4 **Ostbevern**, Ger.
41/G1 **Oste** (riv.), Ger.
42/B1 **Ostend** (Oostende), Belg.
38/F2 **Osterburg**, Ger.
41/F4 **Ostercappeln**, Ger.
40/D1 **Osterems** (chan.), Neth.
37/E4 **Östergötland** (co.), Swe.
45/K2 **Osterhofen**, Ger.
41/F2 **Osterholz-Scharmbeck**, Ger.
41/H5 **Osterode**, Ger.
38/F3 **Osterode am Harz**, Ger.
37/E3 **Östersund**, Swe.
37/D4 **Østfold** (co.), Nor.
41/E2 **Ostfriesland** (reg.), Ger.
37/F3 **Östhammar**, Swe.
48/C2 **Ostia Antica** (ruins), It.
45/J4 **Ostiglia**, It.
39/K4 **Ostrava**, Czh.
41/E2 **Ostrhauderfehn**, Ger.
42/C3 **Ostricourt**, Fr.
50/D4 **Oštri Rt** (cape), Yugo.
39/K2 **Ostróda**, Pol.
54/F2 **Ostrogozhsk**, Rus.
39/L2 **Ostrołęka**, Pol.
39/L2 **Ostrołęka** (prov.), Pol.
45/K1 **Ostrov**, Czh.
52/F4 **Ostrov**, Rus.
39/L3 **Ostrowiec Świętokrzyski**, Pol.
39/L2 **Ostrów Mazowiecka**, Pol.
39/J3 **Ostrów Wielkopolski**, Pol.
39/J3 **Ostrzeszów**, Pol.
41/H1 **Oststeinbek**, Ger.
48/E2 **Ostuni**, It.
49/G2 **Osum** (riv.), Alb.
51/G4 **Osŭm** (riv.), Bul.
64/B5 **Ōsumi** (isls.), Japan
64/B5 **Ōsumi** (pen.), Japan
64/B5 **Ōsumi** (str.), Japan
46/C4 **Osuna**, Sp.
95/B2 **Osvaldo Cruz**, Braz.
33/G3 **Oswaldkirk**, Eng,UK
33/F4 **Oswaldtwistle**, Eng,UK
110/E3 **Oswego**, NY,US
33/E6 **Oswestry**, Eng,UK
39/K3 **Oświęcim** (Auschwitz), Pol.
64/F2 **Ōta**, Japan
64/C3 **Ōta** (riv.), Japan
64/C3 **Ōtake**, Japan
65/G2 **Ōtakine-yama** (mtn.), Japan
45/K2 **Otava** (riv.), Czh.
65/G2 **Ōtawara**, Japan
50/F3 **Oţelu Roşu**, Rom.
79/L6 **Otepa**, FrPol.
101/N8 **Oteros** (riv.), Mex.
62/D2 **Otgon**, Mong.
62/D2 **Otgon Tenger** (peak), Mong.
106/D4 **Othello**, Wa,US
31/U9 **Othis**, Fr.
49/F3 **Othonoí** (isl.), Gre.
85/F4 **Oti** (riv.), Gui.
75/R11 **Otira**, NZ
87/C5 **Otjikango**, Namb.
87/C5 **Otjinene**, Namb.
87/C5 **Otjiwarongo**, Namb.
87/B4 **Otjokavare**, Namb.
33/G4 **Otley**, Eng,UK
66/A3 **Otog Qi**, China
107/L3 **Otoskwin** (riv.), On,Can
65/N10 **Otowa**, Japan
37/C4 **Otra** (riv.), Nor.
55/J1 **Otradnyy**, Rus.
49/F2 **Otranto** (str.), Alb., It.
39/J4 **Otrokovice**, Czh.
64/D3 **Ōtsu**, Japan
37/D3 **Otta**, Nor.
110/F2 **Ottawa** (cap.), Can.
103/H3 **Ottawa** (isls.), NW,Can
110/E2 **Ottawa** (riv.), On, Qu,Can
110/B3 **Ottawa**, Il,US
109/J3 **Ottawa**, Ks,US
110/C3 **Ottawa**, Oh,US
34/C5 **Otter** (riv.), Eng,UK
33/F1 **Otterburn**, Eng,UK
41/F1 **Otterndorf**, Ger.
41/G2 **Ottersberg**, Ger.
31/M7 **Ottershaw**, Eng,UK
34/C5 **Ottery Saint Mary**, Eng,UK
42/D2 **Ottignies-Louvain-La-Neuve**, Belg.
45/J2 **Ottobrunn**, Ger.
107/K5 **Ottumwa**, Ia,US
43/G5 **Ottweiler**, Ger.
77/B3 **Otway** (cape), Austl.
97/J8 **Otway** (bay), Chile
97/K8 **Otway** (sound), Chile
77/B3 **Otway Nat'l Park**, Austl.
39/L2 **Otwock**, Pol.
69/C1 **Ou** (riv.), Laos
112/E3 **Ouachita** (riv.), Ar, La,US
109/J4 **Ouachita** (mts.), Ar, Ok,US
82/C3 **Ouadane**, Mrta.
83/J5 **Ouaddaï** (reg.), Chad
85/E3 **Ouagadougou** (cap.), Burk.
83/K6 **Ouaka** (riv.), CAfr.
84/D2 **Oualâta, Dhar** (hills), Mrta.
44/E3 **Ouanne** (riv.), Fr.
82/C3 **Ouarane** (reg.), Mrta.
82/G1 **Ouargla**, Alg.
82/D1 **Ouarzazate**, Mor.
111/F1 **Ouasiemsca** (riv.), Qu,Can
81/S16 **Ouassel, Nahr** (riv.), Alg.
83/J6 **Oubangui** (riv.), CAfr.
85/E3 **Oubritenga** (prov.), Burk.
65/L10 **Ōuda**, Japan
85/E3 **Oudalan** (prov.), Burk.
40/B5 **Oud-Beijerland**, Neth.
40/A5 **Ouddorp**, Neth.
40/D5 **Oude IJssel** (riv.), Neth.
42/C2 **Oudenaarde**, Belg.
40/B5 **Oudenbosch**, Neth.
42/B1 **Oudenburg**, Belg.
40/E2 **Oude Pekela**, Neth.
44/C3 **Oudon** (riv.), Fr.
88/C4 **Oudtshoorn**, SAfr.
40/B6 **Oud-Turnhout**, Belg.
84/E2 **Oued el Hadjar** (well), Mali
81/R16 **Oued Rhiou**, Alg.
82/D1 **Oued Zem**, Mor.
85/F5 **Ouémé** (prov.), Ben.
85/F4 **Ouémé** (riv.), Ben.
79/V13 **Ouen** (isl.), NCal.
81/W18 **Ouenza**, Alg.
81/M13 **Ouerrha** (riv.), Mor.
44/A2 **Ouessant** (isl.), Fr.
82/J7 **Ouesso**, Congo
85/H5 **Ouest** (prov.), Camr.
101/G4 **Ouest** (pt.), Haiti
81/M13 **Ouezzane**, Mor.
83/J6 **Ouham** (riv.), CAfr., Chad
42/C5 **Ouichy-le-Château**, Fr.
81/P13 **Oujda**, Mor.
37/J2 **Oulangan Nat'l Park**, Fin.
77/A2 **Oulnina** (peak), Austl.
37/H2 **Oulu**, Fin.
37/H2 **Oulu** (prov.), Fin.
37/H2 **Oulujärvi** (lake), Fin.
81/V18 **Oum El Bouaghi**, Alg.
82/D1 **Oum er Rhia** (riv.), Mor.
83/J5 **Oum Hadjer**, Chad
52/E2 **Ounasjoki** (riv.), Fin.
35/F2 **Oundle**, Eng,UK
83/K4 **OuniangaKebir**, Chad
43/E2 **Oupeye**, Belg.
43/F4 **Our** (riv.), Eur.
44/F3 **Ource** (riv.), Fr.
42/C5 **Ourcq** (riv.), Fr.
37/H1 **Øure Anarjokka Nat'l Park**, Nor.
37/F1 **Øure Dividal Nat'l Park**, Nor.
83/J3 **Ouri**, Chad
94/B2 **Ouricuri**, Braz.
95/B2 **Ourinhos**, Braz.
85/H3 **Ourofané**, Niger
95/G7 **Ouro Fino**, Braz.
95/D2 **Ouro Preto**, Braz.
43/E3 **Ourthe** (riv.), Belg.
33/H4 **Ouse** (riv.), Eng,UK
35/G5 **Ouse** (riv.), Eng,UK
44/B3 **Oust** (riv.), Fr.
47/Q11 **Outão**, Port.
110/E2 **Outaouais** (riv.), Qu,Can
111/G1 **Outardes** (riv.), Qu,Can
111/G1 **Outardes Quatre** (res.), Qu,Can
84/D2 **Outeid Arkas** (well), Mali
36/A2 **Outer Hebrides** (isls.), Sc,UK
46/A1 **Outes**, Sp.
106/G3 **Outlook**, Sk,Can
42/A2 **Outreau**, Fr.
111/N6 **Outremont**, Qu,Can
79/V12 **Ouvéa** (atoll), NCal.
45/H4 **Ovada**, It.
79/Y18 **Ovalau** (isl.), Fiji
91/B3 **Ovalle**, Chile
46/A2 **Ovar**, Port.
43/G2 **Overath**, Ger.
40/B5 **Overflakkee** (isl.), Neth.
42/D2 **Overijse**, Belg.
40/D3 **Overijssel** (prov.), Neth.
40/D4 **Overijssels** (can.), Neth.
109/J3 **Overland Park**, Ks,US
115/K7 **Overlea**, Md,US
96/C5 **Overo** (peak), Arg.
43/E1 **Overpelt**, Belg.
35/E1 **Overseal**, Eng,UK
35/H1 **Overstrand**, Eng,UK
35/E4 **Overton**, Eng,UK
33/F6 **Overton**, Wal,UK
108/D3 **Overton**, Nv,US
37/G2 **Övertorneå**, Swe.
46/C1 **Oviedo**, Sp.
37/J1 **Øvre Pasvik Nat'l Park**, Nor.
87/C1 **Owando**, Congo
65/N9 **Owariasahi**, Japan
64/E3 **Owase**, Japan
109/J3 **Owasso**, Ok,US
107/K4 **Owatonna**, Mn,US
110/E3 **Owego**, NY,US
67/B6 **Owen** (shoal)
75/R11 **Owen** (peak), NZ
32/A2 **Owenkillew** (riv.), NI,UK
108/C3 **Owens** (riv.), Ca,US
110/C4 **Owensboro**, Ky,US
110/D2 **Owen Sound**, On,Can
108/C2 **Owhyee** (mts.), Id,US
115/K7 **Owings Mills**, Md,US
106/F4 **Owl Creek** (mts.), Wy,US
110/C3 **Owosso**, Mi,US
108/C2 **Owyhee** (riv.), Id, Or,US
108/C2 **Owyhee** (lake), Or,US
60/E1 **Owzan** (riv.), Iran
107/H3 **Oxbow**, Sk,Can
107/K2 **Oxford** (lake), Mb,Can
35/E3 **Oxford**, Eng,UK
35/E3 **Oxford** (can.), Eng,UK
116/E6 **Oxford**, Mi,US
113/F3 **Oxford**, Ms,US
110/C4 **Oxford**, Oh,US
35/E3 **Oxfordshire** (co.), Eng,UK
31/M7 **Oxhey**, Eng,UK
76/E7 **Oxley** (cr.), Austl.
115/A2 **Oxnard**, Ca,US
115/K8 **Oxon Hill-Glassmanor**, Md,US
31/M8 **Oxshott**, Eng,UK
31/N8 **Oxted**, Eng,UK
65/F2 **Oyabe**, Japan
65/F2 **Oyama**, Japan
65/M10 **Ōyamada**, Japan
65/L10 **Ōyamazaki**, Japan
93/H3 **Oyapock** (riv.), FrG.
82/H7 **Oyem**, Gabon
106/F3 **Oyen**, Ab,Can
85/F5 **Oyo**, Nga.
85/F4 **Oyo** (state), Nga.
65/L10 **Ōyodo**, Japan
64/B5 **Ōyodo** (riv.), Japan
115/G5 **Oyster Bay**, NY,US
41/G2 **Oyten**, Ger.
67/D6 **Ozamiz**, Phil.
44/D2 **Ozanne** (riv.), Fr.
109/J3 **Ozark** (plat.), US
113/G4 **Ozark**, Al,US
112/E3 **Ozark**, Ar,US
112/E3 **Ozark** (mts.), Ar, Mo,US
109/J3 **Ozarks, Lake of the** (lake), Mo,US
50/E1 **Ózd**, Hun.
57/S4 **Ozernoy** (cape), Rus.
106/B3 **Ozette** (lake), Wa,US
107/L3 **Ozhiski** (lake), On,Can
48/A2 **Ozieri**, It.
39/K3 **Ozimek**, Pol.
31/U10 **Ozoir-la-Ferrière**, Fr.
112/C4 **Ozona**, Tx,US
39/K3 **Ozorków**, Pol.
31/U11 **Ozouer-le-Voulgis**, Fr.
64/C4 **Ōzu**, Japan

P

45/J2 **Paar** (riv.), Ger.
88/B4 **Paarl**, SAfr.
39/K3 **Pabianice**, Pol.
70/E3 **Pābna**, Bang.
92/F6 **Pacaás Novos** (mts.), Braz.
92/F6 **Pacaás Novos Nat'l Park**, Braz.
93/H4 **Pacajá** (riv.), Braz.
94/C2 **Pacajus**, Braz.
92/C5 **Pacasmayo**, Peru
48/C4 **Paceco**, It.
92/C6 **Pachacamac** (ruins), Peru
48/D4 **Pachino**, It.
70/C3 **Pachmarhī**, India
28/B4 **Pacific** (ocean)
106/B3 **Pacific** (ranges), BC,Can
116/K11 **Pacifica**, Ca,US
115/B2 **Pacifico** (mtn.), Ca,US
102/D4 **Pacific Rim Nat'l Park**, BC,Can
72/D5 **Pacinan** (cape), Indo.
72/D5 **Pacitan**, Indo.
47/P10 **Paço de Arcos**, Port.
72/B4 **Padang**, Indo.
72/B4 **Padangpanjang**, Indo.
72/A3 **Padangsidempuan**, Indo.
31/N7 **Paddington**, Eng,UK
35/G4 **Paddock Wood**, Eng,UK
41/F5 **Paderborn**, Ger.
61/J3 **Pad Īdan**, Pak.
33/F4 **Padiham**, Eng,UK
50/E3 **Padina**, Yugo.
37/E2 **Padjelanta Nat'l Park**, Swe.
45/J4 **Padova** (Padua), It.
87/B2 **Padrão, Ponta do** (pt.), Ang.
112/D5 **Padre Island Nat'l Seashore**, Tx,US
46/A1 **Padrón**, Sp.
88/D4 **Padrone** (cape), SAfr.
34/B5 **Padstow**, Eng,UK
45/J4 **Padua** (Padova), It.
110/B4 **Paducah**, Ky,US
112/C3 **Paducah**, Tx,US
64/A2 **Paektŏk-san** (mtn.), SKor.
63/K3 **Paektu-San** (mtn.), NKor.
63/J4 **Paengnyŏng** (isl.), SKor.
50/B3 **Pag** (isl.), Cro.
67/D6 **Pagadian**, Phil.
72/B4 **Pagai Selatan** (isl.), Indo.
72/A4 **Pagai Utara** (isl.), Indo.
78/D3 **Pagan** (isl.), NMar.
108/E3 **Page**, Az,US
79/H6 **Pago Pago** (cap.), ASam.
108/F3 **Pagosa Springs**, Co,US
110/C1 **Pagwachuan** (riv.), On,Can
72/B3 **Pahang** (riv.), Malay.
108/D3 **Pahrump**, Nv,US
108/C3 **Pahute Mesa** (upland), Nv,US
66/C5 **Pai** (lake), China
49/L7 **Paiania**, Gre.
34/C6 **Paignton**, Eng,UK
37/H3 **Päijänne** (lake), Fin.
69/C3 **Pailin**, Camb.
104/T10 **Pailolo** (chan.), Hi,US
52/D3 **Paimio**, Fin.
96/C2 **Paine**, Chile
97/J7 **Paine** (peak), Chile
110/D3 **Painesville**, Oh,US
34/C2 **Painscastle**, Wal,UK
107/J2 **Paint** (lake), Mb,Can
108/E4 **Painted** (des.), Az,US
112/D4 **Paint Rock**, Tx,US
110/D4 **Paintsville**, Ky,US
36/C3 **Paisley**, Sc,UK
70/C4 **Paithan**, India
37/G2 **Pajala**, Swe.
39/K3 **Pajęczno**, Pol.
94/C3 **Pajeú** (riv.), Braz.
101/E6 **Pajonal Abajo**, Pan.
72/B3 **Pakanbaru**, Indo.
76/E6 **Pakenham**, Austl.
97/J7 **Pakenham** (cape), Chile
49/J5 **Pákhnes** (peak), Gre.
53/X9 **Pakhra** (riv.), Rus.
61/H3 **Pakistan**
50/B3 **Paklenica Nat'l Park**, Cro.
71/G3 **Pakokku**, Burma
106/F3 **Pakowki** (lake), Ab,Can
61/K2 **Pākpattan**, Pak.
71/H6 **Pak Phanang**, Thai.
50/B3 **Pakrac**, Cro.
50/D2 **Paks**, Hun.
69/D3 **Pakxe**, Laos
82/H6 **Pala**, Chad
47/N9 **Palacio Real**, Sp.
47/G2 **Palafrugell**, Sp.
48/D4 **Palagonia**, It.
48/E1 **Palagruža** (isls.), Cro.
49/F3 **Palaiokastritsa**, Gre.
31/S10 **Palaiseau**, Fr.
70/D4 **Pālakolla**, India
47/G2 **Palamós**, Sp.
72/D4 **Palangkaraya**, Indo.
70/B3 **Pālanpur**, India
104/T10 **Palaoa** (pt.), Hi,US
87/E5 **Palapye**, Bots.
70/C5 **Palar** (riv.), India
46/B1 **Palas de Rey**, Sp.
116/P15 **Palatine**, Il,US
113/H4 **Palatka**, Fl,US
78/C4 **Palau** (terr.), US
67/C6 **Palawan** (isl.), Phil.
67/C5 **Palawan** (passage), Phil.
70/C6 **Pālayankottai**, India
48/D4 **Palazzolo Acreide**, It.
82/G8 **Palé**, EqG.
73/F3 **Paleleh**, Indo.
72/B4 **Palembang**, Indo.
96/B4 **Palena** (riv.), Chile
46/C1 **Palencia**, Sp.
111/Q9 **Palermo**, On,Can
48/C3 **Palermo**, It.
112/E4 **Palestine**, Tx,US
112/E3 **Palestine** (lake), Tx,US
61/K5 **Pālghar**, India
64/A2 **P'algong-san** (mtn.), SKor.
95/B3 **Palhoça**, Braz.
70/B2 **Pāli**, India
97/K8 **Pali Aike Nat'l Park**, Chile
50/D4 **Palić**, Yugo.
104/V13 **Palikea** (peak), Hi,US
49/H3 **Palioúrion, Ákra** (cape), Gre.
115/F5 **Palisades Park**, NJ,US
70/B3 **Pālitāna**, India
50/C3 **Paljenik** (peak), Bosn.
70/C6 **Palk** (str.), India, SrL.
45/J3 **Palla Bianca** (Weisskugel) (mt.), Aus., It.
37/H1 **Pallas-Ounastunturin Nat'l Park**, Fin.
37/H1 **Pallastunturi** (peak), Fin.
75/S11 **Palliser** (cape), NZ
75/H3 **Palm** (isls.), Austl.
94/A4 **Palma** (riv.), Braz.
47/G3 **Palma**, Sp.
46/C4 **Palma del Río**, Sp.
48/C4 **Palma di Montechiaro**, It.
94/D3 **Palmares**, Braz.
95/B3 **Palmas**, Braz.
84/D5 **Palmas** (cape), Libr.
101/F3 **Palma Soriano**, Cuba
113/H4 **Palm Bay**, Fl,US
76/H8 **Palm Beach**, Austl.
115/B1 **Palmdale**, Ca,US
95/B3 **Palmeira**, Braz.
94/C3 **Palmeira dos Índios**, Braz.
94/A3 **Palmeiras** (riv.), Braz.
87/B2 **Palmeirinhas, Ponta das** (pt.), Ang.
47/Q10 **Palmela**, Port.
98/V **Palmer** (arch.), Ant.
98/V **Palmer Land** (reg.), Ant.
76/C3 **Palmerston** (cape), Austl.
79/J6 **Palmerston** (atoll), Cookls.
75/R12 **Palmerston**, NZ
76/B2 **Palmerston Nat'l Park**, Austl.
75/S11 **Palmerston North**, NZ
113/H5 **Palmetto**, Fl,US
113/H4 **Palm Harbor**, Fl,US
48/D3 **Palmi**, It.
96/C2 **Palmilla**, Chile
92/C3 **Palmira**, Col.
108/C4 **Palm Springs**, Ca,US
79/J4 **Palmyra** (isl.), PacUS
60/C2 **Palmyra** (ruins), Syria
70/E3 **Palmyras** (pt.), India
32/E2 **Palnackie**, Sc,UK
70/C3 **Palni**, India
67/D5 **Palo**, Phil.
116/K12 **Palo Alto**, Ca,US
101/N8 **Palo Bola**, Mex.
109/G3 **Palo Duro** (cr.), Ok, Tx,US
45/J4 **Palon** (peak), It.
112/D3 **Palo Pinto**, Tx,US
47/E4 **Palos, Cabo de** (cape), Sp.
116/Q16 **Palos Hills**, Il,US
115/B3 **Palos Verdes Estates**, Ca,US
100/D5 **Palo Verde Nat'l Park**, Mex.
70/D2 **Pālpa**, Nepal
91/C1 **Palpalá**, Arg.
73/G4 **Palpetu** (cape), Indo.
59/D2 **Palu**, Turk.
67/D5 **Paluan**, Phil.
72/C3 **Pamangkat**, Indo.
44/D5 **Pamiers**, Fr.
68/B4 **Pamir** (riv.), Afg., Taj.
68/B4 **Pamir** (reg.), China, Taj.
113/J3 **Pamlico** (riv.), NC,US
113/J3 **Pamlico** (sound), NC,US
112/C3 **Pampa**, Tx,US
96/E2 **Pampa Humida** (plain), Arg.
96/E3 **Pampas** (plain), Arg.
96/D3 **Pampa Seca** (plain), Arg.
92/D2 **Pamplona**, Col.
46/E1 **Pamplona**, Sp.
51/K5 **Pamukova**, Turk.
67/E6 **Panabo**, Phil.
108/D3 **Panaca**, Nv,US
70/C6 **Panadura**, SrL.
51/G4 **Panagyurishte**, Bul.
72/B5 **Panaitan** (isl.), Indo.
70/B4 **Panāji**, India
101/E6 **Panama**
101/E6 **Panama** (can.), Pan.
101/E6 **Panamá** (cap.), Pan.
101/F6 **Panama** (gulf), Pan.
101/F6 **Panama** (isth.), Pan.
113/G4 **Panama City**, Fl,US
108/C3 **Panamint** (range), Ca,US
45/J4 **Panaro** (riv.), It.
67/D5 **Panay** (isl.), Phil.
108/C3 **Pancake** (range), Nv,US
50/E3 **Pančevo**, Yugo.
50/E4 **Pančicev vrh** (peak), Yugo.
51/H3 **Panciu**, Rom.
87/E4 **Pandamatenga**, Bots.
91/B2 **Pan de Azúcar Nat'l Park**, Chile
70/C4 **Pandharpur**, India
97/G2 **Pando**, Uru.
71/F2 **Pandu**, India
52/E5 **Panevėžys**, Lith.
68/D3 **Panfilov**, Kaz.
69/B1 **Pang** (riv.), Burma
79/H7 **Pangai**, Tonga
49/J2 **Pangaíon** (peak), Gre.
87/G1 **Pangani** (riv.), Tanz.
35/E4 **Pangbourne**, Eng,UK
72/A3 **Pangkalanberandan**, Indo.
73/F4 **Pangkalaseang** (cape), Indo.
72/C4 **Pangkalpinang**, Indo.
108/D3 **Panguitch**, Ut,US
73/F2 **Pangutaran**, Phil.
67/D6 **Pangutaran** (isl.), Phil.
112/C3 **Panhandle**, Tx,US
73/J4 **Paniai** (lake), Indo.
104/R10 **Paniau** (peak), Hi,US
78/F7 **Panié** (peak), NCal.
70/C2 **Pānīpat**, India
61/K1 **Panj** (Pyandzh) (riv.), Afg., Taj.
70/D3 **Panna**, India
76/F7 **Pannikin** (isl.), Austl.
95/B2 **Panorama**, Braz.
33/E6 **Pant**, Eng,UK
35/G3 **Pant** (riv.), Eng,UK
93/G7 **Pantanal Matogrossense Nat'l Park**, Braz.
48/B4 **Pantelleria** (isl.), It.
31/T10 **Pantin**, Fr.
46/B1 **Pantón**, Sp.
100/B3 **Pánuco**, Mex.
100/B3 **Pánuco** (riv.), Mex.
71/H2 **Panzhihua**, China
94/C3 **Pão de Açúcar**, Braz.
48/E3 **Paola**, It.
109/J3 **Paola**, Ks,US
108/F3 **Paonia**, Co,US
82/J6 **Paoua**, CAfr.
69/C3 **Paoy Pet**, Camb.
50/C2 **Pápa**, Hun.
100/D5 **Papagayo** (gulf), CR
100/B3 **Papantla de Olarte**, Mex.
79/X15 **Papara**, FrPol.
79/X15 **Papeete** (cap.), FrPol.
41/E2 **Papenburg**, Ger.
40/B5 **Papendrecht**, Neth.
79/X15 **Papenoo**, FrPol.
79/X15 **Papetoai**, FrPol.
59/J4 **Paphos**, Cyp.
109/H2 **Papillion**, Ne,US
49/G2 **Papingut, Maj'e** (peak), Alb.
73/H4 **Papisoi** (cape), Indo.
78/D5 **Papua** (gulf), PNG
78/D5 **Papua New Guinea**
95/C1 **Pará** (riv.), Braz.
94/A1 **Pará** (state), Braz.
95/K7 **Paracambi**, Braz.
94/A5 **Paracatu**, Braz.
94/A5 **Paracatu** (riv.), Braz.
67/B4 **Paracel** (isls.)
58/N7 **Parace Vela** (Okino-Tori-Shima) (isl.), Japan
50/E4 **Paraćin**, Yugo.
47/N8 **Paracuellos**, Sp.
94/C1 **Paracuru**, Braz.
95/C1 **Pará de Minas**, Braz.
70/E3 **Paradip**, India
106/F2 **Paradise Hill**, Sk,Can
94/A1 **Paragominas**, Braz.
113/F2 **Paragould**, Ar,US
92/F6 **Paraguá** (riv.), Bol.
92/F2 **Paragua** (riv.), Ven.
95/H6 **Paraguaçu**, Braz.
94/B4 **Paraguaçu** (riv.), Braz.
95/B2 **Paraguaçu Paulista**, Braz.
93/G6 **Paraguai** (riv.), Braz.
101/G5 **Paraguaná** (pen.), Ven.
91/E2 **Paraguarí**, Par.
90/D5 **Paraguay**
92/C2 **Paraíba** (state), Braz.
95/D2 **Paraíba do Sul** (riv.), Braz.
94/A2 **Paraibano**, Braz.
95/H8 **Paraibuna** (riv.), Braz.
94/A3 **Paraim** (riv.), Braz.
93/J6 **Paraíso do Norte de Goiás**, Braz.
95/G7 **Paraisópolis**, Braz.
85/F4 **Parakou**, Ben.
93/G2 **Paramaribo** (cap.), Sur.
94/B2 **Parambu**, Braz.
92/C2 **Paramillo Nat'l Park**, Col.
94/B4 **Paramirim** (riv.), Braz.
115/B3 **Paramount**, Ca,US
115/F5 **Paramus**, NJ,US
57/R4 **Paramushir** (isl.), Rus.
95/B3 **Paraná** (state), Braz.
90/D5 **Paraná** (riv.), SAm.
95/B3 **Paranaguá**, Braz.
95/B1 **Paranaíba**, Braz.
95/B1 **Paranaíba** (riv.), Braz.
95/B2 **Paranapanema** (riv.), Braz.
95/B3 **Paranapiacaba** (range), Braz.
90/D4 **Paranatinga** (riv.), Braz.
93/H8 **Paranavai**, Braz.
73/F2 **Parang**, Phil.
95/C1 **Paraopeba**, Braz.
93/J8 **Parapanema** (riv.), Braz.
75/S11 **Paraparaumu**, NZ
92/F7 **Parapetí** (riv.), Bol.
95/J8 **Parati**, Braz.
95/H8 **Paratinga** (riv.), Braz.
31/T10 **Paray-Vieille-Poste**, Fr.
70/C4 **Parbhani**, India
38/F2 **Parchim**, Ger.
39/M3 **Parczew**, Pol.
59/M8 **Pardes Hanna-Kardur**, Isr.
70/B3 **Pārdi**, India
95/G6 **Pardo** (riv.), Braz.
39/H3 **Pardubice**, Czh.
72/D5 **Pare**, Indo.
92/F6 **Parecis** (mts.), Braz.
47/P10 **Parede**, Port.
96/C2 **Paredones**, Chile
110/E1 **Parent** (lake), Qu,Can
73/E4 **Parepare**, Indo.
47/L6 **Parets del Vallès**, Sp.
49/G3 **Párga**, Gre.
101/J5 **Paria** (gulf), Trin., Ven.
108/E3 **Paria** (riv.), Az, Ut,US
101/J5 **Paria** (pen.), Ven.
101/J6 **Pariaguán**, Ven.
72/B4 **Pariaman**, Indo.
92/E7 **Parinacota** (peak), Bol.
93/G4 **Parintins**, Braz.
42/B6 **Paris** (cap.), Fr.
112/E3 **Paris**, Ar,US
110/B4 **Paris**, Tn,US
112/E3 **Paris**, Tx,US
31/T10 **Paris** (inset) (cap.), Fr.
108/F2 **Park** (range), Co,US
108/D4 **Parker**, Az,US
109/F3 **Parker**, Co,US
110/D4 **Parkersburg**, WV,US
77/D2 **Parkes**, Austl.
35/H3 **Parkeston**, Eng,UK
110/B2 **Park Falls**, Wi,US
32/B2 **Parkgate**, NI,UK
34/A5 **Park Head** (pt.), UK
35/E5 **Parkhurst**, Eng,UK
116/C3 **Parkland**, Wa,US
107/K4 **Park Rapids**, Mn,US
116/Q15 **Park Ridge**, Il,US
115/F4 **Park Ridge**, NJ,US
107/J3 **Park River**, ND,US
115/K7 **Parkville**, Md,US
116/L9 **Parkway-Sacramento**, Ca,US
46/D2 **Parla**, Sp.
70/D4 **Parlakhemundi**, India
70/C4 **Parli**, India
45/J4 **Parma**, It.
110/D3 **Parma**, Oh,US
31/S9 **Parmain**, Fr.
94/B1 **Parnaíba**, Braz.
94/B1 **Parnaíba** (riv.), Braz.
49/H3 **Parnassos Nat'l Park**, Gre.
49/H3 **Párnis** (peak), Gre.
49/H4 **Párnon** (mts.), Gre.
52/E4 **Pärnu**, Est.
75/G5 **Paroo** (riv.), Austl.
49/J4 **Páros** (isl.), Gre.
88/B4 **Parow**, SAfr.
108/D3 **Parowan**, Ut,US
96/C3 **Parral**, Chile
76/H8 **Parramatta**, Austl.
100/A2 **Parras de la Fuente**, Mex.
34/D4 **Parrett** (riv.), Eng,UK
100/E6 **Parrita**, CR
103/H2 **Parry** (bay), NW,Can
102/F1 **Parry** (chan.), NW,Can
103/R7 **Parry** (isls.), NW,Can
110/D2 **Parry Sound**, On,Can
45/J3 **Parseierspitze** (peak), Aus.
107/H4 **Parshall**, ND,US
115/F5 **Parsippany**, NJ,US
106/C2 **Parsnip** (riv.), BC,Can
109/J3 **Parsons**, Ks,US
52/C2 **Pårtefjället** (peak), Swe.
44/C3 **Parthenay**, Fr.
48/C3 **Partinico**, It.
63/L3 **Partizansk**, Rus.
110/D1 **Partridge** (riv.), On,Can
70/C4 **Partūr**, India
93/H4 **Paru** (riv.), Braz.
70/D4 **Pārvathīpuram**, India
35/G3 **Parwich**, Eng,UK
88/D2 **Parys**, SAfr.
111/K1 **Pasadena**, Nf,Can
115/B2 **Pasadena**, Ca,US
115/K7 **Pasadena**, Md,US
112/E4 **Pasadena**, Tx,US
92/C4 **Pasaje**, Ecu.
69/C3 **Pa Sak** (riv.), Thai.
96/C3 **Pasaman** (peak), Indo.
113/F4 **Pascagoula**, Ms,US
51/H2 **Paşcani**, Rom.
106/D4 **Pasco**, Wa,US
97/J7 **Pascua** (riv.), Chile
42/B3 **Pas-de-Calais** (dept.), Fr.
42/B3 **Pas-en-Artois**, Fr.
67/D5 **Pasig**, Phil.
71/G2 **Pāsighāt**, India
59/E2 **Pasinler**, Turk.
39/K1 **Pasłęk**, Pol.
39/L2 **Pasłęka** (riv.), Pol.
50/B4 **Pašman** (isl.), Cro.
61/H3 **Pasni**, Pak.
91/E2 **Paso de Los Libres**, Arg.
96/C2 **Paso del Planchón** (peak), Chile
108/B4 **Paso Robles** (El Paso de Robles), Ca,US
114/M3 **Pass** (peak), Yk,Can
115/F5 **Passaic**, NJ,US
115/F5 **Passaic** (riv.), NJ,US
95/J7 **Passa Quatro**, Braz.
45/K2 **Passau**, Ger.
42/C2 **Passendale**, Belg.
48/D4 **Passero** (pt.), It.
91/F2 **Passo Fundo**, Braz.
95/A3 **Passo Fundo** (res.), Braz.
85/E3 **Passoré** (prov.), Burk.
95/C2 **Passos**, Braz.
45/G4 **Passy**, Fr.
92/C4 **Pastaza** (riv.), Ecu., Peru
92/C3 **Pasto**, Col.
114/F3 **Pastol** (bay), Ak,US
72/D5 **Pasuruan**, Indo.
50/D2 **Pásztó**, Hun.
96/D4 **Patagonia** (reg.), Arg.
72/B4 **Patah** (peak), Indo.
70/B3 **Pātan**, India
115/K7 **Patapsco** (riv.), Md,US
115/G5 **Patchogue**, NY,US
34/D3 **Patchway**, Eng,UK
33/G3 **Pateley Bridge**, Eng,UK
47/E3 **Paterna**, Sp.
115/F5 **Paterson**, NJ,US
61/L2 **Pathānkot**, India
106/G5 **Pathfinder** (res.), Wy,US
72/D5 **Pati**, Indo.
92/C3 **Patía** (riv.), Col.
61/L2 **Patiāla**, India
73/F2 **Patikul**, Phil.
70/E2 **Patna**, India
32/D1 **Patna**, Sc,UK
73/F1 **Patnongon**, Phil.
59/E2 **Patnos**, Turk.
95/A3 **Pato Branco**, Braz.
113/G2 **Patoka** (riv.), In,US
49/F2 **Patos**, Alb.
94/C2 **Patos**, Braz.
95/B4 **Patos** (lake), Braz.
95/C1 **Patos de Minas**, Braz.
49/G3 **Pátrai**, Gre.
49/G3 **Patrai** (gulf), Gre.
97/J7 **Patricio Lynch** (isl.), Chile
33/H4 **Patrington**, Eng,UK
95/C1 **Patrocínio**, Braz.
69/C5 **Pattani**, Thai.
69/C3 **Pattaya**, Thai.
41/G4 **Pattensen**, Ger.
48/D3 **Patti**, It.
34/D1 **Pattingham**, Eng,UK
70/C5 **Pattukkottai**, India
114/N4 **Pattullo** (mtn.), BC,Can
94/C2 **Patu**, Braz.
100/E4 **Patuca** (pt.), Hon.
100/D5 **Patuca** (riv.), Hon.
115/K8 **Patuxent** (riv.), Md,US
44/C5 **Pau**, Fr.
94/C4 **Pau Brasil**, Braz.
94/C2 **Pau dos Ferros**, Braz.
92/E5 **Pauini** (riv.), Braz.
95/F7 **Paulínia**, Braz.
94/C3 **Paulo Afonso**, Braz.
94/C3 **Paulo Afonso Nat'l Park**, Braz.
115/E6 **Paulsboro**, NJ,US
109/H4 **Pauls Valley**, Ok,US
34/D4 **Paulton**, Eng,UK
71/G4 **Paungde**, Burma
68/C5 **Pauri**, India
45/H4 **Pavia**, It.
51/G4 **Pavlikeni**, Bul.
68/C1 **Pavlodar**, Kaz.
114/F4 **Pavlof** (vol.), Ak,US
54/E2 **Pavlograd**, Ukr.
52/J5 **Pavlovo**, Rus.
45/J4 **Pavullo nel Frignano**, It.
72/D4 **Pawan** (riv.), Indo.
109/H3 **Pawhuska**, Ok,US
69/B2 **Pawn** (riv.), Burma
109/H3 **Pawnee** (riv.), Ks,US
110/C3 **Paw Paw**, Mi,US
115/G5 **Pawtucket**, RI,US
49/F3 **Paxoí** (isl.), Gre.
49/G3 **Paxoí** (Yáïos), Gre.
72/B4 **Payakumbuh**, Indo.
96/C3 **Payén, Altiplanicie del** (plat.), Arg.
106/D4 **Payette**, Id,US
106/D4 **Payette** (riv.), Id,US
53/P1 **Pay-Khoy** (mts.), Rus.
103/J3 **Payne** (lake), Qu,Can
97/F2 **Paysandú**, Uru.
97/F1 **Paysandú** (dept.), Uru.
31/T9 **Pays de France** (plain), Fr.
44/C3 **Pays de la Loire** (reg.), Fr.
108/E4 **Payson**, Az,US
108/E2 **Payson**, Ut,US
96/C3 **Payún** (peak), Arg.
59/D3 **Pazarcık**, Turk.
51/G4 **Pazardzhik**, Bul.
54/D5 **Pazaryeri**, Turk.
95/A2 **Peabiru**, Braz.
102/E3 **Peace** (riv.), Ab, BC,Can
113/H5 **Peace** (riv.), Fl,US
106/D1 **Peace River**, Ab,Can
106/D3 **Peachland**, BC,Can
113/G3 **Peachtree City**, Ga,US
33/G5 **Peak District Nat'l Park**, Eng,UK
104/W13 **Pearl** (har.), Hi,US
113/F4 **Pearl** (riv.), La, Ms,US
113/F3 **Pearl**, Ms,US

153

Pearl – Ponta

115/B1 Pearland, Ca,US
79/H2 Pearl and Hermes (reef), Hi,US
104/W13 Pearl City, Hi,US
67/B3 Pearl River (inlet), China
115/F4 Pearl River, NY,US
112/D4 Pearsall, Tx,US
103/R7 Peary (chan.), NW,Can
109/H4 Pease (riv.), Tx,US
35/E2 Pebworth, Eng,UK
50/E4 Peć, Yugo.
53/N2 Pechora, Rus.
53/M1 Pechora (bay), Rus.
53/M2 Pechora (riv.), Rus.
109/G5 Pecos (riv.), NM, Tx,US
112/C4 Pecos, Tx,US
109/F4 Pecos Nat'l Mon., NM,US
42/C3 Pecquencourt, Fr.
50/D2 Pécs, Hun.
101/E6 Pedasí, Pan.
77/C4 Pedder (lake), Austl.
101/G4 Pedernales, DRep.
95/B2 Pederneiras, Braz.
115/C3 Pedley, Ca,US
94/B5 Pedra Azul, Braz.
95/G7 Pedreira, Braz.
94/B2 Pedreiras, Braz.
70/D6 Pedro (pt.), SrL.
101/F4 Pedro Cays (isls.), Jam.
92/E3 Pedro II, Braz.
91/E1 Pedro Juan Caballero, Par.
95/C1 Pedro Leopoldo, Braz.
95/A4 Pedro Osório, Braz.
94/B2 Pedro Segundo, Braz.
36/D3 Peebles, Sc,UK
76/F6 Peel (isl.), Austl.
102/G1 Peel (sound), NW,Can
114/L2 Peel (riv.), Yk,Can
32/D3 Peel, IM,UK
33/F1 Peel Fell (mtn.), Eng,UK
43/E1 Peer, Belg.
75/R11 Pegasus (bay), NZ
45/J2 Pegnitz, Ger.
45/J2 Pegnitz (riv.), Ger.
47/E3 Pego, Sp.
33/G1 Pegswood, Eng,UK
69/B2 Pegu, Burma
69/B2 Pegu (mts.), Burma
69/B2 Pegu (riv.), Burma
69/B2 Pegu (Bago) (div.), Burma
35/H4 Pegwell (bay), Eng,UK
96/E2 Pehuajó, Arg.
96/C2 Pehuenche (pass), Chile
66/B3 Peijiachuankou, China
41/H4 Peine, Ger.
37/H4 Peipus (lake), Est., Rus.
95/K6 Peixe (riv.), Braz.
95/C2 Peixoto (res.), Braz.
72/C5 Pekalongan, Indo.
72/B3 Pekan Nanas, Malay.
110/B3 Pekin, Il,US
96/C5 Pelada (plain), Arg.
48/C5 Pelagie (isls.), It.
50/F3 Peleaga, Vîrful (peak), Rom.
111/D3 Pelee (isl.), On,Can
110/D3 Pelee (pt.), On,Can
101/J5 Pelée (mt.), Mart.
111/R9 Pelham, On,Can
113/G3 Pelham, Al,US
39/H4 Pelhřimov, Czh.
106/E2 Pelican (mts.), Ab,Can
107/H2 Pelican (lake), Sk,Can
107/H2 Pelican Narrows, Sk,Can
84/A4 Pelindã, Ponta de (pt.), GBis.
50/E5 Pelister Nat'l Park, Macd.
50/C4 Pelješac (pen.), Cro.
114/M3 Pelly (riv.), Yk,Can
102/H2 Pelly Bay, NW,Can
114/L3 Pelly Crossing, Yk,Can
49/G3 Peloponnisos (reg.), Gre.
48/D3 Peloritani (mts.), It.
95/A4 Pelotas, Braz.
95/B3 Pelotas (riv.), Braz.
39/K2 Pelplin, Pol.
73/F5 Pemali (cape), Indo.
72/A3 Pematangsiantar, Indo.
81/G5 Pemba (isl.), Tanz.
106/C3 Pemberton, BC,Can
106/E2 Pembina (riv.), Ab,Can
107/J3 Pembina (riv.), Can., US
107/J3 Pembina, ND,US
110/E2 Pembroke, On,Can
34/B3 Pembroke, Wal,UK
31/P8 Pembury, Eng,UK
96/B3 Pemuco, Chile
46/A2 Penafiel, Port.
96/C9 Peñaflor, Chile
46/D2 Peñalara (mtn.), Sp.
94/A1 Penalva, Braz.
95/B2 Penápolis, Braz.
46/C2 Peñaranda de Bracamonte, Sp.
47/E2 Peñarroya (mtn.), Sp.
46/C3 Peñarroya-Pueblonuevo, Sp.
34/C4 Penarth, Wal,UK
97/L8 Peñas (cape), Arg.
97/J6 Penas (gulf), Chile
46/C1 Peñas (cape), Sp.
96/B3 Penco, Chile
49/L6 Pendelikón (mtn.), Gre.
94/C2 Pendências, Braz.
85/F4 Pendjari (riv.), Ben., Burk.
85/F4 Pendjari Nat'l Park, Ben.
33/F4 Pendle (hill), Eng,UK
106/D4 Pendleton, Or,US
106/D4 Pend Oreille (lake), Id,US
106/D3 Pend Oreille (riv.), Id, Wa,US
46/A2 Peneda-Gerês Nat'l Park, Port.
94/C3 Penedo, Braz.
34/C1 Penegoes, Wal,UK
110/E2 Penetanguishene, On,Can
70/C4 Penganga (riv.), India
31/N7 Penge, Eng,UK
67/C3 Penghu (Pescadores) (isls.), Tai.
95/B3 Penha, Braz.
106/E2 Penhold, Ab,Can
46/C4 Penibético, Sistema (range), Sp.
46/A3 Peniche, Port.
94/A3 Penitente (mts.), Braz.
34/D1 Penkridge, Eng,UK
32/E5 Penmaenmawr, Wal,UK
44/A3 Penmarch, Fr.
44/A3 Penmarc'h, Pointe de (pt.), Fr.
48/D1 Penna, Punta della (cape), It.
50/C5 Penne (pt.), It.
70/C5 Penner (riv.), India
110/E3 Penn Hills, Pa,US
45/G4 Pennine Alps (mts.), It., Swi.
33/F2 Pennine Chain (range), Eng,UK
115/F5 Pennington, NJ,US
115/E6 Pennsauken, NJ,US
110/E3 Pennsylvania (state), US
103/S7 Penny (str.), NW,Can
110/E3 Penn Yan, NY,US
110/G2 Penobscot (riv.), Me,US
101/E6 Penonomé, Pan.
32/E1 Penpont, Sc,UK
32/D5 Penrhyn Mawr (pt.), Wal,UK
79/K5 Penrhyn (Tongareva) (atoll), Cookls.
76/G8 Penrith, Austl.
33/F2 Penrith, Eng,UK
34/A6 Penryn, Eng,UK
98/X Pensacola (mts.), Ant.
113/G4 Pensacola, Fl,US
107/G3 Pense, Sk,Can
31/P8 Penshurst, Eng,UK
34/B5 Pensilva, Eng,UK
113/J3 Pentagon, Va,US
78/F6 Pentecost (isl.), Van.
94/C1 Pentecoste, Braz.
51/H3 Penteleu (peak), Rom.
106/D3 Penticton, BC,Can
34/B5 Pentire (pt.), UK
36/D3 Pentland (hills), Sc,UK
34/C3 Pentyrch, Wal,UK
96/C2 Peñuelas Nat'l Park, Chile
34/A6 Penwith (pen.), Eng,UK
33/E6 Pen-y-Cae, Wal,UK
33/F3 Pen-y-Ghent (mtn.), Eng,UK
32/E5 Pen-y-Gogarth (pt.), Wal,UK
34/C2 Pen y Gurnos (mtn.), Wal,UK
55/H1 Penza, Rus.
34/A6 Penzance, Eng,UK
55/G1 Penza Obl., Rus.
45/J3 Penzberg, Ger.
57/S3 Penzhina (bay), Rus.
57/S3 Penzhina (riv.), Rus.
110/B3 Peoria, Il,US
43/E2 Pepinster, Belg.
115/F5 Pequannock, NJ,US
75/G2 Pera (head), Austl.
72/B4 Perabumulih, Indo.
47/M9 Perales (riv.), Sp.
111/H1 Percé, Qu,Can
44/D2 Perche (hills), Fr.
39/J4 Perchtoldsdorf, Aus.
74/C4 Percival (lakes), Austl.
76/C3 Percy (isls.), Austl.
94/A3 Perdida (riv.), Braz.
47/F1 Perdido (mtn.), Sp.
92/C3 Pereira, Col.
95/B2 Pereira Barreto, Braz.
96/E2 Pergamino, Arg.
45/K5 Pergola, It.
111/G1 Péribonca (riv.), Qu,Can
44/D4 Périgueux, Fr.
101/G6 Perija, Sierra de (range), Col., Ven.
60/D6 Perim (isl.), Yem.
49/J3 Peristéra (isl.), Gre.
49/L6 Peristéri, Gre.
97/K6 Perito Moreno Nat'l Park, Arg.
70/C5 Periyakulam, India
115/E5 Perkasie, Pa,US
43/F5 Perl, Ger.
100/E5 Perlas (lag.), Nic.
100/E5 Perlas (pt.), Nic.
38/F2 Perleberg, Ger.
53/N4 Perm', Rus.
53/M4 Perm' Obl., Rus.
94/C3 Pernambuco (state), Braz.
44/F4 Pernes-les-Fontaines, Fr.
50/F4 Pernik, Bul.
52/D3 Perniö, Fin.
42/B4 Péronne, Fr.
53/X9 Perovo, Rus.
44/E5 Perpignan, Fr.
115/C3 Perris, Ca,US
44/B2 Perros-Guirec, Fr.
111/N7 Perrot (isl.), Qu,Can
102/F2 Perry (riv.), NW,Can
113/H4 Perry, Fl,US
113/H3 Perry, Ga,US
109/H3 Perry, Ok,US
115/K7 Perry Hall, Md,US
112/C2 Perryton, Tx,US
109/K3 Perryville, Mo,US
31/S9 Persan, Fr.
60/F3 Persepolis (ruins), Iran
34/D2 Pershore, Eng,UK
60/E3 Persian (gulf), Asia
59/D2 Pertek, Turk.
110/E2 Perth, On,Can
36/D2 Perth, Sc,UK
115/F5 Perth Amboy, NJ,US
44/F5 Pertuis, Fr.
44/C3 Pertuis Breton (inlet), Fr.
48/A2 Pertusato (cape), Fr.
92/C5 Peru
110/B3 Peru, Il,US
110/C3 Peru, In,US
50/D4 Perućačko (lake), Bosn.
48/C1 Perugia, It.
95/G9 Peruíbe, Braz.
42/C2 Péruwelz, Belg.
59/E3 Pervari, Turk.
53/J5 Pervomaysk, Rus.
54/D2 Pervomaysk, Ukr.
53/N4 Pervoural'sk, Rus.
72/B4 Pesagi (peak), Indo.
45/K5 Pesaro, It.
67/C3 Pescadores (Penghu) (isls.), Tai.
48/D1 Pescara, It.
55/J4 Peschanyy, Mys (cape), Kaz.
53/L2 Pesha (riv.), Rus.
61/K2 Peshāwar, Pak.
51/G4 Peshtera, Bul.
110/B2 Peshtigo (riv.), Wi,US
94/C3 Pesqueira, Braz.
44/C4 Pessac, Fr.
44/D5 Pessons, Pic dels (peak), And.
50/D2 Pest (co.), Hun.
52/G4 Pestovo, Rus.
59/K5 Petah Tiqwa, Isr.
113/F4 Petal, Ms,US
49/J4 Petalión (gulf), Gre.
116/J10 Petaluma, Ca,US
43/E4 Pétange, Lux.
100/B4 Petapa, Mex.
101/H5 Petare, Ven.
87/F3 Petauke, Zam.
110/E2 Petawawa (riv.), On,Can
110/E2 Petawawa, On,Can
107/L4 Petenwell (lake), Wi,US
110/E2 Peterborough, On,Can
35/F1 Peterborough, Eng,UK
36/E2 Peterhead, Sc,UK
98/T Peter I (isl.), Ant.
28/E9 Peter I (isl.), Nor.
33/G2 Peterlee, Eng,UK
96/C2 Peteroa (vol.), Arg.
106/F1 Peter Pond (lake), Sk,Can
110/E4 Petersburg, Va,US
35/F5 Petersfield, Eng,UK
41/F4 Petershagen, Ger.
48/E3 Petilia Policastro, It.
111/H2 Petitcodiac, NB,Can
101/G4 Petite Riviere de l'Artibonite, Haiti
43/F5 Petite-Rosselle, Fr.
42/C6 Petit Morin (riv.), Fr.
37/J3 Petkeljärven Nat'l Park, Fin.
70/B3 Petlād, India
100/D3 Peto, Mex.
96/C2 Petorca, Chile
110/C2 Petoskey, Mi,US
57/M2 Petra (isls.), Rus.
86/C2 Petra (Baṭrā) (ruins), Jor.
47/E3 Petrel, Sp.
48/C2 Petrella (peak), It.
51/F5 Petrich, Bul.
108/E4 Petrified Forest Nat'l Park, Az,US
51/F3 Petrila, Rom.
52/F4 Petrodvorets, Rus.
51/F4 Petrokhanski Prokhod (pass), Bul.
94/C3 Petrolândia, Braz.
94/B3 Petrolina, Braz.
56/G4 Petropavlovsk, Kaz.
57/R4 Petropavlovsk-Kamchatskiy, Rus.
95/K7 Petrópolis, Braz.
51/F3 Petroşani, Rom.
50/D3 Petrovaradin, Yugo.
51/F1 Petrovsk, Rus.
62/F1 Petrovsk-Zabaykal'skiy, Rus.
52/G3 Petrozavodsk, Rus.
33/F2 Petterill (riv.), Eng,UK
35/F5 Petworth, Eng,UK
52/F2 Petzeck (peak), Aus.
114/G4 Peulik (mtn.), Ak,US
96/C2 Peumo, Chile
35/G5 Pevensey, Eng,UK
116/P13 Pewaukee (lake), Wi,US
35/E4 Pewsey, Eng,UK
53/K2 Peza (riv.), Rus.
44/E5 Pézenas, Fr.
43/G5 Pfälzer Wald (for.), Ger.
41/G6 Pfieffe (riv.), Ger.
45/H2 Pforzheim, Ger.
45/H2 Pfungstadt, Ger.
69/C1 Phak (riv.), Laos
70/B2 Phalodi, India
69/C3 Phanat Nikhom, Thai.
69/B4 Phangan (isl.), Thai.
69/C3 Phang Hoei (range), Thai.
69/C3 Phanom Dongrak (mts.), Camb., Thai.
69/E4 Phan Rang, Viet.
69/E4 Phan Thiet, Viet.
112/D5 Pharr, Tx,US
69/C5 Phatthalung, Thai.
69/C2 Phaya Fo (peak), Thai.
69/B2 Phayao, Thai.
113/G3 Phenix City, Al,US
88/C2 Phepane (dry riv.), SAfr.
69/B3 Phet Buri, Thai.
69/C2 Phetchabun, Thai.
69/C2 Phichit, Thai.
113/F3 Philadelphia, Ms,US
115/E6 Philadelphia, Pa,US
80/B4 Philae (ruins), Egypt
107/H4 Philip, SD,US
42/D3 Philippeville, Belg.
110/D4 Philippi, WV,US
78/B3 Philippine (sea), Asia
67/D5 Philippines
101/J4 Philipsburg, NAnt.
106/E4 Philipsburg, Mt,US
40/B5 Philipsdam (dam), Neth.
109/H3 Phillipsburg, Ks,US
115/E5 Phillipsburg, NJ,US
69/C3 Phimai (ruins), Thai.
69/C2 Phitsanulok, Thai.
69/D4 Phnom Penh (Phnum Penh) (cap.), Camb.
69/D3 Phnum Tbeng Meanchey, Camb.
69/C5 Pho (pt.), Thai.
79/H5 Phoenix (isls.), Kiri.
108/D4 Phoenix (cap.), Az,US
113/H2 Phoenix (peak), NC,US
79/H5 Phoenix (Rawaki) (atoll), Kiri.
115/E5 Phoenixville, Pa,US
69/C1 Phongsali, Laos
69/C2 Phou Bia (peak), Laos
69/D2 Phou Huatt (peak), Viet.
69/C1 Phou Loi (peak), Laos
69/D2 Phou Xai Lai Leng (peak), Laos
69/C2 Phrae, Thai.
69/C3 Phra Nakhon Si Ayutthaya, Thai.
69/B4 Phra Thong (isl.), Thai.
69/C4 Phsar Ream, Camb.
69/D2 Phuc Loi, Viet.
71/J3 Phuc Yen, Viet.
69/C2 Phu Hin Rong Kla Nat'l Park, Thai.
69/E4 Phu Hoi, Viet.
69/B5 Phuket, Thai.
69/B5 Phuket (isl.), Thai.
69/C2 Phu Kradung Nat'l Park, Thai.
70/D3 Phulabāni, India
69/D2 Phu Loc, Viet.
69/D1 Phu Luong, Viet.
69/D1 Phu Luong (peak), Viet.
69/D1 Phu Ly, Viet.
69/C4 Phumi Banam, Camb.
69/C4 Phumi Choan, Camb.
69/D3 Phumi Kampong Trabek, Camb.
69/D4 Phumi Krek, Camb.
69/D3 Phumi Labang Siek, Camb.
69/D3 Phumi Prek Preah, Camb.
69/C3 Phumi Samraong, Camb.
69/C3 Phumi Toek Sok, Camb.
69/E3 Phu My, Viet.
69/E3 Phu Nhon, Viet.
69/D2 Phu Phan Nat'l Park, Thai.
69/C4 Phu Quoc (isl.), Viet.
69/D4 Phu Rieng Sron, Viet.
69/C2 Phu Rua Nat'l Park, Thai.
69/D1 Phu Tho, Viet.
69/D2 Phu Vang, Viet.
66/D4 Pi (riv.), China
94/C4 Piaçabuçu, Braz.
45/H4 Piacenza, It.
94/C2 Piancó, Braz.
48/A1 Pianosa (isl.), It.
39/L2 Piaseczno, Pol.
51/H2 Piatra Neamţ, Rom.
94/B3 Piauí (riv.), Braz.
94/B2 Piauí (state), Braz.
45/K3 Piave (riv.), It.
101/N9 Piaxtla (riv.), Mex.
48/D4 Piazza Armerina, It.
83/M6 Pibor Post, Sudan
110/C1 Pic (riv.), On,Can
101/P8 Picacho del Centinela (peak), Mex.
42/B4 Picardy (Picardie) (reg.), Fr.
113/F4 Picayune, Ms,US
48/E2 Piccolo (lag.), It.
96/C2 Pichidegua, Chile
96/C2 Pichilemu, Chile
111/R8 Pickering, On,Can
33/H3 Pickering, Eng,UK
33/H3 Pickering, Vale of (val.), Eng,UK
107/L3 Pickle Lake, On,Can
47/S12 Pico (isl.), Azor.,Port.
92/F3 Pico da Neblina Nat'l Park, Braz.
100/A4 Pico de Tancitaro Nat'l Park, Mex.
115/B3 Pico Rivera, Ca,US
94/B2 Picos, Braz.
96/D5 Pico Truncado, Arg.
42/B4 Picquigny, Fr.
110/E3 Picton, On,Can
111/J2 Pictou, NS,Can
34/D5 Piddle (riv.), Eng,UK
70/D6 Pidurutagala (peak), SrL.
45/G4 Piedmont (reg.), It.
116/K11 Piedmont, Ca,US
97/F2 Piedras (pt.), Arg.
92/D6 Piedras (riv.), Peru
33/K3 Piekary Śląskie, Pol.
88/B4 Piekenierskloof (pass), SAfr.
37/H3 Pieksämäki, Fin.
37/J3 Pielinen (lake), Fin.
39/L4 Pieniński Nat'l Park, Pol.
47/K6 Piera, Sp.
109/H2 Pierce, Ne,US
106/F2 Pierceland, Sk,Can
107/H4 Pierre (cap.), SD,US
31/T10 Pierrefitte-sur-Seine, Fr.
111/N7 Pierrefonds, Qu,Can
42/C5 Pierrefonds, Fr.
44/F4 Pierrelatte, Fr.
31/S9 Pierrelaye, Fr.
83/E3 Pietermaritzburg, SAfr.
87/E5 Pietersburg, SAfr.
89/E2 Piet Retief, SAfr.
51/G2 Pietrosul (peak), Rom.
106/E2 Pigeon (lake), Ab,Can
107/L3 Pigeon (riv.), Can., US
110/B4 Piggott, Ar,US
100/E3 Pigs (bay), Cuba
96/E3 Pigüé, Arg.
100/C4 Pijijiapan, Mex.
40/B4 Pijnacker, Neth.
78/D4 Pikelot (isl.), Micr.
109/F3 Pikes (peak), Co,US
115/K7 Pikesville, Md,US
110/D4 Pikeville, Ky,US
67/D6 Pikit, Phil.
39/J2 Piła, Pol.
39/J2 Piła (prov.), Pol.
88/P12 Pilanesberg (range), SAfr.
91/E2 Pilar, Par.
73/F1 Pilar, Phil.
92/F8 Pilaya (riv.), Bol.
116/D1 Pilchuck (riv.), Wa,US
90/C5 Pilcomayo (riv.), SAm.
31/P7 Pilgrims Hatch, Eng,UK
67/D5 Pili, Phil.
54/B2 Pilica (riv.), Pol.
49/H3 Pilion (peak), Gre.
50/D2 Pilis, Hun.
39/K5 Pilisvörösvár, Hun.
70/C2 Pilkhua, India
77/C4 Pillar (cape), Austl.
33/E2 Pillar (mtn.), Eng,UK
116/K12 Pillar (pt.), Ca,US
94/A5 Pilões (mts.), Braz.
113/G2 Pilot (peak), Tn,US
45/K2 Pilsen (Plzeň), Czh.
108/E4 Pima, Az,US
70/B4 Pimpri-Chinchwad, India
101/M7 Pinacote (mt.), Mex.
97/J7 Pinaculo (peak), Arg.
67/D5 Pinamalayan, Phil.
72/A2 Pinang (isl.), Malay.
59/D2 Pınarbaşı, Turk.
100/E3 Pinar del Río, Cuba
51/H5 Pınarhisar, Turk.
92/C4 Piñas, Ecu.
67/D4 Pinatubo (mt.), Phil.
107/K3 Pinawa, Mb,Can
33/H6 Pinchbeck, Eng,UK
106/E3 Pincher Creek, Ab,Can
110/D3 Pinconning, Mi,US
48/E2 Pîncota, Rom.
111/N7 Pincourt, Qu,Can
39/L3 Pińczów, Pol.
95/H7 Pindamonhangaba, Braz.
94/A2 Pindaré (riv.), Braz.
94/A1 Pindaré-Mirim, Braz.
61/K2 Pindi Gheb, Pak.
49/G3 Pindos Nat'l Park, Gre.
49/G2 Pindus (mts.), Gre.
70/B3 Pindwāra, India
113/F4 Pine (hills), Ms,US
107/G4 Pine (hills), Mt,US
115/F6 Pine Barrens (reg.), NJ,US
112/E3 Pine Bluff, Ar,US
107/G5 Pine Bluffs, Wy,US
47/G2 Pineda de Mar, Sp.
106/F5 Pinedale, Wy,US
107/J3 Pine Falls, Mb,Can
52/J2 Pinega (riv.), Rus.
115/F6 Pine Hill, NJ,US
107/L2 Pineimuta (riv.), On,Can
98/T Pine Island (bay), Ant.
110/A2 Pine Island, Mn,US
88/L10 Pinelands, SAfr.
107/H5 Pine Ridge, SD,US
45/G4 Pinerolo, It.
89/E3 Pinetown, SAfr.
69/B2 Ping (riv.), Thai.
66/C4 Pingdingshan, China
66/D3 Pingdu, China
78/F4 Pingelap (atoll), Micr.
66/C5 Pingjing Guan (pass), China
66/D2 Pingquan, China
66/C3 Pingshan, China
67/D3 Pingtung, Tai.
65/C3 Pingxiang, China
67/B2 Pingxiang, China
69/D1 Pingxiang, China
66/C3 Pingxing Guan (pass), China
63/J4 Pingyang, China
95/G7 Pinhal, Braz.
47/Q10 Pinhal Novo, Port.
95/B3 Pinhão, Braz.
94/A1 Pinheiro, Braz.
95/D1 Pinheiros, Braz.
49/G3 Piniós (riv.), Gre.
49/G4 Piniós (riv.), Gre.
40/C2 Pinkegat (chan.), Neth.
108/B3 Pinnacles Nat'l Mon., Ca,US
41/G1 Pinnau (riv.), Ger.
41/G1 Pinneberg, Ger.
96/C3 Pino Hachado (pass), Arg.
116/K10 Pinole, Ca,US
108/C4 Pinos (peak), Ca,US
100/E3 Pinos (Juventud) (isl.), Cuba
46/D4 Pinos-Puente, Sp.
100/E4 Pinotepa Nacional, Mex.
73/E4 Pinrang, Indo.
78/F7 Pins, Ile des (isl.), NCal.
54/C1 Pinsk, Bela.
96/C3 Pinto, Chile
47/N9 Pinto, Sp.
108/D3 Pioche, Nv,US
94/B2 Pio IX, Braz.
48/B1 Piombino, It.
56/J2 Pioner (isl.), Rus.
39/L3 Pionki, Pol.
94/F2 Piorini (riv.), Braz.
39/K3 Piotrków (prov.), Pol.
39/K3 Piotrków Trybunalski, Pol.
94/A1 Pio XII, Braz.
70/B2 Pīpār, India
108/D3 Pipe Spring Nat'l Mon., Az,US
107/H3 Pipestone (cr.), Mb, Sk,Can
107/L2 Pipestone (riv.), On,Can
107/J4 Pipestone, Mn,US
107/J4 Pipestone Nat'l Mon., Mn,US
61/K2 Piplān, Pak.
111/G1 Pipmuacan (res.), Qu,Can
110/C3 Piqua, Oh,US
95/H7 Piquete, Braz.
95/A3 Piquiri (riv.), Braz.
95/B1 Piracanjuba, Braz.
95/C2 Piracicaba, Braz.
94/B1 Piracuruca, Braz.
95/A4 Piraí, Braz.
95/B3 Piraí do Sul, Braz.
49/H4 Piraiévs, Gre.
95/B2 Piraju, Braz.
95/B2 Pirajuí, Braz.
97/J7 Pirámide (peak), Chile
96/E2 Pirané, Arg.
95/D2 Piranga (riv.), Braz.
94/C2 Piranhas (riv.), Braz.
94/C2 Piranji (riv.), Braz.
95/C1 Pirapora, Braz.
95/B2 Pirapòzinho, Braz.
95/B2 Pirássununga, Braz.
96/C1 Pircas (peak), Arg.
95/B1 Pires do Rio, Braz.
51/F5 Pirin, Bul.
51/F5 Pirin (mts.), Bul.
51/F5 Pirin Nat'l Park, Bul.
94/B2 Piripiri, Braz.
94/B3 Piritaba, Braz.
43/G5 Pirmasens, Ger.
39/G3 Pirna, Ger.
50/F4 Pirot, Yugo.
54/E2 Piryatin, Ukr.
45/J5 Pisa, It.
73/E2 Pisau, Tanjong (cape), Malay.
92/D2 Pisba Nat'l Park, Col.
115/F5 Piscataway, NJ,US
92/C6 Pisco, Peru
92/C6 Pisco (riv.), Peru
45/L2 Písek, Czh.
61/J2 Pishīn, Pak.
91/C2 Pissis (peak), Arg.
42/B4 Pissy, Fr.
116/P15 Pistakee (lake), Il,US
48/E2 Pisticci, It.
45/J5 Pistoia, It.
46/C1 Pisuerga (riv.), Sp.
39/L2 Pisz, Pol.
108/B2 Pit (riv.), Ca,US
92/C3 Pitalito, Col.
95/B3 Pitanga, Braz.
79/N7 Pitcairn Islands (terr.), UK
37/G2 Piteå, Swe.
37/F2 Piteälv (riv.), Swe.
51/G3 Piteşti, Rom.
44/E2 Pithiviers, Fr.
36/D2 Pitlochry, Sc,UK
115/E6 Pitman, NJ,US
36/D2 Pitmedden, Sc,UK
96/B3 Pitrufquén, Chile
78/H8 Pitt (lake), Austl.
36/C2 Pittenweem, Sc,UK
116/L10 Pittsburg, Ca,US
109/J3 Pittsburg, Ks,US
112/E3 Pittsburg, Tx,US
110/E3 Pittsburgh, Pa,US
111/F3 Pittsfield, Ma,US
111/G2 Pittsfield, Me,US
95/C2 Piũí, Braz.
92/B5 Piura, Peru
70/D2 Piuthān, Nepal
49/F1 Piva (riv.), Yugo.
101/G5 Pivijay, Col.
50/D4 Pivsko (lake), Yugo.
53/K4 Pizhma (riv.), Rus.
48/E3 Pizzo, It.
48/C1 Pizzuto (peak), It.
88/D3 P. K. Le Rouxdam (res.), SAfr.
111/L2 Placentia (bay), Nf,Can
115/C3 Placentia, Ca,US
67/D5 Placer, Phil.
31/T9 Plailly, Fr.
69/C3 Plai Mat (riv.), Thai.
115/F5 Plainfield, NJ,US
112/C3 Plains, Tx,US
115/F5 Plainsboro, NJ,US
110/A2 Plainview, Mn,US
115/G5 Plainview, NY,US
112/C3 Plainview, Tx,US
109/H3 Plainville, Ks,US
31/R10 Plaisir, Fr.
73/E5 Plampang, Indo.
94/A4 Planaltina, Braz.
95/D1 Planalto do Brasil (plat.), Braz.
101/F6 Planeta Rica, Col.
112/D3 Plano, Tx,US
113/H5 Plantation, Fl,US
113/H4 Plant City, Fl,US
113/F4 Plaquemine, La,US
46/B2 Plasencia, Sp.
48/C4 Platani (riv.), It.
97/F2 Plata, Río de la (estuary), Arg.
85/H4 Plateau (state), Nga.
101/G6 Plato, Col.
109/J2 Platte (riv.), Mo,US
109/H2 Platte (riv.), Ne,US
107/J5 Platte, SD,US
110/B3 Platteville, Wi,US
45/K2 Plattling, Ger.
110/F2 Plattsburgh, NY,US
45/K1 Plauen, Ger.
50/D4 Plav, Yugo.
100/D4 Playa de los Muertos (ruins), Hon.
92/B4 Playas, Ecu.
108/E5 Playas (lake), NM,US
69/E3 Play Cu (Pleiku), Viet.
107/J2 Playgreen (lake), Mb,Can
116/K11 Pleasant Hill, Ca,US
116/L11 Pleasanton, Ca,US
112/D4 Pleasanton, Tx,US
116/Q14 Pleasant Prairie, Wi,US
115/G4 Pleasantville, NY,US
69/E3 Pleiku (Play Cu), Viet.
38/G3 Pleisse (riv.), Ger.
77/G5 Plenty (riv.), Austl.
75/S10 Plenty (bay), NZ
107/G3 Plentywood, Mt,US
44/B2 Plérin, Fr.
39/J3 Pleszew, Pol.
111/G1 Plétipi (lake), Qu,Can
41/E6 Plettenberg, Ger.
51/G4 Pleven, Bul.
50/B3 Plitvice Lakes Nat'l Park, Cro.
45/L4 Plitvička Jezera Nat'l Park, Cro.
50/D4 Pljevlja, Yugo.
50/B4 Ploča, Rt (pt.), Yugo.
39/K2 Płock, Pol.
39/K2 Płock (prov.), Pol.
50/C4 Ploćno (peak), Bosn.
44/B3 Ploemeur, Fr.
51/H3 Ploieşti, Rom.
38/F1 Plön, Ger.
106/G2 Plonge (lake), Sk,Can
39/L2 Płońsk, Pol.
39/H3 Ploučnice (riv.), Czh.
44/B2 Ploufragan, Fr.
44/A2 Plougastel-Daoulas, Fr.
51/G4 Plovdiv, Bul.
51/G5 Plovdiv (reg.), Bul.
110/B2 Plover, Wi,US
32/A2 Plumbridge, NI,UK
52/D5 Plungé, Lith.
101/J4 Plymouth (cap.), Monts.
34/B6 Plymouth, Eng,UK
34/B6 Plymouth (sound), Eng,UK
110/C3 Plymouth, In,US
111/G3 Plymouth, NH,US
110/C3 Plymouth, Wi,US
34/C2 Plynlimon (mtn.), UK
45/K2 Plzeň (Pilsen), Czh.
39/J2 Pniewy, Pol.
85/E4 Pô, Burk.
45/J4 Po (riv.), It.
45/J4 Po (val.), It.
95/G8 Poá, Braz.
68/D3 Pobedy, Pik (peak), Kyr.
39/J2 Pobiedziska, Pol.
113/F2 Pocahontas, Ar,US
94/A2 Poção de Pedra, Braz.
106/E5 Pocatello, Id,US
54/D1 Pochep, Rus.
45/K2 Pöcking, Ger.
78/E6 Pocklington (reef), PNG
33/H4 Pocklington, Eng,UK
94/B4 Poções, Braz.
95/H6 Poço Fundo, Braz.
109/J4 Pocola, Ok,US
93/G7 Poconé, Braz.
115/E4 Pocono (lake), Pa,US
95/G6 Poços de Caldas, Braz.
39/K3 Poddębice, Pol.
39/M3 Podlasie (reg.), Pol.
52/H5 Podol'sk, Rus.
84/B2 Podor, Sen.
52/G3 Podporozh'ye, Rus.
50/C3 Podravska Slatina, Cro.
50/E4 Podujevo, Yugo.
45/J5 Poggibonsi, It.
49/G2 Pogradec, Alb.
114/F5 Pogromni (vol.), Ak,US
64/A2 P'ohang, SKor.
111/G2 Pohénégamook, Qu,Can
37/G3 Pohjanmaa (reg.), Fin.
78/E4 Pohnpei (isl.), Micr.
115/E5 Pohopoco Mtn. (ridge), Pa,US
98/H Poinsett (cape), Ant.
102/E2 Point (lake), NW,Can
113/F4 Point au Fer (isl.), La,US
101/J4 Pointe-à-Pitre, Guad.
111/N7 Pointe-Claire, Qu,Can
111/F2 Pointe-du-Lac, Qu,Can
87/B1 Pointe-Noire, Congo
47/G4 Pointe Pescade, Cap de la (cape), Alg.
101/J5 Point Fortin, Trin.
77/E1 Point Lookout (peak), Austl.
110/D3 Point Pelee Nat'l Park, On,Can
115/F5 Point Pleasant, NJ,US
110/C4 Point Pleasant, Oh,US
110/D4 Point Pleasant, WV,US
31/S10 Poissy, Fr.
44/D3 Poitiers, Fr.
44/C3 Poitou (hist. reg.), Fr.
44/C3 Poitou-Charentes (reg.), Fr.
37/J3 Pojois-Karjala (prov.), Fin.
94/C4 Pojuca, Braz.
70/B2 Pokaran, India
70/D2 Pokhara, Nepal
55/K1 Pokhvistnevo, Rus.
69/E4 Po Klong Garai Cham Towers, Viet.
83/L7 Poko, Zaire
45/L1 Polabská Nížina (reg.), Czh.
46/C1 Pola de Laviana, Sp.
46/C1 Pola de Lena, Sp.
46/C1 Pola de Siero, Sp.
54/A2 Pol'ana (peak), Slvk.
39/K2 Poland
39/L3 Pol'aniec, Pol.
53/P2 Polar Urals (mts.), Rus.
59/C2 Polatlı, Turk.
39/J2 Pol'czyn-Zdrój, Pol.
61/J1 Pol-e-Khomri, Afg.
35/E1 Polesworth, Eng,UK
50/E2 Polgár, Hun.
49/J4 Políaigos (isl.), Gre.
48/D3 Policastro (gulf), It.
39/H2 Police, Pol.
48/E2 Policoro, It.
49/H2 Políkhni, Gre.
67/D4 Polillo (isl.), Phil.
48/E3 Polistena, It.
39/J3 Polkowice, Pol.
47/G3 Pollensa, Sp.
67/E6 Polomolok, Phil.
97/G2 Polonia (cape), Uru.
70/D6 Polonnaruwa, SrL.
54/C2 Polonnoye, Ukr.
52/F5 Polotsk, Bela.
34/B6 Polperro, Eng,UK
51/G4 Polski Trŭmbesh, Bul.
106/E4 Polson, Mt,US
54/E2 Poltava, Ukr.
54/E2 Poltava Obl., Ukr.
52/F3 Polvijärvi, Fin.
52/G1 Polyarnyy, Rus.
79/J3 Polynesia (reg.)
95/D2 Pomba (riv.), Braz.
94/C2 Pombal, Braz.
46/A3 Pombal, Port.
39/H2 Pomerania (reg.), Pol.
39/H1 Pomeranian (bay), Ger., Pol.
95/B3 Pomerode, Braz.
32/B2 Pomeroy, NI,UK
106/D4 Pomeroy, Wa,US
78/E5 Pomio, PNG
115/C2 Pomona, Ca,US
51/H4 Pomorie, Bul.
113/H5 Pompano Beach, Fl,US
48/D2 Pompei (ruins), It.
95/C1 Pompeu, Braz.
115/F4 Pompton Lakes, NJ,US
85/E4 Pô Nat'l Park, Burk.
109/H3 Ponca City, Ok,US
101/H4 Ponce, PR
110/E1 Poncheville (lake), Qu,Can
103/J1 Pond (inlet), NW,Can
70/B5 Pondicherry (terr.), India
70/C5 Pondicherry (terr.), India
70/D4 Pondicherry (terr.), India
46/B1 Ponferrada, Sp.
89/E2 Pongolo (riv.), SAfr.
84/E4 Poni (prov.), Burk.
39/M3 Poniatowa, Pol.
106/E2 Ponoka, Ab,Can
52/H2 Ponoy (riv.), Rus.
42/D3 Pont-à-Celles, Belg.
94/C5 Ponta da Baleia (pt.), Braz.
47/S12 Ponta da Pico (mtn.), Azor.,Port.
47/T13 Ponta Delgada, Azor.,Port.

Ponta – Quiri

47/U15 **Ponta do Sol,** Madr.,Port.
95/B3 **Ponta Grossa,** Braz.
95/B1 **Pontalina,** Braz.
43/F6 **Pont-à-Mousson,** Fr.
93/G8 **Ponta Porã,** Braz.
34/C3 **Pontardawe,** Wal,UK
34/B3 **Pontardulais,** Wal,UK
45/G3 **Pontarlier,** Fr.
31/T10 **Pontault-Combault,** Fr.
110/E1 **Pontax** (riv.), Qu,Can
113/F4 **Pontchartrain** (lake), La,US
44/B3 **Pontchâteau,** Fr.
44/E4 **Pont-du-Château,** Fr.
48/C2 **Pontecorvo,** It.
46/A3 **Ponte de Sor,** Port.
33/G4 **Pontefract,** Eng,UK
33/G1 **Ponteland,** Eng,UK
95/D2 **Ponte Nova,** Braz.
34/C2 **Ponterwyd,** Wal,UK
34/D1 **Pontesbury,** Eng,UK
92/G7 **Pontes e Lacerda,** Braz.
46/A1 **Pontevedra,** Sp.
110/B3 **Pontiac,** Il,US
116/F6 **Pontiac,** Mi,US
72/C4 **Pontianak,** Indo.
44/B2 **Pontivy,** Fr.
31/S9 **Pontoise,** Fr.
113/F3 **Pontotoc,** Ms,US
34/C2 **Pontrhydfendigaid,** Wal,UK
34/D3 **Pontrilas,** Eng,UK
42/B5 **Pont-Sainte Maxence,** Fr.
44/F4 **Pont-Saint-Esprit,** Fr.
34/B3 **Pontyates,** Wal,UK
34/C3 **Pontyclun,** Wal,UK
34/C3 **Pont y Cymmer,** Wal,UK
34/C3 **Pontypool,** Wal,UK
34/C3 **Pontypridd,** Wal,UK
48/C2 **Ponziane** (isls.), It.
34/E5 **Poole,** Eng,UK
35/E5 **Poole** (bay), Eng,UK
70/B4 **Poona,** India
92/E7 **Poopó** (lake), Bol.
92/C3 **Popayán,** Col.
42/B2 **Poperinge,** Belg.
77/B2 **Popilta** (lake), Austl.
77/B2 **Popio** (lake), Austl.
107/K2 **Poplar** (riv.), Mb, On,Can
107/G3 **Poplar,** Mt,US
107/G3 **Poplar** (riv.), Mt,US
109/K3 **Poplar Bluff,** Mo,US
113/F4 **Poplarville,** Ms,US
82/J6 **Popokabaka,** Zaire
78/D5 **Popondetta,** PNG
51/H4 **Popovo,** Bul.
39/L4 **Poprad,** Slvk.
39/L4 **Poprad** (riv.), Slvk.
93/J6 **Porangatu,** Braz.
70/A3 **Porbandar,** India
46/C4 **Porcuna,** Sp.
114/K2 **Porcupine** (riv.), Yk,Can, Ak,US
76/B3 **Porcupine Gorge Nat'l Park,** Austl.
107/H2 **Porcupine Plain,** Sk,Can
45/K4 **Pordenone,** It.
37/G3 **Pori,** Fin.
75/R11 **Porirua,** NZ
52/E4 **Porkhov,** Rus.
101/J5 **Porlamar,** Ven.
34/C4 **Porlock,** Eng,UK
63/N2 **Poronaysk,** Rus.
98/J **Porpoise** (bay), Ant.
46/A1 **Porriño,** Sp.
37/H1 **Porsangen** (fjord), Nor.
37/D4 **Porsgrunn,** Nor.
59/B2 **Porsuk** (riv.), Turk.
92/F7 **Portachuelo,** Bol.
32/B3 **Portadown,** NI,UK
32/C3 **Portaferry,** NI,UK
110/C3 **Portage,** Mi,US
110/B3 **Portage,** Wi,US
107/J3 **Portage la Prairie,** Mb,Can
106/B3 **Port Alberni,** BC,Can
46/B3 **Portalegre,** Port.
46/B3 **Portalegre** (dist.), Port.
109/G4 **Portales,** NM,US
88/D4 **Port Alfred,** SAfr.
106/B3 **Port Alice,** BC,Can
106/C3 **Port Angeles,** Wa,US
101/F4 **Port Antonio,** Jam.
36/C2 **Port Appin,** Sc,UK
112/E4 **Port Arthur,** Tx,US
111/K1 **Port au Choix,** Nf,Can
74/F6 **Port Augusta,** Austl.
101/G4 **Port-au-Prince** (cap.), Haiti
32/C3 **Portavogie,** NI,UK
41/F4 **Porta Westfalica,** Ger.
71/F5 **Port Blair,** India
112/E4 **Port Bolivar,** Tx,US
84/E5 **Port-Bouët,** IvC.
103/K2 **Port Burwell,** Qu,Can
111/H1 **Port-Cartier,** Qu,Can
113/H5 **Port Charlotte,** Fl,US
115/G5 **Port Chester,** NY,US
110/D3 **Port Clinton,** Oh,US
111/R10 **Port Colborne,** On,Can
111/Q8 **Port Credit,** On,Can
111/S8 **Port Darlington,** On,Can
77/C4 **Port Davey** (har.), Austl.
101/G4 **Port-de-Paix,** Haiti
72/B3 **Port Dickson,** Malay.
114/M4 **Port Edward,** BC,Can
94/B4 **Porteirinha,** Braz.
93/H4 **Portel,** Braz.
110/D2 **Port Elgin,** Can.
88/D4 **Port Elizabeth,** SAfr.
32/D3 **Port Erin,** IM,UK
88/L10 **Porterville,** SAfr.
108/C3 **Porterville,** Ca,US
44/F4 **Portes-lès-Valence,** Fr.
82/B3 **Port-Étienne,** Mrta.
44/D5 **Portet-sur-Garonne,** Fr.
34/B3 **Port Eynon,** Wal,UK
34/B3 **Port Eynon** (pt.), Wal,UK
87/A1 **Port-Gentil,** Gabon
35/C3 **Port Glasgow,** Sc,UK
32/B2 **Portglenone,** NI,UK
34/C3 **Porth,** Wal,UK
85/G5 **Port Harcourt,** Nga.
106/B3 **Port Hardy,** BC,Can
111/J2 **Port Hawkesbury,** NS,Can
34/C4 **Porthcawl,** Wal,UK
74/B4 **Port Hedland,** Austl.
34/A6 **Porthleven,** Eng,UK
34/B2 **Porthmadog,** Wal,UK
115/A2 **Port Hueneme,** Ca,US
116/H6 **Port Huron,** Mi,US
46/A4 **Portimão,** Port.
34/B5 **Port Isaac,** Eng,UK
34/D4 **Portishead,** Eng,UK
115/G5 **Port Jefferson,** NY,US
77/C4 **Portland** (cape), Austl.
101/F4 **Portland** (pt.), Jam.
34/D6 **Portland** (pt.), Eng,UK
114/N4 **Portland** (inlet), BC,Can, Ak,US
110/C3 **Portland,** In,US
111/G3 **Portland,** Me,US
106/C4 **Portland,** Or,US
113/G2 **Portland,** Tn,US
34/D5 **Portland, Isle of** (pen.), Eng,UK
112/D4 **Port Lavaca,** Tx,US
74/F6 **Port Lincoln,** Austl.
89/S15 **Port Louis** (cap.), Mrts.
77/E1 **Port Macquarie,** Austl.
32/B5 **Portmarnock,** Ire.
106/B3 **Port McNeill,** BC,Can
111/H1 **Port-Menier,** Qu,Can
78/D5 **Port Moresby** (cap.), PNG
111/G1 **Portneuf** (riv.), Qu,Can
48/A1 **Porto** (gulf), Fr.
46/A2 **Porto,** Port.
46/A2 **Porto** (dist.), Port.
95/B4 **Pôrto Alegre,** Braz.
87/B3 **Porto Amboim,** Ang.
94/D3 **Pôrto Calvo,** Braz.
45/K5 **Portocivitanova,** It.
94/C3 **Pôrto da Fôlha,** Braz.
48/C4 **Porto Empedocle,** It.
48/B1 **Portoferraio,** It.
95/C2 **Pôrto Ferreira,** Braz.
94/A2 **Porto Franco,** Braz.
101/J5 **Port-of-Spain** (cap.), Trin.
45/K4 **Portogruaro,** It.
45/J4 **Portomaggiore,** It.
93/J6 **Porto Nacional,** Braz.
85/F5 **Porto-Novo** (cap.), Ben.
113/H4 **Port Orange,** Fl,US
48/C1 **Porto San Giorgio,** It.
48/B1 **Porto Santo Stefano,** It.
94/C5 **Porto Seguro,** Braz.
48/A2 **Porto Torres,** It.
95/B3 **Porto União,** Braz.
92/F5 **Porto Velho,** Braz.
92/B4 **Portoviejo,** Ecu.
32/C2 **Portpatrick,** Sc,UK
77/C3 **Port Phillip** (bay), Austl.
74/F6 **Port Pirie,** Austl.
32/B1 **Portrush,** NI,UK
86/C2 **Port Said** (Būr Sa'īd), Egypt
113/G4 **Port Saint Joe,** Fl,US
44/F5 **Port-Saint-Louis-du-Rhône,** Fr.
113/H5 **Port Saint Lucie,** Fl,US
32/D3 **Port Saint Mary,** IM,UK
35/E5 **Portsea** (isl.), Eng,UK
114/M4 **Port Simpson,** BC,Can
35/F5 **Portslade by Sea,** Eng,UK
35/E5 **Portsmouth,** Eng,UK
111/G3 **Portsmouth,** NH,US
110/D4 **Portsmouth,** Oh,US
110/E4 **Portsmouth,** Va,US
77/E2 **Port Stephens** (bay), Austl.
32/B1 **Portstewart,** NI,UK
86/D5 **Port Sudan** (Būr Sūdān), Sudan
34/C3 **Port Talbot,** Wal,UK
106/C3 **Port Townsend,** Wa,US
46/A3 **Portugal**
46/D1 **Portugalete,** Sp.
101/H6 **Portuguesa** (riv.), Ven.
115/G5 **Port Washington,** NY,US
110/C3 **Port Washington,** Wi,US
32/D2 **Port William,** Sc,UK
91/E2 **Posadas,** Arg.
46/C4 **Posadas,** Sp.
50/C3 **Posavina** (val.), Bosn., Cro.
73/F4 **Poso** (lake), Indo.
63/K5 **Posŏng,** SKor.
94/A4 **Posse,** Braz.
116/C2 **Possession** (sound), Wa,US
112/C3 **Post,** Tx,US
52/E5 **Postavy,** Bela.
82/F3 **Poste Maurice Cortier** (ruins), Alg.
82/F3 **Poste Weygand** (ruins), Alg.
106/D4 **Post Falls,** Id,US
88/C3 **Postmasburg,** SAfr.
50/B3 **Postojna,** Slov.
88/D2 **Potchefstroom,** SAfr.
109/J4 **Poteau,** Ok,US
48/D2 **Potenza,** It.
48/C1 **Potenza** (riv.), It.
106/D4 **Potholes** (res.), Wa,US
94/B2 **Poti** (riv.), Braz.
55/G4 **Poti,** Geo.
45/J5 **Poti, Alpe di** (peak), It.
115/J7 **Potomac,** Md,US
110/E4 **Potomac** (riv.), Md, Va,US
92/E7 **Potosí,** Bol.
109/K3 **Potosi,** Mo,US
91/C2 **Potrerillos,** Chile
38/G2 **Potsdam,** Ger.
110/F2 **Potsdam,** NY,US
31/N6 **Potters Bar,** Eng,UK
35/F2 **Potterspury,** Eng,UK
35/F2 **Potton,** Eng,UK
70/D6 **Pottuvil,** SrL.
110/F3 **Poughkeepsie,** NY,US
32/B5 **Poulaphouca** (res.), Ire.
33/G5 **Poulter** (riv.), Eng,UK
33/F4 **Poulton-le-Fylde,** Eng,UK
45/G4 **Pourri** (mtn.), Fr.
95/H7 **Pouso Alegre,** Braz.
69/C3 **Pouthisat,** Camb.
69/C3 **Pouthisat** (prov.), Camb.
39/K4 **Považská Bystrica,** Slvk.
46/A2 **Póvoa de Varzim,** Port.
52/G5 **Povorino,** Rus.
63/L3 **Povorotnyy, Mys** (cape), Rus.
103/J2 **Povungnituk** (riv.), Qu,Can
107/G4 **Powder** (riv.), Mt, Wy,US
108/E3 **Powell** (lake), Az, Ut,US
106/F4 **Powell,** Wy,US
106/B3 **Powell River,** BC,Can
111/R9 **Power** (res.), NY,US
34/C1 **Powys, Vale** (val.), Wal,UK
93/H7 **Poxoréo,** Braz.
67/C2 **Poyang** (lake), China
33/F5 **Poynton,** Eng,UK
46/A1 **Poyo,** Sp.
50/E3 **Požarevac,** Yugo.
100/B3 **Poza Rica,** Mex.
50/E4 **Požega,** Yugo.
39/J2 **Poznań,** Pol.
39/J2 **Poznań** (prov.), Pol.
46/D4 **Pozo Alcón,** Sp.
46/C3 **Pozoblanco,** Sp.
47/N9 **Pozuelo de Alarcón,** Sp.
48/D4 **Pozzallo,** It.
48/C1 **Pozzoni** (peak), It.
39/K2 **Prabuty,** Pol.
69/B4 **Pracham Hiang** (pt.), Thai.
45/L2 **Prachatice,** Czh.
69/C3 **Prachin Buri,** Thai.
69/C3 **Prachin Buri** (riv.), Thai.
69/B4 **Prachuap Khiri Khan,** Thai.
39/J3 **Praděd** (peak), Czh.
94/C5 **Prado,** Braz.
115/C3 **Prado** (dam), Ca,US
45/L1 **Prague (Praha)** (cap.), Czh.
45/L1 **Praha** (reg.), Czh.
51/G3 **Prahova** (co.), Rom.
80/K11 **Praia** (cap.), CpV.
47/S12 **Praia de Victória,** Azor.,Port.
95/G9 **Praia Grande,** Braz.
110/B3 **Prairie du Chien,** Wi,US
111/N6 **Prairies** (riv.), Qu,Can
107/J4 **Prairies, Coteau des** (upland), US
112/E4 **Prairie View,** Tx,US
69/B3 **Pran Buri** (res.), Thai.
70/D4 **Prānhita** (riv.), India
72/A3 **Prapat,** Indo.
69/D3 **Prasat Preah Vihear,** Camb.
39/K3 **Praszka,** Pol.
95/B1 **Prata,** Braz.
45/J5 **Prato,** It.
48/C1 **Pratola Peligna,** It.
97/J7 **Pratt** (isl.), Chile
109/H3 **Pratt,** Ks,US
113/G3 **Prattville,** Al,US
46/B1 **Pravia,** Sp.
34/C6 **Prawle** (pt.), Eng,UK
73/E5 **Praya,** Indo.
51/G3 **Predeal,** Rom.
107/H3 **Preeceville,** Sk,Can
33/F5 **Prees,** Eng,UK
33/F4 **Preesall,** Eng,UK
38/F1 **Preetz,** Ger.
39/L1 **Pregolya** (riv.), Rus.
110/E1 **Preissac** (lake), On,Can
69/D4 **Prek Pouthi,** Camb.
47/L7 **Premiá de Mar,** Sp.
39/G2 **Prenzlau,** Ger.
39/J4 **Přerov,** Czh.
45/J3 **Presanella** (peak), It.
33/F5 **Prescot,** Eng,UK
110/F2 **Prescott,** On,Can
108/D4 **Prescott,** Az,US
50/E4 **Preševo,** Yugo.
91/D2 **Presidencia Roque Sáenz Peña,** Arg.
94/A2 **Presidente Dutra,** Braz.
95/A2 **Presidente Epitácio,** Braz.
95/B2 **Presidente Prudente,** Braz.
96/B5 **Presidente Ríos** (lake), Chile
95/B2 **Presidente Venceslau,** Braz.
112/B4 **Presidio,** Tx,US
51/H4 **Preslav,** Bul.
31/U10 **Presles-en-Brie,** Fr.
39/L4 **Prešov,** Slvk.
49/G2 **Prespa** (lake), Eur.
111/G2 **Presque Isle,** Me,US
33/E5 **Prestatyn,** Wal,UK
85/E5 **Prestea,** Gha.
34/D2 **Presteigne,** Wal,UK
45/K2 **Přeštice,** Czh.
77/G5 **Preston,** Austl.
33/F4 **Preston,** Eng,UK
34/D5 **Preston,** Eng,UK
106/F5 **Preston,** Id,US
110/D4 **Prestonsburg,** Ky,US
33/F4 **Prestwich,** Eng,UK
36/C3 **Prestwick,** Sc,UK
35/F3 **Prestwood,** Eng,UK
94/A3 **Prêto** (riv.), Braz.
94/A5 **Prêto** (riv.), Braz.
88/E2 **Pretoria** (cap.), SAfr.
41/F4 **Preussisch Oldendorf,** Ger.
49/G3 **Préveza,** Gre.
114/D4 **Pribilof** (isls.), Ak,US
50/D4 **Priboj,** Yugo.
45/L2 **Příbram,** Czh.
108/E3 **Price,** Ut,US
108/E3 **Price** (riv.), Ut,US
113/F4 **Prichard,** Al,US
46/C4 **Priego de Córdoba,** Sp.
88/C3 **Prieska,** SAfr.
106/D3 **Priest** (lake), Id,US
106/D3 **Priest River,** Id,US
46/C1 **Prieta** (mtn.), Sp.
39/K4 **Prievidza,** Slvk.
38/F2 **Prignitz** (reg.), Ger.
50/C3 **Prijedor,** Bosn.
50/D4 **Prijepolje,** Yugo.
55/H3 **Prikaspian** (plain), Kaz., Rus.
55/H3 **Prikumsk,** Rus.
50/E5 **Prilep,** Macd.
54/E2 **Priluki,** Ukr.
48/C2 **Prima Porta,** It.
97/J7 **Primero** (cape), Chile
35/E1 **Primethorpe,** Eng,UK
57/P5 **Primorsk Kray,** Rus.
54/F3 **Primorsko-Akhtarsk,** Rus.
106/F2 **Primrose** (lake), Ab, Sk,Can
43/F5 **Prims** (riv.), Ger.
102/E1 **Prince Albert** (pen.), NW,Can
102/E1 **Prince Albert** (sound), NW,Can
107/G2 **Prince Albert,** Sk,Can
107/G2 **Prince Albert Nat'l Park,** Sk,Can
102/D1 **Prince Alfred** (cape), NW,Can
103/J2 **Prince Charles** (isl.), NW,Can
29/L8 **Prince Edward** (isls.), SAfr.
111/J2 **Prince Edward Island** (prov.), Can.
111/J2 **Prince Edward Island Nat'l Park,** PE,Can
106/C2 **Prince George,** BC,Can
103/R7 **Prince Gustav Adolf** (sea), NW,Can
98/C **Prince Harold** (coast), Ant.
102/G1 **Prince Leopold** (isl.), NW,Can
40/C2 **Princenhof** (lake), Neth.
74/G2 **Prince of Wales** (isl.), Austl.
102/G1 **Prince of Wales** (isl.), NW,Can
102/E1 **Prince of Wales** (str.), NW,Can
114/M4 **Prince of Wales** (isl.), Ak,US
98/C **Prince Olav** (coast), Ant.
103/R7 **Prince Patrick** (isl.), NW,Can
102/G1 **Prince Regent** (inlet), NW,Can
114/M4 **Prince Rupert,** BC,Can
35/F3 **Princes Risborough,** Eng,UK
98/A **Princess Astrid** (coast), Ant.
76/A1 **Princess Charlotte** (bay), Austl.
103/S6 **Princess Margaret** (range), NW,Can
98/Z **Princess Martha** (coast), Ant.
98/B **Princess Ragnhild** (coast), Ant.
106/A2 **Princess Royal** (isl.), BC,Can
101/J5 **Princes Town,** Trin.
106/C3 **Princeton,** BC,Can
110/B3 **Princeton,** Il,US
110/C4 **Princeton,** In,US
110/C4 **Princeton,** Ky,US
107/K4 **Princeton,** Mn,US
115/F5 **Princeton,** NJ,US
110/D4 **Princeton,** WV,US
114/J3 **Prince William** (sound), Ak,US
82/G7 **Príncipe** (isl.), SaoT.
114/K3 **Prindle** (vol.), Ak,US
106/C4 **Prineville,** Or,US
40/B5 **Prinsenbeek,** Neth.
40/C2 **Prinses Margriet** (can.), Neth.
100/E5 **Prinzapolka,** Nic.
48/D4 **Priolo di Gargallo,** It.
46/A1 **Prior** (cape), Sp.
52/F3 **Priozersk,** Rus.
54/C2 **Pripet** (marshes), Bela., Ukr.
50/E4 **Priština,** Yugo.
38/G2 **Pritzwalk,** Ger.
44/F4 **Privas,** Fr.
55/H2 **Privolzhskiy,** Rus.
55/K1 **Priyutovo,** Rus.
50/E4 **Prizren,** Yugo.
50/C3 **Prnjavor,** Bosn.
72/D5 **Probolinggo,** Indo.
112/D3 **Proctor** (lake), Tx,US
70/C5 **Proddatūr,** India
43/D3 **Profondeville,** Belg.
100/E6 **Progreso,** Pan.
97/T12 **Progreso,** Uru.
63/K2 **Progress,** Rus.
55/H4 **Prokhladnyy,** Rus.
68/E1 **Prokop'yevsk,** Rus.
50/E4 **Prokuplje,** Yugo.
71/G4 **Prome,** Burma
95/D2 **Promissão,** Braz.
95/B2 **Promissão** (res.), Braz.
94/C3 **Propriá,** Braz.
39/J2 **Prosna** (riv.), Pol.
114/L3 **Prospector** (mtn.), Yk,Can
67/E6 **Prosperidad,** Phil.
39/J4 **Prostějov,** Czh.
39/K3 **Prószowice,** Pol.
51/H4 **Provadiya,** Bul.
45/G5 **Provence** (mts.), Fr.
44/F5 **Provence** (reg.), Fr.
45/G4 **Provence-Alpes-Côte d'Azur** (reg.), Fr.
92/F6 **Providência** (mts.), Braz.
100/E5 **Providencia** (isl.), Col.
44/E2 **Provins,** Fr.
108/E2 **Provo,** Ut,US
47/T13 **Provoação,** Azor.,Port.
106/F2 **Provost,** Ab,Can
50/C4 **Prozor,** Bosn.
95/B2 **Prudentópolis,** Braz.
33/G2 **Prudhoe,** Eng,UK
114/J1 **Prudhoe** (bay), Ak,US
39/J3 **Prudnik,** Pol.
43/F3 **Prüm** (riv.), Ger.
39/K1 **Pruszcz Gdański,** Pol.
39/L2 **Pruszków,** Pol.
51/J2 **Prut** (riv.), Eur.
98/F **Prydz** (bay), Ant.
112/E2 **Pryor** (cr.), Ok,US
39/L2 **Przasnysz,** Pol.
39/H3 **Przemków,** Pol.
39/M4 **Przemyśl,** Pol.
39/M4 **Przemyśl** (prov.), Pol.
39/M3 **Przeworsk,** Pol.
68/C3 **Przheval'sk,** Kyr.
52/C5 **Przylądek Rozewie** (cape), Pol.
39/L3 **Przysucha,** Pol.
49/J3 **Psará** (isl.), Gre.
52/F4 **Pskov** (lake), Est., Rus.
52/F4 **Pskov,** Rus.
52/F4 **Pskov Obl.,** Rus.
39/K4 **Pszczyna,** Pol.
49/G2 **Ptolemaís,** Gre.
50/B2 **Ptuj,** Slov.
69/C2 **Pua,** Thai.
92/D5 **Pucallpa,** Peru
116/G7 **Puce,** On,Can
66/B4 **Pucheng,** China
96/Q9 **Puchuncaví,** Chile
51/G3 **Pucioasa,** Rom.
39/K1 **Puck,** Pol.
35/G3 **Puckeridge,** Eng,UK
96/C3 **Pucón,** Chile
37/H2 **Pudasjärvi,** Fin.
34/D5 **Puddletown,** Eng,UK
33/G4 **Pudsey,** Eng,UK
71/H2 **Pudu** (riv.), China
70/C5 **Pudukkottai,** India
100/B4 **Puebla,** Mex.
100/B4 **Puebla** (state), Mex.
46/A1 **Puebla del Caramiñal,** Sp.
109/F3 **Pueblo,** Co,US
100/C5 **Pueblo Nuevo Tiquisate,** Guat.
96/C2 **Puente Alto,** Chile
46/A1 **Puenteareas,** Sp.
46/A1 **Puente Caldelas,** Sp.
46/A1 **Puente-Ceso,** Sp.
96/C2 **Puente del Inca,** Arg.
46/A1 **Puentedeume,** Sp.
46/C4 **Puente-Genil,** Sp.
46/B1 **Puentes de García Rodríguez,** Sp.
104/R10 **Pueo** (pt.), Hi,US
108/E4 **Puerco** (riv.), Az, NM,US
108/F4 **Puerco** (riv.), NM,US
96/B5 **Puerto Aisén,** Chile
92/C3 **Puerto Asís,** Col.
92/E2 **Puerto Ayacucho,** Ven.
100/D4 **Puerto Barrios,** Guat.
101/H5 **Puerto Cabello,** Ven.
100/E5 **Puerto Cabezas,** Nic.
101/H5 **Puerto Cumarebo,** Ven.
47/X16 **Puerto de la Cruz,** Canl.
46/A1 **Puerto del Son,** Sp.
100/B4 **Puerto Escondido,** Mex.
91/F2 **Puerto Iguazú,** Arg.
101/J5 **Puerto La Cruz,** Ven.
100/D4 **Puerto Lempira,** Hon.
46/C3 **Puertollano,** Sp.
46/E4 **Puerto Lumbreras,** Sp.
96/D4 **Puerto Madryn,** Arg.
92/E6 **Puerto Maldonado,** Peru
96/B4 **Puerto Montt,** Chile
100/D3 **Puerto Morelos,** Mex.
97/J7 **Puerto Natales,** Chile
101/F6 **Puerto Obaldía,** Pan.
101/G4 **Puerto Plata,** DRep.
67/C6 **Puerto Princesa,** Phil.
96/B4 **Puerto Quellón,** Chile
46/B4 **Puerto Real,** Sp.
101/H4 **Puerto Rico** (commonwealth), US
100/C5 **Puerto San José,** Guat.
92/G7 **Puerto Suárez,** Bol.
101/N9 **Puerto Vallarta,** Mex.
96/B4 **Puerto Varas,** Chile
96/C5 **Pueyrredón** (lake), Arg.
32/D5 **Puffin** (isl.), Wal,UK
55/J1 **Pugachev,** Rus.
116/C2 **Puget** (sound), Wa,US
48/E2 **Puglia** (reg.), It.
44/E5 **Puigmal** (mtn.), Fr.
47/G1 **Puigsacalm** (mtn.), Sp.
72/C5 **Pujut** (cape), Indo.
79/J6 **Pukapuka** (isl.), CookIs.
79/M6 **Puka Puka** (atoll), FrPol.
79/M6 **Pukarua** (isl.), FrPol.
110/C1 **Pukaskwa Nat'l Park,** On,Can
73/F1 **Pulanduta** (pt.), Phil.
78/D4 **Pulap** (atoll), Micr.
113/G3 **Pulaski,** Tn,US
110/D4 **Pulaski,** Va,US
39/L3 **Puławy,** Pol.
35/F5 **Pulborough,** Eng,UK
64/A3 **Pulguk-sa,** SKor.
40/D7 **Pulheim,** Ger.
73/G3 **Pulisan** (cape), Indo.
106/D4 **Pullman,** Wa,US
45/G3 **Pully,** Swi.
39/G3 **Pulsnitz** (riv.), Ger.
39/L2 **Pułtusk,** Pol.
78/D4 **Puluwat** (atoll), Micr.
34/C2 **Pumpsaint,** Wal,UK
71/F2 **Pumu** (pass), China
79/X15 **Punaauia,** FrPol.
92/E7 **Punata,** Bol.
61/K2 **Pūnch,** India
72/B3 **Punggai** (cape), Malay.
87/E1 **Punia,** Zaire
68/C5 **Punjab** (state), India
61/K2 **Punjab** (plains), Pak.
61/K3 **Punjab** (prov.), Pak.
92/D7 **Puno,** Peru
100/B4 **Punta Allen,** Mex.
97/K8 **Punta Arenas,** Chile
101/G5 **Punta Cardón,** Ven.
101/J6 **Punta de Mata,** Ven.
100/D4 **Punta Gorda,** Belz.
100/E5 **Punta Gorda** (bay), Nic.
113/H5 **Punta Gorda,** Fl,US
101/M7 **Punta Peñasco,** Mex.
100/E6 **Puntarenas,** CR
46/B4 **Punta Umbría,** Sp.
104/S10 **Puolo** (pt.), Hi,US
92/D6 **Puquio,** Peru
56/H3 **Pur** (riv.), Rus.
92/C3 **Puracé Nat'l Park,** Col.
34/D5 **Purbeck, Isle of** (pen.), Eng,UK
109/H4 **Purcell,** Ok,US
96/B3 **Purén,** Chile
109/G3 **Purgatoire** (riv.), Co,US
70/D3 **Purī,** India
52/E4 **Purikari** (pt.), Est.
31/N8 **Purley,** Eng,UK
40/B3 **Purmerend,** Neth.
70/C3 **Pūrna,** India
70/C3 **Pūrna** (riv.), India
91/B5 **Purranque,** Chile
35/E3 **Purton,** Eng,UK
92/F4 **Purús** (riv.), Braz.
51/G4 **Pŭrvomay,** Bul.
72/C5 **Purwokerto,** Indo.
70/C4 **Pusad,** India
64/A3 **Pusan,** SKor.
72/A2 **Pusat Gayo** (mts.), Indo.
52/F4 **Pushkin,** Rus.
50/E2 **Püspökladány,** Hun.
96/C2 **Putaendo,** Chile
72/D4 **Puting** (cape), Indo.
100/B4 **Putla,** Mex.
96/B4 **Putomayo** (riv.), Col.
56/K3 **Putorana** (mts.), Rus.
96/C4 **Putrachoique** (peak), Arg.
70/C6 **Puttalam,** SrL.
42/D1 **Putte,** Belg.
40/C4 **Putten,** Neth.
40/B5 **Putten** (isl.), Neth.
43/F5 **Püttlingen,** Ger.
84/C5 **Putu** (range), Libr.
92/D4 **Putumayo** (riv.), SAm.
72/D3 **Putussibau,** Indo.
104/T10 **Puu Kukui** (peak), Hi,US
42/D1 **Puurs,** Belg.
66/B3 **Pu Xian,** China
116/C3 **Puyallup,** Wa,US
116/C3 **Puyallup** (riv.), Wa,US
66/C4 **Puyang,** China
44/E4 **Puy de Barbier** (peak), Fr.
44/E4 **Puy de Sancy** (peak), Fr.
96/B4 **Puyehué** (vol.), Chile
96/B4 **Puyehué Nat'l Park,** Chile
44/D5 **Puymorens, Col de** (pass), Fr.
47/E3 **Puzal,** Sp.
87/E2 **Pweto,** Zaire
32/D6 **Pwllheli,** Wal,UK
61/K1 **Pyandzh (Panj)** (riv.), Afg., Taj.
52/F2 **Pyaozero** (lake), Rus.
71/G4 **Pyapon,** Burma
56/J2 **Pyasina** (riv.), Rus.
55/G3 **Pyatigorsk,** Rus.
44/F4 **Pyfara** (mtn.), Fr.
37/H3 **Pyhä-Häkin Nat'l Park,** Fin.
37/H3 **Pyhäjärvi,** Fin.
37/H2 **Pyhätunturi** (peak), Fin.
69/B2 **Pyinmana,** Burma
34/C3 **Pyle,** Wal,UK
63/K4 **Pyŏngt'aek,** SKor.
63/K4 **P'yŏngyang** (cap.), NKor.
114/M4 **Pyramid** (mtn.), BC,Can
115/B1 **Pyramid** (lake), Ca,US
108/C3 **Pyramid** (lake), Nv,US
47/E1 **Pyrenees** (range), Eur.
44/C5 **Pyrénées Occidentales Nat'l Park,** Fr.
39/H2 **Pyrzyce,** Pol.
53/Q4 **Pyshma** (riv.), Rus.
69/B2 **Pyu,** Burma

Q

59/L6 **Qā'al Jafr** (salt pan), Jor.
59/K5 **Qabāṭiyah,** WBnk.
82/H1 **Qābis,** Tun.
60/F1 **Qā'emshahr,** Iran
49/G1 **Qafa e Malit** (pass), Alb.
82/G1 **Qafṣah,** Tun.
63/J2 **Qagan** (lake), China
66/C2 **Qahar Youyi Qianqi,** China
62/D4 **Qaidam** (basin), China
59/M8 **Qalansuwa,** Isr.
59/F3 **Qal'at Dizah,** Iraq
59/H6 **Qallīn,** Egypt
59/K5 **Qalqīlyah,** WBnk.
60/F5 **Qamar, Ghubbat al** (bay), Yem.
59/N8 **Qanah, Wādī** (dry riv.), WBnk.
61/J2 **Qandahār,** Afg.
59/E3 **Qarah Qōsh,** Iraq
81/W17 **Qar'at al Ashkal** (lake), Tun.
83/Q6 **Qardho,** Som.
60/E2 **Qareh Chāy** (riv.), Iran
68/F4 **Qarqan** (riv.), China
49/G2 **Qarrit, Qaf'e** (pass), Alb.
48/B4 **Qarṭājannah** (ruins), Tun.
86/B2 **Qārūn, Birkat** (lake), Egypt
60/E2 **Qaşr-e-Shīrīn,** Iran
86/A3 **Qaşr Farāfirah,** Egypt
59/L5 **Qaṭanā,** Syria
60/F3 **Qatar**
86/A2 **Qattara** (depr.), Egypt
59/L4 **Qaṭṭīnah** (lake), Syria
70/A2 **Qāzi Ahmad,** Pak.
60/F1 **Qazvīn,** Iran
49/F2 **Qendrevica** (peak), Alb.
61/G3 **Qeshm** (isl.), Iran
60/E1 **Qezel** (riv.), Iran
71/J2 **Qi** (riv.), China
66/D4 **Qian** (can.), China
66/D5 **Qian** (riv.), China
66/D5 **Qianqiu Guan** (pass), China
66/E2 **Qian Shan** (peak), China
66/B5 **Qifeng Guan** (pass), China
62/D4 **Qilian** (mts.), China
62/D4 **Qilian** (peak), China
59/N9 **Qilt, Wādī** (dry riv.), WBnk.
68/F4 **Qimantag** (mts.), China
66/B4 **Qin** (mts.), China
66/C4 **Qin** (riv.), China
86/C3 **Qinā,** Egypt
86/C3 **Qinā** (gov.), Egypt
67/B1 **Qing** (riv.), China
66/E3 **Qingdao,** China
62/D4 **Qinghai** (lake), China
62/D4 **Qinghai** (mts.), China
67/C2 **Qingjiang,** China
67/A2 **Qingshui** (riv.), China
67/B2 **Qingzhou,** China
66/D3 **Qinhuangdao,** China
66/C3 **Qinyuan,** China
67/B4 **Qiongshan,** China
63/J2 **Qiqihar,** China
59/K5 **Qiryat Ata,** Isr.
59/K5 **Qiryat Bialik,** Isr.
59/K6 **Qiryat Gat,** Isr.
59/M9 **Qiryat Mal'akhi,** Isr.
59/K5 **Qiryat Shemona,** Isr.
59/K5 **Qiryat Yam,** Isr.
63/L2 **Qitaihe,** China
66/C4 **Qi Xian,** China
63/L2 **Qixing** (riv.), China
60/F2 **Qom,** Iran
60/F2 **Qom** (riv.), Iran
70/E2 **Qomolangma (Everest)** (peak), China
61/J1 **Qondūz** (riv.), Afg.
67/C2 **Qu** (riv.), China
111/F3 **Quabbin** (res.), Ma,US
35/F3 **Quainton,** Eng,UK
41/E3 **Quakenbrück,** Ger.
115/E5 **Quakertown,** Pa,US
62/H5 **Quan** (riv.), China
112/D3 **Quanah,** Tx,US
66/B4 **Quanbao Shan** (mtn.), China
69/E3 **Quang Ngai,** Viet.
69/D2 **Quang Trach,** Viet.
69/D2 **Quang Tri,** Viet.
34/C4 **Quantocks** (hills), Eng,UK
67/B2 **Quanzhou,** China
107/G3 **Qu'Appelle** (riv.), Mb, Sk,Can
107/H3 **Qu'Appelle,** Sk,Can
107/G3 **Qu'Appelle** (dam), Sk,Can
103/K2 **Quaqtaq,** Qu,Can
42/C3 **Quaregnon,** Belg.
72/E4 **Quarles** (mts.), Indo.
45/J5 **Quarrata,** It.
48/A3 **Quartu Sant'Elena,** It.
115/B1 **Quartz Hill,** Ca,US
81/W17 **Quballāt,** Tun.
61/G1 **Qūchān,** Iran
77/D2 **Queanbeyan,** Austl.
103/J3 **Québec** (prov.), Can.
111/G2 **Québec** (cap.), Qu,Can
95/J7 **Quebra-Cangalha** (mts.), Braz.
96/B4 **Quedal** (pt.), Chile
34/D3 **Quedgeley,** Eng,UK
102/C3 **Queen Charlotte** (isls.), BC,Can
102/C3 **Queen Charlotte** (sound), BC,Can
106/B3 **Queen Charlotte** (str.), BC,Can
112/E3 **Queen City,** Tx,US
103/R7 **Queen Elizabeth** (isls.), NW,Can
98/G **Queen Mary** (coast), Ant.
98/P **Queen Maud** (mts.), Ant.
102/F2 **Queen Maud** (gulf), NW,Can
98/Z **Queen Maud Land** (reg.), Ant.
74/D2 **Queens** (chan.), Austl.
103/S7 **Queens** (chan.), NW,Can
32/E1 **Queensberry** (mtn.), Sc,UK
33/G4 **Queensbury,** Eng,UK
33/E5 **Queensferry,** Wal,UK
76/B3 **Queensland** (state), Austl.
111/R9 **Queenston,** On,Can
75/Q12 **Queenstown,** NZ
88/D3 **Queenstown,** SAfr.
96/B4 **Queilén,** Chile
93/H4 **Queimada,** Braz.
94/C3 **Queimadas,** Braz.
87/G4 **Quelimane,** Moz.
46/A3 **Queluz,** Port.
35/E3 **Quenington,** Eng,UK
96/F3 **Quequén,** Arg.
96/F3 **Quequén Grande** (riv.), Arg.
100/A3 **Querétaro,** Mex.
100/A3 **Querétaro** (state), Mex.
100/E5 **Quesada,** CR
46/D4 **Quesada,** Sp.
66/C4 **Queshan,** China
106/C2 **Quesnel,** BC,Can
106/C2 **Quesnel** (lake), BC,Can
69/E3 **Que Son,** Viet.
109/F3 **Questa,** NM,US
61/J2 **Quetta,** Pak.
96/B5 **Queulat Nat'l Park,** Chile
92/C4 **Quevedo,** Ecu.
100/C5 **Quezaltenango,** Guat.
67/E6 **Quezon,** Phil.
67/D5 **Quezon City,** Phil.
66/D4 **Qufu,** China
87/B3 **Quibala,** Ang.
92/C2 **Quibdó,** Col.
44/B3 **Quiberon** (bay), Fr.
87/B2 **Quiçama Nat'l Park,** Ang.
41/G1 **Quickborn,** Ger.
43/G5 **Quierschied,** Ger.
108/D4 **Quijotoa,** Az,US
96/B4 **Quilán** (cape), Chile
96/Q9 **Quilicura,** Chile
107/G2 **Quill** (lakes), Sk,Can
92/D6 **Quillabamba,** Peru
92/E7 **Quillacollo,** Bol.
96/B4 **Quillagua** (pt.), Chile
96/C3 **Quilleco,** Chile
96/C2 **Quillota,** Chile
70/C6 **Quilon,** India
96/C2 **Quilpué,** Chile
44/A3 **Quimper,** Fr.
113/G4 **Quincy,** Fl,US
110/B4 **Quincy,** Il,US
111/G3 **Quincy,** Ma,US
106/D4 **Quincy,** Wa,US
31/T10 **Quincy-sous-Sénart,** Fr.
69/E3 **Qui Nhon,** Viet.
108/C2 **Quinn** (riv.), Nv,US
46/D3 **Quintanar de la Orden,** Sp.
100/D4 **Quintana Roo** (state), Mex.
96/Q9 **Quintero,** Chile
96/D2 **Quinto** (riv.), Arg.
94/C3 **Quipapá,** Braz.
101/N8 **Quiriego,** Mex.
96/B3 **Quirihue,** Chile
87/H3 **Quirimba** (arch.), Moz.

155
Quiri – Rolde

95/B1 **Quirinópolis**, Braz.
101/J6 **Quiriquire**, Ven.
111/H2 **Quispamsis**, NB,Can
91/D2 **Quitilipi**, Arg.
113/H4 **Quitman**, Ga,US
113/F3 **Quitman**, Ms,US
112/E3 **Quitman**, Tx,US
92/C4 **Quito** (cap.), Ecu.
94/C2 **Quixadá**, Braz.
94/C2 **Quixeramobim**, Braz.
71/H2 **Qujing**, China
62/C4 **Qumar** (riv.), China
102/G2 **Quoich** (riv.), NW,Can
32/C3 **Quoile** (riv.), NI,UK
88/B4 **Quoin** (pt.), SAfr.
59/L4 **Qurnat as Sawdā'** (mtn.), Leb.
86/C3 **Qūş**, Egypt
62/F4 **Quvu** (mts.), China
69/C1 **Quynh Nhai**, Viet.
66/C3 **Quzhou**, China
67/C2 **Quzhou**, China
50/D5 **Qyteti Stalin**, Alb.

R

45/L3 **Raab** (riv.), Aus.
37/H2 **Raahe**, Fin.
40/D4 **Raalte**, Neth.
40/B5 **Raamsdonk**, Neth.
59/M8 **Ra'anana**, Isr.
103/S7 **Raanes** (pen.), NW,Can
83/P8 **Raas Jumbo**, Som.
50/B3 **Rab** (isl.), Cro.
50/C2 **Rába** (riv.), Hun.
48/D5 **Rabat**, Malta
81/L13 **Rabat** (cap.), Mor.
78/E5 **Rabaul**, PNG
45/K4 **Rabbi** (riv.), It.
39/K4 **Rabka**, Pol.
70/C4 **Rabkavi**, India
111/S8 **Raby** (pt.), On,Can
45/G4 **Racconigi**, It.
113/F4 **Raccoon** (pt.), La,US
103/L4 **Race** (cape), Nf,Can
69/D4 **Rach Gia**, Viet.
69/D4 **Rach Gia** (bay), Viet.
39/K3 **Racibórz**, Pol.
116/Q14 **Racine**, Wi,US
50/D2 **Ráckeve**, Hun.
51/G2 **Rădăuţi**, Rom.
45/K2 **Radbuza** (riv.), Czh.
33/F4 **Radcliffe**, Eng,UK
33/G6 **Radcliffe on Trent**, Eng,UK
50/A2 **Radenthein**, Aus.
41/E6 **Radevormwald**, Ger.
110/D4 **Radford**, Va,US
70/B3 **Rādhanpur**, India
106/G2 **Radisson**, Sk,Can
31/N6 **Radlett**, Eng,UK
51/G4 **Radnevo**, Bul.
39/L3 **Radom**, Pol.
39/L3 **Radom** (prov.), Pol.
50/F4 **Radomir**, Bul.
39/K3 **Radomsko**, Pol.
50/F5 **Radoviš**, Macd.
34/D4 **Radstock**, Eng,UK
52/D5 **Radviliškis**, Lith.
34/C3 **Radyr**, Wal,UK
39/K2 **Radziejów**, Pol.
39/L2 **Radzymin**, Pol.
39/M3 **Radzyń Podlaski**, Pol.
103/H3 **Rae** (isth.), NW,Can
102/E2 **Rae** (riv.), NW,Can
70/D2 **Rāe Bareli**, India
113/J3 **Raeford**, NC,US
43/F2 **Raeren**, Belg.
40/D5 **Raesfeld**, Ger.
74/C5 **Raeside** (lake), Austl.
91/D3 **Rafaela**, Arg.
59/K6 **Rafah**, Gaza
61/G2 **Rafsanjān**, Iran
106/E5 **Raft** (riv.), Id, Ut,US
83/L6 **Raga**, Sudan
97/J8 **Ragged** (pt.), Chile
32/A1 **Raghtin More** (mtn.), Ire.
34/D3 **Raglan**, Wal,UK
37/E2 **Rago Nat'l Park**, Nor.
31/P8 **Ragstone** (range), Eng,UK
48/D4 **Ragusa**, It.
41/F4 **Rahden**, Ger.
61/K3 **Rahīmyār Khān**, Pak.
115/F5 **Rahway**, NJ,US
79/K6 **Raiatea** (isl.), FrPol.
70/C4 **Raichūr**, India
70/D3 **Raigarh**, India
108/E3 **Rainbow Bridge Nat'l Mon.**, Ut,US
33/F4 **Rainford**, Eng,UK
31/P7 **Rainham**, Eng,UK
106/C4 **Rainier** (mt.), Wa,US
113/G3 **Rainsville**, Al,US
33/G5 **Rainworth**, Eng,UK
107/K3 **Rainy** (lake), Can., US
107/K3 **Rainy** (riv.), Can., US
110/A1 **Rainy River**, On,Can
70/D3 **Raipur**, India
38/F1 **Raisdorf**, Ger.
116/E8 **Raisin** (riv.), Mi,US
37/G3 **Raisio**, Fin.
42/C3 **Raismes**, Fr.
79/L7 **Raivavae** (isl.), FrPol.
72/A3 **Raja** (pt.), Indo.
70/D4 **Rājahmundry**, India
70/C5 **Rājampet**, India
72/D3 **Rajang** (riv.), Malay.
61/K3 **Rājanpur**, Pak.
70/C6 **Rājapālaiyam**, India
70/B4 **Rājāpur**, India
70/B2 **Rājasthān** (state), India
61/L3 **Rajgarh**, India
70/C3 **Rājgarh**, India
70/C3 **Rājkot**, India
70/D3 **Rāj-Nāndagaon**, India
61/L2 **Rājpura**, India
70/E3 **Rājshāhi**, Bang.
70/B3 **Rājula**, India
79/J5 **Rakahanga** (atoll), Cookls.
61/K1 **Rakaposhi** (mtn.), Pak.
71/F4 **Rakhine** (state), Burma
61/H3 **Rakhshān** (riv.), Pak.
87/D5 **Rakops**, Bots.
51/G4 **Rakovski**, Bul.
52/E4 **Rakvere**, Est.
113/J3 **Raleigh** (cap.), NC,US
78/F4 **Ralik Chain** (arch.), Mrsh.
106/F3 **Ralston**, Ab,Can
94/A4 **Ramalho** (mts.), Braz.
59/K6 **Rām Allāh**, WBnk.
70/B4 **Ramas** (cape), India
59/K5 **Ramat Gan**, Isr.
59/M8 **Ramat HaSharon**, Isr.
79/Z17 **Rambi** (isl.), Fiji
42/A6 **Rambouillet**, Fr.
34/B6 **Rame** (pt.), UK
70/E2 **Rāmechhāp**, Nepal
70/C6 **Rāmeshwaram**, India
60/E2 **Rāmhormoz**, Iran
59/K6 **Ramla**, Isr.
86/C2 **Ramm, Jabal** (mt.), Jor.
32/A4 **Ramor, Lough** (lake), Ire.
71/F4 **Ramree** (isl.), Burma
60/F1 **Ramsar** (Sakht Sar), Iran
33/F4 **Ramsbottom**, Eng,UK
35/E4 **Ramsbury**, Eng,UK
110/D2 **Ramsey** (lake), On,Can
35/F2 **Ramsey**, Eng,UK
32/D3 **Ramsey**, IM,UK
34/A3 **Ramsey** (isl.), Wal,UK
35/H4 **Ramsgate**, Eng,UK
43/G5 **Ramstein-Miesenbach**, Ger.
78/D5 **Ramu** (riv.), PNG
70/E3 **Rānāghāt**, India
96/C2 **Rancagua**, Chile
44/B2 **Rance** (riv.), Fr.
95/B2 **Rancharia**, Braz.
106/G4 **Ranchester**, Wy,US
70/E3 **Rānchī**, India
116/M9 **Rancho Cordova**, Ca,US
115/C2 **Rancho Cucamonga** (Cucamonga), Ca,US
115/B3 **Rancho Palos Verdes**, Ca,US
96/B4 **Ranco** (lake), Chile
83/P5 **Randa**, Djib.
115/K7 **Randallstown**, Md,US
32/B2 **Randalstown**, NI,UK
48/D4 **Randazzo**, It.
88/P13 **Randburg**, SAfr.
37/D4 **Randers**, Den.
115/F5 **Randolph**, NJ,US
39/H2 **Randow** (riv.), Ger.
76/H8 **Randwick**, Austl.
69/C2 **Rang** (peak), Thai.
71/F3 **Rāngāmāti**, Bang.
73/E4 **Rangasa** (cape), Indo.
108/E2 **Rangely**, Co,US
112/D3 **Ranger**, Tx,US
75/R11 **Rangiora**, NZ
79/L6 **Rangiroa** (atoll), FrPol.
69/B2 **Rangoon** (div.), Burma
69/B2 **Rangoon** (Yangon) (cap.), Burma
70/E2 **Rangpur**, Bang.
70/C5 **Rānībennur**, India
112/C4 **Rankin**, Tx,US
69/B4 **Ranong**, Thai.
43/G3 **Ransbach-Baumbach**, Ger.
111/S9 **Ransomville**, NY,US
42/D1 **Ranst**, Belg.
73/F4 **Rantekombola** (peak), Indo.
110/B3 **Rantoul**, Il,US
69/D2 **Rao Co** (peak), Laos
45/G2 **Raon-L'Étape**, Fr.
78/H7 **Raoul** (isl.), NZ
66/C3 **Raoyang**, China
79/L7 **Rapa** (isl.), FrPol.
96/Q10 **Rapel** (lake), Chile
96/B5 **Raper** (cape), Chile
107/H4 **Rapid City**, SD,US
110/E4 **Rappahannock** (riv.), Va,US
70/D2 **Rapti** (riv.), India
115/F5 **Raritan** (bay), NJ,US
115/F5 **Raritan** (riv.), NJ,US
79/K6 **Raroia** (atoll), FrPol.
79/J7 **Rarotonga** (isl.), Cookls.
96/E4 **Rasa** (pt.), Arg.
59/E3 **Ra's al 'Ayn**, Syria
83/J7 **Ra's al Unūf**, Libya
81/Q16 **Râs el Ma**, Alg.
81/T16 **Râs el Oued**, Alg.
86/C2 **Ras Gharib**, Egypt
32/B2 **Rasharkin**, NI,UK
59/K5 **Rāshayyā**, Leb.
59/H6 **Rashīd** (Rosetta), Egypt
60/E1 **Rasht**, Iran
50/E4 **Raška**, Yugo.
102/G2 **Rasmussen** (basin), NW,Can
47/P10 **Raso** (cape), Port.
74/C5 **Rason** (lake), Austl.
55/G1 **Rasskazovo**, Rus.
45/H2 **Rastatt**, Ger.
41/F2 **Rastede**, Ger.
114/E6 **Rat** (isls.), Ak,US
72/B5 **Rata** (cape), Indo.
71/F3 **Ratangarh**, India
69/B3 **Rat Buri**, Thai.
70/C2 **Rāth**, India
107/K5 **Rathbun** (lake), Ia,US
38/G2 **Rathenow**, Ger.
32/B3 **Rathfriland**, NI,UK
32/B1 **Rathlin** (isl.), NI,UK
32/B1 **Rathlin** (sound), NI,UK
78/F4 **Ratik Chain** (arch.), Mrsh.
40/D6 **Ratingen**, Ger.
70/C3 **Ratlām**, India
70/B4 **Ratnāgiri**, India
70/D6 **Ratnapura**, SrL.
109/F3 **Raton**, NM,US
37/E3 **Rättvik**, Swe.
38/F2 **Ratzeburg**, Ger.
72/B3 **Raub**, Malay.
96/F3 **Rauch**, Arg.
37/D3 **Raufoss**, Nor.
95/D2 **Raul Soares**, Braz.
35/F2 **Raunds**, Eng,UK
75/S10 **Raupehu** (vol.), NZ
70/D3 **Raurkela**, India
48/C4 **Ravanusa**, It.
40/C6 **Ravels**, Belg.
33/E3 **Ravenglass**, Eng,UK
45/K4 **Ravenna**, It.
45/H3 **Ravensburg**, Ger.
33/G5 **Ravenshead**, Eng,UK
110/D4 **Ravenswood**, WV,US
61/K2 **Rāvi** (riv.), India, Pak.
50/B2 **Ravne na Koroškem**, Slov.
79/H5 **Rawaki** (Phoenix) (atoll), Kiri.
61/K2 **Rāwalpindi**, Pak.
39/L3 **Rawa Mazowiecka**, Pol.
39/J3 **Rawicz**, Pol.
106/G5 **Rawlins**, Wy,US
33/G5 **Rawmarsh**, Eng,UK
96/D4 **Rawson**, Arg.
33/F4 **Rawtenstall**, Eng,UK
111/K2 **Ray** (cape), Nf,Can
72/D4 **Raya** (peak), Indo.
70/D4 **Rāyadrug**, India
70/D4 **Rāyagada**, India
63/K2 **Raychikhinsk**, Rus.
35/G3 **Rayleigh**, Eng,UK
106/E3 **Raymond**, Ab,Can
112/D5 **Raymondville**, Tx,US
107/G3 **Raymore**, Sk,Can
69/C3 **Rayong**, Thai.
55/H4 **Razdan**, Arm.
51/J3 **Razelm** (lake), Rom.
51/H4 **Razgrad**, Bul.
49/K1 **Razgrad** (reg.), Bul.
51/F5 **Razlog**, Bul.
44/A2 **Raz, Pointe du** (pt.), Fr.
44/C3 **Ré** (isl.), Fr.
34/D2 **Rea** (riv.), Eng,UK
35/F4 **Reading**, Eng,UK
69/C3 **Reang Kesei**, Camb.
79/M6 **Reao** (atoll), FrPol.
74/C6 **Rebecca** (lake), Austl.
63/N2 **Rebun** (isl.), Japan
45/K5 **Recanati**, It.
74/C6 **Recherche** (arch.), Austl.
43/F6 **Réchicourt-le-Château**, Fr.
54/D1 **Rechitsa**, Bela.
94/D3 **Recife**, Braz.
88/D4 **Recife** (cape), SAfr.
41/E5 **Recke**, Ger.
41/E5 **Recklinghausen**, Ger.
38/G2 **Recknitz** (riv.), Ger.
69/B2 **Reclining Buddha** (Shwethalyaung) (ruins), Burma
91/E2 **Reconquista**, Arg.
60/C4 **Red** (sea), Afr., Asia
71/H3 **Red** (riv.), China, Viet.
32/B1 **Red** (bay), NI,UK
109/J5 **Red** (riv.), US
112/D2 **Red** (hills), Ks,US
39/K1 **Reda**, Pol.
115/F5 **Red Bank**, NJ,US
108/B2 **Red Bluff**, Ca,US
109/G4 **Red Bluff** (lake), NM, Tx,US
35/F3 **Redbourn**, Eng,UK
31/P7 **Redbridge** (bor.), Eng,UK
33/G2 **Redcar**, Eng,UK
106/F3 **Redcliff**, Ab,Can
76/F6 **Redcliffe**, Austl.
109/H2 **Red Cloud**, Ne,US
106/E2 **Red Deer**, Ab,Can
106/F3 **Red Deer** (riv.), Ab,Can
107/H2 **Red Deer** (lake), Mb,Can
107/H2 **Red Deer** (riv.), Mb, Sk,Can
108/B2 **Redding**, Ca,US
35/E2 **Redditch**, Eng,UK
107/J4 **Redfield**, SD,US
116/F7 **Redford**, Mi,US
31/N8 **Redhill**, Eng,UK
104/T10 **Red Hill** (peak), Hi,US
111/K1 **Red Indian** (lake), Nf,Can
43/G6 **Réding**, Fr.
107/K3 **Red Lake**, On,Can
107/K3 **Red Lake** (riv.), Mn,US
115/J7 **Redland**, Md,US
76/F7 **Redland Bay**, Austl.
115/C2 **Redlands**, Ca,US
106/F4 **Red Lodge**, Mt,US
106/C4 **Redmond**, Or,US
116/C2 **Redmond**, Wa,US
44/B3 **Redon**, Fr.
46/A1 **Redondela**, Sp.
46/B3 **Redondo**, Port.
115/B3 **Redondo Beach**, Ca,US
114/H3 **Redoubt** (vol.), Ak,US
107/J3 **Red River of the North** (riv.), Can., US
107/K5 **Red Rock** (lake), Ia,US
34/A6 **Redruth**, Eng,UK
86/D4 **Red Sea** (hills), Sudan
102/D2 **Redstone** (riv.), NW,Can
107/K2 **Red Sucker** (lake), Mb,Can
107/H3 **Redvers**, Sk,Can
85/E4 **Red Volta** (riv.), Burk., Gui.
106/E2 **Redwater**, Ab,Can
108/B2 **Redway**, Ca,US
109/G2 **Red Willow** (cr.), Ne,US
110/A2 **Red Wing**, Mn,US
116/K12 **Redwood City**, Ca,US
107/K4 **Redwood Falls**, Mn,US
108/A2 **Redwood Nat'l Park**, Ca,US
110/C3 **Reed City**, Mi,US
35/H1 **Reedham**, Eng,UK
108/C3 **Reedley**, Ca,US
110/B3 **Reedsburg**, Wi,US
106/B5 **Reedsport**, Or,US
77/B3 **Reedy** (cr.), Austl.
78/F6 **Reef** (isls.), Sol.
75/R11 **Reefton**, NZ
36/A4 **Ree, Lough** (lake), Ire.
35/H1 **Reepham**, Eng,UK
40/D5 **Rees**, Ger.
108/C3 **Reese** (riv.), Nv,US
40/D3 **Reest** (riv.), Neth.
33/G3 **Reeth**, Eng,UK
40/B4 **Reeuwijk**, Neth.
112/D4 **Refugio**, Tx,US
39/H2 **Rega** (riv.), Pol.
95/E1 **Regência, Pontal de** (pt.), Braz.
94/B2 **Regeneração**, Braz.
45/K2 **Regensburg**, Ger.
45/K2 **Regenstauf**, Ger.
76/H8 **Regents Park**, Austl.
82/F2 **Reggane**, Alg.
40/D4 **Regge** (riv.), Neth.
48/D3 **Reggio di Calabria**, It.
45/J4 **Reggio nell'Emilia**, It.
51/G2 **Reghin**, Rom.
107/G3 **Regina** (cap.), Sk,Can
108/F3 **Regina**, NM,US
107/G3 **Regina Beach**, Sk,Can
95/C3 **Registro**, Braz.
45/J2 **Regnitz** (riv.), Ger.
46/B3 **Reguengosde Monsaraz**, Port.
41/G4 **Rehburg-Loccum**, Ger.
43/F5 **Rehlingen-Siersburg**, Ger.
87/C5 **Rehoboth**, Namb.
55/M9 **Rehovot**, Isr.
43/G2 **Reichshof**, Ger.
106/F3 **Reid** (lake), Sk,Can
113/J2 **Reidsville**, NC,US
31/N8 **Reigate**, Eng,UK
42/D5 **Reims**, Fr.
97/J7 **Reina Adelaida** (arch.), Chile
41/H1 **Reinbek**, Ger.
107/J2 **Reindeer** (isl.), Mb,Can
107/H1 **Reindeer** (lake), Mb, Sk,Can
107/H1 **Reindeer** (riv.), Sk,Can
46/C1 **Reinosa**, Sp.
37/G1 **Reisduoddarhal'di** (peak), Nor.
40/D2 **Reitdiep** (riv.), Neth.
106/F5 **Reliance**, Wy,US
81/R16 **Relizane**, Alg.
41/G1 **Rellingen**, Ger.
43/G2 **Remagen**, Ger.
94/B3 **Remanso**, Braz.
31/S11 **Remarde** (riv.), Fr.
72/D5 **Rembang**, Indo.
81/Q16 **Remchi**, Alg.
93/H3 **Rémire**, FrG.
45/H2 **Rems** (riv.), Ger.
41/E6 **Remscheid**, Ger.
66/B5 **Ren** (riv.), China
96/C2 **Renca**, Chile
113/F2 **Rend** (lake), Il,US
38/E1 **Rendsburg**, Ger.
45/G3 **Renens**, Swi.
110/E2 **Renfrew**, On,Can
72/B4 **Rengat**, Indo.
96/C2 **Rengo**, Chile
54/D3 **Reni**, Ukr.
40/C5 **Renkum**, Neth.
78/F6 **Rennell** (isl.), Sol.
44/C2 **Rennes**, Fr.
45/J4 **Reno** (riv.), It.
108/C3 **Reno**, Nv,US
88/C3 **Renoster** (riv.), SAfr.
88/D2 **Renoster** (riv.), SAfr.
66/D3 **Renqiu**, China
110/C3 **Rensselaer**, In,US
46/E1 **Rentería**, Sp.
116/C3 **Renton**, Wa,US
111/P6 **Repentigny**, Qu,Can
33/G6 **Repton**, Eng,UK
106/D3 **Republic**, Wa,US
109/H2 **Republican** (riv.), Ks, Ne,US
76/C3 **Repulse** (bay), Austl.
92/D4 **Requena**, Peru
47/E3 **Requena**, Sp.
96/C2 **Requinoa**, Chile
96/B5 **Rescue** (pt.), Chile
55/D5 **Resen**, Macd.
95/J7 **Resende**, Braz.
108/E4 **Reserve**, NM,US
91/E2 **Resistencia**, Arg.
50/E3 **Reşiţa**, Rom.
102/G1 **Resolute**, NW,Can
103/K2 **Resolution** (isl.), NW,Can
34/C3 **Resolven**, Wal,UK
95/D1 **Resplendor**, Braz.
42/B4 **Ressons-sur-Matz**, Fr.
111/H2 **Restigouche** (riv.), NB,Can
107/H3 **Reston**, Mb,Can
115/J8 **Reston**, Va,US
116/C2 **Restoration** (pt.), Wa,US
100/C5 **Retalhuleu**, Guat.
42/D4 **Rethel**, Fr.
49/J5 **Réthimnon**, Gre.
43/E1 **Retie**, Belg.
50/F3 **Retrezap Nat'l Park**, Rom.
89/R15 **Réunion** (dpcy.), Fr.
47/F2 **Reus**, Sp.
43/C6 **Reusel**, Neth.
33/G2 **Reuterstadt Stavenhagen**, Ger.
45/H2 **Reutlingen**, Ger.
52/H5 **Reutov**, Rus.
44/D5 **Revel**, Fr.
106/D3 **Revelstoke**, BC,Can
76/H8 **Revesby**, Austl.
42/D4 **Revin**, Fr.
68/B4 **Revolyutsii, Pik** (peak), Taj.
37/G1 **Revsbotn** (fjord), Nor.
70/D3 **Rewa**, India
70/C2 **Rewāri**, India
114/J3 **Rex** (mtn.), Ak,US
106/F5 **Rexburg**, Id,US
42/B2 **Rexpoëde**, Fr.
101/F6 **Rey** (isl.), Pan.
35/H2 **Reydon**, Eng,UK
108/B3 **Reyes** (pt.), Ca,US
59/D3 **Reyhanlı**, Turk.
30/A2 **Reykjanestá** (cape), Ice.
37/N7 **Reykjavík** (cap.), Ice.
100/B2 **Reynosa**, Mex.
44/C3 **Rezé**, Fr.
52/E4 **Rēzekne**, Lat.
45/H3 **Rhaetian Alps** (mts.), It., Swi.
34/C2 **Rhayader**, Wal,UK
41/F5 **Rheda-Wiedenbrück**, Ger.
40/D5 **Rheden**, Neth.
35/F2 **Rhee** (Cam) (riv.), Eng,UK
42/F2 **Rheinbach**, Ger.
40/D5 **Rheinberg**, Ger.
41/E4 **Rheine**, Ger.
82/E2 **Rhemiles** (well), Alg.
40/C5 **Rhenen**, Neth.
38/D3 **Rhine** (riv.), Eur.
41/E5 **Rhine-Herne** (can.), Ger.
110/B2 **Rhinelander**, Wi,US
43/F3 **Rhineland-Palatinate** (state), Ger.
81/R16 **Rhiou** (riv.), Alg.
43/D3 **Rhisnes**, Belg.
34/C1 **Rhiw** (riv.), Wal,UK
111/G3 **Rhode Island** (state), US
59/B3 **Rhodes** (isl.), Gre.
59/B3 **Rhodes** (Ródhos), Gre.
51/F4 **Rhodope** (mts.), Bul.
34/C3 **Rhondda**, Wal,UK
44/F4 **Rhône** (riv.), Fr., Swi.
44/F4 **Rhône-Alpes** (reg.), Fr.
42/C3 **Rhonelle** (riv.), Fr.
33/E6 **Rhosllanerchrugog**, Wal,UK
34/B3 **Rhossili**, Wal,UK
32/E5 **Rhuddlan**, Wal,UK
41/H5 **Rhume** (riv.), Ger.
81/V17 **Rhumel** (riv.), Alg.
32/E6 **Rhyddhywel** (mtn.), Wal,UK
34/B2 **Rhydowen**, Wal,UK
32/E5 **Rhyl**, Wal,UK
34/C3 **Rhymney**, Wal,UK
94/C3 **Riachão do Jacuípe**, Braz.
94/B4 **Riacho de Santana**, Braz.
115/C2 **Rialto**, Ca,US
46/A1 **Rianjo**, Sp.
72/B3 **Riau** (isls.), Indo.
46/A1 **Ribadavia**, Sp.
46/B1 **Ribadeo**, Sp.
46/C1 **Ribadesella**, Sp.
89/H8 **Riban'i Manamby** (mts.), Madg.
33/F4 **Ribble** (riv.), Eng,UK
33/E1 **Ribe**, Den.
33/E1 **Ribe** (co.), Den.
95/B3 **Ribeira** (riv.), Braz.
94/C3 **Ribeira do Pombal**, Braz.
47/T13 **Ribeira Grande**, Azor.
80/J9 **Ribeira Grande**, CpV.
94/D3 **Ribeirão**, Braz.
95/B2 **Ribeirão do Pinha**, Braz.
95/C2 **Ribeirão Preto**, Braz.
42/C4 **Ribemont**, Fr.
48/C4 **Ribera**, It.
92/E6 **Riberalta**, Bol.
38/G1 **Ribnitz-Damgarten**, Ger.
110/E2 **Rice** (lake), On,Can
110/B2 **Rice Lake**, Wi,US
102/C2 **Richards** (isl.), NW,Can
111/G2 **Richardson** (lakes), Me,US
43/C2 **Richel** (isl.), Neth.
108/D3 **Richfield**, Ut,US
32/B3 **Richhill**, NI,UK
106/D4 **Richland**, Wa,US
113/H3 **Richland Balsam** (peak), NC,US
110/B3 **Richland Center**, Wi,US
112/D4 **Richland Creek** (res.), Tx,US
77/D2 **Richmond**, Austl.
111/F2 **Richmond**, Qu,Can
33/G3 **Richmond**, Eng,UK
116/K11 **Richmond**, Ca,US
110/C4 **Richmond**, In,US
110/C4 **Richmond**, Ky,US
112/E4 **Richmond**, Tx,US
110/E4 **Richmond** (cap.), Va,US
116/C2 **Richmond Beach-Innis Arden**, Wa,US
111/R8 **Richmond Hill**, On,Can
76/G8 **Richmond-Raaf**, Austl.
31/N7 **Richmond upon Thames** (bor.), Eng,UK
31/M7 **Rickmansworth**, Eng,UK
40/B5 **Ridderkerk**, Neth.
110/E2 **Rideau** (lake), On,Can
108/C4 **Ridgecrest**, Ca,US
115/F5 **Ridgewood**, NJ,US
33/G2 **Riding Mill**, Eng,UK
107/H3 **Riding Mtn. Nat'l Park**, Mb,Can
45/K2 **Ried im Innkreis**, Aus.
43/F5 **Riegelsberg**, Ger.
43/E2 **Riemst**, Belg.
39/G3 **Riesa**, Ger.
97/J8 **Riesco** (isl.), Chile
88/D3 **Riet** (riv.), SAfr.
41/F5 **Rietberg**, Ger.
48/C1 **Rieti**, It.
33/G3 **Rievaulx**, Eng,UK
106/C4 **Riffe** (lake), Wa,US
108/F3 **Rifle**, Co,US
37/N6 **Rifsnes** (pt.), Ice.
52/E4 **Riga** (Rīga) (cap.), Lat.
106/F5 **Rigby**, Id,US
61/H2 **Rīgestan** (reg.), Afg.
105/D4 **Riggins**, Id,US
70/D3 **Rihand Sāgar** (res.), India
37/H3 **Riihimäki**, Fin.
98/C **Riiser-Larsen** (pen.), Ant.
37/J2 **Riisitunturin Nat'l Park**, Fin.
50/B3 **Rijeka**, Cro.
40/B4 **Rijnsburg**, Neth.
40/D4 **Rijssen**, Neth.
40/B4 **Rijswijk**, Neth.
79/M7 **Rikitea**, FrPol.
51/F4 **Rila** (mts.), Bul.
49/H1 **Rilski Manastir**, Bul.
79/K7 **Rimatara** (isl.), FrPol.
39/L4 **Rimavská Sobota**, Slvk.
60/D3 **Rīma, Wādī** (dry riv.), SAr.
106/E2 **Rimbey**, Ab,Can
83/J5 **Rimé** (wadi), Chad
45/K4 **Rimini**, It.
51/H3 **Rîmnicu Sărat**, Rom.
51/G3 **Rîmnicu Vîlcea**, Rom.
111/G1 **Rimouski**, Qu,Can
62/D1 **Rinchinlhümbe**, Mong.
46/C4 **Rincón de la Victoria**, Sp.
100/D5 **Rincon de la Vieja Nat'l Park**, CR
101/P9 **Rincón de Romos**, Mex.
32/C3 **Ringboy** (pt.), NI,UK
37/D4 **Ringkøbing**, Den.
33/G6 **Ringmer**, Eng,UK
115/F5 **Ringoes**, NJ,US
32/B1 **Ringsend**, NI,UK
37/D4 **Ringsted**, Den.
40/B4 **Ringvaart** (can.), Neth.
37/F1 **Ringvassøy** (isl.), Nor.
77/G5 **Ringwood**, Austl.
35/E5 **Ringwood**, Eng,UK
115/F4 **Ringwood**, NJ,US
49/J4 **Rinia** (isl.), Gre.
32/C2 **Rinns, The** (pen.), Sc,UK
41/G4 **Rinteln**, Ger.
92/C5 **Río Abiseo Nat'l Park**, Peru
92/C4 **Riobamba**, Ecu.
95/L7 **Rio Bonito**, Braz.
92/E6 **Rio Branco**, Braz.
97/G2 **Río Branco**, Uru.
95/B3 **Rio Branco do Sul**, Braz.
110/C4 **Río Bravo del Norte** (Rio Grande) (riv.), Mex., US
96/B4 **Río Bueno**, Chile
95/D2 **Rio Casca**, Braz.
97/T12 **Riochuelo**, Uru.
96/C2 **Río Clarillo Nat'l Park**, Chile
95/J7 **Rio Claro**, Braz.
96/D3 **Río Colorado**, Arg.
96/D2 **Río Cuarto**, Arg.
94/B4 **Rio de Contas**, Braz.
95/K7 **Rio de Janeiro**, Braz.
95/K7 **Rio de Janeiro** (state), Braz.
106/B5 **Rio Dell**, Ca,US
95/B3 **Rio do Sul**, Braz.
47/Q10 **Rio Frio**, Port.
97/K7 **Río Gallegos**, Arg.
97/L8 **Río Grande**, Arg.
95/A5 **Rio Grande**, Braz.
112/C4 **Rio Grande** (riv.), Mex., US
112/D5 **Rio Grande City**, Tx,US
95/G8 **Rio Grande da Serra**, Braz.
100/E5 **Río Grande de Matagalpa** (riv.), Nic.
94/C2 **Rio Grande do Norte** (state), Braz.
94/B2 **Rio Grande do Piauí**, Braz.
95/A4 **Rio Grande do Sul** (state), Braz.
101/G5 **Riohacha**, Col.
101/E6 **Río Hato**, Pan.
92/C5 **Rioja**, Peru
92/F4 **Rio Jaú Nat'l Park**, Braz.
94/D3 **Rio Largo**, Braz.
46/A3 **Rio Maior**, Port.
44/E4 **Riom**, Fr.
106/D3 **Riondel**, BC,Can
96/C4 **Río Negro** (prov.), Arg.
97/F2 **Río Negro** (dept.), Uru.
97/F2 **Río Negro** (res.), Uru.
48/D2 **Rionero in Vulture**, It.
95/C1 **Rio Paranaíba**, Braz.
95/A4 **Rio Pardo**, Braz.
91/E2 **Río Pilcomayo Nat'l Park**, Arg.
94/A5 **Rio Prêto** (mts.), Braz.
108/F4 **Rio Rancho**, NM,US
94/C3 **Rio Real**, Braz.
44/F3 **Riorges**, Fr.
96/E1 **Río Segundo**, Arg.
96/B5 **Río Simpson Nat'l Park**, Chile
96/D2 **Río Tercero**, Arg.
94/D2 **Rio Tinto**, Braz.
95/B1 **Rio Verde**, Braz.
100/B3 **Rioverde**, Mex.
93/H7 **Rio Verde de Mato Grosso**, Braz.
50/E3 **Ripanj**, Yugo.
31/M8 **Ripley**, Eng,UK
113/F3 **Ripley**, Ms,US
113/F3 **Ripley**, Tn,US
47/G1 **Ripoll**, Sp.
47/G1 **Ripoll** (riv.), Sp.
47/L6 **Ripollet**, Sp.
33/G3 **Ripon**, Eng,UK
107/L5 **Ripon**, Wi,US
48/D4 **Riposto**, It.
33/G4 **Ripponden**, Eng,UK
34/C3 **Risca**, Wal,UK
63/N2 **Rishiri** (isl.), Japan
59/K6 **Rishon LeZiyyon**, Isr.
44/D2 **Risle** (riv.), Fr.
50/B3 **Risnjak** (peak), Cro.
50/B3 **Risnjak Nat'l Park**, Cro.
51/G3 **Rîşnov**, Rom.
112/E3 **Rison**, Ar,US
37/D4 **Risør**, Nor.
31/T11 **Ris-Orangis**, Fr.
92/D2 **Ritacuba** (peak), Col.
78/C2 **Ritaiō** (isl.), Japan
41/F2 **Ritterhude**, Ger.
65/L9 **Rittō**, Japan
106/D4 **Ritzville**, Wa,US
45/J4 **Riva**, It.
96/E2 **Rivadavia**, Arg.
45/G4 **Rivarolo Canavese**, It.
100/D5 **Rivas**, Nic.
44/F4 **Rive-de-Gier**, Fr.
96/B5 **Rivera** (isl.), Chile
91/E3 **Rivera**, Uru.
97/G1 **Rivera** (dept.), Uru.
75/H7 **Riverina** (reg.), Austl.
116/F7 **River Rouge**, Mi,US
106/B3 **Rivers** (inlet), BC,Can
107/H3 **Rivers**, Mb,Can
85/G5 **Rivers** (state), Nga.
88/C4 **Riversdale**, SAfr.
115/C3 **Riverside**, Ca,US
76/G8 **Riverstone**, Austl.
107/J3 **Riverton**, Mb,Can
75/Q12 **Riverton**, NZ
106/F5 **Riverton**, Wy,US
111/H2 **Riverview**, NB,Can
116/F7 **Riverview**, Mi,US
113/H5 **Riviera Beach**, Fl,US
115/K7 **Riviera Beach**, Md,US
111/G2 **Rivière-du-Loup**, Qu,Can
88/L11 **Riviersonderendreeks** (mts.), SAfr.
45/G4 **Rivoli**, It.
42/D2 **Rixensart**, Belg.
60/E4 **Riyadh** (Ar Riyāḑ) (cap.), SAr.
59/E2 **Rize**, Turk.
66/D4 **Rizhao**, China
48/E3 **Rizzuto** (cape), It.
37/D4 **Rjukan**, Nor.
84/B2 **Rkîz** (lake), Mrta.
37/D3 **Roa**, Nor.
35/F2 **Roade**, Eng,UK
36/D2 **Roadside**, Sc,UK
101/J4 **Road Town** (cap.), BVI
108/E3 **Roan** (plat.), Co,US
33/F1 **Roan Fell** (hill), Sc,UK
113/H2 **Roan High** (peak), NC,US
44/F3 **Roanne**, Fr.
113/G3 **Roanoke**, Al,US
113/J2 **Roanoke** (riv.), NC, Va,US
110/E4 **Roanoke**, Va,US
113/J2 **Roanoke Rapids**, NC,US
100/D4 **Roatán** (isl.), Hon.
77/C4 **Robbins** (isl.), Austl.
77/B1 **Robe** (peak), Austl.
36/A4 **Robe** (riv.), Ire.
43/E6 **Robert-Espagne**, Fr.
112/C4 **Robert Lee**, Tx,US
114/E4 **Roberts** (mtn.), Ak,US
35/G5 **Robertsbridge**, Eng,UK
37/G2 **Robertsfors**, Swe.
70/E3 **Robertsganj**, India
88/B4 **Robertson**, SAfr.
111/F1 **Roberval**, Qu,Can
33/H3 **Robin Hood's Bay**, Eng,UK
74/B5 **Robinson** (ranges), Austl.
110/C4 **Robinson**, Il,US
116/C3 **Robinson** (pt.), Wa,US
90/B6 **Robinson Crusoe** (isl.), Chile
76/C4 **Robinson Gorge Nat'l Park**, Austl.
107/H3 **Roblin**, Mb,Can
92/G7 **Roboré**, Bol.
106/D2 **Robson** (peak), BC,Can
112/D5 **Robstown**, Tx,US
112/C3 **Roby**, Tx,US
46/A3 **Roca, Cabo da** (cape), Port.
100/B4 **Roca Partida** (pt.), Mex.
93/M4 **Rocas**, Braz.
45/G4 **Rocciamelone** (peak), It.
44/E5 **Roc de France** (mtn.), Fr.
97/G2 **Rocha**, Uru.
97/G2 **Rocha** (dept.), Uru.
33/F4 **Rochdale**, Eng,UK
34/B6 **Roche**, Eng,UK
44/C4 **Rochefort**, Fr.
35/G4 **Rochester**, Eng,UK
110/C3 **Rochester**, In,US
116/F6 **Rochester**, Mi,US
107/K4 **Rochester**, Mn,US
111/G3 **Rochester**, NH,US
110/E3 **Rochester**, NY,US
116/F6 **Rochester Hills**, Mi,US
35/G3 **Rochford**, Eng,UK
110/B3 **Rock** (riv.), Il, Wi,US
106/C4 **Rock** (cr.), Or,US
30/B3 **Rockall** (isl.), UK
114/L3 **Rock Creek**, Yk,Can
76/H8 **Rockdale**, Austl.
98/R **Rockefeller** (plat.), Ant.
110/B3 **Rockford**, Il,US
111/G2 **Rock Forest**, Qu,Can
107/G3 **Rockglen**, Sk,Can
76/C3 **Rockhampton**, Austl.
113/H3 **Rock Hill**, SC,US
74/B6 **Rockingham**, Austl.
113/J3 **Rockingham**, NC,US
110/B3 **Rock Island**, Il,US
110/F2 **Rockland**, On,Can
111/G2 **Rockland**, Me,US
77/B3 **Rocklands** (res.), Austl.
113/H4 **Rockledge**, Fl,US
112/D4 **Rockport**, Tx,US
112/C4 **Rocksprings**, Tx,US
106/F5 **Rock Springs**, Wy,US
115/J7 **Rockville**, Md,US
115/G5 **Rockville Center**, NY,US
112/D3 **Rockwall**, Tx,US
113/G3 **Rockwood**, Tn,US
99/E4 **Rocky** (mts.), NAm
110/D4 **Rocky** (peak), Ky,US
77/C4 **Rocky Cape Nat'l Park**, Austl.
111/K1 **Rocky Harbour**, Nf,Can
110/D2 **Rocky Island** (lake), On,Can
113/J3 **Rocky Mount**, NC,US
113/J3 **Rocky Mount**, Va,US
106/E2 **Rocky Mountain House**, Ab,Can
109/F2 **Rocky Mountain Nat'l Park**, Co,US
115/H5 **Rocky Point**, NY,US
43/G5 **Rodalben**, Ger.
111/K1 **Roddickton**, Nf,Can
34/D1 **Roden** (riv.), Eng,UK
116/K10 **Rodeo**, Ca,US
44/E4 **Rodez**, Fr.
59/B3 **Ródhos** (Rhodes), Gre.
45/K2 **Roding**, Ger.
31/P7 **Roding** (riv.), Eng,UK
41/G4 **Rödinghausen**, Ger.
49/F2 **Rodonit, Kep i** (cape), Alb.
29/N6 **Rodrigues** (isl.), Mrts.
32/B2 **Roe** (riv.), NI,UK
74/C3 **Roebuck** (bay), Austl.
40/D6 **Roer** (riv.), Neth.
40/C6 **Roermond**, Neth.
42/C2 **Roeselare**, Belg.
116/D2 **Roesiger** (lake), Wa,US
103/H2 **Roes Welcome** (sound), NW,Can
54/D1 **Rogachev**, Bela.
37/C4 **Rogaland** (co.), Nor.
50/D4 **Rogatica**, Bosn.
112/E2 **Rogers**, Ar,US
110/D4 **Rogers** (peak), Va,US
110/D2 **Rogers City**, Mi,US
113/H2 **Rogersville**, Tn,US
44/F2 **Rognon** (riv.), Fr.
39/J2 **Rogoźno**, Pol.
108/B2 **Rogue** (riv.), Or,US
83/L6 **Rohl** (riv.), Sudan
61/J3 **Rohri**, Pak.
69/C2 **Roi Et**, Thai.
42/C4 **Roisel**, Fr.
31/T10 **Roissy**, Fr.
31/T9 **Roissy-en-France**, Fr.
96/E2 **Rojas**, Arg.
100/B3 **Rojo** (cape), Mex.
101/H4 **Rojo** (cape), PR
72/B3 **Rokan** (riv.), Indo.
76/A1 **Rokeby-Croll Creek Nat'l Park**, Austl.
84/C4 **Rokel** (riv.), SLeo.
65/L10 **Rokkō-san** (peak), Japan
95/B2 **Rolândia**, Braz.
40/D3 **Rolde**, Neth.

156

Rolla – Saint

106/C2 Rolla, BC,Can
109/K3 Rolla, Mo,US
107/J3 Rolla, ND,US
116/P15 Rolling Meadows, Il,US
76/C4 Roma, Austl.
44/E4 Romagnat, Fr.
43/E5 Romagne-sous-Montfaucon, Fr.
113/J3 Romain (cape), SC,US
103/K3 Romaine (riv.), Qu,Can
51/H2 Roman, Rom.
73/G5 Romang (isl.), Indo.
73/G5 Romang (str.), Indo.
51/F3 Romania
44/F4 Romans-sur-Isère, Fr.
114/E3 Romanzof (cape), Ak,US
48/C2 Roma (Rome) (cap.), It.
43/F5 Rombas, Fr.
67/D5 Romblon, Phil.
113/G3 Rome, Ga,US
110/F3 Rome, NY,US
116/P16 Romeoville, Il,US
48/C2 Rome (Roma) (cap.), It.
31/P7 Romford, Eng,UK
44/E2 Romilly-sur-Seine, Fr.
40/D6 Rommerskirchen, Ger.
35/G4 Romney Marsh (reg.), Eng,UK
54/E2 Romny, Ukr.
38/E1 Rømø (isl.), Den.
44/D3 Romorantin-Lanthenay, Fr.
35/E5 Romsey, Eng,UK
116/F7 Romulus, Mi,US
69/D2 Ron, Viet.
106/E4 Ronan, Mt,US
93/H6 Roncador (mts.), Braz.
101/F5 Roncador Cay (isl.), Col.
48/C1 Ronciglione, It.
42/C2 Roncq, Fr.
46/D4 Ronda, Sp.
37/D3 Rondane Nat'l Park, Nor.
93/H7 Rondonópolis, Braz.
71/J2 Rong (riv.), China
107/G2 Ronge (lake), Sk,Can
78/F3 Rongelap (atoll), Mrsh.
78/F3 Rongerik (atoll), Mrsh.
79/X15 Roniu (peak), FrPol.
115/G5 Ronkonkoma, NY,US
39/H1 Rønne, Den.
37/E4 Ronneby, Swe.
98/U Ronne Entrance (inlet), Ant.
41/G4 Ronnenberg, Ger.
42/C2 Ronse, Belg.
93/H6 Ronuro (riv.), Braz.
88/P13 Roodeport-Maraisburg, SAfr.
88/B2 Rooiberg (peak), Namb.
70/C2 Roorkee, India
40/B5 Roosendaal, Neth.
98/N Roosevelt (isl.), Ant.
92/F6 Roosevelt (riv.), Braz.
102/D3 Roosevelt (mtn.), BC,Can
108/E2 Roosevelt, Ut,US
114/L4 Root (mtn.), Ak,US
116/Q14 Root (riv.), Wi,US
46/D4 Roquetas de Mar, Sp.
92/F2 Roraima (peak), Guy.
107/J3 Rorketon, Mb,Can
81/W17 Rosa (cape), Alg.
96/E2 Rosario, Arg.
94/A1 Rosário, Braz.
101/N9 Rosario, Mex.
97/F2 Rosario, Uru.
91/D2 Rosario de la Frontera, Arg.
97/S11 Rosario del Tala, Arg.
91/F3 Rosário do Sul, Braz.
101/M8 Rosarito, Mex.
47/G1 Rosas (gulf), Sp.
92/C3 Rosa Zárate, Ecu.
41/G6 Rosdorf, Ger.
79/J6 Rose (isl.), ASam.
114/M4 Rose (pt.), BC,Can
107/J3 Roseau (riv.), Can., US
101/J4 Roseau (cap.), Dom.
107/K3 Roseau, Mn,US
89/S15 Rose Belle, Mrts.
106/C5 Roseburg, Or,US
115/K7 Rosedale, Md,US
113/F3 Rosedale, Ms,US
36/D2 Rosehearty, Sc,UK
116/P16 Roselle, Il,US
115/F5 Roselle, NJ,US
111/N6 Rosemère, Qu,Can
112/E4 Rosenberg, Tx,US
38/G5 Rosenheim, Ger.
47/G1 Roses, Sp.
48/D1 Roseto degli Abruzzi, It.
106/G3 Rosetown, Sk,Can
59/H6 Rosetta (Rashīd), Egypt
116/M9 Roseville, Ca,US
116/G6 Roseville, Mi,US
59/M8 Rosh Ha'Ayin, Isr.
59/K5 Rosh HaNiqra (pt.), Isr.
51/G3 Roşiori de Vede, Rom.
38/G1 Roskilde, Den.
38/F1 Roskilde (co.), Den.
54/E1 Roslavl', Rus.
40/C5 Rosmalen, Neth.
31/T10 Rosny-sous-Bois, Fr.
48/D4 Rosolini, It.
44/B3 Rosporden, Fr.
43/G2 Rösrath, Ger.
98/M Ross (isl.), Ant.
98/P Ross (sea), Ant.
107/J2 Ross (isl.), Mb,Can
45/K3 Rossa (peak), It.
33/E4 Rossall (pt.), Eng,UK
48/E3 Rossano, It.
78/E6 Rossel (isl.), PNG
98/N Ross Ice Shelf, Ant.
111/H2 Rossignol (lake), NS,Can
36/H6 Rosskeeragh (pt.), Ire.
106/D3 Rossland, BC,Can
32/A3 Rosslea, NI,UK
84/B2 Rosso, Mrta.
34/D3 Ross on Wye, Eng,UK
54/F2 Rossosh', Rus.
114/M3 Ross River, Yk,Can
107/F2 Rosthern, Sk,Can
38/G1 Rostock, Ger.
54/F3 Rostov, Rus.
55/G2 Rostov Obl., Rus.
32/B3 Rostrevor, NI,UK
113/G3 Roswell, Ga,US
109/F4 Roswell, NM,US
45/H2 Rot (riv.), Ger.
78/D3 Rota (isl.), NMar.
46/B4 Rota, Sp.
41/G2 Rotenburg, Ger.
41/G7 Rotenburg an der Fulda, Ger.
43/F2 Rötgen, Ger.
38/E3 Rothaargebirge (mts.), Ger.
33/G1 Rothbury, Eng,UK
33/G5 Rother (riv.), Eng,UK
35/F5 Rother (riv.), Eng,UK
33/G5 Rotherham, Eng,UK
36/D2 Rothes, Sc,UK
43/E2 Rotheux-Rimière, Belg.
35/F2 Rothwell, Eng,UK
73/F6 Roti (isl.), Indo.
75/S10 Rotorua, NZ
43/D2 Rotselaar, Belg.
45/K2 Rott (riv.), Ger.
43/F6 Rotte (riv.), Fr.
40/B5 Rotterdam, Neth.
40/D2 Rottumeroog (isl.), Neth.
40/D2 Rottumerplaat (isl.), Neth.
45/H2 Rottweil, Ger.
78/G6 Rotuma (isl.), Fiji
42/C2 Roubaix, Fr.
47/F4 Roubion (riv.), Fr.
44/D2 Rouen, Fr.
110/F2 Rouge (riv.), Qu,Can
116/F6 Rouge (riv.), Mi,US
113/G2 Rough (riv.), Ky,US
76/C4 Round Hill (pt.), Austl.
32/B1 Round Knowe (mtn.), NI,UK
116/P15 Round Lake, Il,US
116/P15 Round Lake Beach, Il,US
108/C3 Round Mountain, Nv,US
112/D4 Round Rock, Tx,US
106/F4 Roundup, Mt,US
34/E4 Roundway (hill), Eng,UK
76/G8 Rouse Hill, Austl.
43/E5 Rouvres-en-Woëvre, Fr.
110/E1 Rouyn-Noranda, Qu,Can
37/H2 Rovaniemi, Fin.
69/D3 Rovieng Tbong, Camb.
45/J4 Rovigo, It.
54/C2 Rovno, Ukr.
54/C2 Rovno Obl., Ukr.
74/B3 Rowley (shoals), Austl.
103/J2 Rowley (isl.), NW,Can
84/B4 Roxa (isl.), GBis.
67/C5 Roxas, Phil.
67/D4 Roxas, Phil.
73/F1 Roxas City, Indo.
113/J2 Roxboro, NC,US
101/J5 Roxborough, Trin.
84/A3 Roxo (cape), Sen.
109/F4 Roy, NM,US
108/D2 Roy, Ut,US
45/G4 Roya (riv.), Fr.
36/B4 Royal (can.), Ire.
102/H4 Royale (isl.), Mi,US
35/E2 Royal Leamington Spa, Eng,UK
35/G4 Royal Military (can.), Eng,UK
88/E3 Royal Natal Nat'l Park, SAfr.
76/H9 Royal Nat'l Park, Austl.
116/F6 Royal Oak, Mi,US
35/G4 Royal Tunbridge Wells, Eng,UK
44/C4 Royan, Fr.
35/F2 Royston, Eng,UK
33/F4 Royton, Eng,UK
50/E4 Rožaje, Yugo.
39/L4 Rožňava, Slvk.
42/D4 Rozoy-sur-Serre, Fr.
39/M3 Roztoczański Nat'l Park, Pol.
112/E3 R.S. Kerr (lake), Ok,US
55/G1 Rtishchevo, Rus.
33/E6 Ruabon, Wal,UK
87/B4 Ruacana (falls), Ang.
87/B4 Ruacana, Namb.
87/F2 Ruaha Nat'l Park, Tanz.
60/E5 Rub' al Khali (des.), SAr.
31/U11 Rubelles, Fr.
54/F2 Rubezhnoye, Ukr.
47/G2 Rubí, Sp.
115/C3 Rubidoux, Ca,US
94/B5 Rubim, Braz.
68/D1 Rubtsovsk, Rus.
108/D2 Ruby (mts.), Nv,US
108/D2 Ruby Valley, Nv,US
40/B5 Rucphen, Neth.
39/K2 Ruda Woda (lake), Pol.
33/G6 Ruddington, Eng,UK
39/G2 Rüdersdorf, Ger.
39/M3 Rudnik, Pol.
55/M1 Rudnyy, Kaz.
56/F1 Rudolf (isl.), Rus.
38/F3 Rudolstadt, Ger.
60/F1 Rūdsar, Iran
33/H3 Rudston, Eng,UK
32/B1 Rue (pt.), NI,UK
31/S10 Rueil-Malmaison, Fr.
44/D4 Ruelle-sur-Touvre, Fr.
50/F4 Ruen (Rujen) (peak), Bul., Mac.
83/M5 Rufā'ah, Sudan
49/F3 Ruffano, It.
87/G2 Rufiji (riv.), Tanz.
96/E2 Rufino, Arg.
35/E2 Rugby, Eng,UK
107/J3 Rugby, ND,US
34/E1 Rugeley, Eng,UK
39/G1 Rügen (isl.), Ger.
40/D6 Ruhr (riv.), Ger.
41/D6 Ruhrgebiet (reg.), Ger.
109/F4 Ruidoso, NM,US
40/D3 Ruinen, Neth.
31/M7 Ruislip, Eng,UK
101/N9 Ruiz, Mex.
50/F4 Rujen (Ruen) (peak), Bul., Macd.
83/J8 Ruki (riv.), Zaire
87/F2 Rukwa (lake), Tanz.
50/D3 Ruma, Yugo.
83/L6 Rumbek, Sudan
101/G3 Rum Cay (isl.), Bahm.
111/G2 Rumford, Me,US
39/K1 Rumia, Pol.
34/C4 Rumney, Wal,UK
63/N3 Rumoi, Japan
87/F3 Rumphi, Malw.
115/F5 Rumson, NJ,US
42/D1 Rumst, Belg.
32/B1 Runabay Head (pt.), NI,UK
33/F5 Runcorn, Eng,UK
83/L7 Rungu, Zaire
87/F2 Rungwa, Tanz.
87/F2 Rungwe (peak), Tanz.
115/E6 Runnemede, NJ,US
115/C2 Running Springs, Ca,US
62/D3 Ruo (riv.), China
62/E4 Ruoqiang, China
72/B3 Rupat (isl.), Indo.
51/F2 Rupea, Rom.
42/D1 Rupel (riv.), Belg.
110/E1 Rupert (riv.), Qu,Can
106/E5 Rupert, Id,US
103/J3 Rupert House (Waskaganish), Qu,Can
43/G2 Ruppichteroth, Ger.
43/F1 Rur (riv.), Ger.
79/K7 Rurutu (isl.), FrPol.
87/F4 Rusape, Zim.
35/E4 Rushall, Eng,UK
107/K4 Rush City, Mn,US
35/F2 Rushden, Eng,UK
110/C4 Rushville, In,US
109/G2 Rushville, Ne,US
112/E4 Rusk, Tx,US
33/H5 Ruskington, Eng,UK
94/C2 Russas, Braz.
76/F7 Russell (isl.), Austl.
107/H3 Russell, Mb,Can
107/H1 Russell (lake), Mb,Can
102/F1 Russell (isl.), NW,Can
113/H3 Russell (lake), Ga, SC,US
109/H3 Russell, Ks,US
113/G3 Russellville, Al,US
112/E3 Russellville, Ar,US
110/C4 Russellville, Ky,US
56/* Russia
108/B3 Russian (riv.), Ca,US
51/J5 Rustavi, Geo.
88/D2 Rustenburg, SAfr.
112/E3 Ruston, La,US
46/C4 Rute, Sp.
73/F5 Ruteng, Indo.
87/F5 Rutenga, Zim.
108/D3 Ruth, Nv,US
41/F6 Rüthen, Ger.
33/E5 Ruthin, Wal,UK
111/F3 Rutland, Vt,US
35/F1 Rutland Water (res.), Eng,UK
68/C5 Rutog, China
87/E1 Rutshuru, Zaire
40/D3 Ruurlo, Neth.
48/E2 Ruvo di Puglia, It.
59/F3 Ruwāndūz, Iraq
94/B4 Ruy Barbosa, Braz.
55/H1 Ruzayevka, Rus.
39/K4 Ružomberok, Slvk.
87/E1 Rwanda
77/D2 Ryan (mt.), Austl.
32/C2 Ryan, Loch (inlet), Sc,UK
54/F1 Ryazan', Rus.
52/J5 Ryazan' Obl., Rus.
54/G1 Ryazhsk, Rus.
52/G1 Rybachiy (pen.), Rus.
68/C3 Rybach'ye, Kyr.
52/H4 Rybinsk, Rus.
52/H4 Rybinsk (res.), Rus.
39/K3 Rybnik, Pol.
51/J2 Rybnitsa, Mol.
106/D2 Rycroft, Ab,Can
76/H8 Ryde, Austl.
35/E5 Ryde, Eng,UK
35/G5 Rye, Eng,UK
35/G5 Rye (bay), Eng,UK
33/H3 Rye (riv.), Eng,UK
108/C2 Rye Patch (res.), Nv,US
39/L3 Ryki, Pol.
55/J2 Ryn-Peski (des.), Kaz.
65/F1 Ryōtsu, Japan
65/M9 Ryōzen-yama (peak), Japan
39/K2 Rypin, Pol.
54/B2 Rysy (peak), Slvk.
33/G2 Ryton, Eng,UK
35/E2 Ryton on Dunsmore, Eng,UK
39/H1 Rytterknægten (peak), Den.
65/G3 Ryūgasaki, Japan
65/M9 Ryūō, Japan
39/M3 Rzeszów, Pol.
39/L3 Rzeszów (prov.), Pol.
52/G4 Rzhev, Rus.

S

41/G4 Saale (riv.), Ger.
38/F3 Saalfeld, Ger.
45/K3 Saalfelden am Steinernen Meer, Aus.
106/C3 Saanich, BC,Can
43/F5 Saar (riv.), Ger.
43/F5 Saarbrücken, Ger.
52/D4 Saaremaa (isl.), Est.
43/F5 Saarland (state), Ger.
43/F5 Saarlouis, Ger.
69/D3 Sab (riv.), Camb.
101/J4 Saba (isl.), NAnt.
50/D3 Šabac, Yugo.
47/G2 Sabadell, Sp.
64/E3 Sabae, Japan
73/E2 Sabah (state), Malay.
72/A2 Sabang, Indo.
101/F6 Sabanita, Pan.
83/M6 Sabat (riv.), Eth., Sudan
61/H2 Sāberi, Hāmūn-e (lake), Afg.
82/H2 Sabhā, Libya
86/B3 Sabie, Egypt
89/F2 Sabie (Sabierivier) (riv.), Moz., SAfr.
47/E1 Sabiñánigo, Sp.
100/A2 Sabinas, Mex.
100/A2 Sabinas (riv.), Mex.
100/A2 Sabinas Hidalgo, Mex.
112/E4 Sabine (lake), La, Tx,US
112/E4 Sabine (riv.), La, Tx,US
109/J5 Sabine Pass (waterway), La, Tx,US
48/C1 Sabini (mts.), It.
95/D1 Sabinópolis, Braz.
60/F4 Sabkhat Maṭṭī (salt marsh), UAE
73/F1 Sablayan, Phil.
111/J3 Sable (isl.), Can.
111/H3 Sable (cape), NS,Can
113/H5 Sable (cape), Fl,US
44/C3 Sablé-sur-Sarthe, Fr.
46/B2 Sabor (riv.), Port.
73/H4 Sabra (cape), Indo.
98/J Sabrina (coast), Ant.
61/G1 Sabzevār, Iran
106/D4 Sacajawea (peak), Or,US
108/E4 Sacaton, Az,US
46/A3 Sacavém, Port.
48/C2 Sacco (riv.), It.
51/G3 Săcele, Rom.
107/L2 Sachigo (lake), On,Can
107/L2 Sachigo (riv.), On,Can
111/H2 Sackville, NB,Can
31/S10 Saclay, Fr.
111/G3 Saco, Me,US
95/C1 Sacramento, Braz.
116/M9 Sacramento (cap.), Ca,US
108/B2 Sacramento (riv.), Ca,US
109/F4 Sacramento (mts.), NM,US
46/D4 Sacratif (cape), Sp.
104/W12 Sacred (falls), Hi,US
33/G2 Sacriston, Eng,UK
48/E2 Sacro (peak), It.
46/A1 Sada, Sp.
106/C2 Saddle (hills), Ab, BC,Can
33/G4 Saddleworth, Eng,UK
69/D4 Sa Dec, Viet.
61/K3 Sādiqābād, Pak.
71/G2 Sadiya, India
65/F2 Sado (isl.), Japan
46/A3 Sado (riv.), Port.
64/B4 Sadowara, Japan
70/B2 Sādri, India
82/H1 Safāqis, Tun.
81/X18 Safāqis (gov.), Tun.
60/E3 Saffānīyah, Ra's as (pt.), SAr.
37/E4 Säffle, Swe.
108/E4 Safford, Az,US
35/G2 Saffron Walden, Eng,UK
82/D1 Safi, Mor.
61/H2 Safid (mts.), Afg.
61/J1 Safīd (riv.), Afg.
61/K1 Safid Khers (mts.), Afg., Taj.
59/L4 Ṣāfītā, Syria
52/G5 Safonovo, Rus.
52/E4 Safranbolu, Turk.
70/E2 Saga, China
64/B4 Saga, Japan
64/A4 Saga (pref.), Japan
65/G1 Sagae, Japan
71/G3 Sagaing, Burma
71/F3 Sagaing (div.), Burma
65/H7 Sagami (bay), Japan
65/H7 Sagami (riv.), Japan
65/F3 Sagami (sea), Japan
65/F3 Sagamihara, Japan
65/H7 Sagamiko, Japan
70/C3 Sāgar, India
114/J2 Sagavanirktok (riv.), Ak,US
73/F1 Sagay, Phil.
110/D3 Saginaw, Mi,US
110/D3 Saginaw (bay), Mi,US
103/K3 Saglek (bay), Nf,Can
48/A1 Sagone (gulf), Fr.
46/A4 Sagres, Port.
68/E2 Sagsay (riv.), Mong.
101/F3 Sagua de Tánamo, Cuba
108/E4 Saguaro Nat'l Mon., Az,US
111/G1 Saguenay (riv.), Qu,Can
82/C2 Saguia el Hamra (wadi), Mor., WSah.
47/E3 Sagunto, Sp.
31/R9 Sagy, Fr.
70/E2 Sa'gya, China
55/K2 Sagyz (riv.), Kaz.
59/L6 Saḥāb, Jor.
86/B5 Sahaba, Sudan
101/F6 Sahagún, Col.
60/E1 Sahand (mtn.), Iran
82/G3 Sahara (des.), Afr.
61/L3 Sahāranpur, India
70/E2 Saharsa, India
70/E2 Sāhibganj, India
61/K2 Sāhīwāl, Pak.
82/H2 Ṣaḥrā Awbārī (des.), Libya
83/K2 Sahra' Rabyānah (des.), Libya
100/A3 Sahuayo, Mex.
70/D2 Sai (riv.), India
65/E2 Sai (riv.), Japan
81/R16 Saïda, Alg.
70/D2 Saidpur, India
64/C2 Saigō, Japan
69/D4 Saigon (Ho Chi Minh City), Viet.
64/C4 Saijō, Japan
64/A4 Saikai Nat'l Park, Japan
64/B4 Saiki, Japan
70/C4 Sailu, India
37/J3 Saimaa (lake), Fin.
42/C4 Sains-Richaumont, Fr.
36/D3 Saint Abb's Head (pt.), Sc,UK
44/E5 Saint-Affrique, Fr.
34/A6 Saint Agnes, Eng,UK
111/L2 Saint Alban's, Nf,Can
31/N6 Saint Albans, Eng,UK
31/M6 Saint Albans (val.), Eng,UK
111/F2 Saint Albans, Vt,US
110/D4 Saint Albans, WV,US
106/E2 Saint Albert, Ab,Can
34/D5 Saint Aldhelm's Head (pt.), Eng,UK
42/C3 Saint-Amand-les-Eaux, Fr.
44/E3 Saint-Amand-Montrond, Fr.
111/G1 Saint-Ambroise, Qu,Can
89/R15 Saint-André, Reun.
44/F2 Saint-André-les-Vergers, Fr.
36/D2 Saint Andrews, Sc,UK
84/B5 Saint Ann (cape), SLeo.
101/F4 Saint Ann's Bay, Jam.
44/B2 Saint Anne, Chl,UK
111/Q9 Saint Anns, On,Can
34/A3 Saint Ann's (pt.), UK
111/L1 Saint Anthony, Nf,Can
106/F5 Saint Anthony, Id,US
111/N6 Saint-Antoine, Qu,Can
42/D6 Saint-Armand-sur-Fion, Fr.
31/R11 Saint-Arnoult-en-Yvelines, Fr.
32/E5 Saint Asaph, Wal,UK
34/C4 Saint Athan, Wal,UK
44/B2 Saint Aubin, Chl,UK
111/N6 Saint-Augustin, Qu,Can
113/H4 Saint Augustine, Fl,US
34/B6 Saint Austell, Eng,UK
44/B3 Saint-Avé, Fr.
43/F5 Saint-Avold, Fr.
44/D5 Saint-Barthélemy, Pic de (peak), Fr.
32/E3 Saint Bees, Eng,UK
32/E3 Saint Bees Head (pt.), Eng,UK
111/M6 Saint-Benoît, Qu,Can
89/R15 Saint-Benoît, Reun.
111/P7 Saint-Blaise, Qu,Can
88/C4 Saint Blaize (cape), SAfr.
34/D3 Saint Briavels, Eng,UK
31/T10 Saint-Brice-sous-Forêt, Fr.
34/A3 Saint Brides (bay), Wal,UK
44/B2 Saint-Brieuc, Fr.
44/B2 Saint-Brieuc (bay), Fr.
111/P6 Saint-Bruno-de-Montarville, Qu,Can
111/M6 Saint-Canut, Qu,Can
111/R9 Saint Catharines, On,Can
101/J5 Saint Catherine (mt.), Gren.
35/E5 Saint Catherine's (pt.), Eng,UK
44/F4 Saint-Chamond, Fr.
116/P16 Saint Charles, Il,US
110/E4 Saint Charles, Md,US
109/K3 Saint Charles, Mo,US
31/S11 Saint-Chéron, Fr.
116/G7 Saint Clair (lake), On,Can, Mi,US
116/H6 Saint Clair (riv.), On,Can, Mi,US
116/G6 Saint Clair Shores, Mi,US
44/F3 Saint-Claude, Fr.
34/B3 Saint Clears, Wal,UK
31/S10 Saint-Cloud, Fr.
107/K4 Saint Cloud, Mn,US
34/B6 Saint Columb Major, Eng,UK
111/N7 Saint-Constant, Qu,Can
107/K4 Saint Croix (riv.), Mn, Wi,US
101/H4 Saint Croix (isl.), USVI
114/M3 Saint Cyr (mtn.), Yk,Can
31/S10 Saint-Cyr-l'École, Fr.
31/S11 Saint-Cyr-sous-Dourdan, Fr.
34/A3 Saint David's, Wal,UK
34/A3 Saint David's Head (pt.), Wal,UK
31/T10 Saint-Denis, Fr.
89/R15 Saint-Denis (cap.), Reun.
45/G2 Saint-Dié, Fr.
44/F2 Saint-Dizier, Fr.
44/E3 Saint-Doulchard, Fr.
110/F2 Sainte-Agathe-des-Monts, Qu,Can
111/H1 Sainte-Anne-des-Monts, Qu,Can
111/N6 Sainte-Anne-des-Plaines, Qu,Can
111/G2 Sainte-Foy, Qu,Can
109/K3 Sainte Genevieve, Mo,US
31/T11 Sainte-Geneviève-des-Bois, Fr.
111/P6 Sainte-Julie-de-Verchères, Qu,Can
111/J2 Saint Eleanors, PE,Can
114/K3 Saint Elias (mts.), Can., US
114/K4 Saint Elias (cape), Ak,US
114/K3 Saint Elias (mt.), Ak,US
114/K3 Saint Elias-Wrangell Nat'l Park and Prsv., Ak,US
111/H1 Sainte-Marguerite (riv.), Qu,Can
111/G2 Sainte-Marie, Qu,Can
89/J7 Sainte Marie, Nosy (isl.), Madg.
45/G5 Sainte-Maxime, Fr.
42/C5 Sainte-Erme-Outre-et-Ramecourt, Fr.
107/J3 Sainte Rose du Lac, Mb,Can
44/C4 Saintes, Fr.
111/M6 Sainte-Scholastique, Qu,Can
44/E5 Saint-Estève, Fr.
111/N6 Sainte-Thérèse, Qu,Can
44/F4 Saint-Étienne, Fr.
44/D2 Saint-Étienne-du-Rouvray, Fr.
111/N6 Saint-Eustache, Qu,Can
31/T11 Saint-Fargeau-Ponthierry, Fr.
111/F1 Saint-Félicien, Qu,Can
32/C3 Saintfield, NI,UK
44/E2 Saint-Florentin, Fr.
44/E3 Saint-Florent-sur-Cher, Fr.
83/K6 Saint-Floris Nat'l Park, CAfr.
44/E4 Saint-Flour, Fr.
88/D4 Saint Francis (cape), SAfr.
109/K4 Saint Francis (riv.), Ar, Mo,US
109/G3 Saint Francis, Ks,US
116/Q14 Saint Francis, Wi,US
113/F4 Saint Francisville, La,US
113/F2 Saint Francois (mts.), Mo,US
44/D5 Saint-Gaudens, Fr.
111/H2 Saint George, Nb,Can
111/K1 Saint George (cape), Nf,Can
114/E4 Saint George (isl.), Ak,US
108/A2 Saint George (pt.), Ca,US
113/H3 Saint George, SC,US
108/D3 Saint George, Ut,US
111/K1 Saint George's, Nf,Can
111/J2 Saint Georges (bay), NS,Can
111/G2 Saint-Georges, Qu,Can
101/J5 Saint George's (cap.), Gren.
32/C6 Saint George's (chan.), Ire., UK
31/S10 Saint-Germain-en-Laye, Fr.
31/T11 Saint-Germain-lès-Corbeil, Fr.
31/U10 Saint-Germain-sur-Morin, Fr.
42/A5 Saint-Germer-de-Fly, Fr.
42/C3 Saint-Ghislain, Belg.
44/F5 Saint-Gilles, Fr.
44/C3 Saint-Gilles-Croix-de-Vie, Fr.
44/D5 Saint-Girons, Fr.
34/B3 Saint Govan's Head (pt.), Wal,UK
31/S10 Saint-Gratien, Fr.
76/F6 Saint Helena (isl.), Austl.
88/B4 Saint Helena (bay), SAfr.
80/B6 Saint Helena (isl.), UK
116/J9 Saint Helena (mtn.), Ca,US
77/D4 Saint Helens (pt.), Austl.
33/F5 Saint Helens, Eng,UK
106/C4 Saint Helens, Or,US
106/C4 Saint Helens, Mount (vol.), Wa,US
44/B2 Saint Helier, Chl,UK
44/C3 Saint-Herblain, Fr.
111/M6 Saint-Hermas, Qu,Can
70/E3 Sainthia, India
111/G1 Saint-Honoré, Qu,Can
111/P7 Saint-Hubert, Qu,Can
111/F2 Saint-Hyacinthe, Qu,Can
110/C1 Saint Ignace (isl.), On,Can
110/C2 Saint Ignace, Mi,US
76/H8 Saint Ives, Austl.
34/A6 Saint Ives, Eng,UK
35/F2 Saint Ives, Eng,UK
111/P7 Saint-Jacques-le-Mineur, Qu,Can
102/C3 Saint James (cape), BC,Can
107/K5 Saint James, Mn,US
115/G5 Saint James, NY,US
111/G1 Saint-Jean (lake), Qu,Can
111/H1 Saint-Jean (riv.), Qu,Can
44/C4 Saint-Jean-d'Angély, Fr.
44/D3 Saint-Jean-de-la-Ruelle, Fr.
44/C5 Saint-Jean-de-Luz, Fr.
111/G2 Saint-Jean-Port-Joli, Qu,Can
111/F2 Saint-Jean-sur-Richelieu, Qu,Can
111/N6 Saint-Jérôme, Qu,Can
106/D4 Saint Joe (riv.), Id,US
111/H2 Saint John, NB,Can
111/H2 Saint John (riv.), Can., US
44/B2 Saint John, Chl,UK
101/J4 Saint John's (cap.), Anti.
32/C3 Saint John's (pt.), IM,UK
108/E4 Saint Johns, Az,US
105/K6 Saint Johns (riv.), Fl,US
111/F2 Saint Johnsbury, Vt,US
110/B1 Saint Joseph (lake), On,Can
89/R15 Saint-Joseph, Reun.
110/C2 Saint Joseph (isl.), Mi,US
110/C3 Saint Joseph (riv.), Mi,US
109/J3 Saint Joseph, Mo,US
44/E5 Saint-Juéry, Fr.
44/D4 Saint-Junien, Fr.
34/A6 Saint Just, Eng,UK
34/A6 Saint Just in Roseland, Eng,UK
77/F5 Saint Kilda, Austl.
36/A2 Saint Kilda (isl.), Sc,UK
101/J4 Saint Kitts and Nevis
111/P6 Saint-Lambert, Qu,Can
107/J3 Saint Laurent, Mb,Can
111/N6 Saint-Laurent, Qu,Can
42/B3 Saint-Laurent-Blangy, Fr.
93/H2 Saint-Laurent du Maroni, FrG.
111/J1 Saint Lawrence (gulf), Can.
111/L2 Saint Lawrence, Nf,Can
111/G1 Saint Lawrence (riv.), Can., US
114/D3 Saint Lawrence (isl.), Ak,US
110/E2 Saint Lawrence Islands Nat'l Park, Can.
111/M7 Saint-Lazare, Qu,Can
77/G5 Saint Leonard (mtn.), Austl.
111/N6 Saint-Léonard, Qu,Can
89/R15 Saint-Leu, Reun.
31/S9 Saint-Leu-la-Forêt, Fr.
44/C2 Saint-Lô, Fr.
111/N7 Saint Louis (lake), Qu,Can
107/G2 Saint Louis, Sk,Can
89/R15 Saint-Louis, Reun.
84/A2 Saint-Louis, Sen.
84/B3 Saint-Louis (reg.), Sen.
106/A2 Saint Louis (riv.), Mn,US
109/K3 Saint Louis, Mo,US
111/H2 Saint-Louis-de-Kent, NB,Can
101/G4 Saint-Louis du Nord, Haiti
111/P7 Saint-Luc, Qu,Can
101/J5 Saint Lucia
89/F3 Saint Lucia, Lake (lag.), SAfr.
44/C3 Saint-Maixent-l'École, Fr.
107/J3 Saint Malo, Mb,Can
44/B2 Saint-Malo, Fr.
44/B2 Saint-Malo (gulf), Fr.
31/T10 Saint-Mandé, Fr.
44/F5 Saint-Mandrier-sur-Mer, Fr.
31/U9 Saint-Mard, Fr.
35/H4 Saint Margaret's at Cliffe, Eng,UK
106/D4 Saint Maries, Id,US
107/J3 Saint Martin (lake), Mb,Can
101/J4 Saint-Martin (isl.), Fr.
42/A2 Saint-Martin-Boulogne, Fr.
42/C6 Saint-Martin-d'Ablois, Fr.
44/F4 Saint-Martin-d'Hères, Fr.
31/T9 Saint-Martin-du-Tertre, Fr.
84/A3 Saint Mary (cape), Gam.
76/G8 Saint Marys, Austl.
110/D3 Saint Mary's, Nf,Can
111/J2 Saint Marys (riv.), NS,Can
114/F3 Saint Marys, Ak,US
113/H4 Saint Marys, Ga,US
110/E3 Saint Marys, Pa,US
111/N7 Saint-Mathieu, Qu,Can
114/D3 Saint Matthew (isl.), Ak,US
113/H3 Saint Matthews, SC,US
78/E5 Saint Matthias (isls.), PNG
31/T10 Saint-Maur-des-Fossés, Fr.
110/F1 Saint-Maurice (riv.), Qu,Can
34/A6 Saint Mawes, Eng,UK
43/F6 Saint-Max, Fr.
34/C3 Saint Mellons, Wal,UK
42/D6 Saint-Memmie, Fr.
31/S11 Saint-Michel-sur-Orge, Fr.
44/B3 Saint-Nazaire, Fr.
35/F2 Saint Neots, Eng,UK
43/E2 Saint-Nicolas, Belg.
31/S10 Saint-Nom-la-Bretèche, Fr.
42/B2 Saint-Omer, Fr.
42/A4 Saint-Omer-en-Chaussée, Fr.
31/S9 Saint-Ouen-l'Aumône, Fr.
111/G2 Saint-Pamphile, Qu,Can
111/G2 Saint-Pascal, Qu,Can
31/U9 Saint-Pathus, Fr.
28/H5 Saint Paul (isls.), Braz.
106/F2 Saint Paul, Ab,Can
29/N7 Saint Paul (isl.), FrAnt.
85/F5 Saint Paul (cape), Gha.
84/C5 Saint Paul (riv.), Gui., Libr.
89/R15 Saint-Paul, Reun.
114/E4 Saint Paul (isl.), Ak,US
109/J3 Saint Paul, Ks,US
107/K4 Saint Paul (cap.), Mn,US
44/C5 Saint-Paul-lès-Dax, Fr.
76/B1 Saint Pauls (peak), Austl.
44/F4 Saint-Paul-Trois-Châteaux, Fr.
107/K4 Saint Peter, Mn,US
93/M3 Saint Peter and Saint Paul (rocks), Braz.
44/B2 Saint Peter Port, Chl,UK
35/H4 Saint Peter's, Eng,UK
53/V7 Saint Petersburg (inset), Rus.
113/H5 Saint Petersburg, Fl,US
52/F4 Saint Petersburg (Leningrad), Rus.
52/G3 Saint Petersburg Obl., Rus.
111/P7 Saint-Philippe-de-La Prairie, Qu,Can
101/J5 Saint-Pierre, Mart.
89/R15 Saint-Pierre, Reun.
111/K2 Saint Pierre & Miquelon (dpcy.), Fr
44/D3 Saint-Pierre-des-Corps, Fr.
44/C5 Saint-Pierre-du-Mont, Fr.
31/T11 Saint-Pierre-du-Perray, Fr.
107/J3 Saint Pierre-Jolys, Mb,Can
44/B2 Saint-Pol-de-Léon, Fr.
42/B1 Saint-Pol-sur-Mer, Fr.
44/E5 Saint-Pons (mtn.), Fr.
31/S9 Saint-Prix, Fr.
42/C4 Saint-Quentin, Fr.
45/G5 Saint-Raphaël, Fr.
44/F5 Saint-Rémy-de-Provence, Fr.
31/S10 Saint-Rémy-lès-Chevreuse, Fr.
42/A3 Saint-Riquier, Fr.
44/B2 Saint Sampson's, Chl,UK
42/C3 Saint-Saulve, Fr.
113/H4 Saint Simons Island, Ga,US

157
Saint – Santo

31/U9 Saint-Soupplets, Fr.
111/H2 Saint Stephen, NB,Can
34/B6 Saint Stephen in Brannel, Eng,UK
110/D3 Saint Thomas, On,Can
101/H4 Saint Thomas (isl.), USVI
111/N7 Saint-Urbain-Premier, Qu,Can
44/F3 Saint-Vallier, Fr.
42/B2 Saint-Venant, Fr.
74/F6 Saint Vincent (gulf), Austl.
77/C4 Saint Vincent (pt.), Austl.
101/J5 Saint Vincent & the Grenadines
43/F3 Saint Vith, Belg.
31/T11 Saint-Vrain, Fr.
106/F2 Saint Walburg, Sk,Can
31/T9 Saint-Witz, Fr.
70/D2 Sāipal (mtn.), Nepal
78/D3 Saipan (isl.), NMar.
65/F2 Saitama (pref.), Japan
64/B4 Saito, Japan
69/B3 Sai Yok Nat'l Park, Thai.
92/E7 Sajama Nat'l Park, Bol.
50/E1 Sajószentpéter, Hun.
88/C3 Sak (riv.), SAfr.
65/H7 Sakado, Japan
65/J7 Sakae, Japan
65/M9 Sakahogi, Japan
65/F2 Sakai, Japan
64/C3 Sakaide, Japan
64/C3 Sakaiminato, Japan
107/H3 Sakakawea (lake), ND,US
103/J3 Sakami (lake), Qu,Can
51/K5 Sakarya (prov.), Turk.
59/B2 Sakarya (riv.), Turk.
63/M4 Sakata, Japan
64/C4 Sakawa, Japan
57/Q4 Sakhalin (gulf), Rus.
57/Q4 Sakhalin (isl.), Rus.
60/F1 Sakht Sar (Ramsar), Iran
54/E3 Saki, Ukr.
67/D3 Sakishima (isls.), Japan
55/L1 Sakmara (riv.), Rus.
69/D2 Sakon Nakhon, Thai.
61/J3 Sakrand, Pak.
65/F2 Saku, Japan
65/J7 Sakura, Japan
65/L10 Sakurai, Japan
80/K10 Sal (isl.), CpV.
55/G3 Sal (riv.), Rus.
39/J4 Šal'a, Slvk.
37/F4 Sala, Swe.
48/D2 Sala Consilina, It.
91/E2 Saladas, Arg.
96/F2 Saladillo, Arg.
96/D3 Salado (riv.), Arg.
96/F2 Salado (riv.), Arg.
100/B2 Salado (riv.), Mex.
90/C5 Salado del Norte (riv.), Arg.
85/E4 Salaga, Gha.
73/G4 Salahatu (mtn.), Indo.
50/F2 Sălaj (co.), Rom.
82/J5 Salal, Chad
86/D4 Şalālah, Sudan
96/D5 Salamanca (plain), Arg.
96/C1 Salamanca, Chile
100/A3 Salamanca, Mex.
46/C2 Salamanca, Sp.
110/E3 Salamanca, NY,US
83/J6 Salamat (riv.), Chad
49/H3 Salamís, Gre.
49/L7 Salamís (isl.), Gre.
59/L4 Salamīyah, Syria
69/C1 Sala Mok, Laos
46/B1 Salas, Sp.
55/K1 Salavat, Rus.
78/B5 Salayar (isl.), Indo.
28/D7 Sala y Gomez (isls.), Chile
44/E3 Salbris, Fr.
34/C6 Salcombe, Eng,UK
77/C3 Sale, Austl.
81/L13 Salé, Mor.
33/F5 Sale, Eng,UK
73/G3 Salebabu (isl.), Indo.
56/G3 Salekhard, Rus.
70/C5 Salem, India
110/C4 Salem, In,US
109/K3 Salem, Mo,US
111/G3 Salem, NH,US
106/C4 Salem (cap.), Or,US
110/D4 Salem, Va,US
48/C4 Salemi, It.
48/F2 Salentina (pen.), It.
48/D2 Salerno, It.
48/D2 Salerno (gulf), It.
35/G3 Sales (pt.), UK
33/F5 Salford, Eng,UK
50/D1 Salgótarján, Hun.
94/C3 Salgueiro, Braz.
109/F3 Salida, Co,US
59/B2 Salihli, Turk.
87/F3 Salima, Malw.
86/B4 Salīmah (oasis), Sudan
46/B1 Salime (res.), Sp.
101/G3 Salina (pt.), Bahm.
48/D3 Salina (isl.), It.
109/H3 Salina, Ks,US
108/E3 Salina, Ut,US
100/B4 Salina Cruz, Mex.
94/B5 Salinas, Braz.
100/A3 Salinas, Mex.
108/B3 Salinas, Ca,US
108/B3 Salinas (riv.), Ca,US
47/G3 Salinas, Cabo de (cape), Sp.
109/F4 Salinas Nat'l Mon., NM,US
48/D2 Saline (marsh), It.
109/J4 Saline (riv.), Ar,US
109/G3 Saline (riv.), Ks,US
93/J4 Salinópolis, Braz.
103/J2 Salisbury (isl.), NW,Can
35/E4 Salisbury, Eng,UK
34/D4 Salisbury (plain), Eng,UK
110/F4 Salisbury, Md,US
113/H3 Salisbury, NC,US
94/B3 Salitre (riv.), Braz.
37/J2 Salla, Fin.
45/G4 Sallanches, Fr.
40/D4 Salland (reg.), Neth.
84/B4 Sallatouk (pt.), Gui.
42/B3 Sallaumines, Fr.
47/F2 Sallent, Sp.
109/J4 Sallisaw, Ok,US
86/D5 Sallūm, Sudan
70/D2 Sallyāna, Nepal
32/B5 Sally Gap (pass), Ire.
43/F3 Salm (riv.), Ger.
59/F2 Salmās, Iran
106/D4 Salmon (riv.), Id,US
106/D3 Salmon Arm, BC,Can
108/D2 Salmon Falls (riv.), Id, Nv,US
106/E4 Salmon River (mts.), Id,US
37/G3 Salo, Fin.
44/F3 Salon (riv.), Fr.
44/F5 Salon-de-Provence, Fr.
83/K8 Salonga Nat'l Park, Zaire
49/H3 Salonika (Thermaic) (gulf), Gre.
49/H2 Salonika (Thessaloníki), Gre.
50/E2 Salonta, Rom.
46/B3 Salor (riv.), Sp.
84/B3 Saloum, Vallée du (wadi), Sen.
55/G3 Sal'sk, Rus.
48/C4 Salso (riv.), It.
88/C3 Salt (riv.), SAfr.
108/E4 Salt (riv.), Az,US
91/C1 Salta, Arg.
34/B6 Saltash, Eng,UK
33/H2 Saltburn, Eng,UK
36/B4 Saltee (isls.), Ire.
37/E2 Saltfjorden (fjord), Nor.
34/D4 Saltford, Eng,UK
113/H4 Saltilla (riv.), Ga,US
100/A2 Saltillo, Mex.
108/E2 Salt Lake City (cap.), Ut,US
96/E2 Salto, Arg.
95/C2 Salto, Braz.
48/C1 Salto (riv.), It.
91/E3 Salto, Uru.
97/F1 Salto (dept.), Uru.
91/E3 Salto Grande (res.), Arg., Uru.
108/C4 Salton Sea (lake), Ca,US
95/A3 Salto Santiago (res.), Braz.
113/H3 Saluda (riv.), SC,US
67/D6 Salug, Phil.
70/D4 Sālūr, India
93/H2 Salut (isls.), FrG.
45/G4 Saluzzo, It.
97/J7 Salvación (bay), Chile
94/C4 Salvador, Braz.
46/A3 Salvaterra de Magos, Port.
46/A1 Salvatierra de Miño, Sp.
58/J8 Salween (riv.), Asia
55/J5 Sal'yany, Azer.
110/D4 Salyersville, Ky,US
39/H5 Salza (riv.), Aus.
41/E4 Salzbergen, Ger.
45/K3 Salzburg, Aus.
45/K3 Salzburg (prov.), Aus.
41/H4 Salzgitter, Ger.
41/G4 Salzhemmendorf, Ger.
41/F5 Salzkotten, Ger.
38/F2 Salzwedel, Ger.
46/C1 Sama, Sp.
72/C4 Samak (cape), Indo.
73/F2 Samales (isls.), Phil.
70/D4 Sāmalkot, India
86/B2 Samālūt, Egypt
101/H4 Samaná (cape), DRep.
59/C3 Samandağı, Turk.
59/H6 Samannūd, Egypt
67/E5 Samar (isl.), Phil.
55/J1 Samara, Rus.
55/K1 Samara (riv.), Rus.
55/J1 Samara Obl., Rus.
63/M2 Samarga (riv.), Rus.
59/N8 Samaria (reg.), WBnk.
59/N8 Samaria Nat'l Park, WBnk.
49/H5 Samarias Gorge Nat'l Park, Gre.
73/E4 Samarinda, Indo.
56/G6 Samarkand, Uzb.
60/D2 Sāmarrā', Iraq
61/K3 Samasata, Pak.
70/D3 Sambalpur, India
87/C2 Samba Lucala, Ang.
89/H7 Sambao (riv.), Madg.
72/D4 Sambar (cape), Indo.
72/C3 Sambas, Indo.
89/J6 Sambava, Madg.
54/B2 Sambor, Ukr.
97/F2 Samborombón (bay), Arg.
69/D3 Sambor Prei Kuk (ruins), Camb.
42/C3 Sambre (riv.), Belg.,Fr.
42/C4 Sambre à l'Oise, Canal de (can.), Fr.
64/A2 Samch'ŏk, SKor.
87/G1 Same, Tanz.
69/C4 Samit (cape), Camb.
69/C3 Samkos (peak), Camb.
116/C2 Sammamish (lake), Wa,US
64/A3 Samnangjin, SKor.
50/B3 Samobor, Cro.
51/F4 Samokov, Bul.
47/Q10 Samora Correia, Port.
59/A3 Sámos, Gre.
49/J2 Samothráki (isl.), Gre.
96/D2 Sampacho, Arg.
72/D4 Sampit, Indo.
72/D4 Sampit (riv.), Indo.
112/E4 Sam Rayburn (res.), Tx,US
69/C1 Sam Sao (mts.), Laos, Viet.
76/E6 Samson (mtn.), Austl.
69/D2 Sam Son, Viet.
76/E6 Samsonvale (lake), Austl.
59/D2 Samsun, Turk.
69/B4 Samui (isl.), Thai.
65/H7 Samukawa, Japan
55/J4 Samur (riv.), Azer., Rus.
69/C3 Samut Prakan, Thai.
69/C3 Samut Sakhon, Thai.
69/C3 Samut Songkhram, Thai.
69/D3 San (riv.), Camb.
63/H5 San (riv.), China
84/D3 San, Mali
39/M3 San (riv.), Pol.
50/C3 Sana (riv.), Bosn.
46/A1 San Adrián, Cabo de (cape), Sp.
80/D4 Sanaga (riv.), Afr.
67/E6 San Agustin (cape), Phil.
47/N8 San Agustin de Guadalix, Sp.
114/F5 Sanak (isl.), Ak,US
73/G4 Sanama (isl.), Indo.
90/B5 San Ambrosio (isl.), Chile
60/E1 Sanandaj, Iran
116/K11 San Andreas (lake), Ca,US
100/E5 San Andrés, Col.
100/E5 San Andrés (isl.), Col.
108/F4 San Andres (mts.), NM,US
97/S12 San Andrés de Giles, Arg.
46/C1 San Andrés del Rabanedo, Sp.
100/B4 San Andrés Tuxtla, Mex.
112/C4 San Angelo, Tx,US
116/J11 San Anselmo, Ca,US
97/F3 San Antonio (cape), Arg.
96/C2 San Antonio, Chile
101/M9 San Antonio, Mex.
115/C2 San Antonio (mt.), Ca,US
108/F4 San Antonio, NM,US
112/D4 San Antonio, Tx,US
112/D4 San Antonio (riv.), Tx,US
47/F3 San Antonio Abad, Sp.
96/F2 San Antonio de Areco, Arg.
101/J5 San Antonio del Golfo, Ven.
96/D4 San Antonio Oeste, Arg.
112/E4 San Augustine, Tx,US
70/C3 Sānāwad, India
48/D2 San Bartolomeo in Galdo, It.
48/C1 San Benedetto del Tronto, It.
115/C2 San Bernardino, Ca,US
115/C2 San Bernardino (mts.), Ca,US
96/C2 San Bernardo, Chile
101/F6 San Bernardo (pt.), Col.
101/N8 San Blas, Mex.
113/G4 San Blas (cape), Fl,US
112/E3 San Bois (mts.), Ok,US
45/J4 San Bonifacio, It.
92/E6 San Borja, Bol.
111/S9 Sanborn, NY,US
116/K11 San Bruno, Ca,US
100/A2 San Buenaventura, Mex.
115/A2 San Buenaventura (Ventura), Ca,US
96/C3 San Carlos, Chile
100/A2 San Carlos, Mex.
100/E5 San Carlos, Nic.
67/D4 San Carlos, Phil.
97/G2 San Carlos, Uru.
108/E4 San Carlos (lake), Az,US
116/K11 San Carlos, Ca,US
101/H6 San Carlos, Ven.
96/C4 San Carlos de Bariloche, Arg.
101/G6 San Carlos del Zulia, Ven.
49/F2 San Cataldo, It.
96/C2 San Clemente, Chile
46/D3 San Clemente, Sp.
108/C4 San Clemente (isl.), Ca,US
91/D3 San Cristóbal, Arg.
100/E3 San Cristóbal, Cuba
100/D5 San Cristobal (vol.), Nic.
78/F6 San Cristobal (isl.), Sol.
92/D2 San Cristóbal, Ven.
100/C4 San Cristóbal de las Casas, Mex.
101/F3 Sancti Spíritus, Cuba
106/F2 Sand (riv.), Ab,Can
88/D3 Sand (riv.), SAfr.
109/G2 Sand (hills), Ne,US
64/D3 Sanda, Japan
32/C1 Sanda (isl.), Sc,UK
69/D3 Sandan, Camb.
51/F5 Sandanski, Bul.
33/F5 Sandbach, Eng,UK
41/F2 Sande, Ger.
37/D4 Sandefjord, Nor.
98/Q Sanders (coast), Ant.
112/C4 Sanderson, Tx,US
113/H3 Sandersville, Ga,US
76/F6 Sandgate, Austl.
32/D2 Sandhead, Sc,UK
111/Q8 Sandhill, On,Can
35/F4 Sandhurst, Eng,UK
97/L8 San Diego (cape), Arg.
108/C4 San Diego, Ca,US
112/D5 San Diego, Tx,US
59/B2 Sandıklı, Turk.
115/C2 San Dimas, Ca,US
48/D4 San Dimitri, Ras (pt.), Malta
100/E3 Sandino, Cuba
73/E3 Sandkan, Malay.
37/C4 Sandnes, Nor.
37/E2 Sandnessjøen, Nor.
87/D2 Sandoa, Zaire
39/L3 Sandomierz, Pol.
45/K4 San Donà di Piave, It.
84/B3 Sandougou (riv.), Gam., Sen.
35/E5 Sandown, Eng,UK
106/D3 Sandpoint, Id,US
77/F5 Sandringham, Austl.
35/G1 Sandringham, Eng,UK
110/D3 Sandusky, Mi,US
110/D3 Sandusky, Oh,US
37/D4 Sandvika, Nor.
37/F3 Sandviken, Swe.
76/B2 Sandwich (cape), Austl.
35/H4 Sandwich, Eng,UK
76/D4 Sandy (cape), Austl.
107/K2 Sandy (lake), On,Can
35/F2 Sandy, Eng,UK
108/E2 Sandy, Ut,US
107/H2 Sandy Bay, Sk,Can
115/F5 Sandy Hook (bay), NJ,US
113/G3 Sandy Springs, Ga,US
43/E4 Sanem, Lux.
48/C2 San Felice Circeo, It.
96/C2 San Felipe, Chile
101/M7 San Felipe, Mex.
92/E1 San Felipe, Ven.
90/A5 San Félix (isl.), Chile
97/S12 San Fernando, Arg.
96/C2 San Fernando, Chile
100/B3 San Fernando, Mex.
67/D4 San Fernando, Phil.
46/B4 San Fernando, Sp.
115/B2 San Fernando, Ca,US
101/H6 San Fernando de Apure, Ven.
47/N9 San Fernando-de-Henares, Sp.
37/E3 Sånfjällets Nat'l Park, Swe.
114/K3 Sanford (mtn.), Ak,US
113/H4 Sanford, Fl,US
111/G3 Sanford, Me,US
113/J3 Sanford, NC,US
91/D3 San Francisco, Arg.
101/M7 San Francisco, Mex.
67/E6 San Francisco, Phil.
108/E4 San Francisco (riv.), Az, NM,US
116/K11 San Francisco, Ca,US
116/K11 San Francisco (bay), Ca,US
101/G5 San Francisco, Ven.
100/D5 San Francisco de la Paz, Hon.
101/N8 San Francisco del Oro, Mex.
101/G4 San Francisco de Macorís, DRep.
96/C2 San Francisco de Mostazal, Chile
115/B2 San Gabriel, Ca,US
115/B2 San Gabriel (mts.), Ca,US
115/C2 San Gabriel (riv.), Ca,US
70/B4 Sangamner, India
110/B3 Sangamon (riv.), Il,US
61/H2 Sangān (mtn.), Afg.
92/C4 Sangay Nat'l Park, Ecu.
46/A1 Sangenjo, Sp.
66/C2 Sanggan (riv.), China
72/D3 Sanggau, Indo.
82/J7 Sangha (riv.), CAfr., Congo
61/J3 Sanghar, Pak.
73/F3 Sangihe (isls.), Indo.
92/D2 San Gil, Col.
48/E2 San Giorgio Ionico, It.
48/C4 San Giovanni Gemini, It.
48/E3 San Giovanni in Fiore, It.
45/J4 San Giovanni in Persiceto, It.
62/D2 Sangiyn Dalay (lake), Mong.
64/A2 Sangju, SKor.
73/E3 Sangkulirang, Indo.
70/B4 Sāngli, India
82/H7 Sangmélima, Camr.
65/L10 Sangō, Japan
108/C4 San Gorgonio (peak), Ca,US
109/F3 Sangre de Cristo (mts.), Co, NM,US
101/J5 Sangre Grande, Trin.
48/D2 Sangro (riv.), It.
92/G6 Sangue (riv.), Braz.
85/E4 Sanguie (prov.), Burk.
101/M8 San Hipólito (pt.), Mex.
88/E3 Sani (pass), SAfr.
100/D4 San Ignacio, Belz.
92/E6 San Ignacio, Bol.
92/F7 San Ignacio, Bol.
96/B3 San Ignacio, Chile
101/M8 San Ignacio, Mex.
101/N9 San Ignacio, Mex.
64/D3 San'in Kaigin Nat'l Park, Japan
101/F6 San Jacinto, Col.
115/C3 San Jacinto (riv.), Ca,US
96/C2 San Javier, Chile
47/E4 San Javier, Sp.
65/F2 Sanjō, Japan
92/F6 San Joaquín, Bol.
108/B3 San Joaquin (val.), Ca,US
96/E1 San Jorge, Arg.
96/D5 San Jorge (cape), Arg.
96/D5 San Jorge (gulf), Arg.
101/M7 San Jorge (bay), Mex.
47/F2 San Jorge (gulf), Sp.
96/D4 San José (gulf), Arg.
100/D4 San Jose, Belz.
100/E6 San José (cap.), CR
101/M8 San José (isl.), Mex.
67/D4 San Jose, Phil.
47/F3 San José, Sp.
97/F2 San José (dept.), Uru.
97/T11 San José (riv.), Uru.
116/L12 San Jose, Ca,US
101/G5 San José, Ven.
101/J6 San José de Amacuro, Ven.
67/D5 San Jose de Buenavista, Phil.
92/F7 San José de Chiquitos, Bol.
101/M8 San José de Gracia, Mex.
101/J6 San José de Guanipa, Ven.
101/H6 San José de Guaribe, Ven.
91/C3 San José de Jáchal, Arg.
101/N9 San José del Cabo, Mex.
96/Q9 San José de Maipo, Chile
97/F2 San José de Mayo, Uru.
101/M8 San José de Pimas, Mex.
96/C1 San Juan, Arg.
97/M8 San Juan (cape), Arg.
96/C1 San Juan (prov.), Arg.
91/C3 San Juan (riv.), Arg.
100/E5 San Juan (riv.), CR, Nic.
101/G4 San Juan, DRep.
101/H4 San Juan (cap.), PR
108/F3 San Juan (mts.), Co,US
108/E3 San Juan (riv.), Co, Ut,US
112/A2 San Juan (basin), NM,US
91/E2 San Juan Bautista, Par.
47/E3 San Juan de Alicante, Sp.
46/B4 San Juan de Aznalfarache, Sp.
101/P10 San Juan de Lima (pt.), Mex.
100/E5 San Juan del Norte, Nic.
101/P9 San Juan de los Lagos, Mex.
101/H6 San Juan de los Morros, Ven.
97/K7 San Julián, Gran Bajo de (val.), Arg.
91/D3 San Justo, Arg.
84/C4 Sankanbiriwa (peak), SLeo.
84/C4 Sankoroni (riv.), Gui., Mali
45/L3 Sankt Andrä, Aus.
43/G2 Sankt Augustin, Ger.
45/H3 Sankt Gallen, Swi.
43/G5 Sankt Ingbert, Ger.
45/K3 Sankt Johann im Pongau, Aus.
45/K3 Sankt Johann in Tirol, Aus.
45/L2 Sankt Pölten, Aus.
45/L3 Sankt Veit an der Glan, Aus.
43/G5 Sankt Wendel, Ger.
101/M9 San Lázaro (cape), Mex.
116/K11 San Leandro, Ca,US
92/E6 San Lorenzo, Bol.
97/J6 San Lorenzo (peak), Chile
92/C3 San Lorenzo, Ecu.
92/B4 San Lorenzo (cape), Ecu.
48/A3 San Lorenzo (cape), It.
101/N8 San Lorenzo, Mex.
116/K11 San Lorenzo, Ca,US
46/C2 San Lorenzo de El Escorial, Sp.
46/B4 Sanlúcar de Barrameda, Sp.
101/N9 San Lucas, Mex.
101/N9 San Lucas (cape), Mex.
96/D2 San Luis, Arg.
96/D2 San Luis (mts.), Arg.
96/D2 San Luis (prov.), Arg.
101/F3 San Luis, Cuba
100/D4 San Luis, Guat.
112/B2 San Luis (val.), Co,US
108/B4 San Luis Obispo, Ca,US
100/A3 San Luis Potosi, Mex.
100/A3 San Luis Potosí (state), Mex.
101/M7 San Luis Río Colorado, Mex.
108/E4 San Manuel, Az,US
101/F6 San Marcos, Col.
100/B4 San Marcos, Mex.
112/D4 San Marcos, Tx,US
67/D4 San Mariano, Phil.
45/K5 San Marino
45/K5 San Marino (cap.), SMar.
96/C2 San Martín, Arg.
97/J7 San Martín (lake), Arg.
92/F6 San Martín (riv.), Bol.
96/C4 San Martín de los Andes, Arg.
85/E3 Sanmatenga (prov.), Burk.
116/K11 San Mateo, Ca,US
112/B3 San Mateo (mts.), NM,US
96/D4 San Matías (gulf), Arg.
92/G7 San Matías, Bol.
66/B4 Sanmenxia, China
92/F6 San Miguel (riv.), Bol.
100/D5 San Miguel, ESal.
100/A3 San Miguel de Allende, Mex.
96/F2 San Miguel del Monte, Arg.
91/C2 San Miguel de Tucumán, Arg.
67/C2 Sanming, China
65/L9 Sannan, Japan
83/M5 Sannār, Sudan
48/D2 Sannicandro Garganico, It.
108/C4 San Nicolas (isl.), Ca,US
96/E2 San Nicolás de los Arroyos, Arg.
100/A2 San Nicolás de los Garzas, Mex.
57/P2 Sannikova (str.), Rus.
31/S10 Sannois, Fr.
65/F2 Sano, Japan
39/M4 Sanok, Pol.
96/B4 San Pablo, Chile
67/D5 San Pablo, Phil.
116/K11 San Pablo, Ca,US
116/K10 San Pablo (bay), Ca,US
96/F2 San Pedro, Arg.
100/D4 San Pedro, Belz.
96/C2 San Pedro, Chile
91/C1 San Pedro (vol.), Chile
84/D5 San Pédro, IvC.
91/E1 San Pedro, Par.
46/B3 San Pedro (range), Sp.
108/E4 San Pedro (riv.), Az,US
115/B3 San Pedro (bay), Ca,US
100/C4 San Pedro Carchá, Guat.
100/A2 San Pedro de las Colinas, Mex.
92/C5 San Pedro de Lloc, Peru
47/E4 San Pedro del Pinatar, Sp.
101/H4 San Pedro de Macorís, DRep.
100/B4 San Pedro Pochutla, Mex.
100/D4 San Pedro Sula, Hon.
48/A3 San Pietro (isl.), It.
32/E1 Sanquhar, Sc,UK
92/C3 Sanquianga Nat'l Park, Col.
101/L7 San Quintín, Mex.
101/L7 San Quintín (cape), Mex.
96/C2 San Rafael, Arg.
116/J11 San Rafael, Ca,US
108/E3 San Rafael (riv.), Ut,US
101/G5 San Rafael, Ven.
97/G2 San Ramón, Uru.
116/L11 San Ramon, Ca,US
91/D1 San Ramón de la Nueva Orán, Arg.
45/G5 San Remo, It.
46/C4 San Roque, Sp.
96/B3 San Rosendo, Chile
112/D4 San Saba, Tx,US
109/H5 San Saba (riv.), Tx,US
100/D5 San Salvador (cap.), ESal.
97/S11 San Salvador (riv.), Uru.
91/C1 San Salvador de Jujuy, Arg.
101/G3 San Salvador (Watling) (isl.), Bahm.
48/D1 San Salvo, It.
46/E1 San Sebastián, Sp.
46/D2 San Sebastián de los Reyes, Sp.
45/J4 San Sebastiano, It.
48/D2 San Severo, It.
62/F2 Sant, Mong.
100/D5 Santa Ana, ESal.
101/M7 Santa Ana, Mex.
115/C3 Santa Ana, Ca,US
115/C3 Santa Ana (mts.), Ca,US
101/H5 Santa Ana, Ven.
95/D1 Santa Bárbara, Braz.
96/B3 Santa Bárbara, Chile
100/D5 Santa Bárbara, Hon.
101/N8 Santa Bárbara, Mex.
115/A2 Santa Barbara, Ca,US
115/A2 Santa Barbara (chan.), Ca,US
92/E3 Santa Bárbara, Ven.
95/C2 Santa Bárbara d'Oeste, Braz.
67/D6 Santa Catalina, Phil.
108/C4 Santa Catalina (gulf), Ca,US
108/C4 Santa Catalina (isl.), Ca,US
95/B3 Santa Catarina (isl.), Braz.
95/B3 Santa Catarina (state), Braz.
95/B3 Santa Cecília, Braz.
101/F3 Santa Clara, Cuba
46/A4 Santa Clara (res.), Port.
116/L12 Santa Clara, Ca,US
115/B2 Santa Clara (riv.), Ca,US
101/J6 Santa Clara, Ven.
115/B2 Santa Clarita, Ca,US
47/G2 Santa Coloma de Farners, Sp.
47/L7 Santa Coloma de Gramanet, Sp.
46/A1 Santa Comba, Sp.
97/K7 Santa Cruz (prov.), Arg.
97/K7 Santa Cruz (riv.), Arg.
92/F7 Santa Cruz, Bol.
94/C2 Santa Cruz, Braz.
96/C2 Santa Cruz, Chile
100/D5 Santa Cruz, CR
67/D5 Santa Cruz, Phil.
67/E6 Santa Cruz, Phil.
78/F6 Santa Cruz (isls.), Sol.
108/B3 Santa Cruz, Ca,US
115/A2 Santa Cruz (isl.), Ca,US
47/S12 Santa Cruz da Graciosa, Azor.,Port.
47/R12 Santa Cruz das Flores, Azor.,Port.
94/C4 Santa Cruz da Vitória, Braz.
100/C4 Santa Cruz del Quiché, Guat.
101/F3 Santa Cruz del Sur, Cuba
47/X16 Santa Cruz de Tenerife, Canl.
94/C2 Santa Cruz do Capibaribe, Braz.
95/B2 Santa Cruz do Rio Pardo, Braz.
91/F2 Santa Cruz do Sul, Braz.
47/L7 Sant Adrià de Besòs, Sp.
96/D5 Santa Elena (peak), Arg.
100/D5 Santa Elena (cape), CR
46/A1 Santa Eugenia de Ribeira, Sp.
47/F3 Santa Eulalia del Río, Sp.
96/E1 Santa Fé, Arg.
96/E2 Santa Fé (prov.), Arg.
46/D4 Santa Fé, Sp.
113/H4 Santa Fe (riv.), Fl,US
109/F4 Santa Fe (cap.), NM,US
95/B2 Santa Fe do Sul, Braz.
48/D3 Sant'Agata di Militello, It.
95/B1 Santa Helena de Goiás, Braz.
94/A1 Santa Inês, Braz.
94/C4 Santa Inês, Braz.
97/J8 Santa Inés (isl.), Chile
95/G8 Santa Isabel, Braz.
100/E5 Santa Isabel, Col.
78/E5 Santa Isabel (isl.), Sol.
82/G7 Santa Isabel, Pico de (peak), EqG.
97/F2 Santa Lucía, Uru.
97/G2 Santa Lucía (riv.), Uru.
94/C3 Santa Luz, Braz.
94/A1 Santa Luzia, Braz.
94/C2 Santa Luzia, Braz.
95/D1 Santa Luzia, Braz.
80/J10 Santa Luzia (isl.), CpV.
96/E2 Santa Magdalena, Arg.
101/M8 Santa Magdalena (isl.), Mex.
101/M9 Santa Margarita (isl.), Mex.
91/F2 Santa Maria, Braz.
94/A4 Santa Maria (hills), Braz.
96/C2 Santa María, Chile
96/B3 Santa María (isl.), Chile
47/T13 Santa Maria (isl.), Azor.,Port.
108/B4 Santa Maria, Ca,US
46/B4 Santa María, Cabo de (cape), Port.
48/D2 Santa Maria Capua Vetere, It.
94/C3 Santa Maria da Boa Vista, Braz.
94/A4 Santa Maria da Vitória, Braz.
49/F3 Santa Maria di Leuca (cape), It.
95/D1 Santa Maria do Suaçi, Braz.
101/G5 Santa Marta, Col.
95/B4 Santa Marta Grande, Cabo de (cape), Braz.
115/B2 Santa Monica, Ca,US
115/B3 Santa Monica (bay), Ca,US
115/B2 Santa Monica Mts. Nat'l Rec. Area, Ca,US
94/A4 Santana, Braz.
94/B1 Santana (isl.), Braz.
47/P11 Santana, Port.
47/V15 Santana, Madr.,Port.
94/B1 Santana do Acaraú, Braz.
94/C3 Santana do Ipanema, Braz.
91/E3 Santana do Livramento, Braz.
92/C3 Santander, Col.
46/D1 Santander, Sp.
48/A3 Sant'Antioco, It.
115/A2 Santa Paula, Ca,US
47/E3 Santa Pola, Sp.
47/E3 Santa Pola, Cabo de (cape), Sp.
94/B2 Santa Quitéria, Braz.
93/H4 Santarém, Braz.
46/A3 Santarém, Port.
46/A3 Santarém (dist.), Port.
94/A2 Santa Rita, Braz.
94/D2 Santa Rita, Braz.
94/A3 Santa Rita de Cássia, Braz.
95/H7 Santa Rita do Sapucaí, Braz.
96/D3 Santa Rosa, Arg.
96/D4 Santa Rosa (val.), Arg.
91/F2 Santa Rosa, Braz.
92/C4 Santa Rosa, Ecu.
108/B3 Santa Rosa, Ca,US
108/B4 Santa Rosa (isl.), Ca,US
109/F4 Santa Rosa, NM,US
108/C2 Santa Rosa (range), Nv,US
96/D2 Santa Rosa de Calamuchita, Arg.
100/D5 Santa Rosa de Copán, Hon.
95/C2 Santa Rosa de Viterbo, Braz.
101/M8 Santa Rosalía, Mex.
101/H6 Santa Rosalía, Ven.
100/D5 Santa Rosa Nat'l Park, CR
115/B2 Santa Susana (mts.), Ca,US
93/J6 Santa Teresa (riv.), Braz.
97/G2 Santa Teresa Nat'l Park, Uru.
93/H6 Santa Teresinha, Braz.
97/F3 Santa Teresita, Arg.
95/B1 Santa Vitória, Braz.
97/G2 Santa Vitória do Palmar, Braz.
47/L7 Sant Boi de Llobregat, Sp.
47/F2 Sant Carles de la Ràpita, Sp.
47/G2 Sant Celoni, Sp.
47/G2 Sant Cugat del Vallès, Sp.
113/H3 Santee (dam), SC,US
113/J3 Santee (riv.), SC,US
101/P10 San Telmo (pt.), Mex.
45/J4 Santerno (riv.), It.
48/D3 Sant'Eufemia (gulf), It.
47/G2 Sant Feliu de Guíxols, Sp.
47/G2 Sant Feliu de Llobregat, Sp.
47/F1 Sant Gervàs (peak), Sp.
91/F2 Santiago, Braz.
96/C2 Santiago (cap.), Chile
97/J7 Santiago (cape), Chile
101/G4 Santiago, DRep.
112/B5 Santiago (riv.), Mex.
100/E6 Santiago, Pan.
100/E6 Santiago (mt.), Pan.
67/D4 Santiago, Phil.
115/C3 Santiago (peak), Ca,US
112/C4 Santiago (mts.), Tx,US
46/A1 Santiago de Compostela, Sp.
101/F4 Santiago de Cuba, Cuba
91/D2 Santiago del Estero, Arg.
96/Q9 Santiago (inset) (cap.), Chile
101/N9 Santiago Ixcuintla, Mex.
100/B4 Santiago Jamiltepec, Mex.
101/N8 Santiago Papasquiaro, Mex.
96/Q9 Santiago, Región Metropolitana de (reg.), Chile
45/H3 Säntis (peak), Swi.
47/K6 Sant Jeroni (mtn.), Sp.
47/K6 Sant Llorenc del Munt Nat'l Park, Sp.
65/K9 Santō, Japan
94/C4 Santo Amaro, Braz.
95/G8 Santo Amaro (isl.), Braz.
94/C3 Santo Amaro das Brotas, Braz.
95/B2 Santo Anastácio, Braz.

Santo – Shar'y

159

Shash – Sonid

83/N6 Shashemenē, Eth.
66/C5 Shashi, China
108/B2 Shasta (dam), Ca,US
108/B2 Shasta (peak), Ca,US
54/B2 Shatskiy Nat'l Park, Ukr.
82/G1 Shaṭṭ al Jarīd (dry lake), Tun.
109/H3 Shattuck, Ok,US
106/F3 Shaunavon, Sk,Can
35/E4 Shaw, Eng,UK
110/B2 Shawano, Wi,US
111/M6 Shawbridge, Qu,Can
34/D1 Shawbury, Eng,UK
111/F2 Shawinigan, Qu,Can
109/H4 Shawnee, Ok,US
59/E3 Shaykhān, Iraq
54/C1 Shchara (riv.), Bela.
54/F1 Shchekino, Rus.
53/X9 Shchelkovo, Rus.
54/F2 Shchigry, Rus.
68/B1 Shchuchinsk, Kaz.
83/P6 Shebelē Wenz (riv.), Eth.
61/J1 Sheberghān, Afg.
110/C3 Sheboygan, Wi,US
111/H2 Shediac, NB,Can
32/A4 Sheelin, Lough (lake), Ire.
114/F2 Sheep (mtn.), Ak,US
40/D5 's-Heerenberg, Neth.
33/G5 Sheffield, Eng,UK
113/G3 Sheffield, Al,US
35/F2 Shefford, Eng,UK
83/P6 Shēh Husēn, Eth.
97/K7 Shehuen (riv.), Arg.
110/C1 Shekak (riv.), On,Can
61/K2 Shekhūpura, Pak.
55/H4 Sheki, Azer.
57/T2 Shelagskiy (cape), Rus.
111/H3 Shelburne, NS,Can
113/F3 Shelby, Ms,US
106/F3 Shelby, Mt,US
113/H3 Shelby, NC,US
113/F2 Shelbyville (lake), Il,US
110/C4 Shelbyville, In,US
113/G3 Shelbyville, Tn,US
57/R3 Shelekhov (gulf), Rus.
114/H4 Shelikof (str.), Ak,US
107/G2 Shellbrook, Sk,Can
110/B2 Shell Lake, Wi,US
107/K5 Shell Rock (riv.), Ia,US
116/A3 Shelton, Wa,US
55/J4 Shemakha, Azer.
114/A5 Shemya (isl.), Ak,US
107/K5 Shenandoah, Ia,US
110/E4 Shenandoah Nat'l Park, Va,US
84/B5 Shenge (pt.), SLeo.
68/E3 Shengli Daban (pass), China
66/B5 Shennongjia, China
35/E1 Shenstone, Eng,UK
63/J3 Shenyang, China
71/K3 Shenzhen, China
70/B2 Sheoganj, India
70/C2 Sheopur, India
54/C2 Shepetovka, Ukr.
112/E4 Shepherd, Tx,US
78/F6 Shepherd (isls.), Van.
35/G4 Sheppey (isl.), Eng,UK
35/E1 Shepshed, Eng,UK
34/D4 Shepton Mallet, Eng,UK
103/H1 Sherard (cape), NW,Can
34/D5 Sherborne, Eng,UK
84/B5 Sherbro (isl.), SLeo.
111/G2 Sherbrooke, Qu,Can
33/G2 Sherburn, Eng,UK
85/H4 Shere (hill), Nga.
70/D3 Sherghāti, India
112/E3 Sheridan, Ar,US
106/G4 Sheridan, Wy,US
35/H1 Sheringham, Eng,UK
112/D3 Sherman, Tx,US
40/C5 's-Hertogenbosch, Neth.
106/E2 Sherwood Park, Ab,Can
30/C2 Shetland (isls.), Sc,UK
55/J4 Shevchenko, Kaz.
66/D4 Sheyang (riv.), China
107/J4 Sheyenne (riv.), ND,US
66/C4 Shi (riv.), China
116/E6 Shiawassee (riv.), Mi,US
65/F2 Shibata, Japan
86/B2 Shibīn al Kaum, Egypt
107/L2 Shibogama (lake), On,Can
64/B5 Shibushi (bay), Japan
68/B1 Shiderty (riv.), Kaz.
64/D3 Shido, Japan
34/D1 Shifnal, Eng,UK
65/L9 Shiga, Japan
64/E3 Shiga (pref.), Japan
65/M10 Shigaraki, Japan
66/C3 Shigu Shan (mtn.), China
68/E3 Shihezi, China
49/F2 Shijak, Alb.
66/C3 Shijiazhuang, China
61/J3 Shikārpur, Pak.
65/M9 Shikatsu, Japan
65/H7 Shiki, Japan
64/C4 Shikoku (isl.), Japan
64/C4 Shikoku (mts.), Japan
63/P3 Shikotan (isl.), Rus.
33/G2 Shildon, Eng,UK
62/H1 Shilka, Rus.
63/H1 Shilka (riv.), Rus.
61/L2 Shilla (mtn.), India
59/N8 Shillo, Naḥal (dry riv.), WBnk.
71/F2 Shillong, India
62/D2 Shilüüstey, Mong.
65/M10 Shima (pen.), Japan
64/B4 Shimabara, Japan
64/D3 Shimamoto, Japan
64/C3 Shimane (pref.), Japan
63/K1 Shimanovsk, Rus.
65/M9 Shimasahi, Japan
83/Q5 Shimber Berris (peak), Som.
71/H2 Shimian, China
65/F3 Shimizu, Japan
65/F3 Shimoda, Japan
65/F2 Shimodate, Japan
70/C5 Shimoga, India
65/L10 Shimoichi, Japan
64/A5 Shimo-koshiki (isl.), Japan
64/B4 Shimonoseki, Japan
65/F2 Shinano (riv.), Japan
61/H2 Shindand, Afg.
64/D4 Shingū, Japan
64/C3 Shinji (lake), Japan
53/N4 Shinjō, Japan
65/M9 Shinkawa, Japan
65/E2 Shinminato, Japan
65/M9 Shinsei, Japan
87/F1 Shinyanga, Tanz.
65/G1 Shiogama, Japan
64/D4 Shio-no-misaki (cape), Japan
31/P8 Shipbourne, Eng,UK
33/G4 Shipley, Eng,UK
111/H2 Shippegan, NB,Can
65/M9 Shippo, Japan
108/E3 Shiprock, NM,US
35/E2 Shipston on Stour, Eng,UK
68/C5 Shipuqi Shankou (pass), China
60/F2 Shīr (mtn.), Iran
65/H8 Shirahama, Japan
64/E3 Shirakawa-tōge (pass), Japan
65/F3 Shirane-san (mtn.), Japan
65/H6 Shiraoka, Japan
60/F3 Shīrāz, Iran
59/H6 Shirbīn, Egypt
33/G1 Shiremoor, Eng,UK
66/C5 Shirjiu (lake), China
65/J7 Shiroi, Japan
65/G2 Shiroishi, Japan
65/F2 Shirone, Japan
65/H7 Shiroyama, Japan
61/G1 Shīrvān, Iran
66/D2 Shi San Ling, China
114/F5 Shishaldin (vol.), Ak,US
62/D1 Shishhid (riv.), Mong.
66/C5 Shishou, China
65/J7 Shisui, Japan
70/C2 Shivpurī, India
66/B4 Shiyan, China
62/F4 Shizuishan, China
63/N3 Shizunai, Japan
65/F3 Shizuoka, Japan
65/F3 Shizuoka (pref.), Japan
49/F1 Shkodër, Alb.
49/G2 Shkumbin (riv.), Alb.
114/C2 Shmidta, Mys (pt.), Rus.
77/D2 Shoalhaven (riv.), Austl.
107/H3 Shoal Lake, Mb,Can
76/C3 Shoalwater (bay), Austl.
64/C3 Shōbara, Japan
64/D3 Shōdō (isl.), Japan
35/G3 Shoeburyness, Eng,UK
70/C4 Sholāpur, India
59/N8 Shomron (ruins), WBnk.
65/M9 Shonai (riv.), Japan
65/J7 Shōnan, Japan
70/C4 Shorāpur, India
35/F5 Shoreham by Sea, Eng,UK
116/P16 Shorewood, Il,US
116/Q13 Shorewood, Wi,US
61/K2 Shorkot, Pak.
76/F6 Shorncliffe, Austl.
113/G3 Short (peak), Tn,US
78/E5 Shortland (isl.), Sol.
35/E5 Shorwell, Eng,UK
108/C3 Shoshone (mts.), Nv,US
106/F4 Shoshone (riv.), Wy,US
106/F5 Shoshoni, Wy,US
54/E2 Shostka, Ukr.
35/H3 Shotley, Eng,UK
33/G2 Shotton, Eng,UK
65/H7 Shōwa, Japan
108/E4 Show Low, Az,US
54/D2 Shpola, Ukr.
112/E3 Shreveport, La,US
34/D1 Shrewsbury, Eng,UK
34/D1 Shropshire (co.), Eng,UK
33/F6 Shropshire Union (can.), Eng,UK
66/D4 Shu (riv.), China
66/D5 Shu (riv.), China
63/K3 Shuangyang, China
63/L2 Shuangyashan, China
59/H6 Shubrā Khīt, Egypt
59/K6 Shu'fāṭ, WBnk.
66/D5 Shuiyang (riv.), China
61/K3 Shujāābād, Pak.
62/D4 Shule (riv.), China
114/G4 Shumagin (isls.), Ak,US
51/H4 Shumen, Bul.
53/K5 Shumerlya, Rus.
68/B2 Shunak, Gora (peak), Kaz.
66/C3 Shuo Xian, China
61/G2 Shūr (riv.), Iran
87/F4 Shurugwi, Zim.
68/F1 Shushenskoye, Rus.
60/E2 Shūshtar, Iran
106/D3 Shuswap (lake), BC,Can
83/N5 Shuwak, Sudan
52/J4 Shuya, Rus.
69/A1 Shwebo, Burma
69/B2 Shwemawdaw Pagoda (ruins), Burma
68/C5 Shyok (riv.), India
61/H2 Siāh (mts.), Afg.
72/B3 Siak (riv.), Indo.
61/K2 Siālkot, Pak.
67/E6 Siargao (isl.), Phil.
67/D6 Siasi, Phil.
73/F2 Siaton (pt.), Phil.
73/G3 Siau (isl.), Indo.
52/D5 Šiauliai, Lith.
67/D5 Sibalom, Phil.
55/L1 Sibay, Rus.
50/B4 Šibenik, Cro.
56/K3 Siberia (reg.), Rus.
61/J3 Sibi, Pak.
83/N7 Sibiloi Nat'l Park, Kenya
87/B1 Sibiti, Congo
51/G3 Sibiu, Rom.
51/G2 Sibiu (co.), Rom.
35/G3 Sible Hedingham, Eng,UK
72/A3 Sibolga, Indo.
71/F2 Sibsāgar, India
73/F2 Sibuco, Phil.
73/F2 Sibuko, Phil.
73/F1 Sibuyan (isl.), Phil.
67/D5 Sibuyan (sea), Phil.
106/D3 Sicamous, BC,Can
71/H2 Sichuan (prov.), China
48/C4 Sicilia (reg.), It.
48/C3 Sicily (isl.), It.
48/B4 Sicily (str.), It., Tun.
100/D4 Sico (riv.), Hon.
92/D6 Sicuani, Peru
50/D3 Šid, Yugo.
31/P7 Sidcup, Eng,UK
70/C4 Siddipet, India
48/E3 Siderno Marina, It.
95/B4 Siderópolis, Braz.
115/C1 Sidewinder (mtn.), Ca,US
49/F3 Sidhári, Gre.
70/D3 Sidhi, India
49/H2 Sidhirókastron, Gre.
70/B3 Sidhpur, India
81/S16 Sidi Aïssa, Alg.
86/A2 Sīdī Barrānī, Egypt
81/Q16 Sidi Bel-Abbes, Alg.
81/W18 Sīdī Bū Zayd (gov.), Tun.
82/C2 Sidi Ifni, Mor.
81/M13 Sidi Kacem, Mor.
59/H6 Sīdī Sālim, Egypt
98/R Sidley (mtn.), Ant.
76/A1 Sidmouth (cape), Austl.
34/C5 Sidmouth, Eng,UK
106/C3 Sidney, BC,Can
107/G4 Sidney, Mt,US
109/G2 Sidney, Ne,US
110/C3 Sidney, Oh,US
113/G3 Sidney Lanier (lake), Ga,US
59/K5 Sidon (Ṣaydā), Leb.
82/J1 Sidra (gulf), Libya
41/F3 Siede (riv.), Ger.
39/M2 Siedlce, Pol.
39/L2 Siedlce (prov.), Pol.
43/G2 Sieg (riv.), Ger.
43/G2 Siegburg, Ger.
43/H2 Siegen, Ger.
39/M2 Siemianówka (lake), Pol.
39/M2 Siemiatycze, Pol.
69/D3 Siempang, Camb.
69/C3 Siemreab, Camb.
45/J5 Siena, It.
44/C2 Sienne (riv.), Fr.
33/K3 Sieradz, Pol.
39/K3 Sieradz (prov.), Pol.
43/F5 Sierk-les-Bains, Fr.
39/K2 Sierpc, Pol.
112/B4 Sierra Blanca, Tx,US
92/D3 Sierra de la Macarena Nat'l Park, Col.
100/A2 Sierra del Carmen Nat'l Park, Mex.
101/M7 Sierra de San Pedro Mártir, Mex.
96/D4 Sierra Grande, Arg.
87/B4 Sierra Leone
84/B4 Sierra Leone (cape), SLeo.
115/B2 Sierra Madre, Ca,US
100/B4 Sierra Madre del Sur (mts.), Mex.
101/N8 Sierra Madre Occidental (range), Mex.
100/B3 Sierra Madre Oriental (mts.), Mex.
100/A2 Sierra Mojada, Mex.
108/B3 Sierra Nevada (range), Ca,US
101/G5 Sierra Nevada de Santa Marta, Col.
101/G6 Sierra Nevada Nat'l Park, Ven.
108/E5 Sierra Vista, Az,US
45/G3 Sierre, Swi.
47/M8 Siete (peak), Sp.
96/C2 Siete Tazas Nat'l Park, Chile
49/J4 Sífnos (isl.), Gre.
81/Q16 Sig, Alg.
51/F2 Sighetu Marmaţiei, Rom.
51/G2 Sighişoara, Rom.
33/F1 Sighty Crag (hill), Eng,UK
81/T15 Sigli (cape), Alg.
72/A2 Sigli, Indo.
45/H2 Sigmaringen, Ger.
52/C4 Sigtuna, Swe.
70/D3 Sihorā, India
37/H3 Siilinjärvi, Fin.
59/E3 Siirt, Turk.
102/D3 Sikanni Chief (riv.), BC,Can
70/C2 Sīkar, India
84/D4 Sikasso, Mali
84/D4 Sikasso (reg.), Mali
109/K3 Sikeston, Mo,US
63/M2 Sikhote-Alin' (mts.), Rus.
49/J4 Síkinos (isl.), Gre.
70/E2 Sikkim (state), India
50/D3 Siklós, Hun.
46/B1 Sil (riv.), Sp.
100/A3 Silao, Mex.
67/D5 Silay, Phil.
71/F3 Silchar, India
51/J5 Şile, Turk.
35/E1 Sileby, Eng,UK
39/H3 Silesia (reg.), Pol.
82/F3 Silet, Alg.
59/C3 Silifke, Turk.
70/E2 Silīguri, India
68/E5 Siling (lake), China
79/H6 Silisili (peak), WSam.
51/H3 Silistra, Bul.
51/J5 Silivri, Turk.
37/D4 Silkeborg, Den.
33/G2 Silksworth, Eng,UK
47/E3 Silla, Sp.
52/E4 Sillamäe, Est.
46/A1 Silleda, Sp.
33/E2 Silloth, Eng,UK
112/E2 Siloam Springs, Ar,US
60/D1 Silopi, Turk.
112/E4 Silsbee, Tx,US
33/G4 Silsden, Eng,UK
82/J4 Siltou (well), Chad
39/L1 Šilutė, Lith.
59/E2 Silvan, Turk.
70/B3 Silvassa, India
106/D5 Silver (cr.), Or,US
108/B2 Silver (lake), Or,US
107/L4 Silver Bay, Mn,US
108/E4 Silver City, NM,US
114/L3 Silver Creek, Yk,Can
33/F3 Silverdale, Eng,UK
116/B2 Silverdale, Wa,US
116/C2 Silver Lake-Fircrest, Wa,US
115/J8 Silver Spring, Md,US
35/E2 Silverstone, Eng,UK
34/C5 Silverton, Eng,UK
108/F3 Silverton, Co,US
106/C4 Silverton, Or,US
112/C3 Silverton, Tx,US
46/A4 Silves, Port.
48/D1 Silvi, It.
108/C2 Silvies (riv.), Or,US
81/W17 Silyānah (gov.), Tun.
72/D3 Simanggang, Malay.
94/C3 Simão Dias, Braz.
110/E2 Simard (lake), Qu,Can
59/B2 Simav, Turk.
55/J1 Simbirsk, Rus.
55/H1 Simbirsk Obl., Rus.
110/D3 Simcoe, On,Can
110/E2 Simcoe (lake), On,Can
83/N5 Simēn (mts.), Eth.
50/F3 Simeria, Rom.
72/A3 Simeulue (isl.), Indo.
54/E3 Simferopol', Ukr.
66/E5 Siming (mtn.), China
51/F5 Simitli, Bul.
115/B2 Simi Valley, Ca,US
61/L2 Simla, India
50/F2 Şimleu Silvaniei, Rom.
45/G3 Simme (riv.), Swi.
43/F2 Simmerath, Ger.
43/G4 Simmerbach (riv.), Ger.
94/C4 Simões Filho, Braz.
100/C4 Simojovel, Mex.
106/D2 Simonette (riv.), Ab,Can
88/B4 Simonstown, SAfr.
40/D1 Simonszand (isl.), Neth.
72/A3 Simpang-kiri (riv.), Indo.
43/E2 Simpelveld, Neth.
74/F4 Simpson (des.), Austl.
102/H2 Simpson (pen.), NW,Can
102/G2 Simpson (riv.), NW,Can
39/H1 Simrishamn, Swe.
73/E3 Simunul, Phil.
83/Q6 Sinadhago, Som.
60/B3 Sinafir (isl.), SAr.
86/C2 Sinai (pen.), Egypt
101/N8 Sinaloa (state), Mex.
101/F6 Sincelejo, Col.
113/H3 Sinclair (lake), Ga,US
106/G5 Sinclair, Wy,US
94/B4 Sincorá (mts.), Braz.
70/C2 Sind (riv.), India
61/J3 Sind (prov.), Pak.
67/D6 Sindañgan, Phil.
72/C5 Sindangbarang, Indo.
45/H2 Sindelfingen, Ger.
46/A4 Sines, Port.
46/A4 Sines, Cabo de (cape), Port.
84/D5 Sinfra, IvC.
72/B3 Singapore
72/B3 Singapore (cap.), Sing.
69/C3 Sing Buri, Thai.
45/H3 Singen, Ger.
51/G2 Sîngeorz-Băi, Rom.
87/F1 Singida, Tanz.
49/H2 Singitic (gulf), Gre.
71/F4 Singkang, Indo.
72/C3 Singkawang, Indo.
72/B4 Singkep (isl.), Indo.
77/D2 Singleton, Austl.
48/A2 Siniscola, It.
83/M5 Sinjah, Sudan
59/E3 Sinjār, Iraq
86/D5 Sinkāt, Sudan
42/C3 Sin-le-Noble, Fr.
70/B4 Sinnar, India
48/E2 Sinni (riv.), It.
50/E2 Sînnicolau Mare, Rom.
86/B2 Sinnūris, Egypt
84/C5 Sino (co.), Libr.
51/J3 Sinoe (lake), Rom.
93/G6 Sinop, Braz.
59/C1 Sinop, Turk.
72/D3 Sintang, Indo.
42/D2 Sint-Genesius-Rode, Belg.
42/D1 Sint-Gillis-Waas, Belg.
42/D1 Sint-Katelijne-Waver, Belg.
42/C1 Sint-Laureins, Belg.
101/J4 Sint Maarten (isl.), NAnt.
40/C5 Sint-Michielsgestel, Neth.
42/D1 Sint-Niklaas, Belg.
40/C5 Sint-Oedenrode, Neth.
112/D4 Sinton, Tx,US
42/D2 Sint-Pieters-Leeuw, Belg.
46/A3 Sintra, Port.
47/P10 Sintra (mts.), Port.
43/E2 Sint-Truiden, Belg.
101/F6 Sinú (riv.), Col.
63/J3 Sinŭiju, NKor.
43/G2 Sinzig, Ger.
50/D2 Sió (riv.), Hun.
73/F2 Siocon, Phil.
50/D2 Siófok, Hun.
87/D4 Sioma Ngwezi Nat'l Park, Zam.
45/G3 Sion, Swi.
44/E4 Sioule (riv.), Fr.
107/J5 Sioux City, Ia,US
107/J5 Sioux Falls, SD,US
110/B1 Sioux Lookout, On,Can
48/E1 Šipan (isl.), Cro.
66/F2 Siping, China
107/J2 Sipiwesk (lake), Mb,Can
98/Q Siple (coast), Ant.
98/R Siple (isl.), Ant.
113/G3 Sipsey (riv.), Al,US
72/A4 Sipura (isl.), Indo.
95/B2 Siqueira Campos, Braz.
100/E5 Siquia (riv.), Nic.
37/C4 Sira (riv.), Nor.
48/D4 Siracusa (Syracuse), It.
70/E3 Sirājganj, Bang.
106/C2 Sir Alexander (peak), BC,Can
59/D2 Şiran, Turk.
74/F3 Sir Edward Pellew Group (isls.), Austl.
51/H2 Siret, Rom.
51/H3 Siret (riv.), Rom.
72/D3 Sirik (cape), Malay.
69/C2 Sirikit (res.), Thai.
94/D3 Sirinhaém, Braz.
71/H4 Sirit (res.), Thai.
114/B5 Sirius (pt.), Ak,US
102/D2 Sir James MacBrien (peak), NW,Can
61/G3 Sīrjān, Iran
77/D4 Sir John (cape), Austl.
59/E3 Şirnak, Turk.
70/B3 Sirohi, India
70/C3 Sironj, India
49/J4 Siros (isl.), Gre.
70/C2 Sirsa, India
70/B5 Sirsi, India
50/C3 Sisak, Cro.
69/D3 Sisaket, Thai.
71/H4 Si Sa Ket, Thai.
69/B2 Si Satchanalai (ruins), Thai.
107/H2 Sisipuk (lake), Mb, Sk,Can
69/C3 Sisophon, Camb.
107/J4 Sisseton, SD,US
85/E4 Sissili (prov.), Burk.
113/H2 Sissonville, WV,US
71/F3 Sitākunda, Bang.
47/F2 Sitges, Sp.
49/H2 Sithoniá (pen.), Gre.
49/K5 Sitia, Gre.
114/M2 Sitidgi (lake), NW,Can
114/L4 Sitka, Ak,US
39/K4 Sitno (peak), Slvk.
69/B2 Sittang (riv.), Burma
40/C7 Sittard, Neth.
35/G4 Sittingbourne, Eng,UK
71/F3 Sittwe (Akyab), Burma
50/D3 Sivac, Yugo.
70/C6 Sivakāsi, India
59/D2 Sivas, Turk.
59/D3 Siverek, Turk.
59/D2 Sivrihisar, Turk.
42/D3 Sivry-Rance, Belg.
83/L2 Sīwah, Egypt
70/D2 Siwān, India
32/A2 Sixmilecross, NI,UK
114/K3 Sixtymile, Yk,Can
62/C3 Siziwang, China
37/D5 Sjælland (isl.), Den.
50/D4 Sjenica, Yugo.
37/M6 Sjönfridh (peak), Ice.
37/P7 Skaftafell Nat'l Park, Ice.
37/D4 Skagen, Den.
37/D4 Skagens (cape), Den.
37/D4 Skagerrak (str.), Eur.
37/P6 Skálfandafljót (riv.), Ice.
39/J4 Skalica, Slvk.
45/K2 Skalice (riv.), Czh.
49/J3 Skantzoura (isl.), Gre.
37/E4 Skaraborg (co.), Swe.
39/L3 Skarżysko-Kamienna, Pol.
39/K4 Skawina, Pol.
102/D3 Skeena (range), BC,Can
106/A2 Skeena (riv.), BC,Can
33/J5 Skegness, Eng,UK
37/G2 Skellefteå, Swe.
37/F2 Skellefteälv (riv.), Swe.
33/G4 Skelmanthorpe, Eng,UK
33/F4 Skelmersdale, Eng,UK
33/H2 Skelton, Eng,UK
33/G2 Skerne (riv.), Eng,UK
32/B4 Skerries, Ire.
49/G4 Skhiza (isl.), Gre.
109/H3 Skiatook, Ok,US
33/F2 Skiddaw (mtn.), Eng,UK
37/D4 Skien, Nor.
39/L3 Skierniewice, Pol.
39/K3 Skierniewice (prov.), Pol.
81/V17 Skikda, Alg.
49/G4 Skinári, Ákra (cape), Gre.
33/H4 Skipsea, Eng,UK
33/F4 Skipton, Eng,UK
33/F3 Skirfare (riv.), Eng,UK
49/J3 Skíros (isl.), Gre.
37/D4 Skjeberg, Nor.
52/B2 Skjelåtinden (peak), Nor.
37/D5 Skjern, Den.
34/A3 Skokholm (isl.), Wal,UK
116/Q15 Skokie, Il,US
34/A3 Skomer (isl.), Wal,UK
69/D3 Skon, Camb.
49/H3 Skópelos (isl.), Gre.
54/F1 Skopin, Rus.
55/F5 Skopje (cap.), Macd.
37/E4 Skövde, Swe.
63/J1 Skovorodino, Rus.
111/G2 Skowhegan, Me,US
114/L3 Skukum (mtn.), Yk,Can
109/K2 Skunk (riv.), Ia,US
39/H2 Skwierzyna, Pol.
116/D2 Skykomish (riv.), Wa,US
97/J8 Skyway (sound), Chile
37/D5 Slagelse, Den.
33/F4 Slaidburn, Eng,UK
39/L4 Slaná (riv.), Slvk.
36/B4 Slaney (riv.), Ire.
52/F4 Slantsy, Rus.
51/G3 Slatina, Rom.
99/F3 Slave (riv.), Can.
85/F5 Slave Coast (reg.), Afr.
106/E2 Slave Lake, Ab,Can
68/C1 Slavgorod, Rus.
50/C3 Slavonia (reg.), Cro.
50/C3 Slavonska Požega, Cro.
50/D3 Slavonski Brod, Cro.
54/C2 Slavuta, Ukr.
54/F2 Slavyansk, Ukr.
54/F3 Slavyansk-na-Kubani, Rus.
39/J1 Sławno, Pol.
107/K5 Slayton, Mn,US
33/H6 Sleaford, Eng,UK
40/D3 Sleen, Neth.
103/H3 Sleeper (isls.), NW,Can
107/K4 Sleepy Eye, Mn,US
32/A4 Sliabh na Caillighe (mtn.), Ire.
113/F4 Slidell, La,US
40/B5 Sliedrecht, Neth.
48/D5 Sliema, Malta
32/A3 Slieve Beagh (mtn.), NI,UK
32/C3 Slieve Binnian (mtn.), NI,UK
32/C3 Slieve Croob (mtn.), NI,UK
32/C3 Slieve Donard (mtn.), NI,UK
32/B3 Slieve Gullion (mtn.), NI,UK
32/A1 Slieve Snaght (mtn.), Ire.
36/A3 Sligo, Ire.
36/A3 Sligo (bay), Ire.
51/H4 Sliven, Bul.
51/H4 Slivnitsa, Bul.
111/S10 Sloan, NY,US
53/L4 Slobodskoy, Rus.
51/H3 Slobozia, Rom.
40/D2 Slochteren, Neth.
54/C1 Slonim, Bela.
40/C3 Slotermeer (lake), Neth.
31/M7 Slough, Eng,UK
39/K4 Slovakia
50/B3 Slovenia
50/B2 Slovenska Bistrica, Slov.
39/L4 Slovenské Rudohorie (mts.), Slvk.
39/J1 Słowiński Nat'l Park, Pol.
39/H2 Słubice, Pol.
54/C2 Sluch' (riv.), Ukr.
39/J2 Słupca, Pol.
39/J1 Słupia (riv.), Pol.
39/J1 Słupsk, Pol.
39/J1 Słupsk (prov.), Pol.
54/C1 Slutsk, Bela.
62/E1 Slyudyanka, Rus.
31/N8 Smallfield, Eng,UK
103/K3 Smallwood (res.), Nf,Can
107/G2 Smeaton, Sk,Can
50/E3 Smederevo, Yugo.
50/E3 Smederevska Palanka, Yugo.
37/E3 Smedjebacken, Swe.
54/D2 Smela, Ukr.
81/V17 Smendou (riv.), Alg.
40/D3 Smilde, Neth.
98/V Smith (pen.), Ant.
106/B3 Smith (inlet), BC,Can
103/J2 Smith (isl.), NW,Can
106/F4 Smith (riv.), Mt,US
106/B2 Smithers, BC,Can
113/J3 Smithfield, NC,US
108/E2 Smithfield, Ut,US
110/E4 Smith Mtn. (lake), Va,US
110/E2 Smiths Falls, On,Can
115/G5 Smithtown, NY,US
111/Q9 Smithville, On,Can
109/J4 Smithville, Ok,US
77/E1 Smoky (cape), Austl.
106/D2 Smoky (riv.), Ab,Can
109/H3 Smoky (hills), Ks,US
109/G3 Smoky Hill (riv.), Ks,US
106/E2 Smoky Lake, Ab,Can
37/C3 Smøla (isl.), Nor.
52/G5 Smolensk, Rus.
52/F5 Smolensk Obl., Rus.
49/G2 Smólikas (peak), Gre.
51/G5 Smolyan, Bul.
98/U Smyley (isl.), Ant.
113/G3 Smyrna, Ga,US
32/D3 Snaefell (mtn.), IM,UK
114/M2 Snake (riv.), Yk,Can
106/D4 Snake (riv.), US
109/G2 Snake (riv.), Ne,US
75/Q12 Snares (isls.), NZ
40/C2 Sneek, Neth.
40/C2 Sneekermeer (lake), Neth.
88/D3 Sneeuberg (mts.), SAfr.
88/B4 Sneeuberg (peak), SAfr.
111/Q8 Snelgrove, On,Can
35/G1 Snettisham, Eng,UK
39/H3 Sněžka (peak), Czh.
50/B3 Snežnik (peak), Yugo.
39/L2 Śniardwy (lake), Pol.
35/G4 Snodland, Eng,UK
37/D3 Snøhetta (peak), Nor.
116/C2 Snohomish, Wa,US
116/C2 Snohomish (riv.), Wa,US
116/D2 Snoqualmie (riv.), Wa,US
37/E2 Snøtind (peak), Nor.
32/D5 Snowdon (mtn.), Wal,UK
32/D5 Snowdonia Nat'l Park, Wal,UK
108/E4 Snowflake, Az,US
107/H2 Snow Lake, Mb,Can
114/K2 Snowy (peak), Ak,US
77/D3 Snowy River Nat'l Park, Austl.
112/C3 Snyder, Tx,US
89/H7 Soalala, Madg.
89/J7 Soanierana-Ivongo, Madg.
33/G6 Soar (riv.), Eng,UK
45/L2 Soběslav, Czh.
73/K4 Sobger (riv.), Indo.
61/J3 Sobhādero, Pak.
94/B3 Sobradinho (res.), Braz.
94/B1 Sobral, Braz.
65/M9 Sobue, Japan
39/L2 Sochaczew, Pol.
54/F4 Sochi, Rus.
79/K6 Society (isls.), FrPol.
95/G7 Socorro, Braz.
108/F4 Socorro, NM,US
112/B4 Socorro, Tx,US
58/E8 Socotra (isl.), Yem.
69/D4 Soc Trang, Viet.
46/D3 Socuéllamos, Sp.
37/H2 Sodankylä, Fin.
106/F5 Soda Springs, Id,US
65/H7 Sodegaura, Japan
37/F3 Söderhamn, Swe.
37/F4 Södertälje, Swe.
83/N6 Sodo, Eth.
41/F5 Soest, Ger.
40/C4 Soest, Neth.
41/E3 Soeste (riv.), Ger.
89/J6 Sofia (riv.), Madg.
51/F4 Sofia (Sofiya) (cap.), Bul.
50/F4 Sofiya (reg.), Bul.
92/D2 Sogamoso, Col.
37/B3 Sognafjorden (fjord), Nor.
37/C3 Sogn og Fjordane (co.), Nor.
62/J4 Sogollé (well), Chad
63/K5 Sŏgwip'o, SKor.
35/G2 Soham, Eng,UK
42/D2 Soignies, Belg.
31/U11 Soignolles-en-Brie, Fr.
42/C5 Soissons, Fr.
31/T11 Soisy-sur-Seine, Fr.
64/C3 Sōja, Japan
70/B2 Sojat, India
55/J1 Sok (riv.), Rus.
69/C3 Sok (pt.), Thai.
65/H7 Sōka, Japan
63/K4 Sokch'o, SKor.
59/B3 Söke, Turk.
62/F1 Sokhor (peak), Rus.
50/E4 Sokobanja, Yugo.
85/F4 Sokodé, Togo
52/J4 Sokol, Rus.
39/M2 Sokółka, Pol.
45/K1 Sokolov, Czh.
39/M2 Sokołów Podlaski, Pol.
85/G4 Sokoto (plains), Nga.
85/G4 Sokoto (riv.), Nga.
85/G3 Sokoto (state), Nga.
37/C4 Sola, Nor.
67/D4 Solana, Phil.
94/D2 Solânea, Braz.
92/C2 Solano (pt.), Col.
46/C4 Sol, Costa del (coast), Sp.
47/P10 Sol, Costa do (reg.), Port.
109/J2 Soldier (riv.), Ia,US
101/G5 Soledad, Col.
115/B2 Soledad (canyon), Ca,US
101/J6 Soledad, Ven.
100/A3 Soledad Diez Guiterrez, Mex.
95/A4 Soledade, Braz.
35/E5 Solent (chan.), Eng,UK
43/E4 Soleuvre (mtn.), Lux.
59/E2 Solhan, Turk.
54/C1 Soligorsk, Bela.
35/E2 Solihull, Eng,UK
53/N4 Solikamsk, Rus.
55/K2 Sol'-Iletsk, Rus.
41/E6 Solingen, Ger.
37/F3 Sollefteå, Swe.
47/G3 Sóller, Sp.
41/G5 Solling (mts.), Ger.
37/D3 Søln (peak), Nor.
44/F3 Solnan (riv.), Fr.
72/B5 Solo (riv.), Indo.
72/B4 Solok, Indo.
100/C5 Sololá, Guat.
78/E5 Solomon (sea), PNG, Sol.
112/D2 Solomon (riv.), Ks,US
78/E6 Solomon Islands
55/L4 Solonchak Goklenkui (salt marsh), Trkm.
45/G3 Solothurn, Swi.
52/G2 Solovetskiy (isls.), Rus.
47/F2 Solsona, Sp.
50/D2 Solt, Hun.
50/B4 Šolta (isl.), Cro.
41/G3 Soltau, Ger.
50/D2 Soltvadkert, Hun.
50/E5 Solunska (peak), Macd.
34/A3 Solva (riv.), Wal,UK
108/B4 Solvang, Ca,US
37/E4 Sölvesborg, Swe.
32/E2 Solway Firth (inlet), Eng, Sc,UK
87/E3 Solwezi, Zam.
65/G2 Sōma, Japan
59/A2 Soma, Turk.
42/C3 Somain, Fr.
81/G4 Somalia
111/F1 Somaqua (riv.), Qu,Can
50/D3 Sombor, Cro.
101/P9 Sombrerete, Mex.
95/B4 Sombrio, Braz.
33/G5 Somercotes, Eng,UK
40/C6 Someren, Neth.
37/G3 Somero, Fin.
106/E3 Somers, Mt,US
102/G1 Somerset (isl.), NW,Can
34/D4 Somerset (co.), Eng,UK
110/C4 Somerset, Ky,US
115/F5 Somerset, NJ,US
111/S9 Somerset, NY,US
77/C4 Somerset-Burnie, Austl.
88/D4 Somerset East, SAfr.
88/B4 Somerset West, SAfr.
35/F2 Somersham, Eng,UK
111/G3 Somersworth, NH,US
34/D4 Somerton, Eng,UK
108/D4 Somerton, Az,US
115/F5 Somerville, NJ,US
109/H5 Somerville (lake), Tx,US
51/F2 Someş (riv.), Rom.
51/G2 Someşul Mare (riv.), Rom.
81/T15 Sommam (riv.), Alg.
44/D1 Somme (bay), Fr.
42/B4 Somme (dept.), Fr.
42/A3 Somme (riv.), Fr.
42/D6 Somme (riv.), Fr.
42/D5 Somme-Soude (riv.), Fr.
50/C2 Somogy (co.), Hun.
100/D5 Somoto, Nic.
35/F5 Somptin, Eng,UK
37/D5 Sønderborg, Den.
88/L11 Sonderend (riv.), SAfr.
38/E1 Sønderjylland (co.), Den.
45/H3 Sondrio, It.
70/C2 Sonepat, India
70/D3 Sonepur, India
69/E3 Song Cau, Viet.
69/D4 Song Dinh, Viet.
87/G3 Songea, Tanz.
66/F1 Songhua (riv.), China
68/B3 Song-Kel' (lake), Kyr.
69/C5 Songkhla, Thai.
69/C2 Songkhram (riv.), Thai.
63/J2 Songling, China
69/C1 Song Ma, Viet.
87/F4 Songo, Moz.
66/C4 Song Shan (peak), China
63/K4 Songt'an, SKor.
66/C3 Songzi Guan (pass), China
69/E3 Son Ha, Viet.
62/G3 Sonid Youqi, China

160

Sonid – Surig

62/G3 **Sonid Zuoqi**, China
69/C1 **Son La**, Viet.
61/J3 **Sonmiāni** (bay), Pak.
45/J1 **Sonneberg**, Ger.
35/F4 **Sonning**, Eng,UK
38/G5 **Sonntagshorn** (peak), Ger.
93/J5 **Sono** (riv.), Braz.
94/A5 **Sono** (riv.), Braz.
64/D3 **Sonobe**, Japan
116/K10 **Sonoma**, Ca,US
116/J10 **Sonoma** (mts.), Ca,US
101/M8 **Sonora** (riv.), Mex.
101/M8 **Sonora** (state), Mex.
108/B3 **Sonora**, Ca,US
112/C4 **Sonora**, Tx,US
101/M7 **Sonoyta** (riv.), Mex.
60/E2 **Sonqor**, Iran
40/D5 **Sonsbeck**, Ger.
46/D3 **Sonseca**, Sp.
100/D5 **Sonsonate**, ESal.
78/C4 **Sonsorol** (isls.), Palau
50/D3 **Sonta**, Yugo.
69/D1 **Son Tay**, Viet.
41/G6 **Sontra**, Ger.
73/G3 **Sopi** (cape), Indo.
69/C1 **Sopka**, Laos
61/K2 **Sopore**, India
51/G4 **Sopot**, Bul.
39/K1 **Sopot**, Pol.
50/C2 **Sopron**, Hun.
34/D3 **Sôr** (riv.), Wal,UK
48/C2 **Sora**, It.
63/K4 **Sŏrak-san** (mtn.), SKor.
111/F2 **Sorel**, Qu,Can
59/M9 **Soreq, Nabel** (dry riv.), Isr.
45/H4 **Soresina**, It.
44/F5 **Sorgues**, Fr.
59/C2 **Sorgun**, Turk.
46/D2 **Soria**, Sp.
97/F2 **Soriano** (dept.), Uru.
72/A3 **Sorikmerapi** (peak), Indo.
55/K3 **Sor Karatuley** (salt pan), Kaz.
55/K3 **Sor Kaydak** (salt marsh), Kaz.
55/K3 **Sor Mertvyy Kultuk** (salt marsh), Kaz.
42/D4 **Sormonne** (riv.), Fr.
38/F1 **Sorø**, Den.
95/C2 **Sorocaba**, Braz.
55/K1 **Sorochinsk**, Rus.
51/J1 **Soroki**, Mol.
78/D4 **Sorol** (atoll), Micr.
73/H4 **Sorong**, Indo.
83/M7 **Soroti**, Ugan.
37/G1 **Sørøya** (isl.), Nor.
37/G1 **Sørøysundet** (chan.), Nor.
41/E6 **Sorpestausee** (res.), Ger.
46/A3 **Sorraia** (riv.), Port.
48/D2 **Sorrento**, It.
87/B5 **Sorris-Sorris**, Namb.
48/A2 **Sorso**, It.
67/D5 **Sorsogon**, Phil.
52/F3 **Sortavala**, Rus.
52/D4 **Sõrve** (pt.), Est.
41/H5 **Söse** (riv.), Ger.
54/F1 **Sosna** (riv.), Rus.
96/C2 **Sosneado** (peak), Arg.
53/M3 **Sosnogorsk**, Rus.
53/L4 **Sosnovka**, Rus.
39/K3 **Sosnowiec**, Pol.
101/G4 **Sosúa**, DRep.
42/D6 **Soude** (riv.), Fr.
101/J4 **Soufrière** (mt.), Guad.
101/J5 **Soufrière** (mt.), StV.
81/V17 **Souk Ahras**, Alg.
43/G1 **Soultz-sous-Forets**, Fr.
85/E3 **Soum** (prov.), Burk.
43/E2 **Soumagne**, Belg.
88/E3 **Sources, Mont aux** (peak), Les.
93/J4 **Soure**, Braz.
46/A2 **Soure**, Port.
81/S15 **Sour El Ghozlane**, Alg.
107/H3 **Souris**, Mb,Can
111/J2 **Souris**, PE,Can
107/H3 **Souris** (riv.), Can., US
84/E3 **Sourou** (prov.), Burk.
82/D2 **Sous** (wadi), Mor.
94/C2 **Sousa**, Braz.
46/B3 **Sousel**, Port.
88/C3 **Sout** (riv.), SAfr.
76/G8 **South** (cr.), Austl.
111/H2 **South** (mts.), NS,Can
103/H2 **South** (bay), NW,Can
75/Q12 **South** (cape), NZ
75/Q11 **South** (isl.), NZ
87/D6 **South Africa**
31/M7 **Southall**, Eng,UK
35/E2 **Southam**, Eng,UK
90/* **South America**
103/H2 **Southampton** (cape), NW,Can
103/H2 **Southampton** (isl.), NW,Can
110/D2 **Southampton**, On,Can
35/E5 **Southampton**, Eng,UK
71/F5 **South Andaman** (isl.), India
113/J2 **South Anna** (riv.), Va,US
113/H3 **South Augusta**, Ga,US
103/K3 **South Aulatsivik** (isl.), Nf,Can
74/E5 **South Australia** (state), Austl.
113/F3 **Southaven**, Ms,US
32/D3 **South Barrule** (mtn.), IM,UK
110/C3 **South Bend**, In,US
31/P8 **Southborough**, Eng,UK
110/E4 **South Boston**, Va,US
35/F5 **Southbourne**, Eng,UK
34/C6 **South Brent**, Eng,UK
111/F2 **South Burlington**, Vt,US
113/H3 **South Carolina** (state), US
58/L8 **South China** (sea), Asia
107/H4 **South Dakota** (state), US
34/D5 **South Dorset Downs** (uplands), Eng,UK
35/F5 **South Downs** (hills), Eng,UK
29/S8 **South East** (cape), Austl.
77/C3 **South East** (pt.), Austl.
101/G3 **Southeast** (pt.), Bahm.
114/E3 **Southeast** (cape), Ak,US
116/P16 **South Elgin**, Il,US
33/G4 **South Elmsall**, Eng,UK
32/C1 **Southend**, Sc,UK
35/G3 **Southend-on-Sea**, Eng,UK
59/K6 **Southern** (dist.), Isr.
84/B5 **Southern** (prov.), SLeo.
75/Q11 **Southern Alps** (range), NZ
79/J6 **Southern Cook** (isls.), CookIs.
102/G3 **Southern Indian** (lake), Mb,Can
113/J3 **Southern Pines**, NC,US
32/D1 **Southern Uplands** (mts.), Sc,UK
35/G1 **Southery**, Eng,UK
77/C4 **South Esk** (riv.), Austl.
74/D3 **Southesk Tablelands** (plat.), Austl.
116/F7 **Southfield**, Mi,US
35/H4 **South Foreland** (pt.), Eng,UK
108/F3 **South Fork**, Co,US
113/F2 **South Fulton**, Tn,US
31/N7 **Southgate**, Eng,UK
115/B3 **South Gate**, Ca,US
116/F7 **Southgate**, Mi,US
98/X **South Georgia** (isl.), UK
34/C4 **South Glamorgan** (co.), Wal,UK
34/C6 **South Hams** (plain), Eng,UK
35/F5 **South Hayling**, Eng,UK
110/E4 **South Hill**, Va,US
40/B5 **South Holland** (prov.), Neth.
116/Q16 **South Holland**, Il,US
31/N8 **South Holmwood**, Eng,UK
33/G4 **South Kirkby**, Eng,UK
63/K4 **South Korea**
108/C3 **South Lake Tahoe**, Ca,US
87/F3 **South Luangwa Nat'l Park**, Zam.
98/K **South Magnetic Pole**, Ant.
116/Q14 **South Milwaukee**, Wi,US
35/G3 **Southminster**, Eng,UK
34/C6 **South Molton**, Eng,UK
107/J2 **South Moose** (lake), Mb,Can
114/M5 **South Moresby Nat'l Park Rsv.**, BC,Can
33/G5 **South Normanton**, Eng,UK
31/P7 **South Ockenden**, Eng,UK
98/W **South Orkney** (isls.), UK
55/G4 **South Ossetian Aut. Obl.**, Geo.
31/M7 **South Oxhey**, Eng,UK
34/D5 **South Petherton**, Eng,UK
76/E6 **South Pine** (riv.), Austl.
115/F5 **South Plainfield**, NJ,US
109/G2 **South Platte** (riv.), Co, Ne,US
98/A **South Pole**, Ant.
33/E4 **Southport**, Eng,UK
113/J3 **Southport**, NC,US
115/F5 **South River**, NJ,US
98/Y **South Sandwich** (isls.), UK
116/K11 **South San Francisco**, Ca,US
106/F3 **South Saskatchewan** (riv.), Ab, Sk,Can
98/W **South Shetland** (isls.), UK
33/G2 **South Shields**, Eng,UK
109/H2 **South Sioux City**, Ne,US
70/E3 **South Suburban**, India
75/R10 **South Taranaki** (bight), NZ
33/F2 **South Tyne** (riv.), Eng,UK
73/F2 **South Ubian**, Phil.
31/N7 **Southwark** (bor.), Eng,UK
33/H5 **Southwell**, Eng,UK
77/C4 **South West** (cape), Austl.
77/C4 **South West Nat'l Park**, Austl.
35/H2 **Southwold**, Eng,UK
35/G3 **South Woodham Ferrers**, Eng,UK
76/C4 **Southwood Nat'l Park**, Austl.
33/G5 **South Yorkshire** (co.), Eng,UK
51/G2 **Sovata**, Rom.
48/E3 **Soverato Marina**, It.
39/L1 **Sovetsk**, Rus.
52/D5 **Sovetsk**, Rus.
52/L4 **Sovetsk**, Rus.
63/N2 **Sovetskaya Gavan'**, Rus.
33/G4 **Sowerby Bridge**, Eng,UK
88/D2 **Soweto**, SAfr.
52/J2 **Soyana** (riv.), Rus.
64/A2 **Soyang** (lake), SKor.
44/D4 **Soyaux**, Fr.
98/E **Soyuz**, Ant.
54/D1 **Sozh** (riv.), Eur.
43/E3 **Spa**, Belg.
98/U **Spaatz** (isl.), Ant.
46/C2 **Spain**
33/H6 **Spalding**, Eng,UK
116/C3 **Spanaway**, Wa,US
101/F4 **Spanish Town**, Jam.
108/C3 **Sparks**, Nv,US
113/H2 **Sparta**, NC,US
115/F4 **Sparta**, NJ,US
113/G3 **Sparta**, Tn,US
110/B3 **Sparta**, Wi,US
113/H3 **Spartanburg**, SC,US
49/H4 **Sparta** (Spárti), Gre.
81/M13 **Spartel** (cape), Mor.
48/A3 **Spartivento** (cape), It.
48/E4 **Spartivento** (cape), It.
106/E3 **Sparwood**, BC,Can
63/L3 **Spassk-Dal'niy**, Rus.
49/H5 **Spátha, Ákra** (cape), Gre.
36/C2 **Spean** (riv.), Sc,UK
36/C2 **Spean Bridge**, Sc,UK
107/H4 **Spearfish**, SD,US
33/F5 **Speke**, Eng,UK
74/F7 **Spencer** (cape), Austl.
74/F6 **Spencer** (gulf), Austl.
114/E2 **Spencer** (pt.), Ak,US
107/K5 **Spencer**, Ia,US
41/F4 **Spenge**, Ger.
33/G2 **Spennymoor**, Eng,UK
49/H3 **Sperkhiós** (riv.), Gre.
32/A2 **Sperrin** (mts.), NI,UK
36/D2 **Spey** (riv.), Sc,UK
45/H2 **Speyer**, Ger.
111/Q8 **Speyside**, On,Can
48/E3 **Spezzano Albanese**, It.
103/H2 **Spicer** (isl.), NW,Can
41/E1 **Spiekeroog** (isl.), Ger.
45/G3 **Spiez**, Swi.
40/B5 **Spijkenisse**, Neth.
114/K2 **Spike** (mtn.), Ak,US
50/A2 **Spilimbergo**, It.
33/J5 **Spilsby**, Eng,UK
48/A2 **Spina, Bruncu** (peak), It.
61/J2 **Spin Būldak**, Afg.
43/E5 **Spincourt**, Fr.
106/D2 **Spirit River**, Ab,Can
106/G2 **Spiritwood**, Sk,Can
39/L4 **Spišská Nová Ves**, Slvk.
35/E5 **Spithead** (chan.), Eng,UK
56/B2 **Spitsbergen** (isl.), Sval.
45/K3 **Spittal an der Drau**, Aus.
107/K2 **Split** (lake), Mb,Can
50/C4 **Split**, Cro.
45/H3 **Splugenpass** (Passo dello Spluge) (pass), It., Swi.
106/D4 **Spokane** (riv.), Id, Wa,US
106/D4 **Spokane**, Wa,US
48/C1 **Spoleto**, It.
110/B3 **Spoon** (riv.), Il,US
110/B2 **Spooner**, Wi,US
107/K3 **Sprague**, Mb,Can
40/C5 **Sprang-Capelle**, Neth.
67/B5 **Spratly** (isls.)
39/H2 **Spree** (riv.), Ger.
45/K4 **Spresiano**, It.
43/E3 **Sprimont**, Belg.
113/G4 **Spring** (cr.), Ga,US
112/E4 **Spring**, Tx,US
111/K1 **Springdale**, Nf,Can
112/E2 **Springdale**, Ar,US
41/G4 **Springe**, Ger.
109/F3 **Springer**, NM,US
108/E4 **Springerville**, Az,US
109/G3 **Springfield**, Co,US
110/B4 **Springfield** (cap.), Il,US
111/F3 **Springfield**, Ma,US
109/J3 **Springfield**, Mo,US
110/D4 **Springfield**, Oh,US
106/C4 **Springfield**, Or,US
113/G2 **Springfield**, Tn,US
115/J8 **Springfield**, Va,US
111/F3 **Springfield**, Vt,US
111/H2 **Springhill**, NS,Can
112/E3 **Springhill**, La,US
88/E2 **Springs**, SAfr.
107/H3 **Springside**, Sk,Can
77/G5 **Springvale**
107/K5 **Spring Valley**, Mn,US
115/F4 **Spring Valley**, NY,US
41/E6 **Sprockhövel**, Ger.
35/H1 **Sprowston**, Eng,UK
110/E4 **Spruce** (peak), WV,US
115/E5 **Spruce Run** (res.), NJ,US
40/B5 **Spui** (riv.), Neth.
33/J4 **Spurn Head** (pt.), Eng,UK
106/C3 **Squamish**, BC,Can
48/E3 **Squillace** (gulf), It.
49/F2 **Squinzano**, It.
50/D3 **Srbobran**, Yugo.
69/C4 **Sre Ambel**, Camb.
50/D3 **Srebrenica**, Bosn.
51/G4 **Sredna** (mts.), Bul.
51/G4 **Srednogorie**, Bul.
69/D3 **Sre Khtum**, Camb.
39/J2 **Śrem**, Pol.
50/E3 **Sremčica**, Yugo.
50/D3 **Sremska Mitrovica**, Yugo.
69/C3 **Sreng** (riv.), Camb.
69/D3 **Sre Noy**, Camb.
69/D3 **Srepok** (riv.), Camb.
63/H1 **Sretensk**, Rus.
61/K3 **Sri Dungargarh**, India
61/K3 **Sri Gangānagar**, India
70/D4 **Srikākulam**, India
70/D6 **Sri Lanka**
61/K2 **Srīnagar**, India
70/B4 **Srīvardhan**, India
39/J3 **Środa Śląska**, Pol.
39/J2 **Środa Wielkopolska**, Pol.
76/A2 **Staaten River Nat'l Park**, Austl.
37/H1 **Stabbursdalen Nat'l Park**, Nor.
40/B6 **Stabroek**, Belg.
41/G1 **Stade**, Ger.
42/C2 **Staden**, Belg.
40/D3 **Stadskanaal**, Neth.
41/G4 **Stadthagen**, Ger.
40/D5 **Stadtlohn**, Ger.
45/H3 **Stäfa**, Swi.
39/G1 **Staffanstorp**, Swe.
33/F6 **Stafford**, Eng,UK
34/D2 **Stafford & Worcester** (can.), Eng,UK
33/F5 **Staffordshire** (co.), Eng,UK
48/B4 **Stagnone** (isls.), It.
33/G2 **Staindrop**, Eng,UK
31/M7 **Staines**, Eng,UK
31/T10 **Stains**, Fr.
116/M12 **Stakes** (mtn.), Ca,US
54/F2 **Stakhanov**, Ukr.
34/D5 **Stalbridge**, Eng,UK
35/H1 **Stalham**, Eng,UK
103/S6 **Stallworthy** (cape), NW,Can
39/M3 **Stalowa Wola**, Pol.
33/F5 **Stalybridge**, Eng,UK
51/G4 **Stamboliyski**, Bul.
35/F1 **Stamford**, Eng,UK
115/G4 **Stamford**, Ct,US
33/H4 **Stamford Bridge**, Eng,UK
37/E1 **Stamsund**, Nor.
32/B4 **Stamullin**, Ire.
88/E2 **Standerton**, SAfr.
33/F4 **Standish-with-Langtree**, Eng,UK
35/G4 **Stanford le Hope**, Eng,UK
31/P6 **Stanford Rivers**, Eng,UK
37/D3 **Stange**, Nor.
89/E3 **Stanger**, SAfr.
33/F2 **Stanhope**, Eng,UK
115/F5 **Stanhope**, NJ,US
108/B3 **Stanislaus** (riv.), Ca,US
51/F4 **Stanke Dimitrov**, Bul.
77/C4 **Stanley** (peak), Austl.
111/H2 **Stanley**, NB,Can
70/C5 **Stanley** (res.), India
33/G2 **Stanley**, Eng,UK
107/H3 **Stanley**, ND,US
83/L8 **Stanley** (falls), Zaire
50/E4 **Stanovo**, Yugo.
57/N4 **Stanovoy** (range), Rus.
31/P8 **Stansted**, Eng,UK
35/G3 **Stansted Mountfitchet**, Eng,UK
35/G2 **Stanton**, Eng,UK
115/C3 **Stanton**, Ca,US
110/D4 **Stanton**, Ky,US
112/C3 **Stanton**, Tx,US
31/M7 **Stanwell**, Eng,UK
40/D3 **Staphorst**, Neth.
35/E4 **Stapleford**, Eng,UK
31/P7 **Stapleford Abbotts**, Eng,UK
35/G4 **Staplehurst**, Eng,UK
39/L3 **Starachowice**, Pol.
50/E3 **Stara Pazova**, Yugo.
50/F3 **Stara Planina** (mts.), Yugo.
52/F4 **Staraya Russa**, Rus.
51/G4 **Stara Zagora**, Bul.
79/K5 **Starbuck** (isl.), Kiri.
76/B1 **Starcke Nat'l Park**, Austl.
39/H2 **Stargard Szczeciński**, Pol.
113/H4 **Starke**, Fl,US
113/F3 **Starkville**, Ms,US
54/F3 **Staroderevyan-kovskaya**, Rus.
54/E1 **Starodub**, Rus.
39/K2 **Starogard Gdański**, Pol.
54/F3 **Staroshcher-binovskaya**, Rus.
34/C6 **Start** (bay), Eng,UK
34/C6 **Start** (pt.), Eng,UK
39/L3 **Staszów**, Pol.
110/E3 **State College**, Pa,US
115/F5 **Staten** (isl.), NY,US
113/H3 **Statesboro**, Ga,US
113/H3 **Statesville**, NC,US
38/E3 **Staufenberg**, Ger.
34/D3 **Staunton**, Eng,UK
110/E4 **Staunton**, Va,US
34/D2 **Staunton on Wye**, Eng,UK
37/C4 **Stavanger**, Nor.
33/F3 **Staveley**, Eng,UK
33/G5 **Staveley**, Eng,UK
55/G3 **Stavropol'**, Rus.
55/G3 **Stavropol' Kray**, Rus.
77/B3 **Stawell**, Austl.
106/C4 **Stayton**, Or,US
108/F2 **Steamboat Springs**, Co,US
41/H3 **Stederau** (riv.), Ger.
77/F5 **Steele** (cr.), Austl.
107/J4 **Steele**, ND,US
89/E2 **Steelpoortrivier** (riv.), SAfr.
40/B5 **Steenbergen**, Neth.
108/C2 **Steens** (mtn.), Or,US
103/J1 **Steensby** (inlet), NW,Can
40/D3 **Steenwijk**, Neth.
74/A5 **Steep** (pt.), Austl.
107/G1 **Steephill** (lake), Sk,Can
34/C4 **Steep Holm** (isl.), Eng,UK
33/J5 **Steeping** (riv.), Eng,UK
114/J2 **Steese Nat'l Rec. Area**, Ak,US
102/F1 **Stefansson** (isl.), NW,Can
96/C5 **Steffen** (peak), Chile
45/G3 **Steffisburg**, Swi.
50/A2 **Steiermark** (prov.), Aus.
45/J2 **Steigerwald** (for.), Ger.
38/F4 **Stein**, Ger.
43/E2 **Stein**, Neth.
107/J3 **Steinbach**, Mb,Can
41/F5 **Steinhagen**, Ger.
41/G5 **Steinheim**, Ger.
41/G4 **Steinhuder Meer** (lake), Ger.
37/D2 **Steinkjer**, Nor.
42/D1 **Stekene**, Belg.
111/J2 **Stellarton**, NS,Can
41/H2 **Stelle**, Ger.
88/B4 **Stellenbosch**, SAfr.
45/H5 **Stello** (mtn.), Fr.
45/J3 **Stelvio Nat'l Park**, It.
38/F2 **Stendal**, Ger.
51/G4 **Steneto Nat'l Park**, Bul.
37/D4 **Stenungsund**, Swe.
55/H5 **Stepanakert**, Azer.
77/B1 **Stephens Creek**, Austl.
111/K1 **Stephenville**, Nf,Can
112/D3 **Stephenville**, Tx,US
109/G2 **Sterling**, Co,US
112/C4 **Sterling City**, Tx,US
116/F6 **Sterling Heights**, Mi,US
55/K1 **Sterlitamak**, Rus.
45/J3 **Sterzing** (Vipiteno), It.
106/E2 **Stettler**, Ab,Can
110/D3 **Steubenville**, Oh,US
35/F3 **Stevenage**, Eng,UK
107/J2 **Stevenson** (lake), Mb,Can
114/H4 **Stevenson** (str.), Ak,US
110/B2 **Stevens Point**, Wi,US
106/E4 **Stevensville**, Mt,US
40/C3 **Stevinsluizen** (dam), Neth.
74/E2 **Stewart** (cape), Austl.
114/L3 **Stewart** (riv.), Yk,Can
75/Q12 **Stewart** (isl.), NZ
114/L3 **Stewart Crossing**, Yk,Can
114/L3 **Stewart River**, Yk,Can
32/B2 **Stewartstown**, NI,UK
107/K5 **Stewartville**, Mn,US
35/F5 **Steyning**, Eng,UK
45/L2 **Steyr**, Aus.
45/L3 **Steyr** (riv.), Aus.
40/C2 **Stiens**, Neth.
109/J4 **Stigler**, Ok,US
114/M4 **Stikine** (riv.), BC,Can
107/K4 **Stillwater**, Mn,US
108/C3 **Stillwater** (range), Nv,US
109/H3 **Stillwater**, Ok,US
109/J4 **Stilwell**, Ok,US
32/D1 **Stinchar** (riv.), Sc,UK
112/C3 **Stinnett**, Tx,US
50/F5 **Štip**, Macd.
45/F5 **Stiring-Wendel**, Fr.
36/D2 **Stirling**, Sc,UK
111/L2 **St. John's** (cap.), Nf,Can
37/D3 **Stjørdal**, Nor.
35/E4 **Stockbridge**, Eng,UK
39/J4 **Stockerau**, Aus.
37/F4 **Stockholm** (cap.), Swe.
33/F5 **Stockport**, Eng,UK
33/F4 **Stocks** (res.), Eng,UK
33/G5 **Stocksbridge**, Eng,UK
116/M11 **Stockton**, Ca,US
109/J3 **Stockton** (lake), Mo,US
112/C4 **Stockton** (plat.), Tx,US
33/G2 **Stockton-on-Tees**, Eng,UK
69/D3 **Stoeng Treng**, Camb.
34/B6 **Stoke** (pt.), Eng,UK
33/F5 **Stoke-on-Trent**, Eng,UK
77/B4 **Stokes** (pt.), Austl.
50/C4 **Stolac**, Bosn.
43/F2 **Stolberg**, Ger.
57/P2 **Stolbovoy** (isl.), Rus.
88/K10 **Stompneuspunt** (pt.), SAfr.
33/F6 **Stone**, Eng,UK
36/D2 **Stonehaven**, Sc,UK
35/E4 **Stonehenge** (ruins), Eng,UK
34/D3 **Stonehouse**, Eng,UK
107/J3 **Stonewall**, Mb,Can
111/Q9 **Stoney Creek**, On,Can
107/J2 **Stony** (pt.), Mb,Can
115/G5 **Stony Brook**, NY,US
107/J3 **Stony Mountain**, Mb,Can
115/G4 **Stony Point**, NY,US
56/K3 **Stony Tunguska** (riv.), Rus.
110/D1 **Stooping** (riv.), On,Can
103/S7 **Stor** (isl.), NW,Can
41/G1 **Stör** (riv.), Ger.
37/F2 **Stora Sjöfallets Nat'l Park**, Swe.
37/F2 **Storavan** (lake), Swe.
38/F1 **Store Bælt** (chan.), Den.
37/D3 **Støren**, Nor.
77/C4 **Storm** (bay), Austl.
107/K5 **Storm Lake**, Ia,US
32/C2 **Stormont**, NI,UK
35/F5 **Storrington**, Eng,UK
37/F1 **Storsteinsfjellet** (peak), Nor.
38/F1 **Storstrøm** (co.), Den.
35/G3 **Stort** (riv.), Eng,UK
37/F2 **Storuman**, Swe.
106/G4 **Story**, Wy,US
97/J7 **Stosch** (isl.), Chile
35/F2 **Stotfold**, Eng,UK
107/H3 **Stoughton**, Sk,Can
34/D5 **Stour** (riv.), Eng,UK
35/E2 **Stour** (riv.), Eng,UK
35/H3 **Stour** (riv.), Eng,UK
35/F4 **Stour** (riv.), Eng,UK
34/D2 **Stourbridge**, Eng,UK
35/G4 **Stour, Great** (riv.), Eng,UK
34/D2 **Stourport on Severn**, Eng,UK
35/G2 **Stowmarket**, Eng,UK
35/E3 **Stow on the Wold**, Eng,UK
32/A2 **Strabane** (dist.), NI,UK
36/C2 **Strachan**, Sc,UK
36/C2 **Strachur**, Sc,UK
45/H4 **Stradella**, It.
40/D6 **Straelen**, Ger.
45/K2 **Strakonice**, Czh.
51/H4 **Straldzha**, Bul.
38/G1 **Stralsund**, Ger.
88/B4 **Strand**, SAfr.
32/C3 **Strangford**, NI,UK
32/C3 **Strangford Lough** (inlet), NI,UK
52/C4 **Strängnäs**, Swe.
32/B1 **Stranocum**, NI,UK
32/C2 **Stranraer**, Sc,UK
107/G3 **Strasbourg**, Sk,Can
45/G2 **Strasbourg**, Fr.
110/D3 **Stratford**, On,Can
75/R10 **Stratford**, NZ
115/E6 **Stratford**, NJ,US
35/E2 **Stratford upon Avon**, Eng,UK
36/C3 **Strathaven**, Sc,UK
32/D1 **Strathclyde** (reg.), Sc,UK
106/E3 **Strathmore**, Ab,Can
34/B5 **Stratton**, Eng,UK
45/K2 **Straubing**, Ger.
37/M6 **Straumnes** (pt.), Ice.
39/G2 **Strausberg**, Ger.
115/B2 **Strawberry** (peak), Ca,US
74/E6 **Streaky** (bay), Austl.
116/P15 **Streamwood**, Il,US
31/N7 **Streatham**, Eng,UK
35/E3 **Streatley**, Eng,UK
110/B3 **Streator**, Il,US
45/L2 **Středočeská Žulová Vrchovina** (mts.), Czh.
45/L2 **Středočeský** (reg.), Czh.
39/K4 **Středoslovenský** (reg.), Slvk.
34/D4 **Street**, Eng,UK
111/Q8 **Streetsville**, On,Can
51/F3 **Strehaia**, Rom.
52/H2 **Strel'na** (riv.), Rus.
33/F5 **Stretford**, Eng,UK
35/G2 **Stretham**, Eng,UK
40/B5 **Strijen**, Neth.
49/H2 **Strimón** (gulf), Gre.
49/H2 **Strimónas** (riv.), Gre.
97/K7 **Strobel** (lake), Arg.
49/G4 **Strofádhes** (isls.), Gre.
48/D3 **Stromboli** (isl.), It.
37/D4 **Strømmen**, Nor.
37/D4 **Strömstad**, Swe.
37/E3 **Strömsund**, Swe.
39/J3 **Stronie Śląskie**, Pol.
34/D3 **Stroud**, Eng,UK
50/E5 **Struga**, Macd.
88/C4 **Struisbaai** (bay), SAfr.
32/A2 **Strule** (riv.), NI,UK
49/H2 **Struma** (riv.), Bul., Gre.
34/A2 **Strumble Head** (pt.), Wal,UK
50/F5 **Strumica**, Macd.
37/C3 **Stryn**, Nor.
39/J3 **Strzegom**, Pol.
39/H2 **Strzelce Krajeńskie**, Pol.
76/A5 **Strzelecki** (cr.), Austl.
77/D4 **Strzelecki** (peak), Austl.
39/J3 **Strzelin**, Pol.
39/L4 **Strzyżów**, Pol.
106/B2 **Stuart** (lake), BC,Can
106/B2 **Stuart** (riv.), BC,Can
113/H5 **Stuart**, Fl,US
110/E4 **Stuarts Draft**, Va,US
39/G1 **Stubbenkammer** (pt.), Ger.
35/E5 **Studland**, Eng,UK
35/E2 **Studley**, Eng,UK
39/J4 **Stupava**, Slvk.
52/H5 **Stupino**, Rus.
107/J3 **Sturgeon** (bay), Mb,Can
110/B1 **Sturgeon** (lake), On,Can
110/C2 **Sturgeon Bay**, Wi,US
110/E2 **Sturgeon Falls**, On,Can
110/C3 **Sturgis**, Mi,US
107/H4 **Sturgis**, SD,US
34/D5 **Sturminster Newton**, Eng,UK
35/H4 **Sturry**, Eng,UK
76/A5 **Sturt** (des.), Austl.
77/B1 **Sturt** (peak), Austl.
77/B1 **Sturt Nat'l Park**, Austl.
88/D4 **Stutterheim**, SAfr.
45/H2 **Stuttgart**, Ger.
113/F3 **Stuttgart**, Ar,US
54/C2 **Styr** (riv.), Ukr.
45/L3 **Styria** (prov.), Aus.
95/D1 **Suaçui Grande** (riv.), Braz.
86/D5 **Suakin** (arch.), Sudan
67/D3 **Suao**, Tai.
72/C5 **Subang**, Indo.
48/C1 **Subasio** (peak), It.
81/W18 **Subayṭilah**, Tun.
72/C3 **Subi** (isl.), Indo.
50/D2 **Subotica**, Yugo.
115/F5 **Succasunna-Kenvil**, NJ,US
51/H2 **Suceava**, Rom.
51/G2 **Suceava** (co.), Rom.
39/L3 **Suchedniów**, Pol.
36/A4 **Suck** (riv.), Ire.
92/E7 **Sucre** (cap.), Bol.
92/G5 **Sucunduri** (riv.), Braz.
95/B2 **Sucuriú** (riv.), Braz.
31/T10 **Sucy-en-Brie**, Fr.
52/H4 **Suda** (riv.), Rus.
83/L5 **Sudan**
82/H5 **Sudan** (phys. reg.), Afr.
110/D2 **Sudbury**, On,Can
35/G2 **Sudbury**, Eng,UK
41/H2 **Sude** (riv.), Ger.
39/H3 **Sudeten** (mts.), Czh., Pol.
40/D5 **Südlohn**, Ger.
85/H5 **Sud-Ouest** (prov.), Camr.
83/L6 **Sue** (riv.), Sudan
47/E3 **Sueca**, Sp.
51/G4 **Süedinenie**, Bul.
86/C2 **Suez** (can.), Egypt
86/C2 **Suez** (gulf), Egypt
86/C2 **Suez** (As Suways), Egypt
59/K5 **Ṣūf**, Jor.
115/F4 **Suffern**, NY,US
35/G2 **Suffolk** (co.), Eng,UK
110/E4 **Suffolk**, Va,US
109/K2 **Sugar** (riv.), Il, Wi,US
112/E4 **Sugar Land**, Tx,US
75/J6 **Sugarloaf** (pt.), Austl.
34/C3 **Sugar Loaf** (mtn.), Wal,UK
113/H2 **Sugarloaf** (peak), Ky,US
62/F1 **Sühbaatar**, Mong.
45/J1 **Suhl**, Ger.
59/B2 **Şuhut**, Turk.
67/B3 **Sui** (riv.), China
69/B4 **Sui** (pt.), Thai.
93/H6 **Suia-Missu** (riv.), Braz.
63/L2 **Suibin**, China
63/L3 **Suifenhe**, China
63/K2 **Suihua**, China
63/K2 **Suileng**, China
42/D5 **Suippe** (riv.), Fr.
36/B4 **Suir** (riv.), Ire.
116/K10 **Suisun City**, Ca,US
65/L10 **Suita**, Japan
115/K8 **Suitland-Silver Hill**, Md,US
62/G5 **Suizhou**, China
70/B2 **Sūjāngarh**, India
72/C5 **Sukabumi**, Indo.
72/C4 **Sukadana**, Indo.
72/C4 **Sukadana** (bay), Indo.
65/G2 **Sukagawa**, Japan
54/E1 **Sukhinichi**, Rus.
52/J4 **Sukhona** (riv.), Rus.
69/B2 **Sukhothai**, Thai.
55/G4 **Sukhumi**, Geo.
61/J3 **Sukkur**, Pak.
64/C4 **Sukumo**, Japan
73/G4 **Sula** (isls.), Indo.
53/L2 **Sula** (riv.), Rus.
61/J3 **Sulaimān** (range), Pak.
73/E4 **Sulawesi** (Celebes) (isl.), Indo.
86/B4 **Sulb Temple** (ruins), Sudan
32/D3 **Sulby** (riv.), IM,UK
39/H2 **Sulechów**, Pol.
39/H2 **Sulęcin**, Pol.
39/L2 **Sulejówek**, Pol.
41/F3 **Sulingen**, Ger.
62/D4 **Sulin Gol** (riv.), China
37/F2 **Sulitjelma** (peak), Nor.
92/B4 **Sullana**, Peru
106/F3 **Sullivan** (lake), Ab,Can
110/C4 **Sullivan**, In,US
110/E1 **Sullivan Mines**, Qu,Can
34/C4 **Sully**, Wal,UK
48/C1 **Sulmona**, It.
109/J4 **Sulphur** (riv.), Ar, Tx,US
112/E4 **Sulphur**, La,US
109/H4 **Sulphur**, Ok,US
112/E3 **Sulphur Springs**, Tx,US
73/E2 **Sulu** (sea), Malay., Phil.
67/D6 **Sulu** (arch.), Phil.
59/C2 **Suluova**, Turk.
83/K1 **Sulūq**, Libya
43/G2 **Sülz** (riv.), Ger.
43/G5 **Sulzbach**, Ger.
45/J2 **Sulzbach-Rosenberg**, Ger.
98/P **Sulzberger** (bay), Ant.
98/Q **Sulzberger Ice Shelf**, Ant.
50/E3 **Šumadija** (reg.), Yugo.
92/D3 **Sumapaz Nat'l Park**, Col.
72/B4 **Sumatra** (isl.), Indo.
72/E5 **Sumba** (isl.), Indo.
72/E5 **Sumba** (str.), Indo.
55/L5 **Sumbar** (riv.), Trkm.
72/E5 **Sumbawa** (isl.), Indo.
73/E5 **Sumbawa Besar**, Indo.
87/F2 **Sumbawanga**, Tanz.
87/B3 **Sumbe**, Ang.
62/F2 **Sümber**, Mong.
114/M4 **Sumdum** (mtn.), Ak,US
94/C2 **Sumé**, Braz.
50/C2 **Sümeg**, Hun.
72/D5 **Sumenep**, Indo.
55/J4 **Sumgait**, Azer.
33/G3 **Summer Bridge**, Eng,UK
106/D3 **Summerland**, BC,Can
111/J2 **Summerside**, PE,Can
110/D4 **Summersville**, WV,US
113/G3 **Summerville**, Ga,US
113/H3 **Summerville**, SC,US
115/F5 **Summit**, NJ,US
116/C3 **Sumner**, Wa,US
64/D3 **Sumoto**, Japan
39/J4 **Šumperk**, Czh.
113/H3 **Sumter**, SC,US
54/E2 **Sumy**, Ukr.
54/E2 **Sumy Obl.**, Ukr.
106/E4 **Sun** (riv.), Mt,US
65/M9 **Sunami**, Japan
77/C3 **Sunbury**, Austl.
35/F4 **Sunbury on Thames**, Eng,UK
63/K5 **Sunch'ŏn**, SKor.
108/D4 **Sun City**, Az,US
115/C3 **Sun City**, Ca,US
111/G3 **Suncook**, NH,US
72/B5 **Sunda** (str.), Indo.
107/G4 **Sundance**, Wy,US
70/E3 **Sundarbans** (reg.), Bang., India
70/D3 **Sundargarh**, India
61/L2 **Sundarnagar**, India
88/D4 **Sundays** (riv.), SAfr.
33/G2 **Sunderland**, Eng,UK
41/F6 **Sundern**, Ger.
77/D1 **Sundown Nat'l Park**, Austl.
106/E3 **Sundre**, Ab,Can
37/F3 **Sundsvall**, Swe.
72/B4 **Sungaipenuh**, Indo.
72/B2 **Sungai Petani**, Malay.
59/C2 **Sungurlu**, Turk.
112/B4 **Sunland Park**, NM,US
37/D3 **Sunndalsøra**, Nor.
37/E4 **Sunne**, Swe.
35/F4 **Sunninghill**, Eng,UK
116/K12 **Sunnyvale**, Ca,US
65/H8 **Su-no-saki** (cape), Japan
110/B3 **Sun Prairie**, Wi,US
115/B3 **Sunset Beach**, Ca,US
77/B2 **Sunset Country** (reg.), Austl.
108/E4 **Sunset Crater Nat'l Mon.**, Az,US
77/F5 **Sunshine**, Austl.
57/P3 **Suntar-Khayata** (mts.), Rus.
41/G4 **Süntel** (mts.), Ger.
85/E5 **Sunyani**, Gha.
87/F2 **Suo** (peak), Zam.
64/B4 **Suo** (sea), Japan
69/D1 **Suoi Rut**, Viet.
37/H3 **Suomenselkä** (reg.), Fin.
69/D4 **Suong**, Camb.
92/C6 **Supe**, Peru
110/C2 **Superior** (lake), Can., US
108/E4 **Superior**, Az,US
106/E4 **Superior**, Mt,US
110/B2 **Superior**, Wi,US
110/A2 **Superior** (upland), Wi,US
69/C3 **Suphan Buri**, Thai.
73/J4 **Supiori** (isl.), Indo.
60/E2 **Sūq ash Shuyūkh**, Iraq
59/L4 **Şuqaylabīyah**, Syria
66/D4 **Suqian**, China
97/F3 **Sur** (pt.), Arg.
43/E4 **Sûr** (riv.), Belg.
108/B3 **Sur** (pt.), Ca,US
55/H1 **Sura** (riv.), Rus.
72/D5 **Surabaya**, Indo.
70/D4 **Surada**, India
72/D5 **Surakarta**, Indo.
67/D6 **Surallah**, Phil.
39/K4 **Šurany**, Slvk.
70/B3 **Surat**, India
70/B2 **Suratgarh**, India
69/B4 **Surat Thani**, Thai.
43/G6 **Surbourg**, Fr.
97/J7 **Sur, Campo de Hielo** (glacier), Chile
50/E3 **Surčin**, Yugo.
50/F4 **Surdulica**, Yugo.
43/E4 **Sûre** (riv.), Belg., Lux.
70/B3 **Surendranagar**, India
44/C3 **Surgères**, Fr.
56/H3 **Surgut**, Rus.
70/D3 **Sūri**, India
47/F2 **Súria**, Sp.
67/E6 **Surigao**, Phil.

161

Surin – Terno

69/C3 **Surin,** Thai.
93/G3 **Suriname**
68/A4 **Surkhob** (riv.), Taj.
115/K8 **Surrattsville** (Clinton), Md,US
106/C3 **Surrey,** BC,Can
31/M8 **Surrey** (co.), Eng,UK
82/J1 **Surt,** Libya
37/D3 **Sur-Trøndelag** (co.), Nor.
59/K5 **Şūr** (Tyre), Leb.
94/D2 **Surubim,** Braz.
59/D3 **Sürüç,** Turk.
65/F3 **Suruga** (bay), Japan
31/T9 **Survilliers,** Fr.
81/X18 **Sūsah,** Tun.
81/X17 **Sūsah** (gov.), Tun.
64/C4 **Susaki,** Japan
60/E2 **Sūsangerd,** Iran
108/B2 **Susanville,** Ca,US
59/D2 **Suşehri,** Turk.
66/B4 **Sushui** (riv.), China
114/J3 **Susitna** (riv.), Ak,US
65/F3 **Susono,** Japan
110/E3 **Susquehanna** (riv.), US
111/H2 **Sussex,** NB,Can
35/F4 **Sussex, Vale of** (val.), Eng,UK
40/C6 **Susteren,** Neth.
57/Q3 **Susuman,** Rus.
76/H9 **Sutherland,** Austl.
50/D4 **Sutjeska Nat'l Park,** Bosn.
61/K2 **Sutlej** (riv.), India, Pak.
33/H6 **Sutterton,** Eng,UK
31/N7 **Sutton** (bor.), Eng,UK
33/J6 **Sutton Bridge,** Eng,UK
35/E1 **Sutton Coldfield,** Eng,UK
33/G5 **Sutton in Ashfield,** Eng,UK
33/J5 **Sutton on Sea,** Eng,UK
33/H5 **Sutton on Trent,** Eng,UK
88/D4 **Suurberge** (mts.), SAfr.
78/G6 **Suva** (cap.), Fiji
65/F2 **Suwa,** Japan
39/M1 **Suwałki,** Pol.
39/M2 **Suwałki** (prov.), Pol.
113/H4 **Suwannee** (riv.), Fl,US
79/J6 **Suwarrow** (atoll), Cookls.
59/K5 **Şuwaylih,** Jor.
66/D4 **Suzhou,** China
66/E5 **Suzhou,** China
65/E2 **Suzu,** Japan
64/E3 **Suzuka,** Japan
65/M10 **Suzuka** (range), Japan
65/E2 **Suzu-misaki** (cape), Japan
45/J4 **Suzzara,** It.
56/C2 **Svalbard** (arch.), Nor.
69/D4 **Svay Rieng,** Camb.
37/E4 **Svealand** (reg.), Swe.
38/F1 **Svendborg,** Den.
103/S7 **Svendsen** (pen.), NW,Can
37/E4 **Svenljunga,** Swe.
53/P4 **Sverdlovsk** (Yekaterinburg), Rus.
103/S7 **Sverdrup** (chan.), NW,Can
103/R7 **Sverdrup** (isls.), NW,Can
56/H2 **Sverdrup** (isl.), Rus.
54/D1 **Svetlogorsk,** Bela.
55/G3 **Svetlograd,** Rus.
50/E4 **Svetozarevo,** Yugo.
37/P7 **Svíahnúkar** (peak), Ice.
50/E3 **Svilajnac,** Yugo.
51/H5 **Svilengrad,** Bul.
51/G4 **Svishtov,** Bul.
39/J4 **Svitavy,** Czh.
63/K1 **Svobodnyy,** Rus.
51/F4 **Svoge,** Bul.
37/E1 **Svolvær,** Nor.
57/Q2 **Svyatyy Nos** (cape), Rus.
35/E1 **Swadlincote,** Eng,UK
35/G1 **Swaffham,** Eng,UK
76/D3 **Swain** (reefs), Austl.
113/H3 **Swainsboro,** Ga,US
79/H5 **Swains Island** (atoll), ASam.
87/C2 **Swa-Kibula,** Zaire
87/B5 **Swakopmund,** Namb.
33/G3 **Swale** (riv.), Eng,UK
35/H4 **Swalecliffe,** Eng,UK
35/G4 **Swale, The** (chan.), Eng,UK
40/D6 **Swalmen,** Neth.
106/D2 **Swan** (hills), Ab,Can
107/H2 **Swan** (riv.), Mb, Sk,Can
100/E4 **Swan** (isls.), Hon.
35/E5 **Swanage,** Eng,UK
77/B2 **Swan Hill,** Austl.
31/P7 **Swanley,** Eng,UK
35/G4 **Swanley Hextable,** Eng,UK
107/H2 **Swan River,** Mb,Can
31/P7 **Swanscombe,** Eng,UK
34/C3 **Swansea,** Wal,UK
34/C3 **Swansea** (bay), Wal,UK
115/E6 **Swarthmore,** Pa,US
88/D3 **Swart Kei** (riv.), SAfr.
39/J2 **Swarzędz,** Pol.
88/B2 **Swarzrand** (mts.), Namb.
32/B2 **Swatragh,** NI,UK
35/E5 **Sway,** Eng,UK
89/E2 **Swaziland**
37/E3 **Sweden**
106/C4 **Sweet Home,** Or,US
112/C3 **Sweetwater,** Tx,US
106/F5 **Sweetwater** (riv.), Wy,US
88/C4 **Swellendam,** SAfr.
39/J3 **Świdnica,** Pol.
39/M3 **Świdnik,** Pol.
39/H2 **Świdwin,** Pol.
39/J3 **Świebodzice,** Pol.
39/H2 **Świebozin,** Pol.
39/K2 **Świecie,** Pol.
106/G3 **Swift Current,** Sk,Can
35/E3 **Swindon,** Eng,UK
33/H6 **Swineshead,** Eng,UK
39/H2 **Świnoujście,** Pol.
33/G5 **Swinton,** Eng,UK
45/G3 **Swiss** (plat.), Swi.
43/F2 **Swist Bach** (riv.), Ger.
45/G3 **Switzerland**
32/B5 **Swords,** Ire.
52/G3 **Syamozero** (lake), Rus.
39/J3 **Syców,** Pol.
77/D2 **Sydney,** Austl.
111/J2 **Sydney,** NS,Can
76/H8 **Sydney** (inset), Austl.
79/H5 **Sydney** (Manra) (atoll), Kiri.
111/J2 **Sydney Mines,** NS,Can
41/F3 **Syke,** Ger.
53/L3 **Syktyvkar,** Rus.
113/G3 **Sylacauga,** Al,US
37/E3 **Sylarna** (peak), Swe.
71/F3 **Sylhet,** Bang.
38/E1 **Sylt** (isl.), Ger.
53/N4 **Sylva** (riv.), Rus.
110/D3 **Sylvania,** Oh,US
116/F6 **Sylvan Lake,** Mi,US
49/L6 **Syntagma Square,** Gre.
115/G5 **Syosset,** NY,US
98/C **Syowa,** Ant.
109/G3 **Syracuse,** Ks,US
110/E3 **Syracuse,** NY,US
48/D4 **Syracuse** (Siracusa), It.
56/G5 **Syrdar'ya** (riv.), Asia
60/C1 **Syria**
71/G4 **Syriam,** Burma
53/L3 **Sysola** (riv.), Rus.
35/E1 **Syston,** Eng,UK
55/J1 **Syzran',** Rus.
50/E1 **Szabolcs-Szatmár-Bereg** (co.), Hun.
39/J2 **Szamotuły,** Pol.
50/E2 **Szarvas,** Hun.
50/D2 **Százhalombatta,** Hun.
39/H2 **Szczecin,** Pol.
39/H2 **Szczecin** (prov.), Pol.
39/J2 **Szczecinek,** Pol.
39/L2 **Szczytno,** Pol.
50/E2 **Szeged,** Hun.
50/E2 **Szeghalom,** Hun.
50/E2 **Szegvár,** Hun.
50/D2 **Székesfehérvár,** Hun.
50/D2 **Szekszárd,** Hun.
50/D2 **Szentendre,** Hun.
50/E2 **Szentes,** Hun.
50/E1 **Szerencs,** Hun.
39/M1 **Szeskie** (peak), Pol.
50/C2 **Szigetvár,** Hun.
50/E2 **Szolnok,** Hun.
50/C2 **Szombathely,** Hun.
39/H3 **Szprotawa,** Pol.
39/K2 **Sztum,** Pol.
39/J2 **Szubin,** Pol.
39/L3 **Szydłowiec,** Pol.

T

67/D5 **Tabaco,** Phil.
61/G2 **Ţabas,** Iran
100/C4 **Tabasco** (state), Mex.
94/A3 **Tabatinga** (mts.), Braz.
106/E3 **Taber,** Ab,Can
47/E3 **Tabernes de Valldigna,** Sp.
94/C2 **Tabira,** Braz.
78/G5 **Tabiteuea** (atoll), Kiri.
67/D5 **Tablas** (isl.), Phil.
88/B4 **Table** (bay), SAfr.
88/L10 **Table** (mtn.), SAfr.
109/J3 **Table Rock** (lake), Ar, Mo,US
46/B1 **Taboada,** Sp.
45/L2 **Tábor,** Czh.
87/F2 **Tabora,** Tanz.
84/D5 **Tabou,** IvC.
79/K4 **Tabuaeran** (Fanning) (atoll), Kiri.
67/D4 **Tabuk,** Phil.
60/C3 **Tabūk,** SAr.
94/C2 **Tabuleiro do Norte,** Braz.
78/F6 **Tabwemasana** (mtn.), Van.
101/F6 **Tacarcuna** (mt.), Pan.
68/D2 **Tacheng,** China
67/D3 **Tachia** (riv.), Tai.
64/A4 **Tachibana** (bay), Japan
65/F3 **Tachikawa,** Japan
67/D3 **Tachoshui,** Tai.
45/K2 **Tachov,** Czh.
67/E5 **Tacloban,** Phil.
92/D7 **Tacna,** Peru
116/C3 **Tacoma,** Wa,US
92/E7 **Tacora** (vol.), Chile
47/X16 **Tacoronte,** Canl.,Sp.
97/G1 **Tacuarembó,** Uru.
97/G2 **Tacuarembó** (dept.), Uru.
65/F2 **Tadami** (riv.), Japan
65/L10 **Tadaoka,** Japan
33/G4 **Tadcaster,** Eng,UK
82/F2 **Tademaït** (plat.), Alg.
70/D4 **Tādepallegūdem,** India
79/V12 **Tadine,** NCal.
35/E4 **Tadley,** Eng,UK
60/C2 **Tadmur,** Syria
65/M9 **Tado,** Japan
64/C3 **Tadotsu,** Japan
70/C5 **Tādpatri,** India
82/H2 **Tadrart** (mts.), Alg., Libya
31/N8 **Tadworth,** Eng,UK
63/K4 **T'aebaek** (mts.), NKor., SKor.
63/K4 **Taech'ŏn,** SKor.
63/K4 **Taegang-got** (pt.), NKor.
64/A3 **Taegu,** SKor.
63/K4 **Taejŏn,** SKor.
34/B3 **Taf** (riv.), Wal,UK
46/E1 **Tafalla,** Sp.
34/C3 **Taff** (riv.), Wal,UK
91/C2 **Tafí Viejo,** Arg.
60/F2 **Taft,** Iran
61/H3 **Taftān** (mtn.), Iran
65/M9 **Taga,** Japan
54/F3 **Taganrog,** Rus.
54/F3 **Taganrog** (gulf), Rus., Ukr.
84/C2 **Tagant** (reg.), Mrta.
61/G1 **Tagarav** (peak), Trkm.
64/B4 **Tagawa,** Japan
67/D6 **Tagbilaran,** Phil.
45/G5 **Taggia,** It.
82/E1 **Taghit,** Alg.
114/M3 **Tagish,** Yk,Can
45/K3 **Tagliamento** (riv.), It.
42/D5 **Tagnon,** Fr.
73/F2 **Tagolo** (pt.), Phil.
78/E6 **Tagula** (isl.), PNG
67/E6 **Tagum,** Phil.
53/P4 **Tagun** (riv.), Rus.
46/B3 **Tagus** (riv.), Port., Sp.
72/B3 **Tahan** (peak), Malay.
65/N10 **Tahara,** Japan
82/G3 **Tahat** (peak), Alg.
81/R16 **Tahat, Oued et** (riv.), Alg.
79/L6 **Tahenea** (atoll), FrPol.
79/L6 **Tahiti** (isl.), FrPol.
112/E3 **Tahlequah,** Ok,US
114/J3 **Tahneta** (pass), Ak,US
108/C3 **Tahoe** (lake), Ca, Nv,US
112/C3 **Tahoka,** Tx,US
85/G3 **Tahoua,** Niger
85/G3 **Tahoua** (dept.), Niger
106/B3 **Tahsis,** BC,Can
86/B3 **Taḩtā,** Egypt
79/L6 **Tahuata** (isl.), FrPol.
73/G3 **Tahulandang** (isl.), Indo.
66/L8 **Tai** (lake), China
63/H4 **Tai'an,** China
79/X15 **Taiarapu** (pen.), FrPol.
66/C3 **Taibai Shan** (mtn.), China
67/D3 **Taichung,** Tai.
66/C3 **Taihang** (mts.), China
67/D3 **Taihsi,** Tai.
65/L10 **Taima,** Japan
36/C2 **Tain,** Sc,UK
67/D3 **Tainan,** Tai.
49/H4 **Taínaron, Ákra** (cape), Gre.
84/D5 **Taï Nat'l Park,** IvC.
94/B4 **Taiobeiras,** Braz.
79/L5 **Taiohae,** FrPol.
67/D2 **Taipei** (cap.), Tai.
63/J2 **Taiping** (peak), China
72/B3 **Taiping,** Malay.
64/C3 **Taisha,** Japan
65/L10 **Taishi,** Japan
67/C2 **Taishun,** China
96/B5 **Taitao** (pen.), Chile
67/D3 **Taitung,** Tai.
67/D3 **Taiwan**
67/C3 **Taiwan** (str.), China, Tai.
49/H4 **Taíyetos** (mts.), Gre.
66/C3 **Taiyuan,** China
66/D4 **Taizhou,** China
66/E2 **Taizi** (riv.), China
72/C4 **Tajam** (peak), Indo.
82/H3 **Tajarhī,** Libya
56/H6 **Tajikistan**
65/F2 **Tajima,** Japan
65/E3 **Tajimi,** Japan
65/L10 **Tajiri,** Japan
46/C3 **Tajo** (Tagus) (riv.), Sp.
60/F1 **Tajrīsh,** Iran
100/C4 **Tajumulco** (vol.), Guat.
46/D2 **Tajuña** (riv.), Sp.
69/B2 **Tak,** Thai.
65/G2 **Takahagi,** Japan
64/D3 **Takahama,** Japan
64/C3 **Takahashi,** Japan
64/C3 **Takahashi** (riv.), Japan
65/G2 **Takahata,** Japan
65/L10 **Takaishi,** Japan
64/D3 **Takamatsu,** Japan
65/M10 **Takami-yama** (peak), Japan
64/B4 **Takanabe,** Japan
65/E2 **Takaoka,** Japan
75/R10 **Takapuna,** NZ
65/L10 **Takarazuka,** Japan
79/L6 **Takaroa** (isl.), FrPol.
65/F2 **Takasaki,** Japan
65/M9 **Takashima,** Japan
65/L10 **Takatori,** Japan
64/D3 **Takatsuki,** Japan
65/E2 **Takayama,** Japan
64/E3 **Takefu,** Japan
64/C3 **Takehara,** Japan
60/E1 **Tākestān,** Iran
64/B4 **Taketa,** Japan
65/M10 **Taketoyo,** Japan
69/D4 **Takev,** Camb.
71/H4 **Ta Khli,** Thai.
83/R2 **Takht-e Jamshīd** (Persepolis) (ruins), Iran
65/M10 **Taki,** Japan
102/E2 **Takijuq** (lake), NW,Can
63/N3 **Takikawa,** Japan
65/K10 **Takino,** Japan
106/B2 **Takla** (lake), BC,Can
68/D4 **Takla Makan** (des.), China
85/E5 **Takoradi,** Gha.
59/H6 **Talā,** Egypt
33/E5 **Talacre,** Wal,UK
96/Q9 **Talagante,** Chile
70/B3 **Talāja,** India
85/G2 **Talak** (reg.), Niger
87/C2 **Tala Mugongo,** Ang.
72/B4 **Talang** (peak), Indo.
43/F5 **Talange,** Fr.
44/F3 **Talant,** Fr.
92/B4 **Talara,** Peru
68/B3 **Talas** (riv.), Kaz.
59/C2 **Talas,** Turk.
73/G3 **Talaud** (isls.), Indo.
46/C3 **Talavera de la Reina,** Sp.
70/D6 **Talawakele,** SrL.
83/M5 **Talawdī,** Sudan
46/C3 **Talayuela,** Sp.
74/D2 **Talbot** (cape), Austl.
96/C2 **Talca,** Chile
96/B3 **Talcahuano,** Chile
70/E3 **Tālcher,** India
68/C3 **Taldy-Kurgan,** Kaz.
44/C4 **Talence,** Fr.
56/H5 **Talgar,** Kaz.
34/C3 **Talgarth,** Wal,UK
73/F4 **Taliabu** (isl.), Indo.
83/M6 **Tali Post,** Sudan
73/E5 **Taliwang,** Indo.
59/H6 **Ţalkhā,** Egypt
113/G3 **Talladega,** Al,US
59/E3 **Tall 'Afar,** Iraq
113/G4 **Tallahassee** (cap.), Fl,US
113/F3 **Tallahatchie** (riv.), Ms,US
59/N9 **Tall 'Āsūr** (Ba'al Hazor) (mtn.), WBnk.
115/E6 **Talleyville,** De,US
52/E4 **Tallinn** (cap.), Est.
59/E3 **Tall Kayf,** Iraq
113/H3 **Tallulah** (falls), Ga,US
113/F3 **Tallulah,** La,US
83/N5 **Talo** (peak), Eth.
70/B3 **Taloda,** India
61/J1 **Tāloqān,** Afg.
91/B2 **Taltal,** Chile
102/E2 **Taltson** (riv.), NW,Can
69/C4 **Talumphuk** (pt.), Thai.
61/L2 **Talwāra,** India
65/H7 **Tama,** Japan
65/H7 **Tama** (riv.), Japan
65/M10 **Tamaki,** Japan
85/E4 **Tamale,** Gha.
78/G5 **Tamana** (atoll), Kiri.
80/C2 **Tamanghasset,** Alg.
34/B5 **Tamar** (riv.), Eng,UK
50/D2 **Tamási,** Hun.
100/B3 **Tamazunchale,** Mex.
65/L9 **Tamba,** Japan
65/L9 **Tamba** (hills), Japan
84/B3 **Tambacounda,** Sen.
84/B3 **Tambacounda** (reg.), Sen.
84/C3 **Tambaoura, Falaise de** (escarp.), Mali
72/C3 **Tambelan** (isls.), Indo.
73/E5 **Tambora** (peak), Indo.
77/C3 **Tamboritha** (peak), Austl.
55/G1 **Tambov,** Rus.
55/G1 **Tambov Obl.,** Rus.
46/A1 **Tambre** (riv.), Sp.
83/L6 **Tambura,** Sudan
35/E1 **Tame** (riv.), Eng,UK
46/B2 **Támega** (riv.), Port.
85/H2 **Tamgak** (peak), Niger
84/B3 **Tamgue, Massif du** (reg.), Gui., Sen.
70/C5 **Tamil Nadu** (state), India
69/E3 **Tam Ky,** Viet.
69/D2 **Tam Le,** Viet.
113/H5 **Tampa,** Fl,US
37/G3 **Tampere,** Fin.
100/B3 **Tampico,** Mex.
72/A3 **Tampulonanjing** (peak), Indo.
100/B3 **Tamuín,** Mex.
100/B3 **Tamulipas** (state), Mex.
77/D1 **Tamworth,** Austl.
35/E1 **Tamworth,** Eng,UK
71/K3 **Tan** (riv.), China
83/N5 **Tana** (lake), Eth.
80/F5 **Tana** (riv.), Kenya
37/H1 **Tana** (riv.), Nor.
64/D4 **Tanabe,** Japan
95/B2 **Tanabi,** Braz.
37/J1 **Tanafjorden** (fjord), Nor.
114/C6 **Tanaga** (isl.), Ak,US
48/D2 **Tanagro** (riv.), It.
65/G2 **Tanagura,** Japan
69/C5 **Tanah Merah,** Malay.
74/E3 **Tanami** (des.), Austl.
69/D4 **Tan An,** Viet.
114/J3 **Tanana** (riv.), Ak,US
45/H4 **Tanaro** (riv.), It.
70/C2 **Tānda,** India
70/D2 **Tandā,** India
84/D3 **Tanda** (lake), Mali
83/M5 **Tandaltī,** Sudan
51/H3 **Ţăndărei,** Rom.
96/F3 **Tandil,** Arg.
61/J3 **Tando Ādam,** Pak.
61/J3 **Tando Allāhyār,** Pak.
61/J3 **Tando Muhammad Khān,** Pak.
77/B2 **Tandou** (lake), Austl.
32/B3 **Tandragee,** NI,UK
64/B5 **Tanega** (isl.), Japan
69/B2 **Tanem** (range), Burma, Thai.
82/E3 **Tanezrouft** (des.), Alg., Mali
66/C3 **Tang** (riv.), China
66/C4 **Tang** (riv.), China
87/G2 **Tanga,** Tanz.
89/H8 **Tangainony,** Madg.
87/F2 **Tanganyika** (lake), Afr.
93/G6 **Tangará da Serra,** Braz.
114/G1 **Tangent** (pt.), Ak,US
38/F2 **Tangerhütte,** Ger.
81/M13 **Tanger** (Tangier), Mor.
68/E5 **Tanggula** (mts.), China
68/F5 **Tanggula Shankou** (pass), China
81/M13 **Tangier** (Tanger), Mor.
116/B3 **Tanglewilde-Thompson Place,** Wa,US
68/E5 **Tangra** (lake), China
67/D6 **Tangub,** Phil.
73/H5 **Tanimbar** (isls.), Indo.
67/D6 **Tanjay,** Phil.
72/A3 **Tanjungbalai,** Indo.
72/C5 **Tanjungkarang-Telukbetung,** Indo.
72/C4 **Tanjungpandan,** Indo.
72/A3 **Tanjungpura,** Indo.
61/K2 **Tānk,** Pak.
78/F6 **Tanna** (isl.), Van.
65/L9 **Tannan,** Japan
68/F1 **Tannu-Ola** (mts.), Mong., Rus.
85/E5 **Tano** (riv.), Ghana, IvC.
59/H6 **Ţanţā,** Egypt
83/M1 **Tantā,** Egypt
82/C2 **Tan-Tan,** Mor.
100/B3 **Tantoyuca,** Mex.
70/D4 **Tanuku,** India
87/F2 **Tanzania**
65/H7 **Tanzawa-yama** (peak), Japan
67/B2 **Tao** (riv.), China
69/B4 **Tao** (isl.), Thai.
63/J2 **Tao'er** (riv.), China
48/D4 **Taormina,** It.
109/F3 **Taos,** NM,US
82/E3 **Taoudenni,** Mali
81/N13 **Taourirt,** Mor.
67/B2 **Taoyuan,** China
67/D3 **Taoyuan,** Tai.
52/E4 **Tapa,** Est.
100/C5 **Tapachula,** Mex.
93/G4 **Tapajós** (riv.), Braz.
93/G3 **Tapanahoni** (riv.), Sur.
92/E5 **Tapauá** (riv.), Braz.
67/D5 **Tapaz,** Phil.
95/B4 **Tapejara,** Braz.
95/B4 **Tapes,** Braz.
72/B3 **Tapis** (peak), Malay.
85/F3 **Tapoa** (prov.), Burk.
50/C2 **Tapolca,** Hun.
110/E4 **Tappahannock,** Va,US
115/G4 **Tappan,** NY,US
115/G4 **Tappan Zee** (reach), NY,US
116/C3 **Tapps** (lake), Wa,US
70/B3 **Tāpti** (riv.), India
86/B5 **Taqab,** Sudan
86/D5 **Taqātu' Hayyā,** Sudan
95/B4 **Taquara,** Braz.
95/B4 **Taquari,** Braz.
93/G7 **Taquari** (riv.), Braz.
95/B2 **Taquaritinga,** Braz.
95/B2 **Taquarituba,** Braz.
68/B3 **Tar** (riv.), Kyr.
50/D4 **Tara** (riv.), Bosn., Yugo.
56/H4 **Tara,** Rus.
85/H4 **Taraba** (riv.), Nga.
59/K4 **Ţarābulus** (Tripoli), Leb.
82/H1 **Ţarābulus** (Tripoli) (cap.), Libya
32/B4 **Tara, Hill of** (hill), Ire.
73/E3 **Tarakan,** Indo.
46/D2 **Tarancón,** Sp.
87/G1 **Tarangire Nat'l Park,** Tanz.
48/E2 **Taranto,** It.
48/E3 **Taranto** (gulf), It.
92/C5 **Tarapoto,** Peru
44/F4 **Tarare,** Fr.
44/F5 **Tarascon,** Fr.
92/D5 **Tarauacá,** Braz.
79/M7 **Taravai** (isl.), FrPol.
78/G4 **Tarawa** (atoll), Kiri.
46/E2 **Tarazona,** Sp.
46/E3 **Tarazona de la Mancha,** Sp.
68/D2 **Tarbagatay** (mts.), Kaz.
61/K2 **Tarbela** (res.), Pak.
44/D5 **Tarbes,** Fr.
113/J3 **Tarboro,** NC,US
50/A2 **Tarcento,** It.
44/E3 **Tardes** (riv.), Fr.
44/D4 **Tardoire** (riv.), Fr.
63/M2 **Tardoki-Jani** (peak), Rus.
77/E1 **Taree,** Austl.
81/V18 **Tarf** (lake), Alg.
86/C2 **Ţarfā', Wādī al** (dry riv.), Egypt
86/B4 **Tarfâwi, Bîr** (well), Egypt
32/D2 **Tarf Water** (riv.), Sc,UK
82/H1 **Tarhūnah,** Libya
46/C4 **Tarifa,** Sp.
92/F8 **Tarija,** Bol.
73/J4 **Tariku** (riv.), Indo.
73/J4 **Tariku-taritatu** (plain), Indo.
62/B4 **Tarim** (basin), China
68/D3 **Tarim** (riv.), China
61/J2 **Tarin** (riv.), Afg.
73/J4 **Taritatu** (riv.), Indo.
54/E3 **Tarkhankut, Mys** (cape), Ukr.
85/E5 **Tarkwa,** Gha.
67/D4 **Tarlac,** Phil.
92/C6 **Tarma,** Peru
44/D5 **Tarn** (riv.), Fr.
62/E2 **Tarna** (riv.), Mong.
61/J2 **Tarnak** (riv.), Afg.
39/L3 **Tarnobrzeg,** Pol.
39/L3 **Tarnobrzeg** (prov.), Pol.
39/L3 **Tarnów,** Pol.
39/L3 **Tarnów** (prov.), Pol.
68/D5 **Taro** (lake), China
45/J4 **Taro** (riv.), It.
82/D1 **Taroudannt,** Mor.
113/H4 **Tarpon Springs,** Fl,US
33/F5 **Tarporley,** Eng,UK
48/B1 **Tarquinia,** It.
47/F2 **Tarragona,** Sp.
47/F2 **Tàrrega,** Sp.
115/G4 **Tarrytown,** NY,US
59/C3 **Tarsus,** Turk.
52/E4 **Tartu,** Est.
59/K4 **Ţarţūs,** Syria
59/K4 **Ţarţūs** (dist.), Syria
65/M9 **Tarui,** Japan
64/B5 **Tarumizu,** Japan
69/B5 **Tarutao Nat'l Park,** Thai.
62/D2 **Tarvagatay** (mts.), Mong.
33/F5 **Tarvin,** Eng,UK
69/D3 **Ta Seng,** Camb.
68/E2 **Tashanta,** Rus.
56/F5 **Tashauz,** Trkm.
55/L4 **Tashauz Obl.,** Trkm.
68/A3 **Tashkent** (cap.), Uzb.
68/B3 **Tash-Kumyr,** Kyr.
72/C5 **Tasikmalaya,** Indo.
59/C3 **Taşkent,** Turk.
59/C2 **Taşköprü,** Turk.
75/* **Tasman** (sea)
77/C4 **Tasman** (pen.), Austl.
75/R11 **Tasman** (bay), NZ
77/C4 **Tasman Head** (cape), Austl.
77/C4 **Tasmania** (state), Austl.
50/F2 **Tăşnad,** Rom.
50/D2 **Tata,** Hun.
82/D2 **Tata,** Mor.
50/D2 **Tatabánya,** Hun.
110/D2 **Tatachikapika** (riv.), On,Can
79/M6 **Tatakoto** (isl.), FrPol.
62/D4 **Tatalin** (riv.), China
63/N2 **Tatar** (str.), Rus.
53/L5 **Tatar Aut. Rep.,** Rus.
56/H4 **Tatarsk,** Rus.
82/H1 **Tatāwīn,** Tun.
65/F3 **Tateyama,** Japan
65/E2 **Tate-yama** (mtn.), Japan
102/E2 **Tathlina** (lake), NW,Can
84/B2 **Tatilt** (well), Mrta.
102/G3 **Tatnam** (cape), Mb,Can
85/H3 **Tatokou,** Niger
39/K4 **Tatranský Nat'l Park,** Slvk.
39/K4 **Tatrzański Nat'l Park,** Pol.
31/P8 **Tatsfield,** Eng,UK
65/E3 **Tatsuno,** Japan
33/H5 **Tattershall,** Eng,UK
59/E2 **Tatvan,** Turk.
94/B2 **Tauá,** Braz.
95/H8 **Taubaté,** Braz.
45/H2 **Tauberbischofsheim,** Ger.
45/K3 **Tauern, Hohe** (mts.), Aus.
45/K2 **Taufkirchen,** Ger.
109/K3 **Taum Sauk** (peak), Mo,US
71/G3 **Taungdwingyi,** Burma
69/B1 **Taunggyi,** Burma
61/K2 **Taunsa,** Pak.
111/S8 **Taunton,** On,Can
34/C4 **Taunton,** Eng,UK
111/G3 **Taunton,** Ma,US
45/H1 **Taunusstein,** Ger.
75/S10 **Taupo,** NZ
75/S10 **Taupo** (lake), NZ
39/M1 **Tauragė,** Lith.
75/S10 **Tauranga,** NZ
44/D3 **Taurion** (riv.), Fr.
59/C3 **Taurus** (mts.), Turk.
46/E2 **Tauste,** Sp.
44/C2 **Taute** (riv.), Fr.
79/X15 **Tautira,** FrPol.
78/E5 **Tauu** (isls.), PNG
108/E3 **Tavaputs** (plat.), Ut,US
113/H4 **Tavares,** Fl,US
59/B3 **Tavas,** Turk.
53/Q4 **Tavda** (riv.), Rus.
35/H1 **Taverham,** Eng,UK
31/S9 **Taverny,** Fr.
79/Z17 **Taveuni** (isl.), Fiji
46/B4 **Tavira,** Port.
34/B5 **Tavistock,** Eng,UK
69/B3 **Tavoy,** Burma
63/L3 **Tavrichanka,** Rus.
59/B2 **Tavşanlı,** Turk.
34/B5 **Tavy** (riv.), Eng,UK
34/B4 **Taw** (riv.), Eng,UK
65/L10 **Tawaramoto,** Japan
110/D2 **Tawas City,** Mi,US
73/E3 **Tawau,** Malay.
34/C3 **Tawe** (riv.), Wal,UK
67/C6 **Tawi-tawi** (isl.), Phil.
86/D5 **Ţawkar,** Sudan
82/G1 **Tawzar,** Tun.
100/B4 **Taxco,** Mex.
61/K2 **Taxila** (ruins), Pak.
68/C4 **Taxkorgan** (Taxkorgan Tajik Zizhixian), China
36/D2 **Tay** (riv.), Sc,UK
36/C2 **Tay, Loch** (lake), Sc,UK
109/H2 **Taylor,** Ne,US
110/B4 **Taylorville,** Il,US
57/L2 **Taymyr** (isl.), Rus.
56/K2 **Taymyr** (pen.), Rus.
56/K2 **Taymyr** (riv.), Rus.
56/J2 **Taymyr Aut. Okr.,** Rus.
69/D4 **Tay Ninh,** Viet.
56/K4 **Tayshet,** Rus.
67/C5 **Taytay,** Phil.
56/J3 **Taz** (riv.), Rus.
81/M13 **Taza,** Mor.
81/M13 **Tazekka** (peak), Mor.
113/H2 **Tazewell,** Tn,US
110/D4 **Tazewell,** Va,US
83/K2 **Tāzirbū** (oasis), Libya
100/D5 **Tazumal** (ruins), ESal.
55/H4 **Tbilisi** (cap.), Geo.
87/B1 **Tchibanga,** Gabon
82/H6 **Tcholliré,** Camr.
39/K1 **Tczew,** Pol.
92/E4 **Tea** (riv.), Braz.
33/H5 **Tealby,** Eng,UK
75/Q12 **Te Anau,** NZ
75/Q12 **Te Anau** (lake), NZ
115/F5 **Teaneck,** NJ,US
100/C4 **Teapa,** Mex.
75/S10 **Te Araroa,** NZ
75/S10 **Te Aroha,** NZ
75/S10 **Te Awamutu,** NZ
72/B4 **Tebak** (peak), Indo.
81/W18 **Tébessa,** Alg.
81/W18 **Tebessa** (mts.), Alg., Tun.
85/F2 **Tebesselamane** (well), Mali
91/E2 **Tebicuary** (riv.), Par.
72/A3 **Tebingtinggi,** Indo.
55/H4 **Tebulos-mta** (peak), Rus.
47/E5 **Tech** (riv.), Fr.
44/J3 **Techirghiol,** Rom.
96/C4 **Tecka** (riv.), Arg.
101/P10 **Tecomán,** Mex.
101/N9 **Tecuala,** Mex.
51/H3 **Tecuci,** Rom.
116/G7 **Tecumseh,** On,Can
110/D3 **Tecumseh,** Mi,US
109/H2 **Tecumseh,** Ne,US
61/H1 **Tedzhen,** Trkm.
56/G6 **Tedzhen** (riv.), Trkm.
33/G2 **Tees** (bay), Eng,UK
33/G2 **Tees** (riv.), Eng,UK
92/F4 **Tefé,** Braz.
92/E4 **Tefé** (riv.), Braz.
72/C5 **Tegal,** Indo.
40/D6 **Tegelen,** Neth.
82/H2 **Tegheri** (well), Libya
32/E6 **Tegid, Llyn** (lake), Wal,UK
85/H3 **Tégouma** (wadi), Niger
100/D5 **Tegucigalpa** (cap.), Hon.
102/G2 **Tehek** (lake), NW,Can
60/F1 **Tehrān** (cap.), Iran
68/C5 **Tehri,** India
100/B4 **Tehuacán,** Mex.
100/C4 **Tehuantepec** (gulf), Mex.
100/C4 **Tehuantepec** (isth.), Mex.
47/X16 **Teide** (peak), Canl.,Sp.
34/B2 **Teifi** (riv.), Wal,UK
83/L4 **Teiga** (plat.), Sudan
34/C5 **Teignmouth,** Eng,UK
46/B3 **Tejo** (Tagus) (riv.), Port.
109/H2 **Tekamah,** Ne,US
75/R9 **Te Kao,** NZ
100/D3 **Tekax,** Mex.
68/C3 **Tekeli,** Kaz.
68/D3 **Tekes** (riv.), China
60/C6 **Tekezē Wenz** (reg.), Eth.
83/N5 **Tekezē Wenz** (riv.), Eth., Sudan
68/D4 **Tekiliktag** (peak), China
51/H5 **Tekirdağ,** Turk.
70/D4 **Tekkali,** India
75/S10 **Te Kuiti,** NZ
70/D3 **Tel** (riv.), India
100/D4 **Tela,** Hon.
81/Q16 **Télagh,** Alg.
55/H4 **Telavi,** Geo.
59/K5 **Tel Aviv** (dist.), Isr.
59/K5 **Tel Aviv-Yafo,** Isr.
47/X17 **Telde,** Canl.
84/E2 **Télé** (lake), Mali
68/G2 **Telem** (lake), Mong.
95/B3 **Telemaco Borba,** Braz.
37/D4 **Telemark** (co.), Nor.
73/E3 **Telen** (riv.), Indo.
51/G4 **Teleorman** (co.), Rom.
82/G3 **Telertheba** (peak), Alg.
93/G5 **Teles Pires** (riv.), Braz.
34/D1 **Telford,** Eng,UK
45/J3 **Telfs,** Aus.
41/E5 **Telgte,** Ger.
84/B4 **Télimélé,** Gui.
59/N9 **Tel Jericho Nat'l Park,** WBnk.
106/B2 **Telkwa,** BC,Can
81/Q16 **Tell Atlas** (mts.), Alg.
110/C4 **Tell City,** In,US
70/C5 **Tellicherry,** India
108/F3 **Telluride,** Co,US
59/N7 **Tel Megiddo Nat'l Park,** Isr.
62/D2 **Telmen** (lake), Mong.
72/B3 **Telok Anson,** Malay.
68/E1 **Telotskoye** (lake), Rus.
52/D5 **Telšiai,** Lith.
39/G2 **Teltow** (reg.), Ger.
85/E5 **Tema,** Gha.
110/D2 **Temagami** (lake), On,Can
88/E2 **Tembisa,** SAfr.
101/J6 **Temblador,** Ven.
87/C2 **Tembo,** Zaire
34/D2 **Teme** (riv.), Eng,UK
50/D3 **Temerin,** Yugo.
72/B3 **Temerloh,** Malay.
68/B1 **Temirtau,** Kaz.
111/F1 **Témiscamie** (riv.), Qu,Can
110/E2 **Témiscaming,** Qu,Can
62/E1 **Temnik** (riv.), Rus.
79/M7 **Temoe** (isl.), FrPol.
108/E4 **Tempe,** Az,US
48/A2 **Tempio Pausania,** It.
112/D4 **Temple,** Tx,US
32/B2 **Templepatrick,** NI,UK
77/G5 **Templestowe,** Austl.
39/G2 **Templin,** Ger.
100/B3 **Tempoal,** Mex.
87/C3 **Tempué,** Ang.
54/F3 **Temryuk,** Rus.
42/D1 **Temse,** Belg.
96/B3 **Temuco,** Chile
75/R11 **Temuka,** NZ
82/D5 **Tena Kourou** (peak), Burk.
70/D4 **Tenāli,** India
69/B3 **Tenasserim** (range), Burma
69/B4 **Tenasserim** (Thanintharyi) (div.), Burma
40/D2 **Ten Boer,** Neth.
34/D2 **Tenbury,** Eng,UK
34/B3 **Tenby,** Wal,UK
83/P5 **Tendaho,** Eth.
65/G1 **Tendō,** Japan
82/G3 **Ténéré du Tafassasset** (des.), Niger
85/H2 **Ténéré, 'Erg du** (des.), Niger
47/X16 **Tenerife** (isl.), Canl.
81/R15 **Ténès,** Alg.
47/L6 **Tenes** (riv.), Sp.
69/B1 **Teng** (riv.), Burma
73/E4 **Tenggarong,** Indo.
62/E4 **Tengger** (des.), China
68/A1 **Tengiz** (lake), Kaz.
45/G4 **Tenibres** (peak), It.
91/D1 **Teniente Enciso Nat'l Park,** Par.
50/D3 **Tenja,** Cro.
85/E4 **Tenkodogo,** Burk.
113/F2 **Tennessee** (riv.), US
113/G3 **Tennessee** (state), US
96/C2 **Teno,** Chile
37/H1 **Tenojoki** (riv.), Fin.
100/C4 **Tenosique,** Mex.
65/L10 **Tenri,** Japan
65/E3 **Tenryū** (riv.), Japan
35/G4 **Tenterden,** Eng,UK
69/B2 **Ten Thousand Buddhas, Cave of,** Burma
73/F3 **Tentolomatinan** (peak), Indo.
46/A1 **Teo,** Sp.
100/A3 **Teocaltiche,** Mex.
95/A2 **Teodoro Sampaio,** Braz.
95/D1 **Teófilo Otoni,** Braz.
101/P9 **Tepatitlán de Morelos,** Mex.
101/P9 **Tepic,** Mex.
39/G3 **Teplice,** Czh.
101/M7 **Tepoca** (cape), Mex.
79/L6 **Tepoto** (isl.), FrPol.
101/P9 **Tequila,** Mex.
47/G1 **Ter** (riv.), Sp.
85/F3 **Téra,** Niger
46/B1 **Tera** (riv.), Sp.
40/B4 **Ter Aar,** Neth.
79/K4 **Teraina** (Washington) (atoll), Kiri.
48/C1 **Teramo,** It.
59/E2 **Tercan,** Turk.
47/S12 **Terceira** (isl.), Azor.,Port.
96/E2 **Tercero** (riv.), Arg.
51/K2 **Terderovsk** (bay), Ukr.
55/H4 **Terek** (riv.), Rus.
94/B2 **Teresina,** Braz.
95/L7 **Teresópolis,** Braz.
42/C4 **Tergnier,** Fr.
62/D4 **Tergun Daba** (mts.), China
40/B5 **Terheijden,** Neth.
52/G1 **Teriberskiy, Mys** (pt.), Rus.
40/C2 **Terkaplesterpoelen** (lake), Neth.
51/H5 **Terkirdağ** (prov.), Turk.
61/J1 **Termez,** Uzb.
48/C4 **Termini Imerese,** It.
100/C4 **Términos** (lag.), Mex.
108/B2 **Termo,** Ca,US
48/D1 **Termoli,** It.
34/D1 **Tern** (riv.), Eng,UK
73/G3 **Ternate,** Indo.
40/A6 **Terneuzen,** Neth.
48/C1 **Terni,** It.
44/F3 **Ternin** (riv.), Fr.
42/B3 **Ternoise** (riv.), Fr.
54/C2 **Ternopol',** Ukr.
54/C2 **Ternopol' Obl.,** Ukr.

Terpe – Trebu

163
Trede – Valle

34/C3 **Tredegar**, Wal,UK
34/C2 **Trefeglwys**, Wal,UK
32/E5 **Trefnant**, Wal,UK
34/C2 **Tregaron**, Wal,UK
97/G2 **Treinta y Tres**, Uru.
97/G2 **Treinta y Tres** (dept.), Uru.
45/G4 **Tré-la-Tête** (mtn.), Fr.
44/C3 **Trélazé**, Fr.
34/B3 **Trelech**, Wal,UK
96/D4 **Trelew**, Arg.
44/D4 **Trélissac**, Fr.
38/G1 **Trelleborg**, Swe.
32/D6 **Tremadoc** (bay), Wal,UK
31/T10 **Tremblay-lès-Gonesse**, Fr.
32/B4 **Tremblestown** (riv.), Ire.
106/B2 **Trembleur** (lake), BC,Can
43/D2 **Tremelo**, Belg.
48/D1 **Tremiti** (isls.), It.
108/D2 **Tremonton**, Ut,US
111/F1 **Trenche** (riv.), Qu,Can
39/K4 **Trenčín**, Slvk.
96/E2 **Trenque Lauquen**, Arg.
33/H5 **Trent** (riv.), Eng,UK
33/F6 **Trent and Mersey** (can.), Eng,UK
45/J3 **Trentino-Alto Adige** (reg.), It.
45/J3 **Trento**, It.
110/E2 **Trenton**, On,Can
113/H4 **Trenton**, Fl,US
113/G3 **Trenton**, Ga,US
116/F7 **Trenton**, Mi,US
109/J2 **Trenton**, Mo,US
115/F5 **Trenton** (cap.), NJ,US
113/F3 **Trenton**, Tn,US
34/C3 **Treorchy**, Wal,UK
49/F2 **Trepuzzi**, It.
97/T11 **Tres Arboles**, Uru.
96/E3 **Tres Arroyos**, Arg.
95/H6 **Tres Corações**, Braz.
95/B2 **Trés Irmáos** (res.), Braz.
91/D2 **Tres Isletas**, Arg.
95/B2 **Três Lagoas**, Braz.
95/C1 **Três Marias**, Braz.
95/C1 **Três Marias** (res.), Braz.
101/N9 **Tres Marías** (isls.), Mex.
96/B5 **Tres Montes** (cape), Chile
96/C4 **Tres Picos** (peak), Arg.
96/E3 **Tres Picos** (peak), Arg.
95/H6 **Três Pontas**, Braz.
96/D5 **Tres Puntas** (cape), Arg.
95/K7 **Três Rios**, Braz.
45/J2 **Treuchtlingen**, Ger.
38/G2 **Treuenbrietzen**, Ger.
45/H4 **Treviglio**, It.
45/K4 **Treviso**, It.
34/A5 **Trevose Head** (pt.), Eng,UK
115/J7 **Triadelphia** (res.), Md,US
76/B2 **Tribulation** (cape), Austl.
49/F3 **Tricase**, It.
70/C5 **Trichūr**, India
73/J4 **Tricora** (peak), Indo.
67/B5 **Trident** (shoal)
42/A5 **Trie-Château**, Fr.
31/S10 **Triel-sur-Seine**, Fr.
43/F4 **Trier**, Ger.
48/E2 **Triggiano**, It.
51/G4 **Triglav** (peak), Bul.
50/A2 **Triglav** (peak), Slov.
50/A2 **Triglav Nat'l Park**, Slov.
48/D2 **Trigno** (riv.), It.
46/B4 **Trigueros**, Sp.
49/G3 **Tríkala**, Gre.
49/G3 **Trikhonis** (lake), Gre.
45/G3 **Trimbach**, Swi.
33/G2 **Trimdon**, Eng,UK
70/D6 **Trincomalee**, SrL.
93/J7 **Trindade**, Braz.
39/K4 **Trinec**, Czh.
35/F3 **Tring**, Eng,UK
96/E3 **Trinidad** (isl.), Arg.
92/F6 **Trinidad**, Bol.
97/J7 **Trinidad** (gulf), Chile
97/F2 **Trinidad**, Uru.
109/F3 **Trinidad**, Co,US
101/J5 **Trinidad and Tobago**
93/N8 **Trinidade**, Braz.
111/L2 **Trinity** (bay), Nf,Can
114/H4 **Trinity** (isls.), Ak,US
108/B2 **Trinity** (riv.), Ca,US
108/C2 **Trinity** (range), Nv,US
112/E4 **Trinity** (riv.), Tx,US
86/D5 **Trinkitat**, Sudan
89/S15 **Triolet**, Mrts.
49/H4 **Trípolis**, Gre.
82/H1 **Tripolitania** (reg.), Libya
59/K4 **Tripoli** (Ţarābulus), Leb.
82/H1 **Tripoli** (Ţarābulus) (cap.), Libya
70/C6 **Tripunittura**, India
71/F3 **Tripura** (state), India
28/J7 **Tristan da Cunha** (isls.), StH.
84/B4 **Tristao** (isls.), Guin.
96/D4 **Triste** (peak), Arg.
89/D4 **Tri Ton**, Viet.
41/H1 **Trittau**, Ger.
70/C6 **Trivandrum**, India
39/J4 **Trnava**, Slvk.
78/E5 **Trobriand** (isls.), PNG
42/A5 **Troesne** (riv.), Fr.
45/L3 **Trofaiach**, Aus.
48/D2 **Troia**, It.
47/Q11 **Tróia**, Port.
43/G2 **Troisdorf**, Ger.
43/G6 **Troisfontaines**, Fr.
81/N13 **Trois Fourches, Cap des** (cape), Mor.
111/G1 **Trois-Pistoles**, Qu,Can
111/F2 **Trois-Rivières**, Qu,Can
53/P5 **Troitsk**, Rus.
37/E4 **Trollhättan**, Swe.
93/G4 **Trombetas** (riv.), Braz.
81/H6 **Tromelin** (isl.), Reu.
37/F1 **Troms** (co.), Nor.
37/F1 **Tromsø**, Nor.
96/C4 **Tronador** (peak), Arg., Chile
37/D3 **Trondheim**, Nor.
48/C1 **Tronto** (riv.), It.
59/J4 **Troodos** (mts.), Cyp.
32/D1 **Trool, Loch** (lake), Sc,UK
36/C3 **Troon**, Sc,UK
48/D3 **Tropea**, It.
108/D3 **Tropic**, Ut,US
32/B1 **Trostan** (mtn.), NI,UK
31/Q8 **Trottiscliffe**, Eng,UK
102/D2 **Trout** (lake), NW,Can
107/K3 **Trout** (lake), On,Can
33/F3 **Troutbeck**, Eng,UK
106/E1 **Trout Lake**, BC,Can
34/D4 **Trowbridge**, Eng,UK
113/G4 **Troy**, Al,US
116/F6 **Troy**, Mi,US
110/F3 **Troy**, NY,US
113/G1 **Troy**, Oh,US
51/G4 **Troyan**, Bul.
51/G4 **Troyanski Prokhod** (pass), Bul.
44/F2 **Troyes**, Fr.
49/K3 **Troy** (Ilium) (ruins), Turk.
50/E4 **Trstenik**, Yugo.
114/M3 **Truitt** (peak), Yk,Can
100/D4 **Trujillo**, Hon.
92/C5 **Trujillo**, Peru
46/C3 **Trujillo**, Sp.
101/G6 **Trujillo**, Ven.
78/E4 **Truk** (isls.), Micr.
115/G4 **Trumbull**, Ct,US
34/D2 **Trumpet**, Eng,UK
69/D1 **Trung Khanh**, Viet.
111/J2 **Truro**, NS,Can
34/A6 **Truro**, Eng,UK
108/F4 **Truth Or Consequences**, NM,US
39/H3 **Trutnov**, Czh.
44/E4 **Truyère** (riv.), Fr.
32/D6 **Trwyn Cilan** (pt.), Wal,UK
51/G4 **Tryavna**, Bul.
37/E3 **Trysil**, Nor.
39/J2 **Trzcianka**, Pol.
39/H1 **Trzebiatów**, Pol.
39/J3 **Trzebnica**, Pol.
39/J2 **Trzemeszno**, Pol.
50/B2 **Tržič**, Slov.
62/D3 **Tsagaan Bogd** (peak), Mong.
62/G2 **Tsagaan-Ovoo**, Mong.
62/E1 **Tsagaan-Üür**, Mong.
89/J6 **Tsaratanana Massif** (plat.), Madg.
88/B2 **Tsarisberge** (mts.), Namb.
68/F2 **Tsast Uul** (peak), Mong.
88/E3 **Tsatsana** (peak), Les.
87/D5 **Tsau**, Bots.
87/G1 **Tsavo**, Kenya
87/G1 **Tsavo East Nat'l Park**, Kenya
87/G1 **Tsavo West Nat'l Park**, Kenya
68/B1 **Tselinograd**, Kaz.
62/F2 **Tsenhermandal**, Mong.
62/D2 **Tsetsen-Uul**, Mong.
87/B1 **Tshela**, Zaire
87/D2 **Tshibwika**, Zaire
87/D2 **Tshikapa**, Zaire
83/K6 **Tshuapa** (riv.), Zaire
81/G6 **Tsiafajavona** (peak), Madg.
53/L2 **Tsil'ma** (riv.), Rus.
55/G2 **Tsimlyansk** (res.), Rus.
89/H9 **Tsiombe**, Madg.
89/H7 **Tsiribihina** (riv.), Madg.
89/H7 **Tsiroanomandidy**, Madg.
88/C4 **Tsitsikamma Forest & Coastal Nat'l Park**, SAfr.
55/G4 **Tskhinvali**, Geo.
52/G4 **Tsna** (riv.), Rus.
62/D2 **Tsogt**, Mong.
62/F3 **Tsogt-Ovoo**, Mong.
62/F3 **Tsogttsetsiy**, Mong.
62/F2 **Tsöh** (riv.), Mong.
88/D3 **Tsomo** (riv.), SAfr.
64/E3 **Tsu**, Japan
64/A3 **Tsu** (isls.), Japan
65/F2 **Tsubame**, Japan
64/E2 **Tsubata**, Japan
65/G2 **Tsuchiura**, Japan
65/M10 **Tsuchiyama**, Japan
63/M3 **Tsugaru** (str.), Japan
65/L10 **Tsuge**, Japan
65/H7 **Tsukui**, Japan
64/B4 **Tsukumi**, Japan
87/C4 **Tsumeb**, Namb.
65/K10 **Tsuna**, Japan
65/F3 **Tsuru**, Japan
64/E3 **Tsuruga**, Japan
65/H7 **Tsurugashima**, Japan
65/E2 **Tsurugi**, Japan
64/D4 **Tsurugi-san** (mtn.), Japan
65/M9 **Tsushima**, Japan
64/D3 **Tsuyama**, Japan
72/C5 **Tua** (cape), Indo.
46/B2 **Tua** (riv.), Port.
96/B4 **Tuamapu** (chan.), Chile
79/L6 **Tuamotu** (arch.), FrPol.
66/B4 **Tuan** (riv.), China
72/A3 **Tuan** (pt.), Indo.
69/C1 **Tuan Giao**, Viet.
72/A3 **Tuangku** (isl.), Indo.
69/D2 **Tuan Thuong**, Viet.
67/D4 **Tuao**, Phil.
54/F3 **Tuapse**, Rus.
108/E3 **Tuba City**, Az,US
72/D5 **Tuban**, Indo.
60/D6 **Tuban** (riv.), Yem.
95/B4 **Tubarão**, Braz.
40/D4 **Tubbergen**, Neth.
45/H2 **Tübingen**, Ger.
42/D2 **Tubize**, Belg.
84/C5 **Tubmanburg**, Libr.
78/H6 **Tubou**, Fiji
83/K1 **Ţubruq** (Tobruk), Libya
79/K7 **Tubuaā** (isls.), FrPol.
79/K7 **Tubuaī** (isl.), FrPol.
94/C3 **Tucano**, Braz.
39/J2 **Tuchola**, Pol.
108/E4 **Tucson**, Az,US
109/G4 **Tucumcari**, NM,US
101/H6 **Tucupido**, Ven.
101/J6 **Tucupita**, Ven.
93/J4 **Tucuruí**, Braz.
93/H4 **Tucuruí** (res.), Braz.
46/E1 **Tudela**, Sp.
31/P8 **Tudeley**, Eng,UK
44/E5 **Tude, Rochers de la** (mtn.), Fr.
88/E3 **Tugela** (falls), SAfr.
89/E3 **Tugela** (riv.), SAfr.
113/H2 **Tug Fork** (riv.), WV,US
67/D4 **Tuguegarao**, Phil.
73/F5 **Tukangbesi** (isls.), Indo.
52/D4 **Tukums**, Lat.
72/D4 **Tukung** (peak), Indo.
116/C3 **Tukwila**, Wa,US
100/B3 **Tula**, Mex.
54/F1 **Tula**, Rus.
68/F4 **Tulagt Ar** (riv.), China
100/B3 **Tulancingo**, Mex.
54/F1 **Tula Obl.**, Rus.
108/C3 **Tulare**, Ca,US
109/F4 **Tularosa**, NM,US
109/F4 **Tularosa** (val.), NM,US
88/L10 **Tulbagh**, SAfr.
92/C3 **Tulcán**, Ecu.
51/J3 **Tulcea**, Rom.
51/J3 **Tulcea** (co.), Rom.
112/C3 **Tulia**, Tx,US
114/E5 **Tulik** (vol.), Ak,US
78/E5 **Tulin** (isls.), PNG
59/K5 **Ţūlkarm**, WBnk.
113/G3 **Tullahoma**, Tn,US
36/B4 **Tullamore**, Ire.
44/D4 **Tulle**, Fr.
39/J4 **Tulln**, Aus.
52/G1 **Tuloma** (riv.), Rus.
109/J3 **Tulsa**, Ok,US
92/C3 **Tuluá**, Col.
57/L4 **Tulun**, Rus.
100/D5 **Tuma** (riv.), Nic.
108/E5 **Tumacacori Nat'l Mon.**, Az,US
93/H3 **Tumac-Humac** (mts.), Braz.
92/C3 **Tumaco**, Col.
67/D4 **Tumauini**, Phil.
83/J8 **Tumba** (lake), Zaire
92/B4 **Tumbes**, Peru
69/C3 **Tumbot** (peak), Camb.
63/K3 **Tumen**, China
101/J6 **Tumeremo**, Ven.
70/C5 **Tumkūr**, India
36/C2 **Tummel** (riv.), Sc,UK
63/M1 **Tumnin** (riv.), Rus.
72/B2 **Tumpat**, Malay.
73/F4 **Tumpu** (peak), Indo.
77/D2 **Tumut**, Austl.
116/B3 **Tumwater**, Wa,US
59/D3 **Tunceli**, Turk.
87/F2 **Tunduma**, Tanz.
87/G3 **Tunduru**, Tanz.
68/C1 **Tundyk** (riv.), Kaz.
50/H4 **Tundzha** (riv.), Bul., Turk.
70/C4 **Tungabhadra** (res.), India
70/C4 **Tungabhadra** (riv.), India
77/C3 **Tungamah**, Austl.
56/K3 **Tunguska, Lower** (riv.), Rus.
56/K3 **Tunguska, Stony** (riv.), Rus.
81/X17 **Tūnis** (cap.), Tun.
48/B4 **Tunis** (gov.), Tun.
81/X17 **Tunis** (gulf), Tun.
82/G1 **Tunisia**
92/D2 **Tunjá**, Col.
94/A2 **Tuntum**, Braz.
103/K3 **Tunungayualuk** (isl.), Nf,Can
96/C2 **Tunuyán**, Arg.
96/C2 **Tunuyán** (riv.), Chile
108/B3 **Tuolumne** (riv.), Ca,US
69/D2 **Tuong Duong**, Viet.
71/J3 **Tuoniang** (riv.), China
68/F5 **Tuotuo** (riv.), China
95/B2 **Tupã**, Braz.
95/B1 **Tupaciguara**, Braz.
79/K6 **Tupai** (isl.), FrPol.
113/F3 **Tupelo**, Ms,US
95/B2 **Tupi Paulista**, Braz.
96/C1 **Tupiza**, Bol.
110/F2 **Tupper Lake**, NY,US
96/C2 **Tupungato** (peak), Arg., Chile
70/F2 **Tura**, India
53/Q4 **Tura** (riv.), Rus.
63/L1 **Turana** (mts.), Rus.
75/S10 **Turangi**, NZ
56/G5 **Turan Lowland** (plain), Uzb.
101/F5 **Turbaco**, Col.
61/H3 **Turbat**, Pak.
101/F6 **Turbo**, Col.
51/F2 **Turda**, Rom.
79/M7 **Tureia** (atoll), FrPol.
39/K2 **Turek**, Pol.
56/G4 **Turgay Obl.**, Kaz.
110/E1 **Turgeon** (riv.), Qu,Can
51/H4 **Türgovishte**, Bul.
59/A2 **Turgutlu**, Turk.
59/D2 **Turhal**, Turk.
47/E3 **Turia** (riv.), Sp.
94/A1 **Turiaçu** (riv.), Braz.
45/G4 **Turin** (Torino), It.
83/N7 **Turkana** (lake), Eth., Kenya
68/A3 **Turkestan**, Kaz.
50/E2 **Túrkeve**, Hun.
59/C2 **Turkey**
56/F6 **Turkmenistan**
101/G3 **Turks and Caicos** (isls.), UK
37/G3 **Turku** (Åbo), Fin.
37/G3 **Turku Ja Pori** (prov.), Fin.
108/B3 **Turlock**, Ca,US
101/H5 **Turmero**, Ven.
32/D1 **Turnberry**, Sc,UK
100/D4 **Turneffe** (isls.), Belz.
40/B6 **Turnhout**, Belg.
106/F1 **Turnor Lake**, Sk,Can
39/H3 **Turnov**, Czh.
51/G4 **Turnu Măgurele**, Rom.
62/B3 **Turpan**, China
68/E3 **Turpan** (depr.), China
100/F4 **Turquino** (pk.), Cuba
36/D2 **Turriff**, Sc,UK
84/B5 **Turtle** (isls.), SLeo.
106/F2 **Turtleford**, Sk,Can
33/F4 **Turton**, Eng,UK
68/C3 **Turugart Shankou** (pass), China
95/J6 **Turvo** (riv.), Braz.
113/G3 **Tuscaloosa**, Al,US
48/B1 **Tuscano** (arch.), It.
45/J5 **Tuscany** (reg.), It.
108/C2 **Tuscarora**, Nv,US
113/G3 **Tuskegee**, Al,US
115/C3 **Tustin**, Ca,US
39/K3 **Tuszyn**, Pol.
52/H4 **Tutayev**, Rus.
33/G6 **Tutbury**, Eng,UK
70/C6 **Tuticorin**, India
50/E4 **Tutin**, Yugo.
72/D3 **Tutong**, Bru.
51/H3 **Tutrakan**, Bul.
109/H3 **Tuttle Creek** (lake), Ks,US
79/H6 **Tutuila** (isl.), ASam.
114/F2 **Tututalak** (mtn.), Ak,US
62/F2 **Tuul** (riv.), Mong.
37/H3 **Tuusula**, Fin.
56/K4 **Tuva Aut. Rep.**, Rus.
78/G5 **Tuvalu**
60/E4 **Ţuwayq, Jabal** (mts.), SAr.
33/H5 **Tuxford**, Eng,UK
101/N9 **Tuxpan**, Mex.
100/B4 **Tuxtepec**, Mex.
100/C4 **Tuxtla Gutiérrez**, Mex.
46/A1 **Túy**, Sp.
69/D2 **Tuyen Hoa**, Viet.
69/D1 **Tuyen Quang**, Viet.
69/E3 **Tuy Hoa**, Viet.
53/M5 **Tuymazy**, Rus.
60/E2 **Tūysarkān**, Iran
59/C2 **Tuz** (lake), Turk.
108/D4 **Tuzigoot Nat'l Mon.**, Az,US
60/D2 **Ţūz Khurmātū**, Iraq
50/D3 **Tuzla**, Bosn.
52/G4 **T'ver**, Rus.
52/G4 **T'ver Obl.**, Rus.
52/G4 **Tvertsa** (riv.), Rus.
51/G4 **Tvŭrditsa**, Bul.
39/J3 **Twardogóra**, Pol.
35/D3 **Tweed** (riv.), UK
77/E1 **Tweed Heads**, Austl.
40/D4 **Twente** (can.), Neth.
40/D4 **Twente** (reg.), Neth.
110/G9 **Twenty Mile** (riv.), On,Can
109/G5 **Twin Buttes** (res.), Tx,US
106/E5 **Twin Falls**, Id,US
41/G6 **Twiste** (riv.), Ger.
41/F3 **Twistringen**, Ger.
75/R11 **Twizel**, NZ
81/G3 **Two Buttes** (riv.), Co,US
77/D3 **Twofold** (bay), Austl.
107/L4 **Two Harbors**, Mn,US
106/F2 **Two Hills**, Ab,Can
110/C2 **Two Rivers**, Wi,US
35/E1 **Twycross**, Eng,UK
35/F4 **Twyford**, Eng,UK
34/C1 **Twymyn** (riv.), Wal,UK
32/D2 **Twynholm**, Sc,UK
39/K3 **Tychy**, Pol.
35/G1 **Tydd Saint Giles**, Eng,UK
110/E2 **Tyendinaga**, On,Can
113/H3 **Tyger** (riv.), SC,US
33/F4 **Tyldesley**, Eng,UK
112/E3 **Tyler**, Tx,US
63/N1 **Tymovskoye**, Rus.
45/L2 **Týn**, Czh.
109/H2 **Tyndall**, SD,US
36/C2 **Tyndrum**, Sc,UK
33/F2 **Tyne** (riv.), Eng,UK
33/G2 **Tyne & Wear** (co.), Eng,UK
33/G1 **Tynemouth**, Eng,UK
60/C2 **Tyre**, Leb.
59/K5 **Tyre** (Şūr), Leb.
63/L2 **Tyrma** (riv.), Rus.
55/G4 **Tyrnyauz**, Rus.
77/B2 **Tyrrell** (cr.), Austl.
77/B2 **Tyrrell** (lake), Austl.
48/B2 **Tyrrhenian** (sea), It.
115/J8 **Tysons Corner**, Va,US
55/J3 **Tyub-Karagan** (pt.), Kaz.
55/J3 **Tyulen'i** (isls.), Kaz.
55/H3 **Tyuleniy** (isl.), Rus.
53/Q4 **Tyumen'**, Rus.
53/Q4 **Tyumen' Obl.**, Rus.
68/C3 **Tyup**, Kyr.
34/B3 **Tywi** (riv.), Wal,UK
34/B1 **Tywyn**, Wal,UK
87/F5 **Tzaneen**, SAfr.

U

79/M5 **Ua Huka** (isl.), FrPol.
79/L5 **Ua Pou** (isl.), FrPol.
92/G4 **Uatumã** (riv.), Braz.
92/E3 **Uaupés** (riv.), Braz.
50/E3 **Ub**, Yugo.
95/D2 **Ubá**, Braz.
43/F2 **Übach-Palenberg**, Ger.
53/Q5 **Ubagan** (riv.), Kaz.
94/C4 **Ubaitaba**, Braz.
94/B1 **Ubajara**, Braz.
94/B1 **Ubajará Nat'l Park**, Braz.
83/J7 **Ubangi** (riv.), Zaire
94/C4 **Ubatã**, Braz.
95/H8 **Ubatuba**, Braz.
67/D5 **Ubay**, Phil.
45/G4 **Ubaye** (riv.), Fr.
40/C5 **Ubbergen**, Neth.
64/B4 **Ube**, Japan
46/D3 **Úbeda**, Sp.
92/G7 **Uberaba** (lake), Bol.
95/C1 **Uberaba**, Braz.
43/F5 **Überherrn**, Ger.
95/B1 **Uberlândia**, Braz.
73/J4 **Ubia** (peak), Indo.
69/D3 **Ubon Ratchathani**, Thai.
46/C4 **Ubrique**, Sp.
92/D5 **Ucayali** (riv.), Peru
38/C3 **Uccle**, Belg.
53/N5 **Uchaly**, Rus.
53/X8 **Uchinskoye**, Rus.
63/N2 **Uchiura** (bay), Japan
38/F2 **Uchte** (riv.), Ger.
57/P4 **Uchur** (riv.), Rus.
43/F5 **Uckange**, Fr.
39/G2 **Uckermark** (reg.), Ger.
35/G5 **Uckfield**, Eng,UK
106/B3 **Ucluelet**, BC,Can
62/F1 **Uda** (riv.), Rus.
70/B3 **Udaipur**, India
37/D4 **Uddevalla**, Swe.
37/F2 **Uddjaure** (lake), Swe.
40/C5 **Uden**, Neth.
40/C5 **Udenhout**, Neth.
70/C4 **Udgīr**, India
61/L2 **Udhampur**, India
45/K3 **Udine**, It.
70/B5 **Udipi**, India
53/L4 **Udmurt Aut. Rep.**, Rus.
69/C2 **Udon Thani**, Thai.
39/H2 **Ueckermünde**, Ger.
65/F2 **Ueda**, Japan
83/K7 **Uele** (riv.), Zaire
41/H3 **Uelzen**, Ger.
65/F3 **Uenohara**, Japan
41/G1 **Uetersen**, Ger.
41/H4 **Uetze**, Ger.
53/M5 **Ufa**, Rus.
53/N5 **Ufa** (riv.), Rus.
35/E3 **Uffington**, Eng,UK
87/F1 **Uganda**
49/F3 **Ugento**, It.
45/G4 **Ugine**, Fr.
63/N2 **Uglegorsk**, Rus.
52/H4 **Uglich**, Rus.
45/L4 **Ugljan** (isl.), Cro.
54/E1 **Ugra** (riv.), Rus.
62/F2 **Ugtaaltsaydam**, Mong.
39/J4 **Uherské Hradiště**, Czh.
45/K2 **Úhlava** (riv.), Czh.
87/C2 **Uíge**, Ang.
55/K2 **Uil** (riv.), Kaz.
88/L11 **Uilkraal** (riv.), SAfr.
55/G4 **Uilpata, Gora** (peak), Rus.
108/E2 **Uinta** (mts.), Ut,US
94/C2 **Uiraúna**, Braz.
64/A2 **Ŭisŏng**, SKor.
88/D4 **Uitenhage**, SAfr.
40/B3 **Uitgeest**, Neth.
40/B4 **Uithoorn**, Neth.
78/F4 **Ujae** (atoll), Mrsh.
78/F4 **Ujelang** (atoll), Mrsh.
50/E2 **Újfehértó**, Hun.
65/L10 **Uji**, Japan
65/L10 **Ujitawara**, Japan
70/C3 **Ujjain**, India
73/E5 **Ujung Pandang**, Indo.
53/M3 **Ukhta**, Rus.
108/B3 **Ukiah**, Ca,US
52/E5 **Ukmergė**, Lith.
54/D2 **Ukraine**
62/F2 **Ulaanbaatar** (cap.), Mong.
62/C2 **Ulaangom**, Mong.
62/D2 **Ulaanhus**, Mong.
62/F1 **Ulan-Burgasy** (mts.), Rus.
63/J2 **Ulanhot**, China
62/F1 **Ulan-Ude**, Rus.
68/F5 **Ulan Ul** (lake), China
87/G2 **Ulaya**, Tanz.
64/A2 **Ulchin**, SKor.
50/D5 **Ulcinj**, Yugo.
62/G2 **Uldz** (riv.), Mong.
63/H2 **Ulgain** (riv.), China
70/B4 **Ulhāsnagar**, India
62/D2 **Uliastay**, Mong.
83/L8 **Ulindi** (riv.), Zaire
78/D3 **Ulithi** (atoll), Micr.
46/A1 **Ulla** (riv.), Sp.
77/D2 **Ulladulla**, Austl.
37/F1 **Ullsfjorden** (fjord), Nor.
33/F2 **Ullswater** (lake), Eng,UK
64/B2 **Ullŭng** (isl.), SKor.
45/H2 **Ulm**, Ger.
64/A3 **Ulsan**, SKor.
32/A3 **Ulster** (reg.), Ire.
100/D4 **Ulúa** (riv.), Hon.
60/D1 **Uludoruk** (peak), Turk.
59/C3 **Ulukışla**, Turk.
62/B2 **Ulungur** (lake), China
62/B2 **Ulungur** (riv.), China
74/E5 **Uluru** (Ayers Rock) (peak), Austl.
68/A2 **Ulutau, Gora** (peak), Kaz.
33/E3 **Ulverston**, Eng,UK
77/C4 **Ulverstone**, Austl.
52/F4 **Ul'yanovka**, Rus.
112/C2 **Ulysses**, Ks,US
100/D3 **Umán**, Mex.
54/D2 **Uman'**, Ukr.
94/C2 **Umarizal**, Braz.
70/D4 **Umarkot**, India
61/L2 **Umāsi La** (pass), India
78/D5 **Umboi** (isl.), PNG
48/C1 **Umbria** (reg.), It.
45/K5 **Umbro-Marchigiano, Appenino** (range), It.
56/B3 **Ume** (riv.), Swe.
37/G3 **Umeå**, Swe.
37/F2 **Umeälv** (riv.), Swe.
89/E3 **Umfolozi** (riv.), SAfr.
89/E3 **Umgeni** (riv.), SAfr.
61/F4 **Umm as Samīm** (salt dep.), Oman
83/M4 **Umm Durmān** (Omdurman), Sudan
59/K5 **Umm el Fahm**, Isr.
86/C4 **Umm Hibal, Bi'r** (well), Egypt
83/M5 **Umm Ruwābah**, Sudan
114/E5 **Umnak** (isl.), Ak,US
106/C5 **Umpqua** (riv.), Or,US
88/E3 **Umtata**, SAfr.
91/F1 **Umuarama**, Braz.
88/E3 **Umzimvubu** (riv.), SAfr.
50/B3 **Una** (riv.), Bosn., Cro.
75/R11 **Una** (peak), NZ
94/A5 **Unaí**, Braz.
114/E5 **Unalaska** (isl.), Ak,US
60/C2 **'Unāzah, Jabal** (mtn.), SAr.
108/E3 **Uncompahgre** (plat.), Co,US
107/H4 **Underwood**, ND,US
79/Z17 **Undu** (pt.), Fiji
54/E1 **Unecha**, Rus.
114/F4 **Unga** (isl.), Ak,US
87/H1 **Ungama** (bay), Kenya
103/K3 **Ungava** (bay), Qu,Can
103/J2 **Ungava** (pen.), Qu,Can
54/C3 **Ungeny**, Mol.
94/B2 **União**, Braz.
95/B3 **União da Vitória**, Braz.
94/C3 **União dos Palmares**, Braz.
114/E4 **Unimak** (isl.), Ak,US
92/F4 **Unini** (riv.), Braz.
109/K3 **Union**, Mo,US
115/F5 **Union**, NJ,US
106/D4 **Union**, Or,US
113/H3 **Union**, SC,US
116/K11 **Union City**, Ca,US
115/F5 **Union City**, NJ,US
113/F2 **Union City**, Tn,US
100/E3 **Unión de Reyes**, Cuba
113/G3 **Union Springs**, Al,US
110/E4 **Uniontown**, Pa,US
111/R8 **Unionville**, On,Can
109/J2 **Unionville**, Mo,US
60/F4 **United Arab Emirates**
36/* **United Kingdom**
102/* **United States**
103/T8 **United States** (range), NW,Can
106/F2 **Unity**, Sk,Can
112/D4 **Universal City**, Tx,US
70/B3 **Unjha**, India
41/E5 **Unna**, Ger.
70/D2 **Unnāo**, India
38/F3 **Unstruct** (riv.), Ger.
59/D2 **Ünye**, Turk.
64/A4 **Unzen-Amakusa Nat'l Park**, Japan
64/B4 **Unzen-dake** (mtn.), Japan
53/K4 **Unzha** (riv.), Rus.
65/E2 **Uozu**, Japan
101/J6 **Upata**, Ven.
87/E2 **Upemba Nat'l Park**, Zaire
88/C3 **Upington**, SAfr.
70/B3 **Upleta**, India
31/P7 **Upminster**, Eng,UK
104/U10 **Upolu** (pt.), Hi,US
79/H6 **Upolu** (isl.), WSam.
108/C2 **Upper** (lake), Ca,US
113/H1 **Upper Arlington**, Oh,US
106/D3 **Upper Arrow** (lake), BC,Can
45/K2 **Upper Austria** (prov.), Aus.
115/E6 **Upper Darby**, Pa,US
35/G5 **Upper Dicker**, Eng,UK
85/E4 **Upper East** (reg.), Gha.
75/S11 **Upper Hutt**, NZ
109/J2 **Upper Iowa** (riv.), Ia,US
106/C5 **Upper Klamath** (lake), Or,US
32/B2 **Upperlands**, NI,UK
110/C2 **Upper Peninsula** (pen.), Mi,US
107/L5 **Upper Peoria** (lake), Il,US
107/K3 **Upper Red** (lake), Mn,US
35/E3 **Upper Thames** (val.), Eng,UK
85/E4 **Upper West** (reg.), Gha.
35/F1 **Uppingham**, Eng,UK
37/F4 **Uppsala**, Swe.
37/F3 **Uppsala** (co.), Swe.
114/D3 **Upright** (cape), Ak,US
76/B2 **Upstart** (bay), Austl.
107/G4 **Upton**, Wy,US
34/D2 **Upton upon Severn**, Eng,UK
60/E2 **Ur** (ruins), Iraq
65/H7 **Uraga** (chan.), Japan
94/A1 **Uraim** (riv.), Braz.
56/F3 **Ural** (mts.), Rus.
56/F5 **Ural** (riv.), Rus., Kaz.
55/J2 **Ural'sk**, Kaz.
55/J2 **Ural'sk Obl.**, Kaz.
102/F3 **Uranium City**, Sk,Can
92/F3 **Uraricoera** (riv.), Braz.
65/F3 **Urawa**, Japan
56/G3 **Uray**, Rus.
65/H7 **Urayasu**, Japan
110/B3 **Urbana**, Il,US
110/D3 **Urbana**, Oh,US
33/G3 **Ure** (riv.), Eng,UK
100/E6 **Ureña**, CR
100/B3 **Ures**, Mex.
65/M10 **Ureshino**, Japan
59/D3 **Urfa**, Turk.
41/G6 **Urft** (riv.), Ger.
56/G5 **Urgench**, Uzb.
37/H1 **Urho Kekkosen Nat'l Park**, Fin.
92/F2 **Urimáan**, Ven.
101/N8 **Urique** (riv.), Mex.
40/C3 **Urk**, Neth.
59/A2 **Urla**, Turk.
51/H3 **Urlaţi**, Rom.
63/L2 **Urmi** (riv.), Rus.
60/D1 **Urmia** (lake), Iran
33/F5 **Urmston**, Eng,UK
50/E4 **Uroševac**, Yugo.
32/E1 **Urr Water** (riv.), Sc,UK
93/J6 **Uruaçu**, Braz.
100/A4 **Uruapan**, Mex.
92/D6 **Urubamba** (riv.), Peru
92/G4 **Urubu** (riv.), Braz.
94/C1 **Uruburetama**, Braz.
94/C4 **Uruçuca**, Braz.
94/A2 **Uruçuí**, Braz.
94/A3 **Uruçuí** (mts.), Braz.
94/A5 **Uruçuí** (riv.), Braz.
94/A3 **Uruçuí Prêto** (riv.), Braz.
91/E2 **Uruguaiana**, Braz.
91/E3 **Uruguay**
91/E2 **Uruguay** (riv.), SAm.
62/B3 **Ürümqi**, China
57/R5 **Urup** (isl.), Rus.
95/B4 **Urussanga**, Braz.
63/H1 **Uryumkan** (riv.), Rus.
55/G2 **Uryupinsk**, Rus.
51/H3 **Urziceni**, Rom.
31/R9 **Us**, Fr.
64/B4 **Usa**, Japan
53/N2 **Usa** (riv.), Rus.
59/B2 **Uşak**, Turk.
97/N7 **Usborne** (peak), Falk.
64/B4 **Ushibuka**, Japan
65/J7 **Ushiku**, Japan
68/C2 **Ushtobe**, Kaz.
97/K8 **Ushuaia**, Arg.
70/C6 **Usilampatti**, India
31/H3 **Usinsk**, Rus.
34/D3 **Usk**, Wal,UK
34/D3 **Usk** (riv.), Wal,UK
51/J5 **Üsküdar**, Turk.
41/G5 **Uslar**, Ger.
54/F1 **Usman'**, Rus.
62/E1 **Usol'ye-Sibirskoye**, Rus.
67/D5 **Uson**, Phil.
96/C2 **Uspallata** (pass), Arg., Chile
44/E4 **Ussel**, Fr.
44/F3 **Usses** (riv.), Fr.
63/L2 **Ussuri** (Wusuli) (riv.), Rus., China
63/L3 **Ussuriysk**, Rus.
48/C3 **Ustica** (isl.), It.
57/L4 **Ust'-Ilimsk**, Rus.
39/H3 **Ústí nad Labem**, Czh.
39/J1 **Ustka**, Pol.
57/S4 **Ust'-Kamchatsk**, Rus.
68/D2 **Ust'-Kamenogorsk**, Kaz.
57/L4 **Ust'-Kut**, Rus.
62/E1 **Ust'-Ordynskiy**, Rus.
39/M4 **Ustrzyki Dolne**, Pol.
53/K3 **Ust'ya** (riv.), Rus.
55/K4 **Ustyurt** (plat.), Kaz., Uzb.
68/D3 **Usu**, China
64/B4 **Usuki**, Japan
100/D5 **Usulután**, ESal.
100/C4 **Usumacinta** (riv.), Mex.
108/E3 **Utah** (state), US
108/D2 **Utah** (lake), Ut,US
65/L10 **Utano**, Japan
109/G3 **Ute** (cr.), NM,US
52/E5 **Utena**, Lith.
69/C3 **Uthai Thani**, Thai.
110/F3 **Utica**, NY,US
46/E3 **Utiel**, Sp.
107/K2 **Utik** (lake), Mb,Can
106/E2 **Utikuma** (lake), Ab,Can
78/G3 **Utirik** (atoll), Mrsh.
78/G5 **Utiroa**, Kiri.
70/D2 **Utraulā**, India
40/C4 **Utrecht**, Neth.
40/C4 **Utrecht** (prov.), Neth.
46/C4 **Utrera**, Sp.
65/F2 **Utsunomiya**, Japan
69/C2 **Uttaradit**, Thai.
68/C5 **Uttarkashi**, India
70/C2 **Uttar Pradesh** (state), India
33/G6 **Uttoxeter**, Eng,UK
101/H4 **Utuado**, PR
78/F6 **Utupua** (isl.), Sol.
79/K6 **Uturoa**, FrPol.
62/G2 **Uulbayan**, Mong.
62/E1 **Üür** (riv.), Mong.
62/C1 **Üüreg** (lake), Mong.
62/C1 **Uus** (lake), Mong.
37/H3 **Uusimaa** (prov.), Fin.
92/E3 **Uva** (riv.), Col.
112/D4 **Uvalde**, Tx,US
53/K4 **Uval, Northern** (hills), Rus.
55/G2 **Uvarovo**, Rus.
68/F1 **Uvs Nuur** (lake), Mong.
64/C4 **Uwajima**, Japan
83/L6 **Uwayl**, Sudan
31/M7 **Uxbridge**, Eng,UK
66/B3 **Uxin Qi**, China
100/D3 **Uxmal** (ruins), Mex.
53/P5 **Uy** (riv.), Kaz., Rus.
62/E2 **Uyanga**, Mong.
62/C2 **Üyench**, Mong.
92/E8 **Uyuni**, Bol.
56/G5 **Uzbekistan**
54/B2 **Uzhgorod**, Ukr.
54/F1 **Uzlovaya**, Rus.
51/H5 **Uzunköprü**, Turk.

V

38/C3 **Vaal** (riv.), SAfr.
88/E2 **Vaaldam** (res.), SAfr.
43/F2 **Vaals**, Neth.
43/E2 **Vaalsberg** (hill), Neth.
37/G3 **Vaasa** (prov.), Fin.
37/G3 **Vaasa** (Vasa), Fin.
40/C4 **Vaassen**, Neth.
50/D2 **Vác**, Hun.
116/K10 **Vaca** (mts.), Ca,US
95/B4 **Vacaria**, Braz.
116/L10 **Vacaville**, Ca,US
103/J2 **Vachon** (riv.), Qu,Can
45/H3 **Vaduz** (cap.), Lcht.
52/J3 **Vaga** (riv.), Rus.
50/B3 **Vaganski vrh** (peak), Cro.
53/R4 **Vagay** (riv.), Rus.
37/E4 **Vaggeryd**, Swe.
39/J4 **Váh** (riv.), Slvk.
79/M6 **Vahitahi** (isl.), FrPol.
61/K5 **Vaijāpur**, India
109/F3 **Vail**, Co,US
42/C5 **Vailly-sur-Aisnes**, Fr.
31/T10 **Vaires-sur-Marne**, Fr.
78/G5 **Vaitupu** (isl.), Tuv.
59/D2 **Vakfıkebir**, Turk.
56/J3 **Vakh** (riv.), Rus.
61/K1 **Vākhān** (mts.), Afg.
61/J1 **Vakhsh** (riv.), Trkm.
40/C5 **Valburg**, Neth.
52/G4 **Valdai** (hills), Rus.
43/F6 **Val-de-Bide**, Fr.
46/C3 **Valdecañas** (res.), Sp.
31/T10 **Val-de-Marne** (dept.), Fr.
37/F4 **Valdemarsvik**, Swe.
47/M8 **Valdemorillo**, Sp.
46/D3 **Valdepeñas**, Sp.
46/C2 **Valderaduey** (riv.), Sp.
96/E4 **Valdés** (pen.), Arg.
96/B3 **Valdivia**, Chile
42/A5 **Val-d'Oise** (dept.), Fr.
110/E1 **Val d'Or**, Qu,Can
113/H4 **Valdosta**, Ga,US
46/A1 **Valdoviño**, Sp.
106/D5 **Vale**, Or,US
106/D2 **Valemount**, BC,Can
95/K7 **Valença**, Braz.
94/B2 **Valença do Piauí**, Braz.
47/E3 **Valencia**, Sp.
47/E3 **Valencia** (aut. comm.), Sp.
47/F3 **Valencia** (gulf), Sp.
101/H5 **Valencia**, Ven.
46/B3 **Valencia de Alcántara**, Sp.
42/C3 **Valenciennes**, Fr.
51/H3 **Vălenii de Munte**, Rom.
94/B2 **Valentim** (mts.), Braz.
109/G2 **Valentine**, Ne,US
112/B4 **Valentine**, Tx,US
31/T10 **Valenton**, Fr.
45/H4 **Valenza**, It.
101/G6 **Valera**, Ven.
52/E4 **Valga**, Est.
95/G7 **Valinhos**, Braz.
44/D5 **Valier** (mtn.), Fr.
48/A2 **Valinco** (gulf), Fr.
50/D3 **Valjevo**, Yugo.
43/E2 **Valkenburg**, Neth.
40/C6 **Valkenswaard**, Neth.
100/D3 **Valladolid**, Mex.
46/C2 **Valladolid**, Sp.
47/E3 **Vall de Uxó**, Sp.
47/N8 **Vallecas**, Sp.
45/G5 **Vallecrosia**, It.

Valle – Waite

165

Waiye – Windo

79/Z17 **Waiyevu**, Fiji
65/E2 **Wajima**, Japan
83/P7 **Wajir**, Kenya
73/G4 **Waka** (cape), Indo.
64/D3 **Wakasa**, Japan
64/D3 **Wakasa** (bay), Japan
107/G2 **Wakaw**, Sk,Can
64/D3 **Wakayama**, Japan
64/D4 **Wakayama** (pref.), Japan
78/F3 **Wake** (isl.), PacUS
112/D2 **Wakeeney**, Ks,US
33/G4 **Wakefield**, Eng,UK
110/B2 **Wakefield**, Mi,US
71/G4 **Wakema**, Burma
64/D3 **Waki**, Japan
63/N2 **Wakkanai**, Japan
65/H7 **Wakō**, Japan
110/D1 **Wakwayowkastic** (riv.), On,Can
51/G3 **Walachia** (range), Rom.
51/G3 **Walachia** (reg.), Rom.
39/J3 **Wałbrzych**, Pol.
39/J3 **Wałbrzych** (prov.), Pol.
35/E4 **Walbury** (hill), Eng,UK
40/A5 **Walcheren** (isl.), Neth.
42/D3 **Walcourt**, Belg.
39/J2 **Wałcz**, Pol.
43/G2 **Waldbröl**, Ger.
41/G6 **Waldeck**, Ger.
109/F2 **Walden**, Co,US
106/G2 **Waldheim**, Sk,Can
45/G2 **Waldkirch**, Ger.
45/L2 **Waldviertel** (reg.), Aus.
73/F4 **Walea** (str.), Indo.
73/F4 **Waleabahi** (isl.), Indo.
103/H2 **Wales** (isl.), NW,Can
36/C4 **Wales**, UK
98/T **Walgreen** (coast), Ant.
107/J3 **Walhalla**, ND,US
113/H3 **Walhalla**, SC,US
87/E1 **Walikale**, Zaire
88/L11 **Walker** (bay), SAfr.
108/C3 **Walker** (lake), Nv,US
108/C3 **Walker** (riv.), Nv,US
110/D2 **Walkerton**, On,Can
106/E4 **Wallace**, Id,US
116/H6 **Wallaceburg**, On,Can
33/E5 **Wallasey**, Eng,UK
106/D4 **Walla Walla**, Wa,US
116/F6 **Walled** (lake), Mi,US
116/F6 **Walled Lake**, Mi,US
41/F4 **Wallenhorst**, Ger.
42/C3 **Wallers**, Fr.
35/E3 **Wallingford**, Eng,UK
79/H6 **Wallis** (isls.), Wall.
78/G6 **Wallis & Futuna** (terr.), Fr.
106/D4 **Wallowa** (mts.), Or,US
33/G2 **Wallsend**, Eng,UK
33/E3 **Walney, Isle of** (isl.), Eng,UK
115/C2 **Walnut**, Ca,US
108/E4 **Walnut Canyon Nat'l Mon.**, Az,US
116/K11 **Walnut Creek**, Ca,US
113/F2 **Walnut Ridge**, Ar,US
114/F4 **Walrus** (isls.), Ak,US
34/E1 **Walsall**, Eng,UK
103/K2 **Walsingham** (cape), NW,Can
35/G1 **Walsingham**, Eng,UK
41/G3 **Walsrode**, Ger.
113/H3 **Walterboro**, SC,US
113/G4 **Walter F. George** (res.), Al, Ga,US
31/P6 **Waltham Abbey**, Eng,UK
31/N7 **Waltham Forest** (bor.), Eng,UK
35/G3 **Waltham Holy Cross**, Eng,UK
33/F4 **Walton-le-Dale**, Eng,UK
35/F4 **Walton on Thames**, Eng,UK
35/H3 **Walton on the Naze**, Eng,UK
41/E5 **Waltrop**, Ger.
87/B5 **Walvisbaai**, SAfr.
87/C3 **Wama**, Ang.
83/L7 **Wamba**, Zaire
40/C5 **Wamel**, Neth.
33/E2 **Wampool** (riv.), Eng,UK
106/G5 **Wamsutter**, Wy,US
66/D5 **Wan** (riv.), China
75/Q11 **Wanaka**, NZ
115/F4 **Wanaque**, NJ,US
115/F4 **Wanaque** (res.), NJ,US
63/L2 **Wanda** (mts.), China
71/G3 **Wanding**, China
31/N7 **Wandsworth** (bor.), Eng,UK
69/B2 **Wang** (riv.), Thai.
75/S10 **Wanganui**, NZ
77/C3 **Wangaratta**, Austl.
45/H3 **Wangen**, Ger.
41/E1 **Wangerooge** (isl.), Ger.
73/F6 **Wanggamet** (peak), Indo.
69/B4 **Wang Hip** (peak), Thai.
66/E5 **Wangpan** (bay), China
73/F4 **Wani** (peak), Indo.
65/M9 **Wanouchi**, Japan
68/D5 **Wanquan** (lake), China
33/G1 **Wansbeck** (riv.), Eng,UK
31/P7 **Wanstead**, Eng,UK
35/E3 **Wantage**, Eng,UK
62/F5 **Wanxian**, China
43/E2 **Wanze**, Belg.
110/C3 **Wapakoneta**, Oh,US
107/G2 **Wapawekka** (lake), Sk,Can
106/D2 **Wapiti** (riv.), Ab, BC,Can
73/J4 **Wapoga** (riv.), Indo.
109/K3 **Wappapello** (lake), Mo,US
107/K5 **Wapsipinicon** (riv.), Ia,US
65/H7 **Warabi**, Japan
70/C4 **Warangal**, India
35/F2 **Warboys**, Eng,UK
41/G6 **Warburg**, Ger.
74/F5 **Warburton** (cr.), Austl.
43/F3 **Warche** (riv.), Belg.
75/R11 **Ward**, NZ
35/G4 **Warden** (pt.), Eng,UK
41/F2 **Wardenburg**, Ger.
70/C3 **Wardha**, India
33/F3 **Ward's Stone** (mtn.), Eng,UK
35/F3 **Ware**, Eng,UK
42/C2 **Waregem**, Belg.
34/D5 **Wareham**, Eng,UK
42/E2 **Waremme**, Belg.
38/G2 **Waren**, Ger.
41/E5 **Warendorf**, Ger.
35/F3 **Wargrave**, Eng,UK
69/D3 **Warin Chamrap**, Thai.
32/B3 **Waringstown**, NI,UK
33/F1 **Wark**, Eng,UK
39/L3 **Warka**, Pol.
75/R10 **Warkworth**, NZ
34/D2 **Warley**, Eng,UK
31/N8 **Warlingham**, Eng,UK
107/G2 **Warman**, Sk,Can
88/D2 **Warmbad**, SAfr.
41/G6 **Warmebach** (riv.), Ger.
41/H5 **Warme Bode** (riv.), Ger.
39/K1 **Warmia** (reg.), Pol.
34/D4 **Warminster**, Eng,UK
115/E5 **Warminster**, Pa,US
108/E2 **Warner** (mts.), Ca,US
113/H3 **Warner Robins**, Ga,US
38/G2 **Warnow** (riv.), Ger.
40/D4 **Warnsveld**, Neth.
74/F5 **Warrandirinna** (lake), Austl.
77/G5 **Warrandyte**, Austl.
76/B4 **Warrego** (range), Austl.
75/H5 **Warrego** (riv.), Austl.
114/M2 **Warren** (pt.), NW,Can
112/E3 **Warren**, Ar,US
116/F6 **Warren**, Mi,US
107/J3 **Warren**, Mn,US
115/F5 **Warren**, NJ,US
110/D3 **Warren**, Oh,US
110/E3 **Warren**, Pa,US
32/B3 **Warrenpoint**, NI,UK
109/J3 **Warrensburg**, Mo,US
88/D3 **Warrenton**, SAfr.
110/E4 **Warrenton**, Va,US
116/P16 **Warrenville**, Il,US
33/F5 **Warrington**, Eng,UK
113/G4 **Warrington**, Fl,US
77/B3 **Warrnambool**, Austl.
107/K3 **Warroad**, Mn,US
77/D1 **Warrumbungle Nat'l Park**, Austl.
110/C3 **Warsaw**, In,US
109/J3 **Warsaw**, Mo,US
39/L3 **Warsawa** (prov.), Pol.
39/L2 **Warsaw** (Warszawa) (cap.), Pol.
39/H5 **Warscheneck** (peak), Aus.
33/G5 **Warslow**, Eng,UK
33/G5 **Warsop**, Eng,UK
41/F6 **Warstein**, Ger.
39/H2 **Warta** (riv.), Pol.
76/D5 **Warwick**, Austl.
35/E2 **Warwick**, Eng,UK
111/G3 **Warwick**, RI,US
35/E2 **Warwickshire** (co.), Eng,UK
108/E2 **Wasatch** (range), Ut,US
108/C4 **Wasco**, Ca,US
107/K4 **Waseca**, Mn,US
102/F1 **Washburn** (lake), NW,Can
33/G4 **Washburn** (riv.), Eng,UK
107/M3 **Washi** (lake), On,Can
33/F5 **Washingborough**, Eng,UK
33/G2 **Washington**, Eng,UK
106/C4 **Washington** (state), US
115/J8 **Washington** (cap.), DC,US
110/B3 **Washington**, Il,US
110/C4 **Washington**, In,US
113/J3 **Washington**, NC,US
111/G2 **Washington** (mtn.), NH,US
115/F5 **Washington**, NJ,US
110/D3 **Washington**, Pa,US
116/C2 **Washington** (lake), Wa,US
110/C2 **Washington** (isl.), Wi,US
110/D4 **Washington Court House**, Oh,US
79/K4 **Washington** (Teraina) (atoll), Kiri.
109/H4 **Washita** (riv.), Ok, Tx,US
35/G1 **Wash, The** (bay), Eng,UK
39/M2 **Wasilków**, Pol.
110/E1 **Waskaganish** (Rupert House), Qu,Can
114/G4 **Waskey** (mtn.), Ak,US
40/B4 **Wassenaar**, Neth.
40/D6 **Wassenberg**, Ger.
45/H1 **Wasserkuppe** (peak), Ger.
104/C4 **Wassuk** (range), Nv,US
33/E3 **Wast Water** (lake), Eng,UK
110/E1 **Waswanipi** (lake), Qu,Can
73/E4 **Watampone**, Indo.
65/M10 **Watarai**, Japan
65/F2 **Watarase** (riv.), Japan
65/G1 **Watari**, Japan
34/C4 **Watchet**, Eng,UK
35/E3 **Watchfield**, Eng,UK
35/G2 **Waterbeach**, Eng,UK
111/F3 **Waterbury**, Ct,US
111/Q9 **Waterdown**, On,Can
113/H3 **Wateree** (lake), SC,US
113/H3 **Wateree** (riv.), SC,US
36/B4 **Waterford**, Ire.
116/F6 **Waterford**, Mi,US
34/A6 **Watergate** (bay), Eng,UK
107/J2 **Waterhen** (lake), Mb,Can
106/F2 **Waterhen** (riv.), Sk,Can
42/D2 **Waterloo**, Belg.
110/D3 **Waterloo**, On,Can
109/J2 **Waterloo**, Ia,US
110/B4 **Waterloo**, Il,US
42/D2 **Waterloo Battlesite**, Belg.
35/E5 **Waterlooville**, Eng,UK
42/D2 **Watermael-Boitsfort**, Belg.
106/E3 **Waterton Lakes Nat'l Park**, Ab,Can
110/F3 **Watertown**, NY,US
107/J4 **Watertown**, SD,US
110/B3 **Watertown**, Wi,US
89/E2 **Waterval-Bo**, SAfr.
111/G2 **Waterville**, Me,US
106/C4 **Waterville**, Wa,US
31/M7 **Watford**, Eng,UK
107/H4 **Watford City**, ND,US
33/G5 **Wath-upon-Dearne**, Eng,UK
101/G3 **Watling** (San Salvador) (isl.), Bahm.
35/F3 **Watlington**, Eng,UK
69/B2 **Wat Mahathat**, Thai.
109/H4 **Watonga**, Ok,US
73/G3 **Watowato** (peak), Indo.
69/D3 **Wat Phu**, Laos
107/G3 **Watrous**, Sk,Can
83/L7 **Watsa**, Zaire
110/C3 **Watseka**, Il,US
102/D2 **Watson Lake**, Yk,Can
108/B3 **Watsonville**, Ca,US
45/J3 **Wattens**, Aus.
42/C2 **Wattignies**, Fr.
35/G1 **Watton**, Eng,UK
42/C2 **Wattrelos**, Fr.
69/C2 **Wat Xieng Thong**, Laos
113/H5 **Wauchula**, Fl,US
116/P15 **Wauconda**, Il,US
74/C4 **Waukarlycarly** (lake), Austl.
116/Q15 **Waukegan**, Il,US
116/P13 **Waukesha**, Wi,US
34/C3 **Waun Fâch** (mtn.), Wal,UK
34/C1 **Waun Oer** (mtn.), Wal,UK
110/B3 **Waupun**, Wi,US
109/H4 **Waurika**, Ok,US
110/B2 **Wausau**, Wi,US
110/C3 **Wauseon**, Oh,US
116/P13 **Wauwatosa**, Wi,US
35/H2 **Waveney** (riv.), Eng,UK
33/E2 **Waver** (riv.), Eng,UK
77/G5 **Waverly**, Austl.
113/G2 **Waverly**, Tn,US
42/D2 **Wavre**, Belg.
42/B2 **Wavrin**, Fr.
83/L6 **Wāw**, Sudan
110/C2 **Wawa**, On,Can
110/E1 **Wawagosic** (riv.), Qu,Can
112/D3 **Waxahachie**, Tx,US
43/F3 **Waxweiler**, Ger.
113/H4 **Waycross**, Ga,US
116/F7 **Wayne**, Mi,US
109/H2 **Wayne**, Ne,US
115/F5 **Wayne**, NJ,US
113/H3 **Waynesboro**, Ga,US
113/F4 **Waynesboro**, Ms,US
110/E4 **Waynesboro**, Pa,US
110/E4 **Waynesboro**, Va,US
109/J3 **Waynesville**, Mo,US
113/H3 **Waynesville**, NC,US
42/C3 **Waziers**, Fr.
65/L10 **Wazuka**, Japan
38/K2 **Wda** (riv.), Pol.
85/F3 **W du Niger Nat'l Park**, Afr.
72/A2 **We** (isl.), Indo.
35/G4 **Weald, The** (reg.), Eng,UK
33/G2 **Wear** (riv.), Eng,UK
33/F2 **Wear Head**, Eng,UK
109/H4 **Weatherford**, Ok,US
112/D3 **Weatherford**, Tx,US
33/F5 **Weaver** (riv.), Eng,UK
108/B2 **Weaverville**, Ca,US
107/J4 **Webster**, SD,US
107/K5 **Webster City**, Ia,US
83/M7 **Webuye**, Kenya
98/W **Weddell** (sea), Ant.
97/M7 **Weddell** (isl.), Falk.
77/C2 **Weddin Mountains Nat'l Park**, Austl.
41/G1 **Wedel**, Ger.
41/G3 **Wedemark**, Ger.
34/D4 **Wedmore**, Eng,UK
34/D1 **Wednesbury**, Eng,UK
34/D1 **Wednesfield**, Eng,UK
108/B2 **Weed**, Ca,US
35/E2 **Weedon Bec**, Eng,UK
113/H4 **Weeki Wachee Springs**, Fl,US
34/B5 **Week Saint Mary**, Eng,UK
40/D4 **Weerselo**, Neth.
40/C6 **Weert**, Neth.
40/C4 **Weesp**, Neth.
40/D6 **Wegberg**, Ger.
39/L1 **Węgorzewo**, Pol.
39/M2 **Węgrów**, Pol.
41/G6 **Wehre** (riv.), Ger.
63/H4 **Wei** (riv.), China
63/H3 **Weichang**, China
38/G3 **Weida**, Ger.
45/K2 **Weiden**, Ger.
66/D3 **Weifang**, China
63/J4 **Weihai**, China
45/H1 **Weilburg**, Ger.
43/F2 **Weilerswist**, Ger.
45/J3 **Weilheim**, Ger.
38/F3 **Weimar**, Ger.
45/H3 **Weingarten**, Ger.
39/J4 **Weinviertel** (reg.), Aus.
110/D3 **Weirton**, WV,US
106/D4 **Weiser**, Id,US
106/D4 **Weiser** (riv.), Id,US
66/D4 **Weishan** (lake), China
43/F4 **Weiskirchen**, Ger.
113/G3 **Weiss** (lake), Al,US
45/J2 **Weissenburg im Bayern**, Ger.
38/F3 **Weissenfels**, Ger.
43/G3 **Weissenthurm**, Ger.
43/F3 **Weisser Stein** (peak), Ger.
45/J3 **Weisskugel** (Palla Blanca) (mt.), Aus., It.
45/G3 **Weissmies** (peak), Swi.
39/H3 **Weisswasser**, Ger.
45/L3 **Weiz**, Aus.
71/J3 **Weizhou** (isl.), China
39/K1 **Wejherowo**, Pol.
110/D4 **Welch**, WV,US
83/N5 **Weldiya**, Eth.
35/F2 **Weldon**, Eng,UK
83/M6 **Welel** (peak), Eth.
35/E4 **Welford**, Eng,UK
31/N6 **Welham Green**, Eng,UK
70/D6 **Weligama**, SrL.
43/E2 **Welkenraedt**, Belg.
88/D3 **Welkom**, SAfr.
111/R10 **Welland**, On,Can
111/R10 **Welland** (can.), On,Can
35/F1 **Welland** (riv.), Eng,UK
111/R10 **Wellandport**, On,Can
43/E2 **Wellen**, Belg.
74/F3 **Wellesley** (isls.), Austl.
35/F2 **Wellingborough**, Eng,UK
77/C3 **Wellington** (inlet), Austl.
103/S7 **Wellington** (chan.), NW,Can
97/J7 **Wellington** (isl.), Chile
75/R11 **Wellington** (cap.), NZ
88/B4 **Wellington**, SAfr.
34/C5 **Wellington**, Eng,UK
34/D2 **Wellington**, Eng,UK
112/D2 **Wellington**, Ks,US
112/C3 **Wellington**, Tx,US
74/C5 **Wells** (lake), Austl.
106/C2 **Wells**, BC,Can
34/D4 **Wells**, Eng,UK
106/E5 **Wells**, Nv,US
35/G1 **Wells-next-the-Sea**, Eng,UK
110/D4 **Wellston**, Oh,US
45/L2 **Wels**, Aus.
34/C1 **Welshpool**, Wal,UK
41/E5 **Welver**, Ger.
35/F3 **Welwyn**, Eng,UK
35/F3 **Welwyn Garden City**, Eng,UK
33/F6 **Wem**, Eng,UK
87/F1 **Wembere** (riv.), Tanz.
106/D2 **Wembley**, Ab,Can
34/B6 **Wembury**, Eng,UK
103/J3 **Wemindji**, Qu,Can
42/D2 **Wemmel**, Belg.
106/C4 **Wenatchee**, Wa,US
67/B4 **Wenchang**, China
85/E5 **Wenchi**, Gha.
41/H4 **Wendeburg**, Ger.
43/G2 **Wenden**, Ger.
35/F3 **Wendover**, Eng,UK
108/D2 **Wendover**, Nv,US
34/A6 **Wendron**, Eng,UK
34/D2 **Wenlock Edge** (ridge), Eng,UK
41/F6 **Wenne** (riv.), Ger.
41/G4 **Wennigsen**, Ger.
33/F3 **Wennington**, Eng,UK
33/F3 **Wensleydale** (val.), Eng,UK
35/H1 **Wensum** (riv.), Eng,UK
33/G4 **Went** (riv.), Eng,UK
67/D2 **Wenzhou**, China
38/G3 **Werdau**, Ger.
83/Q6 **Werdēr**, Eth.
41/E6 **Werdohl**, Ger.
40/B5 **Werkendam**, Neth.
41/E5 **Werl**, Ger.
41/E3 **Werlte**, Ger.
41/E6 **Wermelskirchen**, Ger.
41/E5 **Werne an der Lippe**, Ger.
45/J2 **Werneck**, Ger.
41/H5 **Wernigerode**, Ger.
77/D2 **Werong** (peak), Austl.
41/G6 **Werra** (riv.), Ger.
41/F4 **Werre** (riv.), Ger.
77/E1 **Werrikimbe Nat'l Park**, Austl.
33/F5 **Werrington**, Eng,UK
41/E5 **Werse** (riv.), Ger.
45/H2 **Wertheim**, Ger.
41/F4 **Werther**, Ger.
40/C3 **Wervershoof**, Neth.
42/C2 **Wervik**, Belg.
40/D5 **Wesel**, Ger.
41/E5 **Wesel-Datteln-Kanal** (can.), Ger.
41/F2 **Weser** (riv.), Ger.
41/G4 **Wesergebirge** (ridge), Ger.
112/D5 **Weslaco**, Tx,US
88/D2 **Wes-Rand**, SAfr.
74/F2 **Wessel** (cape), Austl.
74/F2 **Wessel** (isls.), Austl.
34/D4 **Wessex** (reg.), Eng,UK
107/J4 **Wessington Springs**, SD,US
77/C4 **West** (pt.), Austl.
116/P13 **West Allis**, Wi,US
113/H3 **West Augusta**, Ga,US
115/G5 **West Babylon**, NY,US
59/K5 **West Bank** (occ. zone)
110/B3 **West Bend**, Wi,US
70/E3 **West Bengal** (state), India
35/G3 **West Bergholt**, Eng,UK
110/C2 **West Branch**, Mi,US
33/G6 **West Bridgford**, Eng,UK
35/E1 **West Bromwich**, Eng,UK
34/D4 **Westbury**, Eng,UK
115/G5 **Westbury**, NY,US
116/P16 **West Chicago**, Il,US
31/M8 **West Clandon**, Eng,UK
34/B3 **West Cleddau** (riv.), Wal,UK
113/H3 **West Columbia**, SC,US
33/G2 **West Cornforth**, Eng,UK
115/C2 **West Covina**, Ca,US
40/A6 **Westdorpe**, Neth.
30/F3 **West Dvina** (riv.), Eur.
112/B2 **West Elk** (mts.), Co,US
40/D3 **Westerbork**, Neth.
31/P8 **Westerham**, Eng,UK
41/E4 **Westerkappeln**, Ger.
38/E1 **Westerland**, Ger.
43/D1 **Westerlo**, Belg.
86/B3 **Western** (des.), Egypt
85/E5 **Western** (reg.), Gha.
84/B4 **Western** (area), SLeo.
74/C4 **Western Australia** (state), Austl.
64/A3 **Western Channel** (str.), Japan, SKor.
56/C4 **Western Dvina** (riv.), Lat., Rus.
70/B4 **Western Ghats** (mts.), India
82/B3 **Western Sahara**
79/H6 **Western Samoa**
62/C1 **Western Sayan** (mts.), Rus.
40/A6 **Westerschelde** (chan.), Neth.
41/E2 **Westerstede**, Ger.
110/D3 **Westerville**, Oh,US
40/C5 **Westervoort**, Neth.
43/G2 **Westerwald** (for.), Ger.
41/F4 **Westfalica, Porta** (pass), Ger.
97/M8 **West Falkland** (isl.), Falk.
107/J4 **West Fargo**, ND,US
78/D4 **West Fayu** (isl.), Micr.
115/F5 **Westfield**, NJ,US
42/B2 **West Flanders** (prov.), Belg.
110/B4 **West Frankfort**, Il,US
40/C2 **West Frisian** (isls.), Neth.
34/C3 **West Glamorgan** (co.), Wal,UK
35/F1 **West Glen** (riv.), Eng,UK
31/P7 **West Ham**, Eng,UK
115/G4 **West Haverstraw**, NY,US
113/F3 **West Helena**, Ar,US
36/D2 **Westhill**, Sc,UK
31/Q7 **West Horndon**, Eng,UK
31/M8 **West Horsley**, Eng,UK
33/F4 **Westhoughton**, Eng,UK
111/Q8 **West Humber** (riv.), On,Can
101/F4 **West Indies** (isls.), NAm.
75/J4 **West Islet** (isl.), Austl.
115/G5 **West Islip**, NY,US
108/E2 **West Jordan**, Ut,US
31/P8 **West Kingsdown**, Eng,UK
33/E5 **West Kirby**, Eng,UK
116/F7 **Westland**, Mi,US
106/E2 **Westlock**, Ab,Can
87/E3 **West Lunga Nat'l Park**, Zam.
32/A4 **Westmeath** (co.), Ire.
113/F3 **West Memphis**, Ar,US
35/G3 **West Mersea**, Eng,UK
35/E2 **West Midlands** (co.), Eng,UK
115/F4 **West Milford**, NJ,US
115/B3 **Westminster**, Ca,US
31/N7 **Westminster Abbey**, Eng,UK
31/N7 **Westminster, City of** (bor.), Eng,UK
116/Q16 **Westmont**, Il,US
115/E6 **Westmont** (Haddon), NJ,US
33/F3 **Westmoreland** (reg.), Eng,UK
111/N7 **Westmount**, Qu,Can
109/J3 **Weston**, Mo,US
110/D4 **Weston**, WV,US
88/P13 **Westonaria**, SAfr.
34/D4 **Weston-super-Mare**, Eng,UK
34/D4 **Weston Zoyland**, Eng,UK
115/F5 **West Orange**, NJ,US
113/H5 **West Palm Beach**, Fl,US
31/Q8 **West Peckham**, Eng,UK
113/G4 **West Pensacola**, Fl,US
109/K3 **West Plains**, Mo,US
113/G3 **West Point** (lake), Al, Ga,US
113/F3 **West Point**, Ms,US
109/H2 **West Point**, Ne,US
75/R11 **Westport**, NZ
115/G4 **Westport**, Ct,US
106/B2 **West Road** (riv.), BC,Can
116/L9 **West Sacramento**, Ca,US
111/S10 **West Seneca**, NY,US
56/H3 **West Siberian** (plain), Rus.
35/F4 **West Sussex** (co.), Eng,UK
31/P7 **West Thurrock**, Eng,UK
108/E2 **West Valley City**, Ut,US
106/C3 **West Vancouver**, BC,Can
110/D4 **West Virginia** (state), US
34/B4 **Westward Ho!**, Eng,UK
115/F5 **Westwood**, NJ,US
33/G4 **West Yorkshire** (co.), Eng,UK
112/B2 **Wet** (mts.), Co,US
73/G5 **Wetar** (isl.), Indo.
73/G5 **Wetar** (str.), Indo.
106/E2 **Wetaskiwin**, Ab,Can
87/G2 **Wete**, Tanz.
110/E1 **Wetetnagami** (riv.), Qu,Can
33/F2 **Wetheral**, Eng,UK
33/G4 **Wetherby**, Eng,UK
77/B2 **Wetherell** (lake), Austl.
41/E6 **Wetter**, Ger.
42/C1 **Wetteren**, Belg.
41/E4 **Wettringen**, Ger.
42/C2 **Wevelgem**, Belg.
78/D5 **Wewak**, PNG
109/H4 **Wewoka**, Ok,US
36/B4 **Wexford**, Ire.
32/B6 **Wexford** (co.), Ire.
31/M8 **Wey** (riv.), Eng,UK
35/H1 **Weybourne**, Eng,UK
31/M7 **Weybridge**, Eng,UK
107/H3 **Weyburn**, Sk,Can
34/D5 **Weymouth**, Eng,UK
34/D5 **Weymouth** (bay), Eng,UK
75/S10 **Whakatane**, NZ
33/G5 **Whaley Bridge**, Eng,UK
33/F4 **Whalley**, Eng,UK
75/R10 **Whangarei**, NZ
33/G3 **Wharfe** (riv.), Eng,UK
112/D4 **Wharton**, Tx,US
107/G5 **Wheatland**, Wy,US
35/E3 **Wheatley**, Eng,UK
116/P16 **Wheaton**, Il,US
34/D1 **Wheaton Aston**, Eng,UK
115/J7 **Wheaton-Glenmont**, Md,US
113/G3 **Wheeler** (lake), Al,US
109/F3 **Wheeler** (peak), NM,US
108/D3 **Wheeler** (peak), Nv,US
116/Q15 **Wheeling**, Il,US
110/D3 **Wheeling**, WV,US
33/F3 **Whernside** (mtn.), Eng,UK
33/G2 **Whickham**, Eng,UK
116/B1 **Whidbey** (isl.), Wa,US
108/B2 **Whiskeytown-Shasta-Trinity Nat'l Rec. Area**, Ca,US
33/G2 **Whitburn**, Eng,UK
111/S8 **Whitby**, On,Can
33/H3 **Whitby**, Eng,UK
33/F6 **Whitchurch**, Eng,UK
35/E4 **Whitchurch**, Eng,UK
35/F3 **Whitchurch**, Eng,UK
34/C4 **Whitchurch**, Wal,UK
98/D **White** (isl.), Ant.
74/D4 **White** (lake), Austl.
111/K1 **White** (bay), Nf,Can
110/C1 **White** (lake), On,Can
52/H2 **White** (sea), Rus.
114/L4 **White** (riv.), Ak,US
113/F3 **White** (riv.), Ar,US
108/E2 **White** (riv.), Co, Ut,US
110/C4 **White** (riv.), In,US
109/J5 **White** (lake), La,US
109/K4 **White** (riv.), La, Mo,US
109/G2 **White** (riv.), Ne, SD,US
108/D3 **White** (riv.), Nv,US
112/C3 **White** (riv.), Tx,US
110/D4 **White** (peak), Va,US
111/K1 **White Bear** (riv.), Nf,Can
107/G3 **White City**, Sk,Can
106/E2 **Whitecourt**, Ab,Can
33/E1 **White Esk** (riv.), Sc,UK
107/K4 **Whiteface** (riv.), Mn,US
33/F4 **Whitefield**, Eng,UK
110/C2 **Whitefish** (bay), On,Can, Mi,US
106/E3 **Whitefish**, Mt,US
114/L2 **Whitefish Station**, Yk,Can
34/B3 **Whiteford** (pt.), Wal,UK
107/G2 **White Fox**, Sk,Can
106/E4 **Whitehall**, Mt,US
115/E5 **Whitehall** (Fullerton), Pa,US
32/E2 **Whitehaven**, Eng,UK
32/C2 **Whitehead**, NI,UK
114/L3 **Whitehorse** (cap.), Yk,Can
35/E3 **Whitehorse** (hill), Eng,UK
115/K7 **White Marsh**, Md,US
114/J2 **White Mountains Nat'l Rec. Area**, Ak,US
107/K3 **Whitemouth** (riv.), Mb,Can
83/M5 **White Nile** (riv.), Sudan
115/K7 **White Oak**, Md,US
110/A1 **White Otter** (lake), On,Can
115/G4 **White Plains**, NY,US
110/C1 **White River**, On,Can
108/E4 **Whiteriver**, Az,US
112/B3 **White Rock**, NM,US
108/F4 **White Sands**, NM,US
108/F4 **White Sands Nat'l Mon.**, NM,US
97/K8 **Whiteside** (chan.), Chile
106/F4 **White Sulphur Springs**, Mt,US
110/D4 **White Sulphur Springs**, WV,US
113/J3 **Whiteville**, NC,US
85/E4 **White Volta** (riv.), Burk., Gha.
107/L3 **Whitewater** (lake), On,Can
107/H3 **Whitewood**, Sk,Can
32/D2 **Whithorn**, Sc,UK
34/B3 **Whitland**, Wal,UK
33/G1 **Whitley Bay**, Eng,UK
108/C3 **Whitney** (mtn.), Ca,US
109/H4 **Whitney** (lake), Tx,US
34/B6 **Whitsand** (bay), Eng,UK
35/H4 **Whitstable**, Eng,UK
76/C3 **Whitsunday I. Nat'l Park**, Austl.
115/B3 **Whittier**, Ca,US
35/F1 **Whittlesey**, Eng,UK
33/G5 **Whitwell**, Eng,UK
33/F4 **Whitworth**, Eng,UK
102/F2 **Wholdaia** (lake), NW,Can
74/F6 **Whyalla**, Austl.
69/B2 **Wiang Ko Sai Nat'l Park**, Thai.
110/D2 **Wiarton**, On,Can
42/C2 **Wichelen**, Belg.
109/H3 **Wichita**, Ks,US
109/H4 **Wichita** (mts.), Ok,US
109/H4 **Wichita** (riv.), Tx,US
112/D3 **Wichita Falls**, Tx,US
108/D4 **Wickenburg**, Az,US
35/G3 **Wickford**, Eng,UK
77/C3 **Wickham** (cape), Austl.
35/H2 **Wickham Market**, Eng,UK
32/B6 **Wicklow** (co.), Ire.
32/B5 **Wicklow** (mts.), Ire.
32/B5 **Wicklow Gap** (pass), Ire.
32/C6 **Wicklow Head** (pt.), Ire.
41/F4 **Wickriede** (riv.), Ger.
33/F5 **Widnes**, Eng,UK
43/G2 **Wied** (riv.), Ger.
41/G2 **Wiedau** (riv.), Ger.
41/F2 **Wiefelstede**, Ger.
41/F4 **Wiehengebirge** (ridge), Ger.
43/G2 **Wiehl**, Ger.
39/L4 **Wieliczka**, Pol.
42/C2 **Wielsbeke**, Belg.
39/K3 **Wieluń**, Pol.
39/J4 **Wien** (prov.), Aus.
39/J5 **Wiener Neustadt**, Aus.
39/J4 **Wien** (Vienna) (cap.), Aus.
45/L2 **Wienerwald** (reg.), Aus.
39/M3 **Wieprz** (riv.), Pol.
40/D4 **Wierden**, Neth.
40/B3 **Wieringermeerpolder** (polder), Neth.
40/C3 **Wieringerwerf**, Neth.
39/K3 **Wieruszów**, Pol.
45/H1 **Wiesbaden**, Ger.
45/G3 **Wiese** (riv.), Ger.
56/H2 **Wiese** (isl.), Rus.
41/E2 **Wiesmoor**, Ger.
41/E3 **Wietmarschen**, Ger.
41/G3 **Wietze**, Ger.
41/G3 **Wietze** (riv.), Ger.
39/K1 **Wieżyca** (peak), Pol.
33/F4 **Wigan**, Eng,UK
113/F4 **Wiggins**, Ms,US
35/E5 **Wight, Isle of** (isl.), Eng,UK
35/E1 **Wigston**, Eng,UK
33/E2 **Wigton**, Eng,UK
32/D2 **Wigtown**, Sc,UK
32/D2 **Wigtown** (bay), Sc,UK
40/C5 **Wijchen**, Neth.
40/D4 **Wijhe**, Neth.
40/C5 **Wijk bij Duurstede**, Neth.
83/N5 **Wik'ro**, Eth.
109/H2 **Wilber**, Ne,US
33/H4 **Wilberfoss**, Eng,UK
106/D4 **Wilbur**, Wa,US
109/J4 **Wilburton**, Ok,US
56/G1 **Wilczek** (isl.), Rus.
88/E4 **Wild Coast** (reg.), SAfr.
41/F3 **Wildeshausen**, Ger.
111/Q8 **Wildfield**, On,Can
107/J4 **Wild Rice** (riv.), Mn,US
45/J3 **Wildspitze** (peak), Aus.
115/K8 **Wild World**, Md,US
88/E2 **Wilge** (riv.), SAfr.
98/F **Wilhelm II** (coast), Ant.
93/G3 **Wilhelmina** (mts.), Sur.
40/C5 **Wilhelminakanaal** (can.), Neth.
41/G2 **Wilhelmsburg**, Ger.
41/F1 **Wilhelmshaven**, Ger.
113/H2 **Wilkesboro**, NC,US
98/J **Wilkes Land** (reg.), Ant.
106/F2 **Wilkie**, Sk,Can
98/V **Wilkins** (sound), Ant.
114/N4 **Will** (mtn.), BC,Can
106/C4 **Willamette** (riv.), Or,US
77/C2 **Willandra Nat'l Park**, Austl.
106/B4 **Willapa** (bay), Wa,US
33/F5 **Willaston**, Eng,UK
108/E4 **Willcox**, Az,US
41/G5 **Willebadessen**, Ger.
42/D1 **Willebroek**, Belg.
101/H5 **Willemstad** (cap.), NAnt.
31/N7 **Willesden**, Eng,UK
77/B3 **William** (peak), Austl.
108/D4 **Williams**, Az,US
110/C4 **Williamsburg**, Ky,US
110/E4 **Williamsburg**, Va,US
106/C2 **Williams Lake**, BC,Can
110/D4 **Williamson**, WV,US
77/F5 **Williamstown**, Austl.
111/S10 **Williamsville**, NY,US
40/D6 **Willich**, Ger.
115/F5 **Willingboro**, NJ,US
33/G2 **Willington**, Eng,UK
33/G6 **Willington**, Eng,UK
112/E4 **Willis**, Tx,US
75/J3 **Willis Islets** (isls.), Austl.
106/C2 **Williston** (lake), BC,Can
113/H4 **Williston**, Fl,US
107/H3 **Williston**, ND,US
34/C4 **Williton**, Eng,UK
108/B3 **Willits**, Ca,US
107/K4 **Willmar**, Mn,US
106/C2 **Willow** (riv.), BC,Can
106/D4 **Willow** (cr.), Or,US
116/Q16 **Willowbrook**, Il,US
107/G3 **Willow Bunch**, Sk,Can
115/E5 **Willow Grove**, Pa,US
106/C2 **Willow River**, BC,Can
108/B3 **Willows**, Ca,US
74/D4 **Wills** (lake), Austl.
116/Q15 **Wilmette**, Il,US
31/P7 **Wilmington**, Eng,UK
115/E6 **Wilmington**, De,US
113/J3 **Wilmington**, NC,US
110/D4 **Wilmington**, Oh,US
113/H4 **Wilmington Island**, Ga,US
33/F5 **Wilmslow**, Eng,UK
43/H2 **Wilnsdorf**, Ger.
40/B6 **Wilrijk**, Belg.
41/G2 **Wilseder Berg** (peak), Ger.
103/H2 **Wilson** (cape), NW,Can
115/B2 **Wilson** (mt.), Ca,US
113/J3 **Wilson**, NC,US
111/S9 **Wilson**, NY,US
115/E5 **Wilson**, Pa,US
77/C3 **Wilsons Promontory Nat'l Park**, Austl.
35/E4 **Wilton**, Eng,UK
35/E4 **Wiltshire** (co.), Eng,UK
31/N7 **Wimbledon**, Eng,UK
34/E5 **Wimborne Minster**, Eng,UK
42/A2 **Wimereux**, Fr.
88/D3 **Winburg**, SAfr.
34/D4 **Wincanton**, Eng,UK
35/E3 **Winchcombe**, Eng,UK
35/G5 **Winchelsea**, Eng,UK
35/E4 **Winchester**, Eng,UK
110/C4 **Winchester**, Ky,US
113/G3 **Winchester**, Tn,US
110/E4 **Winchester**, Va,US
106/F5 **Wind** (riv.), Wy,US
107/G5 **Wind Cave Nat'l Park**, SD,US
113/H3 **Winder**, Ga,US
33/F3 **Windermere**, Eng,UK
33/F3 **Windermere** (lake), Eng,UK
87/C5 **Windhoek** (cap.), Namb.
107/K5 **Windom**, Mn,US

166

Windo – Zand

108/E4 **Window Rock,** Az,US
106/F5 **Wind River** (range), Wy,US
35/E3 **Windrush** (riv.), Eng,UK
76/G8 **Windsor,** Austl.
111/L1 **Windsor,** NF,Can
111/H2 **Windsor,** NS,Can
116/F7 **Windsor,** On,Can
111/G2 **Windsor,** Qu,Can
35/F4 **Windsor,** Eng,UK
101/K5 **Windward** (isls.), NAm.
101/G4 **Windward** (passage), NAm.
106/D3 **Winfield,** BC,Can
109/H3 **Winfield,** Ks,US
35/F3 **Wing,** Eng,UK
33/G2 **Wingate,** Eng,UK
42/C1 **Wingene,** Belg.
111/R10 **Winger,** On,Can
35/H4 **Wingham,** Eng,UK
74/C4 **Winifred** (lake), Austl.
107/M2 **Winisk,** On,Can
107/M2 **Winisk** (lake), On,Can
107/M2 **Winisk** (riv.), On,Can
107/J3 **Winkler,** Mb,Can
85/E5 **Winneba,** Gha.
110/B3 **Winnebago** (lake), Wi,US
108/C2 **Winnemucca,** Nv,US
107/J5 **Winner,** SD,US
116/Q15 **Winnetka,** Il,US
106/F4 **Winnett,** Mt,US
112/E4 **Winnfield,** La,US
107/J3 **Winnipeg** (cap.), Mb,Can
107/J2 **Winnipeg** (lake), Mb,Can
107/K3 **Winnipeg** (riv.), Mb, On,Can
107/J3 **Winnipeg Beach,** Mb,Can
107/J3 **Winnipegosis,** Mb,Can
107/H2 **Winnipegosis** (lake), Mb,Can
112/F3 **Winnsboro,** La,US
113/H3 **Winnsboro,** SC,US
111/Q9 **Winona,** On,Can
107/L4 **Winona,** Mn,US
40/E2 **Winschoten,** Neth.
34/D4 **Winscombe,** Eng,UK
33/F5 **Winsford,** Eng,UK
34/D4 **Winsley,** Eng,UK
35/F3 **Winslow,** Eng,UK
108/E4 **Winslow,** Az,US
113/H2 **Winston-Salem,** NC,US
40/D2 **Winsum,** Neth.
41/F6 **Winterberg,** Ger.
88/D4 **Winterberge** (mts.), SAfr.
34/D3 **Winterbourne,** Eng,UK
113/H4 **Winter Haven,** Fl,US
113/H4 **Winter Park,** Fl,US
40/D5 **Winterswijk,** Neth.
45/H3 **Winterthur,** Swi.
111/G2 **Winthrop,** Me,US
116/Q15 **Winthrop Harbor,** Il,US
38/F3 **Wipper** (riv.), Ger.
41/H2 **Wipperau** (riv.), Ger.
41/E6 **Wipperfürth,** Ger.
33/G5 **Wirksworth,** Eng,UK
33/E5 **Wirral** (pen.), Eng,UK
35/G1 **Wisbech,** Eng,UK
110/B2 **Wisconsin** (state), US
110/B2 **Wisconsin Rapids,** Wi,US
107/J4 **Wishek,** ND,US
39/K4 **Wisła,** Pol.
39/K1 **Wiślany** (lag.), Pol.
39/K2 **Wisła** (Vistula) (riv.), Pol.
39/L4 **Wisłok** (riv.), Pol.
39/L4 **Wisłoka** (riv.), Pol.
38/F2 **Wismar,** Ger.
43/G5 **Wissembourg,** Fr.
43/G2 **Wissen,** Ger.
35/G1 **Wissey** (riv.), Eng,UK
88/E2 **Witbank,** SAfr.
88/A2 **Witberg** (peak), Namb.
35/G3 **Witham,** Eng,UK
33/H5 **Witham** (riv.), Eng,UK
34/C5 **Witheridge,** Eng,UK
33/J4 **Withernsea,** Eng,UK
114/J3 **Witherspoon** (mtn.), Ak,US
113/H4 **Withlacoochee** (riv.), Fl, Ga,US
33/F4 **Withnell,** Eng,UK
88/D3 **Wit Kei** (riv.), SAfr.
39/J2 **Witkowo,** Pol.
35/E3 **Witney,** Eng,UK
39/H2 **Witnica,** Pol.
43/E2 **Wittem,** Neth.
41/E6 **Witten,** Ger.
38/G3 **Wittenberg,** Ger.
38/F2 **Wittenberge,** Ger.
45/G3 **Wittenheim,** Fr.
35/F1 **Wittering,** Eng,UK
41/H3 **Wittingen,** Ger.
43/F4 **Wittlich,** Ger.
41/E1 **Wittmund,** Ger.
39/G1 **Witton** (pen.), Ger.
38/G2 **Wittstock,** Ger.
88/P12 **Witwatersrand** (reg.), SAfr.
41/G6 **Witzenhausen,** Ger.
34/C4 **Wiveliscombe,** Eng,UK
75/J5 **Wivenhoe** (lake), Austl.
35/G3 **Wivenhoe,** Eng,UK
116/E6 **Wixom,** Mi,US
39/L2 **Wkra** (riv.), Pol.
39/K1 **Władysławowo,** Pol.
39/K2 **Włocławek,** Pol.
39/K2 **Włocławek** (prov.), Pol.
39/K2 **Włocławskie** (lake), Pol.
39/M3 **Włodawa,** Pol.
39/K3 **Włoszczowa,** Pol.
34/C1 **Wnion** (riv.), Wal,UK
35/F2 **Woburn Sands,** Eng,UK
77/C3 **Wodonga,** Austl.
39/K4 **Wodzisław Śląski,** Pol.
40/B4 **Woerden,** Neth.
43/G6 **Woerth,** Fr.
40/C3 **Wognum,** Neth.
43/F5 **Woippy,** Fr.
73/H5 **Wokam** (isl.), Indo.
63/K2 **Woken** (riv.), China
31/M8 **Woking,** Eng,UK
35/F4 **Wokingham,** Eng,UK
111/S9 **Wolcottsville,** NY,US
31/N8 **Woldingham,** Eng,UK
78/D4 **Woleai** (atoll), Micr.
114/H2 **Wolf** (mtn.), Ak,US
109/G3 **Wolf** (cr.), Ok, Tx,US
110/B2 **Wolf** (riv.), Wi,US
114/F3 **Wolf Creek** (mtn.), Ak,US
106/E4 **Wolf Creek,** Mt,US
38/G3 **Wolfen,** Ger.
41/H4 **Wolfenbüttel,** Ger.
41/G6 **Wolfhagen,** Ger.
107/G3 **Wolf Point,** Mt,US
41/H4 **Wolfsburg,** Ger.
39/G1 **Wolgast,** Ger.
39/H2 **Woliński Nat'l Park,** Pol.
102/E2 **Wollaston** (pen.), NW,Can
102/F3 **Wollaston** (lake), Sk,Can
97/L8 **Wollaston** (isl.), Chile
35/F2 **Wollaston,** Eng,UK
77/D2 **Wollemi Nat'l Park,** Austl.
77/D2 **Wollongong,** Austl.
88/D2 **Wolmaransstad,** SAfr.
45/J3 **Wolnzach,** Ger.
82/C6 **Wologizi** (range), Libr.
39/L2 **Wołomin,** Pol.
39/J3 **Wołów,** Pol.
88/L10 **Wolseley,** SAfr.
33/G2 **Wolsingham,** Eng,UK
39/J2 **Wolsztyn,** Pol.
42/D2 **Woluwé-Saint-Lambert,** Belg.
40/D3 **Wolvega,** Neth.
34/D1 **Wolverhampton,** Eng,UK
35/F2 **Wolverton,** Eng,UK
110/D2 **Woman** (riv.), On,Can
34/D1 **Wombourne,** Eng,UK
33/G4 **Wombwell,** Eng,UK
116/P15 **Wonder** (lake), Il,US
77/C1 **Wongalarroo** (lake), Austl.
77/C3 **Wonnangatta-Moroka Nat'l Park,** Austl.
63/K4 **Wŏnsan,** NKor.
107/H2 **Wood** (lake), Sk,Can
106/G3 **Wood** (mtn.), Sk,Can
114/K3 **Wood** (mtn.), Yk,Can
111/Q8 **Woodbridge,** On,Can
35/H2 **Woodbridge,** Eng,UK
115/F5 **Woodbridge,** NJ,US
102/E2 **Wood Buffalo Nat'l Park,** Ab, Yk,Can
111/Q9 **Woodburn,** On,Can
32/C2 **Woodburn,** NI,UK
106/C4 **Woodburn,** Or,US
115/E6 **Woodbury,** NJ,US
116/Q16 **Wood Dale,** Il,US
76/D4 **Woodgate Nat'l Park,** Austl.
33/H5 **Woodhall Spa,** Eng,UK
116/F7 **Woodhaven,** Mi,US
116/L9 **Woodland,** Ca,US
109/F3 **Woodland Park,** Co,US
78/E5 **Woodlark** (isl.), PNG
115/K7 **Woodlawn,** Md,US
35/F4 **Woodley,** Eng,UK
115/G5 **Woodmere,** NY,US
116/P16 **Woodridge,** Il,US
74/E5 **Woodroffe** (peak), Austl.
33/F6 **Woodseaves,** Eng,UK
111/H2 **Woodstock,** NB,Can
35/E3 **Woodstock,** Eng,UK
116/P15 **Woodstock,** Il,US
110/E4 **Woodstock,** Va,US
113/F4 **Woodville,** Ms,US
112/E4 **Woodville,** Tx,US
109/H3 **Woodward,** Ok,US
34/D5 **Wool,** Eng,UK
34/D4 **Woolavington,** Eng,UK
33/G1 **Woolsington,** Eng,UK
31/P7 **Woolwich,** Eng,UK
109/H1 **Woonsocket,** SD,US
33/F6 **Woore,** Eng,UK
110/D3 **Wooster,** Oh,US
35/E3 **Wootton Basset,** Eng,UK
88/B4 **Worcester,** SAfr.
34/D2 **Worcester,** Eng,UK
111/G3 **Worcester,** Ma,US
34/D2 **Worcester & Birmingham** (can.), Eng,UK
45/K3 **Wörgl,** Aus.
32/E2 **Workington,** Eng,UK
33/G5 **Worksop,** Eng,UK
106/G4 **Worland,** Wy,US
28/* **World**
40/B4 **Wormer,** Neth.
31/N6 **Wormley,** Eng,UK
45/H2 **Worms,** Ger.
45/J2 **Wörnitz** (riv.), Ger.
41/F2 **Worpswede,** Ger.
33/G4 **Worsbrough,** Eng,UK
116/Q16 **Worth,** Il,US
35/F5 **Worthing,** Eng,UK
107/K5 **Worthington,** Mn,US
78/F3 **Wotho** (atoll), Mrsh.
78/G4 **Wotje** (atoll), Mrsh.
34/D3 **Wotton under Edge,** Eng,UK
40/C4 **Woudenberg,** Neth.
40/C5 **Woudrichem,** Neth.
40/B5 **Wouw,** Neth.
73/F4 **Wowoni** (isl.), Indo.
33/H5 **Wragby,** Eng,UK
57/T2 **Wrangel** (isl.), Rus.
114/A5 **Wrangell** (cape), Ak,US
114/K3 **Wrangell** (mts.), Ak,US
114/K3 **Wrangell-Saint Elias Nat'l Park & Prsv.,** Ak,US
33/J5 **Wrangle,** Eng,UK
109/G2 **Wray,** Co,US
31/M7 **Wraysbury,** Eng,UK
33/H6 **Wreake** (riv.), Eng,UK
75/K4 **Wreck** (reef), Austl.
88/B3 **Wreck** (pt.), SAfr.
34/D1 **Wrekin, The** (hill), Eng,UK
33/F5 **Wrenbury,** Eng,UK
33/F5 **Wrexham,** Wal,UK
107/G5 **Wright,** Wy,US
115/F5 **Wrightstown,** NJ,US
115/C2 **Wrightwood,** Ca,US
35/G3 **Writtle,** Eng,UK
39/J3 **Wrocław,** Pol.
39/J3 **Wrocław** (prov.), Pol.
31/P8 **Wrotham,** Eng,UK
102/D1 **Wrottesley** (cape), NW,Can
34/D1 **Wroxeter,** Eng,UK
35/H1 **Wroxham,** Eng,UK
39/J2 **Września,** Pol.
39/J3 **Wschowa,** Pol.
71/K2 **Wu** (riv.), China
66/C3 **Wu'an,** China
66/C5 **Wuchang** (lake), China
63/K2 **Wudalianchi,** China
66/B4 **Wudang Shan** (mtn.), China
66/B3 **Wuding** (riv.), China
66/C5 **Wuhan,** China
66/D5 **Wuhu,** China
62/F3 **Wujia** (riv.), China
40/E6 **Wülfrath,** Ger.
67/B2 **Wuling** (mts.), China
85/H5 **Wum,** Camr.
41/F2 **Wümme** (riv.), Ger.
70/C3 **Wūn,** India
41/F5 **Wünnenberg,** Ger.
41/G4 **Wunstorf,** Ger.
108/E4 **Wupatki Nat'l Mon.,** Az,US
41/E6 **Wüpper** (riv.), Ger.
41/E6 **Wuppertal,** Ger.
68/C4 **Wuqia,** China
43/F2 **Würm** (riv.), Ger.
85/G3 **Wurno,** Nga.
43/F2 **Würselen,** Ger.
45/H2 **Würzburg,** Ger.
63/H5 **Wushan** (lake), China
66/C5 **Wusheng Guan** (pass), China
68/C3 **Wushi,** China
41/G6 **Wüstegarten** (peak), Ger.
63/L2 **Wusuli** (Ussuri) (riv.), China, Rus.
66/C3 **Wutai Shan** (peak), China
84/C4 **Wuteve** (peak), Libr.
40/B6 **Wuustwezel,** Belg.
66/D5 **Wuwei,** China
66/E5 **Wuxi,** China
66/C5 **Wuxue,** China
67/C2 **Wuyi** (mts.), China
63/K2 **Wuyur** (riv.), China
69/E2 **Wuzhi** (mts.), China
66/D2 **Wuzhi Shan** (peak), China
71/K3 **Wuzhou,** China
116/F7 **Wyandotte,** Mi,US
77/D2 **Wyangale** (dam), Austl.
115/F4 **Wyckoff,** NJ,US
34/D3 **Wye** (riv.), UK
34/D4 **Wylye** (riv.), Eng,UK
33/G6 **Wymeswold,** Eng,UK
35/H1 **Wymondham,** Eng,UK
113/F3 **Wynne,** Ar,US
76/F6 **Wynnum,** Austl.
107/G3 **Wynyard,** Sk,Can
106/F5 **Wyoming** (state), US
110/C3 **Wyoming,** Mi,US
106/F5 **Wyoming** (peak), Wy,US
108/E2 **Wyoming** (range), Wy,US
77/B2 **Wyperfeld Nat'l Park,** Austl.
33/F4 **Wyre** (riv.), Eng,UK
39/L2 **Wyszków,** Pol.
110/D4 **Wytheville,** Va,US

X

69/D4 **Xa Binh Long,** Viet.
100/B4 **Xadani,** Mex.
68/E5 **Xainza,** China
70/E2 **Xaitongmoin,** China
89/F2 **Xai-Xai,** Moz.
69/D1 **Xam Nua,** Laos
69/D3 **Xan** (riv.), Viet.
40/D5 **Xanten,** Ger.
49/J2 **Xánthi,** Gre.
95/A3 **Xanxerê,** Braz.
83/Q7 **Xarardheere,** Som.
69/E4 **Xa Song Luy,** Viet.
87/C3 **Xassengue,** Ang.
69/D3 **Xa Tho Thanh,** Viet.
93/J6 **Xavantes** (mts.), Braz.
95/B2 **Xavantes** (res.), Braz.
69/D4 **Xa Vo Dat,** Viet.
68/D3 **Xayar,** China
100/D3 **Xel-há** (ruins), Mex.
110/D4 **Xenia,** Oh,US
69/D2 **Xeno,** Laos
66/E2 **Xi** (lake), China
63/E3 **Xi** (riv.), China
63/F5 **Xi** (riv.), China
63/H5 **Xi** (riv.), China
67/B3 **Xi** (riv.), China
71/H2 **Xiaguan,** China
67/C3 **Xiamen,** China
66/B4 **Xi'an,** China
67/B2 **Xiang** (riv.), China
66/C4 **Xiangfan,** China
69/C2 **Xiang Khoang** (plat.), Laos
67/B2 **Xiangtan,** China
67/B2 **Xiangxiang,** China
66/C5 **Xianning,** China
66/C5 **Xiantao,** China
62/F5 **Xianyang,** China
66/C3 **Xiao** (riv.), China
67/B2 **Xiao** (riv.), China
71/H2 **Xiao** (riv.), China
63/J1 **Xiaobole** (peak), China
66/C5 **Xiaogan,** China
63/K2 **Xiao Hinggang** (mts.), China
66/D3 **Xiaoqing** (riv.), China
66/L9 **Xiaoshan,** China
66/C3 **Xiaowutai Shan** (peak), China
71/F2 **Xibaxa** (riv.), China
66/C4 **Xicheng Shan** (mtn.), China
100/B3 **Xicohténcatl,** Mex.
100/B3 **Xicotepec,** Mex.
66/C4 **Xifei** (riv.), China
62/F4 **Xifeng,** China
63/J3 **Xifeng,** China
67/A2 **Xifeng,** China
70/E2 **Xigazê,** China
62/E5 **Xihan** (riv.), China
68/F4 **Xijir Ulan** (lake), China
66/E2 **Xiliao** (riv.), China
67/C2 **Xin** (riv.), China
66/D5 **Xin'an** (riv.), China
66/D5 **Xin'anjiang** (res.), China
67/B3 **Xinfengjiang** (res.), China
66/E2 **Xingcheng,** China
87/C2 **Xinge,** Ang.
66/D4 **Xinghua,** China
68/D3 **Xingjiang Uygur Aut. Reg.,** China
63/L3 **Xingkai** (lake), China
66/C3 **Xingtai,** China
93/H4 **Xingu** (riv.), Braz.
66/C4 **Xingyang,** China
62/E4 **Xining** (Xining Shi), China
66/C3 **Xinji,** China
58/J5 **Xinjiang** (reg.), China
66/D4 **Xintai,** China
66/C4 **Xinxiang,** China
66/C4 **Xinyang,** China
67/B2 **Xinyu,** China
68/D3 **Xinyuan,** China
62/E5 **Xiqing** (mts.), China
94/B3 **Xique-Xique,** Braz.
67/B2 **Xiu** (riv.), China
70/E2 **Xixabangma** (peak), China
71/J3 **Xiyang** (riv.), China
66/E3 **Xizhong** (isl.), China
67/C2 **Xu** (riv.), China
66/C2 **Xuanhua,** China
66/C4 **Xuchang,** China
83/P7 **Xuddur** (Oddur), Som.
66/E5 **Xuedou** (peak), China
62/D4 **Xugin Gol** (riv.), China
66/B4 **Xun** (riv.), China
67/B3 **Xun** (riv.), China
63/K2 **Xunke,** China
66/D4 **Xuyi,** China
66/D4 **Xuzhou,** China

Y

62/E6 **Ya'an,** China
82/G7 **Yabassi,** Camr.
83/N7 **Yabēlo,** Eth.
100/E5 **Yablis,** Nic.
62/F1 **Yablonovyy** (ridge), Rus.
65/G2 **Yabuki,** Japan
67/A2 **Yachi** (riv.), China
65/J7 **Yachiyo,** Japan
95/A4 **Yacuí** (riv.), Braz.
92/F8 **Yacuiba,** Bol.
70/C4 **Yādgīr,** India
65/L9 **Yagi,** Japan
82/J5 **Yagoua,** Camr.
62/D4 **Yagradagzê** (peak), China
97/G2 **Yaguarón** (riv.), Uru.
65/N10 **Yahagi** (riv.), Japan
59/C2 **Yahyalı,** Turk.
65/F2 **Yaita,** Japan
65/F3 **Yaizu,** Japan
63/J2 **Yakeshi,** China
106/C4 **Yakima,** Wa,US
106/C4 **Yakima** (riv.), Wa,US
85/E3 **Yako,** Burk.
83/K7 **Yakoma,** Zaire
51/F4 **Yakoruda,** Bul.
64/B5 **Yaku-Kirishima Nat'l Park,** Japan
65/K9 **Yakuno,** Japan
114/K4 **Yakutat** (bay), Ak,US
57/N3 **Yakut Aut. Rep.,** Rus.
57/N3 **Yakutsk,** Rus.
69/C5 **Yala,** Thai.
109/K4 **Yalobusha** (riv.), Ms,US
82/J6 **Yaloké,** CAfr.
71/H2 **Yalong** (riv.), China
54/E3 **Yalta,** Ukr.
63/J3 **Yalu** (riv.), China, NKor.
64/B4 **Yamaga,** Japan
65/G1 **Yamagata,** Japan
65/F1 **Yamagata** (pref.), Japan
64/B3 **Yamaguchi** (pref.), Japan
56/G2 **Yamal** (pen.), Rus.
56/G3 **Yamal-Nenets Aut. Okr.,** Rus.
65/F3 **Yamanashi** (pref.), Japan
76/B2 **Yamanie Falls Nat'l Park,** Austl.
53/N5 **Yamantau, Gora** (peak), Rus.
65/N9 **Yamaoka,** Japan
65/L10 **Yamashiro,** Japan
65/L10 **Yamato-Kōriyama,** Japan
64/D3 **Yamatotakada,** Japan
65/M10 **Yamazoe,** Japan
83/L7 **Yambio,** Sudan
51/H4 **Yambol,** Bul.
69/B1 **Yamethin,** Burma
73/K4 **Yamin** (peak), Indo.
76/A4 **Yamma Yamma** (lake), Austl.
65/G1 **Yamoto,** Japan
84/D5 **Yamoussoukro** (cap.), IvC.
108/F2 **Yampa** (riv.), Co,US
70/C2 **Yamuna** (riv.), India
61/L2 **Yamunānagar,** India
71/E2 **Yamzho Yumco** (lake), China
66/B3 **Yan** (riv.), China
70/D6 **Yan** (riv.), SrL.
57/P3 **Yana** (riv.), Rus.
64/B4 **Yanagawa,** Japan
64/C4 **Yanai,** Japan
53/M4 **Yanaul,** Rus.
66/C4 **Yancheng,** China
66/E4 **Yancheng,** China
79/T12 **Yandé** (isl.), NCal.
71/G4 **Yandoon,** Burma
83/K7 **Yangambi,** Zaire
71/G2 **Yangbi** (riv.), China
66/L8 **Yangcheng** (lake), China
67/C2 **Yangdang** (mts.), China
66/C2 **Yanggao,** China
63/K4 **Yanggu,** SKor.
69/B2 **Yangon** (Rangoon) (cap.), Burma
66/C3 **Yangquan,** China
71/K3 **Yangshan,** China
71/K3 **Yangshuo,** China
66/D5 **Yangtze** (Chang) (riv.), China
83/P5 **Yangudi Rassa Nat'l Park,** Eth.
64/A1 **Yangyang,** SKor.
66/C2 **Yangyuan,** China
66/D4 **Yangzhou,** China
63/K3 **Yanji,** China
85/H4 **Yankari Game Rsv.,** Nga.
107/J5 **Yankton,** SD,US
66/C3 **Yanmen Guan** (pass), China
66/E3 **Yantai,** China
66/C2 **Yantong Shan** (mtn.), China
77/G5 **Yan Yean** (res.), Austl.
64/D3 **Yao,** Japan
82/H7 **Yaoundé** (cap.), Camr.
78/C4 **Yap** (isls.), Micr.
92/E3 **Yapacana Nat'l Park,** Ven.
73/J4 **Yapen** (isl.), Indo.
73/J4 **Yapen** (str.), Indo.
115/H5 **Yaphank,** NY,US
101/M8 **Yaqui,** Mex.
101/N8 **Yaqui** (riv.), Mex.
35/E5 **Yar** (riv.), Eng,UK
101/F3 **Yara,** Cuba
73/J4 **Yaramaniapuka** (mtn.), Indo.
53/K4 **Yaransk,** Rus.
59/B3 **Yardımcı** (pt.), Turk.
35/H1 **Yare** (riv.), Eng,UK
65/E2 **Yari-ga-take** (mtn.), Japan
51/J5 **Yarımca,** Turk.
68/C4 **Yarkant** (riv.), China
111/H3 **Yarmouth,** NS,Can
52/H4 **Yaroslavl',** Rus.
52/H4 **Yaroslavl' Obl.,** Rus.
77/G5 **Yarra** (riv.), Austl.
92/C2 **Yarumal,** Col.
78/G6 **Yasawa Group** (isls.), Fiji
54/C1 **Yasel'da** (riv.), Bela.
65/H7 **Yashio,** Japan
65/K10 **Yashiro,** Japan
55/L2 **Yasnyy,** Rus.
69/D3 **Yasothon,** Thai.
60/F4 **Yas, Sir Bani** (isl.), UAE
65/M9 **Yasu,** Japan
65/M10 **Yasu** (riv.), Japan
64/C3 **Yasugi,** Japan
92/C4 **Yasuni Nat'l Park,** Ecu.
65/G2 **Yatabe,** Japan
59/B3 **Yatağan,** Turk.
34/D3 **Yate,** Eng,UK
35/F4 **Yateley,** Eng,UK
85/E3 **Yatenga** (prov.), Burk.
109/J3 **Yates Center,** Ks,US
102/G2 **Yathkyed** (lake), NW,Can
65/M9 **Yatomi,** Japan
65/E2 **Yatsuo,** Japan
64/B4 **Yatsushiro,** Japan
59/K6 **Yaṭṭah,** WBnk.
34/D4 **Yatton,** Eng,UK
92/D5 **Yavari** (riv.), Peru
70/C3 **Yavatmāl,** India
56/H2 **Yavay** (pen.), Rus.
101/F6 **Yaviza,** Pan.
59/M9 **Yavne,** Isr.
65/J7 **Yawahara,** Japan
65/L10 **Yawata,** Japan
64/C4 **Yawatahama,** Japan
100/C4 **Yaxchilán** (ruins), Mex.
35/F2 **Yaxley,** Eng,UK
61/F2 **Yazd,** Iran
113/F3 **Yazoo** (riv.), Ms,US
113/F3 **Yazoo City,** Ms,US
45/L2 **Ybbs** (riv.), Aus.
69/B3 **Ye,** Burma
33/G4 **Yeadon,** Eng,UK
34/B6 **Yealmpton,** Eng,UK
69/C4 **Yeay Sen** (cape), Camb.
68/C4 **Yecheng,** China
47/E3 **Yecla,** Sp.
54/F1 **Yefremov,** Rus.
55/G3 **Yegorlak** (riv.), Rus.
59/M8 **Yehud,** Isr.
83/M7 **Yei,** Sudan
53/P4 **Yekaterinburg Obl.,** Rus.
53/P4 **Yekaterinburg** (Sverdlovsk), Rus.
53/M5 **Yelabuga,** Rus.
55/G2 **Yelan',** Rus.
54/F1 **Yelets,** Rus.
57/Q4 **Yelizavety** (cape), Rus.
57/R4 **Yelizovo,** Rus.
81/R16 **Yellel,** Alg.
63/J4 **Yellow** (sea), Asia
113/G4 **Yellow** (riv.), Al, Fl,US
107/G3 **Yellow Grass,** Sk,Can
63/H4 **Yellow** (Huang) (riv.), China
102/E2 **Yellowknife** (cap.), NW,Can
102/E2 **Yellowknife** (riv.), NW,Can
107/G4 **Yellowstone** (riv.), Mt,US
106/F4 **Yellowstone** (lake), Wy,US
106/F4 **Yellowstone Nat'l Park,** Wy,US
112/E2 **Yellville,** Ar,US
34/B6 **Yelverton,** Eng,UK
62/D4 **Yema** (riv.), China
60/E5 **Yemen**
54/F2 **Yenakiyevo,** Ukr.
71/F3 **Yenangyaung,** Burma
69/D1 **Yen Bai,** Viet.
85/E4 **Yendi,** Gha.
68/C4 **Yengisar,** China
54/E4 **Yenice** (riv.), Turk.
59/C2 **Yeniceoba,** Turk.
51/J5 **Yenişehir,** Turk.
56/J3 **Yenisey** (riv.), Rus.
56/K4 **Yeniseysk,** Rus.
69/D1 **Yen Minh,** Viet.
74/C5 **Yeo** (lake), Austl.
34/D5 **Yeo** (riv.), Eng,UK
61/K4 **Yeola,** India
34/D5 **Yeovil,** Eng,UK
76/C3 **Yeppoon,** Austl.
49/H3 **Yerakovoúni** (peak), Gre.
42/A4 **Yères** (riv.), Fr.
55/H4 **Yerevan** (cap.), Arm.
108/C3 **Yerington,** Nv,US
59/C2 **Yerköy,** Turk.
68/C1 **Yermak,** Kaz.
56/H4 **Yermentau,** Kaz.
59/K6 **Yeroḥam,** Isr.
31/T10 **Yerres,** Fr.
31/U11 **Yerres** (riv.), Fr.
92/C6 **Yerupaja** (peak), Peru
59/K6 **Yerushalayim** (Jerusalem) (cap.), Isr.
71/G3 **Yesagyo,** Burma
68/A1 **Yesil',** Kaz.
59/D2 **Yeşilirmak** (riv.), Turk.
55/G3 **Yessentuki,** Rus.
34/D5 **Yetminster,** Eng,UK
44/B3 **Yeu** (isl.), Fr.
70/B3 **Yevla,** India
55/H4 **Yevlakh,** Azer.
54/E3 **Yevpatoriya,** Ukr.
54/G3 **Yeya** (riv.), Rus.
54/F3 **Yeysk,** Rus.
66/C4 **Yi** (riv.), China
97/G2 **Yi** (riv.), Uru.
49/H2 **Yiannitsá,** Gre.
49/J4 **Yíaros** (isl.), Gre.
66/B5 **Yichang,** China
67/B2 **Yichun,** China
67/C2 **Yihuang,** China
63/K2 **Yilan,** China
59/D2 **Yıldızeli,** Turk.
63/J1 **Yilehuli** (mts.), China
66/B4 **Yima,** China
63/J2 **Yimin** (riv.), China
62/F3 **Yin** (mts.), China
62/F4 **Yinchuan,** China
74/C6 **Yindarlgooda** (lake), Austl.
66/C4 **Ying** (riv.), China
66/C5 **Yingcheng,** China
63/J3 **Yingkou,** China
67/C2 **Yingtan,** China
68/D3 **Yining,** China
83/M6 **Yirol,** Sudan
66/F2 **Yitong** (riv.), China
66/C4 **Yiyang,** China
67/B2 **Yiyang,** China
66/D4 **Yizheng,** China
32/E6 **Y Llethr** (mtn.), Wal,UK
37/G3 **Ylöjärvi,** Fin.
112/D4 **Yoakum,** Tx,US
64/D3 **Yodo** (riv.), Japan
57/P4 **Yoduma** (riv.), Rus.
82/J4 **Yogoum** (well), Chad
72/D5 **Yogyakarta,** Indo.
106/D3 **Yoho Nat'l Park,** BC,Can
82/J7 **Yokadouma,** Camr.
64/E3 **Yōkaichi,** Japan
64/D3 **Yokawa,** Japan
64/E3 **Yokkaichi,** Japan
65/F3 **Yokohama,** Japan
65/H7 **Yokohama** (inset), Japan
65/F3 **Yokosuka,** Japan
82/H6 **Yola,** Nga.
69/C2 **Yom** (riv.), Thai.
87/B1 **Yombi,** Gabon
67/A3 **Yon** (riv.), China
44/C3 **Yon** (riv.), Fr.
64/C3 **Yonago,** Japan
65/G2 **Yonezawa,** Japan
67/C2 **Yong'an,** China
64/A3 **Yŏngch'ŏn,** SKor.
71/G3 **Yongde,** China
66/H7 **Yongding** (riv.), China
64/A2 **Yŏngdŏk,** SKor.
71/J3 **Yongfu,** China
64/A2 **Yŏngju,** SKor.
66/C3 **Yongnian,** China
64/A2 **Yŏngwŏl,** SKor.
67/B2 **Yongzhou,** China
115/G5 **Yonkers,** NY,US
44/E2 **Yonne** (riv.), Fr.
65/H7 **Yono,** Japan
68/C4 **Yopurga,** China
115/C3 **Yorba Linda,** Ca,US
74/G2 **York** (cape), Austl.
74/C2 **York** (sound), Austl.
111/R8 **York,** On,Can
111/H1 **York** (riv.), Qu,Can
33/G4 **York,** Eng,UK
113/F3 **York,** Al,US
109/H2 **York,** Ne,US
113/H3 **York,** SC,US
110/E4 **York** (riv.), Va,US
74/F6 **Yorke** (pen.), Austl.
107/J1 **York Landing,** Mb,Can
33/G4 **York Minster,** Eng,UK
33/F3 **Yorkshire Dales Nat'l Park,** Eng,UK
33/H3 **Yorkshire Wolds** (hills), Eng,UK
107/H3 **Yorkton,** Sk,Can
33/G3 **York, Vale of** (val.), Eng,UK
100/D4 **Yoro,** Hon.
65/M9 **Yorō,** Japan
65/J7 **Yōrō** (riv.), Japan
65/M10 **Yoroi-zaki** (pt.), Japan
62/F2 **Yöröö,** Mong.
33/F6 **Yorton,** Eng,UK
85/F4 **Yorubaland** (plat.), Nga.
108/C3 **Yosemite Nat'l Park,** Ca,US
64/C4 **Yoshida,** Japan
64/D3 **Yoshii** (riv.), Japan
65/H7 **Yoshikawa,** Japan
64/D3 **Yoshimo** (riv.), Japan
65/L10 **Yoshino,** Japan
64/E3 **Yoshino-Kumano Nat'l Park,** Japan
53/L4 **Yoshkar-Ola,** Rus.
63/K5 **Yŏsu,** SKor.
63/N3 **Yōtei-san** (mtn.), Japan
65/J7 **Yotsukaidō,** Japan
67/A2 **You** (riv.), China
67/A3 **You** (riv.), China
77/D2 **Young,** Austl.
97/F2 **Young,** Uru.
111/R9 **Youngstown,** NY,US
110/D3 **Youngstown,** Oh,US
63/L2 **Youyi,** China
92/E2 **Yoví** (peak), Ven.
59/C2 **Yozgat,** Turk.
116/E7 **Ypsilanti,** Mi,US
32/D6 **Yr Eifl** (mtn.), Wal,UK
108/B2 **Yreka,** Ca,US
42/B2 **Yser** (riv.), Fr.
39/G1 **Ystad,** Swe.
34/C3 **Ystalyfera,** Wal,UK
34/C3 **Ystradgynlais,** Wal,UK
34/C3 **Ystrad Mynach,** Wal,UK
34/C2 **Ystwyth** (riv.), Wal,UK
36/D2 **Ythan** (riv.), Sc,UK
71/J3 **Yu** (riv.), China
67/D3 **Yū** (peak), Tai.
66/C5 **Yuan** (lake), China
67/B2 **Yuan** (riv.), China
71/H3 **Yuan** (riv.), China
66/C3 **Yuanping,** China
108/B3 **Yuba City,** Ca,US
63/N3 **Yūbari,** Japan
115/C2 **Yucaipa,** Ca,US
100/D4 **Yucatan** (pen.), Mex.
100/D3 **Yucatan** (state), Mex.
100/D3 **Yucatan** (chan.), NAm.
108/D4 **Yucca,** Az,US
66/C3 **Yuci,** China
66/D5 **Yuexi,** China
71/H2 **Yuexi,** China
67/B2 **Yueyang,** China
53/K3 **Yug** (riv.), Rus.
53/P1 **Yugorskiy** (pen.), Rus.
50/D3 **Yugoslavia**
66/L9 **Yuhang,** China
65/F2 **Yūki,** Japan
102/B2 **Yukon** (riv.), Can., US
114/K2 **Yukon-Charley Rivers Nat'l Prsv.,** Ak,US
114/L3 **Yukon Crossing,** Yk,Can
102/C2 **Yukon Territory** (terr.), Can.
59/F3 **Yüksekova,** Turk.
60/D1 **Yüksekova,** Turk.
64/B4 **Yukuhashi,** Japan
74/E5 **Yulara,** Austl.
69/E2 **Yulin,** China
71/K3 **Yulin,** China
66/B3 **Yulin** (riv.), China
66/D5 **Yuling Guan** (pass), China
108/D4 **Yuma,** Az,US
109/G2 **Yuma,** Co,US
96/B3 **Yumbel,** Chile
87/E1 **Yumbi,** Zaire
92/C3 **Yumbo,** Col.
62/D4 **Yumen,** China
66/C5 **Yun** (riv.), China
59/B2 **Yunak,** Turk.
92/E7 **Yungas** (reg.), Bol.
96/B3 **Yungay,** Chile
71/H3 **Yunnan** (prov.), China
66/D4 **Yuntai Shan** (peak), China
66/D2 **Yunwu Shan** (peak), China
66/D4 **Yunyan** (riv.), China
66/C3 **Yunzhong Shan** (mtn.), China
71/J2 **Yuping,** China
66/H7 **Yuqiao** (res.), China
64/D3 **Yura** (riv.), Japan
56/J4 **Yurga,** Rus.
92/C5 **Yurimaguas,** Peru
68/C4 **Yurungkax** (riv.), China
53/N5 **Yuryuzan'** (riv.), Rus.
66/D3 **Yutian,** China
43/F5 **Yutz,** Fr.
66/C3 **Yu Xian,** China
66/C4 **Yu Xian,** China
67/D1 **Yuyao,** China
63/N2 **Yuzhno-Sakhalinsk,** Rus.
54/D2 **Yuzhnyy Bug** (riv.), Ukr.
31/R10 **Yvelines** (dept.), Fr.
45/G3 **Yverdon,** Swi.
31/S10 **Yvette** (riv.), Fr.
43/D3 **Yvoir,** Belg.
44/E3 **Yzeure,** Fr.

Z

81/N13 **Za** (riv.), Mor.
40/B4 **Zaandam,** Neth.
39/L2 **Ząbki,** Pol.
39/J3 **Ząbkowice Śląskie,** Pol.
61/H2 **Zābol,** Iran
39/J4 **Zábřeh,** Czh.
39/K3 **Zabrze,** Pol.
100/D5 **Zacapa,** Guat.
100/A4 **Zacapú,** Mex.
100/A3 **Zacatecas,** Mex.
101/P9 **Zacatecas,** Mex.
100/A3 **Zacatecas** (state), Mex.
100/D5 **Zacatecoluca,** ESal.
113/F4 **Zachary,** La,US
100/B3 **Zacualtipán,** Mex.
50/B3 **Zadar,** Cro.
69/B4 **Zadetkyi** (isl.), Burma
62/D5 **Zadoi,** China
46/B3 **Zafra,** Sp.
39/H3 **Żagań,** Pol.
81/X17 **Zaghwān',** Tun.
81/W17 **Zaghwān'** (gov.), Tun.
50/B2 **Zagorjeob Savi,** Slov.
50/C3 **Zagreb** (cap.), Cro.
60/E1 **Zagros** (mts.), Iran
68/E5 **Za'gya** (riv.), China
61/H3 **Zāhedān,** Iran
70/C4 **Zahirābād,** India
59/K5 **Zaḩlah,** Leb.
60/D5 **Zahrān,** SAr.
80/E5 **Zaire**
80/E4 **Zaïre** (Congo) (riv.), Zaire
50/F4 **Zaječar,** Yugo.
62/E1 **Zakamensk,** Rus.
59/E3 **Zākhū,** Iraq
49/G4 **Zákinthos,** Gre.
49/G4 **Zákinthos** (isl.), Gre.
39/K4 **Zakopane,** Pol.
83/J5 **Zakouma Nat'l Park,** Chad
49/J5 **Zakro** (ruins), Gre.
50/C2 **Zala** (co.), Hun.
50/C2 **Zala** (riv.), Hun.
50/C2 **Zalaegerszeg,** Hun.
46/C3 **Zalamea de la Serena,** Sp.
63/J2 **Zalantun,** China
50/C2 **Zalaszentgrót,** Hun.
50/F2 **Zalău,** Rom.
82/J2 **Zalṭan** (well), Libya
40/C5 **Zaltbommel,** Neth.
65/H7 **Zama,** Japan
87/F4 **Zambezi** (riv.), Afr.
87/D3 **Zambezi,** Zam.
87/E3 **Zambia**
67/D6 **Zamboanga,** Phil.
39/M2 **Zambrów,** Pol.
47/P11 **Zambujal de Cima,** Port.
85/G3 **Zamfora** (riv.), Nga.
69/B3 **Zami** (riv.), Burma
92/C4 **Zamora,** Ecu.
92/C4 **Zamora** (riv.), Ecu.
100/A4 **Zamora,** Mex.
46/C2 **Zamora,** Sp.
39/M3 **Zamość,** Pol.
39/M3 **Zamość** (prov.), Pol.
46/D3 **Záncara** (riv.), Sp.
68/C5 **Zanda,** China
40/A5 **Zandkreekdam** (dam), Neth.
40/B4 **Zandvoort,** Neth.

Zanes – Żywie

Acknowledgements

OXFORD UNIVERSITY PRESS ADVISORS

Dr C. Board
Department of Geography
London School of Economics and Political Science

Dr A. S. Goudie
Professor of Geography
University of Oxford

COMPUTERIZED CARTOGRAPHIC ADVISORY BOARD

Mitchell J. Feigenbaum, Ph.D
Chief Technical Consultant
Toyota Professor, The Rockefeller University
Wolf Prize in Physics, 1986
Member, The National Academy of Sciences

Judson G. Rosebush, Ph.D
Computer Graphics Animation
Producer, Director and Author

Gary Martin Andrew, Ph.D
Consultant in Operations Research,
Planning and Management

Warren E. Schmidt, B.A.
Former U.S. Geological Survey,
Chief of the Branch of Geographic
and Cartographic Research

HAMMOND PUBLICATIONS ADVISORY BOARD

UNITED STATES AND CANADA
Daniel Jacobson
Professor of Geography and Education,
Adjunct Professor of Anthropology,
Michigan State University

LATIN AND MIDDLE AMERICA
John P. Augelli
Professor and Chairman,
Department of Geography-Meteorology,
University of Kansas

WESTERN AND SOUTHERN EUROPE
Norman J. W. Thrower
Professor, Department of Geography,
University of California, Los Angeles

NORTHERN AND CENTRAL EUROPE
Vincent H. Malmstrom
Professor, Department of Geography,
Dartmouth College

SOUTH AND SOUTHEAST ASIA
P. P. Karan
Professor, Department of Geography,
University of Kentucky

EAST ASIA
Christopher L. Salter
Professor and Chairman,
Department of Geography,
University of Missouri

AUSTRALIA, NEW ZEALAND
& THE PACIFIC AREA
Tom L. McKnight
Professor, Department of Geography,
University of California, Los Angeles

POPULATION AND DEMOGRAPHY
Kingsley Davis
Distinguished Professor of Sociology,
University of Southern California
and Senior Research Fellow,
The Hoover Institution,
Stanford University

BIBLICAL ARCHAEOLOGY
Roger S. Boraas
Professor of Religion,
Upsala College

FLAGS
Whitney Smith
Executive Director,
The Flag Research Center,
Winchester, Massachusetts

LIBRARY CONSULTANT
Alice C. Hudson
Chief, Map Division,
The New York Public Library

SPECIAL ADVISORS

DESIGN CONSULTANT
Pentagram

CONTRIBUTING WRITER
Frederick A. Shamlian

HAMMOND INCORPORATED

Charles G. Lees, Jr., V.P.
Editor in Chief, Cartography

William L. Abel, V.P.
Graphic Services

Chingliang Liang
Director, Technical Services

Martin A. Bacheller
Editor-In-Chief, Emeritus

Joseph F. Kalina, Jr.
Managing Editor

Phil Giouvanos
Manager, Computer Cartography

Shou-Wen Chen
Cartographic Systems Manager

Ernst G. Hofmann
Nadya Sazanets
Topographic Specialists

Michael E. Agishtein, Ph.D
Advanced Systems Development

Lauren Kaligo
Manager, Information & Statistics